CHILDBIRTH EDUCATION:

PRACTICE, RESEARCH, AND THEORY

FRANCINE H. NICHOLS, RNC, Ph.D., AACE

Associate Professor of Nursing, The Wichita State University,
Wichita, Kansas;
Faculty, ASPO/Lamaze Childbirth Educator Certification Program

SHARRON SMITH HUMENICK, RN, Ph.D., AACE

Associate Professor of Nursing, University of Wyoming,
Laramie, Wyoming;
Faculty, ASPO/Lamaze Childbirth Educator Certification Program

1988 W. B. SAUNDERS COMPANY Philadelphia, London, Toronto, Montreal, Sydney, Tokyo

W. B. SAUNDERS COMPANY
Harcourt Brace Jovanovich, Inc.

The Curtis Center
Independence Square West
Philadelphia, PA 19106

Library of Congress Cataloging-in-Publication Data

Nichols, Francine H.
Childbirth education.

1. Childbirth—Study and teaching. I. Humenick, Sharron Smith. II. Title. [DNLM: 1. Labor. 2. Parents—education. 3. Pregnancy, WQ 300 N618c]
RG973.N53 1988 618.4 87-24323

Childbirth Education: Practice, Research, and Theory ISBN 0-7216-6779-1

Last digit is the print number: 9 8 7 6 5 4 3 2 1

This book is dedicated to all childbirth educators
and expectant parents,
together with our families—
Gary L., Gary E., and David Nichols
and
Mike, Christine, and Michael Humenick

CONTRIBUTORS

VIRGINIA AUKAMP, R.N., Ph.D., ACCE

Assistant Professor of Nursing, University of Missouri–Columbia, Columbia, MO

The Learner; The Teacher

ELISABETH BING, ACCE

Faculty Emeritus, ASPO/Lamaze Childbirth Educator Certification Program; Director, The Elisabeth Bing Center for Parents, New York, NY

Sexuality

MARTHA BUTLER, R.N., M.N.

Nursing Program Director, Southwestern College, Department of Nursing, Winfield, KS

Coaching: The Labor Companion

JOYCE DiFRANCO, R.N., B.S., ACCE

Faculty, ASPO/Lamaze Childbirth Educator Certification Program; Instructor, UCLA Extension Division of Health Sciences; Private Practice, Childbirth Education, Los Angeles, CA

Relaxation: Biofeedback; Relaxation: Music

MARGARET R. EDWARDS, R.N., M.S.N.

Associate Professor, School of Nursing, College of Pharmacy and Health Sciences, Northeast Louisiana University, Monroe, LA

Group Process

DONNA HOHMANN EWY, Ed.D., ACCE

Faculty, ASPO/Lamaze Childbirth Educator Certification Program; Co-ordinator, Adolescent Parenting Program, Boulder Valley Schools; Coordinator, Lutheran Medical Center, Boulder, CO

The Early Parenting Experience

ARLENE FREDERICK, R.N., Ed.D., ACCE

Faculty, ASPO/Lamaze Childbirth Educator Certification Program; Director of Nursing Education, William S. Hall Psychiatric Institute, Columbia, SC

The Learner; The Teacher

EILEEN FREDERICK, R.N., M.S., ACCE

Faculty, ASPO/Lamaze Childbirth Educator Certification Program; Perinatal Education Coordinator, Lake Forest Hospital, Lake Forest, IL

Coaching: The Labor Companion

SUSAN GENNARO, R.N., D.S.N., ACCE

Robert Wood Johnson Clinical Nurse Scholar, University of Pennsylvania, Philadelphia, PA

The Childbirth Experience

DONNA J. HAWLEY, R.N., Ed.D.

Associate Professor, Department of Nursing, The Wichita State University, Wichita, KS

Marketing Strategies

SUZANNA MAY HILBERS, R.P.T., ACCE

Faculty, ASPO/Lamaze Childbirth Educator Certification Program; Senior Therapist, Lakeshore Hospital, Birmingham, AL

Relaxation: Paced Breathing Techniques

SHERRY LYNN MIMS JIMENEZ, R.N., ACCE

Freelance Health Writer, San Antonio, TX

Supportive Pain Management Strategies

LINDA CORSON JONES, R.N., Ph.D., ACCE

Associate Professor and Co-ordinator, Parent-Child Health Nursing, Louisiana State University Medical Center School of Nursing, Graduate Program, New Orleans, LA

Support Systems

RUTH JUNGMAN, M.M., ACCE

Faculty, ASPO/Lamaze Childbirth Educator Certification Program; Childbirth Education Consultant, University of Texas Health Science Center at San Antonio, School of Nursing, San Antonio, TX

Relaxation: Acupressure

MARILYN MAILLET LIBRESCO, B.A., M.S., ACCE

Faculty, ASPO/Lamaze Childbirth Educator Certification Program; Health Educator, Kaiser Permanente Medical Center, Hayward, CA

Philosophy; Relaxation: Progressive and Selective Relaxation

JUDITH A. LOTHIAN, R.N., M.A., ACCE

Faculty, ASPO/Lamaze Childbirth Educator Certification Program; Private Practice, Childbirth Education, Brooklyn, NY

Relaxation: Therapeutic Touch

DOROTHY LUTHER, R.N., Ph.D.

Associate Professor, College of Nursing, University of Kentucky, Lexington, KY

Coaching: The Labor Companion

SUSAN McKAY, R.N., Ph.D., ACCE

Associate Professor of Nursing, University of Wyoming; Visiting Associate Professor of Nursing, University of Colorado, Laramie, WY

Consumer-Provider Relationships

MARY LOU MOORE, R.N.C., Ph.D., FAAN, ACCE

Research Instructor, Department of Obstetrics and Gynecology, Bowman Gray School of Medicine, Winston-Salem, NC

Conflict Resolution and Negotiation

ALICE K. NAKAHATA, R.P.T., M.A., ACCE

Faculty, ASPO/Lamaze Childbirth Educator Certification Program; Childbirth Educator, University of California at San Francisco Hospital; Parent Educator, San Francisco Community College Centers, San Francisco, CA

Exercise

SIGRID NELSSON-RYAN, R.N., ACCE

Faculty, ASPO/Lamaze Childbirth Educator Certification Program; Private Practice, Childbirth Education, Briarcliff Manor, NY

Positioning: Second Stage Labor

MINELLA PAVLIK, R.N., M.S.N., ACCE

Faculty, ASPO/Lamaze Childbirth Educator Certification Program; Parent Education Coordinator, St. David's Community Hospital, Austin, TX

Positioning: First Stage Labor

CELESTE PHILLIPS, R.N., Ed.D.

Maternity Nursing Instructor, Cabrillo College; Principal, Phillips and Fenwick, Inc., Specialists in Women's Health Care, Santa Cruz, CA

Marketing Strategies

ANNE TUCKER ROSE, R.N., M.S., ACCE

Faculty, ASPO/Lamaze Childbirth Educator Certification Program; Assistant Professor, Department of Nursing, Hudson Valley Community College, Troy, NY

Relaxation: Paced Breathing Techniques

ELAINE SCHROEDER-ZWELLING, R.N., Ph.D., ACCE

Faculty, ASPO/Lamaze Childbirth Educator Certification Program; Assistant Professor of Nursing, Ohio State University, Columbus, OH

The Pregnancy Experience; The Unexpected Childbirth Experience

PAMELA SHROCK, R.P.T., Ph.D., ACCE

Faculty, ASPO/Lamaze Childbirth Educator Certification Program; Lecturer in Human Sexuality, Northwestern University Medical School; Perinatal Educator, Prentice Womens Hospital, Staff Therapist, Adult Sexuality Program, Northwestern University Memorial Hospital, Psychologist in Private Practice, Chicago, IL

The Basis of Relaxation

SANDRA APGAR STEFFES, R.N., M.S., ACCE

Faculty, ASPO/Lamaze Childbirth Educator Certification Program; Program Co-ordinator, UCLA Extension Health Sciences; Private Practice, Childbirth Education, Early Parenting, and Lactation, Pacific Palisades, CA

Philosophy; Relaxation: Imagery

JOSEPH F. STEINER, Pharm. D.

Professor, Schools of Human Medicine and Pharmacy, University of Wyoming, Wyoming Medical Center, Casper, WY

Pharmaceutical Pain Management Strategies

SUSAN H. STEINER, R.N.C., B.S.N.

Clinical Instructor in Obstetrics, University of Wyoming School of Nursing; OB/GYN Nurse Practitioner, Family Nurse Practitioner, University of Wyoming Family Practice Residency Program, Casper, WY

Pharmaceutical Pain Management Strategies

NORMA NEAHR WILKERSON, R.N., Ph.D.

Associate Professor, University of Wyoming School of Nursing; Consultant, Ivinson Memorial Hospital Maternal Child Nursing, Laramie, WY

Nutrition; Sexuality; Setting Up a Practice

JOAN MARIA YOUMANS, R.N., M.N.

Clinical Educator, Birth Center, Penrose Community Hospital, Colorado Springs, CO

The Early Parenting Experience

FOREWORD

For the first time in the history of nursing, evidence of a research data base for practice has emerged. It is indeed fitting that childbirth education is the subject of the first text to support an approach to practice evolved from research findings. The movement of childbirth education from a "specific methods" focus to a practice based on testing of hypotheses composed of principles that incorporate well-defined concepts is exciting.

Childbirth education is an interdisciplinary field to which people from many disciplines have made major contributions. It remains, however, closely aligned with nursing because historically it has been and remains an integral part of nursing. This text offers something for all who are interested in childbirth education regardless of their discipline—nursing, medicine, physical therapy, education, psychology, or sociology. The beginning childbirth educator will find a lucid and readable foundation for practice. The experienced practitioner will find a critical analysis of current beliefs, information on which to further refine practice, and guidelines for the development and testing of new initiatives.

From a nursing perspective, if nursing is to document its impact on the health of society, what better place to begin than the education for expectant couples? This text defines the role of the childbirth educator, critically reviews childbirth education techniques, and analyzes the relationship between strategies used to prepare expectant couples for childbirth and outcomes of the process.

This text was written, in collaboration with colleagues from other disciplines, by a new generation of nurses: those who are clinically competent as well as disciplined in the development of science. The authors are nurse-scientists who have provided a new beginning for the profession. Readers are provided with a comprehensive review of the major facets of childbirth education. Practice implications are then developed on the basis of these research findings, and areas for further investigation are suggested. The critical analysis of the literature presented about specific techniques used to prepare couples for childbirth is, in and of itself, a monumental accomplishment.

The Nurses' Association of the American College of Obstetrics and Gynecology, Committee on Research, published *research priorities for obstetrical, gynecological and neonatal nursing research* in 1985. *Childbirth Education: Practice, Research, and Theory* reflects a scholarly response to these priorities and addresses many of the topics identified. Its publication three years following the identification of the priorities is a formidable accomplishment.

What Doctors Nichols and Humenick have provided in this volume is an important proclamation about the state of the art and science in nursing today. Their book is an indispensable guide for discussion; it is not a mere review of tradition but a completely articulated, accurate summary and a trustworthy analysis of the field of childbirth education. The authors and contributors are to be commended as they lead nursing forward and provide a basis on which to document our contribution to the health of society. This book should be read by all who are concerned about the nature and purpose of the childbirth educator.

Rosanne C. Perez-Woods, EdD, RN, CPNA
Neihoff Chair and Professor of Maternal Child Health Nursing
Neihoff School of Nursing, Loyola University of Chicago

PREFACE

During the last decade, there has been a proliferation of published information on childbirth education, both research and anecdotal, that often espoused different methods and recommended conflicting practices. Heated debate ensued on the merits of various prepared childbirth techniques. Questions of ''Why?'' and ''Why not?'' resounded from expectant parents, obstetrical care providers, childbirth educators, and childbirth researchers. The appropriateness of basing childbirth education solely on any one of the specific methods introduced several decades ago was being challenged.

In response to this situation, an ASPO/Lamaze National and University Faculty Conference, ''The Scientific Basis of Prepared Childbirth Techniques,'' was held in 1983. In preparation, faculty members reviewed and critically analyzed the research literature on prepared childbirth techniques and other aspects of childbirth education. During the conference, research on specific practices and related issues was discussed, debated, and clarified, and the current scientific basis of childbirth education was identified. The conception of this book took place when, at the close of the conference, faculty members voiced a common concern—the need to share the information with those in the childbirth education community. As this book evolved, new research findings on prepared childbirth techniques were included and the literature was reviewed on additional topics related to childbirth education by other contributing authors.

This book represents the results of our efforts to present the information in a manner that will be readily available to childbirth educators and other professionals interested in childbirth education. We believe that all childbirth educators, regardless of the method of childbirth preparation they teach, will find the information useful because the research and theory on childbirth education on which the book is based cuts across philosophical lines.

Why, the reader might ask, is it so important to establish the scientific basis and efficacy of childbirth education? Today, obstetrical care providers are bombarded with "scientific" and legal reasons to routinely use technology and medical interventions, as if every birth was a high-risk event. At the same time there is increasing emphasis on family-centered maternity care, the benefits of prepared childbirth techniques and a physiological approach to childbirth as well as the importance of individualized, participatory family-centered birth experiences for expectant parents. However, these dimensions may become overshadowed or even lost in this era of "high-tech" obstetrics. It is not enough for the childbirth educator to intuitively value the psychosocial aspects of the birth experience and a low-risk approach to birth with the use of technology based on individual need. To advocate effectively for humanistic prepared childbirth experiences, the childbirth educator must understand the scientific basis of prepared childbirth and must be able to support her position with research findings. It takes a well-informed, scientifically based and articulate childbirth educator to teach consumer-oriented childbirth classes today. Childbirth educators also need to be able to document their contributions to the health of the childbearing family as clearly as the efficacy of medical intervention is expected to be documented.

We have tried to achieve a balance between the academic and the applied. Research findings have been analyzed and summarized, and then practical implications for childbirth education are presented. The book can be used to gain an understanding of the scientific basis of childbirth education and its importance to practice; to identify areas of needed research; to learn practical strategies for teaching classes, working with other health professionals, and for setting up and marketing a practice; and to examine the role of the childbirth educator and professional issues related to the practice of childbirth education.

This book reflects the authors' insights at a point in time. As research increases and issues are clarified, the practice of childbirth education will continue to evolve as others contribute their insights and recommendations. We hope that this book will promote vigorous debate and discussion and stimulate research to test the concepts and principles of childbirth education presented here, further refining our knowledge base for practice.

FRANCINE H. NICHOLS

SHARRON S. HUMENICK

ACKNOWLEDGMENTS

Many people—expectant parents, childbirth educators, obstetrical care providers, and childbirth researchers—have contributed to this book, often without being aware of it. They motivated us to critically examine the practice of childbirth education and to document what we believe. Numerous other individuals made significant contributions to the book in various ways. Their assistance was sincerely appreciated.

Sincere thanks go to the following individuals: Our contributing authors, whose work exemplifies the significance and richness of childbirth education; Nancy McKelvey, who proposed and organized the conference that was the impetus for this book; Jim McCall, whose tangible and intangible support has made a difference in childbirth education; the many childbirth educators who critiqued early drafts of chapters; Carynne Corvaia of Writers in Residence, Wichita, Kansas, for her suggestions on writing style and organization of chapters; Mary Brucker, RN, CNM, Dallas, TX; Delores F. Jeffers, RN, MSN, ACCE, Perinatal Clinical Specialist, Tampa General Hospital, Tampa, FL; Cynthia Hoy, RN, ACCE, Head Nurse, Obstetrics, Bishop Clarkson Memorial Hospital, Omaha, NE; and Margaret Imle, RN, PhD, Associate Professor of Family Nursing, The Oregon Health Sciences University, Portland, OR, who critically reviewed the manuscript, raised pointed questions, and contributed many ideas that were incorporated into the book; Joan Moon and Eylene Teichgraeber, who provided quotes, checked references, and helped with other editorial tasks; and Toni Combow, Kathy Lydon, Juarlene Woodard, and Dora Zeimans, who typed chapters and handled correspondence.

We are indebted to the following individuals and organizations who provided pictures for the book: Alice Berman of ASPO/Lamaze; Susan Biasella; Richard Blinkoff; Jamie Bolane of Childbirth Graphics, Ltd.; Gini Burns; Century Manufacturing Company; Caroline Donahue; Equicore Health Plan, Inc., Wichita, KS; Donna and Rodger Ewy of Educational

Graphic Aids, Inc.; Loel Fenwick of Borning Corporation; Los Alamitos Medical Center, Los Alamitos, CA; Judith Lothian; March of Dimes Birth Defects Foundation; Alice Nakahata and Deanna Sollid of Babes; National Library of Medicine; The Birth Center, Penrose Community Hospital, Colorado Springs, CO; Marjorie Pyle of Lifecircle; Mark Salmanson of St. David's Community Hospital, Austin, TX; Anne Rose; Harvey Wang; The Word Publishing Company; and Bill Youmans.

Sincere appreciation goes to the Office of Research Administration, The Wichita State University, who provided a development grant for this project, to Martha S. Shawver, past Chairperson of the Department of Nursing, The Wichita State University, who provided support for the project in numerous ways, and to our faculty colleagues who listened, made suggestions, and provided resources during this project.

In the preparation of this book, special thanks goes to Ilze Rader, editor at W. B. Saunders, who provided invaluable suggestions and constructive feedback and whose advice was always right on the mark. This book evolved beyond that which we originally envisioned due to Ilze's expert guidance and her belief in the significance of the project. We thank Edna Dick, manuscript editor, for her superb editing and careful attention to detail, and for her unfailing calmness as we dealt with the details of the production process. To the other W. B. Saunders staff who made their own unique contributions, we are appreciative.

Three organizations deserve special recognition because of their contributions to childbirth education and to this book: the American Society for Psychoprophylaxis in Obstetrics (ASPO/Lamaze), the International Childbirth Education Association (ICEA), and the Nurses' Association of the American College of Obstetricians and Gynecologists (NAACOG). They have brought the needs of expectant parents to the attention of the public and obstetrical health care providers. Many changes in the obstetrical health care system have occurred because of their actions.

Finally, we wish to acknowledge our appreciation for the courage of the pioneers of childbirth education who spoke out for the importance of childbirth education at a time when it was considered part of the counterculture. They provided the "beginning" that made our task easy by comparison.

CONTENTS

INTRODUCTION

Of all of life choices, none are more important to society, none has more far reaching consequences, none represents a more complete blending of social, biological, and emotional forces than bringing another life into the world.[1]

Victor Fuchs

Childbirth education is an exciting specialty area of health care which is moving from a focus on ''specific methods'' as originally proposed by Dick-Read, Lamaze, and Bradley to an ''eclectic approach'' that is scientifically based. We are continuing to document with research those elements that are the most important for preparing expectant parents for childbirth. We are gaining a greater understanding of the effects of choice and alternative coping strategies on parents' childbirth experiences. From this we will continue to see a blurring of the lines of distinction between the traditional methods of childbirth preparation as childbirth educators use these research findings as a basis for their classes. Childbirth educators may receive preparation for teaching from different organizations espousing specific methods, and some distinction will remain. However, we predict that increasingly childbirth educators will teach expectant parents using a variety of approaches.

It has been observed that experienced childbirth educators tend to refine and shift their class content to reflect their own interests and expertise, the needs of their type of clients, and the introduction of new material.[2] Each class eventually becomes a unique blend of content based on characteristics of the instructor, the expectant parents, the knowledge available, and the community in which the classes are taught. How can the childbirth educator be helped to create the best blend for her situation?

It is the purpose of this book to help the childbirth educator work her way through the ''kaleidoscope'' of influences on childbirth education. The childbirth educator should feel confident that the approaches she has chosen are scientifically based and work well for her and her clients. Developing a curriculum for childbirth classes that can effectively prepare individuals for the childbirth and early parenting experiences is a challenging and complex task. The use of a conceptual framework, however, can greatly simplify that task.

Why Use a Conceptual Framework for Curriculum Development?

A conceptual framework describes the important elements of a curriculum and identifies their relationships to one another. It is a map that organizes the pieces into an orderly pattern. It provides a systematic way of viewing the influences on the curriculum rather than using a ''hit-or-miss'' approach. A conceptual framework also guides the selection of content and teaching strategies used in classes. Thus, using a conceptual framework helps ensure that the curriculum is planned in a systematic and comprehensive manner.

The childbirth educator using a conceptual framework can more easily analyze and evaluate the parts of the curriculum to determine if revisions are needed. Using a conceptual framework to plan and evaluate a curriculum for childbirth classes increases the likelihood that the curriculum will be one of excellence and thus will meet the needs of expectant parents and will help achieve both the clients' and childbirth educator's goals.

THE CONCEPTUAL FRAMEWORK

The conceptual framework (Fig. I–1), describes broad categories that influence the curriculum for childbirth education classes. These elements can be divided into inputs, process and product and are set within the context of a sociocultural-technical-legal-health care system.

Inputs

There are four factors—the childbirth educator, the expectant parents, the knowledge base, and the community context—which are the inputs into childbirth education classes.

- *The childbirth educator* is an individual who brings her own philosophy, which is based on a values system, to the classroom. This influences whether she plays out her role in a highly professional manner and whether she considers consumer advocate and change agent to be parts of her role.
- *The expectant parents* are individuals with ideas about health providers and health care. Through reading research and through experience, the childbirth educator can predict a great deal about their typical needs related to pregnancy, childbirth, and early parenting. She recognizes that in addition to their need for information about birth, they are at a point in their lives when they may be very open to adopting a more wellness-oriented lifestyle.
- *The knowledge base* for both optimizing the childbirth experience and promoting wellness in the family consists of information and specific skills. This knowledge base is continually expanding and changing.
- *The community context* is the environment in which childbirth education takes place. To function effectively in the community, the childbirth educator will need to know about consumer-provider relationships, conflict resolution and negotiation, business management principles, and marketing strategies.

Process

The *process* of childbirth education typically takes place in a classroom setting. The *classroom experience* is composed of the interactions between learner behaviors and teacher behaviors. Through this classroom experience expectant parents acquire knowledge and coping skills that will increase their competence in the pregnancy, childbirth, and early parenting experiences.

Product

The *product* or *outcomes* of childbirth education are both the short-term and long-term effects of childbirth education classes. Short-term effects are those measured at the completion of the classes, such as skill levels (ability to perform relaxation and breathing techniques) and attitudinal changes reflecting increased feelings of competence and preparedness for childbirth. Long-term effects are those that are measured after the birth experience, most typically by a postpartum evaluation form

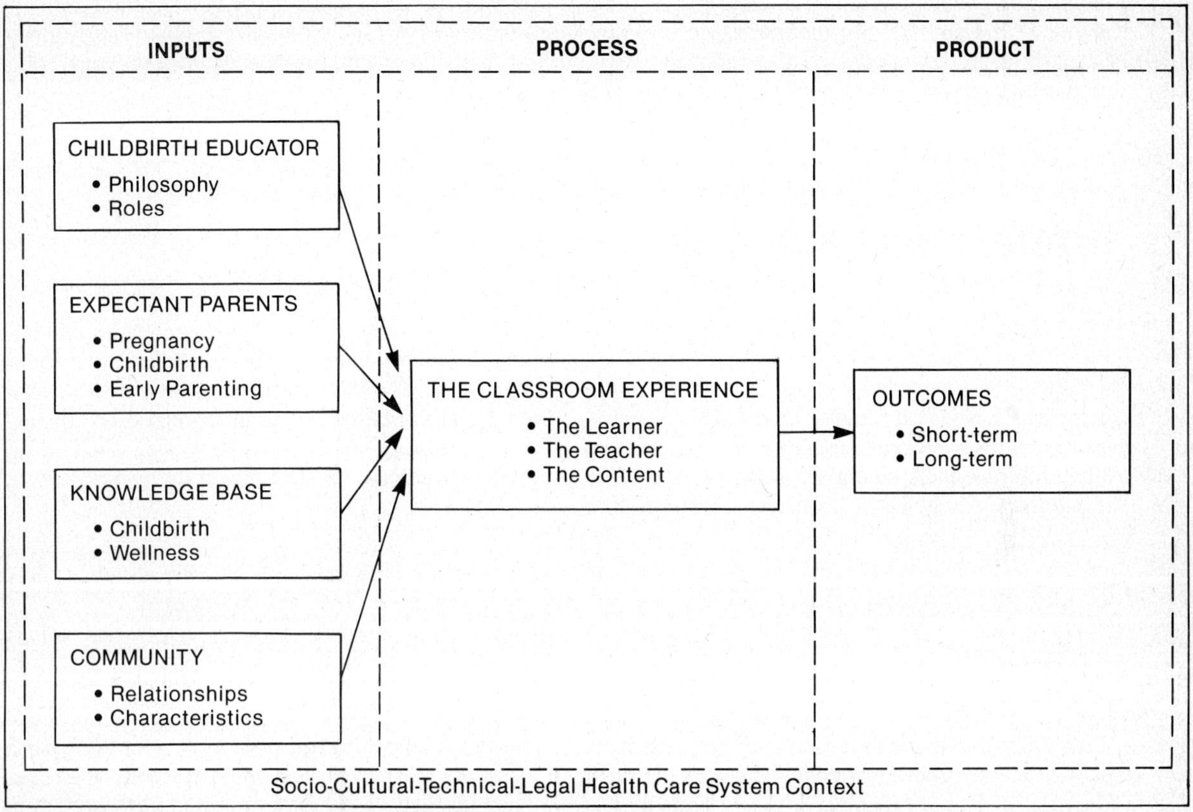

FIGURE I–1. A conceptual framework for childbirth education classes. (Adapted from S. Humenick and F. Nichols: A Conceptual Framework for Childbirth Education Classes. Paper presented at ASPO/Lamaze National and University Faculty Conference on the Scientific Basis of Prepared Childbirth Techniques, Columbus, Ohio, 1983.)

wherein the parents describe their birth experience and the effectiveness of prepared childbirth techniques for them. The variables that are most commonly measured in research studies are self-esteem, childbirth satisfaction, active participation during childbirth (i.e., control), pain levels as measured by the amount of medication taken during childbirth, and fetal and obstetrical variables.

IMPLICATIONS FOR PRACTICE

New childbirth educators can use the conceptual framework presented here to aid in planning their classes. Experienced childbirth educators are encouraged to use the framework for evaluating and revising classes.

Start by identifying each factor and the characteristics that affect your teaching. For example, describe your typical learner. What is the educational level, age, learning style, motivation to come to class, and type of desired childbirth experience?

If you don't know some of the answers, develop a plan to find out this information. Once you have listed the characteristics of your community, learners, knowledge base, and your teaching style, begin to think about the implications for your classes. This activity is most productive when brainstorming with other childbirth educators in your community.

IMPLICATIONS FOR RESEARCH

In addition to its usefulness for curriculum development, a conceptual framework is useful for designing or interpreting research. For example, many early research studies on childbirth preparation classes appeared to make the assumption that all childbirth education classes were the same. The researchers neglected to consider that variation which might take place between one class and another. In reality there may be important differences in the type of clients, teacher behaviors, and content taught in classes. The interpretation of the results of studies depends on how well such influences were considered in the study design.

SUMMARY

Childbirth education is complex. Like most areas of health care, the knowledge base and the birth settings and expectant parents are continually changing. As a result, there is a need to periodically review and update the material you present in your classes. The information in this book is intended to provide a guide for such review and a base for curriculum planning, evaluation and revision.

The book is divided into sections that are organized using the conceptual framework presented in this chapter. Thus the reader will examine the childbirth educator in Section 1, the expectant parents in Section 2, the knowledge base in Sections 3 and 4, the classroom experience in Section 5, and the community context in Section 6. At the beginning of each section there is a brief overview that is intended to further expand each segment of the conceptual framework.

The task of describing aspects of herself, her learners, and her community that influence her classes is an individual activity for the childbirth educator. However, keeping up with the ever changing knowledge base reported in the research literature is a difficult job more easily accomplished when childbirth educators work together. In this book, the contributing authors have combed the research literature, summarized their findings, and clearly described how the childbirth educator can make use of these findings. We hope you will find the book interesting as well as very helpful in teaching your childbirth education classes.

References

Shrock, P., Simken, P., and Shearer, M. Teaching prenatal exercises. Part II—Exercises to Think About Twice. *Birth* *8*(3), Fall 1981.

Beginning Quote

Fuchs, V. *How We Live*. Cambridge, MA: Harvard University Press, 1983.

Section

1

THE CHILDBIRTH EDUCATOR

The childbirth educator plays an important role in preparing expectant parents for childbirth and in promoting family health and wellness during the childbearing years. In this book the authors have focused on childbirth education for expectant couples and the role of the childbirth educator, along with strategies used in preparing for childbirth. However, we want to emphasize that the practice of childbirth education is broad; it extends from the preconception period through the early parenting period and includes other family members as well as the expectant parents.

The values and beliefs of the childbirth educator—i.e., her *philosophy* as it pertains to expectant parents, childbirth, childbirth education, and teaching—all influence the teaching process. Therefore, Chapter 1 deals with developing a philosophy of childbirth education. Philosophy is viewed by some people as ''high brow'' and impractical. Actually, a clearly identified philosophy is very useful because it provides strength and direction for practice. The childbirth educator who has not identified those principles that lead toward and support ''good'' childbirth and parenting experiences or who has not examined her beliefs about what constitutes ''good'' childbirth education in general is not prepared to identify which content is most appropriate for her childbirth education classes or those changes in her community that would support better childbirth experiences for families. Each childbirth educator is encouraged to do some ''soul searching'' about her beliefs and values related to childbirth education and reflect on how these influence her classes. Also, in Chapter 1 the philosophy on which this book is based is made explicit so that readers will know the philosophy of childbirth education that guided the organization and development of this book.

In Chapter 2 the various roles of the childbirth educator are described, and teachers are encouraged to examine their vision of their potential roles in society. We believe that no one is more prepared to work with expectant parents and other family members from preconception through parenting than the well-prepared and experienced childbirth educator. Also, we believe that no one is more qualified to speak for the needs of the American family, or has a greater responsibility to do so, than the professional childbirth educator. In the past, childbirth educators have been instrumental in improving the birth experiences of expectant parents and maternity care services for the American family through determined efforts and commitment to that cause. We encourage all childbirth educators to be committed to continuing this tradition.

The authors recognize there is a growing number of men who are childbirth educators. However, since the majority of childbirth educators are women, we have used the feminine pronoun when referring to the childbirth educator in order to eliminate the awkwardness of using both the feminine and masculine pronouns.

chapter 1

PHILOSOPHY

FRANCINE H. NICHOLS, SHARRON S. HUMENICK, MARILYN LIBRESCO, and SANDRA APGAR STEFFES

A childbirth educator's philosophy determines how any specific situation is approached and directly influences her behaviors in childbirth education classes and her interactions with expectant parents and with other health care professionals.

Francine Nichols

Who should control the birth experience—expectant parents, health care providers, or some negotiated combination of both? What is a reasonable balance between the use of technology and the reliance on the laboring woman's natural forces? Is the childbirth educator's role that of *crusader* for change, *negotiator* and *collaborator* for change, or *conformist* who follows agency policies even if they are in conflict with the needs of expectant parents and the expected practices of family-centered maternity care?

How much should the childbirth educator try to influence expectant couples' decisions about the childbirth experience? Should the childbirth educator *tell* expectant parents what childbirth options they should *demand* for their birth experience? Should the childbirth educator *present* birth options that are or should be available in the community and *guide* expectant parents in making an *informed decision* about what is best for their particular situation? Or should the childbirth educator *prepare* couples for how birth is accomplished in a particular agency so that they will more readily *comply* with agency policies? In the case of a shortage of childbirth preparation classes, is it better to turn expectant couples away from classes rather than overload existing classes and possibly diminish the quality of education provided? These are examples

Every time you express an opinion on a subject or make an evaluation of a situation, you are stating your philosophy on the subject.

Box 1–1

WHAT DO YOU BELIEVE?

1. CHILDBIRTH IS:	**A NO-RISK EVENT**	**USUALLY NORMAL**	**A HIGH- RISK EVENT**
Comments that indicate this philosophy	"Too much is made of the problems encountered during childbirth. It's just negative energy to worry. Everything will be OK."	"The body has a wisdom and mostly that wisdom prevails."	"All this talk about the beauty of birth is fine in theory, but who will speak for the baby? Each birth is a close call."
2. DURING CHILDBIRTH:	**INTERVENTION IS UNNECESSARY**	**INTERVENTION IS OCCASIONALLY NEEDED**	**ROUTINE INTERVENTION IS NEEDED**
Comments that indicate this philosophy	"Intervention simply justifies the existence and cost of hospitals. They make the physician instead of the woman the focus of birth."	"While most births are normal, an approach of watchful waiting is not unreasonable."	"It is a disservice to the mother and her baby not to offer her all that science can provide. Routine monitoring and astute surveillance are essential to detect problems. A low-risk birth is a postpartum diagnosis."
3. THE CURRICULUM FOR CHILDBIRTH EDUCATION CLASSES SHOULD BE BASED ON:	**THE CHILDBIRTH EDUCATOR'S PERSONAL KNOWLEDGE AND PHILOSOPHY**	**THE CHILDBIRTH EDUCATOR'S PERSONAL KNOWLEDGE AND PHILOSOPHY AND CONSUMER INPUT**	**BIRTHING AGENCY'S PHILOSOPHY AND PRACTICES**
Comments that indicate this philosophy	"Clients pay me for my knowledge and benefit from my experience. They want the bottom line, and I'm the best one to give it."	"My job is to balance the information and to provide a forum. They are responsible for their own learning."	"I'm paid by the hospital. It's unethical to undermine it in the name of consumer advocacy and to set up clients unrealistically."
4. TEACHING CHILDBIRTH EDUCATION CLASSES IS:	**A VOLUNTEER ACTIVITY**	**A PROFESSIONAL ACTIVITY**	**A STRICTLY BUSINESS ACTIVITY**
Comments that indicate this philosophy	"I set class fees to just cover costs, but I feel guilty and uncomfortable with even that. Childbirth education is that important to me!"	"Childbirth education is a profession . . . with all the rights and responsibilities of any other profession. I am committed to it, and expect to be respected for my expertise."	"As with any other career, adequate compensation prevents burnout. A lot of my energy goes to making a profit so that I can justify my time."

Box 1–1 Continued

5. IN THE COMMUNITY THE CHILDBIRTH EDUCATOR'S ROLE SHOULD BE THAT OF:	**A CONFORMIST**	**A CHANGE AGENT**	**A CRUSADER**
Comments that indicate this philosophy	**"Each community and agency has its own values and norms and its members know what's best. Who am I to say what changes should be made?"**	**"There's a lot of change needed and my goal is to improve birthing practices and birthing options for women. However, I believe it is best to work within the health care system, as well as in the community. True, change is slower, but it is longer lasting."**	**"Childbirth educators who work in hospitals have 'sold out' to the medical establishment! What is needed are vocal teachers who lead the crusade to improve birthing settings and practices for expectant parents."**
6. THE CHILDBIRTH EDUCATOR'S NEED FOR CONTINUING EDUCATION IS:	**NOT NECESSARY**	**MINIMAL**	**CONTINUAL**
Comments that indicate this philosophy	**"I'd like to take some workshops, but I don't have the time and they are so expensive. Besides, the basics of birthing don't really change."**	**"I'd like to do more; but I read a lot, and I attend at least one conference a year."**	**"I attend every seminar I can in order to stay current and credible. Also, I want to know more than just what is expected."**

of philosophical questions. The answers are primarily a matter of beliefs or values as opposed to the issues of science or knowledge. Every childbirth educator will face these and similar questions. The answers one gives to such questions are a reflection of one's philosophy of childbirth education.

Every time the childbirth educator expresses an opinion on a subject or makes an evaluation of a situation, she is stating her philosophy on the matter, a universal and almost inevitable activity.[2] A philosophy is an *attitude* which is reflected in one's view of people and the universe. An individual's *beliefs and values* as well as the *depth of understanding* about an event determine to a great extent how one *thinks* about a phenomenon or situation. The way one thinks about a situation is a strong determinant of one's *actions*.[4] Thus, the childbirth educator's philosophy about childbirth, childbirth education, expectant parents, the childbirth educator, and teaching all influence the practice of childbirth education. The childbirth educator who has not examined her beliefs and values (her philosophy) is primarily functioning at an intuitive level. In this situation, the childbirth educator risks being reactive and overly emotional, erratic and undirected, and unsure of herself. All childbirth educators will benefit from examining their beliefs, values, actions, and decisions that reflect the philosophy they will use in childbirth education classes and in interactions with other health professionals. This clarification of values can be done by using an exercise such as "What Do You Believe?" (Box 1–1). This presents a few of the concepts that should be considered. Participation in a discussion group with other childbirth educators can also be valuable; beliefs, values, actions, and decisions are analyzed and each childbirth educator identifies a personal philosophy of childbirth education.

WHAT IS PHILOSOPHY?

Philosophy has been defined as "pursuit of wisdom; a search for a general understanding of values and reality by chiefly speculative rather than observational means; an analysis of the grounds of and concepts expressing fundamental beliefs; a theory underlying or regarding a sphere of activity or thought; and the most general beliefs, concepts, and attitudes of an individual or groups."[5] Philosophy is rational and reasoned inquiry about human activity. *It often does not provide as many answers as it generates questions.*[2] Philosophy involves three areas: concern with knowledge, values, and being or one's beliefs about why one exists.[4] These three areas of philosophy can be related to childbirth education as follows:

AREAS OF PHILOSOPHY	CHILDBIRTH EDUCATION
Knowledge	Based on research and theory related to childbirth and childbirth education.
Values	Governed by a code of ethics.
Existence	Concerned with the needs of expectant parents, childbirth practices, and the development of a scientifically based practice.

Using this framework, "Philosophy of childbirth education" can be defined as the intellectual and affective outcomes of the childbirth educator's efforts to:

- Understand the processes of pregnancy, childbirth, and early parenting and their impact on individuals, the community, and society.
- Apply a personal belief system about childbirth, expectant parents' roles in childbirth, childbirth education, and teaching.
- Approach childbirth education as a scientific discipline whose major concerns are helping expectant parents prepare for an optimal birthing experience and learning skills that will enhance wellness throughout life.

A philosophy provides the basis for ethical decision-making,[4] a process that is often a source of stress for the childbirth educator. The ethical decision-making process is a rigorous, logical analysis of the situation and includes analyzing, weighing, justifying, choosing, and evaluating competing and often diametrically opposed reasons for an action. A personal philosophy consistent with a philosophy of a profession can be a *source of strength,* as other health professionals, the community, and society recognize the values for which an individual stands and the roles that the individual fulfills. The profession's code of ethical conduct provides general principles to guide and evaluate the actions of the childbirth educator (Box 1–2). The code of ethics is an expression of the philosophy of the profession. Through its ethical code the profession's commitment to the childbearing family becomes a matter of public record to expectant parents, other health care professionals, and members of the profession. Every member of the profession has a personal obligation to uphold and adhere to the code and to influence other members to do likewise.

The Importance of Philosophy

The benefits of philosophy[2] for childbirth educators are that it:

- Provides a comprehensive view of expectant parents and their universe.
- Develops the childbirth educator's ability to deal

Box 1–2

CODE OF ETHICS
FOR CHILDBIRTH EDUCATORS

- **The childbirth educator respects the uniqueness of each expectant parent and family member and provides services without regard for social or economic status, or personal characteristics and goals.**
- **The childbirth educator assumes responsibility and accountability for individual judgments and actions.**
- **The childbirth educator collaborates with other health professionals and concerned persons in promoting local, state, and national efforts to meet the health, safety, and educational needs of the FAMILY during the childbearing years.**
- **The childbirth educator is a consumer advocate who promotes informed decision-making, the independence and competence of clients, and the collaboration of clients with the health care team.**
- **The childbirth educator maintains competence in the practice of childbirth education and incorporates new knowledge as it develops into the practice of childbirth education.**
- **The childbirth educator participates in the efforts of the profession to implement and improve the standards of childbirth education and maternity care services.**
- **The childbirth educator participates in activities that contribute to the ongoing development of the body of knowledge for childbirth education.**
- **The childbirth educator uses informed judgment and individual competence and qualifications as criteria in accepting responsibilities or in seeking consultation.**
- **The childbirth educator safeguards clients' rights to privacy by protecting information of a confidential nature.**
- **The childbirth educator acts to protect the client and the public when health care and safety are affected by incompetent, unethical, or illegal practice of any person.**

with abstract ideas and concepts, to ask intelligent questions, and to formulate rational answers.

- Gives direction for practice and assists in choosing of desirable goals, means and purposes, and provides a basis for ethical decision-making.

DEVELOPING A PHILOSOPHY OF CHILDBIRTH EDUCATION

To develop a "philosophy of childbirth education" the childbirth educator needs to examine attitudes and beliefs.

- *What is your view of childbirth?* Is childbirth a normal physiological process in which medical intervention typically is not needed or is childbirth a high-risk event that warrants high levels of medical surveillance and often intervention, and can be termed low risk only "after" the birth? What is the balance between use of technology and reliance on the laboring woman's natural forces? Who should control the birth experience, expectant parents, health care providers, or a negotiated combination of both?
- *What is the ultimate purpose of childbirth education?* Is the primary purpose to prepare ex-

pectant couples intellectually for childbirth (that is, to provide information; to arm them with pain management skills for childbirth (for example, relaxation and breathing techniques), or both? How much emphasis should be given to the emotional preparation of expectant parents for childbirth? What importance is placed on helping expectant couples clarify their values about childbirth-related issues, such as medication or breastfeeding? Is the same emphasis appropriate for all clients? Your answers to these questions will determine how you structure classes and the content that you will include in them.

Should childbirth education be used to change social systems through influencing and changing individuals or the health care system? It is apparent that when learning occurs with individuals, change in the social system can be brought about through collective action. The issue is whether or not the purpose of childbirth education should extend beyond the classroom and the individual learner.

The childbirth educator must also examine the efficacy of childbirth education in preparing parents for birth. To what extent and in what situations can childbirth educators make claims regarding the efficacy of childbirth education? To what extent does the childbirth educator base her teaching on research and theory related to childbirth education and sound educational principles?

- *What is your role as a childbirth educator?* For example, are you a *crusader* for better birth experiences for expectant parents, a *negotiator* and *collaborator* who assists expectant parents to have the type of birth experience they desire and works with the health care system to achieve this goal, or a *conformist* who teaches only information that reflects the philosophy and approach of a specific agency? Do you teach expectant parents how to make "informed" decisions about subjects such as medication, or do you tell them how things "will" or "should" go during birth? (This can range from telling an expectant mother that she "should not take medication" to telling her that "you will get your epidural when you are dilated 5 centimeters.")

  What is your personal commitment to childbirth education? Do you teach because you are committed to the importance and value of childbirth education or do you teach classes primarily because it is a part of your job? An overcommitment can lead to burnout while a lack of commitment has a detrimental effect on teaching and students' learning. Should information collected during class (or problems that are identified during class) be released to anyone else, such as the physician, midwife, or birthing agency? Most would agree that expectant parents have the right to privacy and confidentiality. However, is it ever acceptable to release any information? If so, under what circumstances?

  Last, how does your role as a childbirth educator differ from that of other health professionals? What type of educational preparation is necessary to prepare a skilled childbirth educator? How important do you believe it is to be certified as a childbirth educator by a professional organization? What importance do you place on continuing education in the field of childbirth education?

- *What are your expectations of clients who attend classes?* Do you expect women to come to class motivated to seek a birth experience in which there is minimal medication and medical intervention or do you expect that women will need and want to use medication and medical intervention? Do you expect clients to take responsibility for learning and decision-making, or do you as the "expert" assume full responsibility for decision-making? The middle-ground is to assist expectant parents to make decisions using information and guidelines provided by the childbirth educator. What are your feelings about expectant parents who want to relinquish all control to the physician and welcome the use of technological interventions during birth? For example, how do you respond to the woman who wants an epidural as soon as she can get one?

- *What are your beliefs about teaching?* Should the teacher always respond to the "felt" needs of expectant parents? What is the balance between teaching what the couples *want* to know and what the couples *need* to know about childbirth? Should the teacher ever abandon the goal of fostering self-directed learning in order to achieve a specific learning outcome? Should expectant parents be expected, that is, should they feel compelled, to participate during classes?

Who controls the curriculum of the childbirth education classes? Is the content governed by the importance of the information to the preparation for childbirth or is the content governed by the policies and procedures of a specific group or agency? What is the balance between no input and censorship of the curriculum? Who should make the final decision as to what is taught in your childbirth education classes?

How central is the woman to her own birth? How much emphasis should the childbirth educator put on helping the woman to trust her own instincts rather than to structure her behavior during childbirth? What is the balance between structure and freedom in teaching childbirth education classes?

As a beginning, the childbirth educator may find it helpful to examine her beliefs about some general but very important concepts which influence the practice of childbirth education (see Box 1–1).

Box 1–3

A PHILOSOPHICAL STATEMENT

THE PROBLEM OF CHILDBIRTH EDUCATORS' PERSONAL OPINIONS

Sherry Lynn Mims Jiménez, RN, ACCE

Personal opinion of the teacher is not a valid part of the adult educational process. The process of adult education relies on the strengths and weaknesses of the learner, and on her past experiences, to assist her in considering, choosing and using appropriate behaviors to reach her goal. The role of the teacher is to facilitate this process by providing access to complete and accurate information about available alternative routes to reach the goal, as well as the possible risks and benefits of each route. The teacher also helps the learner choose and practice skills designed to help her cope with the risks of her chosen route, while fully reaping the benefits of it. In her role of concerned counselor and teacher, the childbirth educator has important influence on both the decisions the client makes and on *how she feels about the decision and its results.* If the client perceives that the teacher has a strong opinion regarding a topic or issue, even though the atmosphere is "supportive and non-judgmental," the seed of self-doubt has been planted. If later, the client chooses to abdicate her right and responsibility and makes her decision based on the teacher's opinion, she will have learned nothing of lasting value. The teacher who freely gives advice and opinions instead of education and counsel, fosters a dependent relationship with her client. This may not do any harm, though many nurses have reported cases in which the patient who coped well in class could not cope in labor because her teacher was not there. Even when no problems are evident from this style of teaching, very little growth will be seen either.

The client must choose her own causes. Some instructors ask, "Who will change obstetric practices if not educated parents who select their caregivers?" I agree with the philosophy, but not with instructors who feel free, and perhaps even righteous, in drawing the client into the causes that concern the teacher. Although such consumerism is laudable, it may be a disservice to the very consumers who rely on childbirth educators for accurate, unbiased information. In the classroom I am not an activist, but an educator. There, my first concern is to help pregnant people or couples evaluate and meet those goals that are important to them. Whether their ideas coincide or conflict with mine, if I use my influence to advance my own causes, I am violating my client's trust—*no matter how noble the cause.* If I do not feel I can support the decisions my client makes, and if I feel they may be detrimental to her, her family or her baby, it is my duty to help her re-examine the options and risks of what she wants to do, and to do so in the light of current, valid research. If the conflict remains, I must decide either to let her, as an adult, make and follow through on her decision, or to tell her that I cannot support her decision, but I respect her right to make it, and ask her to seek another teacher.

But, when I leave the classroom, I become the change-seeking activist in the community along with my colleagues and other health care providers. I have seen in the past the effects of teachers who draw clients into their battles, when the client may have had no difficulty with a particular issue. Sometimes there is a small change for the better in that particular birth or that hospital, but in the long run, the only thing that has happened is the hospital or doctor has given in to a patient who gave in to a teacher. No real change comes from this except perhaps beautiful birthing rooms with a staff who wishes the doors would be locked, or classes designed to teach hospital cooperation in order to avoid having patients unduly swayed by a childbirth educator.

From Jiménez, S. The Problem of Childbirth Educators' Personal Opinions. *Birth* 11(2):113, Summer 1984.

Box 1–4

A PHILOSOPHY OF CHILDBIRTH EDUCATION: THE BELIEF SYSTEM ON WHICH THIS BOOK IS BASED

This book is based on a philosophy of childbirth education that includes the following essential elements: childbirth, childbirth education, expectant parents, and childbirth educator.

Childbirth

Pregnancy, childbirth, and the early parenting experiences are significant events in the lives of those who experience them. The meaning of childbirth is as individual as the goals of individual childbearing women and their families. Each pregnancy and birth is unique and has physiological, psychological, spiritual, and social importance. Childbirth is a normal physiological process that generally does not require medical intervention. It is an experience that can influence the mental and social health of women and family members. Childbirth should be accomplished in a manner that not only promotes biological safety but enhances the emotional and spiritual aspects inherent in birth as well.

Childbirth Education

Childbirth education is a dynamic process in which expectant parents learn cognitive information about physical and emotional aspects of pregnancy, childbirth, and early parenting, coping skills, and labor support techniques. Values clarification and informed decision-making are emphasized throughout the educational process. The focus of the classes is on preparing expectant parents and family members intellectually, emotionally, and physically (for the expectant woman) for childbirth, and promoting wellness behaviors of clients as a lifestyle. The practice of childbirth education is broad; it extends from preconception through the early parenting period and includes other family members as well as expectant parents. The goal of childbirth education is to promote the competence of expectant parents in meeting the challenges of childbirth and early parenting. Individuals are assisted to identify their own unique goals for childbirth, balance these goals within the existing health care system and their own personal situation, and move toward the fulfillment of their goals.

Expectant Parents

Expectant parents come to childbirth education classes from broad segments of society, with different types of learning styles and with different levels of motivation to learn. Individuals hold their own personal belief system about birth, but by coming to class acknowledge the need to explore these values and attitudes and to gain additional information in order to achieve a higher goal. They expect their values, goals, and attitudes to be treated with dignity and respect regardless of how different or similar they may appear to other members of the class.

Childbirth Educator

The childbirth educator is a professional practitioner who is accountable to clients and the public for maintaining high standards for childbirth education and for promoting the improvement of maternity care services. The childbirth educator, while being caring and supportive, also promotes independence and competence in her clients. The childbirth educator is a consumer advocate who promotes informed decision-making and responsible choice related to obstetrical health care. The childbirth educator's role as a teacher is that of a facilitator. The childbirth educator must be knowledgable about teaching and be able to use this information skillfully in the classroom. The childbirth educator collaborates with other health professionals in the care of clients.

The childbirth educator should possess a broad knowledge base from the biological and behavioral sciences, and should be knowledgeable about obstetrical practices and the scientific basis for childbirth education. This is best accomplished by a specialized course of study designed for the preparation of childbirth educators, in addition to a basic professional degree. The childbirth educator should be able to discuss theoretical and technical aspects of childbirth education with a variety of health professionals, as well as field questions from clients. Childbirth educators need curiosity and openness to new ideas balanced by cautiousness as they review alternative therapies presented for their consideration as potential additions to the field of childbirth education.

The childbirth educator can communicate effectively with physicians, other health care professionals, consumer groups, and the media. Childbirth educators need the ability to be assertive, to support their decisions effectively with sound rationale, and to negotiate and deal constructively with controversy. The childbirth educator requires a broad experimental base. She benefits by observing many births under a variety of circumstances, especially the birth experiences of clients she has taught in class. The childbirth educator has a responsibility to remain current in the field through continuing education and through belonging to her professional association.

TABLE 1–1. MODELS OF HELPING AND COPING IN CHILDBIRTH

DIMENSIONS OF MODEL	TYPES OF MODELS			
	MORAL MODEL	COMPENSATORY MODEL	MEDICAL MODEL	ENLIGHTENMENT MODEL
Responsibility for Problem	Each person's troubles are of his own making.	People are not blamed for problem but are seen as suffering from a lack of resources and services to which they are entitled.	People are not responsible for their problems. Individuals with problems are expected to adopt sick-role behavior.	People are blamed for causing their problems.
Responsibility for Solution	Each person must find his own solution.	People have the responsibility to solve their own problems by seeking and using help from peers, subordinates, or professional helpers.	Persons are not responsible for finding a solution and are expected to seek and use expert help.	Persons are not responsible for solving their problems.
Role of Helper	Help may be given by *peers* who provide strong emotional support or who exhort the individual to change and improve.	Provides resources or opportunities that the person needs. The responsibility for deciding what will be helpful and if it will be used lies with the recipient of the help.	Help is given by experts who know what the problem is, prescribe the appropriate solution, and determine if the solution has been successful.	This model serves to *enlighten* persons about the true nature of their problems and the course of action that is needed to deal with their problems. The helper tells clients what they should do and why.
Value of Model	Compels individuals to take action on their own behalf and assume full responsibility for change.	Preferred by people who want to prepare themselves to solve their own problems. Increases competence of the individual.	This model allows people to claim and accept help without being blamed for problem.	This model is helpful when people are unable to control what they believe is undesirable behavior on their part.
Problems of Model	The belief that people always get what they deserve or deserve what they get. Conducive to loneliness.	People continually are responsible for solving their own problems even when the problems were not created by them. People may become bitter or have a paranoid view of the world.	This model fosters dependency rather than competency and compliance with agency policies.	This may induce guilt in those persons for whom the solution does not work.
Example	Mutual self-help groups. Couples who take full responsibility for their pregnancy and birth and choose to deliver at home with the help of family and friends.	Prepared childbirth classes and LaLeche groups that are based on consumer advocacy and informed decision-making.	This is the predominant philosophy of obstetrical health care providers.	*Early* natural childbirth and LaLeche groups whose goals were to *enlighten* expectant parents on the benefits of natural childbirth and breastfeeding. They had strong overtones of crusading and gathering support for the cause.

Adapted from Cronenwett, L. and Brickman, P. Models of Helping and Coping in Childbirth. *Nursing Research* 32 (2):84–88, 1983.

Next, the childbirth educator should consider each question posed carefully, write the answer down, and formulate a personal philosophy of childbirth education. It is a challenging and often difficult process! Sometimes you may find it is helpful to discuss the questions with other childbirth educators prior to developing your own philosophy. However, be sure that the philosophy you write down really reflects your own values. It is sometimes helpful to start with just one part of the philosophy, perhaps the part that seems easier to put into words. Jimenez[3] wrote a philosophical statement on the role of the childbirth educator in the classroom which describes her beliefs (Box 1–3). You may want to use this as a model in initially developing your philosophy, because it is often easier to write your philosophy by concentrating on one part at a time. We wrote a philosophy of childbirth education (Box 1–4) that reflects our personal philosophies of childbirth education and is also the belief system on which this book is based. You may find it helpful to examine it as you develop your own personal philosophy of childbirth education.

Expectations and Reality: A Philosophical Dilemma

Cronenwett and Brickman[1] classified four existing models of helping and coping (Table 1–1) that health care providers and clients use and that differ according to who assumes responsibility for the *origin of the problem* and who had the responsibility for finding a *solution to the problem*. They are the moral model (the client is responsible for both), the compensatory model (the client is not blamed for problems, but is responsible for solutions), the medical model (the client is not responsible for either), and the enlightenment model (the client is blamed for problems, but is not responsible for solutions). The basic assumptions from which individuals operate have consequences for their own behavior as well as the behavior of people who they influence. It is a reality that the childbirth educator's expectations of expectant parents preparing for childbirth may not match the expectations of the clients who attend class. Indeed, it is very likely that clients with varying and often conflicting expectations will be in the same class. First, analyze which helping model you must generally use when teaching expectant parents. Then, carefully determine the expectations of each individual who attends classes. Identifying your own belief system will enable you to understand problems that may arise in class and that are due to differences in expectation. Also, only after you have determined the client's expectations can you develop a plan to help expectant parents meet their own unique needs. Respect for the individual's right to approach childbirth with a perspective that is different from the teacher's is paramount.

IMPLICATIONS FOR PRACTICE

Developing a personal philosophy of childbirth education has profound implications for the childbirth educator:

- It provides strength and direction for practice.

> I have gained this by philosophy: that I do without being commanded what others do only from fear of law.
>
> ARISTOTLE[1]

- It requires the childbirth educator to view her class and other activities as a personal statement of her philosophy, that is, her beliefs and values. While she may adhere to an established code of ethics, the *what, how, why,* and *when* she includes information and learning experiences in classes reflect her personal belief system. It raises into question the use of "canned" or published childbirth education curriculum, the "cloning" of a mentor's childbirth education program, or the use of an agency's teaching syllabus without critical evaluation of the appropriateness of the content and teaching strategies, and the need for modifications so that the curriculum will meet the needs of the specific class to be taught.

- It establishes a community of childbirth educators who are linked to one another through knowledge and belief systems. The development of agreed-upon philosophical positions results in collegial exchange and periodic examination of those positions and establishes the need and direction for planned change at the local, state, or national levels.
- It establishes a set of expectations with other professionals in the health care community and with clients about the *content* and *intent* of childbirth education. Thus, the childbirth educator is accountable to peers, clients, and society.

> The philosophy which is so important in each of us is not a technical matter; it is our more or less dumb sense of what life honestly and deeply means. It is only partly got from books; it is our individual way of just seeing and feeling the total push and pressure of the cosmos.
>
> WILLIAM JAMES[1]
>
> On dark days, my philosophy gives me strength and keeps me going in the right direction.
>
> A CHILDBIRTH EDUCATOR

SUMMARY

Periodic examination of one's philosophy is essential because an individual's beliefs and values do change. They are influenced by many factors: feelings, increased knowledge, recent experiences and events, and the level of ego involvement. As the childbirth educator grows and develops as a professional, her attitudes, beliefs, knowledge, and skills change. In addition, the clients that she teaches and the setting in which she teaches also change. Thus, periodically, the childbirth educator also needs to examine the philosophical positions of her clients, other health care professionals, and birthing agencies in the community. Clarifying commonalities of goals and differences in beliefs and expectations is helpful. For while one may not agree with the beliefs and values of clients, other health care professionals, or birthing agencies, identifying these differences enables one to determine what specific problems exist and to look realistically for possible approaches or solutions to those problems. During a periodic evaluation the childbirth educator can also examine changes that have occurred in the community and evaluate its readiness for future changes in maternity care services. Finally, the childbirth educator who has a clearly identified philosophy of childbirth education and who is able to articulate it to other health professionals will find that it provides strength and direction for practice.

References

1. Cronenwett, L., and Brickman, P. Models of Helping and Coping in Childbirth. *Nursing Research 32*(2):84–88, 1983.
2. Howick, W. H. *Philosophies of Education*. Danville, IL: The Interstate Printers and Publishers, Inc., 1980.
3. Jimenez, S. The Problem of Childbirth Educators' Personal Opinions. *Birth 11*(2):113, 1984.
4. Leddy, S., and Pepper, M. *Conceptual Basis of Professional Nursing*. Philadelphia: J. B. Lippincott, 1985.
5. *Webster's New Collegiate Dictionary*, 1977.

Beginning Quote

Nichols, F. Developing a Philosophy of Childbirth Education. Unpublished paper. Wichita, KS; St. Mary of the Plain College, 1983.

Boxed Quote

1. Bartlett, J. *Familiar Quotations*. Boston: Little, Brown and Company, 1980.

chapter 2

ROLES

FRANCINE H. NICHOLS

In the past we have had a light which flickered, in the present we have a light which flames, and in the future there will be a light which shines over all land and sea.

Winston Churchill

The primary role of the childbirth educator is that of teacher (see Chapter 26). However, to enact that role in the most effective manner, skills in the roles of leader, decision-maker, change agent, consumer advocate, consultant, and entrepreneur are also needed. Armed with expertise in these roles, the childbirth educator can better fulfill the responsibility of her position in the community.

The Concept of Role

The concept of role can be defined as an expected set of behaviors that are attributed to an individual on the basis of a specific office or position. Every society has defined expectation of specific role behaviors of members who fulfill certain positions of responsibility. An individual's perceived role in society greatly influences how the individual communicates with other members of society. There are three elements of role that influence an individual's interactions with other members of society: role prescription, role description, and role expectations.[9] These are defined as follows:

- *Role prescription:* the *formal*, explicit statement of what behaviors *should* be performed by persons in a given role.
- *Role description:* a report of the behaviors that *actually are* performed by persons in a given role.
- *Role expectations:* the images or general impressions that people have about the behaviors that are performed by persons in a given role.

In the ideal relation between an individual and society, there is agreement on the role prescriptions, descriptions, and expectations. This agreement on role behavior reduces uncertainty, increases purposeful communications with other members of society, and results in more effective outcomes. However, disagreement on role behavior leads to ambiguous or confusing messages and role conflict in which an individual, for example, a childbirth educator receives different messages from several sources—community, client, other health professions—that are not consistent with her own perceptions of her role functions. This results in increased tension and anxiety that can lead to ineffective interactions with other members of society.[9] Thus, a thorough understanding of role theory can enable the childbirth educator to personally clarify her role as childbirth educator and to identify discrepancies between this role as she perceives it and how it is perceived by clients, other health professionals, and society in general. After discrepancies are identifed, the childbirth educator can develop a plan of action to solve the problem.

The role of childbirth educator has many components, such as that of leader, decision-maker, change agent, consumer advocate, consultant, and entrepreneur. In this chapter, each of these roles is examined and their contributions to the overall role of the childbirth educator are discussed. As you will see, there is considerable overlap among these various roles.

ROLES OF THE CHILDBIRTH EDUCATOR

Leader

One role inherent in the role of childbirth educator is that of leader. A leader is an individual who displays the *characteristics of leadership*. Leadership is defined as the ability to inspire and influence others to the attainment of goals through formal and informal procedures. Bass wrote in Stogdill's *Handbook of Leadership* that leadership has been seen as the focus of group process, as a personality attribute, as the art of inducing compliance, as an exercise of influence, as a particular kind of act, as a form of persuasion, as a power relation, as an instrument in goal attainment, as an effect of interaction, as a differentiated role, and as initiation of a structure. What is known is that effective leadership can be learned. There are four components of leadership: the management of attention, the management of meaning, the management of trust, and the management of self.[1]

Management of Attention. Leaders have an ability to draw individuals to them because they have a vision and a dream, and they communicate commitment.

Management of Meaning. Leaders have the ability to communicate their dream and vision to others and are able to get people to understand and support their cause.

Management of Trust. Leaders are reliable and predictable. You always know what a leader stands for; they can be trusted.

Management of Self. Leaders know their own strengths and weaknesses. They know how to use their skills effectively and they nurture their strengths.

Styles of Leadership

Leaders can interact with individuals and groups in many different ways, some of which are more effective than others. An individual's leadership style is the *way* in which he or she uses personal influence to achieve desired goals. Each individual develops a characteristic style of trying to influence others. Learning how to analyze the situation and how to use the appropriate leadership style for that situation will enable an individual to interact with others in a more productive and harmonious manner.

Styles of leadership range from very conservative to very liberal. While there are different ways of classifying leadership styles, three major styles have emerged: authoritarian, democratic, and permissive, e.g., laissez-faire. A comparative summary of these styles is shown in Table 2–1. The style of leadership is characterized by one's use of authority in interactions with individuals and groups.[16] A leadership style that is best for one situation is not necessarily appropriate for another situation. Thus, the effective childbirth educator will study the situation, the tasks to be accomplished, and the persons to be led, and then will adopt a leadership style that complements the situation. To refine her leadership skills, the

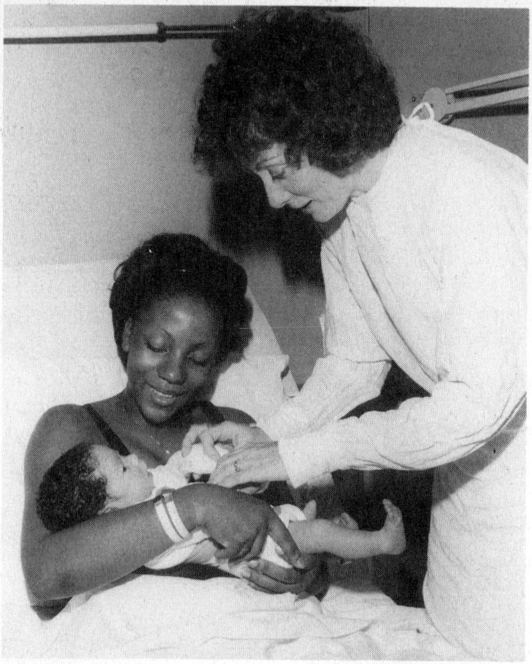

Childbirth educators serve in positions of leadership in birthing agencies as well as in the community. They are involved in educational programs for the childbearing family, the development of approaches to increase breastfeeding education and support, and fostering the philosophy of family-centered maternity care. (Courtesy of Caroline M. Donahue, ACCE, and The Brooklyn Hospital, Brooklyn, New York.)

childbirth educator is encouraged to begin by critically examining her current leadership style through an assessment of her use of authority in interactions with individuals and groups. Using a continuum that ranges from autocratic to permissive (laissez-faire) styles of leadership, developed by Tannenbaum and Schmidt,[16] the childbirth educator can determine her typical leadership style. Then, the childbirth educator can go on to evaluate and refine her skills in the areas of analyzing different situations, determining which style of leadership is needed in the situation, and putting that style of leadership in action to accomplish desired outcomes.

Decision-Maker

Many childbirth educators find themselves caught between the policies of physicians or hospitals and their clients; they are expected to be loyal and supportive of the views and needs of both groups. More and more childbirth educators in leadership positions are beginning to question the *placement* of childbirth educators in the organizational structure of the health care system or agency and are seeking expanded decision-making in the system. A thorough understanding of the nature of decisions and the decision-making process will increase the ability of the childbirth educator to function more effectively as a decision-maker.

There are two basic categories of decisions: nonroutine, which are nonrecurring and uncertain; and routine, which are recurring and certain.[17] The routine decisions tend to have predictable outcomes and are decisions that for the childbirth educator would involve scheduling of classes, purchasing of supplies for classes, and developing guidelines and policies for classes. The nonroutine decisions often have unpredictable outcomes and generally require more analysis and attention and creativity in problem-solving. Examples of nonroutine decisions are conflict with a physician over what is taught in classes, birthing agency and office nurses who are unsupportive of childbirth education, couples who may have unrealistic expectations for the childbirth experience, and revisions of the childbirth education curriculum or expansion of the childbirth education program to include other types of classes. Differentiating between routine and nonroutine decisions is important so that the appropriate amount of time and energy can be devoted to those decisions (nonroutine) that require the greatest amount of judgment and creativity. Childbirth educators who focus primarily on routine decisions will find that they neglect long-range planning, development of strategies, and often handling of problems until they become crises. The outcome of this behavior for the childbirth educator can be devastating.

The Decision-Making Process

Decision-making is an integral part of all of the activities of the childbirth educator. Many decisions can be made easily with what appears to be minimal thought because they are common occurrences (routine decisions). Other more complex decisions require much thought, and the childbirth educator will benefit from using a decision-making model

TABLE 2–1. COMPARATIVE SUMMARY OF AUTHORITARIAN, DEMOCRATIC, AND PERMISSIVE STYLES OF LEADERSHIP

AUTHORITARIAN	DEMOCRATIC	PERMISSIVE
Conservative	Participative	Ultraliberal
Organizational goals	Group goals	Individual goals
Defensive	Open	Open
Restrictive	Facilitating	Permissive
Coercive, pressure	Freeing	Abdicating
Discouraging	Encouraging	Frustration, conflict
Rejecting	Accepting	Accepting and rejecting
Sameness	Variety	Differences
Inequality	Equality	Equality
Fearing	Trusting	Indifferent
Constant surveillance	Available supervision	Supervision as requested
Force	Encouragement, assistance	Self-direction
Obedience	Freedom of choice	Freedom of choice
Competition	Cooperation, group loyalty	Limited group alliance
Exploitation	Opportunity	Uncontrolled
Threat	Challenge	Permissive
Praise	Recognition	Acceptance
Punishment	Self-discipline	Self-gratification
Reward	Satisfaction	Acceptance

From Douglass, L. *The Effective Nurse: Leader and Manager,* 2nd ed. St. Louis: C. V. Mosby, 1984, p. 22.

to get a clearer picture of the available choices and to improve her performance as a decision-maker.

The decision-making process includes six functions: setting objectives, searching for alternatives, evaluating and comparing alternatives, making a choice (selecting an alternative), implementing the decision, and evaluation. The decision-making process also involves three components: taking corrective action if needed to ensure implementation of the choice, continuing search for alternatives, and revision of objectives on the basis of outcomes of the process.[17]

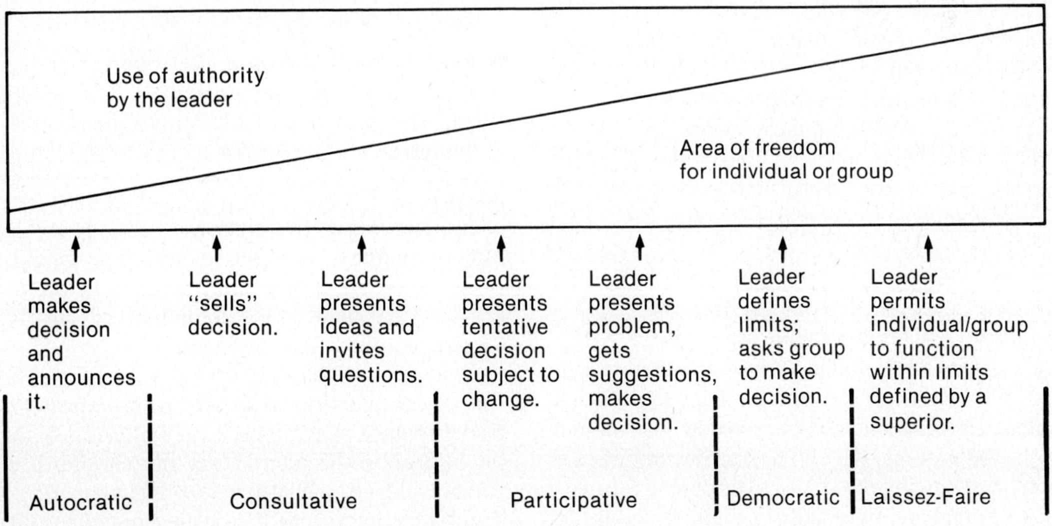

FIGURE 2–1. Continuum of leader decision-making authority. (Adapted from Tannenbaum, R. and Schmidt, W. How to choose a leadership pattern. *Harvard Business Review* 51:162, May/June 1973.)

Setting Objectives. The first step in the decision-making process is to set objectives for the desired outcome. They should be specific and have measurable results and a deadline for completion. The success of the childbirth educator's decision will be measured by the degree to which the objectives are met.

Searching for Alternatives. A search for alternatives is organized and may include a review of the literature on the subject, talking with colleagues or consultants about the problem, reviewing resources in the community or agency, or contacting professional organizations such as American Society for Psychoprophylaxis in Obstetrics (ASPO/Lamaze), International Childbirth Education Association (ICEA), or Nurses Association of the American College of Obstetricians and Gynecologists (NAACOG) for position papers, standards, or other information on the subject. The initial information can usually be acquired with a moderate amount of effort. Thereafter, the cost of time and energy increases when it is compared with the amount of additional information that is obtained. When the cost of getting additional data outweighs the value of the information obtained, the childbirth educator should stop looking for additional information and focus on the list of alternatives that have been developed. It is a fact of life that one will never have all the information needed or wanted on which to make a decision—one has to make the best decision using the information that has been gathered.

Evaluating and Comparing Alternatives. At this point the childbirth educator compares all the possible alternatives, weighs their potential effectiveness, and chooses three or four that have the greatest potential for meeting the objective. This selection process involves the skills of judgment, analysis, and sometimes compromise with other individuals concerned about the outcome.

Making a Choice—Choosing Among Alternatives. This step is often viewed as the most difficult and significant part of the decision-making process. However, it is best viewed as just another step in the process; the childbirth educator should focus on reviewing the alternatives objectively. Alternatives that are marginally acceptable should be discarded first. The remaining alternatives should be scrutinized in terms of information to support potential general effectiveness and cost-effectiveness. Jones[7] identified five difficulties that decision-makers may encounter when selecting among alternatives and suggests actions that can be taken:

- *Two or more alternatives appear equal.* If this happens, the choice does not make a difference. The childbirth educator can use a toss of a coin or put two slips of paper with an alternative written on each in a hat and draw one out. While certainly not scientific, this still is an appropriate way of making a decision when alternatives appear equal and saves time and energy because energies can be directed toward the next step.

- *No one alternative appears to have the potential to meet the objective.* In this situation, the childbirth educator may have to use a combination of two or three alternatives in order to meet the objective.

- *The undesirable consequences of any of the choices is overwhelming.* In this situation, an individual can easily become immobilized. The childbirth educator may find that a revision of the objective is necessary or perhaps a renewed search for other alternatives should be started.

- *The overabundance of alternatives is confusing.* The choice can be limited by putting similar alternatives together and considering them as a group in terms of potential effectiveness.

- *None of the objectives appears to have potential for accomplishing the objectives.* The childbirth educator will have to continue the search for additional alternatives or consider modifying the objective.

Implementing the Decision. This is the most time-consuming step and requires a commitment to action. After careful consideration of the time, cost, and acceptance by other individuals involved, the alternative is implemented.

Evaluation. The outcome of a decision is a result of the function of the decision's quality and its acceptance at the time it is implemented. After implementing the alternative, the childbirth educator evaluates the alternative by comparing the actual outcomes with the desired outcomes. If an outcome is not satisfactory, the decision-making process starts anew.

Personal Values and Decision-Making

The values and personality of the childbirth educator significantly influence the entire decision-making process. The unwillingness to act and to take risks, the inability to remain objective, the inability to tolerate frustration when searching for alternatives and high expectations of perfectionism all negatively influence the decision-making process and make the process of choosing alternatives more complex than it really is. The amount of available information, time, and money also are factors that influence the decision-making process. However, if decision-making is approached objectively using the decision-making model that has been described, the outcomes of the decision process should be more productive and satisfactory for the childbirth educator.

Change Agent

A change agent is "a person or group who initiates changes or assists others in making modifications in themselves or the system."[8] The change agent generates ideas, introduces the innovation, develops a climate for planned change by overcoming resistance, marshals forces for acceptance, and implements and evaluates change.[9] As a change agent the childbirth educator works with clients and maternity care agencies to identify areas that need change and to facilitate desired changes that will improve maternity health care services for the family.

There are two types of change agents: formal change agents and informal change agents. A formal change agent has a designated role and position within the system and has the specific authority to plan and initiate change. The informal change agent generally does not have formal authority within the system, but the individual's opinion is respected by members of the system. An informal change agent must use persuasion and informal sanction from the group or individual targeted for change. Understanding the process of change can provide the childbirth educator with an important tool for planning and implementing significant innovations in maternity health care services.

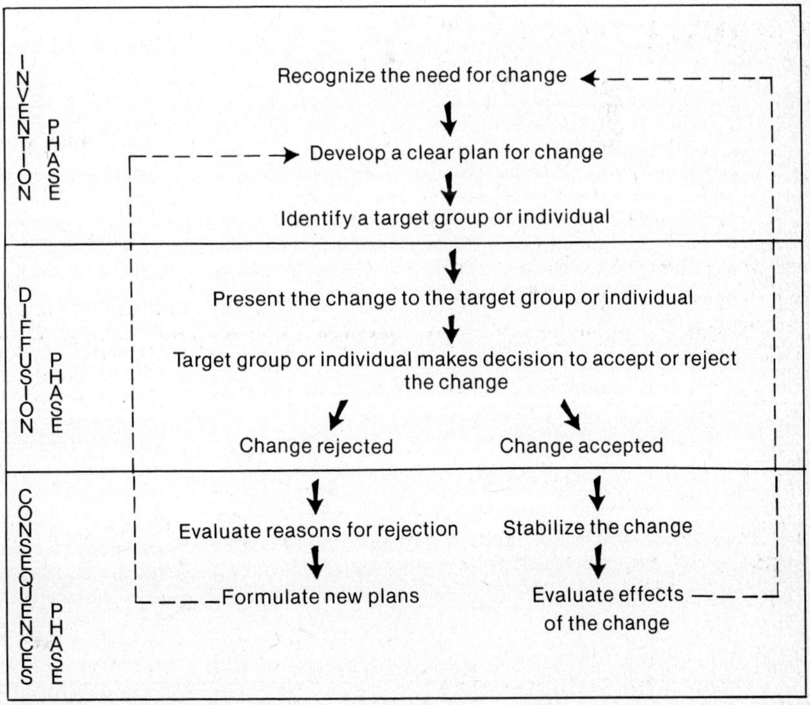

FIGURE 2–2. The process of planned change.

To modify a system and improve its functioning, the process of planned change, a deliberate process, is used. This process consists of three phases:

- *Invention:* the creation or development of new ideas.
- *Diffusion:* the communication of new ideas to a member of a system.
- *Consequences:* the changes within a system that happen as a result of the adoption or rejection of the innovation.[14]

The six critical steps in planned change process are shown in Figure 2–2.[8] They are recognizing the needs for change, developing a clear plan for change, identifying a target group or individual, presenting the change to the target group or individual, target group or individual making decision to accept or reject the change, and evaluating the effects of the change.

Steps in Planned Change Process

Recognizing the Need for Change. After the childbirth educator has identified and analyzed the need for change, the target individual or group must be helped to recognize this need for change. The childbirth educator persuades the group or individual of the necessity for and nature of the needed change. Some persuasion principles that have been shown to be effective in convincing individuals and groups of needed changes are shown in Table 2–2. Understanding the psychological principles of influencing people and using them in an ethical and professional manner during the process of planned change will enable the childbirth educator to more easily achieve the stated objective.

Developing a Clear Plan for Change. The childbirth educator develops a specific plan for initiating the change and enlists the cooperation of the target individual or group. Usually, the target group or individual will be more receptive to the change if they assist with the development of the plan.

Identifying a Target Group or Individual. Next, the childbirth educator identifies an opinion leader (an individual to whom other individuals within the group look for advice and information) and convinces the opinion leader of the need for and value of the planned change, and enlists his or her support in implementing change.

Presenting the Change to the Target Group or Individual. The method chosen for introducing change to the target individual or group will

TABLE 2–2. THE PRINCIPLES OF PERSUASION

Consistency. After committing themselves to a position, even in some trivial way, people are more likely to agree to perform behaviors consistent with that position. When people decide to comply with a request, they check to see if they have already done something that is consistent with the request. For example, in one Cancer Society charity drive it was found that homeowners who had previously gone on record as supporting the Cancer Society (by accepting and wearing a small lapel pin for a day) were nearly twice as likely as usual to give a monetary donation a week later when the charity drive began. It is important to recognize, however, that not all small, initial commitments are equally good at producing consistent future behavior. They are most effective in this regard when they are active, public, and not coerced.

Reciprocity. One question people ask themselves before agreeing to another's request is, "Do I owe this person something?" If the answer is yes, they frequently comply, often when they would have otherwise declined and even when what they agree to do is larger than what they received earlier.

Social Validation. People are more influenced to perform an action or hold a belief when they see that others are doing so. An important piece of evidence people look for in deciding what is appropriate conduct for themselves in a situation is how others are acting. It is for this reason that advertisers love to include the words "fastest growing" or "largest selling" in their product descriptions. They don't have to say directly that the product is good; they only need say that others think so, which seems proof enough.

Authority. People are more willing to follow the suggestions of someone they perceive to be a legitimate authority in terms of knowledge and trustworthiness. Demonstrating knowledge can usually be accomplished by showing evidence of superior experience, training, skill, or information. Establishing trustworthiness is trickier. One device, in pitching a story to an editor, for example, is to back off from this week's pitch but promise real newsworthiness with the following week's item, that is, not be an always positive representative. To wit: "I know this item isn't exactly what you want, but wait until you see what we will have next week!"

Scarcity. People try to seize those items and opportunities that are scarce or dwindling in availability. This accounts for the success of the "deadline," "limited number," and "can't-come-back-later" sales tactics. Research indicates that people want a scarce item more than ever when they are in competition with others for it, or when they believe they have an exclusive.

—R.C.

From Cialdini, R. Persuasion Principles. *Public Relations Journal* 41:12, October 1985.

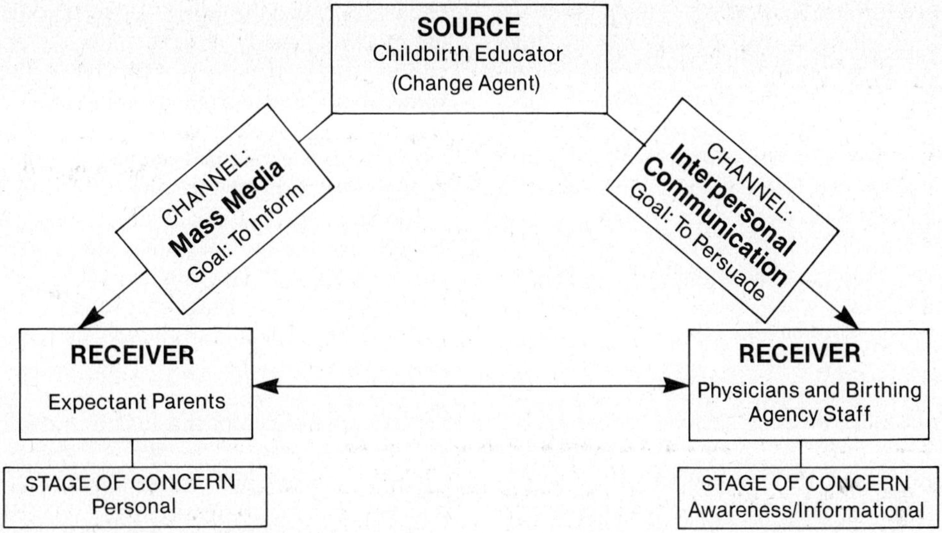

FIGURE 2–3. Communication channels should be selected based on the interest of the listener.

vary depending on the specific situation. The channel for introducing change will depend on an individual's interest in the topic (see Fig. 2–3). If the target audience has a *personal* interest, an informational approach is appropriate. If the target audience has little interest and personal concern, a persuasion approach must be used.[14] In some situations, such as a presentation to physicians, hospital administrators, or maternal-child nursing managers, an audiovisual presentation may be the most effective method to convey your message. You can present data to support the need for change and the benefits to the individual and organization in an orderly and persuasive manner and then have a discussion period at the end of the presentation. In other situations, such as working with a small group (a few of the staff nurses in the birth unit) or talking with an individual, a more informal presentation is the most appropriate. You can furnish them with a "fact sheet" in which the main points you want to make are listed along with references that support them. Change is never easy and the childbirth educator should anticipate common responses to change and plan for them accordingly (Table 2–3).

There are five types of strategies for introducing change: confrontation, prescriptive, acceptant, catalytic, and the theory-principles approach. The *confrontation* strategy involves creating an atmosphere of tension and forcing the target group or individual to consider change. This approach is

TABLE 2–3. FACTORS TO BE CONSIDERED DURING CHANGE

1. There is an almost universal tendency to seek to maintain the status quo on the part of those whose needs are being met by it.
2. Resistance to change increases in proportion to the degree to which it is perceived as a threat.
3. Resistance to change increases in response to direct pressure for change.
4. Resistance to change decreases when it is perceived as being favored by trusted others such as highly prestigious figures whose judgment is respected and people of like mind.
5. Resistance to change decreases when those involved are able to foresee how they may establish a new equilibrium as good as, or better than, the old.
6. Commitment to change increases when those involved have the opportunity to participate in the decision to make the change and in its implementation.
7. Temporary alterations in most situations can be accomplished by the use of direct pressures, but these changes are accompanied by heightened tension in the total situation and therefore yield a highly unstable situation in which major changes may occur suddenly and often unpredictably.

From Gawlinski, A. and Rasmussen, S. Improving documentation through the use of change theory. *Focus on Critical Care* 11:12, 1984.

often uncomfortable for both the change agent and the target group or individual, and in most situations will not be the strategy that childbirth educators will want to choose in introducing change. The *prescriptive* approach requires formal power within an organization or setting. While it is tolerated better by the target group or individual, it is often ineffective because the change target was not actively involved in the invention phase of the change process. Unless the childbirth educator has some formal power within the organization or community, the prescriptive approach is not an appropriate choice. Even if it is a possible choice, the childbirth educator needs to weigh carefully the benefits and risks of using such an approach. For example, it is quite possible to ''win the battle'' (the approval and implementation of a birthing room) but to ''lose the war'' (the birthing room is rarely used because physicians do not want their patients using it).

In the *acceptant* approach the childbirth educator focuses on creating an atmosphere for change to occur and in the *catalytic* approach the childbirth educator helps members of the target group in collecting information and clarifying their perceptions of the problem, and then voices the legitimate need for change. The last two are generally the most appropriate strategies for the childbirth educator to use in introducing change to an individual, group, or within the community.

The *theory-principles* approach consists of educational activities aimed at assisting clients to gain knowledge of existing theory and principles about a specific area (for example, scientific information about the benefits of a physiological approach to childbirth). Childbirth educators are using this approach when they present in-service education programs in birthing agencies. Change that occurs using this approach depends on clients gaining insight into the problem and internalizing and using the theory-principles to guide their practice.

Target Group or Individual Makes Decision to Accept or Reject the Change as Implemented. The decision of the target group or individual to accept the change depends on a variety of factors. First, it will depend on how well the change has been implemented in the particular setting. Second, it will depend to a great extent on the interactions among members of the group, the opinion leader of the group, and the change agent. Individuals and groups who readily accept change have specific characteristics; they have a greater ability to deal with the total picture (more abstract thinkers), they are less autocratic, more logical, and more analytical, they are risk takers, and have positive attitudes toward the change and education.[8]

If the target individual or group *accepts* the change, the change agent then takes steps to *stabilize the change*. This can be done by reinforcing the benefits of the change and making the change more visible. The childbirth educator then moves on to the evaluating step of the planned change process. If the target individual or group *rejects* the change, the childbirth educator goes directly to the *evaluating step* of the planned change process and examines possible reasons why the change was rejected.

Evaluating the Effects of the Change. The outcomes of planned change can either be positive or negative. Careful planning prior to the introduction of change will decrease negative consequences; the potential advantages and disadvantages of planned change should be predicted and considered when selecting a change alternative. The short-term and long-term consequences of change should be examined carefully and recommendations for future actions developed. If the change has been rejected, the change agent returns to the second step of the planned change process—that is, develop a clear plan for change—and starts anew. If the change has been accepted, the change agent can focus on refinement of the existing change or move on to another area in which change is needed (return to step 1 of the planned change process).

Planned Change and Leadership. Kemp[8] emphasizes that leadership is an essential element in every step of the planned change process. The change agent needs effective leadership skills in order to successfully implement planned change. It is also of interest that change agents who are ''people-oriented'' tend to be more successful than change agents who are ''agency-oriented.'' The reasons why ''people-oriented'' change agents are more effective are because they tend to elicit feedback from others about the change, have excellent rapport with the target individual or group, have high credibility with the target individual or group, and usually base the planned change on people's needs.

In the role of change agent, childbirth educators will be more effective and see successful outcomes for their efforts to introduce change if they structure their efforts using the planned change process. If they are "people-centered" and focus on the needs of the childbearing family, they can increase the success of their planned-change activities even further. Childbirth educators will need to assess what type of strategy they usually use to introduce change and determine whether it is the most effective approach to take. Childbirth educators will usually find that they are most effective when using the acceptant and catalytic strategies for introducing change. With these strategies they work with individuals and groups within the health care system to achieve the desired goal. Use of the confrontation or prescriptive approaches which involves telling or attempting to force individuals or groups in the health care system to use particular strategies to achieve one's desired goal is rarely effective.

Consumer Advocate

Advocacy is the "act of informing and supporting a person so that he can make the best decisions possible for himself."[9] Consumer advocacy is an important role of the childbirth educator; clients are encouraged to participate in decisions involving their well-being and that of their unborn child. In this role childbirth educators accept the obligation to keep the clients first in priority at all times. However, the greatest challenge that the childbirth educator faces today is how to be an advocate for expectant couples without being an adversary of other members of the maternity health care team, especially physicians.

In the advocacy role, collaborative relationships with clients and other health care professionals are essential. There are four behaviors that are components of the advocacy roles: mutuality, facilitation, protection, and coordination.[9]

Mutuality. The most important principle of mutuality is that the childbirth educator and expectant parents are equal and responsible for outcomes. While the childbirth educator has expertise in pregnancy, childbirth, and parenting, clients have expertise in understanding and evaluating their situation and in choosing what is best for themselves. The childbirth educator and client together explore the particular situation and desired goals and examine alternative decisions. However, decisions related to the childbearing period are made by clients and the role of the childbirth educator is to support clients in their decisions. In this stage, the childbirth educator provides expectant parents with *technical and informational supports and assists them in gaining information and access to desired maternity care services.*

Facilitation. In the role of advocate, the childbirth educator serves as a facilitator. Expectant parents are viewed as having strengths and the role of the childbirth educator is to help them function at their best. This is best accomplished by assisting expectant parents to understand certain tasks such as relaxation or the process of birth, ensuring success during the learning process, providing an environment of trust and respect that is conducive to learning, and offering information and emotional support.

Protection. A responsibility of a consumer advocate is the protection of clients' rights. The primary role of the childbirth educator is "to provide consumers with the necessary skills and information to secure and defend for themselves their rights in health care."[6] In addition, the childbirth educator monitors the quality of maternity care services and attempts to resolve situations in which conflicts exist between the rights of expectant parents and policies and procedures of health care agencies. The childbirth educator does not act as an adversary to other health care professionals but rather works with other health care professionals to bring about needed changes that will improve maternal health care of expectant parents.

Coordination. The most common role of the consumer advocate is that of coordination. The childbirth educator works with expectant parents, physicians, and maternity care staff and often coordinates the various needs and expectations of each individual.

Consumer Advocacy and the Change Agent

Understanding the process of planned change and functioning skillfully as a change agent are essential to function effectively as a consumer ad-

Childbirth educators function in a consumer-advocate role in many ways. This childbirth educator (*left*) appears regularly on a live television talk show to discuss topics related to pregnancy, childbirth, and parenting with the show's cohosts (*center* and *right*). During the show, viewers call in to ask questions about the subject. (Courtesy of Susan Biasella, ACCE, and WEWS-TV5, Cleveland, Ohio.)

vocate. The childbirth educator should use data as a basis for recommending change. Consumer advocacy is far more effective if the childbirth educator works from a position of strength armed with solid facts about the situation rather than opinions and the sincere belief that the changes will improve the quality of health care for expectant parents, and uses a collaborative approach and negotiates to resolve conflicts in order to avoid adversary relationships.

Consultant

A consultant assists individuals to "figure out the nature and elements of problems with which they are confronted and ways of dealing with these problems."[2] In the consultant role, the childbirth educator collaborates with other health professionals in designing educational programs that will improve family health. She also facilitates organizational problem-solving in implementing contemporary maternity care services by offering alternative perspectives on the problem and suggesting alternative approaches to its solution. To function effectively as a consultant, the childbirth educator must have:[2]

- *Process expertise*. In addition to providing sound technical assistance, she must have the ability to analyze organizational attitudes toward change and facilitate the implementation of planned change and resolve conflicts in a sensitive manner.
- *Content expertise*. She must have the ability to provide specific information, advice, and resources on a particular topic requested by an agency.
- *Support skills*. This involves the ability to work effectively with people and also provide support. In this role the childbirth educator functions as an observer, documentor, listener, resource person, counselor, and coordinator. Empowering others through mutual respect and active support is a key characteristic of an accomplished consultant.

In the role of consultant, the childbirth educator functions as a change agent, initiating change, facilitating the change efforts of others, or helping others to respond to changes within the system.

Networking

Networking, the process of developing and using your contacts for information, advice, and moral support as you pursue your career,[12] is a strategy frequently used by consultants. Consultants also use networking to link up clients with other individuals who have faced similar problems or have implemented an innovation successfully. Indeed, networking is vital to the growth and development of all childbirth educators, regardless of their chosen role. A network is an effective strategy for developing a power base within a community or organization (Fig. 2–4). Developing a network is not difficult; however, it does take planning and time to nourish. The first step is to identify your *professional goals*. This will provide a sense of direction and purpose for developing your network. The second step is to identify your existing net-

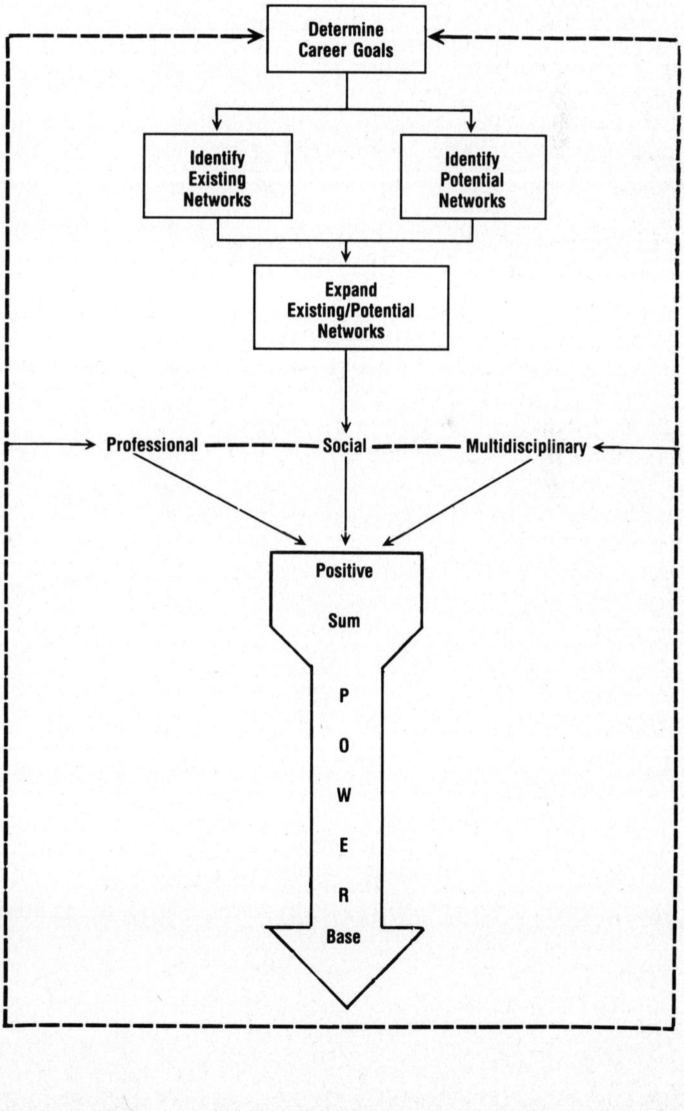

FIGURE 2–4. The nature of a network. A network is an effective way to develop a power base in a community or organization. (From Persons, B. and Weick, L. Networking: A Power Strategy. *Nursing Economics* 3:53, January/February 1985. Reproduced with permission of Anthony J. Jannetti, Inc., publisher, *Nursing Economics*, January/February 1985.)

works and your potential networks. Evaluate these networks in terms of your professional goals. What are their strengths and weaknesses? Where do you need to spend additional time and effort in developing or nourishing your network? The next step is to expand both existing and potential networks. In expanding your network, three groups of colleagues should be included: social and community contacts, professional contacts within childbirth education, and professional contacts outside of childbirth education (such as physicians, nurses, politicians, university professors, and hospital administrators). A broad base of individuals from whom you can gain support and assistance will help you establish a power base that will enable you to be more successful in attaining your professional goals.

Expanding Your Network. Your networking activities should begin in your community and agency. Make a list of those persons in the community or agency who can be helpful to you in achieving your professional goals. Be sure to include all persons who may be helpful to you, not just necessarily those who are accorded status and power within the organization. For example, a physician's office nurse is a key individual in helping you with things such as information, and a secretary in an agency can often help you get a foot in the door or give you some needed information. Also, evaluate your abilities and how you can contribute to the relationship. Persons and Wieck[12] emphasize:

> Know and be known! Hiding your abilities and skills will not gain professional recognition or power. Acknowledging your professional competence can instill the self-confidence necessary to strive for visibility.

Ways to develop and expand your network are shown in Figure 2–5. You can expand your network by demonstrating professional competence; serving on task forces, committees, and agency and community projects; by being an active member

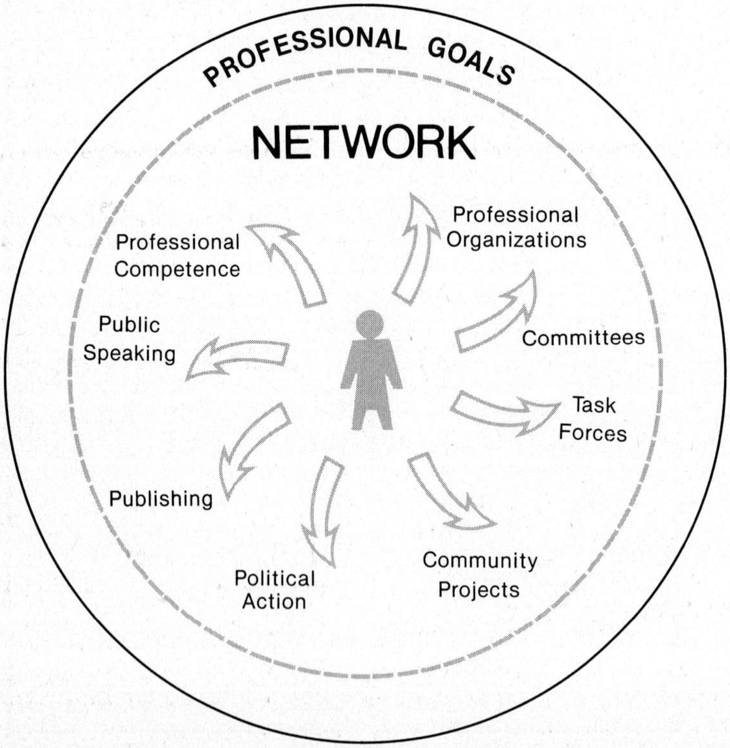

FIGURE 2–5. Ways to develop and expand your network.

of your professional organization (ASPO/Lamaze, ICEA, or NAACOG); and through public speaking, writing for publication, and political action.[12,15]

At periodic intervals, you should assess your networking activities and the status of your network. How effective is your network in your community, state, and nationally? How many new contacts have you made during the past few months? Have you taken enough time to nurture contacts through phone calls, letters, and attending professional or social events? Have you responded to network members regarding their support and suggestions? Again, the power of a network is being a contributing part of the network structure. The rules for a productive network are simple but essential:[10]

- *Keep a Focus*. Keep sight of the reason for your network. If the intent becomes unclear, chances are that network will cease to meet its members' needs.
- *Stay in Touch*. Networks cannot survive without communication. Make it a point to "touch base" with other members every few weeks or months.
- *Keep It Small*. Small, well-focused networks are more successful than large, diffuse ones. You may have several networks which could overlap, but each one is more workable than a giant network.
- *Keep It Simple and Cheap*. The lack of complexity and low cost of a network will increase its strength, endurance, and effectiveness.
- *Reciprocate*. Networking is a *reciprocal* relationship. Both individuals in a networking relationship have the responsibility to share information and provide support. Without reciprocation a network will die.

Entrepreneur

An entrepreneur is an individual who organizes and manages a business. The entrepreneur creates products, such as prepared childbirth classes or sibling classes, for new and existing markets; creates markets for new and existing products, such as pregnancy and postpartum fitness classes; and creates new ways for delivering products and reaching markets, such as starting a maternity wear shop or a health spa where childbirth education classes are also taught.[11]

Many childbirth educators are entrepreneurs. This childbirth educator started her own business. She offers maternity clothing, breastfeeding consultant services, and a variety of educational services for the childbearing family, including prepared childbirth classes and breastfeeding seminars. (Courtesy of Gini Burns, ACCE.)

The entrepreneur is a risk taker, an innovator who expands the horizons of current practices and challenges others to change. One of the skills of an entrepreneur is progressive marketing of programs and the ability to motivate individuals to attend classes[11] (see Chapter 32 for an in-depth discussion of marketing strategies). For the childbirth educator to enact this role successfully the following qualities are needed: vision, ingenuity, the ability to respond to the unique needs of individuals, and the ability to change current practices to meet emerging needs.

Manager

No childbirth educator can escape the role of manager. For the childbirth educator, management is an integral aspect of the entrepreneur role. To implement a childbirth education program, the educator must be a manager of logistics and resources. Successful enactment of the manager role requires the childbirth educator to perform the five traditional managerial functions: planning, organizing, staffing, directing, and controlling.[11] In administering the program, the childbirth educator oversees day-to-day operations, manages budget, personnel, and materials, keeps records, and maintains a system of quality control. The identification of new teaching resource material and the purchase of these materials requires attention and time, as well as management of the learning environment. Teaching childbirth education classes is a business, and the childbirth educator will be more successful if she uses sound business principles in structuring her practice.

IMPLICATIONS FOR RESEARCH

While there is considerable research on the various roles that have been discussed in this chapter, no research was found that has been done looking at childbirth educators. The number of research questions is limitless. As a start, the following questions may be examined:

- What roles do childbirth educators fulfill most effectively?
- What is the best way to help childbirth educators develop expertise in the various roles?

> Unless you try to do something beyond what you have already mastered, you will never grow.
>
> RONALD E. OSBORN[1]
>
> One of the greatest pains to human nature is the pain of a new idea. It . . . makes you think that after all, your favorite notions may be wrong, your firmest beliefs ill-founded . . . Naturally, therefore, common men hate a new idea, and are disposed more or less to ill-treat the original man who brings it.
>
> WALTER BAGEHOT[2]
>
> Man's mind, once stretched by a new idea, never regains its original dimensions.
>
> OLIVER WENDELL HOLMES[1]
>
> To get the bad customs of a country changed and new ones, though better, introduced, it is necessary to first remove the prejudices of the people, enlighten their ignorance, and convince them that their interests will be promoted by the proposed changes; and this is not the work of a day.
>
> BENJAMIN FRANKLIN[2]
>
> No problem can stand the assault of sustained thinking.
>
> VOLTAIRE[1]

SUMMARY

The effective childbirth educator plays many different roles skillfully. She chooses the role that is best for the particular task or situation. Childbirth educators are encouraged to examine each role and develop a broader vision of their potential roles in society. Each role has specific components. Childbirth educators will find that with practice they can develop expertise in each of the roles.

References

1. Bennis, W. The four competencies of leadership. *Training and Development Journal* 38:15, August 1984.
2. Carrillo, R. P., Lumbley, L. J., and Westbrook, J. D. Effective networking: The roles of the consultant. *Consultation* 3:37, Spring 1984.
3. Cialdini, R. Persuasion principles. *Public Relations Journal* 41:12, October 1985.
4. Douglass, L. M. *The Effective Nurse: Leader and Manager.* St. Louis: C. V. Mosby, 1984.
5. Gawlinski, A. and Rasmussen, S. Improving documentation through the use of change theory. *Focus on Critical Care* 11:12, 1984.
6. Hamilton, P. Consumerism and the Childbearing Experience. *NAACOG Update Series,* 5:22, 1987.
7. Jones, M. *Executive Decision Making*. Homewood, IL: Richard D. Irwin, 1962.
8. Kemp, V. H. An overview of change and leadership. *Topics in Clinical Nursing* 6:1, April 1984.
9. Leddy, S. and Pepper, J. M. *Conceptual Bases of Professional Nursing*. Philadelphia: J. B. Lippincott, 1985.
10. McConkey, D. M. and Crandall, D. P. A consultant's network can improve his net work . . . and more! *Consultation* 3:30, Spring 1984.
11. O'Connor, A. B. *Nursing Staff Development and Continuing Education*. Boston: Little, Brown and Company, 1986.
12. Persons, C. B. and Wieck, L. Networking: A power strategy. *Nursing Economics* 3:53, January-February 1985.
13. Rogers, E. M. *Diffusin of Innovations*. New York: The Free Press, 1983.
14. Rogers, E. M. and Shoemaker, F. F. *Communication of Innovations: A Cross Cultural Approach,* 2nd ed. New York: The Free Press, 1971.
15. Sharp, N. The role of the childbirth educator as a political activist. *NAACOG Update Series* 5 (20), 1986.
16. Tannenbaum, R. and Schmidt, W. How to choose a leadership pattern. *Harvard Business Review* 51:162, May/June 1973.
17. Taylor, A. The decision-making process and the nursing administrator. *Nursing Clinics of North America* 18:439 1983.

Beginning Quote

Bartlett, J. *Familiar Quotations*. Boston: Little, Brown and Company, 1968.

Boxed Quotes

1. *Motivational Quotes*. Downers Grove, IL: Graphicenter, Inc., 1984.
2. Rogers, E. M. Diffusion of Innovations. New York: The Free Press, 1983.

Section

2

THE EXPECTANT PARENTS

Pregnancy, childbirth, and early parenting experiences are important milestone events in the lives of those who experience them. Once a pregnancy occurs, the related stressors and support systems that evolve have long-term implications for both individual and family health. A short-term goal of childbirth education is to help families optimize childbearing experiences. Through those same good experiences, the long-term goal is to contribute to the ongoing physical and mental health of families.

Each pregnancy and birth are unique, as are the families having the experiences. Thus there is no standard "cookbook" formula for meeting the needs of expectant parents. There is, however, a wealth of research describing the common needs of childbearing families. A review of the literature on the experiences of pregnancy, childbirth, and early parenting appears in the next three chapters of this book for the purpose of enhancing the childbirth educator's ability to anticipate the probable needs of expectant parents entering classes. Using this information as a guideline, a general plan can be developed for the classes to be followed by a more personalized plan once the actual classes begin.

The authors wish to especially call the reader's attention to the literature describing the meaning of childbearing experiences to individuals and families. It is healthy when parents respond as if their pregnancy or their baby is an extra-special event. Health care providers, including childbirth educators, who work with many expectant parents may inadvertently begin to respond to expectant parents in an assembly line fashion—this negates the parents' important perspective of their pregnancy, birth, and child as special.

It is the hope of the authors that through reading this description of childbearing experiences each reader will be aided in the quest to plan excellent, comprehensive classes. Just as important, the authors hope the reader will keep alive the ability to marvel with each parent at the wonder of it all.

chapter 3

THE PREGNANCY EXPERIENCE

ELAINE SCHROEDER-ZWELLING

A woman does contemplate the outcomes of the childbearing in its meaning to her and to her world. Having a child is perceived not only as an act of acquisition. Becoming a mother is unlike taking a role where self and relationships with others remain constant, unchanged. From onset to destination, childbearing requires an exchange of a known self in a known world for an unknown self in an unknown world.

Reva Rubin

The event of conception, the development of a pregnancy, the process of birth, and the transition to parenthood mark a year of extreme significance for a woman and her partner. For many parents, this childbearing year is perceived to be one of the most important years experienced in their lifetime. The experience of pregnancy often becomes all-consuming, for it can alter and influence all aspects of life. Pregnancy is not only a physical experience but also a holistic experience that influences the psyche, social interaction, and cognitive processes.

Pregnancy affects not only the woman who is directly experiencing it but all those around her. Pregnancy, birth, and the transition to parenthood are major developmental tasks accomplished during the life span, moving the expectant parents from being a dyad to a childrearing family. Health care professionals who have contact with parents during this childbearing year have a unique opportunity to positively shape the nature of the pregnancy experience.

This chapter explores all aspects of the pregnancy experience. What is the impact of the physical changes experienced during pregnancy? How do expectant parents respond emotionally during pregnancy? How does culture influence the pregnancy experience? What are the intellectual needs of expectant parents? And how can the childbirth educator incorporate information on all aspects of the pregnancy experience into her teaching?

REVIEW OF THE LITERATURE

The Physical Experience

The physical changes occurring within the woman's body and the resultant minor discomforts she experiences may be viewed as the most concrete, and perhaps the most observable, changes during pregnancy. Because of these changes, pregnancy is often viewed as primarily a physical experience. The family and friends of the pregnant woman are most likely to inquire about the physical changes and symptoms that she is experiencing. When a pregnant woman is asked how she is feeling, her response is likely to be about the physical manifestations of pregnancy. The topics of discussion most often heard among pregnant women and their friends are symptoms such as morning sickness, fatigue, urinary frequency, backache, stretch marks, or weight gain. The physical changes of pregnancy are those that women most often discuss or question with their physicians and health care providers (Table 3–1).

Numerous medical and nursing textbooks clearly outline the hormonal influences on all systems of the body during pregnancy and discuss the clinical manifestations of these influences.[34,37] From a biological point of view, pregnancy and birth represent the primary function of the female reproductive system and should be considered a normal process.[37] The many changes that occur in maternal physiology during pregnancy are most apparent in the reproductive organs but involve all other body systems as well. Physiological changes and physical symptoms that at any other time would be considered to be abnormal pathology are accepted as normal during pregnancy.

The physiological changes are often rapid in

TABLE 3–1. CHANGES DURING PREGNANCY

Physical	Emotional	Sociocultural	Cognitive
FIRST TRIMESTER			
Fatigue Breast tenderness Urinary frequency Morning sickness ↓ Sexual libido	Ambivalence ↑ Lability Dreams/fantasies Acceptance of pregnancy	Withdrawal from usual interests and relationships Taking on maternal role (i.e. mimicry, role play, fantasy, integration) Health vs. illness behavior	Interest in own physical changes and symptoms, and management of same
SECOND TRIMESTER			
↑ Energy ↑ Skin pigmentation, striae, and linea nigra Quickening ↑ Weight gain ↑ Sexual libido	Ambivalence ↑ Lability Dreams/fantasies Altered body image Fetal embodiment Introversion	Develop new interests and relationships relevant to childbearing Taking on maternal role Health vs. illness behavior	Interest in fetal growth and development
THIRD TRIMESTER			
Fatigue Urinary frequency ↑ Weight gain Backache Leg cramps Ligament pain Shortness of breath Lightening Braxton-Hicks contractions ↓ Sexual libido	↑ Lability Dreams/fantasies Altered body image Preparation to give up fetus Eagerness for birth	Taking on maternal role Health vs illness behavior	Interest in labor and birth Interest in practical aspects of parenting

their onset and change from one trimester to the next. Even though all of the symptoms are considered to be normal, they can cause great anxiety in the woman or her partner.[11] Although many symptoms can be alleviated or will disappear, the discomforts the woman experiences can spoil the pleasure of being pregnant. However, when the baby is happily anticipated, the discomforts tend to be perceived as an irritating imposition, and measures to minimize them usually have some success.[22]

The expectant father may also experience physical symptoms during the pregnancy. Men have reported such symptoms as morning sickness, increased fatigue, increased hunger, and weight gain. The manifestation of these physical symptoms may be related to the couvade phenomenon. The term couvade comes from the French word meaning "to brood" or "to hatch." It most frequently refers today to the physical symptoms experienced by an expectant father during his partner's pregnancy—for example, the symptoms of morning sickness, heartburn, or increased weight gain that some expectant fathers report. In some tribal cultures the couvade phenomenon may even include a ritualistic acting-out of the contractions of labor by the father while his partner is giving birth. The trend in this country toward a more active role of the father during pregnancy and birth may enhance the couvade phenomenon.[1,8,17,33]

Sexuality

Both expectant mothers and fathers are concerned about sexuality during pregnancy. The sexuality that is usually so important to the partners as a means of satisfaction, affirmation, and communication of love between them may become an issue because of the woman's physical changes and the psychological demands on both partners.[14]

During pregnancy, particularly the first trimester, the woman may not feel up to lovemaking because of her physical symptoms. Fatigue or nausea may make intercourse seem to be too much of an effort. As the pregnancy progresses she may worry about the possibility of infection or preterm labor and may experience discomfort during intercourse. Secretion of colostrum from the breasts, the increasingly distended waistline, and marked venous engorgement of the vaginal vault may adversely influence the couple's sexual interest. Both partners may worry about harming the baby during lovemaking. However, some partners also report that lovemaking during pregnancy is enhanced, particularly during the second trimester when the woman is feeling her best physically. Freedom from worry about birth control and joy about the pregnancy are the reasons given for these positive responses.[3,14,48]

Unfortunately, sexuality in pregnancy is often given little attention by health care providers during the antepartal period, and expectant parents are very hesitant to express their concerns. Too often when advice is given it is scant, inconsistent, based on tradition rather than scientific study, and imparted with embarrassment.[14] Solberg and coworkers reported that physicians rarely gave their patients information regarding sexual activities, except advice to abstain.[47] A study by Quirk showed that only 4 per cent of expectant women were advised about sexual intercourse by nurses, and 66 per cent received no information during pregnancy from any health professional.[36] There is also disagreement in the literature regarding what advice should be given.[14] Research does not support the need for a healthy woman to refrain from sexual activity at any time during her pregnancy unless she has a poor obstetrical history of abortions and preterm labors, has ruptured membranes, or is in labor.[47,48] The influence of the physical and psychological changes of pregnancy on sexuality and the role of health care providers are discussed in detail in Chapter 23.

The Emotional Experience

Pregnancy has been called the fulfillment of the deepest and most powerful wish of a woman, an expression of creation and self-realization.[12] Somewhat in contrast, pregnancy has also been identified as a developmental crisis, a critical life period in which psychic conflicts of previous developmental phases may be revived, often enabling new solutions to be found and psychological growth to occur.[2,5,31] *Despite the fact that pregnancy is often viewed as a physical experience, in the literature it is most often defined as a psychological or emotional experience.* There is a certain distinctive quality of inner experience during pregnancy that

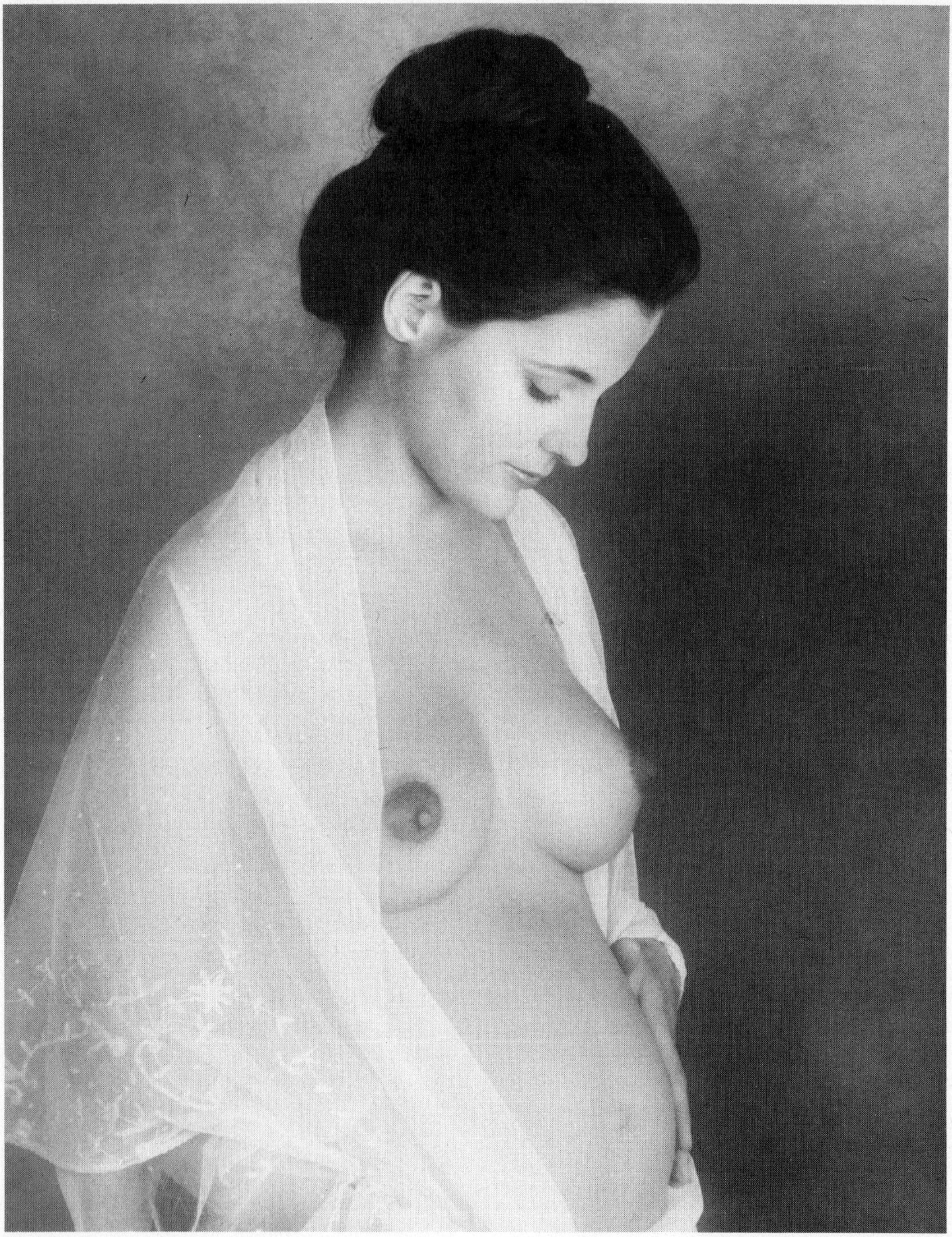

Pregnancy can be fulfillment of the deepest and most powerful wish of a woman, an expression of creation and self-realization. (Photograph by Richard Blinkoff.)

sets it apart from life at any other time (see Table 3–1).

Several authors discuss the emotional lability of the pregnant woman,[8,20,22] which may be manifested by increased sensitivity to routine happenings in her daily life. She may be more quickly disgusted by what seems ugly and cruel and more readily thrilled by beauty and tenderness. She is particularly receptive and may cry more easily in movies, react more strongly to trivial events, and be prone to sudden bouts of anxiety or anger. The pregnant woman's emotional highs and lows will be greater than usual, will come and go more quickly, and will pass through extremes at a pace that may be confusing and distressing to her and her family.[8]

Ambivalence

Ambivalence is another emotional response observed in many pregnant women. They may react with ambivalence to the news that they are pregnant, even if the pregnancy was planned and positively anticipated. Surprise or shock may be the initial reaction, followed by very mixed feelings. Rubin states that most women want a child "someday," but "someday" lies somewhere in the future, not "now." Rubin believes that few women who become pregnant feel ready "now."[41] For one reason or another, at first a woman may feel that now is not the time to have a baby. She or her partner may want to finish school, further a career, or improve their financial situation. Initial rejection of the pregnancy is common, Caplan states, but it is usually replaced by acceptance by the end of the first trimester.[5]

Ambivalence may be expressed occasionally throughout pregnancy as a wish not to be pregnant, and is often associated with speculation about the immensity of the responsibility of parenthood. Brown discusses the ambivalence that both expectant mothers and fathers feel in the third trimester of pregnancy as they face new roles as parents.[4] Women in particular may become concerned about the rigors of juggling career and motherhood. They may have doubts and fears about the ability to deal with labor and birth. Ambivalence is considered normal in the first trimester and may occur intermittently later in pregnancy. Continued and intense ambivalence throughout pregnancy may indicate unresolved conflicts or rejection of the pregnancy.[22]

Maternal Identity

A great deal has been written about alterations that occur in a woman's identity and body image during pregnancy. With each childbearing experience there is an incorporation into a woman's self system of a new personality dimension that Rubin identifies as maternal identity.[43] This psychological incorporation of a maternal identity begins anew and develops independently with each pregnancy experience. At the onset of pregnancy, the woman's interpersonal relationship with family, work, and social interests are likely to be in balance. This balance provides the woman with some sense of her identity. At the completion of pregnancy, the sense of equilibrium and established identity may be greatly altered. Existing relationships are often changed in order for the woman to develop a new relationship with her infant. Thus, pregnancy can be thought of as a period of emotional or psychological adjustment and preparation, enabling the woman to accept a child into her identity and life system. The formation of a maternal identity is extremely important during pregnancy, for it serves to bind the woman to the child she is carrying. Two concepts related to maternal identity are maternal tasks and maternal attachment.

According to Rubin, a woman strives to accomplish two major tasks during pregnancy: conserving the intactness of her own identity and family system while at the same time orchestrating the assimilation and accommodation of the infant into that same self and family system (Table 3–2).[43] Rubin sees these tasks as being accomplished in four ways. First, the woman seeks to ensure a safe passage for her child by collecting data, seeking medical care, reading, or attending childbirth classes. Second, she seeks others' acceptance of the coming child, particularly that of her husband and immediate family. Third, she develops an affiliative awareness of and relationship to the infant. This "binding-in" most often begins after the woman

TABLE 3–2. MATERNAL TASKS OF PREGNANCY

- Ensuring a safe passage for infant
- Seeking acceptance for infant
- Developing a relationship to infant ("binding-in")
- Giving of self

TABLE 3–3. TASKS OF PRENATAL ATTACHMENT

- Planning, confirming, and accepting pregnancy
- Recognizing fetal movement
- Developing an affiliative response to fetus
- Incorporating fetus into body image (''fetal embodiment'')
- Recognizing fetus as separate being
- Preparing to give up fetus
- Birth

has experienced quickening. The final task is that of giving of one's self. This is viewed as the most intricate and complex task of pregnancy, for the progressive physical, emotional, and social demands and deprivations of pregnancy are not easily endured with self-sacrifice unless the woman can readily identify a purpose for them.

The other aspect of maternal identity discussed in the literature is attachment to the infant. The attachment process begins long before the infant is born. Several authors agree that the woman must complete a series of adaptive tasks in order to be able to effectively assume her mothering relationship with her infant (Table 3–3). These tasks are identified as planning, confirming, and accepting the pregnancy; recognizing fetal movement; developing an affiliative response to the fetus; incorporating the fetus into the body image; separating the self from the fetus and recognizing it as a separate being; preparing to give up the fetus; and birth and assigning a reality-based identity to the neonate after birth through the process of caretaking.[5,7,8,21]

This prenatal attachment process can often be observed. A pregnant woman frequently interacts with her baby in utero through such activities as rubbing her abdomen to quiet a kicking fetus, touching or stroking fetal parts, talking or singing to the fetus, selecting pet names, or offering the fetus food when she eats.[6,22,23] Carter-Jessop has demonstrated that maternal prenatal attachment can be promoted through a planned intervention that encourages a women to daily feel for the fetal parts and position, to increase her awareness of fetal activity and how she can affect that activity, and to rub, stroke, and massage her abdomen over the fetus.[6]

Body Image Changes

A woman's body image, which is a component of her identity, is also altered during pregnancy.

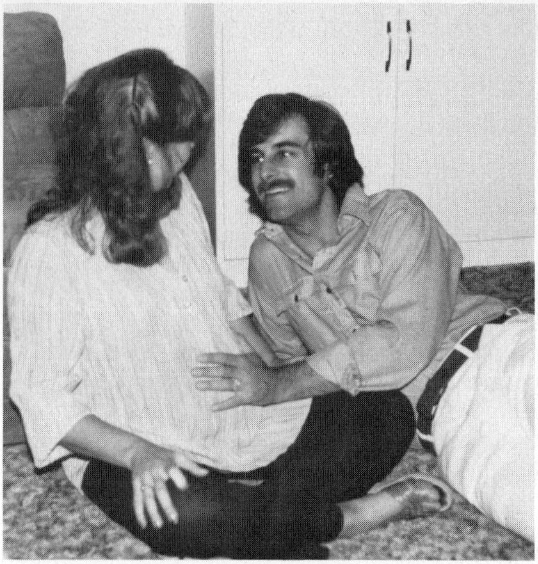

A woman's feelings about her altered physical state during pregnancy may be positive or negative and are influenced by many factors such as the reactions of significant others and society, age, developmental stage, and perceptions of physical changes. (Photo by Marjorie Pyle,© Lifecircle, Costa Mesa, CA.)

Whether the change in her mental picture of her body's appearance is positive or negative depends on the influence of such factors as age, developmental stage, perception of physiological changes, and the reactions of significant others and society. Body image during pregnancy is also influenced by a growth in size, a change in the woman's perception of her body's boundaries, changes in posture and movement, and the experience of physical discomforts or pain.[43] If a pregnant woman views her changing body as useful by bringing a wanted child into the world, she is likely to have a positive body image. If, on the other hand, she sees her body as being big, awkward, and in the way of her normal activities, her body image will be negative.[30] Although pregnancy is often viewed as the ultimate in femininity and although the pregnant woman may be happy that her body is functionally capable of bearing a child, her body image may not mirror these positive attitudes.

Unfortunately, the body image of many pregnant women is not good and it becomes progressively worse as the pregnancy advances. Pregnant women often describe themselves with such negative terms as "blimp, whale, watermelon, barn, or elephant."[8,22] This negative self-image is very likely a cultural response in a country where slimness is idealized. By the media's standards of ideal, the pregnant woman is overweight and has curves in many of the wrong places, and usually can't fit into the latest fashions. The expectant mother is also likely to react more strongly to her view of her body than is the nonpregnant woman[30] because of the influence of pregnancy on her emotional balance.

Fantasy Life

Colman and Colman's view of pregnancy as an altered state of consciousness supports another emotional aspect of pregnancy: dreams or fantasies.[8] Clinicians and researchers have been aware for some time that women may experience disturbing fantasies during pregnancy. Rubin describes changes in fantasy patterns that occur throughout the three trimesters of pregnancy and often cause anxiety.[43] Sherwin categorized the dreams experienced by pregnant women and found them to be either associated with positive emotions such as pleasure, joy, and peace, or negative states of guilt, fear, and panic.[45] The most common areas of dreams and fantasies were about having an abnormal infant, being attacked, being enclosed or drowning, forgetting or losing things, being unprepared, sexual encounters, and restoring or resolving old crises. Colman and Colman point out that many dreams occurring during pregnancy have highly positive themes, such as anticipation, joy at the fullness of life, the love of a man, unity with a world alive with growing things, or playing with a grown child.[8]

Fathers' Emotions

Pregnancy is an emotional experience for fathers also. Ambivalence is common as men attempt to balance the joy of impending fatherhood with the concerns of financial adjustments and increasing responsibility. Sexual issues may arise for men as well as women during pregnancy. Changes in his partner's appearance and sexual responsiveness may influence a man's sexual reactions. He may dream about changes in his own body, or about becoming pregnant himself. He may feel intense envy and jealousy. The expectant father may experience a new sense of tenderness and protectiveness toward his partner as the pregnancy nears completion, and begin to anticipate the birth of the child. Most expectant fathers do not imagine the baby as a newborn but see themselves walking with their two-year-old or playing ball with a teenager.[1,8,17]

Research by May suggests that there is a pattern of emotional development during pregnancy in first-time fathers.[26] This pattern consists of three phases. The first is the "announcement phase," a time when the male first discovers the pregnancy and begins to adjust to it. The second phase, "the moratorium," is the phase when fathers may put aside conscious thought about the pregnancy. This phase usually corresponds to the period when the man cannot see much evidence of the pregnancy. The third phase, the "focusing phase," begins as the father identifies the pregnancy as real and important in his life. Communication between the expectant mother and father during pregnancy is essential in helping them bridge the gap between their concurrent emotional response to the major changes that pregnancy imposes on their relationship.

The Sociocultural Experience

Pregnancy is just as much a sociocultural experience as it is a physical and emotional experience. The expectant parents' responses and behaviors during pregnancy and childbirth and the development of their parental roles are all shaped by the society in which they live (see Table 3–1). Jordan compared pregnancy and childbirth in four different cultures and concludes that these events include not only medical-physiological aspects but also social-ecological factors which make the childbearing year a biosocial event.[18]

A woman's behavior (her response to the physical and emotional manifestations of her pregnancy) is greatly influenced by sociocultural factors. Whether she responds to her pregnancy with "health" behavior or "illness" behavior depends on the way in which pregnancy and childbirth are viewed within her culture. Health behavior is likely to occur if the woman and her social system view pregnancy as a normal, positive experience. The primary role assumed in health behavior is the "at-risk" role and includes behavior directed at maintaining health or preventing illness.[49] During pregnancy, the at-risk role would include such health behaviors as seeing a physician or nurse-midwife at regular intervals for assessment, following a nutritious diet, exercising regularly, and getting sufficient rest. The physiological changes and minor discomforts of pregnancy would be viewed as occasionally bothersome but not incapacitating.

On the other hand, a woman's social system might influence her to respond to her pregnancy with illness behavior. This response is likely to occur if the woman or those around her view pregnancy as a deviation from health or if the pregnancy, for some reason, is not viewed positively. Minor discomforts are more likely to be viewed as major deviations, and as incapacitating. The primary role assumed in illness behavior is that of the sick role.[34] There are ''privileges'' of the sick role that include exemption from normal role responsibilities, exemption from responsibility for one's health, and the need to be dependent and cared for. A number of individual and cultural variables can influence the adoption of health or illness behavior during pregnancy. The socioeconomic status of the woman and her family, the woman's age, her female sexual orientation, her educational preparation for pregnancy and birth, the influences of family and friends, her relationship with her physician or midwife, and the attitudes of individuals within her maternity care system will all shape the way she responds to her pregnancy.

Whether she responds to pregnancy with health or illness behavior, development of the maternal role occurs in all women. It can be viewed from a psychological perspective as a component of identity formation during pregnancy and as a social process. Early in pregnancy a woman begins to develop a sense of being different and unique. If this feeling produces a gradual sense of alienation from her usual interests, relationships, and activities, she may begin to withdraw. Midway through her pregnancy, she begins to develop new interests and relationships that are relevant only to pregnancy and childbearing. The pregnant woman is often drawn to the company of other women and may develop a concern with the past and with her relationship with her own mother.[8,41]

There is contradiction in the literature over whether pregnancy and the transition to parenthood constitute a crisis situation for a family.[13,16,24,44] Certainly the changes precipitated by alterations in family structure and roles during pregnancy and early parenthood are a stressful developmental event. Whether or not this normal developmental task becomes a crisis depends upon expectant parents' resources and their perception or interpretation of the event. The age of the woman will also influence her response to the pregnancy.[17,29]

The characteristics of the parents' social network and the social support they receive have been shown to influence adjustment outcomes. The literature identifies the size, composition, and cohesion of social networks as important factors. A study by Cronenwett found that the mean social network size for expectant parents was 8.5 people, composed primarily of relatives.[10] Of three types of social support—emotional, cognitive, and general socializing—emotional support was found to be the best predictor of satisfaction with the parenting role and infant care for both mothers and fathers. Crawford found that network size may be negatively related to maternal role attainment.[9] As the size of social support networks increases, the possibility that advice from various support people will be incongruent and lead to conflict also increases. Chapter 22 contains a comprehensive discussion of social support during childbearing.

Maternal Role Acquisition

Rubin studied the socialization process by which the maternal role is acquired and identified several distinct components of this process.[39,43] The first is mimicry or replication. The pregnant woman copies and adapts behaviors and practices of other women in the same situation. For example, the wearing of maternity clothes, the adopting of certain gestures or postures during pregnancy, or the use of particular speech patterns (high-pitched voice, pet names, babytalk) toward the infant may all be copied because the woman sees them as symbols of the status of motherhood that she desires to obtain. A woman's own mother and her female peers are the most common models for the development of maternal behavior.[40]

Another component of the socialization process is role play. Role play is somewhat similar to mimicry but differs in that it goes beyond symbolic behaviors into an actual acting out of a role. Pregnant women often search for situations or subjects that allow them to role-play mothering. Requesting to feed a neighbor's infant his bottle, playing with a toddler in the park, or offering to babysit for a friend's children all allow the expectant woman to "try on" the role of mother. Her past experiences will shape her role play. If she has been well nurtured, then she has a good role model on which to build her own motherhood identity.

Rubin[39,43] and Lederman[22] both discuss fantasy as a major component in the development of the maternal role. The woman begins to image how it will be with her child. These fantasies may occur during the day while the woman is awake or in her dreams at night. She may envision herself as a mother, think about those characteristics she wishes to have as a mother, and anticipate changes in her life that will be necessary when assuming the mothering role. Part of this fantasy also deals with the grief of letting go of former identities and roles that are incompatible with the new role of mother.

Resolution of role conflicts and "dedifferentiation," that is, the examining and evaluating of the "goodness of fit" of the new maternal role, are the final steps in this developmental process.[43] At this stage the woman is beyond copying behavior or trying on and imagining roles and is ready to integrate all the components of the mothering role that she values. She is able to make decisions and act independently on the basis of the knowledge and self-confidence she has gained as a result of earlier steps in the role acquisition process. Her mothering role becomes a compromise between her own personality and identity and the influences of the society in which she carries out that role.

The Cognitive Experience

The literature contains very little about the intellectual component of pregnancy, probably because cognition is so intertwined with the emotional or psychological nature of pregnancy. However, the number of books about pregnancy and childbirth available in bookstores today, and the tremendous growth in the demand for childbirth education classes, support the notion that pregnancy is a cognitive as well as an emotional experience (see Table 3–1).

The fact that pregnancy has an intellectual component is evidenced by many couples' desire to understand all that is happening to them during this important period in their lives. This desire is very clearly illustrated in Marjorie Karmel's classic story about her transformation from a woman who wanted to know as little as possible about her pregnancy and forthcoming birth to one with a voracious appetite for information.[19] For many women and men, the need to talk with others, to ask questions, and to obtain knowledge is strong. Studies of pregnant women have shown that they are far more open and receptive to learning new information than individuals who are in a nonpregnant state.[8] Pregnant women's willingness to talk personally about their experiences is an expression of the universal need to explain the unknown.

Whether questions are answered and whether knowledge is obtained from within the family system, from reading, from health care providers, or from childbirth classes depends on the individual characteristics and resources of each expectant mother and father. Expectant parents today seek knowledge in order to decrease their fears and anxieties and to achieve a sense of control about what will be happening to them during pregnancy and birth. More and more women are becoming assertive about their desires for knowledge. The literature suggests that the childbirth educator's role should also include facilitating assertiveness to help expectant parents communicate with their physician or other health care providers.[28] When combined with good listening skills, assertive behavior can encourage a positive relationship between the expectant woman and her physician or midwife. This can lead to better health care based on decisions that have been made in a collaborative manner.

There is some controversy in the literature about the actual availability of options in our maternity care system today and whether parents really are able to make choices.[28,32,38] However, it is generally agreed that expectant parents have a need and a right to be informed about options. They need to have an opportunity to consider and discuss their choices so that they can make responsible decisions about their pregnancy and birth experiences.

IMPLICATIONS FOR PRACTICE

A thorough understanding of the physical, emotional, sociocultural, and intellectual aspects of pregnancy is an essential first step for a childbirth educator. A knowledge of the general characteristics of pregnant clients and their partners will guide the childbirth educator in the developing of course objectives, content, and teaching methods. This foundation will need to be continually expanded by reading current literature and research and regularly observing expectant parents. The childbirth educator should address all four aspects of the pregnancy experience—physical, emotional, sociocultural and cognitive—in a childbirth education course.

Meeting Physical Needs

Since the physical nature of pregnancy is often a major focus for expectant parents, a large proportion of a childbirth course should deal with physical issues. It is ideal if the childbirth educator can offer an early pregnancy course to deal with early pregnancy issues as well as a later course for preparation for birth and parenthood. Much of the information about the physical nature of pregnancy is more meaningful if presented in the first or second trimesters when expectant parents are beginning to experience physical changes. More time also can be devoted to these issues in an early pregnancy course. If an early course is not possible, however, this information can and must be presented succinctly in a later pregnancy course.

By using creative teaching methods in early class sessions, the educator can assess which physical changes and discomforts are of concern to expectant parents. This might be done in the first class by using an introduction strategy, in which each class member is asked to share one "good" thing and one "bothersome" thing about this pregnancy. Very often the "negative" aspects expectant parents identify are the physical changes or symptoms of pregnancy. The childbirth educator can then respond with factual information about the physical concerns that are shared. This strategy also allows expectant parents to recognize that they are not the only ones experiencing bothersome physical discomforts. This reinforces the fact that physical changes are "normal," and their anxiety often decreases.

The childbirth educator may design a part of one class session as a structured lecture format to provide cognitive information about the physiological changes and resultant minor discomforts in pregnancy. Understanding the cause of these discomforts decreases expectant parents' anxiety. Visual aids such as the Maternity Center Birth Atlas and Schuchardt Charts or the ASPO/Lamaze Birth Series will increase class members' understanding. This information can be greatly enhanced by interspersing the lecture with demonstration and student participation of comfort measures for selected minor discomforts. For example, principles of good posture and the pelvic rock exercise can be introduced when discussing low backache during pregnancy; pelvic floor (Kegel) exercises could be introduced when discussing urinary frequency and urgency.

Because sexuality during pregnancy and the postpartum period may not be discussed by other health care providers, the childbirth educator should allow time to present information and discuss expectant parents' questions. Class members are more likely to be comfortable with this discussion after they have developed a relationship with their teacher and each other. If the childbirth educator is comfortable discussing sexuality and uses a professional approach, the expectant parents will also be comfortable. Handouts and a lending library of reading materials will add to expectant parents' knowledge, allowing them to be responsible for some of their learning and allowing the educator to make the best use of time in the course.

Meeting Emotional Needs

Although information about emotional changes in pregnancy can be presented in a lecture format, expectant parents are usually quite eager to discuss

TABLE 3–4. CONCERNS OF EXPECTANT FATHERS

- Financial responsibilities
- Ability to fulfill role as father
- Sexual relationships during pregnancy
- Effect of child on relationship with partner
- Role during childbirth education classes
- Role during childbirth
- Safety of partner and child during childbirth

the emotional changes they are experiencing. The introduction strategy or structured small group discussions will often reveal an expectant mother's emotional lability, and the ambivalence being experienced by both women and men. Expectant parents may share these emotional changes in a humorous or teasing manner; however, this humor may actually be a cover for feelings that do not really seem so funny. It is important to discuss the expectant fathers' emotional changes as well as the expectant mothers. Class members receive a great deal of comfort by hearing that other expectant parents are experiencing similar emotional responses to pregnancy.

If the subject of dreams and fantasies does not surface during the class discussions, the childbirth educator should make a point to introduce it. It is helpful for parents to share dreams and to realize that dreams and fantasies are common. The childbirth educator's role is not to interpret these dreams but to acknowledge that they are not unusual during pregnancy and allow an opportunity for parents to express concerns about troublesome dreams.

A childbirth educator can enhance maternal attachment in several ways. A brief overview of fetal growth and development, supplemented with visual aids, allows the expectant parents to focus on their baby as a developing human being. They can be encouraged and instructed to palpate the expectant mother's abdomen to identify fetal parts and position. This might be suggested during a discussion of fetal growth and development or when the teacher presents information about fetal position in regard to the labor and birth process. Knowing that the infant in utero can respond to sound and touch can encourage expectant parents to communicate with their infants long before birth. If any of the women in the class have had ultrasound scans, they can be asked to share the picture with the other class members. This can also help expectant parents to identify with a baby in utero. Asking them to share the female and male names they have chosen is another way to acknowledge the fetus as a reality. This sharing of names might be done at the completion of a final labor rehearsal in which the parents have just "given birth" to their babies.

The childbirth educator can greatly enhance a pregnant woman's body image by presenting body awareness relaxation strategies, visual imagery, instruction regarding posture and body mechanics, and encouraging her to practice relaxation techniques, good posture, and exercise daily. If the pregnant woman has a cognitive understanding of her bodily changes and then actively participates in techniques or exercises that will enhance her sense of well-being, her feelings about her body are likely to be more positive. All the relaxation and muscle-toning exercises that are a part of childbirth education today will provide these added benefits. The teacher's own attitudes and manner will also influence a pregnant woman's developing body image. If the teacher obviously views the pregnant body as being beautiful and miraculous in its ability to give life, parents will begin to feel this way also.

Meeting Sociocultural Needs

A positive approach in presenting information about the physical and emotional aspects of pregnancy, labor, and birth will support a woman's demonstration of health behavior rather than illness behavior. Reinforcing the importance of antepartal care, providing information about nutrition and exercise, and offering strategies for dealing with minor discomforts all encourage women to approach their pregnancies from a perspective of health.

If time permits, it is helpful to provide an opportunity for expectant parents to discuss the changes that have occurred in family roles and structure as a result of the pregnancy. Both women and men find it helpful to verbalize their thoughts and feelings about the ways in which their relationship is changing and what changes they anticipate they will need to make as they assume the roles of mother and father or as they integrate another child into the family system. As expectant parents learn about the immediate postpartum pe-

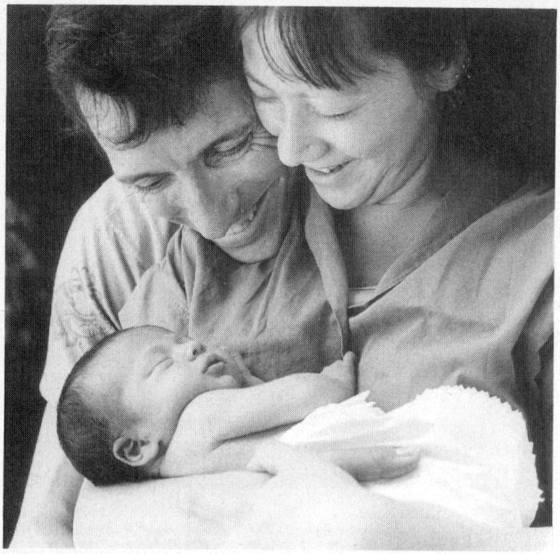

Expectant parents often think only about the joys of having a new baby. During childbirth education classes the changes in family roles and structure that occur at the birth of a baby should be discussed. Expectant parents can be encouraged to identify ways to make these changes and role transition easier. (Photograph © Harvey Wang.)

riod, they can be encouraged to identify ways to make their role transitions easier and use their social network most effectively. For example, the childbirth educator can divide class members into small groups to participate in postpartum planning. Each group can be given a different hypothetical family situation including information about the size of the family, its composition and support structures, the type of dwelling (i.e., a one- versus a two-floor plan, number of bathrooms, and so on), financial resources, and the nature of the situation when the mother arrives home with the new baby. Each group can be instructed to develop a plan for the first week at home, including where mother and baby will stay in the home, who will assume responsibility for cooking, laundry, and housekeeping, how the family and support structure can best be used, how the needs of the family can be met within the budget, and how various needs of the newborn will be met. The groups can then share the plans they developed. This strategy allows parents to brainstorm about ways to best use their social support structure, to share ideas with each other, and to receive input from the teacher.

Meeting Cognitive Needs

A childbirth education course meets expectant parents' cognitive needs in a wide variety of ways. In addition to the information the teacher presents in class and the information couples share with each other in discussion, other sources of knowledge include handouts, books, visual aids, slides, films, or hospital tours. All of this learning cannot be expected to take place within the structured class period or to be directly provided by the teacher. Because expectant parents are adult learners, they can be stimulated and encouraged to meet their cognitive needs by assuming some of the responsibility for their learning outside of class.

In addition to her role as facilitator in providing expectant parents with the information they need to meet their cognitive needs during pregnancy, the childbirth educator also serves as the expectant parents' advocate as the couples interact with the health care system. In this role it is important for childbirth educators to help their clients become responsible and assertive consumers who make informed choices. They should encourage expectant parents to communicate with their health care providers in a positive and assertive manner, neither passively or aggressively. McKay offers a number of excellent suggestions and examples for incorporating the teaching of assertive behavior into a childbirth course.[28] By using self-assessment questionnaires, discussions regarding the nature of relationships between providers and consumers, and role play situations, educators can help expectant parents to identify the components of assertive communication and positive ways to implement them. This aspect of cognitive development is an important one, for many people feel intimidated by health care providers. As a result, their needs and desires are not communicated. Dissatisfaction or anger with the treatment received is often the outcome. To prevent this negative experience, the childbirth educator can help expectant parents identify their rights and responsibilities as consumers and to learn and practice, within the safety of the class setting, positive assertive communication.

Another component of teaching assertive behavior is to inform parents of their choices and options regarding the childbirth experience. The thought of having health care choices may be an entirely new and somewhat foreign concept to many expectant parents. A number of people may feel that it is much easier to entrust all decision-making to the physician or other health care providers. Despite this attitude, it is important for the childbirth educator to at least introduce the concept of responsible choice and to stimulate parents' thinking. Parents need to know that there are controversies about whether choices really do exist in maternal-newborn care,[28,32,38] that there is no one "right" way to accomplish the goal of a safe birth, and that there are wide differences in the types of services available today in maternity care. Without this understanding by consumers, a health care system in which choices are readily available will never come to pass.

A teaching strategy that can help parents to think about options and at least provides a basis for communication with their physician or midwife is the development of a *birth plan*.[46] The birth plan is a list of options that parents identify that they would prefer for their birth experience, such as no enema or prep, ambulation during labor, music during labor, squatting for the birth, and so on. It can also include options about a cesarean birth and a plan for action should complications arise for the mother or newborn. The birth plan is developed based on information that has been gathered about the options available in the community. Expectant parents should discuss their birth plan with the caregivers several times during pregnancy, and it should serve as a reference for those providing care for the parents during labor and birth. A birth plan needs to be based on trust between the provider and consumer, and may even serve to help develop that trust. The health care provider can also benefit from the birth plan. Open communication leads to clarification of misunderstandings, and expectant parents and health care providers can negotiate and resolve any differences. This may increase the parents' satisfaction and may potentially increase the health care provider's satisfaction with his or her professional role.

> Pregnancy, with its heightened emotions, often brings us in touch with feelings that don't fit our self-image, our accepted range of feelings. An inner attitude of acceptance can help such feelings pass quickly or help parts of ourselves to grow and transform.
>
> RAHIMA BALDWIN AND TERRA PALMARINI[1]
>
> . . . the questions 'Who am I?' and 'What will I be?' are paramount in pregnancy, as in adolescence when critical decisions about the future invite confrontation. In continuing and repeated attempts to fathom the unknown, the gravida asks herself 'What kind of a mother should I, can I, will I be?'
>
> REGINA LEDERMAN[2]
>
> . . . a first pregnancy may be a lonely time . . . Much of the need for aloneness concerns itself with the matter of looking ahead—daydreaming, weaving fantasies about the infant, seeing themselves in the new role of mother. The women were in the process of giving up much that had been meaningful in the past and at the same time reorganizing their psychological resources to look toward the future.
>
> PAULINE SHERESHEFSKY, HAROLD PLOTSKY, AND ROBERT LOCKMAN[3]

IMPLICATIONS FOR RESEARCH

A great deal has been written about the nature of pregnancy. Yet very little is based upon formal research studies. Even less research exists to identify the effects of childbirth education on the physical, emotional, sociocultural, and cognitive aspects of pregnancy. These areas provide a fertile ground for the development of research questions. Research about pregnancy and childbirth education would contribute to a knowledge base that would guide all those who strive to make the childbearing year a positive one. Questions that need to be answered are:

- What is the relationship between a woman's knowledge about pregnancy and her degree of physical discomfort?
- What variables influence health versus illness behavior during pregnancy?
- Does knowledge regarding sexuality during pregnancy influence the development of body image?
- What is the relationship between sexual activity during pregnancy and complications occurring in pregnancy?
- Do dreams and fantasies of men and women during pregnancy influence the development of maternal and paternal roles?
- What is the relationship between expectant parents' social structure and the adaptation to pregnancy and parenthood?
- What is the incidence of the male couvade phenomenon, and how does it influence paternal adaptation to pregnancy and parenthood?
- How do fathers develop a relationship with their infants?
- How can childbirth educators teach assertive communication skills to expectant parents?
- What are the benefits of teaching expectant parents to use assertive communication and to make responsible choices?
- Do expectant parents use assertive communication skills to obtain a positive birth experience?
- Does expectant parents' knowledge about options and choices for childbirth influence the nature of the birth experience?

These research questions are only a small number of those that can be generated regarding the pregnancy experience. By continuing to raise questions and generate new knowledge, childbirth educators can strive to make the experience of pregnancy an optimal one.

SUMMARY

Pregnancy, birth, and the transition to parenthood are multifaceted experiences. The physical nature of pregnancy influences both women and their partners. The emotional responses of parents include developmental tasks that must be accomplished in order to take on the role of parenting. Society and culture shape the responses and behaviors of expectant parents during pregnancy and childbirth. For many men and women, the desire for knowledge about pregnancy and birth is strong and serves to make the experience a more positive one. Childbirth educators are challenged to assess parental needs relating to the physical, emotional, sociocultural, and cognitive aspects of pregnancy and to design a childbirth education course to meet expectant parents' needs in all these areas.

References

1. Antle, K. Psychologic involvement in pregnancy by expectant fathers. *JOGN Nursing* 4:40, 1975.
2. Bibring, G. L. Some considerations of the psychological processes in pregnancy. *Psychoanalytic Study of the Child* 14:113, 1959.
3. Bing, E., and Colman, L. L. *Making Love During Pregnancy.* New York: Bantam Books, Inc., 1977.
4. Brown, S. Late-pregnancy ambivalence. *Childbirth Educator* 3:37, 1984.
5. Caplan, G. Psychological aspects of maternity care. *American Journal of Public Health* 47:25, 1957.
6. Carter-Jessop, L. Promoting maternal attachment through prenatal intervention. *Maternal Child Nursing* 6:107, 1981.
7. Cohen, R. Some maladaptive syndromes of pregnancy and the puerperium. *Obstetrics and Gynecology* 27:562, 1966.

8. Colman, A. D., and Colman, L. L. *Pregnancy: The Psychosocial Experience*. New York: Herder and Herder, 1971.
9. Crawford, G. A. Theoretical model of support network conflict experienced by new mothers. *Nursing Research* 34:93, 1985.
10. Cronenwett, L. R. Network structure, social support, and psychosocial outcomes of pregnancy. *Nursing Research* 34:93, 1985.
11. David, M. L. and Doyle, E. W. First trimester pregnancy. *American Journal of Nursing*: 76:1945, 1976.
12. Deutsch, H. *The Psychology of Women: Motherhood*. Vol. 2. New York: Grune and Stratton, 1945.
13. Dyer, L. Parenthood as crisis. *Marriage and Family Living* 25:196, 1963.
14. Ellis, D. J. Sexual needs and concerns of expectant parents. *JOGN Nursing* 10:306, 1980.
15. Hill, R. *Family Under Stress*. Westport, CT: Greenwood Press, 1949.
16. Hobbs, D. F. Parenthood as Crisis. *Journal of Marriage and Family* 27:367, 1965.
17. Hott, J. R. The crisis of expectant fatherhood. *American Journal of Nursing* 76:1436, 1976.
18. Jordan, B. *Birth in Four Cultures*. Montreal, Canada: Eden Press Women's Publications, 1980.
19. Karmel, M. *Thank You, Dr. Lamaze*. Philadelphia: J. B. Lippincott, 1959.
20. Kitzinger, S. *The Experience of Childbirth*. Baltimore: Penguin Books, Inc., 1967.
21. Klaus, M., and Kennell, J. *Maternal Infant Bonding*. St. Louis: C. V. Mosby, 1976.
22. Lederman, R. P. *Psychosocial Adaptation in Pregnancy*. Englewood Cliffs, NJ: Prentice-Hall, Inc., 1984.
23. Leifer, M. Psychological changes accompanying pregnancy and motherhood. *Genetic Psychology Monographs* 95:55, 1977.
24. LeMasters, E. Parenthood as crisis. *Journal of Marriage and Family Living* 19:352, 1956.
25. May, A. K. Active involvement of expectant fathers in pregnancy: some further considerations. *JOGN Nursing* 7:7, 1978.
26. May, A. K. Three phases in the development of father involvement in pregnancy. *Nursing Research* 31:337, 1982.
27. McKay, S. Assertive childbirth. *Childbirth Educator* Winter: 33, 1985a.
28. McKay, S. The limits of choice in childbirth. *Genesis* February/March: 8, 1985b.
29. Mercer, R. *First-time Motherhood: Experiences from Teens to Forties*. New York: Springer Publishing Co., 1986.
30. Moore, D. S. The body image in pregnancy. *Journal of Nurse Midwifery* 22:17, 1978.
31. Nadelson, C. ''Normal'' and ''special'' aspects of pregnancy. *Obstetrics and Gynecology* 41:611, 1973.
32. Norton, K. Beyond ''choice'' in childbirth. *Birth* 10:179, 1983.
33. Olds, S. B., London, M. J., and Ladewig, P. A. *Maternal Newborn Nursing: A Family Centered Approach*. Menlo Park, CA: Addison-Wesley Publishing Co., 1984.
34. Parsons, T. *The Social System*. Glencoe, Ill.: The Free Press, 1951.
35. Pritchard, J. A., MacDonald, P. C., Gant, N. F. *Williams Obstetrics,* 17th ed. Norwalk, CN: Appleton-Century-Crofts, 1985.
36. Quirk, B. H. The nurse's role in advising patients on coitus during pregnancy. *Nursing Clinics of North America* 8:501, 1973.
37. Reeder, S. J., Mastroianni, L., and Martin, L. L. *Maternity Nursing*. 15th ed., Philadelphia: J. B. Lippincott, 1983.
38. Richards, M. P. M. The trouble with choice in childbirth. *Birth* 9:253, 1982.
39. Rubin, R. Attainment of the maternal role. Part I: Processes. *Nursing Research* 16:3, 1967a.
40. Rubin, R. Attainment of the maternal role. Part II: Models and referrants. *Nursing Research* 16:342, 1967b.
41. Rubin, R. Cognitive style in pregnancy. *American Journal of Nursing* 70:502, 1970.
42. Rubin, R. Fantasy and object constancy in maternal relations. *Maternal Child Nursing* 1:101, 1972.
43. Rubin, R. *Maternal Identity and the Maternal Experience*. New York: Springer Publishing Co., 1984.
44. Russel, T. Transition to Parenthood: Problems and gratification. *Journal of Marriage and the Family* 36:294, 1974.
45. Sherwin, L. N. Fantasies during the third trimester of pregnancy. *Maternal Child Nursing* 5:398, 1981.
46. Simkin, P. The birth plan: Vehicle for trust and communication. *Birth* 10:184, 1983.
47. Solberg, D. A., et al. Sexual behavior in pregnancy. *New England Journal of Medicine* 288:1098, 1973.
48. Swanson, J. The marital sexual relationship during pregnancy. *JOGN Nursing* 10:267, 1980.
49. Wu, R. *Behavior and Illness,* Englewood Cliffs, NJ: Prentice-Hall, Inc., 1973.

Beginning Quote

Rubin, R. *Maternal Identity and the Maternal Experience*. New York: Springer Publishing Co., 1984, p. 52.

Boxed Quotes

1. Baldwin, R., and Palmarini, T. *Pregnant feelings*. Berkeley, CA: Celestial Arts, 1986, p. 12.
2. Lederman, R. *Psychosocial Adaptation in Pregnancy*. Englewood Cliffs, NJ: Prentice-Hall, Inc., 1984, p. 62.
3. Shereshefsky, P., and Yarrow, L. *Psychological Aspects of a First Pregnancy and Early Postnatal Adaptation*. New York: Raven Press, 1973, p. 86.

chapter 4

THE CHILDBIRTH EXPERIENCE

SUSAN GENNARO

Giving birth can be a shock from which a woman never recovers. . . . It can also be a moment of pure ecstasy and the beginning of a greatly enhanced sense of self-worth.

Fredelle Maynard

Birth and death are transcendent events and have meaning far beyond the physiological processes that occur on these occasions. Birth has been universally ritualized and has, throughout history, been a matter of concern for religion, philosophy, and the law.[46] The childbirth experience is a unique event that, because of its physiological, psychological, spiritual, and social importance, is perhaps best understood from the perspective of many disciplines. Therefore, research from sociology, nursing, medicine, psychology, and anthropology will be presented in this chapter.

REVIEW OF THE LITERATURE

Childbirth is in part a physiological process in which (assuming a vaginal delivery) the uterus contracts, the cervix softens and opens, the fetus descends through the pelvis, and the mother helps push a new member of the human race out into the world. Birth is physically a time-limited event. Friedman[26] carefully quantified the average labor and delivery as 14 hours for a first childbirth and eight hours for multiparas. However, the time that a woman spends in childbirth has an effect long after the physical experience is over. Childbirth forever shapes women's thoughts of themselves and may affect relationships with other family members.[1,21,31,50,51] It is clearly much more than just an eventful day in the life of a woman; it is an experience that has far-reaching potential for affecting the mental and social health of women and family members. Childbirth must be accomplished in a manner that promotes more than biological safety.

Childbirth, because of its significance in a woman's life, has long been viewed by some researchers as a developmental task of pregnant women. Childbirth has also been conceptualized as a crisis.[7,19,21,67] However, researchers working within a framework of childbirth as crisis impose values regarding adaptive (good) and nonadaptive (bad) behavior on the data they collect. Thus, childbirth and mothering are often evaluated in terms of what a woman's feelings and behaviors should be rather than what her feelings and behaviors actually are. Imposing one's values on behavior is a problem that needs to be considered in all research studies, regardless of the framework that is used. Social desirability may cloud reality, thus creating a flaw in some of the research available on childbirth.[58]

A mother's personal history helps shape her perception of the childbirth experience.[15] The childbearing woman's feelings of self, her social support, and the significant life events she has experienced may all affect her childbirth.[11,35,38,40,57] The childbirth experience is affected not only by the woman's personal history but also by history in general, since history affects the norms of society, including norms surrounding the childbirth experience.[13,27]

Childbirth was, throughout much of history, an experience for and of women. Birthing in the colonial United States, for example, was attended by female midwives.[13] In 1900 less than 5 per cent of U.S. women delivered in hospitals. The medicalization of childbirth started as women began going to hospitals to give birth. By 1975, 95 per cent of U.S. women had hospital deliveries.[30] Advances in the treatment of conditions such as pregnancy-induced hypertension fostered institutionalization of childbirth, as did advances in surgical techniques and in anesthesia.[30] For the high-risk mother and fetus, U.S. medicine in the 1980's brings a level of safe care unimaginable even a decade or two

Labor is an intense emotional and physical experience. (Courtesy of Ida and Douglas Bird. Photo Copyright 1981, Hella Hammid.)

ago. However, critics have raised questions about depersonalization and the increased incidence of intervention common to obstetrical practice in the U.S. today.[2,30,61,64] Questions are also raised as to the appropriateness of treating all childbirth as a high-risk experience. Most women in the U.S. go to an institution that is totally devoted to sickness to deliver their infants. This fact coupled with the predominance of physiological research in childbirth on pain and complications leads to the conclusion that in the U.S. childbirth is viewed as an illness.[48] Gordon and Haire[30] suggest that lower infant mortality rates in countries such as the Netherlands and Sweden, where low-risk women are delivered by midwives and childbirth is not a medically oriented experience, should make U.S. women *question the legitimacy and necessity of the current style of childbirth for low-risk women.*

Since the childbirth experience is influenced by so many factors including personal history, contemporary norms, and physiological and psychological factors, the meaning of childbirth is as individual as the goals of individual childbearing women and their support persons. Childbirth educators have sought to give women a more active role in the birth experience while at the same time helping women to understand the physiology of childbirth and appropriate interventions that may be encountered in a hospital setting.[15,46] Perhaps the most valuable goal of childbirth education is to help individuals meet their own unique goals and therefore fulfill their own personal destinies.

Culture and Childbirth

Birth is viewed as an important event by all cultures, but the norms surrounding birth are culturally diverse. Mead and Newton[47] provide an interesting overview of cultural differences regarding childbirth. Differences in attitudes can be seen in how childbirth is viewed. Is it a normal physiological function or an illness? Contemporary Americans are not the only people who tend to view childbirth as a sickness. The Aracanian Indians of South America and the Cuna Indians of Panama regard childbirth as abnormal. In fact, the Cuna Indians seek help from the medicine man daily throughout their pregnancies and are medicated throughout labor.

Some cultures such as the ancient Egyptians, ancient Mexicans, and the Navajo show a great frankness regarding childbirth. In other cultures such as the Cuna and in contemporary United States, childbirth has been cloaked with privacy and considered an event appropriate for viewing only by medical personnel and, in the U.S., by fathers (although this is changing to a limited extent). The sexual implications of birth are strongly aligned to the secrecy in which birth is cloaked. In the U.S. and in England, as Oakley[58] corroborates in her research, sexually allied emotions in either the parturient or attendant are taboo. This taboo is not found in some areas, such as Laos, Burma, Jamaica, or rural India.[3]

In many cultures women are praised for their achievement in birthing a baby. In other cultures this achievement is shared with or attributed to the obstetrician. In the United States, for example, the common prevailing philosophy is that a woman is *delivered* of her child as opposed to *giving birth*.

Birth may be considered to be dirty or defiling. Postpartum purification ceremonies are reported to occur with the Hottentots, village people in Jordan, and in the Caucasia region of Russia. The ancient Hebrews had a purification rite; in Vietnam and other areas of Asia women are considered to be impure during and after birth.

Just as attitudes regarding labor and its conduct differ among cultures, so do behaviors in terms of labor management, as Mead and Newton[47] also clearly demonstrate. In many primitive cultures sensory stimulation such as music (used by Laotians, the Navajo, and the Cuna of Panama), heat (used by the Comanche and the Tewa) or abdominal stimulation (used by the Kurtatchi, the Yahgan of Tierra del Fuego, the Punjabs, and the Kazakhs of Kasakhstan in Asia) are employed during labor. In some cultures physical activity by the mother is severely limited (as with the Hottentots), whereas in other cultures activity is encouraged (the Tuareg of the Sahara walk throughout labor). Currently in many hospitals in the U.S., activity is generally limited once the parturient enters the hospital, although this is changing in some places as the advantages of the upright position become recognized.

Clearly, although childbirth is a universal phenomenon, the context in which a woman labors and delivers is very much influenced by her cultural milieu. Brown[9,10] provides an interesting view of how anthropologists unfamiliar with the United States might view childbirth there:

> During labor, the Vestal Virgins assume their positions around the woman, leading her in a variety of magical incantations with rhythmic breathing to blow off the magic spirits of pain. Finally when the time of delivery is near, the Vestal Virgins position the woman in one of the most torturous of the culture's institutions, a special apparatus used only at the time of birth. In it the woman is made to lie flat on her back with her legs and feet raised at a 90-degree angle and bent at the knee. It is thought that if a woman is able to deliver her baby in this almost impossible position, she will have passed the first initiation rites of motherhood.

Childbirth and Enjoyment

Much of the research on childbirth focuses primarily on "problems" such as pain or obstetrical complications rather than on positive aspects such as enjoyment. Humenick[37] questions the prevailing norm among health care professionals that the critical element responsible for a "good birth experience" is the reduction of pain. Rather, she asks:

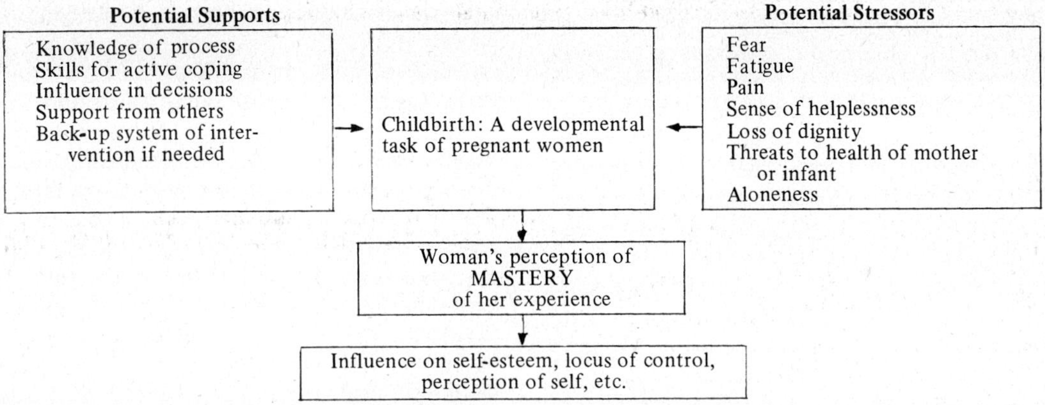

FIGURE 4–1. Mastery: The key to childbirth satisfaction. (From Humenick, S. Mastery: The Key to Childbirth Satisfaction? A Review. *Birth and the Family Journal* 8:79, 1981.)

Should not the goals of health care professionals be to enhance the parturient's control or feelings of mastery and accomplishment in labor? She describes a "mastery model of childbirth" derived from a review of research literature (Fig. 4–1).

Several studies examine factors leading to enjoyment in childbirth.[56] Of the 249 women in one study, women with higher social status, greater marital closeness, and less traditional attitudes toward sex roles were found to have greater enjoyment during childbirth. The researchers stated that enjoyment is experienced primarily at birth. High levels of pain may interfere with enjoyment, but enjoyment and pain can easily coexist. Women with low levels of pain do not necessarily have high levels of enjoyment.

Tanzer[71] interviewed 36 women antenatally and postpartally. Seven women reported having rapture or near mystical bliss during childbirth. Words the women used to describe their experience included "joy," "excitement," and "a wonderful free feeling." In this study women with a history of menstrual problems experienced more childbirth pain (a finding supported by Melzack).[49] Women who took childbirth preparation courses expressed more positive feelings about childbirth, and the women who experienced near-bliss during childbirth all had their husbands present. These findings in this early study on childbirth led Tanzer to conclude:

> Our prescription for childbirth would read: 'For positive emotions, take the course. For pain reduction, have a good menstrual history and take the course. For rapture, have your husband present.'

The influence of the husband's presence in childbirth on the woman's positive perception of this event is supported by later studies of Doering and colleagues[20] and of Norr et al.[56]

Leifer[43] studied 19 primiparas throughout pregnancy, childbirth, and the postpartum and found that the labor experience of women who received psychoprophylactic (Lamaze) training was very positive. The parturients' experiences could be summarized as "very hard work but work that was intensely rewarding and satisfying."

Although few studies have been designed specifically to measure the enjoyment experienced during childbirth, many studies have been done to determine the parturients' overall perception of the birth experience. Entwisle and Doering[23] found that women who were two or more weeks post date had significantly less positive views of childbirth than did women who delivered earlier. It is interesting to note that 14 per cent of the 120 women in the study said they were ecstatic at birth.

Mercer[50] found that teenagers rated their childbirth experience less positively than older women. There was no relationship between level of education, marital status, or race and perception of the birth experience in Mercer's 294 subjects.

Mastery and Sense of Control

The amount of pleasure a woman experiences during birth seems to be related to her ability to remain in control and/or to influence what happens to her. This relationship is supported by several studies. Doering and colleagues[19] found that remaining in control is more important to a woman's perception of her childbirth experience than is having less pain. Willmuth[78] studied 1145 women and found that the perception of maintaining control was closely associated with satisfaction. In Willmuth's study control was defined as the woman's ability to meaningfully influence decisions related to care. It should be noted that this definition of control is not the same as "behaving in a controlled manner." The control desired by women in labor is related to *participation in decision-making*. Similarly, Davenport-Slack and Boylan[18] concluded that the most important factor in contributing to a positive experience in labor was a woman's desire to be an active participant. Women who were active participants were much more satisfied with their birth experience than the women who expected to rely on their physicians and on drugs.

Lamaze classes have been shown to significantly increase the extent to which parturients view themselves as agents of control.[24] Mothers' beliefs about their ability to have some control may be influenced prenatally and continue to have effects after the baby is born. Humenick and Bugen[38] studied 37 primiparas and found that the mother's perceived instrumental behaviors (independence, decisiveness, and confidence) during childbirth were significantly correlated with increases prenatally to postpartally in these same behaviors. That women see themselves differently after birth as compared with before birth on this relatively stable personality characteristic supports the contention that birth is a developmental task. Perhaps one reason that women who attend classes have been found to be more satisfied in general with their childbirth experience is that classes enable women to set their own goals and participate more in decision-making during their childbirth experiences.

Pain Research

Many researchers and care providers have not considered the importance of active participation and mastery to birth satisfaction. They, then, may operate from an implicit model that equates birth satisfaction primarily with the reduction of pain. Even though this model is not supported by research, it is a commonly held viewpoint. The pain experience in childbirth is of significance and has been extensively researched. Entwisle and Doering[23] conducted a longitudinal study of 120 couples during pregnancy, childbirth, and in the postpartum, and discovered that 29 per cent of the parturients found childbirth to be more painful than expected, whereas 22 per cent found childbirth to be less painful. On the average the first stage of labor was characterized as being of moderate to bad pain whereas the second stage was characterized as being slightly or moderately painful. Transition (8 to 10 centimeters of dilatation) was labeled as most painful by 38 per cent of the parturients, 4 per cent said childbirth was painless, and 12 per cent said the pain they experienced was from interventions such as intravenous infusions performed by caregivers.

Melzack's research corroborates the variability of the pain experienced in childbirth.[49] Melzack measured pain using the McGill pain questionnaire (MPQ) while parturients were in labor. Thus the methodological concern with the appropriateness of measuring remembered pain rather than actual pain was avoided and pain was measured with a tool that had documented psychometric properties. Eighty-seven primiparas rated childbirth pain as either very mild (9.2 per cent), moderate (29.5 per cent), severe (37.9 per cent), or extremely severe (23.4 per cent). This distribution is very similar to the findings of a study by Nettelbladt et al.[54] Multiparas in Melzack's study had lower pain scores than primiparas: 24.1 per cent had mild pain, 29.6 per cent had moderate pain, 35.2 per cent had severe pain, and 11.1 per cent had very severe pain.

Melzack[49] found that the pain a woman experienced and her stage of labor were not well correlated. Some women had high levels of pain early in labor while others had low pain scores throughout labor. Melzack concluded that pain in labor is highly individual not only as to when the pain is felt but also as to where in the body pain is experienced. Melzack also concluded that Lamaze childbirth preparation decreased childbirth pain (by as much as 30 per cent) but that the parturient's pain experience was still appreciable. Epidural

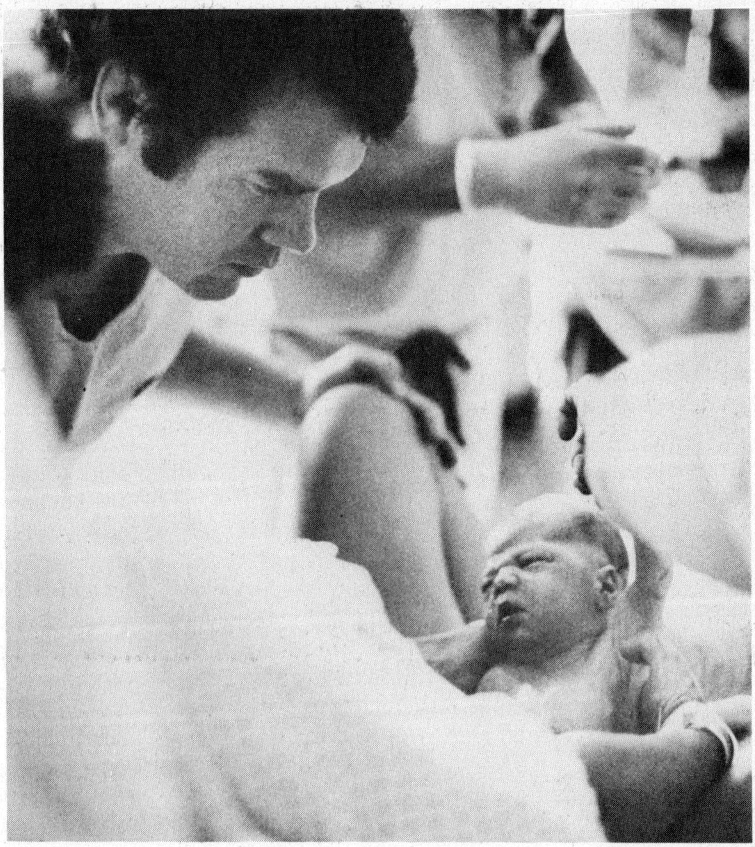

Abbey's birth. (Copyright © The Borning Corporation. Reprinted/reproduced with permission from The Borning Corporation.)

blocks gave more total pain relief than psychoprophylactic methods but were associated with a 10 per cent failure rate and obstetrical complications.

Niven and Gijsbers[55] also used the MPQ to measure childbirth pain both while women were in labor and 24 to 48 hours after they delivered. While pain was found to be severe in the 29 study subjects, again it was highly variable. Patients who had previously experienced significant levels of pain unrelated to childbirth had less pain than subjects who had not had this experience.

Epidural Anesthesia

Many of Melzack's findings[49] were corroborated in a study in England.[52] Pain in 1000 women was measured during the early postpartum period using a visual linear analogue scale. Over half (536) of the patients had epidural anesthesia and 80 patients had no analgesia or anesthesia. Patients who had an epidural had significantly longer labor and more assisted deliveries (51 per cent of the epidural group had forceps deliveries) than patients who did not have epidurals. Although patients with epidurals had the lowest average pain scores, one-third of mothers in all groups experienced more pain than they had expected. Only 35 per cent of the mothers in the study reported having a pain-free labor; this finding led the researchers to conclude that modern techniques can diminish but not abolish pain in childbirth. In a follow-up study a year later 626 of the 1000 subjects responded to a questionnaire about labor satisfaction.[53] The investigators found that although mothers still reported that epidurals were effective in reducing pain, 16 per cent of the subjects who received epidurals were dissatisfied with the childbirth experience. Patients who refused anesthesia had more pain but also had higher satisfaction scores both immediately after labor and one year later.

Bennett and coworkers[5] found that 11 per cent of the women in their study who had epidurals were dissatisfied with the childbirth experience both immediately and three weeks after birth. Conversely, in another study there was no initial difference at birth in perceptions of the childbirth experience between mothers who received epidurals, mothers who received no anesthesia or analgesia, and mothers with analgesia for labor and local anesthesia for birth. However, within two days after delivery mothers with epidurals had less positive feelings about childbirth than did the other two groups.[66]

Poore and Foster[60] found epidural anesthesia was associated with significantly longer labors, higher use of oxytocin during labor, more forceps deliveries, and more postpartum bladder catheterizations. Women who received epidurals were younger and more passive in decision-making about childbirth than were women who did not have epidurals. As in all studies of epidural anesthesia and childbirth it is not possible to tell if women with longer labors experienced more pain and therefore had more epidurals, or if epidurals caused longer labors. However, it may be concluded that satisfaction with the childbirth experience may not be closely related to the efficacy of pain relief.

Childbirth Preparation Efficacy

A large number of studies have been conducted on the efficacy of childbirth preparation classes.[5,6,14,18,22,36,39,42,59,63,65,72,74,75] Cogan[16] in a scholarly review of this research concludes that childbirth preparation does have positive effects on the birth experience, including (1) a reduced pain experience, (2) reduced use of medicine during parturition, (3) less use of forceps, and (4) more positive attitudes about the labor experience. Beck and Hall[4] also reviewed the research in this area. As they point out, the validity of much of the research done on the effectiveness of psychoprophylaxis has been questioned because of methodological flaws, including use of inappropriate tools, bias in sample selection, and lack of control groups including one that receives an attention-placebo treatment (two control groups, one of which receives class instruction in an unrelated topic and one that receives no class instruction). Table 4–1 lists 15 studies that compare childbirth outcomes in prepared and nonprepared couples.

The methodological flaws that Beck and Hall[4] discuss are present to some extent in all the studies. However, the study by Timm[72] does support Cogan's[16] conclusions. The Timm study is methodologically one of the soundest done on the efficacy of the psychoprophylactic method. Timm had an adequate sample size (118), random assignment to group, and an attention-placebo treatment (one control group went to knitting classes; another control group received no instruction). One limitation in methodology is that Timm does not mention having used obstetricians who were unaware of the patient's level of preparation. It is possible, therefore, that some of the variability in childbirth outcome in this study resulted from differences in how obstetricians knowingly treated prepared and nonprepared couples rather than in differences produced in couples by class attendance. Timm found that PPM training does result in positive outcomes for the parturient and her baby (see Table 4–1).

Other variables that make it difficult to compare results of attending childbirth classes across studies is the variability in instructors and the uniqueness of the goals and motivation of subjects attending classes.[17] Reasons that women choose to participate in Lamaze classes are highly individual and include positive factors such as a desire to participate actively in childbirth and negative factors such as fears of anesthesia, death, and losing control.[25]

Demographic differences in women who choose to attend classes and those who do not attend classes have been found. Therefore, the results of studies that do not adequately control for biases in sample selection are suspect. Users of prepared childbirth techniques tend to be better educated, of a higher socioeconomic status, and are older than nonusers.[5,12,45,77] However, prenatal classes have also been found to be beneficial to high-risk indigent women.[79]

Other outcomes of childbirth preparation have also been studied. In general, prenatal education

TABLE 4–1. OUTCOMES OF CHILDBIRTH PREPARATION

AUTHOR	NO. OF SUBJECTS	RELIABLE VALID TOOL*	CONTROLS	RESULTS
Bennett et al. (1985)[5]	398	—	Not matched	Same length of labor; same incidence of complications
Patton et al. (1985)[59]	128	—	Matched age, risk, SES, ethnicity	Same length of labor; increased satisfaction
Moore (1983)[51]	105	Yes	Matched age, SES, education	Same marital satisfaction; less medication
Timm (1979)[72]	108	Yes	Random assignment	Less medication, complications, fetal distress; same length of labor
Charles et al. (1978)[14]	249	—	Yes; not matched	Less pain; more enjoyment; less anesthesia
Hughey et al. (1978)[36]	1000	—	Matched age, race, parity	Same length of labor; less fetal distress
Scott and Rose (1976)[65]	258	—	Matched SES, age, EDC	Less anesthesia, analgesia, use of forceps; same length of labor
Davenport–Slack and Boylan (1974)[18]	75	—	Not matched	Same pain, length of labor
Enkin et al. (1972)[22]	120	Yes	Matched age, parity; EDC, motivation	Less medication; same length of labor
Huttel et al. (1972)[39]	72	—	Random assignment	Same pain, length of labor, use of forceps, complications
Tanzer (1968)[71]	36	—	Not matched	Less pain, more satisfaction
Bergstrom-Walen (1963)[6]	250	Yes	No	Less pain; less anxiety; shorter labor
Rodway (1957)[63]	2700	—	Matched age	Same pain, length labor, anesthesia, complications
Laird and Hogan (1956)[42]	532	—	Not matched	Same length of labor; same incidence of complications
Van Eps (1955)[75]	800	—	Not matched	More satisfaction
Van Auken and Tomlinson (1955)[74]	400	—	Not matched	Shorter labor; less anesthesia

*— Indicates reliability and validity not discussed.

does not affect infant birthweight,[59,62,72] but reactions to the birth experience and to the baby may be more positive in couples attending classes.[5,19] Many studies have shown the number of obstetrical complications are not lower in prepared women,[5,39,42] although Timm did find fewer obstetrical complications in her prepared subjects.[72]

Studies are currently being performed to determine what specific aspects of Lamaze training are most effective in pain relief. Relaxation training has been found to be one very important component of the Lamaze method.[28] Manderino and Bzdek[44] found subjects who received both information on and modeling of the procedures they were to undergo reported less pain than subjects who received only information or modeling. Sensory transformation—that is, using the imagination to transform stimuli into a pleasant feeling—has been found to be a very effective method of pain relief.[29] Imagery provided greater pain relief than focal point visualization and relaxation or breathing techniques when each of the three pain management methods was evaluated separately.[70] One limitation that each of these studies share, however, is that they were performed on nulliparous college students in a laboratory setting rather than on women in labor. Although current research supports the efficacy of Lamaze preparation in pain management, the specific aspects of this training that are the most important remain to be defined.

Other Variables Associated with Childbirth Pain and Maternal Coping

Childbirth education classes and pharmacological methods of anesthesia and analgesia are not the only variables that have been associated with reduced pain in childbirth. Women with lower levels of anxiety have been found to experience lower levels of pain.[41] Women whose husbands were present at labor and birth reported less pain.[33] Women with low levels of education[54] and younger women[18] reported experiencing more pain in childbirth.

Standley and Nicholson[68] developed a model for looking at maternal coping during the childbirth experience (Fig. 4–2). It depicts the relationship between the psychological, physiological, and environmental factors that can be tested. The outcome measures were identified as *childbirth competence,* "a woman's ability to control her behavior and assist in the labor and delivery of her child without showing signs of psychological distress or functional inability," and *postpartum childbirth affect,* "how a woman feels physically and emotionally immediately after birth." The woman's childbirth competence is influenced by general determinants such as background and personal characteristics and factors related to her pregnancy and physical and social environment and her cognitive appraisal of childbirth, which is related to her expectations for childbirth, her psychophysiological adaptability, and by stimuli in the childbirth environment. A woman's interactions with others in the environment influence her coping ability during childbirth.

Obstetrical Complications

Another physiological area that has been well researched (aside from pain) is obstetrical complications. Studies of the management or incidence of particular obstetrical complications are not of interest here. Rather, the incidence of obstetrical complications in low-risk patients is the area of interest. Entwisle and Doering[23] found that 29 per cent of their sample developed complications during childbirth. In another longitudinal study of childbearing couples a high (55 per cent) incidence of obstetrical complications occurred that led the researchers to conclude that antenatally parents need to receive information about obstetrical complications they might experience during the intrapartum period. This is further discussed in Chapter 27.

Routine Interventions

In 1933, the White House Conference on Child Health and Protection Report entitled "Fetal, New

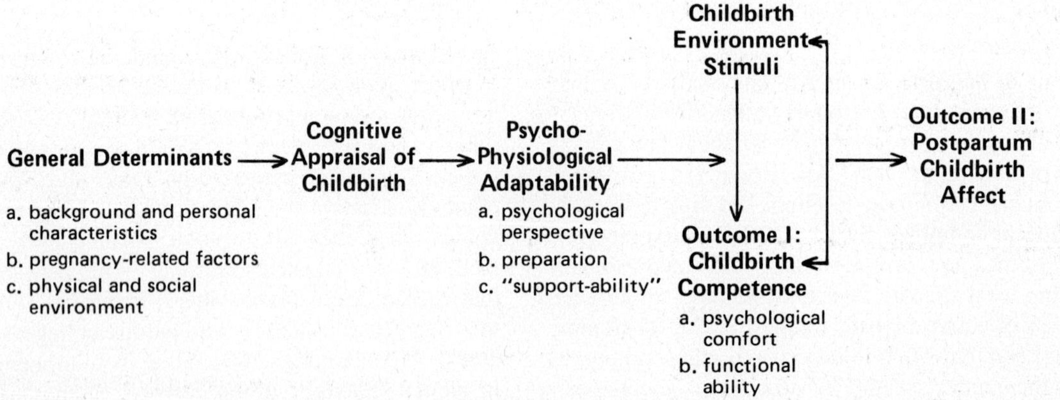

FIGURE 4–2. A model of maternal coping during labor and delivery and evaluation of the childbirth experience. (From Standley, K. and Nicholson, J. Observing the Childbirth Environment: A Research Model. *Birth and the Family Journal* 7:15, 1980.)

Born, and Maternal Mortality and Morbidity'' stated that the principal reason for increased maternal and infant mortality was excessive intervention.[8] Today, the use of routine interventions during childbirth continues to increase. It is clear that obstetrical interventions are not independent of each other. For example, Brackbill and co-workers[8] described the ''intervention daisy chain,'' in which ''accepting the first intervention increases the probability that a second intervention will be 'necessary,' which in turns increases the probability of a third, and so on.''

One concrete example of the effect one intervention has on another is the use of fetal monitoring. The debate over whether or not fetal monitoring should be used routinely is not new and continues. Advocates point to the small percentage of infants who have improved outcomes as a result of monitoring, and opponents speak of monitor misuse and an increased cesarean birth rate.

The effect one intervention can have on another is evident. However, new questions are being asked regarding how health care providers should determine ''routine care.'' Some of these questions are best summarized in a Hastings conference on values in childbirth technology.[69] Routine interventions often involve costly technology. Can we afford the cost? Changes in third party payment and the realities of spiralling health care costs are making it painfully clear that Americans are going to have to make health care decisions based on economics. If a limited sum is available for maternal-infant health programs and prenatal care is not available for many women living in disadvantaged urban and isolated rural areas, how do we spend our money? Do we provide more intensive health care to those already receiving care or do we try to provide more care to more individuals?

Additionally, in examining cost benefit ratios, how do we know if our routine interventions are really beneficial? As the Hastings Conference participants have queried:[69]

> . . . how suspicious should medicine itself be of new forms of treatment and diagnosis where their effects are untested, particularly in a normally nonpathological process like pregnancy and childbirth? Pain-killing drugs, anesthesia, induced labors, and restricted diets are often introduced for well-defined therapeutic ends and quickly become routine practices, even in normal pregnancies. Only when problems appear are they given the critical scrutiny they should have had in the first place.

Which of the routine interventions we now use could be placed in the category of inadequately tested? Are we sure that routine interventions are beneficial?

Lastly, questions are raised about patient autonomy and the protection of the fetus. Is the routine care we provide really beneficial for both mother and baby? Verney[76] in an examination of this issue concluded:

> Medical technology has greatly added to our knowledge of fetal development and our capacity to ''see'' the unborn child. It has also improved the outcome in high-risk pregnancy. The question is whether the benefits from this explosion of gyngadgetry outweighs the risks.
>
> First, we hospitalized birth; now we have mechanized it. Obstetrics today is rushing headlong toward ''guaranteed safe no-risk'' birth. In pursuing this goal, we have created new problems that may prove worse than the ones the high-tech procedures were supposed to solve.
>
> Current evidence does not favor the unrestrained use of technical procedures. Rather, it would be prudent at present to limit diagnostic tests and monitoring devices in obstetrics to a narrow segment of the spectrum of conditions in high-risk pregnancies.

IMPLICATIONS FOR PRACTICE

Fostering Mastery and Increasing Childbirth Satisfaction

One of the most important services childbirth education classes can provide is a forum for dialogue about childbirth so that attendees can be assisted in formulating their own individual goals. Small class sizes and classes in which communication between class members and the instructor is open and unrestricted foster decision-making and goal setting.

Goals are variable. One person's goal may be focused primarily on having a live baby; she may see the medicalization of childbirth as helping to achieve that goal and thus may welcome the technology so routinely associated with birth today. Another person may have great concerns about the effects of obstetrical interventions during childbirth and might wish to discuss how to keep interventions such as fetal monitoring and use of intravenous lines to a safe minimum. Helping individuals formulate goals that are flexible and can be tailored to meet the unique situations to be met in childbirth requires skill on the part of the instructor.

The childbirth educator must be objective, have excellent communication skills, and be an interactive instructor. Lecturing is easier than encouraging class participation and discovery learning. However, being a passive recipient of information does little to help individuals determine how they will participate in childbirth. If classes are designed to help couples take an active role in childbirth, that behavior must be modeled in class and couples must be encouraged to use information to shape classes to fit their needs.

Exercises that can be helpful in facilitating goal setting are having attendees write down and hand in goals for the class series (which the instructor must incorporate). This experience helps couples in designing goals for their birth experience in the form of birth plans.

In helping class attendees to meet their goals, it is important for childbirth educators to realize that there is a certain degree of cultural eccentricity in obstetrical practice. Not all of the practices that are done are advantageous for a mother and a baby's health and welfare. However, encouraging couples to do things a little differently, if changes best meet their individual needs, can create a dilemma. Childbirth educators are not always present with couples during labor and birth. Care providers may not immediately understand how their flexibility might enhance the childbirth situation. Encouraging class attendees to communicate their goals and birth plans with care providers is one step in ensuring that parturients receive support. Over time childbirth educators can help bridge the gap between class and the birthing agency by maintaining positive relationships with care providers, perhaps by volunteering to do inservice education in local hospitals on topics such as the importance of active participation in birth or pain management.

Role playing is a valuable exercise to help class participants develop ways to optimize the support they receive from caregivers if differences between the parturient's needs and situational norms arise. For example, while discussing active labor the instructor might ask each couple to imagine they are now in the hospital and that the instructor is the nurse. The nurse comes into the room to do a vaginal examination and asks the coach to leave. The first few coaches may acquiesce, but then someone asks why leaving is necessary. If a particular couple feels they would not like this separation (which is not necessary for the health and safety of the mother and fetus), constructive ways to resolve this situation can be role played. This exercise need not be time-consuming and at the same time class participants are gaining valuable insight into how they might respond and how they could use negotiation skills in labor. They also are receiving important information on which procedures might be performed in the hospital during active labor.

A variation of this exercise is to let some class members play the role of care providers in mock labor scenarios. Typically they will act out fears they have of care providers' behavior or will devise scenarios of the kind of support they desire from doctors and nurses. This opens up the topic to discussion without the instructor having to suggest that some care is less than flexible. Expectant parents as a group bring this up readily if the stage is set for them to do so. The same kind of insight in negotiating can be emphasized in the discussion.

Pain Management Skills

Another important service childbirth education classes provide is to teach pain management skills, as discussed in Chapter 6. If any pregnant woman in class has had prior pain episodes she should be encouraged early in the class series to identify the techniques that have helped her previously to deal with pain. The study by Niven and Gijsbers,[55] in which women with past pain experiences had less pain in childbirth, indicates that people learn from their past experiences and can use that knowledge with future pain episodes. Pain is a unique experience mediated by the individual's perception of the pain stimuli. Class participants who are taught a wide variety of pain management techniques and who are encouraged to be flexible in their use of these techniques are likely to be successful.[34,28,29,70]

Manderino's and Bzdek's[44] findings regarding the importance of modeling painful procedures support the instructor's use of role playing, audiovisual aids, and demonstrations with equipment used in the hospital. Additionally, showing films of women in labor who are using pain management techniques may be helpful. This study also lends support to having couples participate in mock labors. To foster mastery in labor, however, the instructor might wish to develop some written instructions describing some labor scenarios such as back labor or transition. Each couple could receive a folder. After moving to a separate area the couple would follow the written instructions step by step. The instructor could serve as a nurse, midwife, or physician, and move from area to area modeling care as labor progresses. A discussion of how individuals felt and the variations they experienced in their labor would be useful and would help class participants realize in what ways this exercise mirrors reality.

Coaches or labor partners need to be taught assessment skills and pain management techniques so they can interact with their partner in ways that are most helpful to the pair. Standley[67] demonstrated that some coaches are much more interactive than others during labor. However, regardless of the level of interaction, the social support parturients receive from their partners has been shown to be invaluable in the satisfaction they experience with childbirth.[37,56]

The coaches' assessment skills are honed by developing good communication skills. Coaches and their partners need time after each practice contraction to discuss with each other how well they think particular cognitive strategies, breathing techniques, and relaxation techniques are working, how the parturient feels, and how comfortable she appears. This is particularly important because pain has an affective, cognitive, and behavioral component[34]; if coaches' assessment of pain is based only on their partner's behavior the coach will not receive all the information needed to plan which pain management strategies to implement next during childbirth.

> The experience of bearing a child is central to a woman's life. Years after the baby has been born she remembers acutely the details of her labour and her feelings as the child was delivered. One can speak to any grandmother about birth and almost immediately she will begin to talk about her own labours. It is unlikely that any experience in a man's life is comparably vivid.
>
> SHEILA KITZINGER[1]
>
> Giving birth can be a deeply intimate experience for both partners. It can be a window to intrinsic patterns of the universe, to cycles of life and death that have existed since the first matter crossed the indefinable line and took the form of living cells. One transcends the ordinary, familiar sense of self to achieve an extraordinary understanding of being one with the cosmos. Women sense their autonomy, at the same time they experience being part of all that is, ever has been, ever will be.[2]
>
> LENI SCHWARTZ[2]
>
> A respect for the energy of birth has always existed among women, who have known its beauty and power in their own bodies and have passed on the ancient wisdom of birthing from one generation to the next.[3]
>
> RAHIMA BALDWIN AND TERRA PALMARINI[3]
>
> As the baby births, we fill with layers of emotions . . . joy for the baby, relief that labor is over, empty of the fullness of life within, wonder, thoughts of mothering, weariness, bliss, unreality, disbelief, openness, detachment, awe, discovery.
>
> HARRIETTE HARTIGAN[4]
>
> The knowledge that each and every childbirth is a spiritual experience has been forgotten by too many people in the world today, especially in countries with high levels of technology.
>
> INA MAY GASKIN[5]

Enjoyment of Childbirth

Childbirth generally has a very happy outcome. Like other important achievements in life, the hard work of labor is usually followed by exhilaration and pride in one's accomplishment of a challenging task. However, obstetrical complications do occur[32] and it is important that potential problems or variations in labor and delivery be discussed throughout the class series (see Chapter 19 on the unexpected childbirth experience). The overall class experience should emphasize the positive feelings the parturient can experience while working with her body to bring a new life into the world. The media frequently emphasize the difficult aspects of births and neglect to show the public a balanced view including the joy of the birth process. Childbirth educators may be the group most capable of keeping a balanced view of birth before the public. The variation in experience from birth to birth and the variation in what is important to people make describing birth a complex task.

However, instructors should strive to see that class members complete classes with a healthy respect for the potential rigors of the birth experience balanced with an understanding of the depth of potential joy and satisfaction. Furthermore, it is important that expectant parents understand that the birth experience need not be painless or uncomplicated to be satisfying. If expectant parents are pleased with the role they played in the events associated with their birth experiences, they will most likely find they feel satisfied.

IMPLICATIONS FOR RESEARCH

The framework used to examine childbirth guides the kinds of questions that researchers ask. If childbirth is viewed as an important life event rather than as a crisis,[58] the information gathered about childbirth might focus on variables such as enjoyment, happiness, and satisfaction with birth as well as on factors such as pain, that have been more widely researched.

There is a continued need for methodologically sound studies to examine the childbirth experience of women who do and do not attend prepared childbirth classes. Numerous researchers have found it impossible to randomly assign subjects to classes in their communities now that a high percentage of people take classes. Furthermore, even in studies of randomly assigned or matched groups of subjects, researchers need to control for informal training that may occur through reading materials, audio or video tapes, discussion with friends, or in-labor coaching from birth attendants. More studies need to be conducted on population samples who are not predominantly white and middle class, such as adolescents, the indigent, and on high-risk women.

Perhaps the most important research question at present is which components of prepared childbirth classes are most likely to promote good birth experiences. With changes in the current medical reimbursement schema, all health professionals need to be concerned with proving the worth of their particular services. Certified childbirth educators in private practice are facing competition from ''free'' childbirth education classes conducted by hospital-based instructors who often are not certified. Studies that look at differences in hospital and physician costs and client satisfaction between nonprepared persons and class attendees in childbirth education classes in different settings (agency, private practice and so on) would help certified childbirth educators document the worth of their classes to third party payers and the medical community.

The efficacy of teaching strategies used in childbirth preparation classes needs to be researched. As more research-based information becomes available on factors contributing to satisfaction and enjoyment in childbirth, more research will need to be conducted to determine how these factors can be enhanced in childbirth classes. Additionally, research on what teaching strategies are most effective with particular groups of childbearing women, such as teenagers, is necessary to ensure that all women receive the optimal advantage from childbirth class attendance.

There is also a continued need for studies on the effectiveness of various pain management techniques in labor and how satisfied childbearing women are with these techniques. Again, as research-based information becomes available on effectiveness of pain management techniques, research needs to be performed on how these pain management techniques can best be taught to childbearing women and their coaches in class.

Research on aspects of labor management, such as activity level in labor, needs to be encouraged. As medicolegal issues continue to affect the delivery of obstetrical care in the United States and obstetricians practice defensive medicine, it is likely that obstetrical practice might become more invasive. Research done to evaluate practice that supports physical safety and psychological well-being is necessary to ensure that the gap does not widen between what care providers consider safe and consumers consider satisfying.

In summary, research questions that need to be answered include:

- How can positive outcomes of childbirth be influenced?
- What constitutes a satisfying childbirth experience?
- How does attending childbirth classes affect the labor and birth experience?
- Are childbirth classes cost effective?
- What teaching strategies are most efficacious and for which kinds of class participants?
- What pain management techniques are most effective and for which women?

SUMMARY

Childbirth is a unique event in a woman's life that is influenced by the sum of her past experiences and that may influence many future experiences. Although the childbirth experience is universal and so unites women around the world, it is also highly overlaid by cultural values and norms.

Pain is commonly experienced in childbirth. However, just as childbirth varies greatly from one culture to another, childbirth pain varies greatly from one individual to another. Generally, multiparas seem to experience less pain than primiparas. Women with histories of menstrual pain seem to experience more pain than women without this history. The husband's presence in childbirth seems to decrease pain, and the degree of pain experienced is not well correlated either with enjoyment in labor or satisfaction with childbirth.

Many women report enjoying labor and experiencing rapturous moments at birth. The amount of satisfaction a woman experiences with her labor appears, in large part, to be determined by how much she feels she is in control of her childbirth. Childbirth educators are encouraged to structure their classes so that class members are facilitated

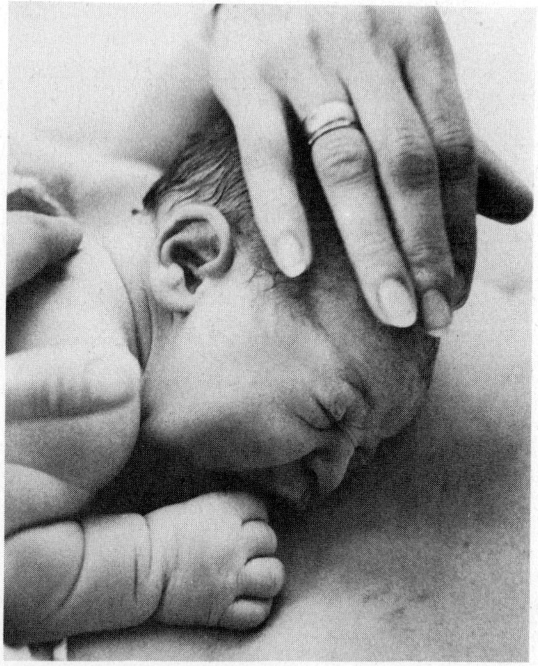

Special moments following birth. (Courtesy of Ida and Douglas Bird. Photo Copyright 1981, Hella Hammid.)

in making decisions, formulating goals, and learning skills to enable them to have a childbirth experience that meets their own individual needs. Based on a sound understanding of the childbirth experience, research is needed on the benefits of childbirth preparation and on how educators can best prepare families for childbirth.

References

1. Areskog, B., Uddenberg, N., and Kjessler, B. Postnatal emotional balance in women with and without antenatal fear of childbirth. *Journal of Psychosomatic Research* 28:213, 1984.
2. Arms, S. *Immaculate Deception*. Boston, MA: Houghton-Mifflin, 1975.
3. Bates, B., and Turner, A. Imagery and symbolism in the birth practices of traditional cultures. *Birth* 12:29, 1985.
4. Beck, N., and Hall, D. Natural childbirth: A review and analysis. *Obstetrics and Gynecology* 52:371, 1978.
5. Bennett, A., Hewson, D., Booker, E., and Holliday, S. Antenatal preparation and labor support in relation to birth outcomes. *Birth* 12:9; 1985.
6. Bergstrom-Walen, J. Efficacy of education for childbirth. *Journal of Psychosomatic Research* 7:131, 1963.
7. Bibring, G. Some considerations of the psychological processes in pregnancy. *Psychological Studies of Children* 14:113, 1959.
8. Brackbill, Y., Rice, J., and Young, D. *Birth Trap: The Legal Low-Down on High-Tech Obstetrics*. St. Louis: G.V. Mosby, 1984.
9. Brown, M.S. Culture and childbearing. In Anne Clark (ed.), *Culture and Childrearing*. Philadelphia: F.A. Davis Co., 1981, pp. 2–35.
10. Brown, M.S. Maternal-child care in Nacerima. *Image* 18:74, 1986.
11. Butani, P., and Hodnett, E. Mothers' perceptions of their labor experiences. *Journal of Maternal Child Nursing* 9:73, 1980.
12. Cave, C. Social characteristics of natural childbirth users and nonusers. *American Journal of Public Health* 68:898, 1978.
13. Chaney, J. Birthing in early America. *Journal of Nurse Midwifery* 25:5, 1980.
14. Charles, A., Norr, K., Block, C., Meyering, S., and Meyers, E. Obstetric and psychological effects of psychoprophylactic preparation for childbirth. *American Journal of Obstetrics and Gynecology* 31:44, 1978.
15. Chertok, L. *Motherhood and Personality*. London: Tavistock Publications, 1969.
16. Cogan, R. Effects of childbirth preparation. *Clinical Obstetrics and Gynecology* 23:1, 1980.
17. Coussens, W., and Coussens, P. Maximizing preparation for childbirth. *Health Care for Women International* 5:335, 1984.
18. Davenport-Slack, B., and Boylan, C. Psychological correlates of childbirth pain. *Psychosomatic Medicine* 36:215, 1974.
19. Doering, S., and Entwisle, D. Preparation during pregnancy and ability to cope with labor and delivery. *American Journal of Health and Social Behavior* 21:12, 1980.
20. Doering, S., Entwisle, D., and Quinlan, D. Modeling the quality of women's birth experience. *Journal of Health and Social Behavior* 21:12, 1980.
21. Dooher, M. Lamaze method of childbirth. *Nursing Research* 29:220, 1980.
22. Enkin, M. W., Smith, S. L., Dermer, S. S., and Emmett, J. O. An adequate controlled study of the effectiveness of PPM training. In Morris, N. (ed.), *Psychosomatic Medicine in Obstetrics and Gynecology*. Basel: Steiner & Co., 1972, pp. 62–67.
23. Entwisle, D., and Doering, S. *The First Birth: A Family Turning Point*. Baltimore: Johns Hopkins University Press, 1981.
24. Felton, G., and Siegelman, F. Lamaze childbirth training and changes in belief about personal control. *Birth and the Family Journal* 5:141, 1978.
25. Friedman, D. D. Motivation for natural childbirth. In Morris, N. (ed.), *Psychosomatic Medicine in Obstetrics and Gynecology*. Basel: Steiner & Co., 1972, pp. 30–34.
26. Friedman, E. A. An objective method of evaluating labor. *Hospital Practice* 5:82, 1970.
27. Gebbie, D. *Reproductive Anthropology—Descent Through Woman*. New York: John Wiley & Sons, 1981.
28. Geden, E., Beck, N., Brouder, G., Glaister, J., and Pohlman, S. Self-report and psychophysiological effect of Lamaze preparation: An analogue of labor pain. *Research in Nursing and Health* 8:155, 1985.
29. Geden, E., Beck, N., Haughe, G., and Pohlman, S. Self-report and psychophysiological effects of five pain coping strategies. *Nursing Research* 33:155, 1984.
30. Gordon, J., and Haire, D. Alternatives in childbirth. In Ahmed, P. (ed.), *Pregnancy, Childbirth and Parenthood*. New York: Elsevier, 1981, pp. 287–313.
31. Grimm, E. Psychological and Social Factors in Pregnancy, Delivery and Outcomes. In Richardson, S. and Guttmacher, A. (eds.), *Childbearing—Its Social and Psychological Aspects*. Baltimore: Williams & Wilkins, 1967, pp. 1–52.
32. Grossman, F., Eichler, L., and Winickoff, S. *Pregnancy, Birth and Parenthood*. San Francisco: Jossey-Bass, 1980.
33. Henneborn, W. J., and Cogan, R. The effect of husband participation on reported pain and probability of medication during labor and birth. *Journal of Psychosomatic Research* 19:215, 1975.
34. Hilbers, S., and Gennaro, S. Non-pharmaceutical pain relief. *NAACOG Update Series* Volume 5, 1986.
35. Hott, J. Best-laid plans: Pre- and postpartum comparison of self and spouse in primiparous Lamaze couples who share delivery and those who do not. *Nursing Research* 29:20, 1980.
36. Hughey, M., McElin, T., and Young, T. Maternal and fetal outcome of Lamaze-prepared patients. *Obstetrics and Gynecology* 51:643, 1978.

37. Humenick, S. Mastery the key to childbirth satisfaction? A review. *Birth and the Family Journal* 8:79, 1981.
38. Humenick, S., and Bugen, L. Mastery: The key to childbirth satisfaction? A study. *Birth and the Family Journal* 8:84, 1981.
39. Huttel, F. A., Mitchell, I., Fisher, W., Meyer, A. Qualitative evaluation of psychoprophylaxis in childbirth. *Journal of Psychosomatic Research* 16:81, 1972.
40. Klein, H., Potter, H., and Dyk, R. *Anxiety in Pregnancy and Childbirth*. New York: Paul B. Hoeber, Inc., 1950.
41. Klusman, L. Reduction of pain in childbirth by the alleviation of anxiety during pregnancy. *Journal of Consulting and Clinical Psychology* 43:162, 1975.
42. Laird, M., and Hogan, M. An elective program on preparation for childbirth at the Sloane Hospital for Women May 1951 to June 1953. *American Journal of Obstetrics and Gynecology* 72:641, 1956.
43. Leifer, M. *Psychological effects of motherhood: A study of first pregnancy.* New York: Praeger Press, 1980.
44. Manderino, M., and Bzdek, V. Effects of modeling and information on reactions to pain: A childbirth preparation analogue. *Nursing Research* 33:9, 1984.
45. McGraw, R., and Abplanalp, J. Selection factors involved in the choice of childbirth method. *Issues in Health Care of Women* 3:359, 1981.
46. Mead, M. Childbirth in a changing world. In Durston, J. (ed.), *Pregnancy, Birth and the Newborn Baby.* Boston: Delacorte Press, 1972, 40–61.
47. Mead, M., and Newton, N. Cultural patterning of perinatal behavior. In Richardson, S. and Guttmacher, A. (eds.), *Childbearing—Its Social and Psychological Aspects*. Baltimore: Williams & Wilkins, 1967, pp. 142–244.
48. Mead, M., and Newton, N. Conception, pregnancy, labor, and the puerperium in cultural perspective. In *Medicine psychosomatique et Maternite (Proceedings of the First International Congress of Psychosomatic Medicine and Childbirth)*. Paris: Gauthier Villars, 1962, pp. 51–54.
49. Melzack, R. The myth of painless childbirth. *Pain* 19:321, 1984.
50. Mercer, R. Relationship of the birth experience to later mothering behaviors. *Journal of Nurse Midwifery* 30:204, 1985.
51. Moore, D. Prepared childbirth and marital satisfaction during the antepartum and postpartum periods. *Nursing Research* 32:73, 1983.
52. Morgan, B., Bulpitt, C. J., Clifton, P., and Lewis, P. J. Effectiveness of pain relief in labour, survey of 1000 mothers. *British Medical Journal* 285:689, 1982.
53. Morgan, B., Bulpitt, C. J., Clifton, P., and Lewis, P. J. Analgesia and satisfaction in childbirth (The Queen Charlotte 1000-mother survey). *Lancet* 1:808, 1982.
54. Nettlebladt, P., Fagerstrom, C., and Uddenberg, N. The significance of reported childbirth pain. *Journal of Psychosomatic Research* 20:215, 1976.
55. Niven, C., and Gijsbers, K. A study of labour pain using the McGill Pain Questionnaire. *Social Science Medicine* 19:1347, 1984.
56. Norr, K., Block, C., Charles A., Meyering, S., and Meyer, T. Explaining pain and enjoyment in childbirth. *Journal of Health and Social Behavior* 18:260, 1977.
57. Nuckolls, K. B., Cassel, J., Kaplan, B. H. Psychosocial aspects of life crisis and the prognosis of pregnancy. *American Journal of Epidemiology* 95:431, 1972.
58. Oakley, A. *Women Confined—Towards a Sociology of Childbirth*. New York: Schocken Books, 1980.
59. Patton, L., English, E., and Hambleton, J. Childbirth preparation and outcomes of labor and delivery in primiparous women. *The Journal of Family Practice* 20:375, 1985.
60. Poore, M., and Foster, J. Epidural and no epidural anesthesia: Differences between mothers and their experience of birth. *Birth* 9:205, 1985.
61. Richards, M. P. M. The trouble with choice in childbirth. *Birth* 9:253, 1982.
62. Robitaille, Y., and Kramer, M. Does participation in prenatal courses lead to heavier babies? *American Journal of Public Health* 75:1186, 1985.
63. Rodway, H. Education of childbirth and its results. *Journal of Obstetrics and Gynaecology of the British Empire* 64:545, 1957.
64. Rothman, B. Awake and aware or false consciousness? In Renalis, S. (ed.), *Childbirth—Alternative to Medical Control*. Austin: University of Texas Press, 1981.
65. Scott, J., and Rose, N. Effect of psychoprophylaxis on labor and delivery in primiparas. *New England Journal of Medicine* 294:1205, 1976.
66. Slavazza, K., Mercer, R., Marut, J., and Schider, S. Anesthesia, analgesia for vaginal childbirth: Differences in maternal perceptions. *JOGN Nursing* 14:321, 1985.
67. Standley, K. Research on childbirth: Toward an understanding of coping. In Ahmed, O. (ed.), *Pregnancy, Childbirth and Parenthood*. New York: Elsevier, 1981, pp. 213–223.
68. Standley, K., and Nicholson, J. Observing the childbirth environment: A research model. *Birth and the Family Journal* 7:15, Spring 1980.
69. Steinfels, M. O. New childbirth technology: A clash of values. *Hastings Center Report* 8(9), February 1978.
70. Stone, C., Demchik-Stone, D., and Horan, J. Coping with pain: A component analysis of Lamaze and cognitive-behavioral procedures. *Journal of Psychosomatic Research* 21:451, 1977.
71. Tanzer, D. Natural childbirth: Pain or peak experience? *Psychology Today* 1:18, 1968.
72. Timm, M. Prenatal education evaluation. *Nursing Research* 28:338, 1979.
73. Tronick, E., Wise, S., Als, H., Adamson, L., Scanlon, J., and Brazelton, T. B. Regional obstetric anesthesia and newborn behavior: Effect on the first ten days of life. *Pediatrics* 58:94, 1976.
74. Van Auken, W., and Tomlinson, D. An appraisal of patient training for childbirth. *American Journal of Obstetrics and Gynecology* 66:100, 1955.
75. Van Eps, L. W. Psychoprophylaxis in labor. *Lancet* 269:112, 1955.
76. Verney, T. The psycho-technology of pregnancy and labor. *Neonatal Network* 4:10, 1985.
77. Whitley, N. A comparison of prepared childbirth couples and conventional prenatal class couples. *JOGN Nursing* 8:109, 1979.

78. Willmuth, L. R. Prepared childbirth: The concept of control. *JOGN Nursing* 4:38, 1975.
79. Zacharias, J. F. Childbirth education classes: Effects on attitudes toward childbirth in high-risk indigent women. *JOGN Nursing* 10:265, 1981.

Beginning Quote

Maynard, F. The emotional highs of successful childbirth. *Woman's Day,* September 1, 1978, p. 70.

Boxed Quotes

1. Kitzinger, S. *The Experience of Childbirth*. London: Victor Gollancz, Ltd., 1972, p. 17.
2. Schwartz, L. *The World of the Unborn*. New York: Marek, 1980.
3. Baldwin, R., and Palmarini, T. *Pregnant Feelings*. Berkeley, CA: Celestial Arts, 1986, p. 2.
4. Hartigan, H. *Women in Birth*. Artemis, 1984, p. 15. (Available from Childbirth Graphics, Ltd., Rochester, NY.)
5. Gaskin, I. M. *Spiritual Midwifery.* Summertown, TN: The Book Publishing Company, 1980, p. 11.

chapter 5

THE EARLY PARENTING EXPERIENCE

DONNA HOHMANN EWY and JOAN MARIA YOUMANS

When I came home from the hospital I stood in the middle of the living room and cried. I just wasn't prepared for the emotions I would experience.

A New Mother

The birth of a new baby has been identified as a critical period for learning, as well as a time of stress in which parents are confronted with new roles, relationships, and daily activities.[59] Resources for resolving stress through learning are often unavailable or inaccessible to new parents.[58] In this day of the nuclear family, many parents receive little or no information during the postpartum period to assist them in making this important psychological, physical, and emotional transition. The mother and father leave the hospital with their infant to begin alone the adventure of parenting a newborn. Yet researchers have found that women who were prepared for the task of mothering were happier; their babies were healthier and their marriages more successful than were those of women who received no preparation for motherhood.[23]

Parents do not automatically have the information and skills that result in accurate expectations of their newborn's ability to respond. Realistic expectations are learned, not instinctual. Many people enter parenthood believing that their baby is a piece of clay to be molded. Few recognize the tremendous potential of their infant. Without information about their baby's innate capabilities, they blunder into parenthood, missing opportunities to enhance their child's development. Parents who learn about children's early abilities can begin to encourage at birth their own child's development.

As childbirth educators increase their understanding of the knowledge and skills required of new parents, they can incorporate this information into their classes. The neonatal period offers the childbirth educator a special opportunity to help parents develop realistic expectations for their newborns and to provide information that will enhance healthy parent-infant relationships. The childbirth educator can also offer parents postpartum support and education.

REVIEW OF THE LITERATURE

Early Parenting Experience

The transition to parenthood has been viewed as a time of problems and gratifications.[67] The potential for growth and achievement of a higher developmental state exists in the transition to parenthood. Many changes accompany transitions to parenthood including reorganization of the family system, role changes, and changes in lifestyle.

The birth of an infant results in reorganization of the family system. Upon the birth of the first child, the family unit usually changes from a couple or two-person family to a three-person or triangular family.[36] Many changes in the roles and responsi-

The birth of an infant results in the reorganization of the family system. (Copyright BABES, Inc.)

bilities of each family member accompany this reorganization.

Parenthood is a new role for the mother and father, with a complete set of new tasks for each.[65] The mother's roles change from being a wife to being a wife and mother. The father's roles change from being a husband to being a husband and father.[36] The mother's roles may change from being a professional working outside the home to being a full-time mother, while the father may suddenly be the sole source of income for the family. Becoming a parent does not involve gradually assuming responsibility as when one takes on a professional role[62]; it is an immediate 24-hour responsibility.

Parents often find that they are not ready for the changes in lifestyle that a new infant brings. The following concerns about these changes have been identified by new parents: little time for themselves as a couple; little time to socialize with friends; more confinement to home; additional economic pressure and expenses with the new baby; loss of sleep; and a decline in housekeeping standards.[26,28,36]

Changes in the lifestyles of new parents often result from trying to balance the three major needs of the new family.

1. The development of a parent-infant relationship, which includes meeting the needs of the infant;
2. The personal needs of each individual parent; and
3. The needs of the couple.[28] The dependency of infants demands that their needs be met first; the parents may have to delay meeting some of their own personal needs.[14]

New parents often find themselves experiencing many conflicting feelings, with all the changes accompanying their transitions to parenthood. New parents express the feelings of joy, anxiety, confusion, overwhelming responsibility, love, helplessness, fear, depression, exhaustion, and guilt in their adjustment to parenthood.[14,26,36,67,71] Parents often experience these feelings as they find themselves with an infant on a 24-hour-a-day basis.[73] In addition, parents often find that their infants are not like their perception of the stereotyped "ideal" infant.[28] Parents need to realize that their conflicts and feelings are a normal part of becoming a parent.

Concerns of Parents of Newborns

Studies have been completed to determine the concerns of new parents after they have been home with their infants.[1,15,25,78] These studies have revealed that the following concerns are common among new mothers in the postpartum period: physiological changes in the mother including return of the body to prepregnancy shape; tiredness and fatigue; infant behaviors such as crying and sleeping; infant growth and development; infant care activities such as feeding, bathing, cord care, and circumcision care.[1,15,25,78]

Infant Crying. Infant crying has been found to be a major concern of parents.[1,11,20,50] New parents often do not have a realistic picture of the amount of crying that occurs in normal newborns.[27] Parents need to know that research has found that responding to infants' needs when they cry will not "spoil" the infant.[6,17,52] Research has also revealed that responding slowly or ignoring an infant's crying often results in an increase in infant fretfulness and crying.[6,76]

Infant crying is often perceived by parents as indicating failure of their parenting ability.[11] Infant crying has been found to evoke a mother's feelings of frustration, nervousness, helplessness, anxiety, guilt about her feelings, and sadness.[27] Infant crying can become a continuing cycle for the infant and parent.[50] For example, the infant cries and the parent becomes tense and anxious and tries to comfort the infant. The infant senses the parent's tension and intensifies the crying. This results in the parent becoming more tense, anxious, and possibly angry. As the parent intensifies the effort to comfort the infant, the infant in turn senses this and cries harder.[50] Parents need to learn various ways to comfort their crying infant and to break the crying cycle; what comforts one infant may not be useful in calming another.[50]

Infant Feeding. Infant feeding is another major concern of new parents.[1,15,51,58] Infant feeding has a profound meaning for parents in relationship to their infant's growth and well-being.[58] Parents often wonder whether their infants are getting too little or too much to eat; they receive a sense of accomplishment when they know their infant is receiving the nourishment needed for growth.

The feeding process is a learning experience for both infant and parent.[70] Parents need to know how to make feeding time a pleasurable and rewarding experience for the infant and parent. Infants may experience frustration associated with feeding if they must wait for a feeding until nearly exhausted from crying, if they are frequently interrupted while sucking, if they are forced to eat too much or if they are not allowed to get enough food, and if they are forced to feed themselves before they develop the necessary skills.[51]

Parents have different concerns about infant feeding. For example, parents who bottle feed their infant may express concern about feeding their infant too often, while breastfeeding mothers may be concerned that their infants are not getting enough to eat at each feeding. In childbirth education classes, parents who will bottle feed their infant may have questions about formula preparation, and mothers who will breastfeed may have questions about breastfeeding techniques.

Therefore, expectant parents should be given general information on infant feeding, and then individual questions on infant feeding should be addressed. General topics on infant feeding may include information on infant sucking and cuddling needs associated with feeding, infant feeding methods (breastfeeding or bottle feeding), and the recommendations of the American Academy of Pediatrics Committee on Nutrition on when solids or supplemental foods should be introduced into an infant's diet. The Committee recommended that solids or supplemental foods should not be introduced into infants' diets until they are four to six months old.[3] Early introduction of solids into an infant's diet has been associated with childhood and adult obesity.[42]

Fatigue. A loss of sleep and its resulting tiredness and fatigue is another concern of new mothers.[15,66] Sleep deprivation and sleep hunger are often severe in the first month postpartum, and they continue for as long as the infant requires any feeding during the night or has an illness or colic.[66] New fathers have also reported a decrease in sleep following the birth of their infant.[26]

New parents need to be assisted in their expectations of what each can do to contribute to household responsibilities.[45] New mothers often need help with finding ways to conserve their energy.[15] In one study, parents who were associated with good postpartum adjustment had given less emphasis to the tidiness of the home after their infant's birth.[24] In addition, these parents had obtained more experienced help with the baby, and the husbands were found to have limited their outside activities and had become more available in their homes.[24] These couples continued to socialize outside their home but less frequently.

Returning to Work. In 1980, more than one million women became pregnant, and more than half of these returned to work within a year of giving birth.[31] Factors that influence a mother's decision to work outside the home include economic necessity, social and sex role factors, and personal factors such as fulfillment and gratification provided to the mother by her career.[35]

Finding optimal child care often represents the biggest headache and heartache for the working mother.[31] Mothers often experience ambivalence about leaving their infant with someone else to return to work.[31] Mothers have often expressed concern that the chosen setting may not be good for the infant. Parents need to examine the advantages and disadvantages of the three major alternatives that exist for child care: care in someone else's home (family day care), care in the mother's home (housekeeper/babysitter), and group care (day care center or nursery).[31]

The Mothering Role

Mercer defined maternal role attainment as "a process in which the mother achieves competence in the role and integrates the mothering behaviors into her established role set so that she is comfortable with her identity as a mother."[47] The attainment of the maternal role progresses through four stages: anticipatory, formal, informal, and personal. Each stage involves interactions between the individual and her external expectations, which include the individual's attempts to influence the expectations of others as well as others' attempts to influence the individual.

The *anticipatory stage* occurs during the pregnancy as the mother begins to learn about expectations of the mothering role, this knowledge being acquired through direct and indirect learning. Social and psychological adjustment to the new role begins during this stage. The *formal stage* begins with the birth of the infant; at this time maternal role behaviors are influenced largely by the consensual expectations of others within the role set. In the *informal stage,* the mother develops her own unique way of dealing with her role as this stage allows for flexibility within the maternal role. In the *final personal stage* the mother feels a congruence of herself and her role as she develops her own mothering style and others accept her individual role performance.[47,80] This process of maternal role attainment has been observed to occur within a range of three to ten months.[47]

Numerous factors have an impact on maternal role attainment, including age, perceptions of the birth experience, early maternal-infant separation, support systems, self-concept and personality traits, maternal illness, childrearing attitudes, their own mothering experience, infant temperament and health, culture, and socioeconomic level.[46] The age of mothers has also been found to have a significant effect on the reported gratification obtained in their mothering roles.[48] The following factors were found to be associated with an easy adaptation to motherhood in ''normal'' primiparous women: previous experience with infants and children, help during the first week at home, satisfaction with nursing care received in the hospital, a perception of the husband as being helpful, and a positive self-concept.[19]

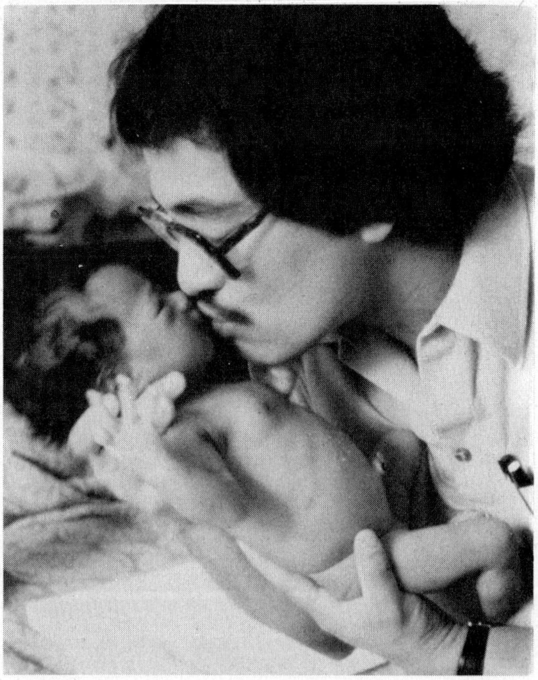

Many fathers take an active role in the care-taking and nurturing of their infants. (Copyright BABES, Inc.)

The Fathering Role

Historically the role of the father has been to provide for and protect his family. Only in recent years has the father's role changed from being the economic provider to being an active participant in the childbearing and childrearing processes.[30] As more mothers are working outside the home, fathers have taken an active role in the physical tasks of raising a child. In addition to taking on physical tasks, fathers appear to be developing special relationships with their children.

Only recently has research begun to look at the fathering role. In reviewing the literature, Hangsleben found the following factors to be related to fathers' adjustments to parenthood: quality of their marital relationships, memories of being fathered as a child, and ability to be involved in the pregnancy and birth.[26] Fathers who reported more changes in lifestyle and greater involvement in caretaking activities experienced more signs of depression, especially irritability, sleep disturbance, and fatigability. This suggested that the early days of fathering can be as stressful to the father's lifestyle as to many mothers. Further research is needed to determine if a process for attaining the fathering role, similar to that for maternal role, exists.

Current research has been focusing on paternal-infant bonding. Taubenheim studied paternal-infant bonding and found that engaging in caretaking activities, such as feeding the newborn, resulted in a higher number of bonding behaviors.[79] Thus, care-taking activities may be an important element in paternal-infant bonding. The behavior of talking about their newborns with another person was frequently noted, and this may be a characteristic of paternal-infant bonding.[79] In another study the attachment process in the father was associated with the amount of caretaking activities, the amount of stimulating play, and the strength of the emotional investment.[55]

The Parent-Infant Interaction Experience

A warm, nurturing, and consistent relationship between parents and infants has been found to be essential for the healthy psychological development of infants.[16,32] The last decade of research on parent-infant relationships shows that its development is a two-sided process, to which both infants and parents contribute actively.[4] This interaction between the parent and child is shown in the Barnard model in Figure 5–1.

Infant Characteristics. The interactions between the parents and child depend on the infant's clarity of cues and responsiveness to the parent. Infants send many types of cues to parents to indicate hunger, irritability, and sleepiness. The more clearly the infant sends the cues, the easier it is to determine the infant's needs. When the infant sends ambiguous or confusing cues, it is frustrating to the parent because determining the baby's wants or needs is difficult. The infant's responsiveness to the parents also influences the parent-infant interaction experience. If the baby is very responsive, i.e., likes to be cuddled or is soothed easily, the experience is a pleasurable one for both parent and infant. If the baby does not respond (for example, is difficult to soothe), the interaction is frustrating for the parent and engenders negative overtones.

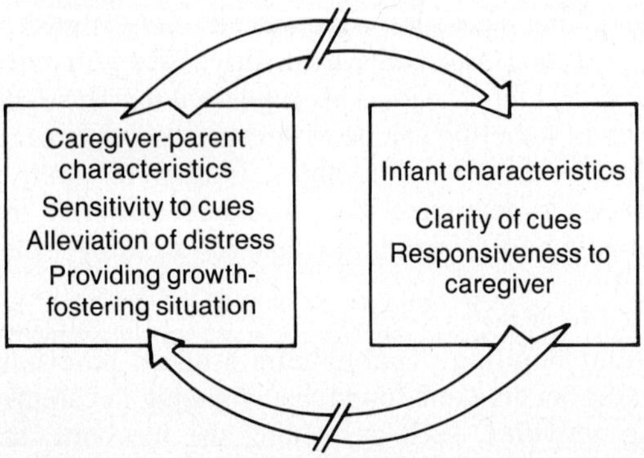

FIGURE 5–1. Barnard model of parent-infant interaction. The infant and the parent each make unique contributions to the parent-infant interaction experience. The infant's tasks are to produce clear cues and to respond to the caregiver. The parent's tasks are to alleviate distress and to provide growth-fostering situations. The system breaks down when the infant or the parent does not respond appropriately and parent-infant interaction is compromised. (From Barnard, K. *Instructor's Learning Resource Manual.* University of Washington, Nursing Child Assessment Satellite Training, 1985.)

Parent Characteristics. There are three major parent characteristics that influence parent-child interactions: parents' sensitivity to child's cues, parents' ability to alleviate the infant's distress, and parents' social and emotional growth-fostering activities. Parents need to be able to recognize their child's needs and identify them accurately. Stress such as financial problems or too many demands on a parent's time can influence sensitivity to an infant's needs.

The parents' ability to alleviate the distress of the infant influences the interaction experience. There are several factors that influence this ability: the parents recognize that the infant has a problem, they know the appropriate actions that can be taken, and they are able to take this information and put it into action. The parents' ability to provide growth-fostering situations also influences interactions. Growth-fostering situations fall into three areas: social (engaging in social interactions), emotional (playing affectionately with the infant and cuddling), and cognitive activities (play activities that promote the child's development). These depend upon the parents' knowledge of child development as well as their available energies for the tasks. From the moment of birth, the infant's senses, reflexes, and behavior help him deal with the environment. They are the "tools" through which the infant expresses satisfaction and displeasure and fosters interaction with the parents.

Infant Characteristics

The Newborn Sensory Capacities. Research indicates that newborns can focus their eyes at birth and prefer the human face, in full-face presentations that allow for direct eye contact.[53] The ability of the newborn to fix and follow the face of the caregiver is the beginning of two-way communication.[53] Infants' sense of smell is also well developed. In one study, infants who were offered two sets of pads containing mother's milk consistently preferred the pad with their own mother's milk.[41] By the fourth day of life a child learns to produce first sounds by mimicking the sounds of human voices. An infant's reflexes—blinks, sneezes, stretches, burps, hiccups, twitches, and jerky movement—help the baby to control the environment. Parents who understand their baby's innate capabilities and resources are better able to "tune in" to their child's cues, and they enjoy their parenting experience more.[13]

Sleep/Wake States. One of the most powerful factors that helps shape the way infants respond is their state of consciousness. Babies experience six basic states of waking and sleeping. The two sleep states have been identified as deep sleep and light sleep. The four awake states are drowsy, quiet alert, active alert, and crying.[8]

Each state is significant in the infant's growth and development, and the states also affect the parents' interaction and stimulation time. Parents who learn to recognize when their baby is most responsive can match their behavior to the infant's needs (Table 5–1). The sleep/wake states are characterized by body activity, eye movements, breathing patterns, and the infant's response to external and internal stimuli.

Babies have a high threshold to sensory stimuli during deep sleep; at that time stimuli must be intense to arouse the infant.[54,57,81] During light sleep infants are more responsive than in deep sleep to internal stimuli (such as hunger), and many times they display movements that mislead the parents into thinking that the infant is hungry.[54] In the drowsy state infants are between sleep and alertness. They are more open to internal and external stimuli. More stimuli can bring them to a full alert state. If left alone, they may return to a deep sleep.[54]

The infant is most open to stimuli during the quiet alert state. This is the state that gives the parents and the infant the most pleasure and positive feedback.[54,57] During the active alert state, the infant may be more sensitive to stimuli such as hunger, fatigue, noise, and excessive handling and may become fussy. If left alone, the infant may start to cry but with intervention can be brought back to the quiet alert state.[54,57,81] As newborns mature, quiet periods become longer.[37] Whether asleep or awake, infants flow between active and quiet periods. Some infants flow smoothly and predictably from state to state, as if they were moving up and down a ladder step by step or two steps at a time.[8] Other infants jump from one extreme to the other, making parenting more difficult.

In the first weeks of life, infants sleep on the average from 16 to 20 hours a day.[37] The average length of a sleep cycle is from 50 to 80 minutes, during which 35 to 60 minutes are spent in light sleep and 15 to 20 minutes in deep sleep[37] (Fig. 5–2).

Knowing that the average sleep/wake cycle is about two hours can help parents develop more realistic expectations of what night feedings and their own sleep patterns will be like. A baby's sleep patterns may be an indicator of maturity, as sleep patterns of premature infants are very different from those of full-term infants.[54]

Being able to determine an infant's state is important in helping parents understand their newborn. Infants use their states to control how much input they receive. Infants who spend long periods in sleep affect their parents differently from infants who spend a great deal of time awake. Babies who spend more time awake interact with their parents more and have more opportunities to receive and process learning experiences.

Reciprocity. A complex code of reciprocal obligations governs interactions between parent and newborn. For example, a parent who looks a baby fully in the face invites the baby into an exchange. When parents respond to their baby as if the infant understands them, the child responds with greater developed skills.[69]

An infant anticipates that interactions will be two-sided, because he has been primed to expect it. Reciprocity in communication, or turn-taking, is a building block of cooperation. Its origins lie in the infant's innate burst-and-pause cycle of activity. When reciprocity is provided, the child's communication skills blossom. The baby eventually turns away from anyone who cannot or will not interact reciprocally.[53]

Play. The infant is a social being with the desire and capacity to learn. What the parents do with their faces, voices, bodies, and hands provides babies with their first experiences in human communication and relationships. Play or interaction between the baby and parent or sibling is a mutual exchange of joy and fun that gives the baby the experience needed to grow and develop socially.[69,75]

TABLE 5–1. INFANT STATE CHART (SLEEP AND AWAKE STATES)

	CHARACTERISTICS OF STATE					
SLEEP STATES	**Body Activity**	**Eye Movements**	**Facial Movements**	**Breathing Pattern**	**Level of Response**	**Implications for Caregiving**
Deep Sleep	Nearly still, except for occasional startle or twitch.	None.	Without facial movements, except for occasional sucking movement at regular intervals.	Smooth and regular.	Threshold to stimuli is very high so that only very intense and disturbing stimuli will arouse infants.	Caregivers trying to feed infants in deep sleep will probably find the experience frustrating. Infants will be unresponsive, even if caregivers use disturbing stimuli (flicking feet) to arouse infants. Infants may only arouse briefly and then become unresponsive as they return to deep sleep. If caregivers wait until infants move to a higher, more responsive state, feeding or caregiving will be much pleasanter.
Light Sleep	Some body movements.	Rapid eye movements (REM), fluttering of eyes beneath closed eyelids.	May smile and make brief fussy or crying sounds.	Irregular.	More responsive to internal and external stimuli. When these stimuli occur, infants may remain in light sleep, return to deep sleep, or arouse to drowsy.	Light sleep makes up the highest proportion of newborn sleep and usually precedes wakening. Due to brief fussy or crying sounds made during this state, caregivers who are not aware that these sounds occur normally may think it is time for feeding and may try to feed infants before they are ready to eat.

AWAKE STATES						
Drowsy	Activity level variable, with mild startles interspersed from time to time. Movements usually smooth.	Eyes open and close occasionally, are heavy-lidded with dull, glazed appearance.	May have some facial movements. Often there are none, and the face appears still.	Irregular.	Infants react to sensory stimuli although responses are delayed. State change after stimulation frequently noted.	From the drowsy state, infants may return to sleep or awaken further. In order to awaken, caregivers can provide something for infants to see, hear, or suck, as this may arouse them to a quiet alert state, a more responsive state. Infants left alone without stimuli may return to a sleep state.
Quiet Alert	Minimal.	Brightening and widening of eyes.	Faces have bright, shining, sparkling looks.	Regular.	Infants attend most to environment, focusing attention on any stimuli that are present.	Infants in this state provide much pleasure and positive feedback for caregivers. Providing something for infants to see, hear, or suck will often maintain a quiet alert state. In the first few hours after birth, most newborns commonly experience a period of intense alertness before going into a long sleeping period.
Active Alert	Much body activity. May have periods of fussiness.	Eyes open with less brightening.	Much facial movement. Faces not as bright as quiet alert state.	Irregular.	Increasingly sensitive to disturbing stimuli (hunger, fatigue, noise, excessive handling).	Caregivers may intervene at this stage to console and to bring infants to a lower state.
Crying	Increased motor activity, with color changes.	Eyes may be tightly closed or open.	Grimaces.	More irregular.	Extremely responsive to unpleasant external or internal stimuli.	Crying is the infant's communication signal. It is a response to unpleasant stimuli from the environment or from within infants (fatigue, hunger, discomfort). Crying tells us infants' limits have been reached. Sometimes infants can console themselves and return to lower states. At other times, they need help from caregivers.

State is a group of characteristics that regularly occur together: body activity, eye movements, facial movements, breathing pattern, and level of response to external stimuli (e.g., handling) and internal stimuli (e.g., hunger).

From Blackburn, S. Sleep and awake states of the newborn. *In* Early Parent-Infant Relationships, Series 1, Module 3. White Plains: The National Foundation—March of Dimes, 1978, with permission of the copyright holder.

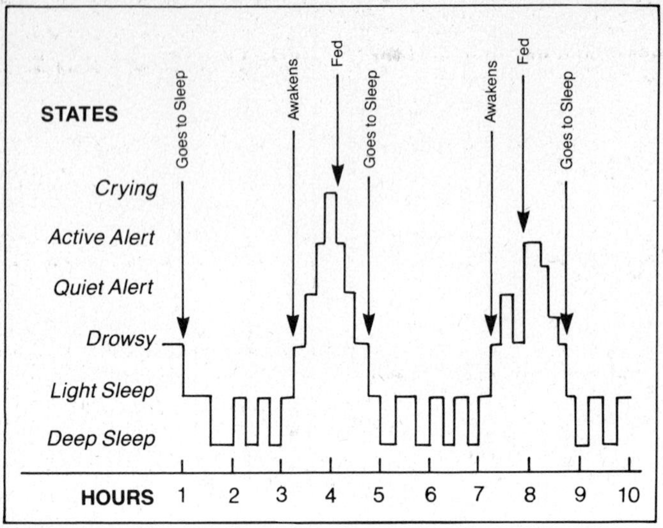

FIGURE 5–2. Diagrammatic example of infant state change. (From Blackburn, S. Sleep and awake states of the newborn. In *Early Parent-Infant Relationships*, Series 1, Module 3. White Plains NY: The National Foundation-March of Dimes, 1978, with permission of the copyright holder.)

Infant Behavior. Parents need to understand the impact of their infant's basic behavior patterns on the mother-father-infant relationship. Although there are as many variations in newborn patterns as there are newborns, certain basic behavior patterns influence the parents' interaction with their infant: predictability, adaptability, activity level, soothability (consolability), ability to shut out annoying stimuli, capacity to respond, and level of irritability.[12]

The interactions between the baby and sibling are fun for both and provide the baby with the experiences to grow and develop socially. (Photograph by Bill Youmans.)

TEMPERAMENTS. Babies come to their parents with differences in temperaments that affect the interaction between the parent and child. The qualities that seem to determine a baby's temperament are the amount of time the baby stays in the alert state, response to visual stimuli, response to auditory stimuli, habituation (the ability to handle obnoxious stimuli), cuddliness, consolability, body movements and activity, level of irritability, and readability of the infant's cues (Table 5–2). When the parents can respond with appropriate behavior they see themselves in a more positive light.

VISUAL RESPONSES. One of the infant's most powerful tools is the ability to see: to focus in and make eye contact with the parents. Within a few days after birth, infants begin to coordinate their vision and hearing.[72] They can brighten, focus, and follow an object.[10] Infants are more open to visual stimuli when they are held upright in a sitting position or held upright against the caregiver's shoulder so they can see around them.[34] Eye-to-eye contact gives important feedback to the parents and helps to establish intimate communication. It also provides special pleasure to parents and elicits caregiving responses.[61]

AUDITORY RESPONSES. Newborns are especially

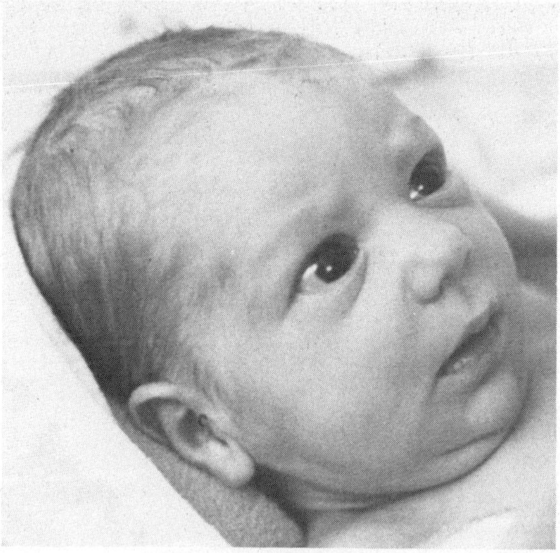

One of the infant's most powerful tools is the ability to focus in and make eye contact with the parents. (Photograph by Rodger Ewy, © Educational Graphic Aids, Inc.)

responsive to the human voice; they can find the general location of a voice and can follow it from side to side.[34,72] Parents find it exciting when their infants respond to their voices.

HABITUATION. Infants come into the world with the ability to tune out annoying stimuli. If they reacted to everything around them, they would be constantly overstimulated. The ability to turn down and tune out stimuli allows the baby to selectively choose and learn from a wide variety of stimuli.[77] Babies such as premature infants who do not have a well-developed ability to habituate and tune out stimuli may be overwhelmed and must be protected from overstimulation.[77]

CUDDLINESS. Babies come with the ability to cuddle and to fit themselves comfortably and affectionately into their parents' arms. Parents enjoy cuddly babies and usually feel rejected by babies who resist being held.[13]

CONSOLABILITY. Most babies are able to be soothed when they are crying and can be brought into other states of alertness or sleeping. Parents view a baby who is easily consoled as an easy-to-handle and enjoyable baby; they are likely to view themselves as "good parents." Babies who are not easily consoled are viewed as "difficult." Since parents often view how well they parent by how well they soothe or console their babies, the factor of consolability or inconsolability has great impact on parental self-esteem.[13]

MOTOR BEHAVIOR AND ACTIVITY. Some infants have smooth, rhythmical movements of their arms, legs, and body, while others may move in jerky, uneven startles. Most infants move from the smooth to the jerky when they are in different states. Parents need assurance that their baby's different movements are normal.[29] Parents of children with unpredictable, jerky, and unsmooth movements need special help in understanding and shaping their infants' movements.

IRRITABILITY. Crying is one way an infant has to respond to stimuli. Those who exhibit more fretfulness and crying and need more frequent consoling by the parents may be perceived as more difficult. Parents need information on a great variety of methods to console the "difficult" infant. They need to know that some infants need more predictable routines, along with quieter, more protected environments. The baby's irritability is a reflection of the baby's temperament and not a comment on the parents' ability to soothe.[13]

READABILITY OF CUES. One of the greatest mysteries new parents must unravel is how to read the cues their baby sends. Some infants send out clearer cues than others. Babies who send out strong, consistent, predictable cues are easier to read than babies who send out inconsistent, unpredictable, or weak cues. Parents need help and support in learning that the kind of cues their baby sends is part of his temperament and not a reflection on their parenting ability.[13]

TABLE 5–2. INFANT STATE-RELATED BEHAVIOR CHART

BEHAVIOR	DESCRIPTION OF BEHAVIOR	INFANT STATE CONSIDERATION	IMPLICATIONS FOR CAREGIVING
Alerting	Widening and brightening of the eyes. Infants focus attention on stimuli, whether visual, auditory, or objects to be sucked.	From drowsy or active alert to quiet alert.	Infant state and timing are important. When trying to alert infants, one may try to: 1. unwrap infants (arms out at least) 2. place infants in upright position 3. talk to infants, putting variation in your pitch and tempo 4. show your face to infants 5. elicit the rooting, sucking, or grasp reflexes. Being able to alert infants is important for caregivers, as alert infants offer increased feedback to adults.
Visual Response	Newborns have pupillary responses to differences in brightness. Infants can focus on objects or faces about 7–8 inches away. Newborns have preferences for more complex patterns, human faces, and moving objects.	Quiet alert.	Newborns' visual alertness provides opportunities for eye-to-eye contact with caregivers, an important source of beginning caregiver-infant interaction.
Auditory Response	Reaction to a variety of sounds, especially in the human voice range. Infants can hear sounds and locate the general direction of the sound, if the source is constant and remains coming from the same direction.	Drowsy, quiet alert, active alert.	Enhances communication between infants and caregivers. The fact that crying infants can often be consoled by voice demonstrates the value this stimulus has to infants.
Habituation	The ability to lessen one's response to repeated stimuli. For instance, this is seen when the Moro response is repeatedly elicited. If a noise is continually repeated, infants will no longer respond to it in most cases.	Deep sleep, light sleep, also seen in drowsy.	Because of this ability families can carry out their normal activities without disturbing infants. Infants are not victims of their environments. Infants can shut out most stimuli, similar to adults not hearing a dripping faucet after a period of time. Infants who have more difficulty with this will probably not sleep well in active environments.
Cuddliness	Infant's response to being held. Infants nestle and work themselves into the contours of caregivers' bodies versus resist being held.	Primarily in awake states.	Cuddliness is usually rewarding behavior for the caregivers. It seems to convey a message of affection. If infants do not nestle and mold, it would be wise to discuss this tendency and show the caregivers how to position infants to maximize this response.
Consolability	Measured when infants have been crying for at least 15 seconds. The ability of infants to bring themselves or to be brought by others to a lower state.	From crying to active alert, quiet alert, drowsy, or sleep states.	Crying is the infant behavior that presents the greatest challenge to caregivers. Parents' success or failure in consoling their infants has a significant impact on their feelings of competence as parents.

Self-Consoling	Maneuvers used by infants to console themselves and move to a lower state: 1. hand-to-mouth movement 2. sucking on fingers, fist, or tongue 3. paying attention to voices or faces around them 4. changes in position.	From crying to active alert, quiet alert, drowsy, or sleep states.	If caregivers are aware of these behaviors, they may allow infants the opportunity to gain control of themselves instead of immediately responding to their cues. This does not imply that newborns should be left to cry. Once newborns are crying and do not initiate self-consoling activities, they may need attention from caregivers.
Consoling by Caregivers	After crying for longer than 15 seconds, the caregivers may try to: 1. show face to infant 2. talk to infant in a steady, soft voice 3. hold both infant's arms close to body 4. swaddle infant 5. pick up infant 6. rock infant 7. give a pacifier or feed.	From crying to active alert, quiet alert, drowsy, or sleep states.	Often parental initial reaction is to pick up infants or feed them when they cry. Parents could be taught to try other soothing maneuvers.
Motor Behavior and Activity	Spontaneous movements of extremities and body when stimulated versus when left alone. Smooth, rhythmical movements versus jerky ones.	Quiet alert, active alert.	Smooth, nonjerky movements with periods of inactivity seem most natural. Some parents see jerky movements and startles as responses to their caregiving and are frightened.
Irritability	How easily infants are upset by loud noises, handling by caregivers, temperature changes, removal of blankets or clothes, etc.	From deep sleep, light sleep, drowsy, quiet alert, or active alert to fussing or crying.	Irritable infants need more frequent consoling and more subdued external environments. Parents can be helped to cope with more irritable infants through the items listed under "Consoling by Caregivers."
Readability	The cues infants give through motor behavior and activity, looking, listening, and behavior patterns.	All states.	Parents need to learn that newborns' behaviors are part of their individual temperaments and not reflections on their parenting abilities or because their infants do not like them. By observing and understanding an infant's characteristic pattern, parents can respond more appropriately to their infant as an individual.
Smile	Ranging from a faint grimace to a full-fledged smile. Reflexive.	Drowsy, active alert, quiet alert, light sleep.	Initial smile in the neonatal period is the forerunner of the social smile at 3–4 weeks of age. Important for caregivers to respond to it.

From Blackburn, S. Sleep and awake states of the newborn. *In* Early Parent-Infant Relationships, Series 1, Module 3, White Plains: The National Foundation–March of Dimes, 1978, with permission of the copyright holder.

IMPLICATIONS FOR PRACTICE

Parents need information, skills, and support to have a successful early parenting experience.[78] The most opportune time to share information is during the prenatal and postpartum periods.[71] The childbirth educator is in a unique position to offer information, share skills, and assist parents to develop a support system.

Support Systems for Parents of Newborns

One of the greatest gifts the childbirth educator brings to parents is the ability to organize a support group during the prenatal period. While childbirth education and parenting classes are helpful, parents may also need to meet together on their own. The childbirth educator may organize a class list from which the parents can choose names and addresses of class members with whom they wish to share babysitting tasks, or perhaps organize a babysitting co-op, mothers' group, or parents' support group.

Childbirth educators can also inform parents of other support systems available to them. Parents can utilize relatives, friends, physicians, nurses, teachers, clergymen, self-help organizations such as LaLeche League, parenting groups, religious groups, childrearing books, community health departments, social workers, and the American Red Cross to address their questions and concerns about themselves and their infant.

Support systems can help parents realize that their feelings, frustrations, and reactions to parenthood are encountered by most new parents.[28] Parenting classes can help them realize that they are not alone and their concerns are shared by many new parents. Support systems can help with some of their daily responsibilities.[28] Friends and relatives can help with the household chores and babysitting to allow the parents more time for rest and other activities. Individuals and groups can provide new parents concrete information regarding care of the infant, care of self, and resources within the community.[28] Support systems can address the various questions and concerns of new parents. A comprehensive discussion of support systems is presented in Chapter 22.

Curriculum for Parent Education

Time will not allow the comprehensive coverage, as presented here, of the early parenting experience in a six-week childbirth preparation course. Also, childbirth educators may find that expectant parents are more interested in information on the newborn and parenting during the second trimester, a time when the pregnancy is real but before the rigors of labor loom quite so large. Another option is to increase the number of classes in the childbirth preparation course. A third option is to offer parenting preparation classes concurrently with childbirth preparation classes.

It is often difficult to get new parents to start attending parenting classes after the birth of their infant. New parents are more likely to continue with parenting classes if they have been involved in the classes before the birth of their baby. Because there are a variety of ways in which information on the early parenting period can be made available for new parents, many different approaches for teaching the information are included in this section. The childbirth educator will have to "pick and choose" those that will best fit the goals and time frame of the particular type of class she is offering.

A curriculum to help prepare couples for the early parenting experience should include information in the following areas: changes in roles, responsibilities, and lifestyle associated with the birth of an infant; concerns of new parents including infant crying, infant feeding, tiredness and fatigue, and returning to work; developing realistic expectations of the newborn's physical appearance; developing appreciation for their newborn's senses (sight, hearing, touch, taste, and smell); developing an appreciation of the newborn's range of reflexes; the basic sleep/wake states and their implications on parent-infant interactions; and developing the skills they need to interpret their baby's basic behavior pattern and recognize what that means to their relationship.

When beginning a discussion on the postpartum period, the childbirth educator can read to the class the description of the early parenting period by Linda B. Pincus found in Box 5–1.

Changes in Roles, Responsibilities, and Lifestyle

The childbirth educator is in an ideal position to help parents explore the changes in roles, responsibilities, and lifestyle that often accompany the birth of an infant. In the prenatal period the instructor can utilize anticipatory guidance in discussing changes that the parents may experience in their adaptation to parenthood. In the postpartum period, the educator can ask the parents to discuss the changes that have occurred with the birth of their infant and their adjustment to the changes.

CLASS CONTENT. Lectures and discussions of changes parents often experience during their transition to parenthood are part of the class. During the prenatal period, class members could discuss changes in their roles, responsibilities, and lifestyles they are anticipating after their infant is born. During the postpartum period, parents could discuss what changes they have been experiencing in their roles, responsibilities, and lifestyles, and how they feel about the changes. The instructor could have the parents draw a diagram of their individual changes in roles and their reorganization of responsibilities within their family, as shown in Figure 5–3.

DEMONSTRATION. In brainstorming sessions, class members could develop several different diagrams depicting changes in roles and responsibilities, and the childbirth educator could draw these diagrams on a blackboard. For example, one diagram could depict a family in which the mother has maintained all her previous roles as housekeeper, full-time accountant, and community leader, and has added the new roles as mother and infant caregiver. The same diagram could depict a change in the father's role from husband to father with no changes in his responsibilities.

GROUP ACTIVITIES. The group could discuss the appropriateness of the husband's and wife's changes in roles and responsibilities depicted in the instructor's diagrams. This could lead to a discussion of how husbands and wives can share the responsibilities of caring for their newborn and other tasks.

Box 5–1

THE NEW BABY
A FANTASY . . . A REALITY

A Fantasy

Ruffles, soft music, cherubic sleeping infant. Small, fragrant being awakens every four hours . . . exactly. Eats well, burps on schedule, returns to peaceful slumber.

Smiling friends . . . helpful (but not too helpful) relatives.

Fitting back into size nine clothes the first day home.

A flat belly.

Husband comes home after work to sparkling house, delicious hot meal. Enjoys noticing wife in sexy black negligee holding sweet-smelling, cooing infant in one hand, scotch and soda for him in the other.

A Reality

Husband goes off to work without breakfast since toaster is lost under dirty dishes.

Wife decides it is not worthwhile to remove rumpled terry robe since size nine clothes fit left leg only.

Hair uncombed, must plan ahead to take shower.

Wife's bottom hurts . . . no need for sexy black negligee.

Baby crying, demanding, unaware his diaper has just been changed.

Relatives bossy, too many visitors.

Occasional thoughts of gently putting baby in bureau drawer, closing it carefully, for just ten minutes.

Always, perpetually, and forever tired.

Husband comes home from work, sees chaos, leaves for McDonald's.

From Pincus, L. Reality versus Fantasy: Preparing parents for the postpartum period. *Genesis* 5:16, June/July 1983.

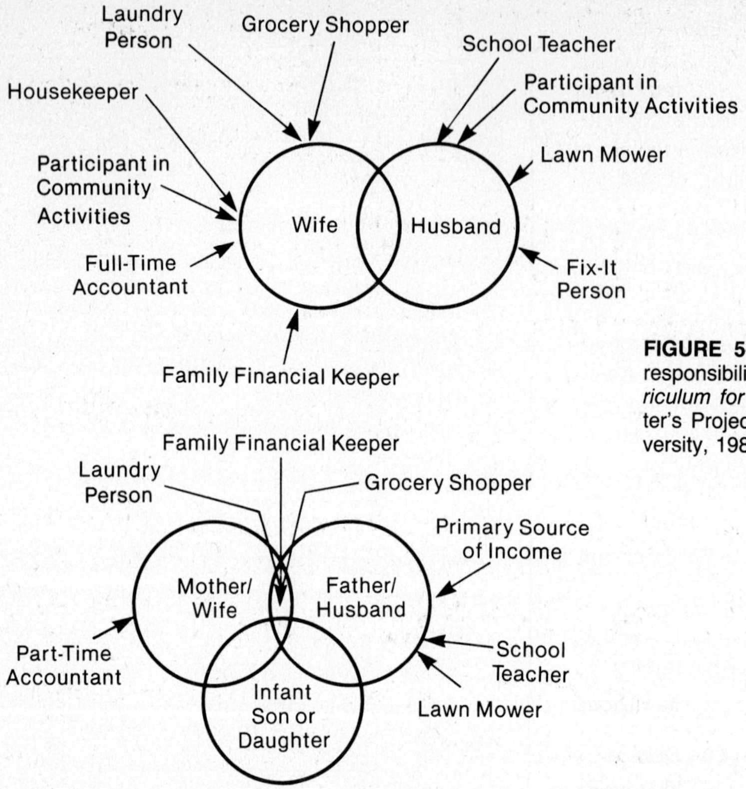

FIGURE 5–3. Role changes—reorganization of responsibilities. (Adapted from Youmans, J. *A Curriculum for Parenting Classes*. Unpublished Master's Project. Wichita, KS: The Wichita State University, 1985.)

Concerns of Parents of Newborns

Infant Crying

Childbirth educators can assist parents in developing a realistic picture of the amount of infant crying that often occurs in "typical" infants. In addition, parents should be aware that infants cry because they want to communicate a need. One of the parent's greatest challenges is to respond with soothing behaviors to their infant's cry. How a newborn reacts to the parents consoling efforts greatly affects the parents' feelings about themselves. The childbirth educator can provide parents with information and skills to help them soothe and console their infants.

CLASS CONTENT. Literature and research on crying in infants and soothing techniques can be discussed in class. Instructors can discuss research in the area of infant crying, which has found that infants whose needs were met immediately when they cried tended to cry less than other infants.[6,11,52,76] Other research has found that infants who cry excessively often had mothers who were extremely inconsistent in regard to frequency, duration, amount, and quality of handling and feeding, and in regard to time elapsed before responding to a crying infant.[76] Infants who continuously fretted and cried after the first few months of life and who fit the stereotype of the "spoiled" child had mothers who ignored their cries or had a long delay in responding to them.[6]

The class members could discuss various ways they know to soothe a crying infant. The members could also discuss how they would reply to someone who told them they were "spoiling" their infants by picking them up every time they cried. The parents may benefit from discussing feelings that infant crying evokes in them such as frustration, nervousness, upset, helplessness, wondering what is wrong, and guilt about feelings.[27]

Have class members fantasize that they are in a strange land in which the language is completely unknown. They need to eat, sleep, express pain, and so on; however, they are imprisoned in a bed, they cannot walk, and they cannot talk. Direct them to try different cries to signal hunger, cold, boredom, tiredness, overstimulation, and pain. How can they make their needs known? How does it feel to be powerless?

DEMONSTRATION. Bring in a baby from a nursery or have parents bring in a baby before feeding time. Explain that most crying is a signal of distress. Have the class brainstorm about why the baby may be crying. Is the baby hungry, uncomfortable, overly excited, lonely, or tired? Ask the parents of the baby how long has it been since the last feeding and how adequate that feeding was. Have parents share their perceptions of the cause of the crying signal. Usually experienced parents are able to hear specific qualities in their baby's cry to help them differentiate the meanings of a particular crying pattern. Have them share this with the group.

Demonstrate that every baby responds differently to different techniques of consoling. While many newborns may be soothed easily, others demand vigorous interventions. Show parents various soothing techniques from the least vigorous interventions to the greatest. First, try leaving the baby alone for a short period of time to show that some babies are capable of soothing themselves. Move into vision of the infant to demonstrate that some babies are consoled when they can see the parent's face. Then try to talk to the baby, crooning or singing. Some babies are soothed by having a hand placed firmly on their belly or having one or both of their arms held firmly to their sides. If these techniques do not work, pick up the baby to show that some babies quiet when they have something interesting to focus on. Other soothing effects can be added: holding, cuddling, crooning, vigorous rocking, tight swaddling; a bottle, breast, or pacifier may then be given.

GROUP ACTIVITIES. Discuss the soothing techniques that parents have built in (rocking, cuddling, unscheduled feeding, mother's voice, warm constant temperature). Have expectant parents go home and keep a list of all the things they do during the week that could soothe their babies (walking, singing, bathing, driving in the car, using vibrations from a clothes dryer—the baby's bed is placed securely on top of a clothes dryer that is turned on ''air only''). Have them report back the next week.

> Those big eyes just looked at me, something very special was happening . . . I was falling in love.
>
> A NEW MOTHER[1]

> Women just do not know *the extent of the impact of the infant on a family's lifestyle*. Being forewarned is being forearmed. Part of the distress from infant-related stress was in the lack of being prepared for the extensive change in mate relationships, schedules, and social time for self and others.[2]
>
> RAMONA MERCER[2]

> Over and over again fathers reported themselves to be profoundly affected by the birth of their infants and to experience a great feeling of satisfaction with themselves for sharing in the birth experience. These men's basic nurturing instincts seemed to allow them to find fathering both stimulating and gratifying. In fact, most of these fathers were just as involved as the mothers in interacting with their infants, although they often left the caretaking responsibilities to the babies' mothers.
>
> CELESTE PHILLIPS AND JOSEPH ANZALONE[3]

> . . . the newborn affects his environment as much as it influences him. With this in mind, young parents need not feel quite so guilty when they find themselves in conflict with their new and precious, but not-so-helpless infant.
>
> T. BERRY BRAZELTON[4]

> Parenting is like the domestic Peace Corps. The hours are long. The work is hard. The pay is zip. . . . What do you get for taking on the most awesome job in the world? Burnt toast crumbs in bed today. A bunch of flowers from your own yard. Maybe a phone call. A bond of love I cannot begin to describe.
>
> ERMA BOMBECK on *Mothers Day*[5]

Ask them to think about how they can use that information when their baby is born.

New parents may feel that learning how to appropriately respond to their child's cry is the most important skill the childbirth educator can teach them. Encourage parents to be ready to recognize their newborn's irritability and respond to it. Encourage them to try different techniques to see what works best with their babies. Assure them that a baby's crying is not the parents' fault, but that the infant's fretfulness and irritability are built in.

Infant Feeding

Parents need to believe that they are capable of providing their infant with the nourishment needed for healthy growth and development. The feeding process is a learning experience for both infant and parent. Childbirth educators can provide parents with general information about infant feeding and then address individual questions and concerns.

CLASS CONTENT. Lecture and discuss general infant feeding concerns of parents, including how much and how often to feed an infant, when to introduce solid foods into the infant's diet, and how to know when the infant is getting too much or too little to eat. Parents' individual questions about infant feeding need to be answered. Class members could also discuss ways to make their infant's feedings a pleasurable experience for themselves and their infant.

DEMONSTRATION. The childbirth educator could show a film on both bottle feeding and breastfeeding an infant, including the benefits of breastfeeding.

GROUP ACTIVITIES. The class members could discuss how they would respond to friends who say that their infant is sucking on his hand after being fed because he is still hungry and is never satisfied.

Fatigue

New parents need help finding ways to conserve energy.[15] Childbirth educators need to assist parents in being realistic in their expectations of what each spouse can do to contribute to infant care needs and household chores. Parents may need help finding people outside their home who can help with some of the household chores, allowing them more time to rest. Mothers will be able to catch up on some sleep during the day if they are not responsible for all the household chores.

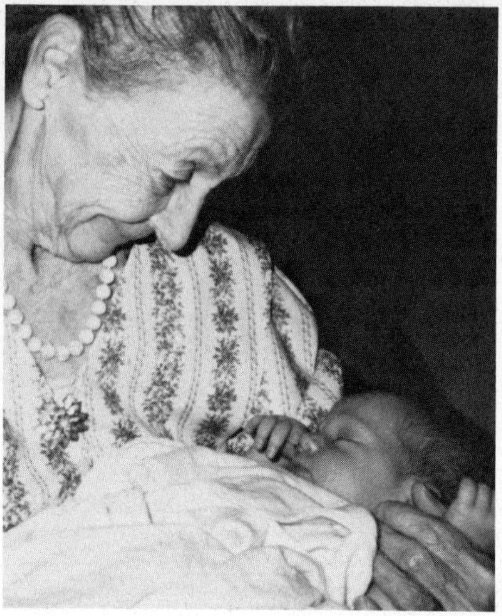

New babies are a source of interest, pride, and concern to many generations within a family. New mothers will benefit when a caring relative helps with household chores or watches the baby while she rests. (Courtesy of Anne Rose.)

CLASS CONTENT. Discuss various ways that parents can decrease their fatigue, including redefining roles and responsibilities, and seeking help outside the home. Also, discuss the need for new mothers to sleep while their infant sleeps; this may mean taking several short naps during the day.

The class members could discuss ways they plan to conserve energy and obtain adequate rest after their infant is born. The members may want to begin to list people they plan to ask to help with their household chores after their infant's birth.

DEMONSTRATION. Childbirth educators may want to have parents with four-month-old infants discuss the loss of sleep and fatigue they experienced as new parents, and what they found helpful in obtaining more rest.

GROUP DISCUSSION. The group could discuss the following factors that have been associated with good postpartum adjustment: less emphasis on the tidiness of the home after an infant's birth; obtaining more experienced help with the infant; husbands limiting outside activities and becoming more available in the home; and couples continuing to socialize outside the home but less frequently.[24]

Returning to Work

Childbirth educators can help parents explore the advantages and disadvantages of various child care options when the mother is planning to return to work. Instructors can also assist parents in developing good screening and interviewing skills they can utilize in selecting child care for their infant. Mothers can be given an opportunity to discuss feelings they may experiencc during their first week at work after the birth.

CLASS CONTENT. Discuss the advantages and disadvantages of the three main alternatives to child care including care in someone else's home (family day care), care in the mother's home (housekeeper or babysitter), and group care (day care center or nursery). In addition, discuss questions the parents can ask when interviewing potential child care agencies or babysitters or both. The parents could be given an opportunity to practice interviewing potential babysitters.

DEMONSTRATION. The childbirth educator could role-play a new mother on her first day at work after her infant's birth. This could include frequent phone calls to check on the infant, crying every time someone asks about the infant, and watching the clock.

GROUP ACTIVITIES. Parents could be given an opportunity to express their feelings about the wife returning to work after the infant's birth. Group members could discuss their experiences in trying to find child care. The group could problem-solve ways to make the first week back on the job less stressful for the mother.

The Parent-Infant Interaction Experience

Appearance of the Newborn

The childbirth educator is in an ideal position to help parents develop realistic expectations of the appearance of their newborn. During childbirth education classes and in the postnatal period, the childbirth educator can use several strategies to help parents explore the possibilities of their newborn's appearance.

Strategies that can be used in childbirth education classes include:

CLASS CONTENT. Present information about and discuss the newborn's appearance. Then have class members discuss how they are expecting their newborn to look and act. Give them newsprint and felt-tip pens to draw their baby. Have them fantasize the gamut of possibilities (from blond to black hair, brown to blue eyes, large to small baby, boy or girl).

The childbirth educator can prepare parents for the birth experience (see Chapter 4): when the baby is suctioned, the cord is cut, and the baby takes the first breath. Familiarize parents with the *Apgar scoring system,* weighing, and measuring. Discuss the issue of keeping the baby warm and give them information on skin-to-skin contact. Give them permission to explore their baby, feel the vernix caseosa, touch the skin, and stroke the hair.

DEMONSTRATION. Show films on newborns. Bring several infants to class or take the class to a newborn nursery. Have class members comment on and discuss the similarities and the differences of newborns. Point out vernix caseosa, swollen caput, puffy face and eyes, abdomen cord, swollen genitals, or other conditions that may give concern.

GROUP ACTIVITIES. Take the drawing of the baby fantasized and share it with the group. Have the group discuss each other's drawings. Are the expectations realistic? If not, why not?

Strategies in the postpartum period can begin with a visit to the parents in the hospital. The childbirth educator can discuss their perceptions of the newborn's appearance. If they have any concerns, the educator can answer their questions. During a postpartum class have parents discuss how their babies are different or similar. Answer any questions. Ask them to write down one concern they have about their baby's appearance. Put the papers in a box. Mix them up and pass them around so other class members can read them.

Sensory Abilities

One of the most interesting areas that childbirth educators can cover is the sensory capacities of the newborn. Even in the uterus the fetus can see, hear, taste, and touch. Newborn's sensory abilities play an important part in fostering interactions with the parents.

Strategies that can be used in childbirth education classes include:

CLASS CONTENT. Share research on sensory capabilities. Discuss books by Brazelton, Sanger, March of Dimes Birth Defects Foundation, and so forth (see References).

Ask class members to fantasize what it is like to be a fetus. Talk about what the baby can see (light and dark), feel (constant swaddling, rocking when the mother walks), and hear (the mother's heartbeat and voice, loud noises, sounds of the amniotic fluid). Emphasize that in the first few days of their infant's life, the more closely parents can reproduce that environment (unscheduled feedings, swaddling, rocking, warm constant temperature, mother's high-pitched voice, rhythmic sounds), the easier their parenting tasks will be.

DEMONSTRATION. Bring a newborn baby to the alert state. Show the class how the newborn can focus at a distance of 8 to 12 inches and prefers the human face. Use bright objects to show how the infant will turn his face to follow the object. Move the object up and down. Explain how different babies enjoy different things and have different abilities to follow through. Ring a bell, use your voice, or shake a rattle and direct the class to watch how the baby focuses on the sound; move the sound from side to side and have the class watch the infant follow it. Assure the parents that different babies prefer different sounds and have different maturity levels in following sounds. Demonstrate a massage session in which you show the class how to touch and massage their babies with warm, gentle, and rhythmic stroking and touching.

Reflexes

Although the newborn's nervous system does not yet give the child control over his reactions, it is fun for parents to look for those reflexes that the newborn is born with and that help him control the environment. Sucking and swallowing, for example, are important for survival. Blinking, sneezing, coughing, and withdrawing help protect the newborn. Other reflexes are forerunners of skills the baby will develop.

Strategies that can be used in prenatal classes include the following:

CLASS CONTENT. Discuss with class members the baby's reflexes that they are aware of during pregnancy, e.g., kicking, hiccupping, jerking, stretching, swimming, sucking, motor tone, withdrawal. Have the class fantasize what it feels like to be in the mother's uterus (call it A Day in the Life of the Fetus).

DEMONSTRATION. Show a film on newborn reflexes such as the Brazelton Assessment film or slides on newborn characteristics. Visit a newborn nursery or have parents bring in a newborn in the alert state (before or after feeding). Demonstrate standing, walking, placing, crawling, righting, doll's eye, rooting, sucking, smother, and withdrawal reflex. Discuss limp versus tense motor tone, cuddling versus withdrawing. Discuss how these reflexes may affect the parenting experience.

GROUP ACTIVITIES. Have the class choose partners. To demonstrate the effect that limp and tense motor tone have in a relationship, have one partner put his arms around the other. Then instruct the other partner to tense up and then withdraw. Then instruct the partner to go limp. Change partners and repeat the exercise. Discuss how motor tone may affect the parent-infant interaction. Have one couple demonstrate cuddling versus withdrawing. Have them share what that may mean to parent-infant interaction.

In postpartum classes, the childbirth educator can provide new parents with information about a newborn's reflexes. The parents can then use the information immediately with their own newborns.

Discuss a baby's basic temperament. Give the parents permission to explore and play with their baby. Show them how to elicit the grasp reflex. Instruct them to hold the newborn in a standing position and see if the child will put one foot in front of the other. Show them that when they put their baby in a sitting position or hold him upright, the baby's eyes will open. (This is helpful for feeding a sleepy newborn.) Place a finger on the side of the baby's cheek and watch him turn and root for the finger. This shows that the parent does not have to stuff the nipple into the baby's mouth. Teach parents with tense or limp babies different techniques to soothe and please. Emphasize that parents may feel rejected if the baby lies passively, slides through their arms, or resists being held by stiffening and thrashing.

Sleep/Wake States

The childbirth educator can help parents learn how to recognize the times when their baby is most responsive to stimulation or consoling and match their actions to the baby's needs. Strategies that can be used in childbirth education classes include:

CLASS CONTENT. Discuss research on the components and significance of the six basic infant states. Have expectant parents keep a log for one week of when their baby appears to be awake or asleep, how long the baby seems to stay awake or asleep, and the sleep/wake intervals. Have couples share this information in the following class. Discuss their expectations of night feeding and their own sleep patterns after the baby is born and help them to develop realistic expectations for the experience.

DEMONSTRATION. Visit a nursery or have parents bring in several newborns. Try to time it so that one baby is brought in after feeding (quiet, active, dozing), another before feeding (alert, fussy, crying), and a third sleeping. Point out breathing, eye movements, physical movements, and reception to stimulation in each state. Demonstrate how to get a dozing baby into the alert state, an alert baby into the dozing state, a fussy baby into an alert or sleeping state. Point out that in the alert state the baby is receptive to learning and new information. The deep quiet state seems to be the time for growth and development. Show the Brazelton Neonatal Assessment Film to demonstrate the various sleep and awake states of infants.

Behavior Patterns

The childbirth educator can use a variety of strategies to help parents understand how their newborn's individual behavior pattern influences the way they react. Since parents also have their own personalities, sometimes a discrepancy may exist between the mother's style and her baby's. A very active mother may be quite disturbed by a quiet baby; while a quiet mother would be contented. On the other hand, a very quiet mother may be distraught by an active baby, and an active mother distressed by a quiet baby. Temperament is part of the personality and cannot be changed, but an understanding mother can work with her baby to develop a mutually satisfying relationship. Strategies that can be used in childbirth education classes include:

CLASS CONTENT. Discuss research on varying behavior patterns in infants and how it affects the parent-infant relationship. Share books written by Brazelton, Sanger, and others.

Ask mothers if they think they are basically active or basically quiet people. Then ask them if they think they are carrying active babies or quiet babies. Ask the active mothers who are carrying quiet babies if they feel that temperament may affect their relationship with the baby. Ask the quiet mothers who are carrying active babies the same question. Help them to think about ways they can cope with a child of opposite temperament.

DEMONSTRATION. Visit a nursery or have parents bring in several newborns. Show expectant parents how some babies prefer visual stimuli while others prefer sounds. Demonstrate how all the babies seem to prefer the human face and voice. Put your face in the baby's line of vision and begin to play with him. Let the class watch as the baby follows your face from side to side. Demonstrate that when you apply a stimulus (such as thumping) to the baby's foot, the child will be annoyed the first time but will eventually tune out the annoying stimulus. Show the babies' different levels of irritability. Demonstrate several soothing techniques and discuss how different babies are soothed by different methods.

GROUP ACTIVITIES. Use several infants to demonstrate the differences between babies. Have class members decide if the newborns are basically active, quiet, or average. Let them explain their decision. Divide the class into two groups: those who perceive themselves as quiet and those who perceive themselves as active. Have quiet couples role-play that they are parents of an active newborn. Let active couples imagine they have a quiet baby. Have each couple discuss the effects on their relationship to the baby and to each other.

The childbirth educator can encourage parents in the postpartum period to stimulate their newborns in order to encourage development. Encourage parents to discover their baby's unique and particular temperament. Explore various techniques to help them interpret their child's uniqueness and to develop a variety of coping mechanisms. Suggest that parents stimulate their child's responses by using brightly colored wallpaper and pleasant, interesting sounds. Remind them that the baby's most interesting toys are his parents' faces, bodies, voices, and touch.

Stimulation

Research shows that what parents do with their faces, voices, bodies, and hands provides the baby with the first experiences in human communication and relationships. Play between parent and infant is a mutual exchange of joy and fun that builds the baby's knowledge of all things human. Give-and-take play provides babies with the experiences they need to grow and develop.

Strategies that can be used in childbirth education classes include:

CLASS CONTENT. Discuss research and information on the significance of play and stimulation with the newborn.

Ask the expectant parents to explore for a week all the things that they do during a day that "turns their fetus on." Have them report their findings at the next class session. Point out that many of the things that stimulate their fetus soothe others. Discuss whether they think this will change when they are interacting with their baby after birth.

DEMONSTRATION. Bring a newborn baby to the alert stage. Place the baby in an en face position. Demonstrate the synchronization between your movements and baby's responses. Point out that the baby's body movements are his means of communication. Show parents that the parent and baby respond to each other rhythmically, taking turns. Demonstrate the attention/inattention cycle in which the baby focuses and then turns away. Ask the group what would happen if the parent kept stimulating the baby when the baby turns away. Ask the group members what would happen if the baby makes gestures to participate and the parent turns away. Show a movie on synchronicity and reciprocity in parent-infant interactions.

GROUP ACTIVITIES. Have a couple come to the front of the class and discuss an interesting subject, such as politics or religion. Direct the class to watch the body movements and give-and-take in a good conversation. Ask group members to pair off and have a conversation about what they did today. Direct one member to monopolize the conversation. Ask the other member how that feels. Have them have a conversation in which both members share equal time. Ask them how that might be similar to the parent-infant interaction process.

Infants learn quickest and remember longest actions that they initiate. A child who is stimulated by the parents quickly learns the reciprocity inherent in communication. The childbirth educator can help parents develop this skill in their newborn.

Encourage parents to explore and play with their babies. Explain that the baby and parent respond to each other rhythmically, taking turns. Ask the parents to initiate play with a touch or eye contact. Encourage parents to watch the baby's face, toes, hands, fingers, and the body rhythm while they wait for a response. Encourage them to "clue into" when the baby has received enough stimulation as shown by withdrawing, perhaps by yawning or turning away.

IMPLICATIONS FOR RESEARCH

Although there has been a great deal of research on the capabilities, resources, and strengths of the newborn, more research needs to be done on parents: their styles, temperaments, resources, and how these factors affect the early parenting experience. Further research is needed on the fathering role and what factors are related to a father's adjustment to parenthood.

Another area of research that should be explored is the effect of siblings on the infant and the effect of the infant on siblings. A fourth area of research that needs to be pursued is the effect of the support network (grandparents, aunts, uncles, neighbors, religious community) on the early parenting experience.

Yet another area of needed research involves the childbirth educator. Questions that require answers are:

- To what extent are childbirth educators involved in the preparation of couples for the parenting experience?
- How does attending childbirth education classes influence early parenting ability?
- What are the best approaches (content, placement, and so on) for including parenting information in childbirth education classes?
- What strategies are most effective for preparing parents for the parenting experience?

SUMMARY

During the early parenting experience mothers and fathers experience many changes in their roles, responsibilities, and lifestyles. Childbirth educators can assist parents by preparing them for these changes and the feelings often associated with the changes. Parents need to be aware that their concerns about infant crying and feeding and their own fatigue and returning to work are shared by many new parents. Parents can be taught the knowledge and skills needed to assist them with their individual concerns and help them meet their own and their infant's needs.

Parents need to be gently guided to discover their baby's individual style and find a "fit" between the baby's and the parent's styles. Parents can be helped to avoid being rigid in either their own requirements or their perceptions of the infant's needs. They should be advised to do what makes them and their baby feel the best and enjoy each other the most. Success comes when the parents and the baby enjoy their interactions. What they do as parents is not as important to their baby as how they do it. Caring about their baby is the most important message they can send.

References

1. Adams, M. Early concerns of primigravida mothers regarding infant care activities. *Nursing Research* 12:72, 1963.
2. Ainsworth, M. Attachment theory and its utility in cross-cultural research. *Culture and Infancy.* New York: Academic Press, 1977.
3. American Acdemy of Pediatrics, Committee on Nutrition. On the feeding of supplemental foods to infants. *Pediatrics* 65:1178, 1980.
4. Barnard, K. E., and Eyres, S. J. *Nursing Child Assessment.* Washington, D.C.: U.S. Public Health Service, Dept. of Health, Education and Welfare, 1977.
5. Barnard, K. L., Blackburn, S., Kang, R., and Spietz, A. *Early Parent-Infant Relationships.* White Plains, NY: The National Foundation/March of Dimes, 1978.
6. Bell, S. M., and Ainsworth, M. D. Infant crying and maternal responsiveness. *Child Development* 43:1171, 1972.
7. Bennett, E. A. Coping in the puerperium: Reported experience of new mothers. *Journal of Psychosomatic Research* 25:13, 1981.
8. Blackburn, S. Part A. Sleep and awake states of the newborn. In Duxbury, M. L. and Carroll, P. (eds.): *Early Parent-Infant Relationships.* White Plains, NY: National Foundation/March of Dimes, 1978, pp. 14–21.
9. Blackburn, S. Part B: State-related behaviors and individual differences. In Duxbury, M. L., and Carroll, P. (eds.): *Early Parent-Infant Relationships.* White Plains, NY: National Foundation/March of Dimes. 1978, pp. 22–38.
10. Brackbill, Y., Douthitt, T. C., and West, H. Neonatal posture, psychological effects. *Neuropaedatrie* April 4, p. 245, 1973.
11. Brazelton, T. B. Crying in infancy. *Pediatrics* 29:579, 1962.
12. Brazelton, T. B. *Neonatal Behavioral Assessment Scale.* Philadelphia: J. B. Lippincott Co., 1973.
13. Brazelton, T. B., Koslowski, B., and Main, M. The origins of reciprocity: the early mother-infant interaction. In Lewis, M., and Rosenblum, L. A. (eds.): *The Effect of the Infant on Its Caregiver.* New York: John Wiley & Sons, 1974, pp. 49–74.
14. Briggs, E. Transition to parenthood. *Maternal Child Nursing Journal* 10:197, 1979.
15. Bull, M. Change in concerns of first-time mothers after one week at home. *Journal of Obstetric, Gynecologic, and Neonatal Nursing* 10:391, 1981.
16. Campbell, B. G., and Taylor, P. M. Bonding and attachment: theoretical issues. In Taylor, P. M. (ed.): *Parent-Infant Relationships.* New York: Grune & Stratton, 1980, pp. 3–23.
17. Clarke-Stewart, A. *Child Care in the Family.* New York: Academic Press, 1977.
18. Condon, W. S. Primary phase organization of infant responding behavior. In *Studies in Mother-Infant Interaction.* New York: Academic Press, 1977, pp. 153–176.
19. Curry, M. A. Variables related to adaptation to motherhood in "normal" primiparous women. *Journal of Obstetric, Gynecologic, and Neonatal Nursing* 12:115, 1983.
20. Davidson, S., and Leonard, L. G. Appearance, behavior and capabilities—teaching new parents infant ABC's. *Canadian Nurse* 77:37, 1981.
21. Emde, R. M., and Scorce, J. F. The rewards of infancy: Emotional availability and reference. In *Frontiers in Infant Psychiatry* New York: Basic Books, 1983.
22. Gordon, A. H., and Jameson, J. C. Infant mother attachment in patients with nonorganic failure to thrive syndrome. *American Journal of Child Psychiatry* 18:251, 1979.
23. Gordon, I. J. Early child stimulation through parent education. ERIC Document, Identification EDO33-912, 1974.
24. Gordon, R. E., and Gordon, K. K. Social factors in prevention of postpartum emotional problems. *Obstetrics and Gynecology* 15:433, 1960.
25. Gruis, M. Beyond maternity: postpartum concerns of moth-

ers. MCN: *American Journal of Maternal Child Nursing* 2:182, 1977.

26. Hangsleben, K. L. Transition to fatherhood—an exploratory study. *Journal of Obstetric, Gynecologic, and Neonatal Nursing 12*:265, 1983.
27. Harris, J. When babies cry. *Canadian Nurse* 75:32, 1979.
28. Hrobsky, D. M. Transition to parenthood. *Nursing Clinics of North America* 12:457, 1977.
29. Johnson, S. H., and Grubbs, J. P. The premature infant's reflex behaviors. *Journal of Obstetric, Gynecologic, and Neonatal Nursing* 3:15–21, 1975.
30. Jones, S. P. First-time fathers: A preliminary study. *Maternal Child Nursing Journal* 9:103–106, 1984.
31. Kelley, M. The workplace—postpartum concerns. *NAACOG Update Series* 2:1, 1985.
32. Klaus, M. H., and Kennell, J. H. *Maternal Infant Bonding*. St. Louis: C. V. Mosby Co., 1976.
33. Klaus, J. H., and Kennell, J. H.: *Bonding—the Beginnings of Parent-Infant Attachment*. New York: C. V. Mosby Co., 1983.
34. Korner, A. F. Early stimulation and maternal care as related to infant capacities and individual. *Early Child Development and Care*. 2:307, 1973.
35. Kutzner, S. K., and Toussie-Wengarten, C. Working parents: the dilemma of child rearing and career. *Topics in Clinical Nursing* 6:30, 1981.
36. LeMasters, E. E. Parenthood as a crisis. *Marriage and Family Living* 19:352, 1957.
37. Lenard, H. B. Sleep studies in infancy. *Acta Paediatrica Scandivanica,* September 1970.
38. Lester, B. N., and Seskind, P. S. A biobehavioral perspective on crying in early infancy. In *Theory and Research in Behavioral Pediatrics,* Vol. 1. New York: Plenum Press, 1982.
39. Lewis, M., and Rosenblum, L. (eds.) *The Effect of the Infant on His Caregiver.* New York: John Wiley and Son, 1974.
40. Lewis, M., and Michalson, L. *Children's Emotions and Moods*. New York: Plenum Press, 1982.
41. MacFarlane, J. A. Parent-infant interaction. Ciba Foundation Symposium No. 33. Amsterdam: Elsevier Publishing Co., 1975.
42. Markesbury, B. A. and Wong, W. M. Watching baby's diet: a professional and parental guide. MCN: *American Journal of Maternal Child Nursing* 4:177, 1979.
43. Meltzoff, A., and Moore, M. The origins of imitation in infancy. In *Advances in Infancy Research*. Norwood, NJ.: Albex Publishing, 1983, pp. 266–311.
44. Mercer, R. T. Teenage motherhood: The first year. I. The teenage mother's view and responses. Part II. How their infants fared. *Journal of Obstetric, Gynecologic, and Neonatal Nursing* 9:16, 1980.
45. Mercer, R. T. The nurse and maternal tasks of early postpartum. *Maternal Child Nursing Journal* 6:341, 1981.
46. Mercer, R. T. A theoretical framework for studying factors that impact on the maternal role. *Nursing Research* 30:73, 1981.
47. Mercer, R. T. The process of maternal role attainment over the first year. *Nursing Research* 34:198, 1985.
48. Mercer, R. T. The relationship of age and other variables to gratification in mothering. *Health Care for Women International* 6:295, 1985.
49. Messer, D. J., and Vietze, P. M.: Timing and transitions in mother-infant gaze. *Infant Behavior and Development* 7:167, 1984.
50. Newton, L. D. Helping parents cope with infant crying. *Journal of Obstetric, Gynecologic, and Neonatal Nursing* 13:199, 1983.
51. O'Grady, R. S. Feeding behavior in infants. *American Journal of Nursing* 71:736, 1971.
52. Ourth, L., and Brown, K. B. Inadequate mothering and disturbance in the neonatal period. *Child Development* 32:287, 1961.
53. Papousek, H., and Papousek, M. Musical elements in the infant's vocalization. In *Advances in Infancy Research Vol. I*. Norwood, NJ: Albex Publishing, 1981, p. 164.
54. Parmelee, A. H., and Stern, E. *Development of States in Infants*. New York: Academic Press, 1972.
55. Pederson, F., and Robson, K. Father participation in infancy. *American Journal of Orthopsychiatry* 39:466, 1969.
56. Pincus, L. B. Reality versus fantasy: preparing parents for the postpartum period. *Genesis* 5:16, 1983.
57. Prechtle, H. F. R. The behavorial states of the newborn. *Brain Research* 6:185, 1974.
58. Pridham, K. F. Infant feeding and anticipatory care: supporting the adaptation of parents to their new babies. *Maternal Child Nursing Journal* 10:111, 1981.
59. Rapoport, R., Rapoport, R. N., Sterlitz, Z., and Kew, S. *Fathers, Mothers and Society.* New York: Basic Books, 1977.
60. Robson, K. S. The role of eye-to-eye contact in maternal-infant attachment. *Journal of Child Psychology and Psychiatry* 8:13, 1967.
61. Robson, K. S., and Moss, H. A. Patterns and determinants of maternal attachment. *Journal of Pediatrics* 77:976, 1970.
62. Rossi, A. S. Transition to parenthood. *Journal of Marriage and the Family* 30:26, 1968.
63. Rubin, R. Basic maternal behavior. *Nursing Outlook* 9:683, 1961.
64. Rubin, R. Puerperal change. *Nursing Outlook* 9:753, 1961.
65. Rubin, R. Attainment of the maternal role. *Nursing Research* 16:342, 1967.
66. Rubin, R. *Maternal Identity and the Maternal Experience*. New York: Springer Publishing Co., 1984.
67. Russell, C. S. Transition to parenthood: Problems and gratifications. *Journal of Marriage and Family* 36:294, 1974.
68. Sander, L. Polarity, paradox, and the organizing process in development. In *Frontiers of Infant Psychiatry.* New York: Basic Books, 1983.
69. Sanger, S., and Keely, J. *You and Your Baby's First Year.* New York: William Morrow and Co., Inc., 1985.
70. Scahill, M. C. Helping the mother solve problems with feeding her infant. *Journal of Obstetric, Gynecologic, and Neonatal Nursing* 4:51, 1975.
71. Sheehan, F. Assessing postpartum adjustment. *Journal of Obstetric, Gynecologic, and Neonatal Nursing* 10:19, 1981.
72. Smart, M. S., and Smart, R. C. *Development and Relationships*. New York: Macmillan Co., 1973.

73. Smith, D., and Smith, H. L. Toward improvements in parenting. *Journal of Obstetric, Gynecologic, and Neonatal Nursing* 7:22, 1978.
74. Snyder, C., Eyres, S. J. and Barnard, K. Mother's prenatal expectations about infant development. MCN: *American Journal of Maternal Child Nursing* 4:185, 1979.
75. Stern, D. The early transition effect. In *Birth Interaction and Attachment*. Skillman, NJ: Johnson & Johnson, 1982.
76. Stewart, A. H., Wieland, I. H., Leider, A. R., Mangham, C. A., Holmes, T. H., and Ripley, H. S. Excessive infant crying (colic) in relation to parent behavior. *American Journal of Psychiatry* 110:687, 1954.
77. Stone, L. J., Smith, H. T., and Murphy, L. B. (eds.). *The Competent Infant-Research and Commentary.* New York: Basic Books, 1973.
78. Sumner, G., and Fritsch, J. Postnatal parental concerns: the first six weeks of life. *Journal of Obstetric, Gynecologic, and Neonatal Nursing* 6:27, 1977.
79. Taubenheim, A. M. Paternal-infant bonding in the first-time father. *Journal of Obstetric, Gynecologic, and Neonatal Nursing*. 10:261, 1981.
80. Thorton, R., and Nardi, P. M. The dynamics of role acquisition. *American Journal of Sociology* 80:870, 1975.
81. Wolff, P. H. Causes, controls and organizations of behavior in neonates. *Psychological Issues* 5, Monograph 17, New York: International Universities Press, 1966.

Boxed Quotations

1. Original
2. Mercer, R. *First-Time Motherhood: Experiences from Teens to Forties*. New York: Springer Publishing Co., 1986, pp. 337–338.
3. Phillips, C. R. and Anzalone, J. T. *Fathering: Participation in Labor and Birth*. St. Louis: C. V. Mosby Co., 1978, p. 145.
4. Brazelton, T. B. *Infants and Mothers: Differences in Development*. New York: Dell Publishing Co., Inc., 1969, pp. xvii–xviii.
5. Bombeck, E. Mothering more than a biological process. The Austin American-Stateman, May 10, 1987, P. E8.

Section

3

SUPPORTIVE TECHNIQUES FOR CHILDBIRTH

Techniques that support the laboring woman as she copes with the challenges of childbirth have been the primary focus of the childbirth movement over the last several decades. Seldom a month goes by in which the literature does not urge the childbirth educator to add still more "important information" to expectant parent classes. The childbirth educator must protect the valuable class time that is needed to effectively teach support techniques to expectant parents and resist the temptation to include all the emerging information. A large portion of this book is devoted to the supportive techniques for childbirth because of their centrality to childbirth education.

When expectant couples come to class, they often think they have come primarily to learn *breathing*. Prepared childbirth has been characterized by the paced breathing techniques it involves because they are the most visible of the various techniques; they involve an outwardly noticeable response to contractions. However, researchers and experienced childbirth educators tend to agree that skilled *relaxation* is actually the primary element for effectively coping with childbirth. Therefore, this section of the book includes seven chapters on relaxation skills. Paced breathing patterns are presented as an aid to relaxation.

This section of the book begins with a chapter on supportive pain management strategies and has a chapter on pharmaceutical pain management strategies near the end. This ordering portrays the philosophy that pharmaceutical intervention does play a role in childbirth, but supportive techniques should be the *primary approach* used to help laboring women cope with childbirth. Relaxation, coaching, and positioning are examples of the first lines of defense in supporting the laboring woman. Pharmaceutical intervention, when used, should augment supportive strategies rather than become a substitute for them.

Because the supportive strategies for coping with labor are ''the reason for being'' of childbirth education, the childbirth educator needs to become familiar with the technical details of each strategy taught. The reader may find the review of the literature in some of these chapters relatively heavy reading. However, we believe that childbirth educators do want to be able to cite the research literature when they find themselves needing to explain or defend their practice. It has been our goal to present as comprehensive a review of the literature as possible while retaining a focus on the implications for practice. In this way we hope to contribute toward a scientific basis as the foundation for childbirth education.

chapter 6

SUPPORTIVE PAIN MANAGEMENT STRATEGIES

SHERRY LYNN MIMS JIMÉNEZ

The outstanding thing about the psychoprophylactic method (prepared childbirth) is that it unites and synthetizes all the natural and harmless means known to render labour and delivery agreeable for the parturient.

Isidore Bonstein

The issue of pain in childbirth has been the focus of debate for centuries in religion and medicine.[7,11] During the latter part of this century childbirth pain has become the focus of research throughout the world, and an entire professional specialization has developed to teach women and their partners how to deal with all aspects of childbirth, including pain.

History is unclear on the date of the first formal childbirth education class.[2] Midwives probably gave informal instruction to their clients long before preparation moved to the classroom. Dick-Read[12] in Great Britain and Velvovsky, Platonov, and Nikolayev[35] in Russia claimed to have been the first to introduce a true method of pain prevention in childbirth. In his first book, *Natural*

Childbirth (1933), Dick-Read makes no mention of childbirth education classes, expecting that instruction will come from the obstetrician.[2] By the publication of the 1953 edition of *Childbirth without Fear*, first published in 1944, Dick-Read had established classes taught by nurses, physical therapists, or midwives.[2] Velvovsky gives 1947 to 1949 as the dates when he and his colleagues developed the system of psychoprophylaxis that apparently included classes from its onset.[35,36]

Whatever the date on which the first formal childbirth education class was held, it probably had as its central goal the prevention or reduction of pain, or both. In the early years the promise was "painless childbirth" and the major proponents of prepared childbirth—Dick-Read, Velvovsky, Lamaze, and Vellay—all agreed on one thing: physiological childbirth should not hurt. In later years Dick-Read conceded that pain was possible in "the last few contractions."[13]

Although some women do experience childbirth without pain, for many the reality does not live up to that old promise, and over the last two and a half decades childbirth education has grown to encompass other skills in family living. However, when childbirth educators meet and the conversation turns to why people attend classes, there is agreement that the greatest motivator for participation is probably the fear of pain. Some women see a reflection of their own self-image in the way they confront and cope with this pain. Others simply want to escape it. It is not unusual to hear from women (or their male partners) who felt cheated because they had been promised painless birth. Some think that, if pain is not a factor of normal birth, and if relaxation and focusing should prevent pain, the presence of pain indicates either that the birth is not normal or that the woman is doing something wrong.

A converse viewpoint held by others is that a certain level of pain is normal and even useful. Pain may motivate a woman to assume a position more advantageous to the descent of the fetus. From an extensive review of the literature on pain during labor, Roberts[30] concludes that the reasons why pain in labor is more distressing for some women cannot be explained, because there is no direct relationship between aversive stimuli and the perception of pain. Furthermore, the distress of labor may be caused not only by pain but by feelings of helplessness and lack of control stemming from repeated painful contractions. Relaxation and breathing may not relieve pain as much as they relieve the distress that accompanies pain. This explains why numerous studies have found that prepared women often use less pain medication and yet do not always report less pain. Roberts reports that a number of studies have shown that the perception of *intensity* of pain is not the same perception as that of *unpleasantness* of the pain.

It is the suffering of pain that most mothers want most to avoid, and it is this suffering aspect that childbirth education can most affect. This distinction often is not understood by expectant parents, researchers, or health professionals, either presently or historically. But, understood or not, the distinction is appreciated by the mother who says, "Yes, I knew the pain was there, but I was able to keep on top of it."

Since before Aristotle's time, people have tried to define pain and to understand its mechanism,[6] but the laboring woman is not interested in debates over which theory is more accurate or which technique more correct. What she wants is an easy, safe, effective way to prevent, reduce, or relieve pain.

Bonica describes the "deleterious effects of parturition pain" in *Obstetric Analgesia and Anesthesia*.[5] He states that persistent pain and stress affect respiration, circulation, endocrine function, and other bodily functions. Studies show that painful contractions cause ventilation to increase five to 20 times the normal rate, resulting in respiratory alkalosis, increased sympathetic activity, and increased release of the hormone norepinephrine. This causes a cardiac output increase of between 50 and 150 per cent and a blood pressure increase of between 20 and 40 per cent. The metabolic rate and oxygen consumption also rise. Since the increased level of norepinephrine release may counteract the effect of oxytocin, contractions may become ineffective, resulting in dystocia.[5] Beck, professor of psychology at the University of Missouri, diagrammed the "psychological-physiological-obstetrical-pediatric chain" that can occur when fear of labor turns into pain (Fig. 6–1).[1,20] Thus, it becomes clear that the laboring woman's desire for safe, effective pain relief is not only valid

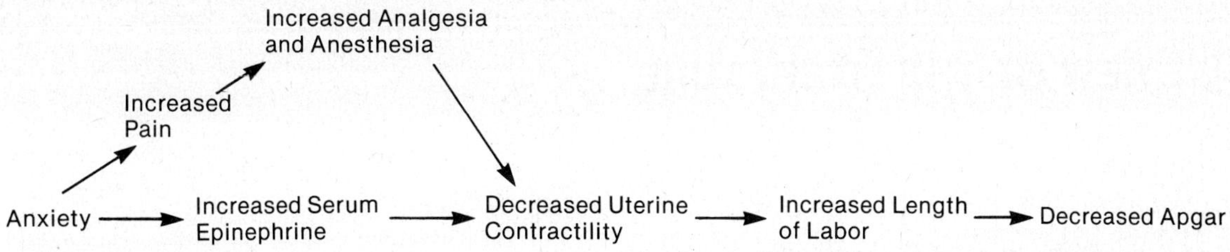

FIGURE 6–1. Beck's pain chain. (From Jiménez, S. Application of the Body's Natural Pain Relief Mechanisms to Reduce Discomfort in Labor and Delivery. In *NAACOG Update Series, Vol 1.* Princeton, NJ: Continuing Professional Education Center, Inc., 1983.)

but imperative for the safety of her and her child. Furthermore, as Beck notes, combating increased pain with increased analgesia and anesthesia can also result in decreased uterine contractions, indicating that the ideal pain relief method would involve a minimum use of pharmaceutical agents.

Current Practice

There are almost as many approaches to labor pain and its management as there are childbirth educators and obstetricians. The following list attempts to give a summary of the overall picture in current childbirth education.

- Pain theories usually are introduced early in the course, often in the first class, and are typically taught as a separate topic. Some teachers integrate this information with practice of pain management techniques. Others refer to the pain theories again as new techniques are taught. Theory may or may not be illustrated by applications in daily activities.
- The most commonly taught theories of pain management seem to be attention-focusing theory and gate-control theory.
- Theory often is taught as if it were fact. This includes theory for the origin of pain as well as its management.
- Although many teachers emphasize correct performance of a specific set of techniques, there is an increasing trend toward helping the learner modify techniques in ways that will enable her to attain mastery in line with her goals.
- There is a trend away from "maintaining control" and toward maintaining harmony with the rhythms of labor.[20]
- Some teachers contend that psychoprophylaxis is not "natural childbirth" and offer women a new set of responses to childbirth and pain. Others believe that psychoprophylaxis should enhance, not replace, the woman's existing pain and stress management systems.
- Some teachers adopt a prescriptive approach, believing that each couple should learn every technique since they may not know which technique will be most effective until labor starts. Others adopt a holistic approach, in which the couple is assisted in choosing the techniques that seem the most comfortable and effective for them.
- For many teachers pain reduction is the central goal of childbirth preparation. Recently Humenick[18] (see Chapter 4) has advocated a model of mastery as the key to childbirth satisfaction that may be closely related to influencing the suffering aspect of pain. This may become the central goal of preparation, with pain intensity reduction as a wonderful side effect.

REVIEW OF THE LITERATURE

Physical Causes of Pain

In the 1985 edition of *Williams Obstetrics,* the chapter on analgesia and anesthesia opens with the following statement: "Labor may subject the nulliparous woman to the most pain that she has ever experienced."[29] In describing the uterine contractions, the author states, "Unique among physiologic muscular contractions, those of labor are painful." Interestingly, that observation, made through the years, has led some physicians to conclude that labor is not "a normal physiological process" and led others to conclude that pain was not a normal feature of the physiological process called birth. Neither conclusion is necessarily correct, however. An emerging view is that a certain level of pain may be a useful aspect of a normal physiological process. Pain may serve to warn the mother to take shelter and obtain assistance, thus helping to ensure that the infant is born in a warm, safe environment. Some of the strategies for coping with this pain such as relaxing, making position changes, and taking shelter may physiologically promote good birth outcomes. The view that some pain may serve a useful purpose is not the same as some traditional or religious beliefs that childbirth *should* be painful.

In *Oxorn-Foote Human Labor and Birth,* the following generally accepted hypotheses as to physical causes of pain in labor are discussed:[28]

1. Hypoxia of the uterine muscle. During contractions the blood supply to the uterus is greatly decreased. If the uterus does not relax sufficiently between contractions, the blood flow may be further compromised, thereby increasing pain. The classic example given to support the hypothesis that uterine hypoxia leads to pain is that of the intense pain resulting from cardiac ischemia. However, since reduced blood flow is not normal in the heart muscle but is normal in the uterine muscle during a labor contraction, this may be an inappropriate analogy.
2. Cervical stretching and pressure on the nerve ganglia of the cervix. The ability of a paracervical block to relieve the pain of contractions supports this theory.
3. Traction on the fallopian tubes, ovaries, and peritoneum.
4. Traction on and stretching of the uterine ligaments.
5. Pressure on the urethra, bladder, and rectum.
6. Distension of the muscles of the pelvic floor and perineum.

Bonica theorizes that "high threshold pain receptors called nociceptors"* are repeatedly stimulated during contractions, thus lowering their threshold and resulting in the stimulus becoming more painful. (Some researchers argue that, by definition, a threshold is constant, but that tolerance is variable. Thus, it may be more accurate to say that the repeated stimulation eventually attains the threshold level of the nociceptors.) Bonica states that another possible source of pain is cellular destruction, which may occur with dilatation and expulsion and which would release "pain-producing substances."[5]

Pain Pathways

Uterine sensory fibers follow the sympathetic nerves along the following route: the cervical plexus to the pelvic plexus (inferior hypogastric plexus), to the middle hypogastric plexus, to the lower and lumbar thoracic sympathetic chain, and to the spinal cord (through white rami communicantes associated with the 10th, 11th, and 12th thoracic and 1st lumbar nerves) (Fig. 6–2). The sensory fibers of the genital tract travel through the pudendal nerve to the posterior of the sacrospinous ligament to the 2nd, 3rd, and 4th sacral nerves.[5]

*Nociceptors or nociceptive receptors are nerve endings possessed by most body tissue which are particularly sensitive to tissue dysfunction. These free nerve endings provide the means by which we are made aware of pain.

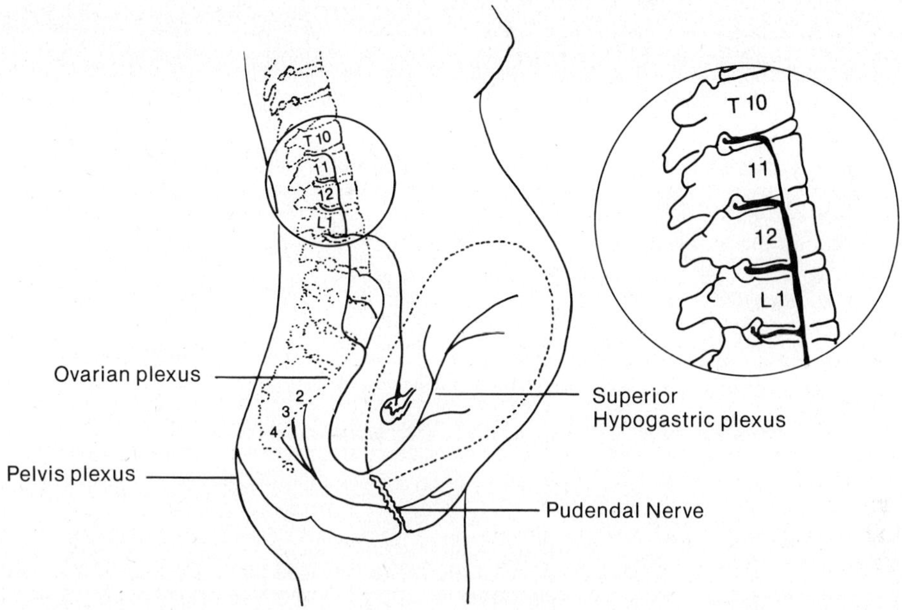

FIGURE 6–2. Pain pathways during childbirth. The uterus, including the cervix, is supplied by sensory (pain) fibers that pass from the uterus to the spinal cord by accompanying sympathetic nerves. The primary pathways (shown as thick lines in the insert) enter the 11th and 12th spinal segments while the secondary auxiliary pathways enter at T–10 and L–1. The pathways from the perineum pass to the sacral spinal cord via the pudendal nerves. (Modified from Bonica, J.J. *Principles and Practice of Obstetric Analgesia and Anesthesia*. Philadelphia: F.A. Davis Co., 1967.)

According to Greenhill and Friedman,[16] although sensory receptors have been identified in the cervix, none have been found within the body of the uterus (Figs. 6–3 and 4).

Aside from physiological factors that cause pain, Bonica cites several physical factors that influence the degree and character of pain in the parturient:

1. Intensity and duration of contractions. (Reports of increasing pain usually correlate with increased strength and length of contractions.)
2. Degree of cervical dilatation, as well as rate of dilatation per contraction. (Women whose labors are quite short often report intense pain, possibly due to the degree of work accomplished with each contraction and the strength of contractions required for a rapid labor. Others report little or no pain under similar circumstances.)
3. Perineal distension. (Some women find the stretching of the perineum to be painful. Others do not. Many experience what has been called ''nature's anesthesia'' as the perineal nerves become numb under the pressure of the baby's head.)
4. Maternal age, condition, and parity. Bonica cites fatigue, malnutrition, and generally poor physical condition as having a strong influence on pain tolerance. He also states that the cervix of a multipara is ''less sensitive than that of a primipara,'' and that the labor of the elderly primipara will be longer and more painful than that of a young primipara.
5. Fetal size and position. (It is well known that the woman whose baby is in a posterior position is likely to report higher and more persistent levels of pain and that the pain often decreases significantly if the baby turns to an anterior position.)

An alternative hypothesis to the generally accepted theories is that pain, as well as dystocia and

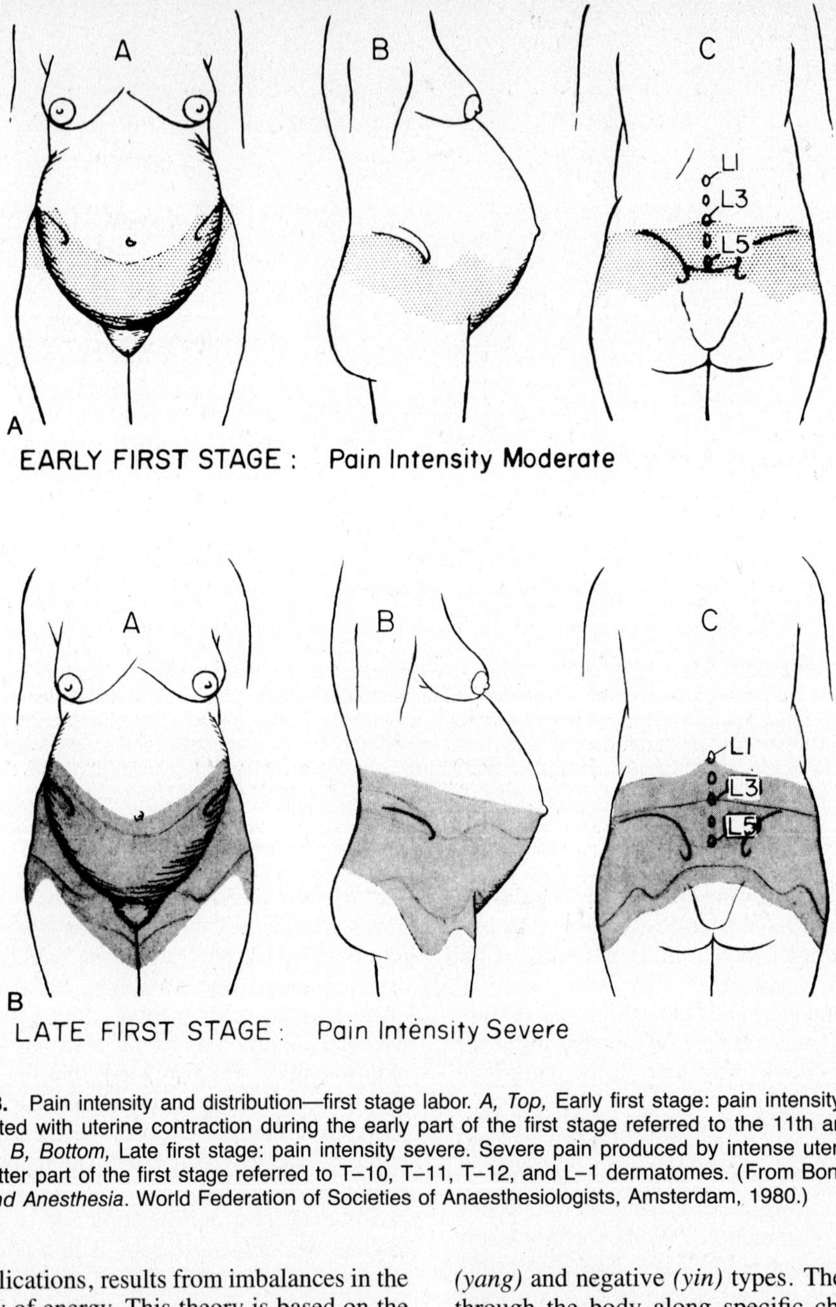

FIGURE 6–3. Pain intensity and distribution—first stage labor. *A, Top,* Early first stage: pain intensity moderate. The pain associated with uterine contraction during the early part of the first stage referred to the 11th and 12th thoracic dermatomes. *B, Bottom,* Late first stage: pain intensity severe. Severe pain produced by intense uterine contractions during the latter part of the first stage referred to T–10, T–11, T–12, and L–1 dermatomes. (From Bonica, J. *Obstetric Analgesia and Anesthesia*. World Federation of Societies of Anaesthesiologists, Amsterdam, 1980.)

other complications, results from imbalances in the body's flow of energy. This theory is based on the Oriental concept of homeostasis, which states that life energy, *chi,** can be divided into positive *(yang)* and negative *(yin)* types. The energy flows through the body along specific channels, called *meridians*. (Points located along the meridians are used in the practice of acupuncture and acupressure. These points, or *tsubos,* have been found to have increased electrical conductivity and decreased electrical resistance.) If the energy flow

*Energy fields are also called "ki" and "prana" by different philosophical and cultural groups.

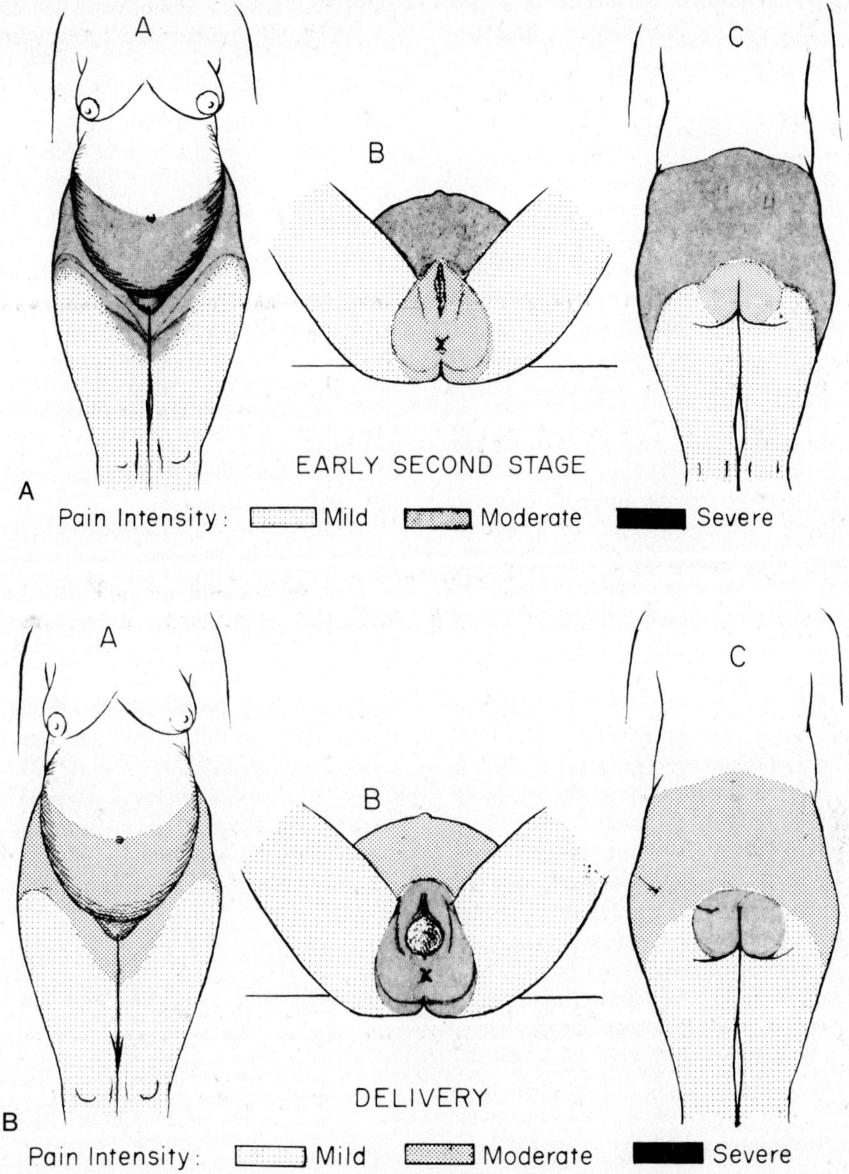

FIGURE 6–4. Pain intensity and distribution, second stage labor. *A, Top,* Early second stage. Distribution of labor pain during the early phase of the second stage. Uterine contractions remain intense and produce severe pain in T–10 to L–1 dermatomes and, at the same time, the presenting part exerts pressure on pelvic structures and thus causes moderate pain in the very low back and perineum and often mild pain in the thighs and legs. *B, Bottom,* Delivery. Distribution of childbirth pain during the later phase of the second stage and in the actual delivery. The perineal component is the primary cause of discomfort. Uterine contractions produce moderate pain. (From Bonica, J. *Obstetric Analgesia and Anesthesia.* World Federation of Societies of Anaesthesiologists, Amsterdam, 1980.)

becomes blocked to an area or if energy is congested in a part of the body, or if there is an imbalance of positive and negative energy, illness or pain results. Because of the transitional nature of pregnancy and birth, it is thought the woman may be more vulnerable to energy imbalances at these times, giving rise to childbirth pain.

Iatrogenic sources of pain must also be addressed here, although they receive little attention in most obstetrical textbooks. Certain obstetrical interventions, whether or not they are indicated, can cause or increase pain to the parturient. Women whose labors are induced often report stronger, more uncomfortable contractions and usually have a more difficult time coping with them due to the abrupt initiation of active labor and the nature of the contractions, which tend to peak rapidly. Women also report increased pain during vaginal examinations done in labor. They are usually directed to lie on their backs during the examination, even though, for most women, this is not a comfortable position when laboring and may even result in maternal hypotension. When the examiner's fingers are inserted into the cervix, a contraction may be brought on or an existing contraction may be intensified. Many women report an increase in the discomfort of contractions after amniotomy, as well. Some have complained of discomfort from tight abdominal fetal monitors and others have reported discomfort from internal monitor leads.

Enemas are well known for increasing the intensity of contractions—if only temporarily—as well as for causing intense contractions of the intestines along with occasional chills and nausea. Other obvious sources of short-lived pain include the needles used to administer pain-relieving medications and other solutions. Forceps and episiotomies may also be painful. Although each of these procedures may be done to help reduce discomfort or time in labor or to ensure the safety or ascertain the condition of the mother or baby, each has been reported as a source of discomfort and for many women they are a source of anxiety, even before the first signs of labor are felt.

Psychological Causes of Pain

In 1933, Dick-Read published his hypothesis that childbirth is not inherently painful. He proposed that the pain of labor was of psychic origin and due largely to cultural myths. Dick-Read believed that this resulted in ''obstruction in the birth canal,''[14] and that this led to pain. He stated that fear, caused by cultural and social myths, causes excitation of the sympathetic nervous system and that this activates contraction of the circular muscle fibers of the uterus. Thus, the lower portion of the uterus works in direct opposition to the upper portion of the organ. According to Dick-Read, this results in excessive tension within the uterus. He believed that ''the uterus is supplied with organs which record pain set up by excessive tension,''[13] and that this is the origin of pain in labor. Most texts agree that the reproductive structures are supplied with nerves that respond to stretching and pressure, often resulting in pain. Dick-Read's theory also may relate to Bonica's ''high threshold mechanical nociceptors.''

Dick-Read was also a proponent of the ischemic pain theory, as described earlier in this chapter, because he thought that it further supported his belief that labor pain is of psychic origin and that it justified his ''fear-tension-pain syndrome.'' He believed that the ischemia arose from prolonged uterine tension, brought on by fear. (According to Beck,[2] the first published reference to the ''fear-tension-pain syndrome'' was in 1947 in *Birth of a Child*. Although *Childbirth Without Fear* was first published in 1944, it was not until the later editions that this theory was included.)

In his ''Historical Perspective'' Beck points out

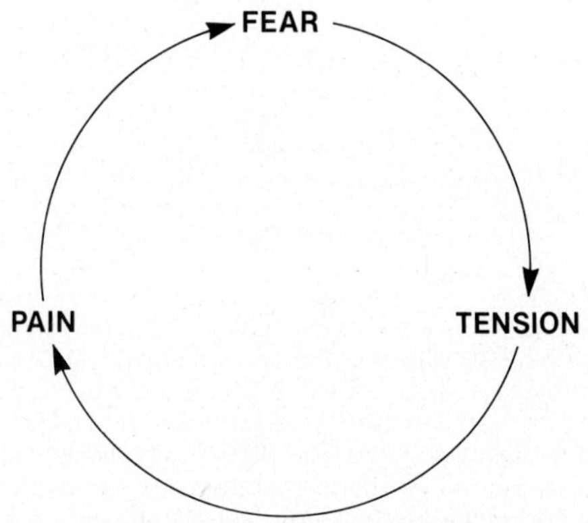

FIGURE 6–5. Fear-tension-pain syndrome.

that Dick-Read showed little interest in testing his theories through research.[2] Dick-Read himself admitted that his colleagues criticized him and said that his theories were unsupported and not "strictly scientific," but he answered their criticisms with report after report of "happy women with their newborn babies in their arms (who said) 'How right you are, doctor, it is so much easier this way.' "[4] A study by Lederman et al.[23] found that increased maternal anxiety correlated significantly with increased levels of plasma epinephrine (a biochemical measure of anxiety), which were significantly related to decreased uterine contractility and lengthened duration of labor. In commenting on this study, Beck concluded that this does not confirm "a simple, direct, and linear relationship between fear, tension, and pain." This is because increased levels of plasma epinephrine are not necessarily associated with pain. This study does, however, support Dick-Read's contention that anxiety (fear) contributes negatively toward the childbirth process.

According to Velvovsky, his colleague Platonov first investigated hypnosuggestion to prevent labor pain in 1920.[34] By 1926 Velvovsky had become "disappointed in hypnosuggestion as a general method of painless childbirth" and began formulating a link between obstetrics and psychoneurology. Velvovsky claimed to have "laid down the principles of the psychoprophylactic system" by 1930 but did not apply them in a practical manner until 1947. His theories gained the support of Nikolayev in 1949, and it was their system that Lamaze observed in 1952. Velvovsky published his theories in 1954 in the book *Painless Childbirth Through Psychoprophylaxis*. He and his co-authors summed up their basic premises as follows:

1. There is no proof that labour pain is necessarily inherent in childbirth. On the contrary, obstetrical science has established that pain is not indispensable to the normal course of labour.
2. The very essence of childbirth, as a physiological act, inclines us to believe that labour pain constitutes a superfluous and acquired phenomenon produced by elements not contained in the nature of parturition.

Velvovsky and Nikolayev based their theories on the work of Pavlov, claiming that pain was not a natural part of labor, but that it was a "conditioned reflex." They held that physiological changes of pregnancy and birth may give rise to noxious stimuli, but that the actual interpretation of these stimuli as pain depends on the central nervous system in general and, specifically, the cerebral cortex. In 1972, Velvovsky further elaborated on causes of pain during physiological labor, dividing them into two groups:

1. Excessive aggravation of neurodynamical interaction in the system of the cortex-subcortex of the brain.
2. The historical psychofixation of the act of labour as a painful act, and as an act of suffering which induced negative emotion to pregnancy and made it a mass phenomenon.[34]

Although Velvovsky acknowledged the existence of pain due to pathological conditions in labor, he placed highest importance on "cortical pain" due to the disturbing effect of "negative emotions" on "the dynamics of the nervous processes." He held that this caused an excitatory-inhibitory imbalance in the cerebral cortex and subcortex allowing "non-pain stimuli to break through to the cerebral cortex . . . (that) are perceived there as pain stimuli."[35]

Beck et al.[2] point out that, like Dick-Read, Velvovsky and his colleagues did not provide valid research to back up their theories—nor did their disciple, Lamaze. Beck also takes exception to their description of pain in labor as a "conditioned response," since pain has always been considered part of the unconditioned response. The fear of labor is more appropriately labeled a conditioned response that leads to increased pain.

In *Obstetric Analgesia and Anesthesia*, Bonica describes "psychologic dimensions" that can influence the degree of pain:

- Anxiety and emotional arousal
- Motivation and affect
- Cognitive-conceptual-judgmental dimensions

It is well known that anxiety and arousal increase muscular tension, thereby increasing nociceptor stimulation. Fear and tension can activate the sympathetic nervous system (SNS), leading to ischemia through vasospasm. According to Bonica, "under appropriate conditions, anxiety, fear, and apprehension may activate certain brain mechanisms that inhibit the efficacy of supraspinal descending inhibitory systems that, in turn, enhance the transmission of nociceptive impulses, resulting in greater pain perception. Thus a 'vicious circle' is initiated . . .''[5] Interestingly, although stated differently and with more research to back it up, this is, in essence, what Dick-Read said 40 years ago when he first described the ''fear-tension-pain syndrome'' as follows: ''The fear of pain actually produces true pain through the medium of pathological tension . . . and once it is established, a vicious circle demonstrating a crescendo of events will be observed . . .''[12]

Stevens states that the mind can perceive pain in a part of the body even ''in the absence of a physical pain stimulus along the pathway of the pain system.''[33] He adds that the degree of perceived pain is not only related to the intensity of the stimulation but also to the woman's ''mental state,'' which ''is able to enhance, diminish, misinterpret, or even create perception of pain.'' In support of this statement, Stevens cites phantom limb pain, studies on the placebo effect in managing postoperative pain, and Pavlov's experiment, in which puppies became conditioned to react happily to a painful shock.

Several studies have been done to investigate the influence of ethnicity on pain perception.[4,9,10,38,39] There seems to be a link between cultural upbringing and expectations and either the perception, interpretation, or expression of pain. This often is a source of problems for health professionals and the pregnant couple, or between the parturient and her partner, for expectations of both pain and behavior may differ on the basis of past experiences and values. This means that those involved in helping the woman prevent, cope with, or reduce her pain may be approaching the pain experience from totally different perspectives. Perhaps the wisest approach is that advocated by McCaffey in *Nursing Management of the Patient in Pain*:[27] ''Pain is whatever the experiencing person says it is and exists whenever he (or she) says it does.''

PAIN MANAGEMENT THEORIES

This section will provide an overview of pain management theories applicable to the childbirth experience. Later chapters will deal in depth with the practical application of these theories.

Cognitive Control. Stevens[33] defines cognitive control as ''a psychological strategy whereby the subject involves his mind in mental activities other than awareness of the incoming pain sensation.'' He divides cognitive control into two categories:

1. Dissociation–The subject focuses on a nonpainful aspect of the source of stimulation. In the case of labor, this might include focusing on the pressure or heat or motion of the uterine contraction or on the work of dilatation and effacement and the downward movement of the baby. Research has shown that this technique increases pain tolerance. Dissociation may influence pain perception by changing cognitive and affective and motivational dimensions of the pain experience or it may work through gate control, through the descending sensory pathways. (Gate control will be explained further later in this section.)
2. Interference–These strategies provide a stimulation outside the source of pain that may interfere with completion of transmission of the pain message or with interpretation of it. Interference strategies can be passive, as in distraction techniques such as watching television, or they can be active, as in attention-focusing strategies (internal or external focal points). Stevens found attention-focusing to be superior to distraction in reducing pain. Controlled breathing, use of focal points, and guided imagery are forms of attention-focusing, and they also are used to enhance relaxation.

Sensory Transformation. In this strategy mothers are taught to transform the pain stimulus into a pleasant feeling. For example, the throbbing resulting from a painful stimulus can be imagined as a pleasant warm feeling. This is in contrast to "pleasant imagery" wherein one might imagine a peaceful beach scene. Geden and colleagues[15] found that, when tested in the laboratory against a pain stimulus designed to deliver pain stimulation of the configuration of painful uterine contractions, sensory transformation was effective, whereas relaxation training, pleasant imagery, and neutral imagery were not. Extending this concept to childbirth preparation, the mother might use sensory training to transform the labor contraction into a strong pleasant embrace from a loved one. This strategy certainly fits with the thought that it is primarily the unpleasantness of pain with which women need to cope.

Relaxation. In one form or another, relaxation is a major component of the three predominant methods of childbirth preparation: those of Dick-Read, Bradley, and psychoprophylaxis (PPM, or Lamaze). According to Stevens,[33] systematic relaxation increases pain tolerance by decreasing mental anxiety and fear, resulting in decreased awareness of the pain stimulus. Benson[3] cites early studies that showed relaxation can decrease sympathetic nervous system (SNS) arousal and activate the parasympathetic nervous system (PNS), resulting in vasodilation, decreased release of catecholamines, and decreased epinephrine and norepinephrine levels. (This is congruent with the earlier cited findings of Lederman.) Thus, relaxation may reduce ischemic pain as well as pain arising from the neurohumeral response to stress. As illustrated in Figure 6–1, this can have a significant effect on the labor process and the infant's well-being, as well as the level of pain.

Relaxation also reduces pain perception by blocking the "vicious circle" described by both Bonica and Dick-Read, in which fear leads to tension, which leads to pain, which reinforces the original fear. Humenick[19] showed that high prenatal relaxation ability correlated with decreased reports of use of medication. Although relaxation is covered here as one of many pain management theories and strategies, all major therapies related to pain reduction incorporate some form of relaxation training, and many of the pain management techniques that will be described here are used, at least partially, to enhance relaxation.

It is interesting to note that relaxation was not a part of the original PPM method as it came from Russia. In fact, Velvovsky et al. devoted several pages of their book[35] to trying to prove that relaxation training is nothing more than hypnosuggestion, and that, as such, it is the opposite of PPM. Velvovsky believed that relaxation led to cortical inhibition, thus reducing the nociceptors' threshold, resulting in increased pain. His system taught cortical excitation techniques that he believed increased this threshold and thereby lowered pain.

Cognitive Rehearsal. This strategy reduces pain by giving the subject information about the pain experience before it occurs. A study by Staub and Kellet[32] found that pain reduction was best when the subject received both subjective and objective descriptions about the expected pain experience. Cognitive rehearsal is a major component of all methods of childbirth preparation, as the teacher describes to the class both the typical course of labor, as well as variations. It is important to keep in mind that the class members must learn what will happen and why, how it will feel, and what they can do about it. Studies show that the information must be realistic—that is, the pain experience must validate the cognitive rehearsal. *If, as in the past, the expectant mother is told that childbirth is not inherently painful and that she can have a painless birth, and if she experiences pain, from that point on her learning experience may become invalid to her and she may be unable to carry out the practiced pain-reducing strategies.*

Physical Rehearsal. Physical rehearsal is common in childbirth classes in the form of a tendon or muscle squeeze. Worthington et al.[37] tested strategies to help women tolerate the pain of ice water. They found that those who practiced with the stress of ice water had improved tolerance over those who used cognitive (imagining the pain) rehearsal or no rehearsal. They comment that childbirth preparation classes often include practice with a painful squeeze of a tendon. They suggest that ice water practice at home might be a better stimulus than a tendon squeeze because the intensity and configuration of tendon squeezes tend to vary widely among individuals. Ice water practice would be standard (0 to 1° C), and a woman could more objectively measure her ability to use her pain-reducing techniques. This is an interesting idea, but the fact that ice water practice is best for preparing for an ice water test does not necessarily indicate that it is preferable for labor rehearsal. Further research in this area is needed.

Modeling. Manderino and Bzdek[25] use the framework of Bandura's social learning theory to discuss vicarious learning. They propose that a pain-reducing effect might be gained from expectant mothers viewing a videotape in which realistic modeling of coping with childbirth is shown. The modeling strategy was tested in a laboratory with student nurses and a Forgione-Barker pain stimulator, which produced pressure on the index finger. Subjects who received both information and modeling rated their pain as significantly less than those who received information alone or modeling alone. Although this concept needs replication in a childbirth setting, there appear to be implications for selecting a childbirth movie. It would seem that the ideal movie is informative and also models coping with a realistic labor.

Desensitization. Desensitizing of the pregnant woman to the fear of childbirth has been a basic function of childbirth education since its inception. Perhaps the only two major points agreed on by Dick-Read, Velvovsky, and Lamaze are that childbirth is not inherently painful and that fear is a major source of pain. The process of desensitization utilizes many strategies to help the woman confront her fears and take an active role in decreasing them. While helping her relax, the teacher offers attention and support, which utilize the Hawthorne effect to increase the woman's confidence. Throughout the series of classes, cognitive rehearsal takes place as the group explores the various routes that labor may take and considers possible coping tools. By combining all or several of the tools discussed in this chapter, the woman determines how she can cope best. Through practice and with the introduction of increasing realistic stressors (descriptions of contractions and possible procedures, thigh pressure, and so on), she learns to relax and to reduce her fear and increase her confidence.

Hawthorne Effect. This effect is seen when the subject receives special attention from the experimenter or teacher and, as a result, performs better. Positive support from those who are viewed as childbirth experts, such as the childbirth educator, nurse, or physician, enables the parturient to cope more effectively, thereby increasing the effectiveness of her pain management strategies. Support from a labor partner such as the husband or another person has also been shown to reduce both pain and length of labor.

Gate Control Theory. Melzack and Wall's gate control theory[6,31] has been used to explain the effectiveness of many prepared childbirth techniques, including massage, pressure, heat and cold applications, breathing patterns, and focusing. First described in 1965, this theory states that the pain stimulus can be modified as it travels through the spinal cord. The pain stimulus is transmitted along the ascending pathway through *small-diameter* neural fibers. When the impulse reaches the substantia gelatinosa, a "highly specialized closed system of cells that extends throughout the spinal cord on both sides,"[6] a gating mechanism can be activated by sensations traveling through *large-diameter* fibers. This modifies or inhibits the pain impulse before it reaches the transmission cells in the dorsal horn. According to Melzack, writing in *Altering the Experience of Pain,*[6] "the substantia gelatinosa cells probably gate impulse transmission from peripheral fibers . . . by blocking impulses at the presynaptic axon terminals or by decreasing the amount of transmitter substance; and post-synaptically, by increasing or decreasing their own level of excitability." The speed at which impulses are conducted depends on the diameter, degree of myelination, and route taken by the nerve fibers.

Figure 6–6 illustrates how gate control might work when massage is used to counter painful uterine contractions. Pressure, heat, and cold, which are transmitted along large-diameter nerve fibers, are able to activate this gating mechanism. However, since large nerve fibers habituate more easily than small fibers, these strategies may provide temporary relief, after which the pain will again be felt.

When this happens, or possibly before it happens, the subject can reactivate the "gate" by changing the location or type of large-fiber stimulation. It is important to note that light touch travels along the same pathway as pain and therefore may increase pain perception.[6] For this reason, fingertip massage, known as *effluerage,* when used lightly is often not appropriate in the prevention of childbirth pain. In fact, many women who are taught to use a light touch in class resort to quite firm pressure in labor. At least one research study

Support during labor has been shown to decrease pain and shorten the length of labor. (Copyright BABES, Inc.)

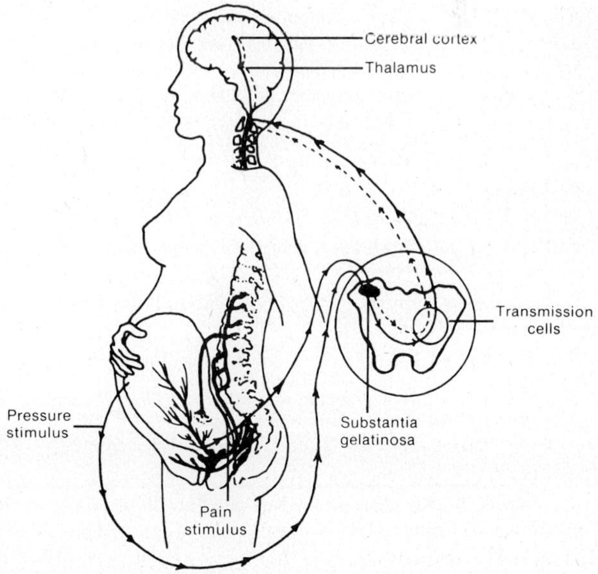

FIGURE 6–6. Schematic diagram of the gate-control theory. The diagram shows the route of the uterine pain impulse as it travels to the spinal cord where, in the substantia gelatinosa (see insert of enlarged vertebra), it is blocked by the large-fiber stimulation provided by the woman's hand massaging her abdomen. The dotted line indicates the path the pain impulse would have taken had the gate been open. (From Jiménez, S. Application of the Body's Natural Pain Relief Mechanisms to Reduce Discomfort in Labor and Delivery. In *NAACOG Update Series, Volume 1,* Princeton, NJ: Continuing Professional Education Center, 1983.)

has found effluerage to be ineffective in pain reduction.[37]

There are several different types of neural receptor systems, including mechanoreceptors, chemoreceptors, and thermoceptors. In Table 6–1, the types of receptor systems are described, their common locations cited, and potential implications for labor pain reduction noted. These interventions were proposed by Hilbers and Gennaro on the basis of an extensive review of neurophysiology.[17] It is not necessary, and in most cases is not useful, to present this anatomical detail to expectant parents. The important general principle is that all of the pain-reducing techniques listed in Table 6–1 have a scientific basis and any of them may help alter the perception of labor pain. A woman and her partner can therefore be encouraged to try a variety of these strategies and to use those that they find

TABLE 6–1. TECHNIQUES FOR PAIN REDUCTION BASED ON PRINCIPLES OF NEUROPHYSIOLOGY

RECEPTOR SYSTEMS	RECEPTOR DESCRIPTION/ FUNCTION	LOCATION	POTENTIAL PAIN-REDUCING TECHNIQUES
A. Mechanoreceptors			
1. Merkel's disks	Well-myelinated receptors; large, fast in transmitting sensations; respond to steady maintained pressure; do not habituate readily, can be used for a long time before pain-reducing potential is diminished.	Most numerous on palms, soles, external genitalia, and lips.	Pressure to lips through kissing, index finger, or Chapstick Pressure to hands from squeezing objects or holding hands with a partner. Pressure to feet through standing or placing feet on a hard surface. Pressure to genitalia from sitting on a firm surface.
2. Meissner's corpuscles	These receptors transmit faster than pain; used primarily to distinguish texture of receptors of objects.	Fingertips and hairless skin.	Move fingertips lightly in circles on sheets. Finger soft textures (velvet). Feel partner's face, effluerage self or sense effluerage by partner, touch message.
3. Pacinian corpuscles	These receptors transmit rapidly and are slow to habituate; largest of the receptors.	Deep layers on the skin; most widely distributed receptor—detect deep pressure and vibration.	Use of vibrating pillows or a cordless vibrator around the pelvis or muscles along spine.
4. Tactile hair end organs	These receptors use the same routes as pain and may thus increase pain.		Avoid tickling or a light moving touch against hair follicles (rubbing someone the wrong way).
5. Joint receptors	Large receptors slow the adapt/ habituate.	In joint capsules, ligaments, and synovial membranes throughout body.	Change position, standing, walking, hugging, rocking, gently shaking joints, pelvic rocking on all fours. May even be stimulated in ribs by breathing techniques.
B. Chemoreceptors			
1. Olfactory	Small fibers going to hypothalamus and limbic system.	Upper part of nostrils.	Provide familiar calming scents such as own pillow case, partner, favorite herb or spice smells. Avoid unfamiliar smells.
2. Taste			Use sucking of object such as wash cloth dipped in flavored water.
C. Thermoceptors	Heat and cold receptors.	Throughout skin.	Ice chips, cold packs, warm showers or baths, warm hair dryers . . . hot and cold alternating. Avoid use on anesthesized tissue.

Data from Hilbers, S., and Gennaro, S. Non-pharmaceutical pain relief. NAACOG Update Series, Vol. 5, Princeton, NJ: Continuing Professional Education Center, 1986.

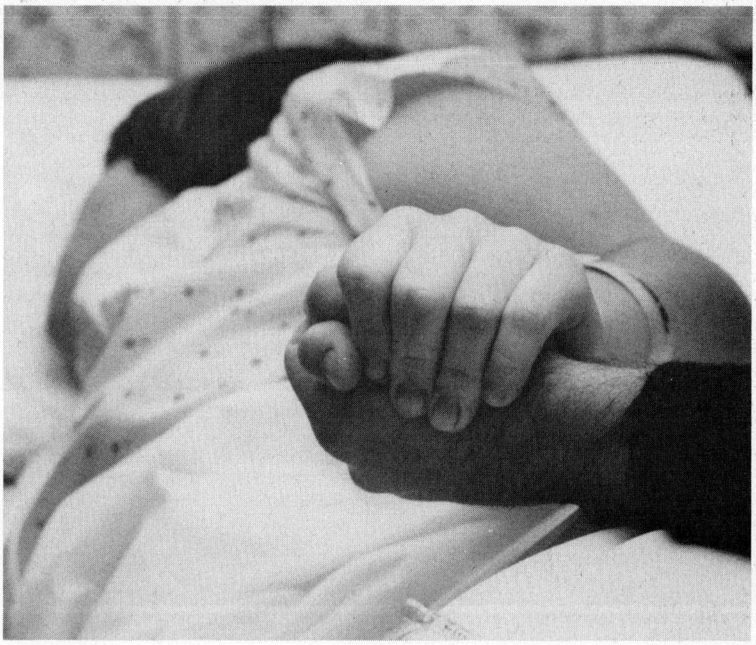

Some laboring women find squeezing a partner's hand helpful because it stimulates mechanoreceptors in the palm of the hand and decreases the perception of pain. (Copyright BABES, Inc.)

helpful. Childbirth educators should be open to observing the effects of many pain-reducing techniques rather than teaching only those techniques associated with a specific childbirth method. For example, childbirth educators may fear that squeezing an object with the hands is antithetical to relaxation. However, Table 6–1 explains why some laboring women find hand squeezing helpful in reducing pain.

As mentioned previously, gate control is thought to work through the descending pathway as well as the ascending pathway. This may account for the effectiveness of a variety of focusing (cognitive) strategies in prepared childbirth such as breathing, music, verbal coaching, and so on. These cognitive strategies may be examples of gate control through a descending pathway.

Endorphin System. The discovery of the *endorphin system* in 1975 increased our understanding of why and how certain pain-prevention techniques (including acupressure and shiatsu) work, as well as why these same techniques, under different circumstances, can be ineffective. When researchers located opiate receptor sites in the brain, this led to the identification of endogenous chemicals that are released from the brainstem and pituitary gland. These small fragments of beta-lipoprotein, a pituitary peptide, were called *enkephalins* (''in the head''). Later, a larger peptide, *endorphin* (''endogenous morphine''), was discovered, and this name has become more generally associated with these natural pain inhibitors. Although pharmacologically different, endorphins and morphine are identical in molecular configuration. They both act by traveling to the opiate receptors, where they fit like a key in a lock, blocking transmission of the pain impulse. Endorphins also can make the subject feel relaxed and drowsy. The endorphin level of the parturient has been found to be much higher than that of a nonlaboring woman, and it continues at a high level for several days postpartum.[22] In a recent study, Newnham found endorphin blood values in women at delivery to be 30 times that of the nonpregnant woman.[24] These levels have been found to be as much as 20 times higher in prolonged, difficult labors as in uncomplicated labors.[22]

Electro-acupuncture stimulation produces an eightfold increase in the natural endorphin level in the general population. This suggests that acupressure and shiatsu may also activate the release of endorphins. (More research is needed into the effects of electro-acupuncture and acupressure on blood values in pregnant women.) Many gate-control strategies also have been shown to have a positive effect on endorphin production.

The administration of exogenous opiates such as Demerol, opiate derivatives, and opiate antagonists has been found to suppress the production of endogenous opioids. In the past it was suggested that this occurs because the exogenous opioids take up all available opiate receptor sites, suggesting to the body that there is no further need to produce endorphin at that time. Recently, several researchers have attributed this reduction of naturally occurring opioids to the effectiveness of the pharmaceutical agent in reducing pain. In a study by Browning[22,25] the endorphin level was significantly lower in women receiving an epidural block than in those who did not receive one. (The difference held true whether or not a woman had been given pethidine as well.) More research is needed to determine the effect of opiates and opiate derivatives on natural pain management. For example, can a small dose of medication reduce the effectiveness of natural coping strategies sufficiently to cause the woman to need more medication?

The antagonistic effect of certain drugs on endorphin may have implications in the postpartum period. In 1979 Kimball published a study that suggested a positive link between naturally occurring endorphins and the release of prolactin.[22] At that time he proposed a further connection between this endogenous opioid and lactation and maternal behaviors. Although further research by Kimball and others has failed to establish a significant correlation between endogenous opioids (endorphins) and mothering behaviors or postpartum emotional moodiness (''blues''), Kimball seems convinced that an endogenous opioid will be found to play an important role in postpartum behaviors.

Regarding endorphin's role in pain management in labor, Newnham found a negative correlation between the woman's estimate of her own labor pain and her postpartum blood values of endogenous opioids, suggesting that women who perceived less pain in childbirth may have been naturally protected by the body's ability to produce its own analgesia.[24] Interestingly, a positive correlation was found in endorphin levels at 36 weeks' gestation and the woman's attitude toward her pregnancy. Women with positive attitudes had higher blood values. No correlation has been found between maternal and fetal postpartum blood values of endogenous opioids, but researchers suggest that endorphins may also play a role in protecting the child from pain during the birth process.

Homeostasis. The ancient idea of homeostasis has endured throughout the centuries as a legitimate medical concept. An equally ancient companion, harmony, has long been relegated to the ranks of ''alternative therapies.'' While homeostasis focuses on achieving or maintaining physical balance, harmony encompasses a balance of the physical, mental, and spiritual. The theories discussed thus far offer support for the need for physical and mental balance. The spiritual component of self is fundamental to a woman's goals and values. Webster's Collegiate Thesaurus lists ''soul'' and ''vital force'' as synonyms for ''spirit,'' and defines ''spiritual'' as ''related to the higher emotions.''[21] It would seem, then, that the woman's spiritual nature has a strong impact on the attitude with which she approaches childbirth and thus would have great importance to both her perception and her interpretation of the sensory experience.

IMPLICATIONS FOR PRACTICE

As evidence continues to reveal the synergism of the triad of mind, body, and spirit, it becomes apparent that childbirth education must provide a holistic approach to the sensory aspects of the birth experience. Although the current trend is to label as holistic any type of alternative therapy, this is a misconception. Holism is simply the consideration of the entire person, her lifestyle, her environment, and her family. Most childbirth educators follow this approach in promoting cognitive and affective learning but then may adopt a prescriptive approach to teaching psychomotor skills. Another myth is that a holistic class is unstructured and permissive. In reality, to ensure the development of effective skills, the teacher must help each couple develop goals and a plan of learning and practice, based on continuing assessment by the teacher and self-assessment by the couple.

In moving away from a prescriptive approach, there must be a de-emphasis on the principle that only one way is *the* correct way and an emphasis on mastery or achievement of goals and related subgoals. Each woman can be encouraged to make each technique her own, so that she is master of the technique and not the reverse. Each woman's perception of and reaction to pain is as different as each woman's life. Thus, her preparation must also be different.

The following guidelines are helpful in promoting mastery of pain management skills:

- When teaching pain theories, offer or ask for examples from daily life, and then relate this to how the theory might be used in labor. For example, gate control can be understood easily when it is likened to the pain relief given by cool, running water on a burned finger. Both the sensation of coolness and the feel of the water as its runs over the skin would, according to this theory, stimulate large nerve fibers, thus closing the gate to the pain message. When the finger is removed from the flow of water, the pain soon returns. Habituation can be explained in the same way: if the burned finger is left in the water for 10 or 15 minutes the pain sensation may return, as the large nerve fibers stop registering the coolness and touch of the water, allowing the pain message through once again.

  After the class members understand how the theory works in daily life and, in fact, has probably already worked many times for each of them, it is a simple step to the process of labor and how to use gate control to manage its pain. A warm shower may ease back labor, a firm pressure may decrease pain in the back. As habituation develops, if pain returns or increases, the woman or her partner will know that it does not mean the technique is ineffective, but that, for now, it must be altered in order to restimulate large nerve fibers. This may mean exchanging the stimulus of firm pressure for stroking or use of an ice pack. Later, as the new strategy begins to wear out, they may try another, or return to the original pain management technique. As the class members develop and refine their skills in understanding and applying each theory, the finer points, such as the ability of cognitive strategies to initiate gate-control mechanisms, should be explored.

- As each labor management skill is explained and demonstrated, briefly review the applicable theory, or ask the class how or why this skill will help. For example, when teaching a new massage technique, ask why it might reduce pain or stress in labor.

- Integrate skills practice with cognitive content to increase relevance and learning. Instead of teaching physical strategies as a separate topic, blend them into each class. As the physical and emotional aspects of early labor are described, ask each couple to assume a comfortable position. When explaining what these first contractions might feel like, have them suggest and try some of the techniques they will use. One might suggest a back rub for tension in early labor. The teacher might add that calm, slow breathing would also help. At this point the class can practice both for a moment before going on, or they may want to continue relaxing as the teacher talks. This immediate application of what they have heard and seen to what they should do will increase their ability to remember and perform it.

- Use judgment in presenting the many different types of pain reduction strategies. While the multimodal approach is appropriate, care must be taken to avoid overwhelming class members. It is not essential that each woman master each strategy. Rather, she should use those strategies that work best for her.

- Promote confidence by having the class practice first in an environment with as little stress as possible. Move slowly and steadily to the addition of simple physical stress, such as thigh pressure, or the practice of relaxing certain body parts while others are working. An example is to relax the upper body and legs during the pelvic

> It is advisable to teach the pregnant woman several techniques in order that she may vary them if any of them cease to be effective.
>
> VELVOVSKY[1]
>
> We took this big shopping list to the hospital of all the different tools we could use during labor. It helped because we both couldn't remember a thing!
>
> A NEW MOTHER
>
> The most positive thing about my labor was how we all worked together. My friend was the breathing coach and my husband gave me support and massage. It helped a lot.
>
> A NEW MOTHER

tilt. Have the class practice relaxing with mental stressors. For example, after they become relaxed, review a topic such as hospital admission, and ask the partners and the women to note how each item discussed affects her relaxation level. The final step is to combine physical and mental stressors during practice. This can be done by reviewing a subject such as transition while the woman receives a physical stimulus such as pressure by the partner or holding a piece of ice in her hand.

- Assist class members to develop a realistic attitude toward pain. It is the body's way of telling us something needs to be done. It is not bad, but it may be unpleasant. A woman who has a painful labor has not failed; she simply has had a painful labor. The expression of pain is not bad, nor does it indicate cowardice or inability to cope. If a woman sitting in a movie theater becomes very cold, she will put on a sweater. If she has none or if the one she has is not sufficient, and if she finds the cold unacceptable, she will complain to someone near her. If necessary, she may complain to the manager, as well. No one will think badly of her, nor will she feel guilty. She was cold and she said so. Pain and cold are both sensory experiences that can be unpleasant. Unfortunately, the growth of prepared childbirth has given some women the false impression that childbirth pain is not inherent, and therefore, if you are in pain, you are inadequate. We must deal with the three phases of pain: anticipation, presence, and aftermath,[26] and we must help our clients deal with them realistically.

- Help the class to understand that pain may not be the foremost problem in each labor. For some women fatigue, nausea, or the feelings of frustration or desperation are stronger than pain. They must learn to cope with these, as well.

- Discover how the woman has managed previous pain and stress and help her integrate new pain management skills into her present system to make both more effective. For example, if a woman ordinarily finds herself humming to ease tension, she can learn to adapt this to the rhythm of paced breathing and rhythmic massage. If she is accustomed to having her husband rub her temples when she is ill, this may be the most effective form of massage for her in labor, *no matter where she is hurting*. The effectiveness of this rubbing can be optimized by matching it to the cadence of paced breathing. By helping the woman and her partner use what they already know and do, the teacher not only increases their ability to learn and to reduce pain and stress but also may help them increase their self-esteem, which may further enhance coping abilities.

- In teaching pharmacological alternatives for pain management, the childbirth educator can emphasize that the choice should be made on the basis of the concept of risk versus benefit, as well as what the woman perceives as an unacceptable level of pain. Each expectant parent can list the physical and emotional risks and benefits to mother and child of each potential alternative and discuss the weight of importance each item carries for them. Some may want to give a number value to each, but others find it difficult to be so definite about something that has not yet happened and which they may never have experienced. Perhaps it is best to leave them with preferences rather than absolute choices, and to help them discuss and practice ways to obtain these preferences as much as is feasible in their situation.

Another strategy that can help couples share their feelings on medication, as well as other interventions, is the *values continuum*. A line is drawn on the chalkboard to represent the importance of avoiding medication. One end of the line is marked "Definitely important" and the other end is marked "Definitely unimportant." Before class or during a break class members are asked to make a mark on the line at the point that best estimates their feelings about medication. This can be done in an inconspicuous way by allowing several time periods during which class members may choose to place their marks. In this way no one feels "put on the spot." If desired, the continuum may be more personal, with couples designing their own values lines for various alternatives and then deciding where on each line their feelings lie. As with any such teaching strategy, the teacher should follow up with a discussion among the class members about what they learned about themselves and their partners, and how this might affect what happens during labor. If some class members are uncomfortable with discussing this with the group, they should not feel pushed to do so, although it should be understood that at some point, if someone has strong feelings about certain options, it will be necessary to make these feelings known to those attending the birth.

A scoreboard exercise is similar to the values continuum. Each person uses 10 or 12 small squares of paper on which to list options in childbirth as they are suggested by the class. These might include having the labor partner remain with the mother throughout the entire labor and birth, having a choice about an enema, or avoiding an epidural. (Some couples see avoiding an epidural or some other intervention as a negative option, preferring to have the choice that it be available for them rather than being shielded from it. It is therefore important that these options not always be presented as procedures that normal people or "good parents" want to avoid. As an educator, the teacher's role is to help her students *discover what they want,* not what she thinks they should want.)

After listing these options, class members arrange their squares in the order of their importance to them, moving them about until they are satisfied. The teacher then asks them to turn face down each option that they could give up and to continue until the only options left face up are those they absolutely must have. At this point each person should share with the partner their scoreboard arrangement. The teacher may ask couples to discuss these by posing questions to each other, such as "What surprised you most about my choices?" or "Why did you omit option 4?" and "What steps should be take to ensure that we receive these options?"

- Couples can learn to cope effectively with medications and anesthesia by discussing or writing a list of their roles during administration of medication, during its effective period, and afterward, when the pain may return.
- Finally, as teachers, we must remain open-minded about new and old concepts of pain and its management. *We must be careful neither to embrace without reservation nor to dismiss without consideration theories and techniques that seem different.*

IMPLICATIONS FOR RESEARCH

The research literature describes various versions of the aforementioned theories of causes of pain and focuses on either the effects or relief of pain. No recent research was found on physical causes of pain in childbirth. The lack of interest in research as to actual causes of pain in labor would seem to come from the strong influence of the DeLee[11] and then the Williams[29] obstetrics textbooks, which described labor as a pathological process. This may also help account for the difficulty that some obstetricians had in the past in accepting the possibility of nonpharmacological prevention or reduction of pain. Some childbirth researchers believe that the predominance of male researchers may affect the level of interest in childbirth pain. A comparison can be made with menstrual cramps, which even today are seen by the majority of physicians either as psychosomatic (and something a woman must learn to live with) or as entirely physical and something for which there must be a pill.

Fortunately, the field of pain research is active and growing, and much of what is being revealed about surgical pain, chronic pain, and pain syndromes (such as migraine or ''cluster'' headaches) is applicable to childbirth. But more specific research is needed into the issues of causes of pain in childbirth and pain prevention, as well as the short-term and long-term effect of pain in the birth experience. To bring this about, our profession must raise the consciousness of the laity and the scientific community to the legitimacy of women's pain in general and childbirth pain in particular. There must be general agreement that childbirth can be painful and that it can be painless. There must be more clarity related to the difference between intensity of pain as opposed to unpleasantness of pain (suffering). Finally, we must observe and listen to the pregnant and laboring woman. She will tell us more about childbirth pain, its causes, its management, and its effects than we can ever learn from books and monitoring devices.

In summary, while extensive research into pain exists, more studies are needed that specifically explore the childbirth pain experience. Some questions that require answers are:

- What is the relative effect of the factors that influence the childbirth pain experience?
- What are the predictors of pain in childbirth?
- Which prepared childbirth strategies are the most effective for reducing pain during childbirth?
- What are the most effective approaches for teaching pain management skill in childbirth education classes?
- What are the short-term and long-terms effects of childbirth pain on the woman as well as her baby?

SUMMARY

In discussing pain, the childbirth educator should focus on the body's natural resources and emphasize the use of supportive pain management techniques for childbirth. We must keep in mind that for some the mastery of childbirth in their own terms is more important than pain relief. We must also respect the woman's right to her feelings about pain, medication, and other aspects of birth. It is critical that discussions about medication during childbirth be conducted in a manner that will not foster a sense of guilt or failure in the woman if she must use medication during childbirth. Couples need to master the skills that are required to manage the pain and stress of childbirth with the dignity and comfort they want, and they need to remain flexible in order to cope with the variety of situations that may arise. The role of the childbirth educator is to present a realistic picture of the childbirth pain experience, assist class members to develop and refine pain management skills for childbirth, and promote expectant parents' confidence that they can cope with the experience of childbirth.

References

1. Beck, N. Cognitive-Behavioral Methods of Pain, Anxiety and Stress Reduction. Paper presented at a continuing education course, American Society for Psychoprophylaxis in Obstetrics, 1982.
2. Beck, N., Geden, E., and Brouder, G. Preparation for Labor: A Historical Perspective. *Psychosomatic Med.* 41:243, 1979.
3. Benson, H. *The Relaxation Response*. New York: William Morrow, 1976.

4. Bogin, M. *The Path to Pain Control*. Boston: Houghton Mifflin, 1982.
5. Bonica, J. *Obstetric Analgesia and Anesthesia*. For the World Federation of Societies of Anaesthesiologists, Amsterdam, 1980.
6. Bonica, J., et al. *Altering the Experience of Pain*. New York: Pfizer Laboratories, 1979.
7. Browning, A. J., et al.: Maternal and cord plasma concentrations of beta-lipotrophin, beta-endorphin, and gamma-lipotrophin at delivery. *British Journal of Obstetrics and Gynecology* 90:1152, 1983.
8. Chabon, I. *Awake and Aware*. New York: Delacorte Press, 1966.
9. Clark, W. *Pain Sensitivity and the Report of Pain*. In Weisenburg, M., and Tursky, B. (eds.) Pain: New Perspectives in Therapy and Research. New York: Plenum Press, 1976.
10. Clark, W., et al. Pain responses in Nepalese porters. *Science* 209:410, 1980.
11. DeLee, J. *Principles and Practice of Obstetrics*. Philadelphia: W.B. Saunders Company, 1918.
12. Dick-Read, G. *Childbirth Without Fear*. New York: Harper and Rowe, 1959.
13. Dick-Read, G. *Childbirth Without Fear*. New York: Harper and Rowe, 1944.
14. Dick-Read, G. *Natural Childbirth*. London: Heinemann, 1933.
15. Geden, E., Beck, N., Hauge, G., and Pohlman, S. Self report and psychophysiological effects of five pain-coping strategies. *Nursing Research* 33(5): 1984.
16. Greenhill, J., and Friedman, E. *Biological Principles and Modern Practice of Obstetrics*. Philadelphia: WB Saunders Company, 1974.
17. Hilbers, S., and Gennaro, S. Non-pharmaceutical pain relief. NAACOG Update Series, Vol. 5, 1986.
18. Humenick, S. Mastery: The Key to Childbirth Satisfaction? A Review. *Birth: Issues in Perinatal Care and Education* 8:79, 1981.
19. Humenick, S. Validation of a Scale to Measure Relaxation in Childbirth Education Classes. *Birth: Issues in Perinatal Care and Education* 8:145, 1981.
20. Jiménez, S. Application of the Body's Natural Pain Relief Mechanisms to Reduce Discomfort in Labor and Delivery. *In* NAACOG Update Series Vol. 1, Princeton: Continuing Professional Education Center, 1983.
21. Kay, M. (ed.) *Webster's Collegiate Thesaurus*. Springfield: G&C Merriam, 1976.
22. Kimball, C. Do endorphin residues of beta-lipotrophin in hormone reinforce reproductive functions? *American Journal of Obstetrics and Gynecology* 134:127, 1979.
23. Lederman, R., Lederman, E., Work, B. A., and McCann, D. S. The relationship of maternal anxiety, plasma catecholamines and plasma cortisol to progress in labor. *American Journal of Obstetrics and Gynecology* 132:495, 1978.
24. Newnham, J., et al. A study of the relationship between beta-endorphin-like immunoreactivity and postpartum "blues." *Clinical Endocrinology* (Oxf) 20:169, 1984.
25. Manderino, M., and Bzdek, V. Effects of modeling and information on reactions to pain: A childbirth-preparation analogue. *Nursing Research* 33:9, 1984.
26. Martin, L. *Health Care of Women*. Philadelphia: J.B. Lippincott, 1978.
27. McCaffey, M. *Nursing Management of the Patient in Pain*. Philadelphia: J.B. Lippincott, 1972.
28. Oxorn, H. Oxorn-Foote Human Labor & Birth. 5th ed. Norwalk, CN: Appleton-Century-Crofts, 1986.
29. Pritchard, J. A., MacDonald, P. C., and Gant, N. L. *Williams Obstetrics*. Norwalk, CN: Appleton-Century-Crofts, 1985.
30. Roberts, J. Factors influencing distress from pain during labor. *Maternal Child Nursing* 8(1): 1983.
31. Seigel, D. The gate-control theory. *American Journal of Nursing* 74:498, 1974.
32. Staub, E., and Kellet, D. Increasing pain tolerance by information about adversive stimuli. *Journal of Perspectives on Social Psychology,* 21:198, 1972.
33. Stevens, R. Psychological Strategies for Management of pain in prepared childbirth, Part I. *Birth; Issues in Perinatal Care and Education* 3:157, 1976–77.
34. Velvovsky, I. Psychoprophylaxis in Obstetrics: A Soviet Method. *In* Howells, J. (ed): *Modern Perspectives in Psycho-obstetrics*. New York: Brunner/Mazel, 1972.
35. Velvovsky, I., Platonov, K., Ploticher, U., and Shugom, E. *Painless Childbirth Through Psychoprophylaxis*. Moscow: Foreign Languages Publishing House, 1960.
36. Wensel, L. *Acupuncture for Americans*. Reston, VA: Prentice-Hall, 1980.
37. Worthington, E. L., Martin, G. A., and Sumate, M. Which prepared childbirth coping strategies are effective? *JOGN Nursing* 11:45, 1982.
38. Zbrowski, M. Cultural Components in Responses to Pain. *Journal of Social Issues*. 8:16, 1952.
39. Zbrowski, M. *People in Pain*. San Francisco: Jossey-Bass, 1969.

Beginning Quote

Bonstein, I. *Psychoprophylactic Preparation for Painless Childbirth*. New York: Grune & Stratton, Inc., 1958, p. 13.

Boxed Quote

1. Velvovsky, I., Platonov, K., Ploticher, V., and Shugom, E. *Painless Childbirth Through Psychoprophylaxis*. Moscow: Foreign Languages Publishing House, 1960, p. 249.

chapter 7

THE BASIS OF RELAXATION

PAMELA SHROCK

Civilization and culture have brought influence to bear on the minds of women and introduced justifiable fears and anxieties concerning labor. Fear and anticipation have given rise to natural protective tensions in the body . . . tension not of the mind only . . . for the protective mechanisms induce muscle tension. Such resistance and tension give rise to pain

Grantly Dick-Read

Fifty years later, the mechanisms of the physiological processes Dick-Read[15] speaks of and ways to modify them are still being studied. New theories are constantly evolving as practitioners seek scientifically based, nonpharmaceutical, and noninvasive means to counter innate physiological responses and reduce pain perception. Although the names and techniques have changed over time, *the most consistently advocated technique for reducing muscle tension and pain in childbirth is relaxation.*

REVIEW OF THE LITERATURE

What is Relaxation?

The American Heritage Dictionary defines relaxation as "relief of muscular and nervous tension, release of fatigue, the state of being relaxed, return to equilibrium, and peace of mind." In the research literature, relaxation is associated with reduction of tension in muscles,[31] lengthening of in-

Relaxation is the most consistently advocated technique for reducing muscle tension and pain in childbirth. (Courtesy of The Book Publishing Company. Summertown, TN)

active muscle and muscle fibers,[23] a protective response that alleviates the "fight-or-flight" response and decreases the heart rate, metabolism, and breathing rate to bring the body into a homogeneous balance,[2] and the shaping of low arousal as the integrated hypothalamic reaction that results in a generalized decrease in sympathetic and nervous system activity.[18]

Humenick[20] proposed the following composite definition of relaxation: ". . . a state of low arousal, the antithesis of the 'fight-or-flight' response. Somatic and autonomic responses such as muscle tension, heart rate, breathing rate, and metabolism are decreased to bring the body into balance."

Uses of Relaxation

Relaxation training has become a standard component of therapy programs in several disciplines—dentistry, medicine, nursing, and psychology—to modify behavior and reduce individuals' symptoms of stress and anxiety.[6,12,17,24,32] When used as a primary treatment strategy for various disorders, relaxation skills have repeatedly been shown effective in reducing tension, anxiety, and pain perception.[3,23] These results have been found when treating the medical conditions of hypertension,[38,41,44] insomnia,[7,45] tension headaches,[35] asthma,[26] as well as the nonpathological condition of childbirth.[1,43]

The Body's Responses to Threat and Fear

When a person is subjected to threats or fear, whether real or anticipated, bodily changes occur as a defense mechanism to signal danger and to allow the individual to fight back or flee. This fight-or-flight mechanism is initiated by the activation of the autonomic nervous system. Considered to be the link between the "psyche and soma" originally, this system was believed to be under unconscious control.[11] When an individual is confronted with anxiety and fear, bodily changes (for example, increased heart rate and breathing rate) occur as a result of the response of the autonomic system. These responses are highly individualized, although there are basic physiological changes common to all.[14]

Protective responses to fear and anxiety are innate and involuntary physiological reactions. Goldstein[16] proposed that the basis of these reactions is the startle or Moro reflex, which inhibits higher nervous centers. In the infant, this innate response occurs before cognition of any threat. As an individual matures, the actual stressful situations are less important in the production of fear and anxiety than the manner in which these situations are perceived and interpreted by the individual. With maturity and understanding, threats can be reduced to manageable levels through the use of cognitive interventions.

Autonomic Nervous System. This complex system consists of two divisions, the sympathetic system and the parasympathetic system, which work in opposition to balance one another.[34] The sympathetic system is the medium for increasing heart rate, raising blood pressure, and releasing epinephrine (adrenalin) into the bloodstream; these reactions mobilize the individual to fight back or flee from danger. The emotions produced when the sympathetic system is stimulated are typically fear, anxiety, and anger.

When an individual is afraid, crude sensory stimuli cause an autonomic reaction that is relayed through the hypothalamus to the reticular activating system of the brain. This regulates alertness and permits fight or flight by stimulating the endocrine system, specifically the adrenal glands, to secrete epinephrine. As a result, blood flow is shifted from the digestive system to the extremities, lungs, and brain. Blood pressure rises, oxygen consumption increases, and stored glucose is released into the bloodstream.

The body reacts in this manner whether the fearful situation occurs in the real world or in the imagination. Impulses are directed to the cerebral cortex for interpretation or conscious awareness. Apprehension levels depend on how the individual interprets potential dangers. Using cognitive thought inherent in development and learning, the cortex can inhibit the intensity of the emotional responses and, with training, the physical responses.[34]

The parasympathetic system stimulates digestive, vegetative, and other maintenance functions of the organism. The feelings associated with these

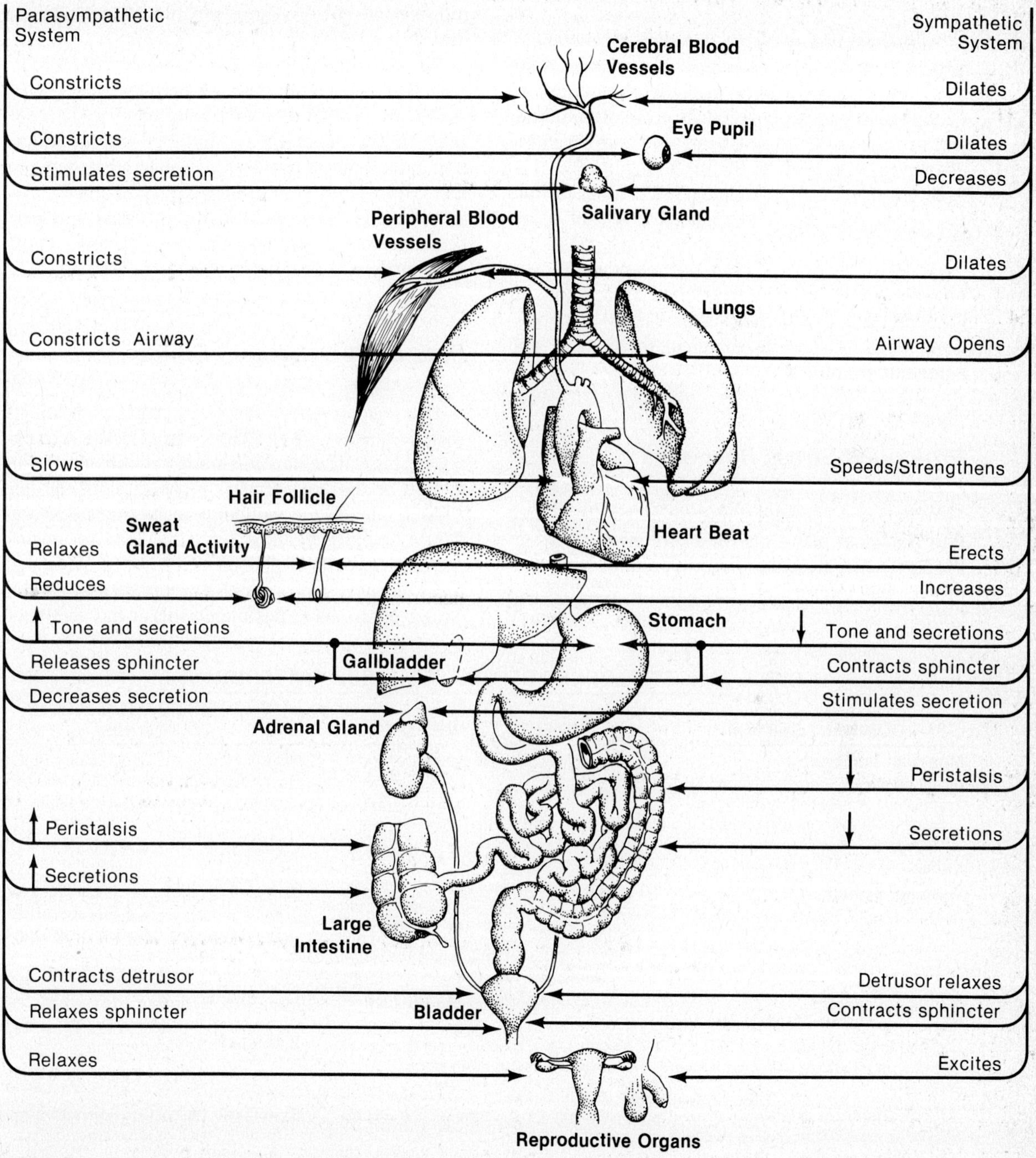

FIGURE 7–1. Autonomic nervous system. (Adapted from Chusid, J. *Correlative Neuroanatomy and Functional Neurology.* 16th ed. Los Altos, CA: Lange Medical Publications, 1984.)

activities are comfortable, pleasurable, and relaxing.[28]

This relaxation response is a reduced metabolic state that results from decreased sympathetic activity and increased parasympathetic stimulation. Feelings associated with relaxation are often subtle, and include a slowing of heart rate and breathing and lowered tension in the skeletal muscles. The benefits of relaxation include lowered heart rate and blood pressure, and reduced levels of blood lactates. Some of the techniques that cause this lowering of excitation with the resulting physiological changes have been elicited by religious or secular training and training programs of relaxation, Yoga, Zen, transcendental meditation, and autogenic training.

Prolonged Stress Response

Wilson and Schneider[47] proposed that there were four dominant pathways for a prolonged stress response: neuromuscular, neurovascular, neurohumeral, and interneural. Each has a selective response that affects specific organs. For each dominant pathway, some specific relaxation techniques have proven more effective than others in decreasing the stress response (Table 7–1).

Whether used as a main treatment or as a component of stress reduction techniques, the central assumption is that relaxation training results in lowering of muscle action and indirectly in the reduction of autonomic activity.[48] When balance between the sympathetic system and parasympathetic system exists an individual is able to relax and rest, heart and breathing rates are slowed, and a sense of security and tranquility ensues.

Role of Relaxation in Childbirth

The psychological aspect of pain in childbirth was recognized in the 1930's when Dick-Read proposed the ''fear-tension-pain'' syndrome,[15] although he did not publish his theory until the late 1940's. The pain a woman perceived in labor was due to socially induced fears that lead to tension and subsequently to pain (see Chapter 6). Although this syndrome was originally described as a vicious circle, others have postulated that it has feedback

TABLE 7–1. PROLONGED STRESS RESPONSE PATTERNS

DOMINANT SYSTEM	POTENTIAL SYMPTOMS	SUGGESTED RELAXATION TECHNIQUES
Muscular response Increased muscle tone may compress veins and lymphatics, resulting in waste product accumulation and leading to further increased muscle tone.	Fatigue, increased susceptibility to infection Muscle spasm in the neck and shoulder Low back pain Tension headaches	Neuromuscular relaxation emphasized with feedback from coach or an electromyograph biofeedback machine
Vascular system	Increased heart rate and blood pressure Cold extremities Sweaty palms May progress to migraines, menstrual cramps, angina	Autogenic training with feedback on hand temperature from sensation, mood ring, thermometer, or Biodot.
Hormonal system Increase in ACTH, adrenalin, norepinephrine and thyroid hormone Decrease in follicle stimulating hormone (FSH)	Hypermotility of stomach, intestines Amenorrhea Retardation of immune response Compulsive eating or anorexia	Meditation (including focal points and concentration on breathing patterns) Body imagery
Neurotransmitter system May be an excess deficiency or alteration of neurotransmitters	Increase in cortical activity, fear, depression Increased use of alcohol, nicotine, and caffeine with higher than average potential for addiction	Systematic desensitization and locus training added to other types of relaxation training

From Humenick, S. Teaching relaxation. *Childbirth Educator* 4:47, 1984.

loops within the circle, recognizing that the interrelationship between fear and anxiety is complex.

Prepared childbirth techniques alleviate or reduce the perception of pain during childbirth through accessing the brain, more specifically the cerebral cortex and the autonomic nervous system (or limbic system). The cerebral cortex is divided into two hemispheres: right and left.

Left Hemisphere. The left hemisphere is thought to be concerned with the somatic aspects of the body, voluntary muscle control, and is the center of concentration for conscious relaxation of striated muscles. This part of the brain is also thought to be involved with cognitive processes—that part of the brain from which rational thought, intellectual analysis, evaluation, calculating, counting, thinking, and verbal skills emanate.

The anxiety and fears a pregnant woman experiences during labor are not different from those of a dental patient anticipating a painful procedure. The resulting tension in jaws, neck, abdomen, pelvic floor, and legs utilizes available oxygen. This decreases oxygen available to the fetus and particularly to the uterine wall, causing uterine hypoxia and pain. Increased lactic acid buildup impinges on pain receptors and magnifies pain perception. During the second stage of labor when the woman attempts to expel the fetus against a tense pelvic floor, unnecessary pain will result. When fear causes fight-or-flight responses, these decrease the laboring woman's confidence, rendering her more dependent and seemingly without a sense of control.

Resistance from a tense abdominal wall further decreases the efficiency of the uterine contractions. Prolonged striated muscle tension will result in generalized fatigue. Fatigue decreases pain threshold and increases pain perception while it reduces the woman's ability to conserve energy for the expulsive efforts needed during second-stage labor.

Conscious relaxation of those muscles not actively involved in uterine cervical dilation is essential to enable the uterus to work unimpeded.[27,46] Viewing the uterine contractions as a positive work force that brings her closer to the goal of birthing her child provides the cognitive understanding of the process and reduces the woman's interpretation of the sensations as ''pains.'' With increased participation through focused attention to conscious release, her voluntary muscles, and her active involvement in the birth process, the woman decreases her sense of dependency on others, increases her own sense of mastery and self-confidence, and allows for increased sharing and intimacy with her labor partner.

The Right Hemisphere. This is described as the creative, symbolic, sensory part of the brain and includes the affective, spiritual aspects of mind functioning, control of involuntary bodily functions, and stimulation of the autonomic nervous system. This includes visual pictures, imagery, music, rhythm, color, odors, taste, and the emotional sensations they evoke.

For labor, the conscious and unconscious and the cognitive and affective must be brought into play, and the brain stimulated in many ways to reduce pain perception. Individuals respond to stress in different ways and thus will benefit from learning different cognitive and affective relaxation techniques for childbirth. A variety of relaxation techniques should be taught in childbirth education classes (Table 7–2).

IMPLICATIONS FOR PRACTICE

Relaxation, the core of the ''therapeutic program,''[3,6,19] has been recognized as effective for a diverse number of conditions and situations. An essential component of all childbirth education classes, relaxation is a coping skill promoted by childbirth education groups of all philosophies—ASPO/Lamaze, ICEA, Dick-Read, Bradley, and holistic groups (see Chapter 6). Class members can use relaxation techniques during pregnancy, childbirth, and the postpartum period. Expectant parents

TABLE 7–2. APPROACHES TO TEACHING RELAXATION

NAME AND TYPE	DESCRIPTION	FEEDBACK
Progressive relaxation (modifies muscular responses)	Consists of systematically tensing and releasing muscles. Developed by Jacobson modified by Wolpe into a 6-week approach with home practice.	Primary feedback initially described as the awareness of participant who focuses on the sensation of tensing and relaxing each muscle. Either a coach or electromyograph can provide feedback.
Neuromuscular dissociation (modifies muscular responses)	Follows progressive relaxation by asking participant to tense some muscles and relax others simultaneously. Introduced in this country by Elisabeth Bing.	Feedback by having the coach check relaxation and tension was introduced by Karmel and Bing—not mentioned in books by either Lamaze or Chabon.
Autogenic training (mental control modifying muscular and autonomic systems responses)	Training through suggestions including "my right arm is heavy" or "my left arm is warm." Includes slowing of the heart and respiration as well as cooling of forehead. Developed by Schultz and Luther.	Feedback initially described as the awareness of the participant with no outside feedback. Has been used with biofeedback equipment, thermometers, etc.
Meditation (modifies vascular and neurotransmitter responses)	Defined by Benson as dwelling on an object (repeating a sound or gazing at an object) while emptying all thoughts and distractions in a quiet atmosphere in a comfortable position. Used in transcendental meditation and yoga.	Concentration on a local point and on breathing patterns would be forms of meditation by Benson's definition. Participant can monitor self but also receives coach's feedback on both activities.
Visual imagery	Includes techniques such as visualizing oneself on a warm beach or as a bag of cement or going down a staircase. Often precedes introduction of other kinds of relaxation. May also be used to visualize and potentially affect specific body parts as in cancer therapy. May be used in desensitization in which one relaxes while visualizing a potentially threatening situation. Used in labor rehearsals.	
Touching, massaging	Touch has always been a way for one person to calm another. There is evidence of actual transfer of energy taking place in some forms of touching in childbirth preparation; touching is associated with muscular relaxation (Sheila Kissinger).	Feedback from coach includes informing when muscle tension is felt, necessitating advanced coaching. Coaches may need first to discern relaxation by moving a limb.
Biofeedback	Electromyograph measures neuromuscular tension. Thermometer measures skin temperature at extremities Galvanic skin reflex records conductivity changes because of action of sweat glands at skin surface. Electroencephalograph distinguishes alpha, beta, and theta waves in the brain.	Feedback from all of these machines is in one or more of these forms: visualization of a meter, listening to a sound, or watching a set of flashing lights.

From Humenick, S. Teaching relaxation. *Childbirth Educator* 4:47, 1984.

can also transfer and integrate this skill easily into life situations, such as stress when the baby is crying or in a job situation.

Teaching relaxation skills requires sufficient class time for learning, practice, consistent evaluation, feedback, and more practice as needed. Because of the tremendous amount of information that childbirth educators include in a childbirth education course, often not enough time is spent on relaxation training. It is important that the childbirth educator devote adequate class time to relaxation training. Relaxation skills are not only of immense value in easing the pain of childbirth but can be adapted and used by both expectant parents in everyday life.

Relaxation training is a self-regulating skill which can only be learned through individual effort. The most important factor in skill acquisition is the amount of time spent practicing the relaxation techniques outside of training sessions.[29] As with all skill acquisition, diligent practice is needed on a daily basis not only to acquire the skill but also to maintain or improve the level of competence.[4,7,9,13,25,33] Thus, the childbirth educator should emphasize the importance of consistent practice to class members.

Relaxation involves not only the physical act of ''letting go'' of tension in the muscles but also the autonomic and somatic systems, and those portions of the brain involved with cognitive, affective, sensual, and psychomotor processes. Relaxation training can therefore be divided into three components: cognitive, affective, and psychomotor.

Cognitive Component

Expectant parents need a basic understanding of what stress is, the physiological changes it causes, and its detrimental effects during pregnancy and childbirth on the physical and emotional status of the expectant mother, the process of labor, and the fetus. If they understand the benefits of relaxation in reducing stress and decreasing pain perception, they may be more motivated to practice and acquire these skills.

Class members should be encouraged to rethink the concept of tension. During uterine contractions, for example, the tension a woman perceives in her uterus should be interpreted as the work of the uterus toward the positive goal of birth, while tension in striated muscles not specifically involved in the process should be recognized and consciously released.[30] The woman should consciously pay attention to the status of her muscles and joints during uterine contractions to allow for the coordination of this process.

The woman can increase her level of concentration during labor, thereby increasing her degree of relaxation, by focusing on an outside object—a ''focal point''—or by visualizing a pleasant scene.[10,36,40,42] Other ways to involve the cognitive processing of the brain and increase relaxation are attention to and evaluation of the rhythm, pace and co-equal quality of comfortable breathing,[2,22] and counting or repetition of nursery rhymes or words such as ''heavy, limp, loose, released,'' and ''warm.''[37]

Affective Component

The affective component can be divided into two parts: the physical environment and the emotional environment. At times these parts are interdependent.

Physical Environment. The physical environment of the classroom and birthing room can positively affect the couple's ability to release tension and enjoy a sense of calm. The physical environment should be without distraction or noise, at a comfortable temperature, and with sufficient space. Positioning of the woman's body is of extreme importance; there should be an ample number of pillows to maintain the woman's body and limbs in a semiflexed position and to provide support behind the back. Other measures that can enhance emotional tranquility include the use of music, a warm tub bath or shower, and warmth from a waterbottle or hands during massage. The atmosphere of the entire room should be one of comfort and support.

Emotional Environment. Before relaxation training can begin, the childbirth educator needs to present factual information to allay couples' fears and anxieties about the unknown. Even with such information, expectant mothers may feel unable to cope with pregnancy and childbirth. Pregnant women often feel vulnerable, and they may not be receptive to the idea of ''releasing'' or ''letting go,'' since this may be perceived as an additional loss of bodily control. Yet receptivity to relaxation training is imperative for skill acquisition; so a feeling of trust in her partner, the instructor, and the other class members must be cultivated in order to increase her trust in her body. Affirming statements also enhance the sense of well-being needed to release protective defenses.

Having her partner assist her in learning and practicing relaxation techniques gives the expectant mother a greater sense of trust, calm, and peacefulness. She becomes conditioned to her partner's instructions: coaxing in a soothing voice; giving verbal cues in a concise, consistent manner; and giving feedback when evaluating relaxation ability, praising her when it is deserved, and offering constructive reminders when indicated. The partner can assist in relaxation training in various ways (Table 7–3) and should assume a shared responsibility for practice of relaxation techniques. This shared responsibility increases the level of trust and develops the teamwork necessary for effective participation in class training and childbirth.

To effectively transfer relaxation training skills from the classroom to childbirth and everyday life, the expectant woman (and her partner) need to become self-reliant and able to use relaxation by themselves, at any time and in any stressful situation. Without this sense of self-sufficiency and acquired skill the woman's ability will be detrimentally influenced if she encounters negative situations during childbirth.

TABLE 7–3. INCLUSION OF PARTNER IN RELAXATION TRAINING

The following are ways the partner can assist in relaxation training, and can be encouraged to become more involved in classes.

- Life skill for partner for stress management
- Team concept
- Increase communication, both verbally and nonverbally
- Encourage touch and massage as means of communication
- Role-reversal and feedback practice for both partners
- Assessment of evaluation of improvement
- Feedback and increased coaxing to release
- Positive encouragement
- Reinforcement of skill mastery
- Increase modes/methods to improve release mastery
- Involve increasingly complex strategies
- Gain feedback on needs and what pleases her in mode varieties
- Practice frequently to help integrate techniques/skills both with partner and for partner
- Application to labor, postpartum period, and parenting
- Application to daily living and stress management

From Shrock, P. Relaxation Skills: Update on Problems and Solutions. *Genesis* 6:8, 1984.

Psychomotor Component

Physical comfort is the most important and basic component of all relaxation skills. A woman needs enough space to attain any position she chooses and to change to other positions as needed. There should be adequate support of limbs in semiflexed positions on a firm surface or supported by pillows. Changing positions is a prerequisite for a safer and more comfortable labor. Practicing relaxation skills in a variety of positions will give a couple excellent preparation for most situations they will encounter during labor.

In order to fully benefit from relaxation training, couples need to develop an ''awareness core'': a sense of self, of muscle and joint tension, of relationship to the environment and the role of the visual, auditory, tactile, and noxious stimulation. Exercises can help couples increase their awareness of breathing and of inner body sounds and help them discern the difference between tense and relaxed muscles.

Understanding the mind-body connection, or neuromuscular reactivation, is essential to learning relaxation skills. Expectant parents must be able to ''tune in'' to their bodies and to distinguish left from right and tensed from released. Awareness exercises that assist couples in increasing their senses of sight, sound, smell, and touch need refining through imagery or visualization.[42]

Other exercises that enhance body awareness include imagining body parts through a ''journey through the body;''[40] using swaying movements or circular exercises,[39] detecting increasing sensitivity to body position or pressure of body parts on the floor or chair; and focusing on chest movements during breathing.

The childbirth educator can encourage the development of an awareness core through progressive relaxation techniques, as well as a variety of other exercises. The goal of all activities is to help couples become more aware of their bodies.

Each person in a childbirth education class must

be allowed to proceed at his or her own rate of learning. The childbirth educator should teach relaxation in a logical and sequential progression from simple to complex techniques, because this provides a foundation for further learning. By learning skills sequentially, couples will be able to master basic skills before progressing on to skills of increasing difficulty (Table 7–4). For example, in teaching awareness, couples move from an awareness of breathing to awareness of inner body

TABLE 7–4. GUIDELINES FOR TEACHING RELAXATION SKILLS

Skill Acquisition
- In every class
- Training and ongoing practice in class and at home
- Self-refinement and modification
- Inclusion of individual coping skills

Cognitive Aspects
- Understanding of physiological changes
- Rationale
- Benefits to mother/baby
- Reconceptualization of tension
- Attention: focus and concentration

Affective

Environment: Physical
- Temperature
- Physical comfort
- Distraction/noise

Environment: Emotional
- Trust
- Receptivity
- Decreasing anxiety

Psychomotor
- Physical comfort (support, flexed limbs)
- Sequential mastery
- Progress only after mastery of skill
- Skill transfer to daily living
- Variety of positions practiced
- All possibilities for labor (sitting, standing, walking, all-fours, kneeling)

Awareness
- Utilize senses/tune in
- Differentiation
- Practice and integration

Progressive Relaxation
- Simple to complex
- One joint to whole limb
- Add breathing
- Add counting

Differential Relaxation
- Simple to complex
- Add cues (visual, verbal, touch, massage)

Skill Integration
- Integrate strategies
- Breathing . . . Expulsion

Practice . . . Evaluation . . . Feedback

Multi-Modal Strategies
- Individual coping mechanisms
- Personal strategies (counting, music, singing, mantras, yoga, warmth, water, touch, energy flow, rhythmic breathing, paced breathing, comfortable breathing)

Cognitive Suggestion
- Attention focus
  - External (focal point)
  - Internal (muscles and joints, breathing, contraction)
  - Fantasy (imagery, visual pictures of event)
- Autogenic training
- Systematic desensitization
- Visualization (own special place, specific suggestion, rehearsal)
- Role play (specific suggestions of stress, one choice of situation)

Evaluation . . . Feedback
- Self-evaluation
  - Body awareness
  - Practice
  - Strategy choices
- Partner
  - Visual
  - Physical
  - Individualized feedback
  - Reinforcement
  - Suggestion for improvement
- Instructor
  - Role model
  - Specific evaluation, feedback and reinforcement
  - Additional strategies and modes
  - Assess coach role and reinforce it

Skill Integration
- Self refinement

Skin Transfer
- Pregnancy
- Postpartum
- Daily living
- Any situation of stress or anxiety

From Shrock, P. Relaxation Skills: Update on Problems and Solutions. *Genesis* 6:8, 1984.

> Pain is all a matter of degree and is relieved more by relaxation than control.
>
> ELIZABETH NOBEL[1]
>
> The most important thing to me was learning how to relax and breathe. I practiced—I was scared!
>
> A NEW MOTHER
>
> Relaxation is for care providers as well as for mothers in labor! The most pleasant part of my baby's birth was the relaxed atmosphere of the Birth Center and all of the staff.
>
> A NEW MOTHER

sounds or focusing on the left arm, then the whole upper torso. The progression to more complex techniques (such as various combinations of limbs in neuro-muscular control; the addition of multimodal strategies such as the addition of paced breathing and/or counting; and the coordinated effect of expulsion when specific muscles are released while others are consciously contracted) should be attempted only after the student has mastered the basic techniques.

The first step toward acquiring the skills of differentiating between contracted and released muscles is to have couples alternately tense then relax one joint, such as the ankle joint; then a whole limb. The next step is to perform these activities in combination with paced breathing and/or counting. The final step is to work up to the coordinated effort of expulsion, when specific muscles are released while others are consciously contracted.

Verbal cues signaling the release of a muscle group need to be concise, consistent, and directed at a specific body part. Coaxing a person to "Release your right arm" is more effective than saying "You must relax." The labor partner should use consistent words and soothing and directive tone of voice. Using a set of commands consistently aids couples in learning the skill and allows for quicker response under stress.

Touch cues that can be used to encourage an expectant parent to relax muscle groups include light to deep stroking of a limb from the proximal to the distal portion or massaging the limb. Following extensive practice, firm pressure or touch and a touch at the jaw, shoulder, or hip will elicit relaxation. All are effective ways of helping an individual achieve a release response of muscle groups.

A variety of techniques should be included in a practice regimen, and the woman needs to tell her partner which ones she prefers. A combination of verbal, touch, and massage cues is helpful and should be used during the practice sessions.

Problems and Solutions

Many couples in childbirth education classes do not master relaxation skills.[21] They do not integrate them with other skills and use them in childbirth to reduce stress and pain. They seem unable to transfer relaxation skills to the postpartum period and into their daily living. Common reasons for the failure of couples to learn relaxation skills are insufficient time to learn the skills, lack of motivation to learn the skills, and the failure of the childbirth educator to teach an "awareness core" of simpler techniques before teaching more complex ones.

Many childbirth education classes begin eight to ten weeks before the woman's due date, and often not enough time is allotted for learning the skills for consistent evaluation, and for needed feedback and practice during class session. Couples' lack of motivation to learn relaxation skills is a common problem encountered in classes. This can be attributed to instructors devoting only short periods of time to relaxation within classes while failing to provide the rationale of the benefits of relaxation for both mother and fetus during pregnancy and childbirth. Instructors frequently demonstrate only the "how-to" of relaxation skills to couples and follow this by a limited practice session rather than conducting actual relaxation training sessions as a integral part of each class.

Many instructors fail to teach an "awareness core" that enables participants to differentiate between tense and released muscles, and do not follow a logical and sequential progression from simple to complex techniques. When the instructor

TABLE 7–5. TEACHING RELAXATION: PROBLEMS AND POSSIBLE SOLUTIONS

The following table is a summary of various teaching problems with possible solutions. The column heads list the problems; the indented phrases that follow list possible solutions.

Skill Demonstration
- Skill acquisition/ongoing practice
- Increased class practice time
- Increased home practice

Use of Tapes and Cassettes
- Instructor teach relaxation/evaluate
- Instructor's own voice on tape
- Instructor encourage self-reliance

Rationale "It's Important"
- Cognitive understanding of stress
- Physiological results, e.g., fatigue
- Emotional results, e.g., ability to cope
- Effect on baby, e.g., available oxygen

Lack of Motivation to Practice
- Benefits . . . physiological
- Emotional . . . baby
- Cognitive understanding of detriments
- Increased class time for practice
- Ongoing evaluation/feedback/reinforcement
- Specific home practice schedule

Non-Receptive Attitude
- Provide environment of trust
- Voice tone and touch cues
- Rationale for relaxation

Lack of Awareness Core
- Include all senses
- Awareness exercises; tune into body

Inability to Differentiate Muscle Tension vs. Release
- Jacobson relaxation/progressive relaxation
- Logical progression
- Sequential mastery
- Increase degree of difficulty

Insufficient Suggestions for Relaxation Competency
- Multimodal approach
- Inclusion of rhythmic breathing
- Hear breathing
- Counting
- Humming/mantra
- Temperature: warmth; water
- Position change
- Touch/massage
- Verbal coaxing
- Cognitive suggestion
- Positive affirmation
- Attention focus: Internal/external
- Visualization
- Biofeedback: Tune into body
- Role-play; Labor rehearsal

Insufficient Evaluation/Feedback: Inability of Partner to Assess; and Nonevaluation of Partner
- Ongoing in class
- Assess partner's ability to evaluate
- Offer specific suggestions
- Individualize to each person/couple
- Role reversal
- Evaluation and suggestions

Skill Integration
- Do not progress until mastery of each step
- Integrate with breathing/expulsion

Skill Transfer to Daily Living
- Specific ideas of daily stress
- Implement in daily life
- Role play/rehearsal

From Shrock, P. Relaxation Skills: Update on Problems and Solutions. *Genesis* 6:8, 1984.

presents complex neuromuscular techniques or multimodal strategies before expectant parents have mastered the basics, they become overwhelmed and discouraged because they cannot do the exercises and soon do not even attempt to master the techniques. Common problem areas that childbirth educators encounter and their possible solutions are shown in Table 7–5.

Evaluation and Feedback

Self-evaluation increases body awareness and leads to self-reliance and future use of relaxation skills. During relaxation training, however, evaluation by an objective partner is essential. Observation of the position of limbs, set of the jaw, and position of the mouth are clues that help the evaluator identify tense areas. It is important that the woman's partner become adept at this phase, for checking the laboring woman's degree of relaxation by lifting limbs is bothersome and distracting. However, during practice sessions, to truly evaluate a woman's relaxation status, checking by lifting and gently moving the limbs back and forth to ascertain the degree of free movement ensures more objective and accurate feedback.

After evaluation, the partner should praise the woman and give suggestions for improvement and refinements of the techniques. At first, 15 minutes per childbirth education class may be needed for couples to develop awareness and learn to release tension. The woman's repetition and consistent practice every day, both alone and with her partner, will allow for proficiency and promote teamwork.

Later, when the basic relaxation techniques become easier, couples should learn to use multimodal strategies or techniques involving the different senses that will ensure a deeper sense of relaxation in situations of acute stress. These multimodal strategies may include warmth in the form of immersion in a bath tub of warm water or the warmth of a partner's hand massaging a limb or body part. Imagery, involving visualizing pleasant scenes, color of choice, shapes or energy fields, and rhythmic sounds (see Chapter 12), lilting music (see Chapter 13), rhymes, and counting can be used to aid in reducing tension. Calming, paced breathing and focusing on the rhythmic sounds of breathing or the air moving in and out of the body are useful in increasing the degree of relaxation (see Chapter 14). Class members should select strategies that are best suited to their individual personalities. Strategies that individuals have used to cope with difficult situations in the past usually work better than strategies selected by the instructor. However, the childbirth educator needs to make couples aware of the large variety of possibilities, and encourage them to experiment with and practice various combinations prior to labor.

The childbirth educator should also suggest ways to integrate relaxation skills into everyday life, citing times when relaxation skills can be of benefit. The group can discuss the merits of relaxation when visiting the dentist or speaking before a group; then the childbirth educator can ask the group to think of times when relaxation skills could be useful during the postpartum period.

IMPLICATIONS FOR RESEARCH

Since relaxation is at the core of the therapeutic basis of childbirth preparation skills, it is imperative that well-designed research studies be encouraged to ascertain which components are the most effective. These components, in turn, can be further studied to measure their benefits to the expectant mother, expectant couples, and the fetus.

Studies are needed in which the terminology of different techniques is consistent and that can be replicated. One of the greatest problems is that a number of different techniques bear the same name, while at the same time one technique may have many different names (e.g., "neuromuscular control," "conscious control," and "differential" or "disassociation").

The procedural components of relaxation training also need to be enumerated and studied:[8] the number of sessions, the length of each session, whether the training was by one instructor or through an audiotape or videotape, the size and description of the relaxation technique taught, how feedback was given, and the resulting comparison with control or other specific relaxation techniques. In order to replicate studies, a researcher must know exactly what information was given to the subjects, by whom the training was given, and where it was given. (Laboratory training and evaluation, while they may be similar, often are not the same as the situation in which an individual may experience stress—for example, childbirth.)

The most fundamental questions today are whether or not relaxation skills do produce physiological effects, under what conditions, whether these benefits can be generalized, and if so, under what constraints. Other questions that require answers are:

- Do individuals relax better in response to a female voice or male voice?
- How effective are group teaching sessions of relaxation training, such as childbirth education classes, when compared with training done on an individual basis?

SUMMARY

People learn new skills and respond to feedback differently. Some are more rational and respond to the cognitive aspects of teaching (explanations of the processes, the facts involved, and rationales). Many are bound up in the environment of the learning situation—the group, the instructor, and the praise of support people. Still others are reflective learners who need to observe demonstrations of techniques and see illustrations of positions on handouts or posters. For some, learning is enhanced by using music, rhythmic chants, counting out loud, or hearing the sighing of their exhaled breath. Tactile people respond best to touch, stroking, feelings of warmth, and changes in physical pressure—alteration of position or immersion in water.

All couples need to participate actively in the new skill, attempt to master it, obtain feedback through evaluation, *practice frequently and consistently,* introduce refinements, and practice, practice, practice—until true mastery has been attained.

References

1. Beck, N. C., and Siegel, L. J. Preparation for childbirth and contemporary research on pain, anxiety, and stress reduction: A review and critique. *Psychosomatic Medicine* 42:429, 1980.
2. Benson, H. *The Relaxation Response*. New York: William Morrow and Co., 1975.
3. Bernstein, D., and Borkovec, T. *Progressive Relaxation Training*. Champaign, IL: Research Press, 1973.
4. Bing, E. *Six Practical Lessons for an Easier Childbirth*. New York: Grosset & Dunlap, 1967.
5. Blanchard, E. B., Theobald, D. E., Williamson, D. A., Silver, B. V., and Brown, D. A. Temperative biofeedback in treatment of migraine headaches. *Archives of General Psychiatry* 35:581, 1978.
6. Blanchard, E. B., and Ahler, T. A. Behavioral treatment of psychophysical disorders. *Behavior Modification* 3:518, 1979.
7. Bootzin, R. Comparison of progressive relaxation and autogenic training as treatment for insomnia. *Journal of Abnormal Psychology* 83:253, 1974.
8. Borkovec, T. D., and Sides, J. K. Critical procedural variables related to physiological effects of progressive relaxation—a review. *Behaviour Research and Therapy* 7:119, 1979.
9. Bradley, R. *Husband-Coached Childbirth*. New York: Harper and Rowe, 1965.
10. Bressler, D. *Free Yourself from Pain*. New York: Simon and Shuster, 1979.
11. Cannon, W. *Bodily Changes in Pain, Hunger, Fear, and Rage*. 2nd ed. New York: Norton Publishing Co., 1927.
12. Carr, R. *Yoga Way to Release Tension*. New York: Harper and Rowe, 1974.
13. Chabon, I. *Awake and Aware*. New York: Dell, 1966.
14. Chusid, J. *Correlative Neuroanatomy and Functional Neurology*. 16th ed. Los Altos, CA: Lange Medical Publications, 1984.
15. Dick-Read, G. *Natural Childbirth*. London: W. Heineman, 1933.
16. Goldstein, K. *The Organism: A Holistic Approach to Biology*. New York: American Book Co., 1939.
17. Grad, R. Effect of electromyographic biofeedback-assisted relaxation training on experience of childbirth. Unpublished doctoral thesis, University of Maryland, 1980.
18. Greenwood, M., and Benson, H. Efficacy of progressive relaxation in systematic desensitization and proposal for alternative competitive response. *Behaviour Research and Therapy* 15:337, 1977.
19. Hillenberg, J. B., and Collins, F. L. Procedural analysis and review of relaxation training research. *Behaviour Research and Therapy,* 20:251, 1982.
20. Humenick, S. The many modes of relaxation. *In* Humenick, S. (ed.) *Expanding Horizons in Childbirth Education,* Vol. 1. Washington, DC: American Society for Psychoprophylaxis in Obstetrics, 1983.
21. Humenick, S., and Marchbanks, P. Validation of a scale to measure relaxation in childbirth education classes. *Birth and Family Journal* 8:3, 1981.
22. Jacobson, E. *How to relax and have your baby.* New York: McGraw-Hill, 1965.
23. Jacobson, E. *Modern treatment of tense patients*. Springfield, IL: Charles C Thomas, 1970.
24. Jaffe, D. T., and Bresler, D. E. The use of guided imagery as an adjunct to medical diagnosis and treatment. *Journal of Humanistic Psychiatry* 20:45, 1980.
25. Kitzinger, S. *Complete Book of Pregnancy.* New York: Random House, 1980.
26. Knapp, T. J., and Wells, L. A. Behaviour therapy for asthma: Review. *Behaviour Research and Therapy* 16:103, 1978.
27. Lamaze, F. *Painless Childbirth*. Chicago: Regney Co., 1970.
28. May, R. *The Meaning of Anxiety.* New York: Norton and Co., 1977.
29. McGuigan, F. J., Sime, W., and Wallace, E.: *Stress and Tension Control*. New York: Plenum Press, 1980.
30. Meichenbaum, D. *Cognitive-behavior Modification: An Integrative Approach*. New York: Plenum Press, 1977.
31. Miller, B., and Keane, C. *Encyclopedia and Dictionary of Medicine and Nursing*. Philadelphia, W.B. Saunders Company, 1972.

32. Nocella, J., and Kaplan, R. Training children to cope with dental treatment. *Journal of Pediatric Psychology* 7:175, 1982.
33. Paul, G., and Trimble, R. Recorded vs. "live" relaxation training and hypnotic suggestion: Comparative effectiveness for reducing arousal and inhibiting stress response. *Behavior Therapy* 1:285, 1970.
34. Pelletier, K. *Mind as Healer, Mind as Slayer.* New York: Dell, 1977.
35. Philips, C., and Hunter, M. Treatment of tension headaches, E.M.G. "normality" and relaxation. *Behaviour Research and Therapy* 19:499, 1981.
36. Samuels, M., and Samuels, N. *Seeing With the Mind's Eye*. New York: Random House Bookworks, 1975.
37. Schulz, J., and Luthe, W. *Autogenic Training*. New York: Grune and Stratton, 1959.
38. Seer, P. Psychological control of essential hypertension. Review of literature and methodological critique. *Psychiatry Bulletin* 86:1015, 1979.
39. Shrock, P. Exercise and physical activity in pregnancy. *In* Sciarra, J. (ed.): Obstetrics and Gynecology, Vol. 2. Philadelphia, J. B. Lippincott, 1985.
40. Shrock, P. Relaxation skills: Update on problems and solutions. *Genesis* 6:Oct./Nov., 1984.
41. Southan, M., Agras, S., Taylor, C. B., and Kraemer, H. Relaxation training. Blood pressure lowering during the day. *Archives of General Psychiatry* 39:715, 1982.
42. Steffes, S. Relaxation plus: Use of imagery and visualization. *In* Humenick, S. S. (ed.): *Expanding Horizons in Childbirth Education*. Washington, DC: ASPO, 1982.
43. Stevens, R. J. Psychological strategies for management of pain in prepared childbirth II. Study of psychoanalgesia in prepared childbirth. *Birth and Family Journal,* 1977.
44. Taylor, C. B., Farquhar, J. W., Nelson, E., and Agras, W. S. Relaxation therapy and high blood pressure. *Archives of General Psychiatry* 34:339, 1977.
45. Turner, R., and Ascher, M. Therapist factor in treatment of insomnia. *Behaviour Research and Therapy* 20:33, 1982.
46. Vellay, P. *Childbirth with Confidence*. New York: McMillan and Co., 1969.
47. Wilson, S., and Schneider, J. The Neurophysiologic Pathways of Distress. *Foundations of Biofeedback*. Practice syllabus from a meeting of the Biofeedback Society of America. Atlanta, GA, May 1980.
48. Wolpe, J. *Psychotherapy by Reciprocal Inhibition*. Stanford, CA: Stanford University Press, 1958.

Beginning Quote

Dick-Read, G. *Natural Childbirth*. London: W. Heineman, 1933.

Boxed Quote

1. Nobel, E. *Childbirth With Insight*. Boston: Houghton Mifflin, 1983.

chapter 8

RELAXATION: Progressive and Selective Relaxation

MARILYN MAILLET LIBRESCO

Your task will be to allow it (the uterus) to work freely while you keep the rest of your body deliberately relaxed.

Elizabeth Bing

Childbirth education developed during the same time period as the practice of deep muscle relaxation. One need only to scan the writings of such promoters of prepared, natural, or painless childbirth as Dick-Read,[8] Lamaze,[23] Bing,[5] Bradley,[7] or Kitzinger[21,22] to understand the central positions that kinesthetic awareness and specific muscle control hold in the construct of childbirth education strategies. Initially the pioneers of prepared childbirth emphasized a modified use of the selective or dissociative relaxation described by Jacobson,[17] which is still in use today. Eventually an abbreviated form of progressive relaxation became the relaxation technique most closely associated with childbirth preparation.

In this chapter "progressive relaxation" is defined and described historically and currently. The literature is reviewed to promote a better understanding of progressive relaxation's usefulness and limitations. Implications of the research are considered, as are guidelines for the use of progressive relaxation in childbirth education. And finally, suggestions for future study are made.

REVIEW OF THE LITERATURE

Definitions: Progressive and Selective Relaxation

The *progressive and selective relaxation of childbirth education* may not be the same progressive and selective relaxation described in the general literature. Traditional progressive relaxation, also known as *jacobsonian relaxation or neuromuscular relaxation,* is a technique used to induce muscle relaxation through a series of muscle contraction and release activities, often requiring months of training. *Selective relaxation,* also termed *dissociative or differential relaxation,* is based on the principles of progressive relaxation and is the process of contracting at an optimal level only those muscles required for the activity at hand.

Work toward the development of progressive and selective relaxation began in 1908 by then Harvard graduate student Edmund Jacobson, whose studies initiated the first psychophysiological research into relaxation. By 1938, Jacobson's efforts culminated in the publication of his technique as a treatment for neuromuscular tension, primarily for hospital patients.[17] For a period of 70 years, Jacobson continued to research and assess this technique, providing invaluable data and insight into the field of stress management and relaxation training.

Definitions: Modified or Abbreviated Progressive Relaxation

Progressive relaxation in its classical form has undergone modification and revision over the years: by Wolpe and Lazarus in 1958,[44] Paul in 1966,[29] and Bernstein and Borkovec in 1973.[4] Although based on the same physiological principles, these modified versions differ markedly from Jacobson's original technique. Typically the modified progressive relaxation technique reported in research is not used in childbirth classes. The relaxation taught in most childbirth classes is more probably a combination of several techniques: modified progressive relaxation, selective relaxation, touch relaxation, visualization, and desensitization and attention-focusing techniques.

Progressive Relaxation: A Physiological Basis

The "flight-or-fight" response first described by Cannon at the turn of the century as an "emergency" reaction prepares an animal—or human—for running or fighting, and remains a part of our evolutionary heritage.[1] When provoked, one becomes ready for action: blood pressure increases, respiratory rate increases, body metabolism rises, and the flow of blood to the limbs intensifies. As Benson[1] has so convincingly described, this usually results in the development of stress and its accompanying physiological consequences, especially if circumstances do not allow the fight or flight to occur. The application of this concept to the woman in labor, in the manner of Dick-Read,[8] is not a difficult connection to make: fear of a contraction or the contractions themselves evoke the fight-or-flight response, with the inability to either flee from or fight the power of the contractions.

As Jacobson pursued his work with neuromuscular tension, he found that in relaxed subjects, even thinking about moving a limb produced tiny muscle tensions.[17–20] Utilizing advances in a technique that was to become known as electromyography (EMG), he was able to record minute muscle tensions in relaxed subjects. Jacobson found that all thought is accompanied by low levels of muscle activity. This is particularly true in the regions of the eyes or speech area or both. Jacobson found that direct relaxation of the skeletal musculature affects the central nervous system and, through hormonal activity, affects many components of the autonomic system.

Noted researcher F.J. McGuigan[24] emphasizes the importance of the complex system of neuromuscular circuitry in understanding how progressive relaxation works. When a muscle contracts, receptors in the muscles are activated and generate volleys of neural impulses that are carried to the brain along afferent neural fibers. This generation and transmission of afferent neural impulses is the "control signal" or the local sign of tension. After reaching the brain, where complex central nervous system activity occurs, the neural impulses return to the muscle along efferent neural fibers, completing a feedback cycle. There the neural impulses generate additional neural impulses to and from the brain, reverberating constantly and rapidly. This high-speed "highway" or circuit of neural impulses creates the muscular tension observed by Jacobson in subjects even considering movement or in a person poised in the classical fight-or-flight reaction. The cycle can be broken. For example, in labor, the muscular part of the circuit can be brought under conscious control and relaxed, thus interrupting the uterine pain circuitry.

Progressive relaxation is based on the ability to act as one's own "internal biofeedback machine."[24] The goal of progressive relaxation is to constantly monitor and release unwanted or unnecessary tensions; it is a continual and automatic process. The ability to make automatic and sensitive observations of one's internal world means that one is receiving physiological input without use of a visual display or machine and acting on that data, continually and without effort, to release tension.[24] The implications for the laboring woman are profound: without aid of machines and with little or no external information, she can be trained to automatically and continually release muscle tension created by the process of labor, thus increasing oxygenation to the musculature and decreasing perception of pain.

Jacobson's Progressive Relaxation: A Description

Jacobson's progressive relaxation involves the recognition and control of decreasingly intense levels of muscle tension. One learns to recognize the control signal from the muscle (the muscle tension) and to release that tension. Training involves increasing the sensitivity to even slight muscle control signals and continually, without effort, releasing the unnecessary tension. Jacobson's term for that release is "going negative."[17] He is adamant that "any attempt to relax is a failure to relax," that the release is a natural result of ceasing to be tense. The key is not learning to relax—the key is learning to recognize the control signal and then to "go negative." The goal is to recognize even the slightest evidence of tension and to be continually releasing unnecessary tension in the course of the day.[18]

Jacobson is equally insistent on several other points significant to the field of childbirth education. One is that it is impossible to conduct relaxation "exercises"—the two terms to Jacobson are mutually exclusive, as are anxiety and relaxation. *Relaxation* involves the natural *lengthening* of the muscle fiber; *exercise* involves the *shortening* of the muscle fiber and an increasing awareness and alertness of the body systems. Similarly, Jacobson wrote at length about the differences between the relaxed state and the hypnotic state, feeling strongly that the hypnotic state increases personal dependence rather than self-reliance and is not always reliable.[18]

Many current teachers of hypnosis, especially those who teach self-hypnosis, disagree strongly with Jacobson on the issue of dependence. Jacobson contends that hypnosis requires instilling the belief that pain will be reduced, whereas muscle relaxation relieves pain mechanically, independent of beliefs. It is worth noting that Jacobson was developing his relaxation technique in the same era that Velvovsky, Nikolayev, and others in Russia were relying heavily on hypnosis in childbirth.

These Soviet scientists later discarded hypnosis as impractical; Jacobson rejected it as inappropriate. Jacobson and his Russian counterparts diverged on another point: while the Russians, as well as Dick-Read and later Lamaze and Bradley, turned to mass education as a means of reducing pain in childbirth, Jacobson thought that there was no need to create "enthusiasm" or to educate the woman in the mechanism of labor; to him, all that was needed was mastery over relaxation techniques.[19]

In this classical form of jacobsonian progressive relaxation, all attention is focused on the recognition of the control signal. There is never a suggestion of the physical sensations or the mental process that may accompany the "going negative" of release, such as "Your hand is heavy" or "Feel the warmth in your hand." The person is the source of all sensation, feeling, and recognition; Jacobson sought to increase self-reliance and decrease personal dependence on a therapist or teacher through this restriction.[19]

Training in the classical form of progressive relaxation may take many months or even years, although Jacobson has reported getting an adequate training effect in some after only one session.[20] The approximately 1030 skeletal muscles in the body are organized into groups, and only one muscle group is under attention in any given session—for example, only the arm muscles are worked on a given day. Each muscle is tensed to the point where the client is able to recognize the control signal, and over time, less and less tension is required for that recognition to occur. The skill that is developed is that of recognizing more and more subtle levels of muscle tension and releasing that tension—hence the term *progressive relaxation*.

In his book *How to Relax and Have Your Baby*,[19] Jacobson is quite specific in detailing his technique. Sessions last between 30 and 40 minutes and are initiated with a period of 3 to 4 minutes of quiet rest with eyes open followed by 3 to 4 minutes of rest with eyes closed. The tension activity is usually repeated three times with tensing of 1 to 2 minutes alternating with release periods of 3 to 4 minutes. The last 20 minutes of the session are devoted to "going negative," with no activity whatsoever, and every third session is totally "going negative" for the entire session. During a tensing activity, the guide or teacher may ask the client to note where the tension is being felt. The client is not asked to describe the quality of that sensation. During a session the teacher may even leave the room; the woman is her own source of information. During the frequent daily practice, clients are told not to use a clock and to rely on their own timing. See Table 8–1 for a summary of Jacobson's progressive relaxation training for childbirth.

TABLE 8–1. SUMMARY OF TRAINING SESSIONS USING JACOBSON'S PROGRESSIVE RELAXATION

CONCENTRATION	SESSIONS
Left arm	1–7
Right arm	8–14
Left leg	15–24
Right leg	25–34
Trunk	35–44
Neck	45–50
Eyes	51–61
Visualization	62–72
Speech	73–88

Adapted from Jacobson, E. *How to Relax and Have Your Baby*. New York: McGraw-Hill, 1965.

Jacobson emphasizes his goal repeatedly: to employ the minimum tension capable of being recognized as a control signal and to release that tension.[19] Especially in the sessions focusing on the neck, eyes, and speech, Jacobson emphasizes differential relaxation, or utilization of only those muscles required at minimal level for the desired activity. The woman in labor, therefore, is using only those muscles required for labor to progress (the uterine muscles and those required to support her body) and is automatically monitoring and releasing even minute levels of tension throughout her labor.

As an aside, in reading Jacobson's work, one cannot help but note that Jacobson positions women for labor practice in the traditional "labor position" (on the back) and raises only the mildest of objections to the routine administration of anesthesia during second-stage labor, probably in accordance with the practice of the times. Also, this classical form of progressive relaxation for childbirth requires that training begin well before the third trimester. Consequently, this pure form of jacobsonian relaxation seldom appears in the descriptive childbirth literature.

Progressive Relaxation: Modifications and Abbreviations

Joseph Wolpe's[44] work with the counterconditioning of fear responses marked the first modification of Jacobson's technique. In what has become known as *systematic desensitization,* the client is exposed—in fantasy—to increasingly fearsome situations while maintaining deep muscle relaxation. At least one researcher has compared Wolpe's fear hierarchy to the emphasis placed in childbirth education on meeting increasingly intense contractions with a relaxation response.[43] To achieve more efficiency with clients, Wolpe condensed Jacobson's technique into six weekly 20-minute sessions with two 15-minute practice sessions daily. This prescription for training and practice may have had some impact on the usual six training sessions, a prescription that was popularized in Bing's[5] *Six Practical Lessons* and became the hallmark of most Lamaze and Bradley classes.

Additional variations on Jacobson's technique have proliferated, often designed for limited experimental projects. Variations have included altering the length of training sessions as well as the number of muscle groups on which the client concentrates. Bernstein and Borkovec[4] raised concerns over a decade ago that such variations, although acceptable for limited experimentation, lack careful assessment of their effectiveness, as well as sufficient detailed description of the method employed and the subjects involved. One result is that evaluations across studies have become difficult to conduct.

Authors Bernstein and Borkovec provide a basis for many of the variations in their work *Progressive Relaxation Training: A Manual for the Helping Professions*. They suggest a procedure for training that involves ten sessions and is outlined in Table 8–2.

Bernstein and Borkovec also suggest a basic six-step procedure for teaching a modified form of progressive relaxation, which is outlined in Table 8–3.

Table 8–4 details the reduction of the 16 muscle groups, to seven and then to four. The authors contend that attention to the muscle groups must always follow the same order. The reader is referred to the entire text of Bernstein and Borkovec[4] for an excellent and detailed description of the rationale and method of the technique.

In addition to differing as to the number of sessions required for training, progressive relaxation methods differ in other significant areas. While Jacobson concentrated on only one muscle group per session, modified techniques focus on all groups during any one session. In Jacobson's classical version, the emphasis is placed solely on the client's experience of muscle relaxation; in the modified versions, some forms of suggestion are included, such as telling the client where she might experience sensation, and modulating and pacing

TABLE 8–2. MODIFIED PROGRESSIVE RELAXATION (BERNSTEIN AND BORKOVEC)

Session 1	Procedure: 16 muscle groups tensed and released twice. Homework of 15 minutes daily practice sessions to be continued throughout training
Session 2 and 3	Repeat as needed
Session 4 and 5	16 muscle groups reduced to 7 groups
Session 6 and 7	7 muscle groups reduced to four groups
Session 8	4 muscle groups plus recall*
Session 9	Recall and counting†
Session 10	Counting only

Adapted from Bernstein, D., and Borkovec, T. Progressive Relaxation Training: A Manual for the Helping Professions. Champaign, IL: Research Press, 1973.

*Recall: Focusing on a muscle group, remembering what tension felt like there, and releasing that tension through recall without ever actually tensing those muscles.

†Counting: Releasing of muscles while teacher/therapist counts from 1 to 10.

TABLE 8–3. BERNSTEIN AND BORKOVEC: SIX-STEP PROCEDURE

1. Focus attention on the muscle group
2. Tense the muscle group at a predetermined signal from teacher: ("When I say now, tense")
3. Maintain the tension for 5 to 7 seconds (shorter duration for foot and leg muscles, due to danger from muscle cramping)
4. Release tension at predetermined signal from teacher ("Relax")
5. Concentrate on relaxed muscles and discriminate differences in sensation from muscle tension and release (30 to 40 seconds)
6. Use the technique in each muscle group twice

Adapted from Bernstein, D., and Borkovec, T. Progressive Relaxation Training: A Manual for the Helping Professions. Champaign, IL: Research Press, 1973.

TABLE 8–4. PROGRESSIVE COMBINING OF MUSCLE GROUPS IN RELAXATION PRACTICE

16 MUSCLE GROUPS	7 MUSCLE GROUPS	4 MUSCLE GROUPS
1. Dominant hand and forearm 2. Dominant biceps	Dominant arm (hand, lower arm, biceps)	Left and right arms
3. Nondominant hand and forearm 4. Nondominant biceps	No dominant arm	
5. Forehead 6. Upper cheeks and nose 7. Lower cheeks and jaws	Face (eyes, eyebrows, nose, and jaws)	Face and neck
8. Neck and throat	Neck and throat	
9. Chest, shoulders and upper back 10. Abdomen	Chest, shoulders, back, and abdomen	Chest, shoulders, back, and abdomen
11. Dominant thigh 12. Dominant calf 13. Dominant calf	Dominant leg (thigh, calf, and foot)	Left and right legs
14. Nondominant thigh 15. Nondominant calf 16. Nondominant foot	Nondominant leg	

Adapted from Bernstein, D., and Borkovec, T. Progressive Relaxation Training: A Manual for the Helping Professions. Champaign, IL: Research Press, 1973.

the voice to the client's breathing patterns. While Jacobson's technique places emphasis on the continual monitoring and releasing of even the slightest tension, modified forms rely more on inducing tension and then releasing it to produce relaxation.[45] Bernstein and Borkovec view their modified progressive relaxation as one among many techniques and encourage its use in conjunction with others.

Selective, Dissociative, or Differential Relaxation

As noted earlier, Jacobson described *selective relaxation* as utilizing only those muscles needed for a particular activity, and then utilizing them to the minimal degree required. This skill is acquired through progressive relaxation training, through sensitization of and differentiation of muscle tension.

Ferdinand Lamaze[23] described a program of neuromuscular education for birth, terming its components "exercises," surely to the dismay of the purist Jacobson. Lamaze required the woman to lie on her back (a position used by most relaxation therapists) to "tone" her muscles by tensing them strenuously and then to stop all contractions and stay relaxed. This procedure, because it considers all muscle groups in one session, qualifies as an abbreviated form of the jacobsonian method described well before Bernstein and Borkovec published their effort to standardize modified progressive relaxation training. Lamaze elaborated on the technique by adding a feedback check that relied on an outside observer and not on the experience of the woman herself, as do both jacobsonian progressive relaxation and Bernstein's and Borkovec's modified version of it. The feedback loop introduced by Lamaze requires that the other person successively move each part of the woman's body with instructions to the woman to neither assist nor resist the mobilization. Lamaze gives further instruction for more complex relaxation assessment, i.e., mobilizing two segments of the body at the same time.

Bing[5] described similar relaxation training, termed *neuromuscular control exercises*. She provided a rationale for learning to recognize and control muscular tension in labor and learning to differentiate which muscle groups are at work and which at rest. She, as did Lamaze, integrates a partner into the practice, who gives commands to "tense" and "release." Checking for relaxation became a method for building the teamwork required during labor. Bing in this early work states that it is impossible for the woman to check on her own relaxation.[5] With the increasing intensity of labor, the woman may not become aware of the tension of unnecessary musculature and can rely on her partner to recognize this tension and to aid her in its release. Bing's introduction of an external information giver or source of feedback (from the labor coach) to the pregnant woman represents a firm departure from jacobsonian and modified forms of progressive relaxation, in which the stated goal is for the woman to become her own monitor for muscular tension and release.

Ewy and Ewy[10] also describe a form of abbreviated progressive relaxation. All the muscles are dealt with in one session, which is followed by practice in neuromuscular dissociation. However, the Ewy's rely more on the woman getting the "feel" of muscle relaxation and contraction, and they do not raise the issue of either internal or external assessment of relaxation during practice for labor. Kitzinger's "residual" and "differential" relaxation,[22] Dick-Read's "residual tension,"[8] and Noble's "active" and "passive" relaxation[28] all refer to learning to recognize unnecessary tension in the body while allowing necessary muscles to work with a minimal amount of tension.

It is difficult to determine how the two forms—progressive relaxation and selective relaxation—are currently being used in childbirth education classes. In many classes, relaxation in class 1 is probably similar to session 1 of Bernstein and Borkovec's modified progressive relaxation in that all muscle groups in the body are reviewed. In subsequent classes, selective relaxation is introduced and use of an external source of assessment (the labor coach) is encouraged. Training similar to Wolpe's desensitization is added to the relaxation training in the form of descriptions of increasingly intense contractions while the woman relaxes.

Research on Relaxation

Jacobson's original progressive relaxation has been researched, reviewed, critiqued, analyzed, revered, and dismissed probably more than any other relaxation technique. Its efficacy has been investigated in terms of effect upon autonomic processes, general tension reduction, and treatment for anxiety, tension headaches, insomnia, and a host of other ailments. Little investigation, however, has focused specifically on its efficacy in childbirth.

In a comprehensive review of the literature, Woolfolk and Lehrer[45] conclude that different relaxation techniques have differential effects on general stress reduction. Consequently, they describe a somatic-cognitive-behavioral distinction between relaxation therapies. They suggest somatic (neuromuscular relaxation) interventions for primarily somatic (muscular) tension. They recommend cognitive interventions for cognitive issues, such as phobias, and they suggest behavioral interventions for behavioral problems. They recommend a combination of techniques of relaxation as more effective than employment of a single technique. Thus there is some support for the eclectic approach to relaxation found in many childbirth classes.

Studies Comparing Jacobsonian and Modified Progressive Relaxation

Few studies have concentrated on differences between these two relaxation techniques, and indeed Bernstein and Borkovec noted that many studies of relaxation do not even describe the technique employed.[4] Woolfolk and Lehrer[45] report only two studies that compare jacobsonian and modified progressive relaxation, although those techniques should be considered as different approaches to relaxation. Unfortunately, both studies utilize a population of college students, who it is noted can attain a level of relaxation relatively easily. Therefore, results of these studies may not be broadly generalized.

So the question of whether Jacobson's extended method of training is superior to the modified forms of progressive relaxation training remains unanswered. However, most training designs, out of expediency, employ some abbreviated form. Childbirth classes seldom, if ever, use traditional progressive relaxation. Many teachers used a modified progressive relaxation, often in combination with other relaxation techniques.

The Research: Efficacy of Progressive Relaxation

Does progressive relaxation training result in the intended outcome? Are the results long-lived and generalizable outside of the training session? To what extent does the use of the technique result in lowered perception of pain or anxiety or both? Are there cautions to be noted in using what is generally thought of as a benign technique? These questions must be addressed in order for helping professionals to employ this technique appropriately, safely, and effectively.

In reviewing the massive amount of literature on progressive relaxation, it becomes evident that certain questions should be kept in mind. Among them:

1. *Who were the subjects?* Woolfolk and Lehrer[45] demonstrated that college students can learn to relax easily. Many studies employ an easily accessible college student population; the results obtained cannot be generalized to expectant parents.
2. *What training method was employed?* Was it Jacobson's progressive relaxation or an abbreviated number of sessions? Was the training taped or live?
3. *What outcome measures were employed?* Generally, EMG biofeedback on the frontalis muscle has been regarded as an indicator of a general relaxation state, although this has been questioned. Bernstein and Borkovec[4] list other outcome indicators: slowed and more quiet breathing, a slack jaw, feet at a 45-degree angle, and the resemblance to peaceful sleep. Jacobson[17–20] and Wolpe[44] both used a signal from the client, usually lifting a finger, but this as well as a verbal indication depends upon the client being able to discern the difference between tension and relaxation. Vital signs (blood pressure, pulse) are a widely used indicator of relaxation. A variety of standardized cognitive tests are also employed: Affect Adjective Checklist (AACL), State-Trait Anxiety Inventory (STAI), Minnesota Multiphasic Personality Inventory (MMPI), Taylor Manifest Anxiety Scale (TMAS), and the Subjective Rating Scale (SRS).
4. *Was there an outcome measure?* In some studies the research assumes that simply being exposed to training ensures skill acquisition.
5. *Were "outside-of-training" measurements considered?* Most outcome measurements are taken during or at the completion of a training session. Notable exceptions are those that deal with insomnia, those in which self-report diaries have been used, as well as reports by family members or roommates. One experimenter, Edelman,[9] interrupted the training to secure measurements, thereby perhaps jeopardizing results. Long-term effects of training become significant factors in determining efficacy, and most studies provide little follow-up data.

In a review of the literature in which an attempt is made to compare technique, subject, and measurement variables, Snyder[37] concludes that there is sufficient evidence that modified forms of progressive relaxation can function significantly enough to warrant a recommendation that they be employed as a nursing intervention. In the 13 studies conducted from 1971 through 1981 that Snyder reviewed, the subjects primarily were persons experiencing some form of medical trauma. Only one study used subjects who were healthy. She reports that in all but one study positive effects were found to be present with the use of modified forms of progressive relaxation training. It is significant to note that many of the studies Snyder considers deal with subjects experiencing pain, and therefore these studies may have direct application to the woman in labor. No studies were found in the literature comparing women's responses with those of men to progressive relaxation training, even though most studies employed a mixed group.

Reviewing the literature in regard to two specific pain areas may have application to the laboring woman. Headache and back pain are areas of distress during both pregnancy and childbirth. Woolfolk and Lehrer[45] report on several reviews that conclude that both progressive relaxation and EMG biofeedback have substantial effect on reducing headache pain, but that neither has an advantage over the other. One study found that muscle tension is not much of a factor in predicting tension headaches and cites environmental stressors, general autonomic arousal, and levels of pain threshold as other factors to be considered. Consequently, they too suggest the use of more than one form of therapy, specifically the use of cognitive strategies in addition to somatic (muscular) forms. Progressive relaxation (jacobsonian) is a highly somatic technique because it focuses solely on the muscles. However, modified forms of progressive relaxation may be considered cognitive as well, since they include varying degrees of suggestion in the therapy.

The literature in terms of back pain is more scarce. Woolfolk and Lehrer in their report on self-treatment say Kravitz determined that people suffering from low back pain involve their back muscles unnecessarily in various muscular activities as compared with those who do not suffer from low back pain. Use of progressive relaxation both with and without biofeedback improved chronic low back pain.[45]

Progressive Relaxation: A Comparison With Other Techniques

Woolfolk and Lehrer[42] in a comprehensive review of stress management techniques examine differences between relaxation techniques. For an in-depth analysis of differences, the reader is referred to their work. They discuss the "specific effects" hypothesis put forth by Davidson and Schwartz in which it is argued that an intervention oriented toward somatic, cognitive, or behavioral therapy will have the greatest effect on symptoms in one of these areas. The idea is to match treatments to presenting problems, although it is recognized that there are overlapping circumstances. Benson,[1] in contrast, argues for a generalized relaxation response. These two theories are not mutually exclusive. Consequently, a look at progressive relaxation in comparison with other techniques used in childbirth education is necessary.

Autogenic Training. Developed in Germany at the turn of the century and popularized by Schultz and Luthe,[34] autogenic training involves a form of passive concentration in which control over autonomic processes is acquired through concentration on visual, auditory, or somatic imagery. Woolfolk and Lehrer[45] found three studies that support the hypothesis that autogenic training appears to have greater impact on autonomic measures such as temperature than does progressive relaxation training. A study by Edelman[9] also supports this finding. Additionally, however, in two studies muscular training such as progressive relaxation training and EMG feedback seems to produce greater muscular tension reduction than does autogenic training. All these findings would seem to support the specific-effects hypothesis.

In contrast, Woolfolk and Lehrer[45] report only one study that failed to show any difference between progressive relaxation and autogenic training and a self-regulation group in blood pressure readings. This finding is supported in a study by Nicassio and Bootzin[27] showing no difference between progressive relaxation and autogenic training on treatment of severe insomniacs. However, the progressive relaxation group did show significant improvement earlier than did the autogenic group. Borkovec and Fowles[6] found no difference between treatment groups using hypnosis, progressive relaxation, and self-regulation. This finding led Nicassio and Bootzin[27] to suggest that results may depend not only on matching treatment to condition but also on matching intensity of treatment to intensity of condition. This has some import for childbirth educators in the design of sequence of relaxation technique.

Hypnosis. Researchers Wideman and Singer[43] report that some investigators suggest that the repetitive instructions of Lamaze training are a form of self-hypnosis. Women who "succeed" using the Lamaze method were thought to be more "hypnotizable" than women who "fail" using the method. They found one study in which an author tested the hypothesis and found that hypnotic susceptibility had no significance on training or on the birth experience of a Lamaze-trained woman.

Paul's studies[29,30] demonstrated that live progressive relaxation was more powerful in reducing levels of physiological arousal and reactivity than was hypnotic suggestion. However, when he substituted taped progressive relaxation for live training,[30] there was no significant difference between the techniques. Borkovec and Fowles[6] found no difference between three training sessions of either progressive relaxation or hypnosis on frontalis measurements, EMG, respiration rate, heart rate, and skin conductance.

Meditation. Woolfolk and Lehrer[45] reviewed studies comparing progressive relaxation and meditation. Their review of the literature indicates that there are some important cognitive and somatic differences between progressive relaxation and mantra meditation, but the differences are neither reliable nor strong. One study found resting heart rates to be lower for long-term practitioners of progressive relaxation than for those using transcendental meditation over time. The reviewing authors note that because the heart rate is in part related to muscular tension, a relaxation technique emphasizing musculature would be expected to have greater effect.

Strong motivational differences have been found between meditation and progressive relaxation.[45] Some individuals are very willing to learn and practice meditation, but for others the thought of participating in meditation may cause anxiety. In contrast, progressive relaxation is usually readily accepted by clients and it is generally not thought to be anxiety producing.

Visualization (A Cognitive Intervention). The literature surveyed by Woolfolk and Lehrer[45] comparing cognitive interventions and progressive relaxation is complex. Some authors have argued that biofeedback adds a cognitive element, as the cognitive mind becomes absorbed with somatic concerns. The separation of the two becomes a difficult task. They report on a study in which insomnia subjects were given taped training in progressive muscular relaxation. The progressive relaxation seemed to control pre-sleep tensions, but not when strong cognitive elements such as worry interfered. The same subjects then received either training in mental relaxation or were in a self-monitoring control group. Mental relaxation involved imaging or visualizing oneself in a relaxing situation. Improvement on insomnia ratings was higher in the mental relaxation group than in the self-control group. This finding seems to support the specific effects theory: that a cognitive-oriented therapy (such as visualization) has greatest effect on cognitive-oriented issues (such as anxiety or worry).

One researcher, Horan,[13] has reported case study use of ''in vivo emotive imagery'' as very useful. He defines in vivo emotive imagery as visualizing pleasant covert events during overt anxiety-arousing situations. His report describes perceiving muscles during labor as causing ''antagonism'' followed by a spontaneous shift to positive imagery. According to Horan, this shift produces tension reduction. This appears to be the same technique as sensory transformation discussed on page 106.

Progressive Relaxation and the Question of Feedback

Since the 1960's, evidence related to the ability of persons trained in biofeedback methods to alter the processes of their bodies has flooded the literature. Such physiological responses as skin temperature, heart rate, vasoconstriction, vasodilation, muscle tension, blood pressure, and brain waves have been affected through successful biofeedback training.[2]

A study specific to childbirth supported the inclusion of the feedback. Schwartz found that a combination of biofeedback training and Lamaze training was more effective than Lamaze training alone.[35] Humenick[14,15] emphasizes the importance of feedback during relaxation training and the importance of pacing the training according to the learner's accomplishments, specifically in terms of childbirth education. Humenick and Marchbanks[15] established the ability of a rater to assess relaxation progress nearly as accurately as a biofeedback machine by comparing rater judgment to biofeedback ratings. These authors conclude that childbirth educators can be trained to accurately evaluate relaxation skill, give feedback, and train labor partners to assess and communicate information on relaxation skills to each other.

Paul and Trimble[30] suggest that immediate feedback to the trainee is the critical element that accounts for the effectiveness of live over taped relaxation training. In their classic study of 30 college women, taped instruction was demonstrated to be less effective than live (therapist-present) training in relaxation. These differences were demonstrated by variation in heart rate, muscle tension, and response to stressful imagery. The authors concluded that adjusting the pace of the training to learner mastery affects the outcome.

Two studies reported by Woolfolk and Lehrer[45] also compared live with taped training and found substantial benefits in the live training. Both studies examined "subject-contingent" (exercise repetition based on learner needs) and "program-contingent" (exercise repetition based on a pre-set program) training. They report that subject-contingent training produced better relaxation as measured by lower EMG levels and skin temperature readings. However, program-contingent instructions were more effective in reducing anxiety. Woolfolk and Lehrer have concluded in reviewing these studies that the relationship between client and therapist—the human factor—may affect training outcomes.

Humenick[15] and Snyder[37] both focus on a significant point. The questions for the therapist or the childbirth educator are neither "How many sessions were conducted?" nor "Was live or taped training used?", but rather "Was there mastery of relaxation skill?" and "Can the therapist, childbirth educator, or learner in some way determine the level of skill attained?"

Progressive Relaxation: Locus of Control and Efficacy

Rosenthal's landmark study indicates that nurturing the expectation that an intervention or a technique will succeed is indeed an important contributory element to its success.[33] A client's locus of control is on a continuum ranging from external (a belief that outside forces such as luck or powerful others determine one's fate) to internal (a belief that one's own efforts strongly affect one's destiny). The effect of positive expectancy may interact with an internal locus of control to potentiate the effect of progressive relaxation training. Woolfolk and Lehrer[45] report mixed findings when the effect of locus of control on relaxation has been studied. In one study they report that those clients scoring high on internal control and high on success expectancy *practiced* relaxation training more than did those who scored low on those scales. However, another study found greater reductions of heart rate and anxiety recording among those with an external locus of control as compared with an internal locus. In contrast, another study indicated that those women scoring high in self-efficacy were less likely to receive medication during labor than were low-scoring women.

Numerous other studies reported by Woolfolk and Lehrer indicate either no difference between external and internal locus of control groups or give a slighter edge to the external locus of control groups when evaluating the effects of progressive relaxation. Differences may be due to study design. For example, in many studies done in a laboratory setting no provision was made for home practice (a factor that would presumably appeal to internal-control locus groups) and feedback typically was given via a biofeedback machine (a factor presumably attractive to an externally oriented person). Thus study design in the laboratory may have biased the findings to make them nongeneralizable to childbirth education classrooms.

The locus of control issue seems to emerge as an important variable to consider when teaching relaxation in childbirth education. If locus of control predicts which strategy is most likely to be effective, assessment of locus of control of class members might be important to childbirth education. For example, a coach providing feedback may be better for women who are oriented toward external locus of control. However, Jacobson's progressive relaxation training, in which the woman is sensitized to assessing her own state of relaxation, may be more effective for women with strong internal locus of control.

Wideman and Singer[43] reviewed studies dealing with information and locus of control. Studies showed that combined coping information and situationally descriptive information was significantly effective in reducing anxiety and pain. Studies that utilized only descriptive procedural information failed to demonstrate results. Wideman and Singer differentiate a second category of descriptive information that is not the describing of procedures but rather describing the sensations to be anticipated. Numerous studies reported by Wideman and Singer demonstrated that patients provided with both sensory and procedural information did better than those receiving only procedural or only sensory information. Incidentally, those receiving solely procedural information did not do as well as those receiving solely sensory information. The addition of information on coping strategies resulted in even better outcomes. *Thus clients appear to do best when they know what to expect, how it may feel, and how they might cope.*

Prepared childbirth training, according to Wideman and Singer,[43] is largely procedurally descriptive as compared with sensory descriptive (although many educators differ on this point). They conclude that when providing information and skills for coping, the addition of both sensory as well as procedural information contributes to the development of an internal locus of control.

Progressive Relaxation: Efficacy in Childbirth

Very little research has been conducted on the effectiveness of alternative childbirth preparation methods. Most existing studies focus on the Lamaze method; only one (Humenick and Marchbanks[15]) examines the efficacy of a specific aspect of the approach of mastery of neuromuscular relaxation technique. All others deal with more general issues or outcomes, i.e., maternal attitudes, use of medication, and so on. Generally, these studies indicate that among Lamaze-prepared women there was an increase in personal control,[11] that prepared women had more positive views toward pregnancy, childbirth and themselves and their partners and children,[41] and that significantly lower levels of anxiety were associated with labor and birth.[46] Scott and Rose[36] indicate that there was a significant decrease in analgesia and anesthesia requirements in Lamaze-trained women. According to Wideman and Singer,[40] at least one study challenges the women's perception of pain at postlabor interviews. However, Humenick's[14] review of the literature found no studies in which a woman's perception of pain in labor was associated with her satisfaction with that labor.

Humenick and Marchbanks[15] rated 31 women (Fig. 8–1) on their mastery of neuromuscular dissociation technique after relaxation training in prepared childbirth classes. They note that high ratings on the more difficult items (that is, skill beyond

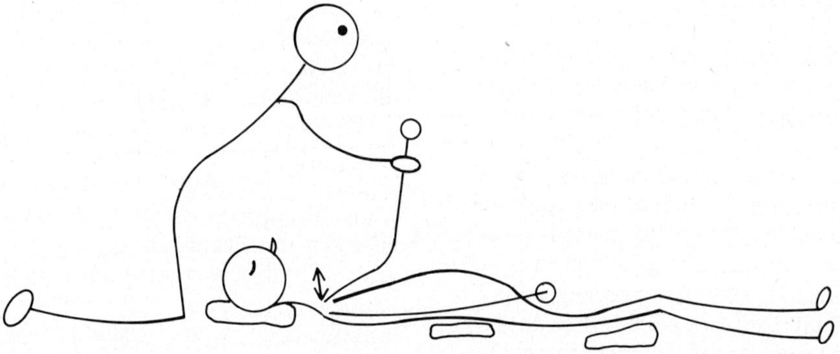

Requests:		Rating of Right Arm Relaxation	
1. Relax your right arm.	Not at all	1 2 3 4 5	Completely
2. Relax your entire body. (Check several limbs.)	Not at all	1 2 3 4 5	Completely
3. Relax while receiving a mildly painful stimulus from squeezing a thigh muscle.	Not at all	1 2 3 4 5	Completely
4. Relax while contracting one limb—your left arm. (Contract by making a fist and lifting your arm 6 inches off the floor.)	Not at all	1 2 3 4 5	Completely
5. Relax while contracting two limbs on the same side of your body, your left arm and leg. (Contract the leg by tensing foot and lifting a few inches off the floor.)	Not at all	1 2 3 4 5	Completely
6. Relax while contracting your left arm and your right leg (two limbs on the opposite sides of the body).	Not at all	1 2 3 4 5	Completely

FIGURE 8–1. The Neuromuscular Dissociation Relaxation Rating Scale (NDRRS). Directions: The woman is positioned on her back with pillows underneath her head and thighs. The rater kneels behind her head. After giving each of the following six requests, the rater lifts the woman's right arm as shown. The rating is based on the heaviness of the woman's arm and its ability to swing freely at the shoulder. (Adapted from Humenick, S., and Marchbanks, P. Validation of a scale to measure relaxation. *Birth and the Family Journal* 8:147, 1981.)

basic relaxation to advanced relaxation demonstrated through skill in neuromuscular dissociation tasks) significantly correlated with reduced medication given in labor. This outcome implies the potential for a causal relationship between a training technique and specific birth result. It is hoped that this promising line of research will be elaborated in future efforts.

Stevens and Heide[39] also isolated components of pain management strategies used commonly in childbirth education. Subjects who used attention focusing and also received feedback on relaxation were able to tolerate pain longer than were other groups. Attention focusing was more effective than relaxation techniques used alone across all groups, indicating that it is an effective strategy.

IMPLICATIONS FOR PRACTICE

Progressive relaxation is and remains the standard against which most relaxation or stress reduction techniques are measured. Considered in isolation as a primarily somatic technique, modified progressive relaxation has been demonstrated to effectively influence primarily the musculoskeletal system. This is important because labor has an important musculoskeletal component. However, when modified progressive relaxation is paired with imagery, it becomes a somatic-cognitive technique and its potency seems to be enhanced. At a time when the childbirth field is flooded with literature on relaxation strategies, modified progressive relaxation has demonstrated its efficacy, not as a panacea, but as a technique that can produce specific and predictable results.

For the childbirth educator, modified progressive relaxation appears to be an appropriate strategy. Although it focuses primarily on the musculoskeletal system, childbirth is above all a physical event. Used in its modified form as described by Bernstein and Borkovec,[4] the childbirth educator could with some assurance predict a general reduction of somatic tension in those who master this skill.

Feedback emerges as an important issue: When is it appropriate for the woman to receive feedback from a trained partner? When should she be her own source of feedback with an internally heightened self-awareness? Do some personality types prefer specific types of feedback? Is a combination of internal and external feedback most useful?

Utilization of modified progressive relaxation in combination with cognitive strategies of suggestion or imagery would seem to potentiate its effect, although this is a matter for continued research. Use of suggestion or imagery is appropriate for the cognitive elements of stress while progressive relaxation is appropriate for the somatic element.

Problems do arise, however, in applying the research to the childbirth education setting. In many studies that consider prepared childbirth, all methods are grouped together. Childbirth education is often considered to be univocal and homogeneous. No differentiation is made between training of the educators, class sizes, number of sessions in the class series, and the amount of time relaxation is practiced in the course and the types taught. There is typically no distinction noted by researchers between methods such as those of Bradley and Lamaze. Similarly, the effect of contributory elements are not considered, such as locus of control, feedback ability of the labor partner (both in assessing relaxation level and ability to communicate information correctly), importance of cognitive information (both procedural and sensoral), respiratory strategies, and both the teacher and client belief and value systems. Nevertheless, modified progressive relaxation training appears to have contributed positively to coping with childbirth.

Additionally, progressive relaxation and its modifications appear safe. Woolfolk and Lehrer[45] do state that several investigators have reported "relaxation-produced anxiety" (a heightened physiological arousal and reactivity). However, this is seen more often with meditation than with progressive relaxation.

A process of autogenic discharge that occurs with autogenic training has been described but does not appear in the literature on progressive relaxation. This discharge takes the form of pain, anxiety, crying, palpitation and/or muscle twitches and is thought to be a process of achieving homeostasis. Woolfolk and Lehrer[45] suggest that these discharges may result from increased somatic awareness, and that anxious persons are likely to interpret heightened physiological awareness as a reason to be more anxious. They conclude that progressive or modified progressive relaxation may be easier to tolerate than some other relaxation strategies because of its direct effect of slowed heart rate and lowered muscle tension. For the childbirth educator who may be considering a sequence of training in multiple relaxation strategies, it may indeed be important to initiate training in modified progressive relaxation first, before adding other strategies.

Guidelines for Practice

The following guidelines for the use of modified progressive relaxation training may be helpful to the childbirth educator:

> Each person needs an inner sense to "feel" when a muscle is tense, and needs to be able to differentiate muscle tension from muscle release. Jacobson and progressive relaxation . . . must be mastered before moving to the more complex neuromuscular relaxation now being taught.
>
> PAMELA SHROCK[1]
>
> Teaching relaxation must take into account couples' existing ability to relax and include a means of assessing what they have learned.
>
> SHARRON HUMENICK[2]
>
> Relaxation is the key to being able to cooperate with labor. Women who keep the necessary tension in the uterus from spreading to other parts of the body have less painful, often shorter, and easier labors than other women.
>
> BETH SHEARER[3]

1. The inclusion of modified progressive relaxation training is important. Although not shown conclusively as the causal factor in reduced need for medication or positive maternal attitude, its use does result in reduced somatic tension outside of childbirth and presumably during childbirth itself.
2. An abbreviated form of progressive relaxation is realistic, given the usual training period. Ideally, training should occur in each class session, but educators may try a minimum of four sessions involving progressive relaxation training. (Many research designs have utilized three or four training sessions.) The first session in which training is provided might follow Bernstein and Borkovec's recipe for training, focusing on all muscle groups. In Session 2 the muscle groups would be reduced to seven; in session 3 they would be reduced to four, and session 4 would utilize counting and recall skills.
3. Daily practice should be encouraged; the usual regimen described in the research was two 15-minute practice sessions daily.
4. Selective relaxation training (dissociative techniques) should begin after progressive relaxation has been mastered. Selective relaxation requires only the use of muscles needed for a particular activity. The ability to differentiate tension from relaxation is a skill required before the use of selective relaxation. Women should be assured that they are not expected to methodically tense and release body parts during labor but rather to release unnecessary tensions during labor. The ability to monitor the body and to release unnecessary tension is the skill used in labor.
5. The laboring woman should be trained in heightened awareness of her own internal world through modified progressive relaxation training. Should she labor without adequate support systems, or should she have a strong internal locus of control, internally provided feedback may enhance the relaxation response as compared with feedback from an external source.
6. Training should be given to the labor partner to enable assessment of muscle tension and the giving of feedback to the woman in a manner that enhances relaxation. All care

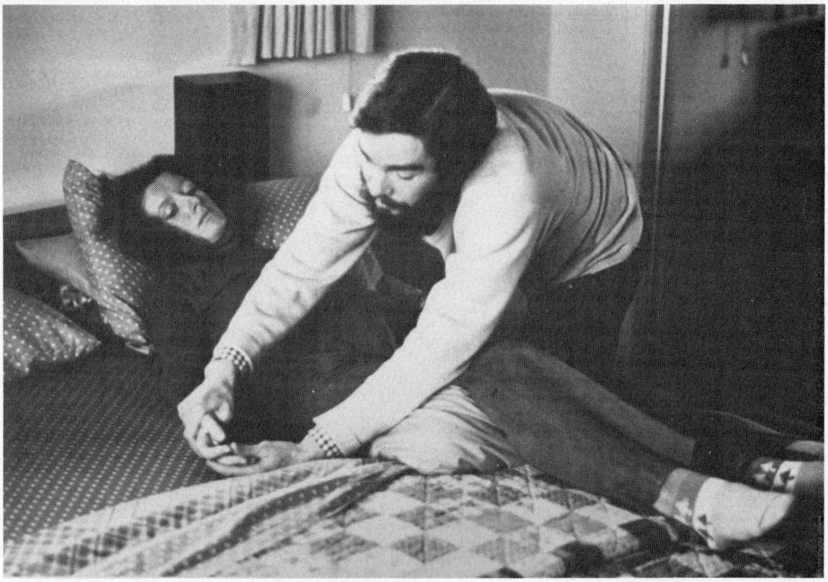

Labor partners need to know how to assess muscle tension and give feedback to the woman in a manner that enhances relaxation. (Photograph by Rodger Ewy, Educational Graphic Aids, Inc.)

should be given to maintain a teamwork approach as opposed to an adversarial one. Some educators prefer to ask coaches to provide "feedback" rather than "check" relaxation, thinking that "check" may be interpreted as an authoritarian role. The labor partner must be seen as supportive by the laboring woman, not as an external judge. He or she should provide feedback as nonjudgmentally as does a biofeedback machine. If the laboring team determines after training that partner feedback does not enhance relaxation, or if she has a strong internal orientation, the woman may become her own source of feedback. She may use the external feedback primarily to further develop her internal feedback.

7. Modified progressive relaxation should be used with other somatic and cognitive strategies in order to potentiate its effect.
8. In a planned sequence of relaxation training, progressive relaxation training should occur near the beginning of the training program, as it appears to be free of relaxation-produced anxieties. As cognitive procedural and sensory descriptive information is added and as progressive relaxation is mastered, other appropriate strategies may be added.

IMPLICATIONS FOR RESEARCH

Several areas of investigation must be addressed:

- Is there a difference between general and specific relaxation response in men and women? R. Estelle Ramey, an endocrinologist and self-identified feminist, indicated in a keynote speech at the 1984 ASPO/Lamaze Annual Conference that most research has not included gender as a factor. Birth is a specifically feminine experience and as such requires sex-specific investigations into coping and relaxation strategies.
- Researchers and childbirth educators themselves must define what they mean by modified progressive relaxation. Is one session of training that covers all muscle groups enough to qualify as even modified progressive relaxation train-

ing? Are taped instructions appropriate for use in classes? How is mastery of the skill best determined?

- The need to isolate factors in childbirth education and to evaluate their efficacy is becoming all too apparent. Training factors of information, support systems, respiratory techniques, and individual and combined relaxation techniques must be separated out and analyzed. Environmental factors of class size, location, instructor preparation and beliefs, and total class hours must be recorded. Childbirth education is a complex and sophisticated undertaking; there are many variables to be considered and researchers can no longer assume all classes are alike.

- The question of locus of control needs to be considered in the study of modified progressive relaxation, as it may have some impact on source of feedback and skill mastery. That is, feedback from an external source, effectively or ineffectively given, may produce increased tension and even antagonism in a woman with a strong internal locus of control. Such a woman may benefit from heightened internal sensory awareness training and function as her own source of feedback.

- Studies considering expectation of effectiveness by the client are needed. The childbirth educator's belief in efficacy of progressive relaxation may also be a significant factor in levels of skill transfer.

- An analysis of situations in which modified progressive relaxation was not useful either in class or in labor needs to be undertaken. What factors led to the lack of success? What strategies should be used?

- Further research into the comparison of jacobsonian versus modified relaxation needs to be conducted. The convenience of modified forms of training has led to their use; that convenience must be supported by research establishing equal effectiveness.

SUMMARY

Although progressive relaxation may not appear at first glance to be as glamorous as some other relaxation strategies, its import cannot be denied. Birth is a highly somatic event, and progressive relaxation is, above all, a somatic relaxation strategy. It historically has been assumed to be the relaxation strategy utilized in childbirth education. However, a close look shows that selective relaxation may typically be added so quickly that even the label modified progressive relaxation may not be entirely appropriate in many of the practice classes. Additionally, other techniques such as visualization that address cognitive as well as somatic issues are currently becoming more fully integrated into the practice of childbirth education. The effectiveness of specific relaxation strategies alone, in combination, and in sequence must receive more intense scrutiny, including progressive relaxation. For now, its central position in childbirth education seems most appropriate.

References

1. Benson, H. *The Relaxation Response*. New York: Avon Books, 1976.
2. Benson, H., Beary, J., and Carol, M. The relaxation response. *Psychiatry* 37:37, 1974.
3. Benson, H., Kotch, J. B., Crassweller, K., and Greenwood, M. Historical and clinical considerations of the relaxation response. *American Scientist* 65:441, 1977.
4. Bernstein, D., and Borkovec, T. *Progressive Relaxation Training: A Manual for the Helping Professions*. Champaign, IL: Research Press, 1973.
5. Bing, E. *Six Practical Lessons for an Easier Childbirth*. New York: Bantam Books, 1969.
6. Borkovec, T. D., and Fowles, D. C. Controlled investigation of the effects of progressive and hypnotic relaxation on insomnia. *Journal of Abnormal Psychology* 82:153, 1973.
7. Bradley, R. *Husband-Coached Childbirth*. New York: Harper and Row, 1965.
8. Dick-Read, G. *Childbirth Without Fear*. New York: Harper and Row, 1959.
9. Edelman, R. Effects of progressive relaxation on autonomic processes. *Journal of Clinical Psychology* 26:421, 1970.

10. Ewy, D., and Ewy, R. *Preparation for Childbirth*. New York: The New American Library, 1972.
11. Felton, G. S., and Segelman, F. B. Lamaze Childbirth Training and Changes in Belief about Personal Control. *Birth and Family Journal* 5:141, 1978.
12. Gregg, R. H. Biofeedback and biophysical monitoring during pregnancy and labor. *In* Basmajian, J.V. (ed): *Biofeedback Principles and Practice for Clinicians*. Baltimore: Williams and Wilkins Co., 1979.
13. Horan, J. J. In vivo emotive imagery: A technique for reducing childbirth discomfort. *Psychological Reprints* 32:1328, 1973.
14. Humenick, S. Assessing the quality of childbirth education: Can teachers change? *Birth and Family Journal* 7:82, 1980.
15. Humenick, S., and Marchbanks, P. Validation of a scale to measure relaxation in childbirth education classes. *Birth and Family Journal* 3:145, 1981.
16. Huttel, F., Mitchell, F., et al. A quantitative evaluation of psychoprophylaxis in childbirth. *Journal of Psychosomatic Research* 16:81, 1972.
17. Jacobson, E. *Progressive Relaxation,* 2nd ed. Chicago: University of Chicago Press, 1938.
18. Jacobson, E. *You Must Relax*. New York: McGraw-Hill, 1957.
19. Jacobson, E. *How to Relax and Have Your Baby.* New York, McGraw-Hill, 1965.
20. Jacobson, E. *Modern Treatments of Tense Patients*. Springfield, IL: Charles C Thomas, 1970.
21. Kitzinger, S. *Education and Counseling for Childbirth*. London: Schocken Books, 1979.
22. Kitzinger, S. *Experience of Childbirth*. London: Penguin, 1967.
23. Lamaze, F. *Painless Childbirth*. New York: Pocket Books, 1965.
24. McGuigan, F. J. Progressive Relaxation: Origins, Principles and Clinical Applications. *In* Woolfolk, R., and Lehrer, P.: *Principles and Practice of Stress Management*. New York: Guilford Press, 1984.
25. McKenna, J. The Mitchell method of physiological relaxation. *Physiotherapy* 64:234, 1978.
26. Mulcahy, R. A., and Janz, N. Effectiveness of raising pain perception threshold in males and females using a psychoprophylactic childbirth technique during induced pain. *Nursing Research* 22:423, 1973.
27. Nicassio, P., and Bootzin, R. A comparison of progressive relaxation and autogenic training as treatment for insomnia. *Journal of Abnormal Psychology* 33:253, 1974.
28. Noble, E. *Essential Exercises for the Childbearing Year.* Boston: Houghton Mifflin Co., 1976.
29. Paul, G. Physiological effects of relaxation training and hypnotic suggestion. *Journal of Abnormal Psychology* 74:425, 1969.
30. Paul, G., and Trimble, R. Recorded vs. live relaxation training and hypnotic suggestion: Comparative effectiveness for reducing physiological arousal and inhibiting stress response. *Behavioral Therapy* 1:285, 1970.
31. Pendleton, L. R., and Tasto, D. L. Effects of metronome-conditioned relaxation, metronome-induced relaxation and progressive muscle relaxation on insomniacs. *Behavior Research and Therapy* 14:165, 1976.
32. Richter, J. and Sloan, R. A relaxation technique. *American Journal of Nursing* 79:1960, 1979.
33. Rosenthal, R., and Jacobson, L. *Pygmalian in the Classroom: Teacher Expectation and Pupils' Intellectual Development*. New York: Holt, Rinehart and Winston, 1968.
34. Schultz, J. and Luthe, W. *Autogenic Therapy (Vol. 1): Autogenic Methods*. New York: Grune and Stratton, 1969.
35. Schwartz, R. A. Biofeedback Relaxation Training in Obstetrics: Its Effects on Perinatal and Neonatal States. (Doctoral Dissertation, California School of Professional Psychology, San Diego, 1979). *Dissertation Abstracts International,* 1980.
36. Scott, J. R., and Rose, N. B. Effect of psychoprophylaxis (Lamaze preparation) on labor and delivery in primiparas. *New England Journal of Medicine* 294:1205, 1979.
37. Snyder, M. Progressive relaxation as a nursing intervention: An analysis. *Advances in Nursing Science* 6:47, 1984.
38. Stevens, R. J. Psychological strategies for management of pain in prepared childbirth. II: A study of psychoanalgesia in prepared childbirth. *Birth and Family Journal* Spring, 1977.
39. Stevens, R. J., and Heide, F., Analgesic characteristics of prepared childbirth techniques: Attention Focusing and Systematic Relaxation. *Journal of Psychosomatic Research* 21:429, 1977.
40. Stone, C., Demchik-Stone, D., and Horan, J. A component analysis of Lamaze and cognitive-behavioral procedures. *Journal of Psychosomatic Research* 21:451, 1977.
41. Tanzer, D., and Block, J. *Why Natural Childbirth?* New York: Schocken Books, 1976.
42. Walsh, P., Dale, A., and Anderson, D. Comparison of biofeedback pulse wave velocity and progressive relaxation in essential hypertension. *Perceptual and Motor Skills* 44:839, 1977.
43. Wideman, M., and Singer, J. The role of psychological mechanisms in preparation for childbirth. *American Psychologist* 39:1357, 1984.
44. Wolpe, J., and Lazarus, A. *Behavior Therapy Techniques*. New York: Pergamon Press, 1966.
45. Woolfolk, R., and Lehrer P. (eds). *Principles and Practice of Stress Management*. New York: Guilford Press, 1984.
46. Zax, M., Sameroff, W. J., and Farnum, J. E. Childbirth education, maternal attitudes, and delivery. *American Journal of Obstetrics and Gynecology* 123:185, 1975.

Beginning Quote

Bing, E. *Six Practical Lessons for an Easier Childbirth*. New York: Grosset & Dunlap, 1967.

Boxed Quotes

1. Shrock, P. Relaxation skills: Update on problems and solutions. *Genesis* 6:10, 1984.
2. Humenick, S. Teaching relaxation. *Childbirth Educator* 3:47, 1984.
3. Shearer, B. Labor and birth in stages. *American Baby's Childbirth* 84:76, 1984.

chapter 9

RELAXATION: Biofeedback

JOYCE DI FRANCO

Every skill that has ever been learned by humans was learned through feedback.

E. Green and A. Green

Biofeedback, a special type of feedback, has been used for centuries to assist individuals in learning complex skills. However, modern biofeedback training that focused on altering the functioning of biological systems did not begin until the late 1950's and early 1960's. The mechanism through which biofeedback works probably varies from one situation to another. Some biofeedback applications involve the acquisition of skills, such as learning to do Kegel exercises more effectively by using a perinometer, while many biofeedback applications appear to be primarily shortcuts to relaxation.[13]

REVIEW OF THE LITERATURE

What is Biofeedback?

Individuals receive feedback in many forms. It comes from those around us both verbally and nonverbally; from our environment; from within ourselves; and at times from specifically designed instruments that measure skin resistance, muscle tension, skin conductivity, and skin temperature. These instruments and the systems they measure are shown in Table 9–1.

Biofeedback is ''the use of monitoring instruments (usually electrical) to detect and amplify internal physiological processes within the body, in order to make this ordinarily unavailable infor-

TABLE 9–1. BIOFEEDBACK INSTRUMENTS

Electromyograph (EMG)	Measures electrical impulses associated with neuromuscular tension. Learning to relax the frontalis muscle, for example, seems to enhance relaxation in head, neck, and upper trunk.
Electrical skin resistance (ESR)	Monitors degree of activity in sympathetic nervous system, giving some indication of degree of arousal. In a decreased state of arousal, there is an increase in skin resistance.[28]
Galvanic skin reflex (GSR)	Records conductivity changes due to the action of sweat glands at skin surface.
The thermistor probe	Measures skin temperature. Provides immediate feedback of the degree of control one has over superficial blood flow and therefore over skin temperature at the extremities. The changes are mentally induced (passive volition) by visualizing hands in warm water, near a warm fire, etc. This is an easily learned response and has the bonus of a sense of potential for self-control. It is believed that when superficial blood flow increases, caused by relaxation of the blood vessels and evidenced by warming of the hands, a concomitant reaction occurs in the rest of the vascular system.

mation available to the individual and literally to feed it back to him in some form.''[4] The information that is fed back must reach the cortex of the brain and be understood by the individual. Then the individual has the *option to change the specific behavior or physiological response*. In summary, biofeedback is a strategy for helping individuals develop an awareness of body process, i.e., ''listening'' to one's body, thus enabling the individual to respond to achieve a change in physiological responses, if desired.

How Does Biofeedback Work?

Green and Green[17] summarized what happens during ''psychophysiological self-regulation'': hidden physiological information is fed back to the cerebral cortex and interpreted by the individual who then responds to achieve a level of homeostasis and inner harmony (Fig. 9–1). They also described the function of biofeedback equipment:

> . . . the mind (or psych, or self, whatever its genesis or definition) chooses and creates a visualization of desired physical, emotional, and mental behavior. This seems to involve the cerebral cortex (the ''thinking brain''). When a specific visualization is repeatedly ''held in the mind'' during deep relaxation, then the brain's limbic system (the so-called ''emotional brain'') accepts the visualization as a program to be implemented. If, in addition to mental and emotional changes, the visualization includes specific overt changes in the so-called involuntary nervous system (the autonomic), the limbic system programs the hypothalamus (the so-called ''mechanical brain'') to bring about these changes, and they begin to be observed in the body. The biofeedback machine merely tells whether or not the visualization is being implemented correctly inside the skin. It is an *outside-the-skin* (external) ''truth'' detector.

FIGURE 9–1. Biofeedback involves listening to your body.

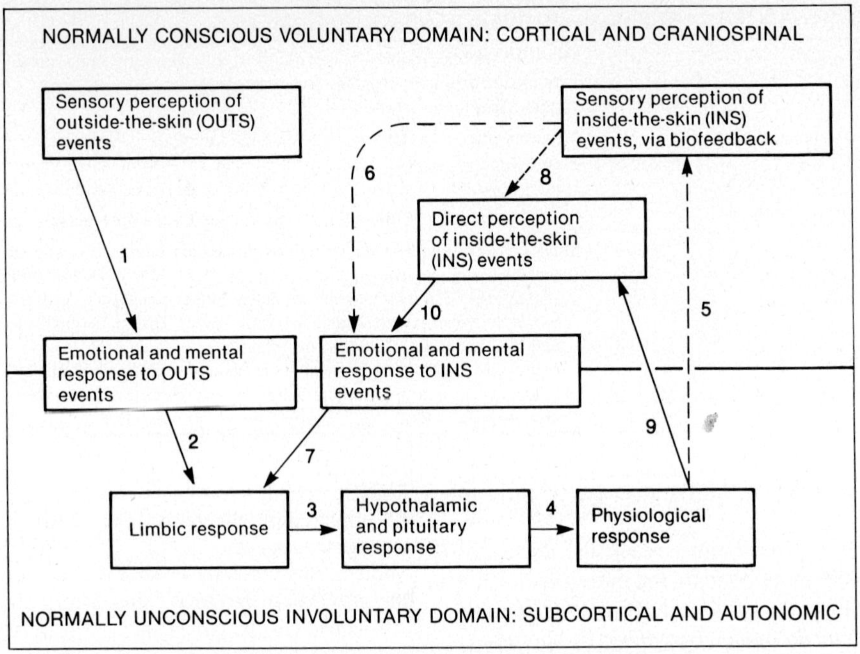

FIGURE 9–2. Diagram of how biofeedback training modifies responses to psychophysiological events. For all events, stressful or otherwise, an individual's sensory perception of outside-the-skin (OUTS) events results in a physiological response along the route of arrows 1 → 2 → 3 → 4. If the individual's physiological response is "picked up" and fed back to the individual via a biofeedback device (arrow 5) and the individual attempts to *change* the behavior using the biofeedback device (arrows 6 → 7), a *new limbic response* develops resulting in modification of the original physiological response. Biofeedback training *increases an individual's sensitivity* to inside-the-skin (INS) events and responses occur via new pathways. When initially using biofeedback, the individual's response to psychophysiological events and processes occurs along the route of arrows 1 → 2 → 3 → 4 → 5 → 8 → 10 → 7. With practice, the individual can perceive these events and processes without the aid of biofeedback (self-regulation) and the individual's response follows the route of arrows 1 → 2 → 3 → 4 → 9 → 10 → 7. (Adapted from Green, E., and Green A. Biofeedback and Transformation. *In* Kunz, D. *Spiritual Aspects of the Healing Arts.* Wheaton, IL: Quest Books, 1985.)

Through biofeedback practice, individuals increase their sensitivity to *inside-the-skin* (internal) events. Eventually, external feedback via biofeedback equipment becomes unnecessary because an individual can directly perceive *inside-the-skin* events and respond to achieve a desired change in physiological processes.[17]

Biofeedback training is often inaccurately called the training of the body; in reality it is "training in self-regulation of the brain, by the mind, with volition."[17] Through the use of biofeedback the individual becomes more aware of the complex interrelationships among the mind, emotions, and body. It is documented that, by using biofeedback, humans can learn to regulate heart rate, blood pressure, and skin temperature and to control headaches and seizure disorders.[31]

Essential Aspects of Biofeedback

There are three essential aspects of biofeedback. First, individuals must have *techniques for gaining control* over their physiological functioning. Second, an individual must learn to *sense physiological states* (such as tension), recognize factors that are related to the physiological state, and learn to respond to achieve a desired state, such as release of tense muscles to achieve a state of relaxation. Third, for biofeedback to be effective, an individual must have a *receptive attitude,* an attitude of openness and ''allowing'' certain responses to come forth, as opposed to an active focus on ''making'' desired responses come forth.[36]

Relaxation Training and Biofeedback

Biofeedback modalities can be classified in two categories: instrumented approaches and noninstrumented approaches. Instrumented approaches include the electromyograph (EMG), electrical skin resistance (ESR), galvanic skin reflex (GSR), and thermistor probes. Noninstrumented approaches are those that involve verbal, touch, and visual feedback without the use of specific biofeedback equipment.

Instrumented Approaches

Electromyograph (EMG). Research focusing on the use of instrumented biofeedback with pregnant women began in the late 1970's (Table 9–2). The results of the majority of these studies indicated that women who had received biofeedback-assisted relaxation training had significantly less muscle tension during labor and shorter length of labor, and used less medication during childbirth.[15,16,20] One study, however, reported no difference in the length of labor and use of medication during childbirth in women who had received biofeedback-assisted relaxation training and women in the control group.[34]

Differences in treatment protocols in the studies make it difficult to compare the results. For example, Gregg[16] used a mastery model in which the women in the experimental group practiced daily beginning first in a quiet environment and then

TABLE 9–2. INSTRUMENTED BIOFEEDBACK STUDIES ON PREGNANT WOMEN

RESEARCHER	DESCRIPTION	FINDINGS
Farrell (1981)[12]	Compared effect of EMG-assisted relaxation training on labor. 60 multiparous women in prepared childbirth classes and 15 multiparous women who did not take classes were subjects.	Significant decrease in average length of first-stage labor in biofeedback-trained groups. No significant difference was found among groups for the length of second-stage labor, analgesia or anesthesia, and infant Apgar scores.
Grad (1980)[15]	Tested the effect of EMG biofeedback-assisted relaxation training on a woman's childbirth experience both objectively and subjectively. 60 women in the third trimester participated.	Biofeedback-trained group remained unmedicated significantly longer. Physician's estimation of the amount of pain and tension experienced was significantly lower for the biofeedback-trained group.
Gregg (1978)[16]	Investigated effects of biofeedback tension-recognition and relaxation training on labor and its management. Data were obtained from 30 biofeedback-trained women and 30 control subjects.	Biofeedback-trained subjects had a significantly shorter first-stage labor. Biofeedback relaxation-trained women used less than 1/10th the amount of sedatives and 1/4th the amount of analgesics as the control group. Biofeedback subjects also reported less pain, less apprehension, and a greater degree of confidence than in previous pregnancies than control subjects.
Humenick and Marchbanks (1981)[20]	Compared the ability of rater using a relaxation rating scale to assess relaxation with EMG biofeedback. 31 women in the third trimester participated.	Authors concluded that childbirth educators can be trained to give reliable feedback to clients on achievement of relaxation. There was a 0.88 correlation between raters and EMG. The mother's report of medication during childbirth was significantly related to prenatal relaxation skill achievement.
St. James-Roberts et al. (1983)[34]	Compared two methods of biofeedback relaxation training, EMG and skin conductance level (SCL), on outcome of labor. 61 women participated.	No difference between control groups and experimental groups on any labor variable. EMG relaxation training fit easily into childbirth education program; SCL did not.

changing time and circumstances of practice. They progressed to practice of relaxation with the EMG feedback, and then returned to the use of the biofeedback equipment for reinforcement or as new circumstances occurred.[1,16] In addition, virtually all of the subjects in the study (both experimental and control subjects) attended childbirth preparation classes in which one would expect that they had learned additional relaxation strategies.

Grad,[15] on the other hand, gave experimental subjects specific instructions on a series of relaxation strategies to be practiced at home. The subjects also augmented relaxation training with EMG biofeedback during each regular prenatal visit in the last trimester of pregnancy. In both studies, women in the experimental groups had significantly shorter labors than women in the control group. In Grad's study,[15] women in the experimental group went without medication a significantly longer period of time than women in the control group. Gregg,[16] however, looked at differences in the amount of medication taken during childbirth and found that women in the biofeedback-trained group took ten to four times less medication than women in the control group.

It should also be noted that the studies varied in which muscle groups were monitored. Gregg[16] monitored the volar surface of the wrists, St. James-Roberts[34] used the midline abdomen, Humenick and Marchbanks[20] used the biceps and trapezius, Farrell[12] monitored the mentalis, and Grad[15] used the frontalis. Jones and Evans[24] and others question whether frontalis EMG biofeedback training effects are indicative of decreased muscle tension and decreased autonomic system arousal. However, this muscle group system is frequently used in biofeedback training.

Studies of nonpregnant subjects using biofeedback and relaxation skills also reveal mixed results (Table 9–3). It is interesting to note that subjects in the experimental groups in both Gregg's[16] study (pregnant sample) and Reynold's[30] study (nonpregnant sample) showed an increase in the ability to achieve a "more relaxed" state. Biofeedback training sessions in both studies were conducted over a period of four to six weeks, included daily home practice, and had a component that focused on developing the ability to transfer information. This format is similar to that which is frequently used in childbirth education classes. Yorde and Witmer[39] found that in using a lecture-discussion format with an experiential component and providing a variety of skills (autogenic training, progressive relaxation, breathing, and guided imagery), the investigators were able to increase stress-coping abilities of subjects. This is also a format that is useful in childbirth education classes.

It is important to remember that biofeedback is a vehicle, not an end, and that learning to make the proper response takes time for the shaping (achieving the desired behavior) to occur.[28] In addition, learning must be reinforced in order to maintain skill levels.[6,31] While questions are often asked about the importance and feasibility of using biofeedback equipment, it seems appropriate to say that biofeedback instruments are valuable because they provide immediate, objective information about body functions. However, because biofeedback equipment is expensive, not readily available in the numbers needed for childbirth education classes, and requires special maintenance, it is seldom used in classes.[20] The childbirth educator may want to become aware of community resources for biofeedback training so that clients who would like to use this modality can be appropriately referred.

Temperature Feedback. Temperature feedback is easy to use and provides an immediate sense of progress. Changes in hand temperature reflect the state of relaxation due to an increased blood flow to the skin. Biodots and finger or temperature bands* reflect color changes that indicate the degree of relaxation and tension and are useful in helping clients learn the skill of relaxation. Although certainly not as accurate as a biofeedback machine, these devices can provide an inexpensive way to measure progress and encourage continued practice at home. One precaution is that these devices will react to extremes in room temperature (very hot, hot, or very cold) when they exist.[11]

Noninstrumented Approaches

Noninstrumented approaches are more accessible to childbirth educators and their clients. These approaches include coach feedback (verbal and

*Biodots are available from the Medical Device Company, 1555 Bellefontaine, North Dr, Indianapolis, IN 46202. Finger or wrist temperature bands are available from Bio Temp Products Inc., 1950 W. 86th Street, Indianapolis, IN 46260.

TABLE 9–3. BIOFEEDBACK STUDIES ON NONPREGNANT WOMEN

RESEARCHER	DESCRIPTION	FINDINGS
Instrumented Biofeedback		
Bowles et al. (1978)[6]	Evaluated two types of relaxation training: progressive relaxation and home practice, and progressive relaxation combined with EMG biofeedback and home practice. Measured EMG levels during training, after training, and the relationship between EMG levels and anxiety. 18 adult women were assigned to either an experimental group (9) or a comparison group (9).	Unable to compare groups because of extreme variance within them. Subject variability within the relaxation-training only group was 60 times higher than variability in the group that received EMG biofeedback plus relaxation training. Pre- and post-EMG measures were significant ($p < 0.01$) for relaxation training and biofeedback group. No significant differences were found between pre- and post-training trait anxiety scores for either group.
Fehring (1983)[13]	Compared the effects of Benson's relaxation technique with Benson's relaxation augmented with GSR biofeedback on the psychological stress symptoms of 78 well college students.	The biofeedback-aided relaxation group had significantly ($p = 0.04$) lower mean state anxiety scores. The biofeedback aided relaxation group had significantly ($p = 0.02$) lower profile of mood scores.
Reynolds (1984)[30]	Compared the efficacy of five relaxation training procedures, four of which used EMG auditory feedback. Sample was composed of 20 university students.	No significant difference was found between groups. There was a significant pre- to post-test difference ($p < 0.001$) and significant groups $\times$ sessions interactions ($p < 0.001$). Author concludes that EMG feedback can be significantly beneficial by facilitating relaxation process.
Steger and Harper (1980)[35]	Compared the efficacy of a comprehensive biofeedback (EMG) and stress management strategy and a self-monitored home relaxation program in treatment of 20 tension headache sufferers.	Both treatment strategies successfully increased patient's ability to relax, but only the comprehensive biofeedback program was successful in reducing reports of headache pain and feelings of psychological distress.
Yorde and Witmer (1980)[39]	Investigated lecture-discussion format to present cognitive and relaxation skills with biofeedback training (EMG) to reduce psychological stress response. 50 subjects divided into 5 groups that consisted of one or a combination of the two treatment conditions.	The lecture/discussion format was effective in reducing the subjects' level of stress. There was no evidence that EMG biofeedback relaxation training contributed to the reduction of stress.
Noninstrumented Biofeedback		
Shapiro and Lehrer[32]	Compared the effects of autogenic training and progressive relaxation on psychophysiological changes of 22 normal subjects	Both procedures were effective in reducing psychopathological symptoms, anxiety, and depression. No significant differences found between groups on physiological variables, heart rate, and skin conductance.
Stevens and Heide (1977)[37]	Examined the effectiveness of attention focusing and systemic relaxation used separately or in combination on pain. 52 subjects were divided into 6 treatment groups.	Attention focusing with systematic relaxation and coach feedback was most effective.
Worthington et al. (1982)[38]	Examined effectiveness of coping strategies taught in childbirth education classes. 104 nulliparous university women served as subjects.	In experiment 1 structured breathing increased pain tolerance more effectively than normal breathing. Effleurage was less helpful than no effleurage. Practice under stress was better than either imaginal practice or no practice. In experiment 2 a combination of structured breathing and attention focal points was better than normal breathing. Coaching was more effective than no coaching. Combination of structured breathing, attention focal points, and coaching produced the strongest treatment effect.

touch), respiration awareness feedback, body awareness feedback, and visual feedback.

Coach Feedback. The literature supports the use of the labor coach as a provider of feedback for the laboring woman.[10] The labor coach can use both verbal and touch feedback to help the laboring woman during childbirth. Both methods require *knowledge* of how each approach can be used as well as *planning* on ways to incorporate them into the support process during childbirth. Coach feedback can aid the woman in learning relaxation and paced breathing techniques during childbirth education classes. Coach feedback can also enhance her ability to use these skills during childbirth. The ability of the coach to provide immediate, clear, objective information is crucial to the success of this approach.

The ability to accurately assess the state of relaxation is a valuable and essential skill for both the childbirth educator and the labor coach. A study conducted by Humenick and Marchbanks[20] indicated that childbirth educators have the potential to be as accurate as an EMG machine in determining the woman's degree of relaxation. If relaxation levels can be accurately assessed by noninstrumented means, verbal feedback is possible. Developing skill in assessing the status of relaxation of the pregnant woman and examining how this skill can be taught most effectively to labor coaches is an area that deserves high priority for the childbirth educator.

Two other studies used nonpregnant subjects in examining the effectiveness of some labor strategies in dealing with pain. Although cold pressor pain using an ice bath is not the same as labor pain, both studies found that coach feedback coupled with other strategies was most effective.[37,38]

Verbal Feedback. In order to be most effective, verbal feedback must be specifically tailored for the individual pregnant woman. Words can be used to create mental pictures of the desired action and thus assist the body in carrying out the desired activity. In addition, voice quality can influence the emotional state of all individuals involved in the childbirth experience. A low-pitched, soothing tone of voice with information presented slowly and definitely conveys calm and confidence. It should be used rather than a high-pitched, harsh voice with information presented in a rapid-fire manner, which often conveys panic and lack of confidence.

In labor, some women find that moaning, verbalization, or screaming is effective in releasing tension. However, this behavior is often viewed as negative by labor attendants. Indeed, our society generally frowns on this response in labor. Negative feedback from labor attendants increases the woman's fears and influences her sense of self-esteem. The laboring woman can direct this verbal release mechanism into purposeful rhythmic moaning or verbalization (as in autogenic training). This can provide the needed release, as well as increase relaxation. The woman's own voice serves as her feedback system.

Touch Feedback. In order to be soothing and promote relaxation, touch must be provided with hands that are warm and that contour to the body part being touched. Touch communicates powerful messages, and persons working with the laboring woman need to be aware of the messages of feedback that are being sent. For example, touch that is soft or slow-moving with a firm pressure typically sends a message of calm while gripping, kneading, or fast movements usually communicate panic and fear.

Respiration Awareness Feedback. Breath awareness has been used by many disciplines (Yoga, Zen) to facilitate relaxation and body awareness. It seems that there is a direct relationship between inhalation and the sympathetic nervous system and exhalation and the parasympathetic nervous system. When one breathes in through the nose, receptors pick up turbulence or the lack of it and that information is processed to the brain. If the breathing is rapid and turbulent, the sympathetic nervous system is aroused and the body begins to ready itself for fight or flight. Conversely, if the breathing is quiet and gentle, reflecting low level of arousal or no turbulence, the parasympathetic nervous system will be stimulated and the relaxation response evoked.[27] Researchers found that when subjects listened to their own amplified breath sounds, they achieved better relaxation than when receiving verbal feedback or direction.[27]

Respiration is a factor in achieving a meditative

state of mind. This meditative state may help laboring women view their contractions as positive, powerful, and a part of themselves rather than imposed from the outside.[29] This mind-set could affect pain interpretation and both internal and external response to it, thus setting in motion a psychological feedback loop. One can view the feedback system inherent in respiration as a key mediating factor in the mind-body paradigm and therefore an essential factor in the search for relaxation mastery.

Body Awareness Feedback. An awareness of body responses and internal feedback systems can enhance relaxation skills. For example, one way for people to relieve tension by using internal feedback systems is to consciously slow and calm their breathing. Being aware of the subtle internal processes in our own bodies requires a quiet state of body awareness that is often at odds with our rushed, modern, "fast food" approach to life.

Body awareness learned via relaxation techniques can help mediate anxiety when it is expressed as muscle tension. Likewise, labor position has been noted to affect the progress of labor and the perception of pain, either positively or negatively.[9] The woman who knows how to use her body appropriately to enhance progress and reduce pain is utilizing positive internal feedback systems that will assist her to have a sense of mastery of the birth process.

Visual Feedback. During labor, an electronic fetal monitor can serve as a visual feedback system for the laboring woman. Often the electronic fetal monitor indicates the beginning of a contraction before the woman is consciously aware of it: this feedback can help her to work with the contraction from its inception.[11]

The expulsive stage of labor is also a time when visual feedback can be beneficial to the laboring woman. Coordinating breath exchange, downward thrust, and muscle activity in order to efficiently move the baby down the birth canal can present a real challenge. The use of visual feedback via a mirror, internal visual feedback (imagery) to "see" the baby moving through the mechanism of labor, or verbal feedback can assist in coordinating these efforts.

Childbirth and Biofeedback

Physiological responses to painful stimuli during childbirth may include skeletal muscle contraction, vasoconstriction, cardiovascular changes, endocrine and visceral responses, as well as outward manifestations such as grimacing, moaning, screaming, and verbalization.[5] These responses tend to influence both labor progress and perception of pain. When fear or pain causes a fight-or-flight response, secretion of the catecholamines epinephrine and norepinephrine increases, and these substances tend to decrease uterine circulation and contractions and hence slow labor progress.[5,14,25]

Women who feel in active control of their lives in general also tend to take control of their actions and behavior in labor and view their contractions as part of themselves.[29] Humenick[21,22] also proposed that women who feel that they have actively participated in their child's birth may show an increased tendency of active control (independence, decisiveness, and confidence) in their lives and thus increased self-esteem. Hypothetically, this could influence how a woman approaches the task of parenting. Biofeedback approaches which include respiration, relaxation, and focusing and imagery skills to reduce fear and anxiety, appropriate labor positions to enhance the labor process and reduce pain, and stimulating of the parasympathetic nervous system and reduction in catecholamine production all contribute to the maintenance of homeostasis.

IMPLICATIONS FOR PRACTICE

Designing an effective childbirth education relaxation program utilizing biofeedback principles requires teaching these skills in a progressive manner. The skills are taught moving from basic to advanced levels, with practice and mastery of skills both emphasized and modeled during classes.[23] As clients note that relaxation, in varied forms, is being presented and practiced throughout the class series, they will be more likely to also place importance on practice of these skills.

Since feedback, in order to be effective, must be immediate and objective, instructors need to be able to observe each couple in order to determine if skill development is occurring, and if not to assist them either in class or by arranging additional help outside of class. Throughout the class series, *attitude feedback* is critical to fostering a positive mind-set of the expectant couple and conveying to them that they have the necessary skills to meet the challenge of childbirth.

> The primary function of biofeedback is to help us tune into our bodies and in so doing reestablish the natural internal harmony that is synonymous with good health.
>
> ROBERT STERN and WILLIAM RAY[1]
>
> Biofeedback is only a learning tool. The aim of training is to learn to produce the state and sense its presence, and then reproduce it without the instrument.
>
> DANIEL GIRDANO and GEORGE EVERLY[2]
>
> One explanation for the action of biofeedback is that it deploys attention away from ego-centered, stress-producing consciousness . . . The feedback and/or the [process or event] it represents becomes the focus of attention.
>
> DANIEL GIRDANO and GEORGE EVERLY[2]

Sequencing of Relaxation Skills

The sequencing of relaxation skills in the classroom will vary to some degree with each instructor depending on her clients, curriculum, and the setting in which classes are taught. The childbirth educator needs to evaluate the vast amount of information often deemed ''essential'' in terms of whether it requires class discussion or could be effectively covered in another manner, such as outside reading. *The maximum amount of class time possible should be used for in-class skills work.*[21]

Beginning skills must be mastered before moving on to more advanced skills (Table 9–4). Class members may enter classes already having mastered some stress reduction skills, and some groups will make faster progress than others. Evaluation of beginning skill levels, then, will be important for the instructor. One means of obtaining that information prior to the start of the class series is with a registration questionnaire or a pre-class phone call. The information could also be elicited as the couples sign in at the first class meeting.

By the time clients have finished the first four or five classes, they should have developed the ability to combine and transfer skills. For example, neuromuscular dissociation skills can be transferred through practice by first contracting body parts to practice later with a pain stimulus. Pressure on a large muscle group, such as the quadriceps, can be used as a pain stimulus to simulate a contraction while practicing pain management skills such as relaxation, focusing, and paced breathing. This provides students with an opportunity to identify strengths and weaknesses and see how skills learned separately fit together. The pain stimulus does not need to be used frequently; rather, its value is its use as an indicator of progress.

Learning Self-Awareness

During this phase, the emphasis is on body awareness feedback and respiration awareness feedback. These are integrated throughout the class

TABLE 9–4. RECOMMENDATIONS FOR FEEDBACK SKILL SEQUENCE

Class I	Progressive relaxation (Bressler style) Progressive neuromuscular relaxation (Contract/Release)
Class II	Review previous skills Introduce touch relaxation and coaching Introduce neuromuscular dissociation skills
Class III	Review previous skills Introduce touch and verbal feedback components of neuromuscular dissociation Introduce imagery
Class IV	Review previous skills Introduce the Neuromuscular Dissociation Relaxation Rating Scale (NDRRS)[20] Introduce temperature feedback Introduce autogenic training phrases
Class V	Introduce concept of transfer and combining skills during review
Class VI	Review all skills (incorporate into labor rehearsal)

sessions. Self-awareness skills begin in class I as progressive relaxation is taught. Noting how muscles feel when being stretched or contracted, as well as describing the sensations of relaxation after a progressive relaxation exercise without the tensing and releasing component such as Bressler's conditioned relaxation,[7] sets in motion a beginning biofeedback loop.

The next step, after allowing time for home practice of progressive and contract-release skills and observation for mastery, may be to add coach touch in a progressive fashion to elicit relaxation. This skill requires information from the teacher about what relaxation looks like and information about how to touch. It also requires information from the pregnant women to their coaches about when touch is soothing, comforting, and relaxing and when it is not.

There is also a vocabulary component in which the coach is helped to develop a repertoire of words that will provide descriptive feedback about how a body part feels when tense and when released. The vocabulary must be specifically tailored for a particular couple so that descriptive terms enhance rather than detract from relaxation. Words that help create mind pictures such as heavy, soft, mushy, warm, and so on as opposed to ''relaxed'' or ''released,'' which describe the endpoint of the action, can be useful. Emphasis must be placed on making the terminology objective as opposed to subjective, and thus avoiding the emotional component that could detract from the effectiveness of this feedback.[20] (''Let your arm become soft and heavy'' as opposed to ''You're not relaxed.'') Using this approach in class first to model appropriate terminology, then giving a homework assignment to develop a list of three to five descriptive terms and ranking them in value is effective. Sharing the lists in class helps reinforce both use and importance of the activity.

Developing Skill

During this phase, the emphasis is on coach feedback, touch feedback, verbal feedback, and visual feedback. Temperature feedback can also be used to improve the ability to achieve a state of relaxation.

Progressing to the next skill level builds on the information the couple has now developed about how their bodies feel when muscles are contracted or relaxed. Neuromuscular dissociation skills require the ability to tense certain part(s) of the body while maintaining relaxation in the rest of the body and is an advanced skill. Again, progressing from the simple to the complex is appropriate. An example is using single body parts and then multiple body parts, and using one side of the body before practicing with the opposite side.

Coach Feedback. The coach can add touch and verbal feedback during the practice of relaxation skills. Also, when determining the degree of relaxation, the coach could rate the relaxation of a body part on a scale of 0 to 5.[20] The next step is to add touch and vocabulary to try to increase re-

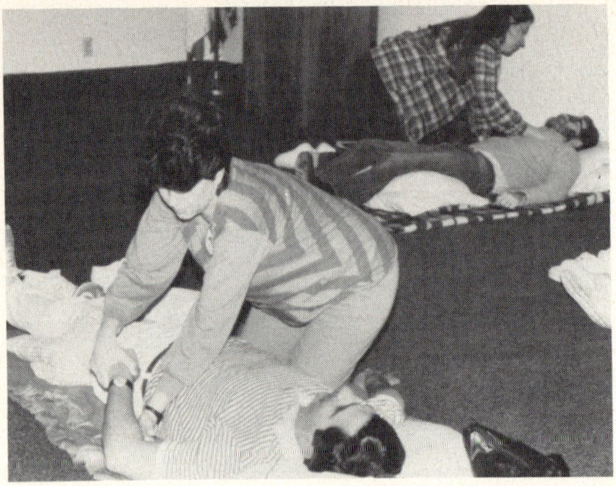

Role reversal assists the pregnant woman's coach to develop an awareness of the difficulty involved in learning relaxation techniques and in how both invasive and soothing touching feels. (Photo by Marjorie Pyle,© Lifecircle, Costa Mesa, CA.)

laxation and rate the part again. Both coach and pregnant woman could rate the part (helping her to increase her awareness skills), and then compare the direction of their ratings, e.g., toward or away from increased relaxation. Feedback from the instructor might be verbal. However, if difficulties are present, the instructor may use her hands over those of the coach to model appropriate touching activities.

Role Reversal. Role reversal, in which the pregnant woman assumes the role of the coach and the coach practices relaxation skills, is helpful, particularly when introducing touch and neuromuscular dissociation skills. Role reversal assists the coach to develop an awareness of the difficulty involved in learning relaxation techniques and in how both invasive and soothing touching feels.

Verbal Feedback. This is yet another approach that increases relaxation. The verbal component of autogenic training can be added to further support self-regulating mechanisms that counter the effects of stress.[32] The woman should be encouraged to use her own voice as a feedback tool, using positive phrases such as "I am calm," "My labor is progressing well," "My hands are warm," and "My body is relaxed." These rhythmic repetitions as well as the content of the phrases can have a relaxing, soothing effect.

Visual Feedback. Expectant parents can use visual feedback strategies to facilitate the dilation of the cervix and promote the progression of labor. The childbirth educator can discuss how to use different types of visual feedback: a fetal monitor, a mirror during the birth process, and internal visual feedback using imagery skills. Incorporating these concepts into a labor rehearsal is also valuable.

Temperature Feedback. The use of temperature feedback can be added by the use of finger or wrist bands or Biodots. These are inexpensive to use and can be useful aids in seeing temperature changes that occur while practicing relaxation techniques. Their use in class can be fun and can also help students identify stress periods in their daily lives and help them practice the stress reduction skills learned in class.

Using Multiple Approaches. Research supports the use of multiple approaches.[39] Clients should practice many skills but should be encouraged to choose the ones that suit them best in their particular situation. Labor is an ever-changing process and an approach that works well during one phase may not be effective during another phase (Table 9–5).

Developing Awareness of Other Feedback Systems. Assisting students to identify feedback systems during the series of classes helps them apply the knowledge they are gaining. Fatigue, for instance, serves to validate the internal work of pregnancy[29] and in late pregnancy may be an alerting factor to slow down the activity level. Having expectant parents monitor stress during the week and consciously deal with it using relaxation and breathing strategies which have been learned and practiced during classes further reinforces classroom activities.

Determining Mastery

Assessing for mastery of relaxation skills may be done in a variety of ways. Visual assessment will reveal slow, quiet breathing with slack jaws. There is a smoothing of the facial muscles and some resemblance to peaceful sleep. As legs relax, feet turn out at a 45-degree angle to each other.[33] When touched, muscles feel loose, limbs are heavy but pliable, and joints move through the range of motion easily.

TABLE 9–5. LABOR FEEDBACK TOOLS

TYPE	WHO	APPLICATION
Touch	Laboring woman Coach/birth attendants	Effleurage Touch relaxation, massage
Verbal	Laboring woman Coach/birth attendants	Rhythmic phrases, moaning Timing contractions, positive feedback
Visual	Laboring woman Coach/birth attendants	Imagery, electronic fetal monitor Mirrors in delivery room; facial/body language
Respiration Awareness	Laboring woman	Focusing on sound of breathing
Body Awareness	Laboring woman	Focusing on tensing muscles and relaxing them; changing position to achieve comfort
Attitude	Laboring woman Coach/Birth attendants	Positive mind-set Reflect positive attitude, confidence, and calmness to laboring woman
Temperature	Laboring woman	Biodots, finger or wrist bands

Feedback and Birth Attendants

Birth attendants can use the various types of feedback to increase the laboring woman's comfort and progress during childbirth. The childbirth educator can provide inservice education for the birth agency staff on the skills and techniques that are taught in childbirth education classes, and demonstrate how staff can provide accurate and effective feedback to the woman during childbirth. An informed staff will ease the transition of couples from the classroom to the birthing agency setting and increase the use and effectiveness of feedback during childbirth.

IMPLICATIONS FOR RESEARCH

In the area of childbirth education, the critical question today for biofeedback is determining the effectiveness of the various methods for *learning* the skill of relaxation and for *improving* the degree of relaxation during childbirth. Much of the previous research needs to be replicated using carefully controlled designs and large samples to validate previous findings. Some of the current research suggests that length and frequency of the use of instrumented biofeedback may influence the effectiveness of this approach; this also warrants investigation. Additional research is needed to answer the following questions:

- Do biofeedback-trained women maintain a higher degree of relaxation during childbirth than women who do not receive biofeedback training?
- Are noninstrumented modes of biofeedback just as effective as instrumented modes of biofeedback in learning relaxation during childbirth education classes?
- What is the most effective way of teaching noninstrumented modes of biofeedback to expectant couples in class?
- Which method of noninstrumented feedback is most effective in the development of relaxation?
- Does a combination of feedback methods work best or is a single method of greater benefit?
- Which students would benefit most from the use of instrumented modes of biofeedback?
- Can a coach or childbirth educator learn to determine the state of relaxation as effectively as EMG or other biofeedback equipment?

- Which type of feedback is most effective in helping the pregnant woman learn to achieve a state of relaxation during classes?
- Which type of feedback is most effective in helping the pregnant woman maintain a state of relaxation during childbirth?
- Which type of feedback is most effective during the expulsion stage of childbirth?
- Does learning biofeedback principles for childbirth help expectant parents to think and act in a more healthy manner?

SUMMARY

Biofeedback is useful in helping expectant parents learn the skill of relaxation as well as achieving a deeper state of relaxation during childbirth. During the expulsion stage of labor, biofeedback assists the woman to push more effectively with contractions. During classes, childbirth educators can help their clients become more aware of internal body processes, to "listen" for changes that are occurring, and to select responses that promote health and well-being. These skills are important in preparing for childbirth and for stress management throughout life.

References

1. Basmajian, J. V. *Biofeedback Principles and Practice for Clinicians*. Williams and Wilkins, 1983.
2. Benson, H. *The Relaxation Response*. New York: Avon Books, 1976.
3. Bing, E. *Six Practical Lessons for an Easier Childbirth*. New York: Grosset and Dunlap, 1977.
4. Birk, L. *Biofeedback: Behavioral Medicine*. New York: Grune & Stratton, 1973.
5. Bonica, J. *Obstetrical Analgesia and Anesthesia*. Amsterdam: World Federation of Societies of Anesthesiologists, 1980.
6. Bowles, C. et al. EMG biofeedback and progressive relaxation training: a comparative study of two groups of normal subjects. *Western Journal of Nursing Research* 1:3, 1979.
7. Bresler, D. *Free Yourself from Pain*. New York: Simon and Schuster, 1979.
8. Brown, B. *Stress and the Art of Biofeedback*. New York: Bantam Books, 1977.
9. Carr, C. Obstetric practices which protect against neonatal morbidity: Focus on maternal position in labor and birth. *Birth and the Family Journal* 7:249, 1980.
10. Chabon, I. *Awake and Aware*. New York: Dell Books, 1966.
11. DiFranco, J. Adaptive biofeedback. *In* Humenick, S. (ed.): *Expanding Horizons in Childbirth Education*. Washington, DC: ASPO/Lamaze, 1983.
12. Farrell, R. Biofeedback as an aid to relaxation in natural childbirth. (Doctoral dissertation, University of California at Irvine, 1981.) *Dissertation Abstracts International 42*:1148B.
13. Fehring, R. Effects of biofeedback-aided relaxation on the psychological stress symptoms of college students. *Nursing Research* 32:362, 1983.
14. Fox, H. The effects of catecholamines and drug treatment on the fetus and newborn. *Birth and the Family Journal* 6:157, 1979.
15. Grad, R. The effect of electromyographic biofeedback assisted relaxation training on the experience of childbirth. (Doctoral dissertation, University of Maryland, 1980,) *Dissertation Abstracts International* 42:562B.
16. Gregg, R. Biofeedback relaxation training effects in childbirth. *Behavioral Engineering* 4:57, 1978.
17. Green, E., and Green, A. Biofeedback and transformation. *In* Kunz, D.: *Spiritual Aspects of the Healing Arts*. Wheaton, IL: Quest Books, 1985.
18. Green, E., and Green, A. *Beyond Biofeedback*. New York, Delacorte Press/Seymour Lawrence, 1977.
19. Humenick, S. (ed.) *Expanding Horizons in Childbirth Education*. Washington, D.C.: ASPO/Lamaze, 1983.
20. Humenick, S., and Marchbanks, P. Validation of a scale to measure relaxation in childbirth education classes. *Birth and the Family Journal* 8:145, 1981.
21. Humenick, S. Mastery, the key to birth satisfaction: a review. *Birth and the Family Journal* 8:79, 1981.
22. Humenick, S., and Burgen, L. Mastery, the key to birth satisfaction: a study. *Birth and the Family Journal* 8:84, 1981.
23. Humenick, S. Teaching relaxation. *Childbirth Educator* 3:47, 1984.
24. Jones, G., and Evans, P. Effectiveness of frontalis feedback training in producing general body relaxation. *Biological Psychology* 12:313, 1981.
25. Levinson, G., and Schnider, S. Catecholamines: the effects of maternal fear and its treatment on uterine function and circulation. *Birth and the Family Journal* 6:167, 1979.

26. McCaffrey, M. The nurse's contribution to pain relief during labor. *In* Reader, S., Mastroanni, L., Martin, L. (eds.): *Maternity Nursing,* 15th ed. Philadelphia: J.B. Lippincott, 1983.
27. Nurenberger, P. *Freedom from Stress*. Honesdale, PA: Himalayan International Institute of Yoga Science and Philosophy, 1981.
28. Olton, D., and Noonberg, A. *Biofeedback Clinical Applications in Behavioral Medicine*. Englewood Cliffs, NJ: Prentice-Hall, 1980.
29. Peterson, G.: *Birthing Normally: A Personal Growth Approach to Childbirth*. Berkeley: Mind-Body Press, 1981.
30. Reynolds, S.B. Biofeedback, relaxation training, and music: Homeostasis for coping with stress. *Biofeedback and Self-Regulation* 9:169, 1984.
31. Runck, B. *Biofeedback Issues in Treatment Assessment*. Rockville, MD: U.S. Department of Health and Human Services, National Institute of Mental Health, 1980.
32. Shapiro, S., and Lehrer, P. Psychophysiological effects of autogenic training and progressive relaxation. *Biofeedback and Self-Regulation* 5:249, 1980.
33. Snyder, M. Progressive relaxation as a nursing intervention: An analysis. *Advances in Nursing Science* 6:47, 1984.
34. St. James-Roberts, I., Hutchinson, C., Haran, F., and Chamberlain, G. Biofeedback as an aid to childbirth. *British Journal of Obstetrics and Gynecology* 90:56, 1983.
35. Steger, J., and Harper, R. Comprehensive biofeedback versus self-monitored relaxation in the treatment of tension headache. *Headache* 18:137, 1980.
36. Stern, R., and Ray, W. *Biofeedback: Potential Limits*. Lincoln: University of Nebraska Press, 1977.
37. Stevens, R.J., and Heide, F. Analgesic characteristics of prepared childbirth techniques: Attention focusing and systematic relaxation. *Journal of Psychosomatic Research* 21:429, 1977.
38. Worthington, E., et al. Which prepared childbirth coping strategies are effective? *JOGN Nursing* 11:45, 1982.
39. Yorde, S., and Witmer, J. M. Educational format for teaching stress management to groups with a wide range of stress symptoms. *Biofeedback and Self-Regulation* 5:75, 1980.

Beginning Quote

Green, E., and Green, A. Biofeedback and transformation. *In* Kunz, D.: *Spiritual Aspects of the Healing Arts*. Wheaton, IL: Quest Books, 1985.

Boxed Quotes

1. Stern, R. M. and Ray, W. J. *Biofeedback: Potential & Limits*. Lincoln, NE: University of Nebraska Press, 1977.
2. Girdano, D., and Everly, G. *Controlling Stress and Tension: A Holistic Approach*. Englewood Cliffs, NJ: Prentice Hall, 1979, pp. 165, 186.

chapter 10

RELAXATION: Therapeutic Touch

JUDITH A. LOTHIAN

The therapeutic use of hands, therefore, appears to be a universal human act: however, it is an act that we have all but forgotten in this scientific age in our adulation of things mechanical, synthetic, and frequently antihuman.

Dolores Krieger

Therapeutic Touch may offer a powerful, noninvasive means of enhancing relaxation, reducing anxiety, and controlling pain. Originally described by Dolores Krieger, a nurse, therapeutic touch is derived from the ancient art of the laying-on of hands. Krieger believes that the universality of laying-on of hands is a fundamental characteristic of people and therefore using hands to help or heal is a natural human potential.[8] Unlike the laying-on of hands, Therapeutic Touch has no religious basis and does not require a declaration of faith from the subject to be effective.[14] It does, however, require the conscious intent of the healer.

"Gestalt-field theory" is the conceptual framework for understanding Therapeutic Touch (see p. 421). Rogers proposes that both man and his environment are energy fields that mutually interact. Healing occurs when one of these energy fields moves in the direction of change while interacting with the other.[20] This view of the world is consistent with modern theoretical physics, Eastern mysticism, and ancient philosophy. In Eastern literature, energy fields are described as *prana,** the life force that flows through the body. Prana is thought to be present in excess in healthy people and deficient in the ill.[14] Healing with Therapeutic Touch is believed to entail the channeling of this energy flow (prana) by the healer for the well-being of the patient. Because we are open systems—that is, mutually interacting systems—the healer may be affected by the healing process also. The healer

*Energy fields are also called "chi" and "ki" by different philosophical or cultural groups.

usually describes a greater sense of inner harmony, while the subject experiences relaxation, flushing, and warmth. The transfer of energy is thought to act as a "booster" to the ill person's own recuperative system.

Therapeutic Touch has been reported to increase human hemoglobin levels,[10] increase the predominance of alpha activity in the brain wave pattern,[9] decrease the state of anxiety,[6,18] decrease pain,[3] and cause a state of generalized relaxation similar to the relaxation response as described by Benson.[9,19] Discomfort, tension, pain, and anxiety are major manifestations in pregnancy, childbirth, and parenting; therefore, Therapeutic Touch may be an effective strategy to integrate with health care of the childbearing family.

REVIEW OF THE LITERATURE

Research in the late 1950's by Grad, a biochemist, and Estabany, a Hungarian immigrant who healed by using touch, demonstrated that wound healing in mice was significantly speeded up in those subjects treated by Estabany's healing touch.[5] In another study, plants watered with water that had been "treated" by Estabany showed increased growth.[4] Smith found that test tubes containing enzyme solution when held by Estabany showed 15 per cent more enzyme activity than those that were not "treated."[20]

Krieger became interested in Estabany's healing powers when she worked on a project with him. Krieger compared the hemoglobin levels of an experimental group of chronically ill individuals who had been treated by Estabany with a control group who had not received any treatment.[10] Pre- and post-test hemoglobin levels showed significant differences in the experimental group. However, Krieger's statistical analysis in the study has been criticized.[1] The study was replicated, controlling for factors thought to affect hemoglobin levels (smoking, yoga, and diet) and again showed significant differences between groups.[11]

Because of these observations, Krieger became convinced that the use of touch in healing is a natural human potential, and called the process "Therapeutic Touch." She described the healer as assuming a meditative state of consciousness and placing the hands on or close to the body of the person to be healed or helped. The healer then "passively listens" with her hands as she scans the body of the patient and gently "attunes" to his or her condition . . . she places her hands over the areas of tension in the patient's body and redirects these energies.[9]

In her studies Krieger found that Therapeutic Touch increased hemoglobin levels[12] and caused a generalized state of relaxation as measured by galvanic skin response, temperature, heart rate, and self-evaluation.[9] Heidt[6] studied the effect of Therapeutic Touch, casual touch, and no touch on the anxiety level of patients in a cardiovascular unit. Subjects who received intervention by Therapeutic Touch had a reduction in post-test state anxiety greater than that seen with casual touch or no touch. In Heidt's study, Therapeutic Touch involved contact.

Quinn[18] replicated Heidt's study using Therapeutic Touch as it is usually practiced—that is, without actual physical contact. Using nurses with several years of experience with Therapeutic Touch, she standardized a treatment called *noncontact Therapeutic Touch* in which the healer's hands are held two to four inches from the subject's body. Subjects who were hospitalized with cardiovascular disease were assigned to either an experimental or control group and compared on the level of acute anxiety. Subjects in the experimental group were treated with noncontact Therapeutic Touch. Subjects in the control group were treated by a second group of nurses with no knowledge of Therapeutic Touch who mimicked the physical actions of the nurses using noncontact Therapeutic Touch. However, their treatment did not include the meditative (centered) state of consciousness, a specific intent to assist the patient, using Therapeutic Touch or a belief in energy exchange between healer and subject. The experimental group showed a significant decrease in anxiety after treatment. This study supported not only the effect of Therapeutic Touch on anxiety but also that no physical contact needs to take place for Therapeutic Touch to be effective.

Not all reports on this modality have been so positive, however, and two recent studies have failed to support its efficacy. In research for her doctoral dissertation, Connell[3] showed that although patients experiencing acute pain did not receive statistically significant pain reduction from Therapeutic Touch, their experience was in the direction of decreased pain. Randolph[19] found that women exposed to a stressful stimulus and treated with Therapeutic Touch did not remain more relaxed than those who simply experienced physical contact.

Keller and Bzdek investigated the effects of Therapeutic Touch and a placebo simulation of Therapeutic Touch.[7] The Therapeutic Touch group experienced a significant sustained reduction in headache pain. Over a four-hour period, the treatment group sustained a 70 per cent pain reduction, about twice the average pain reduction in the control group.

Clark and Clark[1] in "Therapeutic Touch: Is there a scientific basis for practice?" critically reviewed the research on Therapeutic Touch to date. They raise important questions as to the research design, sample selection, control of extraneous variables, and appropriateness of the statistics used in the studies reported by Grad[4,5] and Krieger,[8–15] and also by Smith.[21]

Recent studies by Heidt,[6] Quinn,[18] and Connell[2,3] are more rigorously controlled, but Clark and Clark express concern about the placebo effect. Randolph's[19] double-blind design reduces the possibility of a placebo effect, but Randolph's study did not support an effect from Therapeutic Touch. The result of Keller and Bzdek's[7] study indicated that Therapeutic Touch may have potential beyond the placebo effect in the treatment of tension headache pain.

Philosopher Renee Weber points out that concern with the placebo effect is legitimate if our theoretical framework is the physical-sensory model.[22] Field theory, an open system view of the world, however, is the framework for understanding Therapeutic Touch. Within this system Weber suggests the so-called placebo effect may be an instance of, and indeed evidence for, field interactions. To attribute change to the placebo effect rather than Therapeutic Touch is begging the question.

Studies involving Therapeutic Touch are summarized in Table 10–1. There is some empirical evidence to support the value and use of Therapeutic Touch. In spite of this limited empirical support, interest in and practice of Therapeutic Touch is increasing. The centuries-old tradition of helping by laying-on of hands and the day-to-day successes of therapeutic touch, although not well documented, seem to be largely responsible for the phenomenon.

IMPLICATIONS FOR PRACTICE

Although our current understanding of the how and why of Therapeutic Touch suggests that it is a complex phenomenon, it is relatively simple to teach and to learn. The well-being of both the healer and the subject is usually enhanced in the process of Therapeutic Touch. When added to the demonstrated potential of Therapeutic Touch for reducing anxiety and pain and enhancing relaxation, these features suggest it as a strategy of value for the childbearing family as well as the childbirth educator, nurse, and other members of the health care team.

Knowing and using Therapeutic Touch help the midwife, nurse, physician, and childbirth educator to reduce the client's stress, anxiety, discomfort, and pain. The pregnant woman and her support network can be taught Therapeutic Touch and encouraged to use it as a way of enhancing relaxation,

TABLE 10–1. STUDIES ON THE EFFECTS OF THERAPEUTIC TOUCH (TT)

RESEARCHER	DESCRIPTION	RESULTS
Grad, Cadoret, Paul, 1961[5]	Effect of healing touch on wound healing time. Experimental design: random assignment to 3 groups (2 different healers and 1 control) (N = 300)	Statistically significant, but transient rise in rate on healing in treated mice
Grad, 1963[4]	Effect of healing touch on growth of barley seeds. Double-blind, experimental design: peat pots with 20 barley seeds each randomly assigned to 2 groups, 1% saline solution used to water experimental group (N = 24)	Taller plants and greater yield for 5 days in treated seeds; results transient
Smith, 1971[21]	Effect of healing touch, magnetic field, ultraviolet light, and touch on activity of enzyme trypsin. Experimental design: 3 treatment groups and 1 control group	Rise in enzyme activity with healing touch and magnetic field; no statistical testing for significance of differences
Krieger, 1972[10]	Effect of TT on hemoglobin levels (N = 28)	Significant rise in hemoglobin levels in experimental group
Krieger, 1976[10]	Effect of TT on hemoglobin levels (N = 76). Quasiexperimental design: 2 groups, 1 control and 1 treated with TT; no random assignment and no control for extraneous variables	Significant rise in hemoglobin levels in experimental group
Krieger, 1979[9]	Effect of TT on relaxation as measured by galvanic skin response, temperature, heart rate, self evaluation. Descriptive design, actual numerical results are not reported	Subjects demonstrated relaxation response as measured after treatment. No statistical tests done
Heidt, 1981[6]	Effect of TT, casual touch or no touch on anxiety level of hospitalized cardiovascular patients (N = 90). Quasiexperimental design: 3 matched intervention groups, state anxiety measured pre- and post-treatment with self-evaluation questionnaire	Significantly lower levels of anxiety with TT ($p < 0.01$)
Randolph, 1980[19]	Effect of TT and casual touch on anxiety levels of subjects watching stressful movie (N = 60). Double-blind, experimental design, only examined directing energy, 1st study done with a healthy population	No significant differences in anxiety levels with TT
Quinn, 1984[18]	Effect on noncontact TT vs. noncontact imitation of TT on anxiety levels of hospitalized cardiovascular patients (N = 60). Experimental design: replication of Heidt's study with noncontact TT using 2 groups	Significantly lower state of anxiety with TT ($p < 0.0005$)
Connell, 1984[18]	Effect of TT on postoperative abdominal pain	Decrease in pain but not significant
Keller, Bzdek, 1986[7]	Effect of TT vs. placebo touch on tension headache (N = 60). Experimental design: college students with tension headaches randomly assigned to treatment and placebo groups; McGill-Melzack Pain Questionnaire was given pre- and post-treatment and 4 hours later	Significant decrease in pain ($p < 0.0001$) in TT group; significantly greater decrease in TT group than placebo touch group ($p < 0.01$)

> The safety level of Therapeutic Touch for both healer and healee has been excellent, and this accounts for much of its enthusiastic acceptance. It is a holistic act and its practice can be a significant growth experience ... There are still many unknowns about the dyadic interaction between healer and healee, and intelligent caution is a wise stance. For myself, I still pursue the question, "Why is touch therapeutic?"
>
> DOLORES KRIEGER[1]
>
> During labor it [Therapeutic Touch] was one more tool to help us both cope ... It seemed to help me relax and roll with the contractions.
>
> A NEW MOTHER
>
> When things got tough during labor I did Therapeutic Touch ... My wife didn't want to be actually touched so it was a great way to help her relax.
>
> A NEW FATHER

alleviating the common discomforts of pregnancy, and increasing communication. It is especially helpful for couples who are uncomfortable with physical touch. During labor and birth Therapeutic Touch can be used along with breathing, other relaxation strategies, and concentration to enhance relaxation, decrease pain, and increase communication. In the early months of parenting it is a strategy for calming a crying baby, a distraught wife, or a "blue" mother. The ability to "center" and to elicit the relaxation response through Therapeutic Touch may reduce breastfeeding difficulties.

Perhaps the greatest advantage of Therapeutic Touch is the potential for the healer to be intimately affected in the process. Using Therapeutic Touch is said to enhance the healer's sense of inner harmony, well-being, and relaxation. Instead of becoming emotionally and physically drained, the healer (partner, labor coach, nurse, midwife, childbirth educator, or the mother herself) feels more "whole." It becomes an important way for us to cope at the same time that we are helping. Each of these potential uses of Therapeutic Touch and practical methods for including them in classes is discussed in detail.

Learning Therapeutic Touch

The childbirth educator must first become personally familiar with the techniques and effectiveness of Therapeutic Touch before she can be comfortable teaching it in her classes. Krieger, in *The Therapeutic Touch: How to Use Your Hands to Help or Heal,*[14] describes simple exercises to use when learning to center, assess the energy field, and direct energy. The first step is doing these exercises, practicing Therapeutic Touch, and keeping a journal of your experiences (Box 10–1). Documenting subjective, intuitive feelings during the process of doing Therapeutic Touch as well as documenting how you feel (outcomes) and the effects on the subject is the foundation for increasing sensitivity. Because Therapeutic Touch is such a subjective, intuitive process, careful attention must be paid to feelings—physical and otherwise.

Integrating Therapeutic Touch into the curriculum of childbirth classes is not difficult. It is easily and successfully interwoven with relaxation and breathing strategies within the framework of classes. As with any new technique, beginning slowly, integrating material carefully, and evaluating outcomes is of utmost importance.

The Therapeutic Touch Process

There are four phases in the Therapeutic Touch process:

1. *Centering*. This is physically and psychologically finding within oneself an inner reference of stability. This is sometimes referred to as a *meditative state of consciousness*.
2. *Assessment*. Exercising the natural sensitivity of the hand to assess the energy field of the subject for indications of differences in the quality of energy flow.

3. *Unruffling the Field.* The subject's energy field that the healer may perceive as being nonflowing, sluggish, static or congested is mobilized. This is referred to as "unruffling the field," or freeing bound energy.
4. *Directing Energy.* The conscious direction of energy to assist the subject.

Centering

Centering, the first phase of the process and the most familiar to childbirth educators, is the most important. The concept of centering is much like "focus and relax." It involves focusing attention on releasing all tensions in the body and mind. It is introduced when relaxation is introduced, and it is reinforced as relaxation is practiced and taught in subsequent classes.

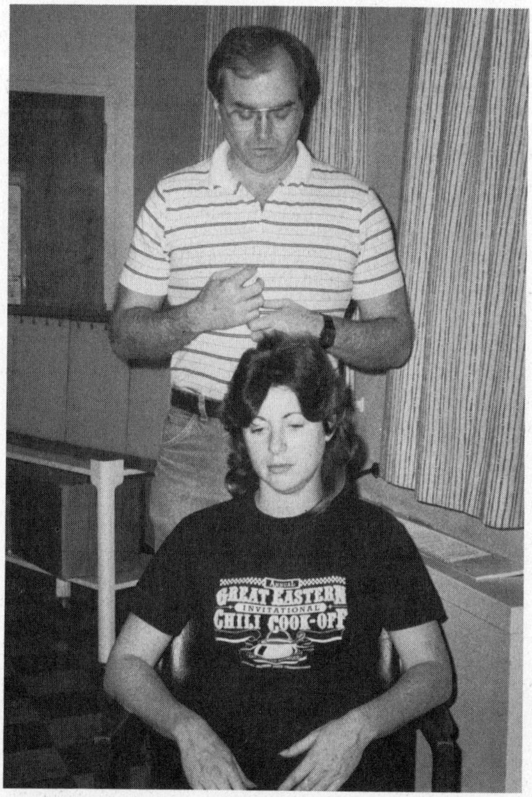

Centering. Preparing one's self physically and psychologically for the process of therapeutic touch. (Photo by Judith A. Lothian.)

Box 10–1

KEEPING A JOURNAL

While doing Therapeutic Touch be aware of how you are feeling subjectively. Look over these questions and use them as a guide. Write down your subjective experiences. Encourage students to share their subjective experiences during Therapeutic Touch and record them also.

1. How do you sense the external environment; i.e., is there any change in the way you perceive things and people about you?

2. Do you feel any different physiologically; i.e., are you aware of any change in heart or respiratory rate, muscle tonus, or energy flow?

3. How would you describe the way you get meaning from your experience; i.e., can you capture the internal dialogue in your head as you explain to yourself what your senses are telling you?

4. Do you notice any changes in your emotions; i.e., do you think you overreact, underreact, not react, react in an entirely different way than usual?

5. How do you use your memory; i.e., are you aware of a continuity of experience?

6. Are you aware of any change in your time sense; i.e., does time speed up or slow down?

7. What sense of identity have you; i.e., what role do you perceive yourself as acting?

8. Are there significant changes in your evaluative and cognitive processes; i.e., are there any important alterations in the rate, logic, or quality of your thought processes?

9. How do you relate to your body image; i.e., what feedback do you get from the movements, postures, and energetic flow of your body?

10. Do you interact differently with the environment; i.e., do you feel involved or detached from objects and living beings around you?

From Krieger, D. *The Therapeutic Touch: How to Use Your Hands to Help or Heal*. Englewood Cliffs, NJ: Prentice-Hall, 1979, pp. 39–40.

The childbirth educator may use the term "center" or simply remind clients to seek a comfortable position, take several deep breaths, and let go of physical and emotional tensions by allowing muscles to become looser and thoughts to flow freely through the mind until a sense of inner quiet has been achieved. While centering is a simple process, it is not easy for the uninitiated. Krieger's guidelines[14] for learning the physical and psychological aspects of centering will be helpful to expectant parents (Box 10–2). The childbirth educator should reassure her clients that this skill improves dramatically with experience. As clients gain skill in centering, they will become able to achieve what Krieger called "instant centering" (Box 10–3). Centering is a vital part of the relaxation techniques traditionally taught in childbirth classes.

Box 10–2

PHYSICAL AND PSYCHOLOGICAL ASPECTS OF CENTERING

1. Sit in a relaxed position, either in a chair or on the floor, so that your body is in alignment.

2. Either lay your hands comfortably on your lap if you are sitting on a chair, or fold you hands one on top the other if you are sitting on the floor or ground with your legs crossed.

3. Slowly move your body one to two inches from side to side two or three times so that when you stop you feel as though your spine is in postural alignment.

4. Now tilt your body back about one to two inches. This should be a comfortable position; your vertebrae should be aligned so that they easily carry the weight of your body.

5. Close your eyes and breathe slowly, evenly, and effortlessly.

6. Feel out—that is, become aware of—your tensions and purposefully relax them. This may be easiest to do upon exhalation.

7. Feel your body to be in balance.

8. Go more deeply within your consciousness. At each deeper level of consciousness, be aware of any tension and release that tension.

9. When you have attained a sense of inner equilibrium, you should feel that you can call upon your physical and psychodynamic energies to command and direct them as you wish—that is, you should feel that you are both aware and in control of your own dynamics.

From Krieger, D. *The Therapeutic Touch: How to Use Your Hands to Help or Heal.* Englewood Cliffs, NJ: Prentice-Hall, 1979, pp. 39–40.

Assessment

The second phase, assessment, is also a familiar one, for childbirth educators have long urged labor partners to look for signs of tension and relaxation. The assessment phase may be introduced when touch relaxation or acupressure massage is presented in class or at any time after the basics of progressive relaxation have been discussed and practiced by all class members. It may be helpful to have parents first experience the energy flow between the hands as described by Krieger.[14]

Experiencing the energy flow between the hands should facilitate the ability to notice differences in the body. The helper must first look closely at the subject, noticing signs of muscle tension, posture, and symmetry or lack of symmetry between one side of the body and the other. Next, the helper's hands are placed about two inches away from the skin and are moved slowly down the body from head to toe, feeling for differences between the left and right sides of the body. Differences might be noticed in terms of temperature, pressure, heaviness, or pushing sensations.

Unruffling the Field

Once the helper has assessed the subject's body, he or she may be encouraged to use the third phase of Therapeutic Touch, "brushing" or "unruffling" the field, for any areas of the body where differences were noted. This phase will probably be less familiar to most childbirth educators and expectant parents. To "unruffle" the field the childbirth educator should demonstrate and instruct the helper to move the hands in a sweeping motion from just above the area of difference toward the subject's feet, keeping the hands about two inches from the skin. The sweeping motion may be repeated several times. This phase seems to be particularly helpful in reducing tension, so the childbirth educator will want to discuss its possible usefulness during pregnancy and labor as the procedure is being practiced. When teaching the technique, the educator can also mention that unruffling the field seems to be especially helpful for soothing babies. She can reiterate this possible benefit when discussing the newborn and the parent-infant attachment process.

Directing Energy

The final phase of Therapeutic Touch is channeling energy from the universe to the subject. An essential part of this process is the *intent* of the helpers to assist or heal the subjects. Conscious intent to help is emphasized throughout the childbirth education course. Both the pregnant woman and her partner are given opportunities to take the role of helper. Such role reversal is a useful and widespread teaching strategy. Each time relaxation is taught, techniques for coping with the pain of contractions are practiced, or acupressure and other forms of touch are used, the childbirth educator should direct her clients to center themselves and then focus caring attention on their partners. Ideally

Box 10–3

INSTANT CENTERING

1. Sit comfortably, but in postural alignment, while doing this Test.

2. Relax. To assure this, I suggest that you check your favorite tension spots and relax those areas of your body. If your neck or shoulder muscles are in tension, strongly depress your shoulders—that is, push your shoulders down so that they are not hunched up toward your neck.

3. Inhale deeply and gently.

4. Slowly exhale.

5. Inhale again—and there you are! It is just here, in this state between breaths which you are now experiencing, that a state similar to the centering experience can be simulated. It is this state of balance, of equipoise, and of quietude that marks the experience of centering.

From Krieger, D. *The Therapeutic Touch: How to Use Your Hands to Help or Heal.* Englewood Cliffs, NJ: Prentice-Hall, 1979, pp. 40–41.

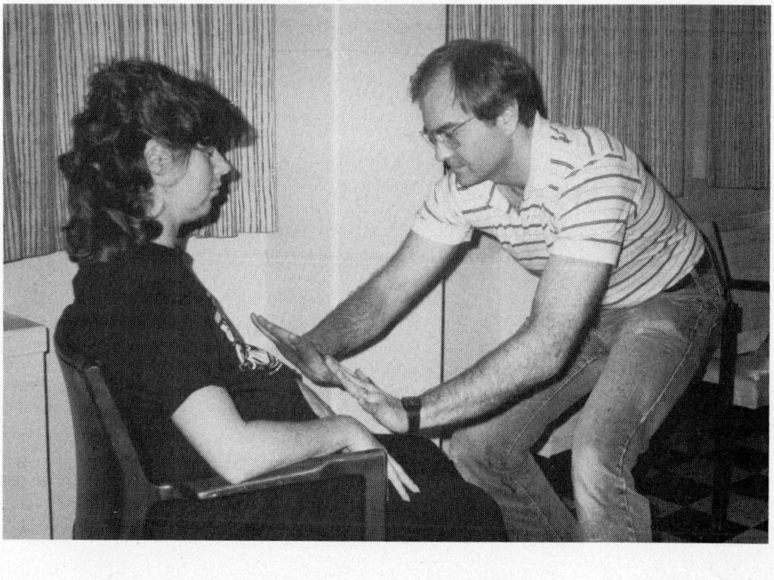

Assessment. Scanning the woman's energy field to determine differences in the quality of the energy flow. (Photo by Judith A. Lothian.)

Box 10–4

EXPERIENCING THE ENERGY FLOW

Therapeutic Touch
Self-Knowledge Test #1:
You Do Not Stop At Your Skin

The first experiential knowing which I'd like to share with you is that you can be consciously aware of the flow of energy into the "empty" space beyond the skin boundaries of your hands. It is very useful to capture first-time experiences as they happen, so, as you do these exercises, keep a pad and pencil handy so that you can take notes for later review.

1. The first step is to sit comfortably with both feet on the ground and simply place your hands so that the palms face each other. Hold your elbows away from the trunk of your body and do not rest your lower arms in your lap. Now bring your palms as close together as you can get them without having them touch each other, so that they are perhaps one-eighth to one-quarter inch apart.

2. The next step is to separate the palms of your hands by about two inches and then slowly bring them back to their original position, about one-eighth to one-quarter inch apart from one another.

3. Now separate your palms by about four inches and, again, slowly bring them back to their original position, as noted above.

4. Repeat this procedure. However, this time, separate your palms by about six inches. Keep your motions slow and steady. As you return your hands to their original position, notice if you begin to feel a build-up of pressure between your hands or if you feel any other significant sensation.

5. Once again separate your palms, this time until they are about eight inches apart. Do not immediately return your hands to their original position. Instead, as you bring your hands close together, at about every two inches, experience the pressure field you have built up by stopping for a moment and slowly trying to compress the field between your hands. You may experience this as a "bouncy" feeling.

6. Spend the next full minute in experiencing this field between your hands and try to determine what other characteristics of the field you feel besides the pressure and the bounciness or elasticity. At the end of the time, write down these other characteristics on a piece of paper.

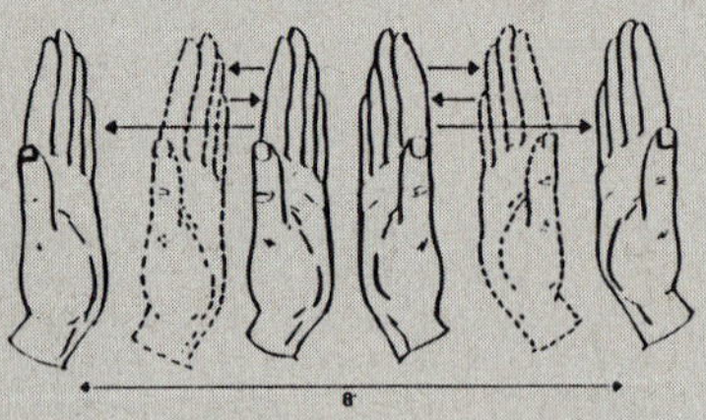

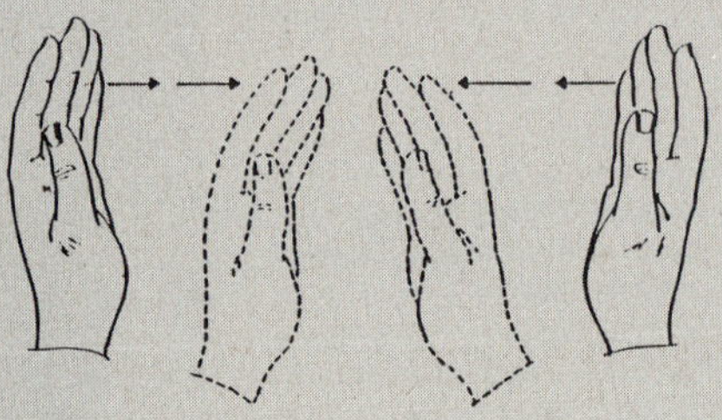

From Krieger, D. *The Therapeutic Touch: How to Use Your Hands to Help or Heal.* Englewood Cliffs, NJ: Prentice-Hall, 1979, pp. 24–25.

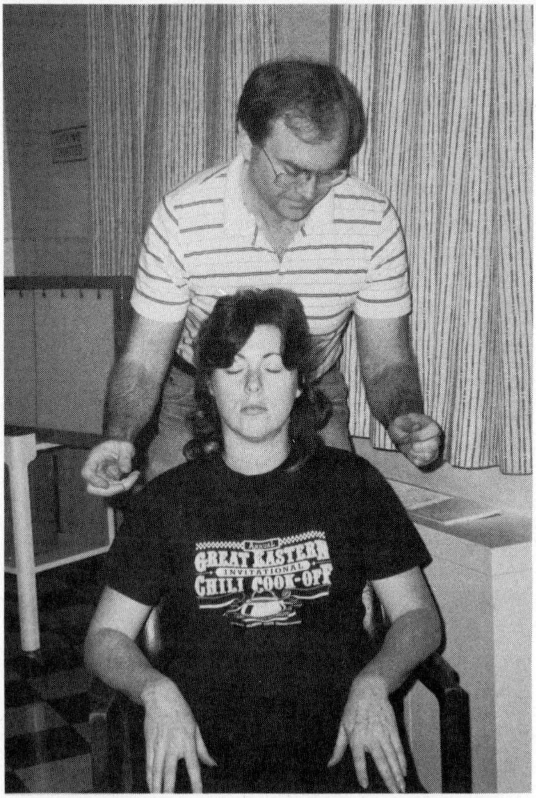

"Unruffling the field." Freeing bound energy from the woman's energy field that was perceived as nonflowing, sluggish, static, or congested. (Photo by Judith A. Lothian.)

each look, each touch, each comfort measure is given with the attitude, "I care about you; I want to help you." Centering and conscious intent to help are of utmost importance throughout the labor process.

Transfer of energy in Therapeutic Touch is accomplished by holding the hands over the body area needing assistance—in labor this may be the uterus or the back. Helpers then visualize the energy surrounding their body, perhaps by visualizing red, blue, or yellow light, and directing that stream of light or energy down the arms, through the palms and to the subject. The objective of the energy transfer is to restore harmony and balance. Since this technique is subjective, the emphasis is on following feelings rather than on the exact placement of the hands or exactly what to visualize when directing the energy. For example, if during the assessment phase the helper has experienced the feeling of cold as the imbalance in an area, then warmth can be directed to the area.

Krieger[14] reports that the person receiving energy in 90 per cent of the cases will breathe more slowly and deeply, sigh, speak in a softer voice, or exhibit a peripheral flush. These are, of course, signs of deepening relaxation. While transfer of energy can be helpful throughout childbirth, it may be most valuable during the late first stage of labor when most women feel very drained and often unable to cope.

The helper may also experience enhanced relaxation and a feeling of inner harmony as a result of the energy transfer. For the labor partner who is expected to encourage, support, and assist the la-

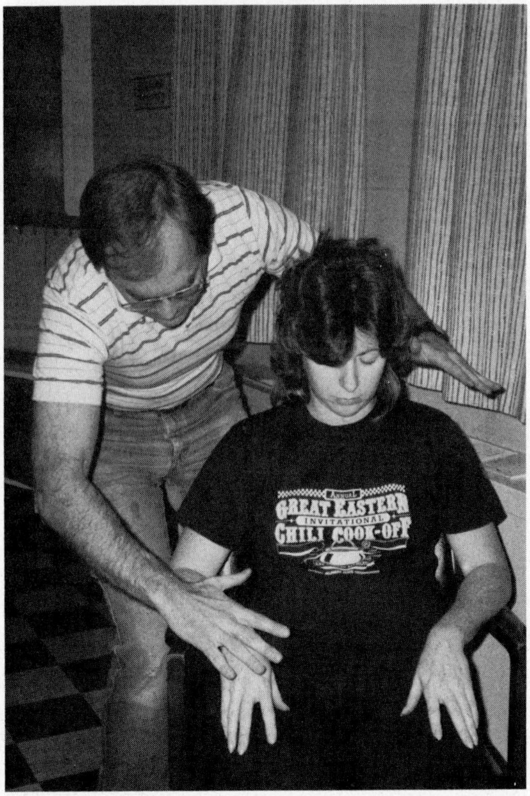

Directing energy. The healer consciously directs his excess body energy to assist the repatterning of that of the woman. (Photo by Judith A. Lothian.)

boring woman and in the process may experience feelings of fatigue, discouragement, and helplessness, Therapeutic Touch can provide important benefits. Therapeutic Touch becomes a tool for the coach to use self-renewal as labor progresses. When the role of the coach is discussed, Therapeutic Touch is again interwoven as a coping strategy for both laboring woman and coach.

When demonstrating baby care techniques and discussing parent-infant interaction, the educator may also wish to demonstrate Therapeutic Touch using a doll. Discussing postpartum adjustments (including how to cope with depression, fatigue, or a crying infant) offers another possibility for the childbirth educator to suggest the use of Therapeutic Touch, in the same way as the use of relaxation, breathing, and massage as life skills are encouraged.

IMPLICATIONS FOR RESEARCH

There is a need for more quantitative and qualitative research to support the effectiveness of Therapeutic Touch. However, traditional quantitative methods may not be the best way to study Therapeutic Touch. Rigorously designed experiential studies using phenomenological or other qualitative designs, in which the human element is not factored out, may capture in a more substantive way the process as well as the outcome of Therapeutic Touch. Perhaps an even greater need is for experiential documentation of how Therapeutic Touch can help the families we teach and support during the experience of childbearing. Specific questions that need to be answered are:

- What is the most effective method of teaching Therapeutic Touch to pregnant women and their coaches during childbirth education classes?
- How effective is Therapeutic Touch for pregnant women during labor?
- What is the range of physiological responses of pregnant women to Therapeutic Touch?
- How does Therapeutic Touch influence the psychological responses of the women during pregnancy and childbirth?
- What is the effect of Therapeutic Touch on the sleep and rest patterns of the newborn?
- Do class members who are trained to use Therapeutic Touch continue to use it as a life skill following childbirth?

SUMMARY

Therapeutic Touch appears to have value for members of the childbearing family and for those committed to helping them. In considering the possibilities of Therapeutic Touch and the inclusion of this technique into the childbirth education curriculum, the most important guideline is to integrate Therapeutic Touch as a component of the coping skills taught to expectant parents. Therapeutic Touch is not just an end in itself. It is a means, an enhancement, an adjunct to the coping skills we teach that has the potential of making those skills more powerful and effective. The childbirth educator is encouraged to practice, teach, and evaluate the efficacy of Therapeutic Touch while actively supporting or participating in carefully constructed scientific studies of its usefulness.

References

1. Clark, P. and Clark, M. Therapeutic Touch: Is there a scientific basis for the practice? *Nursing Research* 33:37, 1984.
2. Connell, M. Therapeutic Touch: The state of the art. *In* Brown, C.: *The Many Facets of Touch*. Skillman, NJ: Johnson & Johnson, 1984.
3. Connell, M. The Effect of Therapeutic Touch on the Experience of Pain in Postoperative Patients. Unpublished doctoral dissertation. New York University, 1984.
4. Grad, B. A telekinetic effect on plant growth. Part 2: Experiments involving treatment of saline in stoppered bottles. *International Journal of Parapsychology* 61:473, 1964.
5. Grad, B., Cadoret, R. J., and Paul, G. S. An unorthodox method of wound healing in mice. *International Journal of Parapsychology* 3:5, 1961.
6. Heidt, P. Effect of Therapeutic Touch on anxiety level of hospitalized patients. *Nursing Research* 30:32, 1981.
7. Keller, E., and Bzdek, V. Effects of Therapeutic Touch on headache pain. *Nursing Research* 35:101, 1986.
8. Krieger, D. Therapeutic Touch: An ancient but unorthodox nursing intervention. *Journal of New York State Nurses Association* 6:6, 1975.
9. Krieger, D., Peper, E., and Ancoli, S. Physiologic indices of Therapeutic Touch. *American Journal of Nursing* 4:660, 1979.
10. Krieger, D. The response of in-vivo human hemoglobin to an active healing therapy by direct laying-on of hands. *Human Dimensions* 1:12, Autumn, 1972.
11. Krieger, D. The relationship of touch with intent to help or to heal, to subjects. In-vivo hemoglobin values: A study in personalized interaction. *In* Proceedings of the American Nurses Association 9th Nursing Research Conference, pp. 39–58, 1973.
12. Krieger, D. Healing by the laying-on of hands as a facilitator of bioenergetic change: The response of in-vivo hemoglobin. *International Journal of Psychoenergetic Systems* 1:121, 1976.
13. Krieger, D. Therapeutic Touch: The imprimatur of nursing. *American Journal of Nursing* 75:784, 1975.
14. Krieger, D. *Therapeutic Touch: How to Use Your Hands to Help or to Heal*. Englewood Cliffs, NJ: Prentice-Hall, 1979.
15. Krieger, D. *The Foundation of Holistic Health Nursing Practices: The Renaissance Nurse*. Philadelphia, J. B. Lippincott, 1981.
16. Lothian, J. Therapeutic Touch: Its application in Lamaze class. *Expanding Horizons in Childbirth Education II*. Washington, D.C.: ASPO/Lamaze, 1985.
17. Miller, L. An explanation of Therapeutic Touch using the science of unitary man. *Nursing Forum* 18:278, 1979.
18. Quinn, J. Therapeutic Touch as energy exchange: Testing the theory. *Advances in Nursing Science*, pp. 42–49, January 1984.
19. Randolph, G. Therapeutic and physical touch: Physiological response to stressful stimuli. *Nursing Research* 33:33, 1984.
20. Rogers, M. *The Theoretical Basis of Nursing*. Philadelphia: F.A. Davis Co., 1970.
21. Smith, M. J. Paranormal effect on enzyme activity. *Human Dimensions* 1:25, Spring 1971.
22. Weber, R. Philosophers on touch. *In* Brown, C.: *The Many Facets of Touch*. Skillman, NJ: Johnson & Johnson, 1984.
23. Wolfson, I. Therapeutic Touch and midwifery. *In* Brown, C.: *The Many Facets of Touch*. Skillman, NJ: Johnson & Johnson, 1984.

Beginning Quote

Krieger, D. *Therapeutic Touch*. Englewood Cliffs, NJ: Prentice-Hall, 1979, p. 16.

Boxed Quote

1. Krieger, D. *Therapeutic Touch*. Englewood Cliffs, NJ: Prentice-Hall, 1979, p. 148.

chapter 11

RELAXATION: Acupressure

RUTH JUNGMAN

It is interesting to note that folk medicine has long since made use of stroking and rubbing the lower part of the abdomen and the small of the back as a means of relieving labour pain.

Velvovsky et al.

A review of the literature indicates that the Russian originators of the psychoprophylactic method of prepared childbirth included some acupressure massage in their approach. In Western practice the technique has been omitted. Research into the effectiveness of acupressure is sparse; however, there is empirical evidence that acupuncture may be an effective tool during labor. Since acupressure can be conceptualized as massage over acupuncture points, childbirth educators may wish to explore the inclusion of this ancient but new technique in their classes.

Most childbirth educators already use some form of touch in their childbirth classes (see Chapter 7). Touch relaxation is one example; however, all too often it is presented late in the course as an additional technique that the couple may or may not find helpful during labor. Massage is another example—although many times it is limited to abdominal effleurage. Massage over acupressure points is yet another form of touch. The majority of childbirth educators are just beginning to become familiar enough with it to incorporate it into their classes.

Most childbirth educators are familiar with unprepared women who intuitively squeeze the caregiver's hands or the bedrails, or may apply fingertip pressure to the abdomen. In some cultures, laboring women have used combs pressed into the palms of their hands to reduce the pain of contractions. Coaches of prepared women have long been taught how to use counterpressure techniques for back labor. Thus the idea that various forms of touch are useful in labor is not a new one.

REVIEW OF THE LITERATURE

Historical Aspects

The Russian theorists of the psychoprophylactic method, Velvovsky, Nikolayev, and their colleagues, recommended both the stroking of certain sections of the abdomen and pressure applied to certain "pain prevention points" located along the small of the back and the anterior superior ilia.[1,22] Lamaze, however, does not mention either stroking or pain prevention points in *Painless Childbirth*.[9] Effleurage, "any stroke that glides over the skin without attempting to move the deep muscle masses,"[19] has been a part of Lamaze childbirth preparation since Bing published her explanation of the method in 1967,[2] in which she described abdominal effleurage. Kitzinger has for many years emphasized the importance of "touch relaxation," that is, releasing muscle tension toward the touch of a support person, as a means of communication between the laboring woman and her partner and as a valuable way to enhance relaxation and pace breathing.[8]

None of these proponents of the use of touch or massage in childbirth preparation have offered any scientific explanation to support their use, nor have they conducted any controlled investigations to evaluate their effectiveness. Empirical evidence of enhanced relaxation and reference to the gate control theory are the only rationale offered.

The effectiveness of acupressure massage—the "pain prevention points" of the Soviet scientists—also lacks the support of definitive scientific research. However, since acupressure is defined as finger pressure or massage over acu*puncture* points,[4] we can look to the research dealing with acupuncture in obstetrics for information on the possible effectiveness of acupressure.

Acupressure Versus Acupuncture

Acupuncture currently is thought by some to produce analgesia and sedation through the release of beta-endorphins.[3,6,7,10,13] In Eastern theory, acupressure is one of several techniques that promote flow of energy (*ki*)* along meridians, the channels that provide energy to body organs and their related structures. Each meridian provides energy to a specific organ and its related structures. *Ki* is thought to be the primal energy that sustains balance and harmony between negative *(yin)* and positive *(yang)* forces and coordinates all functions of the body. A state of health exists when there is balance and harmony. When the flow of *ki* is blocked or sluggish, an imbalance results that leads to disease and pain.

Proponents of the gate control theory might say that acupressure's pain-relieving qualities are based on blocking the gate at the level of the spinal cord (see Chapter 6). Thus the underlying explanation of the mechanism of the pain-decreasing effects of acupressure is not agreed upon.

Effects of Acupressure

Tsueii and her associates reported use of acupressure to effectively stimulate and induce labor and inhibit premature labor.[21] The procedure has been duplicated in other countries.[5,17,23] It has also been shown that "acupuncture needles" are not essential to produce these effects. They are also produced by intense electrical stimulation, heat, and a variety of intense sensory inputs.[13] Since acupressure is an "intense sensory input," it is logical to assume that pressure or massage over acupuncture points may produce the same effects to at least some degree. We may then say that research does suggest the potential efficacy of acupressure, but it should be clear that further research on acupressure is needed.

*Energy fields are also called "chi" or "prana" by different philosophical or cultural groups.

IMPLICATIONS FOR PRACTICE

Rationale for Inclusion in Curriculum

Many childbirth educators and others in the helping professions value the use of touch in their practice based on their observations and experience. This alone is reason for considering incorporating instruction in massage in childbirth education classes. Childbirth educators may wish to increase their knowledge of acupressure so that this particular method of massage may be included as an integral part of their childbirth preparation courses.

It is of interest that those massage and stroking techniques traditionally taught in childbirth preparation classes use the same body areas as do acupressure techniques, although they are based on the Western concept of massage. That is, the body areas stroked and massaged are generally in the same locations as acupressure points. Therefore, teaching and using acupressure is primarily a matter of specifically identifying areas to be massaged so as to take greater advantage of the benefits of massage.

The most effective way to learn more about acupressure and its uses is to become familiar with the basic points illustrated later in this article, and then to use them personally and with family and friends. When the childbirth educator has experienced some of the benefits of acupressure personally, teaching its use to others becomes much easier.

Overview of Applications

Because acupressure is effective for relieving many of the minor discomforts of pregnancy, the childbirth educator may begin to include instruction on its use in early pregnancy classes. (Some forms of acupressure are said to induce labor; therefore, its use in the pregnant woman should be limited to selected points.) In this way the educator can provide noninvasive remedies for the common discomforts of pregnancy while helping the pregnant woman and her partner become accustomed to touching each other in a helping way. In late pregnancy use of selected acupressure points may be taught as part of a pain control routine for labor that also includes relaxation, concentration, and rhythmic breathing. Specific acupressure points for relief of symptoms characteristic of certain phases of labor should be demonstrated in the course when those phases are discussed. Each of these suggestions for practice are developed in detail, and a practical method of including them in classes is emphasized.

Terminology

The childbirth educator may be hesitant to teach acupressure massage because of a lack of familiarity with specific acupressure points or uncertainty about the acceptance of this technique by expectant parents. It should be emphasized that it is not necessary to use the term acupressure if community acceptance of such ideas is generally low. ''Massage points that seem most effective (or helpful) to most people'' or ''pressure point massage'' are acceptable phrases to substitute for the word acupressure. (Although the word acupressure is used throughout this chapter, the term pressure point massage may be more descriptive of the modality when used by care providers who are based in the Western as opposed to the Eastern traditions and philosophy of medicine.)

Concern regarding knowledge of the exact points at which to apply pressure may be alleviated by understanding that an impressive number of studies show that acupressure stimulation need not be applied at the precise points indicated on acupuncture charts. It may be concluded that stimulation is the necessary factor, and the precise site of stimulation is less important than the intensity of the input.[14]

Techniques of Applying Pressure

Acupressure technique fits very well with the philosophy of a labor support person, because the caring attitude of the helper (the person giving the treatment) is an important part of acupressure. When introducing or using any acupressure technique, the childbirth educator should emphasize the importance of the helpers relaxing and focusing their attention on the person being treated.

Pressure is applied with the fingertips or thumbs, either as a nonmoving force or as force applied in very small circles over the acupressure point. Preference of the person being treated will decide exactly how pressure is given. Points are not located directly over a bone; however, pressure is applied toward the bone. When an acupressure point has been located accurately, the treated individual will often describe a sensation of tingling or tenderness. Pressure may be applied for up to five or even ten seconds, and it may be repeated. The amount of pressure used should be decided jointly by the helper and the individual being treated. However, acupressure is rarely a light touch. It does extend into the deeper muscle masses.

Relief of Pregnancy Discomforts

While many childbirth education courses still begin with the participants in the third trimester, the first and second trimesters are the ideal time to begin providing information and self-help suggestions for expectant parents. Most women experience a number of minor discomforts brought on by normal physiological changes during the first and second trimesters. Acupressure massage offers effective relief for many uncomfortable symptoms of early pregnancy. The childbirth educator may demonstrate and discuss the relief measures given below as she covers the discomforts caused by physical changes and the importance of other healthful practices such as exercise and proper nutrition.

Dizziness or Faint Feeling. To relieve dizziness or a faint feeling, apply firm pressure with the fingernail on the midline one-third of the distance between the nose and the lips (Fig. 11–1).

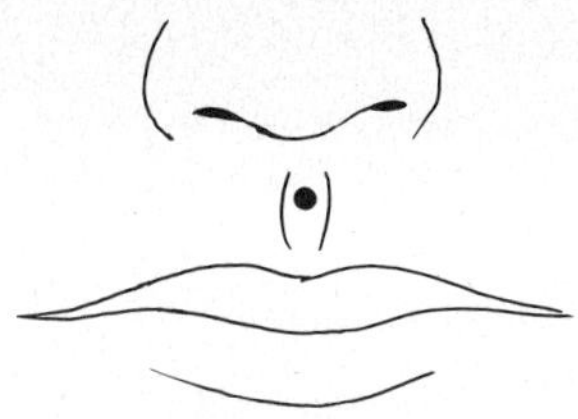

FIGURE 11–1. Acupressure point for syncope.

Headaches. Gentle but firm fingertip pressure over the temples, very firm thumb or fingertip pressure just below the skull on either side of the cervical vertebrae, and firm fingertip pressure on the suprascapular point will help relieve headaches. Pressure should be applied for three to five seconds on each point and may be repeated. This headache relief technique is an especially effective and nonthreatening way to begin teaching the pregnant woman and her partner to touch in a helping way, because it can be done with the two participants seated one behind the other (Fig. 11–2).

> A century ago our ancestors were busy trying to import material treasures of the Orient. Today we find another kind of importing also going on. . . . Health arts, including acupressure . . . are designed to strengthen and energize the body and mind. All are treasures which we in the West can also use to achieve a happier and healthier state of being.
>
> IONA TEEGUARDEN[1]
>
> Most laboring women like to maintain physical contact with someone who cares about them. Touching has many forms—hand holding, a hand on the shoulder or leg, stroking, or slow massage.
>
> BETH SHEARER[2]
>
> In late labor, when my husband pressed the points along my spine, I felt his love and energy flow from his hands into my body and it gave me strength to keep going.
>
> A NEW MOTHER[3]

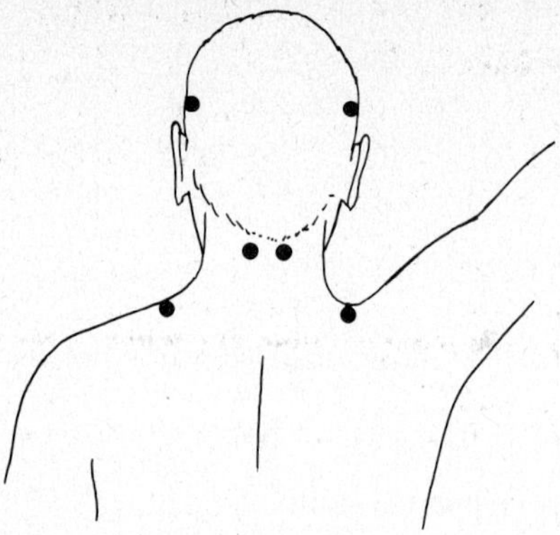

FIGURE 11–2. Acupressure headache relief points.

Sciatic Nerve Pain and Leg Cramps. During the third trimester sciatic nerve pain and leg cramps are common discomforts. These symptoms also respond well to acupressure treatment. To relieve sciatica, firm pressure is applied to the point located about five centimeters from the anterior superior iliac spine and near the greater sciatic notch.[15] These points are also useful for relief of backache during labor (Fig. 11–3).

To relieve leg cramps, pressure is applied with the thumbs in a firm stroking action down the middle of the back of the lower leg and with firm, localized pressure over the points shown on the foot (Fig. 11–4).

Relaxation and Pain Control During Labor

Because acupressure has potential to produce analgesia and sedation, it may be taught as an integral

FIGURE 11–3. Acupressure point for relief of sciatica.

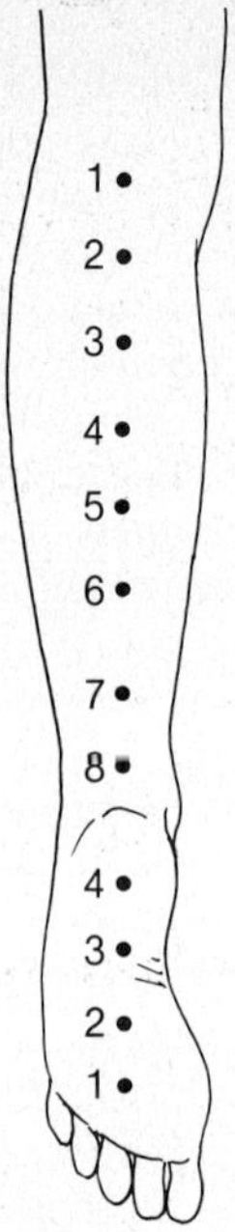

FIGURE 11–4. Acupressure points for relief of leg cramps.

part of a pain control routine for labor. As soon as progressive relaxation has been introduced and experienced in class, a complete acupressure release treatment can be practiced as a means of enhancing or deepening the state of relaxation achieved by the progressive technique. The release treatment should begin with the head, neck, and suprascapular points discussed earlier. The helper may then proceed by applying firm, heavy pressure to the points on either side of the spine, beginning at the level of the shoulder blades (Fig. 11–5). The helper should be careful to apply pressure on the ridges of muscle on either side of the spine, not on the spine directly. Pressure is applied to each point for three to five seconds. The points are located approximately an inch apart down the length of the spine to the level of the iliac crest and then follow the iliac crest outward to the sides.

To release the legs, thumb pressure is applied in a firm stroking action down the midline of the back of the thigh and lower leg, followed by very firm pressure on the foot points (Fig. 11–5).

The arms may be further relaxed by massaging the points down the center of the top of the arm from the shoulder to within about two inches of

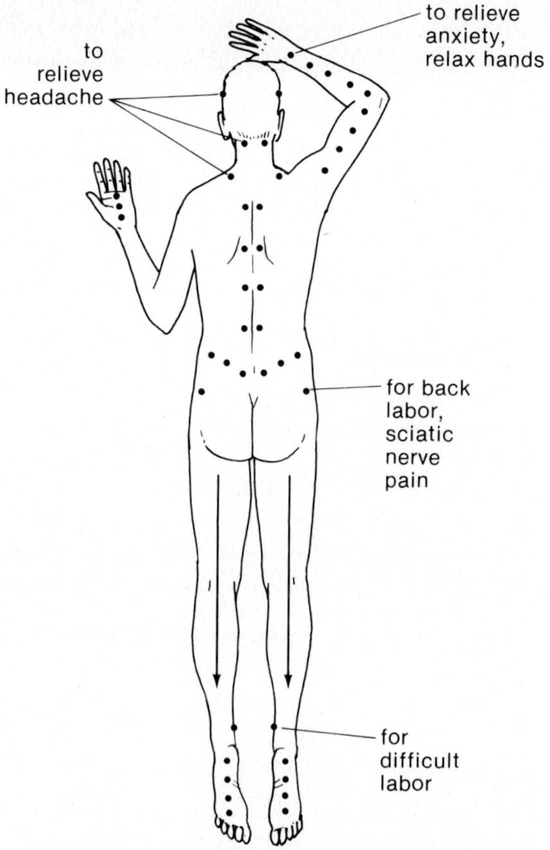

FIGURE 11–5. Acupressure points for back massage. (From Jungman, R. *Education for Childbirth: A New Lamaze Handbook.* Published privately by Education for Childbirth, 6102 Broadway, San Antonio, Texas 78209.)

the wrist (Fig. 11–5). Note that the final arm point, approximately two inches from the wrist, is a point for relieving anxiety. This point may be especially useful at certain times during labor.

There are three points on the palm of the hand: the center of the base of the hand, the center of the palm, and at the base of the middle finger. These points are useful for relaxing the hand (Fig. 11–6).

Expectant parents should be encouraged to practice and experiment with the acupressure release treatment as they practice relaxation at home. The childbirth educator should emphasize in class that a pain control routine for contractions during labor will include relaxation, concentration, paced breathing, and massage of various pressure points.

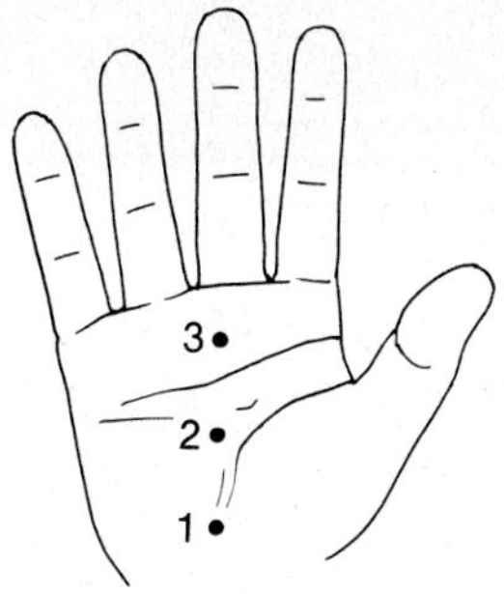

FIGURE 11–6. Acupressure palm points.

The educator must assist the helper to recognize the areas of the body that need assistance with relaxation at any given point as well as to offer suggestions for massage points useful for specific symptoms during labor. In this way the educator will help the laboring couple increase their repertoire of effective coping techniques.

The very strong contractions of late first-stage often cause a woman to grab and squeeze something with her hands. This would be an appropriate time to massage the palm and the *Ho-Ku* points. When accompanied by strong lower abdominal pressure, these same contractions make it quite difficult for a laboring woman to release the tension in her hips, legs, and feet. The massage points on the soles of the feet, in particular the one just behind the ball of the foot, should receive very firm pressure to assist in relaxing the lower part of the body.

The *Ho-Ku* point at the end of the crease between the thumb and forefinger is another point recommended to provide relief of headaches and an increased sense of well-being. Apply gentle pressure with the thumb, pressing toward the forefinger of the person being treated (Fig. 11–7). The *Ho-Ku* point should not be used by a woman who is less than 38 weeks' pregnant because of the possibility of inducing labor.

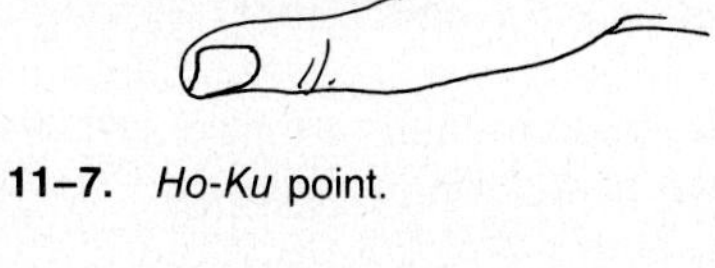

FIGURE 11–7. *Ho-Ku* point.

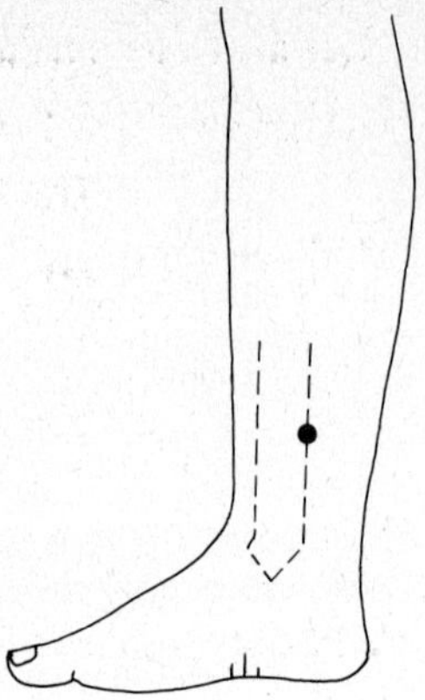

FIGURE 11–8. *San-Yin-Chiao* point.

San-Yin-Chiao, the point for difficult labor (Fig. 11–8) that lies approximately three finger widths above the inner ankle, is appropriate at any time contractions are ineffective. This information should be provided in class; however, care should be taken to emphasize that pressure over *San-Yin-Chiao* should not be applied to a woman who is less than 38 weeks' pregnant. This point in combination with *Ho-Ku* has been shown to be effective for inducing labor.[17,21,23]

The most important guideline the childbirth educator must remember for using acupressure during pregnancy and birth is to consider it an integral part of an approach to dealing with discomfort and pain, which also includes relaxation, concentration, and breathing patterns. In this way expectant parents will be able to make the best use of this valuable technique.

Contraindications. The contraindications to acupressure can be grouped in two areas:

- *Loss of skin integrity.* Acupressure should not be applied to any site where there is red, swollen, broken, or infected skin.
- *Selected points which should not be used during pregnancy.* The *Ho-Ku* and *San-Yi-Chiao* should not be used during pregnancy because of the potential to induce labor.

When initially discussing acupressure, the childbirth educator should present the contraindications to it along with the rationale for her statements. At the conclusion of the activity, the childbirth educator should again summarize the contraindications to ensure that class members understand them. The contraindications should also be included on the instruction sheet on acupressure that expectant parents receive in class.

IMPLICATIONS FOR RESEARCH

It is obvious that there are significant gaps in research, especially in regard to acu*pressure* as opposed to acu*puncture*. Some suggested research questions are:

- To what extent can expectant parents be taught to use acupressure effectively during pregnancy and childbirth?
- How effective is acupressure in decreasing pain during childbirth?
- Under what conditions is acupressure most effectively used in childbirth?
- Which pressure points are most effective in decreasing pain during childbirth?
- What is the physiological basis of acupressure for pain reduction in pregnancy and childbirth?
- What are the perceptions of expectant parents who have used some form of acupressure during pregnancy or childbirth?
- What, if any, side effects are associated with the use of acupressure during pregnancy and childbirth?
- How does the use of acupressure vary among cultures during pregnancy and childbirth?

Childbirth educators may wish to begin collecting this information as small pilot studies to prepare for eventually collaborating with childbirth researchers who systematically study acupressure.

SUMMARY

Expectant parents can use acupressure as an integral part of a pain control routine for coping with childbirth. It is noninvasive, easy to learn, and effective. When using acupressure during labor, the partner's touch also conveys caring and support to the laboring woman, both of which are important in helping her meet the challenge of childbirth. Acupressure is another important tool that educators can include in prepared childbirth classes when teaching expectant parents supportive pain management strategies.

References

1. Beck, N., Geden, E., and Brouder, G. Preparation for labor: A historical perspective. *Psychosomatic Medicine* 41:243, 1979.
2. Bing, E. *Six Practical Lessons for an Easier Childbirth.* New York: Grosset & Dunlap, 1967.
3. Bonica, J. *Obstetric Analgesia and Anesthesia.* Amsterdam, World Federation of Societies of Anaesthesiologists, 1980, pp. 74–76.
4. Chan, P. *Finger Acupressure.* Los Angeles: Price/Stern/Sloan, 1980.
5. Duparc, F. The induction of labor by acupressure electrostimulation. *Journale de Gynecologie, Obstetrique et Biologie de la Reproduction* 8:755, 1979.
6. Electro-acupuncture and peripheral beta-endorphin and ACTH levels. *Lancet (letter)* 2:535, 1979.
7. Hyodo, M., and Gega, O. Use of acupuncture anesthesia for normal delivery. *American Journal of Chinese Medicine* 5:63, 1977.
8. Kitzinger, S. *Complete Book of Pregnancy and Childbirth.* New York: Knopf, 1981.
9. Lamaze, F. *Painless Childbirth.* New York: Pocket Books, 1972.
10. Lo, C., and Chung, Q. Sedative effect of acupuncture. *American Journal of Chinese Medicine* 7:253, 1979.
11. MacHovec, F., and Man, S. Acupuncture and hypnosis compared. *American Journal of Clinical Hypnosis* 21:45, 1978.
12. Melzack, R., Stillwell, D., and Fox, E. Trigger points and acupuncture points for pain: Correlations and implications. *Pain* 3:3, 1978.
13. Melzack, R., and Wall, P. Acupuncture and transcutaneous electrical nerve stimulation. *Postgraduate Medical Journal* 60:893, 1984.
14. Melzack, R., and Wall, P. Acupressure and related forms of folk medicine. *In* Melzack, R., and Wall, P. (eds.): *Textbook of Pain.* Edinburgh: Churchill Livingstone, 1984.
15. Namikoshi, T. *Complete Book of Shiatzu Therapy.* New York: Japan Publications/Harper & Row, 1981.
16. Siegele, D. The gate control theory. *American Journal of Nursing* 74:498, 1974.
17. Sottili, G. Acupuncture and labor. *Minerva Medica* 71:3743, 1980.
18. Stepanova, I. Use of acupressure in obstetrics. *Akush Ginekol (Moskow)* 10:51, 1977.
19. Tappan, F. *Healing Massage Techniques.* Reston, VA: Reston Publishing Co., 1978.
20. Teeguarden, I. *Acupressure Way of Health.* New York: Japan Publications/Harper & Row, 1976.
21. Tsueii, J., Lai, Y., and Sharma, S. The influence of acupuncture stimulation during pregnancy. *Obstetrics and Gynecology* 50:479, 1977.
22. Velvovsky, I., Platonov, K., Ploticher, V., Shugom, E. (eds.). *Painless Childbirth Through Psychoprophylaxis.* Moscow: Foreign Languages Publishing House, 1960.
23. Yip, S., Pang, J., and Sung, M. Induction of labor by acupuncture electro-stimulation. *American Journal of Chinese Medicine* 4:251, 1976.

Beginning Quote

Velvovsky, L., Platonov, K., Ploticher, V., and Shugom, E. *Painless Childbirth Through Psychoprophylaxis.* Moscow: Foreign Languages Publishing House, 1960, p. 254.

Boxed Quotes

1. Teeguarden, I. *Acupressure Way of Health: Jim Shin Do.* New York: Japan Publications/Harper & Row, 1978.
2. Shearer, B. Labor and birth in stages. *American Baby's Childbirth* 84(1):73, 1984, p. 76.
3. Jiménez, S. Acupressure and Shiatsu for pregnancy-related discomforts. *NAACOG Update Series* Vol. 5, No. 17. Princeton, NJ: Continuing Professional Education Center, Inc., 1986, p. 3.

chapter 12

RELAXATION: Imagery

SANDRA APGAR STEFFES

With each contraction, I saw my cervix like a kaleidoscope I had when I was a kid. As the contractions got harder the colors and designs got more intense and the tiny hole in the middle just got bigger and bigger.

A New Mother

Since the inception of the childbirth education movement, imagery has been a part of the educational process. While the word *imagery* was not specifically used, some of the general concepts associated with imagery can be found in the early literature. The early childbirth educational texts promoted birth as an activity that could be accomplished with little or no pain and described how this could be achieved. There was a general consensus among the authors that the mind was a very important aspect of the method. The theories of the use and control of the mind during labor reflect the current research of that day. There are some indications that imagery was also at work.

REVIEW OF THE LITERATURE

Velvovsky et al. mention in several sections of their text that "emotions lead to a number of changes in the state and activity of different internal organs" and that laboring women need positive input.[38] The authors throughout the text discuss various mental states and their positive benefits for the laboring woman. Lamaze in his text emphasizes that the mind of the laboring woman needs to be in a state of equilibrium. When describing a contraction he is quite graphic, likening the contracting uterus to the ebb and flow of a tide.[24] Bing points out that the laboring woman should visualize the pictures and diagrams that show contractions so that it will be clear. She also mentions that it helps to imagine the wave of a contraction and ride the wave with the breath.[5] These are some examples from early texts associated with the Lamaze method. Each of the authors was very specific about control, commonly citing education, respiration, exercises, relaxation, and focusing the mind. Although the ''how'' of focusing varied, the idea of using the mind predominated.

Imagery is a well-known function of the mind. While the concept may be foreign to some, imagery is really an activity people do on and off during the day. This activity is usually referred to as daydreaming, ''zoning out,'' having premonitions, and other terminology that indicates a temporary shift away from immediate activities of the here and now. This daydreaming activity is considered a normal and necessary part of human life.

Imagery has been described as a conscious experience. Unlike daydreaming, the conscious use of imagery involves a certain level of discipline. Imagery allows the individual to work directly with imaginal material to extract meaning and benefits.[10] Benefits associated with the use of imagery appear to be very broad. Blattner lists such things as relief from intractable pain, improvement of vision, as well as relief from anxiety.[6] Hill and Smith indicated that imagery has been useful for such physical illnesses as headaches, hypertension, and cancer.[20]

Blattner also comments on how expectant parents can benefit from using imagery techniques. She indicates that parents can learn more about certain feelings and images and can learn to create the images they want to hold.[6] It would appear that the benefits associated with the relaxation response are also present during the imagery experience.[3] Bressler indicates that imagery appears to allow the individual access to the autonomic nervous system.[7] Bressler and others have concluded that an individual is therefore given access to those functions—blood pressure, heart rate, and so on—that had previously been believed to be involuntary.[1,3,7,11,22,40] The entire issue of the benefits of imagery for the general public has been based to date primarily on clinical observation. This conclusion is supported by Sheikh, who strongly emphasizes the need for systemic research on the therapeutic outcome of various imagery approaches.[35]

Specific to childbirth education there have been a few researchers who have studied the effectiveness of various prepared childbirth strategies, including focusing and imagery. Stone et al. studied the active elements of the Lamaze childbirth technique. They reported marginally significant superiority of the imagery technique over the Lamaze focal-point visualization.[37] Stevens and Heide studied the effectiveness of prepared childbirth strategies on individuals' perception and endurance of pain. They found that the best overall strategy was the focus plus feedback relaxation and the next most successful was basic relaxation and attention focus.[36] Worthington et al. found, when studying coping strategies in childbirth, that combined structured breathing, attention focal points, and coaching produced the strongest treatment.[41]

Geden et al. studied a variety of cognitive-behavior pain-coping strategies associated with labor preparation. The major treatment components were relaxation training, pleasant imagery, sensory transformation, neutral imagery, and combined strategies. During the pleasant imagery the subjects were asked to sit quietly and imagine a pleasant scene; this was facilitated by listening to a reading of a descriptive sensory narrative of a beach scene. During sensory transformation subjects were taught to use imagination to transform the experience of the laboratory pain stimulus into a pleasant feeling. The subjects were asked to imagine and concentrate on the expected throbbing sensation generated by the pain stimulator and were read a narrative that guided them in restructuring the stimulus into a pleasant, warm feeling.[16]

The researchers found that subjects using sensory-transformation reported significantly less pain than control subjects. No other significant treatment effects were found. The researchers hypothesized that the beneficial effects of the treatment procedures such as pleasant imagery tend to be transitory as opposed to those of sensory transformation, which tend to be longer lasting and as a consequence are more appropriate for labor preparation.[16]

Cogan reviewed the literature on the effects of childbirth preparation. She found that among women with childbirth education tension and anxiety were lessened and there was less increase in maternal blood pressure during late labor.[9] Wideman and Singer in their comprehensive review of the literature on the psychoprophylactic (Lamaze) method found that there were few empirical studies on the training regimen. These researchers stated the following: "The research reviewed in this article does not provide evidence on which to accept or reject the notion that the Lamaze method will reduce pain and discomfort of childbirth."[39]

In the general research literature concerning imagery and the childbirth preparation research literature, the specific benefits that imagery may provide in relation to childbirth preparation are undetermined. While clinical experience seems to indicate that imagery does have specific benefits, research is still lacking.

IMPLICATIONS FOR PRACTICE

Designing an Imagery Program

When designing an imagery session for childbirth education there are five general areas that need to be considered: orientation, setting, the technique, processing of information, and follow-up.

Orientation. At times in childbirth classes it appears easier to just include comments on using imagery, a brief description of it, and some type of practice. However, some students may not have a perspective that enables them to understand the full benefit that can be derived from incorporating imagery into their childbirth experience and therefore may disregard its usefulness. Orientation to the subject is therefore vital. The individual students' backgrounds will influence the amount of orientation required. With a class already familiar with imagery skills, only a brief orientation is necessary, while a class unfamiliar with imagery will require a more in-depth orientation. Orientation not only includes the why's associated with an activity but also helps to motivate the student and to increase acceptance. Cogan notes that motivation of the participant is an important factor for positive effects of childbirth preparation.[9]

When imagery is introduced into a childbirth class it should be introduced as any other skill. Using the term *skill* may help students relate what they already know about how to learn a new skill to this material. For example, when mastering a new skill there is usually rationale for doing the skill, some type of demonstration, return demonstration and discussion on how to improve the skill, and then some practice. All of these elements can be utilized with imagery in childbirth classes.

The first area that needs to be considered is theoretical: how imagery is believed to help. Discussing benefits helps to motivate the students. Motivation will also increase the interest of the group and may aid in their learning. The childbirth educator might want to include a section on the potential uses of imagery. For example, imagery can be a useful activity in reducing stress during the latter part of the pregnancy. It can also be useful during labor and birth as a tool for reducing stress, as a pain management strategy, and may serve as a facilitator of the labor process. During labor and birth, a certain amount of normal stress occurs. Then, added to normal stress, there is potential for iatrogenically imposed stress that often accompanies going to a hospital or being in a strange place and receiving care from unknown persons. Imagery techniques may be useful along with other prepared childbirth techniques to reduce some of this stress.

Once some level of interest has been established, the instructor should discuss how a person *may* feel while experiencing an imagery session without telling people how to feel. This can be accomplished by describing a range of experiences. Some instructors have found that not suggesting anything also is effective and then during the group processing each student can describe what occurred. The instructor may want to experiment with these different possibilities.

The childbirth educator may need to address the

issue of losing control, since this is a common experience expressed by many who are new to imagery. She may wish to use the analogy of swimming. There is a point when people start to learn to swim when they have to let go and let the water hold them up. It is not that there is a losing of control, but a gaining of the sense of the support of the water. It is the same when a person moves into a relaxed state. The moment comes when there is a sense of loss. The loss is not necessarily a loss in itself but is really the gaining of an insight, or mentally moving into another dimension. Trying too hard or attempting to make things happen can also block this process. As a childbirth educator you may find that it is necessary to let the students know that they will be safe and that any information or images that appear during an imagery session will only be helpful.

The next point to consider is what to do with the eyes. Some people feel strange about closing their eyes at first and prefer to leave their eyes open. It is usually easier to do imagery with the eyes closed because with closed eyes sensations and/or pictures form more readily. With the eyes open students are often visually distracted by activity going on in the room or pictures on the walls. On the other hand, it can be counterproductive to lie tensely with the eyes closed ready to pop right open. Therefore, just mention the benefits of closing the eyes, and let the class members decide for themselves.

In class there will be certain students who are good at visualizing actual pictures and other students who experience sensations and feelings. Some students who experience only sensations may fear they did not do something correctly because they did not "see" pictures or their picture was not a full-color sound production as they see on television. Samuels describes two types of people: one as "visualizers" and the other type as "sensitives." Visualizers see pictures while sensitives feel something happening. Samuels suggests that most people are somewhere between the two.[30] Forisha believes that some individuals experience more imagery than others.[12] This information can help the class participants accept what they are doing as fine and may avoid comparisons and feelings of failure. The childbirth educator should avoid setting any type of goal for what the class does or does not have to accomplish. By having no expectations for a desired achievement level, ideas of "correctness" can be avoided. If some people are interested in becoming skilled at actually seeing pictures, there are certain exercises that will sharpen this ability, described later in this chapter.

> A vivid imagination compels the whole body to obey it.
>
> ARISTOTLE[1]
>
> Mental imagery can actually bring about physiological changes and alter the course of labor.
>
> SUZANNA MAY HILBERS[1]
>
> Young women are exposed to negative imagery through legends of suffering (in childbirth) from personal sources, even through religious history. An important part of natural childbirth involves educating the mother towards a positive image of childbirth.
>
> Paraphrased from GRANTLY DICK-READ[2]

Another experience of some people when involved in imagery is that the mind begins to wander. Thoughts of what they have to do tomorrow or the grocery list start to come and the student finds these thoughts to be quite distracting. Instead of trying to force these thoughts out of the mind or forget them completely, suggest that the students develop a technique for managing this. One such suggestion is to have a mental shelf and to put on the shelf everything that is to be remembered later. Another is to mentally make a note and put the note on a shelf. Sometimes just stopping and asking "Why is my mind wandering?" may help clarify things for the students. Some people find that when they start an imagery session a portion of their mind starts saying things like "This is dumb" and "I do not want to do it."

Bressler calls this "the little voice in your head that talks to you constantly."[7] The student needs to honor this voice and give it some space. Students may find it helpful to imagine the voice telling an audience everything that is stupid about what they are doing. The audience can be as small as one or as large as a thousand. By giving the voice an audience, the student may find that the voice is no longer a problem. Generally, this technique is helpful and worth trying. In some cases such a technique may make things worse. The students need to know that if they do not want to participate, this is fine. If these suggestions for wandering minds and "little voices" are not effective, the instructor can encourage participants to develop a method that works for them.

Setting. When conducting an imagery session, the instructor needs to create an environment that is conducive to relaxation. This includes such things as ensuring that there is adequate floor space for each participant to stretch out without the fear of intruding on the space of others. The supine position has been found to facilitate the experience of vivid imagery.[33] Since supine hypotension may be a problem for the pregnant participants, they should assume a left-sided or a more upright position. Basically the participant should try to assume a position that leads to decreased tension in the head and neck.[33] The instructor or students will need to bring in adequate pillows or bolsters, if these are not provided, to aid in the assuming of comfortable positions. It also helps if the participants wear loose, nonrestrictive clothing.[20] The noise level should be low, allowing each participant to listen to the childbirth educator's voice or to their own inner voice. If the noise level is a problem, the addition of music may help. Lights also need to be controlled. Soft, nonglaring lights seem to work the best. The temperature of the room needs to be warm, for many people report feeling cooler as they start to relax.

The instructor needs to find a place in the room where all the participants can hear her instructions without strain. The instructor should also avoid moving around for this can cause distractions to the participants. Basically, imagery manifests itself when the participant is awake and when external stimuli are not functionally operative.[33]

Another element to consider is movement. If an individual does not want to participate that is perfectly fine, but ask this person not to walk around in the room while other people are involved in a relaxed state or involved in imagery. However, movement as part of becoming more relaxed is common. Many times people will find that as they become more relaxed they need to shift their bodies around. Shifting kinds of movement are part of moving into a more relaxed state. When starting a relaxation session the childbirth educator should include instructions on shifting. This shifting may include the need to move the head, readjust the pillows, or get the body repositioned.

Techniques (Active vs. Passive). The literature describes two basic types of imagery techniques. The first type has been labeled by a variety of different terms—*active, programmed,* or *direct visualization*. The second type has been referred to as the *receptive, passive,* or *permissive* technique. In an actual imagery session these two techniques often seem to overlap. The following is a description of how these techniques differ theoretically. Several authors describe programmed visualization as an activity that involves people picturing themselves experiencing a specific situation or enjoying such things as increased health, strength, or energy[6,7,32] (see examples in Boxes 1, 2, and 3). The general consequence is that the person is actively involved in the imagery experience and that there is a direction with a certain amount of choice concerning the activity. The passive or receptive technique has been described as one in which the person in a relaxed state allows whatever imagery that may occur to arise.[6] This has been further described as allowing the mind to wander and create many images, with the person simply becoming the observer.[23]

The active technique differs from the passive one in possible benefits achieved. The use of active imagery has been indicated as a technique that is useful in achieving goals and making changes.[32] Other benefits are that the active technique may strengthen the power of concentration, sharpen the ability to visualize, and heighten dream recall.[23] The passive technique has been credited with aiding the ability to access inner feelings and ideas as well as to detect underlying fears, motivations, fantasies, or all these.[23,32] The decision of which technique to use in childbirth education will vary, depending on the size of the group, the preference of the group and instructor, and the type of outcome desired.

Regardless of which technique is used—active, passive, or a combination of both—it is important to have a plan before starting an imagery session. When working with the passive technique, the childbirth educator and the group should decide on the general area of interest that needs to be explored. From this point, move on to the formulation of the question or statement to be used. The group members will also have to decide if they all want to use the same question or statement or a different question or statement. It is usually easier if all use the same question or statement, but if you have a group that objects to this, then each person can make up his or her own question or statement. The use of the passive technique in a childbirth class seems to take more time than the active technique. The extra time usually includes making decisions about the area to be explored and formulation of the question or statement. After the exercise, extra time may also be required for processing, since each person will have individual responses that may need to be explored.

For the active technique, there are a variety of planned texts available.[20,23,32,33] After finding out the likes and dislikes of the group, you might consider creating a text suitable for the classroom situation. For example, going to an imagery beach for a group who has little beach experience may not be as restful as an imagery trip to the mountains.

When doing an actual imagery exercise, regardless of the technique type, always start with some type of relaxation activity. Relaxation has been indicated as the most important prerequisite in achieving vivid imagery.[3,10,13,23,32,33] Therefore, before introducing any imagery techniques in a childbirth class, the instructor will have to assess the ability of the class not only to relax but also to maintain a relaxed state. With students who are able to relax fairly easily and quickly, just asking them to get into a relaxed position is sufficient. The students already know how to arrange themselves in the room, make space for themselves and for each other, and arrange their pillows to help increase relaxation. After the class is in relaxing position, the instructor can start with any relaxation technique. One easy method is to have the participants close their eyes and take three breaths.[31] First they breathe in, and as they breathe out, they let go of the tension, breathing in and letting go again and breathing in and letting go of any final tension. This technique is effective only if the students have practiced it as part of previous relaxation exercise.

From here, move on to ''grounding'' the participants within the room. Have the class members notice where they are lying, what position their bodies have assumed, where their feet and hands are lying on the floor, the room they are in, and the location of the room. This grounding technique will help participants feel secure and give them a type of anchor so they can move mentally away from the place where they are resting and then mentally move back to the same place when the session has ended.

After this grounding has occurred, next ask the participants to clear their minds. If you have talked about what to do with the wandering mind or the ''grocery list'' mind, the class already knows some techniques for handling these situations. Allow some time when you ask them to clear their minds to take care of any of these activities. Remind the class to create a passive nonjudgmental attitude in which random thoughts can be observed or simply allowed to occur.[20] After allowing a few moments for clearing, suggest to the participants that their mind is a screen and on the screen certain impressions will appear. You might want to avoid the ''seeing'' at first. However, once the class gets used to the fact that the word *seeing* does not mean that they have to actually ''see'' something, the use of this word becomes broader—broader in that they can feel and sense. Participants may just know something is there but they do not actually have to see as they do with the eyes open.

After the mind is made a blank screen, the next activity is to provide a suggestion as to what is on the screen. If you use the passive technique, a question or statement is used. The question or statement can be asked in a variety of forms. The participants can just ask the question in their own minds, they could see a skywriting plane fly by with the question attached, they could visualize a sheet of paper and write the question, they could see themselves typing the question, or they could create a sense that the question is being asked. Anything that works for the individual should be encouraged. The participant may have to ask the question several times slowly. Then there is a period of waiting for the answer.

The answer usually comes in a form that may not seem to be an answer, such as a voice talking, a picture, an object, or a general feeling that this was the answer. Also, sometimes no answer comes at all or what comes does not make any sense to the participant. Crampton suggests that if people get a symbol they do not understand, they should then ask for an image of a real-life situation in which the same feeling exists.[10] With the no-answer situation, the participant can just accept this or may want to review the question or statement for clarity. The formulation of the question is just as important as asking it and waiting for the answer. The question has to be clear and the answer within their realm to know. Asking if there will be an earthquake tomorrow may not be an appropriate question, but asking them about their state of health or how it can be enhanced may be more appropriate.

When using the active technique, first start by making suggestions as to what might be on the screen. In the beginning keep the suggestions vague and then move into more details.

From this point you ask the participants to picture themselves on the screen. Then start making suggestions about what may be present. The details of these suggestions may include as many of these senses as possible as well as the kinesthetic sense. Try to make suggestions about taste, touch, sight, sound, and smell and include motion and movement as well. Samuels suggests using such phrases as "look at the surroundings, listen to the music, smell the air, feel the breeze."[32]

Once the participants are "in the imagery," the instructor will guide them through the activity. Mentally they go some place, they do the activity, and then they need to come back.

On the return section, the instructor will want to pay particular attention. With the passive technique or imagery in which the participant is not in the picture, the return may be as simple as asking the class to return to the ordinary and slowly counting from one to three.[32] With the active technique, in which the participants have been asked to enter the picture, the return needs to be slower. The general idea is to lead the participants back past the same things that they encountered on the way in. So if they started in a field, going over a wall past flowers and past a brook to the resting place, then they come back past the brook by the flowers, over the wall into the field and back to the room again. Once the participants are back in the room, then they move their bodies, extremities first. At this point the instructor can start to check to see where people are in the imagery itself. Some people return more slowly than others, so during the return part the instructor needs to allot plenty of time. This time includes participants acting on the suggestion that as part of the imagery, when returning, they can go back again any time they wish. Occasionally some participants seem to fall asleep; this is perfectly acceptable. People who do fall asleep tend to wake up spontaneously when the rest of the class starts to move.

Next, slowly suggest movement. First ask the class to move their feet and hands and check to see who is mentally back in the room and who is lingering in the imagery. The instructor may need to keep slowly suggesting a variety of movements for the extremities. As these suggestions are heard by more participants, the instructor will notice more and more people responding. If the instructor finds someone who is not responding, gently projecting the voice may help. The instructor can also move carefully next to the person who is not responding and suggest directly that the participant say goodbye to the imagery; remind the participant that returning anytime is OK, and to begin to notice the room, the carpet, and the pillows. Once there is movement by most of the participants, the instructor can suggest that people stretch and when their eyes are ready they will open by themselves.

Processing and Follow-up. Once everyone is back in the room and all eyes are open, the next phase in the imagery experience is processing. Woolfolk and Lehrer comment that in human visualizing events, imagining sources of stimulation can create as great a physiological response as the actual experience of the event. For many, imagining squeezing lemon juice under the tongue produces salivation as effectively as actually doing so.[40] For first-time participants, the response is usually one of surprise at how real the imagined things seemed.

The instructor may find at first a silence in the class. During this silence participants are usually remembering the pleasant feelings or reflecting on the process or both. This silence allows the participant to acquire more information and may help in gaining a better understanding of the inner process.[10] Some participants may wish to write the experience down, so having paper and pencils available can facilitate this. Many people do not feel comfortable sharing their experience with the group as a whole. The instructor may wish to have the participants share with their partners or in small groups.

To help put closure on the experience the instructor can explore with the group at large their general feelings regarding the experience and allow time for the group to share as a whole. It is important that each person has time to make some sense of the experience. Crampton warns that information gained from an imagery session needs to be used. If an individual opens up to the wealth of knowledge without utilization, this can undermine the will and dissipate the energy of that person.[10]

Before ending the imagery session the instructor needs to let the participants know that if they feel the need for further discussion during the week, they can contact her. Because sometimes after an imagery session a participant may find the need for further discussion, it is helpful if the instructor is available.

Exercises to Enhance Imagery Skills

Introduction of imagery specifically into a childbirth preparation class is done as a part of relaxation, using the exercises discussed. When working with new skills there is usually a progression in skills from simple to complex. The teacher needs to gauge the progress of the group as a whole as well as the mastery level of each individual participant so as to determine an appropriate level for the class. This often becomes a juggling act for the teacher, for as in all skill-related activities students will progress at various rates. Some of the students will come into class being somewhat familiar with imagery activities and for others this will be the first time these activities are encountered. Also, some students may find more value in learning the activity and thus work harder than others do. It then becomes the task of the teacher to help motivate and create an environment in which all can progress. With imagery the students may find it a somewhat unusual activity at first. The thought that there are exercises that can enhance the skill may not be treated as seriously as the assignment of a physical exercise. However, just as physical exercises can led to physical skill improvement, mental exercises associated with imagery can lead to improvement in the ability to utilize imagery skills and thus increase relaxation during childbirth.

Several authors have extensively discussed mental exercises that enhance the ability to use imagery.[23,30,33] The following is one technique described by Joy.

> Once one has reached a relaxed, quiet state of mind, one was to image a large black curtain on which one was to begin the process of pinning up numbers one by one, from one to one hundred. The numbers were to be large, golden in color and perfect. They could not be hazy . . . (or) waver. One could not take down a number until it had been on the black curtain in clear detail and bright color for at least five seconds. Note that the numbers did not just appear on and disappear from the screen . . . the individual pins up and takes down each number. The hands that pinned up the number and the pin used to hang the number on the curtain must be seen as clearly as the numbers themselves.[23]

Joy felt that using this technique not only sharpens the visualizing mechanism of the mind but vastly strengthens the power of concentration.[23] The Samuels in their *The Well Body Book* include a section on imagery exercises (Fig. 12–1).

The Samuels believe that the exercises in Figure 12–1 can ''expand the visualizing powers and develop the ability to create images of actions, objects and people in the mind's eye at will.''[30] It has been suggested that the ability to control the images is as important as the actual image itself.[33]

A modification of these two exercises that may be useful in childbirth education classes is as follows. After orientation to the subject instruct the class in the following:

1. Close the eyes and relax.
2. Create a black screen.
3. In the middle of the screen create a triangle.
4. Color the triangle red.
5. Hold the image.
6. Take the triangle away.
7. Clear the screen.
8. Open the eyes (see Box 12–1 for specific words to do the exercise in a class).

In a ''usual'' class there are always a wide variety of experiences when practicing imagery exercises. Some people have a gray screen; others

VISUALIZATION EXERCISE

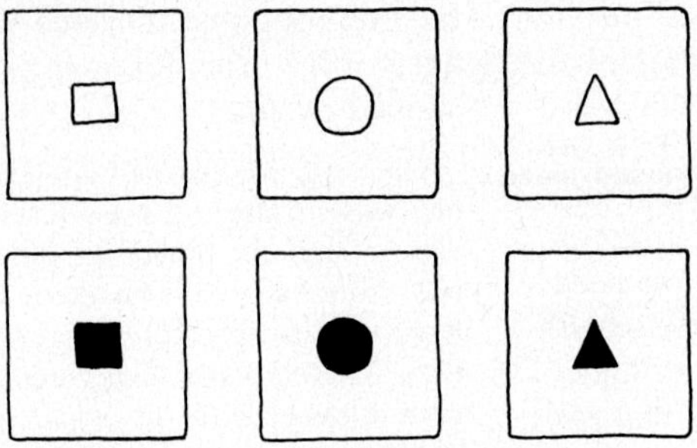

FIGURE 12–1. Visualization exercise. (From Samuels, M., and Bennett, H. *The Well Body Book.* New York: Random House, 1973.)

Sit in a comfortable chair, arms and legs uncrossed. Take three or four deep breaths. Exhale slowly and relax yourself.

Close your eyes. Picture a home movie screen in your mind, or picture a plain, white sheet of paper about two feet square. You may find it necessary to get an actual piece of paper and fasten it on the wall; stare at it for five seconds, close your eyes and try to visualize it for five seconds, then open your eyes and stare at the paper for five seconds, and so on until you can actually see the screen (paper) in your mind's eye.

Change the color of the screen in your mind to red. Hold it in your mind for five seconds.

Change the color of your screen to blue. Hold it for five seconds.

Change the color of your screen to yellow. Hold it for five seconds.

Change the color of your screen to black. Then change it back to white.

Now picture a red square in the center of your white screen for five seconds.

Change the color of your square to yellow.

Change the color of your square to blue.

Change the color of your square to black.

Bring your white screen back.

Now picture a red circle in the center of your white screen for five seconds.

Change the color of your circle to yellow.

Change the color of your circle to blue.

Change the color of your circle to black.

Remove the circle entirely, leaving the white screen.

Now picture a red triangle in the center of your white screen for five seconds.

Change the color of your triangle to yellow.

Change the color of your triangle to blue.

Change the color of your triangle to black.

Now picture your screen white all over.

Change your white screen to black.

Open your eyes. You have now completed the visualization exercise.

have jet black or blue-black or any other variety or shade of black. The same is true for the triangle and the color red. There is always incredible richness and variety when the first imagery experiences are shared in class. Each person is asked to continue practicing at home and when the task becomes easy, change the color of the triangle. After a week of practice the students can share their progress, exchange stories of how the shades of colors or shapes vary. Many students also report that when

Box 12–1

TRIANGLE

I would like to get you into a relaxed place. Take a breath in and as you breathe out, relax your body. Breathe in again and this time as you breathe out . . . slowly feel yourself melting, melting into a state of relaxation.

Breathe once again and breathe out, letting go of any unnecessary tension.

I would like you to image a black screen . . . see it as black as can be . . . think only black . . . just let the color black form in your mind . . . try not to look, just let it come . . . this black is deep black . . . hold the blackness . . . and now if you will in the middle of this black screen find a triangle . . . slowly starting to form . . . slowly starting to take shape . . . a triangle that has three sides with three points . . . each side comes together and makes a clear distinct image. . . .

You have a black screen . . . with a triangle . . . with three sides . . . with three points . . . with three angles. . . . Now watch the triangle fill in with the color red . . . it's a wonderful red. . . . The kind of red you have always liked . . . a deep, clear red . . . see the red triangle on the black screen. . . . Hold this and watch. . . .

Now I want you to take away the color red . . . take away the triangle . . . take away the black screen . . . slowly breathe in . . . breathe out . . . and when you are ready let your eyes open.

Triangle. (From Samuels, M., and Samuels, N. *Seeing with the Mind's Eye*. New York, Random House, 1975.)

they are feeling happy and content the exercise is easier.

When practicing a relaxation imagery *The Garden of Rest,*[31] the description in Box 12–2, lends itself to the childbirth education class. Both the pregnant woman and her partner can practice this in class. *Garden of Rest* is also easy to do at home and may be useful for postpartum relaxation.

Another imagery exercise that works both for class and during labor is *The Golden Ball*. This particular exercise can be done with the labor contractions. During labor, the laboring woman's part-

Box 12–2

THE GARDEN OF REST

Start by getting yourself comfortable and being in a relaxed position

slowly start your breathing

breathe in . . . and breathe out . . .

as you breathe in, think about how relaxed you are and as you breathe out feel the tension moving out of your body.

Notice yourself lying on the floor . . . feel the pillows, feel the fuzzy carpet . . . if you need to move yourself do so now . . .

breathe in again and feel relaxed

breathe out and let any leftover tensions disappear

keeping slowly breathing in . . . and slowly breathing out . . .

Notice if you will . . . a field . . . it is a great wonderful field . . . the kind of field you may have remembered in your childhood . . . a perfect field for playing in . . .

filled with growing things . . . see the colors in the field, feel the gentle wind blow, watch the grasses move . . .

Now notice the fact that you are standing in the middle of your field.

As you stand there you can feel the earth beneath your feet . . . you look up to the sky. You see the clearness of the sky.

As you breathe in you smell the aromas that come from the field.

Look around . . .

Are there flowers growing? . . . Are there grasses growing? . . .

Notice if the sun is shining and how it feels when the sun shines on you . . .

Can you hear the sound of the wind gently blowing?

Does it make the grasses and flowers move? . . . Does it bring the smell of the grasses to your nose? . . .

Start walking in your field . . . and feel how wonderful it is . . . all full of wonderful things to see, to smell, and to touch and as you walk you notice that over in the corner there is a wall . . .

It is a lovely wall . . . as you slowly approach this wall you notice the texture and consistency.

You find yourself wanting to go over this wall . . . and so you do without any hesitation . . . easily and comfortably you go over the wall and find yourself in a wonderful garden . . .

Box 12–2 Continued

This garden is designed by you for you . . . it is full of things that you most like in a garden . . . the trees are the kind of trees that you want . . . the flowers are flowers that you would plant in your garden . . . look at the flowers, see their petals, notice the color of the flowers . . . these are the flowers that are for you . . . Smell the flowers . . . They carry a rich aroma, a sweetness that only your special flowers have . . .

As you look around your garden you see a path . . . a perfect path for your feet . . . a perfect path for you to walk on that leads through your garden . . .

Past your trees, past your flowers, past the things that you love to see in a garden, and as you walk . . . you find a small stream . . . a perfect little brook with water moving so smoothly and so clearly . . . you can hear the water running . . . see its sparkling clearness . . . you stop for a moment and enjoy a drink of the cold clear water . . .

Then you move on . . . along your path in your garden . . . where you come to a wonderful place, a perfect place for resting . . . this was put there by you for you to rest.

So you stop in the middle of your garden and enjoy this wonderful resting place and your resting place is the perfect place to relax . . . a place comfortably molded for your body . . . perfect in every way . . . you can see your garden . . . you can see your flowers . . . you can see your trees . . . the sky is clear . . . the sun is shining and all is well . . . as you breathe in you feel relaxed and know that this is a restful and peaceful state, a wonderful state, a wonderful place to be. . . .

And now it is time for you to leave your garden. You get up from the wonderful place where you were resting, saying goodbye to your resting place you start back along the little path . . . Pass the trees that you love so well and pass the perfect flowers that bloom for you. . . .

You turn and you say goodbye to the lovely brook, knowing that any time you wish you can return and rest in this resting place, knowing that any time you wish you can return and drink from your brook, and knowing that any time you wish you can return to see your flowers and watch the trees moving in the wind . . . so you slowly move along your path, saying goodbye but knowing that you can return. . . .

You come to the wall and you once more turn and face your garden . . . goodbye . . . goodbye . . . and you know that you may return whenever you wish.

You go back over the wall . . . back to the wonderful field . . . looking at the wall knowing that your garden is there peacefully secured and you know any time you wish you can return.

As you walk back through your field the wall goes farther and farther away, but you know you can return. . . .

And now find yourself resting again in the room . . . you can feel your hands and your feet on the floor . . . you can feel your body comfortably resting.

You notice that your feet can move . . . you wiggle your toes . . . you make little circles with your ankles . . . you stretch your legs . . . you move your hands . . . you find your whole body starting to move again . . .

And when you are ready, you let your eyes tell you when they want to open . . . and you enjoy the peaceful feeling you have.

The garden of rest. (Adapted from Samuels, M., and Samuels, N. *Seeing with the Mind's Eye*. New York, Random House, 1975.)

Box 12–3

THE GOLDEN BALL

We are going to practice now what I just talked about in terms of integrating the image of the golden ball with the slow breathing. Remember as you think about inhaling think about breathing in light, energy, and clear cool air, and as you breathe out you are going to think about the discomforts and any pain or tension that you may be experiencing traveling down your legs through a special conduit and out through the bottoms of your feet.

Begin with . . .

Contraction begins . . . inhale . . . exhale . . . relax . . . and focus . . .

slowly start to breathe in . . . and slowly let the air out . . . as you are breathing in, think about a large golden ball floating over your body.

This ball is there just for you . . . to provide you with energy . . . energy to help manage your labor . . . as you breathe in slowly imagine this wonderful ball . . . filling your body with cool clean sparkling radiant energy . . . and as you breathe out all your worries and tensions travel down through your legs and out through the bottom of your feet.

Contraction is half over

you are breathing in . . . and you are breathing out . . . slowly . . . slowly . . . allowing yourself to experience the energy from the golden ball . . .

Contraction ends

cleansing breath

breathe in . . . breathe out

ner can give verbal cues to help enhance the experience. The words that can be used in class are found in Box 12–3.

Passive or receptive visualizations are best made up by the participants themselves. The participants know best what they want to work on. For possible suggestions that may be useful in class see Table 12–1.

Specific imagery techniques that involve the actual contracting of the uterus or dilation of the cervix can be discussed in class, but *should not actually be practiced.* During labor, however, some women have reported that visualizing the uterus working hard and feeling fine about this was most helpful. During class the participants may want to plan possible activities to include during their labor. Actual practice prior to labor of the cervix dilating, the uterus contracting, or the baby descending the birth canal *should not be done.* Since the use of imagery accesses the autonomic nervous system, it is theoretically possible that visualizing the uterus at work could actually start the labor process.

When using the active or the passive technique, the childbirth instructor will find that imagery can be an effective tool in class. During the latter months of pregnancy the stress-reducing aspects of imagery as well as the increased feelings of well-being experienced by the participants can be beneficial. During labor not only the stress-reducing aspects but also the turning of negative images into positive thoughts, actions, or feelings may give the laboring woman and her partner a sense of control and feelings of well-being as well as pain relief.

Specialized functions are commonly referred to as right and left hemisphere functions of the brain. In general, logical and analytical functions have been labeled as "left brain" and imaging or creative functions have been labeled as "right brain." Some researchers now question the accuracy of purported functions of right and left hemispheres, but most generally agree that two classifications of functions do exist. Hilbers and Gennaro[19] suggest that techniques that involve both the right and left hemisphere of the brain may maximize the brain's ability to cope with, or endure, pain.

Hilbers and Gennaro have listed 11 brief exercises that combine imaging with a left hemisphere activity such as counting or reciting (Table 12–2). Using these examples, the childbirth educator can encourage expectant parents to think of other examples that combine left and right hemisphere activities. Favorite images, songs, or verses of class members may be used to create a strategy particularly appealing to them.

TABLE 12–1. USING RECEPTIVE VISUALIZATION BEFORE THE BIRTH

There are a number of questions that generally come to mind when a woman finds she is expecting a baby. Receptive visualization can help her find the answers within herself. To do this she should follow the receptive visualization exercise, looking for images relating to the questions that concern her. The expectant father can also use this technique to explore concerns he has about the coming baby.

SUBJECTS TO THINK ABOUT	EXAMPLES OF SPECIFIC QUESTIONS AND CONCERNS	TYPICAL POSITIVE OR NEGATIVE IMAGES THAT MAY COME TO MIND
Nutrition	What foods does my body crave? What foods don't interest me now?	Milk, leafy green salads, lean meats, seafood Alcohol, pasta, hot chili
Exercise	What kind of exercise appeals to me now?	Walking, swimming
Sleep	Am I getting enough sleep? Do I need naps?	Feeling sleepy in the afternoon
Sex of the baby	What sex will the baby be?	Image of a girl; image of a boy
Kind of delivery	What kind of delivery would be ideal for me?	A natural delivery with no drugs; a delivery that uses some kind of anesthesia so I don't feel the contractions
Method of feeding the baby	What method of feeding the baby makes me feel the happiest?	Nursing the baby; feeding the baby with a bottle only; nursing and occasionally using formula to give me time off
Preparations for the baby	What things do I feel are important to do before the baby is born?	Get a dresser? Buy a special cradle? Set up a whole room? Buy new clothes? Borrow well-loved baby articles from friends?

From Samuels, M. and Samuels, N. *The Well Baby Book,* New York: Summit Books, 1979.

TABLE 12–2. EXAMPLES OF COMBINATION STRATEGIES FOR USE DURING CHILDBIRTH

The first strategy of each sentence is a left hemisphere function and the last part of each sentence is a right hemisphere function.

1. Count the ripples as you imagine throwing rocks in a pond.
2. Sequentially order colors of the rainbow and imagine breathing in color.
3. Remember words of a favorite verse and visualize them on the wall.
4. Remember the words to the song, "Old McDonald Had a Farm," while imagining the smell, feel, and color of each animal.
5. Count the bubbles as you imagine blowing bubbles.
6. Count your steps as you imagine walking or dancing.
7. Count the berries you pick while you imagine smelling, feeling, and tasting them.
8. Count your strokes as you imagine swimming in a pool.
9. Recite or read positive verbal statements while imagining the sensations of the relaxation response.
10. Intentionally change positions to turn your baby while imagining goldfish lazily turning in a bowl.
11. Respond to touch and verbal instructions to release specific muscles while imaging dew and warm sun on a velvety opening rose.

From Hilbers, S. and Gennaro, S. Non-Pharmaceutical Pain Relief. *NAACOG Continuing Education Update Series* Vol. 5. Princeton, NJ: Continuing Professional Education Center, Inc., 1986. The NAACOG Update Series is a program sponsored by NAACOG and published by CPEC, Inc.

Contraindications and Cautions

While it may appear that the use of imagery is safe for all, there are many references in the literature that suggest a certain level of caution needs to be considered.[3,7,10,20,29,33,40] This caution is twofold in nature. One relates to specific personality types in whom imagery may exacerbate an already existing condition and the other relates to possible negative side effects on an otherwise normal person.

As early as 1974 Benson and colleagues listed two factors that needed to be watched for: the kind of person or persons that might be involved in using the relaxation response and the total time actually spent in a relaxation state.[3] These precautions were confirmed by Bressler.[7] Imagery should not be used with psychotics and prepsychotic persons. No more than two 20-minute imagery sessions a day were recommended. For persons spending excessive amounts of time in the relaxation state there could be consequences such as withdrawal from everyday life, insomnia, or hallucinations.[3] An additional consequence suggested by Hill and Smith was disorders that could be affected by a change in metabolic rate (for example, diabetes, hypertension, hyper- or hypothyroidism, chronic respiratory disease). Individuals with these conditions should be monitored by their primary caregiver prior to initiation of relaxation self-care practices.[20]

Rossman also expresses a caveat associated with the use of imagery. He states that generally the use of imagery is more of an issue of responsibility. Since imagery is not useful to everyone, Rossman thinks that generally people will self-select in regard to their interest, level of understanding, and intuition during the imagery exercises. Rossman further states that practitioners need to use their clinical judgment when introducing a patient to imagery techniques. For example, patients who are overly involved in fantasy may not be good candidates. He also confirms the idea that psychotics and prepsychotics needed to be handled very carefully.[29] However, these typically are not people seen in childbirth education classes, so this should not be a problem.

Rossman does verify that over the last two years over 1000 people have purchased the audiotape *Imagine Health* and there have been no adverse effects reported from either the professional or the lay community. He also reports that other professionals who have published guided imagery instructions for self-care that have 10,000 users have not seen any detrimental effects.[29] The warnings that are listed in the literature usually refer to possibilities derived from clinical judgment and are not research-based.

In the preface of the *Anthology of Imagery Techniques,* Sheikh adds a note of caution: ''Since they (imagery) are powerful tools, they should not be used indiscriminately. At times, they pierce resistances surprisingly quickly and uncover deeply disturbing emotional content with which the individual may be unprepared to cope.''[33]

On the basis of these thoughts from experts who work daily with imagery in clinical settings, it would be wise for the childbirth educator to limit the use of imagery in the classroom to stress-reducing images and activities that are self-regulating (the participant is in control). She should avoid using imagery techniques that lead to deep psychological probing or releasing of material that is inappropriate either in childbirth class or beyond that scope of practice for a childbirth educator.

There are some additional considerations that need to be discussed with expectant parents in childbirth classes. These basically fall into three areas—physical considerations, activity during the discussion after imagery, and actual technique. Before people enter the relaxed state involved in imagery they need reassurance that their bodies will not be physically disturbed. The participants also need to know that they are not going to be stepped on by passersby or by the instructor walking around the class. They need to know that they are not going to be unnecessarily disturbed by loud or erratic noises. When classes are held in a home there should not be pets or children running through the room.

In the hospital during labor, unnecessary noises, physical intrusions, and people walking around will likely be part of the environment. Intrusions, however, can be controlled in the classroom as well as in the birthing agency. Just as noise in the classroom can be smoothed out by the use of music, the same would be true in the labor room.[26,28] In labor, music from ear phones may be particularly useful. When the laboring woman is in a relaxed state and using imagery, before being examined or before having any procedures done she should return to the here-and-now state, find out about the procedure and what will take place, and then, if appropriate, use the relaxation state in order to cope with that procedure. The laboring woman can ask her partner to help with this so she can rest assured that someone will not just come into the room and start a procedure while she is involved in imagery.

Another consideration is activity during the discussion phase after imagery in a class setting. Some people may want the instructor to interpret the relevance or value of what they saw. This is a trap that many instructors fall into. It is virtually impossible to tell the true meaning of what a person is visualizing. The instructor is likely to cause the person unnecessary worry or to become involved in activities that are really beyond the scope or interest of a childbirth class. The participants need to discover for themselves what it is they saw and what it means to them personally. Obviously if persons want to talk about their experience in the classroom and this is an appropriate area, discussion can take place. If, however, the instructor thinks the content is unsuitable for classroom discussion or beyond her individual skills, she would talk to the person individually and possibly recommend a competent therapist for further work.

The last precaution relates to the actual imagery activity itself. When leading a visualization or imagery exercise, the instructor needs to use broad as well as gentle words—words that lead the participants to fill in the detail for themselves but also words that create a positive picture. In the middle of a particularly lovely scene, do not introduce a negative aspect or what may appear to be a negative aspect. For instance, if everyone is resting peacefully on the beach, enjoying the sunshine, and listening to the water, suggesting that a tidal wave was coming or a flock of birds was going to fly over to peck at the participants' feet would be introducing into the imagery session scenes that may be very negative. Negative scenes may come to the participants by themselves, but they need no additional help from the instructor. Feedback from the class will help the instructor to shape the imagery experience so the negative aspects can be avoided.

In addition to negative content, the instructor will need to consider the use and non-use of certain content in the classroom. It bears repeating that use of labor rehearsal in a relaxed state where visualization of the actual labor is going on is something that is definitely not recommended. When people are in a relaxed state, as research has shown, they are able to control certain autonomic functions of the body as in blood pressure and temperature control. It could therefore be assumed that there is the possibility that a person may be able to control the onset of labor as well. Labor rehearsal is therefore not recommended for a classroom imagery exercise in which premature labor induction could be a problem.

To summarize, imagery can be done in a childbirth education class as long as the instructor pays attention to certain physical considerations, leaves interpretation of the scene to the individual, uses methods that are gentle and kind, and provides content with a positive outcome.

IMPLICATIONS FOR RESEARCH

There is most definitely a need for more research on the use of imagery in childbirth education. Examples of research questions are:

- How beneficial is imagery in childbirth education? What is the nature of the benefits?
- How extensively or frequently do expectant parents experience negative aspects or problems with visualization in childbirth education classes?
- Can imagery be used to induce overdue labor?
- Can imagery be useful in delaying preterm labor?
- Are combined "right brain–left brain" imagery exercises more effective than a single strategy?

SUMMARY

Although the use of imagery in childbirth education is relatively new, aspects of visualization have been historically associated with prepared childbirth. Research in this area is scant. However, reports of clinical experience suggest that many thousands of people use imagery in an effort to promote health without adverse effects. With a few simple precautions, imagery is one of the tools that can be added to those from which expectant parents may choose to use as they cope with the stresses of pregnancy and childbirth.

References

1. Barber, T. X. Changing "unchangeable" bodily processes by (hypnotic) suggestions: A new look at hypnosis, cognitions, imagining and the mind–body problem. *Advances* 1:7, Spring 1984.
2. Benson, H. Your innate asset for combating stress. *Harvard Business Review* 52:49, 1974.
3. Benson, H., Beary, J. F., and Carol, M. P. The relaxation response. *Psychiatry* 37:37, 1974.
4. Benson, H. *The Relaxation Response*. New York: Avon, 1975.
5. Bing, E. *Six Practical Lessons for an Easier Childbirth*. New York: Grosset, 1967.
6. Blattner, B. *Holistic Nursing*. Englewood Cliffs, NJ: Prentice-Hall, 1981.
7. Bressler, D. *Free Yourself from Pain*. New York: Simon & Schuster, 1979.
8. Bry, A. *Visualization—Directing the Movies of Your Mind*. New York: Barnes & Noble Books, 1979.
9. Cogan, R. Effects of childbirth preparation. *Clinical Obstetrics and Gynecology* 23:1, 1980.
10. Crampton, M. Answers from the Unconscious. *Synthesis* 1:140, 1975.
11. Flynn, P. *Holistic Health*. Bowie, MD: Robert J. Brady Co., 1980.
12. Forisha, B. Relationship between creativity and mental imagery: A question of cognitive styles? *In* Sheikh, A. A. (ed.) *Imagery: Current Theory, Research and Application*. New York: John Wiley & Sons, 1983.
13. Gawain, S. *Creative Visualization*. New York: Bantam Books, 1978.
14. Gawain, S. Creative Visualization. *In* Bliss, S. (ed.) *The New Holistic Health Handbook: Living Well In A New Age*. Lexington, MA: The Stephen Greene Press, 1985.
15. Gawain, S. *Creative Visualization Workbook*. Mill Valley, CA: Whatever Publishing, Inc., 1982.
16. Geden, E., Beck, N., Hauge, G., and Pohlman, S. Self-report and psychophysiological effects on five pain-coping strategies. *Nursing Research* 33:260, 1984.
17. Gendlin, E. *Focusing*. New York: Everest House, 1981.
18. Gordon, R. L. *Self-Care and Wellness*. Los Angeles: Learning for Health, 1981.
19. Hilbers, S., and Gennaro, S. *Non-pharmaceutical pain relief*. NAACOG Continuing Education Update Series, Vol. 5. Princeton, NJ: Continuing Professional Education Center, Inc., 1986.
20. Hill, L. and Smith, N. *Self-Care Nursing*. Englewood Cliffs, NJ: Prentice-Hall, Inc., 1985.
21. Jacobson, E. *How to Relax and Have Your Baby*. New York: McGraw-Hill, 1965.
22. Jaffe, D. T., and Bressler, D. E. The use of guided imagery as an adjunct to medical diagnosis and treatment. *Journal of Humanistic Psychology* 20:45, 1980.
23. Joy, W. B. *Joy's Way*. Los Angeles: J. P. Tarcher Inc., dist. by St. Martin's Press, New York, 1979.
24. Lamaze, F. *Painless Childbirth*. Chicago: Henry Regnery Co., 1956.
25. Lefer, L. The blossoming of the rose. *Synthesis* 3:124, 1977.
26. Livingston, J. C. Music for the Childbearing Family. *JOGN Nursing* 8:363, 1979.
27. Pelletier, K. *Mind As Healer Mind As Slayer*. New York: Dell, 1977.
28. Rider, M., Floyd, J. W., and Kirkpatrick, J. The effect of music, imagery, and relaxation on adrenal corticosteroids and the re-entrainment of circadian rhythms. *Journal of Music Therapy* XXII(1):46, 1985.
29. Rossman, M. L. Imagine health! Imagery in medical self-care. From Sheikh A. A. (ed.) *Imagination and Healing*. Farmingdale, NY: Baywood Publishing Co., 1984.
30. Samuels, M. and Bennett, H. *The Well Body Book*. New York: Random House, 1973.
31. Samuels, M. and Samuels, N. *Seeing With the Mind's Eye*. New York: Random House, 1975.
32. Samuels, M. and Samuels, N. *The Well Baby Book*. New York: Summit Books, 1979.
33. Sheikh, A. A. *Anthology of Imagery Techniques*. Milwaukee, WI: American Imagery Institute, 1986.
34. Sheikh, A. A. *Imagery: Current Theory, Research and Application*. New York: John Wiley & Sons, 1983.
35. Sheikh, A. A. (ed.) *Imagination and Healing*. Farmingdale, NY: Baywood Publishing Co., 1984.
36. Stevens, R. J., and Heide, F. Analgesic characteristics and prepared childbirth techniques: Attention focusing and systematic relaxation. *Journal of Psychosomatic Research* 21:429, 1977.
37. Stone, C., Demchik-Stone, D., and Horan, J. Coping with pain: A component analysis of Lamaze and cognitive-behavioral procedures. *Journal of Psychosomatic Research* 21:451, 1977.
38. Velvovsky, I., Platonov, K., Ploticher, V., and Shugom, E. *Painless Childbirth Through Psychoprophylaxis*. Moscow: Foreign Languages Publishing House, 1960.
39. Wideman, M. and Singer, J. The role of psychological mechanisms in preparation for childbirth. *American Psychologist* 29:1357, 1984.
40. Woolfolk, R. L., and Lehrer, P. M. *Principles and Practices of Stress Management*. New York: The Guilford Press, 1984.
41. Worthington, E., Martin, G., and Shumate, M. Which prepared childbirth coping strategies are effective? *JOGN Nursing* 11:45, 1982.

Boxed Quotes

1. Jones, C. *Mind Over Labor*. New York: Viking, 1987, p. 12.
2. Dick-Read, G. *Childbirth Without Fear*. New York: Harper & Row, 1953, p. 14.

chapter 13

RELAXATION: Music

JOYCE DI FRANCO

Music penetrates into the secret places of the soul.
Plato

Music has been noted for centuries as a therapeutic agent. Pythagorus is said to have believed that music and diet could cleanse both body and soul, and he founded a school of philosophy based on music and numbers.[15,26] Standley indicates that the Kahum papyrus, the oldest known history of medical practices, documents the use of incantations and chanting to heal the sick.[38]

Increasingly, music is used during childbirth education classes to enhance relaxation and during childbirth to decrease anxiety and pain. This chapter examines the properties of music, the research on music therapy, and the application of music in childbirth education classes and during childbirth.

REVIEW OF THE LITERATURE

Modern, systematic research of the uses of music and its effects on human physiology began in the nineteenth century. Much of this research was centered on its use in the dental field for pain relief, although those in other disciplines have also reviewed the therapeutic properties of music. Effects studied have included cardiovascular physiology, respiration, reduction of anxiety, psychological response to pain, and effects on the autonomic nervous system.[32,35,38] All of these parameters are of

TABLE 13–1. RESEARCH STUDIES USING MUSIC WITH OBSTETRICAL PATIENTS

STUDY	SUBJECTS	TYPE OF MUSIC	DEPENDENT VARIABLES	RESULTS
Burt and Korn (1964)	200 women assigned to experimental (music, white noise, suggestion) or control (no contact) group.	Taped listening	Effectiveness of audio analgesia; use of other analgesia; amount of medication. (Behavioral observation and self-report)	Effect size: Music .66* Use of other analgesia .39* Amount of medication .35*
Clark, et al. (1981)	20 patients of one obstetrician assigned to experimental (music therapy training) or control group (no music).	Music-assisted relaxation training; autogenic, guided imagery and music, and progressive relaxation. personal preference; music therapist attended labor.	Level of childbirth success as measured by perceived pain, anxiety during childbirth, length of labor and 6 other variables. (Self-report)	Moderate positive correlation (.61) between music training and level of childbirth success; slightly stronger correlation (.66) between Lamaze practice and successful childbirth; music therapy home practice was a significant predictor of a successful childbirth experience.
Codding (1982)	20 women assigned to experimental (music and Lamaze classes) or control (no music) group.	Taped listening	Perceived pain (Self-report)	Pain effect size .59*
Durham and Collins (1986)	30 women randomly assigned to experimental (music in addition to prepared childbirth classes) or control (prepared childbirth classes only) group.	"Top 40" used in class and available in labor areas; personal preference.	Pain as measured by frequency of medication use. (Hospital labor record)	No significant difference between experimental and control groups.

Hanser et al. (1983)	7 women in Lamaze classes. Repeated measures design with each subject serving as own control.	Personal preference. Music therapist attended labor.	Pain responses of subjects as recorded by music therapist. (Behavioral Observation)	All subjects displayed fewer pain responses while music was playing during labor. Those subjects who used music for rhythm or attention-focusing reported the greatest benefits. Effect size: .90*
Sammons (1984)	54 women in Lamaze classes randomly assigned to experimental (music) or control (no music) group.	Exposure to taped music during one active rehearsal of all breathing patterns (experimental group) and personal preference during labor.	Frequency of music use; factors affecting use of music during labor. (Self-report)	Trend toward music use by experimental group (non-significant). Predominant reasons subjects used music were to establish a favorable mood and to aid relaxation.
Shea and Davis (1986)	20 women. Experimental group attended Lamaze classes in which music was used.	Taped listening; personal preference.	Perceived relaxation; perceived anxiety; factors affecting use of music during childbirth. (Self-report)	71% of experimental group (music) perceived themselves as relaxed versus 23% of control group (no music); 86% of experimental group reported less anxiety with music; use of music was affected by type of labor.
Winokur (1984)	31 women were assigned to experimental (music and Lamaze classes) or control (no music).	Taped listening; personal preference.	Perceived relaxation; length of labor; use of pain medication. (Self-report)	Effect size: Relaxation 1.32* Length of labor .99* Use of medication .98*

*As reported by Standley, J. Music Research in Medical/Dental Treatment: Meta-Analysis and Clinical Applications. *Journal of Music Therapy*, 23:56, 1986. The effect size was determined using procedures identified by Glass and associates. The effect size is the difference between the means of the experimental and control groups in standard score form. An effect size of +1.00 would indicate that the experimental group scored one standard deviation better than the control group.

interest to the childbirth educator, but studies specifically focusing on the effects of music on childbirth are the most valuable and these studies are now appearing in the literature. A summary of these studies appears in Table 13–1.

Standley, using a meta-analysis approach to review the effects of music in the medical and dental literature, reports that using music enhanced the medical objectives no matter how they were measured.[38] Common measurements included psychological and self evaluation and physiological and behavioral observation. Pulse rate was stated to be the dependent variable most affected by music and the length of labor, the least affected. The effects were smallest for neonatal, cancer, and obstetrical patients. The small effects in obstetrical patients would seem to be consistent with Melzack's analysis of pain in childbirth,[25] using the McGill Pain Questionnaire, which identifies the pain of childbirth as being one of the most severe recorded using this tool.

The Properties of Sound

A review of how sound is received and processed assists in understanding the contributions of music to pain relief. The sense of hearing is one that cannot be turned off. Sound is transmitted via sensory impulses directly from the cochlea in the ear to the thalamus and then to the cerebral cortex. The elements of sound—rhythm, pitch, and intensity—are mediated by the thalamus and consequently affect the autonomic nervous system. Even when conscious processing does not occur, music accesses the brain via the thalamus, evoking an emotional response. This has been demonstrated when severely mentally retarded, senile, and some comatose patients have responded to music even though cognitive processes were inaccessible.[38,43]

Rider et al.[32] stated that a relationship between music/relaxation techniques and physical health may exist. This research focused on the connection between music and relaxation and the immunological system as accessed by the hypothalamus. The authors concluded: "The connection between music/GI (guided imagery)/PMR (progressive muscle relaxation) and health is very likely a mechanism involving a (neural) hypothalamic-frontolimbic loop and a (neuroendocrine) hypothalamic-immunological loop." This can be seen in Figure 13–1.

Studies using music for its anxiety-reducing properties with surgery patients have indicated when blood analysis was done that stress hormones were suppressed.[42] Reduction of circulating stress hormones and their effect on both the labor process and the fetus are of significant importance to the childbirth educator.

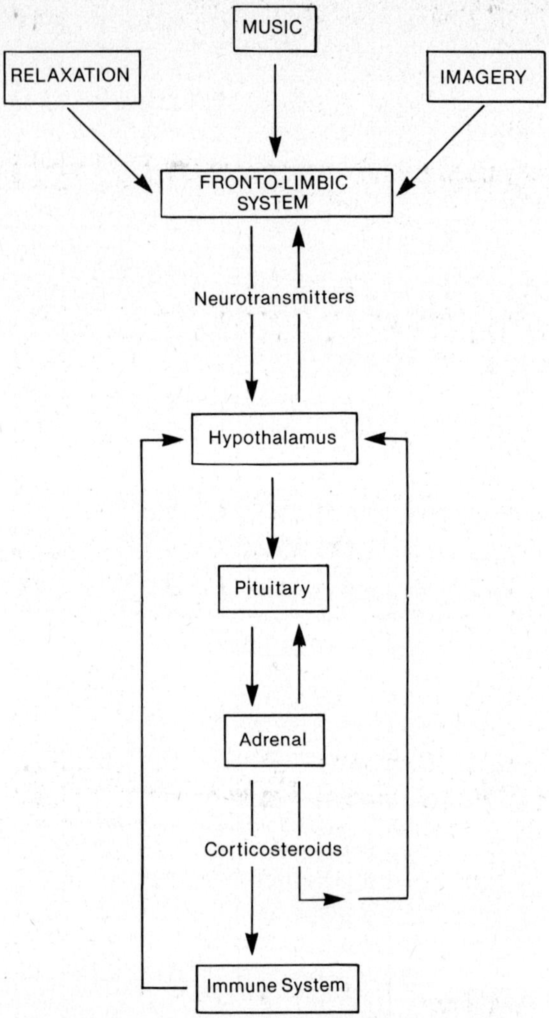

FIGURE 13–1. Music, imagery, and progressive relaxation affect corticosteroid output and consequently the immune system. (From Rider, M., Floyd, J. and Kirkpatrick, J. The effect of music, imagery and relaxation on adrenal corticosteroids and the re-entrainment of circadian rhythms. *Journal of Music Therapy* 22:46, 1985.)

There are others who believe that music affects us via the concept of hemispheric specialization.

According to this concept, the left brain processes analytical, cognitive activities and the right brain processes artistic, imaginative activities (see Chapter 12). Halpern[16] believes that music is able to activate the flow of stored memory material across the corpus callosum so right and left hemispheres of the brain work in harmony rather than conflict. Scarletti[35] makes an assumption based on research by Cook in 1973 and Roederer in 1975 that sedative music will produce a right hemispheric shift, thus inhibiting left hemispheric functioning, and Woolfolk and Lehrer[46] state that meditation also reflects a left-to-right hemispheric shift. Music appears to have application to health and more specifically to childbirth education. This is because the effect on the autonomic nervous system via the thalamus and hypothalamus might be utilized for arousal of the sympathetic nervous system or activation of the parasympathetic system, and there may be a relationship to the hormonal and immunological systems.

The Elements of Music

A review of the elements of music reveals that rhythm is the most basic force.[43] The human biological rhythm corresponds to a 4:4 musical beat; the body, when exposed to noncompatible rhythms, tries to balance itself by adapting to the new rhythm. This may be an aspect of the general adaptation syndrome first described by Hans Seyle. If the new rhythm is not compatible, dysfunction may occur.[16,30] Chants and songs of primitive rhythm may be soothing and calming or they may be rousing. Rhythm may be smooth and flowing as in a dactylic or 3:4 beat, or it may be choppy as in much of "hard rock" music, which generally employs a stopped anapestic rhythm. Halpern[16] and others believe the stopped anapestic rhythm is antagonistic to biological rhythms.

Repetition is another common denominator found in primitive, folk, and lullaby music. The rhythmic repetition seems to have a physiologically and psychologically calming effect on people. This may be related to the phylogenetic principle, in which the individual repeats in condensed form the evolutionary development of the race, or a Jungian concept of collective unconscious in which the early memories of the race influence an individual.[43,46]

Pitch and intensity are two other elements important to the impact of music. The effect of pitch on human physiology varies. Low pitches have a relaxing effect, while high-pitched tones are associated with strong nervous stimuli. Intensity increases respiratory activity, especially when it is high (loud) and when combined with high pitch and fast rhythm. Overstimulation of the auditory nerves can cause pain.[23,38] Sometimes high-intensity music is used to induce relaxation. The effect of this approach on the fetus is unknown, although an increase of external sound above 85 decibels is known to increase the fetal heart rate within five seconds.[23] Thus, caution should be exercised by the pregnant woman when considering this type of activity.

Listening Styles

Since we cannot "close our ears," we tend not to focus on each and every sound that confronts us in our daily living. Listening becomes a selective process. We listen to music in a variety of ways or styles. Sometimes we listen by allowing the sound to "wash over" us. When utilizing this style, attention is paid to the total effect of the music. Some describe this as a feeling of floating—of being carried or supported by the music. Others describe it as being totally immersed in or being bathed or massaged by the music. This is a somewhat passive listening style.

Another approach is to listen actively for the major and minor melody lines and rhythmic patterns, *listening for their recurrence and variations*.[38] This might be described as a semianalytical listening style. A more analytical form of listening is often employed by those who have musical training. In this style the listener *analyzes* the arrangement and the musical form itself. If one were to relate these listening styles to the concept of hemispheric specialization, the "wash-over" listener would perhaps be functioning in the right brain and the analytical one in the left.

The musical selection itself may dictate to some degree the way in which we listen. We are all familiar with the concept of "elevator music" or Muzak, which functions primarily as background but which may affect productivity and other elements in varying ways. Clark et al.[7] suggest that the degree of intrusiveness of a piece affects how we listen. According to them, intrusiveness refers to the qualities of an individual piece of music which allow it to penetrate listeners' awareness and to hold their attention or which allow it to distract the listener from other stimuli. Qualities of rhythms, tempo, dynamic level, timbre, tonal density, and tonal combination contribute to the concept of musical intrusiveness.

Some researchers[9] have studied the effect of rock music on children with attention-deficit disorder. Rock music was chosen for its intrusiveness. The music reduced the amount of motor activity but did not increase attention span. Gaston[13] reported that response to stimulative music results in enhanced body energy and stimulation of striated muscles. Application of this information to the childbirth setting has the potential to improve relaxation and respiration skills as well as provide added interest and stimulation to the program.

IMPLICATIONS FOR PRACTICE

The use of music for women during childbirth is not new; its soothing properties have been known for centuries. Hall[15] notes that it was customary for the Greeks to play songs on the lute to expectant mothers. The melodies were gentle and calculated to evoke a mood of peace and security for the baby. Today, many childbirth educators use music to teach relaxation skills and many women manage labor by breathing to the rhythms of familiar songs. A review of the varied applications to modern childbirth education may expand and stimulate its use.

Emotional Impact

Music, because it is processed through both the primitive, emotional brain and the cerebral cortex, carries with it an emotional impact that may occur because of previous experience and memory or because a particular tone or sequence of notes creates an unexpected emotional response. Bonny[3] and others have found that certain music can create a generalized response in some populations. It is wise to listen to musical selections prior to the birth experience to test response so that unexpected or unwanted reactions can be minimized. At times, a particular piece of music will be selected for the verbal message it conveys much as one would use affirmations or a mantra, a chant used during meditation.

Guided Imagery

Pairing guided imagery and music can enhance the vividness of the image through the use of environmental sounds conducive to the particular image. The combination of imagery and music can enhance relaxation, thus improving the potential for achieving the desired state. GIM (guided imagery and music) is described by Bonny[3] and Bonny and Savary.[4] The state is identified as being similar to dreaming while being awake and aware, or daydreaming with purpose.

Imagery is used in childbirth education in several ways. First, it can produce a state in which the woman uses imagery skills to imagine herself in a place where she is safe, secure, and totally able to relax. She might use this to enhance relaxation during the prenatal period and use it during labor to cope with difficult contractions. She may, in this state, be consciously doing what many people do unconsciously when confronting pain . . . imagining themselves somewhere else. Another application is to use imagery to set a positive tone during pregnancy by imagining managing labor, birth, and parenting in a positive, successful way to create a positive mind set.[33] Imagery can also be used to create a desired result in labor by imagining the cervix dilating, contractions growing stronger, and the baby moving through the proper maneuvers in the pelvis (see Chapter 12). (This should be done only during actual labor, however.) Music can be used to enhance the imagery process and assist in accessing the right brain.

Aid to Relaxation

Relaxation skills are frequently taught using music to assist in learning the skills (both basic and advanced) and as a conditioned response.[38] For example, music might be employed while verbally taking a student through a progressive relaxation exercise. After practice and mastery, the verbal component from the instructor might be deleted so that the student is mentally doing a progressive relaxation along with the music or cued by it. The next step would be to use the music as a signal to totally relax; a conditioned response has been developed. As with all conditioned responses, *practice* and *repetition* are key elements. Therefore, the music selected must be a style that will not cause boredom over a period of time. Popular music does not seem to have the endurance of classical or new age styles.[15–17] The music selected must also fit personal preferences in order to produce maximum benefit.[7,18,34,37]

> The music helped me concentrate.
>
> A NEW MOTHER
>
> As soon as that particular music started I completely relaxed.
>
> A NEW MOTHER
>
> The music made our labor room a quiet, serene oasis in the midst of chaos.
>
> A NEW MOTHER
>
> Images became clearer as the music helped me imagine a peaceful quiet place where I could completely relax.
>
> A NEW MOTHER
>
> Because it is nonverbal, music can move through the auditory cortex directly to the center of emotional responses. Also it may be able to activate the flow of stored memory across the corpus callosum so that right and left hemispheres of the brain work in unity rather than in conflict. Further calming, quieting music may help produce the large molecules called peptides that relieve pain by acting on specific receptors in the brain.
>
> HELEN L. BONNY[1]

Distraction or Attention-Focusing Device

Music may be used as a distraction or an attention-focusing device. There is some dispute over which strategy is most effective. Stevens[40] describes both approaches as cognitive control strategies, with distraction being more passive and attention-focusing more active and therefore more effective. Wepman identifies attention-focusing as an effective means to reduce pain.[44] Sears[36] notes that music requires a person to become more aware of sensory data. In their study, Hanser et al.[18] found that women who used music or rhythm or both as an attention-focusing device during labor received the greatest benefit. A meditative state that some women are able to employ during labor—with or without music—requires increased mental activity, which results in keeping the person mentally alert yet physically relaxed.[46] Davenport-Slack[10] cited prepared childbirth techniques as functioning as distractors, and Standley[38] notes that dental studies report that music may serve as a distractor from pain.

It may be that whether one uses a more passive (music to create an environment) or active (use of earphones) approach will be dictated by the amount of cognitive control required and by the intrusiveness of the music selected. Additionally, to avoid habituation and the resultant decreased pain relief, a variety of styles and selections of music should be included. Intermittent use will also be helpful.

Aid to Respiration

Breathing to the rhythm of music has been used historically. However, with the emphasis on individual pacing of respiration, this might be a more difficult application today. In some studies, some of the women were noted to synchronize their breathing with the beat of the music.[7] In another study, music therapists observed the pace of breathing of the subjects and matched music to that pace. They had their subjects practice breathing with the preselected music for each phase of labor. Four out of seven subjects stated that music "cued correct breathing."[18] Sammons[34] indicates that one of her subjects who had anticipated that music would assist with pace of breathing found that it did not. Livingston[23] suggests the selection of music that increases in pace as well as intensity as labor progresses.

Attempting to artificially pace respiration to rhythm of music would seem to have the potential to cause stress. The effort required to stay on the pace dictated by the music could be fatiguing and out of harmony with mind and body. However, when the rhythm of the music and the pace of breathing are synchronous, the repetitive rhythm could be soothing. The basic approach to labor is relaxation with slow paced breathing. At times, however, during labor an increased pace of breathing may be needed to activate the sympathetic nervous system and to reduce habituation. In those studies in which music was used as a structural aid to breathing, the pregnant women were being taught *rapid breathing*. Several of these studies also used music therapists to assist in selecting music on the basis of the women's preferences and pace of breathing.

One would assume that this approach might reduce some stress because of the selection of music that was more physiologically appropriate.[7,18] As has been noted before, a variety of styles and pace of music would need to be used to match the changing strategies employed throughout labor. Use of headphones, easy access to volume control, and varied music also provide a sense of control, which is known to be a factor in satisfaction and self-esteem.

Rhythm

While rhythm can be utilized by playing music with a well-defined beat, perhaps more useful in terms of individualizing pace is to utilize affirmations, mantras, and chants in which the laboring woman controls this aspect. Positive side effects to this approach are the positive messages constantly being replayed to the person, e.g., "My body tension is released," "Out, baby," thus producing a rhythm that becomes more compelling as body and mind work in harmony and a merging of the two occurs.[46] Hamel[17] speaks of a "magical monotony to produce timelessness," which describes this merging and which may translate in the birth experience as increased focusing and decreased pain.

Some women find that repeating a phrase or a mantra aloud is not acceptable and choose to set up the rhythm in their minds; others choose to make a sound on the "exhale" of the respiratory cycle. Still others utilize tapes and listen to chants or mantras already prerecorded. These could be commercially available tapes or tapes that the couple has made at home. For some, the woman's use of verbalized sound may be interpreted as an expression of severe pain or unacceptable behavior. Staff and coaches alike may need help in accepting this "controlled sound" and understanding its benefit as a means of rhythm, release, and relaxation.

For Cesarean Birth

Music has been used with patients prior to the administration of anesthesia for cesarean births. Goroszeniuk and Morgan[14] describe providing taped music for women to listen to while an epidural anesthetic was being administered for cesarean birth and finding that 75 per cent of the women described it as being very beneficial. The music was stopped at the moment of birth so the woman could hear the baby's first cry and was then resumed if she wanted to continue to listen to the tape while the surgery was completed. Locsin[24] used audioanalgesia for postoperative obstetrical and gynecological patients and discovered less medication use and decreased observable pain reactions during the first 48 hours after surgery.

For the Postpartum Period

The postpartum period also lends itself to the use of music. It is especially helpful for women establishing breastfeeding, enabling them to relax and allow the physiological process to function more effectively. Any postpartum pain might also be reduced by the use of music, and depending on the selection, could potentially give the woman and the family an emotional lift.

Standley[38] cites mixed results in two studies on newborns. Both studies used lullabies; one with normal newborns to three days of age (Owens[28]), which found no significant variables, and one using premature infants (Chapman[6]), which found a 16 per cent decrease in length of time it took the infants to reach discharge weight. Traditionally, mothers have rocked and sung to their offspring to soothe and quiet them, to put them to sleep, and for play.

Selecting Music

Music should be selected on the basis of its ability to produce feelings of energy, harmony, or balance for the person listening to it. Some music will be chosen because it enhances deep relaxation. A common piece chosen for this purpose is the "Canon in D" by Pachelbel. Characteristics that seem to produce relaxation in this piece are that it is composed using a musical progression in fifths and is based on eight bars that repeat 28 times, thus giving listeners a sense of always knowing where they are within the piece. This may give a feeling of security and may allow relaxation to occur.

Sometimes music will be selected to "set the tone" or create an atmosphere in the labor or birth room. Often, when music is being used for this purpose, busy staff enter the room bringing with them the sense of hurry, and the atmosphere within the room quickly brings them to a more relaxed state, slowing their movements, and engendering a state of respect for the event that is taking place. This relaxed, quiet state also helps the laboring woman and her coach to remain calm. Selections that might be useful for this purpose are one of Steve Halpern's "Antifrantic" series, such as "Soft Focus" or "Spectrum Suite." This music is composed using no melody line and does not utilize the orthodox 60 beats per minute. It is very calming and nonintrusive. The childbirth educator could demonstrate use of this music in class by playing it while students arrive and pointing out how quiet the environment becomes as people become aware of it.

Music that is chosen for distraction or as an attention-focusing device, or for producing energy will probably have an increased pace with perhaps a more defined rhythm. Sections of the music from "Chariots of Fire" have been used for this purpose, as well as for pushing. Most of the studies reviewed noted that expectant parents were encouraged to select their own music, since personal preference varies widely. Christenberry, as reported by Standley,[38] lists using personal preference for music first on his list of important variables to maximize music effectiveness when used for painful medical treatment. Other items on his list include beginning music prior to beginning painful procedures, using earphones, and teaching clients to associate music with pain reduction.

Integration into Class

In the childbirth education setting a similar approach can be used. Introducing music as another strategy just as you would relaxation and breathing techniques gives it status as a pain-relieving approach. Standley[38] reports that some dental studies suggest that auditory stimuli may directly suppress pain neurologically. The childbirth educator can demonstrate the use of music by playing it in class, citing various applications and discussing how the group responded to a particular selection. Point out the various styles of listening and have the students identify their usual style and encourage them to try other styles. Suggestions for using music during childbirth education classes are shown in Table 13–2.

Shea and Davis[37] used students from four childbirth educators, all of whom believed in the efficacy of music and used it often in class. Seventy-one per cent of the music users reported being more relaxed in labor. The classes these women attended paired music and relaxation practice, and music, relaxation, and breathing practice in class and encouraged couples to take their tapes with them to the birthing facility. In two other studies both instructors and hospital staff indicated a desire to continue use of music after the study period ended. They acknowledged its soothing effect and its ability to produce a "common ground" effect in prepared childbirth classes.[12,18]

Sammons[34] states that perhaps a more definitive statement by the instructor would increase music

TABLE 13–2. SUGGESTIONS FOR USING MUSIC

I. In prepared childbirth classes:
   A. Introduce music as another strategy just as you would relaxation or breathing techniques.
   B. Demonstrate its use by using it in class frequently, reflecting various applications, and discussing how the group responded.
   C. Integrate it into practice of techniques and have a lending library of tapes if possible.
   D. Encourage students to bring tapes to class to share.
   E. Visit your local hospitals and birthing centers and share with the staff your use of music and pave the way for your students to take their music into the birthing setting with them.

II. Criteria for Selection
   A. The music should produce:
      1. energy
      2. harmony
      3. balance
   B. Different styles of music are selected to produce a desired effect:
      1. deep relaxation
      2. an atmosphere of relaxed calm in the room
      3. energy to eliminate boredom and reduce habituation.

III. To help achieve deep relaxation with music:
   A. Use music that is physiologically compatible.
   B. Select a position that will allow the body to "let go" (all body parts flexed and well-supported.)
   C. Select an environment (or create one) that is conducive to relaxation (warm, indirect lighting, "cozy" atmosphere)
   D. Have students imagine:
      1. Your body bathed in music
      2. Your body being massaged by the music
      3. You are the instrument that is making the sound and you can feel its vibrations
   E. Have students listen to the spaces between the sounds.
   F. Students should let the music dictate depth and pace of breathing.

use in labor; presenting the use of music as a pain-relief strategy would meet that criterion. Shea and Davis[37] found that the music group in their study used more techniques during labor and that they reported that using music did not distract from other techniques. In fact, in the Clark et al.[7] study it was found that "music therapy patients reported significantly greater length of Lamaze home practice sessions than did non-music therapy controls." Perhaps this is a result of the pleasant effect of relaxation when music is included or it may be due to increased involvement of the clients in their own care as they actively select their own music. Encouraging students to bring their tapes to class to share also fosters increased participation and acceptance of responsibility for self-care.

Providing a library of tapes for clients to borrow will allow them to try out various styles of music at home before purchasing, potentially reducing costs to them. A regular, inexpensive tape recorder can be used. Earphones are not essential, although because the earphones block out many environmental sounds and the stimulus is presented directly, some think it is more effective when using music as an attention-focusing device. The laboring woman can also increase or decrease the volume at will. Most earphones allow enough sound to penetrate so that the coach's comments can be heard.

Visiting local birthing facilities to discuss the uses of music during labor and sharing ideas on logistics for use may help pave the way for clients who wish to use it. Sammons[34] found that both the type of labor and perceived acceptance or nonacceptance by hospital staff affected use of this medium. Some hospitals have built-in tape equipment in the rooms and have tapes available for their patients to borrow. Others do not support the use of music and make it difficult for patients to use it. This may be an item clients would want to add to their list of questions when determining which birthing facility to select.

Identifying how music can be used if a cesarean birth occurs and its use in the postpartum period for women who give birth vaginally or via cesarean birth can foster a sense of control as well as a connection to the other couples in the class regardless of route of birth. Childbirth educators who extend their practice into the neonatal period and beyond could continue to encourage music use for its relaxation, rhythm, and as a means to foster continued interaction between parent and child.

The childbirth educator who has never used music may want to invest in one or two tapes initially. Some tapes are composed specifically for use in childbirth and others specifically for relaxation. The tape resource list (Table 13–3) may be of value in locating a beginning library. She may also want to observe other instructors who use music or attend continuing education courses on the subject. Those who already use music may want to expand and experiment and learn from the kinds of music their couples use in labor and the ways in which they thought their selections helped or hindered them. This kind of information could be gathered through the birth report.

TABLE 13–3. TAPE BIBLIOGRAPHY

NEW AGE

Allen, Marcus, Jon Bernoff, Dallas Smith, Bell Tega

Petals, Breathe, Summer Suite

Dream Weaver Music
Rising Sun Records
P.O. Box 524
Mill Valley, CA 94942

Vibes, piano, acoustic and electronic instruments

Akerman, William

Balancing, Childhood and Memory

Windham Hill
Box 9388
Stanford, CA 94305

Guitar

Aura, Williams

Dreamer

Aura Communications
1775 Old Country Rd. #9
Belmont, CA 94002

Acoustic guitar, zither, harps, cymbals, tympani

Ball, Patrick

Celtic harp

Fortuna Records
Box 1116
Novato, CA 94947

Wire-strung celtic harp

Bearns and Dexter

The Golden Voyage Vol. I, III, IV

Awakening Productions, Inc.
4132 Tuller Ave.
Culver City, CA 90230

Environmental sounds with classical guitar, french horns, strings, vibraphone, synthesizers

Bergman, Steve

Sweet Baby Dreams, Lullabies from Around the World

Steve Bergman
P.O. Box 4577
Carmel, CA 93921

Orchestrated lullaby music with maternal heartbeat

Gibson, Dan

Solitudes (series)

Holborn Records
510 Coronation Dr.
West Hill, Ontario, Canada

The Moss Music Group, Inc.
48 W. 38th St.
New York, NY 10018

Halpern, Steve

Antifrantic Series: Dawn, Zodiac Suite, Spectrum Suite, Soft Focus Connection (with Paul Horn)

Halpern Sounds
1775 Old Country Rd. #9
Belmont, CA 94002

Piano, acoustic piano, electric violin, flute, bamboo flute, zither, wind chimes

Highstein, Max

The Healer's Touch

Inner Directions
P.O. Box 66392
Los Angeles, CA 90066

Piano, synthesizers, wind chimes, flute, oboe, cello, English horn, clarinet

Jones, Michael

Seascapes, Pianoscapes

Naranda Publications, Inc.
Postbus 6037
2001 HA, Holland

Naranda Publications, Inc.
1845 N. Farwell Ave.
Milwaukee, WI

Piano

Kelly, Georgia

Seapeace, Birds of Paradise, Ancient Echoes

Heru Records
P.O. Box 954
Topanga, CA 90290

Harp

Table continued on following page

TABLE 13–3. TAPE BIBLIOGRAPHY *Continued*

NEW AGE

Deuter, Chaitanya Hara

Cicada, Nirvana

Kuckuck Schallplatten/Musicverlag
Habsburgerplatz 2
800 München 40, West Germany

Recorder, harp

Meers, Jerrolyn and Dean Babcock

Sonic Light

Sonic Light Music
12025 Lucile St.
Culver City, CA 90230

Piano, guitar

Moon, Guy

Baby Peace

Family Wise Collaborative, Inc.
Tucson, AZ

Phillips, Janet Rabin

Birthnotes Music During Childbirth

Birthnotes
P.O. Box 4281
Greensboro, NC 27404
(Discount for bulk orders to Childbirth Educators)

Flute, orchestra, organ

Kitaro

Silk Road

Gramma Vision Records
260 W. Broadway
New York, NY 10013

Synthesizers, acoustic guitar, drums, percussion

Rowland, Mike

Fairy Ring

Sonia Gaia Productions
1845 Farwell Avenue
Milwaukee, WI 53202

Piano, synthesized strings

Schemuel, Ben, Marc Joseph, Wallace, Amy

The Baby Music

Spherica
P.O. Box 7621
Berkeley, CA 94707

Whitesides-Woo, Rob

Miracles

427 Linnie Canal
Venice, CA 90291

Harps, strings, winds

GREGORIAN/POLYPHONIC

Caeli, Regina

Gregorian Chant

Benedictine Monks of the Abbey
Saint Maurice and Sanit Maur of Ciervaux (Luxembourg)

Phillips 7311073

Trappist Monk's Choir

Chants from Assisi

Talbot, Michael

Come to the Quiet

Sparrow Records
8025 Deering Ave.
Canoga Park, CA 91304

Verbal meditation

CLASSICAL

Bach

Air for the G String,
Jesu, Joy of Man's Desiring,
Mass in B Minor

Brahms

Lullaby

Handel

Water Music

Humperdink

Childrens' Prayer from the opera
Hansel and Gretel

TABLE 13–3. TAPE BIBLIOGRAPHY *Continued*

CLASSICAL

Debussy *Clair de Lune, Prelude to an Afternoon of a Faun*	Gluck *Dance of the Blessed Spirits*
Pachelbel *Canon in D*	Vivaldi *The Four Seasons*

CONTEMPORARY (POPULAR)

Diamond, Neil *Jonathan Livingston Seagull* Soundtrack	Vangelis *Chariots of Fire* Soundtrack
Galway, James *Songs of the Seashore and other Melodies of Japan* RCA	Winston, George *December, Autumn* Windham Hill Box 9388 Stanford, CA 94305 Piano
Somewhere in Time Soundtrack	

FOR CHILDREN

Discovery Music *Lullaby Magic, Morning Magic*	(Both have a vocal and an instrumental side and have a copy of the words so you can sing along.)
Discovery Music 4130 Greenbush Ave. Sherman Oaks, CA 91423 (818) 905-9794	

For additional ideas see Lingerman, H. The Healing Energies of Music. Wheaton, IL: The Theosophical Publishing House, 1983. Ideas are listed in the text and in an appendix.

IMPLICATIONS FOR RESEARCH

There are many areas that need further research. Many of the studies cited had very small samples, therefore results must be viewed with caution and studies must be replicated. Questions that need to be answered include the following:

- To what extent does music enhance relaxation?
- Does the use of a music therapist influence the effectiveness of music during childbirth?
- Is music effective when used to cue breathing or does it produce additional stress?
- Are some styles of music better for use in labor than others?
- Is music more useful in certain phases and stages of labor than in others?

SUMMARY

Research supports the effectiveness of music in increasing relaxation and reducing responses to pain during childbirth. Incorporating music into childbirth education classes is easy and assists in creating an atmosphere of relaxation for couples. Music has implications beyond birth into the period of parenting. Childbirth educators are giving increased attention to the role of music during classes, childbirth, and the early parenting period.

References

1. Allen, M., and Gawain, S. *Reunion Tools for Transformation: A Guide to Meditation and Relaxation*. Mill Valley, CA: Whatever Publishing, 1979.
2. Bauman, E., et al. *The Holistic Health Handbook*. Berkeley, CA: And/Or Press, 1979.
3. Bonny, H. L. *The Role of Taped Music Programs in the GIM Process*. Baltimore: ICM Publications, 1978.
4. Bonny, H. L., and Savary, L. *Music and Your Mind: Listening with a New Consciousness*. Hagerstown, MD: Harper and Row, 1973.
5. Bressler, D. *Free Yourself From Pain*. New York: Simon and Schuster, 1979.
6. Chapman, J. S. The relation between auditory stimulation of short gestation infants and their gross motor limb activity. Unpublished doctoral dissertation. New York University, 1975.
7. Clark, M., McCorkle, R., and Williams, S. Music therapy–assisted labor and delivery. *Journal of Music Therapy* 18:88, 1981.
8. Codding, P. A. An exploration of the uses of music in the birthing process. Unpublished Master's thesis. Florida State University, 1982.
9. Cripe, F. Rock music as therapy for children with attention-deficit disorder: An exploratory study. *Journal of Music Therapy* 23:30, 1986.
10. Davenport-Slack, B. A comparative evaluation of obstetrical hypnosis and antenatal childbirth training. *International Journal of Experimental Hypnosis* 23:266, 1975.
11. Di Motto, J. Relaxation. *American Journal of Nursing* 84:754, 1984.
12. Durham, L., and Collins, M. The effect of music as a conditioning aid in prepared childbirth education. *JOGN Nursing* 15:268, 1986.
13. Gaston, E. T. Dynamic music factors in mood change. *Music Educators' Journal* 37:42, 1951.
14. Goroszeniuk, T., and Morgan, B. Music during epidural cesarean section. *Practitioner* 28:441, April, 1984.
15. Hall, M. *The Therapeutic Value of Music Including the Philosophy of Music*. Los Angeles: Philosophical Research Society, 1982.
16. Halpern, S., and Savary, L. *Sound Health*. Philadelphia: Harper & Row, 1985.
17. Hamel, P. M. *Through Music to the Self*. Longmead, Great Britain: Element Books Ltd., 1986.
18. Hanser, S., Larson, S., and O'Connell, A. Music therapy–assisted labor: effects on relaxation of expectant mothers. *Journal of Music Therapy* 20:50, 1983.
19. Humenick, S. Review: relaxation tapes for childbirth preparation. *Birth* 9:4, 1982.
20. Kibler, V., and Rider, M. Effects of progressive muscle relaxation and music on stress as measured by finger temperature response. *Journal of Clinical Psychology* 39:213, 1983.
21. Leonidal, J. Healing power of chants—universal adjuvant therapy. *New York State Journal of Medicine* 6:966, 1981.
22. Lingerman, H. *The Healing Energies of Music*. Wheaton, IL: The Theosophical Publishing House, 1983.
23. Livingston, J. Music for the childbearing family. *JOGN Nursing* 8:363, 1979.
24. Locsin, R. The effect of music on the pain of selected postoperative patients. *Journal of Advanced Nursing* 6:19, 1981.
25. Melzack, R. The myth of painless childbirth. *Pain* 19:321, 1984.
26. Moore, M., and Moore, L. *The Complete Book of Holistic Health*. Englewood Cliffs, NJ: Prentice-Hall, 1983.
27. Nurenberger, P. *Freedom From Stress: A Holistic Approach*. Honesdale, PA: Himalayan International Institute of Yoga Science and Philosophy, 1981.
28. Owens, I. D. The effects of music on the weight loss, crying, and physical movement of newborns. *Journal of Music Therapy* 16:83, 1979.
29. Palmer, H. Can we call birth normal? *In* Humenick, S. (ed.) *Expanding Horizons in Childbirth Education*. Washington, DC: ASPO/Lamaze, 1983.
30. Pelletier, K. Mind As Healer Mind As Slayer. New York: Dell, 1977.
31. Reynolds, S. Biofeedback, relaxation training, and music: Homeostasis for coping with stress. *Biofeedback and Self-Regulation* 9:169, 1984.
32. Rider, M., Floyd, J., and Kirkpatrick, J. The effect of music, imagery, and relaxation on adrenal corticosteroids and the re-entrainment of circadian rhythms. *Journal of Music Therapy* 22:46, 1985.
33. Samuels, M., and Samuels, N. *Seeing With the Mind's Eye*. New York: Random House-Bookworks, 1975.
34. Sammons, L. The use of music by women during childbirth. *Journal of Nurse-Midwifery* 29:266 July-Aug, 1984.
35. Scarletti, J. The effect of EMG biofeedback and sedative

music, EMG biofeedback only, and sedative music only on frontalis muscle relaxation ability. *Journal of Music Therapy* 21:67, 1984.

36. Sears, W. W. Processes in music therapy. *In* Gaston, E. T. (ed.) *Music in Therapy.* New York: The Macmillan Co., 1968.
37. Shea, E., and Davis, D. The perceived effectiveness of music as a relaxation technique in labor. Unpublished, 1986.
38. Standley, J. Music research in medical/dental treatment: meta-analysis and clinical applications. *Journal of Music Therapy* 23:56, 1986.
39. Steffes, S. Relaxation plus: The use of guided imagery or visualization. *In* Humenick, S. (ed.) *Expanding Horizons in Childbirth Education*. Washington, DC: ASPO/Lamaze, 1983.
40. Stevens, R. J. Psychological strategies for management of pain in prepared childbirth. I. A review of the research. *Birth and Family Journal* 1:157, 1976.
41. Tame, D. *The Secret Power of Music*. New York: Destiny Books, 1984.
42. Tanioka, F., et al. Hormonal effect of anxiolytic music in patients during surgical operations under epidural anesthesia. *In* Droh, R. and Spintge, R. (eds.), *Angst, Schmerz, Music in der anasthesic*. Basel: Editions Roche, 1985.
43. Weigl, V. The rhythmic approach in music therapy. *In* Schneider, E. (ed.) *Music Therapy 1962*. Twelfth Book of the Proceedings of the National Association for Music Therapy, Inc. Lawrence, KS: National Assoc. for Music Therapy, Inc., 1963.
44. Wepman, B. J. Psychological components of pain perception. *Dental Clinics of North America* 22:101, 1978.
45. Winokur, M. A. The use of music as an audio-analgesia during childbirth. Unpublished Master's thesis, The Florida State University, 1984.
46. Woolfolk, R., and Lehrer, P. (eds.). *Principles and Practice of Stress Management*. New York: Guilford Press, 1984.

Boxed Quotes

1. Bonny, H. Music and sound in health. *In* Hastings, Fadiman, and Gordon, *Health for the whole person*. Boulder, CO: Westview Press, 1981.

chapter 14

RELAXATION: Paced Breathing Techniques

ANNE TUCKER ROSE and SUZANNA M. HILBERS

. . . the learning of a short series of (paced) breathing exercises can have significant facilitative effects on reducing autonomic responsivity to a stressful stimulus.

Harris et al.

Prepared childbirth today is so closely allied to changes in the respiratory patterns that, in thinking of this topic, one automatically thinks of variations in breathing. Breathing techniques were perceived as being so basic to prepared childbirth that during its beginnings these techniques were often referred to as "*the* breathing." Breathing was taught in a specified way, with demonstrations by the childbirth educator and return demonstrations by the expectant mothers, each of whom behaved as their role model—the instructor—had performed. Class members relaxed together in the same positions and breathed alike in unison.

This is in no way a criticism of those early beginnings; this structured approach served a valuable purpose. The breathing patterns were recognizable in the obstetrical area, they generated camaraderie and strength of purpose for the couples, and they provided an indication to the birthing agency staff of the expectant parents' intentions for their birth experience. At that time most women during childbirth were passive and welcomed medication. Those first prepared women were considered by the medical establishment to be "radical" and "demanding." Laboring women were expected to cooperate and accept the ministrations of the caregivers without question. The concepts of patients' rights and consumerism were almost unknown and were given little attention.

The Problem

As childbirth education spread and expectant mothers accepted classes as an integral part of planning for the birth of their babies, the standard organization of classes and the structured performance became less appropriate. In any given class, the couples came from a cross section of society and it soon became apparent to many that some of the behaviors being taught were not always applicable to all students. Therefore, different authors and childbirth educators called the breathing patterns by different names and described them in whatever way seemed best to explain them to expectant parents. According to presently accepted standards, many of these changes were not appropriate, but they were understandable given the times and the needs of the clients.

The overall effect of teacher-made changes, however, was to create a Tower of Babel—many different names were used all over the country to describe a variety of breathing patterns. It is still possible today to find instruction manuals that describe breathing patterns called "hah-hee," "hee-hee," "choo-choo," or "sniff-puff." One instruction manual acknowledges this confusing situation with the statement that "childbirth educators do not teach the same breathing patterns."[15] While this is true, many childbirth educators taught the same breathing techniques but called them by different names. At the same time, reports of a physiological or psychological basis were virtually nonexistent.

As childbirth education became the norm rather than the exception, the need for consistency in breathing patterns and terminology has become more imperative. The mobility of our country's population required that a couple prepared in New York City for a first baby find similar classes in San Francisco for a second. The American Society for Psychoprophylaxis in Obstetrics (ASPO/Lamaze) is perceived by many as the interpreter of Lamaze childbirth education theory; thus the organization was often requested to respond to complaints from clients and other childbirth educators about the inconsistency and incongruity of breathing techniques. Also, from a scientific perspective, there was a need to establish the physiological basis for the breathing techniques and develop guidelines for practice. By the early 1980's, it was evident that there was a critical need for consistency and a scientific basis for childbirth education.

In July 1983, an ASPO/Lamaze National and University Faculty Conference on the scientific basis of prepared childbirth techniques was held in Columbus, Ohio, to examine and redefine the Lamaze method of childbirth education. The faculty reviewed and critically analyzed the scientific literature related to prepared childbirth. Each prepared childbirth strategy was evaluated, with the goal of deciding whether there was a sound scientific rationale for its use in childbirth education. These principles were incorporated into the knowledge base that provided the foundation for the Lamaze method of childbirth education, and provide guidelines for the contemporary practice of childbirth education, regardless of the method, because they are scientifically based.

REVIEW OF THE LITERATURE

Historical Perspective

The Evolution of Childbirth Education. The Popular Health Movement of 1830 to 1840 favored preventive care, including improved personal hygiene, diet, and instruction in human physiology, and rejected the drastic "cures" and interventions available from the medical community.[7] At that time, upper-class women were not expected to do much more than to plan the work of their servants.

They were considered delicate and prone to disorders of all kinds. Normal functions—menstruation, pregnancy and childbirth, and menopause—were treated as illnesses. Consequently, women spent long hours "resting" in order to treat "nerves," fainting ("vapors"), and "hysteria"—disorders that had become so much a part of their lives. A short-lived attempt was made to change the focus of health care from illness to wellness in the mid 1880's, but it failed.

Poor women, on the other hand, rarely received medical care. Although they were considered "sturdy," most were in poor health due to long working hours, poor diet, and the prevalence of communicable diseases—especially tuberculosis—which was common. For childbirth, they did receive care from midwives and often would seek advice from them about health problems as well.

The medical advice of those times included warnings against intellectual activity, claiming that it would result in corresponding loss of reproductive ability.[6] While working-class and poorer women were doing the work needed by a growing nation, upper-class urban women became progressively more sheltered and dependent.

After the turn of the century and during World War I, women in the United States and Western Europe began to liberate themselves from their physical, emotional, and financial dependency upon others. In the 1940's they enthusiastically accepted Dick-Read's suggestion in his book, *Childbirth Without Fear,* that childbirth could be a healthy, joyous event. Inherent in that belief is the concept that women need to know how their bodies function, an idea that history suggests has not always been popular.

Dick-Read's description of the education of expectant mothers gives us a clue as to its simplicity compared to our classes today:

> It is necessary, therefore, to explain what is meant by "education." There is no rule of thumb to such teaching, for no two women will or can accept facts in the same words. It is not a question of social class, for similar varieties of women are represented in all classes of society, and judgment must be used in each case. The same applies to the ability to attain relaxation; some are better than others, and the results vary accordingly.[5]

The sharing of information has expanded so much that even Dick-Read and Lamaze would probably be amazed at the level of sophistication of expectant parents and the complicated and detailed physiological information routinely provided in childbirth classes today.

Relaxation. Dick-Read believed that relaxation was an important part of childbirth preparation. To relaxation he attributed "peace of mind," muscular control, and a new interpretation of the sensations experienced during labor.[5]

Lamaze referred to the value of relaxation in physiological terms, stressing that the uterus must "be given the best possible conditions for its work," including relaxation of specific muscles so as to avoid pressure on the cervix and the uterus. He emphasized that muscular relaxation has a use from the beginning to the end of labor during contractions. From the time dilatation has reached the size of a quarter until the end, it (relaxation) should be adhered to between contractions as well.[14] Thus, the woman was taught to focus on relaxation throughout the process of labor. Relaxation is so important to thorough and complete preparation for childbirth that its inclusion in *each class session* is essential; it is a critical element of preparation for childbirth. (See Chapters 7 through 13 on relaxation.)

Breathing Patterns. Early theorists encouraged deep abdominal breathing throughout labor. The basis of this was a belief that some components of the pain in labor were due to muscular interference on the contracting uterus. They emphasized abdominal breathing in order to raise the abdominal muscles, thus enlarging the abdominal cavity and allowing the contracting uterus to rise unimpeded during a contraction.[2] But the hypothesis that pain occurred as a result of the pressure of the diaphragm and abdominals on the uterus has been discarded in favor of a more comprehensive theory which includes lactic acid buildup, mechanical deformation, and endocrine responses. This is still consistent with Dick-Read's fear-tension-pain syndrome.[5] There is little doubt that tension increases the need for oxygen, increases the production of catecholamines and lactic acid, increases the work of the body, and impedes labor, all of which lead to the increased perception of pain.

Lamaze focused on the contractions of normal labor, referring to the changes in frequency and intensity and suggesting that the woman be allowed to "adapt herself." The human body can pass from a state of rest to one of activity only by going through consecutive stages.[14] A large part of his book *Painless Childbirth* dealt with theories, experiments, and outcomes of Pavlov and his colleagues, their mentors, and their students. Lamaze emphasized the importance of preconceived attitudes to pregnancy and labor. He called the resultant behavior a collection of ''harmful conditioned reflexes,'' and he argued that reorganization of the activities of the mind was necessary.[14] Lamaze concluded that more than one type of breathing pattern would be useful to the laboring woman as she progressed through labor. He described two different patterns: a simple slow, deep rhythm and a more challenging ''shallow and quickened'' breathing pattern.[14] Those first descriptions were actually too sketchy to provide an image of the actual techniques; it was left to Bing[2] and others to describe the breathing patterns adequately.

Prepared childbirth today is based on the contributions of Dick-Read, Pavlov, and Lamaze and involves all three aspects identified by these pioneers—education, relaxation, and breathing techniques. However, today breathing techniques are viewed as a strategy that enhances relaxation, and the concept of support has been added as an integral aspect of all childbirth education classes.

Limited, if any, research related to prepared childbirth was available in the early years of childbirth education. What was known about respiratory physiology was confined to an understanding of how to combat the effects of pulmonary illness. It was only during the last decades when enthusiasm for exercise and sports became commonplace that interest in normal respiratory physiology—especially as applied to work—has been generated. Although not specifically designed for laboring women, if we consider the broad definition of work as including the activity of all muscles to expend or transfer energy, both voluntary and involuntary, it is then possible to draw some conclusions about childbirth as work and the respiratory response to that labor.

Lamaze's most unique and significant contribution to the childbirth education movement is his observation that within the obstetrical ''first stage'' of labor there were phases—changes in the nature of the contractions which were indicative of progress and which could be seen as distinct. He described these phases in terms of the frequency, duration, and intensity of the contractions of the uterus and the changing behavioral responses of the laboring woman.[14] He linked these changes to progress through the first stage. Until that time, the first stage had been perceived only in its entirety, measured in terms of cervical dilatation. In obstetrical textbooks today the first stage of labor is still seen as the principal measure of progress. The Friedman curve[20] is based on *time* and *cervical dilatation* and it is upon this curve that progress in labor is determined. Once it has been determined that the woman is in ''true labor,'' often little attention is paid to other physical and behavioral manifestations that a woman is experiencing during the first stage of labor. Frequency, duration, and intensity of contractions are considered worthy of note primarily because of their relationship to cervical dilatation. If labor does not adhere to the norm, if the dilatation is not accomplished within the number of hours deemed appropriate, this woman may be declared to be experiencing ''failure to progress'' and to be in need of intervention. Although most nursing texts give attention to affective changes during the first stage, for the most part, the medical model, the advancement of cervical dilatation, is *the* yardstick of progress in labor.

Lamaze's perception of changes within the first stage of labor led to a greater awareness of and a better way of caring for the laboring woman. No longer just one stage to be endured, labor became a series of events, moving from the simple to the complex, the effortless to the arduous. Nursing care during labor became more individualized largely as a result of the application of theory to his observations—early labor was distinctly different from transition and required different and creative approaches. Support for a woman in transition was specifically different from the support given to her during an earlier phase of labor. A woman was no longer just ''in labor''—she was in a specific phase of labor and different interventions and approaches were indicated. In fact, the term ''transition'' has become part of everyday clinical terminology, despite the fact that it does not appear in the medical obstetrical textbooks. Lamaze described at the end of the stage of dilatation what he termed a physiological phenomenon. This corresponds, he said, to a tug-of-war between the head seeking to enter the pelvis and the as yet incompletely dilated cervix. The uterine contraction loses its regular rhythm of the stage of dilatation; it is no longer the type of contraction that causes dilatation, and not yet the type that leads to expulsion of the child.[14]

The Search

With the identification of the problem—confusion involving breathing patterns in existence, the shortage of rationales for their use, and the lack of credible names—and with an appreciation of the historical background, the ASPO/Lamaze National Faculty began searching for those principles already recognized as having a relationship to changes in respiratory rhythm. First, the literature of a number of other disciplines (especially human respiratory physiology), was meticulously reviewed and analyzed.

Despite the fact that breathing patterns are generally accepted as a valuable tool to the enhancement of relaxation and to pain relief, modification in respiratory rate and depth is given little attention in the obstetrical literature. For example, in a recent obstetrical textbook, Oxorn's description of the use of breathing patterns is limited to: "The patient is trained in breath control."[19]

Physiology of Normal Respiration

Breathing rates typically vary from 12 to 16 breaths a minute. The frequency and depth of respirations are influenced by the individual's metabolism, body fat, circulatory status, and health of the lungs. Breathing through the nose, where the mucous membranes warm, filter, and humidify, the air is calming and this is the norm for many individuals. Some individuals automatically switch from nose to mouth breathing when under stress or during exercise in order to get increased oxygen into the system more quickly. During pregnancy and/or labor, the nasal mucous membranes may become engorged and this can determine a preference for nasal or mouth breathing. The size and position of the baby will affect the placement of the diaphragm and hence respiration. Pregnant women usually perceive an increase in respiratory effort. However, the respiratory rate remains the same.[20] Thus, there are many factors that influence how an individual woman will demonstrate paced breathing patterns.

Respiration modulates and is modulated by both the central nervous system and the autonomic nervous system. The heart rate increases with inspiration and decreases with expiration. Similarly, as the number of inspirations increases, the heart rate increases and as the number decreases the heart rate decreases.[8] Respiration functions under both conscious and unconscious control. However, respiration is one of the easiest involuntary activities to alter with conscious control. *Respiration can be thought of as an emotional change agent.* Breathing in a relaxed manner can potentially reduce the incidence of panic responses to stressful stimuli such as labor contractions.

Before one breathing pattern is advocated over another, it is also necessary to examine what is normal in terms of this mechanical act and its effect upon the absorption of oxygen and the elimination of carbon dioxide in the body. Change should always be made with respect and appreciation for the body's never-ending drive toward homeostasis. "Above all, do no harm" must apply here, also.

During normal quiet breathing, *inspiration,* movement of air into the lungs, is accomplished as the diaphragm contracts to lengthen the thoracic cavity, resulting in a decrease in alveolar pressure.[12] Air, outside of the body at atmospheric pressures, flows into the lungs down the gradient created principally by diaphragmatic contraction alone. The best example of this phenomenon is the hypodermic syringe. When the plunger is pulled back, a partial vacuum is created and air moves into the barrel.

Expiration during quiet breathing, on the other hand, is largely passive and is accomplished by elastic recoil of the lungs and structures of the thoracic wall. The thin film of fluid lining the alveoli and the elastic connective tissue in the lung itself contribute to this elastic recoil as the pressure gradient is reversed slightly, causing the air to flow out. Nevertheless, the structures of the thoracic wall in conjunction with the diaphragm, the abdominals, the external intercostals, and (in some persons) the scaleni muscles are capable of strong contraction when called upon to increase the volume of air as during exercise or the acts of coughing and straining.[23] The total volume of air inhaled and exhaled with each breath during quiet breathing is

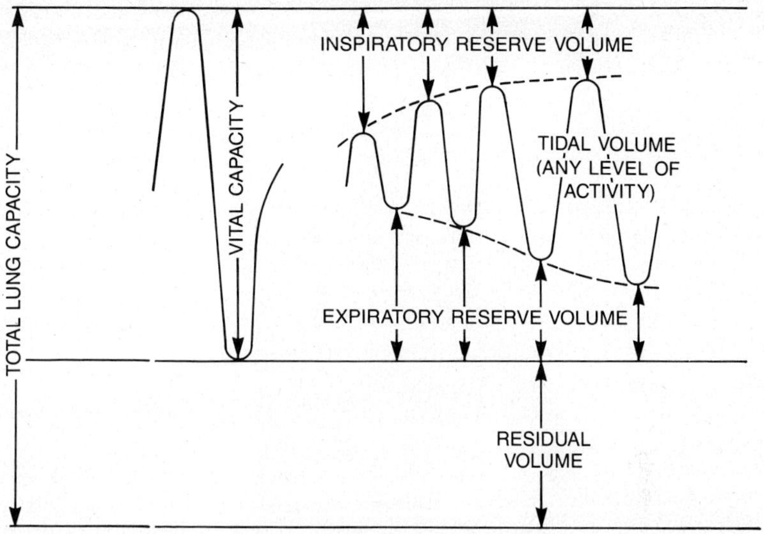

FIGURE 14–1. The various compartments and subdivisions of lung volumes. (Adapted from Dempsey, J. and Rankin, J. Physiologic adaptations of gas transport systems to muscular work in health and disease. *American Journal of Physical Medicine* *46*:582, 1963.)

known as the *tidal volume* (VT) and is usually between 400 and 500 ml. The normal resting VT is greater in larger persons, can be increased by regular exercise, and is decreased with advancing age.

There is, of course, a volume of air available over and above that which is inspired and expired during a single breath. This inspiratory reserve consists of 2500 to 3500 ml of air, while the expiratory reserve is about 1000 ml. These reserves give us the ability to deepen inspirations and expirations as necessary. The absolute maximum amount of air that can be moved in and out of the lungs during a single breath is known as the *vital capacity,* a total of the tidal volume and the inspiratory and expiratory reserves.[9] Finally, after maximal expiration, another 1000 ml remains in the lungs; this is known as *residual volume*.

There is, however, no actual oxygen exchange unless the inspired air reaches the pulmonary arterioles, where this exchange of oxygen is referred to as *alveolar ventilation*. This is the volume of fresh atmospheric air entering the alveoli during each inspiration. Therefore, if an inspiration does not move fresh atmospheric air into the alveoli, it could be said that no ventilation has taken place.[12]

Since there cannot be oxygen exchange in areas that do not contain alveoli, that portion of the respiratory system in which no oxygen is removed from air while it remains in those structures is called the *anatomical dead space*. Classified in these conducting airways are the nose, the pharynx, and the trachea, none of which have the capacity to permit gas exchange with the blood. The approximate total volume of this dead space is 150 ml.[9] When the amount of fresh atmospheric air entering the lungs to take part in alveolar ventilation is considered, the volume of the anatomical dead space must be substracted from the tidal volume. Given an average VT of 500 ml, such an equation would read:

500 ml − 150 ml = 350 ml.[23]

The significance of these measurements becomes obvious when changes in respiratory rate are examined. An average respiratory rate of 12 per minute results in an alveolar ventilation volume of 4200 ml/min (12 × 350 ml = 4200 ml). If the respiratory rate increases in frequency without a corresponding increase in the depth of the respirations, the result will be a dramatic drop in the alveolar ventilation volume despite the rate increase. Imagine a breath so shallow as to have a VT of 300 ml:

300 ml − 150 ml dead space
= 150 ml × 18 rpm = 2700 ml.

Furthermore, if respirations increase in frequency and become so shallow that tidal volume equals

Respiration can be thought of as an emotional change agent. Breathing in a relaxed manner can potentially reduce the incidence of panic responses to stressful stimuli such as labor contractions. (Photo by Rodger Ewy, Educational Graphic Aids, Inc.)

anatomical dead space, no alveolar ventilation will occur regardless of the respiratory rate.[23]

Increased ventilation that is adequate to cause loss of significant amounts of carbon dioxide is known as *hyperventilation,* but not all increases in respiratory rate result in hyperventilation.[23] Exercise results in significant increases in respiratory rate, as does increased body temperature, protective reflexes (coughing and sneezing), pain, epinephrine secretion, and reflexes from joints and muscles.[23] It is only when carbon dioxide is blown off faster than it is produced that hyperventilation results.[23] In other words, the respirations that result in hyperventilation must be both rapid and deep at the same time.

Of all the criticism of prepared childbirth education, probably the most common complaint has been that the more rapid breathing patterns (paced modified and paced patterned) lead to hyperventilation. Despite the requirement of *depth* and *rapidity* of ventilation in order for hyperventilation to occur, many women using paced breathing are needlessly urged by well-meaning caregivers to slow down or cease these patterns while in labor. However, laboring women using paced breathing techniques properly are less likely to hyperventilate than unprepared women.

In studies of subjects breathing very deeply and quickly for two to three minutes (much longer than the average contraction), the episode of hyperventilation was followed by depressed breathing or apnea, then by periodic breathing, and finally by respiration that slowly became normal. This respiratory depression is caused solely by loss of carbon dioxide. Increased ventilation carried out using air containing as little as 5 per cent carbon dioxide did not result in subsequent respiratory changes (apnea and periodic breathing). It is this hypocapnia that also gives rise to the cerebral symptoms and neurological changes that can be observed in cases of true hyperventilation. Dizziness and lightheadedness are reported and consciousness may be dulled because of cerebral vasoconstriction. Vasoconstriction also results in numbness and tingling of extremities. Tetany may appear; it is usually considered to be the result of a lowering of the calcium concentration in the blood and tissue fluids. It produces stiffness of the face and lips, carpopedal spasm, and increased excitability of the motor nerves. Spasm of the facial muscles upon tapping the facial nerve (Chvostek's sign) is positive.[12]

Concerted efforts, through continuing education programs and new employee orientation sessions, are needed to ensure that caretakers of laboring women know that paced breathing techniques, *performed properly,* will not result in hyperventilation. If, for some reason, hyperventilation does occur during labor, simple remedies are available, such as rebreathing some exhaled carbon dioxide from cupped hands or breathing normally while compressing one nostril with the index finger.

Changes in Respiratory Function During Pregnancy

During pregnancy the oxygen needs of the pregnant woman increase because of her increased basal metabolic rate and increased tissue mass. At term, the pregnant woman uses approximately a 20 per cent greater total amount of oxygen than the nonpregnant woman, and a corresponding increase in carbon dioxide occurs. The respiratory center is believed to become more sensitive to carbon dioxide because of the high levels of progesterone during pregnancy. This results in an increase of approximately 50 per cent in minute ventilation and a decrease in arterial P_{CO_2} below that of the nonpregnant woman. In order to maintain adequate ventilation, the pregnant woman breathes deeper and her respiratory rate increases slightly. During pregnancy, the woman is typically in a state of mild respiratory alkalosis that is compensated by a mild metabolic acidosis.[9,20]

Paced Breathing

A redefinition of prepared childbirth breathing patterns in a way that was consistent with the scientific literature was necessary. The terms chosen also needed to be clear, concise, and easy to recall. After a variety of names were considered, the term "paced breathing" was chosen as the most appropriate designation for all prepared childbirth breathing techniques. There was already precedent for the use of the term. *Paced breathing* is a generic term that describes the type of breathing used in studies on responses to stress,[10] in attempts to relieve pain,[3] and in investigation into the role of respiration and responses of the autonomic nervous system.[22]

The implication of the word *paced* was also considered—that of moving ahead, as paces are steps—to proceed. "Pacing oneself" also implies self-regulation in order to conserve energy. Both of these usages are positive images for labor. Within the paced breathing, three adjectives were chosen to designate the difference between the three breathing patterns, names which most accurately described the specific breathing patterns: slow paced breathing, modified paced breathing and patterned paced breathing. Additionally, the "cleansing breath," which has been taught from the early days of prepared childbirth as a prefatory breath and as a signal for the onset and the conclusion of contractions, was retained as an important aspect of all breathing patterns.

The "Cleansing" Breath

The name *cleansing breath* has its origin in the practice of Yoga and other eastern disciplines which rely on breathing for relaxation.[21] In this instance the descriptive word "cleansing" refers to the cleansing of the mind. The expectant mother is encouraged to set aside worries and concerns—all negative distractions that would keep her from total relaxation. Initially in the classroom it may require deliberate efforts and practice on her part until eventually the cleansing breath becomes synonymous with a "tranquil state of mind."[17] Some of these disciplines emphasize concentrating on a single object and others, focusing on a completely clear mind or the suggestion that attention be focused upon a problem in order to solve it positively. It is in these ancient theories that the origin of the use of visualization or focusing upon an object—the so-called *concentration or focal point* as used in childbirth preparation—can be found. Originally taught in this context (the preparation of the mind and body for relaxation), it quickly became a valuable signal to the coach and other caregivers of the laboring woman of the boundaries of each contraction.

There is also evidence that the cleansing breath plays a role in enhancing oxygenation. The contractions of the gravid uterus during labor, like all forms of work, result in the expenditure of energy as the outcome of the oxidation of fuel, at a rate in proportion to the intensity of the work.[4] This performance of work results in some degree of oxygen debt to the working muscles as a result of the initial lag in delivery of oxygen acquired by breathing. The body's capacity for storage of oxygen is limited; ultimately the oxygen necessary for aerobic processes must be derived from the atmosphere. During the time that the work is occurring this oxygen debt cannot be paid but must be made up during the recovery period.[4] It can therefore be hypothesized that any breathing technique or pattern that improves the delivery of oxygen either as the work begins or as soon as it ends could be considered a contribution to repayment of the oxygen indebtedness. For this reason, the cleansing breath should be effortless and as deep as is comfortable. It can best be described as like a sigh—a deep, relaxed breath designed to ventilate well and serve as a signal for relaxation at the same time.

The exact physiological effect of the cleansing breath on the woman's respiratory status during labor has yet to be determined. However, the cleansing breath is important as a signal for relaxation and serves to uncouple the stimulus of the contraction from the tendency toward an alarm response. The depth of the cleansing breathing should be to the woman's level of comfort. She should avoid a breath that is too deep and that stimulates the stretch receptors in the intercostal muscles leading to an alarm response rather than the desired relaxation response.

Slow Paced Breathing

There is ample evidence to demonstrate that slow deep breathing enhances relaxation and that relaxation of the body, such as occurs during sleep, results in a slowing and deepening of respirations. Thus, the adjective "slow" to describe the first paced breathing pattern is appropriate. References to slow deep breathing are consistently found in research on relaxation. In works describing Yoga, Zen, and other forms of meditation, the control of respirations is considered the "key mediating factor between mind and body."[18]

Investigations of the Zen monks and Yogis as they meditated demonstrated the presence of increased alpha waves, brain waves usually associated with a feeling of well-being.[1] A number of psychological and physiological studies have demonstrated the relationship between slow deep breathing and relief from tension and pain. In one investigation comparing respiratory patterns to visual and auditory stimuli, it was reported that high ego strength was associated with slow deep breathing.[8] In another, when the behavioral traits of 160 men and women were compared to their respiratory patterns, it was demonstrated that individuals whose habitual breathing patterns were slow and of large tidal volume were found to be confident, emotionally stable, and physically and intellectually active.[8]

It may be inferred from these studies that the sense of mastery and self-control associated with practiced breathing regulation is responsible for this positive mental attitude, and that this plays an important role in the ability to cope with tension and the perception of pain.

In 1976 Harris et al. studied three groups of 13 male students to determine if autonomic response could be reduced by the use of a slower respiratory rate. The respiration control group was directed to breathe at 8 RPM, a rate that was synchronized to a light that went off and on at four-second intervals. They practiced for ten minutes and were then subjected to electric shock while their cardiac rates (determined by the activity of both the parasympathetic and the sympathetic nervous systems) and electrodermal responses (sympathetic only) were measured. The respiration control group demonstrated that even this pattern after a short practice time can have significant facilitative effects on reducing autonomic responsivity to a stressful stimulus.[10]

McCaul and co-workers used electric shocks on 105 male subjects to study the effect of a slow respiratory rate on physiological arousal and self-evaluation of anxiety. They concluded that paced respirations are effective as a coping strategy, physical arousal was reduced as measured by skin resistance and finger pulse volume.[16]

It is important to note that none of these studies used a respiratory rate chosen for its appropriateness to the individuals in the study. In these reports the rate was chosen because it was one half the average rate of all persons or because of prior data indicating that slow breathing exerted a significant regulatory effect upon cardiac rate. There was no effort to design a rate that was specific to the individual.

Early prepared childbirth references described this breathing pattern as "slow chest." However, there was no evidence to suggest that "chest" (thoracic) breathing was superior to or more effective than "abdominal" breathing. In reality, it is very difficult for anyone to breathe *entirely* with the chest *or* the abdomen without training. The body is constructed in such a way that to move one causes movement, however slight, of the other. Additionally, there is evidence that "thoracic" breathing plays a role in activating the autonomic nervous system, consequently keeping that system in a state of arousal and counteracting any positive effects to be gained by relaxation.[22]

It is even possible that emphasis on chest breathing results in deliberate overexpansion of the chest. Directives such as "Breathe like a bellows" cause tension not only of intercostal muscles but of the throat and face as well; this is combined with a tendency to hold the breath in an effort to slow the breathing to someone else's norm. In the past, some directions for this breathing included inhaling and exhaling to a particular number of seconds, a breathing exercise which is commonly used in Yoga but which requires practice and motivation and commitment to meditation as a discipline in and of itself. It is not necessary to encourage such rigid breathing in a class consisting of expectant parents who have had no other training in breathing. To do so may only serve to encourage them to adopt a rhythm other than their own comfortable one. In the past, such rigid adherence to a formula left the couples and the teacher with no way to respond to individual needs and differences.

The slow deep breathing pattern was termed *slow paced breathing*. It should be at a rate that is comfortable for each woman and that provides adequate oxygenation for the work of labor and supports the relaxation response. Clinically one-half the normal respiratory rate places most women at 6-9 breaths per minute, which is consistent with traditional childbirth breathing techniques. As discussed earlier, Vander et al.[23] provide compelling arguments against any respiratory rate of *less* than one half the normal rate as being too slow to provide adequate alveolar ventilation. Accordingly, the guideline that was adopted is that the respiratory rate for slow paced breathing shall be no *less* than *one half the woman's normal rate*. The childbirth educator will need to teach couples strategies for determining the normal rate in the classroom and for dealing with individual differences early in the class series.

Some childbirth educators claim that if a woman is adequately relaxed, slow paced breathing will occur naturally and thus need not be taught. Others find that introducing slow breathing enhances relaxation and is therefore important to teach. Both ideas may be correct. Some women may respond best to the first approach wherein slow paced breathing is an *affirmation of relaxation,* while others may respond to using deliberate, slow breathing as an *aid to relaxation*. In either case the goal is for the expectant mother to be able to achieve both relaxation and slow breathing simultaneously. Finding the best approach or combination of approaches is the challenge that the childbirth educator faces.

Whether the woman chooses to inspire and expire through the nose or mouth or in any combination is her personal choice. Switching from nose to mouth breathing decreases the work of breathing due to the turbulence and subsequent airflow resistance resulting from the movement of air through the nasal cavities.[13] It is estimated that about 50 per cent of the total airway resistance is encountered in these passageways.[12] On the other hand, those who meditate argue the value of nasal breathing, attributing to it regulation of emotional and physiological states.[18]

If the woman chooses to use mouth breathing, either during practice or actual labor, the childbirth educator should teach ways to protect these mucous membranes from the drying effects of this type of breathing. The most obvious answer is, of course, to provide moisture in the form of liquids. Clear liquids including Jello, crushed ice, and ice pops can be used at home, especially for primaparas who are unlikely to deliver very quickly. In the hospital, clear liquids, rinsing the mouth with water or mouthwash, and brushing the teeth will help. The woman can provide her own mouth spray to provide moisture. One approach that can be used is to suggest that the expectant mother place her tongue gently against the roof of the mouth during the breathing, relax the lower jaw and allow the air to move around the tongue. In this way, the tongue traps moisture and is not as subject to extreme drying. If the tongue is placed behind the upper teeth and the air allowed to flow *around* it, it should be done so gently and merely placed there so that this muscle remains relaxed.

In the performance of slow paced breathing, the woman may appear to the observer to be using mainly the chest or the abdomen or both. Confining the movement to either is inappropriate since *maintenance of relaxation* is the primary goal. Similarly, pursed lip breathing or forced exhalation (candle blowing) should not be used because it causes tension in face and throat and prolonged contraction of intercostal muscles and diaphragm. Any deliberate alteration of expiration results in an act that is no longer passive, as it is designed to be. The exception includes persons trained previously in Yoga who demonstrate an evenness of inspiration and expiration. Because of the enhanced relaxation and improved oxygenation that occurs with slow paced breathing, it is preferable for the woman to be encouraged to use this breathing pattern for as long as possible during labor, changing patterns only when absolutely necessary to maintain relaxation and increase comfort. Furthermore, throughout labor and before changing breathing patterns, expectant mothers should be checked for the need to change position, urinate, relax, or manipulate the environment to minimize distractions and decrease pain.

However, with time, habituation may make slow paced breathing less effective. Habituation describes the diminution of response to a repeated stimulus such as a breathing pattern. Positioning, and environmental changes, and imagery as well as other stimuli will retard habituation to slow paced breathing, but eventually the laboring woman will probably need something else. Slow paced breathing can then be modified by introducing other stimuli such as attention focusing or other repetitive patterns of breathing that will cause an alerting response.

Modified and Patterned Paced Breathing

When work becomes more physically or emotionally demanding or stressful, the rate of respirations increase. An increased need for oxygen results from increased work and the stress response produced by the autonomic nervous system. This need is responsible for the increased respiratory rate, increased heart rate, increased blood pressure, and increased muscle tension. Modified paced breathing was selected to mediate the stress response by pacing the respirations at a controlled rate. In turn, respiratory rate, heart rate, blood pressure, and muscle tension decrease and a state of increased relaxation is achieved. *Modified paced breathing* was so named because it is a modification of the initial slow pace. *Patterned paced breathing,* a more rhythmic pattern, provides a mechanism for *increased attention focusing* by the laboring woman. Because the patterns of modified and patterned paced breathing are deliberately contrived, they must be learned and practiced to be used effectively. If slow paced breathing does not afford relief, these patterns provide a rhythm upon which the woman can concentrate and gives her the ability to work with the contractions and thus cope effectively with her labor. The use of paced breathing patterns, other relaxation techniques, and support of loved ones and caregivers improves the laboring woman's ability to relax, and increases her confidence that she can cope with childbirth.

Only one study could be found in which such a respiratory pattern was used during painful stimuli in an attempt to assess its use in reducing the intensity of the stimuli. Cogan and Kluthe in 1981[3] reported on a study in which 12 male and 12 female student volunteers in three groups were provided with 20 minutes of training in relaxation, 20 minutes of training in patterned breathing mirroring the increasing-decreasing intensity pattern of an inflated blood pressure cuff (which was used as the painful stimulus), and 20 minutes of learning patterned finger tapping. The breathing rates ranged from 30 exchanges a minute at the beginning and ending of the 45-second time period to 120 exchanges a minute during the central 15 seconds of each time period. The investigators found that relaxation seemed to contribute directly to pain reduction while the breathing as described and finger tapping were associated with intermediate ratings.[3]

Respiratory rates this high, however, cast some doubt as to the worthiness of this demonstration. It would seem that the subjects would experience some sense of hypoxia or anxiety or both in this instance. Such studies serve to remind us that there is a great need for continued research to increase understanding of the phenomena observed in the clinical area.

Experiments in respiratory physiology demonstrate that as the respiratory rate increases, the tidal volume decreases because there is not time enough between respirations to empty the lungs adequately. This results in decreased alveolar ventilation.[23] Therefore, the depth of any shallow breathing taught must take into consideration anatomical dead space plus alveolar ventilation. The rate of both modified paced and patterned paced breathing patterns should be enough to require concentration, but not so frequent as to be tiring or to result in a decrease in alveolar ventilation to unacceptable levels. In the absence of precise data on the effects of breathing patterns on the blood gas levels of pregnant women, a recommendation was made that the respiratory rate *not exceed twice the woman's normal rate*. This rate has been observed empirically to be a safe, comfortable upper limit. The depth of each respiration, even if reduced so that the tidal volume is less than the 500 ml considered usual, will provide sufficient alveolar ventilation, as long as it is at least slightly more than twice as great as the anatomical dead space.

The following is an example of modified paced breathing at a rate of 24 RPM (the tidal volume of each breath is arbitrarily placed at 325 ml):

VT 325 ml × 24 RPM
= 7800 ml/min pulmonary ventilation
7800 ml − (150 ml dead space × 24 RPM = 3600 ml) = 4200 ml/min alveolar ventilation

A comparison of these calculations with those given earlier in describing normal respirations demonstrate that the outcomes are the same:

VT 500 ml × 12 RPM = 6000 − (150 × 12 = 1800) = 4200 ml/min.[23]

In the teaching of breathing techniques, a delicate balance is aimed for—a breath deep enough to cause adequate alveolar ventilation but not so shallow as to move only anatomical dead space. Obviously, the breath should not be so rapid and so deep as to cause hyperventilation.

Modified paced breathing is performed as an upper chest breath that is not confined to the throat, nor does it move the entire chest wall vigorously. The laboring woman should appear relaxed and comfortable. Women should understand that any feeling of air hunger or a need to sigh or "catch a breath" is probably a sign that tidal volume is inadequate; the depth of the respiration is too shallow and should be deepened. Telling a pregnant woman to breathe to her level of comfort, i.e., to a level where she feels she is being adequately oxygenated, may help her determine how deeply she needs to breathe to satisfy her own physiological needs. The choice of mouth or nose breathing is again left up to each woman, along with instruction on protection of mucous membranes in the event of mouth breathing. In either event, the coach can readily observe, give feedback, and assist the woman to refine the breathing pattern using these guidelines.

Sounds or suggestion of a sound ("hee" or "hah") should be avoided because these are made by tightening the vocal cords and contracting the intercostal muscles. This threatens the ability to continue relaxation. *Relaxation is the foundation upon which all childbirth preparation techniques, and especially paced breathing patterns, are built.* Often, the breathing is so quiet that only the coach, having practiced with the woman, is aware of the patterns she has chosen.

It is not necessary to practice increasing and decreasing the speed of the modified paced breathing. In all probability that phenomenon will occur naturally in labor as the intensity of the contraction increases. The teacher should describe its occurrence or use ice as an uncomfortable stimulus, at which time respiratory speed variation often occurs automatically. The instructor can use that opportunity to explain how adaptation occurs.

The third type of breathing technique is patterned paced breathing. This term emphasizes the variety of patterns which may be designed. It is performed in exactly the same way as modified paced breathing with the addition of a *slightly* emphasized exhalation at regular intervals. Probably the most common rhythm taught initially is 4–1, meaning four comparatively shallow upper chest breaths plus one similar inspiration followed by an exhalation. The exhalation could be described as the drifting or sighing of air outward with only minimal emphasis and returning again to the original pattern without hesitation or breath holding. Vigorous "candle blowing" is not necessary and is probably counterproductive. When using modified paced and patterned breathing techniques, the emphasis is on maintaining a relaxed posture while using the breathing pattern as a means of attention focusing.

During the two and one half decades that prepared childbirth education has been available in the United States, a great many varieties of patterns for transitional labor have been invented, most by ingenious couples. These invented patterns were a natural development of the expectant parents' understanding of how the breathing pattern helped the laboring woman. All such patterns, the use of alternate numbers (4–1, 6–1, 4–1, 6–1), "pyramids" (6–1, 5–1, 4–1, 3–1, 2–1, 3–1, 4–1, 5–1, 6–1) and random numbers may be appropriate for some or even many women. They can be described by the instructor or they can be practiced as part of the classroom exercise leaving the couples to choose those which appeal to them. They are simply variations of patterned paced breathing. The guidelines which apply here are the same as for all alterations in respiratory rate and depth—that alveolar ventilation not be compromised.

A review of birth reports and letters from prepared women indicates that due to the emphasis on using slow paced breathing as long as possible, women resort to modified paced and patterned paced breathing only when the slower breathing no longer affords relief regardless of dilatation. Women and their coaches often report a wide variety in the uses of the breathing patterns in actual labor, which is to be expected as we encourage flexibility and emphasize individual differences. Slow paced breathing is the basic respiratory skill that is most effective in enhancing the relaxation response. Modified and patterned paced breathing are used for their alerting or habituation reduction effects. Once this has been accomplished, a return to slow paced breathing may be useful. Each breathing technique may be used at various points in labor without reference to any specific phase of labor. Thus, all three breathing patterns are valuable, while the decision as to how best to use them is in the hands of the expectant parents.

All other aids to concentration—the focal point, imagery, effleurage, and massage—are superimposed over relaxation and breathing patterns. However, they are no less important and references to them are only excluded from this chapter because they are dealt with in more detail in other chapters. They too are tools, applied by couples in whatever way best helps them cope with the stresses of labor.

Objectives for Using Paced Breathing Techniques During Childbirth

Paced breathing patterns are used to maximize respiratory efficiency during childbirth and modulate autonomic nervous system responses to both physical and psychological stress. The objectives for their use identified when the paced breathing patterns were first described by Hilbers,[11] include the following:

- Maintain adequate oxygenation of mother and fetus
- Increase physical and mental relaxation and decrease pain and anxiety;
- Enhance opening of airways through the use of relaxed breathing patterns.
- Eliminate inefficient use of muscles to decrease the oxygen cost of breathing
- Provide a means of attention focusing; and
- Control of inadequate ventilation patterns that are symptoms of pain and stress.

These continue to be valuable guidelines as we gain more and more scientific information about the use of respiratory techniques to assist laboring women to cope effectively during childbirth.

IMPLICATIONS FOR PRACTICE

Perhaps the most challenging aspect of the changes in breathing patterns is in the area of teaching strategies. If childbirth educators accept the concept of *individuality* as guiding them as they lead expectant parents to an understanding not only of the process of childbirth but also of their own unique ways of coping, then their teaching becomes a constantly changing dynamic reaction to the class members. Expectant parents' readiness to learn must be assessed along with their motivation or lack thereof, and these feelings discussed. The women's physical characteristics, body type, weight, state of health and nutrition, and the size and position of the baby all need to be considered when teachers individualize their teaching. Breathing patterns are, after all, only one aspect of the physiology of each expectant mother. A "recipe approach," in which the teacher teaches all classes the same way while observing outcomes in the hope that by the last class everyone will look approximately the same, is not appropriate.

A typical class emphasizing individual differences will find women sitting up and lying down, eyes open or closed, breathing at rates that vary, with mouths closed or lips parted. An imaginary picture of expectant mothers lined in a row all doing the same thing at the same time is no longer valid. Each couple is encouraged to practice in a variety of ways to increase options during labor. The instructor may find couples spending more time in talking to each other and in experimenting with breathing and positioning. She becomes more of a facilitator and resource person, introducing principles and topics for discussion and observing how couples apply that knowledge. The teacher who is more comfortable being in control at all times will undoubtedly have difficulty adjusting to these suggestions. The childbirth educator used to being on "center stage" may find herself having to bring the class together from time to time, in order to present new topics as the couples get into lively discussions with each other about comfort positions and relaxation techniques.

The educator in her role as facilitator, while challenged to observe every aspect of the expectant parent, is also expected to find ways to help each individual discover the best way to learn. Additionally, the effect of individual differences on breathing patterns makes it evident that greater emphasis must be placed upon teaching the labor coach how to help the woman deal with labor—discovering, understanding, and applying basic principles while maintaining an awareness of the expectant mother's uniqueness. (For more information on coaching, see Chapter 17.)

In an effort to provide some guidelines on developing strategies, the place to begin is with *normal respirations,* remembering that no one approach will work well for everyone at all times. It is not difficult to teach expectant parents about normal respirations. Start simply with inspiration and expiration. Direct them to place their hands on each other's chest to feel the rise and fall of breathing. Facing each other, have them breathe in rhythm with each other; these methods quickly help them to see and feel what respirations are all about. These simple exercises also give permission for couples to touch each other in class, while the instructor is able to observe their readiness to cooperate and to work together.

Coaches should observe normal respiratory patterns at a time when the woman is *not* relaxed, so that the rate and depth is not distorted by relaxation techniques. Immediately after returning from a break after mild exertion is a good time. Measure one minute's time and have the coaches count respirations during that minute to obtain an "average" rate for their partner. They should know that this

> It might be thought that one could safely leave breathing to chance and that most women in labor breathe all right anyway . . . it is important not only to learn how to breathe in an easy, relaxed, rhythmic way but to allow for a margin of error in the stress of labour, and particularly near full dilatation.
>
> SHEILA KITZINGER[1]
>
> Investigators have found that learned patterned breathing is associated with pain reduction in both laboratory and clinical settings.
>
> ROSEMARY COGAN AND KARL KLUTHE[2]
>
> Many practitioners of yoga believe tht one breathes life energy called *prana* into the whole body, not just air into the lungs. Directing this life energy to fill a particular area of the body with the in-breath and imagining tension draining out of that area with the out-breath is a powerful means of feeling revitalized and relaxed.
>
> CARL JONES[3]
>
> When I increased my presentation of meditation and relaxation techniques, the couples found their own breathing patterns.
>
> JEAN BATTAGIN[4]
>
> My room was next to the birthing room. I heard four women deliver their babies. I don't think I could go through any kind of labor or delivery without knowing how to breathe.
>
> A NEW MOTHER

rate is probably distorted, as the woman, knowing that someone is observing closely, cannot help but become self-conscious about her breathing.

Instruct them to observe again during the week when the woman is unaware, to determine more accurately each woman's average respiratory rate. It is important not to underestimate the importance of the value of the discovery of this basic information by the expectant parents. The *process* of completing this "assignment" prepares them for creative problem-solving, but some couples require more time to become alert to their own physiology. Thus coaches should observe the woman's responses during practice sessions. If, for instance, the woman was to breathe very slowly, at a rate less than one half normal, she would experience the need for more or deeper respirations over one minute's time. This useful observation would lead both individuals to the conclusion that an adjustment in respiratory rate is necessary under certain circumstances.

During the teaching of slow paced breathing, the instructor simply draws upon the coach's understanding of the partner's normal respiratory rate and how she appears when ventilation is inadequate, to describe this breathing pattern. Instructing the woman to breathe deeply while slowing her respiratory rate down to one half her normal rate while the coach times her for one minute, concurrently keeping her appraised of her progress, most often is all that is necessary. The coach encourages her to increase or slow down on the basis of his or her understanding and observation of her "average" respiratory rates as she *paces* her breathing through a mock or simulated contraction.

As the couples work together—discovering principles, sharpening their skills, learning to observe and to respond to each other's needs—the instructor provides opportunities for them to increase their self-esteem and their sense of mastery. She also encourages them to become comfortable with touching and communicating with each other. These are appropriate times to integrate other aspects of training, such as relaxation, massage, use of focal points, and visualization.

A coach's ability to observe and help the woman can be improved by having the coach measure the length of her torso. This measuring of the distance from the rib cage to the point where the femur inserts into the hip gives the coach an awareness of the space in which the fetus lies. (Paper tape measures made by the Hollister Co. are perfect for this purpose.) Coaches observe and compare their awareness of the differences between their partner and other expectant mothers in the class leading them to discover principles with minimal lecture. Classes become more dynamic and discussion more lively. Couples learn to apply what they know to other situations. They can anticipate changes in respiratory effort during exertion after engagement of the baby and see the relationship between that effort, a large baby, and a woman whose torso is comparatively short. They view their partner and baby as a unique dyad unlike any other in the room.

As expectant parents proceed through this process of discovery, they begin to anticipate applications to labor and often invent appropriate approaches for their own situation. As a result, these adult learners are allowed to proceed at their own pace; they also come to realize that they have the inherent ability to devise appropriate ways of coping.

During practice of various methods of relaxation, attention should be paid to breathing and the effects of slow paced breathing on relaxation as well as to its corollary, the effects of relaxation on breathing. The importance of practicing relaxation cannot be overemphasized, and *every* class should include not only adequate time for relaxation but also specific time for the teacher and/or the coach to lead the relaxation practice.

To prepare class members for the concepts of modified and patterned paced breathing, the instructor can suggest that coaches watch their partner as she engages in more strenuous activities. As they note changes in respiratory rate and depth with activity they can more easily understand the role of respirations during rest and activity, and more importantly, they can monitor their own partner through each of the kinds of breathing patterns with a minimum of intervention by the instructor. Using this information they calculate appropriate rhythms and rate with *their partner.*

Teachers who have used flexible approaches to teaching breathing techniques have observed that the respiratory rates chosen by couples are usually not much different from those taught in a structured approach. However, the underlying philosophy of *discovering what is effective for them* is very much different and prepares couples for *problem-solving* during their own unique birth experience.

Initial reactions to paced breathing patterns elicited a great deal of concern from childbirth educators who wanted to know the *right way* to do the "new" breathing patterns and who believed that these patterns should be taught in a structured manner. Years of demonstrating "the breathing" and watching return demonstrations by couples dutifully mimicking their instructors convinced teachers that couples learned very well that way. Undoubtedly they did, but they did *not* learn to use what was appropriate for them, and they were not prepared for problem-solving. They simply reproduced the behavior their instructor wanted.

It is possible to lead couples through the breathing without demonstrating it. It is also possible to demonstrate it without promoting one rigid way of doing it so that couples can modify it to their needs. Teachers are urged to develop methods of instruction which meet these goals. It requires flexibility and creativity to find those methods that meet the needs of expectant parents and the educator's objectives.

In the same way, charts that suggest optimal times or approximate dilatation of the cervix during which to use a specific breathing pattern also reduce the couples' ability to choose what works best for them. These directives also lead them to believe that they should conform to certain expectations and may cause them to question their ability to make independent judgments. The goal is to provide information that will allow couples to choose the method of coping with childbirth which is most appropriate for them.

However, labor charts describing the phases and stages of labor and breathing patterns that laboring women commonly use can be an important adjunct to childbirth education classes. Care must be exercised to keep the charts from becoming a directive to which the couples feel they must adhere. In keeping with the emphasis on individuality, couples should be reminded that during the first stage labor three principles apply: first, that when choosing a paced breathing pattern, always move from *simple to complex*; second, use *the slowest breathing pattern* that supports relaxation and decreases pain during labor, changing only when it is no longer effective; and third, that all breathing is done in such a way that *adequate oxygenation of mother and fetus is maintained*. During second stage labor, two primary principles apply: first, the breathing pattern should *enhance the bearing-down effort;* and, as in first stage labor, all breathing is done in such a way that *adequate oxygenation of mother and fetus is maintained*. Breathing patterns for second stage labor are discussed in Chapter 16.

The effectiveness of paced breathing patterns will be increased when childbirth educators place their emphasis on (1) constant appraisal of *individual differences;* (2) *mastery* of the ability to relax in the face of discomfort; (3) *proficiency in performing breathing patterns* to enhance relaxation, and as a means of increased attention focusing if needed; and (4) the ability of couples to identify difficulties and to find new and innovative solutions to their problems.

IMPLICATIONS FOR RESEARCH

Most of the studies on prepared childbirth presently available were conducted retrospectively by examining charts or birth reports to ascertain length of labor, use of medications, complications, and the woman's satisfaction with her birth experience. There is a great need for studies that focus on *observation* of the woman's use of breathing patterns, including ways to measure their efficacy and their effects upon the mother's physiology. The effects of all breathing patterns on alveolar ventilation must be systematically studied. Blood gas measurements on control subjects under stressful and nonstressful conditions need to be collected and data compared to experimental groups.

Before we can draw any conclusions about the value of prepared childbirth, we need to validate the existing research on the use of breathing techniques to relieve pain with our clinical observations of laboring women. Experiential documentation varies widely from the results obtained under experimental conditions. However, attempts to apply the information gathered from the research conducted so far on prepared childbirth are difficult at best. These studies are seriously flawed when compared with the experience of the laboring woman. Most often ''training'' in breathing pattern(s) occurs over 10 to 20 minutes' time in the research situation.

Expectant parents need time to assimilate all that has been taught them and time to practice under simulated conditions, but little has been studied in regard to optimal practice time. If 10 minutes is not enough time, what minimal amount of time spent will give the best results? Labor unit nurses often report much success teaching slow paced breathing to unprepared mothers already in labor, but less success teaching modified or patterned breathing in late labor. If we accept that practice is necessary, more studies need to be designed to ascertain how much.

One of the attributes of labor that lends itself so well to the use of breathing techniques is that contractions extend through approximately one minute's time. Even when they are longer, the woman can usually maintain her breathing pattern with support and encouragement. Studies done using other kinds of pain—dental work, for instance—do not specify the length of time the painful stimuli last. There is every indication that painful stimulus used is not comparable to labor in either intensity or duration.

A better understanding of how increased attention focusing using modified and patterned paced breathing functions to ''dampen'' painful stimuli is needed. Although birthing centers are becoming more popular, we do not know if women laboring in what are purported to be less stressful places choose different breathing patterns or use the patterns at different times during their labors than women delivering in traditional settings. How much anxiety is actually created by the setting and which aspects of childbirth preparation make the greatest contribution to reducing stress?

As birthing agency staff members have become familiar with modified and patterned paced breathing, they are much less likely to declare that the mother is hyperventilating. However, the actual incidence of true hyperventilation in labor needs to be documented, and comparisons made of prepared women with untrained laboring women.

Further complicating the entire picture of prepared childbirth research is the problem of the many different types of classes, most usually called ''Lamaze.'' There are many that do not meet the standards established by organizations such as ASPO/Lamaze. The results of one study cannot be compared with another. Quality control may be our next most important issue. If childbirth educators do not take the lead in ensuring that childbirth preparation includes at least minimum standards, then consumers will surely do so. Experience has demonstrated that in some other professions, legislative standard-setting has left much to be desired.

Only careful, systematic and scientifically designed research to reflect clinical proof of the physiological benefits of the breathing techniques and other aspects of childbirth preparation will result in the acceptance of childbirth education as a valid alternative to medical intervention during normal labor. We are in danger of substituting an appreciation for what the laboring woman is able to do for herself with an enthusiasm for technology, replacing competency and self-satisfaction with intervention and dependency.

There is a critical need for research in all areas related to prepared childbirth breathing patterns. Several questions that should possibly be addressed first are:

- What is the effectiveness of the different paced breathing patterns in increasing relaxation and decreasing pain of the laboring woman?
- What are the physiological effects of the different paced breathing patterns on the laboring woman?
- What are the most effective approaches for teaching paced breathing techniques in childbirth education classes?
- How much home practice time is needed for women to become proficient in executing paced breathing patterns?
- Can paced breathing patterns be taught effectively to untrained women during labor?

SUMMARY

Prepared childbirth is moving toward center; research is being conducted, it is an accepted part of all maternity nursing texts, references to it are made in other textbooks and articles on a variety of disciplines, and teacher certification programs for childbirth educators are in great demand.

Different methods of childbirth preparation place varying emphasis on the use of breathing patterns as coping tools for the laboring woman. While the concept of individuality is an overriding one, all breathing techniques taught in classes should be based on the scientific literature and should include room for each couples' uniqueness.

The maintenance of relaxation, proper oxygenation and the use of attention focusing, if needed, is the goal. Ultimately, it is the laboring woman who chooses from among all the coping techniques taught those that will best assist her as she embarks on one of the greatest adventures of her life.

References

1. Benson, H. *The Relaxation Response*. New York: William Morrow and Company, Inc., 1975.
2. Bing, E., Karmell, M., and Tanz, A. *A Practical Training Course for the Psychoprophylactic Method of Childbirth*. New York, (privately published), 1961.
3. Cogan, R., and Kluthe, K. The role of learning in pain reduction associated with relaxation and patterned breathing. *Journal of Psychomatic Research* 25:535, 1981.
4. Dempsey, J., and Rankin, J. Physiologic adaptations of gas transport systems to muscular work in health and disease. *American Journal of Physical Medicine* 46:582, 1963.
5. Dick-Read, G. *Childbirth Without Fear*. New York: Harper and Brothers, 1944.
6. Ehrenreich, B., and English, D. *Complaints and Disorders*. Old Westbury, NY: The Feminist Press, 1973.
7. Ehrenreich, B., and English, D. *Witches, Midwives, and Nurses*. Old Westbury, NY: The Feminist Press, 1973.
8. Grossman, P. Respiration, Stress and Cardiovascular Function. *Psychophysiology* 20:284, 1983.
9. Guyton, A. *Textbook of Medical Physiology*. Philadelphia: W. B. Saunders Company, 1987.
10. Harris, V., Katkin, E., Lick, J. and Habberfield, T. Paced respiration as a technique for the modification of autonomic response to stress. *Psychophysiology* 13:386, 1976.
11. Hilbers, S. Paced Breathing: Terminology Changes and Teaching Techniques. *Genesis* 5:16, December 1983/January 1984.
12. Jensen, D. *Principles of Physiology*. New York: Appleton-Century-Crofts, 1980.
13. Judy, W. Physiology of Exercise. *Physiology*. Boston: Little Brown and Co., 1984.
14. Lamaze, F. *Painless Childbirth*. New York: Simon & Schuster, 1965.
15. Lawson, P., and Simon, F. *Childbirth Preparation Manual*. Waban, MA: (privately published), 1978.
16. McCaul, K., Solomon, S., and Holmes, D. Effects of paced respiration and expectations on physiological and psychological responses to threat. *Journal of Personality and Social Psychology* 37:564, 1979.
17. Nakamura, T. *Oriental Breathing Therapy*. Tokyo: Japan Publications, 1981.
18. Nuernberger, P. *Freedom from Stress*, Honesdale, PA: Himalayan International Institute of Yoga Science and Philosophy, 1981.
19. Oxorn, H. *Oxorn-Foote Human Labor and Birth*. New York: Appleton-Century-Crofts, 1986.
20. Pritchard, J., MacDonald, P., and Gant, N. *Williams Obstetrics*. Norwalk, Connecticut: Appleton-Century-Crofts, 1985.
21. Soleferis, A. Tranquility and Insight, Boston: Shambhala, 1986.
22. Stern, R., and Anschel, C. Deep inspirations as stimuli for responses of the autonomic nervous system. *Psychophysiology* 5:132, 1981.
23. Vander, A., Sherman, J., and Luciano, D. *Human Physiology*. New York: McGraw-Hill, 1980.

Beginning Quote:

Harris, V., Katkin, E., Lick, J. and Habberfield, T. Paced respiration as a technique for the modification of autonomic response to stress. *Psychophysiology* 13:386, 1976, p. 386.

Boxed Quotes:

1. Kitzinger, S. *The Experience of Childbirth*. Baltimore: Penguin Books, Inc., 1972, p. 110.
2. Cogan, R., and Kluthe, K. The role of learning in pain reduction associated with relaxation and patterned breathing. *Journal of Psychosomatic Research* 25:535, 1981.
3. Jones, C. *Mind Over Labor*. New York: Viking, 1987, p. 58.
4. Battagin, J. Lamaze childbirth—more than breathing lessons. *Genesis* 6:23, 1984.

chapter 15

POSITIONING: First Stage Labor

MINELLA PAVLIK

So uterine contraction has now a new sense; it is no longer a sign of destiny that has to be obeyed, but a signal for adapting oneself.

Pierre Vellay

In the past 10 to 15 years professionals as well as consumers have begun to question the various positions a woman assumes during labor. The findings of researchers regarding the benefits of the upright position and mobility during labor have increased awareness of the importance of alternative positions and mobility for the woman during the laboring process. It is of utmost importance that childbirth educators present up-to-date information to their clients regarding the advantages and disadvantages of various labor positions. Research has shown that positioning during the first stage of labor affects maternal and fetal well-being, the laboring process, and maternal comfort.[5,9,13,19,24,25,35]

The first stage of labor begins with the first true contraction and ends with complete dilatation of the cervix. It is the longest of the three stages. According to Friedman,[14] the mean length of the first stage of labor is about 11 hours in a nullipara, whereas in a multipara it is approximately 8 hours. However, in the literature investigators have been careful to point out that marked individual variations exist.[30] During this stage numerous physiological and psychological changes are occurring within the woman's body. Positioning during the first stage of labor should be compatible with these changes. The position (positions) assumed should promote labor efficiency, safety, and comfort.

Maternal position during labor is a contemporary issue as well as a historical issue in obstetrical practice.[32] What determines the position (positions) that women assume during labor? Why do some women automatically think that labor means going to bed? Are some positions more effective than others in relation to comfort, maternal and fetal well-being, and labor efficiency? What are childbirth educators doing in their classes to educate couples about labor positions? What teaching strategies best facilitate the couple's use of this information during the actual labor process? This chapter focuses on a comprehensive view of information and content related to positioning in labor that is important for the childbirth educator to know and to share with couples in class.

REVIEW OF THE LITERATURE

Influencing Factors

The position a woman chooses to labor in is influenced by a number of factors. From the beginning of time, custom, convenience, and social attitudes have all contributed to the woman's laboring position.[12,20,21,40] In a historical review of nursing practices pertaining to women's positions for childbirth, Roberts[33] identified two major factors that seemed to have influenced the positions women assume in labor up to the present day. These are:

1. Concomitant obstetrical practices, hospitalization for birth, medication for pain relief, and fetal monitoring
2. Prerogative of the physician in determining the nature of obstetrical practices and influencing the role and actions of nurses.[33]

Obstetrical Practices. These practices continue to influence labor positions assumed in birthing agencies. Fetal monitoring, epidural anesthesia, and induced labor are all examples of obstetrical practices that influence the patient to remain in bed during the labor process. Health professionals often find it more convenient to evaluate uterine activity and fetal status when the woman is in the recumbent position.[6] This is especially true when continuous fetal monitoring is ordered. There are high-risk situations in which patients should be confined to bed. However, even when continuous monitoring is indicated, when epidural anesthesia is in effect, or when Pitocin is being administered, women still can be encouraged to move and change positions frequently.[21]

Radiotelemetry monitoring, which does not require leads attached to a machine, provides continuous fetal heart rate monitoring without constraining devices. The laboring woman can remain fully mobile while uninterrupted fetal surveillance is being provided.[13] Although this sophisticated and rather costly monitoring device is being used on a very selective basis in hospitals in the United States, it is a concept of perinatal care that may find wider usage in the future. Notelovitz states that telemetry monitoring is the answer for obstetricians who object to ambulation once the fetal membranes are ruptured. Telemetry provides an effective means of providing continuous fetal surveillance for detection of potential problems even though the mother is fully mobile.[13,27] Hodnett reported that women monitored with radiotelemetry remained out of bed more during labor and required less anesthesia.[16] In addition, these women indicated more positive labor experiences and more positive feelings of control during labor than those monitored with standard devices.

Research Findings. Research within the past 10 years has also influenced the use of alternative positions during labor. Many studies have demonstrated the physiological and psychological benefits of the upright position during labor.[5,9,13,19,24,25,35] These studies have suggested greater comfort for the laboring woman, stronger and more efficient contractions, and shorter duration of labor with use of the upright position. A lower incidence of abnormal fetal heart rate patterns and a greater sense of control and self-confidence in relation to the birth experience have also been reported.[13] Although three studies indicated no particular maternal or fetal benefits when women used the upright position during labor, the authors concluded that no harm was noted from using ambulation.[6,23,42] Thus, research findings in general support the benefits of upright positions in labor.

Birth Environment. The choice of position is often made on the basis of the freedom the woman feels in her birth environment to assume a position that promotes the greatest comfort during contractions as well as the encouragement she receives from her birth companion and/or caregivers to seek out alternative positions during labor. The home birth movement and the development of alternative birthing centers have provided such a labor environment.[22] This type of environment allows couples to become actively involved in decisions concerning care.

As a result of such developments, consumers and health care professionals have begun to question immobility in labor. In response to criticism

Birthing beds to accommodate a variety of positioning options are available in many birthing agencies. (Photo by Mark Salmanson, St. David's Community Hospital, Austin, TX)

of traditional policies, many hospitals are providing labor lounges or more homelike facilities (birthing suites or LDR [labor, delivery, and recovery] rooms) to enhance the comfort of the laboring couple. The LDR room is a relatively new concept for all laboring women—both low-risk and high-risk—who will be giving birth vaginally and who want a peaceful and attractive, homelike atmosphere. This concept differs from the early birthing room alternative, which was designed primarily for only those low-risk women who desired minimal or no medical intervention. Special labor beds that are designed to accommodate a variety of positioning options are available in many LDR and birthing rooms. The comfort of the laboring woman, the characteristics of her labor, and the infant's well-being should be the primary factors that influence birth environments and obstetrical practices rather than the convenience of the birth attendant. These factors require continued attention from care providers as changes occur in the obstetrical health care system.

Historical Aspects

As early as 1748 the value of ambulation of women in early labor was addressed by William Smellie, as cited in Flynn et al.[13] Throughout history practitioners have addressed the use of a variety of positions during labor such as standing, being suspended, sitting erect, squatting, kneeling, being supine, and many other variations. Positions varied from culture to culture as well as within the same society. Birth chairs and stools were used in various cultures from earliest times. These were designed to provide support for the mother's back as well as to make use of the forces of gravity.[12,40] One author mentions that there was no one best position or method.[12]

The recumbent position for birth was introduced in the United States by Dewees in the mid 1800's. By the end of the 19th century this position was the preferred one. More and more women were attracted to hospitals after 1900 because hospitals offered ''painless birth'' that was not available in the majority of home births.[40] During the first half of the 20th century, the use during labor of drugs such as scopolamine and general anesthetics contributed to immobility during labor and even restraint during the birth process.[21,40] In recent years obstetrical practices that confine laboring women to bed have become widespread. As mentioned previously, use of epidural anesthesia, reliance on uterine and fetal monitors, and induction or augmentation of labor have all contributed to immobility in labor. Subsequently, women began to automatically assume that labor meant going to bed.[34]

Advantages and Disadvantages of Various Positions

Supine. As researchers began to investigate the effects of various medications on the fetus and on labor, the importance of position became evident.[34] Throughout the literature, it is pointed out that the recumbent position during labor is physiologically disadvantageous and can lead to problems such as a narrowing of the birth canal, compression of the maternal aorta and inferior vena cava, loss of pelvic mobility, loss of the benefit of gravity, and diminished efficiency of contractions.[4,9,11,17,18,27,30] The supine hypotensive syndrome occurs in 10 to 20 per cent of pregnant women when they are in a supine position. The weight of the pregnant uterus compresses the ascending vena cava; this in turn diminishes blood return to the right atrium with a resultant drop in cardiac output and maternal blood pressure.[17,30] Moreover, fetal oxygenation is dependent on uterine blood flow. Therefore, fetal hypoxia, bradycardia, and acidosis may develop when the laboring woman is in the dorsal or supine position[15,41] (see Fig. 15–1). Although health professionals find the supine position more convenient in assessing contractions and fetal heart tones, it often causes greater discomfort to the woman.[5,13,24] This is especially true when the woman is experiencing back labor due to a posterior presentation.[3,4,38]

Lateral. In contrast, a sidelying position is known particularly for its beneficial effects in correcting or preventing supine hypotensive syndrome as well as enhancing patient comfort during back labor. Advantages of the lateral position are less danger of aspiration of vomitus, decreased pressure of the pregnant uterus on the inferior vena cava,

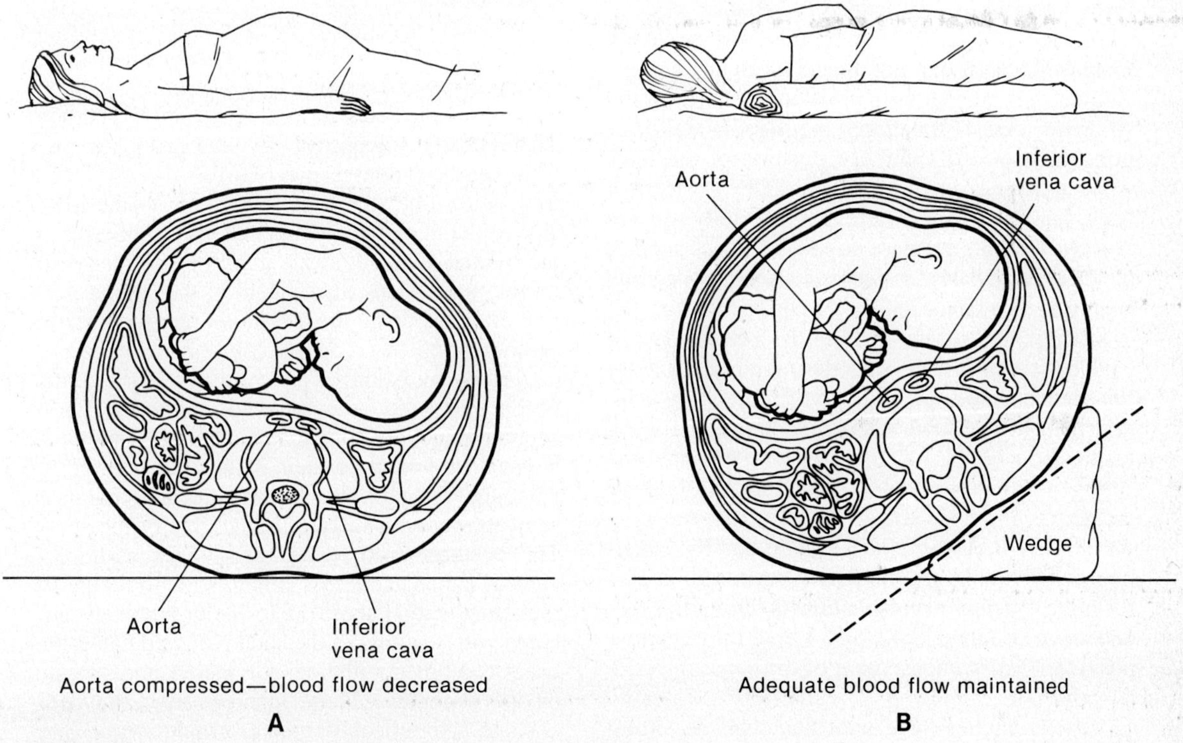

FIGURE 15–1. Aortocaval compression. When the pregnant woman is supine, aortocaval compression occurs (A). Aortocaval compression can be relieved by placing a wedge under the right hip to displace the uterus to the left. (Based on Obstetric anesthesia: What's the wisest choice? *Contemporary OB/GYN 18*:148, 1981.)

and decreased pressure of the presenting part on the sacral area. There are also other advantages involving the urinary tract and the cardiovascular and respiratory systems.[4] The left lateral position is favored in conditions such as pregnancy-induced hypertension, congestive heart failure, shock, and other obstetrical complications such as abruptio placentae, in which maintenance or increase of uterine blood flow benefits the mother or baby or both.[4,7]

The lateral position is also preferred when either caudal or epidural anesthesia is used. Serious hypotension may result because of vasodilatation caused by the anesthetic. Prehydration and the lateral position are recommended before vasopressor medications are administered.[29] Notelovitz comments that a left lateral tilt position promotes uteroplacental circulation during a cesarean delivery and that it is now widely accepted and routinely used by virtually all anesthetists and obstetricians.[27]

In a study by Caldeyro-Barcia et al., the lateral position (right or left) tended to produce less frequent but stronger uterine contractions that were more efficient in dilating the cervix than when the woman was in a dorsal position.[5] Andrews and Andrews[2] demonstrated that the Sims lateral position maintained the anterior position of the fetus when assumed on the opposite side of the fetal back. It is important to note that this study was not done on laboring women; however, it does support the theoretical basis for the use in labor of maternal posturing to aid in rotating a malpresentation.[2]

Sitting. The sitting position has been shown to have certain positive effects during labor. Contractions tended to be more effective in the sitting position than in the supine position. However, when contrasted with the standing or lateral position, the sitting position resulted in contractions of lower intensity and less effect in dilating the cervix.[19,24,25,35] It is interesting to note that the squatting position enlarges the pelvic outlet and allows for more efficient expulsive efforts during the second stage of labor; however, use of the squatting position prior to engagement of the caput impedes descent.[27]

Various studies have indicated that the sitting position or semirecumbent position did promote comfort.[5,9,19,25] Childbirth educators often recommend the tailor-sitting position to promote comfort in early labor. Bing[3] and Simkin et al.[38] recommend sitting or variations of the sitting position as a means to provide relief from back pain.

Ambulant. The standing and/or ambulant position for labor has been shown to contribute to shorter duration of labor with decreased pain and improved comfort levels.[5,13,24] This position has a number of additional benefits. It facilitates application of the presenting part against the cervix, it provides better alignment of the presenting fetal part with the pelvic inlet, and it encourages descent of the fetus because of gravity.[22] In addition, the upright position offers the potential for greater intimacy and interaction between the laboring woman and her partner.[35] A disadvantage to the ambulant position is that it may be tiring when used over long periods of time.[42]

Positions and Fetal Rotation

Although research is lacking regarding the effects of position on fetal rotation during labor, various postures are known to result in spontaneous rotation of the fetus to a more desirable position. Theoretically, except for the fetal head, the back is the heaviest, densest part of the fetal body. Therefore, with time, the back will rotate to the lower side of the maternal abdomen. This rotation places the lighter, more buoyant small parts of the fetus on the upper side. Subsequently, the supine position often results in the infant assuming a posterior position.[2]

A study by Andrews and Andrews[2] showed that four postures did facilitate rotation from a posterior or transverse position to an anterior position in women who were in their 38th week or more of pregnancy.[2] Again, it is important to note that these subjects were not in labor at the time of the study. The postures were hands and knees with back arched, hands and knees combined with the pelvic rock, hands and knees with lower back arched combined with stroking of the abdomen, and hands and knees combined with both pelvic rock and stroking on the abdomen. These four positions did demonstrate a significantly greater proportion of anterior fetal rotations than the control position of sitting in a chair. There were no significant differences in the effectiveness of the four postures. As mentioned previously, this study also suggested that the Sims position is effective in maintaining anterior positions when assumed on the opposite side of the fetal back.[2] These positions also promote comfort by relieving the pressure of the hard round part of the fetal occiput on the sacral nerves when the woman is experiencing back labor due to an occiput posterior or occiput transverse position.[3,38] (See Table 15–1 for advantages and disadvantages of various positions.)

Review of Related Studies

Numerous studies have been done regarding positioning during the first stage of labor. Roberts et al.[35] summarized the designs and results of nine controlled trials of the effects of various maternal positions in labor (Table 15–2). The findings from these studies are mixed.

Three of the studies[6,23,42] did not indicate any advantage to being in an upright position in relation to the duration of labor, amount of analgesia required, or type of delivery. However, studies by Mitre[25] and Liu[19] reported a shortening of the first stage of labor when women labored in an upright sitting position as compared with those in a supine position. Subjects in Mitre's study also reported an "increased tolerance of labor" in the sitting position.

Three studies indicated that the progress of labor was facilitated by an upright ambulatory position.[9,13,24] Subjects in the study by Mendez-Bauer and colleagues reported greater comfort and less pain when in the standing position.[24] In the study by Flynn and co-workers the ambulatory subjects required significantly less analgesia. Although not statistically significant, more women in the recumbent group required augmentation with oxytocics than those in the ambulant group.

Only one study[13] demonstrated any advantage of the upright position in regard to the fetus. In Flynn and co-workers' study[13] Apgar scores were significantly higher at one and five minutes in the ambulant group. Also, there was greater beat-to-beat variability and significantly less fetal heart rate decelerations in this group as compared with the recumbent group.

Mixed results may be attributed to a variety of factors. As is true in most research involving human subjects, methodological problems tend to arise in research design and variables are often difficult to control. For example, subjects did not always adhere to their assigned positions during data collection. In Chan's study[6] women had difficulty maintaining the upright position throughout labor. Most preferred to assume a recumbent position during the latter part of the first stage. In the study of Williams et al., 87.5 per cent of the "ambulant" women requested to return to bed "early in the active phase of labor." In addition, these women objected to being primarily confined to one position during their labors.[35,42]

In many of the investigations, positions were not always clearly defined or were inconsistent.[35] For example, in Chan's study the upright subjects either sat or stood, while the recumbent subjects were sidelying or supine. McManus[23] allowed the subjects in the upright group to be up and about but also allowed them to sit in bed propped with pillows. Williams and co-workers[42] did not operationally define "conventional recumbent position."

In order to eliminate confounding variables that were evident in some of the previous reviewed studies, Roberts et al.[35] studied the effects of a specific position on certain features of labor using the laboring woman as her own control. This type of study eliminates confounding obstetrical and individual differences between laboring women. These researchers compared the effects of sitting alternated with the sidelying position and the supine position alternated with the sidelying position on contraction intensity and frequency, uterine activity and efficiency, and maternal comfort.

Results of this study indicated that contractions were significantly more frequent in the sitting position than in the sidelying position, whereas uterine activity and efficiency were significantly greater in the sidelying position in both the early and later phases of labor. This study also showed that uterine efficiency in each position was affected by the position of alternation. These results suggested that alternating positions may promote more labor efficiency than assuming one "best" position during the entire labor process.[35]

It was also noted in this study that women preferred the sitting position in the first half of the

Text continued on page 246

TABLE 15–1. POSITIONS FOR THE FIRST STAGE OF LABOR

POSITION	ADVANTAGES	DISADVANTAGES
Supine	Convenient for the caregiver[38]; convenient for fetal monitoring; restful for some women[38]	Supine hypotensive syndrome[4,11,17,18,20,30]; increased back discomfort[3,4,24,38]; contractions longer, less efficient, more uncomfortable[4,5,9,24,27]; psychologically vulnerable[38]
Standing	Facilitates application of presenting part against cervix[20,24,32]; facilitates alignment of presenting part with pelvic inlet[27]; contractions less painful and more productive[5,24]; offers potential for greater intimacy and interaction between laboring woman and partner[35]; shorter labor compared with supine position[5,9,24]; takes advantage of gravity and direction of expulsive forces[17,20,24]	May be tiring over long periods[38]; not possible when regional anesthesia such as epidural or caudal is in effect; continuous electronic fetal monitoring may be difficult unless internal or telemetry monitoring is used; telemetry is expensive and not available in most birthing facilities
Standing and leaning forward	Promotes comfort[38]; takes advantage of gravity[24]; contractions less painful and more efficient[5]; facilitates alignment of the presenting part with angle of fetus[20]; provides restful position especially during contractions[36]; decreases back labor by causing the pressure of the fetus to fall away from the mother's back[26]	May be tiring over long periods of time[38]; not possible when regional anesthesia is in effect; external continuous fetal monitor may be difficult to keep in place
Ambulating	Takes advantage of gravity and direction of expulsive forces[17,20,22]; promotes fetal alignment with angle of pelvis[22]; contractions less painful and more efficient[5,13]; shortened duration of labor[5,13,24]; decreased incidence of fetal heart abnormalities[13]; need for analgesia significantly less than recumbent position[13]; Apgar scores higher than in recumbent position[13]	May be tiring over long periods of time[42]; not possible when regional anesthesia is in effect; continuous electronic fetal monitoring not possible unless telemetry monitoring available
Note: It is suggested by one authority (Notelovitz) that if the fetal head is not well applied to the cervix, ambulation may not advance labor. This may be the reason why some researchers[23,42] have not found ''walking the patient'' to be effective.		
Sitting upright	Promotes comfort[5,9,25]; facilitates some use of gravity[38]; can be used with continuous fetal monitoring; averts supine hypotension[20]; shortened duration of labor when compared with supine position[25]	May slow labor if not alternated with other positions[35]; contractions of lower intensity and less effective than in standing or lateral position[19,24,25,35]; may increase suprapubic pain[36]
Semisitting (30–45-degree angle)	Aligns pelvic brim at right angles to vertical axis of uterus[19,27]; maximizes thrust and direction of uterine contractions' force on fetus so as to enhance passage through pelvic canal[19,27]; increases intensity of contractions when compared with recumbent position[19]; greater frequency and regularity of contractions as compared with recumbent position[19]; shorter labor when compared with recumbent position[19]; can be used with fetal monitor	May increase back discomfort; may slow labor process if not alternated with other positions[35]; contractions of lower intensity and less effective than standing or lateral positions[35]

TABLE 15–1. POSITIONS FOR THE FIRST STAGE OF LABOR *Continued*

POSITION	ADVANTAGES	DISADVANTAGES
Tailor-sitting	Promotes comfort[36]; facilitates uterus falling forward thus averting supine hypotension[36]; can be used with fetal monitor; promotes some use of gravity	May possibly slow labor if not alternated with other positions; lack of research to validate advantages and/or disadvantages[36]
Sitting (Leaning forward with support)	Promotes comfort[8]; allows uterus to fall forward with support; facilitates uterus falling forward, averting supine hypotension and back discomfort[26]; promotes some use of gravity; can be used with continuous fetal monitoring; provides access to back and sacrum for counterpressure and/or massage	May slow labor if not alternated with other positions[35]
Hands and knees	Fosters anterior rotation of fetus in the occiput posterior position[26]; decreases back labor by causing fetal weight to fall away from mother's back[26]; allows for pelvic tilt to decrease back discomfort[26]; vaginal exams possible; relieves rectal pressure; facilitates pelvic rocking and pelvic mobility[8]	Wrist fatigue[26]; tiring for long periods; embarrassing for some women; may be difficult to keep fetal monitor in place; not possible when regional anesthesia in effect
Kneeling (Leaning forward, with support)	Encourages rotation of fetal head if fetus is in occiput posterior position[38]; decreases back labor by causing fetal weight to fall away from mother's back[26]; less strain on wrists and hands[26]; provides access to back and sacrum for counterpressure and/or massage	May be difficult to keep fetal monitor in place; may be tiring; not possible when regional anesthesia in effect
Lateral (Left lateral is the preferred side because of the location of the vena cava; however, the right side may be effective in some situations.)	Used to prevent or correct supine hypotension[4,21]; enhances comfort[22,32]; maximizes fetoplacental perfusion[18,30,32]; promotes venous return, cardiac output, and fetal oxygenation[32]; used during cesarean delivery to promote fetoplacental circulation[27]; lessens danger of aspiration[4]; produces less frequent but stronger and more efficient uterine contractions when compared with supine position[5]; vaginal exams, fetal monitoring, regional anesthesia and other interventions possible; decreases back labor[26]	Is more effective when alternated with other positions[35]
Squatting (Feet flat, heels down)	Takes advantage of gravity Increases dimensions of pelvis to its maximum[20,22,27]	Squatting before engagement may impede descent[27]; may be tiring; may be embarrassing for some women
Alternating positions (Walking and standing/sitting alternated with sidelying)	Roberts[35] suggests that changing maternal positions throughout labor increases efficiency of uterine contractions. Clinicians and researchers report that many women prefer ambulation in early phases of labor and as labor progresses tend to assume positions that minimize or deter fatigue and discomfort.	

TABLE 15–2. SUMMARY OF RESEARCH FINDINGS: EFFECTS OF MATERNAL POSITION DURING FIRST STAGE OF LABOR

STUDY	DESIGN	SUBJECTS	SIZE	POSITIONS
Chan (1963)[6]	Randomized clinical trial	Primigravidas in whom elective cesarean birth not done	100 100	Erect standing up or sitting in chair or bed Lying flat in bed supine or lateral
Mitre (1974)[25]	Randomized clinical trial	Nulliparas in early labor; normal term; no stimulation of labor required	50 50	Sitting after amniotomy and head engaged—allowed to lie down from time to time Supine and allowed to turn onto side
Liu (1974)[19]	Randomized clinical trial	Primigravidas; normal; no stimulation of labor; no medication	30	Semiupright in bed (30 degrees)
Mendez-Bauer (1975)[24]	Subjects as own control	Nulliparas; normal from 3 cm	20	Standing alternating with supine
McManus and Calder (1978)[23]	Randomized clinical trial	10 primigravidas and 10 multigravidas in each group; all subjects induced with PGE_2 or oxytocin after amniotomy	20 20	Recumbent lateral Upright—in bed and out
Diaz et al. (1980)[9]	Randomized clinical trial	Normal term; no medication; matched for parity	143 181	Vertical—movement was sitting, standing, walking Horizontal

TABLE 15–2. SUMMARY OF RESEARCH FINDINGS: EFFECTS OF MATERNAL POSITION DURING FIRST STAGE OF LABOR *Continued*

VARIABLES	FINDINGS		SUMMARY OF FINDINGS	COMMENTS
Mode of delivery	No difference		No advantage to being upright in terms of mode of delivery, length of labor, or amount of medication used	Propped position considered to be "awkward" and "inconvenient" for the obstetrician[35] Difficult to ensure that subjects remained in assigned positions[35]
Duration of 1st, 2nd, and 3rd stages	No significant differences			
Complaints of discomfort	More complaints in propped position			
Amount of analgesia	More given in erect group			
Fetal results	No difference		Mean time in active labor phase for sitting group significantly ($p<0.05$) less than for supine; no difference in Apgar scores.	Study criticized by some researchers in that details missing such as not operationally defining "active phase of labor," not explaining frequency and/or timing of amniotomy, use of medication, attendance at childbirth classes, etc.[2]
Time in active labor (hours)	Sitting $\bar{X} = 5.47 \pm 1.71$ Supine $\bar{X} = 7.25 \pm 1.64$			
Apgar scores	Sitting 7–10, $\bar{X} = 9$ Supine 6–10, $\bar{X} = 9$			
Comfort	Patients reported "increased" tolerance of labor in sitting		Questionnaire related to comfort indicated "increased tolerance" to labor in sitting position	
Uterine contractions	Semi-upright	Supine		
Duration—seconds	$\bar{X} = 72.38$	$\bar{X} = 56.86$	Duration not significant; intensity of contractions significantly ($p<0.05$) higher in semiupright group	Carefully controlled research design; supine position of control group not operationally defined (lateral or supine)
Intensity—mm Hg	56.62	42.61		
Frequency—per 20 min (External monitor)	7.77	7.37	Greater regularity of frequency of contractions in semiupright group a factor	No mention of amniorrhexis, which could have affected labor duration[27]
Duration of labor—min			Labor significantly $p<0.05$ shorter in both 1st and 2nd stages of semiupright group	Timing began at 4 cm rather than from onset of first true contraction
1st stage from 4 cm	167.67	253.40		
2nd stage	34.00	74.67		
Apgar score	8.7	8.4	No difference in Apgar scores	
Uterine contractions	Standing	Supine		
Intensity—mm HG	40.89	30.86	Intensity of contractions significantly $p<0.05$ higher in standing position	Timing began at 2–3 cm; no statement as to whether amniorrhexis spontaneous or artificial; high incidence of amniorrhexis may have influenced duration of labor[27]
Frequency—per 10 min	4.17	4.42	No difference in frequency	
Uterine activity—mu (Internal monitor)	160.34	128.89	Uterine activity increased significantly $p<0.05$ in standing position	
Uterine efficiency	274.25	160.07	Uterine efficiency significant $p<0.05$	
Comfort	More	Less	More comfort reported in standing position	
Amount of oxytocin stimulation required	No difference		Results did not demonstrate any advantage to being upright in terms of oxytocin stimulation required, length of labor, mode of delivery, amount of medication used, or fetal condition	Poor description and control of positions used; uncontrolled obstetrical variables that influence labor outcome.[35] Some authorities commented that sample size was inadequate to determine statistical differences between groups[27]
Length of labor induction (delivery interval)	No difference			
Mode of delivery	No difference			
Amount of analgesia	No difference			
Fetal condition	No difference			
Spontaneous rupture of fetal membranes	No difference		No difference in spontaneous ROM; vertical position resulted in a shorter median duration $p<0.002$ of 1st stage; no effect on fetal head molding and caput succedaneum or on Type I or Type II heart decelerations	Large homogeneous sample; carefully controlled research design. First stage of labor operationally defined beginning at 4–5 cm and ending at 10 cm. The fact that 95% of subjects chose to be vertical when given a choice indicated they were probably more comfortable when upright
Median labor duration	Horizontal	Vertical		
Active phase	180 min	135 min		
Incidence of caput succedaneum	No difference			
Apgar score	No difference			
48-hr neurological examination	No difference			

Continued on following page

TABLE 15–2. SUMMARY OF RESEARCH FINDINGS: EFFECTS OF MATERNAL POSITION DURING FIRST STAGE OF LABOR *Continued*

STUDY	DESIGN	SUBJECTS	SIZE	POSITIONS
Flynn et al. (1978)[13]	Randomized clinical trial	Normal term; matched for parity; station in ambulant group significantly higher at start of data gathering	34 34	Ambulant Recumbent (lateral position)
Williams et al. (1980)[42]	Randomized clinical trial	Low-risk parturients	48 55	Ambulant Recumbent
Read et al. (1981)[31]	Randomized clinical trial	Patients with arrested active labor Ruptured membranes	6 8	Oxytocin in bed Ambulant (walking, standing, or occasionally sitting)
Roberts et al. (1983)[35]	Subjects as own control	Nulliparas at term Normal	19 11	Sitting alternated with sidelying (either side) Supine (head and shoulder) propped (15–20 degrees) alternated with sidelying

TABLE 15–2. SUMMARY OF RESEARCH FINDINGS: EFFECTS OF MATERNAL POSITION DURING FIRST STAGE OF LABOR *Continued*

VARIABLES	FINDINGS	SUMMARY OF FINDINGS	COMMENTS
	Ambulant / Bed		
Duration of labor from 2 cm—mean	4.1 hr / 6.7 hr	Duration of labor significantly p < 0.001 shorter, need for analgesia significantly (p < 0.001) less, incidence of fetal heart abnormalities significantly less in ambulant group; Apgar scores at 1 and 5 min were significantly higher in ambulant group; contractions were less frequent and more intense in ambulant group; although not statistically significant, more in recumbent group required augmentation with oxytocics	First study to use continuous monitoring by radiotelemetry
Need for analgesia	14 / 34		
Fetal heart rate:			
Accelerations	10 / 1		
Decelerations	4 / 17		
Beat-to-beat variations	>8 bpm / <8 bpm		
Apgar–1 min	8.8 / 7.5		
5 min	9.9 / 9.4		
Contractions:			
Frequency per 30 min	8.5 / 10.1		
Intensity–mm Hg	55.3 / 46.54		
Basal tone	11 / 11.4		
Need for augmentation	6 / 12		
Length of labor	No difference	No difference in length of first or second stage of labor, incidence of fetal distress, or mode of delivery observed between 2 groups	Difficult to control positions; majority of ambulant patients (87.5%) asked to return to bed in early labor; although all ambulatory patients returned to bed before 2nd stage they found ambulation very acceptable during early 1st stage
Mode of delivery	No difference		
Incidence of fetal distress	No difference		
Changes in labor progress and uterine contractility	Both approaches effective	Initially a greater increase in ambulant group; no statistically significant differences found, but results suggest that ambulation may have been more efficacious	Small sample; further study indicated
Uterine contractions	Sitting / Sidelying		
Intensity mm Hg	32 / 39 p<0.01	Contractions significantly more intense and more frequent when sitting; uterine activity and efficacy were significantly greater while sidelying; women preferred sitting position in 1st half of labor and sidelying in late labor	Overall results indicate that position change is important in achieving efficient uterine contractions[35]
Frequency per 10 min	3.4 / 2.9 p<0.01		
Uterine activity	98 / 108 p<0.05		
Uterine efficacy	175 / 311 p<0.01		
Most comfort or preferred position	+ early / + late (first stage labor)		
	Supine / Sidelying		
Intensity mm Hg	38 / 47 p <0.01	Contractions significantly more intense and less frequent but not significantly while sidelying; no statistically significant difference in uterine activity efficacy or comfort when comparing sidelying and supine positions	
Frequency per 10 min	4.2 / 3 NS		
Uterine activity	153 / 160 NS		
Uterine efficacy	309 / 234 NS		
Most comfort or preferred position	NS / NS		

Adapted from Roberts, J., Mendez-Bauer C. and Wodell, D. The effects of maternal position on uterine contractility and efficiency. *Birth* 10:243, 1983.

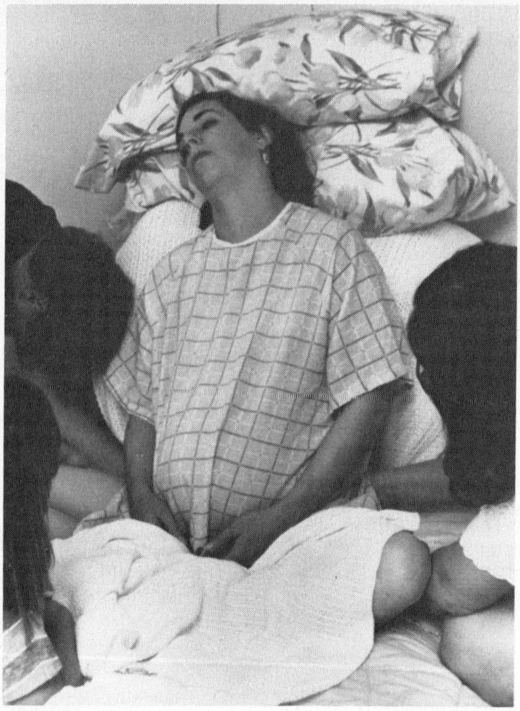

Progress in labor is facilitated by an upright position. (Photo by Rodger Ewy, Educational Graphic Aids, Inc.)

first stage of labor, while the sidelying position was preferred in the second half of the first stage. There was no significant difference in the women's preferences between sidelying and supine positions in the first stage of labor. Roberts'[35] study suggests that if the woman's chosen position for labor is not promoting effective contractions, alternating various positions may enhance uterine efficiency.

Summary of Studies

As seen from the various studies reviewed, objective data to support any one "best" position during labor are limited. Many of the investigators of the studies reviewed recommended further research or replication or both in order to better understand the physiological and psychic effects of maternal position in labor. At this time there is no fixed approach. Even in the three studies reporting no advantages to being upright in labor, no adverse effects were evident.[6,23,42] In fact, Williams et al.[42] concluded that ambulation should be encouraged and facilities for ambulation should be available for those desiring it. Authorities[30] are now suggesting that women in labor be allowed to *assume any position that promotes comfort as long as it is not medically contraindicated because of various complications*.

Roberts'[35] study suggested that *position change* may be more important than a single "best" position. It is unlikely that a woman would assume one position throughout her labor without some attempt at alteration. It has been observed by clinicians and researchers that many women prefer ambulation in the early phases of labor; however, as labor progresses women tend to assume positions that minimize or deter their fatigue and discomfort. Notelovitz[27] and Sumner[22] both recommend full mobility and vertical positioning during labor for those patients without complications. Notelovitz goes on to recommend that during the latter phase of labor or when the woman prefers to rest in bed, a "sitting position with the back at a 45-degree angle to the horizontal" with a wedge or pillow positioned under the woman's right side to maintain a left lateral tilt be used.[27] Odent, a French physician, encourages laboring women to "listen to their own bodies and find alternative positions by themselves."[28] It has also been pointed out in the literature[32] that the choice of position in labor should be made on the basis of the efficiency of contractions, the phase of labor, the well-being of mother and fetus, and her preference.

Current Practice in Childbirth Education

In a study conducted of comfort measures during labor, Tryon[39] identified controlled breathing techniques, back massage, and *positioning* as the most frequently used measures to promote comfort in labor. These techniques are considered a part of the essential content in childbirth education classes. Comfortable positioning is also considered to be an important prerequisite for achieving relaxation.[36] This is an important concept because relaxation is considered to be at the core of all other skills, including breathing and expulsion techniques, being taught in childbirth education classes today.[37]

In childbirth education classes content regarding labor positions tends to vary from a brief verbal description to actual demonstration and practice. In general, the importance of assuming a comfortable position in labor is emphasized when various measures are discussed that promote comfort during labor. Use of items such as pillows, wedges, and beanbag chairs are recommended to enhance comfort. In addition, the woman is reminded to "tune into her body" during the labor process in order to assist her in selecting a position of comfort. Positioning is also explained and demonstrated when back labor is discussed. Labor partners are given specific instructions as to how to promote comfort during the various phases of labor. It is certainly evident that childbirth educators are aware of positioning as a comfort measure. However, the advantages and disadvantages of various positions in relation to labor efficiency and maternal and fetal well-being are often neglected topics. Research information is also a topic that is not dealt with in the majority of classes.

Couples need information on maternal positioning based on sound principles in order to discuss options with their birth attendants prior to the birth experience. Couples also need objective information that can serve as a basis for negotiation and active participation in their care during the actual birth experience.

Since change from traditional practice is often difficult, educating the consumer is extremely important in order that alternatives may be available to the laboring mother.[21] The modern childbirth educator must be able to transfer knowledge developed by scientific research to her practice. This knowledge base enables the educator not only to respond to questions from her clients but also to discuss theoretical and technical aspects of childbirth education with health professionals in practice settings.

IMPLICATIONS FOR PRACTICE

The transfer of knowledge developed by scientific research to practice situations often requires patience, time, and education.[21] A rolc of the childbirth educator is to work with all members of the childbirth team to implement practices supported by research. Providing information to couples in childbirth classes, participating in staff development programs, providing up-to-date information to the medical community, and being a resource person to the labor and delivery staff are all ways in which the childbirth educator can promote acceptance of new ideas and findings.

In view of the reviewed studies, the childbirth educator should discuss with couples the rationale regarding the effects of various positions not only on the mother's comfort but also on the fetus and labor. The benefits and disadvantages of the various positions should be presented in order that couples may have a sound basis for discussing options with their physicians or birth attendants prior to labor. In order to present this type of information, the educator must keep abreast of research findings. This type of information encourages couples to check out policies and procedures regarding ambulation when selecting a hospital or birthing center. Labor itself is not the best time for asserting negotiating skills and/or developing birth plans.

Information taught in childbirth classes regarding the effects of varying positions will be helpful to the mother in her choice of positions during the actual labor process. It is important that she be made aware that she can help herself during labor. If no contraindications exist, she should be allowed to choose the position that is most comfortable for her. Information obtained in classes on labor positions also guides the mother's partner in supporting her choices as well as offering suggestions of positions that promote comfort, enhance labor, and maintain fetal well-being.

The caregiver during labor and birth will greatly influence the laboring woman's choice of

> My back was killing me and I stayed in the tailor-sit position. It took a lot of pressure off.
>
> A NEW MOTHER
>
> My husband and I danced through labor until I hit transition. Being out of bed and free to move around made the labor easier.
>
> A NEW MOTHER
>
> A nurse on the second shift changed my position and alleviated a lot of pain. She had me sit Indian style and lean on her shoulder as she stood at the side of the bed.
>
> A NEW MOTHER

positions. If childbirth professionals are aware that positioning can increase labor efficiency and comfort and improve fetal well-being, they will be more likely to encourage mobility or a variety of positioning options or both. In addition, if the nurse is aware that evidence exists that fetal monitoring, use of IV's, and even ruptured membranes when the head is engaged need not be deterrents to movement and ambulation,[13] she may be more likely to implement these practices. Keeping professionals abreast of the latest technology such as telemetry monitoring devices will possibly influence the purchase of such equipment when the updating of maternity units takes place.

Physician approval is also an important factor in the type of position allowed during labor. Presenting research findings and discussing the validity of findings with physicians may facilitate usage of the information. Providing the birthing agency staff with current articles on research and trends in obstetrical care to share with team members is one method of promoting utilization of research to practice settings. In some areas couples are being provided with such information by their childbirth educators and are encouraged to share the material with their birth attendants.

In spite of the high technology in obstetrical care, one does note a more humanistic approach being taken today toward the laboring couple in maternity units. More and more hospitals are providing labor lounges, birthing rooms, and/or a more homelike environment in which women in labor can walk and visit with spouses, children, family members, and friends. Monitoring may be done intermittently, or if it is continuous, women are encouraged to assume positions to promote comfort. Wedges, beanbag chairs, birthing beds, birthing chairs, and other comfort devices are being made available in the labor setting to accommodate a wide variety of position options that may promote comfort of the mother as well as physiologically enhance the labor progress. In addition, new methods of monitoring without constraining devices are being utilized more and more. Couples should be encouraged to check out facilities and policies regarding birth practices within their communities prior to their birth experience.

Teaching Strategies

A variety of teaching strategies may be used in childbirth classes for teaching positions for the first stage of labor. It is important for the childbirth educator to keep in mind that individuals learn in different ways. Discussion, demonstration, return demonstration, slides, films, posters, and tactile stimulation are just some of the strategies that may be used to incorporate content into classes in order to accommodate the different learning styles of individuals.

Verbal content should include a description of specific positions with rationale as to the advantages and disadvantages of their use during the first stage of labor. Cognitive learners respond readily to facts and reasons. These individuals are more likely to request or assume various positions during the actual labor experience if they are aware of the benefits to the birth experience. Rationale should be validated with supporting theory or research or both.

There are a number of excellent posters, slides, and handouts available from various media companies that depict various positions to promote comfort in labor. Reflective learners respond well to visualization. For example, visual presentations utilizing posters, photographs, or projected transparencies might show positions for sitting in a chair, resting in bed with the head elevated and pillows for support, sitting on the commode, ambulating with an IV, or resting against a wall.

Other individuals learn best by actual performance. Demonstration with return demonstration depicting comfortable positions such as the woman sitting between her partner's legs may be used in practice sessions. The partner may sit in a chair with the mother on the floor between her partner's legs. In order to enhance comfort of this position, pillows may be used to cushion her buttocks and support her back. Variations of this position, such as the partner sitting at the head of the bed with the woman resting her back against his chest, should be discussed for use during the actual labor process. Role playing or labor rehearsals depicting situations in which couples must make decisions regarding positions that not only provide the most comfort but are also beneficial to both the laboring woman and the fetus can be most helpful in preparing clients for the actual labor experience.

Various positions should be discussed and used during practice sessions throughout the class series. Positioning may be introduced during the first session when the importance of exercise and comfort is explained. This session often includes various positions such as tailor-sitting, sidelying, and the hands-and-knees posture. In addition, relaxation sessions are an opportune time for the woman to be encouraged to become more aware of her own body's signals. It is important to remind couples that *comfortable positioning is a prerequisite for achieving relaxation not only in class but also in labor.*[36]

In class sessions in which the early phase of labor is discussed, positions that promote descent should be described. Upright positions that may be suggested include walking, resting against a wall or on the labor partner, or standing in a warm shower. It is important to emphasize *a change of positions frequently* (approximately every 30 minutes) in order to enhance comfort and prevent tiring. Mentioning that ambulation is recommended to distinguish between true and false labor provides a basis for couples when they must assess whether labor has actually begun. Whereas ambulation usually causes false labor contractions to cease, it stimulates uterine contractions in true labor.

Box 15–1

RECOMMENDATIONS FOR TEACHING POSITIONING FOR FIRST STAGE LABOR

Women who attend childbirth education classes need knowledge based on recent research findings regarding the advantages and disadvantages of positions used during first stage labor. This knowledge will enable women to discuss various options with their physician or midwife prior to labor. In addition, the information will offer various options for the woman to experiment with in labor. Thus, the woman will have increased control over the progress and comfort of her childbirth experience. Education of both professionals and clients should assist in the using of positions that physiologically and psychologically enhance the progress of labor as well as promoting comfort and safety for both mother and baby.

Recommendations for teaching positioning for first stage labor are:

1. **Include content in childbirth education classes regarding the benefits and disadvantages of various positions for labor.**
2. **Demonstrate with return demonstration various positions that may be used by the laboring woman.**
3. **Emphasize that these positions are appropriate and helpful for a laboring woman.**
4. **Encourage discussion with physicians and/or birth attendants regarding various options.**
5. **Encourage expectant couples to check out hospitals or birthing centers about policies and facilities relating to ambulation.**
6. **Encourage individuals to become actively involved in decisions concerning positioning during actual labor. Emphasize tuning into body.**
7. **Discuss complications that may alter choice of positions.**
8. **Conduct continuing education programs for health professionals.**
9. **Keep abreast of current research.**

Box 15–2

PROTOCOL FOR BACK LABOR FOR USE IN BIRTHING AGENCIES

NURSING DIAGNOSIS: Alteration in comfort due to back labor which is defined as "a grating back pain which increases in intensity during contractions and may not completely disappear during contractions."[1]

EXPECTED OUTCOME: Patient will verbalize a decrease in the pain associated with back labor after interventions for back labor have been initiated. Patient will demonstrate the ability to cope more effectively with her back labor.

INTERVENTION:

1. Instruct patient on the possible causes of back labor, coping strategies that can be used, and then develop a plan to cope with back labor.

2. Assess if fetus is in occiput posterior position to determine a possible cause of back labor and the need for interventions that favor anterior rotation.

3. Instruct patient on use of relaxation techniques and slow, paced breathing (not less than one-half normal respiratory rate)[2] to achieve a relaxed state during labor.

4. Instruct patient that she may need to increase respiratory rate (not greater than twice normal rate)[2] and modify pattern of breathing to maintain a relaxed state during the later part of labor.

5. Instruct patient's coach in the use of counterpressure to the sacral area. The coach should be instructed to use the heel of one hand to apply firm pressure to the area where the patient feels the most discomfort.

6. Encourage the patient to let her coach know the amount and type of counterpressure that relieves the greatest amount of her pain.

7. Encourage and assist the patient to assume a position in which the pressure of the fetus falls away from her back. Th three primary positions are sidelying, upright leaning forward, and on her hands and knees.

8. If fetus is in the occiput posterior position, assist the patient with interventions that foster anterior rotation. These interventions include frequent position changes from sidelying to hands and knees to lying on the other side at least every 30 minutes.

9. Apply warm, moist heat to patient's lower back and assess if this decreases the back discomfort. A small towel can be used to apply the heat.

10. Apply cold to patient's lower back and assess if this decreases the back discomfort. An ice bag or rubber glove filled with ice chips can be used to apply the cold.

11. Provide support, encouragement, and assist patient in utilizing different coping techniques during contractions.

EVALUATION:

1. Patient will use a variety of techniques to cope more effectively with her back labor.

2. Patient will use various labor positions to foster anterior rotation of fetus.

3. Patient will demonstrate an increased ability to cope with her back labor.

4. Patient's support person will play an active role in assisting the patient during her contractions and back labor.

DOCUMENTATION:

Care plan–Nursing diagnosis
Expected outcome
Interventions
Evaluation
Discharge planning

Problem list–Nursing diagnosis, and time and date problem identified
Time and date problem resolved

Progress notes–Document initial assessment of problem identified
Time and date problem resolved

REFERENCES:

1. Nichols, F. Back labor. NAACOG Update Series, Vol. 5., No. 4. Princeton, NJ: Continuing Professional Education Center, Inc., 1986.

2. Hilbers, S. Paced breathing: Terminology changes and teaching techniques. *Genesis* 5:16, December 1983/ January 1984.

3. Carpenito, L. *Nursing Diagnosis: Application to Clinical Practice.* Philadelphia: J.B. Lippincott, 1983.

Courtesy of Joan M. Youmans, R.N., M.N., Clinical Educator, Birth Center, Penrose Community Hospital, Colorado Springs, CO.

Another important point to mention is that many women prefer ambulation during early labor; however, as labor progresses, they may wish to assume positions that promote relaxation and minimize fatigue. Class content should include suggestions regarding position changes for those laboring mothers who prefer to rest in bed as labor progresses or are confined to bed for various reasons. It is important to point out that *movement is essential whether the mother is in bed or up and about.* Suggestions might include rotating sides or assuming an elevated position in bed (35- to 45-degree angle). If the mother finds the supine position most comfortable, Notelovitz suggests that a wedge be placed under her right hip to maintain a tilt to the left.[27]

When discussing the effects of the occipital posterior or transverse positions on labor, explanation, demonstration, and return demonstration of various techniques for relieving the resulting backache and/or facilitating fetal rotation may be done in class and practice situations. Nichols defines back labor ". . . as dull, aching, or grating back pain which increases in intensity during contractions and may not completely disappear between contractions."[26] In a study by Cogan, counterpressure was identified as the most effective measure for dealing with back labor; however, the next most effective measure identified was changing positions.[8]

Positions to decrease discomfort or encourage rotation of the fetus or both should be taught and practiced in class. Childbirth educators need to focus on information that will assist the couple in early identification of "back labor" and strategies to cope with this devastating problem if it should actually occur. Presenting factual information as well as a variety of techniques for coping with back labor in childbirth education classes assists couples in developing a plan to successfully meet the challenge in labor. Knowing about various choices can give couples more of a sense of control over back labor and can lead to a more positive birth experience.[26]

Suggestions of positions that can cause the weight of the fetus to move away from the woman's back include pelvic rocking on hands and knees, leaning forward with support in either a standing, sitting, or kneeling position, and sidelying. In order to prevent wrist fatigue with the hands-and-knees position, the woman should be encouraged to support herself on her forearms or fists rather than on the palms of her hands.

Leaning forward with support allows the fetus to fall away from the woman's back and increases comfort during back labor. (Copyright, BABES, Inc.)

Pelvic rocking in a hands-and-knees position aids in the rotation of the fetus to an anterior position. (Copyright, BABES, Inc.)

Information regarding the use of the pelvic tilt to relieve back discomfort should be discussed, demonstrated, and practiced in class. This technique can be used in the sidelying position or in the hands-and-knees position. Another option is the use of a passive pelvic tilt, which is done for the woman by her partner.[26]

Suggestions of positions that facilitate rotation of the fetus from the occiput posterior, or transverse position to the anterior position should also be included in class presentations. Frequent position changes from sidelying to hands and knees to lying on the other side should be done every 30 minutes. Andrews recommends pelvic rocking and stroking in combination with a hands-and-knees posture to rotate a fetus to an anterior position.[1] In addition to arming couples with a variety of tools for coping with back labor, the childbirth educator should emphasize the importance of attaining a good state of relaxation throughout labor, because increased muscular tension may impede rotation.[26]

In order to prepare couples for all aspects of the laboring process, the childbirth educator should include discussion of positions that may be necessary if complications occur. Premature labor, bleeding, pregnancy induced hypertension and other maternal and fetal complications may influence the position the woman is allowed to assume. The rationale for adhering to certain positions should be given. For example, the left lateral position is often the one of choice in that it enhances maternal-fetal placental perfusion.

Suggesting to women to use the lateral position or Sims position during the final weeks of pregnancy also promotes comfort as well as prevents supine hypotension. If the pregnant woman is aware of the signs and symptoms of this syndrome, she will be more likely to recognize and report these untoward effects if she has to remain in the supine position for long periods of time such as during prenatal checks or during procedures such as ultrasound or amniocentesis. These procedures tend to aggravate supine hypotension. Using the left lateral position except for the actual time of these tests or examinations will assist in avoiding this problem.[18]

Instructors should not assume that couples will understand and remember all terms. Therefore, written information should be given to couples to reinforce classroom instruction. This type of information will assist the partner or coach to recall information during the actual laboring experience. This also gives couples information that enables them to discuss various options with their physicians and/or birth attendants prior to labor.

Couples also need to be reminded that a variety of factors may influence positions assumed during labor. Roberts[32] includes duration of labor, quality of uterine contractions, maternal hemodynamics, fetal status, and maternal comfort as major considerations.

IMPLICATIONS FOR RESEARCH

Findings have been mixed in the various studies investigating both the physiological and psychological effects of maternal positioning during the first stage of labor. No one approach has been demonstrated as the ''best,'' although the literature definitely cites the disadvantages of the supine position. Evidence that certain positions do influence labor efficiency, maternal and fetal well being, and maternal comfort bears close scrutiny.

There were problems in most studies with scientific design or methodology or both. For example, assigned positions were not always consistently maintained by the laboring women,[6,23,42] and obstetrical variables such as amniotomy and induced labor were often not fully described as to their influence on study outcome.[19,23–25] Positions were not always clearly defined.[19,42] Studies varied as to when the first stage of labor was initiated. For example, in one study[24] timing was initiated when the cervix was 2 to 3 centimeters dilated and in another[25] no definition of the ''phase'' was given. There is a need for standardization and replication of studies before comparisons and generalizations can be made regarding the results.

Information about specific positions and their influence on labor and the outcome of birth needs further understanding. Various studies are being replicated or at least the study design is being utilized in different settings using different samples or populations and being conducted by different investigators.[9,23–25]

More detailed studies on positioning and its effects on comfort in labor need to be addressed. Most of the conclusions on comfort were based on observation or direct questioning rather than on valid and reliable assessment tools.

Although studies on positioning in labor have increased during the past ten years, there are still many unanswered questions that need to be investigated more thoroughly in order to give childbirth educators a sound research base to guide their practice. On the basis of theoretical background and prior research results relating to positioning during labor research, questions can be grouped in four areas: maternal comfort, maternal and fetal well-being, labor efficiency, and education. Questions that lend themselves to investigation and/or replication include the following:

Maternal comfort:

- What position (positions) enhance the comfort of the laboring woman?
- What position (positions) alleviate back labor discomfort?
- What position (positions) promote psychological well being?

Maternal and fetal well being:

- What are the benefits of utilizing the left lateral position as opposed to the right lateral position for avoiding compression of the vena cava?
- What position (positions) promote fetal well-being?
- What position (positions) facilitate anterior fetal rotation during labor?

Labor efficiency:

- What effects do various positions have on labor progress?
- What effects do variations of positions have on labor progress (i.e., tailor-sitting versus sitting in a chair or in a semi-Fowler's position in bed, and so on)?
- What position (positions) are most effective in suppressing premature labor?
- What are the effects of ambulation on labor progress in comparison to labor augmentation with Pitocin?

Childbirth education:

- What effect does content presented in childbirth education classes have in position choices during the labor process?
- What teaching strategies are the most effective in presenting content on positioning in childbirth education classes?

- How does having a plan for back labor influence a couple's ability to cope with it?

The mixed findings of researchers challenges more in-depth investigation by health professionals. Childbirth educators need to take an active role in research in this area by collaborating with researchers, educators, and members of the health care team.

SUMMARY

More research is needed to better understand the physiological and psychological effects of maternal position on labor process. In view of the mixed findings of researchers regarding positioning and its effects on the laboring experience, women should be encouraged to assume positions that promote comfort, enhance labor efficiency, and result in a safe and satisfying birth experience.[34] Couples attending childbirth education classes should have current information regarding the advantages and disadvantages of positions. Such awareness provides a basis for active participation by couples in health care decisions regarding their birth experience.

References

1. Andrews, C. M. Changing fetal position. *Journal of Nurse-Midwifery* 25:7, 1980.
2. Andrews, C., and Andrews, E. Nursing, maternal postures, and fetal position. *Nursing Research* 32:336, 1983.
3. Bing, E. *Six Practical Lessions for an Easier Childbirth.* New York: Bantam Books, 1969.
4. Bond, S. Reevaluating position for labor—lateral vs. supine. *JOGN Nursing* 2:29, 1973.
5. Caldeyro-Barcia, R. The influence of maternal position on time of spontaneous rupture of the membranes, progress of labor, and fetal head compression. *Birth and the Family Journal* 6:7, 1979.
6. Chan, D. Positions in labour. *British Medical Journal* 1:100, 1963.
7. Chelsey, L. C. *Hypertensive Disorders in Pregnancy.* New York: Appleton-Century-Crofts, 1978.
8. Cogan, R. Backache in prepared childbirth. *Birth and the Family Journal* 3:75, 1976.
9. Diaz, A. G., Schwarcz, R., Fescina, R., and Caldeyro-Barcia, R. Vertical position during the first stage of the course of labor, and neonatal outcome. *European Journal of Obstetrics and Gynaecology* 11:1, 1980.
10. Dunn, P. M. Posture in labor (letter). *Lancet* 1:496, 1978.
11. Dunn, P. M. Obstetric delivery today: For better or for worse? *Lancet* 1:790, 1976.
12. Engelman, G. J. *Labor Among Primitive Peoples,* 2nd ed. St. Louis: J. H. Chambers & Co., 1882.
13. Flynn, A. M., Kelly, J., Hollis, G., and Lynch, P. F. Ambulation in labor. *British Medical Journal* 2:591, 1978.
14. Friedman, E. A. *Labor: Clinical Evaluation and Management,* 2nd ed. New York: Appleton-Century-Crofts, 1978.
15. Goodlin, R. C. Importance of the lateral position during labor. *Journal of Obstetrics and Gynecology* 37:698, 1971.
16. Hodnett, E. Patient control during labor, effects of two types of fetal monitors. *JOGN Nursing* 11:94, 1982.
17. Howard, B. K., Goodson, J., and Mengert, W. Supine hypotensive syndrome in late pregnancy. *Obstetrics Gynecology* 1:1371, 1953.
18. Kelley, M. Maternal position and blood pressure during pregnancy and delivery. *American Journal of Nursing* 82:809, 1982.
19. Liu, Y. C. Effects of an upright position during labor. *American Journal of Nursing* 74:2202, 1974.
20. Liu, Y. C. Position during labor and delivery: History and perspective. *Journal of Nurse-Midwifery* 24:23, 1979.
21. McKay, S. Maternal position during labor and birth. *JOGN Nursing* 9:288, 1980.
22. McKay, S. (ed.) Maternal position during labor and birth. *ICEA Review* 2, 1978.
23. McManus, T. J., and Calder, A. A. Upright posture and the efficiency of labor. *Lancet* 1:72, 1978.
24. Mendez-Bauer, C., Arroyo, J., and Ramos, C. G. Effects of standing position on spontaneous uterine contractility and other aspects of labor. *Journal of Perinatal Medicine* 3:89, 1975.
25. Mitre, I. N. The influence of maternal position on duration of the active phase of labor. *International Journal of Gynaecology and Obstetrics* 12:181, 1974.
26. Nichols, F. Back labor. *NAACOG Update Series* 5:2–8. Princeton: Continuing Professional Education Center, Inc., 1986.
27. Notelovitz, M. Commentary on maternal position during labor and birth. *ICEA Review* 2, 1978.
28. Odent, M. The evolution of obstetrics at Pithiviers, France. *Birth and the Family Journal* 8:7, 1981.

29. Ostheimer, G. Obstetric anesthesia: What's the wisest choice? *Contemporary Obstetrics and Gynecology* 18:148, 1981.
30. Pritchard, J., McDonald, P., and Gant, N. *Williams Obstetrics,* 17th ed. Norwalk, CN: Appleton-Century-Crofts, 1985.
31. Read, J. A., Miller, F., and Paul, R. Randomized trial of ambulation versus oxytocin for labor enhancement: A preliminary report. *American Journal of Obstetrics and Gynecology* 139:669, 1981.
32. Roberts, J. Alternative positions for childbirth. Part 1. First stage of labor. *Journal of Nurse-Midwifery* 25:11, 1980.
33. Roberts, J. Maternal positions for childbirth—a historical review of nursing care practices. *JOGN Nursing* 8:24, 1979.
34. Roberts, J. Which position for the first stage? *Childbirth Educator* 1:35, 1982.
35. Roberts, J., Mendez-Bauer, C., and Wodell, D. The effects of maternal position on uterine contractility and efficiency. *Birth* 10:243, 1983.
36. Roberts, J., Malasanos, L., and Mendez-Bauer, C. Maternal positions in labor: Analysis in relation to comfort and efficiency. *In* Roff, B. S. (ed.) *Perinatal Parental Behavior.* White Plains, NY: March of Dimes Birth Defects Foundation XVII:97, 1981.
37. Shrock, P. Relaxation skills: Update on problems and solutions. *Genesis* 6:8, 1984.
38. Simkin, P., Whalley, J., and Keppler, A. *Pregnancy, Childbirth and the Newborn.* Deephaven, MN: Meadowbrook Press, Inc., 1984.
39. Tryon, P. Use of comfort measures as support during labor. *Nursing Research* 15:109, 1966.
40. Wertz, R. W., and Wertz, D. C. *Lying-in: A History of Childbirth in America.* New York: Free Press, 1977.
41. Whitley, N. *A Manual of Clinical Obstetrics.* Philadelphia: J. B. Lippincott, 1985.
42. Williams, R. M., Thom, M., and Studd, J. W., et al. A study of the benefits and acceptability of ambulation in spontaneous labor. *British Journal of Obstetrics and Gynaecology* 87:122, 1980.
43. Young, D. *Changing Childbirth.* New York: Childbirth Graphics Ltd., 1982.

Beginning Quote

Vellay, P. *Childbirth with Confidence.* New York: Macmillan, 1965, p. 114.

chapter 16

POSITIONING: Second Stage Labor

SIGRID NELSSON-RYAN

But after they have had a baby they realize that it is more a matter of breathing and coordination than of straining and making terrific muscular efforts to expel the baby.

Sheila Kitzinger

Traditionally in Western society, physicians have hastened to deliver the baby once full dilation is achieved. Active management of second stage labor has been marked by exhorting the parturient to maximum bearing down effort in a dorsal, propped position as soon as the cervix was dilated, accompanied by prolonged breath-holding.[13,24,37,47] The mother, viewed as a patient, has been transferred to the delivery room when caput became visible and placed in the lithotomy position on the delivery table with her legs in stirrups. A regional or local block has been administered, an episiotomy performed, and the baby delivered. The above is still a common scenario, but one that is changing. The management of second stage of labor has been the subject of increasing discussion among professionals. Some nurse midwives, physicians, and childbirth educators are asking if second stage labor is being overmanaged.[4,8,11,35–38,42,59,60]

During recent years, several trends have become apparent. A more physiologically oriented management of labor, marked by flexible positioning, less forceful breathing patterns, and an increased emphasis on relaxation, has been advocated.[8,12,48] Freedom of position to accommodate the dynamic physiological changes during second stage is being tried. Permitting the woman to bear down spontaneously, using breath holding only as the urge demands, is occurring.[27,60] While advocating conscious relaxation of the pelvic floor to minimize trauma to maternal tissue, many birth attendants are encouraging the woman to have faith in her natural body process.[43,46,53] Perineal massage is an adjunct being used to minimize the need for an episiotomy.[30,52] The birth attendant's role in a normal birth becomes that of guidance to facilitate a birth without trauma rather than use of routine intervention.

REVIEW OF THE LITERATURE

The major medical obstetrical textbooks such as *Williams Obstetrics* still depict women giving birth on a delivery bed in the lithotomy position. It is surprising that other positions used for giving birth have not yet been discussed in the literature that is used in the training of new obstetricians in Western society today. The lithotomy position is a relatively recent arrival on the scene. Englemann did a survey of cultural practices in positioning for birth in the many primitive societies he investigated.[17] One of the most frequent positions a birthing woman assumed was an upright position. Kneeling and squatting were also common. More recent reviewers of posturing and practices during labor among primitive people have further documented a variety of positions assumed by women giving birth.[17,25,50] Paciornik[44] and Odent,[43] modern obstetricians and students of anthropology, are proposing *recognition of women's inherent ability to birth their babies.*

Effects of Maternal Positioning

Roberts and Mendez-Bauer reported on a literature review of maternal positions in labor and concluded that customs, rather than scientific knowledge, have dictated current obstetrical positions.[51] Camacho Carr,[12] Nagai,[40] and Berg[3] all found that women accepted or actually preferred an upright position over a recumbent position for second stage labor.

Anatomical and physiological studies have shown the efficacy of an active, gravity-assisted position for giving birth.[57] The uterine contents press on the proprioceptors in the cervix and later in the pelvic floor, eliciting the Ferguson reflex, thus causing release of a surge of pituitary oxytocin. Additionally, there is also a relaxation of the pelvic joints, as reported by Young.[61] These are significant factors in a more efficient and easier second stage of labor.

Gold showed through x-ray studies, published in 1950, that the pelvic drive is more efficient in an upright position or when the uterus is tilted forward.[19] He suggested that keeping the parturient on her feet as long as possible during first stage labor would result in an advantageous drive and a more efficient second stage of labor. In a study presented at the XIth World Congress of Obstetrics and Gynecology in Berlin in September 1985, Borell of Sweden discussed his research with pelvic diameters, which was a continuation of a previous study.[6]

Borell's study showed the symphysis pubis to have an average downward displacement of 2.5 centimeters during the descent. During the actual birth and for some time afterward, the symphysis pubis displaced upward an additional 2 centimeters from the original position. This serves to increase the anteroposterior sagittal diameter. Thus the pelvic structure has the potential for considerable adjustment during birth and can be regarded as a variable with which to work rather than a given dimension. Caldeyro-Barcia reiterated the factors that Gold reported from his radiological study.[9] Caldeyro-Barcia also contended that there is a much greater uterine pressure while the woman is upright, which would explain a more efficient second stage in that position.

Liu reviewed the effect of upright position during labor and its relationship to physics, citing Newton's law of motion and gravity.[33] She points out that in the anterior occiput delivery of a woman in the horizontal position, the weight of the fetal brain substance sinks toward the frontal lobes because they are in the most dependent position. In contrast, in a squatting or modified upright position, the occipital fontanel bears the mass of weight. She proposes that this older part of the brain, more developed at birth, is better able to withstand stress and less likely to suffer damage than the newer developing frontal lobes, although she has offered no research to date to support this contention.

Atwood divided birthing positions anatomically into two categories, differentiating upright, active positions from neutral or more horizontal positions.[1] He states that it is possible to draw a connecting line between the third and fifth lumbar ver-

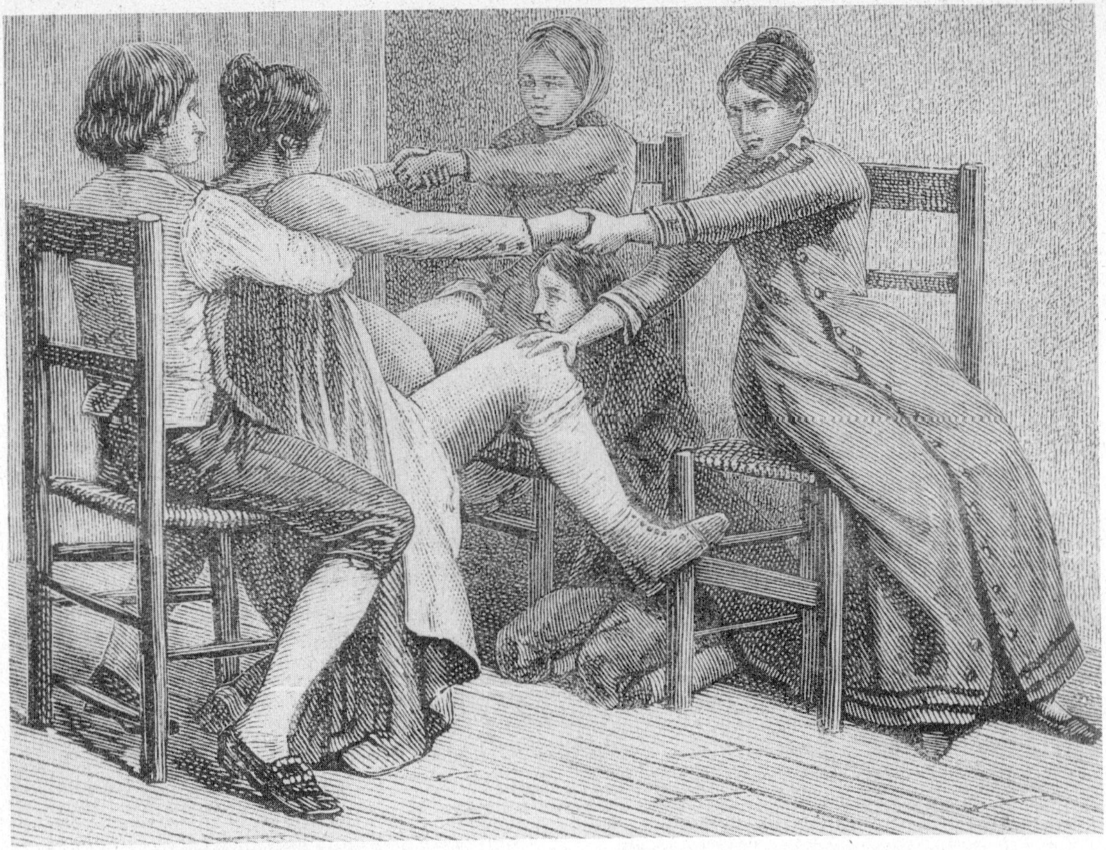

Pioneer birth scene, Paris 1887. (Courtesy of the National Library of Medicine.)

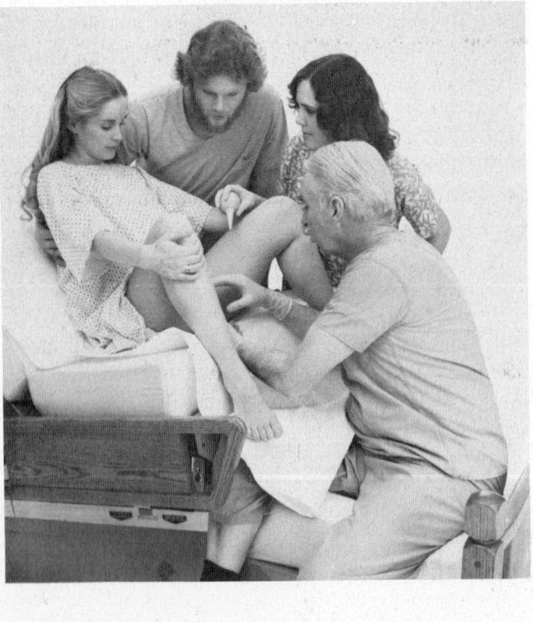

Contemporary birth scene. (Copyright © The Borning Corporation. Reprinted/reproduced with permission from The Borning Corporation.)

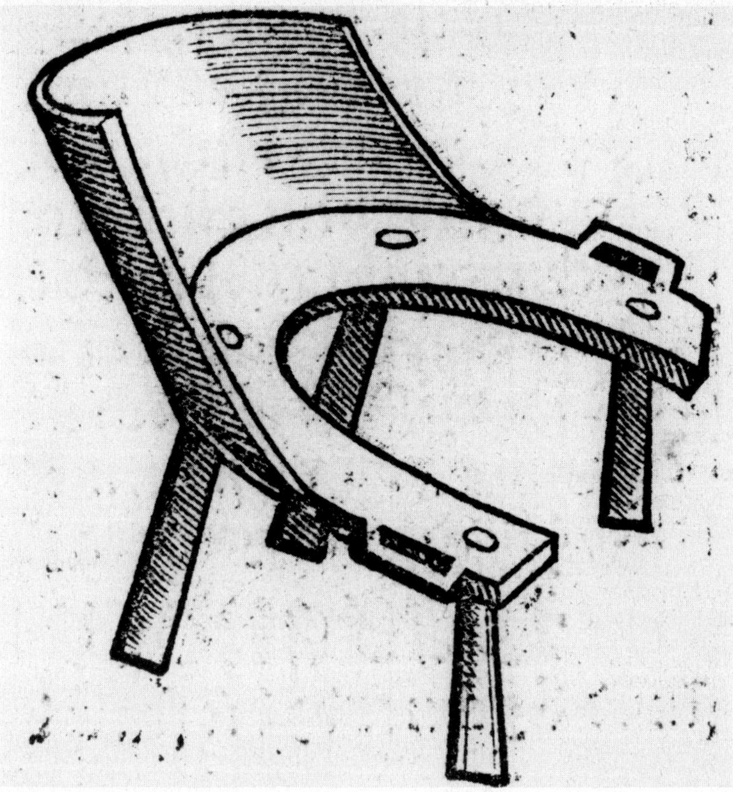

Primitive birthing stool. (Courtesy of the National Library of Medicine.)

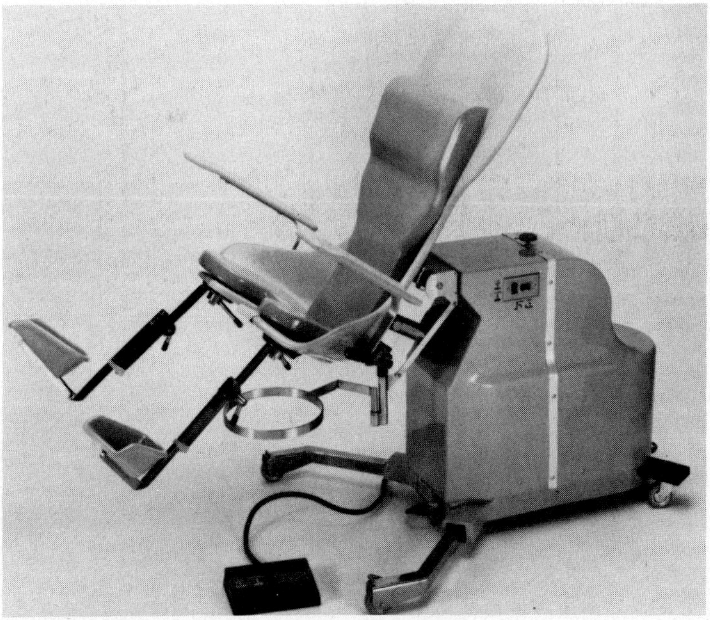

Contemporary birthing chair. (Courtesy of Century Manufacturing Company.)

tebrae. When this line is *nearly vertical*, it is called the *active or upright position* and is achieved when the woman is *standing, sitting, squatting,* or *kneeling*. A *neutral position* occurs when a *nearly horizontal* line can be drawn between the third and fifth lumbar vertebrae. This occurs when the mother is in the *lateral, prone, dorsal, lithotomy,* or *semirecumbent position,* as well as the position on *hands and knees*. Although there is a place for these positions during birth, one of the disadvantages of the neutral positions is that the mother is unable to utilize gravity during second stage labor. Childbirth educators should note that the semirecumbent position often practiced in childbirth classes falls into the latter group. It is also noted that other authors using terms such as upright position may not be using Atwood's definition. In fact, some researchers do not operationally define their use of terms describing positions.

Haukeland in Norway studied old-fashioned birth chairs and designed an adjustable delivery chair.[20] He reports that back pain was reduced and spontaneous births increased using the chair; he suggests its use as one alternative rather than as a routine. A study by Hillan and colleagues presented at the International Conference of Midwives, Sydney, Australia, 1984, reported a shorter active second stage using a birth chair and a seated position.[21] This randomized study of 500 women reported that the upright position facilitated second stage labor without forceps even when lumbar epidural anesthesia was used.

Caldeyro-Barcia[7–11] and Humphrey[24] discuss altered fetal blood gases and the adverse effects of labor on the maternal blood circulation and fetal oxygenation when labor is conducted in the dorsal position. They report that active labor tends to be shorter and more efficient in an upright position. The proposed effects of a dorsal second stage position as proposed by Dunn[16] are outlined in Figure 16–1. Roberts and Von Lier compared advantages and disadvantages of many positions as shown in Table 16–1.

In summary, the results of studies on positioning in second stage have been mixed. There is unequivocal evidence, however, that the dorsal position (which fails to use the forces of gravity), may cause maternal hypotension and fetal hypoxia, may require more strenuous pushing, and may hamper infant descent. Studies on positioning during sec-

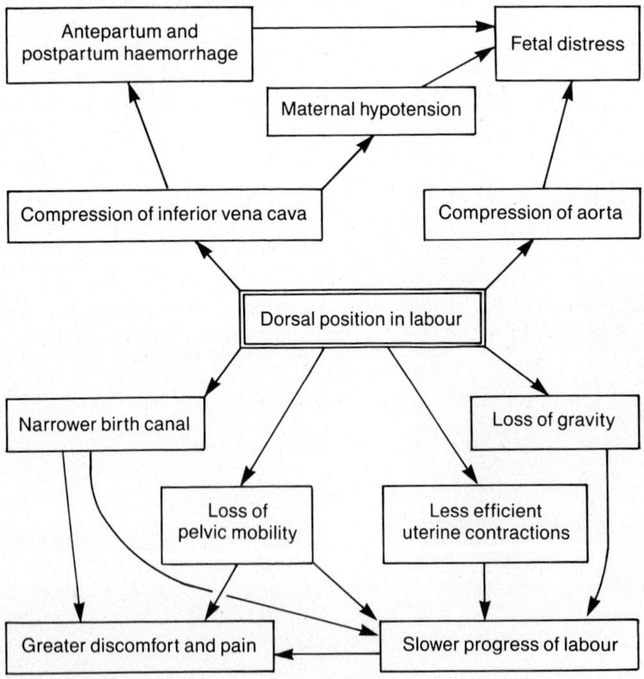

FIGURE 16–1. Consequence of the dorsal position during labor. (From Dunn, P. Obstetric Delivery Today: For Better or Worse. *Lancet* April 10, 1976, 792.)

TABLE 16–1. ADVANTAGES AND DISADVANTAGES OF SECOND STAGE POSITIONS

MOTHER	FETUS	BIRTH ATTENDANT
Lithotomy Position (on back with knees bent or up on chest)		
Advantages		
• Some women say they like the security of stirrups for their legs, particularly if they have used stirrups previously.	• Easy to listen to fetal heart rate	• More control of birth situation; useful if woman is ''out of control'' • Obstetric intervention easiest: forceps, episiotomy, repair of lacerations, anesthesia • More comfortable, less back strain • Asepsis
Disadvantages		
• Adverse effects on blood flow (hemodynamics): The weight of the uterus compresses large blood vessels so as to decrease blood flow to the uterus and ultimately decrease oxygen to the baby. • Less active participation with baby and birth attendant • Stirrups can promote blood clots if legs are in them a long time. • Decreased ability to push • Sense of vulnerability • Possible inhalation of vomit	• Changes in mother's blood flow can cause fetal distress or a depressed baby at birth • Difficult for mother to see or hold baby after birth	• Cannot easily interact with woman and is less able to elicit her cooperation
Standing (weight on feet)		
Advantages		
• Reported improved uterine contractability for first stage—unknown for second stage • Avoidance of negative hemodynamic changes • Can watch birth • May increase help of gravity	• Unknown	• Ease in interacting with woman
Disadvantages		
• Fatigue • Needs two supporters • Hypothesized increased blood loss, uterine prolapse, edema of cervix and vulva	• May fall to ground unless ''caught''	• Difficult to control baby's head and watch perineum • Difficult to assist with delivery
Sitting (weight on buttocks)		
Advantages		
• Shorter second stage: comfortable • Most efficient for expulsive efforts • Maintains some advantages of squatting; increases pelvic diameter • Easy to interact with baby and others • Grunting may aid delivery.	• Probably less negative hemodynamic effects than lithotomy, thus less fetal distress • Easy to listen to fetal heart rate	• Good access to perineum for control of delivery • Able to use interventions such as episiotomy, forceps, or pudendal anesthesia easily
Disadvantages		
• Needs back support • Might induce edema of vulva or cervix		• Some attendants may not want the mother's active participation in the birth.

Table continued on following page

TABLE 16–1. ADVANTAGES AND DISADVANTAGES OF SECOND STAGE POSITIONS *Continued*

MOTHER	FETUS	BIRTH ATTENDANT
Hands and Knees (kneeling with weight supported by hands or elbows)		
Advantages		
• No weight on inferior vena cava; thus, probably less fetal distress • Advocated for aiding delivery of shoulder • Useful for relieving pressure on umbilical cord if trapped or prolapsed	• May be useful in rotating occiput posterior positions or in delivery of shoulders when they are "tight"	• Good visualization of perineum and control of expulsion of presenting part • Optimal control for breech delivery, according to some practitioners
Disadvantages		
• Very tiring; bean bags and pillows useful for maintaining position or for rest between contractions • Difficult to interact with baby and birth attendant, but can turn immediately after delivery and hold baby • Cramps in arms and legs	• Difficult to monitor baby unless one uses fetal scalp electrode	• Must reorient landmarks and adapt hand maneuvers for delivery • Usually turn woman to recumbent position for delivery of placenta, repair of lacerations, and rest
Dorsal Recumbent (on back with legs extended or knees flexed)		
Advantages		
• Less tension on perineum • Less pressure on legs • No stirrups; thus less likely to develop thrombosis	• Easy to listen to fetal heart rate	• Easy access to perineum • Able to do pudendal anesthesia or episiotomy easily
Disadvantages		
• Same blood flow changes as lithotomy • Difficult to participate in birth • Decreased ability to push	• Fetal distress can occur because of hemodynamic changes • Difficult for mother to hold her baby after birth	• Cannot easily interact with woman • Forceps delivery more difficult to do since there is less counter-pressure on fetus
Lateral Recumbent (Sims) (on either side with thighs flexed)		
Advantages		
• Corrects or avoids adverse hemodynamic effects of lithotomy position • May prevent some perineal lacerations because of less tension on perineum • May help to rotate occiput posterior presentations • May be helpful in relieving a shoulder dystocia • Comfortable for many mothers and conducive to resting between contractions since contractions are less frequent	• Promotes maximum uterine blood flow and thus fetal oxygenation	• Conducive for controlled delivery • Preferred by some British practitioners
Disadvantages		
• Least efficient for expulsive efforts; this *may* be desirable to avoid a precipitous delivery for a repeat mother. • Needs someone to hold leg up for delivery	• More difficult to listen to fetal heart tones	• Some practitioners consider position awkward. • Unable to see and interact with mother as easily; cannot see her face directly • Difficult to repair episiotomy or use forceps

TABLE 16–1. ADVANTAGES AND DISADVANTAGES OF SECOND STAGE POSITIONS *Continued*

MOTHER	FETUS	BIRTH ATTENDANT
Squatting (weight on feet with knees bent)		
Advantages		
• Good expulsive effort; shorter second stage • Pressure of the thighs against the abdomen may aid in expulsion by increasing intra-abdominal pressure and promoting longitudinal alignment of the fetus with the birth canal. • Improves pelvic bone diameter. Anterior-posterior diameter of outlet increased by 0.5–2 cm; transverse diameter is also increased. • Avoids adverse hemodynamic effects of lithotomy • Facilitates interaction with birth attendant and baby, and others present	• Promotes fetal descent and rotation	• Some visibility of perineum • Maternal effort is maximized in accomplishing the birth.
Disadvantages		
• Legs can become fatigued, especially if woman is not supported. • Uterine prolapse may be more likely due to strenuous bearing-down effort. • May promote increased perineal and cervical edema. • Rapid descent and expulsion of fetus may be accompanied by vaginal and perineal lacerations. • Increased blood loss possible	• Rapid expulsion may result in sudden reduction in intracervical pressure and cause cerebral bleeding in the brain of a premature infant whose skull bones are not yet firm	• Cannot intervene easily in this position to help control the expulsion of the baby or to aid the birth with an episiotomy or pudendal nerve block

From Roberts, J., and Von Lier, D. Debate: Positions for second stage. *Childbirth Educator* 3:36, 1984.

ond stage labor have generated reports of shorter, easier labors or no difference between upright and other recumbent positions.[3,4,12,15,57] Roberts and coworkers[38,48] are currently investigating self-regulation in second stage in which women are supported to choose the position they find most comfortable. Their study will provide insight into the contention that women left free to choose will select a position advantageous to their particular situation.

Duration of Second Stage Labor

It has been traditional to limit second stage labor to a maximum of two hours for fear of fetal hypoxia. More recently, some investigators have challenged this view, stating that monitoring equipment that detects signs of fetal distress allows for constant surveillance of infants during second stage, thus eliminating the need to routinely restrict the time of second stage labor for all births. Research on the duration of second stage labor is summarized in Table 16–2.

Mahan and McKay[35] conclude from reviewing this research literature that there are five signs that indicate that intervention *may* be needed in second stage. These are (1) abnormal fetal heart rate patterns (especially loss of variability), (2) duration over two hours in primigravidas or one hour in multiparas, (3) neonatal pH levels of less than 7.2, (4) poor-quality contractions, and (5) arrested descent and rotation. They also remind the practitioner that full dilation may not always be accompanied by adequate fetal descent to initiate a bearing-down reflex. The use of gravity in the squatting position or with the woman seated on a

TABLE 16–2. DURATION FINDINGS COMPARED

STUDY	SUBJECTS	PURPOSE	DURATION (minutes)	COMMENTS
Agboda and Agobe (1976)	602 black parturients, both primigravidas and multiparas, in spontaneous labor with no augmentation, epidural anesthesia, assisted delivery or cesarean sections	Study the mean, median and modal durations of labor in Nigerian women (prospective)	Primiparas: mean 25.48, median 20.43 Multiparas: mean 14.53, median 12.54	Highly significant positive correlation in primiparas and multiparas between durations of first and second stage labor
Bergsjo & associates (1979)	2,242 Parturients with spontaneous onset of labor	Reassess duration of labor (prospective)	Primiparas: median 16 Multiparas: median 10 90th Percentile: primiparas 44, multiparas 22	Weak but significant correlation between duration of active phase (4 to 10 cm) and second stage. Approximately 20% of primigravidas and 6% to 8% of multiparas had labor terminated by operative intervention
Bergsjo and Halle (1980)	635 Parturients with vaginal delivery, including both spontaneous and induced labor	Obtain an estimate of true duration of second-stage labor (prospective)	Spontaneous labor Para 0: mean 34 6, median 31.3 Para 1: mean 17.4, median 14.3 Para 2+: mean 15, median 11.7 Induced labor Para 0: mean 32.9, median 27.5 Para 1+: mean 16.4, median 14.4	Authors observe that interferences, such as cesarean section, made it impossible to obtain a true biological picture of second stage labor
Beynon (1957)	100 Normal primigravidas in labor given no pushing instructions, compared with 393 controls instructed in pushing	Assess effects of giving no suggestions to push unless labor was not progressing satisfactorily (prospective)	Mean duration for 83 parturients delivering spontaneously was 63 minutes	No data given about labor duration in remainder of study group (six had forceps and 11 needed directions in forced pushing) or for controls.
Cohen (1977)	4,403 Nulliparas	Determine whether duration of second stage labor influences perinatal outcome or maternal or puerperal morbidity (retrospective)	0–29 (14.15%) 30–59 (28.55%) 60–89 (22.87%) 90–119 (13.6%) 120–149 (9.65%) 150–179 (5.4%) 180+ (5.8%)	No significant increase in frequency of perinatal mortality, neonatal morbidity, or low 5-minute Apgars with long second stages. An increase in postpartal hemorrhage after more than 3 hours of second stage labor attributable to patients being delivered by midforceps

Duignan & associates (1975)	1,306 White, Asian and black parturients	Establish characteristics of normal labor (prospective)	Primiparas: mean 41.5 Multiparas: mean 17.4	Duration of second stage longer in white primiparas than in either Asian or black primiparas
Golditch and Kirkman (1975)	801 Pregnancies resulting in delivery of infants weighing 4,100 gm (9 lb) or more, matched for gestational age and delivery method with control group of 1,000 randomly selected women with infants weighing 2,500 to 4,000 gm	Evaluate approach to management of labor and delivery on outcomes for mother and baby (retrospective)	Large-infant group Primiparas: mean 71.8 Multiparas: mean 33.8 Controls Primiparas: mean 56 Multiparas: mean 16	Second stage labor duration significantly shorter in control group
Kadar and Romero (1983)	149 Primigravidas requiring instrumental delivery for midcavity arrest of fetal head in second stage, compared with 1,259 primigravidas delivering spontaneously	Compare frequency of subsequent childbearing and method of subsequent delivery (retrospective)	Primigravidas: 95th percentile for spontaneous deliveries was 105 minutes	Significant correlation between birthweight and mean duration of second stage in spontaneously delivering primigravidas found after stratifying birthweights between 2,500 and 4,500 gm into 500 gm intervals
Lederman & associates (1978)	32 Primigravidas with no medical or obstetric complications	Examine relationships among maternal anxiety, selected stress-related biochemical factors, and progress in three defined labor phases (retrospective)	75 (Mean and median)	Larger means possible due to skewing effects of extreme scores
Niswander and Gordon (1972)	29,989 Women with vertex presentation and vaginal deliveries	Examine labor variables as part of the Collaborative Perinatal Study (retrospective)	Primigravidas: 62% of whites and 81% of blacks had second-stage duration of 60 minutes or less. By 2 hours, 87% of whites and 95% of blacks had delivered Later births: 97% of whites and 98% of blacks had delivered by 1 hour	Researchers concluded there is increased fetal risk with second stage labors less than 30 minutes and increased incidence of adverse effects when second stage is longer than 2 hours
Perry and Porter (1979)	20 Primigravidas and 20 multiparas	Examine relationship between pushing technique and duration of second stage labor (prospective)	Prenatally educated in pushing technique Primiparas: mean 45 Multiparas: mean 13 No prenatal training in pushing technique Primiparas: mean 68 Multiparas: mean 18	Mean for women not instructed in pushing is very close to that reported by Beynon

Table continued on following page

TABLE 16–2. DURATION FINDINGS COMPARED *Continued*

STUDY	SUBJECTS	PURPOSE	DURATION (minutes)	COMMENTS
Roemar et al. (1977)	3,925 Women with vaginal singleton deliveries (total study population 4,081)	Review of duration of second stage labor (retrospective)	Primiparas: mean 33.1, mean for active pushing 12.9 (95th percentile for primiparas 105) Para 2: mean 13.8, mean active pushing 7.6 Para 3: mean 10.6, mean active pushing 6.3	Authors suggest that second stage labor not exceed 45 minutes
Scott and Rose (1976)	129 Lamaze-educated primigravidas, compared with 129 matched controls who did not take Lamaze classes	Investigate whether prepared childbirth classes had measurable physical advantages (prospective)	Lamaze-educated: mean 51.9 Control group: mean 56.89	Significantly more Lamaze-educated women delivered spontaneously. No significant difference in length of labor between groups
VanCoeverden et al. (1978)	1,006 Women with spontaneous labors	Obtain data on duration of various normal labor stages in white patients in Cape Town, South Africa	Primiparas: mean 27.4 Para 2: mean 13.9 Para 3: mean 13.3 95th Percentile for para 1: 48; for para 2: 30	Correlation found between duration of first and second stage labor in para 1 and para 2 subjects
Wood et al. (1973)	11 Women in each of two comparison groups (parity not identified)	Study fetal condition according to whether delivery was speeded or conducted normally (prospective)	Speeded labors: mean 48 min 18 sec Normals: mean 58 min 32 sec	Intervals between head being in view and start of delivery and time taken for delivery of fetus significantly shorter in "speeded" group. Not surprising, since early episiotomy, encouraged pushing, and forceps with delays were part of speeded management strategy
Yeates and Roberts (1984)	Ten nulliparas; five pushed in traditional manner with sustained breathholding and five spontaneously	Use study to focus on effects of spontaneous bearing-down efforts	Spontaneous bearing down: mean 67.4 Directed bearing down: mean 74.2	Mean time close to that of Beynon, who also examined spontaneous bearing down

From Mahan, C., and McKay, S. Are we overmanaging second stage labor? *Contemporary OB/GYN*, 24:37, 1984 toilet may enhance descent and elicit the bearing-down reflex.

Respiratory and Bearing-down Effort

According to Noble, exertion, whether in exercise, karate, weightlifting, or childbirth is performed on the outward breath. This allows the muscles to contract efficiently.[42] She states that partial closure of the glottis results in characteristic noises of second stage labor and assists the abdominals in their role of forced exhalation. She recommends that vocalization be encouraged in childbirth.

The contrasting pushing effort with glottis closed is called a Valsalva maneuver. This causes a high intrathoracic pressure that prevents venous return to the heart and causes a falling blood pressure, a fall in cardiac output, and disrupted blood flow to the uterus. This in turn has been hypothesized to potentially lead to fetal hypoxia as shown in Figure 16–2. Neither Barnett and Humenick[2] nor Knauth and Haloburo[31] found a significant difference in length of second stage labor with open glottis breathing.

When women are not directed to hold their breath, they tend to exhale forcefully with pushing or to hold their breath only briefly.[27,28,42] Many care providers are uncomfortable with women vocalizing during birth. They may interpret the sounds as an indication of maternal pain, which they feel obligated to relieve. They may fear that the noise generated will leave a poor impression on other laboring women or on other nearby care providers. Most of all, they may not be able to distinguish the noise of vigorous pushing from a cry for help from the woman. Newton and Newton have likened

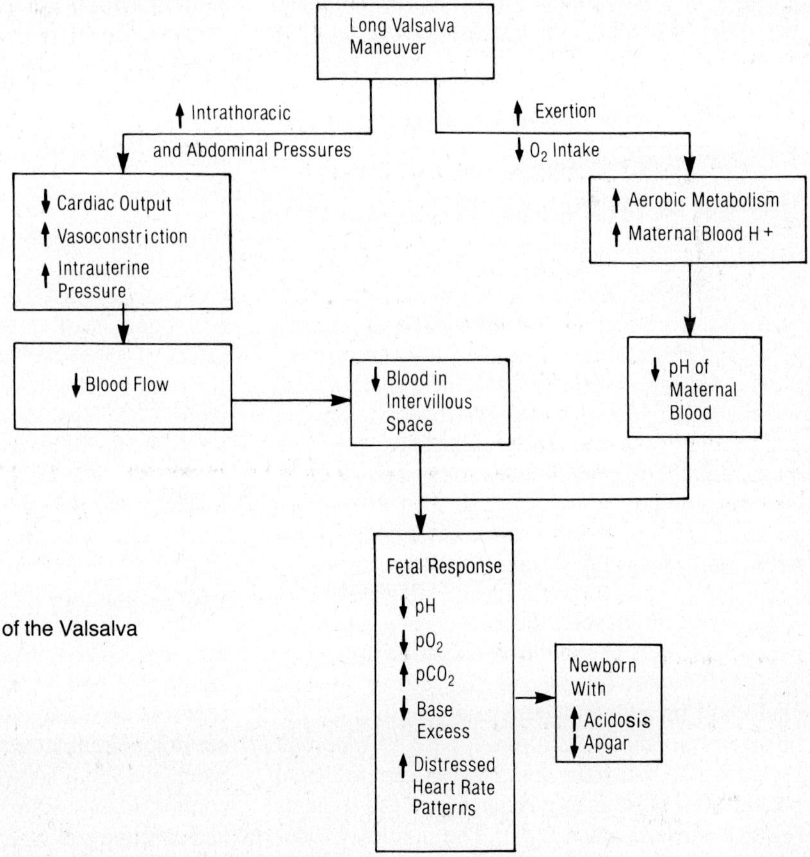

FIGURE 16–2. Consequences of the Valsalva maneuver.

aspects of second stage labor to sexual orgasm and noted the similarity of sounds.[41] This similarity may also make care providers uncomfortable with labor sounds and lead them to find reasons to promote breath holding and its accompanying silence during second stage.

Episiotomy

Cogan and Edmunds examined the research on use of episiotomy.[14] They report evidence that an episiotomy may reduce the laceration rate and shorten second stage labor. However, this procedure may also increase blood loss and postpartum and coital pain. Many women use perineal massage during pregnancy to soften perineal resistance during birth and make an episiotomy less needed. The issue on the need for episiotomy is not so much a question of whether it can sometimes be beneficial but rather whether or not it should be routinely used.

Second Stage Environment

Kelly[26] and Lederman et al.[32] have described the relationship of anxiety to plasma catecholamines and plasma cortisol. It appears that these hormones are increased with maternal anxiety and have potential to slow labor. The presence of family members in many cases may lower maternal anxiety and thus account for the findings of Sosa and colleagues that supportive companionship is associated with lowered perinatal problems, easier labors, and less use of anesthesia.[54]

Odent[43] in his article on the evolution of obstetrics at Pithiviers, France, encourages each woman to be aware of her feelings during birth and let her phylogenic brain take over. Peterson also discusses the importance of the woman using her intuitive self to birth her baby and how emotional and psychological factors can cause a dysfunctional labor.[46] Thus there is a growing awareness that *the birth environment may be as important as birthing techniques*.

IMPLICATIONS FOR PRACTICE

The childbirth educator needs to keep informed of research supporting physiological management of second stage labor.[5,9,18,22,23,51,56] In childbirth education classes, she needs to teach the anatomy and physiology of second stage labor in clear, concise, and meaningful terms. The childbirth educator can encourage the woman to listen to her body signals and sensations.[29,30,43,46] She can also advise the woman that expressing herself emotionally, verbally, and physically during expulsion is helpful and a typical part of second stage labor.[28,42]

In childbirth classes, the expectant mother and her support person should be taught to use relaxation techniques for second stage.[26,32,54] Several choices of breathing patterns and positions for expulsive effort should be offered.[39,45] It is important to teach the rationale for various physiological positions for pushing as well as to have the students practice these in class.[1,7,33,34] The childbirth educator can discuss variables that affect the course of progress such as size and position of the baby, effect of analgesia and anesthesia, as well as differences in length of the second stage in multiparas.[15,57,58] Realistic expectations of what kind of support can be expected from care providers is important. The development of a birth plan that includes detailed preferences for second stage is commonly done in childbirth classes. Women should be encouraged to discuss their birth plans with all participants prior to labor.[35,36,51]

The birth attendants need to be provided with the most current research along with information on what is being taught in classes. Childbirth educators can work with care providers to create an environment that promotes choice for expectant parents. (See Chapters 29 on consumer-provider communication and 30 on negotiating.) Flexible and creative use of birthing beds, chairs, or mod-

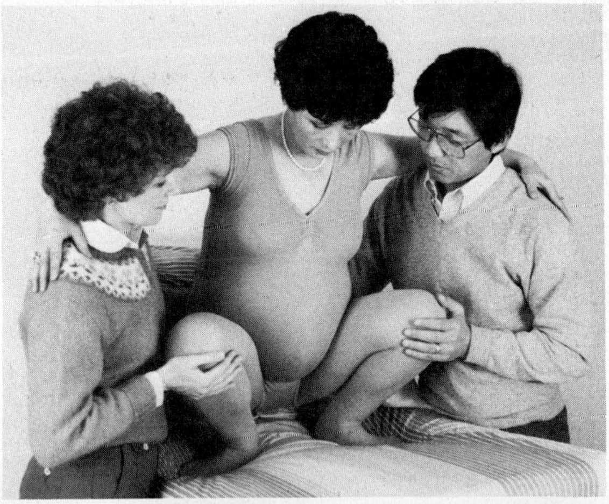

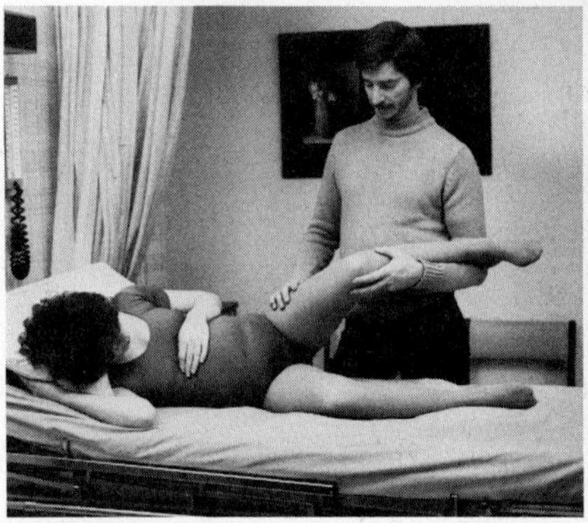

Practicing some of the positions for pushing from Birth Companion by Childbirth Graphics Ltd. (Photos by Childbirth Graphics Ltd.)

ified delivery beds, updated protocols for managing second stage labor,[55] and a positive attitude toward the mother and her support person in regard to choice are all possible, especially in settings where competition for obstetrical clients is keen.

Classroom and Home Practice

The actual class content related to second stage labor will depend on what seems appropriate for a given class. Suggestions for content in the cognitive (intellectual), affective (emotional), and psychomotor domains (skills) are presented in Tables 16–3, 16–4, and 16–5.

During home practice for second stage labor, the woman is encouraged to practice daily a combination of positions, pelvic tilting, and exhalation breathing while practicing very slight pushing. The expectant mother at term can use positive birth imagery during relaxation (see Chapter 12). Gentle perineal massage and release of pelvic floor to touch can be practiced (Box 16–1).

Second Stage Support

During second stage labor, the woman can be encouraged to assume any comfortable position or movement she desires in the absence of contraindications. She can be urged to change position or do some pelvic rocking, especially if there is little progress after one half hour in one position. She should be encouraged and supported in a relaxed

In my opinion, we cannot just tell a woman she may take any position she wants and expect her to be able to stand up, or walk, or get over on all fours, or squat; it may hurt to move in second stage. Therefore, I think our preparation of parents must focus on the need to seek comfort and a more physiologic position than the supine one.

PENNY SIMKIN[1]

. . . one researcher has commented, most odd that, in view of the substantial evidence that "the most unphysiologic thing one can do for either mother or baby is to lie mother flat on her back, it is a sobering thought that as we get more and more involved in . . . monitoring . . . the first thing we do is lie mother flat on her back so that we can drape all our recording gear on her and baby."

A. LILEY cited by Ann Oakley[2]

TABLE 16–3. CLASS CONTENT RELATED TO SECOND STAGE LABOR: COGNITIVE DOMAIN

Maternal: Anatomy and physiology of the pelvic structures, pelvic floor musculature, vaginal canal, and vulva and hormonal influences on these.
- Phases of second stage of labor as well as changes in uterine contractions.
- Positioning and its effect on fetal drive angle and stimulation of proprioceptors in the pelvic floor.
- Effect of gravity and positioning on length of second stage.
- Positioning and maternal ventilation and their effects on maternal and placental circulation.
- Effect of multiparity on duration and sensation of second stage.
- Uterine effort and maternal voluntary effort.
- Physical sensations of birth.
- Perineal massage and episiotomy.
- Effect of anesthesia on descent and rotation of baby.
- Vaginal birth after previous cesarean birth.
- Consumerism (finding own style) for birth.

Fetal: Size, position, presentation, and descent.
- Effect of cord position in relation to above parameters, as well as condition of amniotic membranes.
- Maternal positioning and its effect on fetal blood gases and pH.
- Multiple birth, as well as premature and precipitous birth.
- Operative deliveries such as forceps, vacuum extraction, and cesarean birth.

TABLE 16–4. CLASS CONTENT RELATED TO SECOND STAGE LABOR: AFFECTIVE DOMAIN

Class content should encourage discussion that includes:
- Psychological and emotional changes and responses to second stage.
- Effects of previous birth experiences as well as other related experiences and how it influences the present.
- Awareness—tuning in to the body process of giving birth.
- Effect of physical and emotional environment such as sight, sound (including music), color, touch, and smell.
- Effect of the attitude of the available support system, partner, and medical staff.
- Effect of medical complications and interventions on emotional experience of birth.

and unhurried atmosphere. Relaxation and comfort measures may include use of music, pillows, hot or cold compresses, warm showers or baths, and massage. She should be reassured of her ability to give birth to her baby and helped to imagine the baby's movements toward birth. *She should feel free to make noise, lose control, or do whatever necessary to give birth*. Her ability to give informed consent when procedures and interventions are indicated should be safeguarded.

TABLE 16–5. CLASS CONTENT RELATED TO SECOND STAGE LABOR: PSYCHOMOTOR DOMAIN—SKILLS AND PRACTICE

The class should include practice sessions in the following:
- Practice variations in positioning for pushing, including supported squatting, sitting, standing, kneeling, sidelying, hands-and-knees, as well as propped dorsal recumbent.
- Differentiate muscle groups that need to relax during second stage as well as strengthening of selected muscles through practice.
- A variety of choices in breathing patterns for pushing, including open glottis with grunting at will and short breath-holding periods (5–6 seconds)
- Coordinate breathing patterns with practice of various positions and role-playing for labor.
- Practice imagery of different phases of second stage in conjunction with positioning and breathing. Encourage realistic expectations of the work involved in birth.
- Teach control and modification of body processes as needed through positioning and breathing.
- Discuss practical aspects of prenatal perineal massage and pelvic floor exercises.

Box 16–1

PERINEAL MASSAGE INSTRUCTIONS FOR PREGNANT WOMEN

Perineal massage is a technique used to increase the flexibility of the perineum and decrease the need for episiotomy during childbirth. It also helps the woman to identify the pelvic floor muscles and learn to relax them in response to pressure. Massaging oil into the perineum helps soften and increase the elasticity of the tissue. The woman's ability to relax the pelvic floor muscles also reduces resistance during childbirth and the need for an episiotomy.

GENERAL GUIDELINES

The massage can be done by you or your partner.

Beginning about six weeks before your due date, do the massage once daily for at least five minutes.

Use a lubricant such as wheat germ oil, vitamin E oil (available at health food stores), or other vegetable oils. The oil permits the fingers to glide over the skin. It also helps soften the skin.

A warm bath or warm compresses on your perineum for 5 to 10 minutes before beginning the massage can help you relax, if needed.

A mirror is helpful the first few times you do the massage so that you can see your perineum and what you are doing.

DIRECTIONS

Wash your hands.

Lie in a comfortable, semiseated position against some pillows.

Lubricate your fingers with the oil and rub the oil into the perineum and lower vaginal wall.

Place your thumbs (your partner can use his index fingers) about 1 to 1½ inches into the vagina. Grasp the perineal tissues firmly starting at the center of each side of the vagina and pressing downward toward the rectum. Maintaining a steady pressure, move your fingers upward and slightly outward along the lower sides of the vagina in a rhythmic "U" or sling type movement. At first, the tissue will feel tight, but with time and practice it will relax and stretch. If you have an episiotomy scar, you should concentrate a part of the massage on that area.

As you apply pressure, concentrate on relaxing your muscles.

Increase the pressure on the perineum until you feel a stinging or burning sensation. You will recognize this sensation later as the perineum stretches around the baby's head during birth.

CAUTIONS

The urinary opening should be *avoided* to prevent urinary tract infections.

If you have any infections in the perineal area, check with your physician or midwife *before* starting perineal massage.

Adapted from Schrag, K. Maintenance of pelvic floor integrity during childbirth. *Journal of Nurse-Midwifery* 24:29, 1979, and Fleming, E. *Prenatal Perineal Massage.* Minneapolis, MN: International Childbirth Education Association, Inc., 1986.

IMPLICATIONS FOR RESEARCH

There is a need for continued research to support the move toward a more physiological management of second stage labor. This is especially important in today's legal climate where "sins of omission" may be more damaging to the birth attendant than the "sins of commission" of excessive, iatrogenic intervention. Much of the research to date now needs to be followed by randomized clinical trials; however, this is not always possible from an ethical standpoint. Areas needing more research include:

- The safety and efficacy of upright positions in second stage labor.

- The nature of second stage time-frame averages in low-risk women with healthy infants.
- Controlled studies on the efficiency and results of atraumatic birth techniques (including those involving small lacerations) as compared with episiotomy.
- The efficacy of support measures during second stage labor.
- The cost-to-benefit ratio of single unit labor/delivery/postpartum rooms as compared to traditional birthing units.
- The congruence or lack of congruence between the birthing woman's needs and the desire of several generations of family to be present for the birth.
- The psychological importance to the woman of "giving birth" versus "being delivered."
- The physiological management of birth as opposed to traditional routines, with outcome measures including infant safety and maternal satisfaction.

SUMMARY

A review of second stage labor reveals that this aspect of the birth process is a sensitive one from both an affective and a safety perspective. This has perhaps been one of the slower areas to change since the start of the prepared childbirth movement. Research to date tends to favor those calling for a more physiological approach to second stage when the infant is healthy. Those who would routinely intervene and direct identical positioning and bearing down efforts from all women have little research to support that philosophy. Second stage obstetrics will continue to change as research accumulates and care providers become sensitive to the issues. To the extent that birth practices are as much cultural as logical, one can expect that the change will be slow and that skilled communication and negotiation will be needed to bring that change about.

References

1. Atwood, R. J. Parturitional posture and related birth behavior. *Acta Obstetrics and Gynaecology of Scandinavia* Suppl. 57:1, 1976.
2. Barnett, M., and Humenick, S. Infant outcomes in relation to second stages labor pushing method. *Birth* 9:221, 1982.
3. Berg, G., and Selbring, A. Experience with upright birth. *Lakartidningen* (Physicians Journal, Sweden) 81:115, 117, 1984.
4. Beynon, C. The normal second stage of labor: A plea for its reform. *Journal of Obstetrics and Gynaecology of the British Empire* 64:815, 1957.
5. Bierniarz, J. An arteriographic study. *American Journal of Obstetrics and Gynecology* 100:203, 1968.
6. Borell, W. C., and Fernstrom, I. The mechanism of labor. *Radiologic Clinics of North America* 5:73, 1966.
7. Caldeyro-Barcia, R., Noriega-Guerra, L., Cibils, L. A., et al. Effect of position changes on the intensity and frequency of uterine contraction during labor. *American Journal of Obstetrics and Gynecology* 80:284, 1960.
8. Caldeyro-Barcia, R. The influence of maternal bearing down efforts during the second stage on fetal well being. *Birth and the Family Journal* 6:17, 1979.
9. Caldeyro-Barcia, R. The influence of maternal position during second stage of labor. Kaleidoscope of childbearing. Preparation birth and nurturing. *ICEA Review,* 2, 1978.
10. Caldeyro-Barcia, R. Physiological and Psychological Bases for the Modern and Humanized Management of Normal Labor. Symposium, Recent Progress in Perinatal Medicine, Tokyo, 1979.
11. Caldeyro-Barcia, R. Supine called the worst position during labor and delivery. *OB/GYN News* 1 and 54, June 1975.
12. Camacho Carr, K. Obstetric practices which protect against neonatal morbidity: Focus on maternal position in labor and birth. *Birth and the Family Journal* 7:249, 1980.
13. Clarke, A. P. The influence of the position of the patient in labor in causing uterine inertia and pelvic disturbances. *Journal of the American Medical Association* 16:433, 1981.

14. Cogan, R., and Edmunds, E. The unkindest cut? *Contemporary OB/GYN* 9:55, 1977.
15. Cohen, W. Influence of the duration of second stage of labor. *Obstetrics and Gynecology* 49:266, 1977.
16. Dunn, P. Obstetric delivery today for better or worse. *Lancet* 1:792, 1976.
17. Englemann, G. J. *Labor among Primitive People,* 2nd ed. St. Louis: J.H. Chambers & Co., 1883 or New York: AMS Press, 1882.
18. Flynn, A. M., Kelly, J., Hollins, G., and Lynch, P. F. Ambulation in labour. *British Medical Journal* 2:591, 1978.
19. Gold, E. M. Pelvic drive in obstetrics: An x-ray study of 100 cases. *American Journal of Obstetrics and Gynecology.* p. 890, April 1950.
20. Haukeland, I. An alternative delivery position. *American Journal of Obstetrics and Gynecology* 141:115, 1981.
21. Hillan, E. M., Calder, A. A., and Stewart, P. A randomized study to assess the benefits of delivery in a birthing chair. Int. Congress of Nurse-Midwives. Australia, 1984.
22. Howard, F. H. The physiologic position for delivery. *American Journal of Obstetrics and Gynecology* 78:1141, 1959.
23. Huch, A., and Huch, R. Transcutaneous noninvasive monitoring of po_2. *Hospital Practice* 11:6, 1970.
24. Humphrey, M. D., Chang, A., Wood, E. C., et al. A decrease in fetal pH during the second stage of labor when conducted in the dorsal position. *Journal of Obstetrics and Gynecology of British Commonwealth* 81:600, 1974.
25. Jarcho, J. *Postures and Practices During Labour Among Primitive People.* New York: Paul B. Hoeber, 1934.
26. Kelly, J. Effect of fear on uterine motility. *American Journal of Obstetrics and Gynecology* 83:572, June 1962.
27. Kitzinger, S. Challenges in antenatal education. Part 3. A fresh look at second stage. *Nursing Mirror* 7:17, 1977.
28. Kitzinger, S. *Education and Counseling for Childbirth.* New York: Schocken Books, 1979.
29. Kitzinger, S. *The Complete Book of Pregnancy and Childbirth.* New York: Alfred A. Knopf, 1980.
30. Kitzinger, S., and Simkin, P. (eds.). *Episiotomy and Second Stage of Labor.* Seattle: Pennypress, Inc., 1984.
31. Knauth, D., and Haloburo, E. Effect of pushing techniques in birthing chair on length of second stage of labor. *Nursing Research* 35:49, 1986.
32. Lederman, R., Lederman, W. O, and McCann, D. Relationship of maternal anxiety, plasma catecholamines and plasma cortisol to progress in labor. *American Journal of Obstetrics and Gynecology* 132:5, 1978.
33. Liu, Y. C. Effects of an upright position during labor. *American Journal of Nursing* 74:2202, 1974.
34. Liu, Y. C. Positioning during labor and delivery. History and perspective. *Journal of Nurse-Midwifery* 24:23, 1979.
35. Mahan, C., and McKay, S. Routines: Are we overmanaging second-stage labor? *Contemporary OB/GYN* 24:37, 1984.
36. McKay, S., and Mahan, C. Routines: Laboring patients need more freedom to move. *Contemporary OB/GYN* 24:90, 1984.
37. McKay, S. Second Stage Labor: Has tradition replaced safety? *American Journal of Nursing* 81:1016, 1981.
38. McKay, S. and Roberts, J. Second stage labor: What is normal? *JOGN Nursing* 14:2, 1985.
39. Mengert, W., and Murphy, D. Intra-abdominal pressures created by voluntary muscular effort. *Surgery: Gynecology Obstetrics* 57:745, 1933.
40. Nagai, H. Management of labor. Seminar 18: Alternative in Obstetric Care. *Xth World Congress of Obstetrics and Gynecology.* San Francisco, Oct. 1982.
41. Newton, N., and Newton, M. Mother's reactions to their newborn babies. *Journal of the American Medical Association* 181:206, 1962.
42. Noble, E. Controversies in maternal effort during labor and delivery. *American Journal of Nurse-Midwifery* 26:13, 1981.
43. Odent, M.: The evolution of obstetrics at Pithiviers, France. *Birth and the Family Journal* 8:7, 1981.
44. Paciornik, M., and Paciornik, C. Birth and rooming-in. Lessons learned from Forest Indians from Brazil. *Birth and the Family Journal* 10:2, Summer, 1983.
45. Perry, L., and Potter, C. Pushing technique and the duration of second stage of labor. *West Virginia Medical Journal* 75:32, 1979.
46. Peterson, G. *Birthing normally. A personal growth approach to childbirth.* Berkeley: Mind Body Press, 1981.
47. Pritchard, J. A., MacDonald, P. C., and Gant, N.F.: *Williams Obstetrics.* 17th ed. Norwalk, CN: Appleton-Century-Crofts, 1985.
48. Roberts, J., and Von Lier, D. Debate: Positions for second stage. *Childbirth Educator* 3:36, 1984.
49. Roberts, J., McKay, S., and Noor, K. A Research Proposal to the National Center for Nursing Research of NIH. Funded 9/86.
50. Russell, J. G. B. The rationale of primitive delivery positions. *British Journal of Obstetrics and Gynaecology* 89:712, 1982.
51. Scaer, R., and Korte, D. *A Good Birth, A Safe Birth.* New York: Bantam Books, 1984.
52. Schrag, K. Maintenance of pelvic floor integrity during childbirth. *Journal of Nurse-Midwifery* 24:29, 1979.
53. Silverman, S. Episiotomy—To cut or not to cut? Is there really a question? *The Cybele Report* 6:4, 1985.
54. Sosa, R., Kennell, J., Klaus, M., Robertson, S., and Urrutia, J. The effect of supportive companion on perinatal problems. *New England Journal of Medicine* 303:58, 1980.
55. *Standards for Obstetric, Gynecologic, and Neonatal Nursing,* 3rd ed. Washington, DC: NAACOG, 1986.
56. Ueland, K., and Hansen, J. M. Maternal cardiovascular dynamics. *American Journal of Obstetrics and Gynecology* 103:1, 1969.
57. Valenti, C., Tarquini, G., and Musenga, M. Birth in an upright position. Human reproduction in a changing world. LXI Conference of the Italian Society of Gynecology and Obstetrics. June 1982.
58. WHO Scientific Group: The effects of labour on the fetus

and the newborn. *World Health Organization Technical Report* Ser. o.300, p. 11, 1965.

59. Witzig-Boldt, E. Retarded exhaling instead of holding the breath during expulsion. *Psychosomatic Medicine in Obstetrics and Gynecology,* 3rd International Congress, London. Basel: Karger, 1972.
60. Yeates, D. A., and Roberts, J. E. A comparison of two-bearing-down techniques during the second stage of labor. *Journal of Nurse-Midwifery* 29:3, 1984.
61. Young, J. Relaxation of the pelvic joints in pregnancy: Pelvic arthropathy of pregnancy. *Journal of Obstetrics and Gynaecology of the British Empire* 47:493, 1940.

Beginning Quote

Kitzinger, S. *The Experience of Childbirth*. Baltimore: Penguin Books, Inc., 1972.

Boxed Quotes

1. Simkin, P. Preparing parents for second stage. *Birth: Issues in Prenatal Care and Education* 9:229, 1982.
2. Liley, A. Experiences with uterine and fetal instrumentation. *In* Kaback, M., and Valenti, C. (eds.). *Intrauterine Fetal Visualization: A Multidisciplinary Approach*. Amsterdam: Excerpta Medica, 1976. Cited in A. Oakley, *The Captured Womb*. New York: Basil Blackwell, 1986, p. 183.

chapter 17

COACHING: The Labor Companion

MARTHA BUTLER, DOROTHY LUTHER, and EILEEN FREDERICK

The labor coach is a knowledgeable, supportive benefactor who guides and lovingly directs the woman through childbirth.

Eileen Frederick

Historically, when births began to occur in hospitals, it was because women wanted to have access to anesthesia and analgesia. Women who received "twilight sleep" or "gas" were not responsive to support, and family members were usually excluded. More recently as women began to take a more active role in birth, using prepared childbirth techniques, at least initially family members were discouraged from working together as a team. The reasons for this are only speculative and may include the following: a cultural tradition of birth as women's work; failure of physician and staff to value active participation of both partners; failure of the laboring couple themselves to understand or value the teamwork; reluctance of the birthing agency to relinquish part of their role and authority to a labor companion; and feelings of inadequacy on the part of physicians and staff about their ability to support the couple who chose to work together.

Whatever the initial reasons for discouraging woman-companion teamwork during labor, this trend has all but disappeared. The past two-and-a-half decades have seen a movement toward more active participation of health care consumers in the decision-making process, particularly as it relates to maternity care. Women are requesting active participation during childbirth and are preparing themselves for this.

Although the trend toward a labor companion is a relatively new phenomenon among United States health care institutions, the concept is not new. Throughout history, women have been supported during labor by a companion, usually another woman.[48] What is relatively new, however, is the trend toward encouraging the labor companion to become formally prepared to "coach" the mother through labor and birth, thus taking an active role in the childbirth process.

Terminology: The Dilemma

The decision as to what to call the person who attends childbirth preparation classes with the expectant mother and who will be her companion during labor and birth is often difficult and sometimes controversial, as among some childbirth educators. It is obvious that neither "husband" nor "father" are accurate terms in many cases. Other names for this person have been suggested: partner, significant other, friend, support person, companion, labor assistant, trainer, monitrice, ombudsman, and advocate. Throughout this chapter, various terms are used; however, the coaching role is identified with each one.

REVIEW OF THE LITERATURE

The Concept of Coaching

The term coach has held numerous meanings throughout history: instructor, as of athletes, actors, or singers;[17,26,30,33] tutor, or one who prepares a student in a subject;[20,26,27] one who directs team strategy, as in sports;[11] and to give instructions, directions, or prompting to someone who is attempting something.[11,26,41] The word "coach" has also been associated with such ideas as administration and ruling; dominance and supremacy; managing and directing; and force and power.[25] It is these last associations that conflict with the image of a supportive labor companion and require that the use of the term "coach" in labor be clarified.

In the management literature the coach's role is to improve the recipient's skill attainment, quantitatively and qualitatively, through specific, face-to-face interaction called *coaching*.[16] Continuing this idea of transference (bringing about movement of the coachee toward possession of knowledge and skill) as the function of coaching, Stewart writes that the good coach should know exactly what the recipient needs to improve skill attainment and why.[44]

In an analysis of the concept coaching, Luther identified prerequisites, criteria (or activities), and consequences (or outcomes) of the coaching transaction.[26] It is apparent that coaching is a *supportive, two-way interaction* with no implication that the person coached is dictated to or in a position inferior to the coach. The labor coaching transaction is presented in Table 17–1.

Coaching for Childbearing: A Description

Although some very specific behaviors have been enumerated for the labor coach, the concept of coaching is not well defined in the childbirth literature. Expectant fathers' participation in childbirth lacks clarity, due in part to changing expectations and regulations regarding his role in the birthing agency unit. A further explanation for the vagueness of the concept may be that there is often a lack of association between the labor companion's actual behaviors and the mother's perceptions of the helpfulness of those behaviors. In other words, there may be a tendency to define and qualify specific coaching behaviors in terms of the woman's expectations prior to labor and her perceptions of the helpfulness of the behaviors during labor. However, these criteria vary among individuals, thus leading to inconsistencies in definition.[34]

Labor participation by expectant fathers (and other companions) has been described in the childbirth literature as athletic coaching and has been compared to the behaviors of a football coach.[8,9] The coaching roles in athletics and in labor seem

TABLE 17–1. THE LABOR COACHING TRANSACTION

PREREQUISITES		*ACTIVITIES*		*OUTCOMES*
Instruction Realistic, mutually agreed-upon goals Explicit performance criteria For the coach: Knowledge of: Techniques Performance requisites Skill development methods For the woman: Requisite cognitive and psychomotor apparatus Knowledge of requirements for goal attainment Motivation toward goal	→	Two-way interaction Woman responds purposely to labor stimuli The coach: Observes Compares actual with ideal Diagnoses discrepancies Provides feedback Gives prescription The woman: chooses whether to accept prescription retains responsibility for own actions Coach follows up	→	Woman moves toward: Goal attainment Mastery Self-validation

Adapted from Luther, D. A concept analysis of coaching. Unpublished paper, 1983.

to have some common criteria. Specific expectations of an athletic coach are expert knowledge of the sport,[38] a clear-cut goal, and respect for the athlete; and each athlete must be treated as an individual.[47] The athlete needs to understand the task, receive information regarding skill or activity, receive reinforcement for skilled performance,[46] feel loved as a human being, act with independence, and feel some sense of success.[19]

In his book *Husband-Coached Childbirth,* Bradley also points to the similarity of the athletic coach and labor coach. He states:

> Coaches do not function only during the (event). They are essential in the physical preparation of the body during the training course long before the (event). They should also prepare the athlete's mind so that there is a clear conception and understanding of the duties involved. They should by their interest and enthusiasm be a living symbol to the spirit of the player, motivating the individual to want to (participate) at his level best.[5]

TABLE 17–2. WHAT LABOR COACHING IS AND IS NOT

LABOR COACHING IS *NOT*:	LABOR COACHING *IS*:
• Commanding	• Leading
• Controlling	• Guiding
• Dictating	• Supporting
• Managing	• Caring
• Winning at all costs	• Fostering Specific Skills and Confidence

This concept of labor coaching reflects the importance of knowledge and understanding of the woman's needs to successful coaching.

The concept of the labor companion or coach is

Coaching involves providing care and support to the laboring woman. (Copyright BABES, Inc.)

central to prepared childbirth. The labor coach attends classes and learns how to help the woman practice at home and provide support during pregnancy, or as Bradley suggests, long before the event begins.[5] The coach serves as a conditioned stimulus: the sound of his or her voice, the particular words used, and the repetition of practice are important in preparing for childbirth.[48] The labor companion helps the pregnant woman remain relaxed, assists her to use coping tools at her disposal, provides perspective on what is happening, gives her supportive feedback, and comforts her.[50] At birth, the coach keeps the mother informed of the progression of each contraction from beginning to apex to end and provides specific suggestions about the pushing techniques that bring about birth.[31,48]

Role of the Coach

The likeness of labor coaching to athletic coaching is further strengthened in the area of support. The sports coaching literature emphasizes mutual trust and respect and viewing of the athlete as an individual. Winter states that the labor coach's most important task is to give the woman full attention in a loving, supportive manner; in other words, to function in a supportive role.[50] The labor coach is in the unique position of being familiar with the woman's individual concerns and desires, thus creating an atmosphere of mutual trust and respect. Women's needs vary greatly during labor, and some women want and need nothing from the companion but presence. The companion is a stabilizing influence, her link with reality. Other women may need and want more active participation from their labor companion.

The coach, therefore, assumes the role of advocate during labor and delivery.[8] The advocate role during labor is an important function, as it complements the dependency role the woman may assume during labor. The act of labor, in an unfamiliar environment, produces a temporary period during which many women depend on others for

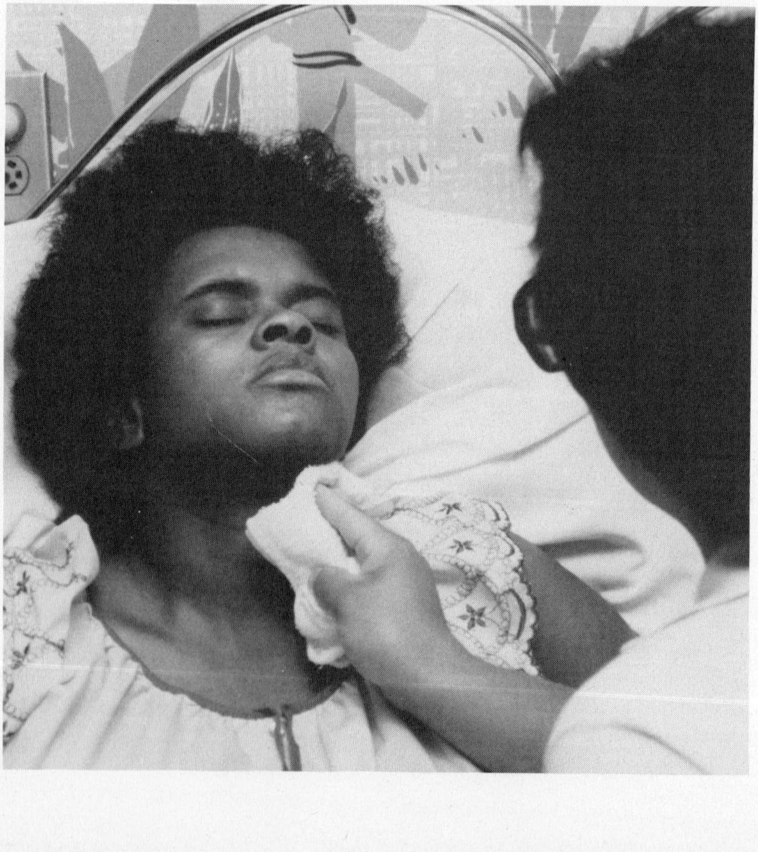

Coaching involves providing comfort measures during childbirth. (Copyright BABES, Inc.)

understanding, encouragement, and direct guidance.[41,51] Labor may demand every ounce of a woman's concentration and she may experience disorientation accompanied by a narrow focusing on the immediate task. The importance of what she is working for is all but forgotten.[30] This is a time when she may benefit from having a trusted advocate, the labor coach, by her side.

In general, the coach's role is that of caring partner, giving feedback to the woman by visual, verbal, and tactile means, and offering her encouragement, reassurance, praise, and reinforcement. The labor coach completes a process involving physical, emotional, and thought responses that approximate the responses of the woman during labor. ElSherif outlines the stages of this process, through which the coach moves during labor:

1. The excitement of early labor;
2. The doubt of midlabor;
3. The immersion (self-absorption) of transition;
4. The exertion of pushing; and
5. The power and pride of achievement at birth.[14]

Coaching vs. Support

The word *support* is frequently used as a synonym for the verb "to coach" in the childbearing literature. Coaching involves many supportive behaviors and the outcomes of a supportive relationship are quite similar to those that we consider optimum for the coaching experience.[21] However, there are some definite differences between the two concepts. Social support has been defined as "behaviors" or "information" that leads one to feel cared for and valued and to have a sense of belonging.[48] Grossman-Schulz and Feeley found that the behaviors most commonly associated with support were empathizing; offering verbal acknowledgment and encouragement, physical presence, and availability; encouraging ventilation; listening; and providing positive reinforcement and reassurance.[21] While communication skills are basic to the concept of support, physical support is not usually cited as supportive behavior.[18]

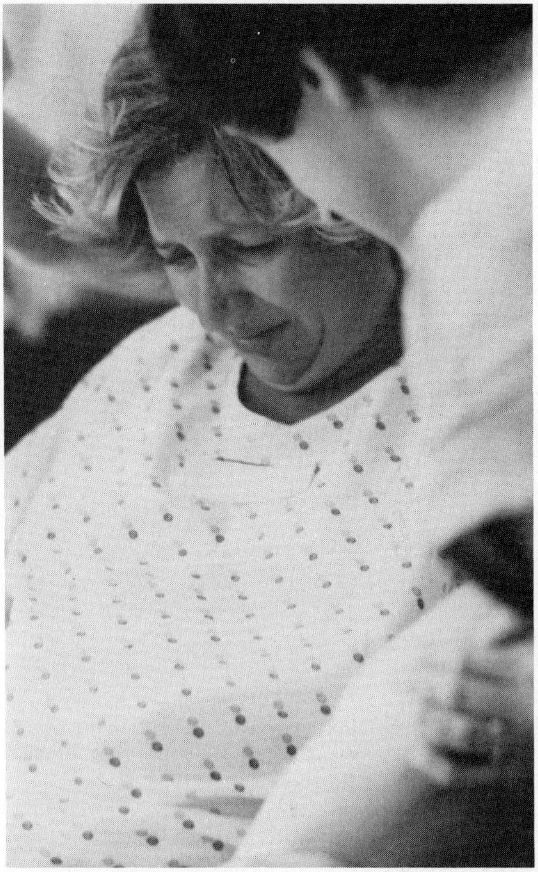

Coaching involves providing feedback and fostering skills. (Copyright BABES, Inc.)

Anderson states that the goal of support during labor is to enhance the woman's participation in childbirth and to foster activity that enables her to cope more effectively.[1] However, no specific behaviors for achieving this goal are suggested. Grossman-Schulz and Feeley found that two behaviors basic to labor coaching—anticipatory guidance and seeking clarification of feelings—were not necessarily cited as supportive behaviors. It seems that support is generally viewed as a skill that involves almost exclusively affective behaviors. Labor coaching involves both affective and psychomotor skills; it consists of clearly identifiable behaviors that include training, teaching, guidance and support. The childbirth literature contains excellent information regarding specific practical suggestions for labor coaching techniques.[4,8,9,24,30,31,50,51]

The labor coach can contribute significantly to the woman's successful use of psychological pain management strategies and her positive feelings about the childbirth experience. (Copyright BABES, Inc.)

Candidates for Coaching: Styles of Involvement

In the United States, the role of labor coach is most commonly fulfilled by the expectant father.[31] The father's special knowledge and understanding can help sustain the woman throughout labor.[24] In addition, the concerned father can easily communicate the kind of childbirth experience the couple desires.[51] However, a close friend, mother, or relative can also fulfill the role of labor coach.[40] Some women want more than one labor support person during childbirth. If there are two or more labor companions, they may give support to the mother at different times or in different ways according to her needs and wishes.

Some expectant mothers may choose the option of enlisting the services of a professional who provides labor support and who is knowledgeable about prepared childbirth. This individual, called a *monitrice,* functions as educator, facilitator, advocate, resource person, and often nurse.[37] Lamaze originated the monitrice concept in France so that women would receive support in the psychoprophylactic method of childbirth. The availability of monitrice services is increasing in the United States.

Regardless of who does the coaching, the coach should be someone who is able to devote complete personal attention to the mother during the childbirth process.[31] While birthing agency staff assume responsibility for the technical aspects of birth, the labor companion brings an invaluable degree of intimacy to the labor situation, and the coach's close relationship with the woman provides insight into her personal strengths and needs: a partner or friend can provide immeasurable support during a distressing moment.[30]

Not all expectant fathers are able or willing to become childbirth coaches. May found that there were several styles of involvement of the partner in the childbirth process. Some expectant fathers preferred to be "onlookers" or "observers" rather than full participants, and according to May, men who adopted these styles remained outside of much of the prenatal decision-making. However, most of these men were pleased to be expecting a baby, were interested in supporting their partners, and wanted to be the best fathers possible. However, some expectant fathers described a feeling of detachment and a lack of enthusiasm.[29]

Nicholson et al. examined the demographic characteristics of new fathers who had participated in childbirth and found that married, middle class fathers with obstetrically low-risk partners consistently reported that they had wanted childbirth to be a "shared emotional experience." These fathers had positive feelings about the experience. Socioeconomic factors and a partner's favorable obstetrical history may influence the type and amount of involvement in childbirth an expectant father is willing to have.[34]

Benefits of the Childbirth Companion

The positive effects of social support on a person's ability to deal with life's events in general and childbirth in particular are well documented in the literature.[48] A comprehensive discussion of social support is included in Chapter 22. Sosa et al. found that women who had human companionship during labor and birth had shorter labors, had fewer problems that required intervention, were more alert following birth, and interacted with their babies more.[43]

Roberts found that the assistance of a significant other, particularly the woman's husband, reduced the distress the expectant mother experienced during childbirth.[39] Butani and Hodnett support this view, asserting that the distress associated with pain during labor seems to be caused not only by the pain but also by feelings of helplessness and lack of control.[6] Women may be able to cope more effectively during childbirth when encouraged by a coach and when taught to use paced breathing and attention-focusing strategies; coaching during labor, therefore, appears to be a very powerful component of prepared childbirth.[52]

Stevens found that the spouse, in providing attention and time to the pregnant woman during childbirth preparation classes and during childbirth, contributes greatly to her use of psychological strategies for pain management. Insufficient attention by staff and/or companion may cause unnecessary requests for chemical analgesics from the woman in childbirth as a subconscious attempt to elicit needed attention and reassurance.[44] Bennett et al. found that women who rated their partner's support more highly were less likely to have used epidural anesthesia and more likely to use nonpharmaceutical pain relief strategies.[3] Less need for medication for pain during labor and birth has thus been attributed to the father's presence.[2]

Overall satisfaction with the childbirth experience is also enhanced by the presence of a labor companion, especially if the expectant father serves as companion. Active father participation in labor may facilitate integration of the childbirth experience and promote paternal self-esteem.[34] Cain et al. reported fathers who were present at cesarean births had positive recollections of the birth and more active decision-making and communication with their partners during childbirth. This in turn resulted in more effective management and reduction of stress.[7] Bennett and co-workers found that labor companions were rated as having provided more practical help and support and having contributed more to feelings of well-being than did any of the medical staff. The majority of women who had labor companions felt that the companion had an effect on how they coped with labor, and higher satisfaction with the childbirth experience was related to higher ratings of companion support.[3] In addition, father presence at birth has been associated with earlier mother-infant contact and with fathers holding their infants sooner.[7] Fathers' feelings of inclusion at birth, then, may be important determinants of subsequent paternal behavior.[36]

Wonnell asserted that the woman's partner is the most capable person to provide support and can enhance the woman's coping. In turn, successfully coping with childbirth gives a woman a tremendous feeling of accomplishment. This increases her confidence in her ability to cope with the maternal role.[51]

Labor coaches fulfill a valuable service to the mother, but they also gain from the experience. Not only does the coach give the mother a sense that "someone cares about me," but the coach experiences a feeling of satisfaction from being a helpful, important part of the process. Fathers who serve as prepared coaches often feel a greater sense of competency than do untrained men and experience less stress due to fear of the unknown.[2]

Preparation for Coaching: Effects

Although the childbirth literature supports that an unprepared labor partner can experience frustration and helplessness as a result of not knowing how to help, it contains little about specific preparation for labor coaches. There are some findings which document the importance of preparation to the mother and to the coach, and describes generally preparation that may be helpful.

Bennett and colleagues studied the effects of amount of prenatal preparation on labor variables and found that women who had received more instruction were more likely to use breathing techniques and receive verbal support and massage from labor coaches for pain relief. Partners were rated as having provided more practical help and support and having contributed more to feelings of well-being during labor than did attending medical personnel, and the extent of this assistance was related to the number of prenatal classes attended.[3]

Stevens proposed that the expectant father can contribute significantly to a woman's successful use of psychological pain management strategies during childbirth and her positive feelings about the experience through the quality of his ''attention to'' the woman during labor and birth.[44] Worthington and co-workers found that coaching, with at least social encouragement and timing of contractions, was quite effective, and when used with visual imagery and relaxation, was even more effective.[52]

Cogan found that prepared women who practiced neuromuscular release for short periods (five to ten minutes per day) reported reliably more pain during the active phase of labor than women who practiced for longer time periods (more than 20 minutes per day). In addition, women who had not practiced at all with their husbands reported reliably more pain during transition than did women who practiced with their husbands.[13]

Campbell and Worthington found that while partners do have a significant role during labor, and special training for partners is usually advocated, men (labor partners) are generally not trained systematically in specific helping behaviors. However, they found that explicit behavioral training for labor coaches in how to help women during childbirth was superior to unstructured discussions on a number of measures. In addition, women whose partners attended structured classes rather than unstructured discussion sessions consistently reported more confidence in their husbands.[8,9] It appears that as the coach's knowledge and positive feelings toward childbirth increase, so does confidence level of the laboring woman. These investigators advocated providing systematic instruction to partners on how to help the laboring woman.

IMPLICATIONS FOR PRACTICE

The literature strongly supports the use of a labor coach. The coach's ability to support and guide the woman during childbirth are increased through childbirth education. Childbirth educators may need to evaluate their teaching styles and methodologies periodically and revise them if necessary so that the following implications for practice are addressed.

Assessment of Learning Needs of Woman and Coach

Learner needs and goals must be determined before any teaching methodology can be effective. This assessment can be done by observing woman-coach interactions, and by asking specific questions. Couples' expectations for childbirth can be influenced by many factors that may have to do with how the coaches see themselves as individuals, especially if the coach is the woman's partner. Variables such as whether the pregnancy was planned, number of other children, financial responsibilities, and beliefs about childbirth and who should be involved are all important factors to be assessed.[14]

Each couple comes to class with different needs and concerns. These should be discussed individually with each couple to determine beginning knowledge level, concerns, expectations, and desired outcomes of the childbirth experience. It is erroneous to assume that all couples want the same thing from the experience, or that both members of a couple always agree on what they want. The type of partner involvement that is most beneficial to father, mother, and infant may depend on specific characteristics of the couple. Such differences should be considered in planning and evaluating childbirth education programs so that instruction regarding coaching techniques can be individualized to the needs of the couple.[34]

It is important to encourage the couple to discuss needs, desires, and concerns between themselves and to encourage values clarification so that they begin to work toward common goals. If each partner knows exactly how the other feels about his or her role and role expectations, anxiety is decreased and cooperation will be enhanced. Some common underlying fears and concerns of the labor coach include:

1. Having to meet the expectations of birthing agency staff;
2. Having to protect the laboring woman against intervention;
3. Fear of doing something ''stupid'' or incorrect; and
4. Feelings of timidity, self-consciousness, or inadequacy.

These concerns can be decreased as the childbirth educator describes what the woman and coach can realistically expect during childbirth and discusses different styles of involvement with the birth process.

> After my daughter was born I just melted. It's bringing tears to my eyes just remembering what it was like, seeing her being born.
>
> A NEW FATHER[1]
>
> My daughter said she wouldn't have made it without me. The nurses said I was one of the best coaches they'd seen. I think my presence kept my daughter from being nervous, which helped with labor.
>
> A NEW GRANDMOTHER[1]
>
> His love and support was manifested in his touch, tone of voice, and caring for me physically. He is very goosey about vomiting, yet held a basin for me in the most calm and loving manner.
>
> A NEW MOTHER[1]
>
> My husband was essential. I fell in love all over again. I can't imagine it without him. I leaned on him with each pain and felt his energy and support and love. The smell of his shirt was comforting. Labor was a very intimate experience.
>
> A NEW MOTHER[1]
>
> The most positive part of childbirth was the togetherness of my husband and me embarking on a new experience.
>
> A NEW MOTHER[1]

Enhancing the Coach's Role During Childbirth

Labor coaches need to receive structured information regarding their role in the birth experience. Once the childbirth educator has determined the coach's concept of his or her role, the discussion of factual information concerning the role will be meaningful. Exploration of the coach's ideas for meeting role expectations can uncover any unrealistic goals or inaccurate information.

The advocacy role of the coach ,should be stressed. It should be made clear that the coach is fulfilling a legitimate role and by participating will enhance the birth experience. The coach needs to understand the dependency role of the mother, and that during this time she will depend on the coach to make their goals and wishes known. Communication skills for use during this time should be stressed. Let the coach know that it will be appropriate to discuss with the staff such things as the mother's feelings about pregnancy, her fears and anxieties, and her expectations about the kind of childbirth experience she desires.[51]

Both the mother and coach need to be advised of the purpose and importance of coping techniques.[4] In addition, the coping techniques that are documented to be most effective should be stressed. These include relaxation with specific and positive feedback from the coach (''Let your body go limp; feel your body getting heavier''); coach-directed visual imagery; coaching that consists of at least social encouragement and timing of contractions (''This contraction's almost over—only ten seconds to go for this one. You're doing great!''); and encouragement for use of structured breathing and attention focal points.[52]

The coach needs to know how to determine the mother's degree of relaxation and to communicate that to her in a positive way rather than ''correcting'' her. The childbirth educator should stress that the emphasis of prepared techniques is not on doing them correctly but on using them to increase the woman's comfort and relaxation. The coach should be encouraged to stay with the woman, since laboring women are much more likely to respond to a familiar voice.[4]

Above all, coaches should be helped to accept their importance in decreasing the woman's feelings of helplessness and increasing her sense of control during childbirth. The coach should also be made aware of the behavioral responses that may be seen during stressful parts of labor: moaning, groaning, screaming, crying, angry outbursts, refusal to use breathing and relaxation techniques, and panic. Techniques for use at this time are summarized in Table 17–3.

Childbirth education classes usually include content that deals with cesarean births. This is important, because planning for vaginal birth and then facing the experience of an emergency cesarean birth can be a frightening situation. All parents need factual and emotional preparation for this possibility.[27] Coaches need to know that the possibility of remaining with the woman throughout the cesarean birth exists in most birthing agencies.

Many physicians and staff nurses recognize the benefit of the coach's calming influence on the woman during the cesarean birth, and do not object to, in fact often welcome, the coach's presence. The coach should be taught specific support behaviors such as touching the woman's face and head, sitting where eye contact is possible, talking together, and sharing their thoughts and concerns. In addition, it is important for coaches and women to know what the surgical suite will look and sound like, and the number of people who will be present. Coaches often feel intimidated in the unfamiliar surroundings of the surgical suite, and will benefit from the support and guidance of the birthing agency staff.

Some partners will make the decision not to participate during childbirth, and are reluctant to attend childbirth education classes. It is important to address the needs of nonparticipating expectant fathers as well as those who do take part. May[29] states that men such as these, who differ from our concept of the ''ideal father,'' may be shortchanged and misunderstood during their interactions with health professionals. These men with detached styles often have unmet needs, which raises the question as to whether value judgments on the part of health care professionals can lead to potentially inadequate care. Often the childbirth educator or the nurse will make a strong argument for the expectant father's presence at birth; this can lead to pressure, guilt feelings, and a sense of inadequacy if the expectant father chooses not to participate. These feelings, in turn, can have an adverse effect on the expectant father's feelings about the pregnancy and birth. May continues to emphasize that health care providers tend to make value judgments as to the quantity and quality of partner involvement rather than accepting individual differences and varying capabilities of each partner.

Childbirth educators can present alternatives to partner-coached childbirth. The most common one is arranging for another support person to function as labor coach, with or without the expectant father's attendance, utilizing a monitrice, friend, or relative.[29] Other ideas are to encourage the partner

TABLE 17–3. COACHING HELP SHEET

ENCOURAGEMENT/MOTIVATION ROUTINE

Assist the laboring woman when discouraged about her labor progress by reminding her of the:

1. Normalcy of her labor pattern and her discouragement.
2. Progress she has made.
3. Techniques—reinforcing the learned behaviors of relaxation, paced breathing, and other coping strategies.
4. Need to take each contraction separately, one at a time, rather than focusing on the entire remaining labor.

Give her:

Attention—lots of it.
Support—both verbal and physical.
Confidence—Remain calm and controlled and communicate to her that she can cope effectively.

PANIC ROUTINE

Assist the laboring woman to cope more effectively during labor.

1. Recognize the signs of panic—inability to use breathing patterns or other coping strategies, and the expression of need for help, or desire to give up.
2. Use eye-to-eye contact. Without words, this says, "I'm here and I can help."
3. Hold her firmly and send message, "I can help you and I know what to do."
4. Engage her total attention: Bring your face within 10 inches of her face. Use your hand to turn her face towards yours. Breathe with her using a loud, throaty sound starting where she is and then changing to a paced breathing pattern to lead her back into the use of appropriate controlled breathing. Move your face to reinforce the breathing pattern.

CONFLICT ROUTINE FOR THE COACH

When the labor coach must make a difficult decision during the labor process:

1. Relax: Take 2 or 3 deep breaths and release your muscles.
2. Realize: Realize what is happening. Think to yourself, "I'm getting upset. I've got to stay calm." Catch the conflict by preparing for it, confronting it early, and coping with feelings of being overwhelmed.
3. Focus: Get your mind off the problem and on to the alternatives.
4. Avoid: Don't get hooked into "tunnel thinking" (focusing on only one solution).
5. Explore: Look at the consequences of each alternative.
6. Decide: Make the best decision you can with the information you have.
7. Forget it: The decision is past and you did your best.

Adapted from Campbell, A., and Worthington, E. Teaching expectant fathers how to be better labor coaches. *MCN: The American Journal of Maternal-Child Nursing* 7:28, 1982.

to become involved in the physical preparations for the baby at home or to make all the necessary arrangements for hospitalization.

Providing an Optimal Learning Experience

Childbirth education classes must focus on needs of the coach as well as those of the mother. If class content includes emotional changes experienced by the mother during pregnancy, then those experienced by the partner should also be discussed. The desired result is to totally involve the expectant father or partner in the classes.[51]

Wonnell advocated offering specific classes for fathers only. This seems to be a strategy that works well, especially when conducted by an enthusiastic father. Coaches need reassurance that what they have learned in the past weeks of class will fit into place as labor progresses and that they will be able to provide the needed support and guidance. Hearing about childbirth from a father's perspective, and from the instructor, can serve as a model for self-disclosure for the coach.[9]

Class sessions should include explicit behavioral training in how to be a helpful coach during labor and birth.[8,9] The group experience allows coaches, particularly expectant fathers, to see how their role fits into their partner's labor and how the event will take shape. The group provides opportunity for coaches to express concerns in a comfortable, nonthreatening atmosphere.[8,9] It is also helpful to utilize role-playing activities so that coaches can actually try out their newly learned skills. Although this experience is limited, it provides them

TABLE 17–4. COACHING INTERVENTIONS

WOMAN'S POTENTIAL BEHAVIORS/FEELINGS	COACH'S RESPONSE
Latent Phase	
Excitement; eagerness to begin work; anticipation Talkativeness Cheerfulness, contentment Perceptual field is broad; focuses on environment Comfort—general Abdominal cramping Mild uterine contractions	Use of humor, if appropriate Movement and ambulation; activity is helpful in stimulating labor Remind woman to drink clear liquids and to eat no fatty or heavy foods Discuss coping tools for use later during labor Be the partner's advocate; make her wishes known to birth attendants Be aware of need to begin use of relaxation and breathing techniques when she can no longer talk or joke her way through the contractions
Active Phase	
Anxiety and apprehension; discomfort and attention to pain, seriousness; ill-defined fears Perceptual field narrows; focuses on self in social behavior Helplessness; tension (grimaces, clenched fists, restlessness, rigidity), dependency; difficulty with concentration Desire for companionship; fear of abandonment; isolation Backache; strengthening of contractions	Give her your undivided attention Verbal support and encouragement: "This contraction is almost over . . . you're doing great!" "Take one contraction at a time." Adapt the environment to provide rest and relaxation: • adjust lights and shades to avoid glare • use quiet music you and she have selected • arrange focal point for easy viewing. Encourage use of: • Attention focal points • Relaxation—give periodic feedback: "Feel your body getting heavier" • Paced breathing techniques—allow her to establish own rate and assist her with breathing patterns, if necessary Use short specific sentences Physical measures, such as: • Gentle touch • Positioning—assist to a position of comfort such as sitting, standing, leaning on you, leaning forward, sidelying, on hands and knees • Cool compresses to her forehead • Counterpressure to her lower back—make sure you are in a comfortable position to do this to prevent a backache of your own • Apply hot or cold compresses to lower back • Effleurage • Massage her aching legs • Offer ice chips, Chapstick, mouthwash, or toothbrushing • Be sure dry pads are kept underneath her • Encourage her to urinate regularly to lessen discomfort and promote labor progress Be alert for signs of progress and communicate these to her: descent of baby in abdomen; location of fetal heart tones in progressively lower areas Remember: Do not become discouraged if she does not respond as expected or tell you how much your support means to her; she is very absorbed in her labor now Take a moment for yourself to consciously relax—take some deep breaths and remember to remain calm. Your partner will depend on and benefit from your presence! Ask for suggestions, help, or relief from the birth attendant if you find yourself getting discouraged, tired, or impatient

TABLE 17–4. COACHING INTERVENTIONS *Continued*

WOMAN'S POTENTIAL BEHAVIORS/FEELINGS	COACH'S RESPONSE
Transitional Phase	
Maximum anxiety and fear: • verbalization of desire to give up • inability to follow breathing routine • emotional outbursts • loss of ability to evaluate situation Narrowed perceptual field; decreased attention span, withdrawal from environment Irritability Periods of disorientation Irrational statements Dependency; inability to make decisions; coping: "I can't" Exhaustion, restlessness, discomfort Diaphoresis Tremors Hot or cold flashes Nausea, vomiting	Realize that she may respond differently now Remain with her constantly; reduce environmental stimuli Remind of breathing techniques if she loses concentration Maintain eye contact—put your face close to hers, tell her to look at you, say "Breathe with me." Use short and simple statements Be alert for signs of panic Interpret directions and information from birth attendants Keep in mind that contractions have reached maximum strength, and relief will come with pushing Encourage rest between contractions Be alert for signs of her urge to bear down: a "catch" in her breath, or a slight grunting sound
Birth	
Renewed energy Exhaustion Possible confusion: inability to remember techniques Desire to push	Assist her in finding a good position for pushing (semireclining, sidelying if tired, modified squatting or hands and knees) Be ready to give step-by-step instructions for pushing if necessary Give specific verbal encouragement for pushing: "Relax your pelvic floor muscles," "Let the baby out" Support her shoulders for pushing Gentle touch to abdomen to help her focus on pushing May need to inform her of contractions if she has had regional anesthesia Apply warm perineal compresses if indicated Remind her to pant or blow as baby's head crowns

some familiarity with the role and may decrease anxiety about expected behaviors during the childbirth process.

The type and amount of practice time a woman and her coach spend prior to labor and birth can have an effect on the woman's coping ability during childbirth. They should be encouraged to practice neuromuscular release together for between five and 20 minutes per day. The implication is that without information about the optimal practice time, teachers may tend to encourage students to practice too extensively, which may discourage students who cannot find sufficient practice time. In addition, an overemphasis on practice time may cause couples to prepare for childbirth mechanically, when they may also need time for accomplishing the psychotherapeutic work of childbirth preparation.[13]

Promoting Collaboration Between Childbirth Educators and Childbirth Practitioners

For the optimal childbirth experience, there must be continuity between expectant couples' childbirth education experiences and the actual childbirth experience. The labor partner must be accepted as a valued, integral part of the team not only by the childbirth educator but also by the nursing and medical staff. Often, however, the focus is on woman and fetus, and labor partners are treated as casual observers rather than the concerned, participating adults they are.[14]

In supporting the coach both prenatally and during labor, both childbirth educators and birth attendants can aim for the following mutual goals:

1. Facilitation of the labor-birth process;

2. Enhancement of the coach's self-esteem;
3. Improvement of the couple's relationship; and
4. Heightening of parent-infant bonding.[14]

Childbirth educators can promote these mutual outcomes by increasing the awareness of the birthing agency staff about childbirth education and prepared childbirth techniques through frequent communication or inservice education offerings. Such offerings can include sharing specific techniques learned by coaches and encouraging birthing agency staff to demonstrate these techniques for couples during labor. Encouraging flexibility in hospital routines and stressing individual needs are also vital in ensuring continuity. Obtaining feedback from birth attendants as to how they perceive couples' use of prepared childbirth techniques would additionally be helpful. Therefore, childbirth educators have the opportunity to enhance the childbirth experience for their clients through collaboration, and should view this as part of their role.

IMPLICATIONS FOR RESEARCH

There exists in the current childbearing literature a dearth of research involving all aspects of coaching. While numerous studies have been done that describe the effects of a supportive companion during labor, there is a lack of information regarding the effects of specific coaching functions and behaviors. Research about coaching could serve to help childbirth educators and childbirth practitioners in their quest to guide expectant parents and coaches more effectively throughout the birth process. Research questions that need to be answered include:

- How is coaching defined by:
  a. Childbirth educators?
  b. Childbirth practitioners?
- What motivates an expectant father/partner/friend to participate in childbirth as a labor coach?
- How much childbirth education is needed for the coach to effectively function during childbirth?
- What types of practice skills in class promote effective coaching behaviors?
- What is the relationship between active coaching during labor and interaction with the neonate?
- In actual clinical settings, what coaching behaviors are effective in promoting:
  a. The woman-coach relationship?
  b. The woman's coping during labor?
- What criteria are necessary to measure the effectiveness of coaching?
- What is the relationship of women's descriptions of helpfulness during labor to coaches' perceptions of the experience?
- What is the relationship between content on coaching presented in class and use of coaching behaviors during childbirth?
- What are some effective alternative methods of coaching for expectant fathers who wish to be "interested observers?"
- What birthing environments facilitate optimal woman-coach interaction?
- Do birthing agency staff and routines inhibit coaching behaviors?
- What differences exist between coaching styles of expectant fathers and other labor coaches (friend, relative, other)?

These are only a few of the research topics that need to be examined. Many more questions need to be raised and addressed so that those who work with prospective labor coaches will have the knowledge base to provide optimal guidance.

SUMMARY

Although the concept of coaching has numerous meanings, the one that has relevance for childbearing connotes help, caring, encouragement, concern, and support. Coaching for childbearing is an integral part of prepared childbirth, and research exists that documents its benefits to mother, coach, and infant. Childbirth educators can guide the labor partner in developing and refining skill in using the techniques of labor coaching. The effective use of coaching techniques is an essential skill for health-care professionals who care for laboring women. Coaching can increase the woman's ability to actively participate in childbirth and work with the contractions of labor and birth as well as enhance the overall quality of the childbirth experience.

Although the term *coach* may have negative connotations for some people *coach* does seem to be the most widely used, best recognized, and most appropriate label for a labor companion who wishes to *give the maximum help in guiding toward a goal*. Because of that name recognition and because of the nature of the role this individual fulfills, the term coach is an appropriate label for the labor companion. Childbirth educators should think of the labor coach as a supportive, encouraging prompter such as a drama, voice, or music coach. In this context, *coach* connotes a knowledgeable, interested benefactor who can guide and direct lovingly toward a desired goal.

References

1. Anderson, C. Operational definition of "support." *Journal of Obstetric, Gynecologic, and Neonatal Nursing* 5:17, 1976.
2. Auvenshine, M., and Enriquez, M. *Maternity Nursing: Dimensions of Change*. Monterey, CA: Wadsworth, Inc., 1985.
3. Bennett, A., Hewson, D., Booker, E., and Holliday, S. Antenatal preparation and labor support in relation to birth outcomes. *Birth* 12:9, 1985.
4. Bloom, K. Assisting the unprepared woman during labor. *JOGN Nursing* 13:303, 1984.
5. Bradley, R. *Husband-Coached Childbirth*. New York: Harper and Row, 1974.
6. Butani, P., and Hodnett, E. Mothers' perceptions of their labor experiences. *Maternal-Child Nursing Journal* 9:38, 1980.
7. Cain, R., Pedersen, F., Zaslow, M., and Kramer, E. Effects of the father's presence or absence during a cesarean delivery. *Birth* 11:10, 1984.
8. Campbell, A., and Worthington, E. Teaching expcctant fathers how to be better childbirth coaches. *MCN: The American Journal of Maternal-Child Nursing* 7:28, 1982.
9. Campbell, A., and Worthington, E. A comparison of two methods of training husbands to assist their wives with labor and delivery. *Journal of Psychosomatic Research* 25:557, 1981.
10. Chute, G. Expectation and experience in alternative and conventional birth. *JOGN Nursing* 14:61, 1985.
11. Cratty, B. *Psychology in Contemporary Sport: Guidelines for Coaches and Athletes*. Englewood Cliffs, NJ: Prentice-Hall, Inc., 1973.
12. Croft, C. Lamaze childbirth education—implications for maternal-infant attachment. *JOGN Nursing* 11:333, 1982.
13. Cogan, R. Practice time in prepared childbirth. *JOGN Nursing* 7:33, 1978.
14. ElSherif, C. Coaching the coach. *JOGN Nursing* 8:87, 1979.
15. *Encyclopedia Britannica, Vol. VII*. Chicago: William Benton, Publisher, 1972.
16. Fournies, F. *Coaching for Improved Work Performances*. New York: Van Nostrand Reinhold Company, 1978.
17. Gallon, A. *Coaching: Ideas and Ideals*. Boston: Houghton-Mifflin Company, 1974.
18. Gardner, K. Supportive nursing: A critical review of the literature. *Journal of Psychiatric Nursing and Mental Health Services* 17:10, 1979.
19. Gaylord, E. *Modern Coaching Psychology*. Dubuque, IA: Wm. C. Brown Book Company, 1967.
20. Gove, P. (ed.). *Webster's Third New International Dictionary of the English Language, Unabridged*. Springfield, MA: G. and C. Merriam Co. Publishers, 1966.
21. Grossman-Schulz, M., and Feeley, N. A working model of support. *Canadian Nurse* 80:42, 1984.
22. Guralnik, D (ed.). *Webster's New World Dictionary of the American Language, 2nd college ed*. New York: The World Publishing Company, 1972.
23. Jimenez, S. Education for the childbearing year—comprehensive application of psychoprophylaxis. *JOGN Nursing* 9:97, 1980.
24. Jones, C. Sharing birth. *American Baby* 47:9, 20, 1985.
25. Laffal, J. *A Concept Dictionary of English*. Essex, CT: Gallery Press, 1973.
26. Luther, D. A concept analysis of coaching. Unpublished paper, 1983.

27. Maloney, R. Childbirth education classes: expectant parents' expectations. *JOGN Nursing* 14:245, 1985.
28. March, F., and March, F. *March's Thesaurus-Dictionary.* Garden City, NJ: Hanover House, 1958.
29. May, K. The father as observer. *MCN: The American Journal of Maternal-Child Nursing* 7:319, 1982.
30. McCabe, K. Labor: The support person's art. *Maternity Center Association Newsletter* 1:1, 3, 1985.
31. McKelvey, N. Working together in labor: The role of the coach. *Lamaze Parent's Magazine* 14, 1983.
32. Morris, W., and Morris, M. *Morris Dictionary of Word and Phrase Origins*. New York: Harper and Row, 1977.
33. National Association for Sport and Physical Education. *Coach's Manual*. Washington, DC: American Alliance for Health, Physical Education and Recreation Publications, 1975.
34. Nicholson, J., Gist, N., Klein, R., and Standley, K. Outcomes of father involvement in pregnancy and birth. *Birth* 10:5, 1983.
35. *The Oxford English Dictionary, vol. II*. Oxford: The Clarendon Press, 1970.
36. Palkovitz, R. Father's birth attendance, early extended contact, and father-infant interaction at five months postpartum. *Birth* 9:173, 1982.
37. Peddicord, K., Curran, P., and Monshower, C. An independent labor-support nursing service. *JOGN Nursing* 13:312, 1984.
38. Poindexter, H., and Mushier, C. *Coaching Competitive Team Sports for Girls and Women*. Philadelphia: W. B. Saunders Company, 1973.
39. Roberts, J. Factors influencing distress from pain during labor. *MCN: The American Journal of Maternal-Child Nursing* 8:62, 1983.
40. Sasmor, J., and Grossman, E. Childbirth education in 1980. *JOGN Nursing* 10:155, 1981.
41. Shields, D. Nursing care in labor and patient satisfaction: a descriptive study. *Journal of Advanced Nursing* 3:535, 1978.
42. Smoyak, S. Teaching as coaching. *Nursing Outlook* 26:361, 1978.
43. Sosa, R., Kennell, J., Klaus, M., Robertson, S., and Urrutia, J. The effect of a supportive companion on perinatal problems, length of labor, and mother-infant interaction. *New England Journal of Medicine* 303:597, 1980.
44. Stevens, R. Psychological strategies for management of pain in prepared childbirth I: a review of the research. *Birth and the Family Journal* 3:157, 1976.
45. Stewart, N. *The Effective Woman Manager.* New York: John Wiley and Sons, 1978.
46. Tutko, T., and Richards, J. *Psychology of Coaching*. Boston: Allyn and Bacon, Inc., 1971.
47. Webster, F. *Coaching and Care of Athletes*. Philadelphia: David McKay Company, 1938.
48. Wideman, M., and Singer, J. The role of psychological mechanisms in preparation for childbirth. *American Psychologist* 39:1357, 1984.
49. Wilson, J. *Thinking with Concepts*. Cambridge: Cambridge University Press, 1963.
50. Winter, C. Coaching Labor. *Lamaze Parent's Magazine* 21, 1985.
51. Wonnell, E. The education of the expectant father for childbirth. *Nursing Clinics of North America* 6:591, 1971.
52. Worthington, E., Martin, G., and Shumate, M. Which prepared-childbirth coping strategies are effective? *JOGN Nursing* 11:45, 1982.

Beginning Quote

Frederick, E. The Labor Coach. Paper presented at the ASPO/Lamaze National and University Faculty Conference on the Scientific Basis of Prepared Childbirth Techniques, Columbus, OH, 1983.

Boxed Quotes

1. Savage, B., and Simkin, D. *Preparation for Childbirth: The Complete Guide to the Lamaze Method*. New York: Ballantine Books, 1987, pp. 305–316.

chapter 18

PHARMACEUTICAL PAIN MANAGEMENT STRATEGIES

SUSAN H. STEINER and JOSEPH F. STEINER

In a study of new mothers, 97 per cent (402) delivering in hospitals received at least one drug with documented adverse fetal effects . . . less than 2 per cent were aware of the drug's hazardous potential for their babies.

Yvonne Brackbill

Use of Analgesia and Anesthesia: The Debate

Debate concerning the use of pharmaceutical pain management strategies during childbirth has continued for over a hundred years. Historically, the successful use of chloroform to achieve a ''painless'' vaginal delivery was reported to the Edinburgh Medical-Chirurgical Society by Scottish obstetrician James Y. Simpson in 1847. Religious leaders were among those protesting against the use of chloroform to induce painless childbirth, citing a Biblical reference indicating that women were intended to ''bring forth their children in sorrow.'' However, Queen Victoria used chloroform in 1853 for the delivery of her eighth child, thus increasing the acceptance of its use.[27] Debates on the pros and cons of labor analgesia and anesthesia have continued ever since.

The debate has been fueled by a recent suggestion that analgesia and anesthesia may be of benefit to the baby. There may be a direct relationship between the mother's stress and fetal asphyxia on the basis of the role of the catecholamines.[19] Catecholamines are the neurotransmitters (hormones) of the sympathetic nervous system, which control the fight-or-flight mechanism of the body. These neurotransmitters are responsible for control of the diameter of blood vessels and lung alveoli, the heart rate, and the distribution of oxygenated blood throughout the body.

The theory is that the anxiety and pain of labor can lead to a large enough release of the catecholamines epinephrine and norepinephrine to cause vasoconstriction of uterine blood vessels, resulting in decreased blood flow to the uterus. The decrease in blood flow leads to a lower level of oxygen in the fetus. Although not directly studied in humans, this phenomenon has been demonstrated in sheep and monkeys. It is thus suggested by some investigators that analgesia and anesthesia, along with reassurance and emotional support for the woman in labor, may make childbirth less stressful for both mother and baby.

On the other side of this argument is the idea that the stress of childbirth is healthy for the infant and that medication may alter this natural response.[22] Researchers Lagercrantz and Slotkin suggest that the presence of catecholamines is actually important to fetal survival and that a surge of these hormones during birth may be protective for the fetus.[20] Such research dates back to the 1960's when it was found that catecholamines are produced in response to hypoxia. In later studies, Lagercrantz found that the catecholamine responses found in a normal birth could cause changes in the fetal heart rate which could be interpreted as fetal distress. However, when definitive biochemical tests were conducted, it was found that asphyxia was present only when the fetal scalp blood pH level was below 7.25. It was further found that when true fetal asphyxia was present, the catecholamine level was far above that found in normal births and, in fact, was similar to the concentration in an adult that would be high enough to precipitate a stroke. Such levels were found in infants who were in the breech position or were strangled by the umbilical cord.

Because of their discoveries, Lagercrantz and Slotkin thought that the high levels of catecholamines found at the time of normal births suggested two protective roles of the catecholamine surge. The first role is to protect the infant during the stress of the birth experience. The second role is to enhance the newborn infant's ability to function effectively in the first few hours of life by facilitating normal breathing, increasing the metabolic rate, and enhancing the blood flow to vital organs.

Without question, the debate over the use of pharmaceutical pain management is far from over. *It is crucial to remember that whatever the mother receives, the baby also receives.* The problem with any pharmaceutical analgesic or anesthetic is that, when used, it is desired that it provide adequate analgesia while not impeding labor or posing any threat to the mother or baby. Certainly not all pharmacological agents can claim to fit such criteria, and in reality all pharmacological agents will pose some risk. It is important, therefore, for those women who do desire pharmaceutical pain management to have the ability to make an informed choice regarding the analgesic or anesthetic method to be employed.

The importance of nonpharmaceutical support measures cannot be overemphasized. The use of relaxation and breathing techniques is a lifelong skill that is of aid during childbirth and invaluable in the future. Lack of fear can be a potent tranquilizer and may decrease the amount of medication desired or eliminate the need for it. As evidenced by responses of women following a childbirth experience, women with good support often prefer to use no pharmaceutical agents for analgesia, relying totally on nonpharmaceutical support measures. The feeling is that analgesia or anesthesia would detract from the childbirth experience and is not worth the risks. On the other hand, for some women the pain interferes with the childbirth experience, and they wish to have the analgesia and anesthesia that may be offered.[29]

It is also important to consider the theories of childbirth satisfaction. As described by Humenick in *Birth and the Family Journal,* there are two theoretical models of childbirth satisfaction: pain management and mastery.[11,12] If one assumes that pain management is the essential element of a satisfactory birth experience, adequate analgesia would provide a logical, although short-term, answer. However, pain management is not the only factor in a satisfactory childbirth experience. Childbirth may be viewed as a developmental task of a pregnant woman and her perception of "mastery" of her experience can affect her self-esteem. The mastery model includes fear, fatigue, a sense of helplessness, loss of dignity, threats to the health of the mother or infant, aloneness, and pain as potential stressors in childbirth. Adequate support in childbirth includes far more than pain management. It includes knowledge of the birth process, coping skills, active participation in decisions, support from others, and a back-up system of obstetrical intervention if needed.

Regarding pain management, each woman has her own perception of pain and coping ability and thus an individual need for pain relief. A woman needs to know that the decision for or against pharmaceutical agents is hers to make. However, to help make this choice, a woman should be cognizant of both the benefits and risks of the various methods and agents used for pharmaceutical pain management. To this end, the risks and benefits of the most commonly employed methods of analgesia and anesthesia are reviewed. However, because of the ever-changing technology and drugs that are used during labor and birth, the technical aspects of analgesia and anesthesia are not covered in this chapter. Childbirth educators are referred to current obstetrical texts and scientific journals as well as birthing agency policies within their community for this information.

REVIEW OF THE LITERATURE

Pharmaceutical pain management can be categorized into two general methods: systemic analgesia and regional or local anesthesia. By definition, analgesia is the "absence of normal sense of pain" with an analgesic being a "medication which relieves pain," but allows for the sense of pain (i.e., it hurts less, but you know it is still painful). Anesthesia is defined as a "partial or complete loss of sensation."[32] An anesthetic is a "medication which produces the loss of feeling."

A brief discussion of some pharmacological factors may be helpful in understanding how drugs may affect the baby. Many studies now record umbilical cord drug levels at birth. The cord venous level reflects the amount of drug transferred from mother to baby, while the cord arterial level reflects the amount of drug left after the uptake of the drug by fetal tissues. Neither value reflects the actual amount of drug circulating in the infant at birth.[17]

Pharmacologically active metabolites are another consideration. A metabolite results from the breaking down of the drug in the body. Many drugs are broken down into forms that are still pharmacologically active, producing either the same or a different effect from the parent drug. Active metabolites can remain in the tissues after the parent drug has been completely excreted. Both meperidine (Demerol) and lidocaine (a commonly used local anesthetic) have active metabolites.[18]

Systemic Analgesia

Systemic medications used during labor include antianxiety agents (tranquilizers, barbiturate sedatives, the narcotic analgesics given by injection, and inhalants such as nitrous oxide). Analgesia is provided by the injectable narcotics and the inhalants (Table 18–1). Although neither the barbiturate sedatives nor the antianxiety agents are analgesics, they are mentioned here because they can be useful in pharmaceutical pain management strategies during labor.

Barbiturate sedatives are sometimes given in the latent phase of labor to allow for rest before the contractions become regular or effective. However, if given during active labor, the barbiturates may increase the perception of pain because pharmacologically they produce algesia (supersensitiveness to pain) rather than analgesia. Antianxiety agents have several uses in pain management strategies. They may be given in the latent phase of labor to decrease anxiety and fear. Also, an analgesic effect may be potentiated by the combination of the antianxiety agent hydroxyzine (Vistaril) and a narcotic analgesic.

Amnesics were once popular to produce a "twilight sleep" from which a woman would wake up with a baby and virtually no remembrance of labor. The combination of scopolamine and morphine was most commonly used for this purpose. Unfortunately, many women suffered from delirium and hallucinations, necessitating close monitoring. Also, infants were often depressed and with both the mother and baby sleeping for hours or lethargic after the birth, and the mother-infant interaction that is so important in the development of a bond between mother and infant was negatively affected.

Injectable Systemic Analgesics

Systemic narcotic medications are often used for pain relief during the first stage of labor. However, if these are given too early in labor, the latent phase may be prolonged. Once labor is well established and the cervix is dilating, a narcotic such as meperidine (Demerol) is frequently given by injection to increase pain tolerance and allow for rest between contractions. Promethazine (Phenergan) is also sometimes given to decrease the possibility of nausea and vomiting. Meperidine in adequate amounts provides good pain relief and has been found to slightly increase uterine activity.[7,26] It is generally preferred over morphine because it causes less nausea and vomiting and does not last as long. It will not penetrate the blood-brain barrier as easily as morphine and therefore does not produce the degree of sedation or respiratory depression.[9,13]

Meperidine may be given by intramuscular or intravenous injection. When given intravenously, the onset of action is faster and less prolonged. Maximum effect from intramuscular administration occurs in about 45 minutes, while the onset for intravenous administration is about five minutes. The duration of action of IM meperidine is up to four hours, whereas the duration of IV meperidine in the same individual is usually shorter. Dosage is often 50 to 100 mg for intramuscular injection and 25 to 50 mg with intravenous injection. Prepared women who use meperidine often prefer 25 mg intramuscularly or 12.5 mg intravenously so that they do not lose the ability to concentrate on the coping techniques they are using.

Timing of the administration of an analgesic is important. It has been found that an infant born two or three hours following the administration of a narcotic has a higher level of drug in the tissues than an infant born within one to two hours or more than three hours after administration.[19]

TABLE 18–1. ANALGESICS USED DURING CHILDBIRTH

I. Injectable Systemic Analgesics
   A. **Narcotic analgesics:** morphine, meperidine (Demerol), nalbuphine (Nubain), butorphanol (Stadol), Fentanyl
      1. Route of administration: intramuscular or intravenous.
      2. Time of administration: during active labor, with general anesthesia, postpartum, or postoperative.
      3. Maternal side effects: dizziness, euphoria, nausea, respiratory depression, hypotension, drowsiness, difficulty in concentrating on her role during labor; drug may cause a decrease in strength and/or frequency of contractions.
      4. Newborn side effects: respiratory depression, poor sucking, decreased motor activity and alertness if given to the mother more than 15 minutes and less than 4 hours before delivery.
   B. **Antianxiety agents:** diazepam (Valium), lorazepam (Atavan), chlordiazepoxide (Librium), hydroxyzine (Vistaril), promethazine (Phenergan)
      1. Route of administration: oral, intramuscular, or intravenous.
      2. Time of administration: latent and active labor, often in conjunction with a narcotic analgesic.
      3. Maternal side effects: drowsiness, confusion, no pain relief if used alone.
      4. Newborn side effects: sleepiness, poor sucking, poor muscle tone, less attentive, more restless; may take several days for effects from large maternal doses to disappear completely.
II. Inhalant Systemic Analgesics
   A. **Nitrous oxide, halothane (Halothane, Fluothane), enflurane (Ethrane)**
      1. Route of administration: inhaled through face mask.
      2. Time of administration: late first stage and second stage of labor.
      3. Maternal side effects: nausea, vomiting (aspiration may occur), accidental deep anesthesia and unconsciousness.
      4. Newborn side effects: decreased alertness, cardiac or respiratory depression.

Potential problems with meperidine affect both mother and baby. Large doses may cause excessive drowsiness, which may decrease the mother's concentration on coping techniques or her ability to push effectively and may cloud the actual birth experience. As mentioned earlier, this ''clouding'' may be considered a benefit by some women, while others would find it an unpleasant side effect.

Effects on the baby include decreased alertness,[10,25] an increase in abnormal reflexes,[10,18] and decreased social responsiveness.[18,25] Higher umbilical cord levels of meperidine have been associated with respiratory depression. Subtle effects lasting up to six weeks include depressed attention, social responsiveness, and ability to self-quiet.[10] Significant negative effects on sucking and alertness have been found up to four and five days after delivery.[10] It is important to note that many of the neurobehavior effects found in various studies were quite subtle and their long-term significance remains unknown at this time. If an infant is having significant respiratory difficulties following use of systemic analgesia for the mother, the drug effects can be neutralized by injecting naloxone (Narcan) into an umbilical vein.[33] Onset of action is within two minutes with a duration of 30 minutes.[25]

Other drugs that are used for systemic analgesia include butorphanol (Stadol) and ketamine. Reports are somewhat varied on these drugs and most authors state that meperidine remains the most commonly used systemic analgesic. Butorphanol is more potent than morphine or meperidine and has an inactive metabolite.

Most of these agents share a profile of actions and side effects similar to meperidine. Ketamine is a short-acting anesthetic that produces a dissociative state. When used, it is generally given as a single intravenous injection just prior to delivery. A dissociative state lasting about 15 minutes is produced. Increased blood pressure may occur. It is important to note, however, that currently ketamine is not suggested for use as an obstetrical analgesic.[15]

Inhalants as Systemic Analgesics

The general anesthetic agents can be given in subanesthestic-analgesic concentrations during the latter part of the first stage and the second stage of labor. A once-popular choice that is no longer used was trichloroethylene (Trilene), which was self-administered. Unfortunately, when a closed circuit system was used to administer Trilene, toxic products were formed and deaths were reported.[25]

The most commonly used mixture now is 50 per cent nitrous oxide and 50 per cent oxygen. It does not interfere with uterine contractions or prolong labor. As long as the oxygen content remains above 30 per cent, marked fetal hypoxia does not occur.[33] Maternal hypoxia also becomes a risk when the oxygen concentration is less than 30 per cent.[25] Advice for administration varies from continuous[21] to intermittent with each uterine contraction.[25,33] Opinions vary on the amount of pain relief afforded by the mixture from inadequate[21] to satisfactory.[25,33] Other agents that are sometimes used include halothane and enflurane. Both of these produce uterine relaxation and thus may prolong labor[13] and increase the chance for hemorrhage.[25] Uterine relaxation, however, may be a benefit if intrauterine manipulation of the fetus is necessary. Renal toxicity can also occur with these agents.

Cyclopropane was once popular. However, it is highly explosive, does not relax the uterus, and unless the administration time is short, the baby may bc depressed and need resuscitation.[25] Methoxyflurane is also not as popular as it once was. It too may decrease uterine activity, increase blood loss, and cause renal toxicity.

One danger of using an inhalant analgesic is the possibility of overdosage.[21] If this occurs, the symptoms include loss of consciousness, involuntary muscle activity, irregular breathing, vomiting, and incontinence.[13] With inhalant administration the woman must have constant medical supervision.

Regional Anesthesia

Because of concern over the potentially negative effects of systemic analgesics, regional anesthesia has been gaining popularity.[2] It allows the woman to be awake and participate in labor and birth without feeling pain while minimizing the amount of drug that the fetus receives. Regional nerve blocks with an anesthetic agent range from local infiltration for an episiotomy to spinal anesthesia (Table 18–2).

Anesthetic Agents

The most commonly used agents are from the local anesthetic classification. They are bupivacaine, chloroprocaine, lidocaine, and mepivacaine.[31] Bupivacaine has a variable onset of action depending upon the route of administration. Pain relief from contractions occurs in three to five minutes, while a sensory block is present in five to ten minutes and a motor block in 15 to 20 minutes. The duration of action is 90 to 180 minutes, with

TABLE 18–2. REGIONAL ANESTHETICS USED IN LABOR AND DELIVERY

Medications: bupivacaine (Marcaine), chloroprocaine (Nesacaine), lidocaine (Xylocaine), mepivacaine (Carbocaine, Isocaine).

1. Route of administration: local infiltration of perineum, pudendal block, paracervical block, caudal or epidural block, spinal or saddle block.
2. Time of administration: varies from late first stage to second stage labor.
3. Maternal side effects: burning or stinging on administration, diminished urge to push, hypotension, central nervous system toxicity if too much is given or if given intravenously.
4. Newborn side effects: decreased muscle tone, fetal depression.

repeat doses given after 120 minutes. Cardiovascular toxicity is possible if a large dose is inadvertently injected intravenously. The drug does not cross the placenta rapidly.

Chloroprocaine is rapidly metabolized in the maternal plasma. It has a rapid onset of action (three to five minutes) and a duration of 40 to 60 minutes. Because of the rapid metabolization, maternal plasma levels are low. Injection may be repeated every 40 to 50 minutes. There is some controversy concerning possible neurotoxic effects of chloroprocaine. Prolonged sensory and motor deficits have been reported after epidural anesthesia.[6] Very small amounts have been found in neonatal blood.

Lidocaine has a rapid onset of action, five to 10 minutes, with a duration of 60 to 75 minutes. Injection may be repeated every 60 minutes. When it is given with epinephrine, a longer duration of action occurs and less drug is needed. Lidocaine is transferred rapidly to the fetus and has been found in infants up to two days after birth.[3]

Mepivacaine also has a fairly rapid onset of action, five to ten minutes, but is metabolized slowly, with high maternal and fetal plasma levels seen. The duration of action is 60 to 70 minutes and a repeat injection can be given in 60 minutes.

Regional anesthesia is not without its problems. The most serious maternal complication is a central nervous system toxicity. Accidental intravenous injection of an anesthetic agent, as well as overdosage, can precipitate a toxic reaction. The symptoms include dizziness, slurred speech, a metallic taste in the mouth, numbness of the tongue and mouth, loss of consciousness, and convulsions. As maternal hypoxia progresses, fetal distress in turn occurs and is manifested by late decelerations or persistent bradycardia. Both the mother and the fetus require constant observation.

Numerous studies have been done to determine the effect of the anesthetic agents on the baby. In 1974, studies by Scanlon and colleagues showed that lidocaine compromised neonatal neurobehavioral function. The infants were described as "floppy but alert."[28] Scanlon also reported that no adverse effects related to bupivacaine were found.[29]

In more recent studies, bupivacaine has been shown to produce depressed motor performance, particularly in the infant at one day of age. Those babies whose mothers were given oxytocin as well seemed to have a greater depression. After one month no differences were seen, but the previously unmedicated mothers reported that their babies were more sociable, easy to care for, and rewarding.[22] In another study[27] infants born after epidural bupivacaine were shown to have adverse effects on motor organization, ability to control their state of consciousness, and physiological response to stress. These effects were found up to six weeks postpartum. Immediately after birth, those infants with the most exposure to bupivacaine were more likely to be cyanotic with decreased alertness.

Another researcher,[1] however, found no deleterious effects on newborn neurobehavior when subjects receiving bupivacaine, chloroprocaine, and lidocaine were compared with a no-drug control group. Yet another study[6] found no neurobehavioral differences between babies whose mothers received epidural lidocaine or bupivacaine, except a decreased sucking response at 24 hours in the bupivacaine group. Thus, it would appear that although there are some subtle neurobehavioral effects from the use of the local anesthetic agents, the extent of their clinical significance is still being debated.

Methods of Regional Anesthesia

A *local infiltration* of the perineum is utilized when an episiotomy is performed or there are lacerations to be repaired. It is given either just before or after delivery. A local block is often the only anesthetic employed in a woman well prepared in supportive pain management strategies. The injection may cause some burning as it is administered but in general is an innocuous form of anesthesia for both mother and baby.

A *pudendal block* is an injection of an anesthetic into the pudendal nerves, usually through the vagina. This block is given in the second stage of labor and effectively numbs the birth canal and perineum for delivery, episiotomy, and repair. The pudendal block is especially helpful for a forceps delivery. This type of block is often used in an otherwise unmedicated labor and birth.

A *paracervical block* is an injection into the nerves on both sides of the cervix. It is given through the vagina in active labor to relieve the discomfort from cervical dilation. Pain relief is afforded until the presenting part of the fetus reaches the lower vagina at which time a pudendal or local infiltration may also be used. The duration of the block is usually one hour and can be repeated if birth is not imminent; however, an overdose can occur this way. Theoretically a woman might receive several injections for a paracervical block followed by more anesthetic agent for birth.

There are several potential problems with a paracervical block. In some women uterine contractions stop for a short time after the injection. Fetal bradycardia may also occur, and if a high dose is used, the infant may be depressed at birth. The injection must be done extremely carefully, for if the needle is inserted too far, the fetus will receive more of the drug than is intended. Convulsions and death may result from an accidental direct fetal injection.

A *spinal block* is an injection of an anesthetic into the spinal fluid through the subarachnoid space. It is a single, low-dose injection of the anesthetic and is given to the woman in a sidelying or sitting position. Spinal anesthesia produces numbness from above the navel to the toes. It can be performed quickly and may be especially useful when an urgent need for instrumental delivery or manual extraction of the placenta occurs.[4] It is given in the second stage of labor once the cervix has fully dilated, usually just before birth. If given prior to this, labor may be disrupted causing potential complications for both the mother and baby. Spinal block anesthesia is also used for cesarean births in some areas.

Possible side effects include maternal hypotension, loss of the urge to push, spinal headache, and difficulty with urination after delivery. Also, paradoxically, hypertension from oxytocin injected after delivery is seen most often in women who have had a spinal or epidural block. There is a rare possibility for nerve injury or meningitis.[23] If maternal hypotension is severe, the baby may become hypoxic. Contraindications to spinal anesthesia include the presence of hemorrhage or severe hypertension and associated hypovolemia. In the presence of these problems, severe drops in blood pressure are seen.[25] A spinal anesthesia should also not be used if the skin is infected around the injection site or if neurological disorders are present.

A saddle block or low spinal is similar to a spinal block except that the anesthetized area extends from the pubis to the toes. The injection is administered in the second stage of labor and used primarily for vaginal deliveries, especially forceps deliveries. Complications and contraindications are the same as for spinal anesthesia.

Epidural anesthesia is considered by many to be relatively safe and effective, allowing for a relatively painless labor and a well-controlled birth over a relaxed perineum usually with low or outlet forceps.[24] As mentioned earlier, there is some thought that epidural anesthesia lowers fetal and maternal catecholamine levels. However, some researchers believe that the catecholamine surge within the normal birth process is protective for the fetus and that its release should not be blocked.

In an epidural block, the local anesthetic is injected into the epidural space of the lumbar region of the spinal column. If the meninges are penetrated, a total spinal block will occur. A caudal anesthesia is essentially the same as a lumbar epidural except that it is given in the caudal canal at the lower end of the sacrum. Most epidurals are placed in the lumbar region because of the safety of the procedure.[2] Epidural anesthesia can be given as a single injection or, more commonly, a catheter can be placed into the epidural space for continuous anesthesia.

An epidural can be given in active labor or just prior to the second stage of labor. An epidural may also be used for a cesarean birth. The woman is placed in a sitting or sidelying position for administration of the anesthetic. Usually, complete pain relief from uterine contractions during birth and repair processes is afforded. The contraindications of epidural anesthesia are the same as those for a spinal block. However, there is some debate over the use of epidurals in the presence of hypertension. Some anesthesiologists prefer to use such anesthesia, believing that cerebrospinal fluid pressure responses to painful uterine contractions are reduced, thereby decreasing the likelihood of hypertensive crisis.

However, epidural anesthesia is not without problems. Inadvertent spinal anesthesia may occur or there may be ineffective anesthesia. According to one author, 85 per cent of women have complete relief, 12 per cent partial relief, and 3 per cent no relief.[25] When anesthetic failures occur, systemic analgesic or another type of regional anesthesia such as a pudendal block is used.

Another complication is maternal hypotension, as a result of vasodilatation, with a subsequent drop in the fetal heart rate. This can usually be prevented by rapid infusion of intravenous fluids such as Ringer's solution to fill the increased vascular space. Also, inadvertent intravenous injection of the local anesthetic can cause central nervous system toxicity, although this is rare, as are systemic reactions to the agent.

There are several common problems with epidural anesthesia which merit discussion. One is shivering and a cold sensation that is caused by a temporary peripheral temperature change.[14] Postpartum urinary retention is not uncommon and catheterization may be required and occasionally headaches may also occur.[8] Labor is sometimes slowed by an epidural, and oxytocin is required more frequently with epidural anesthesia than without. However, it is difficult in some cases to say whether a long labor leads to an epidural or an epidural causes a long labor. Oxytocin, however, does carry the risk of hyperstimulation and subsequent uterine tetany as well as an association with neonatal jaundice.[24] Oxytocin also may increase the woman's desire for analgesic medication and her need for support from her labor coach.

Epidural anesthesia is associated with a higher incidence of forceps deliveries. A diminished urge to push may prolong the second stage of labor. One study showed an incidence of forceps deliveries five times higher in women with epidural anesthesia than in those without anesthesia.[8] Forceps deliveries also carry a risk of injury to the infant.

One final point should be mentioned. With an epidural, the fetus is generally exposed to the anesthetic agent for hours rather than minutes as with a local or pudendal block. One researcher has found that the anesthetic bupivacaine alters red blood cell properties in the fetus. This may be associated with neonatal jaundice, which has a higher incidence in infants delivered after epidural anesthesia.[5]

General Anesthesia

General anesthesia is reserved for cesarean births and in rare cases for very difficult vaginal births. Usually such an anesthetic is used in an emergency when there is not time to administer a regional block. In the case of an elective cesarean birth, a joint decision regarding anesthesia should be made by the woman and her physician.

The inhalant anesthetic agents as well as induction agents such as thiopental are used. Maternal and infant dangers are aspiration of vomitus, neonatal depression, maternal awareness, maternal and fetal hypoxia, maternal hyperventilation with subsequent fetal asphyxia, and decreased uterine contractility that may lead to postpartum hemorrhage.

IMPLICATIONS FOR PRACTICE

Nonpharmaceutical pain management strategies should be emphasized as the first line of defense. If used, the pharmaceutical pain management strategies should be adjuncts to the supportive techniques. However, parents should not be made to feel that they have failed if they choose to use an analgesic or anesthetic, nor should they be frightened of medications. In general, women should be encouraged to take medication only when they need it and then in the smallest dose possible.

Parents should be informed about the benefits and risks of the various methods of pharmaceutical pain management. The data appear insufficient at this time to support the theory that analgesia or anesthesia is necessary for the baby's well-being. Parents should be encouraged to examine their feelings about medication during labor and birth. This includes what they are willing to accept, those methods that would be totally unacceptable, and whether or not they agree with each other. Some thought as to what their goals are for the childbirth experience is also important, as is reflection on any previous labor and birth experience.

Parents should be encouraged to be aware of which pharmaceutical pain management strategies are commonly used in their area, since it does vary. A discussion regarding analgesia and anesthesia should be held with the health care provider and a mutually agreeable individual plan proposed. The mother's health and risk factors of the pregnancy need to be considered. Barring emergency complications, the expectant parents should make the final decision regarding the use of pharmaceutical agents.

However, both the parents and the health care provider must be flexible with the plan. Any decision prior to childbirth can only be tentative, because no one can foresee what may occur during labor or how a particular woman will respond. Some women find labor much easier than anticipated and do not require as much medication as they may have expected. On the other hand, some women may have an extremely difficult labor or a high-risk situation that necessitates the use of medication.

It is an appropriate role for the childbirth educator to help inform the prospective parents of the risks and benefits of analgesia and anesthesia in labor and birth. In general, the major benefit is relief from pain, while the risks are varied for both mother and baby. *Only the expectant parents can ultimately decide what is best for them.*

Teaching about pharmaceutical pain management strategies in class is sometimes a difficult task to accomplish in a balanced manner. Some expectant parents come to class very frightened or anxious about the topic. Some want it discussed early in the series so they can relieve their anxieties and have energy to focus on other topics. Some want the background of attaining skill and confidence in the nonpharmaceutical supportive techniques before they are ready to discuss analgesia and anesthesia. Sometimes teachers find expectant fathers who want to dictate their wife's use or nonuse of medication. Additionally, the teacher often knows by the hospital chosen or birth attendant chosen whether or not the couple is receiving or will receive help with formulating their own plans as opposed to a "packaged plan" urged on all

> The medication took away what control I had and left the pain.
>
> A NEW MOTHER[1]
>
> I had an epidural an hour before my daughter was born. It turned a night that was fast becoming hysterical into an event that I could participate in.
>
> A NEW MOTHER[1]
>
> I was all for medication. I thought painkillers were the answer. Never again! I felt manipulated and out of control.
>
> A NEW MOTHER[1]
>
> After nine hours I was on the edge of hysteria, and my husband was frantic with concern. We decided to go with an epidural—one of the smartest moves I've ever made.
>
> A NEW MOTHER[1]
>
> I feel you lose something with an epidural . . . it took some away from the bond (with baby). Something was lacking.
>
> A NEW MOTHER[2]
>
> After I had the epidural, I didn't have to deal with the pain anymore. I was more alert, could talk with my husband and watch the monitor. Childbirth became more enjoyable.
>
> A NEW MOTHER[2]

clients in that setting. Last but not least, because childbirth educators specialize in nonpharmaceutical supportive pain management strategies, as a group they have stronger feelings about the value of a nonmedicated delivery than does the general public. All these factors contribute to making medication a difficult topic to present comfortably in a balanced manner.

Some childbirth educators present the topic as a values clarification exercise before they discuss the risk-to-benefit considerations of specific types of medication. For example, couples can be asked to visualize a continuum from one to ten on beliefs about medication in labor. Class members can be asked to portray each position. The person representing a one position can describe the extreme view that she wants to know nothing during her labor—just put her out as soon and as completely as possible. Then the person representing position ten can describe an extreme view that no one should take any medication ever for any reason. It should be clear to the class that these views acted out do not need to represent the actors' true views. Next the class members are asked to describe a five position then perhaps a three position followed by an eight position. Then the other positions are filled in. Typically, some rearranging may need to be done because the description of the seven position may be less extreme than the eight position. Eventually the class gets ten value positions described.

After this the teacher helps them to realize that people whose views are represented by one's and ten's seldom come to a childbirth education class. She suggests that these well-meaning people would probably benefit from more information. Depending on the class, the instructor might want to ask members to establish where on the continuum each stands, emphasizing that there is no right or wrong spot. Expectant parents can also describe where they think their care provider stands.

Against this background the class can then discuss the risks and benefits of different medications, including the option of nonpharmaceutical support only. Couples can be encouraged to share their reasons for their views with each other and plan how they will come to an understanding on the topic with their care provider. The childbirth educator's role is to present factual material and to help expectant parents communicate their informed desires to each other and their care providers.

IMPLICATIONS FOR RESEARCH

One important area of research would be more studies to adequately settle the debate regarding the catecholamines. Do they cause fetal asphyxia or are they protective? More data are needed before it can be said that analgesia and anesthesia—particularly epidural anesthesia—is necessary to decrease stress and prevent fetal asphyxia.

Another area of study which merits more work is the neurobehavioral status of the newborn following use of the various analgesic and anesthetic agents. Some of the previous studies have not been able to completely separate one drug group from another. In one study of meperidine, some of the women in both the meperidine and the no-drug control group had actually received epidural anesthesia. Also, some studies have not been controlled for confounding variables such as age of patient, parity, length of labor (which can certainly affect fetal outcome), type of delivery, and combined effects of analgesic drugs. In many, sample size has been too small to be significant. Perhaps longer longitudinal research projects could be undertaken in order to have larger sample groups.

Regarding those studies that investigate the effects of drugs with active metabolites, it may be more meaningful to record the blood levels of the metabolites as well as the parent drug. It might also be interesting to study the amounts of analgesic and anesthetic drugs excreted in breast milk. Many infants are breastfed immediately after birth and this could add to the amount of drug the infant receives and may affect neurobehavior.

Certainly the debate over the various risks and benefits of pharmaceutical pain management strategies will continue. As such, it will be a source of study for years to come. There are many questions related to teaching about medication and anesthesia for childbirth that require answers. Two specific questions that need to be examined are:

- What are the most common fears and concerns that expectant parents have about analgesia and anesthesia for childbirth?
- What are the most effective teaching strategies for presenting information about analgesia and anesthesia in childbirth education classes?

SUMMARY

Pharmaceutical pain management in labor and birth has been a long-debated topic and no doubt will continue to be so. At the heart of the debate is the fact that whatever medication the mother in labor receives, the baby also receives. All drugs have potential side effects and this must be a consideration in the use of analgesia and anesthesia in childbirth. A variety of subtle neurobehavioral effects in infants of mothers receiving medication are described in the literature. Their clinical significance is still under debate.

Two major categories of pharmaceutical pain management strategies are discussed in this chapter: systemic analgesia and regional anesthesia. Today, general anesthesia is usually reserved for cesarean births. Systemic analgesia includes the injectable narcotics and inhalant agents. Regional anesthesia includes local infiltration of the perineum, pudendal block, paracervical block, spinal and low spinal block, and epidural anesthesia. Epidural anesthesia is currently one of the more popular types of pharmaceutical pain management strategies, although its use is not without problems.

It is the role of the childbirth educator to adequately inform prospective parents about the risks and benefits of the various pharmaceutical pain management strategies. Parents also need to explore their feelings about medication during labor and birth and understand that its use is a personal decision. In prepared childbirth, nonpharmaceutical pain management strategies are emphasized as a first line of defense. Pharmaceutical intervention, if needed or desired, should augment supportive strategies rather than become a substitute for them. Expectant parents need to receive adequate and balanced information about pharmaceutical pain management strategies so they can make an informed decision and develop a tentative but flexible plan for childbirth jointly with their care provider.

References

1. Abboud, T. K., Afrasiabi, A., Sarkis, F., et al. Continuous infusion epidural analgesia in parturients receiving bupivacaine, chloroprocaine, or lidocaine—maternal, fetal, and neonatal effects. *Anesthesia and Analgesia* 63:421, 1984.
2. Avard, D. M., and Nimrod, C. M. Risks and benefits of obstetric epidural analgesia: A review. *Birth* 12:215, 1985.
3. Brown, W. U., Bell, G. C., Lurie, A. O., et al. Newborn blood levels of lidocaine and mepivacaine in the first postnatal days following maternal epidural anesthesia. *Anesthesiology* 47:698, 1975.
4. Brownridge, P. Spinal anaesthesia revisited: An evaluation of subarachnoid block in obstetrics. *Anaesthesia and Intensive Care* 12:334, 1984.
5. Clark, D. A., and Landaw, S. A. Bupivacaine alters red blood cell properties—a possible explanation for neonatal jaundice associated with maternal anesthesia. *Pediatric Research* 19:341, 1985.
6. DeJong, R. H. The chloroprocaine controversy. *American Journal of Obstetrics and Gynecology* 140:237, 1981.
7. DeVoe, S. J., DeVoe, K., Jr., Rigsby, W. C., et al. Effects of meperidine on uterine contractility. *American Journal of Obstetrics and Gynecology* 105:1004, 1969.
8. Eggertsen, S. C., and Stevens, N. Epidural Anesthesia and the Course of Labor and Delivery. *Journal of Family Practice* 18:309, 1984.
9. Fishburne, J. I. Systemic analgesia during labor. *Clinical Perinatology* 9:29, 1982.
10. Hodgkinson, R., and Husain, F. J. The duration of effect of maternally administered meperidine on neonatal neurobehavior. *Anesthesiology* 56:51, 1982.
11. Humenick, S. S. Mastery: The key to childbirth satisfaction? a review. *Birth and the Family Journal* 8:79, 1981.
12. Humenick, S. S., and Bugen, L. A. Mastery: the key to

childbirth satisfaction? A study. *Birth and the Family Journal* 8:84, 1981.

13. Jaffe, J. H., and Martin, W. R. Opioid analgesics and antagonists. *In* Gilman, A. G., Goodman, L. S., Rall, T. W., and Murad F. (eds.) *Goodman and Gilman's The Pharmacological Basis of Therapeutics*. New York: MacMillan, 1985.
14. Kapusta, L., Confino, E., Ismajovich, B., et al. *International Journal of Gynaecology and Obstetrics* 23:185, 1985.
15. Kastrup, E. K., Boyd, J. R., and Olin, B. R. (eds). *Drug Facts and Comparisons*. Philadelphia: J. B. Lippincott, 1986.
16. Kileff, M. E., James, F. M., Dewan, D. M., et al. Neonatal neurobehavioral responses after epidural anesthesia for cesarean section using lidocaine and bupivacaine. *Anesthesia and Analgesia* 63:413, 1984.
17. Kuhnert, B. R., Linn, P. L., and Kuhnert, P. M. Obstetric medication and neonatal behavior. Current controversies. *Clinical Perinatology* 12:423, 1985.
18. Kuhnert, B. R., Linn, P. L., Kennard, M. J., et al. Effects of low doses of meperidine on neonatal behavior. *Anesthesia and Analgesia* 64:335, 1985.
19. Kuhnert, B. R., Kuhnert, P. M., Tu, A. S. L., et al. Meperidine and normeperidine levels following meperidine administration during labor. II. Fetus and Neonate. *American Journal of Obstetrics and Gynecology* 133:909, 1979.
20. Lagercrantz, H., and Slotkin, T. A. The "stress" of being born. *Scientific American* 254:100, 1986.
21. McDonald, J. S. Obstetric analgesia and anesthesia. *In* Benson, R. C. (ed). Current Obstetric and Gynecologic Diagnosis and Treatment. Los Altos, CA: Lange Medical Publications, 1982.
22. Murray, A. D., Dolby, R. M., Nation, L. R., et al. Effects of epidural anesthesia on newborns and their mothers. *Child Development* 52:71, 1981.
23. Nichols, F. H. Pain relief in childbirth. *Lamaze Parent's Magazine* 31, 1985.
24. Poore, M. S., and Foster, J. C. Epidural and no epidural anesthesia: Differences between mothers and their experience of birth. *Birth* 12:205, 1985.
25. Pritchard, J. A., MacDonald, P. C., and Gant, N. F. *Williams Obstetrics*. 17th ed. Norwalk, CT: Appleton-Century-Crofts, 1985.
26. Riffel, H. D., Nochimson, D. J., Paul, R. H., and Hon, E.H.G. Effects of meperidine and promethazine during labor. *Obstetrics and Gynecology* 42:738, 1973.
27. Rosenblatt, D. B., Belsey, E.M., Lieberman, B. A., et al. The influence of maternal analgesia on neonatal behavior: II. Epidural Bupivacaine. *British Journal of Obstetrics and Gynaecology* 88:407, 1981.
28. Scanlon, J. W., Brown, W. U., Weiss, J. B., et al. Neurobehavioral responses of newborn infants after maternal epidural anesthesia. *Anesthesiology* 40:121, 1974.
29. Scanlon, J. W., Ostheimer, G. W., Lurie, A. O., et al. Neurobehavioral responses and drug concentrations in newborns after maternal epidural anaesthesia with bupivacaine. *Anesthesiology* 45:405, 1976.
30. Shnider, S. M. Choice of anesthesia for labor and delivery. *Obstetrics and Gynecology* 58(Suppl. 5):25s, 1981.
31. Smith, C. M. Epidural anesthesia in labor. Various agents employed. *JOGN Nursing* 13:17, 1984.
32. Taber, C. W. *Taber's Cyclopedic Medical Dictionary*. 10th ed. Philadelphia: F. A. Davis, 1965.
33. Willson, J. R. Obstetric analgesia and anesthesia. *Obstetrics and Gynecology*, 7th ed. St. Louis: C. V. Mosby, 1983.

Beginning Quote:

Brackbill, Y. Medication in maternity. *Childbirth Educator* 6:30, Winter 1965/1987.

Boxed Quotes

1. Savage, B., and Simkin, D. *Preparation for Childbirth: The Complete Guide to the Lamaze Method*. New York: Ballantine Books, 1987, pp. 247–259.
2. Poore, M.G. Factors Perceived by Women in the Selection of Childbirth Anesthesia, Unpublished Thesis, University of Utah, College of Nursing, August 1983.

chapter 19

THE UNEXPECTED CHILDBIRTH EXPERIENCE

ELAINE SCHROEDER-ZWELLING

The next two months were like a very bad dream. Andrew was holding his own after delivery and was placed in the Intermediate Care section of the Neonatal Unit. My first trip to the Neonatal Nursery was without Tom. He had gone home for a much-needed nap and to be with our two other children. After much hand-washing and gowning, a nurse took me into the nursery. I cried softly when I saw him. He was so beautiful.

Mother of a Premature Infant

Although the majority of all labors and births proceed normally, the possibility of an alteration in the expected normal process does exist. The question of how to discuss the subject of this potential alteration in the classroom setting is often a puzzling one for the childbirth educator. How can one achieve a balance between providing expectant parents with the knowledge base that they would need in coping with a labor alteration and providing the type of information that might serve only to increase their anxiety? How do pregnant women and their partners view an unexpected outcome during labor or birth? Does a deviation from the expected normal process result in a state of crisis for the family, and if so, how can the childbirth educator intervene? In an attempt to answer these questions, this chapter presents a review of the literature relating to crisis theory and parents' reactions to unexpected outcomes of labor and birth. The implications for the practice of childbirth education and for further research are also discussed.

REVIEW OF THE LITERATURE

Crisis Theory

Throughout the life cycle, individuals continually strive to achieve a sense of balance, or equilibrium, in their daily lives. We constantly make minor adaptations in our thinking and in our behavior to achieve this feeling of balance. When a situation occurs which threatens to disrupt this equilibrium, individuals begin to employ their usual problem-solving techniques in order to regain the feeling of balance. If the usual problem-solving techniques fail, a crisis situation is likely to result.[3,4,38] The Chinese character for "crisis" is translated as meaning "danger, yet opportunity."[3,16] This definition brings a great deal of insight to a crisis; it identifies the fact that crisis situations may precipitate disequilibrium within an individual or a family but that they can also result in positive growth.

It is possible that an unexpected occurrence during pregnancy, labor, or birth could result in either manageable stress for the parents or total disequilibrium and the inability to cope effectively. Rapoport contrasts several differences between stress and crisis.[38] In essence, stress can exist for a relatively long period of time without noticeable change in the individual and be manageable because the individual develops adequate coping mechanisms. Many parents no doubt view the normal changes during the childbearing year as stressors, and are able to adapt to them by developing new coping strategies.

On the other hand, a crisis is more likely to be viewed as a hazardous event or a situation blocking one's goals. The event can be perceived as a threat, a loss, or a challenge. The threat may be to fundamental instinctual needs or to the person's sense of integrity, and is usually met with severe anxiety. The loss may be actual or may be experienced as a state of acute deprivation. Loss or deprivation are most often met with depression. If the problem is viewed as a challenge, it is more likely to be met with a mobilization of energy and purposive problem-solving activities. The nature or severity of the unexpected outcome would no doubt have an influence on whether parents view an alteration during childbirth as being merely a stressful event or a crisis situation. It also must be recognized that what constitutes a crisis situation for one individual or family does not necessarily constitute a crisis for others.

Maturational Versus Situational Crises. Crises are identified as being either maturational or situational in their nature. *Maturational* or *developmental crises* are often regarded as "normal" crises because all human beings experience them as they move through the life cycle. They are generally viewed as periods of physical, psychological, and social change that are characterized by common disturbances in thought and feeling.[3,37] For example, adolescence, pregnancy, and menopause are thought of as being normal developmental crises. A *situational* or *accidental crisis* is a stressful external event, not necessarily related to normal development. An *unexpected occurrence* for parents during labor has elements of both a maturational and situational crisis, for it occurs during the normal process of childbirth but yet is an external and unexpected stressful event. Clinical investigators have pointed out that when a situational crisis is superimposed on a normal-phase-of-development crisis, the combined impact of these simultaneous events can often lead to a crisis of major proportions.[3,37]

Variables Influencing Crisis. Hill identifies variables that influence a crisis situation with the use of his well-known ABCX model[9,36] (Fig. 19–1). "A" (the event) interacts with "B" (the person's crisis-meeting resources), which interacts with "C" (the definition the person makes of the event), which produces "X" (the crisis). The hardships of the event, which make up the first variable (A), lie outside the individual's control and are an attribute of the event itself. The second and third variables, the resources and definitions of the event (B and C), lie within the individual and family and therefore can be altered.[9] When applied to the childbearing couple, Hill's model suggests that an unexpected occurrence during labor (A) could result in a state of crisis (X) if the couple is ill-

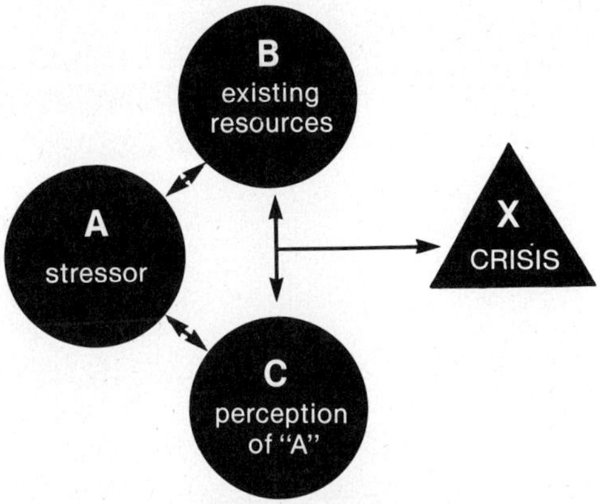

FIGURE 19–1. ABCX model of crisis. (From Burr, W. Families under stress. In McCubbin, H.I., Cauble, A.E., and Patterson, J.M. (eds). *Family Stress, Coping, and Social Support*. Courtesy of Charles C Thomas, Publisher, Springfield, Illinois. 1982.)

prepared and has few resources to deal with the situation (B), or if they define the unexpected situation as being negative (C).

Crisis Intervention

Crisis intervention is the term that is used for the therapeutic counseling given to individuals or families who are experiencing a crisis situation. This approach has evolved from the field of psychotherapy and is a professional intervention method used frequently in the fields of nursing and social work. Because a person in crisis is totally involved in a subjective experience, he or she is psychologically vulnerable and open to outside assistance.

Aguilera et al.[2] discuss the balancing factors that can help an individual regain equilibrium when a stressful event occurs. These balancing factors, illustrated in the Paradigm of Intervention (Fig. 19–2), are the *perception of the event,* the *available situational supports,* and the *coping mechanisms.* It is interesting to note that the balancing factors identified by Aguilera et al. closely parallel the variables-influencing crisis described by Hill in Figure 19–1.

In the upper portion of the Paradigm of Intervention the "normal" initial reaction to stress is illustrated. In column A, the balancing factors are operating and crisis is avoided. However, in column B the absence of one or more of these balancing factors may block resolution of the problem, thus increasing disequilibrium and precipitating crisis.[2] This paradigm can be used during crisis intervention to help with the assessment of the stressful event and the identification of the individual's balancing factors. The minimum goal of crisis intervention is psychological resolution of the person's immediate crisis and restoration to at least the level of function that existed prior to the crisis event. A maximum goal is improvement in functioning above the pre-crisis level.[2,3]

Aguilera et al.[2] identify four steps to be followed when using crisis intervention:

1. Assessment of the individual, his problem, and the factors that are causing the crisis.
2. Planning intervention to return the individual to his pre-crisis level of functioning. It is important to know how much the crisis has disrupted the individual's life and the lives of those around him. Information is also needed about the strengths of the individual, his usual coping skills, and the people in his life who are supports for him.
3. Implementing the planned intervention by helping the individual to gain an intellectual understanding of the crisis and why it occurred, bring his feelings out into the open, and explore new coping mechanisms.
4. Resolution of the crisis and anticipatory planning includes the reinforcing of successful coping mechanisms, making realistic plans for the future, and discussing ways in which the present experience may help in coping with future crises.

Reactions to the Unexpected in Childbirth

Although there are many unexpected events that could occur during the course of pregnancy, labor, and birth, parental reactions and feelings regarding a high-risk pregnancy, cesarean birth, and loss of the infant are those discussed most frequently in the literature. Parents may also find that even minor changes in their anticipated plan for labor can precipitate emotional reactions of loss. Most women

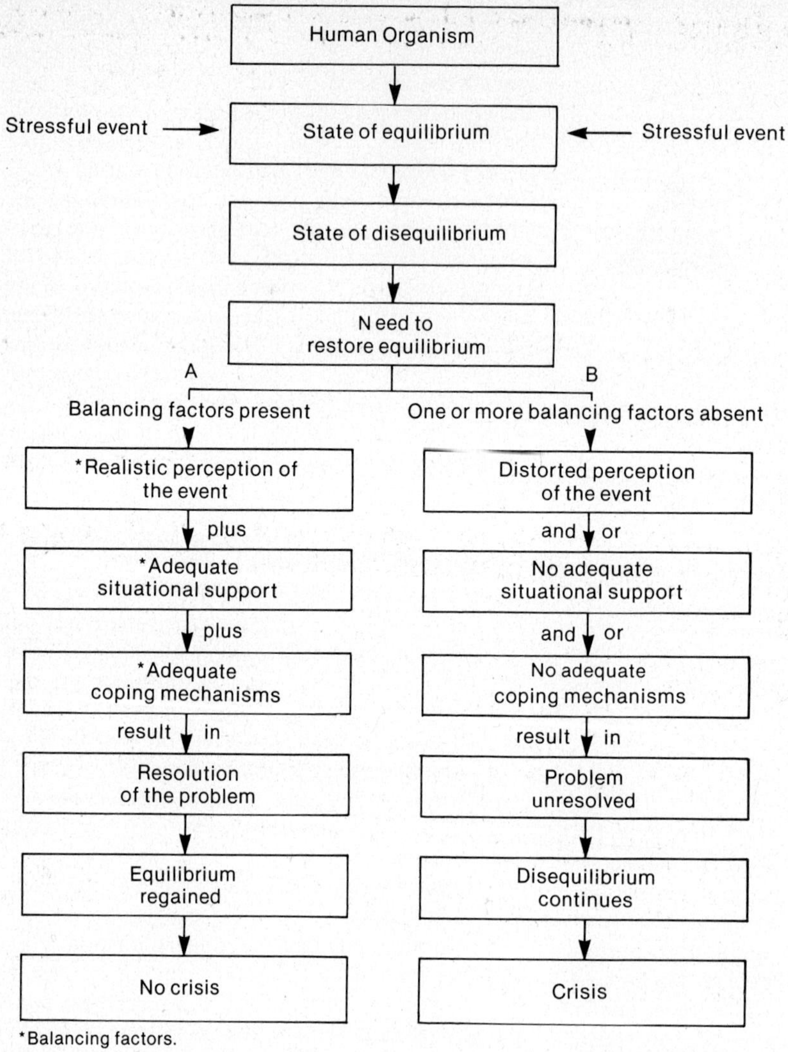

FIGURE 19–2. Paradigm: Effect of balancing factors in a stressful event. (From Aguilera, D.C., Messick, J.M., and Farrel, M.S. *Crisis Intervention: Theory and Methodology.* St. Louis: C.V. Mosby, 1970.)

at some time during pregnancy worry about complications that might occur during childbirth.[8,12,31] For the majority of women, however, these worries are unfounded and quickly forgotten when labor progresses as expected and results in the birth of a healthy infant.

High-Risk Pregnancy and Childbirth

When a woman experiences a high-risk pregnancy, her fears and tensions are magnified. In this situation the possibility of the unexpected occurring during labor is increased. A high-risk pregnancy is complex because the woman must cope simultaneously with two quite distinct crisis situations—the normal developmental crisis of childbearing as well as the recognition that pregnancy may not progress in line with expected "normal" patterns or end with a healthy mother-infant dyad. As a result, the woman's coping abilities become doubly taxed.[42]

The emotional responses of a woman and her family to a high-risk pregnancy can correspond

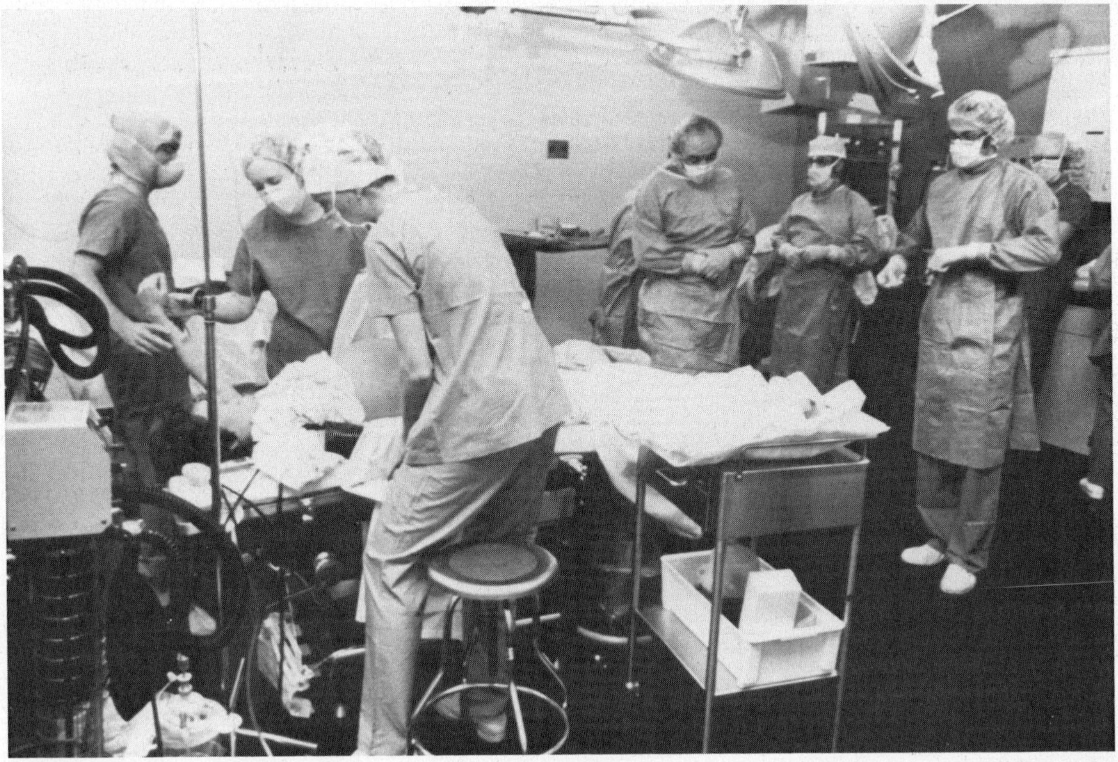

A cesarean birth. An unexpected occurrence for parents during childbirth such as an emergency cesarean birth has elements of both maturational and situational crises. The combined impact of these elements can often lead to a crisis of major proportions. (Photograph by Rodger Ewy, Educational Graphic Aids, Inc.)

with those seen in the grieving process. The diagnosis of a pregnancy as "high-risk" is often a shock to parents. This shock is usually followed by a period of self-questioning, in which parents attempt to determine whether the problem might have been caused by some omission or commission of their own. Parents may experience anger, directed at themselves or at others. Denial may occur and may be a factor if the woman appears to be noncompliant with her health care regimen. Feelings of fear and loss of control can also occur. These reactions may continue throughout the pregnancy and into labor.[42,43]

Cesarean Childbirth

Similar feelings of anxiety, guilt, and loss of control are expressed by many women when delivery of the baby occurs by an unexpected cesarean birth.[14,18,19,30,41] The loss of the planned and anticipated vaginal birth may make cesarean parents feel as though they have lost control of a major event in their lives. They may feel cheated that things did not go as they had hoped, and the fact that they could not be together or share and participate in the experience as they had planned may provoke feelings of anger at those around them. Further strain may arise when parents feel guilty for being disappointed when everyone around them expected them to be happy over the new arrival. Comments such as, "It's so much easier to have a cesarean—you never have to go through labor," "Cesarean babies are so much more beautiful," or "Don't you want to do what's best for the baby?"[30] only compound the guilt parents may be feeling.

Several authors have discussed the fact that

women who have a cesarean birth may express negative feelings about themselves and have a lower level of self-esteem.[13,14,18,39] Rubin[39] contends that the ability to function with control is an important determinant for maintaining self-esteem, and that when there is a loss of control, the risk of maternal role failure is increased. In a study by Cox and Smith,[14] a group of women delivering vaginally were compared with a group who delivered by cesarean in their responses on the Rosenberg Self-Esteem Scale. The comparison between groups showed that the subjects who had cesarean births had significantly lower self-esteem scores than those who had vaginal births. Marut and Mercer[33] also found that women who had cesarean births were generally very critical of themselves and their performance during labor and birth.

Other research findings have demonstrated conflicting outcomes in regard to maternal attitudes and feelings after cesarean birth. Marut and Mercer[33] found that satisfaction with the birth experience was significantly lower among primigravidas with cesarean births than primigravidas with vaginal births. However, Bradley et al.[7] found no significant differences in anxiety levels, depression, or attitudes toward the infant in primiparous women who delivered vaginally or by cesarean birth. Not all feelings expressed by cesarean parents are negative. Reports also indicate some positive reactions, such as feelings of mastery and relief that the birth is over.[19]

If the cesarean birth was an elective one, parents may have worked through many of their negative feelings in advance, although the birth itself may arouse the feelings of loss again in the postpartal period. If the birth was an emergency, the initial shock may be greater for the parents during the postpartum period and they may feel overwhelmed with the mixture of reactions.[30]

Fathers also demonstrate a mixture of reactions and feelings when an unexpected cesarean birth occurs. The literature indicates that negative feelings such as loss, sadness, apprehension, confusion, and helplessness are common in fathers.[1,18,19,34,35] A study by May and Sollid[34,35] found that most negative reactions centered not on the cesarean itself but on policies that excluded fathers from attending the delivery, and on staff behaviors that reflected disregard for the fathers' need to feel included in the birth. However, this same study also revealed that the predominant emotional reaction of fathers to the decision for a cesarean was relief.

The feelings and reactions that have been identified as occurring in parents experiencing a high-risk pregnancy or a cesarean birth are those associated with the grieving process.[27] This process, and the feelings that accompany it, is discussed frequently in the literature in regard to the unexpected loss of the infant.[6,25,28,29]

Death of the Infant

The death of a baby or the birth of a premature or handicapped baby are unexpected occurrences in childbirth that most likely would result in a crisis situation. Throughout pregnancy, parents prepare emotionally for their infant by imagining how the baby will look and behave, and what it will be like to love and be loved by a baby. Parents anticipate the incorporation of a new life into the family and the joys of the events of the child's growth and development. With the loss of these expectations, as a result of the death of the infant or with the birth of a baby that is different from the expected, parents begin a period of grieving.[10,26,45] The death of an infant may be one of the most difficult experiences that parents ever face in their lifetime.

The progression through the grieving process may be complicated by additional factors for parents who have lost an infant. The death of a newborn may not be openly recognized by family and friends in the same way it would be if the death were of an older child or adult. Society often views the loss of a newborn as a "nonevent," an unfortunate occurrence that will quickly be forgotten. Therefore, the family members may be forced to etch out for themselves the way they will publicly acknowledge and respond to their loss. This puts additional stress on the grieving process.[6,17,23]

Another complicating factor is the fact that people move through the stages of the grieving process at their own pace. Thus, the father may be further along in his resolution of the loss of the infant than the mother. This can result in angry feelings between the parents and difficulty in communication.[23]

Interviews with parents who have experienced the loss of an infant reveal a number of factors that facilitated their grieving process:[17,44]

1. Acknowledgment of their infant's death by physician, nurses, friends, and family.
2. Permission to grieve (to cry, to be angry, to feel guilty, to be sad).
3. Being touched and held by others.
4. Being able to see and hold the infant.
5. Facilitation of memories about the baby (being given a picture of the baby, naming the baby, having a copy of the baptismal record, or dressing the baby in his own clothes).
6. The provision of honest, factual information.
7. Increased flexibility of hospital rules and policies.

These factors can help to support parents as they grieve and assist in the resolution of the crisis.

Alterations in Expectations. Feelings of disappointment and grieving responses such as anger, guilt, and depression can even be experienced by parents in response to a labor or birth that did not meet their expectations. These reactions are understandable when viewed as a response to the loss of the planned, anticipated, and fantasized "ideal" labor and birth. Parents may react to such situations as the need for medication or anesthesia that had not been planned, inability to "perform" or "remain in control" as expected, lack of availability of a birthing room or of one's favorite birth attendant to deliver the baby. Although these "losses" may seem minor to others and not worthy of emotional reactions when mother and baby are healthy, they may be significant to the parents and should not be minimized. Parents usually work through these disappointments very quickly and can move on to focusing on the positive aspects of the birth experience.

It would seem that the primary difference between the feelings and reactions that parents demonstrate in response to any unexpected outcome in labor is merely one of degree of intensity. Thus, similar responses might be expected, whether the reaction is to an unexpected cesarean birth, the need for unwanted medication or anesthesia, a long and difficult labor, or the loss of the infant. Whether or not these reactions lead to a crisis sit-

Box 19–1

FIRST THOUGHTS

BY CHERYL WALLERSTEDT, R.N., ACCE
Burleson, Texas

Why do my eyes fill with a mist,
As thick as early morning rain down South?
I have cried till I felt this great fist
Of water would have swept me about.
But still my heart aches because I'm accursed
With an emptiness that will not cease!

The child I could hardly believe was mine;
A miracle so great, so awe-inspiring.
Robbed from me before I had time
To watch him smile. He was expiring.
And I? Never to see him healthy and fine.
Missing the delights of even his first steps.

Am I not to be allowed to give him a mother's love?
Denied the experience of even a child's kiss.
Why at such a tender age was he sent above?
Already, his touch, his angelic face, I miss.
My soul is burning with unquenched love
That cannot be satisfied.

Tears continue to stream down my cheeks and have fell far greater than any waterfall has ever sustained.
But they cannot wash away, expiate or tell
The anguish, the hostility, the hurt, the sorrow, the pain.
I feel burning brighter inside than the flames of hell
For the loss of a son I'd only begun to know.

I feel cheated, deprived, beguiled by life. At the most,
Can only find relief from this devastation so wounding.
In the words written at a great cost
To the poetess, Elizabeth Barrett Browning:
"Tis better to have loved and lost
Than to have never loved at all."

This poem was written on January 14, 1973, six days after the funeral of the Wallerstedt's newborn son.

From Wallerstedt, C. First thoughts. *Genesis*, June/July 1982, p. 15.

Grieving parents. The death of an infant may be one of the most difficult experiences that parents ever face in a lifetime. (Photograph by Rodger Ewy, Educational Graphic Aids, Inc.)

uation depends on the parents' perception and their resources, as identified earlier in this chapter.

Needs of Parents

The primary need expressed by parents who experience an alteration in pregnancy or birth is for honest, factual information.[8,18,19,43] Parents want to know what is happening and why. Parents also want to feel that they continue to have some control—of themselves and of the situation.[30] They want to be given choices or options if at all possible.[30] Remaining together and being able to support each other is important to both mothers and fathers.[30,34,35] Parents say that they need to feel empathy and understanding from those around them.[43] They would also like advice or help in coping with their feelings.[18] Finally, support groups or ''hot lines'' to help parents resolve their feelings about an unexpected outcome have been identified as being helpful.[43]

IMPLICATIONS FOR PRACTICE

The childbirth educator is in an ideal position to provide anticipatory guidance, support, and intervention for expectant parents in regard to unexpected outcomes during pregnancy and birth. Childbirth educators typically spend a number of hours with parents and have the opportunity to form close and trusting relationships with them. The positive influences of childbirth educators have been well documented for many years.[46] Expectant couples often view their childbirth teacher as a primary resource during the childbearing year, and the teacher is likely to be the person who can help parents put their experience into perspective and alleviate any despondency that might interfere with the early weeks of parenthood.

However, many childbirth instructors express discomfort in discussing potential childbirth complications for fear of increasing anxiety. Or they may decline to discuss interventions or alterations in the belief that such discussion will serve only to make parents too complacent and accepting of these occurrences. Expectant parents themselves may prefer to maintain denial and believe that complications only happen to other people.[13,41]

Begin by identifying your own attitudes about unexpected outcomes in labor (i.e., values clarification). Do you feel positively or negatively about such alterations as induction and augmentation, anesthesia, and cesarean birth? Personal attitudes may hinder or assist your presentation and can be unconsciously transmitted to the couples in your class. Do you feel that teaching parents about possible alterations condones their occurrence? The childbirth educator serves as a role model for her students, and it will be difficult for them to develop a positive perception of the event (Hill's ''C'' factor) if she transmits negative feelings.[21,24,41]

Application of Theoretical Models

To identify the role of the childbirth educator as it relates to unexpected outcomes, the ABCX crisis model[9,36] and Aguilera's model of crisis intervention,[2] introduced earlier in this chapter, are helpful. According to Hill,[9,36] the two factors that would influence parents' response to an unexpected occurrence during labor are their existing resources and their perception of the event. One major resource offered through childbirth education is knowledge. Having factual information about potential alterations in the labor and birth process and ways to cope with those alterations will influence the stressor event in a positive way. A second resource is the coping mechanisms of relaxation, massage, and breathing that can be utilized for control in many unexpected occurrences during labor. Another resource that is enhanced with childbirth education is the emotional and social support of the mother and her partner or other family members. The process of childbirth education encourages interaction and supportive communication between the woman and her partner. This preparation would serve as a positive resource in a stressful event during labor.

The parents' perception of a stressful event is also altered through childbirth education. If potential alterations during labor are presented in a positive, matter-of-fact manner, rather than in a negative or frightening light, parents will be able to approach an expected outcome in a more positive way. The decrease in fear that results from knowledge will also allow for a more positive perception. Thus, according to Hill's ABCX crisis model, childbirth educators can exert a major influence on how parents view a stressor event and whether they perceive that event as a crisis situation.

An application of Aguilera's crisis intervention paradigm[2] to the situation of an unexpected occurrence in labor can be seen in Figure 19–3. The childbirth educator can utilize crisis intervention theory from an anticipatory perspective—that is, by preparing parents in advance to be able to identify and then utilize strategies that would be ''balancing factors'' for them should an unexpected situation occur in labor. Childbirth educators, like nurses, are well-suited for the use of crisis intervention strategies, because the primary characteristic necessary is that of closeness.[4] The childbirth educator becomes close psychologically to the parents in her class as she helps them prepare for the birth of their infant. She also is often close in a social sense because of the fact that childbirth educators represent more varied cultural and socioeconomic groups than do professionals in other disciplines. This allows expectant parents to more easily identify with her. The childbirth educator is often in a better position to implement the steps of assessment, intervention, resolution, and anticipatory planning identified by Aguilera.[2] Childbirth educators are also well-trained in positive communication techniques and thus can facilitate adult communication between parents.[16]

Teaching Strategies

A number of teaching strategies for presenting information about unexpected outcomes in labor have been found by childbirth educators to be use-

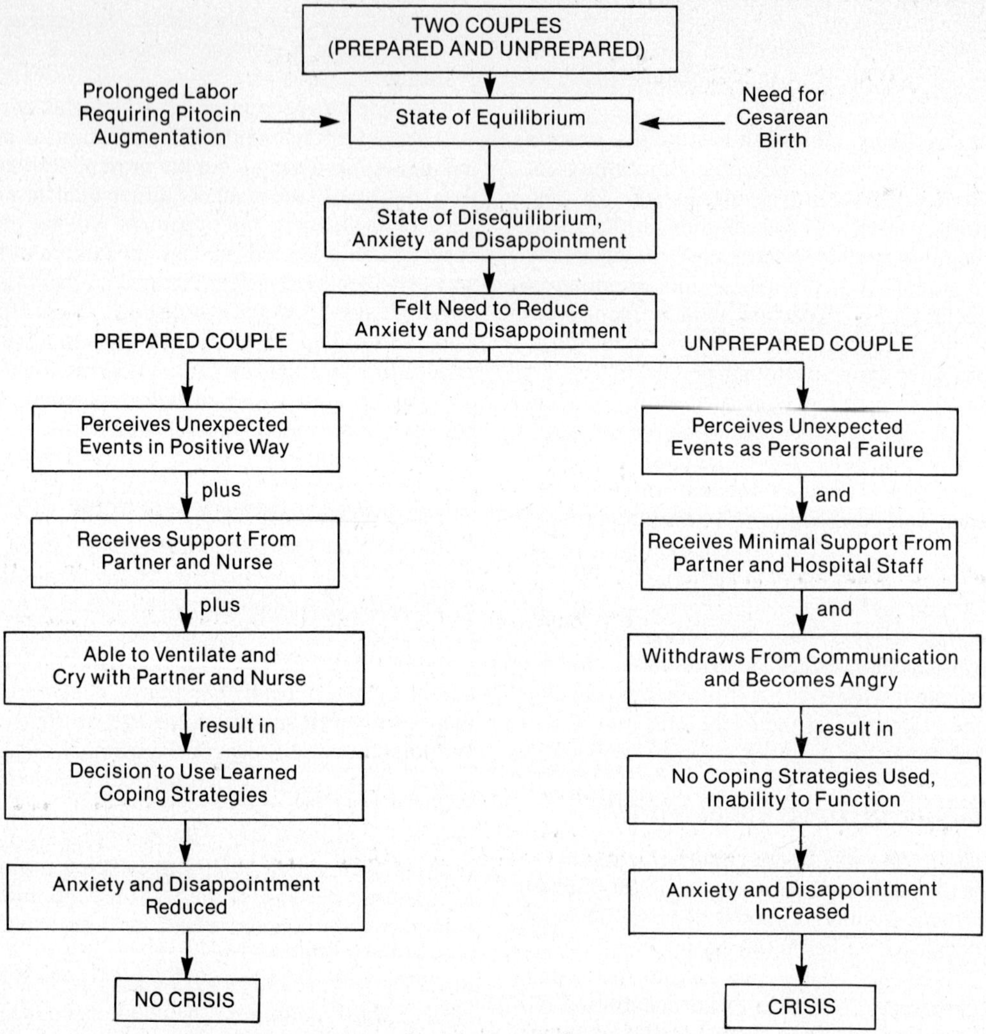

FIGURE 19–3. Aguilara paradigm applied to unexpected outcome in childbirth.

ful. A mixture of several creative approaches is ideal in order to avoid ''blockout'' by expectant parents.[24] Because *denial* is frequently a coping mechanism used by parents when hearing about possible labor alterations, they may not really listen to information presented by the teacher. Parents may actually not want to hear that something could deviate from the well-planned labor and birth they envision. Teaching strategies are suggested in Table 19–1. An elaboration of these principles follows:

1. Present information that defines the labor variation, give statistics of the frequency of occurrence, give reasons for the necessity of an unexpected intervention, include a description of the medical or nursing procedures that might be encountered, and describe both maternal and paternal physical and emotional responses.
2. Integrate the information about labor and birth variations throughout the entire course rather than ''lumping'' it into a single class.

TABLE 19–1. TEACHING STRATEGIES

- Provide factual information
- Integrate information throughout course
- Use positive, not negative, words
- Use visual aids to enhance information
- Provide handouts for later reference
- Encourage formulation of an alternate birth plan
- Include couple who experienced a variation when parents return to class for sharing
- Discuss options and choices relating to variations
- Discuss emotional reactions to an unexpected outcome

Presenting content on variations all at once tends to label them as being different from the ''normal'' labor discussed in all other classes. Lumping also makes it easier for parents to ''tune out'' this information.[13,21]

3. Consider your use of words when discussing possible unexpected outcomes. Be cautious about using the term ''normal'' to describe the labor that progresses as expected, for this then indicates that anything else is ''abnormal.'' ''Typical'' or ''usual'' are less value-laden words. Use the term ''cesarean birth'' rather than ''cesarean section'' because it can feel very dehumanizing to be spoken of as a ''section'' or as being ''sectioned.''
4. Use a variety of visual aids to illustrate and reinforce the points you make. Many professionally made posters are available today to illustrate such labor variations as use of Pitocin for induction, anesthesia, forceps, fetal monitoring, and cesarean birth. Excellent slide programs and films are also available. Visual aids should be used only as an adjunct, never in place of your teaching and discussion.
5. A handout or pamphlet outlining essential facts about labor variations is helpful. Parents can reinforce what they have heard in class by reading the handout at home at their leisure. If information is forgotten, the handout allows parents to have repeated and easy access to it.
6. If you encourage couples to make a birth plan, ask them to formulate an ''alternate birth plan'' as well, identifying in that plan what points would be most important to them in the event of an unexpected variation.[21]
7. If you ask recently delivered parents to return to class to share their birth experience, plan to have at least two couples return. One of the couples should have experienced a labor variation of some type, so that parents in the class can see that such alterations really do occur, that they can be handled, and that the birth experience can still be viewed as a positive one.[13]
8. Discuss the options and choices that would be available in regard to each labor variation. Encourage parents to ask questions of their physician and hospital regarding their options. Emphasize the family-centered com-

> One of the greatest challenges we face as childbirth educators is in getting parents to *listen* to cesarean information.
>
> PATTIE CARROLL KEARNS[1]
>
> Consider having a "baby night" class, which includes information on premature labor, premies, and babies with special health problems. . . . You may be the only support person these parents have.
>
> GALE ORDONEZ[2]
>
> The nursing staff didn't know how to deal with me. The only one who talked to me was a nurse who had lost a child herself. That was helpful—to see someone who had lived through it, because I didn't know how I would. My doctor told me that stillbirths were very rare, that he hardly ever saw them, and that I shouldn't worry about having another child. He tried to be reassuring, but all he did was make me feel like a freak. I felt like I had failed myself and, even more, that I had failed my husband. I apologized to him a hundred times. And it broke his heart to hear me. To him it was a tragedy that happened to both of us, but I felt it was something that was wrong with me.
>
> A GRIEVING MOTHER OF A STILLBORN BABY BOY[3]

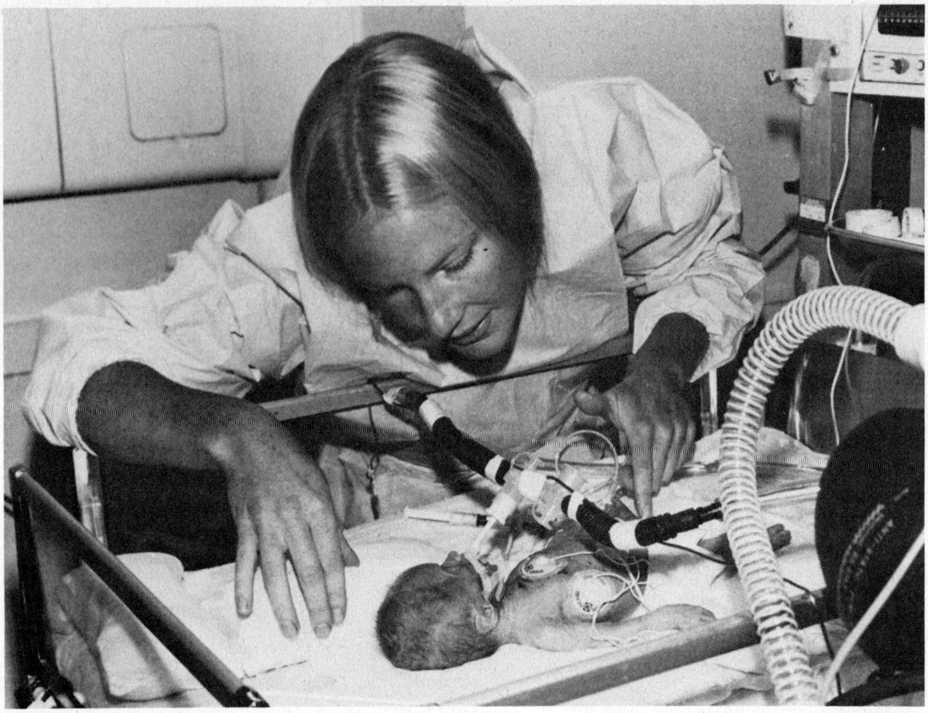

Parents usually respond to the birth of a premature infant with feelings of anxiety and grief. (Courtesy of the March of Dimes Birth Defects Foundation.)

ponents of the childbirth experience that could remain the same, rather than those that might differ if an unexpected event occurred during labor.[5,11]

9. Discuss with parents the reactions and feelings they might experience if an unexpected outcome should occur. You may want to relate these feelings to the process of grieving.[22,29] Rather than introducing the subject by stating, "We are now going to talk about grieving," this discussion can be conducted in a very nonthreatening way and in regard to all unexpected outcomes that might occur. Because a grieving response can result as a reaction to any loss or any outcome that is less than expected, this discussion does not have to be related only to the loss of the infant. Parents might momentarily "grieve" at finding that their child is a boy when they had hoped for a girl or having needed an epidural when they had wanted no anesthesia.

Have couples identify all the things they are hoping for in regard to their birth experience and list them in a column on a blackboard. Numerous responses will be given, ranging from hopes for a healthy baby, to having no pain, to having a preferred physician in attendance (Table 19–2). Once all "hopes" are identified, the couples will identify, with your help, what the "less than expected" outcomes for each hope might be. Place these responses in a second column (Table 19–2). More time should not be spent with the unexpected outcomes regarding the baby than with any of the other issues. The final step is to have parents identify the reactions or feelings they think they might ex-

TABLE 19–2. MODEL FOR DISCUSSION OF GRIEF

HOPING FOR	LESS THAN EXPECTED	TYPICAL FEELINGS
Short labor	Long labor	Fatigue, disappointment
Little pain	More pain	Anger, fear
Little medication and no anesthesia	Medication and anesthesia	Disappointment, self-blame, guilt
Healthy baby	Sick baby; baby with abnormality; baby dies	Denial, anguish, sadness, despair, depression
Girl/boy	Boy/girl	Slight disappointment
Preferred birth attendant	Different birth attendant than expected	Disappointment, anger
Vaginal birth	Cesarean birth	Loss of control, anger, disappointment, self-blame, sadness
Birthing room	Traditional labor room	Anger, disappointment

perience in regard to each less than expected outcome. Place these in a third column. Ask parents to identify actual feelings (fear, anger, sadness), not a process (grief). Then the teacher can summarize this information by relating the identified feelings to loss and the grieving process.[27] It is helpful for parents to realize that it would not be unusual for them to experience such emotional reactions in response to any unexpected outcome. A discussion of coping mechanisms and resources for help and support can be shared by the teacher at this time. This entire discussion takes approximately ten minutes, and is best conducted just prior to a class break.

As information is presented about any of the unexpected outcomes that might occur during labor, it is important to emphasize that the actual birth of one's baby is the most important aspect of the childbirth experience. Whether the birth occurrs vaginally, after a short labor, with minimal pain, with no medication, in a beautiful birthing room, and with one's favorite physician present, or whether there are some unexpected alterations in that perfect plan, is really not the most important issue. In fact, many of those details may be forgotten and may seem unimportant in the years to come. This is not to say that parents should not prepare and strive for their ideal. However, what is most important is that parents feel positive about their birth experience, the efforts they made to prepare for it and cope with it, and the baby that is the result of their efforts. These are the memories that will endure.

Grief Counseling

If the tragic unexpected outcome, neonatal death, should occur for a couple in the class, the childbirth teacher can be an important source of support for the parents. The teacher has the advantage of having already developed a therapeutic relationship with the parents during their pregnancy. Parents are likely to trust that their childbirth educator will understand their grief and not minimize it.[23,29,32]

However, childbirth educators are human—as with most people, they feel helpless when interacting with someone who has experienced such a loss. Many people fear that the "right" thing will not be said or done. The greatest mistake that can be made is to ignore the situation or neglect to offer the parents sympathy and support. The following strategies have been found to be most helpful to grieving parents:[23,29,32,40]

1. Acknowledge the loss. Send a card with a note or make a phone call to let the parents know you have heard about their baby and that you have been thinking about them.
2. Offer your support in a specific way. Ask if a visit from you would be helpful. Determine whether the parents could benefit from such basic help as child care or a few home-cooked

meals. The childbirth educator functions as a networking resource by identification and referral to community agencies and organizations that can assist the parents.

3. Encourage and allow communication. Let the parents know that you are not afraid to talk about their baby and that you will be glad to listen. Grieving parents want to talk about their feelings and their experience. The most important thing the childbirth educator can do is to listen. Do not be afraid of periods of silence. Encourage fathers as well as mothers to express their feelings.
4. Allow the expression of the parents' grief. Comments such as, "Don't cry," "Don't be angry," or "Don't blame yourself" are not helpful. Behaviors such as crying, anger, or self-blame are all part of the normal grieving process and should be openly accepted.
5. Allow the expression of your own grief. Don't be afraid to cry with parents. They will be touched to know you care so much about them. Use physical touch if appropriate to show your feelings.
6. Serve as a resource for parents to local support groups in your community which can provide continuing counseling for those who have lost a baby.[16,22]
7. Plan to make follow-up contact with parents at one month, 6 months, and on the infant's birthday. This contact can be made by telephone or by sending a card or note.

Offering support to grieving parents is never pleasant or easy; however, it is an extension of the role of the childbirth educator. As teachers, we must not only prepare parents for the positive aspects of the childbirth experience and share in the joys they experience, but we must also prepare parents for the unexpected and share in their grief.

IMPLICATIONS FOR RESEARCH

The research that has been done to date on unexpected outcomes of childbirth focuses primarily on the outcomes of cesarean birth. Studies related to the effects of prenatal education about cesarean birth have shown that classes met the perceived needs of participants,[19] that parents did retain the information given about cesarean birth,[15] and that classes positively affected maternal attitudes toward a cesarean birth.[20,46] A number of studies identifying the reactions and feelings of parents following cesarean birth have also been done.[7,14,18,34]

Further research needs to be conducted to replicate the studies that have been done to date. Research should also be directed toward unexpected outcomes other than cesarean birth. The following research questions could be addressed:

- What are the feelings and reactions of parents in response to alterations other than cesarean birth and fetal death? How severe and/or prolonged are these reactions—that is, do other unexpected outcomes result in perceived crisis for parents?
- How does childbirth education influence the resources and perceptions (the balancing factors) of parents to cope with a stressor event and avert crisis?
- Do parents retain information presented to them regarding a variety of potential unexpected outcomes? Is this information recalled when such a stressor event occurs?
- What specific strategies do childbirth educators utilize during the prenatal and postpartal periods to the crisis intervention process?
- How do parents view a discussion in their childbirth class of unexpected outcomes and the grieving process?
- How do parents perceive an unexpected outcome after one, three, and five years have passed?

The childbirth educator is in an ideal position to collect data that can answer these questions. The information obtained by such research will strengthen and improve the teacher's approach in dealing with unexpected outcomes in labor.

SUMMARY

Childbirth educators have an important role to play in preparing parents for the unexpected, as well as the expected, outcomes of labor. Two theoretical models are used as a basis for understanding how an unexpected event can lead to crisis and possibly to grief. Hill's ABCX model shows that the resources and perceptions of parents interact with the unexpected event and determine whether a crisis will result. Aguilera's crisis intervention paradigm illustrates variables that can be influenced by childbirth education to prevent crisis. Parents may experience emotional reactions as a result of an unexpected event, and the childbirth educator can use specific teaching and counseling strategies to meet their needs.

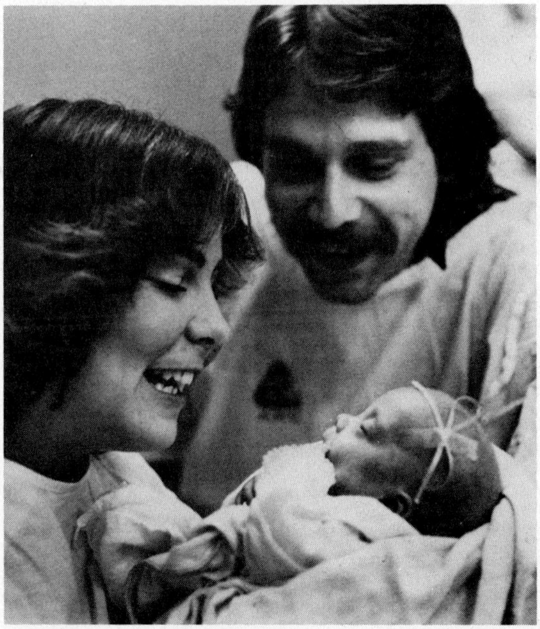

The resources and perceptions of the parents interact with the unexpected event and determine whether a crisis will result. Childbirth educators play an important role in preparing expectant parents for the unexpected childbirth experience. (Courtesy of the March of Dimes Birth Defects Foundation.)

References

1. Affonso, D. D. *Impact of Cesarean Childbirth.* Philadelphia: F. A. Davis, 1981.
2. Aguilera, D. C., Messick, J. M., and Farrel, M. S. *Crisis Intervention: Theory and Methodology.* St. Louis: C. V. Mosby, 1970.
3. Baird, S. F. Crisis intervention strategies. *In* Johnson, S. H. *High-Risk Pregnancy.* Philadelphia: J. B. Lippincott, 1979.
4. Baird, S. F. Crisis intervention theory in maternal-infant nursing. *JOGN Nursing* 5:30, 1976.
5. Berman, A. In the event of a cesarean. *Genesis* 7:21, 1985.
6. Borg, S., and Lasker, J. *When Pregnancy Fails: Families Coping with Miscarriage, Stillbirth, and Infant Death.* Boston: Beacon Press, 1981.
7. Bradley, C. F., Ross, S. E., and Warnyca, J. A prospective study of mother's attitudes and feelings following cesarean and vaginal births. *Birth and the Family Journal* 10:79, 1983.
8. Brown, W. A. Pregnancy fears. *Childbirth Educator* 1:53, 1981.
9. Burr, W. Families under stress. *In* McCubbin, H. I., Cauble, A. E., and Patterson, J. M. *Family Stress, Coping, and Social Support.* Springfield, IL: Charles C Thomas, 1982.
10. Christensen, A. Z. Coping with the crisis of a premature birth—one couple's story. *Maternal Child Nursing* 6:33, 1977.
11. Cohen, N. W. Minimizing emotional sequelae of cesarean childbirth. *Birth and the Family Journal* 4:114, 1977.
12. Colman, A. D., and Colman, L. L. *Pregnancy: The Psychological Experience.* New York: Herder and Herder, 1971.
13. Conner, B.S. Teaching about cesarean birth in traditional childbirth classes. *Birth and the Family Journal* 4:107, 1977.
14. Cox, B. E., and Smith, E. C. The mother's self-esteem after a cesarean delivery. *MCN* 7:309, 1982.
15. Denys, S. N. Do Lamaze parents retain cesarean information? *Genesis* 4:21, 1982.
16. Dzik, R. S. Transactional analysis in crisis intervention. *JOGN Nursing* 5:31, 1976.
17. Estok, P., and Lehman, A. Perinatal death: Grief support for families. *Birth* 10:17, 1983.
18. Erb, L., Hill, G., and Houston, D. A survey of parents' attitudes toward their cesarean births in Manitoba hospitals. *Birth* 10:85, 1983.
19. Fawcett, J., and Burritt, J. An exploratory study of antenatal preparation for cesarean birth. *JOGN Nursing* 14:224, 1985.
20. Hart, G. Maternal attitudes in prepared and unprepared cesarean deliveries. *JOGN Nursing* 9:243, 1980.
21. Hodapp, M. Cesarean information in childbirth classes. *Genesis* 4:19, 1982.

22. Hom, C. Teaching grief in a Lamaze class. *Genesis* 4:23, 1982.
23. Jimenez, S. Grief counseling. *Childbirth Educator* 3:42, 1983.
24. Kearns, P. C. Overcoming blockout. *Genesis* 4:11, 1982.
25. Klaus, M. H., and Kennell, J. H. *Maternal-Infant Bonding*. St. Louis: C. V. Mosby, 1976.
26. Kowalski, K., and Oxborn, M. R. Helping mothers of stillborn infants to grieve. *Maternal Child Nursing* 6:29, 1977.
27. Kübler-Ross, E. *On Death and Dying*. New York: Macmillan, 1969.
28. Kübler-Ross, E. The child will always be there, real love doesn't die. *Psychology Today* 10:48, 1976.
29. Kushner, L. Infant death and the childbirth educator. *MCN* 4:231, 1979.
30. Leach, L., and Sproule, V. Meeting the challenge of cesarean births. *JOGN Nursing* 13:191, 1984.
31. Lederman, R. P. *Psychosocial Adaptation in Pregnancy*. Englewood Cliffs, NJ: Prentice-Hall, 1984.
32. Limbo, R. K., and Wheeler, S. R. Coping with unexpected outcomes. NAACOG Update Series, Vol. 5, Lesson 3, 1986.
33. Marut, J. S., and Mercer, R. T. Comparison of primiparas' perceptions of vaginal and cesarean births. *Nursing Research* 28:260, 1979.
34. May, K. A., and Sollid, D. First-time fathers' responses to unanticipated cesarean birth: An exploratory study. *Genesis* 4:12, 1982.
35. May, K. A., and Sollid, D. Unanticipated cesarean birth from the father's perspective. *Birth* 11:87, 1984.
36. McCubbin, H. I., and Patterson, J. M. Family adaptation to crisis. *In* McCubbin, H. I., Cauble, A. E., and Patterson, J. M. *Family Stress, Coping and Social Support*. Springfield, IL: Charles C Thomas, 1982.
37. Parad, H. J. *Crisis Intervention: Selected Readings*. New York: Family Service Association of America, 1965.
38. Rapoport, L. The state of crisis—some theoretical considerations. *In* Parad, J. H. (ed.) *Crisis Intervention: Selected Readings*. New York, Family Service Association of America, 1965.
39. Rubin, R. Body image and self-esteem. *Nursing Outlook* 16:20, 1968.
40. Shaut, D., and Ligeikis, C. Interacting with bereaved parents. *Genesis* 4:20, 1968.
41. Shearer, B. Teaching about cesareans. *Childbirth Educator* 4:39, 1985.
42. Snyder, D. J. The high-risk mother viewed in relation to a holistic model of the childbearing experience. *JOGN Nursing* 8:164, 1979.
43. Weil, S. G. The unspoken needs of families during high-risk pregnancies. *American Journal of Nursing* 81:2047, 1981.
44. Wooten, B. Death of an infant. *Maternal Child Nursing* 10:257, 1981.
45. Young, R. K. Chronic sorrow: Parents' response to the birth of a child with a defect. *Maternal Child Nursing* 6:38, 1977.
46. Zacharias, J. F. Childbirth education classes: Effects on attitudes toward childbirth in high-risk indigent women. *JOGN Nursing* 10:265, 1981.

Beginning Quote

Redmon, L. Born too soon: One family's story. *Genesis* 5:18, 1983.

Boxed Quotes

1. Kearns, P. Overcoming blackout. *Genesis* 4:25, 1982.
2. Ordonez, G. Informing parents about premature labor and birth. *Genesis* 5:16, 1983.
3. Savage, B., and Simkin, D. *Preparation for Birth: The Complete Guide to the Lamaze Method*. New York: Ballantine Books, 1987, p. 420.

Section 4

PROMOTING WELLNESS

Childbirth education is best known as a means to help parents prepare actively for childbirth. Yet childbirth educators have had a second, less publicized focus, that of helping families move toward wellness. Why is this so?

Pregnancy is a time in people's lives when they are particularly open to considering lifestyle changes. As a society, the United States is currently in the midst of a rather dramatic shift from primarily illness-oriented health care to health care that promotes wellness. Childbirth educators have had years of wellness promotion experience and are intensifying their efforts to take advantage of their unique opportunity to reach families with wellness information.

What are the components of the wellness movement? According to Green,[2] who was speaking about wellness in general and not about childbirth education in particular, they are:

- Learning to recognize and manage stress,
- Acknowledging and learning to deal with feelings,
- Improving interpersonal relationships,
- Attending to illness in a health-promoting way,
- Relating to health care givers with adequate information to enable consumers to participate in making decisions, and
- Use of community self-help groups.

The childbirth literature is replete with articles and suggestions on these topics. These elements have been recommended for inclusion in childbirth education classes for many years. A common expression among some childbirth educators is ". . . psychoprophylaxis is a lifelong skill." This thought gives support to the claim that childbirth educators have long recognized the long-term health implications of their classes beyond childbirth.

It takes little extra time for the childbirth educator as she teaches each skill to point out the carryover into other parts of life. However, it does take conscious planning. "Is the time spent worthwhile?" the childbirth educator might ask. Just what is the potential of the wellness movement?

Almost unlimited potential, according to Ardell.[1] Ardell has described wellness as a superb vehicle for:

- Shaping corporate cultures to be more concerned with people and productivity,
- Changing families from dull, boring groups into invigorating, exciting, and wonderful support groups,
- Changing individuals from a focus on high living, alcohol dependence, and passivity to wholeness, self-responsibility, and energy development,
- Creating community cultures that are supportive of positive health and peace.[1]

This section of the book contains chapters on nutrition, exercise, sexuality, and building support systems during pregnancy. These are examples of childbirth education topics that can be addressed from a lifelong approach because they are also essential components of a healthy lifestyle.

References

1. Ardell, D.B. The history and future of wellness. *Wellness Perspectives* 1(1):3, Winter 1985.
2. Green, K. Health promotion: Its terminology, concepts, and modes of practice. *Health Values: Achieving High Level Wellness* 9(3):8, May June 1985.

chapter 20
NUTRITION

NORMA NEAHR WILKERSON

As a woman nurtures and carries the unborn fetus inside of her, she is already mothering on a biological level. She is nurturing her baby, giving it what it needs through her own body system.

Gayle Peterson

Pregnancy is a time in which an adequate supply of food and the nutrients it contains are absolutely essential to the life and growth of both mother and baby. The woman's body makes a remarkable series of physiological adjustments in order to preserve homeostasis. At the same time her body provides all essential nutrients for the growth and development of the fetus and placenta. Childbirth educators, health professionals, and the lay public have always known that the developing fetus cannot grow and mature normally without an adequate maternal diet. However, specific nutritional recommendations for the pregnant woman have varied greatly from time to time.

Prescientific Nutritional Advice

Before the science of nutrition was applied to pregnancy, many of the recommendations to pregnant women were based on beliefs gained through empiricism or informal observations rather than on research findings from controlled studies. Consequently, advice was not always accurate or health-promoting. For example, in the late 19th century pregnant women were encouraged to eat a fruit diet to decrease pain in childbirth. It was believed that "the fruit diet produced a fetus with small and flexible bones by removing from the mother's diet all substances thought to form bone, particularly wheat.'' A diet of apples, oranges, lemons, potatoes, and rice was believed to produce an infant ''finely proportioned and exceedingly soft, his bones being all in gristle.''[100]

Another example of empirical observation guiding maternal nutrition during pregnancy was the prescription to avoid salty or sour foods. It was believed that such food would cause the infant to be of a ''bad disposition,'' with a salty or sour personality. In other cases, foods such as warm liquids were recommended for their presumed ability to ease the process of labor.[104]

The problems of labor and birth in a given era have also greatly influenced the nutritional recommendations made to pregnant women by the medical community. For example, in the 19th century when rickets was endemic to the population, many women grew up with a contracted or abnormal pelvis. Physicians of this era advocated a low-carbohydrate diet during the last trimester of pregnancy in order to prevent development of large babies that would be much more difficult to deliver.[104]

This trend continued with the concept of limiting weight gain during pregnancy by restricting the total number of calories permitted in order to prevent ''toxemia of pregnancy.'' In Europe during World War I clinicians observed that there was an overall decrease in the incidence of eclampsia. Coincidentally, due to the decreased food supply, pregnant women gained less weight. Physicians concluded that restricting calories would protect pregnant women against the ''toxemias of pregnancy.'' This advice continued through the 1930's, 1940's, and 1950's, and was widely published in medical textbooks.[100] Although not scientifically based, the practice of limiting maternal weight gain to prevent toxemia continues in some obstetrical practices even today.

Early Research

Empirical observations during periods of famine and severe nutritional deprivation during wartime led to an appreciation of the consequences of malnutrition. As Worthington-Roberts reports, recent analyses of systematic and comprehensive data covering periods during both World Wars in England, Germany, and Holland allow researchers to conclude as follows:

1. The number of births is significantly reduced by severe nutritional deprivation at the time of conception.
2. Starvation during the first trimester increases the rates of premature birth, perinatal mortality, congenital malformations of the central nervous system, and death from meningitis in later life.
3. Undernutrition during the third trimester retards fetal growth and increases the incidence of low birth weight infants.[103]

Contemporary researchers fully comprehend the effects of such severe nutritional deprivation on pregnancy and infant outcome. However, the effects of less dramatic and more marginal nutritional deprivation in healthy populations are not as clear. Many nutritional studies have investigated the effects of the maternal diet on pregnancy and infant outcome.

The earliest studies addressed the basic questions of the quality of a pregnant woman's diet. In 1943, Burke and colleagues published a classic study in which the mothers' diets were rated as poor, fair, or good, using Recommended Dietary Allowances to rate the mother's dietary history.[14] Their results showed that mothers with good diets had superior infants; mothers with poor diets had inferior (problem) infants. Later studies focused on the question of whether supplementing the maternal diet with vitamins and minerals could improve infant outcomes. Researchers found that infant mortality and morbidity such as prematurity and toxemia could be reduced by providing both nutritional supplementation and nutritional advice to pregnant women.[8,23]

However, since these early studies were published, we now realize that many variables relate to infant outcome as measured by stillbirth, prematurity, and congenital anomalies. The early studies failed to control for epidemiological factors such as a lifetime of dietary habits, biochemical individuality, environmental factors, and bio-psycho-social stressors that impact on the maternal state of health.

Research cannot isolate diet during pregnancy and identify it as the sole cause of extreme outcomes such as stillbirth and congenital anomaly. For example, in a recent review of studies that investigated the relationship of maternal nutrition to length of gestation, it was concluded that "few dramatic effects of caloric deprivation or supplementation on duration of gestation . . . have been demonstrated."[50]

It has been shown that women living in poverty and chronically deprived of all resources, including optimal nutrition, have a higher incidence of low birth weight infants.[103] Furthermore, some studies, especially those comparing blacks with whites in the United States, show large differences in prematurity rates. However, it is not possible to conclude that diet alone is the factor responsible for such outcomes. There are other major variables associated with such socioeconomically deprived groups: access to health services, exposure to infection, working conditions, levels of stress, sexual practices, maternal age, and habits affecting health such as cigarette smoking and use of alcohol or other drugs.

Focus of Contemporary Research

Much research in biochemical nutrition has been done during the past several decades. However, during the 1950's and 1960's the majority of nutrition in pregnancy research centered on problems and pathology of pregnancy using clinic populations with a high incidence of high-risk pregnancies. In 1970, a landmark report by the National Research Council Committee on Maternal Nutrition made recommendations for future research.[19] Specifically, the committee recommended that studies of the following types, using women in good health as well as impaired health, be undertaken to provide a scientific basis for nutrition policies and practices as they relate to pregnancy and infant outcome.

First, it was recommended that in-depth studies of physiological changes that take place through the reproductive cycle, focusing on maternal-fetal relationships at the biochemical level, should be undertaken. The purpose of these studies is to understand how maternal nutrient intake at different phases of the life cycle influences reproduction. Furthermore, such research could clarify maternal adaptations during pregnancy, fetal growth and development, the sources of metabolites, and the mechanisms that maintain homeostasis. Specific relationships between the nutritional status and diet of the mother during pregnancy and the course and outcome of pregnancy would be documented in these studies.

Longitudinal studies of girls from all socioeconomic groups, beginning at the age of eight and continuing to the end of the natural growth period, were suggested. Epidemiological and field studies were recommended to assess the influences of geographical, social, and economic factors, including food availability, eating habits, and availability of health care.

Finally, the report recommended studies to determine educational methods to teach desirable eating habits to women in the childbearing years. These studies were to be undertaken in schools and clinics that provide health and educational services to children and adolescents. It is emphasized that particular concern be given to socioeconomic status and cultural and ethnic variables that affect food selection and eating habits.[19]

These recommendations emphasize the fact that many factors interact to determine the progress and outcome of any pregnancy. Examples are inherited characteristics, trauma, stress, or illness such as infection during pregnancy; exposure to harmful chemicals including drugs; smoking and drinking during pregnancy; age of the mother and past experiences with childbirth; and nutrition during and before pregnancy. Potentially, women can control some of these factors, such as the age at which they choose to become mothers and the choice to avoid harmful environmental contaminants and drugs. Other factors, such as inherited characteristics, are beyond their control.

However, when it comes to nutrition, women of childbearing age can select a balanced diet and use supplements both prior to and during pregnancy. Their task is to make choices on the basis of the scientific data available. Childbirth educators should base their recommendations on research evidence. The following literature review focuses on the studies that have been done in regard to current recommended daily allowances of nutrients during pregnancy. In addition, the common practices of supplementation with prenatal vitamins, minerals, and iron is reviewed.

Much of the current research in maternal nutrition continues to involve the problems of obstetrical practice, such as pregnancy-induced hypertension and premature rupture of membranes.[102] However, contemporary childbirth educators can base dietary recommendations on clinical studies conducted during the last two decades with relatively healthy populations and using scientific methods to validate empirical clinical observations.

REVIEW OF THE LITERATURE

Current recommended dietary allowances for pregnancy and lactation are summarized in Table 20–1. The most common and valuable food sources for the nutrients are also summarized in Table 20–1. These are the guidelines that most physicians follow in their recommendations on standard prenatal care for nutrition and supplementation.

The review of literature is organized according to the following major classifications: energy requirements, vitamins and minerals, fat-soluble vitamins (A, E, and K), water-soluble vitamins (C and the B complex), iron, zinc, and copper, and alcohol, caffeine, and nicotine.

Energy Requirements

Research has shown that the woman's weight before conception and the amount of weight she gains during pregnancy are independent influences that contribute to infant size in an additive manner.[43,82] If an overweight woman gains an excessive amount of weight during pregnancy, her infant will have a much greater chance of being large for gestational age at birth. Conversely, an underweight woman who does not gain enough weight during pregnancy may deliver an infant who is small for gestational age at birth. Therefore, energy requirements during pregnancy and lactation depend upon maternal weight before conception and to some extent upon weight gain during pregnancy. Table 20–1 lists the recommended dietary energy allowances in additional calories per day assuming that the woman is of normal prepregnancy weight.

Caloric requirements are based on several considerations. First, the mother's diet must be able to provide enough energy to build and sustain new fetal and placental tissue, amniotic fluid, maternal reproductive tissues, extra breast tissue, extra maternal fat and muscle stores, and increased maternal fluid and blood volumes.[16,44,88,92] Second, maternal intake must sustain the new tissue. Therefore, an increased metabolic expenditure of energy requires additional calories. Finally, as the pregnant woman's body enlarges, increased calories are needed for normal activities of daily living.

The amount of voluntary activity in which the pregnant woman engages is the most variable of these considerations. Body movement and functions require additional calories in proportion to the amount of weight the woman gains. Blackburn and Calloway[12] suggest that most pregnant women compensate for extra weight by slowing their pace and diminishing their activities as they gain weight in the last trimester of pregnancy. It is generally recommended that pregnant women can continue their normal activities but should do so in moderation as the pregnancy progresses.

Weight Gain

The National Research Council Committee on Maternal Nutrition considers an average total weight gain of 24 lb (11 kg) as necessary to meet the needs of both mother and fetus during pregnancy.[19,29] Normally, weight gain during the first trimester is minimal (1.5 to 3 lb). Subsequently, there should be a steady progressive weight gain averaging 0.77 to 0.88 lb per week (0.35 to 0.40 kg).[19,29] In addition, it is recommended that women whose prepregnancy weight is 10 per cent or more below the standard for their height and age should gain at a greater rate than the recommended average, up to 30 lb. Women who are overweight by 10 per cent or more at conception should not at-

TABLE 20–1. FOOD SOURCES AND RECOMMENDED DIETARY ALLOWANCE (RDA) FOR NUTRIENTS IN PREGNANCY (P) AND LACTATION (L)

NUTRIENT	RDA-P	RDA-L	FOOD SOURCES
Energy/kcal/day Increased by	150* 350†	500‡	Carbohydrates 45–55% Fat no more than 33% Protein 12–20%
Protein	74 gm	64 gm	Milk, cheese, eggs, meat, fish, poultry, grains, legumes, nuts
Fat-Soluble Vitamins			
Vitamin A (1000 RE–5000 IU)	1000 RE	1200 RE	Green and yellow vegetables, butter, cream, fortified margarine
Vitamin D (2.5 μg–100 IU)	10 μg	10–15 μg	Sunlight, fortified milk, and fortified margarine
Vitamin E	9–16 mg or 13–25 IU	10–15 mg or 13–25 IU	Leafy vegetables, vegetable oils, cereals, meat, fish, poultry, milk, cheese, eggs
Vitamin K	2 μg/kg body wt	2 μg/kg body wt	Green leafy vegetables, fruit, cereals, dairy products, meat, synthesized by flora in gut
Water-Soluble Vitamins			
Vitamin C	80 mg	100 mg	Citrus fruits, strawberries, melons, leafy vegetables, peppers, broccoli, tomatoes, potatoes
Thiamine (B_1)	1.4 mg	1.5 mg	Pork, beef, liver, nuts, legumes, whole grains, enriched flours, yeast, wheat germ, egg yolk
Riboflavin (B_2)	1.5 mg	1.7 mg	Milk, cheese, liver, leafy vegetables, beef, fish, enriched grains, eggs, poultry
Niacin	15 mg	18 mg	Meat, liver, yeast, whole grains, legumes, green vegetables, fish, peanuts
Pyridoxine (B_6)	2.6 mg	2.5 mg	Rice, bran, yeast, corn, wheat, liver, lean meat
Folacin (Folic Acid)	800 μg	500 μg	Leafy vegetables, legumes, liver yeast, lean beef, whole grains, broccoli, asparagus, oranges
Cobalamin (B_{12})	4 μg	4 μg	Liver, milk, cheese, egg, meats
Minerals			
Calcium	1200 mg	1200 mg	Milk, yogurt, cheese, egg yolk, leafy vegetables, whole grains
Phosphorus	1200 mg	1200 mg	Milk, cheese, lean meats, present in nearly all foods
Magnesium	450 mg	450 mg	Vegetables, occurs in most other foods
Iron	18 mg + 30–60 mg supplement	18 mg + 30–60 mg supplement	Liver, meats, eggs, nuts, legumes, dried fruits, leafy vegetables, whole grains, enriched cereals, potatoes
Zinc	20 mg	25 mg	Pork, beef, poultry, seafood, oysters, liver, eggs
Iodine	175 μg	200 μg	Seafood, iodized salt
Copper	3 mg	3 mg	Oysters, nuts, liver, corn oil margarine, dried legumes, some from drinking water depending on piping and hardness
Manganese	2.5–5 mg	2.5–5 mg	Nuts, whole grains, fruits, vegetables
Chromium	50–200 mg	50–200 mg	Meats, cheese, whole grains, condiments
Selenium	50–200 mg	50–200 mg	Seafood, liver, meat, grains, variable with regional soil

*1st trimester.
†2nd and 3rd trimesters.
‡Assuming appropriate weight gain in pregnancy
RDA's based on National Research Council, Recommended Dietary Allowances, 1980.

Abbreviations: gm = gram; mg = milligram; μg = microgram; RE = retinol equivalents; IU = international units

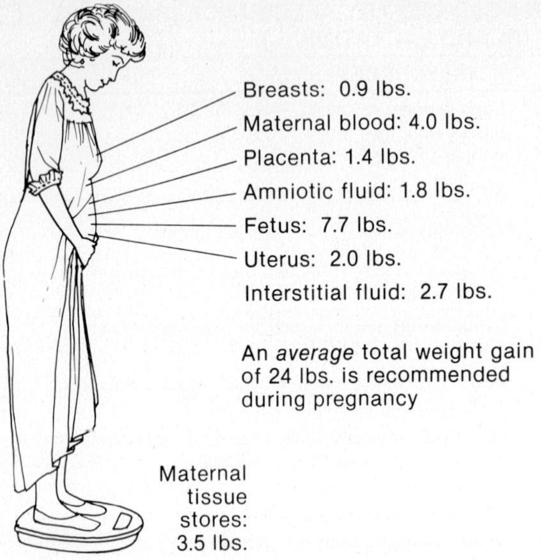

FIGURE 20–1. Weight gain during pregnancy.

tempt to diet and they should gain at least 16 lb (7 to 8 kg).

The pattern of maternal weight gain is more important than the total gain in weight over the entire pregnancy. Erratic gains or losses may signal serious problems. For example, a sudden increase during the latter part of the pregnancy may indicate developing preeclampsia or pregnancy-induced hypertension. Currently, no research evidence suggests that total weight gain greater than 24 pounds is a cause of pregnancy-induced hypertension. Therefore, the previously mentioned practice of limiting weight gain to prevent this complication is not justified.

The Underweight Pregnant Woman

Recently, researchers have studied pregnancy outcomes of underweight women. Findings indicate that underweight women have a significantly increased incidence of anemia, cardiopulmonary problems, endometritis, and premature rupture of membranes.[24] Furthermore, although no difference was found in the incidence of fetal growth retardation and perinatal mortality, there was a higher incidence of prematurity and low Apgar scores. Edwards and colleagues also investigated the mean birthweights of infants born to underweight women and found that the incidence of low birthweight was higher, especially if the underweight women were anemic. This finding was true even if the anemic women gained adequate weight during pregnancy. These infants were followed during the first year of life and found to be below the 25th percentile for weight correlated with height by one year of age. These researchers also concluded, although their data were limited, that neurological development was slower in the infants of underweight women.

Another researcher hypothesized that fetal growth as determined by maternal nutrition is related to maternal blood pressure and uteroplacental perfusion.[63] He found that maternal blood pressure increased with increases in maternal weight before conception and net pregnancy weight gain. Net pregnancy weight gain was defined as the woman's pregnancy weight gain minus the weight of her infant and the placenta.

If women weighed less than 100 lb prior to pregnancy and their net pregnancy weight gains were under 13 lb, their infants showed significant fetal growth retardation. If the women weighed over 100 lb, their net pregnancy weight gain had less influence on the infant's birthweight. From these findings it seems that maternal nutrient stores are particularly vital both prior to conception and during pregnancy. If the woman's stores are depleted prior to pregnancy, it will be particularly difficult for the fetus to compete for needed nutrients from her daily diet. Therefore, a recommendation is for maternal weight to be normal prior to conception.

The Overweight Pregnant Woman

Obstetric complications appear to be the most significant outcome of obesity in pregnancy.[56,69,93] A number of researchers have found significantly higher rates of toxemia, diabetes, pyelonephritis, hypertension, wound complications such as infected episiotomy, thromboembolism, and maternal death from pulmonary embolism among obese women. Obesity is defined as prepregnancy weight 30 per cent or more above the average for height and age.

Infants born to obese women have significantly

higher birthweights than infants of normal-weight women.[25] Edwards and colleagues found that obese women had larger infants even when their total weight gain and caloric intake were below the recommended level for pregnancy.[25] These findings suggest that it may be appropriate to recommend a *well-balanced diet with moderate caloric restriction* in obese pregnant women. Their nutritional stores are apparently used to provide the developing fetus with required nutrients.

Protein

Protein in the maternal diet should be of the highest quality. The maternal diet must provide enough protein for expansion of maternal blood volume, uterus, and breasts. In addition, fetal and placental proteins are formed from the maternal pool of amino acids. Thus, the protein allowance must cover maternal physiological needs as well as the needs for growth and development of the fetus.

Generally, the nutritive value of protein is determined by three factors: its amino acid composition, the percentage of absorbed nitrogen retained by the body when the protein is ingested, and the protein efficiency ratio.[29] The protein efficiency ratio is determined by an animal's rate of growth in relation to the protein ingested. On the basis of this, values for protein quality have been determined. The foods listed in Table 20–1 are sources of high-quality proteins for the maternal diet, and their use should be promoted in childbirth education classes on nutrition. Furthermore, protein-rich foods are usually the same as those that provide adequate amounts of trace nutrients such as zinc and iron, as well as vitamins such as the B complex.

There has been controversy over the past two decades in regard to the amount of dietary protein required by pregnant women. As illustrated in Table 20–1, the current recommendation by the National Research Council is an additional 30 gm per day during pregnancy. The total daily intake for women over 18 years of age should be 0.8 gm per kg per day, plus the additional 30 gm per day to support the pregnancy. The adolescent (15 to 18 years of age) should consume 0.9 gm per kg per day, plus the additional 30 gm per day.

Studies of pregnancy outcome in women who consume inadequate amounts of protein are difficult to interpret. Inadequate protein is usually associated with inadequate intake of total nutrients in poverty situations. Both general malnutrition, with a variety of nutritional deficiencies, and inadequate protein have been associated with toxemia of pregnancy in human and animal studies.[13,54,73] Since the incidence of toxemia continues to be higher in low socioeconomic populations who have relatively poor food supplies, the role of overall malnutrition continues to be a primary area of investigation.

On the other hand, Williams and colleagues[101] reported that women who developed toxemia had higher daily intakes of protein in their diets. In addition, a supplementation study of poor black women in New York[76] found that the use of high protein supplements was associated with a higher rate of premature infants and neonatal death. These studies have created some controversy among researchers regarding the intake of protein in maternal diets.

It is currently suggested that providing protein supplements with more than 20 per cent of calories from protein sources may be a factor in fetal growth retardation. Limiting protein to 20 per cent or less of calories will promote optimal fetal growth and desired increases in birthweights.[77] Even though data are currently limited, this controversy highlights the fact that we do not know as much as we would like to know about prenatal nutrition. The data support the contention that more is not always better. Given the current state of knowledge it seems wise to recommend that the maternal diet be balanced in regard to protein, carbohydrates, and fats.

Vitamins and Minerals

While precise requirements of vitamins and minerals in the human diet are still the subject of intense investigation, recommendations have been stated on the basis of current data from many animal studies and some human studies conducted in both natural and controlled environments. While the concept of biochemical individuality (the theory that ideal nutrient requirements may vary from person to person) is central to research in this area, the related concept of a cellular nutritional link between mother and fetus is also essential in the interpretation of these studies. In other words, individual requirements may be based upon many variables such as lifestyle, exposure to stressors, and inherited characteristics. As one researcher stated, when malnutrition is endemic, the cellular link from generation to generation impedes nutritional evolution. Preconception nutritional screening and therapy may be necessary in order to secure for the baby its full genetic capabilities.

In an excellent review of animal and human research related to vitamin and mineral deficiencies and excesses, abnormalities have been reported ranging from minor to major malformations of every body system.[103] These findings underscore the value of nutritional balance in the maternal diet. The remainder of this review focuses on selected vitamins, minerals, and trace elements that are currently receiving the most research attention.

Fat-Soluble Vitamins (A, E, and K)

Excessive amounts of vitamin A have been associated with vitamin A toxicity in children and adults. Vitamin A toxicity in pregnant women is believed to be responsible for congenital malformations,[11] based on current research showing teratogenic effects with pigs, monkeys, and rats. The allowance during pregnancy is increased from 800 retinol equivalents (RE) to 1000 RE to compensate for fetal storage of the vitamin.[29] (1000 RE is the equivalent of 5000 IU.) Since vitamin A is efficiently stored in the liver, a well-nourished woman will have an adequate supply that can be utilized by her body during pregnancy. The recommended intake can be adequately obtained from a balanced diet. Therefore, some researchers suggest that there is no need for vitamin A supplementation in women who are healthy and have access to a balanced diet.

Table 20–2 summarizes the standard prenatal supplementation commonly prescribed by obstetricians in the United States for pregnant women. It can be seen that the amount of vitamin A in this supplement is over the recommended dietary allowance as described in Table 20–1. While many women may need some supplementation because of inadequate diets, it seems questionable to prescribe a supplement in amounts above the RDA routinely for all pregnant women.

TABLE 20–2. COMPARISON OF TWO STANDARD PRENATAL SUPPLEMENTS* WITH RECOMMENDED DIETARY ALLOWANCES (RDA)

NUTRIENT	DOSE A	DOSE B	PERCENTAGE OF RDA†
Fat-Soluble Vitamins			
Vitamin A	8000 IU	8000 IU	160
Vitamin D	400 IU	400 IU	100
Vitamin E	30 IU	30 IU	100
Vitamin K	none	none	0
Water-Soluble Vitamins			
Vitamin C	90 mg	100 mg	150–167
Thiamine (B_1)	2.55 mg	3.00 mg	150–224
Riboflavin (B_2)	3.00 mg	3.40 mg	150–170
Niacin	20 mg	20 mg	100
Pyridoxine (B_6)	10 mg	4 mg	400–160
Folacin	1 mg	1 mg	125
Cobalamin	12 μg	12 μg	150
Minerals			
Calcium	200 mg	250 mg	15–19
Phosphorus	none	none	0
Magnesium	100 mg	25 mg	22–6
Iron	65 mg	60 mg	361–333
Zinc	none	25 mg	0–167
Iodine	150 μg	0.3 mg	85–170
Copper	none	2 mg	0–66
Manganese	trace	none	trace-0

*Supplements: A = Stuart Natal (Stuart Pharmaceuticals; Wilmington, DE)
B = Materna (Lederle Labs; Pearl River, NY)

†Percentages computed from values published by National Research Council, 1980.

Other researchers have reported that both carotene and vitamin E are increased in breastmilk during the first four days after birth and decline significantly as lactation progesses. In one study the range of vitamin A intake reported by the mothers was from 761 to 1883 IU per day. This intake was well below the recommended dietary allowance as described in Table 20–1. The range of vitamin E intake reported by the women was from 9 to 21 mg per day. It was concluded that elevated milk carotene and vitamin E levels in breastmilk are a compensatory response by the mammary gland. As a relationship between maternal dietary intake of these vitamins and subsequent levels in early breastmilk was not apparent in this study, it was further concluded that these vitamins are stored in the woman's breast tissue during the entire pregnancy. Furthermore, high levels in colostrum may represent a "loading dose" for the neonate.

There has been some interest in preventing hemolytic anemia of infancy due to vitamin E deficiency by providing injectable supplements to the woman before birth. However, since this problem develops when the infant is six to eight weeks old, it is recommended that the infant at risk be given oral supplements after birth.[57]

Vitamin K has been studied as it relates to hemorrhagic disease of the newborn.[67] The normal newborn has a sterile bowel; therefore, vitamin K manufacture by bacteria in the intestine is limited. Currently, the consensus among physicians is to supplement the newborn immediately after birth with an injectable form of synthetic vitamin K rather than administer vitamin K to the woman before birth.

Water-Soluble Vitamins (C and the B Complex)

The current emphasis on vitamin C supplementation for augmenting the immune system in relation to treatment of the common cold has led some women to take extremely large doses (1500 to 3000 mg) on a daily basis. The recommended dietary allowance (Table 20–1) is modest by these standards. The total recommendation of 80 to 100 mg per day is easy to obtain from a balanced diet. As indicated in Table 20–1, vitamin C is present in a variety of fruits and vegetables. The standard prenatal supplement (Table 20–2) provides 100 per cent of the recommended daily allowance. Some researchers report that scurvy developed in the first month of life in newborns of women who ingested massive amounts of vitamin C during pregnancy.[18,66] It is hypothesized that such cases of neonatal scurvy are the result of ineffective fetal metabolism due to dependency on the maternal source of vitamin C.

Although vitamin C deficiencies have not been associated with poor pregnancy outcomes in humans studied, some effects have been reported in women who smoke. Hervada[36] reports both decreased milk production and lower levels of vitamin C in the breastmilk of smoking women.

Folacin (folic acid, folate) requirements have been estimated to double during pregnancy.[29] This is due to the large numbers of red blood cells which the mother must produce as well as the need to support fetal and placental tissue growth.[47] The most frequent problem encountered with deficiencies of folacin are pre-anemic states and various forms of anemia. Women in these pathological states are at greater risk of abruptio placentae, abortion, and fetal growth retardation.[22,32,37]

Folacin deficiencies have also been reported in cases of neural tube defects (spina bifida) that occur very early in the pregnancy.[94] Folacin and vitamin B_6 are also reported to be the vitamins found most frequently at low or unacceptable levels in women of Mexican ancestry in the U.S.[40] Long-term oral contraceptive use has also been found to decrease folacin levels in women of childbearing age. It is recommended that these women be carefully evaluated for folic acid status prior to conception.[103] These findings support the potential need for supplementation during the preconceptional stage of a woman's life, especially if her folic acid status is found to be deficient.

Pyridoxine, or vitamin B_6, has received much attention recently. With the increased use of oral contraceptives there is a greater risk for pyridoxine deficiency in women of childbearing age. Researchers report decreased serum pyridoxine levels in women who have used oral contraceptives for one or more years.[29]

In other studies, pyridoxine levels have been related to infant outcomes. For example, infants had significantly lower one-minute Apgar scores when their mothers had low serum pyridoxine levels.[72] Schuster and colleagues[79] report higher one-minute Apgar scores in infants born to mothers who had supplementation with 7.5 mg or more of pyridoxine during pregnancy.

Recently Kirksey and associates[46] report that low maternal pyridoxine intake may contribute to neurological abnormalities in the breast-fed infant. Animal studies have also demonstrated that litter weights of rats are decreased and neuromotor development is impaired if maternal pyridoxine levels are low.[4,5] Since embryonic brain growth occurs during the first weeks after conception, and fetal brain growth is most rapid during the last trimester, these researchers conclude that maternal supplementation is most necessary before conception. Furthermore, normal maternal pyridoxine levels at birth are associated with adequate birthweight, length, and head circumference.

Evidence has also been presented to demonstrate that unsupplemented lactating mothers have a significantly lower intake of pryridoxine than the recommended dietary allowance. In addition, their breastmilk does not provide the recommended dietary allowance of 0.3 mg per day to their infants.[29,71] Hyperirritability and seizures in the infant have been associated with depressed serum levels of pyridoxine.[80]

In 1979, Greentree named vitamin B_6 the "milk-inhibiting" vitamin and advised that it should be deleted from multivitamin supplements for lactating women.[31] His recommendation was based on research with megadoses of vitamin B_6 (200 to 800 mg per day) in which lactation had been suppressed due to depressed levels of prolactin in supplemented women.

Andon and colleagues[6] studied this issue and report that physiological doses (4 to 10 mg per day) as a supplement do not depress prolactin or suppress lactation. Therefore, it seems that the standard prenatal supplement (Table 20–2) is within physiological norms. Compliance with vitamin B_6 supplementation is particularly relevant if the woman has used oral contraceptives on a long-term basis prior to her pregnancy.

Calcium, Phosphorus, and Vitamin D

The relationships among the minerals calcium and phosphorus and vitamin D have been studied extensively during the past two decades. In 1975, a classic review of calcium metabolism in the pregnant woman, fetus, and newborn was published by Pitkin.[67] These investigations have described calcium homeostasis as a complex, dynamic process. It consists of the relationship between a large source of calcium in the skeleton and a much smaller reserve in extracellular body fluids. The gastrointestinal tract influences calcium metabolism in regard to the amount that is ingested in the diet. The main mechanism of calcium excretion is through the kidneys.

During pregnancy extracellular fluid volume expands, renal function increases, and calcium is transported to the developing fetus as the fetal skeleton mineralizes. Therefore, it can be seen that a woman's calcium requirements increase dramatically during pregnancy. Her diet must not only provide enough calcium for the developing infant, but it must prevent demineralization of her own skeletal system. Most researchers agree that, under normal circumstances, maternal bone mineral content is not significantly decreased during pregnancy.[67,68] If, however, maternal calcium stores are depleted through multiple, closely spaced pregnancies or if her dietary calcium is inadequate, demineralization may occur.

It has been reported that when low calcium intake is combined with lack of sunlight to the exposed skin, as occurs in some Asian cultures, maternal demineralization of skeletal bone (osteomalacia) occurs.[68] Since the circulating form of vitamin D is not substantially decreased by pregnancy itself but by the amount of exposure to ultraviolet light,[68] the importance of vitamin D intake and sunlight to augment calcium metabolism is reinforced.

An ongoing debate in the literature is the potential relationship of inadequate calcium intake to pregnancy-induced hypertension. Some researchers have reported that the incidence of seizures in this complication of pregnancy is decreased with increased calcium intake.[68] In addition, arterial blood pressure has been found to be decreased in calcium-supplemented women and to be increased in unsupplemented women.[68,102]

Others report no significant differences in calcium levels among normal pregnant women, women with chronic hypertension, and women with pregnancy-induced hypertension.[68] These results emphasize the controversy surrounding the role of calcium in hypertension, both in pregnancy and in chronic hypertensives who are not pregnant. Research continues on the role of calcium as a causative factor in the vasoconstriction which occurs with hypertension.

The balance of calcium to phosphorus has been studied for a number of years in relation to the leg cramps that some women experience in pregnancy.[68,103] On the basis of this research, treatment of leg cramps has included limiting the intake of milk to only one or two glasses a day, because of its high phosphorus content. Aluminum hydroxide gel has also been prescribed to make the available phosphate insoluble in the intestinal tract, thereby preventing it from interfering with calcium metabolism. Calcium supplements with nonphosphate calcium salts have also been recommended. The prevailing opinion today is that the amount of milk in the diet should not be limited to treat leg cramps. Instead, calcium-phosphorus balance should be promoted by the avoidance of foods that are high in phosphorus, such as processed meats, salty snacks, and carbonated beverages.[104]

Iron, Zinc, and Copper

The relationship of iron to fetal well-being and maternal health has been well established. Iron deficiency anemia is the most common problem associated with inadequate iron intake in the maternal diet. The demand for iron is significantly increased during pregnancy. Increased iron is required to manufacture red blood cells as the woman's blood volume increases and her bone marrow becomes more active. Additionally, the fetus and placenta must develop from maternal stores of iron and hemoglobin. Finally, the woman must have enough stored iron to compensate for the blood loss associated with childbirth.

When a woman's body stores of iron are depleted, hemoglobin synthesis is reduced. Low hemoglobin increases the workload on the pregnant woman's heart as her body attempts to compensate for reduced oxygen supplies both to placental tissues and to the fetus.[103]

Low hemoglobin has also been associated with complications of pregnancy such as higher rates of spontaneous abortion, stillbirth, perinatal death, low birthweight, and premature birth.[103] Furthermore, as Worthington-Roberts et al. emphasize, the anemic woman is less able to tolerate the stress of perinatal hemorrhage, and she is more likely to develop a postpartum infection.[104]

Another interesting phenomenon associated with iron deficiency is the behavior called *pica*—the eating of clay, starch, or dirt. Kitay and Harbort[47] report that one fourth of pregnant women with iron deficiency anemia engage in pica. Previously, pica was believed to be the cause of iron deficiency anemia. It is now proposed that iron deficiency anemia is a stimulus for this abnormal behavior.[20]

The following conclusions are stated by Crosby[20] regarding pica. First, if either iron deficiency anemia or pica is diagnosed during pregnancy, an assessment should be initiated for the other. The discovery of pica may be the first sign of iron deficiency anemia. In addition, the mother's cultural background may influence the abnormal craving, which is not always for a nonfood substance such as dirt, starch, or clay. Finally, the mother may be inhibited in regard to discussing the behavior because she may experience a sense of guilt or shame in regard to it.

Two additional findings in relation to iron deserve mention here. During an investigation of the bioavailability of zinc it was learned that iron supplements decrease the intestinal absorption of zinc.[33,58,85] Furthermore, investigators report an elevated serum iron level in cases of toxemia.[27] While the significance of these findings in relation to iron supplementation is still under investigation, it seems appropriate to be conservative in the use of iron supplements during pregnancy.

It is generally accepted that the typical U.S. diet is unable to provide the additional iron needed to support a normal pregnancy; therefore, daily iron supplements are recommended.[29] Prenatal supplements of simple ferrous salts from 30 to 65 mg daily are generally prescribed for pregnant women (Table 20–2) by the medical community.

Zinc is essential for normal growth and development of the fetus and for the antibacterial activity of amniotic fluid.[78,87] It is also believed to be important in relation to uterine contractility and the initiation of labor.[107] Serum proteins are responsible for the transport of zinc in the body, and zinc requirements have been found to increase during pregnancy.[107] Therefore, the maternal diet and maternal absorption of zinc are primary factors in its availability.

The role of zinc in pregnancy and infant outcome has received much research attention during the past decade. Depressed serum zinc levels have been associated with infection, fetal distress, and tissue fragility, leading to increased incidence of lacerations of the birth canal during delivery.[62] Depressed zinc levels have also been associated with pregnancy-induced hypertension,[40] fetal malformations,[15,17,38] low birthweight,[59] intrauterine growth retardation, and intrapartum hemorrhage.[58] These reports support the role of zinc in augmenting the immune system, synthesizing protein, improving collagen synthesis and tissue integrity, and diminishing the risk of maternal complications such as toxemia and hemorrhage.

Mukherjee and colleagues,[62] in a well-controlled study of 450 pregnant women, found a significant association between high plasma folate levels and low zinc levels and the occurrence of fetal distress (indicated by meconium in amniotic fluid) and tissue fragility (anal, rectal, and cervical lacerations). These findings are consistent with other experimental findings which indicate that intestinal zinc absorption is decreased with dietary monoglutamyl folate supplementation.[60] As Table 20–2 indicates, standard prenatal supplements commonly provide 1000 μg of folic acid (folacin) as monoglutamyl folate.

As previously discussed, ferrous iron can also inhibit intestinal absorption of zinc.[33] Other researchers report a relationship between high calcium intakes and decreased zinc absorption in both pregnancy and lactation.[49] These observations suggest that excessive self-supplementation with folic acid, calcium, and/or iron could have adverse effects on maternal zinc nutriture leading to complications of pregnancy. Needless to say, this is an area that merits further investigation, especially in view of the fact that these are common components of standard prenatal supplementation.

In regard to zinc supplementation during lactation, it has also been reported that both maternal serum and milk zinc concentrations are highest during early lactation. Colostrum and transitional milk have higher zinc levels than mature milk. *Mature milk* was defined as milk collected one month and beyond during the course of lactation.[49] Mothers in this study were followed for one year and milk samples were included in data analysis up to nine months of lactation. Both maternal serum and breastmilk zinc concentrations decreased as lactation progressed.

Furthermore, the length of time required for serum zinc concentrations to normalize after pregnancy and lactation is not yet known. These findings have implications for women who have another pregnancy prior to completion of breastfeeding a previous infant. In addition, it is suggested that women who plan to breastfeed for more than six months could benefit from increasing their intake of foods high in zinc without increasing their protein intake. If this is not possible, a supplement might be helpful, but it should be within the physiological range of 15 to 25 mg.[49]

Copper has not been studied as extensively as iron and zinc in relation to human pregnancy and infant outcome. It has been reported that zinc and copper compete for intestinal absorption sites in experimental animals.[28] Recently, teratogenic effects of prenatal copper deficiency have also been reported in animals.[41] Researchers in South Wales as reported by Tapper and colleagues[89] described a statistically significant correlation between low copper in drinking water, low maternal serum copper levels, and neural tube defects (spina bifida) in humans. American researchers have not replicated these observations.[98] Finally, it has been suggested that adequate copper in maternal serum is not possible without the use of a supplement.[89]

Even though research in this area is currently inconclusive, one of the examples of a standard prenatal supplement (Table 20–2) does contain 2 mg of copper. The recommended dietary allowance (Table 20–1) is 3 mg. Therefore, the supplement seems to be within a physiological range. These findings suggest a tendency for drug companies to add trace minerals to their supplements in the hope that future research will confirm the need. This could also be translated into a "better safe than sorry" attitude. However, when the relationships among iron, calcium, and folacin are considered as they are reported to inhibit zinc absorption, it might be prudent to limit self-supplementation if the diet is well balanced.

Alcohol, Caffeine, and Nicotine

Any discussion of prenatal nutrition must include current findings in regard to these commonly consumed items. It is now widely accepted that alcohol is teratogenic to the human fetus,[9,10] causing the fetal alcohol syndrome. *Fetal alcohol syndrome* is described as a condition of the newborn associated with a pattern of abnormalities. Impaired growth and development (including microcephaly), eye defects, facial abnormalities (including cleft palate), and other anomalies such as cardiac defects, female genital anomalies, and skeletal-joint abnormalities are seen in the syndrome.[103]

Alcohol consumption has also been associated with intrauterine growth retardation and low birthweight,[106] central nervous system abnormalities, behavioral and learning difficulties,[81] and disturbed infant sleep and wake cycles.[75] Other researchers describe complications of pregnancy such as abruptio placentae and spontaneous abortion due to alcohol consumption.[34,48]

The majority of the research on alcohol in pregnancy has shown negative effects in women who consume large to moderate amounts before and over the entire course of the pregnancy.[105] Whether limited consumption is harmful remains a controversial issue. Some researchers[90] report that ingesting limited amounts of alcohol was not shown to be related to infant birthweight, length, head circumference, or minor physical anomalies commonly associated with the fetal alcohol syndrome. Others have reported fetal growth retardation in infants of alcoholic women who stop drinking during pregnancy.[53]

It is difficult to measure limited, moderate, and heavy use of alcohol in pregnancy. Research in this area uses data reported by the subjects. Alcohol users are notorious for underreporting of the amounts actually ingested. It is impossible ethically to do human research with measured amounts of alcohol. For these reasons, and given current knowledge of fetal alcohol syndrome, it seems prudent to view alcohol as a toxic, teratogenic substance. Its use in pregnancy should not be recommended, and even limited use should be viewed as potentially dangerous.

The relationship of caffeine to pregnancy and infant outcome has also been studied but not as extensively in humans as in research animals. In animal models massive doses of caffeine that would be the equivalent of much more than 30 or 40 cups of coffee per day are used. The results of these studies do indicate that caffeine is teratogenic, causing birth defects such as defective fingers and toes.[103]

Weathersbee and associates[99] surveyed 800 U.S. households in an epidemiological study of caffeine use. They report an increased incidence of stillbirths, spontaneous abortion, and premature birth in women who consumed more than 600 mg of caffeine daily. While research in this area is limited, it seems appropriate to view caffeine as a vasoactive drug, with stimulant properties, which could influence uterine and placental perfusion. Under these circumstances prudent use of caffeine-containing beverages during pregnancy is supported.

Caffeine use during lactation should also be considered. It has been shown that small amounts, 1 per cent or less, of the caffeine a mother ingests in a cup of coffee pass into her breastmilk.[95] A mother who drinks more than 8 to 10 cups of caffeine-containing beverages daily may have an infant who is hyperactive, has difficulty sleeping, and startles more easily.[51] These effects may also be noted in the infant of a mother who consumes caffeine on a regular basis but in smaller amounts. While there appears to be great individual variation among infants to the effects of caffeine, these effects can be compounded by cigarette smoking.[55]

Although a small amount of alcohol in beer or wine may have a beneficial relaxing effect on the nursing mother and augment the letdown reflex, large amounts of caffeine, alcohol, and nicotine have been reported to interfere with the letdown reflex in breastfeeding mothers.[104] The interaction of all of these drugs in a woman who drinks coffee, caffeine-containing soft drinks, and alcohol, and smokes may be of special concern while she is breastfeeding.

Since use of alcohol, caffeine, and nicotine is so interrelated in the lifestyle of those who consume these so-called ''soft drugs,''[30] a brief overview of the effects of nicotine on pregnancy and infant outcome will be described here. In spite of protestations from the U.S. tobacco industry, there is considerable consensus among competent researchers that cigarette smoking has a deleterious effect on human health.

Smoking during pregnancy has been associated with an increased incidence of maternal problems and complications. Researchers report problems such as infertility,[7] spontaneous abortion and congenital malformations,[1,35] decreased maternal hemoglobin levels,[86] decreased placental perfusion,[70] smaller placentas, elevated maternal blood pressure,[96] and complications of labor.[26]

Impaired fetal growth and development has also been associated with maternal smoking. Research in this area suggests that smoking is a factor in an increased incidence of intrauterine growth retardation[61] and low birthweight.[1,45,96] Since these findings were first reported in 1957, more than 45 studies of over a half million births have confirmed them. Furthermore, a dose-response relationship exists. That is to say, the more a woman smokes during pregnancy, the lower the birthweight of her infant. However, if a woman quits smoking during the first trimester of her pregnancy, it is generally believed that her risk of delivering a low birthweight infant is no greater than that of a nonsmoker.

Other fetal effects that have been identified include an increased incidence of congenital malformations[35,65] and fetal heart rate accelerations and decelerations.[52] Smoking has also been implicated in sudden infant death syndrome,[1,45] respiratory distress syndrome,[21] neonatal apnea,[1] and delayed mental development in childhood.[64]

On the basis of these findings, the implications for prenatal education and self-help approaches to intervention during pregnancy to promote cessation of smoking are obvious. The following recommendations are directed to this goal as well as to the goal of promoting health through education related to nutrition.

IMPLICATIONS FOR PRACTICE

Childbirth educators can appreciate the complex physiological and biochemical changes that occur during the course of pregnancy. If all fetomaternal metabolic pathways are to progress normally and produce a healthy infant who can function as a distinct organism at birth, the mother must ingest a wholesome, balanced diet from the moment of conception. Furthermore, the National Research Council (NRC) Committee on Maternal Nutrition has recommended that educators and clinicians give careful attention to the preconception nutrition of women of childbearing age. The relationship of general nutritional health and lifestyle prior to conception and pregnancy outcome is just as important as nutrition during pregnancy.

Childbirth education classes present an opportunity in which the good habits for a lifetime can be encouraged and reinforced. If unhealthy practices have played a part in the lifestyle of those in childbirth education classes, such adult learners are most apt to accept changes for the good of their developing infant.[2] A major goal of the childbirth educator is to reinforce these changes in order to make them permanent habits. Young adults who learn to appreciate the value of good nutrition as a cellular link from generation to generation will be able to teach good habits to their children. The cycle of good nutrition can eventually overcome genetic predispositions to poor nutritional health.

A Balanced Diet

The first major recommendation for childbirth educators is to emphasize the need for a balanced diet in maternal nutrition. Table 20–3 describes a basic food plan that provides the variety required for a balanced diet during pregnancy and lactation. Without variety, balance is not possible.

Furthermore, the maternal diet should contain all the essentials. The fact that a woman is encouraged to gain up to an average of 24 pounds during her pregnancy should not be taken to mean that she can eat all the "empty calorie" and "junk" foods she has learned to avoid. After she has selected all the required nutrients, if more calories remain in her daily allotment, snack foods can be added. Fruit desserts, fruit beverages, nuts, peanut butter, pasta, whole grain baked breads or muffins, and cheese are examples of foods that may be added in moderation. These are not only nutritious snacks, but they are considerably less expensive than processed, commercially prepared snacks such as chips and dips, candy, snack crackers, and ice cream.

Since nutritional requirements are increased during pregnancy, the pregnant woman needs an additional 300 kcal per day. The nursing mother requires even more, 500 kcal per day (Table 20–1). For some women, this may seem like an abnor-

TABLE 20–3. RECOMMENDED BASIC FOOD PLAN FOR PREGNANCY AND LACTATION

TYPE OF FOOD	DAILY AMOUNTS IN SERVINGS Pregnancy	Lactation
Water and other liquids (do not include milk)	6–8 glasses	6–8 glasses
Milk and milk products (excluding cheese)	4 cups	4–5 cups
Protein source (meat; fish; poultry; liver; eggs; hard and soft cheeses; at least one source of vegetable protein such as nuts, beans, lentils, peas)	4 ounces	4–5 ounces
Vegetables		
Dark green, leafy or deep yellow	1/2 cup	1/2 cup
Potato	1 medium	1 medium
Other vegetables	1/2–1 cup	1/2–1 cup
One vegetable should be eaten raw each day		
Whole grain breads and cereals (if not whole grain, use enriched products)	3–4	4–5
Fruits		
Citrus source of vitamin C	1	1
Other fruits	1–2	1–2
Fats		
Including butter, fortified margarine, vegetable oils for cooking, salad dressings, mayonnaise	2–3 Tablespoons to meet individual caloric needs	

Adapted from Sloane, E. *The Biology of Women*, 2nd ed. New York: John Wiley & Sons, 1985.

mally large amount of food to consume. Those who are vitally concerned with weight control and an attractive figure may find it difficult to eat all that is recommended. On the other hand, some women may use pregnancy as an excuse to overeat. Balance and moderation are again the key to success.

The quality of food chosen is extremely important in order to promote weight gain that is not just fat. Childbirth educators can emphasize that the woman is building a new human body within her uterus. She is also adding to her own uterine and breast tissues in order to support the new life within her. Such "person building" is not possible consuming foods laden with empty calories such as doughnuts and potato chips. Foods such as these are primarily sugar and fat. Although they have some nutrient value, they are filling and may diminish the appetite for nutritious fruits, grains, and vegetables.

"You are eating for two," is a common fallacy that pregnant women hear. While it is true that adequate weight gain and extra calories are required, the pregnant woman is actually eating for one (herself) and about one seventh (her fetus). If the total additional caloric requirements are averaged out over the entire pregnancy, the product is approximately 15 per cent more than she would eat normally. With the addition of one-half to two-thirds cup of cooked cereal with a tablespoon of raisins, a slice of whole grain toast with a tablespoon of peanut butter, and a cup of milk to the daily intake, these additional calories might be "spent." Such choices would be excellent examples of quality food selection.

Iron, Zinc, Folacin, Pyridoxine, and Calcium

The nutrients that are the most difficult to obtain during pregnancy are *iron, zinc, folacin, pyridoxine (vitamin* B_6*)*, and *calcium*. Therefore, the childbirth educator should develop strategies for teaching dietary assessment which are particularly relevant to these dietary elements in the woman's self-selected diet. A careful study of Table 20–1 will indicate that the foods high in these nutrients are green leafy vegetables, nuts, legumes, citrus fruits, broccoli, asparagus, whole grains, rice, bran, corn, lean beef, liver, yeast, dried fruits, eggs, potatoes, poultry, pork, seafood (especially oysters), and milk and milk products. Certain foods such as prune juice, dried apricots, molasses, and dried beans and peas are also very high in iron.

Since most of these foods are also quality sources of protein, a woman who eats these nutritious foods

> Look upon meals as important and pleasant pauses in the daily round. . . .eat slowly and enjoy the natural flavors of food of which quality not quantity is the quintessence.
>
> Grantly Dick-Read[1]
>
> As for weight gain, don't fixate on a maximum number of pounds. Every woman's metabolism is different. If you eat well and nutritiously, your weight will take care of itself. Pregnancy is not the time to diet.
>
> Boston Women's Health Collective[2]
>
> Rather than stressing the quantity of food, emphasize the importance of a varied diet and eating small amounts of everything the body needs.
>
> Elizabeth Whelan[3]

will not be as prone to problems such as iron and calcium deficiency, poor weight gain, low birthweight of the infant, infection, and possibly even severe "morning sickness."

Childbirth educators should conceptualize the nausea and vomiting of first trimester pregnancy from a wellness model.[97] Accordingly, "morning sickness," whether it occurs in the morning or at other times of the day or night, is considered to be a normal and predictable sign of pregnancy. It is indicative of a well-implanted placenta. Morning sickness should be viewed as a signal to the woman that her body is preparing for a new phase in her life. Consequently, eating habits must be examined and modified to promote an optimal level of wellness for both mother and baby.

The physiological adjustment mechanisms associated with normal pregnancy appear to induce this phenomenon. As stated by Voda and Randall, "past and present-day clinicians and scholars have postulated that hormones (progesterone, estrogen, testosterone, chorionic gonadotropin, anterior pituitary), disturbed carbohydrate metabolism, vitamin deficiency (B complex), and allergies may cause morning sickness."[97] However, to date, there is no research support for any specific theory relating to the cause of morning sickness. Therefore, these researchers propose a normal physiological etiological model for morning sickness. Voda and Randall[97] suggest that hormonal adjustment mechanisms produce nausea due to fluid retention (hypervolemia) induced by antidiuretic hormone (ADH) and relative sodium depletion (hyponatremia).

The nausea is improved with eating. Nutritional treatment advice has included all of the following: eat small, frequent meals; avoid large amounts of water with meals; do not rise in the morning on an empty stomach (eat a cracker or dry piece of toast first); take bicarbonate of soda, milk of magnesia, or drink ginger ale (to treat gastric acidity); drink herb teas (peppermint, lemon-mint, raspberry, chamomile, and strawberry); avoid fatty foods; eat more complex carbohydrates; take a vitamin B_6 supplement; and increase the protein in the diet.

Women who have tried all of these remedies report varying degrees of satisfaction with them. According to Voda and Randall, the two most frequently mentioned treatments that produced relief were eating frequent, small meals including small amounts of protein and complex carbohydrate, and eating a high protein snack before going to bed.[97] These methods support the advice to "examine your eating habits, and determine a method to eat all essential nutrients in a well-balanced manner."

Milk

Although milk is an important source of calcium, phosphorus, protein, vitamins E, D, and some of the B-complex, it is difficult for many pregnant women to ingest. One quart of milk fulfills a pregnant woman's daily requirement for calcium. Three to four glasses a day are usually recommended. If a woman dislikes milk or has a small appetite, it is even more difficult to drink this much. The childbirth educator can suggest alternate sources of milk protein.

One example is "double milk." To make double milk, add one-third cup of nonfat dry milk to a glass of milk. This produces the nutritional equivalent of two eight-ounce glasses of regular milk. Other nutritional equivalents are one glass of buttermilk, one cup of yogurt, one and one-half cups of ice cream (which contains extra sugar and fat), one and one-half ounces of hard cheese, one-half cup ricotta (semisoft) cheese, or one and one-half cups of cottage cheese.

Protein

Most U.S. women consume enough protein—even, perhaps, too much animal protein and not enough complex carbohydrates. Most pregnant women do not need to increase their consumption of protein, but should be encouraged to examine the sources of protein in their diet. Eggs, fish, or peanut butter on whole wheat bread are examples of alternative sources of protein. Incomplete proteins such as nuts, beans, lentils, rice, corn, and peas can be combined with small amounts of meat to provide excellent sources of complete proteins.

C-reactive protein, an abnormal protein globulin detectable in blood during an active phase of acute illness, has been shown to be elevated in the blood of women under the following conditions: injury and inflammation, increased gestational age of the fetus (postmaturity), and infection.[74] These findings also support the need for pregnant women to consume quality protein in their diet, especially if they are at risk for any complications of pregnancy. However, the need to choose quality sources of protein and increase the amount of complex carbohydrates rather than to eat larger amounts of meat cannot be emphasized enough in childbirth education classes.

Supplementation

Following a thorough review of major supplementation studies, Worthington-Roberts states a general principle as follows:[103] "Overall, the findings appear to suggest that the worse the nutritional condition of the mother entering pregnancy, the more valuable the prenatal diet and/or nutritional supplement will be in improving her pregnancy course and outcome." Childbirth educators should be prepared to promote individual nutritional assessment in their classes. The standard prenatal supplements that are prescribed by the medical community are based upon a general supposition that the maternal diet is inadequate in major nutrients. While it is possible that some women are unable to consume the amount of food required to provide the variety and balance needed for total nutrition, it should not be assumed that all women are alike.

Furthermore, it is true that physicians must meet the needs of the heterogeneous population, including women who are difficult to motivate toward dietary changes conducive to optimal reproductive standards. However, most childbirth educators tend to have students who are motivated to improve their general health as well as promote a healthy pregnancy. Educational levels may be higher among members of prepared childbirth classes. There is a greater tendency for these couples to participate knowledgeably in obstetrical management of the pregnancy. In addition, class members tend to have a greater desire to make informed choices. Therefore, childbirth educators are advised to carefully study the issue of standard prenatal supplementation so they can disseminate the most appropriate individualized information.

Interactions among vitamins, minerals, and trace elements such as zinc and copper must be carefully considered before a woman takes nutritional supplements on her own. Some women believe that "if a little bit is good, a whole lot is better," and may decide to take the nutrients they have heard discussed as essential for one reason or another. For example, if they have heard that Bendectin (now considered unsafe for use in pregnancy) contains vitamin B_6 and was used for control of the nausea of morning sickness, it is possible they might choose to take megadoses of vitamin B_6 to treat this symptom. The result could be a vitamin overdose.

If a woman has been eating a varied, balanced diet, and is not over- or underweight at conception, she should be encouraged to get additional nutrients from foods rather than supplements. Supplements are expensive and may interact to prevent intestinal absorption of the nutrients that are consumed in her daily diet. For example, too much iron, folic acid, and/or calcium may inhibit zinc absorption. If adequate amounts of these nutrients are being consumed, standard prenatal supplementation may not be required.

Supplementation should only be recommended on an individual basis, with consideration for the specific nutrients that are difficult for the woman to obtain in her daily diet. For example, a zinc supplement may be appropriate in communities where fresh seafood is difficult to obtain and for women who refuse to eat fish, pork, or liver.

Iron supplements are notorious for promoting constipation. Pregnant women are sometimes advised to use stool softeners to cope with this problem. If the maternal diet contains adequate amounts of iron-rich foods, the amount of ferrous sulfate prescribed in the supplement may be too much for her biochemical individuality. The resulting constipation may be a signal that the woman is forming complexes in her intestine that are unabsorbable. It may be better to increase her consumption of nuts, leafy vegetables, whole grains, and enriched cereals and decrease the synthetic iron she is taking. Research in this area is scant. However, as previously mentioned, there is some research evidence that too much iron prevents absorption of nutrients such as zinc. How this might relate to constipation remains to be studied.

Classroom Strategies for Childbirth Educators

Creative childbirth educators can develop methods for emphasizing nutrition in their classes. Behavioral and social learning theorists such as Bandura and Sheffield[39] provide some useful principles for application in childbirth education practice.

Bandura's "social learning" process explains that much of adult behavior such as habits involving eating, drinking, and smoking are learned (at least in the beginning) from powerful role models. Since some of these habits can actually become addicting (overeating, constant drinking, and smoking), they continue even after role models from whom they were learned disappear.

Childbirth educators can promote new role models for members of their classes. Emphasizing selecting natural foods and nonalcoholic beverages and giving up smoking within the context of an adult social learning situation, such as a childbirth class, may be a powerful force in changing behavior. Serving nutritious snacks during class breaks and social events such as "new parent and baby" parties is another way in which to emphasize these behaviors.

Sheffield's[39] theory of "imitation" has also been applied to "inoculation" techniques in classroom situations. In order to use these concepts in a childbirth education class, an instructor might adopt the following scenario. Adult learners in the class have been exposed to the social equivalent of "germs" by being pressured to engage in unhealthy eating and drinking habits and in smoking. They have caught "social diseases" such as becoming overweight, drinking too much alcohol, or smoking. The childbirth educator can provide "antibodies" that fight these germs by teaching skills for resisting the temptations to engage in the unhealthy behaviors.

Further "immunization" to continue resisting social pressure to engage in unhealthy food habits can be provided by role-playing social situations and role-modeling healthy practices. Individual class members can be invited to present examples of situations in which it is difficult to choose the healthy alternative. Others can be encouraged to offer suggestions for dealing with these situations. For example, a woman may report that she eats too many fat and salt-containing snacks when they are offered at a party. Suggestions to choose fresh fruits and vegetables, not arrive hungry, and perhaps even provide her own snacks might be appropriately elicited from the group. An important element of these strategies is the fact that group members realize that their concerns and problems dealing with healthy practices are not unique.

Promoting the keeping of food diaries is another way in which childbirth educators can assist their group members to analyze their dietary practices. A diary will also give couples baseline data that they can use for setting their individual nutritional goals. Once members have analyzed their own dietary practices, they can be encouraged to compare their likes and dislikes with the recommendations in Tables 20–1 and 20–2. Further goals can be developed from such an analysis and comparison.

Additionally, gaming and simulation strategies can promote healthy nutrition. Simple games can be devised, such as a trivia-type game about nutritional requirements during pregnancy and lactation. Examples of meal selections can be developed around the basic food groups and written out on cards or exhibited on posters. Group members then discuss their ideas regarding nutrient content of the meals. These methods focus on reinforcing past knowledge as well as teaching new nutritional concepts to adult learners.

Finally, a model for "nutrition education" proposed by Worthington-Roberts et al.[104] may be useful for childbirth educators. In this model educational programs can be of four types: informative, attitudinal, behavioral, and therapeutic. Childbirth educators can develop class goals that focus on one or more of these areas. Needs assessment strategies can be used to define the class knowledge base and individual concerns prior to deciding on particular objectives.

Examples of informative programs would include (1) objectives in which factual information regarding the nutritive requirements of pregnancy and lactation are defined, and (2) objectives dealing with foods which provide the essential nutrients are presented. Attitudinal objectives would include motivating members to identify their values, biases, and beliefs regarding the role of nutrition in their lives. Values clarification strategies could promote attitudinal awareness. Couples would then be prepared to either reinforce or change their motivation for engaging in healthy lifestyle practices.

Behavioral programs, according to this model, focus on teaching methods for implementing nutritional practices into daily living. Members might discuss the problems of buying nutritious food, resisting high-pressure advertising, planning nutritional meals with limited time, brown bagging on a limited budget, or learning how to use exchange lists.

Therapeutic programs can address members' needs for individualized counseling. For example, a couple who is vegetarian may need to learn how to increase the required nutrients within the limits of this diet. Some class members whose dislikes eliminate particular foods, such as milk or fish, from their usual diet may need counseling on potential deficiencies in the maternal diet.

IMPLICATIONS FOR RESEARCH

The National Research Council Committee on Maternal Nutrition made specific recommendations for future research in 1970. Research since has focused on in-depth studies of physiological changes during the reproductive cycle. Fetal-maternal relationships at the biochemical level have been studied intensively. As is the usual case, each investigation not only answers the research questions for which it is designed but provides the basis for asking new questions.

Research on nutritional elements at the biochemical level leads to questions such as the following: How many interactions are occurring among vitamins, minerals, and trace elements due to widespread use of supplements? Is supplementation really necessary in a healthy, well-educated, highly motivated population? Can supplementation overcome nutritional deficiencies that may be beyond our control, such as the deficiencies in foods grown in nutrient-depleted soil and shipped hundreds of miles for purchase? Can we monitor the food we purchase in regard to soil-dependent trace elements such as zinc and selenium? Can a useful system be devised?

The process of nutritional assessment is a primary area of concern for future research. Methods of determining the nutritional status of women of childbearing age other than by using anthropometric measures (height, weight, and skinfold thickness) are required. Is a woman who used oral contraceptives for several years prior to a pregnancy prone to vitamin and mineral deficiencies? Are there noninvasive, economical tests that could be developed to determine biochemical individuality? Some inroads have been made into this area, such as using saliva and hair samples to test for the amount of zinc in the body. These methods are used primarily in the research laboratory and are not well developed for clinical practice.

Finally, the previously mentioned report recommends studies to determine educational methods for promoting healthy eating habits across the life span in order to improve the nutritional status of women of childbearing age. Programs educating teenagers and young adults about the dangers of smoking and alcohol consumption during pregnancy are steps in this direction.[2,3] Researchers report varying degrees of success in regard to altering smoking and alcohol consumption during pregnancy. However, more attention should be given to assessing and altering dietary practices in regard to quality wholesome food choices made by both men and women of childbearing age.

Studies investigating the cultural aspects of food choices are also required. In many instances, women of childbearing age are not given the information required to modify their native diet to meet the demands of pregnancy. For example, it was reported that deficiencies of vitamin B_6 and folacin are two vitamin deficiencies most frequently found among low-income Mexican-American women.[40] Dietary analysis may indicate that their culturally derived food habits cause them to eat less of foods such as lean meat, broccoli, and asparagus that are high in these nutrients. Research studies designed to analyze food habits in this group might lead to culturally acceptable recipes combining rice and corn with small amounts of meat to provide these necessary nutrients.

Finally, childbirth educators who are motivated to incorporate scientifically derived nutritional recommendations into their childbirth classes may eventually form a group from which data will be available for use by researchers. Networking among instructors and researchers will be facilitated. Such networking may eventually provide the stimulus for regional and national conferences in which research-based strategies for effective nutritional education are shared.

In summary, there are many questions that require answers. Additional questions related specifically to childbirth education classes are:

- How much nutritional information do expectant parents receive in childbirth education classes?
- What are the most common methods that childbirth educators use to present nutritional information in childbirth education classes?
- What are the most effective methods of presenting nutritional information in childbirth education classes?
- How much influence does nutritional information received in childbirth education classes have on expectant parents' healthy nutritional habits?

SUMMARY

Pregnancy is a time of complex physiological and biochemical change. A wholesome balanced diet from the moment of conception is essential for the proper functioning of metabolic pathways and to produce a healthy infant. Childbirth education classes provide the opportunity to have expectant parents examine their nutritional habits and discuss current nutritional information. Childbirth educators can then support and promote the woman's good nutritional habits during pregnancy as well as expectant parents' good nutritional practices for a lifetime.

References

1. Abel, E. Smoking and pregnancy. *Journal of Psychoactive Drugs* 66:327, 1984.
2. Allen, C., and Ries, C. Smoking, alcohol, and dietary practices during pregnancy: Comparison before and after prenatal education. *Journal of the American Dietetic Association* 85:605, 1985.
3. Altman, G. Educational strategies for a community program in preventing alcohol use during pregnancy. *Nursing Administration Quarterly* 4:23, 1980.
4. Alton-Mackey, M., and Walker, B. Graded levels of pyridoxine in the rat diet during gestation and the physical and neuromotor development of the offspring. *American Journal of Clinical Nutrition* 25:420, 1973.
5. Alton-Mackey, M., and Walker, B. Physical and neuromotor development of progeny of pyridoxine-restricted rats cross-fostered with control or isonutritional dams. *American Journal of Clinical Nutrition* 31:76, 1978.
6. Andon, M., Howard, M., Moser, P., and Reynolds, R. Nutritionally relevant supplementation of vitamin B_6 in lactating women: Effect on plasma prolactin. *Pediatrics* 76:769, 1985.

7. Baird, D., and Wilcox, A. Cigarette smoking associated with delayed conception. *Journal of the American Medical Association* 253:2679, 1985.
8. Balfour, M. Supplementary feeding in pregnancy. *Lancet* 1:208, 1944.
9. Beagle W. Fetal alcohol syndrome: A review. *Journal of the American Dietetic Association* 79:274, 1981.
10. Beeley, L. Adverse effects of drugs in the first trimester of pregnancy. *Clinical Obstetrics and Gynecology* 8:261, 1981.
11. Bernhardt, I., and Dorsey, D. Hypervitaminosis A and congenital renal anomalies in a human infant. *Obstetrics and Gynecology* 43:750, 1974.
12. Blackburn, M., and Calloway, D. Basal metabolic rate and work energy expenditure of mature pregnant women. *Journal of the American Dietetic Association* 69:24, 1976.
13. Brewer, T. Role of malnutrition in pre-eclampsia and eclampsia. *American Journal of Obstetrics and Gynecology* 125:281, 1976.
14. Burke, B., Beal, V., Kirkwood, S., and Stuart, H. The influence on nutrition upon the condition of the infant at birth. *Journal of Nutrition* 26:569, 1943.
15. Cavdar, A., Babacan, E., Arcasoy, A., and Ertem, U. Effect of nutrition on serum zinc concentration during pregnancy in Turkish women. *American Journal of Clinical Nutrition* 33:542, 1980.
16. Calloway, D. Nitrogen balance during pregnancy. *In* Winick, M. (ed.) *Nutrition in Fetal Development*. New York: John Wiley & Sons, 1974.
17. Cherry, F., Bennett, E., and Bazzano, G. Plasma zinc in hypertension/toxemia and other reproductive variables in adolescent pregnancy. *American Journal of Clinical Nutrition* 34:2367, 1981.
18. Cochrane, W. Overnutrition in prenatal and neonatal life: A problem. *Canadian Medical Association Journal* 93:893, 1965.
19. Committee on Maternal Nutrition, Food and Nutrition Board, National Research Council. *Maternal Nutrition and the Course of Pregnancy: Summary Report*. Washington, DC: National Academy of Sciences, 1970.
20. Crosby, W. Food pica and iron deficiency. *Archives of Internal Medicine* 127:960, 1971.
21. Curet, L., Rao, A., and Zackman, R. Maternal smoking and respiratory distress syndrome. *American Journal of Obstetrics and Gynecology* 147:446, 1983.
22. Dutta, J. Serum folic acid level in abortion. *Journal of the Indian Medical Association* 69:149, 1977.
23. Ebbs, J., Tisdall, F., and Scott, W. The influence of prenatal diet on the mother and child. *Journal of Nutrition* 22:515, 1942.
24. Edwards, L., Alton, I., Barrada, M., and Hakanson, E. Pregnancy in the underweight woman: Course, outcome and growth patterns of the infant. *American Journal of Obsetrics and Gynecology* 135:297, 1979.
25. Edwards, L., Dickes, W., Alton, I., and Hakanson, E. Pregnancy in the massively obese: Course, outcome and obesity prognosis of the infant. *American Journal of Obstetrics and Gynecology* 131:479, 1978.
26. Enkin, M. Smoking and pregnancy—a new look. *Birth* 11:225, 1984.
27. Entman, S., Moore, R., Richardson, L., and Killam, A. Elevated serum iron in toxemia of pregnancy. *American Journal of Obstetrics and Gynecology* 143:398, 1982.
28. Evans, G., Grace, C., and Hahn, C. The effect of copper and cadmium on Zn absorption in zinc deficient and zinc-supplemented rats. *Bioinorganic Chemistry* 3:115, 1974.
29. Food and Nutrition Board. *Recommended Dietary Allowances*, 9th ed. Washington, DC: National Academy of Sciences, 1980.
30. Fried, P., Barnes, M., and Drake, E. Soft drug use after pregnancy compared to use before and during pregnancy. *American Journal of Obstetrics and Gynecology* 151:787, 1985.
31. Greentree, L. Dangers of vitamin B_6 in nursing mothers. *New England Journal of Medicine* 300:141, 1979.
32. Gross, R., Newberne, P., and Reid, J. Adverse effects on infant development associated with maternal folic acid deficiency. *Nutritional Report International* 10:241, 1974.
33. Hambridge, K., Krebs, N., Jacobs, M., Favier, A., Guyette, L., and Ikle, D. Zinc nutritional status during pregnancy: A longitudinal study. *American Journal of Clinical Nutrition* 37:429, 1983.
34. Harlap, S., and Shiono, P. Alcohol, smoking and incidence of spontaneous abortions in the first and second trimester. *Lancet* 2:173, 1980.
35. Hemminki, K., Mutanen, P., and Saloniemi, I. Smoking and the occurrence of congenital malformations and spontaneous abortions: Multivariate analysis. *American Journal of Obstetrics and Gynecology* 145:61, 1983.
36. Hervada, A. Drugs in breastmilk. *Perinatal Care* 2:19, 1978.
37. Hibbard, E., and Smithells, R. Folic acid metabolism and human embryopathy. *Lancet* 1:1254, 1965.
38. Hickory, W., Nanda, R., and Catalanotto, F. Fetal skeletal malformations associated with moderate zinc deficiency during pregnancy. *Journal of Nutrition* 109:883, 1979.
39. Huckabay, L. *Conditions of Learning and Instruction in Nursing*. St. Louis: C. V. Mosby, 1980.
40. Hunt I, Murphy N., Cleaver, A. et al. Zinc supplementation during pregnancy: Effects on selected blood constituents and on progress and outcome of pregnancy in low-income women of Mexican descent. *American Journal of Clinical Nutrition* 40:508, 1984.
41. Hurley, L., and Keen, C. Teratogenic effects of copper. *In* Nriagu, J. (ed.) *Copper in the Environment. Part II. Health Effects*. New York: John Wiley & Sons, 1979.
42. Hyvonen-Dabek, M., Nikkinen-Vilkki, P., and Dabek, J. Selenium and other elements in human maternal and umbilical serum, as determined simultaneously by proton-induced x-ray emission. *Clinical Chemistry* 30:529, 1984.
43. Jacobson, H. Weight and weight gain in pregnancy. *Clinics in Perinatology* 2:233, 1975.
44. King, J. Protein metabolism during pregnancy. *Clinics in Perinatology* 2:243, 1975.
45. King, J., and Fabro, S. Alcohol consumption and cigarette smoking: Effect on pregnancy. *Clinical Obstetrics and Gynecology* 26:437, 1983.
46. Kirksey, A., Roepke, J., Morre, D., and Styslinger, L.

Relationship of vitamin B_6 nutriture during pregnancy and lactation to vitamin B_6 adequacy in the breast-fed infant. *In* Wagner, P., and Kirk, J. (eds.) *Proceedings of the Florida Symposium on Micronutrients in Human Nutrition*. University of Florida, The Institute of Food and Agricultural Sciences, 1981.

47. Kitay, D., and Harbort, R. Iron and folic acid deficiency in pregnancy. *Clinics in Perinatology* 2:255, 1975.
48. Kline, J., Shrout, P., and Stein, Z. Drinking during pregnancy and spontaneous abortion. *Lancet* 2:176, 1980.
49. Krebs, N., Hambridge, K., Jacobs, M., and Rasbach, J. The effects of a dietary zinc supplement during lactation on longitudinal changes in maternal zinc status and milk zinc concentrations. *American Journal of Clinical Nutrition* 41:560, 1985.
50. Kristal, A., and Rush, D. Maternal nutrition and duration of gestation: A review. *Clinical Obstetrics and Gynecology* 27:553, 1984.
51. Lawrence, R. *Breast-feeding: A Guide for the Medical Profession*. St. Louis: C. V. Mosby, 1980.
52. Lehtovirta, P., Forss, M., and Kariniemi, V. Acute effects of smoking on fetal heart-rate variability. *British Journal of Obstetrics and Gynaecology* 90:3, 1983.
53. Little, R., Streissguth, A, Barr, H., and Herman, C. Decreased birth weight in infants of alcoholic women who abstained during pregnancy. *Journal of Pediatrics* 96:974, 1980.
54. Lu, J., Cook, D., Javia, J., et al. Intakes of vitamins and minerals by pregnant women with selected clinical symptoms. *Journal of the American Dietetic Association* 78:477, 1981.
55. Lyon, A. Effects of smoking on breast feeding. *Archives of Disease in Childhood* 58:378, 1983.
56. Maeder, E., Barno, A., and Mecklenburg, F. Obesity: A maternal high risk factor. *Obstetrics and Gynecology* 45:669, 1975.
57. Malone, J. Vitamin passage across the placenta. *Clinics in Perinatology* 2:295, 1975.
58. McMichael, A., Dreosti, I., Gibson, G., Hartshorne, J., Buckley, R., and Colley, D. A prospective study of serial maternal serum zinc levels and pregnancy outcome. *Early Human Development* 7:59, 1982.
59. Meadows, N., Ruse, W., and Smith, M. Zinc and small babies. *Lancet* 2:1135, 1981.
60. Milne, D., Candield, W., Mahalko, J., and Sandstead, H. Effect of oral folic acid supplements on zinc, copper, and iron absorption and excretion. *American Journal of Clinical Nutrition* 40:535, 1984.
61. Mochizuki, M., Maruo, T., and Masuko, K. Effects of smoking on fetoplacental-maternal system during pregnancy. *American Journal of Obstetrics and Gynecology* 149:413, 1984.
62. Mukherjee, M., Sandstead, H., Ratnaparkhi, M., Johnson, L., Milne, D., and Stelling, H. Maternal zinc, iron, folic acid, and protein nutriture and outcome of human pregnancy. *American Journal of Clinical Nutrition* 40:496, 1984.
63. Naeye, R. Nutritional/nonnutritional interactions that affect the outcome of pregnancy. *American Journal of Clinical Nutrition* 34:727, 1981.
64. Naeye, R., and Peters, E. Mental development of children whose mothers smoked during pregnancy. *Obstetrics and Gynecology* 64:601, 1984.
65. Nieburg, P., Marks, J., and McLaren, N. The fetal tobacco syndrome. *Journal of the American Medical Association* 253:2998, 1985.
66. Norkus, E., and Rosso, P. Effects of maternal intake of ascorbic acid on the postnatal metabolism of this vitamin in the guinea pig. *Journal of Nutrition* 111:624, 1981.
67. Pitkin, R. Vitamins and minerals in pregnancy. *Clinics in Perinatology* 2:221, 1975.
68. Pitkin, R. Calcium metabolism in pregnancy and the perinatal period: A review. *American Journal of Obstetrics and Gynecology* 151:99, 1985.
69. Pritchard, J., and McDonald, P. *Williams' Obstetrics*, 15th ed. Norwalk, CT: Appleton-Century-Crofts, 1976.
70. Rauramo, I., Forss, M., and Kariniemi, V. Antepartum fetal heart rate variability and intervillous placental blood flow in association with smoking. *American Journal of Obstetrics and Gynecology.* 146:967, 1983.
71. Reynolds, R., Polansky, M., and Moser, P. Analyzed vitamin B_6 intakes of pregnant and postpartum lactating and nonlactating women. *Journal of the American Dietetic Association* 84:1339, 1984.
72. Roepke, J., and Kirksey, A. Vitamin B_6 nutriture during pregnancy and lactation. I. Vitamin B_6 intake, levels of the vitamin in biological fluids, and condition of the infant at birth. *American Journal of Clinical Nutrition* 32:2249, 1979.
73. Roberts, J., Hill, C., and Riopelle, A. Maternal protein deprivation and toxemia of pregnancy: Studies in the rhesus monkey (Macaca mulatta). *American Journal of Obstetrics and Gynecology* 118:14, 1974.
74. Romen, Y., and Artal, R. C-reactive protein in pregnancy and in the postpartum period. *American Journal of Obstetrics and Gynecology* 151:380, 1985.
75. Rosett, H., Snyder, P., and Sander, L. Effects of maternal drinking on neonate state regulation. *Developmental Medicine and Child Neurology* 21:464, 1979.
76. Rush, D., Stein, Z., and Susser, M. A randomized controlled trial of prenatal nutritional supplementation in New York City. *Pediatrics* 65:683, 1980.
77. Rush, D., Stein, Z., and Susser, M. Controlled trial of prenatal nutrition supplementation defended. *Pediatrics* 66:656, 1980.
78. Schlievert, P., Johnson, W., and Galask, R. Bacterial growth inhibition by amniotic fluid. VI. Evidence for a zinc peptide antibacterial system. *American Journal of Obstetrics and Gynecology* 125:906, 1969.
79. Schuster, K., Bailey, L., and Mahan, C. Effect of maternal pyridoxine HCL supplementation on the vitamin B_6 status of mother and infant and on pregnancy outcome. *Journal of Nutrition* 114:977, 1984.
80. Scriver, C., and Hutchison, J. The vitamin B_6 deficiency syndrome in human infancy: Biochemical and clinical observations. *Pediatrics* 31:240, 1963.
81. Shaywitz, S., Cohen, D., and Shaywitz, B. Behavior and learning difficulties in children of normal intelligence born to alcoholic mothers. *Journal of Pediatrics* 96:978, 1980.
82. Simpson, J., Lawless, R., and Mitchell, A. Responsibility

of the obstetrician to the fetus. II. Influence of pre-pregnancy weight and pregnancy weight gain on birth-weight. *Obstetrics and Gynecology* 45:481, 1975.

83. Simpson, W. A preliminary report on cigarette smoking and the incidence of prematurity. *American Journal of Obstetrics and Gynecology* 73:808, 1957.
84. Sloane, E. *The Biology of Women,* 2nd ed. New York: John Wiley & Sons, 1985.
85. Solomons, N., Pineda, O., Viteri, F., and Sandstead, H. Studies on the bioavailability of zinc in humans: Mechanism of the intestinal interaction of nonheme iron and zinc. *Journal of Nutrition* 113:337, 1983.
86. Stetson, D., and Andrasik, F. Acute effects of cigarette smoking on pregnant women and nonpregnant control subjects. *American Journal of Obstetrics and Gynecology* 148:794, 1984.
87. Tafari, N., Ross, S., Naeye, R., Galask, R., and Zaar, B. Failure of bacterial growth inhibition by amniotic fluid. *American Journal of Obstetrics and Gynecology* 128:187, 1977.
88. Taggart, N., Holiday, R., Billewicz, W., Hytten, F., and Thomson, A. Changes in skinfolds during pregnancy. *British Journal of Nutrition* 21:439, 1967.
89. Tapper, I., Oliva, J., and Ritchey, S. Zinc and copper retention during pregnancy: The adequacy of prenatal diets with and without dietary supplementation. *American Journal of Clinical Nutrition* 41:1184, 1985.
90. Tennes, K., and Blackard, C. Maternal alcohol consumption, birth weight, and minor physical anomalies. *American Journal of Obstetrics and Gynecology* 138:774, 1980.
91. *The Health Consequences of Smoking for Women—A Report of the Surgeon General.* Rockville, MD: U.S. Dept. of Health and Human Services, Public Health Service Office on Smoking and Health, 1981.
92. Thomson, A., and Hytten, F. Calorie requirements in human pregnancy. *Proceedings of the Nutrition Society* 20:76, 1961.
93. Tracy, T., and Miller, G. Obstetric problems of the massively obese. *Obstetrics and Gynecology* 33:204, 1969.
94. Truswell, A. ABC of nutrition: Nutrition for pregnancy. *British Medical Journal* 291:263, 1985.
95. Tyrala, E., and Dodson, E. Caffeine secretion into breast milk. *Archives of Disease in Childhood* 54:787, 1979.
96. van der Velde, W., and Treffers, P. Smoking in pregnancy: The influence on percentile birth weight, mean birth weight, placental weight, menstrual age, perinatal mortality and maternal diastolic blood pressure. *Gynecologic and Obstetric Investigation* 19:57, 1985.
97. Voda, A., and Randall, M. Nausea and vomiting of pregnancy: "Morning sickness." pp. 133–166. *In* Norris, C. (ed.) *Concept Clarification in Nursing*. Maryland: Aspen Systems Corporation, 1982.
98. Wald, N., and Hambridge, M. Maternal serum-copper concentration and neural tube defects. *Lancet* 2:560, 1977.
99. Weathersbee, P., Olsen, I., and Lodge J. Caffeine and pregnancy: A retrospective survey. *Postgraduate Medicine* 62:64, 1977.
100. Wertz, R., and Wertz, D. *Lying–In: A History of Childbirth in America*. London, Collier Macmillan, 1977.
101. Williams, C. Highley, W., Ma, E., Lewis, J., Tolbert, B., Woullard, D., Kirmani, S., and Chung, R. Protein, amino acid and caloric intakes of selected pregnant women. *Journal of the American Dietetic Association* 78:28, 1981.
102. Worley, R. Pathophysiology of pregnancy-induced hypertension. *Clinical Obstetrics and Gynecology* 27:821, 1984.
103. Worthington-Roberts, B. The role of nutrition in pregnancy course and outcome. *Journal of Environmental Pathology and Toxicology* 5:1, 1985.
104. Worthington-Roberts, B., Vermeersch, J., and Williams, S. *Nutrition in Pregnancy and Lactation*. St. Louis: C. V. Mosby, 1981.
105. Wright, J., Macrae, K., and Barrison, I. Effects of moderate alcohol consumption and smoking on fetal outcome. *Ciba Foundation Symposium* 105:240, 1984.
106. Wright, J., Waterson, E., and Barrison, I. Alcohol consumption, pregnancy, and low birthweight. *Lancet* 2:663, 1983.
107. Zimmerman, A., Dunham, B., Nochimson, D., Kaplan, B., Clive, J., and Kunkel, S. Zinc transport in pregnancy. *American Journal of Obstetrics and Gynecology* 149:523, 1984.

Beginning Quote

Peterson, G. *Birthing Normally: A Personal Growth Approach to Childbirth*. Berkley, CA: Mindbody Press, 1984, p. 46.

Boxed Quotes

1. Read, G. *Childbirth without Fear.* New York: Harper & Row, 1953, p. 109.
2. Boston Women's Health Collective. *The New Our Bodies, Ourselves*. New York: Simon & Schuster, Inc., 1984, p. 330.
3. Whelan, E. "Eating Right during Pregnancy." *American Baby,* February 1985, p. 69.

chapter 21

EXERCISE

ALICE K. NAKAHATA

Pregnancy should be the most healthful time in a woman's life. Nature intended it so, and many expectant mothers are finding it possible to enjoy a measure of well-being they never had before through attending exercise classes.

M. Fitzhugh

In 1963 Fitzhugh prefaced her guide to prenatal education, *Preparing for Childbirth,* with these words, and they might well be the advertising on brochures for the many prenatal exercise programs offered today. With the growth of the childbirth education movement and its emphasis on self-responsibility in health care and the rising national interest in fitness, greater numbers of women are motivated to seek special exercise programs as they enter the experience of pregnancy. The hope of an early figure return, the possibility of a more comfortable labor and birth, the sense of well-being that comes from movement—these are but a few of the reasons for undertaking a regular exercise program. Since research in this area has been sparse, validation of these goals has been subjective. However, the range of programs available in books and videotapes over the past few years are testimonies to the keen interest.

It is frequently the childbirth educator who is consulted by her students on recommendations for exercise and physical activity. Because the health of both the unborn child and the woman can be affected by stresses imposed upon the maternal body, exercise needs to be approached with enlightened respect and awareness of possible long-term effects. The purpose of this chapter is to look at the growth of interest in prenatal exercise, to review what information is available from research, and then to consider the implications for physical activity during the gestational period.

REVIEW OF THE LITERATURE

Exercise in Pregnancy: Development

Physical activity as a medical recommendation during pregnancy was advocated in the 1930's in Great Britain.[45] After observing the ease with which more active, working-class women gave birth, physicians began to recommend general physical exercise for the more sedentary upper-class women in the hope of reducing birth complications. Antenatal classes became popular in Great Britain and Sweden, taught primarily by physiotherapists. It is not surprising then that Dick-Read included seven exercises for "physical fitness" in his childbirth preparation instruction. He included these, not because he considered them essential, but to help women "attain the maximum efficiency of both mind and body."[13] The exercises he included were deep breathing while standing, squatting, pelvic tilt on all fours, pelvic floor contractions, and both single and double leg raises.

Heardman, a British physiotherapist of the 1950's, regarded prenatal exercise as training for an athletic event. She conducted one of the earliest studies on the benefits of physical training.[20] In a comparison of 800 trained with an equal number of untrained women, she found the following:

	Trained	Untrained
Average length of labor	16.5	22 hours
Use of forceps	81	144
Number of tears	186	275
Number taking analgesics	476	778
Number with no analgesics	324	22
Postpartum hemorrhages	9	25

It is not clear whether physical exercises were included as part of the breathing and relaxation training of the Psychoprophylactic Method originating in Russia, but Karmel lists several exercises in her book, *Thank You, Dr. Lamaze,* that she credits to the instruction manual by Rennert and Cohen.[28] Like Dick-Read, she advocates single leg raises and pelvic floor contractions but adds passive stretching of the adductors. The single leg raises are done with and without abduction. The original training manual lists the same exercises with the addition of the pelvic tilt.[4]

In subsequent years, exercises have continued to follow these models, with their focus on posture correction and muscle toning to promote comfort for both the pregnancy and birth. Since early childbirth preparation classes were targeted for women in their last trimester of pregnancy, exercises were generally limited in performance level and quantity. Within the last decade, the introduction of early pregnancy classes and the increasing popularity of special prenatal exercise classes have made instruction available for women earlier in pregnancy. A concurrent phenomenon has been the growing national interest in the benefits of aerobic exercise. The transfer of this interest to pregnancy was inevitable, leading to more women pursuing sustained levels of physical activity throughout the entire pregnancy.

Exercise in Pregnancy: Research

The American College of Sports Medicine states that exercise performed three to five times weekly for 15 to 60 minutes at 60 to 90 per cent of an individual's maximum heart rate produces improvements in strength, muscular endurance, and cardiorespiratory functions.[22] How this conditioning guideline can be adapted for pregnancy or even the question of the value of training during gestation is not clear on the basis of current research. Work with laboratory animals, primarily ewes and goats, raises questions about the effects of prolonged raised body temperature and decreased uterine blood flow on the growing fetus.[32] Also in question are the activation of the sympathetic system, leading to uterine stimulation, and the effects of increased fuel demands on fetal growth.

The studies on exercise during pregnancy with pregnant women must be interpreted with caution, since design and subject population are limited by legal and ethical considerations (Table 21–1). Controlling for the many variables of both exercise and pregnancy is difficult. Lotgering et al.[32] point out

TABLE 21–1. SUMMARY OF HUMAN STUDIES ON PREGNANCY AND EXERCISE

RESEARCHER	BRIEF DESCRIPTION	FINDINGS
Artal et al. (1981)[2]	23 women in 3rd trimester checked for cardiovascular and metabolic response before, during, and after 15 min on treadmill	Increased blood pressure, heart rate, and glucagon, norepinephrine, and epinephrine levels; return to baseline within 30 min
Clapp and Dickstein (1983)[8]	Interviewed 336 women over 3 months pregnant. 3 groups: no exercise, minimal exercise, and high level of exercise. Data were compared for fetal and obstetrical outcomes	High level exercise group showed less maternal weight gain, infant weight less, and earlier deliveries than other 2 groups
Collings et al. (1983)[9]	12 women in second trimester pregnancy cycled 3 times weekly for 7–19 weeks at submaximal levels; compared to 8 controls	18% increase in aerobic capacity in exercisers, 4% decrease in controls. Slight increase in FHR during exercise. No difference in fetal growth and birth weight
Dale et al. (1982)[10]	Retrospective study; longitudinal data on 33 runners were compared with 22 nonrunners	Less complications in runners, but there was a trend to have failure to progress in labor. No difference in maternal weight gain and infant birth weight
Dressendorfer and Goodlin (1980)[15]	5 women who swam 3 times weekly were cycle-tested until 80% maximum heart rate was reached; FHR was recorded	Fetal heart rate remained within normal limits
Edwards et al. (1981)[17]	Respiratory studies on 20 women who were cycle-tested in 3rd trimester and at 10–15 weeks postpartum	Expiratory ventilation increase during exercise in pregnancy was higher than postpartum. Increased VO_2, VCO_2, VE at rest during pregnancy over postpartum
Erkkola (1976)[18]	Tested 31 exercisers (active 3 times weekly) for physical work capacity against controls	PWC increased 27% in exercisers; 10% rise in controls. Infants of exercisers were heavier
Hauth et al. (1982)[24]	Assessed FHR on 7 joggers in 3rd trimester after jogging 1.5 mi and 3 flights of stairs	Increased FHR but returned to baseline in 22 min average; nonstress test was reactive; birth outcomes were normal
Hon and Wohlgemuth (1961)[25]	FHR assessed on 26 women on 2-step test for 3 min. FHR taken 30 min pre & post test subjects in supine position	20 women—little change in FHR; 4 of 6 with significant change had problems at birth; exercise may detect uteroplacental insufficiency
Jarrett and Spellacy (1983)[26]	Retrospect study and questionnaire on 67 runners continuing to run through pregnancy were compared on birth data	Miles run had no effect on infant weight or delivery date; no adverse effect on fetal and birth outcome
Knuttgen and Emerson (1974)[29]	Blood and gas analyses of 13 women tested walking and cycling with rest between; tested at 4 wk intervals from 24 wks pregnancy through postpartum	Increased O_2 uptake, hyperventilation, carbohydrate utilization in pregnancy; O_2 utilization increased with body weight
Marsal et al. (1979)[34]	Compared fetal breathing movements and FHR on 2 groups before and after 5 min of cycling	Average maternal heart rate rose 49%. Irregular fetal breathing movements but little change in fetal heart rate suggests fetal breathing is more sensitive to fetal status during exercise
Morris et al. (1956)[35]	Blood flow studies on normal and preeclamptic women, who were cycling 10–16 min	Shift in blood flow from splanchnic area to skeletal muscles; compensatory increase in uterine blood flow after exercise
Pernoll et al. (1975)[40]	Gas analyses on samples before, during, and after cycling 6 minutes on 12 women tested monthly during pregnancy and at 6 months postpartum	Resting VO_2 increase in pregnancy, increase in minute ventilation without significant increase in frequency; O_2 debt with exercise greater in pregnancy than postpartum
Pijpers et al. (1984)[41]	Cardiovascular assessed on 14 women, 2nd trimester after moderate exercise, compared to controls	Significant increase in maternal heart rate, blood pressure during exercise; no significant change in fetal heart rate and mean aortic blood flow velocity

TABLE 21–1. SUMMARY OF HUMAN STUDIES ON PREGNANCY AND EXERCISE *Continued*

RESEARCHER	BRIEF DESCRIPTION	FINDINGS
Pomerance et al. (1974)[43]	Fetal heart rate taken before and after cycling until heart rate 130–180 on 54 women	Of 11 infants with fetal heart rate ± 16, 4 were stressed at birth; suggests that exercise could screen for uteroplacental insufficiency
Sibley et al. (1981)[48]	7 women in 2nd trimester swam 3 times a week for 10 weeks. Tested on treadmill pre and post; gas analyses were compared with controls	7% decrease mean O_2 consumption in swimmers, 10.4% decrease in controls. 6.2% increase in work rate in swimmers, 20.8% decrease in controls. Maternal heart rate, blood pressure, fetal heart rate within normal limits
Tanaka (1984)[50]	Treadmill tested 5 groups: Advanced exercisers, 3rd trim; nonexercisers, 3rd trim; 3-month postpartum exercisers; 3 month nonexercisers; and nonpregnant controls. Gas analyses	No significant difference of maximal O_2 uptake in pregnancy and postpartum exercisers and controls. Significant decrease in nonexercisers during pregnancy and postpartum

FHR = Fetal heart rate; VO_2 = oxygen consumption; VCO_2 = carbon dioxide production; VE = expiratory minute volume; PWC = physical work capacity, O_2 = oxygen.

that physiological differences, such as venous pooling in the upright human and heat elimination through sweating rather than panting, limit applicability of findings from animal studies to pregnant women. In order to view the existing research in perspective, the effects of pregnancy on maternal physiology need to be considered.

Changes in Pregnancy

Musculoskeletal System

The pervasive effect of increased progesterone and estrogen on connective tissue is manifested in many ways throughout the gestational period and for six to seven weeks postpartum.[11] The laxity of ligaments binding joints—particularly in the sacroiliac and pubic areas—allows for the mobility of the pelvic girdle needed for the birth process. However, this same laxity creates instability and strain for the skeletal system, particularly as the uterus increases in size. Subluxation of the sacroiliac joint and sciatic nerve pressure are frequent accompanying conditions. The amount of joint laxity varies with individuals and with parity. One study reported an increase during the last trimester in all subjects experiencing laxity, and an increased occurrence in multiparas over primiparas.[7] During this period, all joints and muscle attachments are more vulnerable to injury, particularly with sudden, forced movements.[16] The abdominal fascia is another area affected greatly. With the pressure of the enlarging uterus, the two bands of the abdominal recti frequently become separated.[37]

Connective tissue relaxation also influences the vascular system. The combination of decreased elasticity of blood vessels, particularly in the lower extremities, and the effects of gravity upon the upright posture for long periods of time predispose to varicosities.[11]

Perhaps the most observable changes of the musculoskeletal system are postural. Weight gain, concentrated primarily in the abdomen and breasts, shifts the center of gravity forward and upward.[11,12,31] Progressive changes over the nine months require ongoing adjustments, particularly in standing activities. Lordosis in the lumbar and cervical areas may become increasingly pronounced, particularly if the abdominal musculature is weak. Accompanying sequelae are thoracic kyphosis with protracted shoulders, a forward head, and hyperextended knees. This posture is often accompanied by traction on the median and ulnar nerves, experienced as numbness, tingling, and pain in the hands or arms.[31] (Increased vascularity and fluid retention can also contribute to these symptoms.)

A less obvious area of stress on musculature is the pelvic floor. As a biped, the pregnant woman supports the weight of the enlarging uterus with this group of muscles. Pressure from the bladder requires the maintenance of tone in this group of muscles to preserve continence.

Cardiovascular and Respiratory Changes

To meet the demands of sustaining the growing fetus, there is an increase in maternal blood volume of 30 to 50 per cent accompanied by an increased stroke volume and heart rate.[5,33] Heart rate increases to a maximum of about 20 beats per minute over nonpregnant values.[3] Cardiac output reaches a maximum at 28 weeks and remains elevated thereafter. Increased plasma volume greater than red cell mass results in the *''physiological anemia''* of pregnancy.[5]

Respiratory alterations include a 4 cm upward compression of the diaphragm, resulting in a decrease in the vertical dimension of the thoracic cavity.[5] A compensatory enlargement of the rib cage due in part to relaxation of ligamentous attachments results in an increased vital capacity. Capillary engorgement throughout the respiratory tract sometimes makes nasal breathing difficult. There is an increase in resting ventilation rate and in tidal volume with a resultant *physiological hyperventilatory state,* considered by some authorities to be progesterone-mediated.[40] With advancing pregnancy, there is increased oxygen consumption and a decline in efficiency of work performed.[2] Near term the oxygen consumption is 16 to 32 per cent above nonpregnant values largely due to the increased uterine tissue mass.

Metabolic Changes

The increasing demand of supporting a growing fetus is also reflected in a higher basal metabolic rate. The energy requirement of a pregnancy is estimated to be about 80,000 kcal. The greatest demand occurs between the 10th and 30th weeks, the need averaging about 390 kcal per day.[3]

Increased metabolism is accompanied by a rise in heat production. The dissipation of heat depends on the mechanisms of radiation, conduction, and evaporation. These occur through the workings of the peripheral circulation and the activity of the sweat glands. Environmental conditions that interfere with these mechanisms, such as hot, humid weather, can result in high maternal core temperatures. This is thought to be reflected in a rise in fetal body temperatures.[32] Possible teratogenic effects of hyperthermia, particularly in the first trimester, have been suggested by some researchers.[3]

Effects on Maternal Physiology

With moderate levels of exercise, there is an expected increase in cardiovascular and respiratory response. Artal reported increases in blood pressure and heart rate with higher levels of glucagon, norepinephrine, and epinephrine after moderate exercise, indicating heightened activity in metabolic and sympathetic systems.[2] All measurements returned to baseline within 30 minutes. Edwards et al. found a higher expiratory ventilation rate during exercise in pregnancy than in postpartum.[17] Knuttgen and Emerson noted an increase in oxygen uptake, hyperventilation, and carbohydrate utilization in pregnancy as compared with postpartum values. Oxygen utilization was greater in treadmill walking than when the cycle ergometer was used. This reflected the increased demands of weightbearing on physical activity.[29] Pernoll et al. also reported increased minute ventilation, increased carbon dioxide production, and increased tidal volume with moderate exercise.[40] Oxygen debt with exercise was greater in pregnant women than in controls. The increase in hyperventilation was not proportional to the severity of exercise.

Several studies suggest that there is a training effect from participating in an ongoing exercise program. Erkkola reported a 27 per cent increase in physical work capacity (exercise tolerance) in women who exercised three times weekly in varied activities.[18] From observations of women cycling three times a week, Collings et al. reported an 18 per cent rise in aerobic capacity as compared to a 4 per cent decline in controls.[9] Sibley noted a 6.2 per cent increase in work rate as tested by treadmill in women who swam three times a week for 10 weeks upon treadmill testing. Controls showed a 20.8 per cent decrease.[48] An unpublished study by Tanaka compared fitness levels of women participating in a maternal aerobics program at 31 weeks' gestation and three months postpartum against nonexercising women of comparable status.[50] There was also a nonpregnant control group. Fitness levels did not differ significantly between the nonpregnant women and the pregnant postpartal exercisers. Fitness levels did differ significantly for the nonexercisers, suggesting that exercise may help to maintain work efficiency at prepregnant levels despite the increasing demands of pregnancy as gestational age advances.

Effects on the Fetus

Of primary concern among researchers is the effect of exercise on the uterine environment, specifically the effects on blood flow and temperature. In studying normal and preeclamptic pregnant women, Morris reported a shift in blood flow from the splanchnic area to the skeletal muscles, causing a 25 per cent reduction in uterine blood flow.[35] However, he also noted compensatory increase in flow following exercise. Animal studies suggest that blood flow redistribution from myometrium to placental cotyledons, increased hemoglobin concentration with concomitant oxygen carrying capacity, and increased oxygen extraction minimize effects of decreased blood flow.[32] In a review of studies on exercise and pregnancy, Lotgering et al. noted that subjects in Morris' study were placed in the supine position, possibly affecting blood flow from aortocaval compression.[32] Pijpers et al. reported no significant changes in fetal heart rates and mean blood flow velocity following exercise in subjects tested at 34 to 38 weeks' gestation.[41]

Monitoring of fetal heart rates during testing on the subjects in the studies on training effects mentioned previously showed rates within normal limits, and return to baseline was within 30 minutes after cessation of exercise.[15,24,48] Two studies used fetal response to exercise to screen for extremes in fetal heart rates.[25,43] A follow-up review of birth data suggested that those responses may have been indicative of uteroplacental insufficiency and a warning of complications at birth. Marsal and colleagues found that fetal breathing movements showed more irregularities following exercise than fetal heart rates, suggesting that breathing movements might be a more sensitive indicator of fetal status.[34]

What these studies seem to indicate is that exercise is tolerated well in a healthy maternal environment. When the health of the mother is not optimal, the stress of exercise may accentuate risk factors.

Endurance Exercise and Birth Outcome

Clapp and Dickstein's prospective study of 336 women who exercised at varying levels of endurance reported a decreased birth weight in infants born to women who continued high-performance activities throughout pregnancy. They were compared to infants born to women who either did no exercise or dropped to a minimal level.[8] High-endurance exercisers also gained less weight and had shorter gestational periods. In contrast, Erkkola noted heavier infants among women who were exercisers when compared with nonexercising controls.[18]

Clapp and Dickstein's findings are also contradicted by Jarrett's retrospective study of 67 women who continued to run through pregnancy.[26] He reported no significant effect of number of miles run on either birth weight or delivery date. However, comparison of this data with averages for all pregnancies revealed a slight decrease in rate of spontaneous abortions, a higher rate of fetal anomalies, and a low incidence of infant and maternal complications. Dale's retrospective study on 33 runners indicated no differences in maternal weight gain and infant birth weight.[10] He noted less complications among runners when compared with nonrunning controls. Both Collings and Sibley found no effects of long-term maternal exercise on birth and fetal outcome.[9,47]

Summary of Research

A review of research studies to date indicates that exercise performed for a moderate duration at a submaximal heart rate level does not compromise the healthy pregnant woman and her fetus and appears to have some beneficial effects. There is some validation for exercising on a regular basis to gain a training effect, thus counteracting the loss of efficiency that accompanies advancing pregnancy. Because of the metabolic and physiological changes imposed by pregnancy, difficulty and duration of exercise sessions should be modified as performance efficiency decreases with gestational age. Switching to a nonweightbearing form of exercise such as swimming may be less stressful while still providing many of the benefits of exercise (see discussion under Recommendations on Sports Activities).

IMPLICATIONS FOR PRACTICE

With the paucity of definitive guidelines from research, recommendations for physical activity continue to rely on the pregnant woman's perception of comfort and her "common sense." How the childbirth educator approaches the question of exercise for her students will be determined by her own educational objectives and by an individualized assessment of the health, gestational period, previous exercise level, and motivation of class members.

Contraindications to Exercise

Assessment of a pregnant woman's health includes determining risk factors. Artal lists the following as contraindications to exercise during pregnancy:[1]

- Risk for premature labor
- Vaginal or uterine bleeding, ruptured membranes
- Nausea, vomiting
- Poor weight gain
- Anemia
- Intrauterine growth retardation
- Hypertension
- Fetal distress
- Pain of any kind: chest, head, back, hips, pubis
- Uterine contractions, regular at 20 minute intervals or shorter
- Dizziness, faintness
- Shortness of breath
- Palpitations, tachycardia
- Difficulty in walking
- Generalized edema
- Decreased fetal activity

Consultation with the health care provider and some degree of caution is necessary for those with orthopedic problems such as back and hip pain and shoulder or other joint problems. Respiratory conditions such as asthma require the same care. Artal also recommends that pregnant women "should avoid exercise during hot or humid weather, maintain water intake, stop frequently to rest, eat adequately before exercise, rest afterward, be aware of fetal activity, and consult the physician if uterine contractions become regular at 15-minute intervals or shorter."[1]

Some generalizations about the selection and performance of exercises can be made, keeping in mind the particular changes of the pregnant body. Pain is a useful alerting mechanism, and movements that hurt are to be avoided. However, even in healthy women, sudden changes of position will cause pain when the round ligaments in the groin area are suddenly stretched by changes in position.[14] Positions that exaggerate the lordotic curve are to be avoided. The back should always be in good alignment when leg and arm movements are performed. Maintaining a pelvic tilt is helpful in ensuring this stability. The supine position with its hypotensive effect should be used minimally, if at all.[5] In evaluation of positions, the influence of gravity should also be considered. In some positions the weight of a body part can make a particular exercise more difficult. This might be beneficial if strength is the goal, or it may be potentially harmful if muscles are too weak to support the adjacent body part. A leg raise from a supine position is an example of the latter.

There is a body of literature that recommends that the knee-chest position not be used during pregnancy and postpartum because of the potential for air embolism.[42] The proximity of the uterine sinuses to the expansive vagina, particularly in that position, make the introduction of air into the circulation possible. There is documentation of postpartum embolism from a few hours after delivery up to the 12th day postpartum.[42] If exercises can be performed in other positions with the same benefits, it may be a more judicious choice to do so.

Conscious, deliberate movements should be emphasized because sudden, jerky movements can stress lax joints and muscle attachments. Bounces and fast swings are therefore to be avoided.[16,53] For the same reasons, forced passive stretches should never be used. In performing all exercises, breathing awareness needs to be emphasized to avoid the Valsalva maneuver, i.e., the breath holding that results in transient hypertension. Conscious exhaling on difficult movements will prevent this.

Artal and Wiswell[3] developed guidelines for exercise during pregnancy on the basis of recommendations of the American College of Obstetricians and Gynecologists and guidelines from the American College of Sports Medicine (Table 21–2).

TABLE 21–2. GUIDELINES FOR EXERCISE DURING PREGNANCY AND THE POSTPARTUM PERIOD

During pregnancy and the postpartum period:

1. Regular exercise (at least 3 times per week) is preferable to intermittent activity. Competitive activities should be discouraged.
2. Vigorous exercise should not be performed in hot, humid weather or during a period of febrile illness.
3. Ballistic movements (jerky, bouncy motions) should be avoided. Exercise should be done on a wooden or a tightly carpeted surface to reduce shock and provide a sure footing.
4. Deep flexion or extension of joints should be avoided because of connective tissue laxity. Avoid activities that require jumping, jarring motions, or rapid changes in direction because of joint instability.
5. Vigorous exercise should be preceded by a 5-minute period of muscular warm-up. This can be accomplished by slow walking or stationary cycling with low resistance.
6. Vigorous exercise should be followed by a period of gradually declining activity that includes gentle static stretching. Stretches should not be taken to the point of maximum resistance, as connective tissue laxity increases the risk of injury.
7. Heart rate should be measured at times of peak activity. Target heart rates and limits established in consultation with the physician should not be exceeded.
8. Care should be taken to rise up from the floor gradually to avoid orthostatic hypotension. Some form of activity involving the legs should be continued for a brief period.
9. Liquids should be taken liberally before, during, and after exercise to prevent dehydration. If necessary, activity should be interrupted to replenish fluids.
10. Women who have led sedentary lives should begin with physical activity of very low intensity and advance activity levels very gradually.
11. Activity should be stopped and a physician consulted if any unusual symptoms appear.

During pregnancy only:

1. Maternal heart rate should not exceed 140 beats/min.
2. Strenuous activities should not exceed 15 min in duration.
3. No exercises should be performed in the supine position after the fourth month of gestation is completed.
4. Exercises that employ the Valsalva maneuver should be avoided.
5. Caloric intake should be adequate to meet not only the extra energy needs of pregnancy but also of the exercise performed.
6. Maternal core temperature should not exceed 38.5° C

From Artal, R., and Wiswell, R.A. *Exercise in Pregnancy.* Baltimore: Williams & Wilkins, 1986.

Exercises For Childbirth Preparation Classes

The selection of exercises as part of the childbirth preparation curriculum will differ from those used in a prenatal exercise class. In most instances, class members will be well into the third trimester and experiencing the full impact of the physiological changes previously discussed. Time for exercise instruction and practice will be limited, since this constitutes only one part of a curriculum that includes information acquisition and the learning of the techniques of breathing and relaxation. Thus, the selection and quantity of exercises are restricted by the limitations of late pregnancy and available class time. It is the opinion of some practitioners that limiting the number of exercises to two or three will result in a more beneficial effect because this small number is more likely to be performed on a daily basis.[44] Other practitioners may include more, reasoning that variety adds to interest as well as benefitting other areas of the body.[47] The discussion that follows attempts to cover a range of exercises included in childbirth preparation classes, leaving selection to the judgment of individual practitioners.

> The advantage of attending a class (exercise class) is that you are stimulated by others also engaged in training for motherhood, with whom you make friends and can compare your babies later on.
>
> KATHLEEN VAUGHN[1]
>
> There is, therefore, room for exercises, always and flowing, which increases in women a happy consciousness of this part of their body as both good, clean and right, and as under their control.
>
> SHEILA KITZINGER[2]
>
> Successfully completing an exercise program will give you a greater sense of control over your body. Being in control, while at the same time being relaxed, will give you confidence and trust you'll need to "let go" for a smoother labor and delivery.
>
> AUTHORS OF THE EXERCISE PLUS PREGNANCY PROGRAM[3]

The primary purpose of exercise is to provide a readiness for labor, to maintain a healthy body image, and to minimize the physical stresses of late pregnancy. These present-day goals are much like those of the early practitioners. Because of more information about body mechanics and muscle physiology, however, greater care and regard for individuality can be used in selecting exercises. There are nine basic muscle groups that may be included in childbirth education classes: pelvic floor contractions; posture re-education, including pelvic tilt; abdominal strengthening; low back and hamstring stretches; neck, shoulder, and upper torso exercises; foot rotation; squatting; and adductor stretches.

Pelvic Floor Contractions (Kegel Exercises)

The pelvic floor muscles form a hammock that extends from the symphysis pubis, which forms the front portion of the pelvic cavity, to the coccyx (tailbone), which articulates with the sacrum, the posterior part of the pelvic cavity. The muscle sheet has three orifices—urethra, vagina, and anus. Muscle fibers circle these openings to form sphincters, with one loop around the urethra and vagina and another loop around the anus. The pelvic floor muscles function to support the pelvic organs—the bladder, uterus, bowels—and maintain their proper placement in the pelvic cavity, and to provide sphincter control for the urethra, vagina, and anus.

During pregnancy, pelvic floor contractions are done to increase the strength of these muscles and provide increased support for the uterus and other pelvic organs, and to develop the ability to relax and control the muscles in preparation for the actual birth of the baby. In the postpartum period, pelvic floor contractions are done to promote healing of perineal tissues, increase strength of the muscles, and promote their return to a "healthy state" and increased urinary control.

Some practitioners caution against doing too many pelvic floor contractions, fearing that the muscle will become rigid and thick. There is little research to support this contention. Although these exercises can be done in any position, antigravity (lying) positions may be helpful in initial learning.

Noble suggests performing pelvic floor contractions in series of five contractions at a time in order to avoid muscle fatigue.[37] This is true theoretically and is appropriate for the prenatal period, in which the emphasis is on developing awareness and control of the muscles. When the emphasis is on strengthening and toning the muscles and increasing urinary control, such as in the postpartum period, or when conducting research, the use of a set protocol of 100 pelvic floor contractions at one time (this takes approximately 20 minutes) has been shown to be effective, and compliance with this exercise protocol was excellent (Fig. 21–1). While muscle fatigue was a problem initially, women were soon able to complete 100 pelvic floor contractions at a time without difficulty. There are numerous protocols for pelvic floor contractions in the literature, and no research exists to support which approach is the most effective. This is an area that requires research in order to establish a scientific basis for practice. Until that time, the choice of protocols will depend upon individual childbirth educators' and class members' preferences.

Anatomical Location of Kegel Muscle
- Attaches at symphysis pubis and coccyx
- Surrounds urethra, vagina, and rectum
- Is about $\frac{3}{4}$ of the way up in vagina

Function of Kegel Muscle
- Serves as the major muscle of support for pelvic floor
- Helps prevent uterine, bladder, and rectal prolapse and stress incontinence
- Contracts vaginally during sexual climax

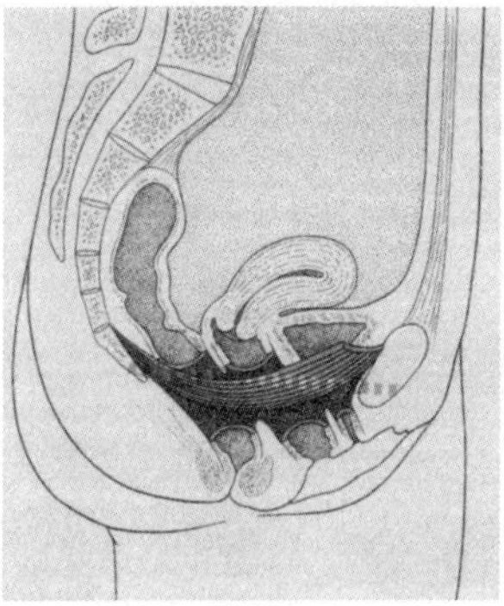

A

The pubococcygeus muscle with good tone and proper position.

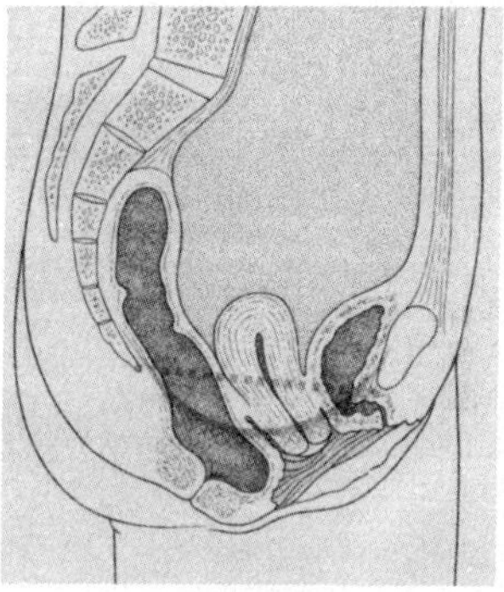

B

The pubococcygeus muscle with poor tone and position. Note the sagging of structures due to weak support.

Potential Problems of Kegel Muscle
- Stretches and sometimes tears slightly during childbirth because it is above level of the episiotomy
- If not exercised, it may not regain tone, which possibly results in structural prolapse and stress incontinence
- Loss of tone decreases sexual enjoyment by decreasing the strength of contractions felt in the vaginal wall during climax

Techniques for Isolating and Identifying Kegel Muscle
- Feel the contraction by running finger along vaginal wall while tightening the muscle
- With knees spread apart, stop the stream of urine when voiding and then resume urination
- Be aware of location and feeling of vaginal contraction during sexual climax
- Use a biofeedback instrument that allows visualization of the contraction (from Farrall Industries, Grand Island, Nebraska)

How to do Kegel Exercises
- During pregnancy to develop awareness, control, and general muscle strengthening, tighten muscles, hold to count of 5 (this can be increased to a count of 10), relax and repeat in a series of 5 contractions at a time
- During postpartum period to strengthen muscles and increase urinary control and for use as a research protocol, tighten muscles, hold to a count of 10, relax, and repeat 100 times
- Women should do Kegel exercises 100 times per day for life

Suggestions to Improve Practice of Kegel Exercises
- Establish a daily practice routine that is adhered to stringently and interferes as little as possible with other activities
- Use a biofeedback instrument for visualization of strength of the contraction (from Farrall Industries, Grand Island, Nebraska)
- Use a vaginal-resistive device during practice, such as a dildo or penis

FIGURE 21–1. Kegel exercise teaching plan. Courtesy of Jane S. Henderson, RN, MN, and Kathleen H. Taylor, RN, C, MS. Based on Henderson, J.S. Effects of a prenatal teaching program on postpartum regeneration of the pubococcygeal muscle. *JOGN Nursing* 12:403, 1983 and Henderson, J.S., and Taylor, K.H. Age as a variable in an exercise program for the treatment of simple urinary stress incontinence. *JOGN Nursing* 16:266, 1987. Figures A and B are from Deutsch, R. *The Key to Feminine Response in Marriage.* New York: Ballantine Books, 1968.

Posture Re-education

An individual assessment of the student will determine if the following exercises are needed, although they can be performed for other benefits listed under the respective rationale. A visual check of the alignment of head, upper trunk, pelvis, and lower extremities will help to determine which exercises are needed. Posture work should also include instruction on good body mechanics, emphasizing the following:

- Bend from the knees and lift, using thigh muscles rather than the back. Consciously tighten abdominals when this is not possible.
- Carry loads as close to the body as possible.
- Legs should be firmly planted in a comfortably wide stance when reaching, in order to provide a broad base for support. Twisting motions are to be avoided.

Pelvic Tilt

The pelvic tilt (Fig. 21–2) is the basis for good postural alignment. It relieves lower back strain and is used to achieve efficient expulsion positions. Since the ultimate goal is to incorporate the pelvic tilt into daily, functional posture, it should be taught in many positions. Women who have weak abdominals or tight back extensors and hamstring muscles will find this position difficult to maintain. Shearer believes that if a woman can hold a pelvic tilt for more than 10 to 15 minutes, there is no need for abdominal strengthening.[44] Pelvic tilts in an all-fours position can be helpful in providing relief for pain in the lower back during late pregnancy and labor.

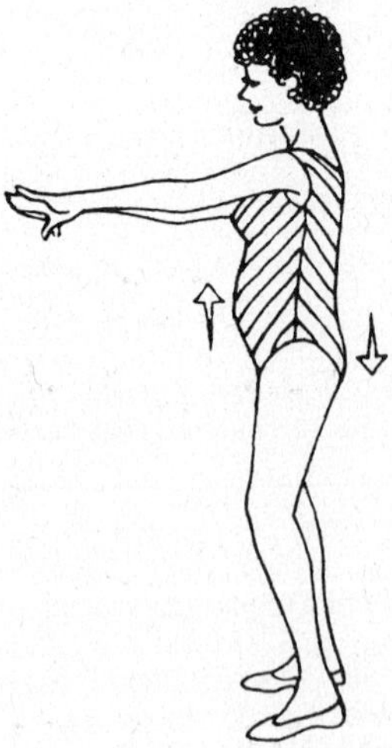

FIGURE 21–2. Pelvic Tilt. (From Nakahata, A., and Sollid, D. *Pre and Post Natal Exercises.* Copyright, Babes, Inc., 1985.)

Abdominal Strengthening

The maintenance of tone in the abdominal muscles is essential for providing adequate support to the spine. With the advance of pregnancy, the spinal column is subjected to ever-increasing stress. This factor, along with having sufficient muscle tone to push effectively in second stage, and the prospect of a speedy recovery postnatally, provide the basic rationale for abdominal exercises.

Exercises can be performed in a variety of ways and positions. One of the simplest is to contract the abdominals during a long exhale. A curl-up from a bent-knee position (Fig. 21–3) is frequently taught in classes. Many childbirth educators prefer to teach let-backs (Fig. 21–4) because this is more comfortable to perform late in pregnancy and allows the client to adjust the movement to her muscle strength. Diagonal curl-ups or let-backs are of value because they involve the oblique muscles, important for maintaining the pelvic tilt and vital for pushing.[37,44] Authorities generally agree that the double-leg raise is to be avoided because of the extreme strain it places on the back and abdomen.[12,43]

Recent electromyographic studies are beginning to examine the effect of positioning and the progression of pregnancy on the abdominal muscles. A study by Booth and co-workers[6] determined that backlying curl-ups were most effective in subjects tested at 38 weeks' gestation. Single-leg raises

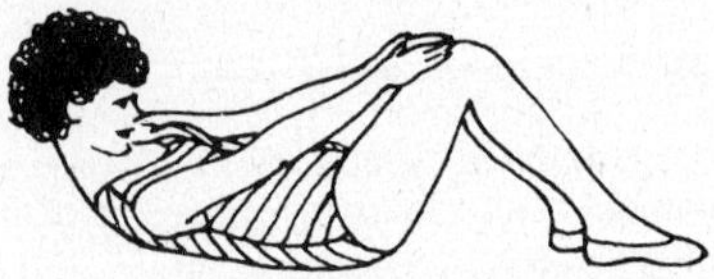

FIGURE 21–3. Curl-up. (From Nakahata, A., and Sollid, D. *Pre and Post Natal Exercises.* Copyright, Babes, Inc., 1985.)

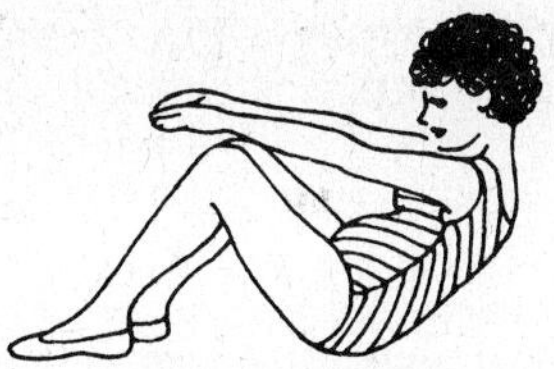

FIGURE 21–4. Let-back. (From Nakahata, A., and Sollid, D. *Pre and Post Natal Exercises.* Copyright, Babes, Inc., 1985.)

were ranked among the most ineffective. Two other studies reported in the *Bulletin of the Ob-Gyn Section of the APTA*[39] noted less activity in both the rectus abdominus and the obliques with both straight and diagonal curl-ups as pregnancy progressed, perhaps due to the extreme stretch to which the muscles are subjected. Until there is more conclusive evidence available, the most effective way to maintain strength in abdominal muscles will be left to the judgment of the childbirth educator. She will base her assessment on such factors as pre-pregnancy muscle tone, size of the uterus, and comfort level of the client.

Before doing any abdominal work, a check for diastasis is essential. This procedure is done by having the pregnant woman lift her head and shoulders from a backlying, bent-knee position. While she maintains this posture, the area round the navel is checked for separation of the recti. Noble states that a separation of more than one inch upon lifting the head from a backlying position requires additional support while exercising.[37] This is done by cupping the two sides of the recti towards the midline with each hand while executing a curl-up.

Lower Back and Hamstring Stretches

These exercises are essential in order to allow enough flexibility for the pelvis to maintain a pelvic tilt with comfort. The exercises need only be done insofar as the tightness of muscles interferes with good posture. A sitting or backlying position offers the most stability for the back (Fig. 21–5). Bending over at the waist from a standing position must be done with care, since the lower back is vulnerable to injury.

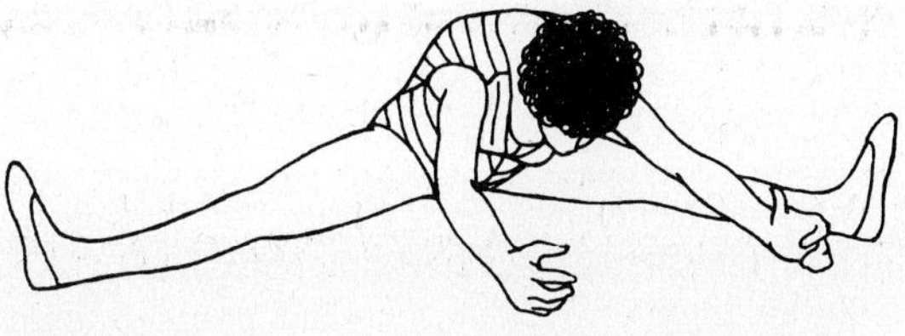

FIGURE 21–5. Lower back and hamstring stretches. (From Nakahata, D. and Sollid, D. *Pre and Post Natal Exercises.* Copyright, Babes, Inc., 1985.)

Neck, Shoulder, Upper Torso Exercises

These exercises release tension, contribute to good posture, and relieve rib cage pressure. Pectoral stretching with attention to actively retracting the shoulders can counteract the "round shoulders" frequently seen in pregnancy. Arm reaches, the "flying" exercise, and neck rolls without hyperextension of the head are some examples of exercises in this category (Fig. 21–6).

FIGURE 26–6. Neck, shoulder, and upper torso exercises. (From Nakahata, A., and Sollid, D. *Pre and Post Natal Exercises.* Copyright, Babes, Inc., 1985.)

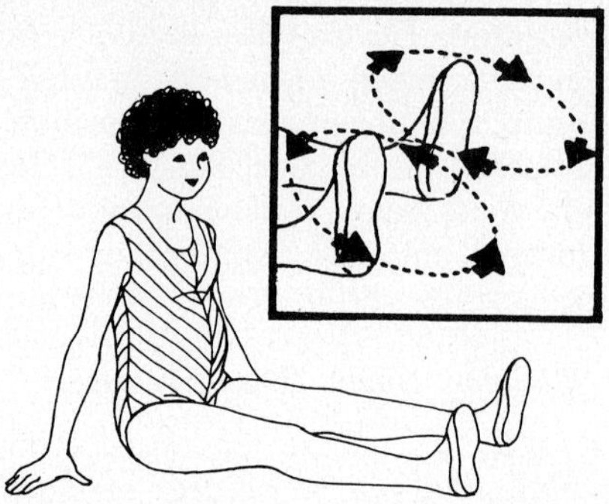

FIGURE 21–7. Foot rotations. (From Nakahata, A., and Sollid, D. *Pre and Post Natal Exercises.* Copyright, Babes, Inc., 1985.)

Foot Rotation

Foot rotation exercises promote venous return and may help to reduce edema. Movement needs to be localized at the ankle joint in order to fully benefit from this exercise (Fig. 21–7). Vigorous extension in rotation should be avoided as it may cause cramping in the calf area.

Squatting

Squatting exercises should be done to increase leg strength so that assuming a squat position for picking up low objects (rather than bending from the waist) and for bearing down during childbirth will be more comfortable. Short periods of squatting with the weight distributed equally over each foot can help the woman become accustomed to this position.[46] Women may need small props under the heels if the Achilles tendons are tight. Prolonged periods of squatting can stress ligaments of the knee and inhibit circulation to the lower extremities. For those with weak quadriceps, a partial squat holding on to a doorknob or chair backrest for support can be a way to begin strengthening the legs.

Adductor Stretches

Adductor stretches are done to increase comfort for expulsion positions. Adductor stretches were considered to be essential by early childbirth educators. With more options for birth positions and with the more active lifestyles of women today, the need for adductor stretches is questionable.[46] If they are used, active movement of the knees outward, rather than passive stretching should be advocated.

Prenatal Exercise Classes

Individual assessment and flexibility of program are absolutely essential in these classes, which precede childbirth education classes. Since these women may be in all stages of pregnancy, the instructor must be ready to suggest modifications or substitutions. Some authorities recommend that women who have not exercised before the pregnancy not enter a program until after the third month because the risk of spontaneous abortion is greater in the first trimester.[52] A health history is important for verifying the health status of the client and also serves to alert the instructor to special problems that might warrant closer observation or require modifications in the exercise program (see Box 21–1).

Most programs begin with a warm-up period in which all major muscle groups are used slowly to allow the muscles and heart to work up to efficiency. There may then be an aerobic component of short duration (5 to 15 minutes), using brisk walking or jogging. Monitoring of maternal heart rate is essential. Many authorities recommend a submaximal target rate of 60 to 70 per cent (220 − age multiplied by 0.60).[9,14] (ACOG recommends less than 140 beats per minute.) During this activity, many women may want to manually support the breasts or uterus.

A strengthening and stretch workout is the core of the class. Variations of exercises and positions mentioned in the previous section are incorporated into the program with the addition of work on toning hips and thighs and chest and maintaining balance. The supine position, particularly after the fifth month, should be used only briefly.[53] As in all physical activity, the cautions about avoiding twisting, bouncing, and jerky movements and being alert to unusual pain, fatigue, or amount of uterine contractions need to be emphasized.

Following the workout, a gradual cooling-down period including gentle stretches is necessary for allowing a slow return to a nonexercise state. A period of relaxation as part of this cooling-down

Box 21–1

PACIFIC PRESBYTERIAN MEDICAL CENTER

EXERCISE FOR PREGNANCY
AND POSTPARTUM RECOVERY

Prenatal/Postpartum History

Name____________________ **Address**____________________

Phone____________________**day** ____________________

____________________**eve.** ____________________

How were you referred to the class?____________________

____

Please answer the following questions, so that we may design the program to meet your specific needs:

1. **Reason for attending:**____________________

   ____

2. **Age:**____________________

3. **Number of weeks pregnant:** ____________________ **Due Date:** __________

4. **Number of pregnancies carried to term:**____________________

5. **Number of cesareans and cause:**____________________

6. **Past or present complications during pregnancy:**____________________

   ____

7. **Number of weeks postpartum:** ____________________ **Delivery Date:** __________

8. **Medical history—Have you had any of the following conditions or problems:**

Cardio-vascular (heart) disease	**yes**______	**no**______
High blood pressure	**yes**______	**no**______
Diabetes	**yes**______	**no**______
Back pain	**yes**______	**no**______
Orthopedic problems	**yes**______	**no**______
Do you smoke?	**yes**______	**no**______

If you answered yes to any of the above, please explain:

____

____

____

Waiver of Claims: I assume full and complete responsibility for any injury or accident which may occur while I am participating or as a result of my participation in the exercise program. I understand that I am participating in this program at my own risk.

Signature/Date ____

Courtesy of Jonna Schengel, RPT, ACCE, and Teresa Corrigan, RN, ACCE, Coordinators of The Family Birthplace Education Program, Pacific Presbyterian Medical Center, San Francisco, CA.

is useful for many reasons. It facilitates recovery from the exertion and serves to acquaint the student with learning the skill of relaxation before she begins her childbirth preparation class.

Many practitioners use music to pace performance as a means to increase the enjoyment of exercise. However, some authorities have made the observation that music may push some women to exceed safe heart levels or encourage bouncing-type movements.[30] Thus, music, if used, requires a judicious appraisal of tempo and duration.

Perhaps one of the most important ingredients of this class is an environment that encourages feedback and allows for a range of performance levels. The instructor's positive, encouraging attitude and her astute professional eye are critical to maintaining a safe, beneficial program. A checklist for consumers on selecting an exercise class is listed in Table 21–3.[46]

Recommendations on Sports Activities

The consensus of experts seems to be that exercise should not exceed pre-pregnancy levels.[27,30,33] High-risk sports such as water skiing and scuba diving should be avoided, along with most contact sports. Heart rate must be monitored and kept at a submaximal level. Women should be advised to expect to decrease the amount of exercise as the pregnancy advances. Switching to nonweightbearing activity is another alternative for late pregnancy.

TABLE 21–3. CHECKLIST FOR SELECTING AN EXERCISE CLASS

1. Instructor's qualifications: Trained by a reputable group/organization; has knowledge of pregnancy, muscle physiology, and kinesiology
2. Instructor's attitudes: Concern for individual client, flexible in ideas, alert to client differences, enthusiastic
3. Environment: Adequate space, well-ventilated, carpeted floor or mats available, temperature adjustable, convenient to bathrooms
4. Class size: Small enough to allow for individual attention, asking questions, observation of incorrect moves and positions
5. Format: Individual assessment, including diastasis check; rationale for each exercise clearly stated; gradual warm-up and cool-down; frequent checks of heart rate; workout of all muscle areas covered in exercises; pace should be slow and methodical; cautions clearly stated

For those who choose to continue jogging, the goal should be to maintain fitness, not to compete or increase mileage. Good supportive footware with shock-absorbing features and a resilient running surface will minimize the jarring effects of weightbearing. Clothes that allow freedom of movement and good breast support will increase comfort. Running should be avoided if temperature or humidity is too high. Conservative authorities recommend limiting mileage to less than two miles per day, a conclusion based on studies that showed both mother and fetus tolerating well this level of activity. Those who are accustomed to greater distances often find themselves reducing mileage as the pregnancy advances.

Bicycling either outdoors or on an indoor stationary cycle is one means of providing aerobic exercise without weightbearing. A standard bicycle may require more attention to balance as the center of gravity changes and weight increases. The 10-speed "crouch" position can aggravate lower back strain.

Swimming or performing exercises in water is also a nonweightbearing activity. The temperature of the water should not exceed 85 to 90° F, in order to maintain body temperature at safe levels. The hydrostatic pressure of the water may have a massaging effect and may be beneficial for those with venous pooling.

The recent popularity of weight training and the use of Nautilus or Universal equipment raises the question of their continued use through pregnancy. As with jogging, maintenance of flexibility and strength should be the goal. In this activity in particular, proper breathing and avoiding the Valsalva maneuver should be emphasized.[3]

A Word About Postpartum

Recommendations for postpartum should be as carefully individualized as for the prenatal period. The ease or difficulty of the birth experience, prior activity levels and fitness, health factors such as blood pressure or diabetes, and fatigue are all considerations. The hormonal effects on connective tissue will not be reversed until six to seven weeks postpartum.[11] Until that time, the risk of injury is still present.

For those with births within the normal range, deep breathing, Kegel exercises, and pelvic tilts can be started within 24 hours. Noble suggests checking for diastasis on the third day.[37] If the gap is more than two fingers wide, she advises carefully performed curl-ups, supporting the two bands of the recti toward the midline. In exercising the abdominal muscles, the intensity can be increased by altering the placement of the arms. Proceeding from arms extended to arms folded over the chest to arms folded behind the head increases the resistance. Lower abdominals and thigh muscles can be strengthened by advancing from bent-knee leg raises or lowers to extended leg raises. Weights can be added to increase resistance further.

The addition of more exercises will depend upon the individual's overall condition, taking into account lochia flow, fatigue, and adjustment to parenthood. The old advice to "Check with your physician" is still valid but not specific enough for some women. Careful monitoring of fatigue levels and lochia flow are good indicators of exercise tolerance level. Return to fitness activities such as jogging should be delayed for about six weeks, and return should be slow and gradual.[30]

Promoting Wellness Through Exercise

The childbirth educator has the opportunity to promote wellness beyond the pregnancy and childbirth period by emphasizing the value of exercise as an essential component of health and well-being. For some women the childbirth preparation class may be the first experience with exercising on a consistent basis. For others who have exercised regularly, it may be one means of maintaining a self-image of a healthy, active body. *The childbirth educator's clarity of presentation, her enthusiasm about the benefits of exercise, and the time she allots to learning will convey the value she places on the role of exercise in health maintenance. Just as relaxation is presented as a life skill, exercise can be described as a life activity.*

An understanding of the mechanism of spinal support and the role of strong abdominals will help to prevent future back problems. Good body mechanics discussed in class will be especially helpful in learning to lift and carry a new and growing infant. An understanding of the role of exercise in fuel metabolism may be the basis for future weight control. If the habit of an aerobic workout three times a week can be developed during pregnancy, there is a good possibility that a similar program will be continued throughout life in order to enjoy the increased stamina and the sense of well-being that comes with such regular activity. An additional incentive for incorporating exercise into a woman's life habits is the recent findings on the role of exercise in preventing osteoporosis after menopause.[23] Thus, the childbirth educator in her role as a primary health information source for pregnancy can be instrumental in helping women to adopt habits that will enhance wellness throughout their lives.

IMPLICATIONS FOR RESEARCH

A survey of existing research makes apparent the critical need for more work on all aspects of pregnancy and physical activity, particularly in studying effects in people. More information is needed on exercise during pregnancy in many areas. Some specific questions are:

- What is the effect of exercise on maternal physiology: cardiovascular, respiratory, metabolic, and endocrine systems?
- What is the effect of exercise on fetal growth, fetal development, and birth outcome?
- What is the effect of exercise on birth: duration of labor and birth, use of medications, complications, and need for medical interventions?
- What is the effect of exercise on maternal recovery: weight loss, return to fitness, lactation, and adjustment to parenthood?

- What is the effect of pre-pregnancy conditioning on exercise tolerance in pregnancy?
- What is the effect of initiating exercise during pregnancy on maternal and fetal health during pregnancy and childbirth?
- What is the effect of frequency and duration of exercise during pregnancy on infant size, labor and birth, and on the training effect of exercise?
- What is the effect of weightbearing versus nonweightbearing exercise on maternal health and specific musculoskeletal changes during pregnancy?
- What is the effect of exercise on women with a multiple pregnancy?
- What is the effect of specific exercises on desired outcomes—e.g., abdominal strengthening and effective pushing, Kegel exercises, and need for episiotomy?

In general, further studies need to be more carefully controlled, to use larger samples, and to provide some longitudinal data on those same subjects. With new, noninvasive techniques of investigation being readily used, the possibility for specific information becomes more realistic.

SUMMARY

Prenatal exercises have been an integral part of preparing for childbirth. Recent interest in fitness has created a desire for increased levels of activity during pregnancy, with a resultant growth of prenatal exercise classes and women continuing to pursue high performance activities throughout the gestational period.

Exercise increases the demands on the pregnant body, raising questions about the risks and benefits to both mother and fetus. Existing studies seem to indicate that moderate levels of exercise are not harmful to the fetus and may be beneficial in maintaining maternal work efficiency. Individual assessment in selecting exercises and close monitoring of performance is essential. More specific guidelines based on further research are needed. The childbirth educator has the opportunity to promote wellness beyond the pregnancy and postpartum periods by emphasizing the importance of exercise as a life-long activity.

References

1. Artal, R. Exercise in pregnancy, notes from presentation. *Technological Approaches to Obstetrics, Benefits, Risks*. San Francisco: Alternative IV, October, 1984.
2. Artal, R., Platt, L., Sperling, M., Kammula, R., Jilek, J., and Nakamura, R. Maternal cardiovascular and metabolic responses in normal pregnancy. *American Journal of Obstetrics and Gynecology* 140:123, 1981.
3. Artal, R., and Wiswell, R. *Exercise in Pregnancy.* Baltimore: Williams & Wilkins, 1986.
4. Bing, E. *A Practical Training Course for the Psychoprophylactic Method of Childbirth*. New York: ASPO, 1969.
5. Bonica, J. *Obstetric Analgesia and Anesthesia*. Amsterdam: World Federation of Societies of Anesthesiologists, 1980.
6. Booth, D., Chennells, M., and Jones, D. Assessment of abdominal muscle exercise in nonpregnant, pregnant, and postpartum, using electromyography. *Australian Journal of Physiology* 26:177, 1980.
7. Calguneri, M., Bird, H., and Wright, V. Changes in joint laxity occurring during pregnancy. *Annals of the Rheumatic Diseases* 41:126, 1982.
8. Clapp, J., and Dickstein, S. Endurance exercise and pregnancy outcome. *Medicine and Science in Sports and Exercise* 16:556, 1984.
9. Collings, C., Curet, L., and Mullin, J. Maternal and fetal responses to a maternal aerobic exercise program. *American Journal of Obstetrics and Gynecology* 145:702, 1983.
10. Dale, E., Mullinax, K., and Bryan, D. Exercise during pregnancy: Effects on the fetus. *Canadian Journal of Applied Sport Sciences* 7:98, 1982.
11. Danforth, D. Pregnancy and labor from the vantage point of the physical therapist. *American Journal of Physical Medicine* 46:653, 1967.
12. DeSanto, P., and Hassid, P. Evaluating exercises. *Childbirth Educator* 26, Spring, 1983.
13. Dick-Read, G. *Childbirth Without Fear.* New York: Harper and Row, 1959.
14. Dilfer, C. *Your Baby, Your Body.* New York: Crown, 1977.

15. Dressendorfer, R., and Goodlin, R. Fetal heart rate responses to maternal exercise testing. *The Physician and Sportsmedicine* 8:91, 1980.
16. Edwards, P., Beresford, P.L., Nadon, C., and Steeves, C. Fitness and pregnancy: A round table discussion. *Canadian Journal of Public Health* 74:86, 1983.
17. Edwards, M., Metcalfe, J., Dunham, J., and Paul, M. Accelerated respiratory response to moderate exercise in late pregnancy. *Respiratory Physiology* 45:229, 1981.
18. Erkkola, R. The influence of physical training during pregnancy on physical work capacity and circulatory parameters. *Scandinavian Journal of Clinical Laboratory Investigation* 36:747, 1976.
19. Fitzhugh, M. *Preparation For Childbirth*. San Jose: Aksarben Press, 1963.
20. Fletcher, W. Exercises in obstetrics. *In* Licht, S. (ed.) *Therapeutic Exercise*. New Haven: E. Licht Publisher, 1958.
21. Fraser, D. Postpartum backache: A preventable condition? *Canadian Family Physician* 22:1434, 1976.
22. George, G., and Berk, B. Exercise before, during and after pregnancy. *Topics in Clinical Nursing* 3:33, 1981.
23. Greenwood, S. *Menopause Naturally*. San Francisco: Volcan Press, 1984.
24. Hauth, J., Gilstrap, L., and Widmer, K. Fetal heart rate reactivity before and after maternal jogging during the third trimester. *American Journal of Obstetrics and Gynocology* 142:545, 1982.
25. Hon, E., and Wohlgemuth, R. The electronic evaluation of fetal heart rate. *American Journal of Obstetrics and Gynecology* 81:361, 1981.
26. Jarrett, J., and Spellacy, W. Jogging during pregnancy: An improved outcome? *Obstetrics and Gynecology* 61:705, 1983.
27. Jopke, T. Pregnancy: A time to exercise judgment. *The Physician and Sportsmedicine* 11:139, 1983.
28. Karmel, M. *Thank You, Dr. Lamaze*. New York: Doubleday, 1965.
29. Knuttgen, H., and Emerson, K. Physiological response to pregnancy at rest and during exercise. *Journal of Applied Physiology* 36:549, 1974.
30. Leaf, D., and Paul, M. Giving birth to a new theory: Is running OK while pregnant? *Runner's World* 70:49, 1983.
31. Little, J. Postural adjustments during pregnancy and implications for the childbearing woman. *Bulletin of Obstetrics and Gynecology* 8:16, 1984.
32. Lotgering, F., Gilbert, R., and Longo, L. The interactions of exercise and pregnancy: A review. *Physiology Review* 65:1, 1985.
33. Maeder, E. Effects of sports and exercise in pregnancy. *Postgraduate Medicine* 77:112, 1985.
34. Marsal, K., Lofgren, O., and Gennser, G. Fetal breathing movements and maternal exercise. *Acta Obstetrics and Gynecology of Scandinavia* 58:197, 1979.
35. Morris, N., Osborn, S., Wright, H., and Hart, A. Effective uterine blood flow during exercise in normal and preeclamptic pregnancies. *Lancet* 2:481, 1956.
36. Nakahata, A., and Sollid, D. *Pre and Post Natal Exercises*. Kentfield, CA: Babes, Inc., 1985.
37. Noble, E. *Essential Exercises for the Childbearing Year*. Boston: Houghton Mifflin, 1976.
38. O'Conner, L. (ed.). Special issue-exercise. *Bulletin of Obstetrics and Gynecology* Vol. 8, 1984.
39. O'Conner, L. (ed.). Continuing education. *Bulletin of Obstretrics and Gynecology,* APTA, Vol. 10, 1986.
40. Pernoll, M., Metcalfe, J., Kovach, P., Wachtel, R. and Dunham, M. Ventilation during rest and exercise in pregnancy and postpartum. *Respiratory Physiology* 25:295, 1975.
41. Pijpers, L., Wladimiroff, J., and McGhie, J. Effect of short-term maternal exercise on maternal and fetal cardiovascular dynamics. *British Journal of Obstetrics and Gynecology* 91:1081, 1984.
42. Pipp, L. The knee-chest position and air embolism: A review of the literature. *Bulletin of Obstetrics and Gynecology* 8:43, 1984.
43. Pomerance, J., Gluck, L., and Lynch, V. Maternal exercise as a screening test for uteroplacental insufficiency. *Obstetrics and Gynecology* 44:383, 1974.
44. Shearer, M. Teaching prenatal exercise: Part 1. Posture. *Birth and the Family Journal* 8:167, 1981.
45. Shrock, P. Exercise and physical activity during pregnancy. *Gynecology Obstetrics* 2:1, 1978.
46. Shrock, P. Questions to ask when choosing a prenatal exercise class. *Genesis* 6:9, 1984.
47. Shrock, P., Simkin, P., and Shearer, M. Teaching prenatal exercise: Part II. Exercises to think twice about. *Birth and the Family Journal* 8:1167, 1981.
48. Sibley, L., Ruhling, R., Cameron-Foster, J., Christensen, C., and Bolen, T. Swimming and physical fitness during pregnancy. *Journal of Nurse Midwifery* 26:3, 1981.
49. Snyder, D., and Carruth, B. Current controversies: Exercising during pregnancy, *Journal of Adolescent Health Care* 5:34, 1984.
50. Tanaka, Y. A new approach to pregnancy and recovery fitness. Presented at Technological Approaches to Obstetrics, Benefits, Risks, Alternatives IV, San Francisco, 1984.
51. Wirth, V., Emmons, P., and Larson, D. Running through pregnancy: Part 1. *Runners World* 55, November, 1978.
52. Woodward, S. How does strenuous maternal exercise affect the fetus? A review, *Birth and the Family Journal* 8:17, 1981.
53. Van Gelder, N. Teaching maternal fitness. *Dance Exercise Today* 3:33, 1985.

Beginning Quote

Fitzhugh, M. *Preparation for Childbirth*. San Jose: Aksarben Press, 1963.

Boxed Quotes

1. Vaugh, K. *Exercises before Childbirth*. London: Faber & Faber, 1951. Cited in Artal, R., and Wiswell, R. *Exercise in Pregnancy*. Baltimore: Williams & Wilkins, 1986.
2. Kitzinger, S. *Exercises for Increased Awareness in Education and Counselling in Childbirth*. London: Bailliere-Tindall, 1977. Cited in Artal, R., and Wiswell, R. *Exercise in Pregnancy*. Baltimore: Williams & Wilkins, 1986.
3. Cedeno, L., Cedeno, O., and Monroe, C. *The Exercise Plus Pregnancy Program*. New York: William Morrow, 1980. Cited in Artal, R., and Wiswell, R. *Exercise in Pregnancy*. Baltimore: Williams & Wilkins, 1986.

chapter 22

SUPPORT SYSTEMS

LINDA CORSON JONES

The supportive sharing by significant persons is not so much a matter of dependence but a necessary condition for the giving of self in the totality required for childbirth.

Reva Rubin

In everyone's life, supportive relationships play an important role in promoting health, preventing medical problems, buffering the effects of stress, and strengthening coping efforts.[8,16,25,26,36] For the childbearing family, supportive relationships influence the number of pregnancy complications, the decision to breastfeed, adjustment to parenthood, and parent-infant interaction. A framework to de-

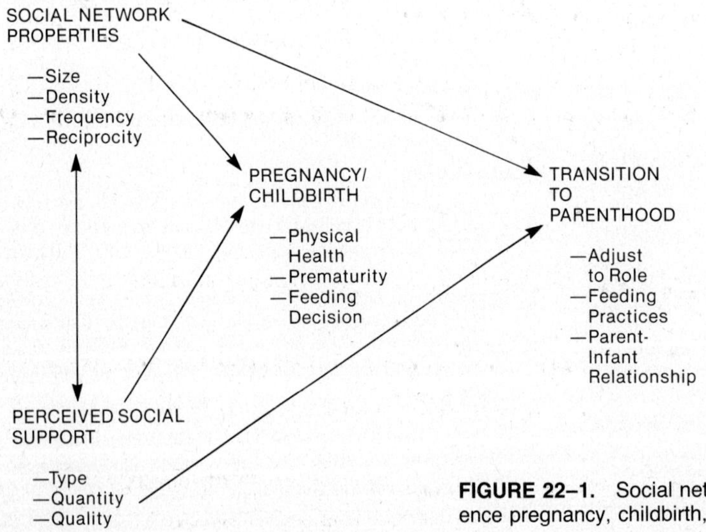

FIGURE 22–1. Social network and social support variables that influence pregnancy, childbirth, and the transition to parenthood.

pict the influence of social network and social support factors on the responses to parenthood is shown in Figure 22–1. This model was used in framing questions for a review of the literature about social support during the childbearing year.

1. What social support resources are available to the childbearing family?
2. What are the benefits of social support for the childbearing family?
3. What are the characteristics of men and women's social networks and social support during the childbearing year?
4. Are different sources and types of support important at different times during the childbearing experience?
5. Is all social support positive, or is there evidence for a "negative side" of support during the childbearing year?
6. Does social support intervention assist the childbearing family?

REVIEW OF THE LITERATURE

What is Social Support?

Social support has been defined as information leading to the belief that one is cared for, loved, esteemed, valued, and part of a network of communication and mutual obligation.[14] Other authors extend the definition of social support to include actual help received and potential help available if it is needed.[12,24] Social support behaviors can be categorized as:[27]

- *Emotional:* Communication of empathy, caring, love, and trust.
- *Instrumental:* Direct aid, such as gifts of money or help with work.
- *Informational:* Sharing information that individuals can use in coping with problems.
- *Appraisal:* Sharing information to help individuals evaluate themselves.

How is Social Support Exchanged?

Social network—the social ties that link individuals—has recently been included in studies of social support and the childbearing family.[20] Anthropologists and sociologists in the 1940's developed social network analysis in order to map power, decision-making, and knowledge diffusion among members of a society.[31,46] Network analysis enables the examination not only of the supportive exchanges between people but also the characteristics of the individuals involved in them. Several features of social networks are frequently discussed:[31]

- *Size:* The number of individuals in a network.
- *Density:* The extent to which members of an individual's social network know and contact one another.
- *Reciprocity:* The extent to which obligations of both give and take are honored.
- *Geographic proximity:* The extent to which an individual's social network lives close.

Social networks can account for the availability and transmission of social support resources for individuals and families.[25] A variety of approaches to mapping the different levels of social networks have been discussed in the literature.[25,26,31,46] Dividing expectant parents' social relationships into network zones illuminates the layers of relationships that they can potentially mobilize for support (Fig. 22–2).

- Spouses and close family members who are most significant to an expectant parent's life occupy the first-order network. Typically, a number of different types of support, such as emotional and instrumental (tangible), are exchanged among individuals within this zone.[20] These relationships represent the most dense component of an

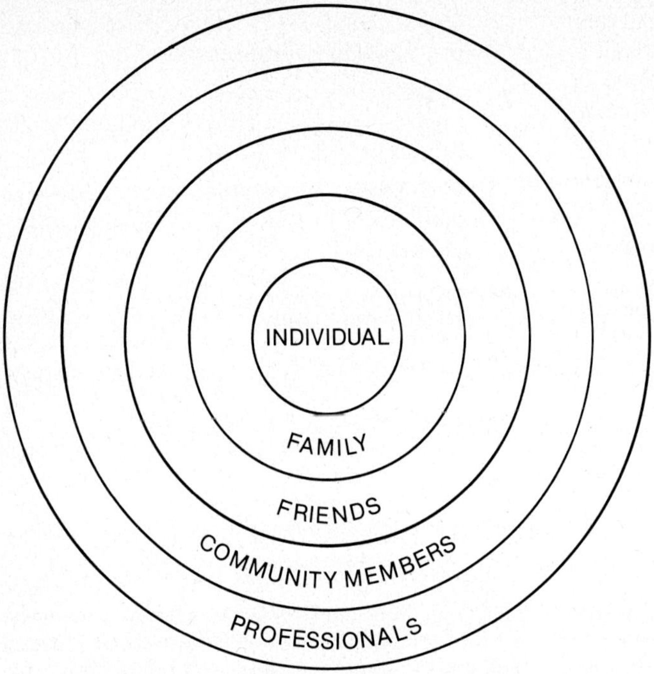

FIGURE 22–2. The social networks of expectant parents.

individual's social network.[31] When an expectant parent has a problem, spouses and family members may be closest in geographic proximity and may know how to help. On the other hand, members of this zone are most likely to be affected by the same problems and may also need support.[25]

- Other relatives and friends with whom there is ongoing contact comprise the second-order network. This network zone may also provide a variety of supportive services.[26] Members of this zone are important sources of support, because they are among the first to hear about any new life events or problems.[25] Unlike the first-order zone, these members are usually somewhat removed from the life events that affect the expectant parents.
- Key community members, including self-help groups such as the LaLeche League, occupy the third-order network. Although members of this network zone are separated from the daily world of the expectant parents and their families, they can provide insight and information that is not available from the expectant parents' usual contacts.[25] Expectant parents may turn to this zone for referral information about the types of professional services to seek for their health beliefs and special needs.
- Professional helpers are the fourth-order network. Although most expectant parents seek assistance from this zone, they also continue seeking support from individuals in the other zones.[25]

Pregnancy and Childbirth

A number of studies demonstrate that supportive relationships influence pregnancy and childbirth (Table 22–1). Women who receive more social support have lower rates of pregnancy and childbirth complications compared with women who have lower levels of support.[7,10,22,32,33,51] Social support was related to better physical and emotional health, greater satisfaction with pregnancy, shorter labor, and fewer premature births. In a similar vein, men who receive emotional support during their wives' pregnancy experience better physical and emotional health.[10]

Social support also plays a role during pregnancy in promoting healthy relationships and practices. Emotionally supportive relationships facilitate the development of parental attachment behaviors toward the unborn child.[17,50] Peers, mothers, and male partners are important sources of informational and emotional support to women when making the decision to choose breastfeeding.[4,43]

Since most studies have examined a remarkably homogeneous population of white middle-income men and women during the third trimester of pregnancy, a composite picture of expectant fathers' and mothers' social networks can be obtained by integrating findings from a number of studies.[7,13,17,20] The typical expectant parent has a social support network of eight to nine members in the first- and second-order zones. The size of the network and the frequency of contact with its members are similar for men and women.

The social networks of both men and women are dominated by relatives. Men obtain much of their support from their wives. Women, however, obtain support from more sources, as compared with men. Relatives provide a great deal of emotional and instrumental support for men, and instrumental support for women. Women's greatest sources of emotional support are relatives, husbands, and other women. Although couples may attend childbirth classes and share in labor and birth, men and women often do not view their spouses as significant sources of informational and appraisal support. For men, co-workers are sources of informational support, and friends are sources of appraisal support. For women, most appraisal and informational support is derived from female co-workers or friends.

Men and women report receiving the same amount of instrumental, informational, and appraisal support. Women, however, receive greater emotional and total support. Men and women differ somewhat in satisfaction with support received from the partner. Men generally are satisfied with the support they receive. Women's satisfaction varies; women under stress report greater dissatisfaction with support from both their partners and others. Men under stress are less satisfied with other people's support, while their satisfaction with their partner's support remains the same.

The primary relationships of mother-daughter and husband-wife are the most influential during pregnancy.[2,3] Social support between husband and wife operates as a reciprocal system.[15] Expectant parents who report giving a great deal of support have partners who also report giving much support. However, paradoxically, many expectant parents report giving increased support while their partners do not recognize the increase in support.[15] One researcher maintained that even though expectant fathers experience more nurturing feelings toward their wives, they may not express them.[49] Expectant parents also may be unclear about the type of support their partners need. Thus, some individuals may be trying to give a great deal of help, but their partners do not perceive the assistance as support.[49]

Mothers who are able to mobilize support from their social networks are more satisfied with their lives and parenting and are more responsive to their infants. (Photograph © Harvey Wang.)

The pregnant woman's mother is an important contributer to the maternal role.[38,40] The pregnant

TABLE 22–1. SUMMARY OF STUDIES ON SOCIAL SUPPORT AND THE CHILDBEARING FAMILY: PREGNANCY AND CHILDBIRTH OUTCOMES

RESEARCHER	DESCRIPTION	FINDINGS
Ballou[2] (1978)	12 primiparous women were followed from 10 weeks of pregnancy to 3 months after childbirth	Women's relationships with their husbands and mothers were very important to them. Women invested a great deal of psychic energy reworking their relationships with their husbands and mothers. Women who had emotionally supportive husbands were better able to resolve dependency issues in mother-daughter relationships.
Baranowski et al.[4] (1983)	358 women were interviewed within 48 hours of giving birth about factors related to choice of feeding	Source of support for promoting breastfeeding varied by ethnic group. Among blacks, support from a close friend was most important. Among Mexican-Americans, support from the women's mother was most important. White women ranked male partner as most important source of support, with best friend ranking second. White women's mothers exerted a negative influence on breastfeeding.
Berkowitz & Kasl[7] (1983)	166 mothers with premature infants were compared to 299 mothers with normal infants	Mothers of normal infants had received slightly more partner support during pregnancy as compared with mothers of premature infants.
Brown[10] (1983)	In latter half of pregnancy, 313 expectant mothers and fathers were questioned about social support and symptomatology in latter half of pregnancy	Social support was related to all dimensions of health in women and to all dimensions, except physical symptoms, in men. Individuals who reported receiving less support experienced more symptoms.
Cranley[17] (1979)	30 women were interviewed during last 6 weeks of pregnancy and 3 days postpartum to determine maternal-fetal attachment	Having a strong social support system of family, friends, and helping professionals was positively associated with maternal-fetal attachment. Support of health care professionals was most highly correlated.
Gladieux[23] (1975)	26 women were interviewed 3 times during pregnancy	Involvement with other pregnant women increased women's satisfaction with pregnancy experience. Support from husbands was important during each trimester in making pregnancy more satisfying.
Norbeck and Tilden[32] (1983)	Socioeconomically diverse group of 117 women were followed from 12–20 weeks of pregnancy through childbirth	48.7% of women experienced complications. High life stress and low social support were significantly related to emotional disequilibrium. Decreased tangible social support in combination with high life stress was associated with increased complications.
Nuckolls et al.[33] (1972)	170 white primiparous Army wives were followed through pregnancy	Social support buffered the effect of negative life events. Women with many psychosocial assets had a complication rate of only 33%, compared to 91% for women with few psychosocial assets.
Richardson[38] (1981)	14 women were interviewed monthly throughout their pregnancy	Relationships with parental figures were more helpful than peer relationships. Although women sought peers in beginning of pregnancy, both pregnant women and peers became involved in their own day-to-day activities and responsibilities as pregnancy advanced.
Rubin[40] (1967)	5 primiparous and 4 multiparous women were studied from first trimester through one month following childbirth	During pregnancy, the women's mothers provided comfort, companionship, and practical advice about body changes during pregnancy. After initially using their mothers' assistance in each phase of pregnancy, the women sought peers for support. Mother-daughter relationships seemed to

TABLE 22–1. SUMMARY OF STUDIES ON SOCIAL SUPPORT AND THE CHILDBEARING FAMILY: PREGNANCY AND CHILDBIRTH OUTCOMES *Continued*

RESEARCHER	DESCRIPTION	FINDINGS
		intensify the pregnant women's sense of maternal inadequacies because the women perceived that their mothers were too competent and knowledgeable.
Sullivan and Jones[43] (1986)	Data from 181 low-income black women were examined to determine variables related to breastfeeding adoption	Support from the women's mothers was important in selecting and continuing breastfeeding. Most women did not consider nurses or other health professionals influential in selecting breastfeeding.
Thrasher[44] (1963)	An ethnographic study of a married graduate student housing complex	Pregnant women had developed strong social networks of many friends and associates who were also pregnant. This helped women compare their pregnancy experiences with those of other women. The pregnant women developed a model of a "typical pregnancy" that had far more symptoms than any individual woman experienced. Each woman who was experiencing pregnancy-related problems was able to rate herself as doing very well.
Weaver and Cranley[50] (1983)	100 husbands who were attending childbirth classes were interviewed during the third trimester of pregnancy	Paternal-fetal attachment exhibited by men was associated with the amount of emotional support they received from their wives.
Weisz[51] (1981)	89 primiparous women were followed from the second trimester of pregnancy through six weeks postpartum	Women with larger social networks had fewer complications.
Zachariah[52] (1985)	115 women were interviewed once during pregnancy	Women derived most of their support from their husbands and mothers. The strength of husband-wife attachment and mother-daughter attachment were positively related to psychological well-being.

woman's mother provides comfort, companionship, and reality testing for the pregnant woman.[40] Maternal support contributes to pregnant women's emotional health.[52]

A social network composed of many friends and associates who are also pregnant is important to expectant women. Involvement in the "subculture of pregnancy" allows expectant women to compare their experiences with other women. This type of support increases pregnant women's satisfaction with the pregnancy experience.[23,44]

Social relationships, while important, can also generate stress.[45] Although no study specifically examined problematic relationships or the costs of receiving social support during pregnancy, a number of conclusions can be drawn from the literature:

- Pregnant women's relationships with their mothers are important but are laced with ambivalence and require a great deal of conciliatory work.[2,3] Women invest a great deal of energy in attempting to resolve relationship problems during pregnancy.[38]

- Expectant fathers' emotional support is important to the well-being of their mates. However, the traditional image of the expectant couple consisting of a support-giving husband and a support-receiving wife must be questioned. Expectant fathers are particularly vulnerable, with stress scores higher than pregnant women.[10] In addition, men receive little naturally occurring support for looking out for their own well-being.

- Pregnancy is a time when the marital relationship is re-evaluated.[29] The existence of a pregnancy may heighten the anxiety and stress of a marital relationship.

- Multiparous women, especially women preg-

TABLE 22–2. SUMMARY OF STUDIES ON SOCIAL SUPPORT AND THE CHILDBEARING FAMILY: PARENTING OUTCOMES

RESEARCHER	DESCRIPTION	FINDINGS
Abernathy[1] (1973)	41 mothers with preschool children were interviewed	Dense social networks were associated with a perception of increased maternal competency. Mothers with less dense networks received a great deal of conflicting child-rearing advice and little feedback about how well they were doing as parents.
Barnard et al.[5] (1984)	A 3-month structured nursing program was used in intervening with 60 infants and their families with physical, health, and social-environmental risks	Some families benefited from the nursing program. The nurses found that they had more difficulty establishing relationships with new mothers during the early postpartum period, as compared to during pregnancy.
Bryant[11] (1982)	76 families enrolled in a public health program were interviewed about infant feeding practices	Having a supportive network of family and friends was related to success in breastfeeding. Absence of a supportive network of family and friends was related to women quitting breastfeeding earlier than they had planned and feeling unhappy about their inability to breastfeed longer. Women's social network had considerable influence on decisions surrounding bottlefeeding, the use of sucrose supplements, and the time to introduce solid foods.
Cohen[15] (1983)	118 mothers completed questionnaires several months after childbirth	Husbands' support was positively related to lower levels of depression in their wives. Support was especially critical in buffering against depression when women were dealing with infant caretaking.
Crnic et al.[18] (1983)	52 mother-premature infant pairs and 53 mother-full-term infant pairs were seen for four months after childbirth	Social support from husbands improved maternal-infant interaction with term and premature infants and increased mothers' satisfaction with life and parenting.
Crockenberg[19] (1981)	48 infant-mother pairs were followed for 1 year after childbirth	Mothers who received more social support had higher levels of maternal-infant attachment. This finding was most significant for attachment between mothers and infants with difficult temperaments.
Cronenwett[21] (1980)	90 women who had participated in a lay postpartum support group program completed questionnaires	Women stated that they joined the parenting groups primarily to share ideas and feelings with other women who were going through the same experiences. When asked to describe why discussion topics were meaningful to them, 73% mentioned the importance of discovering the universal nature of their feelings and receiving reassurance that their own experiences were normal. Women who participated in the groups were somewhat older and better educated.
Cronenwett[20] (1983)	50 primiparous women and their husbands were followed from 3rd trimester of pregnancy to 6 weeks after childbirth	Emotional and instrumental support were positively related to confidence in parenting and satisfaction with parenting. Appraisal support was not related to any parenthood outcomes.
Erickson[22] (1983)	38 primiparous women were followed from the 9th month of pregnancy through several months after childbirth	Women who received social support displayed greater self-confidence in parenting. Husbands' support was positively related to greater self-confidence.
Ladas[28] (1972)	756 women who breastfed their first child completed questionnaires	Women who received informational and emotional support for breastfeeding reported greater satisfaction with it, and breastfed longer than women who received little support.

TABLE 22–2. SUMMARY OF STUDIES ON SOCIAL SUPPORT AND THE CHILDBEARING FAMILY: PARENTING OUTCOMES *Continued*

RESEARCHER	DESCRIPTION	FINDINGS
Lobo[30] (1982)	72 expectant couples were followed from 3rd trimester of pregnancy to 6 weeks after childbirth	For mothers and fathers prenatal support was positively related to confidence in parenthood and infant caretaking.
Oakley[34] (1980)	55 British primiparous women were interviewed several times during pregnancy and following childbirth	Women were identified as victims or victors of childbirth depending on whether or not they experienced depression. Four supports protected women against depression: helpful mates, absence of housing problems, a part-time job, and experience with infants. No mother who had all four supports was a victim; yet 100% of the women lacking all four supports were victims.
Paykel et al.[35] (1980)	120 women were interviewed several weeks after childbirth	Depressed women tended to have husbands who were less communicative and offered little help; these women also had few friends or relatives to confide in.
Raikes[37] (1981)	A cross-sectional study of 42 primiparous mothers 4 months after birth	Network support was significantly related to management of the transition period, perceived mothering competency, infant-mother interaction, and depression. All types of support helped mothers with transition period.
Rumer[41] (1982)	A prospective longitudinal study of expectant couples ($n = 32$) and a comparison group of childless couples ($n = 10$)	Couples having their first child experienced more life change events, had more emotional upset, and had more traditional divisions of household labor than childless couples. Couples having children needed and received more help than childless couples. Amount of social support received after birth was not based on size of couple's support network. Social support was moderately associated with lowered anxiety.
Shereshefsky and Yarrow[42] (1974)	60 expectant couples were followed from the 1st trimester of pregnancy to 6 months after childbirth.	Women who displayed self-confidence in mothering and high-level mother-infant interaction had husbands who were responsive to them and involved with household routines.
Wandersman et al.[48] (1980)	A longitudinal study examining effects of a parent support group. Experimental group consisted of 41 new parents in a parenting group 2 months after delivery and a comparison group of 48 new parents who were interested in the parenting group but could not participate	The importance of types of support may be different for fathers and mothers. For fathers, the combination of participation in the group and a positive relationship with their wives was associated with positive well-being, increased marital interaction, and an increased sense of parental competence 9 months after completion of group. For mothers, having close friends to talk with was related to a sense of well-being.

nant with the second child, report difficult and stressful relationships with their preschool age children.[39,57] Mothers sometimes feel they are betraying their first child by having another child, and young children may regress or act out. The reorganization of parent-child relationships begins during pregnancy and continues during the transition-to-parenthood period.

Transition to Parenthood

It has been well documented that naturally occurring social support eases the adjustment to parenthood (Table 22–2). Women who receive social support, particularly from their husbands, have lower rates of postpartum depression, compared to women with lower levels of support.[15,34,35,37] In addition, women who receive social support believe that they are more competent with parenting and express greater satisfaction with parenting.[1,22,30,37,41,42] Men who receive social support have greater confidence in early parenting and greater parental satisfaction.[20,30,41]

A number of studies have concluded that mothers who are able to mobilize social support from their social networks are more responsive to their infants.[18,19,37,42] Several mechanisms may account for this finding. Social support may increase mothers' satisfaction with their lives and parenting and thereby improve maternal-infant interaction.[18,42] Assistance with household routines and infant caretaking may preserve women's energy, enabling them to be more responsive and synchronous with their infants.[9] Mothers who have difficulty interacting with their infants also have difficulty interacting with adults and thus receive little social support.[5,6]

Parents derive a great deal of their child-rearing information from their social networks.[1,11,28] Parents who are geographically close to friends and relatives turn to their social networks instead of health care professionals for infant care advice.[11] In addition, parents with dense social networks benefit from more consistent advice and clear feedback, compared to parents with less dense social networks.[1] Support groups seem to help new parents, particularly those individuals with few other natural sources of emotional and appraisal support.[21,37,48]

IMPLICATIONS FOR PRACTICE

The childbirth educator is in a pivotal position to help childbearing families obtain the support they need. Childbirth classes can help expectant men and women to assess their support systems, identify ways their network can be strengthened, anticipate the types of support they will need during the transition to parenting, and seek the help they need.

A brief introduction to the concept of social networks can give couples a new way to view their relationships and the importance of social support. Network mapping is an activity that enables parents to identify the people who are most important to their well-being. Ask class members to list the ten people in their lives who help them the most, and then identify which types of support these people provide. Expectant parents can examine how these supportive individuals are connected and the extent to which their supportive relationships are tied in a single sphere of life, such as work, the nuclear family, church, and neighborhood. It is important that expectant parents consider if they will be losing some important sources of support if they quit a job or move into a different neighborhood.

This is a good time to discuss the problems of expectant mothers depending upon only one person, such as the spouse or mother, for the majority of their support. Encouragement to seek many sources of support can balance the woman/partner team emphasis sometimes promoted in classes.

Many expectant parents worry about losing old friends with the arrival of the first baby. Childbirth educators may need to reassure class members that their social life will probably change somewhat, but that most parents with young children do not have fewer relationships with others. In fact, having young children may actually stimulate the development of new relationships.

Expectant parents can be helped to more clearly identify and communicate their needs to their partners by each completing a questionnaire such as the Support During Pregnancy Questionnaire (Table 22–3) and then discussing their responses with their partners, either in class or at home. This strategy emphasizes the needs of both men and women during pregnancy. Class discussion might focus on the reciprocal nature of support (that partners who give more typically also report getting more). Rating the *importance* of various kinds of support rather than checking whether the partner is giving enough of a particular type of support allows for different styles of family functioning. For example,

TABLE 22–3. SUPPORT DURING PREGNANCY QUESTIONNAIRE

You may find that expecting a baby changes the type of help or emotional support you need. Sharing your thoughts with your spouse can be very helpful.

Complete this questionnaire (circle your answers) about how important each of the following types of help are to you and then spend a few minutes sharing your answers with each other. There are no right or wrong answers to this questionnaire.

1. Makes extra efforts to do special things for me.

Not Important — *Somewhat Important* — *Very Important*

2. Spends time preparing the house for the baby.

Not Important — *Somewhat Important* — *Very Important*

3. Listens to my concerns about our relationship.

Not Important — *Somewhat Important* — *Very Important*

4. Physically shows me that he/she loves or cares for me.

Not Important — *Somewhat Important* — *Very Important*

5. Lets me know that I am important.

Not Important — *Somewhat Important* — *Very Important*

6. Boosts me when I feel discouraged.

Not Important — *Somewhat Important* — *Very Important*

7. Talks with me about the baby.

Not Important — *Somewhat Important* — *Very Important*

8. Shows me that other things, in addition to the pregnancy, are also important (work, friends, marriage).

Not Important — *Somewhat Important* — *Very Important*

9. Shares pregnancy with me through doctor visits, classes, etc.

Not Important — *Somewhat Important* — *Very Important*

10. Lets me know that I do some things well.

Not Important — *Somewhat Important* — *Very Important*

a couple may decide that they do not assign much importance to a particular type of helping that is valued by other couples.

Changes in relationships can be discussed with content about other physical and emotional changes during pregnancy. General information about the many changes that relationships undergo during pregnancy may reassure expectant parents that relationship changes are normal. Both positive and negative changes in relationships can be discussed.

Couples who already have a small child may be greatly helped by discussion of the normal ambivalent feelings about having a second child, and of preschoolers displaying regressed or dependent behavior throughout pregnancy and the postpartum period. Handouts outlining specific suggestions for dealing with the reorganization of parent-child relationships might be helpful.

Factual information, such as the following statements, may help expectant parents anticipate their needs for support and mobilize the right amount and type of support:

1. Parents who have a great deal of support are likely to be better off than those who do not.

> Supportive husbands had a calming effect on their wives and . . . their sensitivity to needs erased the gravida's sense of vulnerability.
>
> REGINA LEDERMAN[1]
>
> By the time the baby came there were my children, the housekeeper, my husband, two childbirth teachers, the photographer, my secretary, the nurse, and of course the doctor—how's that for support?
>
> A NEW MOTHER
>
> The most important, the essential, help and support that any grandmother can give her daughter is to build up this confidence in herself, a feeling of rightness about being a mother and of the way she handles her baby, and to help relate herself to the baby.
>
> SHEILA KITZINGER[2]

2. Parents report that during pregnancy they underestimated how much they needed support during the first few months.
3. Lining up someone only for the first week home is probably not enough help.
4. Having family and friends visit is not enough. Parents need relief during the few months so they can rest.
5. Parents need to hear they they are doing a good job, rather than have others doubt their abilities.
6. It is easier to find outlets for recreation and enjoyment before the baby is born.
7. Even very active and supportive new fathers may need their efforts supplemented by other helpers.

The childbirth educator can use group process to effectively portray the helpfulness of a social network. A class warm-up strategy that quickly demonstrates the power of a network for information-seeking is the Cocktail Exercise. Each person writes down one question related to pregnancy, labor and birth, or new parenting that they would like to have answered (such as Which is the best infant car seat to buy?). Then class members circulate and ask others if they have the answer or if they know of someone who does. Within ten minutes, most people will either have the information or the name of someone who can help.

Expectant parents may seek appraisal support during childbirth classes. The childbirth educator can encourage the use of appraisal support by openly acknowledging the social comparison process, remarking with statements such as, "You probably are all guessing which woman will deliver before the course ends," or "You probably have been checking with each other during class breaks to find out if other men and women have experienced the same 'best' and 'worst' parts of the pregnancy experience." Parents can be reassured that their need to compare experiences will continue throughout parenting. The childbirth educator can point out that this comparison of experiences is one of the values of parenting groups.

Informal conversation and sharing can provide class members with important support. Simple steps, such as allowing adequate time for breaks, introducing couples to each other, and pointing out similarities help. A couple from the class whose infant is born before it ends can provide a great deal of informational and emotional support to their "remaining" classmates by reporting on their experience. The new parents may share specific information about support, such as the types of help that they found most effective during labor and birth and early parenting, and whether they have changed their views of the help that was most needed.

A number of topics during the childbirth classes can be presented through information sharing. This strategy encourages expectant parents to independently seek information and it promotes informational support among class members. For example, members can be asked to call or visit various agencies or services that might be helpful to new parents, or they might be asked to check on the pros and cons of various controversial topics such as inductions, cesarean births, routine fetal monitoring, and early discharge. Each person's information can then be briefly shared with the entire class the next week.

IMPLICATIONS FOR RESEARCH

Although research has examined social support and the childbearing family, a number of gaps are evident. The following questions need to be addressed:

- What is the influence of social support on expectant and new fathers?
- What is the influence of social support on individuals from diverse backgrounds, including lower socioeconomic men and women, multiparous women, single women, and remarried couples?
- What aspects of emotional, informational, instrumental (tangible), and appraisal support have the greatest influence during childbearing?
- Under what circumstances does receiving social support produce stress for expectant and new parents?

Longitudinal research examining how social support operates throughout pregnancy and the transition to parenthood is also needed. Studies need to examine network variables, as well as social support. Finally, additional research needs to examine how support interventions, such as parenting groups, pregnancy classes, and support groups, influence childbearing outcomes.

SUMMARY

The multidimensional concepts of social support and social networks provide a new perspective for childbirth education. A rich body of research literature documents that supportive relationships influence the nature of pregnancy and early parenting. Childbirth educators play an important role in helping childbearing families obtain the support they need. Information related to the changing nature of supportive relationships can be included in class content. Specific class activities can be used to help class members identify and access their sources of support. Further research is needed for continuing knowledge development in the area of social support.

References

1. Abernathy, V. Social network and response to the maternal role. *International Journal of Sociology of the Family* 3:86, 1973.
2. Ballou, J. The significance of reconciliative themes in the psychology of pregnancy. *Bulletin of the Menninger Clinic* 42:383, 1978.
3. Ballou, J. W. *The Psychology of Pregnancy.* Lexington, MA: Lexington Books, D. C. Heath Co., 1978.
4. Baranowski, T., Bee, D. E., Rassin, D. K., Richardson, C. J., Brown, J. P., Guenther, N., and Nader, P. R. Social support, social influence, ethnicity and the breastfeeding decision. *Social Science and Medicine* 17:1599, 1983.
5. Barnard, K. E., Snyder, C., and Spietz, A. Supportive measures for high-risk infants and families. *Birth Defects: Original Article Series* 20:291, 1984.
6. Barnard, K. E., and Bee, H. L. The assessment of parent-infant interaction by observation of feeding and teaching. *In* Brazelton, T. B. and Als, H. (eds.). *New Approaches to Developmental Screening*. New York, Elsevier North Holland, Inc. (In press).
7. Berkowitz, G. S., and Kasl, S. V. The role of psychosocial factors in spontaneous preterm delivery. *Journal of Psychosomatic Research* 27:283, 1983.
8. Biegel, D. E., McCardle, E., and Mendelson, S. *Social Networks and Mental Health: An Annotated Bibliography.* Beverly Hills, CA: Sage, 1985.
9. Brazelton, T. B. The importance of mothering the mother. *Redbook* 156:112, 1980.
10. Brown, M.A. *Social Support and Symptomatology: A Study of First-Time Expectant Parents*. Doctoral Dissertation, University of Washington, 1983.
11. Bryant, C. A. The impact of kin, friend, and neighbor networks on infant feeding practices: Cuban, Puerto Ri-

can and Anglo Families in Florida. *Social Science and Medicine* 16:1757, 1982.

12. Caplan, R. D., et al. *Adhering to Medical Regimens: Pilot Experiments in Patient Education and Social Support.* Ann Arbor, MI: Institute for Social Research, 1979.
13. Carveth, W. B., and Gottlieb, B. H. The measurement of social support and its relation to stress. *Canadian Journal of Behavioral Science* 11:179, 1979.
14. Cobb, S. Social support as a moderator of life stress. *Psychosomatic Medicine* 38:300, 1976.
15. Cohen, D. A. *A Multivariate Regression Examination of Stressful Life Events, Social Support, and the Postpartum Depression Syndrome*. Doctoral Dissertation, University of Southern California, 1983.
16. Cohen, S., and Syme, S. L., (eds.) *Social Support and Health*. Orlando, FL: Academic Press, 1985.
17. Cranley, M. S. *The Impact of Perceived Stress and Social Support on Maternal-Fetal Attachment in the Third Trimester.* Doctoral Dissertation, University of Wisconsin-Madison, 1979.
18. Crnic, K. A., Greenberg, M. T., Ragozin, A. S., Robinson, N. M., and Basham, R. B. Effects of stress and social support on mothers and premature and full-term infants. *Child Development* 54:209, 1983.
19. Crockenberg, S. B. Infant irritability, mother responsiveness, and social support influences on the security of infant-mother attachment. *Child Development* 52:857, 1981.
20. Cronenwett, L. R. *Relationships Among Social Network Structure, Perceived Social Support, and Psychological Outcomes of Pregnancy.* Doctoral Dissertation, The University of Michigan, 1983.
21. Cronenwett, L. R. Elements and outcomes of a postpartum support group program. *Research in Nursing and Health* 3:33, 1980.
22. Erickson, E. S. *Transition to Motherhood: Effects of Preparation and Isolation upon a Measure of Mastery in Primiparae*. Doctoral Dissertation, University of Tennessee, 1983.
23. Gladieux, J. D. *Pregnancy—The Transition to Parenthood: Satisfaction with the Pregnancy Experience as a Function of the Marital Relationship and the Social Network.* Doctoral Dissertation, University of California, Berkeley, 1975.
24. Gottlieb, B. H. The development and application of a classification scheme of informal helping behaviors. *Canadian Journal of Behavioral Science* 10:105, 1978.
25. Gottlieb, B. H. *Social Support Strategies: Guidelines for Mental Health Practice*. Beverly Hills, CA: Sage, 1983.
26. Greenblatt, M., Becerra, R. M., and Serafetinides, E. A. Social networks and mental health: An overview. *American Journal of Psychiatry* 139:977, 1982.
27. House, J. S. *Work Stress and Social Support*. Reading, MA: Addison-Wesley, 1981.
28. Ladas, A. K. Information and social support as factors in the outcome of breastfeeding. *Journal of Applied Behavioral Science* 8:110, 1972.
29. Lederman, R. P. Roundtable discussion. *Birth Defects: Original Article Series* 20:121, 1984.
30. Lobo, M. L. *Mothers' and Fathers' Perceptions of Family Resources and Marital Adjustment and their Adaptation to Parenthood*. Doctoral Dissertation, University of Washington, 1982.
31. Mitchell, R. E., and Trickett, E. J. An analysis of the determinants of social networks. *Community Mental Health Journal* 16:27, 1980.
32. Norbeck, J. S. and Tilden, V. P. Life stress, social support, and emotional disequilibrium in complications of pregnancy: A prospective, multivariate study. *Journal of Health and Social Behavior* 24:30, 1983.
33. Nuckolls, K. B., Cassel, J., and Kaplan, B. H. Psychosocial assets, life crisis and the prognosis of pregnancy. *American Journal of Epidemiology* 95:431, 1972.
34. Oakley, A. *Women Confined: Towards a Sociology of Childbirth*. New York: Schocken Books, 1980.
35. Paykel, E. S, Emms, E. M., Fletcher, J., and Rassaby, E. S. Life events and social support in puerperal depression. *British Journal of Psychiatry,* 136:339, 1980.
36. Pilisuk, M. Kinship, social networks, social support and health. *Social Science and Medicine* 12B:273, 1978.
37. Raikes, H. H. *Mothering and Postpartum Social Network Supports*. Doctoral Dissertation, Iowa State University, 1981.
38. Richardson, P. Women's perceptions of their important dyadic relationships during pregnancy. *Maternal-Child Nursing Journal* 10:159, 1981.
39. Richardson, P. Women's perceptions of change in relationships shared with children during pregnancy. *Maternal-Child Nursing Journal* 12:75, 1983.
40. Rubin, R. Attainment of the maternal role: Models and referrants. *Nursing Research* 16:342, 1967.
41. Rumer, R. R. *Couples' Adjustment to First Childbirth*. Doctoral Dissertation, University of North Carolina at Chapel Hill, 1982.
42. Shereshefsky, P. M., and Yarrow, L. J. *Psychological Aspects of a First Pregnancy.* New York: Raven Press, 1974.
43. Sullivan, J., and Jones, L. C. Breastfeeding adoption by low-income black women. *Health Care Women International* 7:295, 1986.
44. Thrasher, J. *The Subculture of Pregnancy in a College Community.* Chapel Hill, NC: Institute for Research in Social Science, 1963.
45. Tilden, V. P. Cost and conflict: The darker side of social support. *Social Support and Health: New Directions for Theory Development and Research*. Rochester, NY: University of Rochester, 1985.
46. Turkat, D. Social networks: Theory and practice. *Journal of Community Psychology* 8:99, 1980.
47. Walz, B. L., and Rich, O. J. Maternal tasks of taking-on a second child in the postpartum period. *Maternal-Child Nursing Journal* 12:185, 1983.
48. Wandersman, L., Wandersman, A., and Kahn, S. Social support in the transition to parenthood. *Journal of Community Psychology* 8:332, 1980.
49. Wapner, J. The attitudes, feelings, and behaviors of expectant fathers attending Lamaze classes. *Birth and the Family Journal* 3:5, 1976.
50. Weaver, R. H., and Cranley, M. S. An exploration of

paternal-fetal attachment behavior. *Nursing Research* 32:68, 1983.
51. Weisz, P. V. *Life Events, Social Support, and Pregnancy Outcome*. Doctoral Dissertation, Washington University, 1981.
52. Zachariah, R. Intergenerational attachment and psychological well-being during pregnancy. *Social Support and Health: New Directions for Theory Development and Research*. Rochester, NY: University of Rochester, 1985.

Beginning Quote

Rubin, R. *Identity and the Maternal Role*. New York: Springer Publishing Company, 1984.

Boxed Quotes

1. Lederman, R. *Psychosocial Adaptation in Pregnancy.* Englewood Cliffs, NJ: Prentice-Hall, 1984.
2. Kitzinger, S. *The Experience of Childbirth*. Baltimore: Penguin Books, Inc., 1972.

chapter 23
SEXUALITY

NORMA NEAHR WILKERSON and ELISABETH BING

> *It is this spirit of hope, this joy in birth as a fulfillment of man and woman's love for each other, that should be the essence of childbirth—childbirth in which a woman finds delight in the rhythmic harmony of her body's functioning. Without this spirit perfect mechanical action in labour is not only made more difficult of attainment, but, even if achieved, is strangely unsatisfying.*
>
> Sheila Kitzinger

Although pregnancy is usually viewed as a fulfilling, joyful time, promoting a closer, more intimate relationship between a woman and her partner, it can also be a developmental crisis in their family life. Pregnancy and the birth of the baby can make a good marriage better, or these events can create tensions causing marital strain, discord, and great unhappiness.

Pregnancy is the outward manifestation of the couple's sexuality, but there are socially reinforced myths, taboos, and fears that affect sexual expression during the time of pregnancy, birth, and postpartum. Sexual intercourse during pregnancy has been forbidden from biblical days and is still forbidden in some primitive societies and in some Eastern cultures. Popular literature continues to promote myths and taboos regarding sexual activity during pregnancy.

For example, Limner, in *Sex and the Unborn Child,*[22] draws a fearful picture of dire societal outcomes due to a ''sick society'' in which men and women are unable to forego momentary pleasures during pregnancy. In Limner's book nearly every known societal problem is attributed to sexual activity during pregnancy! Pregnancy outcomes such as mentally retarded children, defective newborns, and developmental outcomes such as juvenile delinquency are examples of the problems attributed to sexual intercourse during pregnancy.

With misrepresentations such as these and with

myths and general lack of information available to pregnant couples, there is little wonder that they may have unanswered questions about sexuality during pregnancy. Furthermore, lack of understanding of common sexual responses and needs at this time in their lives may prevent couples from experiencing enhanced intimacy in their relationship.

REVIEW OF THE LITERATURE

Childbirth educators require current research-based information in order to serve as counselors to pregnant couples during this time of greatest intimacy of their lives. Research on sexuality during pregnancy began in the 1960's with the work of Masters and Johnson[24] on human sexuality. Since then investigations have focused on the human sexual response during the trimesters of pregnancy, during the birth event itself, and during the postpartum phase.

Research to be discussed in this chapter touches on relevant medical, physiological, and psychological literature. Interrelationships among these important variables are not always documented in a study of human sexual response. Therefore, we present the literature in a format that attempts to clarify these important dimensions in teaching pregnant couples.

Medical Knowledge of Sexuality During Pregnancy

In general, the topic of sexuality during pregnancy and postpartum is no longer totally taboo. However, many women are hesitant to discuss their sexual needs with physicians (who are usually men) during their prenatal care visits. In addition, physicians do not routinely initiate discussion on this topic unless the woman has specific questions, or unless there are specific medical contraindications regarding sexual intercourse. In traditional medical education, physicians have access to very little objective data regarding the ways in which people deal with their sexual needs during pregnancy. Therefore, it is difficult for them to offer advice for maintaining sexual relations during this time.

Furthermore, in studies that have documented physician instruction and counseling on sexual activity during pregnancy, there is little consistency. Table 23–1 summarizes several studies in this regard.

Butler and Wagner[4] attempt to explain the problem of physician reticence by relating it to society's attitude toward sexuality in general, in which a pregnant woman is not viewed as "sexy." According to this belief model, because the pregnant woman is not viewed as a sexual person, she is assumed to be uninterested in teaching, counseling,

Pregnancy can be a fulfilling, joyful time, promoting a closer, more intimate relationship between a woman and her partner. (Photograph by Rodger Ewy, Educational Graphic Aids, Inc.)

TABLE 23–1. PHYSICIAN INSTRUCTION ON SEXUAL ACTIVITY

RESEARCHERS	PERCENTAGE OF SUBJECTS	RECOMMENDATIONS
Masters and Johnson[24] (1966)	69	Warned at sometime during the last trimester not to engage in coitus (abstention); time varied from 1 to 3 months
Solberg et al.[43] (1973)	29	Recommended abstention for times ranging from 2 to 8 weeks before EDC*
	10	Were advised regarding positions of comfort for coitus
	2	Were advised on sexual activities that could be substituted for coitus
Falicov[10] (1973)	26	Recommended abstention 6 to 7 weeks before EDC*
Holtzman[18] (1976)	60	Ranged from: do anything as long as comfortable (n = 10) to abstention for entire pregnancy (n = 3), or from 28th week (n = 1), or from 36th week (n = 1); remaining subjects (n = 15) no advice
Savage[40] (1984)	9	Advised against coitus for medical reasons; additionally found that 33% sought advice from books; 50% received no advice (total sample, 218)

*EDC = Estimated date of confinement or due date.

or advice related to sexuality. Furthermore, Butler and Wagner propose that pregnancy and impending motherhood create unconscious resistance on the part of male physicians, "by mixing the unmixables, lover and mother." Therefore, nurses and childbirth educators (who are usually women) are in the unique position to promote healthy sexuality by addressing these concerns of the pregnant couple.

A majority of the medical advice given over the last five decades has stemmed from medical texts recommending that obstetrical patients abstain from coitus through the latter part of gestation and through the first month or two postpartum. The rationale for this advice stems from increased risk of medical complications without regard to past obstetrical history.

Research has been reported on the effects of sexual activity on the following pregnancy outcomes: premature rupture of membranes, premature birth, fetal heart rate decelerations, fetal hypoxia, meconium staining, low Apgar score, low birthweight, amniotic fluid infection, maternal air embolism, episiotomy healing, and postpartum infection. Cohn,[5] in a thorough review of this literature dating from 1953, supports the following recommendations regarding sexual activity and potential medical complications.

During the first trimester sexual intercourse should be avoided if there is a diagnosis of threatened or inevitable abortion to avoid maternal infection. A history of habitual abortion or incompetent cervix, prior to or without cerclage, also requires abstention from coitus during the first trimester and into the second.[5]

The following medical problems during the second and third trimesters may preclude sexual intercourse: known placenta previa, history of premature labor, premature rupture of membranes, multiple gestation, or ripe cervix several weeks prior to term.[5] During the postpartum period specific concerns regarding episiotomy breakdown and endometritis may warrant abstention until the episiotomy is healed. Studies indicate that most women have a well-healed episiotomy five to seven days postpartum. Participation in sexual intercourse is then a choice based upon personal comfort.

It is extremely important to explain to the woman the exact nature of the medical complication that warrants abstention from sexual intercourse. If the nature of the problem makes vaginal penetration by the penis the primary stressor, other forms of sexual expression are available to the couple. However, if orgasm is a potential stressor due to uterine contractility, the woman should be prepared to abstain from all orgasmic sexual activity, including masturbation. Finally, some research has implicated prostaglandin in semen with premature labor.[44] If this is a potential stressor, a condom may be used during sexual intercourse.

Human Sexual Response During Pregnancy

Sexual health is characterized by knowledge about human sexuality, positive body image, sexual activity consistent with sexual identity, awareness of sexual feelings, effective interpersonal relationships, and a usable value system.[17] The present understanding of sexuality during pregnancy, childbirth, and postpartum will be described within the framework of this definition as well as previous research on human sexuality.

Previous research has described the human sexual response cycle in the following phases: desire, excitement, plateau, orgasm, and resolution.[24] Physical and emotional changes of pregnancy that influence this response cycle are discussed here in the review.

Desire. With regard to sexual desire, the pregnant woman experiences definite changes in her body image. Changes in the outward form of the woman's body are the most obvious physical signs of pregnancy. These influence her attitudinal and perceptual dimensions of body image.[11] There is agreement in the literature that as the woman's body changes, her body image also changes. Ambivalence toward these changes can lead to negative or positive expressions of body image.

For example, some women may perceive themselves as fat, ugly, and generally unattractive during their pregnancy. Others may find their enlarging breasts, rounding abdomens, and fuller shapes more womanly, appealing, and sexually desirable. Negative or positive feelings toward these changes in body image may influence a woman's sexual desire.

In one study of 50 couples, it was found that both husbands and wives demonstrate statistically similar patterns of change in perceived body space during pregnancy.[11] Findings in this study support the *couvade syndrome* extending to perceptual symptoms as well as to physical symptoms such as nausea, vomiting, fatigue, and backache. Thus, objective evidence exists to support the hypothesis that both the woman and her partner have similar experiences during pregnancy. If women can be encouraged to view their bodies as desirable rather than undesirable, their husbands may also incorporate these positive perceptions.

Bing and Colman[3] found that some men frequently find the pregnant partner even more attractive and desirable. They accept the physical changes and feel good about them. Such men and women may find themselves feeling closer and more loving toward each other, as well as desiring sexual relations more frequently.

Excitement. The excitement phase of sexual response is characterized by an increased vasocongestive response in pregnancy. Therefore, orgasm may be reached faster and sexual responses may be more satisfying due to this increased vascularity as well as to increased vaginal lubrication that occurs from the end of the first trimester until the end of pregnancy.

Enlarged breasts, tenderness, turgid nipples, and engorged areolae are frequently present during pregnancy.[24] These symptoms are enhanced by sexual excitement. Women should be encouraged to communicate with their partners how best to adjust to these changes. For some, manual or oral breast stimulation may be painful and uncomfortable. For others, gentle caresses will relieve tension and increase their excitement. Women who perceive their prepregnant breast size as less than adequate may be especially pleased and excited by these changes in their breasts.

Plateau, Orgasm, and Resolution. As tension levels reach the plateau phase of sexual response, the outer third of the vagina becomes extremely engorged forming the orgasmic platform. This reaction is greatly enhanced in pregnancy. As pregnancy advances into the second and third trimesters muscle tension and vasocongestion become so pronounced that some women are more easily aroused during sexual intercourse.[24]

Orgasm may occur more frequently and with greater intensity during pregnancy due to heightened sexual tension described in the previous phases of sexual response. Some women have reported experiencing orgasm for the first time during pregnancy.[19] Internally, the orgasmic platform and the uterus undergo strong contractions similar to labor. The mouth of the cervix opens slightly immediately after orgasm.[24] Masters and Johnson also report that during the last trimester, the woman may experience tonic spasms of the uterus with orgasm rather than the usual rhythmic contractions.

During the resolution phase of sexual response, pelvic vasocongestion is not always completely relieved. The time period for complete resolution is longer than usual, and some pelvic discomfort may be experienced. Some women may find this a positive result as they are more easily aroused for further sexual activity.

Patterns of Sexuality During the Trimesters of Pregnancy

Women's patterns of sexuality during pregnancy have been studied with inconsistent findings. In general, studies support a trend toward declining sexual interest, libido, frequency of coitus, and satisfaction with sexual activity and intercourse in the first and third trimesters.[10,18,24,35,36,38,43] Some of these studies report general increases in sexual interest and activity during the second trimester.[10,24] Bing and Colman[3] have graphed the desires for sexual activity reported throughout pregnancy and the postpartum period (Fig. 23–1).

The four patterns, graphed in the order of their frequency of occurrence, clearly indicate individual variability. These findings support the idea that the effect of pregnancy on sexual desire is not consistent. Falicov[10] hypothesizes an association between a woman's prepregnant level of sexual interest and her level of interest during pregnancy. Further study needs to be done in this area.

The expression of sexuality includes much more than sexual intercourse. Nurturance needs of both partners increase especially during pregnancy.[3,51] Physical closeness is of primary importance. The changes that occur which influence sexuality and sexual activity during the three trimesters of pregnancy and during the postpartum period will be discussed in the following sections.

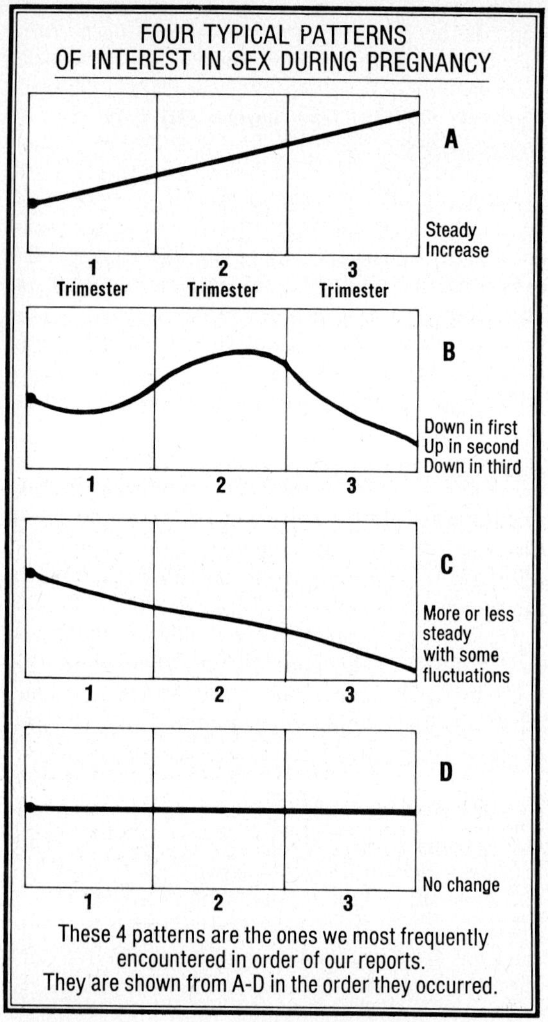

FIGURE 23–1. Four typical patterns of interest in sex during pregnancy. (From Bing, E., and Colman, L.: *Making Love During Pregnancy.* New York: Bantam Books, 1977. Reprinted with permission. All rights reserved.)

Sexuality in the First Trimester

Physical changes such as the discomforts of gastric distress, nausea, vomiting, fatigue, breast tenderness, and increased pelvic congestion may influence a woman's desire for sexual intercourse during this time of pregnancy. Furthermore, women frequently experience increased desire for sleep and need for rest. These factors may diminish sexual responsiveness.[23]

Psychological changes center on the ambivalence characteristic of this time in the pregnancy.[19,29,33] It is normal for many couples to feel the anxiety of ambivalence toward the pregnancy even if the pregnancy was planned and desired.

They may feel anxious and worried about the timing of the pregnancy, their impending parental responsibilities, and a myriad of other concerns such as finances, family relationships, and other social issues.

Ambivalence toward sexual activity may involve concern about the possibility of inducing a miscarriage or hurting the fetus, especially if the couple has had a previous miscarriage or fertility problem. Ambivalence and anxiety may cause even greater stress, and a vicious circle sets in that may further diminish sexual desire.

On the other hand, some women report a heightened sense of femininity and an improved sexual self-image during the first part of their pregnancy. For some women freedom from worry about contraception may add to relaxation and enjoyment of sexual activities, especially as the second trimester approaches. These women generally progress through their pregnancy with increased feelings of sensuality, and often gain a new awareness of their bodies.[19,33]

These same researchers also report that some women, conversely, experience anxiety, defensiveness, and sadness during the first trimester. These negative feelings are sometimes related to a potential loss of independence and changes in lifestyle that threaten self-esteem.

Furthermore, attitudes toward sexuality during pregnancy are influenced by the age of the couple. In 1980, 95 per cent of births in the United States were to women 34 years of age and younger. It is predicted that births to women over 35 will increase by 37 per cent between 1980 and 1990. By 1990, women over 35 will give birth to 46 per cent of the infants born.[1] Women who delay childbearing to further develop their identities and their careers may bring to the childbearing experience both a stable relationship with the infant's father and a mature sense of self. These factors will impact on the nature of their sexuality during the pregnancy.

Masculine attitudes toward the pregnancy may be influenced by the way the woman reacts to the physical changes of pregnancy. If these changes are perceived as normal, positive, and self-actualizing, it will be easier for the man to reflect similar perceptions.[11] If the man values the pregnancy or if it is perceived as proof of his masculinity, he may experience enhanced sexual self-esteem.[16] The man's desire for sexual intercourse may be stable, or it may decrease. His reaction depends upon his perception of the partner's comfort or distress with her pregnancy.

As the couple's pregnancy progresses, emotional acceptance occurs in both the man and the woman. Toward the end of the first trimester, fears of miscarriage decrease and both partners feel more confident to meet each other's sexual needs. It is important for them to realize that, although their desire for coitus may have lessened, there is still a great need for close physical contact. Hugging, holding, caressing, and cuddling may be extremely satisfying forms of sexual expression for both of them.

Sexuality in the Second Trimester

Most researchers agree that the second trimester is the most comfortable time during pregnancy for making love.[3,24,51] Increased vascularity and engorgement of the breasts, labia, and vagina enhance sexual response during pregnancy as was described above. Women often experience heightened sexual tension, more intense orgasms, and more enjoyment of sexual activities. As the fetus grows, the woman usually experiences a general feeling of well-being and satisfaction. She may feel proud of her ability to nurture the life growing within her. Her growing body may also be a source of happiness and pleasure for both partners.

Falicov[10] reports that women who expressed a high interest in sexual activity before pregnancy were more likely to maintain higher levels of interest during pregnancy and postpartum periods. Others report that conflict and guilt play important roles in sexual behavior during pregnancy. If sexual activity is considered to be primarily for procreation, a woman may feel guilty engaging in coitus during pregnancy. Conflict over the roles of mother and wife may also cause guilt from sexual activities.[6]

Colman and Colman[6] also describe high degrees of eroticism in women during second trimester pregnancy. Some are obsessed with bizarre fantasies and so preoccupied with sex that they fear their partners will be frightened by their increased sexual appetite. Bing and Colman[3] report that many women experience their most frequent emotional highs and lows during the second trimester. While these emotional fluctuations were found to have an

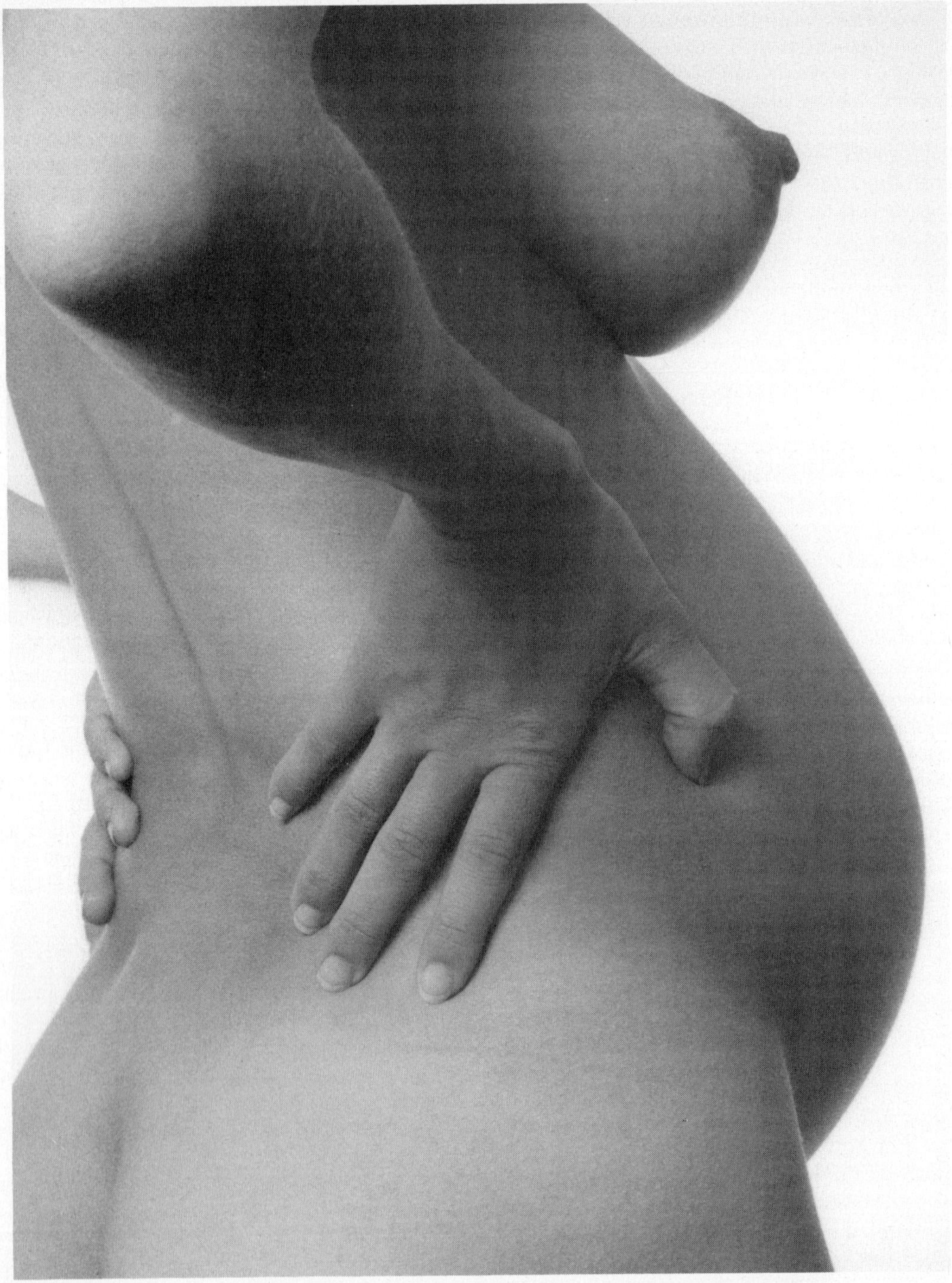

The pregnant woman's growing body may be a source of happiness and pleasure for a couple. For other couples the physical changes of pregnancy may have a negative influence on their feelings of sexuality. (Photograph by Harvey Wang.)

effect on sexual activity, they were not a problem if the couple had been prepared for such mood swings.

Some men report that they do not find the pregnant body attractive; they may actually be repulsed by it. If sexual relations are discontinued by mutual agreement during this time of the pregnancy, there is no problem. Expressions of affection and nurturance will continue to be mutually satisfying. If, however, only one partner desires to discontinue sexual activity because of feelings of guilt, shame, or repulsion, stress will occur.[49]

The man may also be experiencing feelings of increased virility as he shares his partner's pleasure with the growth of the fetus through sight and touch. These enhanced feelings of closeness, affection, and satisfaction may lead the couple to engage in more frequent sexual intercourse. Falicov[10] reported that over 50 per cent of the women in her study valued second trimester sexual interaction as a means of affective communication with their partners rather than for its erotic value.

The degree of variability of male response to second and third trimester pregnancy is illustrated in a study of the reactions of 60 middle-class urban couples to pregnancy.[42] It was reported that 50 per cent of the husbands were fearful of sexual intercourse after fetal movement for fear of harming the baby. A smaller percentage of the husbands were so accepting of the woman's changing body that they desired to take pictures of her. Others did not wish to be seen in public with their pregnant partners for fear of public evidence of "what they had been doing."

Some men may feel lonely and abandoned as they watch their partners becoming increasingly preoccupied by the growing fetus. Mixed feelings regarding the motherliness of his partner may lead the man to gradually withdraw from sexual activity with the woman. The woman's increasing introspection during this time of the pregnancy may also impede the man's sexual responsiveness to her.

Sexuality in the Third Trimester

Studies of sexuality during pregnancy have been hampered in regard to findings in the third trimester. Traditionally, medical advice has been to abstain from intercourse for six to eight weeks before the birth of the infant. It is generally accepted that this may be the reason for consistent findings of decreased sexual activity during the third trimester.[24,43,48]

Physical discomforts such as the size of the woman's abdomen, heartburn, leg cramps, Braxton-Hicks contractions, the weight and position of the fetus, leaking breasts, and more intense uterine contractions with orgasm may all play a part in diminishing sexual activity. At this time emotional factors may lead to decreased frequency of sexual activity if the woman feels less desirable and feels fat, misshapen, and ugly. Changes in self-image may even lead the woman to fear that her partner may seek sexual gratification from other, more desirable women. Indeed, Masters and Johnson[24] reported that some men had their first extramarital affair at this time during the wife's pregnancy.

For the majority of couples, there is no reason to forbid sexual intercourse during the third trimester of pregnancy.[27] Falicov[10] reports that 50 per cent of the women expressed frustration and resentment at having to abstain from sexual activities. By this time in the pregnancy they felt secure and enjoyed their sexual relationship.

Finding new positions may enhance comfort and sexual satisfaction (Fig. 23–2). It is important to emphasize that, even for couples who may have legitimate reasons for abstention, other forms of sexual expression should be encouraged, such as touching, holding, caressing, cuddling, and mutual masturbation. Loving and sexuality do not have to be confined to coitus.

In summary, Bing and Colman[3] in their research identified the primary concerns of pregnant women (Fig. 23–3). It can be seen that throughout the trimesters anxiety and needs for reassurance center on the normal physiological and emotional changes of pregnancy.

The Birth

Today, in some parts of the country, a couple may be able to choose where and how to give birth to their child—whether in a traditional birthing unit, a single-room maternity care unit (LDR or LDR/P room), an out-of-hospital birthing center, or possibly at home. Many hospitals have modified standard intrapartal care in order to facilitate a more relaxed, intimate, home environment. In spite of the trends toward greater freedom of choice and

FIGURE 23–2. Alternate positions for intercourse during pregnancy.

less medical intervention in childbirth, the couple may still have difficulty enjoying and experiencing a satisfying birth.

Newton[33] describes the similarities between undisturbed, undrugged childbirth and orgasmic sexual excitement in lovemaking. By studying these similarities, as presented in Table 23–2, it can be seen that the actual birth experience is in itself the culmination of sexuality. These strong, rhythmic, and energetic responses have the potential for making childbirth a powerfully sensuous experience.

If sexual fulfillment during actual childbirth is to occur, the woman should be assured of a supportive, private, nonthreatening environment. Otherwise, these naturally occurring behaviors may be obscured, inhibited, or actually extinguished.

The woman's partner can also experience the sensuality of childbirth by participating in intimate touching and caressing as he supports her through childbirth. Some practitioners have discovered the benefits to the mother of nipple stimulation and kissing during early labor to relax her and encourage the flow of oxytocin during the labor. Of course, the man's focus is not on the sexual act of intercourse at this time. However, he will be able to identify with his partner in the work of bringing their child into the world by offering complete physical, sensory, and psychological support at such a private time.

Obstetrical management of the birth can be a major factor in helping or hindering the couple as they experience this vital culmination to their sex-

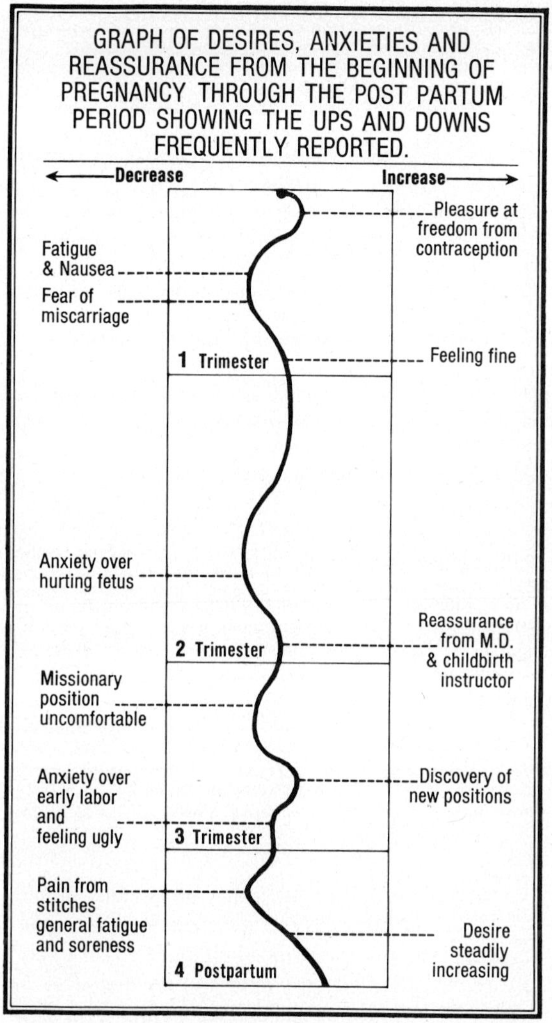

FIGURE 23–3. Graph of desire, anxieties, and reassurance from the beginning of pregnancy through the postpartum period showing ups and downs frequently reported. (From Bing, E., and Coleman, L. *Making Love During Pregnancy.* New York: Bantam Books, 1977. Reprinted with permission. All rights reserved.)

uality. McIntyre[26] has considered approaches to the issues of management of childbirth and proposes two management paradigms: one that views childbirth as a "natural process" and one that treats it as a "process akin to illness." If birthing is considered holistically (as a biocultural, spiritual, family event), the "natural process" viewpoint will be adopted. Conversely, if birthing is considered only from the biomedical point of view, it will be treated as an illness.

Rubin[39] relates the birth event to the postpartum phase of childbearing as an anchor. She states that, "Like a magnet in a field, delivery serves as a point of orientation for both the pregnancy and postpartum phases of childbearing." Pregnancy is confirmation of the couple's sexuality, and birthing is the culmination of their mutual love for each other. They can draw strength from the birth in order to prepare for the postpartum stresses to come.

To promote optimal birth experiences, leading to optimal postpartum health, it is proposed that the following practices be considered: (1) end unnecessary intervention in the management of birth, (2) return normal birth to the home or homelike environments, (3) provide female birth attendants, (4) return control of childbearing to females, and (5) teach realistic information about childbearing to men and women.[34] Furthermore, it is recommended that emotional and physical support and education be provided for younger, less educated, and less prepared couples. Couples identified as "high risk" are often not provided with good family-centered birth experiences. They are at increased risk for high anxiety and subsequent higher incidence of medical interventions such as forceps, birth anesthesia, and cesarean birth.[45] Childbirth educators who promote educational access to information such as this will facilitate rewarding birth experiences for couples.

Postpartum Sexuality

After the birth of the baby most couples find a new set of problems with regard to their sexuality. During the immediate week or two after the birth the mother may have pain and swelling from tissue trauma due to the baby's passage through the birth canal. In addition, if an episiotomy was performed, the perineum will be sore and uncomfortable. As Derthick[7] states, "Crying babies, sleepless nights, spouting nipples, dry vaginas, and sore perineums can do much to compromise the sexual relationship of new parents."

Many couples anxiously anticipate the first time they have sexual intercourse after the birth event.

TABLE 23–2. COMPARISON OF LOVEMAKING AND BIRTHING EXPERIENCES

VARIABLES	BIRTHING	ORGASMIC LOVEMAKING
Breathing, vocalization, and facial expressions	1st stage labor, breathing becomes deeper; 2nd stage tendency to make noises and grunts; as birth climaxes face shows strain	During early stages of sexual excitement fast, deep breathing; gasping occurs as orgasm begins; as orgasm climaxes face becomes tense with a "tortured" expression
Uterine and cervical reactions	Rhythmic uterine contractions during labor; loosening of cervical mucus plug	Uterus contracts rhythmically during sexual excitement; cervical mucus is prepared for sperm
Abdominal muscle reactions and position	Muscles contract periodically in 2nd stage labor; bearing-down urge develops; usual position is on back with legs bent wide apart	Muscles contract periodically during excitement and orgasm; common position for coitus is on back with legs bent wide apart
Central nervous system reactions	Tendency toward uninhibited behavior particularly during transition and 2nd stage labor	Inhibitions and mental blocks often eliminated during sexual excitement and orgasm
Strength and flexibility	Pushing baby through birth canal requires unusual body expansion and strength	Muscular strength increases in sexual excitement; body bending and distorting occurs in unusual ways
Sensory perception	In labor the perineum becomes anesthetized with full dilation; if the woman is unmedicated and is uninhibited by fear, there is tendency to become insensitive to her surroundings; amnesia occurs; suddenly, after the birth she is wide awake and alert	Whole body of sexually aroused person becomes increasingly insensitive to external stimuli; as orgasm approaches loss of sensory perception is almost complete; sensory acuity suddenly returns after orgasm
Emotional response	A flood of joyful emotion occurs after birth of the baby	A strong feeling of well-being often occurs after orgasm

Adapted from Newton, N. Interrelationships between sexual responsiveness, birth, and breastfeeding. In Zubin, J. and Money, J. (eds.) *Contemporary Sexual Behavior: Critical Issues in the 1970s*. Baltimore: Johns Hopkins University Press, 1973, pp. 79–80.

It is normal for them to wonder if their sexual relationship will be the same. If the pregnancy and birth have been shared in a loving, caring relationship, often couples find that their sexual relationship has actually improved.

Traditionally, physicians inform the couple to abstain from intercourse up to the sixth week postpartum. More recently, couples are told they may resume intercourse after all vaginal bleeding has stopped and the discharge is no longer pink-tinged. Furthermore, they should not resume intercourse until the episiotomy is healed. Women vary with regard to meeting these criteria. Normally, it takes from one to three weeks. In one study of 800 women with vaginal delivery and midline episiotomy, it was found that the majority of the women could resume intercourse 14 to 21 days postpartum without endangering the healing process of the perineum.[37]

There are other changes that physicians do not usually explain to the postpartum couple. Kyndely[20] summarizes these changes in an excellent review. Sexual eroticism and tension may be decreased because of steroid starvation. This contributes to postpartum fatigue, exhaustion, mood swings, and reduced vaginal lubrication in response to sexual stimulation. Furthermore, most women experience some fear in resuming intercourse because of possible damage to pelvic structures.

Breastfeeding can be a source of pleasure or stress during the postpartum period. Masters and Johnson[24] reported that some women found the eroticism of breastfeeding pleasurable. Sexual stimulation ranged from excitement to plateau or orgasmic levels for breastfeeding women. Others felt guilty over sexual stimulation from breastfeeding, and decided not to nurse another infant after such experience with a previous child.

A partner's intimate caressing and other expressions of love during labor provide valuable support for the laboring woman. (Photograph by Harvey Wang.)

Furthermore, infants may also respond with sexual satisfaction to breastfeeding.[32] Infants have been observed to respond with rhythmic motion of the hands and feet while breastfeeding. Male infants frequently have penile erections along with their rhythmic sucking. Older infants show signs of eagerness as the breast is prepared for nursing, and they often engage in stroking motions with their hands as they nurse. After nursing, most infants experience total body relaxation characteristic of release of sexual tension in adults after a satisfactory sexual experience.

Breast milk is ejected involuntarily with sexual stimulation in the breastfeeding woman. This can be a source of stress, especially if breast tenderness and cracked nipples are present in the immediate postpartum period. Such changes and events may compromise sexual excitement for the couple.

Finally, postpartum or new baby ''blues'' have been described in the literature following birth. Many variables interact etiologically in the transient depression experienced by many women during this time. Symptoms generally include fatigue, lethargy, irritability, unprovoked and irrational crying, varying levels of anxiety and confusion, some sense of disorganization, and unexplained sadness.[8]

Etiological factors relating to sexuality that have been identified include the following. Some women are concerned about prescribed abstinence from sexual relations with their partners. Masters and Johnson[24] found that women were concerned about their partner's attitudes toward them if they enforced the prescription. Others report that anxiety and fear of resuming sexual relations can exist even with enhanced sexual desire. Thus, a vicious circle of frustration, depression, and desire for sex may occur.[10]

Other women are worried that their vaginal tissues were stretched so much that they will not be able to sexually satisfy their partners or themselves. For this reason they may put off resuming sexual relations and worry over their decision. Fear of becoming pregnant again may also lead to feelings of depression and postponement of sexual activities. Finally, it may be difficult for the new mother to understand how her partner can desire her sexually. Her body image may still be negative because she cannot fit into regular clothes, her weight loss is less than expected, and she has a flabby abdomen and leaking breasts.

Sometimes the new father is reluctant to approach his partner for fear of hurting her. If he witnessed the birth, he may be overly concerned about the stretching, bleeding, and tissue trauma that occurred. Other men feel isolated and alone due to the intense focus of the mother on the needs of the infant. In meeting the newborn's needs for feeding and nurturing, the woman may seem to ignore her partner.

Rubin[39] describes the ''exclusivity and intimacy of the mother-child subsystem'' as a ''territorial problem for the husband becoming a family man and finding the husband-wife relationship relegated to a special subsystem within the family.'' Colman and Colman[6] state that the most common behavioral reaction of men during this time is to simply ''run away.'' They may do so by spending less and less time at home as they involve themselves in outside activities or they may actually begin sexual affairs with other women.

Communication is the key to problem-solving at this time. Both partners must feel free to express the emotions, feelings, and thoughts they are experiencing. As was true during the pregnancy, so it will be true in the postpartum period: ''The specific solution chosen by a couple is probably less important than their method of reaching their solution. Lactating breasts and crying infants can do as much to inhibit a man as a huge belly and a kicking fetus. Again, the honesty of shared feelings is the best way to overcome these touchy problems which are common to all couples.''[6]

Sexuality in Abusive Relationships

Among some couples pregnancy and postpartum changes in the woman can trigger or exacerbate abusive behavior on the part of the man. The physical effects of battering on the woman and the potential for harm to the infant are significant. Emotional trauma is also a result. If the woman is using her energy to resolve conflict with her partner, she will not have enough energy to attach to her infant. Consequently, the potential for maternal-child neglect as well as paternal abuse are factors to consider.

Although an extreme form of behavior, battering is related to sexuality in pregnancy through its negative effects on the intimate relationship between the man and woman. Theories related to pregnancy as a cause for abuse range from pregnancy adding strain to the relationship, jealousy of the baby's presence in the relationship, desires to end the pregnancy, and the woman's increased defenselessness because of the pregnancy.[46]

Abuse is of particular concern to childbirth educators, since many women report that battering began when they first told their partners that they were pregnant.[15,46] If the woman is in an abusive relationship, it will be difficult to engage the couple in a meaningful discussion of their sexual needs. Other indicators of abuse in a relationship may be as follows: the woman's withdrawal from her partner's touch during practice sessions in classes, remaining distant from peers and the childbirth educator, being so monopolized by her partner that she is unable to develop relationships with peers, hints that she wants to talk in private, visible contusions on the arms, appearing hesitant, embarrassed, or evasive regarding the nature of an ache or injury.[25]

It is not the purpose of this chapter to discuss intervention in cases of battering and abuse during pregnancy. However, the childbirth educator may be the first person to develop a supportive, advocacy relationship with an abused woman. The woman may confide in the educator; she will need help and information. Childbirth educators should be prepared to offer supportive care and referral for counseling.

IMPLICATIONS FOR PRACTICE

Childbirth educators are in a unique position for implementing primary prevention through anticipatory guidance of couples during their pregnancy. Even though the topic of sexuality is no longer totally taboo, men and women usually are not eager to discuss the most intimate issues of their sexuality with others. However, with support and guidance from the childbirth educator, they can be encouraged to discuss their concerns. In so doing they will share their fears and anxieties, and realize that their sexual responses and needs are common as well as normal.

Role of the Childbirth Educator

The role of the childbirth educator is twofold: to promote the couple's understanding of the sexual changes of pregnancy and the postpartum period and to facilitate their choices for meeting sexual needs during this time in their lives. In order to fulfill the dimensions of this role, guidelines for practice are organized according to strategies for accomplishing three goals.

First, the childbirth educator must be aware of her own values and attitudes regarding human sexuality. Included in such awareness is the ability to openly discuss the topic of sexuality in her classes. Second, the childbirth educator must develop an adequate knowledge base about sexuality in general and the changes in sexuality during pregnancy and postpartum. Finally, the childbirth educator must develop a repertoire of skills and methods for integrating this content into childbirth classes. She must be able to assess couples' learning needs with respect to their sexuality and develop mutual goals for meeting those needs. If possible, she should evaluate the outcomes and benefits to her students from her counseling.

> You used to see her as a sexy tigress, and suddenly she's a Madonna—inaccessible, even intimidating. In some ways, you're attracted to her as before, but you're also confused.
>
> AN EXPECTANT FATHER
>
> Some men and women react strongly to the presence of the baby—the baby that literally comes between you and your mate when you have sex. You can't ignore it. You can't ask it to leave the room.
>
> ELLEN SUE STERN
>
> On the other hand, the baby's presence may increase your interest in lovemaking. It may enhance the tenderness and passion that you and your mate share during those times. Each act becomes a reaffirmation of the commitment you've made.
>
> ELLEN SUE STERN

Facilitating Discussion of Sexuality in Classes

In order to promote discussion of sexuality, the childbirth educator must be personally aware of her own sexuality. According to Maslow's hierarchy of needs, sexual needs are at the most basic level next to safety and survival. Reproductive anatomy and physiology, the process of labor and birth, the physiology of involution, and contraception are standard content in childbirth classes. However, it is possible to present this information to couples without ever mentioning human sexual response, sexual needs, and issues of sensuality. Such practice exemplifies the way in which a childbirth educator may deny her own sexuality as well as that of the couples in her classes.

Furthermore, the childbirth educator must be prepared to accept the values, attitudes, and beliefs of others in regard to issues of human sexuality in a nonjudgmental manner. Assuming a nonjudgmental attitude precludes the educator from imposing a personal value and belief system upon class members. For example, it may be difficult for an educator to discuss alternatives to coitus for relief of sexual tension. Topics such as oral sexual stimulation, mutual masturbation, individual masturbation, or viewing adult movies may be discussed appropriately to meet couples' needs. It will require great skill on the educator's part to facilitate these discussions if any of these practices are contrary to the educator's personal value system.

Although it can be difficult to initiate discussions regarding lovemaking during pregnancy and postpartum, it is the educator's responsibility to develop appropriate strategies for this purpose. One technique that may encourage couples to discuss their sexual needs uses an indirect approach. Begin by asking couples to describe changes that have occurred in their relationship since the pregnancy began. After a few responses have been elicited, ask, "And what about sex?" Leaving the question open-ended allows for responses that can then be discussed by the entire group. The focus of the discussion should be on commonalities, normalcy of concerns, and reasons for their occurrence.

Sexuality can be a threatening topic and it should be initiated only after the educator has established rapport with the class. There must be adequate time for class members to get to know each other and begin to establish some personal relationships before the topic is presented. Encourage class discussion, but do not put couples "on the spot" if they bring up specific questions. Once it is established that discussing sexual needs is an expectation, the educator can be guided by several principles: Encourage couples to communicate feelings to each other. Give examples of mutual concerns and indicate the way in which communication solved the problem. For example, one husband was concerned about the potential for initiating premature labor by having intercourse during the last trimester of his wife's pregnancy. He was reassured when his wife helped him understand that even if she had an orgasm, intercourse would not initiate labor prior to term during a normal pregnancy. As she approached her due date, if intercourse did initiate labor, what difference would it make?

In addition to communication of feelings, the educator can help couples be creative in exploring new ways of expressing their sexual needs. For example, using body massage, bathing together, experimenting with music, candles, scents, lotions, cuddling, caressing, and mutual masturbation are possibilites.[21] Couples can also be taught perineal massage as a pleasurable method of preparing for the birth, and possibly eliminating the need for an episiotomy.

Other helpful practices that can be discussed within the framework of mutual pleasuring include methods of relaxing the pubococcygeus muscle such as insertion of two fingers into the vagina and gently rotating. This can be done postpartum when the perineum has healed prior to intercourse. It will help eliminate fear of painful intercourse as well as prepare the woman for penetration. Teaching Kegel or perineal squeeze exercises to improve muscle tone can also be done within this framework.

Finally, focus on the couple's need to plan for a good sexual relationship. For example, the woman should plan to have adequate rest. If privacy is a problem and/or the couple is concerned about waking the baby during sexual activity, they can creatively identify locations other than the bedroom and times other than night for enjoying each other. If couples are encouraged to apply problem-solving skills to this area of their lives as they would in financial or career planning, the childbirth educator will help them reinforce coping as they build a stronger relationship with each other.

Developing a Knowledge Base and Strategies for Teaching Sexuality

Issues of sexuality as mentioned in the literature review should be thoroughly studied. If the childbirth educator is to be a resource person, accurate factual information must be learned. In order to integrate the information into scheduled classes the educator must believe in the "naturalness" of the information presented. This approach emphasizes content at the appropriate time in class sequencing. For example, as common changes in the woman's body are discussed with each trimester, changes in sexual interest, sexual response, and sexual needs can be included.

In addition, childbirth educators should concentrate on teaching from a knowledge base other than personal experience. Methods of accomplishing this include extensive reading of material such as *Making Love During Pregnancy*,[3] *Women's Experience of Sex*,[19] *Maternal Emotions*,[33] and *The Parent Manual: A Handbook for a Prepared Childbirth*.[41]

Childbirth educators are encouraged to discuss sexuality with childbearing couples in order to develop greater knowledge and sensitivity toward relevant issues. No question is "too trivial," but it takes a broad, thorough knowledge base to appreciate verbal and nonverbal messages that may be questions in disguise.

For example, a class member who expresses fear may actually be expressing ambivalence toward lovemaking during pregnancy. Rather than express disinterest or disgust with maintaining a sexual relationship during pregnancy, the man may express fear of hurting the woman or the baby. It takes an astute childbirth educator to relieve this type of anxiety. A comment such as, "Many men have been socialized to believe that sex during pregnancy is inappropriate," may be more helpful than a direct question.

Strategies for teaching sexuality should also help couples to enhance their personal relationships with each other. One method of accomplishing this is to help each partner realize that their concerns are not unique and that they are normal. Woolerly and Barkley[50] suggest a method in which the couples are divided into two groups: one group of women and one group of men. The groups are given colored pens and big sheets of newsprint in order to record their data. Each group is asked to appoint a "recorder" who lists the data. The women's group is asked to list the physical changes that they are experiencing in their pregnancy. The men list the emotional changes they are perceiving both in their wives and in themselves.

Both lists are then displayed. Discussion focuses upon possible reasons for the changes that have been listed. Similarities and differences in female and male responses to pregnancy are analyzed. The "normalcy" and "naturalness" of these experiences are stressed. Couples are encouraged to continue discussing changes and perceptions with each other as the pregnancy progresses.

There are few informative films currently available for childbirth educators to use that deal with the issues of sexuality in pregnancy. However, one such resource, *Sex and Pregnancy,*[13] is a 20-minute videotape in which couples express the effects that pregnancy has on their sexual relationships. Use of such media thus further enables couples to realize that their ambivalence regarding lovemaking during pregnancy and fears of sexual activity are common to other couples. The educator could use such a film to initiate further discussion or as a summary after a class discussion.

The motivated childbirth educator has many resources available to learn values clarification skills that are also helpful in dealing with sexuality education in prepared childbirth classes. Basically, in values clarification each partner learns to increase the ability to discuss sexual values. Body image, physical attractiveness, touch, expressions of sexuality, and the true nature of their sexual relationship are examples of values to be clarified.

Education is an area of sexuality that must not be ignored. For many couples, class attendance occurs late in the pregnancy. If the topic is never introduced, important needs will go unmet. Pregnancy is a time to enhance intimacy in the couple's relationship. It presents both challenges to their coping ability and rewards in the learning of new skills as they develop their life together. Ultimately, the family will be a stronger unit if these lessons have been learned well.

IMPLICATIONS FOR RESEARCH

Research on sexuality in pregnancy has been focused primarily on the basic human sexual response as it differs during the trimesters of pregnancy from the nonpregnant state. In addition, studies have investigated the effect of sexual activity on pregnancy outcomes. Medical research that reports negative outcomes such as higher rates of infection, premature labor, premature rupture of membranes, and antepartum hemorrhage[30,31] due to sexual activity has been questioned. These findings were reported from studies that did not control for such variables as social class, maternal age, general health, and risk factors commonly associated with perinatal morbidity.

While it is evident from these studies that sexual stimulation and orgasm during pregnancy are accompanied by uterine contractions, the primary research hypotheses regarding the effects of such uterine activity have been negative. It is time to support research that is designed to identify positive benefits from sexual activity. Research questions such as the following should be studied:

- If a pregnant woman remains sexually active during the third trimester, will uterine contractions gradually efface and dilate the cervix, facilitating a shorter labor?
- Can labor be induced by sexual activity in situations when the fetus is large and the pregnancy is approaching postmaturity?
- Does a sexually satisfied and uninhibited couple have a more relaxed attitude toward labor and delivery?
- Is "failure to progress" related in any way to

the woman's sexual inhibitions, lack of privacy, and lack of intimate support from her partner during labor?

- Is endogenous oxytocin (produced by sexual stimulation) an effective alternative to synthetic drugs such as Pitocin for inducing or augmenting labor or both?

Research has also supported great variability of sexual desire and satisfaction among pregnant women and their partners. Individuality in regard to the ability of pregnant couples to express their sexual feelings and needs is also recognized. Whether a couple perceives their sexual needs to change or remain the same during the pregnancy is not as significant as their ability to communicate in order to get their sexual needs met. Learning to communicate their sexual needs during the pregnancy will provide them with a skill in communicating with each other vital to the postpartum and parenting periods of their lives to come.

Therefore, research is needed to provide strategies for childbirth educators to use in facilitating the couple's recognition of the normalcy of their sexual needs and responses along the continuum of individual variation. Furthermore, research-based tools for assessing values and communication skills with respect to sexuality are needed.

The incidence of postpartum depression in the mild-to-moderate range is estimated at from three to 23 per cent of all births.[8] It is possible that some of these cases are directly related to unresolved conflict over sexuality during the pregnancy and in the immediate postpartum period. Therefore, research should be done to investigate the relevance of sexual counseling to enhance the support system during the prenatal period. Postpartum outcomes on the continuum of postpartum "blues" to postpartum depression and psychosis might be lowered significantly through such intervention. Theoretically, if a pregnant couple learns to communicate sexual needs during the pregnancy, transfer of learning to postpartum feelings and needs will occur.

Finally, an area of need exists with respect to the high-risk mother and her partner. Couples who most commonly benefit from childbirth classes, family-centered birth practices, and sexuality education are from low-risk, higher socioeconomic classes.[28] More research must be done in order to provide a basis for delivery of services to those in greatest need.

How can we teach young, relatively uneducated, and often socially stressed couples to understand and respect each other's sexual needs and responses? How can we identify those at greatest risk? For these couples, the stress of pregnancy on their sexual relationship may precipitate abandonment, separation, neglect, abuse, or divorce. With timely, appropriate educational intervention some of these relationships might be strengthened rather than weakened.

SUMMARY

In summary, childbirth educators can approach pregnancy as a time of heightened feelings in which physical contact and affectionate behaviors are particularly important for the pregnant couple. Rather than creating problems, their sexuality can help solve them. They can achieve greater security, love, and trust from the psychological satisfactions they experience as they engage in intimacy. Intimacy can range from just lying in bed talking and planning for the baby to exploring the pregnant woman's developing body, communicating with the developing fetus, or enjoying each other's bodies through sexual intercourse.

References

1. Adams, M., Oakley, G., and Marks, J. Maternal age and births in the 1980's. *Journal of the American Medical Association* 247:493, 1982.
2. Bing, E. Yes, you can! *Childbirth '85* 2:26, 1985.
3. Bing, E., and Colman, L. *Making Love During Pregnancy.* New York: Bantam Books, 1977.
4. Butler, J., and Wagner, N. Sexuality during pregnancy and postpartum. *In* Green, R. (ed.) *Human Sexuality: A Health Practitioner's Text.* Baltimore: Williams and Wilkins, 1975.
5. Cohn, S. Sexuality in pregnancy: A review of the literature. *Nursing Clinics of North America* 17:91, 1982.

6. Colman, A., and Colman, L. *Pregnancy: The Psychological Experience*. New York: The Seabury Press, 1971.
7. Derthick, N. Sexuality in pregnancy and the puerperium. *Birth and the Family Journal* 1:5, 1974.
8. Duffy, C. Postpartum depression: Identifying women at risk. *Genesis* 5:11, 1983.
9. Ellis, D. Sexual needs and concerns of expectant parents. *JOGN Nursing* 9:306, 1980.
10. Falicov, C. Sexual adjustment during first pregnancy and postpartum. *American Journal of Obstetrics and Gynecology* 117:991, 1973.
11. Fawcett, J. Body image and the pregnant couple. MCN: *American Journal of Maternal-Child Nursing* 3:227, 1978.
12. Fishman, S., Rankin, E., Soeken, K., and Lenz, E. Changes in sexual relationships in postpartum couples. *JOGN Nursing* 15:58, 1986.
13. Glendon Association. *Sex and Pregnancy.* Centre Films, Inc., 1985, 1103 N. El Centro Ave., Hollywood, CA 90038. (213) 466-5123.
14. Hames, C. Sexual needs and interests of postpartum couples. *JOGN Nursing* 9:313, 1980.
15. Greany, G. Is she a battered woman? *American Journal of Nursing* 6:724, 1984.
16. Higgins, L., and Hawkins, J. *Human Sexuality Across the Lifespan*. Monterey, CA: Wadsworth Health Sciences Division, 1984.
17. Hill, L., and Smith, N. *Self-Care Nursing*. Englewood Cliffs, NJ: Prentice-Hall, 1985.
18. Holtzman, L. Sexual practices during pregnancy. *Journal of Nurse Midwifery* 21:22, 1976.
19. Kitzinger, S. *Women's Experience of Sex*. New York: Penguin Books, 1983.
20. Kyndely, K. The sexuality of women in pregnancy and postpartum: A review. *Journal of Gynecologic Nursing* 7:28, 1978.
21. Leander, K., and Grassley, J. Making love after birth. *Birth and the Family Journal* 7:181, 1980.
22. Limner, R. *Sex and the Unborn Child*. New York: Pyramid Books, 1970.
23. Mann, E., and Armistead, T. Pregnancy and sexual behavior. *In* Sadock, B., Kaplan, H., and Freedman, A. (eds.) *The Sexual Experience*. Baltimore: Williams and Wilkins, 1976.
24. Masters, W., and Johnson, V. *Human Sexual Response*. Boston: Little, Brown and Company, 1966.
25. Matteson, P. Pregnant and battered. *Childbirth Educator* 5:46, 1985/1986.
26. McIntyre, S. The management of childbirth: A review of the sociological research issues. *Social Science and Medicine* 11:477, 1977.
27. Mills, J., Harlap, S., and Harley, E. Should coitus late in pregnancy be discouraged? *Lancet* 2:136, 1981.
28. Moore, D. Prepared childbirth and marital satisfaction during the antepartum and postpartum periods. *Nursing Research* 32:73, 1983.
29. Mueller, L. Pregnancy and sexuality. *Journal of Obstetrics and Gynecology and Newborn Nursing* 14:289, 1985.
30. Naeye, R. Coitus associated amniotic fluid infections. *New England Journal of Medicine* 301:1198, 1979.
31. Naeye, R. Coitus and antepartum haemorrhage. *British Journal of Obstetrics and Gynecology* 88:765, 1981.
32. Newton, N. Interrelationships between sexual responsiveness, birth, and breastfeeding. *In* Zubin, J., Money, J. (eds.) *Contemporary Sexual Behavior: Critical Issues in the 1970s*. Baltimore: Johns Hopkins University Press, 1973.
33. Newton, N. *Maternal Emotions*. New York: Paul Hoeber, 1982.
34. Oakley, A. *Women Confined: Towards a Sociology of Childbirth*. New York: Schoken Books, 1980.
35. Perkins, P. Sexuality in pregnancy: What determines behavior. *Obstetrics and Gynecology* 59:189, 1982.
36. Reamy, K., White, S., Daniell, W., and LeVine, E. Sexuality and pregnancy. *Journal of Reproductive Medicine* 27:321, 1982.
37. Richardson, A., Lyon, J., Graham, E., and Williams, N. Decreasing postpartum sexual abstinence time. *Journal of Obstetrics and Gynecology* 126:416, 1976.
38. Robson, K., Brant, H., and Kuma, R. Maternal sexuality during first pregnancy and after childbirth. *British Journal of Obstetrics and Gynecology* 88:882, 1981.
39. Rubin, R. *Maternal Identity and the Maternal Experience*. New York: Springer, 1984.
40. Savage, W. Sexual activity during pregnancy. *Midwife-Health Visitor and Community Nurse* 20:398, 1984.
41. Schuman, T. (ed). *The Parent Manual: A Handbook for a Prepared Childbirth*. Wayne, NJ: Avery Publishing Group, Inc., 1983.
42. Shereshefsky, P., and Yarrow, L. *Psychological Aspects of a First Pregnancy and Early Postnatal Adaptation*. New York: Raven Press, 1973.
43. Solberg, D., Butler, J., and Wagner, N. Sexual behavior in pregnancy. *New England Journal of Medicine* 288:1098, 1973.
44. Speroff, L., and Ramwell, R. Prostaglandins in reproductive physiology. *American Journal of Obstetrics and Gynecology* 107:1111, 1970.
45. Standley, K. Dimensions of prenatal anxiety and their influence on pregnancy outcome. *American Journal of Obstetrics and Gynecology* 135:22, 1979.
46. Stanko, E. *Intimate Intrusions: Women's Experience of Male Violence*. Boston: Routledge and Kegal, Paul of America Ltd., 1985.
47. Swanson, J. The marital sexual relationship during pregnancy. *JOGN Nursing* 9:264, 1980.
48. Tolor, A., and DeGrazia, P. Sexual attitudes and behavior patterns during and following pregnancy. *Archives of Sexual Behavior* 5:539, 1976.
49. Weinberg, J. *Sexuality: Human Needs and Nursing Practice*. Philadelphia: W. B. Saunders Company, 1982.
50. Woolerly, L., and Barkley, N. Enhancing couple relationships during prenatal and postnatal classes. MCN: *American Journal of Maternal-Child Nursing* 6:184, 1981.
51. Zalar, M. Sexual counseling for pregnant couples. MCN: *American Journal of Maternal-Child Nursing* 1:176, 1976.

Beginning Quote

Kitzinger, S. *The Experience of Childbirth*. Baltimore: Penguin Books, Inc., 1972, p. 18.

Boxed Quotes

All from Stern, E. Sex During Pregnancy. *American Baby* March 1987, p. 71.

Section

5

THE CLASSROOM EXPERIENCE

The reasons clients attend prepared childbirth classes have changed. Twenty years ago expectant parents attended classes because they were seeking a particular type of birth experience. These couples, primarily highly educated and from the upper middle class, challenged traditional childbirth practices. Their participation in childbirth education classes and their beliefs about the childbirth experience were considered by many care providers to be "radical and unconventional."

Today, attending classes and preparing for the childbirth experience *is an expected practice*. Clients, with varying levels of motivation, come from a broad segment of society. Many attend classes primarily because it is "the socially acceptable thing to do," or because it is required for husbands, or other support persons, who wish to be present at the birth. Previously, expectant parents came to classes highly motivated to prepare for birth. Now, often one of the major roles of the childbirth educator is to motivate them to practice and prepare for the birth experience. Thus, the changing characteristics of the learner influence the content that needs to be taught and the strategies used for teaching.

There are many more different types of learners in classes today. Teaching classes to single pregnant teens in a clinic situation is strikingly different from teaching couples in an affluent suburb. For example, well-educated couples may want information about the childbirth experience and the reasons why certain techniques are most effective. In contrast, most teens are concerned about the here and now, are not interested in factual knowledge and want something action-oriented. Even more complicated is teaching a class in which the individuals enrolled in the class range from professional couples to the pregnant teen. Providing learning experiences that match the developmental needs of each learner in class is difficult to achieve at times.

The childbirth educator benefits from information about group process, adult learners, individual learning styles, teaching and learning theory, classroom techniques, learning needs of expectant parents, selecting and sequencing class content, and evaluation strategies. The appropriate teaching techniques for a class depend on characteristics of the learner, the teacher, and the material taught. In this section, group process, learner behavior, teacher behavior, class content, and evaluation are discussed in relation to the classroom experience.

chapter 24

GROUP PROCESS

MARGARET R. EDWARDS and FRANCINE H. NICHOLS

To every thing there is a season, and a time to every purpose under Heaven: A time to be born, and a time to die; a time to plant, and a time to pluck up that which is planted . . .

Ecclesiastes 3:1

Life cycles are implicit in all group activities. Every group has a beginning, it may more or less serve a specific purpose, and it has an end. Childbirth education classes consist of persons gathered together in a group to learn how to have the most positive childbirth experience possible for them. Thus far, this book has presented a comprehensive view of the information and skills that are important for the childbirth educator to know and be able to share with the parents in class, and has included some teaching techniques. Knowledge of the life cycles of a group and their influence on group process and activities that are appropriate during each cycle is also important.

This chapter will address the classroom experience from the perspective of group process. How do the class participants interact with each other? How does the childbirth educator interact with the class and its members? What influence do these interactions have on the learning process? Additionally, how can the childbirth educator best facilitate this process of group interaction so that group members benefit not only from the information they learn but also from actively sharing experiences, perceptions, and support with one another? These are the issues of group process.

This chapter will present a review of the literature that relates to group learning, group structure, group development, group process, interpersonal communication in group work, group leadership, and common problems occurring in group work. Guidelines are given for using this information in the practice of childbirth education, and implications for further research are examined.

REVIEW OF THE LITERATURE

What is a "Group?"

In order to discuss the use of groups in the childbirth education setting, one must first establish what is meant by a "group." Although various individuals may think of groups in different ways, the literature offers a common theme from those who study groups. One aspect of this is the fact that a group is more than just a collection of persons. In order to truly constitute a group, those persons must be interdependent and share a common goal.[4,28] Cartwright and Zander examined several definitions of a group before adopting the following definition: "A group is a collection of individuals who have relations to one another that make them interdependent to some significant degree."[4] They further state that "a collection of people who are striving to attain a common goal . . . constitutes a group, since goal-relevant behavior on the part of each person affects the others' likelihood of goal attainment."

Fisher takes this further by suggesting that the individuals in a group possess common characteristics—a sense of membership, shared norms, interdependent goals, and frequent interaction.[12] Miles and Stubblefield go on to a more specialized definition of a learning group, stating that it is "a group organized to acquire understandings, attitudes, or skills about a topic, subject, or performance objective."[25]

The Value of Groups

The use of groups in teaching has many advantages[6,20,22,35] (Table 24–1). Loomis[22] lists several advantages of using groups for helping persons to learn new behaviors. These include the mutual support that is available through a group, improved task accomplishment, socialization, improved learning, increased motivation toward behavior change, and the development of insight into feelings and problems. Lewin states that attitudes of group members often can be changed more easily through group interactions than by direct teaching of the individuals.[20]

The experiential learning derived through group functioning may be as important as the particular information or skills that are being learned. Problem-solving skills may be developed that carry over into other aspects of the participants' lives. The shared group support that can occur during childbirth classes can be particularly beneficial. In fact, because they are involved in a common experience (pregnancy), group members may be better able than the teacher to offer support to one another.[22,35] In the learning group situation, members share perceptions, experiences, and resources, which is not only beneficial, but is also particularly appropriate for adult learners.

Coussens and Coussens look at potential disadvantages in the use of groups in childbirth education, pointing out that group methods may fail to consider individual differences in prior ability or preparation.[6] Individuals come to class with different levels of health, experience, physical capacity, and levels of knowledge. Each of these influences the needs of the class participants, yet all participants usually receive the same or similar training. They also state that group methods frequently used in childbirth education classes may not take into account the differences in motivation for taking a childbirth preparation course.

Group Process

Most of the preceding portions of this book have dealt with the content (the "what") of childbirth

TABLE 24–1. ADVANTAGES OF GROUPS

Mutual support
Improved task accomplishment
Socialization
Improved learning
Increased motivation
Insight development
Attitude changes
Experiential learning
Problem-solving skill development
Sharing of perceptions, experiences, and resources

Expectant parents share common concerns and discuss expectations during small group discussions. (Photograph by Francine Nichols. Courtesy of Equicor Health Plan, Inc., Wichita, KS.)

education classes. The process, on the other hand, is the "who," "why," "when," and "how" of what is said and done to promote effective learning of the content. Murray and Zentner define group process as ". . . the interaction between members and leader(s), each fulfilling certain functions as the group as a whole and individual members proceed through various stages of development."[27]

An effective approach to health education is one that is not only informative but also utilizes student interaction to promote behavioral goals. A group dynamic model can be applied in which attention to process is as important as what is actually being said. The teacher must be aware of how members affect the behavior of one another and of how the teacher affects the behavior of member participants. He or she can then shape class interaction through strategic intervention.[13]

The Importance of Group Process. Group dynamics exert a marked influence on learning in the classroom. The literature contains strong evidence that teaching can no longer be bound simply by the parameters of the content to be learned, augmented by a variety of teaching methods.[38] Loomis and Dodenhoff emphasize that the person doing health-related teaching must have an understanding of what motivates the individuals to come together, what the group's goals are, and the factors that influence the achievement of these goals. The teacher can then influence the direction and effectiveness of the group as a whole, and can also contribute to the learning and satisfaction experienced by individual group members.[23]

Miles and Stubblefield suggest that interaction between the group leader and members and among the members themselves is an important component of the learning experience.[25] This process of interaction creates and develops the group. Furthermore, Fisher proposes that the quality of this interaction determines the effectiveness of the group in meeting its goals as well as the satisfaction with the experience that each member derives from the group.[12]

In task-oriented groups (such as childbirth education classes), the task is clear and acceptable to all members. Accomplishment of the task will provide completion for the classes, and it is toward that end that the group members strive.[35] The entire group may need to focus on group process from time to time, in order to function most effectively in meeting its goals. Miles and Stubblefield remind us, however, that the ultimate goal of the group is the successful accomplishment of their task; effective group process is but a means to that end.[25]

Factors Influencing Group Effectiveness

A variety of factors influence group interaction and the ability of the group to function effectively.

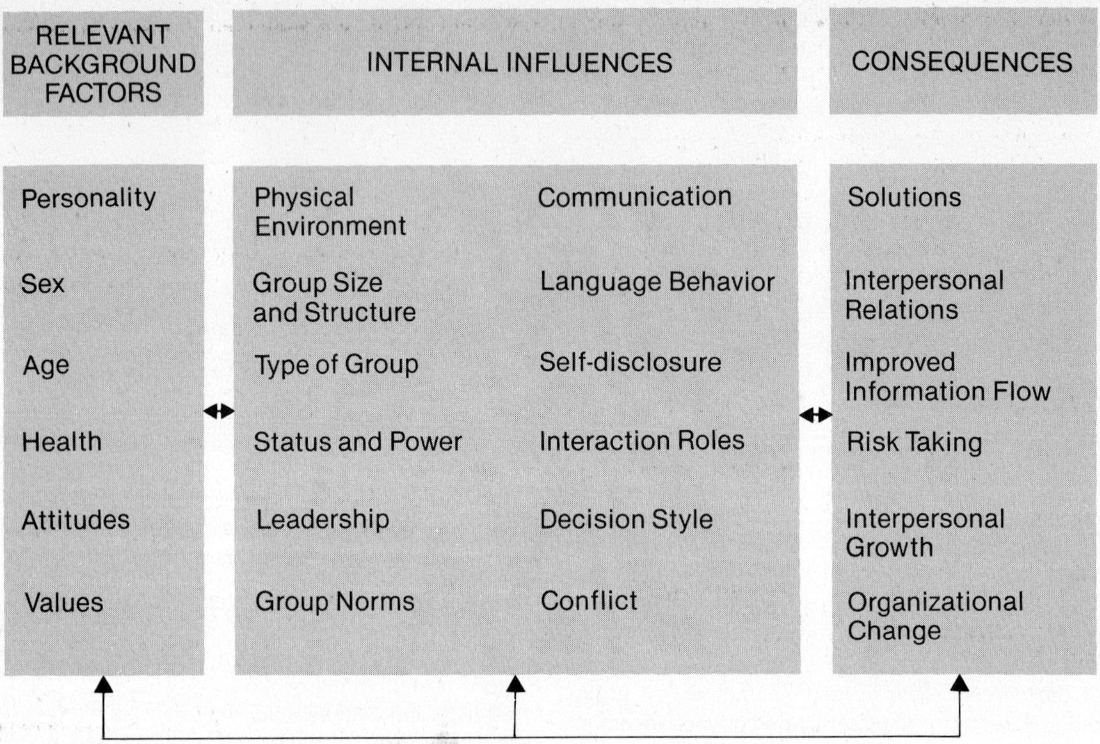

FIGURE 24–1. The Tubbs model of small group interaction. (From Tubbs, S. L.: *A Systems Approach to Small Group Interaction.* Reading, MA: Addison-Wesley Publishing Co., 1978.)

Tubbs[41] proposes looking at small group interaction from a general systems perspective. He suggests that small group interaction occurs in a system of interdependent forces, and that each of these forces must be analyzed in relation to the other forces in order to gain an understanding of small group interaction (Fig. 24–1). In the Tubbs model of small group interaction, three categories of variables are described. The first category, *Relevant Background Factors,* looks at basic attributes of the individual participants. These include personality, sex, age, health, attitudes, and values. The second category, *Internal Influences,* involves influences that can be manipulated in order to change the functioning of the group. These include such things as the type and size of the group, the leadership style, and communication patterns. The third category, the *Consequences* of small group interaction, will vary according to what is involved in the first two categories. The consequences referred to include solutions to problems, interpersonal growth, and organizational change. The Tubbs model can provide a practical and effective means of looking at and analyzing small group interaction and as such can be useful to the childbirth educator in assessing what is happening among the members of the class.

Types of Groups. Miles and Stubblefield categorize different types of learning groups as ''leader-centered,'' ''content-centered,'' and ''group member–centered''[25] (Table 24–2). Prepared childbirth classes in small groups of five to 12 couples are good examples of content-centered groups, while large informational childbirth education programs are, of necessity, leader-centered. Hemphill[17] found that larger groups have a greater tolerance for ''leader-centered'' direction of group activities.

Group Size. Research into group size has shown that the ideal size for a group varies with its type and purpose. For learning, findings indicate that

TABLE 24–2. TYPES OF LEARNING GROUPS

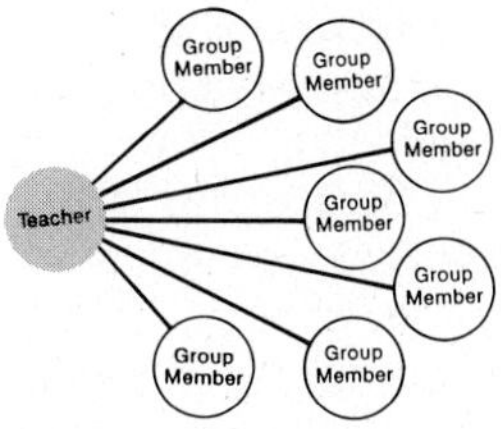

Leader-Centered Group

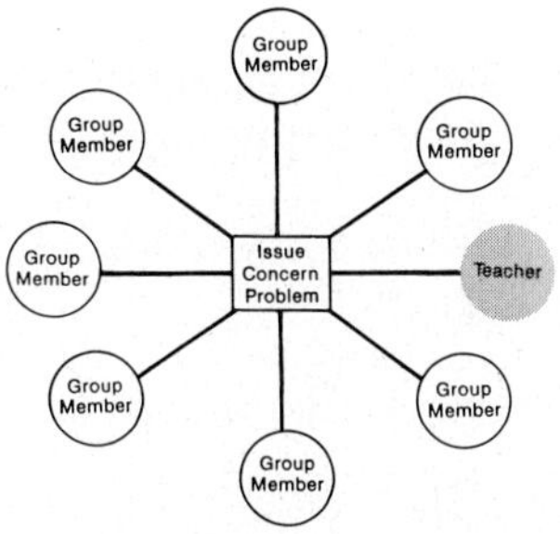

Content-Centered Group

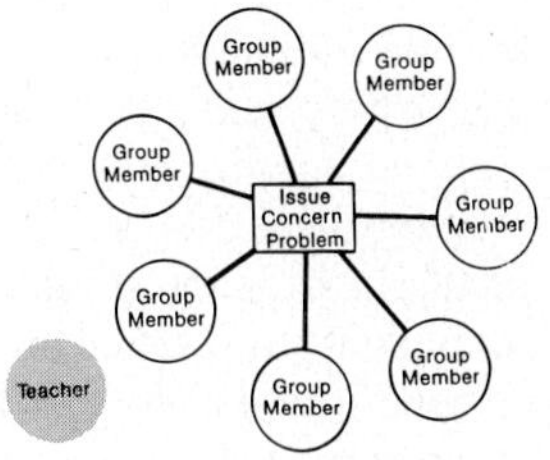

Group Member-Centered Group

	LEADER-CENTERED GROUP	CONTENT-CENTERED GROUP	GROUP-MEMBER–CENTERED GROUP
Group Purpose	To acquire information about a topic.	To acquire information about a topic.	To discuss an issue or topic of concern to members.
Group Leadership	A designated leader, usually a content expert, presents content.	A designated leader, usually a content expert, may also serve as trainer to help group members.	A designated leader who trains group members in process and procedures of group-member-centered discussion, not a content expert; members of the group provide leadership and other service roles.
Content	Source of content usually external to group, usually provided by expert; high emphasis on academic subject matter.	Source of content external to group; secured from expert, readings, or visuals; high emphasis on academic subject matter.	Source of content internal to group; group discusses common need and interests; no emphasis on academic subject matter.
Concern for Group Process	Little emphasis on process; communication flows from leader to group and not among group members; usually little attempt to foster climate of trust and openness.	Group members interact with one another; concern for maintenance and task roles; climate of trust and openness encouraged.	Group members interact with one another, climate of trust and openness deliberately cultivated, group regularly examines process and diagnoses problems in group interaction.

Adapted from Miles, L. and Stubblefield, H. W. Learning groups in training and education. *Small Group Behavior* 13:311, 1982.

participation is more satisfying and group process are more effective in smaller groups.[4,15,38] In this context, small groups are those of approximately five to 12 members, and 20 to 25 is considered a large group. Yalom and Terrazas[24] have proposed groups of four or five individuals as the smallest that can be effective, and Coffey[42] states that 20 or more persons is more of an assemblage and may be unable to function effectively as a group.

Group size is a significant factor in determining group interaction and satisfaction. Interaction between group members and their satisfaction with their participation have been found to decrease as the size of the group increases.[14,34,42] Sasmor and Grossman found that childbirth education groups ranged in size from two to 30, with the majority in the 20 to 30 range, which is inconsistent with principles of group size for effective education.[32] This study looked only at hospital-based classes, however, and did not examine other settings in which childbirth education takes place.

Thelen recommends looking for ways to divide larger classes into small groups.[38] In his ''principle of least group size,'' he proposes forming subgroups within the class. If these subgroups are given clear direction in terms of the task and the processes for accomplishing it, and if they can be helped to recognize the importance of their work to the larger group, these subgroups can be both more effective and more satisfying than the larger group. Thelen cautions that these subgroups must include individuals who have all the socialization and achievement skills required for the particular learning activity at hand.

Subgroups that are larger than necessary result in duplication of skills, less opportunity for the individual to participate, and consequently decreased motivation to be active in the group. Subgroups that are smaller than necessary will be unable to meet all the group needs, resulting in frustration and lack of motivation among the members.

Physical Environment. Marram and Tubbs both point out the importance of physical and environmental conditions to the success of the group. Marram[24] emphasizes that the leader must attend to such physical factors as ventilation, seating arrangements, lighting, spacing of group members in the room, and distracting noises, each of which can affect the moods of group members and can influence their sociability. Tubbs cites several studies that support the assumption that the color and attractiveness of a room influences mood, attitude, and mental functioning.[41]

Group Roles

In addition to characterizing group process by phases of group development, it is helpful to look at the various roles that group members play as they interact with one another. In 1947, the first National Training Laboratory in Group Development analyzed functional member-roles of groups.[2] These member-roles were classified into three broad categories, which were labeled group task roles (helping roles), group building and maintenance roles, and individual roles (hindering roles).

Group task roles are those helping roles that facilitate and coordinate group task accomplishment. They assist the group in problem-solving activities. Group members are performing these roles when they offer information pertinent to the task, explain or elaborate on suggestions previously made, coordinate ideas and activities of group members, or write down suggestions and decisions of the group. Group task roles are important to satisfactory group outcomes.[2]

Group building and maintenance roles assist the group to function effectively. They focus on building and maintaining group-centered attitudes and behaviors. Examples of activities in this category include giving support and positive feedback to others, promoting open communication, and mediating disagreements among members. These group roles are also important to the healthy functioning of the group.[2]

Individual roles, on the other hand, are hindering roles that are deleterious to the healthy functioning of the group. They are irrelevant to the group task and are either nonoriented or negatively oriented to group building and maintenance. They are those roles that members take on in order to satisfy their own personal needs. Examples of these behaviors are domination of the group by interrupting or otherwise manipulating other members, unreasonably negative or stubborn behavior, joking aggressively or belittling others, and expressing insecurity or self-depreciation in order to gain sympathy from other group members.[2]

As they work through the various phases of group process, group members may take on a variety of different roles. Note that an individual can fill more than one role in the group, so it is not necessary to have the same number of members as there are roles. A more detailed description by Benne and Sheats[2] of each of the roles of group members can be found in Table 24–3.

Interpersonal Communication in Group Work

Childbirth education classes involve learning in groups, and whenever groups are involved, the problem of working relationships arises. Interpersonal communication is one of the most important of these relationships. Open communication and an effective flow of information have been found to be major determinants of the quality of the product, task, or goal that any group produces or accomplishes.[1,16] Class members are quick to note the ways in which teachers respond to comments, encourage open communication, and accept opinions that differ from their own. If the teacher communicates a message, whether verbally or nonver-

TABLE 24–3. GROUP ROLES

GROUP TASK ROLES (HELPING ROLES)	GROUP BUILDING AND MAINTENANCE ROLES	INDIVIDUAL ROLES (HINDERING ROLES)
INITIATOR-CONTRIBUTOR: proposes new ideas	ENCOURAGER: gives support and positive feedback to others	AGGRESSOR: belittles and disapproves of others; attacks the group; jokes aggressively
INFORMATION SEEKER: asks for facts and seeks clarification of information	HARMONIZER: tries to keep the peace by mediating disagreements, relieving tension, soothing, and adding humor	BLOCKER: is negative, stubborn and resistant
OPINION SEEKER: asks for clarification of group values related to the task	COMPROMISER: changes his own approach, when involved in conflict, by admitting his error or meeting his opponent half-way, to maintain group harmony	RECOGNITION-SEEKER: calls attention to himself by boasting or acting out
INFORMATION GIVER: offers pertinent facts, generalizations, or personal experiences	GATE-KEEPER or EXPEDITER: promotes open communication, facilitates participation of others, controls or assists outsiders entering the group	SELF-CONFESSOR: vents his personal, non-group oriented feelings to group members
OPINION GIVER: tries to sway the group by stating his beliefs or opinions	STANDARD SETTER or EGO IDEAL: expresses group's standards, and uses them to evaluate the quality of group processes	PLAYBOY: behaves in cynical, nonchalant, or otherwise inappropriate ways, flaunts his lack of involvement in the group
ELABORATOR: expands on group suggestions by giving examples, rationale, or other explanations	GROUP-OBSERVER and COMMENTATOR: records and reports on group process for the purpose of group evaluation	DOMINATOR: asserts his own authority or superiority by interrupting, flattering, or giving directions to the group or its members, or other manipulative behavior
COORDINATOR: tries to pull together the ideas, suggestions, and activities of group members or subgroups	FOLLOWER: is passive and goes along with whatever the group decides or does	HELP-SEEKER: plays on the sympathy of others by expressing insecurity, confusion, or self-deprecation
ORIENTER: summarizes what has happened and clarifes the direction of the group discussion		SPECIAL INTEREST PLEADER: expresses his own prejudices or biases by claiming to speak for a specific group (women, health care professionals, etc.)
EVALUATOR-CRITIC: measures the group's process in relation to group-functioning standards, and measures accomplishment of the group task		
ENERGIZER: attempts to stimulate the group to act, decide, or produce at a higher level		
PROCEDURAL TECHNICIAN: handles routine tasks for the group, such as distributing materials, assisting with refreshments at breaks, etc.		
RECORDER: writes down suggestions and decisions, and acts as the "group memory"		

Adapted from Benne, K. D. and Sheats, P. Functional roles of group members. *Journal of Social Issues* 4:41, 1948.

bally, that open communication is not acceptable, the class will become teacher-dominated, and the potential benefits of group process will be lost for that group.[13]

Although a goal for later sessions is open communication among group members, the leader will need to take a more active role in the early sessions. Research done by Morran et al. indicates that, particularly in the early group sessions, feedback from the leader was more effective than was feedback from members of the group.[26]

Additional results of this study support the assumption that positive feedback is more accepted than negative feedback, and that negative feedback is more difficult to give effectively.[26] Furthermore, research has shown that effective helpers give more positive feedback and ineffective helpers more negative feedback.[18] Positive feedback leads to more open and effective utilization of the skills and resources of the group members, and thus to their greater involvement in group activities and to their greater satisfaction.[5]

Not only can the childbirth educator influence the communication that takes place between herself and the group and within the group, but she is also in a position to enrich communication between partners in the group. Because the approaching arrival of a child and the resultant expansion of the family unit represent major changes in their lives, the couple may benefit greatly from the attention paid to their communication skills by the childbirth educator. With the teacher's help, couples can learn new communication skills that will help them confront their own feelings about becoming parents.[35] Assisting couples to develop more open patterns of communication can enhance their stability and can also help them become more flexible in dealing with change.

Leadership Styles

The three basic leadership styles were first identified in a study conducted by Lewin and colleagues in 1939.[21] These styles are autocratic, democratic, and laissez-faire. The *autocratic leader* sets all goals, determines policy for the group, dictates agendas and activities, and tends to be subjective in offering praise and criticism of group members' efforts. The *democratic leader* allows the group to participate in setting goals and determining policy, agendas, and activities. He or she guides the actions of the group and acts as a resource. This leader is objective in giving praise and criticism. The permissive or *laissez-faire leader* is essentially a nonparticipant in group activities. The group is free to go its own way, with the leader contributing very infrequently.[33]

In selecting a leadership style, it is helpful to know of the experience of others with various styles. Trow and Zander describe student frustration with both autocratic and laissez-faire leadership.[40] Fiedler found that the laissez-faire leader in a task-oriented group loses the esteem of the group.[11] Smith describes how an autocratic stance is ineffective in group work. She suggests that, rather than dictating pre-established group goals, it is better to open discussion, see how many of the leader's goals are suggested by the group, and then offer the remaining ones. A democratic approach, wherein a balance is achieved between giving direction when necessary and allowing the group the freedom to grow, seems to be accepted as the most satisfactory leadership style.[36] In fact, DeTornyay suggests that the democratic leader who encourages group members to share responsibility and participate in group decisions may be able to cause the task-oriented group to be emotionally supportive as well.[7]

Role of the Teacher

The role of the teacher is that of *democratic strategist* or *manager* of the classroom experience.[40] The teacher attends to group process through structuring the learning experience to promote the development of an effective group. A clear understanding of the dynamic forces that affect the class as a group, the phases and stages of group process, and ways to help the group to function effectively is essential in order to be successful as a group leader.

It is important that the teacher be alert to behavioral cues from the group that may indicate that group process needs have not been met. Some examples are the inability to "settle down" and get started on the learning task, group apathy, anxiety, or dissatisfaction with the learning situation. With recognition of these, the teacher can plan specific approaches to resolve these problems, should they occur.

Evaluation of group process is an important aspect of the teacher's role. This can be accomplished in two ways. One is to measure the progress toward group goals; another is to assess improvement in the dynamics of group relationships. There are several sources of this evaluation data. One, of course, is the teacher, who should carry out such evaluation regularly. Another valuable source is the class or group itself. This evaluation is not only an important component of the feedback needed by the teacher but can also serve as a valuable learning experience for the group members. Finally, it is often useful to bring in an outside person to observe in the classroom for the purpose of evaluation.[40] Through frequent evaluation, the teacher can become proficient in using the appropriate strategies to enhance group process in any classroom situation.

Group Characteristics

Cohesiveness. Cohesiveness is an important characteristic of a strong, effective group. Cohesiveness can be defined as the forces that a group exerts on its members to remain in the group.[10] The more cohesive the group, the greater its ability to satisfy the needs of its members.[23] When frustrations are met, highly cohesive groups are much better able to continue movement toward the group goal than are groups of low cohesiveness. Group members are more highly motivated to participate actively, and therefore to learn, in situations in which the group leader and members build a supportive atmosphere in the classroom. This motivation increases as members participate and as the group accepts them as participating members whose contributions are valid and valued.[40]

Goals. The cohesiveness of the group is an important determinant of how well it moves toward its goals. Conversely, group goals and norms are an essential part of group cohesion.[23] Often it is helpful for the teacher/leader and the class participants to formulate a contract together that clarifies realistic objectives and goals.[35] Studies have shown that when group members share in the determination of group goals, and when they have a clear understanding of these goals and the ways to attain them, they then consider themselves co-participants with fellow group members and the group leader, and they feel that they have some control in the situation. This leads to stronger feelings of group-belongingness and greater empathy with the group emotions. Therefore, they are able to accept the group goals as their own personal goals and are more likely to follow through on them.[4,23,29,40]

Participation. An important function of the group leader is to facilitate group participation. Results of a study by Harper and Askling indicate that when a larger proportion of group members actively participate in the group's activities, the quality of the group's product improves.[16] In addition, several authors have demonstrated that increased participation brings increased member satisfaction.[1,3,30,39] Bostram expands on this by reporting that satisfaction from group membership apparently comes more from talking than from listening, and that group members feel greater overall satisfaction when they have not only heard the information they want to learn but have participated actively in discussion as well.[3]

There are several strategies that can be used to minimize the teacher's dominant role and thereby promote increased participation and group interaction in the classroom. These include avoiding standing above the students, which can connote teacher superiority and can inhibit member-to-member participation; moving around the room to support various students; and allowing silence so students can think through what they want to say.[13]

Individual Autonomy

Leavitt suggests that autonomy among group members is another important component of a successful group experience.[19] He suggests that in United States culture, satisfaction in many spheres can be related to independence. Because of our strong needs for autonomy and achievement, our level of satisfaction is influenced positively by increased autonomy and independence in the achievement of our goals. Thus it is important for the leader to help the group members build self-confidence in their own ability to accomplish the goals they have set for themselves.

Finally, it must be emphasized that there is no single combination of roles that a teacher plays or techniques that a teacher uses. Trow and Zander[40] suggest that teachers must constantly reassess which technique will be most effective for any given class, at any given time, in relation to the class goals.

Phases of Group Process

Although every group is unique, the dynamics of all groups are more similar than they are different, and knowledge of the phases of group process will assist the teacher in structuring the best possible learning situation. Several models have been developed to portray the phases of group process. However, a model presented by Stanford and Roark[37] is especially useful because of its detailed description of the phases of group process and the stages or activities that occur within each phase.

There are three phases of group process: the warm-up phase, the work or activity phase, and the integration phase. There are also two continua,

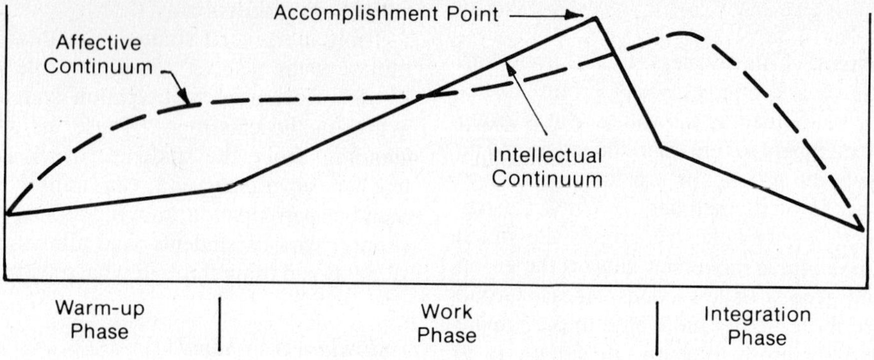

FIGURE 24–2. Characteristics of group process in the classroom. (Adapted from Stanford, G. and Roark, A. *Human Interaction in Education.* Boston: Allyn and Bacon, Inc., 1974.)

the affective continuum and the intellectual continuum, that require careful consideration when planning classroom activities (Fig. 24–2). Each phase of group process can be subdivided into specific stages or activities that occur within each phase (Table 24–4). The phases of group process occur in long-term group activities such as a semester college course or short-term situations such as a six-week prepared childbirth course as well as individual group meetings or classroom experiences.

The primary advantage of understanding the phases and stages of group process is that an educator can select appropriate activities for each phase that will enhance the learning experience; students will not respond well if they are requested to do tasks that do not correspond to the stage they are in, or to start a new activity before they have reached an accomplishment point in the current activity.

Warm-Up Phase. During this phase students must separate from their involvement in previous activities, ''tune in'' to the new situation, and become psychologically and physically prepared to participate in the group activity. The warm-up phase in education is frequently referred to as ''getting them settled down.'' The first task is to divert group members' attention from what they were previously doing. Games, music, or other brief classroom activities are effective approaches to this task. The next task is helping group members ''tune in'' and prepare to participate in the planned group

TABLE 24–4. PHASES AND STAGES OF GROUP PROCESS

PHASES	STAGES		
	1	2	3
Warm-Up Phase	Separates from involvement in previous activities	''Tunes-in'' to new situation or activity	Prepares to become involved in new activity
	1		2
Work Phase	Organizing work, outlining activities, and productive work to accomplish task		Summarizing, reviewing, polishing, and consolidating results
	1	2	3
Integration Phase	Reflecting on personal meaning of the activity, perceptions of activities accomplished.	Summarizing and clarifying what has been accomplished	Discussing significance and usefulness of activity for participant's future, introduction of future activities

Adapted from Stanford, G. and Roark, A. *Human Interaction in Education.* Boston: Allyn and Bacon, Inc., 1974.

activity. Appropriate activities to complete this task are a review of what happened the previous week and a discussion of questions that class members may have, sharing of events that have occurred during the week, and a preview of material to be covered. It is only after these tasks are accomplished that students will be ready to become involved in the classroom activity. Group members usually enter the warm-up phase feeling anxious about the group experience and their readiness to deal with factual information is minimal. Until the warm-up phase has been successfully completed, learning (the intellectual continuum) is limited.

Work or Activity Phase. During this phase the group becomes very task-focused; work is accomplished, and the major amount of learning takes place. This phase can be subdivided into two stages: the building stage, which comprises the majority of the work phase and includes organizing the work, outlining the activities, and accomplishing the task; and the consolidation stage, which is usually of short duration and in which results are summarized, polished, and consolidated. Class members become emotionally involved with the tasks to be accomplished during the work phase and their emotions peak in the integration phase.

Integration Phase. This is a critical phase, and usually is the most troublesome one for teachers. It is more than merely a termination phase and includes clarifying and summarizing what was accomplished. It also includes an emphasis on the group members' perceptions of the activities and the meaning of these activities to them personally. *The degree to which the integration phase is successfully completed is directly related to the amount of satisfaction that class members have with the learning experience.*

Group Problems

Thus far, this chapter has dealt with the literature that can apply to developing and facilitating optimal group process in childbirth education classes. Not always, however, do classes proceed in an optimal fashion. Problems are bound to arise, and the knowledgeable childbirth educator is prepared with an understanding of the types of problems that may arise and a framework from which to deal with these problems.

Zander identifies three problems that can occur as part of group process.[42] These are a reluctance of members to participate, members not having ideas to contribute, and restraints or barriers to free and open discussion. He suggests that a skilled leader will actively plan ways to address these potential sources of inhibition among group members.

Sampson and Marthas suggest seven issues that

TABLE 24–5. AN INTERVENTION MODEL FOR GROUP PROCESS PROBLEMS

DEFINING THE PROBLEM	
1. ISSUE:	Why is this a problem? How does it affect group process?
2. OBSERVATIONS:	What behaviors do I see taking place within the group and its members?
3. DIAGNOSIS:	What does it mean? What can I conclude about the behavior of the group or group members from my observations and my understanding of the issues that are involved?
CHANGING THE GROUP PROCESS	
4. INTERVENTION STRATEGIES:	What are specific techniques that I can use to change the group's interactions and to remedy the problem?
ASSESSING THE EFFECTS	
5. EVALUATION:	What was the effect of the intervention? To what extent was it a success or a failure?

Adapted from Sampson, E. E., and Marthas, M. *Group Process for the Health Professions,* 2nd ed. New York: John Wiley and Sons, 1981.

TABLE 24–6. GROUP PROCESS INTERVENTIONS FOR LEADERS

TYPE OF INTERVENTION	GOALS OF INTERVENTION
Support	Provides supportive climate for group members to express ideas and opinions, including unpopular or unusual points of view. Facilitates members to continue with their current behavior. Helps reinforce positive behavior. Creates a climate that promotes the security of silent members and increases their willingness to participate.
Confrontation	Aids in growth and development of members. Encourages members to use more than one mode of functioning. Helps decrease some types of disruptive behavior. Helps members interact more openly and directly with each other.
Advice and Suggestions	Shares expertise, offers new perspectives. Keeps group's focus on its task and goals.
Summarizing	Assists group to focus on its task by reviewing past actions; sets agenda for future sessions. Identifies unresolved issues that need to be dealt with. Clarifies and organizes what has happened. Identifies themes and patterns of interactions.
Clarifying	Helps decrease distortion in communication. Assists group to focus on substantive issues rather than insignificant or irrelevant issues.
Probing and Questioning	Invites expansion of a point that may have been left incomplete or requires more consideration. Provides more extensive and wider range of information. Encourages members to explore their ideas in greater detail.
Repeating, Paraphrasing, and Highlighting	Supports members to continue with their current behavior; invites further exploration and examination of what is being said. Clarifies important points of a communication, and helps focus on the specific, important, or key aspect of a communication. Increases members' understanding of what is being said or done.
Reflecting: Feelings	Encourages members to consider the feelings that may lie behind what is being said or done. Encourages members to deal with issues they might otherwise avoid or miss.
Reflecting: Behavior	Provides members with information on how their behavior appears to others and enables them to consider it and evaluate its consequences. Increases members' awareness and understanding of others' perceptions and responses to them.
Interpretation and Analysis	Places behavior within a larger context and increases the meaningfulness of the behavior to group members. Summarizes patterns of behavior and provides a useful way of examining them and then making desired changes based on the insights gained.
Listening	Provides an attentive and responsive audience for those talking. Models a helpful way for members to relate to one another; portrays a feeling of sharing and mutual concern. Helps members sharpen their own ideas and thinking as they realize that others are indeed listening and are concerned about what group members are saying.

Adapted from Sampson, E. E., and Marthas, M. *Group Process for the Health Professions,* 2nd ed. New York: John Wiley and Sons, 1981.

group leaders often confront.[31] They include dealing with the following:

1. A group member who dominates or monopolizes the discussion
2. A group member, or even an entire group, that is silent, apathetic, and reluctant to participate
3. Anger, crying, or other emotional outbursts
4. Conflict between group members
5. Behavior that is improper according to group expectations
6. Issues involved in getting a group started
7. Issues involved in ending or terminating the group.

Although it must be emphasized that each situation is unique and calls for sensitivity and understanding on the part of the group leader, an intervention model for approaching these problems can provide a helpful starting point. The intervention model developed by Sampson and Marthas is particularly useful[31] (Table 24–5). In this intervention model, the first step is to define the problem. This involves looking at the issue to determine why it is a problem, how serious it is, and how it may affect group process. It also involves the observation of what associated behaviors are occurring and a diagnosis of the meaning of the behaviors in relation to the issue or problem. The second step is to determine what intervention strategies would be most appropriate, and then to implement these intervention strategies. Various types of leader interventions have been found to be effective in groups (Table 24–6). The final step is to evaluate the effects of the intervention.[31]

IMPLICATIONS FOR PRACTICE

In childbirth education classes, the group is task-oriented because the task—preparation for childbirth—is the reason that expectant parents have chosen to join the group. Accomplishment of the task must be completed within a short time period, typically six weeks. Often, the inexperienced childbirth educator uses primarily lecture and discussion in order to cover class material in the most efficient manner during this limited time period while ignoring critical aspects of group process.

From time to time, however, all childbirth educators must focus on group process if the group is to function most effectively in meeting its goals. The childbirth educator can facilitate the interaction of expectant parents as they learn together in class and can promote the interdependence of group members. This group interdependence can lead to stronger group ties and a more effective and satisfying group learning experience, which in turn can lead to a more positive childbirth experience.

A Content-Centered Group. Childbirth education classes are content-centered groups in which the group leader (childbirth educator) serves as the content expert. Expectant parents are encouraged to take an active role in exploring information and making decisions about their childbirth experience. The childbirth educator is a facilitator and resource person and guides the group process.

During the first class, the group members are usually relatively dependent upon the leader. This stems from their limited knowledge of prepared childbirth and the labor and birth process and from their uncertainty as to their role in class interaction. The childbirth educator can use various approaches, however, to prevent the group from becoming a leader-centered group. For example, the childbirth educator can involve class members in setting the agenda for the classes by asking, ''If you went into labor in the next five minutes, what would you want to know?'' As the class members respond, their answers are written on the blackboard. Typically, the responses of class members are the same as the topics the childbirth educator already planned to cover.

During the discussion, the childbirth educator can point out the similarities in class members' concerns. At the end of the discussion, the childbirth educator indicates to the group when the spe-

> There appears to be some therapeutic value not only in receiving the support of the group but also in being able to share one's own experiences and support with others.
>
> MAXINE LOOMIS[1]
>
> It has been five years since we met in Lamaze classes and we all had our babies and we're still friends.
>
> A CLASS PARTICIPANT
>
> Student satisfaction and sense of accomplishment are closely related to the adequate completion of life cycles in activities. An awareness of life cycles can also be helpful in judging the appropriateness of the time allowed for particular programs or sequences.
>
> G. STANFORD AND A. ROARK[2]

cific topics of interest will be covered during the class series. Topics that were not suggested by class members but which the childbirth educator plans to include in the classes should also be identified. If expectant parents mention concerns that the childbirth educator does not usually include in class, these can be handled either individually or during a future class, depending upon the needs of the group.

The childbirth educator then summarizes the class content and anticipated activities, so expectant parents have a clear understanding of the goals of the course and the outcomes they can anticipate. In essence, through this activity the childbirth educator is assisting expectant parents to establish ties with other group members based on common concerns as well as to set goals for the class.

Another approach that is useful to prevent the group from becoming leader-centered is for the teacher to refer class members' questions or concerns back to the group for an answer. This encourages expectant parents to view themselves as important sources of information and increases communication among class members. Class members often share mutual concerns and frequently contribute innovative and helpful coping strategies that enrich class discussions. Childbirth educators who meet the challenge of promoting cohesion within the group will have taken an important step toward creating a strong and effective group.

The Childbirth Educator as a Group Leader

Periodic self-assessment (Table 24–7) will assist the childbirth educator to function as an effective group leader. This assessment starts prior to the class series as the childbirth educator prepares for the classes. Assessment continues throughout the class series. The childbirth educator should focus on becoming sensitive to the use of group process during the class. Making an audiotape of a class and critically reviewing it using the "Group Process Self-Appraisal Checklist for Childbirth Educators" will also help the teacher to increase skill in the area of group process.

The childbirth educator should do an overall evaluation of group process at the completion of the classes in order to identify strengths and areas that require change in future classes. Recording what was effective with this particular group as well as noting changes that are needed in future classes will assist the childbirth educator in becoming a more effective group leader. As a part of the assessment, the childbirth educator should also note the unique characteristics and personality of this specific group because these influence group process.

The childbirth educator can expect group functioning to vary from group to group. If a group just does not "jell," or if through the eyes of the childbirth educator it is an outright "failure," an assessment of group process is indicated. Along with the interactions within the class, the childbirth educator should examine the characteristics of the group and events surrounding the class series, as these are also important determinants of group process. When the group does not function as anticipated, the childbirth educator should not automatically assume the responsibility for the problem. The childbirth educator and class members share the responsibility for effective group process. All factors that influence group process should be examined carefully in order to determine the source or sources of the problem.

TABLE 24–7. GROUP PROCESS SELF-APPRAISAL CHECKLIST FOR CHILDBIRTH EDUCATORS

PREPARATION

- ☐ Is the group size appropriate for effective interaction?
- ☐ Is the physical environment comfortable, attractive, and conducive to group learning?
- ☐ Are participants preregistered and given the necessary instructions before the first class meeting? (What to bring, what to wear, where to come, what to expect, and so on.)
- ☐ Do I have adequate information about each individual in the group? (Previous childbirth experiences, previous childbirth education, other life and educational experiences, motivation to come to class, problems and special needs)
- ☐ Does the first class focus on activities to foster initial group development?
- ☐ Is each class structured to include a review of previous learning, the presentation of new content, a summary of new learning, and a preview of what is to come next?
- ☐ Is each class structured to allow time for breaks and interaction?
- ☐ Does the last class allow for integration of the material learned and for termination of the group?
- ☐ Do I have a thorough understanding of the material to be presented?
- ☐ Have I prepared questions to guide the discussion?

GROUP LEADERSHIP

- ☐ Do I have a democratic leadership style that balances providing direction for the group when necessary with allowing the group freedom when possible?
- ☐ Do I assist the group to establish clear goals and expectations?
- ☐ Do I use approaches to reduce group members' anxiety about participating in the group?
- ☐ Do I employ strategies to draw out quiet or reluctant individuals in the group?
- ☐ Do I allow periods of silence when appropriate?
- ☐ Do I acknowledge and clarify ideas and feelings expressed by the group?
- ☐ Do I use learners' ideas and experiences in expanding on essential information?
- ☐ Am I sensitive to the nonverbal behavior of individuals within the group?
- ☐ Do I address group problems in a tactful and sensitive manner?
- ☐ Am I flexible in my approach to helping the group achieve its goals?
- ☐ Do I continually evaluate the progress of the group toward meeting its goals?
- ☐ Do I avoid lecturing when another strategy can be used?
- ☐ Do I promote discussion and learner participation in the classroom?
- ☐ Do I always give feedback in a positive manner?
- ☐ Do I use small group activities to promote individual participation?
- ☐ Do I use neutral descriptive terms rather than value-laden words? ("What are your feelings about breast feeding?" instead of "What are the advantages and disadvantages of breast feeding?")

Leadership Style. The effective group leader in childbirth education classes promotes the autonomy of group members and assists group members to increase their decision-making skills and build self-confidence in their own ability to have a positive childbirth experience. This democratic leadership style will also result in more friendliness and motivation within the group, better quality of group work, increased class member satisfaction, and lower absenteeism from class. A task-oriented childbirth education group is more likely to be an emotionally supportive group as well if the childbirth educator uses a democratic leadership style.[41]

Interpersonal Communication. Good interpersonal communication skills are critical if the childbirth educator is to develop a good working relationship with group members. Communication patterns should be open, nonjudgmental and reflective of sincere interest in each individual's opinion even if it differs drastically from the childbirth educator's beliefs about childbirth. It is essential that the group leader periodically evaluate both verbal and nonverbal messages given in class to determine the attitudes that are being conveyed to class members.

Feedback to group members is essential in all areas of the class, but it is especially important for refining skills in the various prepared childbirth techniques—relaxation techniques, breathing techniques, and other pain management techniques. Childbirth educators should give feedback to class members in a positive and descriptive manner as opposed to a negative and evaluative manner. For example, when checking a tense expectant mother for degree of relaxation, the childbirth educator should say, "Let your arm go limp. Feel it getting warm and heavy," instead of "Your arm is too tense. Just let it relax."

Through structured class activities and the process of working together during skills training, couples can be helped to develop more open patterns of communication. This can help them resolve problems, can enhance their relationship, and can make them more realistic and flexible about changes and problems that may occur during the childbearing experience.

Factors Influencing Group Process

A variety of factors influence the group process in any specific group situation. These include background characteristics of the group members such as age, health, and attitudes. The childbirth educator begins assessing these factors when enrolling expectant parents in class and when first planning the classes. In addition, internal influences such as group size, physical environment, group participation, and group problems will affect group process. The childbirth educator must evaluate these factors carefully, and must understand how they can influence group process and therefore group outcomes. Classes can then be tailored to meet the needs of the participants, and internal influences can be changed to promote the best possible learning experience for the group members.

Background Characteristics of Group Members. Expectant parents in childbirth education classes often represent diverse backgrounds. This presents a challenge to the childbirth educator who must attempt to meet the unique individual needs of class members. This diversity can be an advantage for class members, however, because of the variety of experiences and perspectives that class members can offer one another.

There are several background characteristics that the childbirth educator should consider about individual class members. Among these are each individual's age, personality, health, attitudes, value system, and motivation to come to class. This information is essential for the childbirth educator in working with class members during the group experience. For example, the childbirth educator's approach to the expectant father who came to class to get his ''ticket to the delivery room'' will differ from the approach to the one who wants to be part of a ''special birth experience.''

In childbirth education classes, the most significant characteristics of the group members are that they are all involved with a pregnancy and are interested in learning how to participate in and enhance the birth experience. These represent both a common experience and a common goal, and will help group members to establish ties and develop cohesiveness as they work together to prepare for the birth experience.

The behavior of the individual group members gives the group its unique quality and mood. (Photograph by Rodger Ewy, Educational Graphic Aids, Inc.)

Class Size. Childbirth education classes should be small enough to allow the interaction that is so important in an effective and satisfying childbirth education experience—generally five to 10 couples. A class of this size promotes participation and interaction, which in turn enhances learning and member satisfaction.

If the class is larger than the ideal size, the leader should look for ways to implement Thelen's principle of "least group size" during the classes.[41] Careful attention must be paid to the composition of each subgroup in order to ensure that there are the needed expertise and group process skills within each unit to carry out the task assignment. Small groups are best used for values clarification exercises and sharing of feelings about a particular aspect of pregnancy or childbirth. This sharing of feelings, experiences, and often valuable suggestions for coping with problems or changes can increase the cohesiveness of the group. With skill and forethought, the childbirth educator can use small group activities to further facilitate group development, goal attainment, and member satisfaction.

Physical Environment. The physical environment in which the group meetings take place exerts an important influence on the effectiveness of the class. The classroom should be attractive, located in a quiet area, and large enough for the size of the group. Careful attention to such things as temperature, pleasant lighting, comfortable seating, spatial relationship in groupings, rest room accessibility, and availability of amenities such as beverages and nutritious snacks can go a long way toward creating a warm and comfortable learning environment and encouraging successful group interaction.

Breaks during class should be viewed as important interaction time for class members, and not merely as a chance to stretch or attend to personal needs. Thus, there should be adequate time allotted, a refreshment table arranged in a manner to encourage mingling, and possibly a topic assigned for informal discussion during the break period.

Phases of Group Process. The childbirth educator should structure the class series so that the first class focuses on reducing anxiety within the group, assisting group members to get acquainted and identify common concerns, establishing clear goals for the group, and assisting the group to become an effective working unit. Also, during this class it is essential to set forth class expectations, such as "Classes will start and end on time," "It is important to attend every class," and "Class members are encouraged to participate in group discussions in order to increase both individual and group learning."

The most active learning takes place in the following classes, which are usually more content-centered. Here, class members learn new skills in preparation for childbirth and become comfortable enough in the group to share their beliefs and concerns.

The final class is structured to allow for integration of the material that has been learned and termination of the group. Having previous class members return to the first part of the last class with their new babies and share their experiences with the group is an effective way of helping class members to integrate the information that has been learned during the class series. This will also help the expectant parents to develop a more realistic picture of childbirth and of the joys and problems of incorporating a new baby into the family unit, as well as to anticipate potential problem areas during the postpartum period.

A labor rehearsal is another effective approach for clarifying and summarizing what has been learned during the course. A discussion of expectant parents' perceptions of class activities and accomplishments and the meaning of class activities to them personally is critical to the successful completion of the integration phase of group process. While this type of discussion can take place at any time in the last class session, it works very well during the last half of the class and can be used to bring closure to the classroom experience.

During this last class, it is important that no *new* sensitive information—for example, cesarean birth or a discussion about the death of a baby—be presented. Introducing emotion-laden material at this point in the course is not appropriate because the childbirth educator does not have the opportunity to follow up on parents' responses to the information. Also, the group would then leave in a somber mood, as opposed to the upbeat, enthusiastic, and confident mood that is the goal for the final class. If for some reason emotion-laden topics must be addressed either because class members bring them up or because of events that have hap-

Interactions during a refreshment break are an important aspect of the classroom experience. (Photograph by Francine Nichols. Courtesy of Equicor Health Plan, Inc., Wichita, KS.)

pened, the childbirth educator will have to handle them in the most sensitive manner possible, while recognizing that this will most likely affect group process.

Individual Class Sessions. Each class session should follow this same three-phase model. When the class session begins, the *warm-up phase* takes place as the participants ''warm up,'' separate from their previous activities, and prepare to become involved in class activities. In this phase, the childbirth educator should always include a review of the material that was covered in the previous session. In the next phase of the class, the *work phase,* new information is presented and previously learned skills are refined. Following the work phase, each class should end with an *integration phase* to allow the group to wind down, review, summarize, and discuss the significance of what they have learned, preview what they will learn the following week, and provide closure for the class.

Group Roles. Class members function in a variety of roles during the class series and it is important that the childbirth educator identify the particular roles that each individual class member plays within the group (see Table 24–2). In this way the childbirth educator can identify those individuals who contribute to the problem-solving activities of the group through ''group task roles,'' those individuals who contribute to building and maintaining group-centered attitudes and behaviors through ''group building and maintenance roles,'' and those individuals whose behaviors are an attempt to satisfy their own needs and are detrimental to group functioning.

Childbirth educators who are familiar with the

roles people play in groups can recognize these roles as they occur during the class session and can deal with them appropriately, supporting members as they perform group task and maintenance roles, and responding to prevent interference with group process when individuals play roles detrimental to group functioning. The childbirth educator can use this role information in determining individual assignments to different groups during small-group activities and in eliciting specific input from various class members.

Nonverbal behaviors of class members must be assessed. These behaviors, as well as negative roles that individuals may play in the group, usually indicate problems. The childbirth educator must take time to consider these potential group problems and must become comfortable with using a variety of interventions. With such preparation, the childbirth educator will be able to be "pro-active" in confronting and resolving these problems, in order to improve group process, as opposed to being "re-active" and perhaps inappropriately handling sensitive or negative group situations.

Group Participation. Increasing members' participation in the classes results in increased learning of individual group members. Also, group members will feel greater overall satisfaction with their childbirth education experience if the childbirth educator has been successful in facilitating interaction among group members and in promoting discussion in which all group members participate.

How does one go about promoting participation and group interaction in the classroom? It can be accomplished by minimizing the teacher's dominant role by using the following strategies:

1. Get down on the same level as the students. Standing above them connotes teacher superiority and tends to inhibit member-to-member communication.
2. Move around the room to join various students and to support their efforts to get involved in class. Students who might otherwise speak only to the teacher may decide, with the teacher right next to them, to address others around the room.
3. Be willing to allow a reasonable amount of silence. This gives class members a chance to think through what they want to say. When the teacher jumps in to fill every silence, the students will not feel responsible for the silence and will assume a passive role.[13]

The teacher who is successful in helping group members participate more actively during childbirth education classes contributes significantly to their learning and also to their satisfaction with the class experience. This, in turn, will promote carryover, not only of information that they have learned during classes, but also of problem-solving skills and improved communication patterns that will be beneficial in other areas of their lives.

IMPLICATIONS FOR RESEARCH

There has been little systematic research about group process in childbirth education. There are many unanswered questions that need to be explored in order to give childbirth educators a sound research base to guide their practice. Using Tubbs' model of "Small Group Interaction,"[41] research questions can be grouped in three areas: relevant background factors, internal influences, and consequences.

Relevant Background Factors. A definite influence on group functioning is exerted by those attributes of class members that exist prior to the formation of the group and that will continue, possibly in a modified form, after the group no longer exists. Questions that need to be answered are:

- How does the motivation level of individuals to attend class influence their interactions during childbirth education classes?
- How does the diversity of background factors

within a specific group affect group learning and satisfaction?

- Do certain expectant parents benefit from childbirth education classes more than others?
- Can background factors of class members be used to predict the success of class members within the group?

Internal Factors. The nature and functioning of a group can be changed by altering internal factors that influence group process. The following questions need to be investigated:

- How does the organizational setting (health care agency versus independent classes) influence class outcomes?
- What group size promotes the most effective learning in childbirth education classes?
- What impact do the individual characteristics of the childbirth educator (personality, leadership style, age, previous maternal and child health experience, and so on) have on group learning?
- Does the preference of the childbirth educator for certain types of clients influence group functioning and thus group outcomes?
- What is the effect of the coach on the expectant mother's level of learning?
- Which group activities are most successful in promoting interactions among expectant couples?
- Which topics are most effectively taught using small-group activities?
- Which interventions are most effective in dealing with group problems?
- What is it about childbirth education classes that really helps expectant parents?

Consequences. The consequences are the results of the childbirth education experience. Research questions that need to be considered are:

- What is the cost-effectiveness of childbirth education as a preventive health measure?
- What influence does participation in childbirth education classes have on the class member's communication with the obstetrical health care provider?
- Are expectant parents better problem-solvers after participating in childbirth education classes?
- Does the influence of childbirth education classes extend beyond the childbirth experience?
- Do parents learn essential information better when a discussion group learning model is used or when a leader-introduced content model is used?
- Does participation in childbirth education classes increase an individual's ability in the area of interpersonal relationships?
- How can the childbirth educator most effectively promote the wellness behaviors of individuals beyond the childbirth experience?

These are but a few of the questions that we must answer. The waters of group process in childbirth education classes are uncharted and the possible results from well-designed research studies and their implications for the practice of childbirth education are unlimited.

SUMMARY

The challenge to the childbirth educator is demanding but exciting. It is not enough to have expert knowledge about pregnancy and childbirth. In order to be an effective childbirth educator, one must also develop skills in group process. This requires an understanding of the preparations that are necessary before classes begin. It requires an understanding of the factors that influence group process and of techniques that can best promote positive group outcomes. It requires a recognition that group work can best facilitate optimal childbirth education when the childbirth educator thoroughly understands and effectively utilizes the principles of group process. Although this challenge is exacting, the potential benefits are many. Successful classes on a week-by-week basis, favorable evaluation of the series of classes, and positive childbirth experiences among graduates of the classes will amply reward the childbirth educator for having attended to group process, as well as to content, in the childbirth education classes.

References

1. Bavelas, A., Hastorf, A. H., Gross, A. E., and Kite, W. R. Experiments in the alteration of group structure. *Journal of Experimental Social Psychology* 1:55, 1965.
2. Benne, K. D., and Sheats, P. Functional roles of group members. *The Journal of Social Issues* 4(2):41, 1948.
3. Bostram, R. N. Patterns of communicative interaction in small groups. *Speech Monographs* 37:257, 1970.
4. Cartwright, D., and Zander, A. *Group Dynamics: Research and Theory,* 3rd ed. New York: Harper & Row, 1968.
5. Cathcart, R. S., and Samovar, L. A. *Small Group Communication,* 2nd ed. Dubuque, IA: Wm. C. Brown Company Publishers, 1974.
6. Coussens, W. R., and Coussens, P. D. Maximizing preparation for childbirth. *Health Care for Women International* 5:335, 1984.
7. DeTornyay, R. *Strategies for Teaching Nursing.* New York: John Wiley & Sons, 1971.
8. Dinkmeyer, D., and Muro, J. *Group Counseling: Theory and Practice.* Itasca, IL: Free Peacock Publishers, Inc., 1971.
9. Durkin, H. Toward a common basis for group dynamics. *International Journal of Group Psychotherapy* 7:115, 1957.
10. Festinger, L. Informal social communication. *In* Cartwright, D., and Zander, A. (eds.) *Group Dynamics: Research and Theory,* 3rd ed. New York, Harper & Row, 1968.
11. Fiedler, F. Personality and situational determinants of leadership effectiveness. *In* Cartwright, D., and Zander, A. (eds.) *Group Dynamics, Research and Theory,* 3rd ed. New York: Harper & Row, 1968.
12. Fisher, B. A. Communication research and the task-oriented group. *Journal of Communication,* 21:136, 1971.
13. Grubel, M. F. Group dynamic practices applied to health education. *The Journal of School Health* 51:656, 1981.
14. Hare, A. P. A study of interaction and consensus in different sized groups. *American Sociological Review* 17:261, 1952.
15. Hare, A. P. *Creativity in Small Groups.* Beverly Hills: Sage Publications, 1982.
16. Harper, N. L., and Askling, L. R. Group communication and quality of task solution in a media production organization. *Communication Monographs* 47:77, 1980.
17. Hemphill, J. K. Relations between the size of the group and the behavior of "superior" leaders. *Journal of Social Psychology* 32:11, 1950.
18. Kolb, D. A., and Boyatzis, R. E. On the dynamics of the helping relationship. *In* Leavitt, H. J., Pondy, L. R., and Boje, D. M. (eds.) *Readings in Managerial Psychology,* 3rd ed. Chicago: The University of Chicago Press, 1964.
19. Leavitt, H. J. Some effects of certain communication patterns on group performance. *Journal of Abnormal Social Psychology* 46:38, 1951.
20. Lewin, K. Group decision and social change. *In* Newcomb, T. and Hartley, E. (eds.) *Readings in Social Psychology.* New York: Henry Holt, 1947, pp. 330–344.
21. Lewin, K., Lippitt, R. and White, R. K. Patterns of aggressive behavior in experimentally created "social climates." *Journal of Social Psychology* 10:271, 1939.
22. Loomis, M. E. *Group Process for Nurses.* St. Louis: C. V. Mosby, 1979.
23. Loomis, M. E., and Dodenhoff, J. T. Working with informal patient groups. *American Journal of Nursing* 70:1939, 1970.
24. Marram, G. D. *The Group Approach in Nursing Practice.* St. Louis: C.V. Mosby, 1978.
25. Miles, L., and Stubblefield, H. W. Learning groups in training and education, *Small Group Behavior* 13:311, 1982.
26. Morran, D. K., Robison, F. F., and Stockton, R. Feedback exchange in counseling groups: An analysis of message content and receiver acceptance as a function of leader versus member delivery, session, and valence. *Journal of Counseling Psychology* 32:57, 1985.
27. Murray, R. B., and Zentner, J. P. *Nursing Concepts for Health Promotion,* 2nd ed. Englewood Cliffs, NJ: Prentice-Hall, 1979.
28. Perez, P. Group techniques. *Childbirth Educator* 2:35, 1983.
29. Raven, B. H., and Rietsema, J. The effects of varied clarity of group goal and group path upon the individual and his relation to his group. *Human Relations* 10:29, 1957.
30. Riecken, H. W. The effect of talkativeness on ability to influence group solutions of problems. *Sociometry* 21:309, 1958.
31. Sampson, E. E., and Marthas, M. *Group Process for the Health Professions,* 2nd ed. New York: John Wiley and Sons, 1981.
32. Sasmor, J. L., and Grossman, E. Childbirth education in 1980. *JOGN Nursing* 10:155, 1981.
33. Shaw, M. E. *Group Dynamics: The Psychology of Small Group Behavior,* 3rd ed. New York: McGraw-Hill Book Company, 1981.
34. Simmel, G. *The Sociology of Georg Simmel,* translated by Kurt H. Wolf. Glencoe, IL: The Free Press, 1950.

35. Smith, E. D. I. Group process and childbirth education: A position paper. *JOGN Nursing* 7:51, 1978.
36. Smith, L. L. Finding your leadership style in groups. *American Journal of Nursing* 80:1301, 1980.
37. Stanford, G. and Roark, A. *Human Interaction in Education*. Boston: Allyn and Bacon, Inc., 1974.
38. Thelen, H. A. Group dynamics in instruction: principle of least group size. *School Review* 57:139, 1949.
39. Toseland, R., Krebs, A., and Vahsen, J. Changing group interaction patterns, *Journal of Social Service Research* 2:219, 1978.
40. Trow, W. C., Zander, A. E., Morse, W. C., and Jenkins, D. H. Psychology of group behavior: The class as a group. *The Journal of Educational Psychology*, 41:322, 1950.
41. Tubbs, S. L. *A Systems Approach to Small Group Interaction*. Reading, MA: Addison-Wesley, 1978.
42. Zander, A. *Making Groups Effective*. San Francisco: Jossey-Bass, 1982.

Boxed Quotes

1. Loomis, M. *Group Process for Nurses*. St. Louis: C.V. Mosby, 1979, p. 14.
2. Stanford, G. and Roark, A. *Human Interaction in Education*. Boston: Allyn and Bacon, Inc., 1974, p. 55.

chapter 25

THE LEARNER

VIRGINIA AUKAMP, SHARRON S. HUMENICK, and ARLENE FREDERICK

Human behavior is a very broad and complex phenomenon, involving numerous components. It is also a very individualized phenomenon; each person possesses a different "package" of experiences, values, needs, goals, persuasions, and ideas which cause one individual to behave differently (even if only slightly) from another.

Authors of *Adults Teaching Adults*

Expectant parents are unique individuals, and even as a group in childbirth education classes they differ according to geographical location, socioeconomic environment, and from one class to another. Thus, there is no one best way to teach childbirth education classes. Each teacher has to adapt her classes to fit the needs of the class members.

The focus of this chapter is on the learner: the expectant parent. Many known characteristics about expectant parents can form the basis for the initial planning of childbirth preparation classes. There are also a number of theories related to learning or personal development that appear to have implications for understanding the expectant parent in the role of learner. Questions addressed in this chapter are: What is learning? What theories are applicable to learners in childbirth education classes? How do individual learning styles influence class members' responses in the teaching situation and the teacher's selection of teaching strategies?

REVIEW OF THE LITERATURE

What is Learning?

Learning is defined as "a change in human disposition or capability, which persists over a period of time, and which is not simply ascribed to processes of growth." The goal of learning is to increase an individual's competence in a specific area. Behavior changes that result from learning include acquisition of knowledge, skills, insights, and attitudes, which may or may not always be directly observable. However, *effects* of learning can be observed.[12] For example, the childbirth educator can evaluate how well a class member has learned to achieve a state of relaxation—it is directly observable. In contrast, the childbirth educator cannot directly observe how class members process the information presented in class and relate it to their own situation. The teacher can, however, observe the effects of learning as class members increase in the ability to deal with hypothetical problem situations that may occur during childbirth and become more actively involved in planning their birth experience.

Each learner in childbirth education classes is unique and has different life experiences, values, needs, ideas and goals that will influence how he or she will interact during the classroom experience. (Photograph by Marjorie Pyle, © Lifecircle, Costa Mesa, CA.)

The Elements of Learning. Gagne[12] describes four elements present in any learning situation:

- The *learner,* who has the capacity to receive stimuli, interpret stimuli in a meaningful manner, and exhibit actions that show he or she has learned. (In childbirth education, the learner is an expectant parent or a family member.)
- A *stimulus situation,* an event that stimulates the learner's senses. (These are the learning activities initiated by the childbirth educator.)
- The learner's *memory,* in which content is organized, stored, and recovered, i.e., recalled for use. (The childbirth educator strives to organize the learning activities to facilitate the learner's memory process.)
- A *response,* which is the action or performance that results from the stimulus situation and its subsequent transformation. (The childbirth educator builds on activities that enhance both her own and the learner's observation of the learner's responses.)

Learning is a process also requiring *feedback* to provide the learner with information about the effects of his or her performance. The results of this feedback either (1) *confirm* that learning has occurred (reinforcement) and serve to "fix" the learning, making it permanently available, (2) identify *changes* that are needed in the particular activity for learning to occur, or (3) *refute* that learning has occurred. Feedback can come from external sources such as the teacher or coach or internal sources—for example, the sensations the learner experiences.

Major Learning Theories

Research in the area of learning has generated several theories. Knowledge of these theories will assist teachers in understanding learners' capabilities and needs, the process of learning, and how to structure the classroom experience to enhance learning outcomes.

Stimulus-Response Associationism Theory

Of the theories based on stimulus-response associationism, Pavlov's experiments with *classical conditioning* are the best known. The basic principle of this learning theory is conditioning of existing autonomic responses by a signal not normally responsible for the reaction. For example, Pavlov paired two stimuli, meat and bell, to obtain the response of salivation. Eventually a learned response occurred and the bell alone could produce salivation in a dog. Pavlov was the first to scientifically demonstrate that repetition (practice) increases learning.

In childbirth education, a "cleansing breath followed by relaxation" is practiced as a replacement response for tension at the thought of labor contractions. With practice, the verbal cue of "contraction begins" suggests the learned response of a cleansing breath and relaxation rather than tension. Pavlov used a bell as a stimulus, whereas childbirth educators use the words "contraction begins" as a stimulus.

Since Pavlov's early work with classical conditioning, *operant conditioning* has been introduced. The theory of operant conditioning states that any act may be altered in the frequency in which the act occurs by the *consequences* of the act. A reinforcement is anything that encourages repetition of an act. Reinforcements enhance one's feelings of status, worthiness, positive self-image, and self-confidence. In actual labor when relaxation is the response to contractions, the resulting positive benefits of reduced pain tend to reinforce that behavior.

Stimulus-response associationism theories (i.e., classical or operant conditioning) de-emphasize the role of the learner in the learning process. The learner does not have to comprehend the total learning situation. Each individual element of behavior is treated separately, then related to another behavior, until the learner performs the desired behavior. Behaviors that are learned using spaced reinforcement may be difficult to extinguish, while behaviors learned using reinforcement each time disappear quickly if reinforcement is not continued. The type of learning based on stimulus-response associationism is often called *training*. Stimulus-response associationism is clearly applicable in learning skills. However, this theory is not representative of most learning situations that are encountered and its appropriateness for more complex learning is questioned.[12,17]

Gestalt-Field Theory

Gestalt-field theory of learning focuses on man in his environment as a unit participating in what is called *simultaneous mutual interaction*. In one such theory, *cognitive field theory,* Lewin states that reality for any one person is what that individual perceives and experiences it to be. For people, things exist relative to a person's total experience. This explains why two people may hear a childbirth educator say something and what they believe they have heard can be entirely different.

Two principles from Gestalt-field theory that are important for the childbirth educator are (1) the idea that behavior is purposeful or intelligent and (2) the concept of "self." Because behavior is purposeful, holistic human behavior is directed toward goals and need fulfillment. This concept is important to childbirth educators because much of the education for childbirth is directed at helping the learner define goals and needs related to birth and obtaining skills to work toward those goals. Thus, the learner can be expected to learn more efficiently if he or she comprehends how the class activity relates to his or her goals. In Gestalt-field theory, the concept of "self" is emphasized. The self is viewed as an emerging being that is always developing. The growth and development of the self is influenced by the environment in which goal fulfillment is attempted. This concept is supported by research indicating that personal growth can result from a prepared childbirth experience as discussed in Chapter 4.

Gestalt-field theorists describe the continuing development of "self" that occurs:[5]

1. Growth occurs when goal achievement oc-

curs through one's own efforts. Taking responsibility for one's own acts, pride in one's accomplishments, and blame for one's failure all contribute to personal growth.

2. The affirming or revision of one's values and goals takes place through transactions with other people and within one's life space or field.

3. Through learning, the formation of an "ideal self" occurs; it is against this that measurements and evaluations of oneself can be made.

4. One's "self" is prominent in memories of the past and in fantasies and anticipations of the future.

These concepts of the developing self enable the childbirth educator to take a broad view of the potential of childbirth education. Not infrequently, the childbirth educator may find herself being hired to teach classes by an agency administrator or physician who has a much narrower view of preparation for childbirth, such as the need to provide only cognitive information about childbirth in classes. The childbirth educator may need to explain that cognitive information alone is inadequate for preparation for childbirth. Childbirth education is more than imparting cognitive knowledge. It involves training in psychomotor skills and other strategies that will increase expectant parents' ability to cope with childbirth. When done well, childbirth education can enhance personal growth.

Bevis[4] states seven propositions about learning. They are selected from both stimulus-response associationism theory and Gestalt-field theory. These have implications for the childbirth educator in building a curriculum for expectant parents (Table 25–1).

TABLE 25–1. LEARNING THEORY PROPOSITIONS* AND IMPLICATIONS FOR CHILDBIRTH EDUCATION

PROPOSITION	IMPLICATIONS
1. People learn when they encounter a problem or need. This creates anxiety, which in turn produces drive and motivation.	1. The same anxiety that motivates people to attend childbirth classes may interfere with learning unless it is reduced through class activity.
2. Motivation and drive produce a learner need for information, cues, models, or opportunity to discover that enables progression toward goals or problem solutions.	2. The internal motivation of expectant parents to learn about childbirth can be used to promote high interest and goal-seeking in a learner. In the first classes, the teacher should find out what the learner wants to know about childbirth.
3. Progression toward goal achievement is promoted by moving from the familiar to the unfamiliar and actively involving the learner in the learning activities.	3. The teacher can actively involve the learner from the start by taking time to find out what the learner already knows. In future classes, the teacher builds on what expectant parents have already learned.
4. Reinforcement of desired behaviors increases movement toward the goal; conversely, absence of feedback of any kind prevents progress, and consistently negative feedback—deliberate or accidental—leads to frustration, aggression, and avoidance. Progress then halts, and problems are not solved.	4. Reinforcement can be a smile, the use of a name, or the nod of a head. Teachers must assess learner achievement and provide feedback. Reinforcement of desired behavior is an integral part of the class.
5. Repetition with feedback and consequent improvement (practice) accompanied by reinforcement develops behavior habits and patterns.	5. Adequate practice time must be allotted in each class. Class time should also be spent motivating students to practice at home.
6. Spaced and distributed recall or more and varied opportunities for application enable the learner to identify central concepts, verify principles, make generalizations and discriminations, and retain learned behaviors.	6. Rehearsals of many types such as simulations, role play, and quizzes are helpful. Restating general principles at the end of rehearsal is useful. Each class should have a review of previous material learned at the start of class and a summary of major points learned at the close of class.
7. Success (goal achievement) leads to tolerance of failure, realistic self-assessments, realistic goal setting, and continual evaluation.	7. Providing immediate and meaningful feedback throughout classes, when the learner has performed a desired behavior or solved a problem successfully, provides many success opportunities and builds confidence.

*Learning propositions are from Bevis, E. *Curriculum Building in Nursing. A Process,* 3rd ed. St. Louis: C. V. Mosby, 1982.

Social Learning Theory

From the perspective of social learning theory, learning occurs through observing and imitating others and receiving feedback from others. For example, expectant parents watch a demonstration of progressive relaxation in class and then they try it themselves. Feedback from the teacher will help them refine the specific skill. Many cognitive and motor skills from changing a diaper to using more assertive communication skills are acquired at least partially through observing and imitating others and receiving feedback. Social learning theory also deals with self-regulation of behavior through observing and evaluating one's own behaviors. There are four phases in this type of observational learning: the attention, retention, reproduction, and motivational phases.

The *attention* phase is an absolutely essential condition in order for learning to occur. The teacher's first task is to gain the students' attention. Next, the teacher demonstrates the specific task and then assists the students to imitate it. The teacher can enhance learning by providing important cues such as "Concentrate on letting your body limp" or "Place the pillow here." During the *retention* phase, the modeled activity is stored for future use. This will occur most effectively if the students can actively code the task in a verbal statement such as "Take a comfortable, easy breath" or in visual imagery such as picturing themselves ambulating during labor. Learning is also strengthened through practicing the cognitive or motor skill (rehearsal). Students who are actively involved in the learning task will learn more effectively than those who passively watch the teacher model the task.

In the *reproduction* phase, the learning task is practiced until it is an actual reproduction of the modeled activity. During this phase, the teacher evaluates whether or not the students can perform all aspects of the task properly. Feedback from the teacher during this phase will further help students shape their responses until the desired behavior is achieved. In the *motivational* phase, learned behaviors will be performed only if the students find it reinforcing to do so. Thus, structuring the class experience to provide reinforcement is critical in observational learning. Reinforcements may be direct, such as praise from the teacher for the proper performance of a task, or vicarious, such as hearing new parents who return to speak to the class say how much the skills of relaxation or breathing helped during childbirth.

Information Processing Theory

Learning is currently interpreted in terms of information processing theory.[12] This theory proposes that the stimuli from the environment that is encountered by the learner is transformed, or *processed,* in a number of different ways by internal structures, which results in changes occurring—that is, learning. A learner does not merely react to incoming stimuli. Instead, the external stimulation initiates, maintains, or supports the ongoing internal processes that are involved in learning, remembering, or performing. During a single act of learning, several phases of processing may occur. Instruction in the classroom—external stimulation—can be designed to support a single phase of processing or multiple phases of processing.

Information processing starts when *stimulation* from the environment activates an individual's sensory *receptors*. The incoming visual, auditory, or tactile information is transformed into neural information and stored in a structure called the *sensory register* for a brief period of time—one to two seconds at the most. Through the process of selective perception the important aspects of the information are transformed into patterns of information and transferred into the *short-term memory.* Because of the limited capacity of the short-term memory, information is stored there for the very short time of up to 20 seconds. Once the capacity of the short-term memory is exceeded, old information is pushed out so that new information can be added. The silent, mental repetition of information (rehearsal) assists with storing information in the short-term memory for a longer period of time, because it is constantly being added.

Two things may happen after the information has entered the short-term memory. Either a response is generated or the information goes into long-term memory, where it can be retrieved later. If a response is required, the information in short-term memory is fed directly into a *response generator,* a structure that determines the mode (for example, verbal or motor) and pattern (sequence and timing) of response by the *effectors*. Effectors are the muscle systems that exhibit the response—hands, feet, voice, and the like.

When information is transferred from short-term memory to long-term memory, it is *encoded* and transformed into concepts and organized in a meaningful manner. This information can later be retrieved through the use of cues provided by the learner or an external source. During the retrieval process the information may go into either short-term memory or directly to the response generator where the appropriate response is exhibited.

There are two types of control processes that can affect any one or all of the phases of information processing. These are called *executive control processes* and *expectancies*. Executive control processes are cognitive strategies that determine what information received in the sensory register will go into the short-term memory, what information will be stored in long-term memory, how it will be stored, the process used in retrieval of information, and the kind of response that is exhibited. *Expectancies* are the motivation of learners to achieve a specific learning goal. Executive control processes and expectancies determine the manner in which the learner will process information. Gagne has identified nine instructional events that the teacher can use to influence one or more of the internal processes of learning.[12] These are discussed in Chapter 26.

Types of Learning

Gagne[12] describes eight types of learning, each more complex than the preceding type. The first four types of learning—signal, stimulus-response learning, ''chaining,'' and verbal association—are all types of stimulus-response associationism learning. The second four, which are increasingly complex, are discrimination learning, concept learning, rule learning, and problem-solving. The principles of stimulus-response associationism are most useful when teaching psychomotor skills and some cognitive facts. Learning that involves more complex cognitive skills or values is enhanced through use of discrimination learning, concept learning, rule learning, and problem-solving. Examples of Gagne's learning types and their application to childbirth education are given in Table 25–2.

Characteristics of Adult Learners

According to Knowles,[14] the adult differs from the child as a learner. These differences have implications for designing and teaching childbirth education classes. The adult learner:

1. *Is independent and self-directed in learning*. The childbirth educator serves, therefore, as a facilitator, resource person, and encourager in the learning situation as opposed to being the total director of learning.
2. *Has previous experiences that serve as rich resources for learning*. Students learn faster and better when the teacher relates new class material to their past experiences and builds on previous knowledge. Learners can also serve as resources for others in the classroom situation. The teacher is not, therefore, the source of all knowledge in the classroom.
3. *Has a readiness to learn that is based on current social roles and tasks*. Life situations influence the adult's readiness to learn. For example, a stressful life situation of inadequate money can hinder readiness to learn, while other life situations such as pregnancy can increase the adult's eagerness to learn. The childbirth educator needs to be sensitive to the life situations of learners and work with the adult to overcome any barriers to learning.
4. *Wants to learn things that have immediate application*. Adults often are motivated to attend classes because of a particular need. If the class can be structured so that the learner can immediately use some of the information in life situations, this will enhance the learning process. Information presented on the first night of class on coping with the discomforts of pregnancy and how to develop basic relaxation skills are examples of information that the adult learner can use immediately.
5. *Prefers a problem-oriented learning approach as opposed to a subject-oriented learning approach*. Adults want to learn how to solve real-life problems; thus, they are often less interested in information presented in a subject-oriented format. When a childbirth educator teaches fetal development by describing the anatomy and physiology of conception and subsequent development, she is using a subject-centered approach. When she teaches about pregnancy from the perspective of expectant parents' tasks and sensations of pregnancy while weaving in a description of the de-

TABLE 25–2. TYPES OF LEARNING* WITH EXAMPLES IN CHILDBIRTH EDUCATION

TYPES OF LEARNING	EXAMPLE IN CHILDBIRTH EDUCATION
1. Signal learning (early pavlovian conditioning). Association of an available response with a new stimulus.	1. The responding to the verbal stimulus of contraction begins with a cleansing breath and a general ''letting go'' level of relaxation.
2. Stimulus-response learning. This is a refinement of signal learning; response is precise and satisfies a motive. Feedback and reinforcement help shape the desired response; *repetition* of the stimulus response and prompt reinforcement *(contiguity)* enhance learning.	2. The responding to the verbal stimulus of contraction begins with a cleansing breath and an advanced level of learned relaxation skill. Motivating practice and teaching coaches to give prompt, positive reinforcement aid learning.
3. Chaining. Sequential *non-verbal* stimulus response events. Learning the final behavior is dependent on learning earlier responses in the chain.	3. Coordination of second stage pushing efforts is improved by learning proper positioning, the ability to relax the Kegel muscle, to sense the correct direction of the pushing effort, and to use controlled breathing techniques.
4. Verbal association. Learners can name or define terms, although they may not understand them. A verbal sequence links words together to express a fact.	4. For example, couples may learn that expulsion of the baby occurs after complete dilation. Complete is equivalent to 10 centimeters and dilation is opening of the cervix. The previously defined terms *complete* and *dilation* can be linked to define the time for expulsion.
5. Discrimination learning. The learner can differentiate among stimuli used in stimulus-response events.	5. The learner can define the terms *true* and *false labor* and cite the distinguishing differences between them.
6. Concept learning. The learner can classify events using language to represent characteristics of a concept.	6. Expectant parents who have learned the concepts of labor contraction, back labor, and second stage labor can recognize them when they occur regardless of variation in the pattern.
7. Rule learning. This learning implies the linking of concepts—for example, if A is true, then B follows.	7. An example of a common rule among obstetrical care providers is to tell expectant mothers to call if the membranes rupture. A call from a woman with ruptured membranes indicates the rule was learned.
8. Problem solving. This implies applying a combination of rules to a novel situation based on a goal and a repertoire of relevant styles and concepts.	8. A woman with a goal of the least intervention possible in childbirth must be able to combine rules related to activity, position, comfort measures, relaxation, paced breathing, and the like.

*Types of learning are from Gagne, R. M. *The Conditions of Learning*, 3rd ed. New York: Holt, Rinehart and Winston, 1977.

veloping fetus, she is using a problem-centered approach to teaching fetal development. In this approach, learners can more readily apply the information to their own situation.

Time is also very important to adults. Thus, classes should start and end on time. Kidd states that the investment of time in an activity may be as important a decision as the investment of money or effort.[13] Adults need to feel they are getting something of value out of their learning experience. Childbirth classes should be organized so that early in the first class, each learner feels his or her presence in class is important because of the material that was discussed. Ideally, each learner should come away from each class thinking it is a good thing he or she did not miss this class because important things were learned and each minute of class time was well spent.

The adult learner usually responds to the teaching situation by describing how he or she *feels* about the educational experience. The adult will be inclined to continue in class if the learning experience is positive, useful, interesting, and stimulating. However, if the experience is negative, uninteresting, and seen as not useful, the adult learner most likely will not continue attending class.[2]

An educational program that will effectively help expectant parents to acquire problem-solving and psychomotor skills in preparation for childbirth must be structured using the principles, concepts, and conditions for learning that have emerged from the body of literature on adult education (see Table 25–2).

Smith[19] summarized the six conditions under which adults learn best:

1. They feel the need to learn and have input into what, why, and how they will learn.
2. Content and process of the information presented bear a perceived and meaningful relationship to learners' past experiences; these are effectively used as a resource for learning.
3. What is to be learned relates optionally to the individual's developmental changes and life tasks.
4. The amount of autonomy exercised by the learners is congruent with that required by the mode or method utilized.
5. They learn in a climate that minimizes anxiety and encourages freedom to experiment.
6. They learn when their learning styles are taken into account.

Learning Styles

Learning style is the manner in which the learner prefers to approach the learning situation. According to Fry and Kolb,[11] there are four dimensions of learning. These are concrete experience, reflective observation, abstract conceptualization, and active experimentation (Fig. 25–1).

Wilkerson[21] illustrates these in the following examples of teaching breathing patterns or relaxation techniques in childbirth education classes. The *concrete experience* involves the learner becoming fully involved in using eyes, ears, and touch to participate in an experience, such as a demonstration of relaxation. *Reflective observation* follows as the learner interprets this experience. In this phase the learner might consider how the skill can be mastered or under what conditions it will be practiced. As the learner moves on to *abstract conceptualization,* she or he might infer that adequate practice will ensure relaxation competence during labor and result in increased ability to cope with labor pain. In *active experimentation,* the learner may modify approaches to relaxation during actual labor and/or may use these techniques in other stressful situations.

Although each learner uses all four dimensions in learning, individual learners are likely to prefer that learning activities be related to one or two of

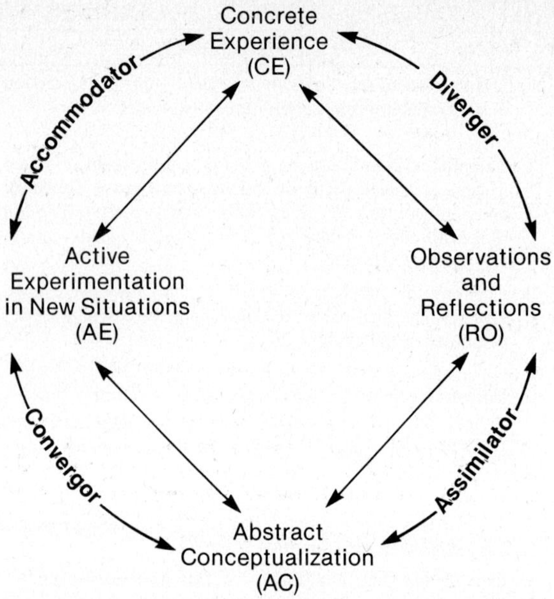

FIGURE 25–1. Learning styles. (Adapted from Fry, R. and Kolb, D. Experiential Learning Theory and Learning Experiences in Liberal Arts Education. *California Management Review* 18, 1976.)

these dimensions. Kolb developed a model of learning preferences that has two dimensions: concrete to abstract, and active to reflective. Kolb has identified four basic learning style preferences[15]:

1. The diverger (likes concrete experiences as opposed to abstract conceptualization and likes reflective observation as opposed to active experimentation).
2. The assimilator (likes abstract conceptualization and reflective observation).
3. The converger (likes abstract conceptualization and active experimentation).
4. The accommodator (likes concrete experiences and active experimentation).

Wilkerson gives examples of approaches that can be used in childbirth education classes for expectant parents with different learning styles.[21]

Divergers view concrete situations from many angles and are strong in imaginative ability. They would be expected to be strong in seeing the outcome of the labor process but have less desire to focus on the details. They may benefit from class time in which members plan how they will incorporate practice time into their life. Divergers do not jump rapidly to conclusions and may become impatient with class members who do. Divergers like reading, listening, and investigating all the possibilities before making a decision. If a diverger is slowing down the pace of the class, the childbirth educator can ask this person to gather additional information in the topic and report back to the class during the next meeting.

Accommodators are strong in planning and getting things done and excel in adapting to situations. They tend to be risk takers and to problem-solve in an intuitive, trial-and-error manner. They are more likely to enjoy role playing. They tend to work well on competitive projects. They may be impatient with repetitive projects unless they can add their own variations. They tend to like audiovisual materials and practical tests. They need an instructor who promotes learner participation and is personally interested in their progress. Accommodators like direct experience; they are not as interested in theory as in applying and doing. They learn best in a class situation in which the childbirth educator promotes learner participation and shows a personal interest in their progress.

Convergers like structured experiences. They tend to make lists and follow them. They are task oriented, unemotional, and conscious of time. They progress in a logical, structured, orderly, and linear fashion. They want to know why before doing something. They like practical reading, listening, group reports, and some team competition. They are willing to share ideas but less likely to share feelings and emotions. Practical applications of role playing or other simulation activities in childbirth education classes must be clear to convergers for them to become involved in such activities.

Assimilators are most likely to be content with knowledge for the sake of knowledge. They synthesize, draw inferences, and excel in explaining the nature of things. Their greatest strength is their ability to create theoretical models of the world around them. They are less concerned with the practical application of theory. Assimilators always consider theory first and may or may not require practical applications to situations. They value organized, structured approaches to learning and will resent a disorganized, poorly executed childbirth education class. They are least likely to take an active part in group work, although they learn from watching others.

Familiarity with Kolb's work can help the childbirth educator understand individual learning style differences. Childbirth education classes are made up of individuals with a variety of learning style preferences, and the partners in each couple often have different individual learning styles. People with different styles can complement each other and combine their strengths. For example, the diverger will be inclined to practice skills and the assimilator to theorize outcomes of faithful practice. Together they can become skilled and transfer the learning to other areas of their lives. The childbirth educator is most effective when her classes are structured to include learning activities that will match learning styles of a variety of learners.

Even when people have strong preferences in their learning styles, they can tolerate less favored activities a part of the time. It helps to balance activities within each class so that each learner relates well to some of the activities. Learning styles are not permanent attributes of all people; some change with time and exposure to other styles. People who represent extremes by virtue of strong preferences when following their natural inclinations may benefit from engaging in a balanced variety of activities in class. The childbirth educator can expect that even in a well-planned class not every portion of the class will appeal to every learner.

It may increase learners' tolerance of a variety of activities and their tolerance of other class members if some explanation of learning style preference is given to the class. It is also possible to administer a brief tool, such as Kolb's *Learning Style Inventory,* which assesses learning styles.[15] Assessment of learning styles can also be done in an informal manner as the teacher observes the responses of the learner. In summary, planning classes so that they accommodate a variety of learning styles and assessment of the learning styles of expectant parents is important to learner motivation and satisfaction.

Pregnancy as a Special Opportunity for Personal Growth

The experience of childbirth can be viewed as a developmental task of pregnant women. A developmental task has been defined as a global behavioral skill or ability that is best learned or accomplished during a specific time period of one's life. Mastery of such a task can promote personal growth and prepares one to deal successfully with later developmental tasks. Pregnancy may be a particularly good time to promote personal growth. Caplan[7] states that pregnant women in psychotherapy can make the amount of progress that might ordinarily be expected to take several years. Thus pregnancy is a time of readiness of psychological change and may be an exceptionally good time to promote competency of the individual.

Less is known about the long-term implications of participating in the childbirth experience for men. It is clear, however, that since men were welcomed as active participants in the birth experience, they have responded in the last three decades in large numbers. From both their behavior and their testimonials one can infer that the childbirth experience has potential for deep meaning to men as well.

Self-Esteem. Learning in general, and childbirth education and positive birth experiences in particular, have considerable potential for increasing an individual's self-esteem. According to Maslow's hierarchy of needs,[15] basic needs are physiological needs and safety needs (see Fig. 25–2). When these are met, according to Maslow, then one can give attention to the higher needs of love and belonging, self-esteem, and the need to have the respect and esteem of others, and then self-actualization.

Childbirth presents issues of physiological needs and safety needs. Expectant parents will need to deal with those issues first. Pregnancy also presents issues of love and belonging, since the new baby will affect the couple's relationship and their roles in society. It is important to focus first on these basic issues and needs of expectant couples during childbirth education classes. However, the potential exists for increasing the self-esteem of the woman through a satisfying birth experience. Active participation in the birth experience, pride in one's ability to problem-solve and to cope effectively with the challenge of the childbirth, and a feeling of competence that the woman experiences can increase her self-esteem.

Competence. The promotion of problem-solving, and therefore competence, is a focus of childbirth education classes. Through preparing for childbirth, class members should gain increased competence specific to coping during childbirth. They often also experience an increased sense of generalized personal competence after childbirth.

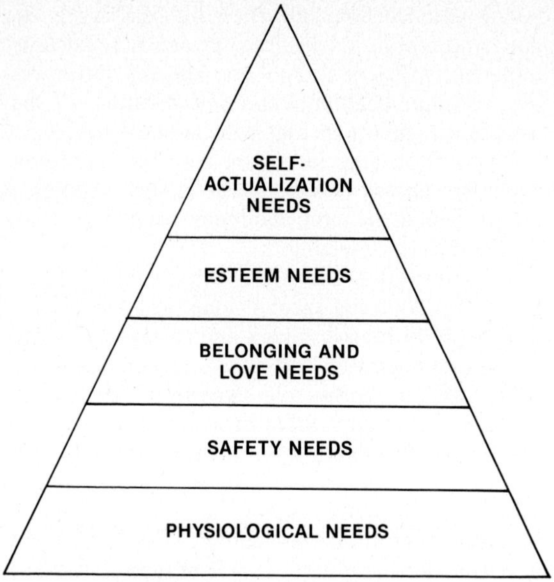

FIGURE 25–2. Maslow's hierarchy of needs.

The first description of the concept of competence was by White, in 1959.[20] He defined competence as an organism's capacity to interact effectively with its environment. White suggested that competence is gained slowly through prolonged feats of learning. Adler[1] provides an excellent analysis of the concept of competence. He proposed that competence includes eight separate elements: performance of social roles, self-concept, interactional functioning, management of effect, navigation of development transitions, management of stressful events, access to available resources, and cognitive functioning. A look at the elements of competence as defined in Table 25–3 illustrates why the task of learning to cope with childbirth is an excellent opportunity to simultaneously promote competence.

Given that labor is a stressful event and that childbirth preparation can promote the development of competence to master the stress of that

TABLE 25–3. ELEMENTS OF COMPETENCE* AND THEIR APPLICATION TO CHILDBIRTH EDUCATION

ELEMENTS OF COMPETENCE	APPLICATION TO CHILDBIRTH EDUCATION
1. *Social role performance* Ability to perform adequately as a student, parent, employee, male or female, etc.	Expectant parents are taking on new roles as parents, and the information learned in classes will increase their ability to function adequately in those roles.
2. *Self-concept* Has self-awareness, self-acceptance, and self-confidence.	The challenge of birth raises these issues for many women. Effectively coping with childbirth using techniques and strategies learned in childbirth education classes can enhance a woman's self-esteem.
3. *Interactional skill* The ability to communicate effectively. Has specific social skills for a variety of situations.	Communication, conflict resolution, and negotiation skills are important in interactions with family members and health care providers. These skills are discussed and practiced in childbirth education classes.
4. *Management of affect* Tolerates moderate amounts of stress. Makes appropriate responses.	The childbirth and new parenting experiences present stresses to deal with. Class experiences assist expectant parents to learn new coping techniques and improve problem-solving skills.
5. *Navigate developmental transitions* Completes developmental tasks and prepares for the next stage.	Childbirth is considered to be a developmental task for most pregnant women. Class discussions on changes during pregnancy, fears and anxieties about childbirth, becoming a parent, changing relationships, and problem-solving approaches will help learners complete this developmental task.
6. *Management of stressful events* Can manage situational crises, such as divorce, illness, physical disability, and poverty.	Pregnancy, childbirth, and the early parenting period can be viewed as stressful events. Expectant parents can learn in classes how to increase their ability to manage these events. Classes should provide an accurate picture of the event, coping strategies that can be used, and information on sources of support.
7. *Access to available resources* Has knowledge of where to go for help. Does not have self-defeating and self-denying attitudes.	Learning about resources is part of effective childbirth preparation. Also, learning how to seek out, request, and obtain support from others is an integral part of classes.
8. *Cognitive skills* Has intellectual skills and problem-solving ability.	Every birth is unique and requires problem-solving based on a repertoire of skills that includes knowledge and understanding of what is happening. These cognitive skills are an important part of childbirth education classes.

*Elements of Competence are from Adler, P. Analysis of the concept of competence. *Community Mental Health Journal* 18:34, 1982.

event, one can view childbirth preparation as promoting increased personal competence, and therefore good mental health. Furthermore, many of the skills learned in childbirth classes are transferable to coping with other life stresses. Thus, it can be asserted that childbirth education has the potential to promote the general development of competence in the learner.

IMPLICATIONS FOR PRACTICE

A variety of types of learning based on different learning theories are used when teaching childbirth education classes. Thus, the childbirth educator must be able to analyze the specific task and select the right approach for teaching that task. Adequate learning will most likely not occur, for example, if psychomotor skills are presented using only lecture and demonstration with token involvement of expectant parents; with this approach, it is highly unlikely that the learners will develop competency in performing the task.

Using stimulus-response associationism, *repetitive practice* and *immediate and positive reinforcement* are essential components of learning and mastering psychomotor skills and must be included in childbirth education classes. The shaping of behavior that occurs through practice and feedback results in different and more polished learned behavior than that which preceded the current learning experience. Additionally, content areas and skills must be appropriately sequenced to facilitate learning. While learning theories provide us a framework for understanding how learning occurs, theories of instruction are also needed because they provide more practical approaches for use in the learning-teaching situation in the classroom.

Gagne's eight types of learning provide the childbirth educator with practical analysis of the problem of instruction in any subject matter.[12] For the purpose of analyzing learning, each single act of learning can be seen as having a beginning (stimulus situation) and an end (response), and two other constant elements: the *learner* and the learner's *memory.* In addition, for optimal learning to occur, *feedback* must be present. When learning does not happen as anticipated, examining these aspects of learning in a systematic manner may provide the childbirth educator with valuable information about the specific problem(s).

There are many different types of performances that are learned and each type has its own unique set of characteristics. In the eight types of learning, there are certain conditions of learning that must be present and the childbirth educator must design classes based on these conditions of learning. Gagne's theory also provides direction for the sequencing of material within classes.[12] For example, before expectant parents can learn to problem-solve situations in labor, they must have previously learned the skills, concepts, and rules related to childbirth. Before they can learn scientific principles, they previously must have learned the relevant concepts underlying these principles.

Expectant Parents as Adult Learners

The individual characteristics of expectant parents are diverse. However, there are principles that apply to all adult learning situations. The teacher should structure the childbirth education course using the principles of adult learning cited earlier in this chapter. These principles provide the rationale for both the inclusion and sequencing of class content. When a new curriculum is established for a prepared childbirth course, it should be built on the principles of adult learning. In established courses, every aspect of the curriculum should be scrutinized to determine if it is compatible with adult learning theory and then revisions made, if indicated.

Creating an Atmosphere That Enhances Learning

At the first class meeting, the childbirth educator is often faced with an anxious group of people with varying motivations. Some expectant parents are eagerly planning a special type of birth experience. Other class members may have come to class only to please a spouse. Some class members (expectant fathers or other support persons) may be in class to gain admission to the delivery room. Others chose to attend class because it was fashionable or because their health care provider suggested or insisted they do so.

Learner anxiety can be decreased and motivation increased if the childbirth educator begins class by acknowledging and accepting that class members have their own reasons for coming, and that whatever the reasons, they and the feelings related to them are all right. Setting an atmosphere in which feelings are acceptable, whatever they are, is an excellent way to increase learner comfort in a class series.

There are other reasons why learners may be highly anxious, especially on the first night of childbirth education classes. Facing labor is anxiety-producing for many. Research has shown that women's anxiety goes up weekly in the last month of pregnancy.[8] Additionally, childbirth has strong sexual connotations and the prospect of discussing such matters in a group is disconcerting to some. High anxiety levels block learning and make it important to use strategies to lower anxiety early in the first class. "Ice breaker" exercises and relaxation techniques are examples. Important content should be reinforced with handouts or repetition or both at a later class, since highly anxious learners will not remember many details of what is said.

The pregnant learner is likely to be tired upon arriving at class. This is especially true of women who are employed outside their homes. Beginning classes with relaxation practice has the potential to refresh them, as well as allow them to separate from their previous activities and increase their readiness to participate in class activities.

If pregnant women are kept in one position too long, they become uncomfortable and their backs may ache. The childbirth educator can tell class members that they are welcome to sit on chairs or get down on mats with pillows and to move back and forth. A circle of chairs with an inner circle of mats or blankets makes this easy. The didactic and discussion parts of classes should be liberally interspersed with activity including exercise, skill practice, and breaks.

The due date of pregnant learners is in reality a time span within two weeks of either side of a date. The learners, like athletes, do not want to peak in their readiness too soon, but neither do they want to give birth before they are prepared. Scheduling classes to enable finishing just prior to delivery can be tricky in ideal circumstances. It can be very difficult when new classes do not begin frequently. Couples should be scheduled to take classes that end just before their due date when possible. The risk of not being able to finish a series is reduced when the course is designed to cover all the content critical to birth by approximately the fourth class in a six-week series, or by two weeks before the end in a longer series. Continued practice of skills, rehearsals, and infant care can be covered in the last classes. In settings when new classes do not start frequently, it is important to work out a system whereby those who finish classes early are motivated to continue practicing.

> By designing educational offerings that consider the nature of the adult learner, the educator can capitalize on the adult's unique learning processes, creating learning experiences that are satisfying for both learner and educator.
>
> ANDREA O'CONNOR[1]
>
> Parents come to us ready for change. Poised between growth and regression, they are more vulnerable to our influence as educators than at any other time in their lives . . . We may as well accept that we cannot make rigid people flexible but we can help them move in that direction.
>
> PATRICIA HASSID[2]

Learning Styles

The learning styles of class members need to be evaluated and class activities structured accordingly. For example, if the childbirth educator has a class primarily composed of professionals, types of activities are indicated that are different from those used when classes are given for a clinic population, who will likely prefer different types of learning activities. A challenge the childbirth educator faces is teaching classes composed of members with widely varying backgrounds. Such classes are best structured to include a wide variety of activities so that the needs of the individual class members can be met.

IMPLICATIONS FOR RESEARCH

Some information exists on the characteristics of couples who attend childbirth education classes; however, additional information is needed to validate previous findings. Although the use of theories of learning, instruction, and the adult learner is essential for guiding the development of the curriculum and for accomplishments of effective learning, almost no research has been done to study the application of these theories in childbirth education classes. The need for such research exists to provide more definitive guidelines for the use of learning principles in childbirth education classes. The following questions are just a few of the many that need to be examined in order to increase the scientific basis of childbirth education:

- What are the characteristics of learners in childbirth education classes? How do these characteristics vary according to the setting of classes—private classes as opposed to agency classes? Have the characteristics of couples attending childbirth education classes changed over the years?
- What are the unique problems (such as fatigue and need for child care for other children) of learners in childbirth education classes?
- Which learning/instructional theories are most appropriate to use as the basis for teaching specific material in childbirth education classes?
- Do childbirth education classes that are taught using the principles of adult learning increase learner competence in desired behaviors?
- Currently, to what extent do childbirth educators base their classes on principles of learning and adult education?
- What are the most common types of learning styles of class members in childbirth education classes? What is the most effective way for the childbirth educator to assess learning styles of individuals in classes?
- How does the match between the teaching style of the teacher and the learning preference of couples influence the effectiveness of childbirth education classes both in class members' learning and teacher satisfaction?

SUMMARY

Childbirth education classes are more than a way to enable the expectant couple to cope with the experience of childbirth, although that usually is the primary focus of the expectant parent. The experience of childbirth is a critical point in life that has the potential to be a special time for individual growth. Childbirth can be seen as one of the key points on the life continuum during which health professionals can foster learning as well as promote the mental health of the individual.

Learners in childbirth education classes have unique characteristics that must be considered when designing and teaching classes. The general principle to be followed is that the classes should be designed to accommodate the learner. The childbirth educator needs to work continually at identifying learner characteristics and modifying classes as appropriate.

Childbirth education classes must be structured on sound learning and instructional theory. Providing a few hours of lecture on childbirth, describing hospital routines, demonstrating relaxation and breathing techniques, and allowing for practice sessions only as time permits is not sufficient for effective childbirth education. An excellent childbirth education class is one that prepares expectant parents adequately for the birth experience and focuses on the health promotion of individuals and the family as well. This type of class will be based on learning principles that emphasize the uniqueness of the adult learner, the differences in learning styles, the need for precise presentation of certain skills and adequate and repetitive practice time, as well as sequencing of knowledge for certain types of content material.

References

1. Adler, P. Analysis of the concept of competence. *Community Mental Health Journal* 18:34, 1982.
2. Axford, R. *Adult Education: The Open Door.* Scranton, PA: International Textbook Co., 1969.
3. Bandura, A. *Social Learning Theory.* Englewood Cliffs, NJ: Prentice-Hall, 1977.
4. Bevis, E.O. *Curriculum Building in Nursing: A Process,* 3rd ed. St. Louis: C. V. Mosby, 1982.
5. Bigge, M. L. *Learning Theories for Teachers.* New York: Harper and Row, 1964.
6. Canfield, A. *Canfield Learning Styles Inventory Form S—A Manual.* Birmingham, MI: A. A. Canfield, 1983.
7. Caplan, G.: *An Approach to Community Mental Health.* New York: Grune and Stratton, 1961.
8. Colman, A. and Colman, L. *Pregnancy the Psychological Experience.* New York: Herder and Herder, 1971.
9. Conti, G. J. The Principles of Adult Learning Scale. *Adult Literacy and Basic Education* 6:135, 1982.
10. Craig, R. (ed.) *Training and Development Handbook,* 2nd ed. New York: McGraw-Hill, 1976.
11. Fry, R., and Kolb, D. Experiential learning theory and learning experiences in liberal arts education. *California Management Review* 18:56, 1976.
12. Gagne, R. M. *The Conditions of Learning,* 4th ed. New York: Holt, Rinehart, and Winston, 1985.
13. Kidd, J. P. *How Adults Learn.* New York: Association Press, 1973.
14. Knowles, M. *The Modern Practice of Adult Education.* Chicago: Association Press, 1980.
15. Kolb, D. Learning style Inventory. Boston, McBer and Co., 1976. (137 Newbury St., Boston, MA 02116. (617)-437-7080.)
16. Maslow, A. *Motivation and Personality.* 2nd ed. New York: Harper and Row, 1970.
17. O'Connor, A. *Nursing Staff Development and Continuing Education.* Boston: Little, Brown and Company, 1986.
18. Rosenshine, B. Recent research on teaching behaviors and student achievement. *Journal of Teacher Education* 26:61, 1976.
19. Smith, R. V. *Learning How to Learn: Applied Theory for Adults.* Chicago: Follett Publishing Co., 1982.
20. White, R. Motivation Reconsidered: The Concept of Competence. *Psychological Review* 66:297, 1959.
21. Wilkerson, N. Assessment of Learning Style for Childbirth Education Classes. *NAACOG Update Series* Vol 5. Princeton, NJ: Continuing Professional Education Center, Inc., 1986.

Beginning Quote

Verduin, J., Miller, H., and Greer, C. *Adults Teaching Adults.* San Diego: University Associates Inc., 1977, p. 9.

Boxed Quotes

1. O'Connor, A. *Nursing Staff Development and Continuing, Education.* Boston: Little, Brown and Company, 1986, p. 158.
2. Hassid, P. Teaching couples to be flexible. *Childbirth Educator* 4:16, 1982.

chapter 26

THE TEACHER

ARLENE FREDERICK, FRANCINE H. NICHOLS, and VIRGINIA AUKAMP

What all the great teachers appear to have in common is love of their subject, and obvious satisfaction in arousing this love in their students, and an ability to convince them that what they are being taught is deadly serious.

Epstein

The childbirth educator fulfills a number of roles within the classroom: educator, manager, and counselor. The major role is that of the *educator* who imparts information, teaches skills, and influences attitudes. In the role of the *manager,* the childbirth educator orchestrates the activities within the class as well as manages the interactions between learner and teacher and among the learners in the group. A third role is that of *counselor.* Class members or couples will frequently ask the childbirth educator for help related to their individual concerns.

In this chapter the following questions are addressed: What is meant by teaching? What are the characteristics of a ''master'' teacher? What role does the teacher play in the classroom? What activities are involved in the process of teaching? What are effective strategies for teaching specific types of information or refining skills? How active should the teacher be as opposed to how active should the learner be in the teaching-learning process?

REVIEW OF THE LITERATURE

Teaching (teacher behavior) is a system of actions designed and intended to bring about learning.[6] Learning is a change in behavior, perception, insight, and attitude, or a combination of these, that can be repeated when the need arises.[1] The role of the teacher in the classroom is an extremely influential one—it can have either a positive or negative effect on students' learning.[8]

Characteristics of Master Teachers

Lowman[11] proposes a two-dimensional model of teaching effectiveness. The first dimension involves the teacher's skill to create *intellectual excitement* in the classroom. The ability to develop *interpersonal rapport* and establish a positive emotional environment in the classroom is the second dimension.

Intellectual Excitement

Creating intellectual excitement depends on the *clarity* of the material that one presents and the *emotional impact* on the learner. *What* the teacher presents influences clarity, while the *way* the material is presented influences the positive emotional impact of the message. Basic to clarity is a solid knowledge of the material that is presented, but comprehensive knowledge of a subject does not assure that the material is presented clearly. Outstanding teachers have the ability to take difficult or confusing concepts and present them in a clear, concise manner using "simple language and concrete images."[11] Teachers who have the ability to create a positive emotional impact use:

> . . . their voices, gestures, and movements to elicit and maintain attention and to stimulate students' emotions. Like other performers, teachers must convey a strong sense of presence, of highly focused energy.[11]

The ability of the teacher to stimulate strong positive emotions about the subject matter and the

TABLE 26–1. TWO-DIMENSIONAL MODEL OF EFFECTIVE TEACHING

	DIMENSION II: INTERPERSONAL RAPPORT		
DIMENSION I: INTELLECTUAL EXCITEMENT	*Low:* Cold, distant, highly controlling, unpredictable	*Moderate:* Relatively warm, approachable, and democratic; predictable	*High:* Warm, open, predictable, and highly student-centered
High: Very clear and exciting	**Intellectual Authority** Creates intellectual excitement and prompts achievement in students who are confident in their own abilities and comfortable with teacher's distant manner. Younger or less able students will probably experience anxiety. More respected than loved by most students.	**Masterful Lecturer** Captivates students by sheer intellectual force and motivates them to learn material because it seems a terribly important and exciting thing to do. Excels in lecture situations but can provide competent instruction in all situations. Has achieved excellence at teaching.	**Master Teachers** Able to perform superbly in both lecture and seminar situations. Modifies approach so as to motivate all students, from the brilliant to the mediocre. Few teachers reach this degree of flexibility.
Moderate: Reasonably clear and interesting	**Adequate** Minimally adequate in lecture classes with relatively compliant students. Needs increased interpersonal skills to expand range of student and situations in which they are effective as a teacher.	**Competent** Effective for most students and in most classroom situations.	**Masterful Facilitator** Most effective in smaller, more advanced classes characterized by considerable discussion but can provide competent instruction in all situations. Stimulates creativity and independent work of high quality. Teacher is often sought out by students for advice. Has obtained excellence at teaching.
Low: Vague and dull	**Inadequate** Unable to present material well or motivate students.	**Marginal** Unable to present material well. May be liked by some students.	**Humanistic** Promotes independent work. Ideal for seminar courses. Inadequate in larger classes requiring lecture. Is less than fully competent.

Adapted from Lowman, J. *Mastering the Techniques of Teaching*. San Francisco: Jossey-Bass, 1984.

learning experience is what separates the competent teacher from the outstanding one.[11]

Interpersonal Rapport

The classroom is a highly emotional interpersonal arena.[11] Couples in childbirth education classes are especially sensitive to the emotional aspects of the classroom experience. The dimension of interpersonal rapport involves the teacher's awareness of interpersonal phenomena and his or her skills at communicating with students in ways that increase *motivation, enjoyment, and independent learning*.[11]

Interpersonal rapport can be enhanced by decreasing activities or behaviors that would stimulate negative emotions (such as increasing anxiety) and communicating to class members that each one is respected as an individual, and that they are competent and are capable of mastering the material presented. Lowman stated that this dimension is not as important to outstanding teaching as is the dimension of intellectual excitement. However, it is the dimension that most strongly affects students' motivation to learn and the climate of the classroom.

The Role of the Teacher

There are three fundamental roles that a teacher plays in order to develop and maintain conditions conducive to learning.[26] These are the *instructional role,* or teacher, which is the focus of this chapter; the *democratic strategist role,* or manager, which is the focus of Chapter 24 on group process; and the *therapist role,* or counselor, which is implicit in the teaching process. The instructional role is the most traditional of the three, but it has changed from the tradition of years past. No longer is the teacher the stern power figure or the supreme academic authority in the classroom. Although he or she is still expected to have superior learning, the teacher acts primarily as a *facilitator,* or resource person, encouraging the students to develop their ability to think and reason.

The second fundamental role of the teacher is that of democratic strategist, or manager of the classroom. It is in this role that the teacher attends to group process and works toward developing an effective group. Here the teacher must have a clear understanding of the forces affecting the class as a group and of ways to help the group to function effectively.

The third role is that of therapist, or counselor. Trow and colleagues suggest that, willing or not, every teacher plays this role. This involves establishing rapport with each group member, creating a supportive atmosphere, and sharing insights into human behavior. Teachers tend to play this role least adequately of all.[26]

Such factors as group apathy, general disturbances in behavior, extreme competitiveness, exclusiveness, and the like provide cues that a shift in roles is needed. The teacher should be alert for these messages, and change roles when the behavior of the group indicates that this is needed.

Evaluation of the appropriate use of teacher roles can be accomplished in several ways. One is to measure the progress toward group goals; another is to assess improvement in the dynamics of group relationships. There are several sources of evaluation data. One, of course, is the teacher, who should carry out such evaluation regularly. Class members are also valuable sources of evaluation data. This evaluation not only is a component of the feedback needed by the teacher but can also serve as a valuable learning experience for group members.

Finally, it is often useful to have an outside person assist in the evaluation process. Through frequent evaluation, the teacher can become proficient in adopting the appropriate role for any classroom situation. An in-depth discussion of evaluation is presented in Chapter 28.

The Process of Teaching

Knowles, who has been called the father of adult education, is best known for his differentiation between androgogy (the education of adults) and pedagogy (the education of children).[9] He explains that teaching adults is different from teaching children: how they learn, why they seek out learning experiences, and when they learn. He describes the overall process of teaching adults from the planning phase to the evaluation phase. Gagné, who has been called an "instructional psychologist," speaks primarily to the implementation phase of

TABLE 26–2. A COMPARISON OF THE TEACHING PROCESS AS SEEN BY TWO THEORISTS

	KNOWLES	GAGNÉ
Planning Phase (Including assessment and diagnosis)	Establish climate Participatory Planning Diagnose needs Formulate objectives Design learning activities	
Implementation Phase	Operation of activities	Gaining attention Informing learner of the objective Stimulating recall of prior knowledge Presenting the stimulus material Providing learning guidance Eliciting performance Providing feedback Assessing performance Enhancing retention and transfer of learning
Evaluation Phase	Rediagnosis	

Based on work of Knowles, M. *The Modern Practice of Adult Education*. Chicago: Association Press, 1980; and Gagné, E. M. *The Conditions of Learning and Theory of Instruction* (4th ed). New York: Holt, Rinehart and Winston, 1985.

the teaching process.[6] He describes a sequence of steps (instructional events) that the teacher should follow when presenting material in the classroom and which will promote more efficient (faster) learning. The work of these two teaching-learning theorists is compared in Table 26–2.

Knowles' Theory of Adult Education

Knowles[9] describes the process of teaching adults as consisting of seven phases:

1. Establishment of a climate conducive to adult learning;
2. Creation of an organizational structure for participative planning;
3. Diagnosis of needs for learning;
4. Formulation of directions for learning (objectives);
5. Development of a design of activities;
6. Operation of the activities;
7. Rediagnosis of needs for learning (evaluation).

Establishing a Climate. The childbirth educator must pay careful attention to establishing a climate conducive to adult learning. The childbirth educator's respect for adult needs will be reflected in the environment (room selected and placement of chairs), the pre-class procedures (registration and pre-class information), and communication patterns (democratic as opposed to authoritarian, clear as opposed to vague). The classroom should ideally be an adequate size to enable couples to sit in a circle yet still have room for floor exercises. The circle is symbolic of equality of the group members, as it was when King Arthur established his round table. Childbirth educators who speak to couples seated in rows and who speak from a podium or from behind a desk are giving an authoritarian message that may impede establishing an atmosphere conducive to adult learning. While not every class can be taught in an ideal room, if location is a continuing problem, the childbirth educator should ask herself whether she should be more creative, more articulate, or more assertive in obtaining better quarters. Chapter 24 includes a comprehensive discussion on factors that influence group process in the classroom.

Participatory Planning. Knowles[9] recommends creating a structure for participatory planning. Even though the curriculum of a childbirth education class is largely set before the series begins, with creativity the registrants can become involved in some aspects of planning prior to arrival.

A sheet can be developed for registrants to complete before class which lists the planned class content and asks which items should receive greatest emphasis, moderate emphasis, and less emphasis. Registrants can also be invited to list any other areas of interest to them. Even if the childbirth educator cannot justify class time to cover in class the suggested added topics, she can locate an article or book on a topic and have it ready to lend or she can refer to some other resource when appropriate. Such personalized touches take educator time and may increase the cost of the class slightly, but they are the hallmarks of excellence.

Needs Diagnosis. The next step, according to Knowles, is the diagnosis of learning needs.[9] A well-defined and efficient method that the childbirth educator can use to determine the learning needs of expectant parents is called the *diagnostic process,* a simplified and pragmatic version of the scientific method of problem-solving. This process has five steps: data collection, diagnosis, planning, teaching, and evaluation (Fig. 26–1).

In the data collection step the childbirth educator gains information about her prospective students in several ways. A registration form can include questions regarding their reproductive history; a scheduled interview can secure information regarding their knowledge base; observing students in class may reveal interpersonal problems. Through analysis of the data gathered the childbirth educator can then diagnose the learning needs of class members.

The learning need(s) can be named on the basis of the data gathered. This diagnosis should be validated with the student. The teacher can use any one of several means (interview, observation, written requests) to be sure the knowledge deficit exists and then can develop a plan to meet the learning need.

Assessment of students' readiness to learn is a part of the data collection step and involves two facets. One is the emotional readiness, or motivation, which determines the student's willingness to put forth the effort necessary to learn. A second facet is experiential readiness, the student's background of experiences, skills, and attitudes and the ability to learn that which is considered desirable. These two facets are closely interrelated.[16] Factors that affect readiness to make a change in health behaviors are beliefs about health, and for expectant parents, beliefs about pregnancy and childbirth (whether it is regarded as an illness or a normal physiological process). Knowledge of these factors and the ability to identify the belief systems and the student's motivation to learn will help the childbirth educator predict the degree of a learner's readiness to change a particular health behavior. In any group of learners there may be as many sources of motivation as there are learners.

Readiness to learn has been defined as a state or condition of being both willing and able to make use of instruction.[16] The degree of readiness to learn depends upon the degree of both willingness and ability. Assessment of the capability to learn should be made concurrently with formulation of class objectives and identification of prerequisite skills. Only when the childbirth educator has de-

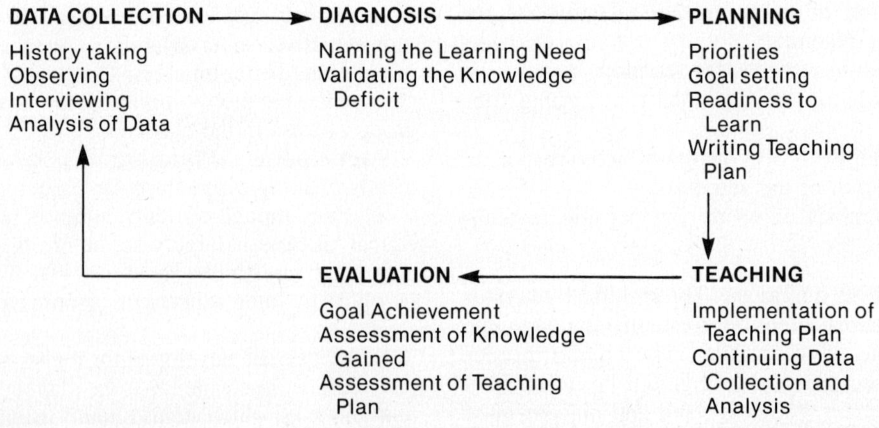

FIGURE 26–1. The diagnostic process. (From Marriner, A. *The Nursing Process a Scientific Approach.* St. Louis: C.V. Mosby Co., 1983.)

termined what is required can she determine whether the student possesses the necessary attributes and abilities and is indeed capable of learning.

Objectives. The formulation of objectives is also an important aspect of course planning. The content of the objectives will be derived from the diagnosis of needs. The basic process of writing objectives is familiar to most educators. Mager's[15] programmed text on objective writing is recommended to readers who are learning to write objectives or who wish to review this skill.[14]

The advantage of using well-defined objectives is that, as with use of a detailed road map, the class with objectives has a clear picture of where it is going. The traveler with a detailed road map can afford to take sidetrips or detours of interest because he can visualize how he can get back on course or make up lost time. Likewise, the teacher with clear objectives can afford to give the class more leeway to pursue special interests because she has no fear that they will become side-tracked and lost.

In Table 26–3, levels of objectives for learning are summarized in the cognitive (intellectual), affective (attitudinal), and psychomotor (motor skill) domains. In Table 26–4, verbs for higher level objectives are listed in each of those domains. The following guidelines are helpful for writing behavioral objectives:

1. State objectives in terms of the *expected behavior* of the learner.
2. State the *action* required. It may be cognitive (''identifies''), psychomotor (''demonstrates''), or affective (''expresses'').
3. State the content or *terminal behavior* (''the phases and stages of labor, slow paced breathing, feelings about cesarean birth'').
4. State the *criterion* for evaluation (''without error, using no less than one-half the normal respiration rate, to other group members'').

TABLE 26–3. TAXONOMIES OF EDUCATIONAL OBJECTIVES

DOMAIN OF LEARNING BEHAVIOR	HIERARCHY OF OBJECTIVE CATEGORY	EXPLANATION
Cognitive domain (intellectual abilities)	Knowledge	Recall or memory of terminology and facts
	Comprehension	Low-level understanding
	Application	Application of ideas, principles, or theories
	Analysis	Analysis of parts, relationships, or organizations
	Synthesis	Creating a unique whole from parts such as a plan
	Evaluation	Quantitative and qualitative judgments
Affective domain (expression of feelings, interest, values, and appreciation)	Receiving (attending)	Willingness to attend
	Responding	Willingness and satisfaction in responding
	Valuing	Acceptance of a value as indicated by behavior
	Organization	Relating the value to those values already held
	Characterization	Values or attitudes clustered to form a basic orientation or value system
Psychomotor domain (motor skills)	Perception	Use of sense organs to become aware of objects, qualities
	Set	Preparedness for a kind of action or experience
	Guided response	Action under instructor guidance
	Mechanism	Habitual learned response with some confidence and skill
	Complex overt response	Performance of a complex motor pattern with high degree of skill

From Libresco, M. Creative Teaching: Beyond lecture and demonstration. *Expanding Horizons in Childbirth Education*. Vol. 1. Washington, DC; American Society for Psychoprophylaxis in Obstetrics, 1983. Adapted from Redman, B. K. *The Process of Patient Teaching in Nursing*. St. Louis: C. V. Mosby, 1972. Based on the works of Bloom, Krathwohl, Simpson.

TABLE 26–4. VERBS FOR BEHAVIORAL OBJECTIVES

1. Knowledge	Defines, describes, identifies, labels, lists, matches, names, outlines, reproduces, selects, states
2. Comprehension	Converts, defends, distinguishes, estimates, explains, extends, generalizes, gives examples, infers, paraphrases, predicts, rewrites, summarizes
3. Application	Changes, computes, demonstrates, discovers, manipulates, modifies, operates, predicts, prepares, produces, relates, shows, solves, uses
4. Analysis	Breaks down, diagrams, differentiates, discriminates, distinguishes, identifies, illustrates, infers, outlines, points out, relates, selects, separates, subdivides
5. Synthesis	Categorizes, combines, compiles, composes, creates, devises, designs, explains, generates, modifies, organizes, plans, rearranges, reconstructs, relates, reorganizes, revises, rewrites, summarizes, tells, writes
6. Evaluation	Appraises, compares, concludes, contrasts, criticizes, describes, discriminates, explains, justifies, interprets, relates, summarizes, supports

Most educators plan broad goals and then write specific objectives under each goal. Another approach that may enhance creativity is for the childbirth educator to work backward.[11] One can write rough objectives, one to a card, on three by five cards. This can be done in a brainstorming fashion, in which for the moment anything goes, regardless of practicality. The cards can then be clustered in more than one way. This process may unleash creativity. From the clusters, one can then write and organize broad goals, filling in missing objectives and discarding impractical ones. This process frees the teacher from thinking she must organize classes just like the ones she has observed.[10]

Designing Learning Activities

The most appropriate learning activities will depend on the objectives, the learners, and the teacher. Ideally, the teacher might plan several strategies for each objective. She would then select the one to be used on the basis of her assessment of the class and class input.

No matter what the method of presentation of the content, the teacher must pay attention to the responses of the students. What does the body language of the students indicate? Are they interested in what is going on in the class or are they sleeping? Do they ask questions or remain sitting in silence? Perhaps the teacher should change the activities for this class if the students do not appear to be responding in a manner indicating that they are interested and appear to be understanding.

Dubin and Taveggia report, after examining 91 comparative studies, "We are able to state decisively that no particular method of college instruction is measurably to be preferred over another, when evaluated by student examination performances."[4] Silvernail also reviewed multiple studies and found inconsistent findings regarding teaching styles as related to student achievement.[23] Lovell summarizes by stating:

> The final choice of methods that the teacher makes will depend upon the aims and objectives he has for his course, the nature of the subject matter and its sequencing, the characteristics of the students, his own skills as a teacher, and the facilities which the teaching environment offers.[12]

Thus, the method the teacher uses should be related to the objectives for the lesson. Knowles provides some general guidelines for this concept in his book, *The Modern Practice of Adult Education*[9] (Table 26–5).

The least effective technique is teacher lecture and explanations. Student involvement seems to be necessary to success in adult learning as it is in all learning. The potential attributes of selected strategies are shown in Table 26–6. Various types of teaching activities are defined and examples are given for their use in childbirth education in Table 26–7. The following comments on several of the teaching strategies listed in Table 26–7 are particularly relevant to the childbirth educator.

Teaching Strategies

Lecture is the most frequently employed teaching technique used to promote cognitive learning. While lecture is not considered the most effective

TABLE 26–5. MATCHING TECHNIQUES TO DESIRED BEHAVIORAL OUTCOMES

TYPE OF BEHAVIORAL OUTCOME	MOST APPROPRIATE TECHNIQUE
Knowledge (generalizations about experience; internalization of information)	Lecture, television, debate, dialogue, interview, symposium, panel, group interview, colloquy, motion picture, slide film, recording, book-based discussion, reading.
Understanding (application of information and generalizations)	Audience participation, demonstration, motion picture, dramatization, socratic discussion, problem-solving discussion, case discussion, critical incident process, case method, games.
Skills (incorporation of new ways of performing through practice)	Role playing, in-basket exercises, games, action mazes, participative cases, T-Group, nonverbal exercises, skill practice exercises, drill, coaching.
Attitudes (adoption of new feelings through experiencing greater success with them than with old)	Experience-sharing discussion, group-centered discussion, role playing, critical incident process, case method, games, participative cases, T-Group, nonverbal exercises.
Values (the adoption and priority arrangement of beliefs)	Television, lecture (sermon), debate, dialogue, symposium, colloquy, motion picture, dramatization, guided discussion, experience-sharing discussion, role playing, critical incident process, games, T-Group.
Interests (Satisfying exposure to new experiences)	Television, demonstration, motion picture, slide film, dramatization, experience-sharing discussion, exhibits, trips, nonverbal exercises.

From Knowles, M. S. *The Modern Practice of Adult Education*. New York: Association Press, 1972, p. 294.

teaching method, it is efficient in terms of time provided that the learner actually receives and understands the message. A lecture can be defined as a carefully prepared oral presentation of a subject given by a qualified person. Types of or vehicles for lectures can be talk, speech, sermon, oration, address, panel, symposium, forum, interview, and dialogue.

Zahn's[27] and Oddi's[19] reviews of the literature on lecture report on the effectiveness of the lecture for imparting information to adult groups. Zahn describes the criteria for an effective lecture. A lecture should be short and carefully constructed, should be simple in language and style, and should present only meaningful and uncomplicated material. In designing an instructional situation, therefore, the particular learning task to be accomplished determines whether the lecture should be used.

Role play encourages active participation, enables problems of human behavior and relationships to be presented, and extends the cognitive into the emotional.[27] Role play is often a constituent element of simulation, but gaming may not involve role play. Simulation and gaming provide a means to involve students in situations similar to those they may face in real life. The students can create learning environments that motivate them as well as expose them to the complexity and dynamics of social situations. Mardment and Bronstein[13] state that there are indications that instructional simulations impart some types of knowledge and skills and influence attitudes and beliefs more successfully than do many conventional methods of instruction. These strategies are therefore particularly useful for affective learning.

Demonstration and return demonstration are particularly useful in psychomotor learning. Of particular concern is the type of feedback given to the learner. Specific feedback is more useful than general feedback. Therefore, ''Your arm is (tense or very relaxed)'' is preferred to ''That's (good, not right).'' Feedback can be corrective (''too fast'') or positive (''just right''). Corrective feedback is important to learning, but the learner needs

TABLE 26–6. POTENTIAL ATTRIBUTES OF SELECTED TEACHING STRATEGIES

POTENTIAL ATTRIBUTES / STRATEGIES	Live Lecture with Visuals	Seminar/Discussion	Live Demonstration with Return Practice	Textbook	Models/Objects	Course Syllabus	16 mm Film	Slides (Multiple/Individual)	Sound Slide/Filmstrip & Built-in Response	Audio Recording	Games (Individual or Group)	Print Programmed Instruction	Video (Lecture Interview)	Role Play (Group)
Provides primarily direct, "hands on" active participation and overt student response		X	X		X						X	X		X
Provides primarily indirect, abstract participation and covert response	X			X		X	X	X	X	X			X	
Provides color stimuli for differentiation	X	X	X	X	X	X	X	X	X		X	X	X	X
Conveys actual movement	X	X	X		X		X				X		X	X
Provides multisensory input	X	X	X		X		X		X		X		X	X
Most suitable for promoting practice of psychomotor skills			X		X		X				X			X
Content can be easily repeated by student			X	X	X	X		X	X	X	X	X	X	
Provides *immediate* feedback, reinforcement, and objectivity		X	X		X						X	X		X
Provides structured organization, step-by-step sequencing, explicit objectives, student response, feedback, reinforcement		X	X								X	X		X
Promotes peer or instructor affiliation and human interaction	X	X	X								X			X
Facilitates face-to-face, oral, two-way communication and interaction	X	X	X								X			X
Reveals information bit-by-bit in sequence	X		X	X		X	X	X	X	X	X	X	X	
Provides for alternative pathways or branching of content		X		X	X			X			X	X		X
Content is in a fixed sequence and not easily reordered by student	X		X			X	X		X	X	X		X	
Content can be easily reordered by student		X		X	X			X				X		X
Rate of presentation can be controlled by student		X	X	X	X	X		X			X	X		X

Adapted from Ostmoe, P. Learning style preferences and selection of learning strategies: Considerations and implications for nurse educators. *Journal of Nursing Education* 23:27, January 1984.

to hear positive feedback more often than corrective. This may mean that the childbirth educator needs to work at pointing out positive performance, especially with a learner who needs a lot of correction. Of course, feedback is not limited to the psychomotor domain of learning. Some general guidelines for giving feedback are shown in Table 26–8.

Teaching strategies can be classified by who controls the generation of the content. Teacher-centered strategies include lecture, demonstration, and questioning. Group-centered strategies include brainstorming, "buzz" sessions, role playing, and peer instruction. Learner-centered strategies include learners doing outside reading and projects and asking questions.

TABLE 26–7. TYPES OF TEACHING ACTIVITIES* AND USE IN CHILDBIRTH EDUCATION

TEACHING ACTIVITIES	EXAMPLES OF USE IN CHILDBIRTH EDUCATION
Brainstorming: Group interaction of a freewheeling, noncritical nature to stimulate creative solutions, evaluative statement not used	Class could be asked to devise strategies to reduce stress in the first 6 weeks postpartum
Buzz Session: Time limited (5–15 minutes) small group work on a clearly identified task	Groups of 4–6 members could be asked to word assertive but not aggressive requests they wish to make of their care providers
Demonstration: A procedure is conducted to teach psychomotor skills; demonstration is return by practice and return demonstration	May be used to teach relaxation, paced breathing, pushing, or any psychomotor skills
Discussion: A teacher- or student-led group deliberation of a question of mutual concern; evaluative statement and feedback on ideas may be included	The teacher may lead the class in a discussion of typical labor experiences, encouraging class members to contribute what they have heard as she described labor
Field Trip: A trip to an unfamiliar unit to observe real-life situations	Class members as a group or individual may visit the maternity unit where birth is planned. Primiparas may arrange to spend some time with a new mother
Games: Structured activities in which learners compete to reach a goal	Crossword puzzles and other games can be used in class.
Interview: A discussion in front of an audience in which the person interviewed answers questions	A recently delivered couple may be interviewed in front of the class about their birth experience and their early parenting experience
Lecture: A carefully organized oral presentation of subject content. Appropriate for topics about which audience can be expected to have little or no knowledge; is followed by questions and answers	A talk on the types of labor medications available and implications of their use
Media Presentation: Slide shows, videotapes, audiotapes, movies shown to the class and followed by discussion	There are numerous films on birth, cesarean birth, new parenting, and breastfeeding that present information effectively
Peer Instruction: Learners teach each other; the process of teaching enhances learning of both	Asking one partner to check the relaxation skill or breathing patterns of the other partner
Questioning: Eliciting learner responses to teacher-posed questions; may be used to stimulate thought or to evaluate learner understanding	Ask the class: "How do you know labor has started?" or "When will you head for the birth place?" or "What should the partner try when in labor the current strategies aren't helping enough?"
Role Playing: Participants enact real life situations without a script; used after class members know each other well	As a group, class can enact a labor with roles of mother, father, contracting uterus, nurse, physician, etc. They often lay some new issues on the table in the process
Simulation: Learners are asked to respond to real life situations and practice solutions	The teacher can lead the class through a labor sequence and ask members to respond to contractions at different stages of labor
Values Clarification: Participants undertake an exercise in which they are encouraged to voice their thinking and reasons or beliefs or attitude	Emotionally laden issues such as use of medications or decisions about breastfeeding lend themselves to values clarification exercises
Visual Aids: Visual presentation of objects that augment teaching	Posters, charts, transparencies, blackboard, knitted uterus, skeletal models, hospital equipment may clarify content

*Adapted from O'Connor, A. *Nursing Staff Development and Continuing Education*. Boston: Little Brown and Company, 1986.

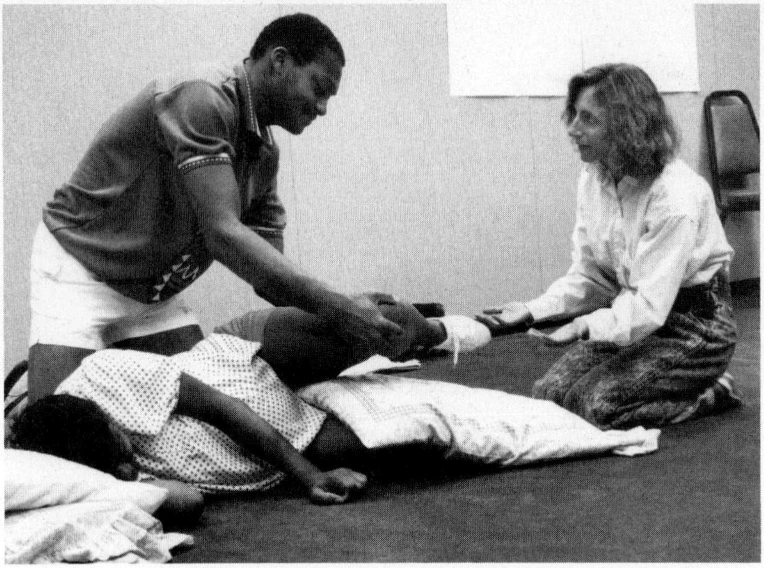

Feedback from the teacher is important in reinforcing correct behavior and in assisting the learner to achieve the desired behavior. (Photograph by Francine H. Nichols. Courtesy of Equicor Health Plan, Inc., Wichita, KS)

Learning activities can also be classified as abstract as opposed to concrete. Abstract learning activities include lectures, buzz sessions, discussion, questioning, and interviewing. Direct concrete experience includes field trips, role playing, simulation, and some types of games. Games and values clarification exercises can be abstract or concrete, depending on the type of activity on the part of the learner.

The general principle in working with a heterogeneous group is to plan each class so that it has a balance of types of activities and thus has appeal for many different types of learners and learning styles. If information is presented in only one manner and it does not ''fit'' the learning style of the learner, essential information will be lost. Thus, the teacher must use a variety of teaching strategies to meet the needs of each learner. Working with more homogeneous groups, the teacher may be able to plan activities specific to the learning needs and styles of the group.

TABLE 26–8. GUIDELINES FOR GIVING FEEDBACK

PRINCIPLE	DESCRIPTION	EXAMPLES
1. Focus feedback on behavior rather than on the person	Use descriptive rather than evaluative words	''Your arm is tense'' not ''That's not right''
2. Focus feedback on observables rather than inference	Describe what is observed rather than why it is believed to have occurred	''I noticed you nodding your head in class'' rather than ''I guess you were bored in class'' or ''I guess you had a hard day today''
3. Focus feedback on sharing of ideas rather than giving advice	Explore alternatives rather than provide solutions	''Can you think of a time in your day when you can practice relaxation?'' rather than ''Practice your relaxation just before you go to bed''
4. Focus feedback on what it may do to the person receiving it	Even worthwhile points to be made must be presented with the recipient in mind; people can handle only so much feedback at one time and some times are better than others for giving or receiving feedback	''Is this a good time to give you some of my observations?'' rather than ''. . . and then after that you also forgot to . . .''

Teachers sometimes assume that because material was presented, it was learned.[10] This faulty assumption puts a tremendous burden on the teacher to transmit information, yet we know that the higher the involvement of the learner, the more the learner will retain. Lectures, slides, and question-and-answer sessions are seen as high-teacher:low-learner involvement activities. These are contrasted with role playing, simulations, life-style exchanges (trade places with new mother), labor games, and the like, which are low-teacher:high-learner involvement strategies.[10] Childbirth classes benefit from a balance of these types of activities. More descriptions of learning activities can be found in *A Handbook of Structured Experiences for Human Relations Training*[21] and *Games Trainers Play.*[17]

No matter which teaching strategy is used, there are various instructional devices that can be used to augment and increase teaching effectiveness with adults. *Audiovisual aids* can be used to assist expectant parents to learn via their senses, thus increasing retention of information. For hearing, audio cassettes, audio recordings, radio, and records can be used. For visual learners, there are devices such as models, charts, diagrams, drawings, graphs, illustrations, photographs, and slides. Visual aids that involve both hearing and seeing are films, tape-slide presentations, television programs, and video recordings. Other learning aids that can be utilized by teachers and learners are articles in journals, books, computer programs, handouts, games, role play and simulations exercises, visits to birthing agencies, and workbooks or worksheets.

Many of these teaching aids are produced commercially; permission for reproduction of materials must be obtained and should be included when acknowledgments are given. If you prepare your own teaching aids, it is wise to look into the copyright laws.

A wide variety of aids and equipment is available to the teacher to assist in enriching the learning experience of students. Because of the numerous methods available, it is important that the techniques used be appropriate to the aims of the material being taught. Snyder and Ylmer[24] have written criteria for selecting instructional techniques:

1. The activities selected should contribute to the accomplishment of specific types of learning objective(s).
2. The advantages and limitations of each technique should be taken into account during the selection process.
3. Specific learner characteristics should be considered—particularly the interest level, the level of independence of learners, the personal preferences of learners' styles of learning, and general ability level in terms of communication skills (speaking, reading, writing, and listening).
4. The familiarity with specific techniques by the teacher affects selection.
5. Costs in terms of time, energy, and money are factors.
6. The size of the learning group should be a consideration.
7. The willingness of the teacher to utilize various techniques has importance.
8. Degree of learner participation sought should be considered.

Operation of Activities. This is the implementation phase of the teaching process. Knowles emphasizes the importance of the previous life experiences of the adult learner on the learning experience.[9] While Knowles provides numerous implications for teaching, two that are specific to the adult learner are included here. First, the practical application of the learning task should be emphasized during the learning experience. Second, the teacher should build on the previous experiences of the learners when presenting new material. A comprehensive discussion of the adult learner can be found in Chapter 25.

Evaluation. It is in this phase that the teacher can determine if the students have mastered the learning objectives. Evaluation is a very important teaching activity and in this book an entire chapter, Chapter 28, has been devoted to this topic.

Gagné's Theory of Instruction

Gagné is the only teaching-learning theorist to specify a sequence of instructional events (activities) that should be followed in teaching students. This model of teaching is based on the information processing theory of learning (see Chapter 25). Each one of the nine instructional events is designed to influence one or more of the internal processes of learning identified in the information processing theory of learning and thus promote more efficient (faster) learning. These events are gaining attention, informing learners of the objective, stimulating recall of prior learning, presenting the stimulus (directing attention), providing learning guidance, eliciting performance, providing feedback, assessing performance, and enhancing retention and transfer.[5]

Gaining Attention. The purpose of this initial event is to stimulate the learner's interest and motivate learning. This involves first *identifying* the motives of the students for participating in the learning situation and then *using* these motivations to help accomplish the learning task. This event involves activities that are selected to match the learners' interests, stimulate their curiosity, create a challenge, or meet specific needs such as affiliative (belonging) or achievement needs. An example of gaining attention is asking expectant parents the following question in the introductory part of the first class: If you went into labor in the next five minutes, what would you want to know?

Informing the Learner of the Objectives. The student is informed about the expected outcome of the learning situation in order to establish expectations about what will be achieved as a result of the learning experience. The following statement is an example of this: ''As a result of participating in these childbirth preparation classes you will gain knowledge about childbirth and thus you will know what to expect, and you will learn techniques and strategies that will enable you to cope more effectively during childbirth.'' This also serves as a stimulus to motivate learners.

Stimulating Recall of Prior Learning. The concept of prerequisite learning (previously learned knowledge must be recalled and is used to learn new information) is a fundamental part of Gagne's theory. New information and skills are anchored to previously learned information and skills. The learner has retrieved the previously learned concepts or rules that are essential to learning the new skill. Statements such as ''Remember how . . .'' or ''You remember what . . .'' are examples of stimulating recall of previously learned information.

Building bridges between old and new information enables learners to consider the interconnections between the new material and what they already know. More effective immediate learning and long-term retention result from teaching methods that involve the presentation and subsequent active recall of material than from methods that rely on presentation alone.

Presenting the Stimulus (Directing Attention). The learning task is presented using the appropriate instructional technique. This event also involves activities that direct the learners' attention to the task. Directing attention has two components. The first is an *alerting* function that leads to students assuming a state of readiness for learning. This can be accomplished by the introduction of novel stimuli, changing voice pitch, or directing learners' attention to specific details. Statements such as ''Look at what happens to the body organs as the fetus grows'' while pointing to a chart, and ''Feel the tension in your arm'' while practicing progressive relaxation are examples of alerting.

The second component of directing attention is identifying for the learner the most important aspects of the material *(selective perception)* that is presented so that these can be stored and processed in *short-term memory*. Statements such as ''It is important to remember . . .'' or ''The essential elements are . . .'' and activities such as circling portions of a diagram or using different colors to highlight important features are examples of this component of directing attention.

Providing Learning Guidance. This instructional event includes activities that affect how the learner transforms *(encodes)* information and stores it in *long-term memory*. There are two approaches that can be used to provide learning guidance—the use of verbal directions and images. The use of *prompts* or *cues* (verbal directions) is an effective means of providing learning guidance for students. Either statements such as ''Labor consists of three stages,'' or questions such as ''What things could you do to . . .?'' can be used to guide learning.

The use of images can enhance the process of encoding and storing of information and provide guidance for learning. Pictures, diagrams, graphs, models, and demonstrations can be used to provide concrete visual images of the information or activity to be learned. Using a knitted uterus to describe effacement and dilatation, using a pelvis and doll to define the term ''station,'' or demonstrating how to do touch relaxation are all ways of guiding learning. Many learning theorists suggest that increased learning results when both verbal directions and images are used to present the learning task.[20]

Eliciting Learner Performance and Providing Feedback. The learner's performance of the educational task is an important aspect of learning. Frequent practice sessions of relaxation techniques throughout the childbirth preparation course are an example of this instructional event. The provision of feedback during the process of learning new information or skills is important in reinforcing a correct performance or shaping a learner's response to achieve the desired performance.

Assessing Performance. The learner's performance of a skill or activity verifies that learning has occurred; it provides objective information about the degree to which the learning objective has been accomplished. This activity serves to establish that the newly learned capability is reasonably stable and also provides additional practice that promotes further retention of what was learned.

Enhancing Retention and Promoting Transfer of Learning. Instruction is designed to promote retention of the learned material and transference of it to a new situation. This can be accomplished using several approaches. The material to be learned can be organized into categories to provide cues for retrieval of information. A review of what has been previously presented in the classroom situation should be spaced throughout the learning experience. Learning is also increased when the student is provided with a variety of new situations in which to practice the learning activity.

IMPLICATIONS FOR PRACTICE

Implementing the Teaching Plan

Building Rapport

The easiest way for the teacher to start building rapport is to learn the students' names and information about them: Which baby is this? Where will the birth take place? Who is the physician? Any particular problems or concerns? This establishes personal contact immediately and communicates to learners that the teacher cares about them and views them as individuals. Another way to build rapport is to be available before class to visit with class members and discuss any questions or concerns they may have. Accessibility to class members will also enhance rapport. Tell them how they can reach you and when the best time is for contact. Anything that the teacher can do to show an interest in class members as individuals will help to build rapport.[11]

Gagné's Instructional Events

The childbirth educator can use specific learning strategies for each of the instructional events outlined by Gagné to promote more efficient (faster) learning.[5,20]

Gaining Attention. Various strategies can be used to gain the learner's attention. These include:

- Asking thought-provoking questions,
- Using visual stimuli such as a picture that captures the essence of the material to be taught or a cartoon that makes a specific point related to the information to be studied,
- Using auditory stimuli such as a forceful statement related to the topic or playing a portion of an audiotape,
- Telling about a life experience, perhaps from a postpartum report, related to the content to be learned or eliciting such an experience from learners in the class.

Informing Learners of the Objectives. While Gagné speaks of "informing" the learner of class objectives,[5] Knowles has pointed out the importance of choices during the learning experiences to the adult learner.[9] Thus, "choosing" class objectives may be a more appropriate term to use for the typical prepared childbirth classes; adult learners are helped to set realistic objectives for their

> The selection and effective implementation of an appropriate teaching strategy are critical to the success of the educational endeavor. Although ideally selection is based on the consideration of all three groups of variables—educational task, learner, teacher—the key determinants of methods should be the behavioral objectives to be achieved by learners.
>
> ANDREA O'CONNOR[1]
>
> The teacher constantly needs feedback from students in order to assess the effectiveness of his teaching. He can easily get this feedback when he uses the discussion method, because of the frequent exchanges among the participants.
>
> RONALD HYMAN[2]
>
> People now-a-days have a strange opinion that everything should be taught by lectures. Now I cannot see that lectures can do more good than reading the books from which the lectures are taken. I know nothing that can be best taught by lectures, except where experiments are to be shown.
>
> SAMUEL JOHNSON[3] IN 1776

own learning experience. Activities that can be used during this instructional event are:

- Provide an opportunity for learners to state what it is they want to learn from the classes.
- Provide clear expectations about the purpose of classes and expected outcomes.
- Assist learners in clarifying expectations about classes.
- Assist learners to develop realistic objectives for their learning experience.
- Assist learner to develop life-long objectives. In the case of childbirth education classes, one objective could be to increase wellness behaviors.

Stimulating Recall of Prior Learning. Expectant parents as adult learners have a wealth of knowledge and skills that they can draw on in learning new content. They may have also acquired some ideas and habits that will need to be unlearned. Strategies that can be used during this instructional step are:

- Help learners to identify what is known and unknown to them about a specific topic.
- Identify practices and ideas that expectant parents will need to unlearn.
- Review material from prior classes.
- Have learners recall experiences or information related to the topic being studied.
- Remind learners what has been previously learned (concept or skill) that is related to the new learning task.

Presenting the Stimulus (Directing Attention). An important aspect of this step is allowing adequate time and using strategies that direct the learners' attention to the learning task. Effective strategies for this instruction event are:

- Present information in small chunks.
- Help learners organize and categorize materials through the use of charts, diagrams, or other aids.
- Present information in several different ways.
- Point out the most important aspects of the information. This can be done verbally, by using charts or pictures, or by demonstration.
- Present information consistent with the learner's level of experience.
- Present information and skills within the context of the life experiences of the learner. The childbirth educator should present information using examples that the learners in class can identify with.
- Help learners to establish the relationship between the learning task and personal experience. How will the information be useful to them?

Providing Learning Guidance. Providing guidance during the learning process is critical to accomplishment of the learning task. Specific strategies that can be used during this instructional event are:

- Present information in a meaningful context—for example, "The transition phase is the last phase of the first stage of labor," assuming that students already have learned the definition of the first stage of labor.
- Use examples of life experiences as cues, prompting devices, or links—for example, "What physical and emotional changes have you noticed since you became pregnant?"
- Suggest ways to practice or learn the information. Giving expectant parents guidelines for home practice and encouraging them to check out books from the lending library are useful ways to increase learning.
- Provide memory aids. These can be handouts that summarize materials, pictures that highlight specific points, or paper and pencil for taking notes.

Eliciting Learner Performance. The purpose of this event is to determine if the material to be learned has been stored in *long-term memory.* The learner is asked to perform the learning task. The following strategies can be used to elicit learner performance:

- Provide clear and concise instructions.
- Elicit performance frequently.
- Pace the learning task to allow for mastery and continuity.

Providing Feedback. Learning is enhanced through feedback about the ability to perform the learning task. Several strategies can be used in providing feedback:

- Discuss the learner's progress toward the learning objective. Provide the learner with a specific description of the *change* (to what extent or type of change) in performance.
- Identify correct and incorrect performance.
- Reinforce correct performance and indicate the behavior necessary to achieve desired performance.
- Point out misperceptions.
- Provide supportive comments for both correct and incorrect performance.

Assessing Performance. It is important to assess student learning *frequently* to determine progress toward the learning objective and to identify areas that need clarification.

- Plan specific class activities to evaluate learner performance (question/answer and practice sessions).
- Ask learners to apply information or skills to past experiences.
- Ask open-ended questions.

Enhancing Retention and Transfer of Learning. This event is the one most likely to be left out of the learning experience. However, it is critical to the learner applying the newly learned information in a variety of situations. Strategies that can be used to enhance retention and transfer of learning are:

- Provide opportunities for the learner to rehearse the application of learning, such as a labor rehearsal.
- Provide novel situations in which learners must adapt newly learned skills to the situation.
- Provide spaced reviews of information with a short interval between reviews. For example, each class should start out with a review of what was learned the previous week.
- Provide summary materials in the form of handouts.
- Have learners speculate about how the new learning could have changed past experiences and its meaning for future experiences.

While many strategies for promoting learning have been identified in this section, many others exist. The teacher is encouraged to think of other ways to promote learning in each of the instructional events in the learning process.

Cultural Differences

Teachers working with different cultural groups must consider the group's cultural beliefs, expectations, and preferences in planning class activities. For childbirth education to be effective the teacher must know the cultural meaning of pregnancy and birth for the target group she wishes to serve and also their perspective on birth. Thornton-Williams lists the following considerations that the childbirth educator should take into account when working with different cultural groups:[25]

- Is the primary orientation of the culture toward a scientific model or social model of birth?
- Is the target population large enough to group classes by ethnicity and/or language?
- Is there a cultural advisor available to the childbirth educator to familiarize her with the group's cultural perspective on pregnancy and birth?
- How does the particular group define pregnancy and birth, as a normal life cycle event or as an illness?
- What proscriptions surround pregnancy, childbirth, and the postpartum period (foods, activities, behaviors and the like)?
- What aspects of pregnancy and birth can be freely discussed with cultural comfort?
- What types of visual aids are culturally acceptable and culturally useful?
- Who is expected to provide support and assistance to the women during pregnancy, childbirth, and the postpartum period?
- What teaching strategies are culturally appropriate?
- What coping techniques for childbirth are culturally acceptable and useful?
- Is the target population an immigrant or refugee group? How does that status affect their health care needs?
- What is the target group's exposure to western culture, especially to western health care?

IMPLICATIONS FOR RESEARCH

Little research has been done in the area of teaching effectiveness in childbirth education. Thus, the research questions that can be generated in this area are endless. The following are just some examples of questions that could be asked:

- What are the characteristics of the childbirth educator who is seen as a ''master teacher?''
- What is the most effective way for the childbirth educator to improve her effectiveness in the classroom?
- When are the most common teaching strategies used by childbirth educators in classes?
- How do childbirth educators structure their classes in order to meet the different needs and learning styles of learners?

SUMMARY

Teaching is a skill that requires thorough knowledge of the subject, the ability to present the information clearly, and the art of establishing a positive emotional climate in the classroom. The role of the teacher in the classroom varies depending on the situation and the learners. Approaching the activity of teaching using the framework discussed in the ''Process of Teaching'' and ''Implementing the Teaching Plan'' sections will increase the teacher's ability to communicate ''the message'' to learners. Teachers will need to use various teaching strategies in order to meet the needs and learning styles of the learners in the classroom.

References

1. Bevis, E. *Curriculum Building in Nursing,* 3rd ed. St. Louis: C. V. Mosby, 1982.
2. Bonner, J. Systematic lesson design for adult learners. *Journal of Instructional Development* 6:34, Fall 1982.
3. Craig, R. *Training and Development Handbook,* 2nd ed. New York: McGraw-Hill Book Company, 1976.
4. Dubin, R. and Taveggia, T. *The Teaching-Learning Paradox*. Eugene, OR: Center for Advanced Study of Educational Administration, University of Oregon, 1968.
5. Gagné, R. M. *The Conditions of Learning and Theory of Instruction*. 4th ed. New York: Holt, Rinehart and Winston, 1985.
6. Guinee, K. *Teaching and Learning in Nursing*. New York, Macmillan Publishing Co., Inc., 1978.
7. Jarvis, P. *Adult and Continuing Education Theory and Practice*. New York: Nichols Publishing Co., 1983, p. 112.
8. King, V., and Gerwig, N. *Humanizing Nursing Education*. Wakefield, MA: Nursing Resources, 1981.
9. Knowles, M. *The Modern Practice of Adult Education*. Chicago: Association Press, 1980.
10. Libresco, M. Creative Teaching: Beyond Lecture and Demonstration. *Expanding Horizons in Childbirth Education,* Vol. 1. Washington, DC: American Society for Psychoprophylaxis in Obstetrics, 1983.
11. Lowman, J. *Mastering The Techniques of Teaching*. San Francisco: Jossey-Bass, 1984.
12. Lovell, R. *Adult Learning*. New York: John Wiley & Sons, 1980, p. 29.
13. Mardment, R., and Bronstein, R. *Simulation Games: Design and Implementation*. Columbus, OH: Charles E. Merrill Publishing Co., 1973, p. 27.
14. Mager, R. *Preparing Instructional Objectives,* 2nd ed. Belmont, CA: Pitman Learning, Inc., 1984.
15. Marriner, A. *The Nursing Process: A Scientific Approach*. St. Louis, C. V. Mosby, 1983.
16. Narrow, B. *Patient Teaching in Nursing Practice: A Patient and Family-Centered Approach*. New York: John Wiley & Sons, 1979.
17. Newstrom, J. *Games Trainers Play*. New York: McGraw-Hill, 1980.
18. O'Connor, A. *Nursing Staff Development and Continuing Education*. Boston: Little, Brown and Company, 1986.
19. Oddi, L. The lecture: An update on research. *Adult Education Quarterly* 33:222, 1983.
20. Ostmoe, P. Learning style preferences and selection of learning strategies: Consideration and implications for nurse educators. *Journal of Nursing Education* 23:27, January 1984.
21. Pfeiffer, J., and Jones, J. *A Handbook of Structured Experiences for Human Relations Training*. La Jolla, CA: University Associates, 1979.
22. Redman, B. *The Process of Patient Teaching in Nursing*. St. Louis: C. V. Mosby Company, 1980.
23. Silvernail, D. *Teaching Styles as Related to Student Achievement*. Washington, DC: National Education Association, 1979, 81–84.
24. Snyder, R., and Ylmer, C. *Guide to Teaching Techniques for Adult Classes*. Englewood Cliffs, NJ: Prentice-Hall Inc., 1972, p. 23.
25. Thornton-Williams, S. Cultural considerations for childbirth education: Outreach efforts for ethnic Chinese and Mien refugees from Southeast Asia. *NAACOG Update Series,* Vol. 5. Princeton, NJ: Continuing Professional Center, Inc., 1987.
26. Trow, W., Zander, A., Morse, W., and Jenkins, D. Psychology of group behavior: The class as a group. *Journal of Educational Psychology* 41:322, 1950.
27. Zahn, J. Differences between adults and youth affecting learning. *Adult Education* 17:75, 1967.

Beginning Quote

Epstein, J. *Masters: Portraits of Great Teachers*. New York: Basic Books, 1981.

Boxed Quotes

1. O'Connor, A. *Nursing Staff Development and Continuing Education*. Boston: Little, Brown and Company, 1986, p. 158.
2. Hyman, R. *Ways of Teaching*. Philadelphia: J. B. Lippincott, 1974.
3. Boswell, J. *The Life of Samuel Johnson,* Oxford edition, Vol. 1. London: Henry Frowde, 1904.

chapter 27

THE CONTENT

FRANCINE H. NICHOLS

Order and simplification are the first steps toward the mastery of a subject . . .

Thomas Mann

Formal childbirth education emerged in the early 1900's as a result of two separate forces with different missions. In 1908, the American Red Cross started classes to meet *public health needs* and to improve the health of women and children. The Maternity Center Association in New York started childbirth education classes in 1919 for similar reasons. Other early childbirth education classes developed in order to meet the *pain reduction needs* of women during childbirth. The contributions of Nikolayev, Dick-Read, and Lamaze in this area form the foundation of most prepared childbirth classes today. Today, classes focus on increasing the ability of the woman to *cope effectively* with childbirth through active participation and increased decision-making during childbirth as well as the use of pain management strategies.

The content of childbirth education has been handed down verbally from generation to generation, from woman to woman, and from childbirth educator to childbirth educator. Throughout the years, this material has been primarily based on the intuitive and empirical experiences of childbirth educators and other individuals and is consistent with a phenomenon that Kirchhoff[48] has described as the "flow of practice into the literature rather than from the literature." Thus, the scientific basis of the content of childbirth education classes has been almost exclusively developed from practice. This useful but unsystematic approach has limited the development of a scientific knowledge base for the practice of childbirth education. A scientific body of knowledge developed from research findings should guide the practice of childbirth education and thus the selection and presentation of the material presented in childbirth education classes.

More recently, increased research in childbirth education, a rapidly expanding body of childbirth-related literature, and increased attention to the importance of childbirth education have done much to promote the development of a scientific basis for childbirth education. However, there is still much to be accomplished. Childbirth educators have a wealth of experiential knowledge about childbirth and parenting and what should be taught in childbirth education classes. This knowledge needs to be documented and verified in a systematic manner through research and developed into a scientific knowledge base for practice.

The childbirth-related content for childbirth education classes and the educational principles on which the classes are based are derived from the literature of many disciplines. Therefore, the task of delineating the type of subject matter, the extent of coverage, the order of presentation, the purpose of teaching the subject matter, and the type of student to be taught is often complex and bewildering. These are the subjects that are addressed in this chapter.

REVIEW OF THE LITERATURE

Historical Overview

Childbirth education classes in the United States grew because expectant parents wanted an active role in "giving birth" and to use medical intervention only if needed. However, individual parents were not able to successfully change the practice of obstetrics. Even when they sought help through the legal system, their attempts to bring about change were often futile.

Thus, groups of parents who wanted to be more active participants in the birth process began to form with the goal of influencing and changing maternity care services. Informal groups led to the development of formal organizations for parents and health professionals, such as the American Society for Psychoprophylaxis in Obstetrics (ASPO/Lamaze) and the International Childbirth Education Association (ICEA). As consumer demands increased, maternity care was advocated, and childbirth education was increasingly seen as an integral part of preparation for childbirth. Today, parents have the opportunity to attend numerous types of educational programs in preparation for childbirth, in a variety of settings—private classes and classes sponsored by community agencies or birthing agencies.

In 1961, the first book on the specific content of prepared childbirth classes, *A Practical Training Course for the Psychoprophylactic Method of Childbirth,* developed by Bing and colleagues, was published.[13] Auerbach's classic book, *Parents Learn Through Discussion: Principles and Practices of Parent Group Education,* published in 1968, provided a comprehensive discussion of the philosophy, goals, and organization of parent education classes.[6] Recently, there has been a proliferation of books and articles related to the content of childbirth and parent education classes.

The childbirth and parent education programs offered today are primarily structured from the perspective of what childbirth educators or other health providers believe that expectant couples need to know.[8,44,49] However, both Koldjeski[49] and Aukamp[8] found discrepancies between what parents thought was important to know and what health professionals considered important for them to know. Koldjeski reported that health professionals emphasized the physical aspects of childbirth while expectant parents' concerns were primarily about the emotional aspects of childbirth—fears and anxieties about pregnancy, labor, and birth. One possible reason for this, according to Imle,[44] is that the ". . . physical aspects are emphasized by caregivers who possess a known medical paradigm, but the nursing paradigm—the human responses to the condition of childbearing—is largely undeveloped." Aukamp emphasized the importance of validating with expectant parents what they needed to know. Articles that present the subject matter that expectant parents believe they need to know are virtually nonexistent in the literature. However, many authors have provided information on professionals' perspectives on the prenatal teaching and counseling needs, learning interests and concerns of expectant parents.

Learning Needs

Pregnancy and Childbirth

The interests and concerns of expectant parents change during the various stages of pregnancy and they seek different kinds of information at different times. During the first trimester of the pregnancy, their primary concerns are about the physical and emotional changes of pregnancy as well as changes in the couple's or family's relationships. During mid-pregnancy, the interests of expectant parents focus on the developing fetus, the characteristics and needs of infants, and the physical and emotional changes of the second trimester of pregnancy. During the third trimester, expectant parents are concerned about labor and birth: What will it be like? Will the woman be able to cope with childbirth? What is the expectant father's role in childbirth? The learning needs of expectant parents for pregnancy and childbirth are summarized in Table 27–1.

Parenting

As expectant parents develop confidence in their ability to cope with the process of childbirth, they are able to devote increased attention to the tasks of parenthood and the needs of the expected infant. This information can be presented in late pregnancy during childbirth education classes and continued throughout the parenting period. The second trimester of pregnancy may also be a good time to present parenting information. This is the time when the pregnancy seems real and yet expectant parents are not highly concerned about the forthcoming childbirth experience. Thus they can more easily focus their attention on learning about the newborn. The goals of parent education are to help parents become familiar with infant characteristics, behavior, growth, and development, and parent-infant interaction; to assist parents to recognize some of the crisis points at different stages in the typical family cycle; to clarify parents' own roles and those of their children within the family and community; and to increase parents' understanding of typical situations and the choices that are available.[6] The early parenting period is often a stressful time and the learning needs and concerns of new parents are well documented in the literature (Table 27–2).

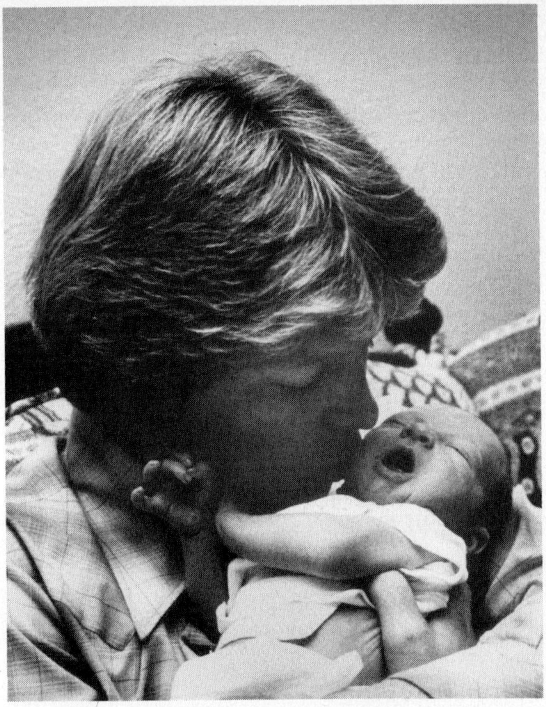

New fathers have unique learning needs. For example, prior to the birth of the infant they usually visualize themselves playing with an older child, sometimes even a teenager. They may need support and guidance in learning how to interact with a newborn. (Photograph by Rodger Ewy, Educational Graphic Aids, Inc.)

Types of Childbirth and Parent Education Classes

Classes that prepare expectant parents for birth are only one component of a comprehensive childbirth and parent education program. Expectant parents and other family members have many and varied learning needs, and different types of childbirth and parent education classes are required to

The goals of parent education are to help parents become familiar with infant characteristics, to understand infant behaviors and growth and development, to learn infant caretaking skills, and to enhance parent-infant interaction. (Courtesy of Janice Riordan.)

meet those needs. In addition to prepared childbirth classes, childbirth educators can offer a wide variety of other types of classes for expectant parents and other family members.

EARLY PREGNANCY CLASSES. These classes are offered during the first three months of pregnancy and provide information about fetal development, physical and emotional changes of pregnancy, human sexuality, the nutritional needs of the mother and fetus, danger signs, drugs and self-medication, and hazards in the environment and workplace. The classes focus on helping women to make lifestyle changes that will promote their health and the health of their unborn baby.[14,15]

MID-PREGNANCY CLASSES. These classes are offered during the second trimester of pregnancy and include subject matter related to the physical and emotional changes of the second trimester, common remedies to relieve maternal discomfort related to the growing fetus, health maintenance, infant feeding, and preparation for the baby.[14,63]

PARENTING CLASSES. These classes may be structured for expectant parents or for parents with newborns. Information that is typically presented in these classes is adjustment to parenthood, coping skills for new parents, infant growth and development, the basics of caring for the newborn, and consumer information that includes selecting and buying baby furniture and toys as well as safety considerations.[6,30,62]

SIBLING PREPARATION CLASSES. These classes focus on preparing siblings for the birth of the new baby. They include a discussion of how the sibling may feel about the new baby and the role of the sibling as a "big brother or sister." The classes also provide basic information about pregnancy, childbirth, and the characteristics and behavior of newborns. A tour of the birthing agency is often included.[27,50,82]

GRANDPARENTING CLASSES. In these classes, current birth practices are discussed and future grandparents learn about childbirth and the newborn. The discussion also focuses on the changing role of grandparents and grandparents' concerns and anxieties about relationships with the expectant parents and grandchildren.[41,47,50,68]

REFRESHER CLASSES. These classes are for expectant parents who have recently attended prepared childbirth classes. Practice of relaxation and paced breathing techniques and other coping skills for childbirth are included. Discussions focus on incorporating the new baby into the family and preparation of siblings. These classes are designed to meet the special needs and concerns of repeat parents.[45,60,71]

CESAREAN BIRTH CLASSES. These classes prepare expectant parents for a cesarean birth. Information about procedures, choices during the birth, coping skills for birth, and the postpartum period and physical recovery is discussed.[33]

VBAC (VAGINAL BIRTH AFTER CESAREAN BIRTH) CLASSES. These classes are designed for women who have had a previous cesarean birth and who want a vaginal birth. They include what to expect, a discussion of feelings and concerns about

TABLE 27–1. LEARNING NEEDS OF EXPECTANT PARENTS: PREGNANCY AND CHILDBIRTH*

FIRST TRIMESTER	SECOND TRIMESTER	THIRD TRIMESTER
• Physical changes of pregnancy[6,19,23,63] • Emotional changes of pregnancy[6,19,63] • Sexuality[63] Changing relationships Sexual concerns • Minor discomforts of pregnancy[23] Frequent urination Nausea Cramps Vaginal discharge Fatigue • Danger signs[19,23,63] Vaginal bleeding Persistent vomiting • Nutrition[19,23,63] • General hygiene[23] Rest and sleep Exercise • Use of drugs[86] Smoking Alcohol OTC drugs Prescription drugs • Fetal development[23] • Financial considerations[23] • How to use the health care system[19] • Resources for pregnancy and childbirth[19,63] • Myths about pregnancy and childbirth[43]	• Physical changes of second trimester[6,19,23,63] • Emotional changes of second trimester[6,63] • Sexuality[5] Changing needs Sexual concerns • Minor discomforts of pregnancy[19,23,63] Backache Varicose veins Braxton-Hicks' contractions Leg cramps Vaginal discharge Constipation Round ligament pain • Danger signs[23,63] Vaginal bleeding Abdominal pain Edema of face, hands, feet Severe headache Visual disturbances Rupture of membranes • Nutrition[19,23,63] • General hygiene[19,23] Rest and sleep Exercise • Use of drugs[86] Smoking Alcohol OTC drugs Prescription drugs • Fetal growth[23,63] • Preparation for newborn[5,63] Feeding methods Physical arrangements Selection of pediatrician Infant care	• Physical changes of third trimester and postpartum period[5,6,17,19,22,23,28,63,88] • Emotional changes of third trimester and postpartum period[5,6,17,19,22,28,63,88] • Sexuality[5,19,23,88] Changing needs Sexual expression (Different methods) Sexual concerns Problem solving • Minor discomforts of pregnancy[5,19,23,88] Frequent urination Backache Dyspnea Varicose veins Braxton Hicks contractions Leg cramps Vaginal discharge Constipation Round ligament pain Fatigue • Danger signs[5,19,23,88] Vaginal bleeding Abdominal pain Edema of face, hands, feet Severe headache Visual disturbances Rupture of membranes (prior to 38 weeks) • Nutrition[5,22,23,88] • General hygiene[5,19,23,88] Rest and sleep Exercise • Use of drugs[5,86,88] Smoking Alcohol OTC drugs Prescription drugs • Fetal growth[5,19,23,63] • Preparation for breastfeeding[5,22,23,88] • Support systems[5,10] • Preparation for childbirth[5,22,23,57,63] Common fears and anxieties Father involvement in childbirth The issue of choice Anatomy and physiology of childbirth Comfort measures Pain management strategies Variations in childbirth Hospital routines Obstetrical interventions Special needs of multiparas

TABLE 27–1. LEARNING NEEDS OF EXPECTANT PARENTS: PREGNANCY AND CHILDBIRTH*
Continued

- Parenting[5,23,88]
  - Life style changes
  - Role changes
  - Role conflict[28,56,80]
  - Balancing family demands[34]
  - Maternal role acquisition[61]
  - Maternal development tasks[61]
- Preparation for newborn[5,19,22,23,63,88] (see Table 27–2)
- Family planning[19,22,23]

*Adapted from Roberts, J. Prenatal teaching guide. *JOGN Nursing* 5:18, 1976. Support for these learning needs by other authors is cited in the table. While there is strong research support for some of these learning needs, others are based on health care professionals' beliefs of what expectant parents need to know. The most appropriate time for the introduction of these topic areas in childbirth education classes is as yet undetermined from a scientific perspective. There is a need for the systematic documentation of the learning needs of expectant parents and the best time during pregnancy to discuss them from the parents' perspective as well as from that of health professionals.

childbirth, and emphasis on prepared childbirth techniques.

CESAREAN PREVENTION CLASSES. Preventing cesarean births is the focus of these classes. Expectant parents learn ways to decrease their chances of having a cesarean, such as using a physiological approach (use of body's natural resources—positioning, ambulation, and the like) to childbirth, and avoiding the use of routine interventions during childbirth.

BREAST-FEEDING CLASSES. These classes provide education and support for the women who plan to breastfeed or are breastfeeding. A major focus of most classes is on problem-solving and practical information and tips that can promote a successful breastfeeding experience.

TABLE 27–2. LEARNING NEEDS OF EXPECTANT PARENTS: PARENTING*

- Parent-infant interaction and attachment[5,22,34,81]
- Infant behavior[17,61,81]
- Infant growth and development[18,40]
- Infant care-taking skills[17,18,22,40,44,81]
- Infant feeding[19,34,81]
- Infant needs[22,28,34]
- Infant health[40,81,84]
- Infant safety[78]
- Circumcision[84]
- Role changes[44,61]
- Parenting care-taking roles[42]
- Resources for new parents[62,84]

*These learning needs were identified from the literature on the interests, learning needs, and concerns of new parents. While some of them are supported by research, others are based on health care professionals' beliefs of what parents need to know. There is a need for the systematic documentation of the learning needs of new parents from their perspective as well as from that of health professionals. The extent to which these topic areas should be included in childbirth education classes is as yet undetermined.

PREPARATION FOR TWINS CLASSES. These classes are designed to meet the special needs of expectant parents who are expecting multiple births. Information includes a discussion of how to prevent preterm labor and helpful information on caring for more than one baby.[46]

PREGNANCY AND POSTPARTUM EXERCISE CLASSES. These classes focus on a physical fitness program specially designed for the pregnant or postpartum woman.

FIRST AID CLASSES. Called ''A Sigh of Relief'' classes by one hospital, these classes are for parents and others who work with children. They include information on safety, first aid, and cardiopulmonary resuscitation (CPR).[38]

CLASSES FOR WORKING PARENTS. These classes include information on balancing the demands of parenthood, family, and career. Specific strategies for coping are discussed. Choosing appropriate day care for the new baby is also examined.[16,66]

ADOLESCENT PREGNANCY CLASSES. These childbirth classes are specially designed to prepare adolescents for coping with childbirth. In addition to the usual childbirth preparation techniques, they include a discussion of options, future goals, and the impact of a new baby on the lifestyle of the teen.

Classes to prepare siblings for the new baby have become an important part of a comprehensive childbirth and parent education program. Some childbirth educators offer two types of sibling classes: one class specifically developed for young children, 3 years and below, and another designed for older children. (Photograph by Francine H. Nichols. Courtesy of Equicor Health Plan, Inc., Wichita, KS.)

ADOPTIVE PARENT CLASSES. These classes are designed for adoptive parents. They include information on parenthood, lifestyle changes, infant characteristics, infant illness, and family coping strategies.[53,72]

CHILDBIRTH CLASSES FOR HANDICAPPED INDIVIDUALS. These classes are developed to meet the needs of a specific population such as blind or deaf individuals and prepare them for the birth experience. Classes are adapted to the special learning needs of these expectant parents.[9]

PRECONCEPTUAL COUNSELING CLASSES. These classes are for individuals who are considering becoming pregnant and starting a family. Discussions center on issues related to pregnancy, childbirth, and being a parent.

Developing the Curriculum for Childbirth Education Classes

Childbirth education has been generally accepted as a worthwhile endeavor in preparing expectant parents for the childbirth experience. However, the content of childbirth education classes varies widely and at times the appropriateness of the selection of particular subject matter is questionable. In fact, some teachers appear to assume that class members need only to have a feast of relevant information about childbirth and related topics laid out for them for childbirth education to be effective. This approach has produced uneven, unpredictable, unclear, and often doubtful results. In order to be most effective, it is necessary that childbirth education classes have a *clear purpose, specific objectives, and careful selection and sequencing of subject matter.*

Determining the Purpose

The childbirth educator should first answer this question: What is the overall purpose of the specific childbirth education classes? Or, stated another way, What is it that you want expectant parents to achieve as a result of attending prepared childbirth classes? You can identify an overall purpose for classes based on your expert judgment as a childbirth educator. However, the overall purpose of the classes should be very specific. A goal of assisting expectant parents to have a positive childbirth experience is inadequate by itself. You also need to be explicit on how it is that they can achieve that end. Another very helpful way to determine a clear purpose is to structure your classes using a theory as a framework. There are a number of theories* that are appropriate frameworks for childbirth education classes. A theory describes, explains, and predicts phenomena and provides the potential to control the outcomes of interventions such as childbirth education classes. A theory also provides a sense of understanding of a phenomenon and is useful in simplifying complex and confusing phenomena.[75] Thus the childbirth educator gains insight into what is happening and can be more flexible in her teaching. A theory also provides direction for the selection of objectives and subject matter for the classes. There is no one best theory, and different theories may work better for different client populations. The advantages of using a theory as a framework for childbirth education classes are shown in Table 27–3.

A summary of theories that can be used as a framework for childbirth education classes is included here. The Competence Model was specifically developed for prepared childbirth classes. The other theories can be easily applied to childbirth education classes. The reader will need to refer to the original source for a complete description of the theory.

Competence Model. Nichols[65] proposed a competence model, adapted from Adler's work, as a framework for prepared childbirth classes. The goal of this model is to increase the competence of the individual in coping with childbirth. Three domains of content are specified in this approach: skills such as relaxation and breathing techniques and expulsion techniques that promote *psychomotor competence;* information and activities that increase the individual's self-confidence and ability to make appropriate responses to stressful situations and thus increase *interpersonal competence* (affective competence); and information and activities that assist the individual to promote *cognitive competence,* the ability to obtain, classify, and interpret information. For adults equal emphasis is placed on all three components. Because teenagers' cognitive developmental stage restricts their ability to translate the information learned to the actual situation of childbirth, for these students less emphasis is placed on cognitive competence and more is placed on developing psychomotor competence for childbirth. A fourth component of the model, *environment,* is viewed as an important influence on the ability of the woman to learn competency strategies during classes and to be able to cope in a competent manner during childbirth.

*In this chapter the terms theory, theoretical framework, and model are used interchangeably; however, these terms are viewed as having different meanings by some theorists.

TABLE 27–3. ADVANTAGES OF USING A THEORY AS A FRAMEWORK FOR CHILDBIRTH EDUCATION CLASSES

CHILDBIRTH EDUCATOR A (DOES NOT USE A THEORY)	CHILDBIRTH EDUCATOR B (USES A THEORY)
Knows current facts about childbirth education.	Knows current facts about childbirth education *and organizes these facts into a meaningful framework.*
Teaches typical childbirth classes.	Teaches typical childbirth classes, *but adapts this teaching to the specific situation using a theory as a framework for childbirth education classes.*
Gives each individual the facts and skills needed to prepare for childbirth.	Gives each individual the facts and skills needed to *understand and respond to this unique childbirth experience.*
Teaches individuals what to do in usual situations that may be encountered.	Teaches individuals the skills of *observation and decision-making that are relevant to both usual and unexpected situations.*

Adapted from Avant, K., and Walker, L. The practicing nurse and conceptual frameworks. *MCN: American Journal of Maternal/Child Nursing* 9:87, 1984.

Psychoeducational Model. Childbirth education classes can be viewed as a psychoeducational intervention (an intervention that includes both psychological and educational approaches). The goal of this approach is to decrease pain, enhance recovery, and improve psychological well-being and satisfaction with health care. This approach includes three domains of content: *information* about the events, procedures, and sensations that may be experienced as well as self-care activities that can be performed, *skills* that can reduce pain or complications, and *psychosocial support* that can reduce anxieties and enhance coping.[25]

Health Education Model. Childbirth education is one type of health education; thus the Health Education Model can serve as an appropriate framework for childbirth education classes. The goal of this model is to improve class members' current and future health status. This approach involves three domains of content: information related to *prevention* (information that should induce or enable changes in class members' behaviors that ultimately have lower levels of morbidity or mortality risks), information that permits individuals to make an *informed choice,* and information that influences class members to assume more *healthy lifestyles.*[31]

Self-Care Theory. The premise of Orem's Self-Care Theory is that individuals are basically capable of caring for themselves and have a need to do so.[69] Thus, the goal of this theory is to promote or enhance the individual's self-care. Orem identified three systems of self-care: *wholly compensatory, partly compensatory,* and *supportive-educative.* In the wholly compensatory system, the individual has no role in her care, for example, if she is physically or mentally totally incapacitated. The individual who requires some assistance but does participate some in her own care demonstrates the partly compensatory system of care. In the supportive-educative system of care, the individual can perform her own self-care given support, guidance, and information as well as the proper environment. In typical childbirth education classes, content would include information and activities that are *supportive* and *educative* in nature and promote the independence of the individual.

Adaptation Theory. Roy views the individual as having four modes of adaptation: physiologic, self-concept, role performance, and interdependence. The purpose of childbirth education classes using this theory would be to promote the expectant parents' positive response, i.e., adaptation, to the childbirth experience in all four modes. Information and activities in classes would focus on *physiological needs* related to childbirth, and maintenance of psychological integrity (*self-concept* needs), *role* functions and changes, and *interdependence* or relationship needs.[77]

Crisis Theory. The goal for this model is to *prevent* the development of a crisis situation or to *promote resolution* of a crisis situation. According to Aquilera and Messick, three balancing factors are necessary: a *realistic perception of the event, adequate situational support,* and *adequate coping mechanisms.*[4] These balancing factors provide the framework for the selection of subject matter for classes, and information relevant to each factor is included in classes. A comprehensive explanation of the use of crisis theory is included in Chapter 19.

Developing the Objectives

Objectives provide the framework for selecting the content to be taught in classes. They should include statements in the cognitive, affective, and psychomotor domains. Objectives for essential content for childbirth education classes in these domains are shown in Table 27–4. These objectives are consistent with the theories that have been discussed in this chapter.

Objectives for the course that flow from a strong theoretical base provide the most guidance and direction for the childbirth educator in terms of *including* or *delimiting* the content for childbirth education classes.[39] After the childbirth educator has decided on a framework for her classes, general objectives that flow from the theoretical framework can be developed for the course. Next, more specific objectives that flow from the general objectives are written for each class. Finally, very specific objectives that flow from the class objectives are developed for each topic presented in class. Guidelines for writing objectives are presented in Chapter 26.

Selecting and Sequencing Content

The next two major tasks facing the childbirth educator are *selecting* and *sequencing* of subject matter.[73]

TABLE 27–4. OBJECTIVES FOR THE ESSENTIAL CONTENT OF A CHILDBIRTH EDUCATION COURSE

ESSENTIAL CONTENT: COGNITIVE DOMAIN

By the end of the course class members will be able to:

1. Describe the common biological, psychological, and social responses to pregnancy, childbirth, and postpartum processes as well as associated comfort measures.
2. Define vocabulary terms useful in facilitating communication with health care providers or in reading literature on childbearing.
3. Use objective information to develop a plan that can serve as a basis for active participation in health care decisions, including commonly encountered interventions.
4. Plan assertive strategies for negotiating support from family members and from health care providers.

ESSENTIAL CONTENT: AFFECTIVE DOMAIN

By the end of the course class members will be able to:

1. View pregnancy and birth as a normal maturational process that includes stressors but also the potential for growth.
2. View themselves as central figures in their own health care and become actively involved in decisions concerning their care.
3. Use values clarification strategies to facilitate making realistic but flexible plans and choices.

ESSENTIAL CONTENT: PSYCHOMOTOR DOMAIN

By the end of the course class members will be able to:

1. Demonstrate physical exercises designed to promote comfort in pregnancy, prepare the body for birth, and promote postpartum recovery.
2. Demonstrate relaxation techniques designed to minimize tension and to promote the body's ability to function at maximum efficiency.
3. Demonstrate techniques using breathing and attention focusing for increasing relaxation.
4. Demonstrate activities that enhance relaxation and comfort in labor, such as positioning, mobility, massages, application of heat or cold, and water therapy.
5. Demonstrate expulsion techniques that support the physiological process of second stage labor.

Selecting Content Areas: What Are the Topics? There are three *sources* of determining appropriate material to be taught in classes. The expertise of the childbirth educator, which stems from her knowledge and experience, is the most frequent source that is used. The expectant parents themselves, through a needs assessment, provide a second source of information. A third source is the identification of class content from a review of the literature, the approach that was used in this chapter to identify learning needs of expectant parents.

There are two primary *approaches* that can be used in selecting subject matter for classes: using a theory as a guide for selection as well as using one's expert judgment as a childbirth educator and rationale from the literature, and selection using one's expert judgment as a childbirth educator and rationale from the literature alone. The advantage of using a theory is that it helps make the difficult decision of what to include or not include in the classes.

Perhaps the easiest way to start the selection of class content is to make a tentative list of all topics that could be included in the childbirth education course. Review the conceptual framework* for childbirth education classes (Figure I–1) that is presented in the introduction to this book (p. 3) and consider the factors presented there and their implications for your unique situation. This will assist you to identify additional subject matter that should be considered for inclusion in classes. From this list the childbirth educator can sort material into two categories: essential and nonessential in light of how important it is for couples to know this information.

The theory you have selected as a framework for the course, the overall objectives for the course, and the more precise class objectives will guide you in deciding what to teach. For example, in

*A conceptual framework for curriculum is like a map that identifies all factors that should be considered when developing, evaluating, or revising educational programs.

crisis theory, an accurate perception of the event is important in preventing or resolving a crisis. This means that couples should have realistic information about events that may occur, such as cesarean birth.

Next, you need to rank the information in terms of how interesting or important you believe it is to expectant parents. It is highly probable that some of the nonessential information you identified may rank very high in terms of importance or interest to expectant parents. As Aukamp pointed out, it is important to verify what you believe are important learning needs with the expectant parents in your classes.[7] All essential information should be included in the classes. However, in terms of balance it is important to include information of high interest and importance to couples, even though you may consider it nonessential. Your final selection of content will depend on your expert judgment as a childbirth educator about what is the *most important* for couples to know in preparation for childbirth, as well as *how interesting and important* specific topics are to expectant parents. A content outline for Lamaze prepared childbirth classes is shown in Table 27–5.

Developing Content Objectives: How Much Do I Want Them To Know? The task here is to decide what type of information you want expectant parents to know. Do you want them to be able to *define* a concept correctly—for example, amniotomy? Or do you want them to be able to *explain* a particular phenomenon, such as transition or second stage labor? Perhaps you want them to *demonstrate* their ability to relax. Whatever it is you want them to be able to do should be clearly stated. This can be a taxing activity that often involves numerous revisions as the overall course develops. This activity is one that requires a strong knowledge base of childbirth education and related areas and maximum creativity.

Realistic Constraints: How Much Can I Include in the Amount of Time I Have? The major constraint on any course is the amount of time allotted for its completion. The first step is to list all class meetings and the amount of time in each session. Each topic is evaluated in terms of the amount of time needed and then tentative topics with teaching strategies are placed in each class session. It is important to schedule time for review and summary in each class period, and allow "catch-up" time in later classes.

One of the biggest problems for the novice childbirth educator is the scheduling of too much subject matter into each class session. In this situation, the childbirth educator will often end up covering everything superficially and nothing in the depth required for learning specific skills or information. A realistic appraisal of what is important for the learner to know using the objectives and theoretical framework of the course is the best approach to this problem. Content may need to be deleted, objectives may need to be refined, or the time frame of the childbirth education classes may need to be expanded.

Sequencing. Posner and Strike[73] point out that educational debates have raged for years on the ordering or sequencing of information. No satisfactory answer has emerged, and it is doubtful that an adequate answer will surface in the near future. In general, content should be *logically arranged with clear distinctions between major and minor points*. Also, topics should flow easily from one to another. Some important guidelines that have been identified for sequencing class content for childbirth education classes are:[5]

- Move from basic to complex.
- Move from known facts to new facts.
- Move from the beginning of a process to its conclusion.
- Move from a chronological point: past to present to future.
- Move from concrete content to abstract levels of understanding, reasoning, and problem solving.
- Group like content.
- Plan content so that each class begins with subject matter that can reduce anxiety and ends with topics that will not produce anxiety.

In skills training, such as relaxation and breathing techniques, sequencing is of utmost importance

TABLE 27–5. CONTENT OUTLINE FOR LAMAZE PREPARED CHILDBIRTH CLASSES

A. Theory of the Lamaze method

B. Anatomy and Physiology as They Relate to:
- Pregnancy
- Labor and birth
- The postpartum period (the mother)
- The newborn

C. Emotional Responses of Expectant Parents to:
- Pregnancy experience
- Childbirth experience
- Early parenting experience (include role changes)

D. Physical Conditioning for Childbirth
- Prenatal exercises
- Posture/body mechanics
- Guidelines for exercises

E. Stages and Phases of Labor
- Overview
- First stage
  - Latent phase
  - Active phase
  - Transition phase
- Second stage
- Third stage
- Woman's physical responses
- Woman's emotional responses
- Coach's role

F. Nonpharmacological Analgesia
- Progressive relaxation
- Touch relaxation
- Imagery
- Focusing techniques
- Effleurage
- Massage
- Comfort measures (back rub, positioning, and the like)
- Support (role of the coach, birthing agency staff, and physician or midwife)

G. Pharmacological Analgesia and Anesthesia
- Types used (describe and explain)
- How and when administered
- Effects on expectant mother and baby

H. Breathing Techniques
- Respiratory theory and principles
- Respiratory techniques
  - Slow paced
  - Modified paced
  - Patterned paced
- Second stage expulsion
  - Physiologic technique
  - Modified valsalval technique

I. Birthing Process
- Vaginal birth
- Cesarean birth
  - Indications
  - Procedures
  - Use of prepared childbirth techniques
  - Coach's role
- Precipitous birth

J. Variations in Labor and Birth
- Back labor
- Amniotomy
- Fetal monitoring
  - External
  - Internal
- Induction and augmentation
- Forceps and vacuum extraction
- Episiotomy (use of perineal massage)

K. Birthing Agency Procedures
- Admission
- Labor and birth
- Postpartum care (mother and baby)
- Parent-infant interaction

L. Provision for Other Content
- Nutrition
- Infant feeding (breast or bottle)
- Signs of premature labor (prevention of prematurity)
- Grieving and loss in unexpected outcomes
- Postpartum "blues"
- Family planning (contraception)

M. Consumer Advocacy (integrated throughout classes)
- Is a balanced viewpoint (positive and negative aspects) of procedures presented?
  - Regarding pregnancy
  - Regarding childbirth
  - Regarding parenting
- Are family-centered options presented?
- Are alternatives to "standard" or "routine" practices that are inconsistent with the philosophy of family-centered maternity care and a physiologic approach to childbirth explored?
- Is the development of effective communication skills promoted between:
  - Pregnant woman and her labor partner?
  - Pregnant woman and her obstetrical care provider?
- Are realistic expectations and birth plans promoted?
- Are information and guidelines provided so that expectant parents can make informed decisions?

From Guidelines for Developing a Teaching Plan, *ASPO/Lamaze Teacher Certification Program for Childbirth Educators*. Washington, DC: American Society for Psychoprophylaxis in Obstetrics, 1987.

TABLE 27–6. SAMPLE TEACHING PLAN

OBJECTIVES*

Students will be able to:
1. Discuss the causes of back labor (cognitive).
2. Demonstrate three strategies to decrease pain in back labor (psychomotor).
3. Share with others, during class, their fears and concerns about coping with back labor (affective).

TOPIC OUTLINE	TEACHING STRATEGIES	EVALUATION
I. Variations in Labor		
A. Back labor	Lecture/Discussion	Students can describe three causes of back labor and five symptoms of back labor
1. Definition		
2. Incidence		
3. Causes	Explain causes of back labor using visual aids	
a. Occiput posterior position		
b. Breech presentation		
c. Dilatation of cervix and descent through the birth canal		
4. Symptoms of back labor	Relate symptoms of back labor to causes of back labor	
a. Low back pain		
b. Premature rupture of membranes		
c. Irregular and ineffective contractions		
d. Failure to progress in labor		
e. Premature urge to bear down		
5. Interventions for back labor	Demonstration/return demonstration	Students can demonstrate three strategies that can be used to decrease the pain of back labor
a. Positioning		
b. Relaxation and paced breathing techniques		
c. Massage and counterpressure		
d. Heat and cold therapy		
6. Coping with back labor	Simulation: "What could you do if you had back labor?"	Students can demonstrate the ability to problem-solve and develop a plan to cope with back labor
a. Accurate perception of the event		
b. Use of coping mechanisms		
c. Situational support (coach's role)		
Time: 15 minutes		

*These are *examples* of three types of objectives (cognitive, psychomotor and affective) that could be used for presenting back labor. It is not necessary to have all three types of objectives for each topic; however, all three types of objectives should be evident in each class. The reference(s) for factual information in the teaching plan should be cited. For example, the information for this topic was based on Nichols, F. "Back Labor," *NAACOG Update Series,* Vol. 5. Princeton, NJ: Continuing Education Center, Inc., 1986.

in order for the individual to learn the skill. The cardinal rules in skills training are to move from *simple to complex* and *never introduce a new procedure until the student has mastered the previous one*.[12] Sequencing of skills is discussed in detail in Chapters 7, 8, and 9.

Writing the Teaching Plan

The development of a well-prepared teaching plan is the hallmark of a professional. It should contain general course objectives and specific objectives for each class. The teaching plan can be presented in column format with the categories Content, Teaching Strategy, and Evaluation Method across the top (Table 27–6). An effective way to organize a teaching plan is place it in a large three-ring notebook and use dividers to separate the classes into sections. Another section can be developed for sample copies of handouts, while yet another section can be used for resource material. Organized in this manner the teaching plan is not only an effective teaching tool but can be an excellent marketing tool as well.

IMPLICATIONS FOR PRACTICE

It is clear that while the literature contains information on the learning needs of expectant parents, systematic documentation of these learning needs specific to childbirth education classes is lacking. Childbirth educators need to keep records on the needs of clients, and as these needs change they can evaluate and refine their classes in order to meet the needs of expectant parents. Childbirth educators can also perform a valuable service to other health professionals by sharing information on learning needs of expectant parents through publications and presentations at professional meetings, or through in-service education programs at birthing agencies.

Careful planning is essential to successful childbirth education classes. Using a theory as a framework, well-thought-out objectives and content based on strong scientific rationale will enhance the success of the classes. The development of a teaching plan for classes enables teachers to have immediate access to lesson plans and other materials for class activities, as well as a professional document to use as a marketing tool for their classes when they talk with other health professionals.

The teacher should also plan alternate activities to be used for teaching on those occasions when things go wrong. (For example, the projector light bulb burned out and another was not available.) These alternates are also useful when the planned activity just does not work with this group. When classes do not turn out as planned, possible reasons for this should be explored. It is more likely that the problem is with the approach, i.e., teaching strategy, than with the content that is presented.

In developing a curriculum for childbirth education classes, two issues almost always emerge:

- Why are classes important? and
- How much time should be devoted to practicing psychomotor skills?

Major Issues

Why Should Expectant Parents Attend Childbirth Education Classes? Some expectant parents, and occasionally some health professionals as well, question the need for attendance at formal childbirth education classes, believing that expectant parents can prepare just as well on their own. The literature indicates that class attendance is important in achieving desired goals. Eble states that "coming to class is essential to mastering the content of a . . . course."[29] Although he was talking about a college course, the principle applies equally to childbirth education.

Lowman concludes that is important for people to come to class for the following reasons:[52]

1. Students are introduced to an informed individual's perspective (the teacher), who models the *thinking skills* that they need in order to evaluate what they hear and read.
2. Hearing what the teacher thinks about a particular content area aids the students in *understanding and evaluating* what they hear and read.
3. Attending classes is *motivational* and stimulates the students to complete outside tasks, such as practicing techniques.
4. And, if nothing else, coming to class regularly *reminds* the students that they are enrolled in a course and have tasks to do, such as practicing techniques at home in preparation for birth.

How Much Time Is Needed for Learning Psychomotor Skills? The answer to this question is not simple. However, if one has the goal of enabling expectant parents to perform the activity easily and competently, repetitive practice is needed. Learning psychomotor skills is a four-step process[85] (Table 27–7) that requires ample practice time and feedback in class for students to learn to use the techniques effectively. Thus, in the planning phase the childbirth educator should pay careful attention to integrating practice work into every class session.

Observation of the skill is the first step. The student watches the activity, paying careful attention to the steps involved and the final product.

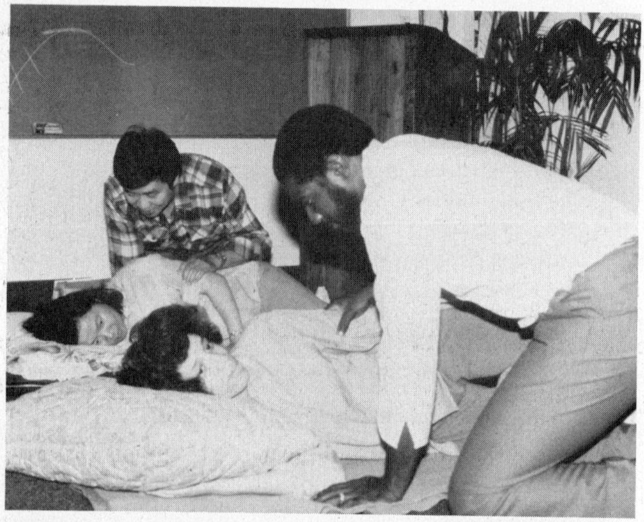

Learning psychomotor skills is a four-step process that requires repetitive practice in class and at home and feedback from the childbirth educator and labor coach for the learner to be able to perform the skills easily, smoothly and with little conscious effort. Thus practice should be integrated into *every* class session. The skill of *relaxation* is the foundation of all prepared childbirth techniques (top left). Consistent and frequent practice of breathing techniques in class (bottom left) and at home (bottom right) is essential for learners in developing and refining the breathing patterns that are most appropriate for them as individuals. (Photographs by Marjorie Pyle, RNC, © Lifecircle, Costa Mesa, CA.)

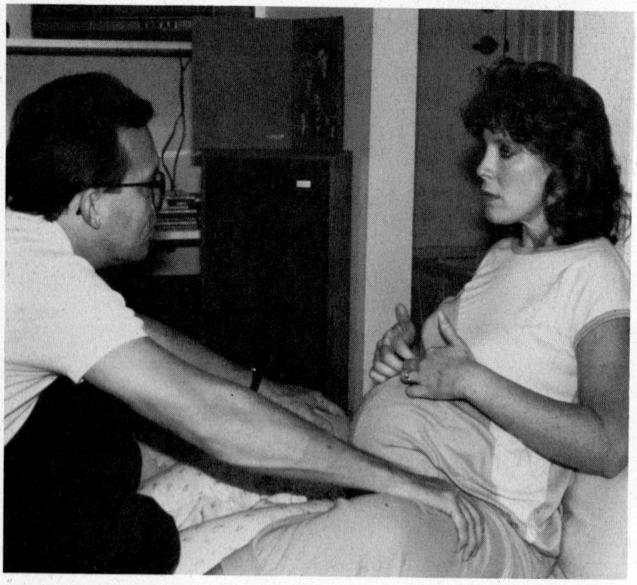

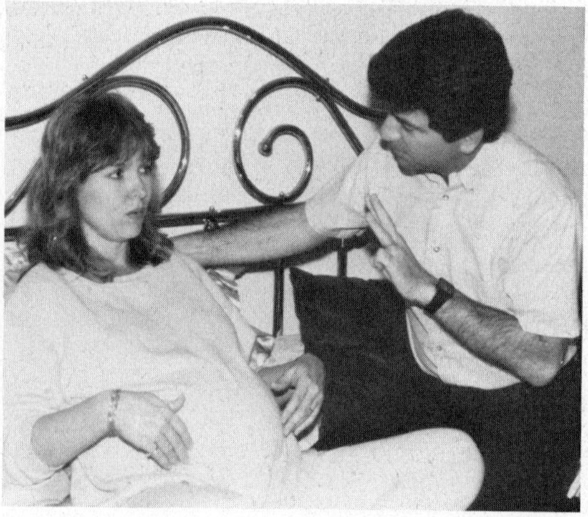

TABLE 27–7. THE PROCESS OF LEARNING PSYCHOMOTOR SKILLS

OBSERVATION
(Individual watches process and pays attention to steps and to finished product.)
↓
IMITATION
(Individual follows directions and carries out steps with conscious awareness. May perform hesitantly.)
↓
PRACTICE
(Individual repeats steps until some or all aspects become habitual, and performs the process smoothly.)
↓
ADAPTATION
(Individual modifies and adapts to suit himself or the situation.)

From Verduin, J., Miller, H., and Greer, C. *Adults Teaching Adults: Principles and Strategies*. San Diego, CA: Learning Concepts, 1977.

> Before launching into course design, think of the complexity of those for whom the course is being planned.
>
> JOSEPH LOWMAN[1]
>
> . . . it should be emphasized again that although thoughtful selection of content and objectives contributes significantly to the course, still, as in warfare and athletics, the value of a battle or game plan depends most on how well it is executed and whether it is flexible when surprises occur.
>
> JOSEPH LOWMAN[1]
>
> There is a tendency . . . to spoon-feed content to learners through highly structured and content-laden offering design. This divests learners of the responsibility for their own learning and impairs their skills in accomplishing learning. Highly structured programming also violates the adult learning principles of involving the learner in the process of learning and drawing on learners' knowledge and experience in developing and conducting educational offerings. Hence, . . . [there should be] an emphasis on selecting teaching-learning processes that will facilitate learners' identification, selection, and sequencing of content to meet their needs.
>
> ANDREA B. O'CONNOR[2]

This step involves learning how to perform each aspect of the skill. The second step is *imitation,* wherein the student follows directions step by step with deliberate awareness. Next, the student *practices* until the skill can be performed easily and smoothly with little conscious effort. This step requires repetitions, with prior imitation of and knowledge of the activity. *Adaptation* is the final category. Only after the first three steps have been mastered can the student use the skill in unique or novel situations. This is the product for which childbirth educators are striving; however, the ''introduction'' of techniques in classes does not allow for the development of the desired product. Using this model for learning psychomotor skills, it is evident that it takes a *minimum of six weeks in classes with adequate feedback* for the pregnant woman to learn the pain management skills of relaxation and paced breathing that will enable her to cope effectively with her contractions during childbirth.

IMPLICATIONS FOR RESEARCH

Problems that need investigation are abundant in the areas of learning needs of expectant parents and curriculum development. Examples of questions that can be asked are:

- What are the learning needs of expectant parents during pregnancy and childbirth, and for parenting?
- How do the learning needs of expectant parents change during the different trimesters of pregnancy?
- How can the childbirth educator most effectively meet the learning needs of expectant parents?
- What is the most effective way for childbirth educators to select the content for childbirth education classes?
- How does basing the class on a specific theory influence class outcomes?
- How does the sequencing of specific content in classes influence the learning and satisfaction of students?
- What is the most effective way of integrating the teaching of psychomotor skills into classes?
- What are the learning needs related to childbirth and new roles of other family members?

Thomas,[83] using the Delphi Technique, identified priorities for prepared childbirth research, many of which are specifically related to the content of childbirth education. This research, which describes areas of agreement and differences, provides further direction for research on the content of childbirth education classes.

SUMMARY

The scientific basis for the content of childbirth education classes has almost exclusively developed from practice. A need exists for systematic documentation through research of the information that is most important for childbirth education classes. Research is also needed on expectant parents' beliefs about what is important to them to know. Most childbirth education programs are primarily structured from the perspective of what childbirth educators or other health professionals think expectant parents need to know. However, it has been pointed out that there are discrepancies between what health professionals believe is important and what expectant parents believe is important. Expectant parents have many and varied learning needs and concerns related to childbirth and parenting. The challenge for the childbirth educator is to choose those topics that are most appropriate for the specific classes that are taught.

In order to be most effective, childbirth education classes need to have a clear purpose, specific objectives, and careful selection and sequencing of subject matter. The use of a theory as a framework for classes is helpful in establishing a clear goal for the classes as well as the development of objectives and the selection of subject matter. Careful sequencing of information enhances the learning of expectant parents while precise sequencing of teaching psychomotor skills is critical to women learning to perform those skills competently. In addition to providing classes for expectant parents, the childbirth educator can play an important role in preparing other family members for childbirth and the new baby by offering a variety of classes structured to meet the unique needs of family members.

References

1. Acevedo, L. My way: Multilingual classes. *Childbirth Educator* 4:14, 1984.

2. Acevedo, L. Teaching Lamaze childbirth to ''non-average'' couples. *Genesis* 4:11, 1982.
3. Adler, P. T. An analysis of the concept of competence in individuals and social systems. *Community Mental Health Journal* 18:34–45, 1982.
4. Aquilera, D., and Messick, J. *Crisis Intervention: Theory and Methodology,* 5th ed. St. Louis: C. V. Mosby, 1986.
5. ASPO/Lamaze. *Faculty Manual for Childbirth Educator Teacher Certification Program*. Washington, DC: The American Society for Psychoprophylaxis in Obstetrics, 1982.
6. Auerbach, A. *Parents Learn through Discussion: Principles and Practices of Parent Group Education*. Malabar, FL: Robert E. Krieger Publishing Co., 1968.
7. Aukamp, V. *Nursing Care Plans for the Childbearing Family.* Norwalk, CN: Appleton-Century-Crofts, 1984.
8. Aukamp, V. *Knowledge Deficit and Anxiety as Nursing Diagnosis in the Third Trimester of Pregnancy: An Exploratory Study to Identify the Defining Characteristics and Contributing Factors*. Unpublished doctoral dissertation. The University of Texas at Austin, 1986.
9. Baranowski, E. Childbirth education classes for expectant deaf parents. *MCN: American Journal of Maternal/Child Nursing* 8:143, 1983.
10. Barnes, F. My way: Prenatal classes as support groups. *Childbirth Educator* 5:39, 1986.
11. Bennett, E. Coping in the puerperium: The reported experience of new mothers. *Journal of Psychosomatic Research* 25:13, 1981.
12. Bernstein, D., and Borkovec, T. *Progressive Relaxation Training: A Manual for the Helping Professions*. Champaign, IL: Research Press, 1973.
13. Bing, E. D. *Six Practical Lessons for an Easier Childbirth*. New York: Grosset and Dunlap, 1967.
14. Bobak, I., and Jensen, M. *Essentials of Maternity Nursing*. St. Louis: C. V. Mosby, 1987.
15. Bretschneider, J., and Minetola, A. Another look at early pregnancy classes. *MCN: American Journal of Maternal/Child Nursing* 8:268, 1983.
16. Bryant, H. Antenatal counseling for women working outside the home. *Birth* 12:227, 1985.
17. Bull, M. Changes in concerns of first-time mothers after one week at home. *JOGN Nursing* 10:391, 1981.
18. Bull, M., and Lawrence, D. Mother's use of knowledge during the first postpartum weeks. *JOGN Nursing* 14:315, 1985.
19. Butnarescu, G., and Tillotson, D. *Maternity Nursing: Theory to Practice*. New York: John Wiley and Sons, 1983.
20. Carter-Jessop, L. Promoting maternal attachment through prenatal intervention. *MCN: American Journal of Maternal/Child Nursing* 6:107, 1981.
21. Celotta, B. New motherhood: A time of crisis? *Birth* 9:21, 1982.
22. Clark, A., and Affonso, D. *Childbearing: A Nursing Perspective*. Philadelphia: F. A. Davis, 1979.
23. Clausen, J., Flook, M., Ford, B., Green, M., and Popiel, E. *Maternity Nursing Today.* New York: McGraw-Hill Book Co., 1976.
24. Delafleur, T. and Payne, J. Role playing in childbirth education classes. *MCN: American Journal of Maternal/Child Nursing* 6:333, 1981.
25. Devine, E., and Cook, T. Clinical and cost-savings effects of psychoeducational interventions with surgical patients: A meta-analysis. *Research in Nursing and Health* 9:89, 1986.
26. Dick-Read, G. *Childbirth Without Fear.* New York: Harper & Row, 1959.
27. Diulio, R. My way: Sibling classes. *Childbirth Educator* 2:43, 1983.
28. Donaldson, N. The postpartum follow-up nurse clinician. *JOGN Nursing* 10:249, 1981.
29. Eble, K. *The Craft of Teaching: A Guide to Mastering the Professor's Art*. San Francisco: Jossey-Bass, 1976.
30. Eden, A. Positive parenting. *Childbirth Educator* 3:22, 1984.
31. Engleman, S., and Forbes, J. Economic aspects of health education. *Social Science Medicine* 22:443, 1986.
32. Ewy, D. *Teaching Strategies: A Practical Guide*. NAACOG Update Series, Vol. 5. Princeton, NJ: Continuing Professional Education Center, Inc., 1986.
33. Fawcett, J., and Burritt, J. An exploratory study of antenatal preparation for cesarean birth. *JOGN Nursing* 14:224, 1985.
34. Gruis, M. Beyond maternity: Postpartum concerns of mothers. *MCN: American Journal of Maternal/Child Nursing* 2:182, 1977.
35. Harrison, M., and Hicks, S. Postpartum concerns of mothers and their sources of help. *JOGN Nursing* 10:361, 1981.
36. Hassid, P. *Textbook for Childbirth Educators*. Philadelphia: J. B. Lippincott, 1984.
37. Hassid, P. My way: Teaching couples to be flexible. *Childbirth Educator* 2:15, 1982.
38. *Healthy Beginnings*. Miami, FL: Baptist Hospital of Miami, 1987.
39. Hiemstra, R. *Lifelong Learning*. Lincoln, NE: Professional Educators Publications, Inc., 1976.
40. Hiser, P. Concerns of multiparas during the second postpartum week. *JOGN Nursing* 16:195, 1987.
41. Horn, M., and Marion, J. Creative grandparenting: Bonding the generations. *JOGN Nursing* 14:233, 1985.
42. Humenick, S., and Bugen, L. Parenting roles: Expectation versus reality. *MCN: American Journal of Maternal/Child Nursing* 12:36, 1987.
43. Huprich, P. Assisting the couple through a Lamaze labor and delivery. *MCN: American Journal of Maternal/Child Nursing* 2:245, 1977.
44. Imle, M. A. Indices to measure concerns of expectant parents in transition to parenthood. (Doctoral Dissertation, University of Arizona). *Dissertation Abstracts International,* 1983.
45. Jimenez, S., Jones, L., and Jungman, R. Prenatal classes for repeat parents: A distinct need. *MCN: American Journal of Maternal/Child Nursing* 4:305, 1979.
46. Jimenez, S., and Jungman, R. Supplemental information for the family with a multiple pregnancy. *MCN: American Journal of Maternal/Child Nursing* 5:320, 1980.
47. Jolles, A. Innovations in Childbirth Classes. *Childbirth Educator* 1:34, 1981.
48. Kirchoff, K. A diffusion survey of coronary precautions. *Nursing Research* 31:196, 1982.
49. Koldjeski, H. D. Concerns of Antepartal Mothers Expressed in Group Teaching Experiences and Implications

for Nursing Practice. *In ANA Clinical Sessions* (American Nurses' Association, San Francisco, 1966). New York: Appleton-Century-Crofts, 1967.
50. Lamp, J. Grandparent and sibling education: A total family concept. *Genesis* 5:9, 1984.
51. Lichtman, R. Postpartum recovery. *Childbirth Educator* 4:17, 1985.
52. Lowman, J. *Mastering the Techniques of Teaching*. San Francisco, CA: Jossey-Bass, 1984.
53. McCaghren, E., and Jackson, M. Maternal adaptation to parenthood: Responses of biological and adoptive mothers. *Genesis* 8:31, December 1986/January 1987.
54. McGraw, R., and Abplanalp, J. Motivation to take childbirth education: Implications for studies of effectiveness. *Birth* 9:179, 1982.
55. McKenzie, C. Comprehensive care during the postpartum period. *Nursing Clinics of North America* 17:23, 1982.
56. Majewski, J. Conflicts, satisfactions, and attitudes during transition to the maternal role. *Nursing Research* 35:10, 1986.
57. Maloney, R. Childbirth education classes: Expectant parents' expectations. *JOGN Nursing* 14:245, 1985.
58. Marquart, R. Expectant fathers: What are their needs? *MCN: American Journal of Maternal/Child Nursing* 1:32, 1976.
59. May, K. The father as observer. *MCN: American Journal of Maternal/Child Nursing* 7:319, 1982.
60. Mercer, R. "She's a multip . . . She knows the ropes." *MCN: American Journal of Maternal/Child Nursing* 4:301, 1979.
61. Mercer, R. The nurse and maternal tasks of early postpartum. *MCN: American Journal of Maternal/Child Nursing* 6:341, 1981.
62. Miller, D., and Baird, S. Helping parents to be parents—A special center. *MCN: American Journal of Maternal/Child Nursing* 2:118, 1978.
63. Moore, M. *Realities in Childbearing*. Philadelphia: W. B. Saunders Company, 1983.
64. Neeson, J., and May, K. *Comprehensive Maternity Nursing*. Philadelphia: J. B. Lippincott, 1986.
65. Nichols, F. The Psychological Effects of Prepared Childbirth in Self-Esteem, Active Participation During Childbirth and Childbirth Satisfaction of Single Adolescent Mothers. (Doctoral Dissertation, The University of Texas at Austin). Dissertation Abstracts International, 1984.
66. O'Brien, M. My way: Mom and dad go back to work. *Childbirth Educator* 6:19, 1986.
67. Olds, S. B., London, M. L., and Ladewig, P. A. *Maternal-Newborn Nursing: A Family-Centered Approach*. Menlo Park, CA: Addison-Wesley Publishing Co., 1984.
68. Olson, M. Fitting grandparents into new families. *MCN: American Journal of Maternal/Child Nursing* 6:419, 1981.
69. Orem, D. *Nursing: Concepts of Practice*, 3rd ed. New York: McGraw-Hill, 1985.
70. Ozurec, L. Childbirth educators: Are they helpful? *MCN: American Journal of Maternal/Child Nursing* 6:329, 1981.
71. Peckham, D. Refresher courses. *Childbirth Educator* 5:47, 1986.
72. Plumez, J. Classes for adoptive parents. *Childbirth Educator* 3:50, 1984.
73. Posner, G. J., and Strike, K. A. A categorization scheme for principles of sequencing content. *Review of Educational Research* 46:665, 1976.
74. Reeder, S., and Martin, L. *Maternity Nursing*. Philadelphia: J. B. Lippincott, 1987.
75. Reynolds, P. A primer for theory construction. Indianapolis: Bobbs-Merrill, 1971.
76. Richards, M. The trouble with "choice" in childbirth. *Birth* 9:253, 1982.
77. Roy, C. *An Introduction To Nursing: An Adaptation Model*, 2nd ed. Englewood Cliffs, NJ: Prentice-Hall, 1984.
78. Sasmor, J. *Childbirth Education: A Nursing Perspective*. New York: John Wiley & Sons, 1979.
79. Shannon-Babitz, M. Addressing the needs of fathers during labor and delivery. *MCN: American Journal of Maternal/Child Nursing* 4:378, 1979.
80. Sheehan, F. Assessing postpartum adjustment: A pilot study. *JOGN Nursing* 10:19, 1981.
81. Sumner, G., and Fritsch, J. Postnatal parental concerns: The first six weeks of life. *JOGN Nursing* 6:27, 1977.
82. Sweet, P. Prenatal classes especially for children. *MCN: American Journal of Maternal/Child Nursing* 6:419, 1981.
83. Thomas, B. Identifying priorities for prepared childbirth education classes. *MCN: American Journal of Maternal/Child Nursing* 6:333, 1981.
84. Van Natta, G. Educational needs of new and expectant fathers. *Genesis* 5:22, October/November, 1983.
85. Verduin, J. R., Miller, H. G., and Greer, C. E. *Adults Teaching Adults: Principles and Strategies*. San Diego, CA: University Associates, 1977.
86. Vogt, B. Pregnancy healthlines. *Childbirth Educator* 6:51, Winter 1986/1987.
87. Walker, B., Erdman, A. Childbirth education programs: The relationship between confidence and knowledge. *Birth* 11:103, 1984.
88. Walls, J. An instruction guide for educating expectant mothers. *MCN: American Journal of Maternal/Child Nursing* 8:274, 1983.
89. Wapner, J. The attitudes, feelings and behaviors of expectant fathers attending Lamaze classes. *Birth and the Family Journal* 3:5, 1976.
90. Whitley, N. *A Manual of Clinical Obstetrics*. Philadelphia: J. B. Lippincott, 1985.
91. Zalar, M. Sexual counseling for pregnant couples. *MCN: American Journal of Maternal/Child Nursing* 1:176, 1976.

Beginning Quote

Bartlett, J. *Familiar Quotations*. Boston: Little, Brown and Company, 1968, p. 937.

Boxed Quotes

1. Lowman, J. *Mastering the Techniques of Teaching*. San Francisco, CA: Jossey-Bass, 1984, p. 147.
2. O'Connor, A. *Nursing Staff Development and Continuing Education*. Boston: Little, Brown and Company, 1986.

chapter 28

PROGRAM EVALUATION

SHARRON SMITH HUMENICK

Hearing is not knowing; knowing is not understanding; understanding is not believing; believing is not doing.

M. Singh

The above maxim points out a dilemma of teaching. Much that occurs in classrooms is based on a premise that providing information will lead to altered behavior. In reality, hearing may lead to knowing, understanding, believing, and doing, but not always, and when it does occur, it occurs to varying degrees. Perhaps the greatest difference between a novice and an accomplished teacher is that the accomplished teacher is aware of the results of her teaching. This awareness comes through the process of informal and/or formal *evaluation*.

There is no one formula for an educational program evaluation. The choice of an evaluation process depends on the goals, philosophy, and methods of the evaluator.[10] The purpose of this chapter is to review and clarify elements of evaluation and then to propose recommendations for evaluation in childbirth preparation classes.

REVIEW OF THE LITERATURE

What Is Evaluation?

Evaluation is a complex concept as evidenced by the following definitions and statements about evaluation.

1. Evaluation is the process of delineating, obtaining, and providing useful information for judging decision alternatives.[12]
2. Evaluation differs from measurement in that while measurement simply documents quantity, evaluation ascribes worth or value.[13]
3. Evaluation seeks information for immediate application, whereas experimental research generally is unconcerned with the immediate use of the information derived from the data.[2]
4. Educational evaluation involves both the systematic collection of information and the ability to judge worth of student knowledge, skills, or attitudes.[8]
5. Low use of evaluation data is a phenomenon discussed widely in the literature. Failing to use collected evaluation data is more than a waste of time and money. It leads to the evaluation process becoming a continual irritant rather than an aid.[1]

Combining these statements, one might define educational evaluation as a process in which judgments are made about the adequacy of a student's achievement or the adequacy of a program. It is based on systematically collected data for use in

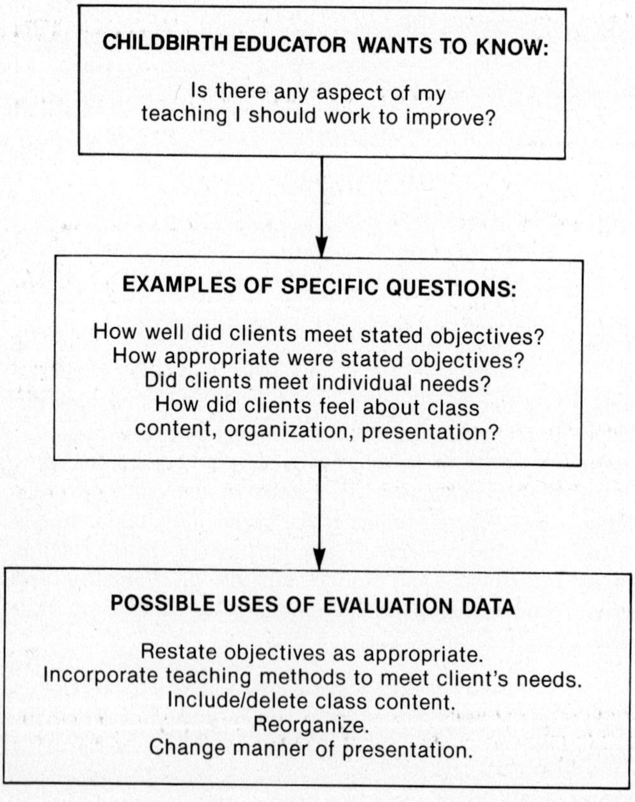

FIGURE 28–1. Overview of evaluation.

immediate application in judging decision alternatives. If the data are not used, the collection process becomes useless and burdensome. Possible uses of evaluation data are shown in Figure 28–1.

When an evaluation process is designed, the following areas are important to consider:

1. The purpose of the evaluation process.
2. The aspects of the program to be evaluated.
3. The sources and timing of data collection.
4. The process or steps of evaluation.
5. The strategies or tools of evaluation.

These five areas are discussed in the next pages as they relate to programs of childbirth education.

The Purpose of Evaluation

Who Cares? Bland and co-workers state that identifying who will use the evaluation information is the most important element and the most consistently ignored step of evaluation.[1] Patton found that the evaluation process was useful only when the person(s) who cared about the information could be identified.[9]

Why Do They Care? Knowing who will use the information is important, but also important is knowing what they will use it for. The approach used by a childbirth educator who wants to evaluate herself to improve her classes may be quite different from the approach used by the administrator of an agency who uses the information as a basis for deciding to retain childbirth educators or set their salary. The approach may be different still for a childbirth educator who as a sponsor-teacher is evaluating a candidate for a certification program.

What are Some Effects of Evaluation? Evaluation is similar to sandpaper in that it serves to shape and smooth the teacher as a result of the process, but it may be uncomfortable or even painful at times. Evaluation can be threatening to even the most self-assured teacher. If the evaluation data must be shared with someone in a supervisory role, the threat is dramatically increased. On the other hand, evaluation can also be wonderfully reassuring and validating. Most people, including childbirth educators, are their own worst critics as contrasted with expectant parents, who tend to be kind in their evaluations.

Evaluation Models. MacNaughton et al. categorize evaluation models using the terms *''traditional, neo-traditional, ends oriented,* and *teacher-concern.''*[7] Each model is broader in scope than the preceding one.

- Traditional (means-oriented) evaluation, they say, focuses solely on teacher behavior and answers such questions as ''Was the lesson well planned?'' or ''Was the delivery style pleasing?''
- Neotraditional evaluation is broader because it includes the learner. Additional questions that focus on the learner are added, such as ''Was the provision of practice time adequate?'' or ''Were the objectives achieved?''
- In the ends-oriented model, learner performance continues as a focus along with an added focus on how to better help the learner meet the objectives.
- A ''teacher-concern evaluation'' model requires a collegial relationship between the evaluator and those being evaluated. This is based on the belief that trust and a nonthreatening atmosphere are important to the teacher's desire to improve.

Program Aspects to be Evaluated

What Is the Question? A question should accompany each aspect of the program that is to be evaluated. As previously mentioned, *one should want an answer to something* before investing the time and effort to collect and analyze evaluation data. I have known of many childbirth educators who confessed to having stacks of evaluations from past classes in their basement or garage. These were being saved because maybe someday someone would get around to analyzing the data. They had subscribed to the idea that evaluation is important, but they collected information for which they personally had no use. A look at such questionnaires found questions more appropriate to a research study with a specific hypothesis than to evaluation, which is to assist with making education program decisions. The following are evaluation questions that childbirth educators may want to ask:

1. To what extent did the learners meet the goals and objectives of the program?

2. To what extent were the goals and objectives appropriate?
3. To what extent did the learning activity serve to facilitate the learner's meeting of the objectives?
4. What attributes of the teacher enhanced or hindered the learning process?
5. How well did the scheduling meet the learner's needs?
6. How well was the program administered?

When asking expectant parents these questions, the childbirth educator will need to restate them in language the couples can easily understand. For example, the question, To what extent did the learner meet the goals and objectives of the program? could be restated as, How well do you believe you will be able to cope with childbirth?

To learn the answers to these questions, the childbirth educator can use a variety of techniques. These are discussed later in this chapter.

The Timing and Sources of Data Collection

The collection of evaluation data can occur at four times. The first time is before the program, is part of planning, and is called *planning evaluation*. It can be based on the written or spoken comments of participants of similar programs in the past, other childbirth educators, books such as this one, or even individuals who have elected not to take part in similar programs in the past. These data are used to predict what the learners of a future class will want and need.

A second time when data is collected is throughout the program. This is called *formative evaluation*. Data are collected from those attending a class presently to determine if their needs are being met while there is still time to make alterations if indicated. Mechanisms can include observation, discussion, quizzes, role playing, and weekly reaction sheets and/or suggestion boxes. Formative evaluation is an integral part of good teaching.

A third time to collect evaluation data is at the end of the program, and this is called *summative evaluation*. At the end of a childbirth education course, the learners are in a position to comment meaningfully on the class activities, the teacher's style or other attributes, and details such as class scheduling and administration. The summative evaluation is usually a questionnaire filled out at the end of class. Knowles suggests another evaluation method in which learners are placed in small groups, with each group given a blank piece of paper.[6] One learner in the group makes an evaluative statement and the rest of the group ranks on a scale of 1–5 how much they agree or disagree with the statement. A recorder lists the statements and the group scores on the statement. Then another learner makes a second statement and the process continues. This evaluation process will be focused on the issues as seen by the class. An advantage of this method is that it may prevent one person's idiosyncratic gripe from carrying much weight, as the group would be expected to mediate atypical statements.

The fourth type of evaluation can be conducted after the birth and is called *follow-up evaluation*. Class members are usually asked to mail an evaluation form back after the birth. At that point they can better evaluate the usefulness of the course. This information is more difficult to collect since a childbirth educator usually has to rely on the parents to mail this form. Self-addressed, stamped envelopes given to the parents as the class ends help get a response. Additionally, follow-up data are sometimes obtained from directly observing couples in labor. This can be very useful as the childbirth educator observes people she taught. Also, comments are sometimes solicited or received from other health professionals who participate in the birth of couples taught by a particular childbirth educator.

The Process of Evaluation

The many authors writing on evaluation describe slightly different steps for evaluation or describe the same steps using different names. What they all have in common, however, is a description of evaluation as an *ordered process*. An example of ordered steps based on Bland is as follows:[1]

1. Identify the decision-makers or information users.
2. Identify the decisions.
3. Design the data collection strategy.

4. Define any deadlines for the decisions to be made and plan a report if indicated before the date.
5. Collect the information, analyze it, and summarize the findings.
6. Use the results to make the changes indicated.

Strategies of Evaluation

Evaluation strategies can be as informal as mental notes of the teacher to herself and as formal as developing a rating scale. Most fall in between and may include interviews, surveys, tests, checklists, or anecdotal notes. At least as much time should go into analyzing and using the information as collecting it. How formal the evaluation becomes depends on the characteristics of the typical class member of a given teacher. A teacher with many pregnant teen class members or blue collar couples would be less likely to use even anonymous written tests than a teacher of primarily white collar couples or college-graduate students. Class members do value formative evaluation of some type and, when it is done collegially, usually view it as personal attention from the instructor.

Cognitive Domain. Objectives in the cognitive domain (intellectual knowledge) are most reliably evaluated in written or oral quizzes or in rehearsal sessions. The problem with oral quizzes to the group is that those who know the answers may answer all the questions and others may still be confused. Humenick reported using a short, anonymous, written quiz with six questions:[4]

1. Name up to three signs that labor is beginning or is about to begin.
2 What is the purpose of having a coach ask a woman to tense an arm while relaxing the rest of her body?
3. Which of the two is usually the most comfortable position for a laboring woman, lying on her side or flat on her back?
4. Name up to five suggestions a coach might make before suggesting medication if a laboring woman finds that her present breathing technique is no longer helping enough.
5. Name up to three things a coach can do to correct or prevent hyperventilation of a laboring woman.
6. How do nurses usually tell when a woman's labor has progressed enough that she should begin pushing her baby out?

Administering this short quiz to the members of ten series of classes of middle-class couples representing five teachers revealed the following: (1) Women scored significantly higher than men. (2) Classes whose teachers had seen the test averaged 90 per cent as compared with a 76 per cent average in classes in which the teachers had not seen the test. (3) The most correctly answered question was number six, which may be the least critical information for couples to know in terms of decision-making on their part. (4) Question numbers four and five were difficult for fathers especially. Although 15 different correct answers to number four were accepted as correct, many fathers could think of only one or two things they would do in spite of the fact that this question is central to the expectant father's role in labor. After each childbirth educator saw the test, in every case her next class scored better. This shows that evaluation can affect teaching and learner outcomes.

Some of the incorrect answers given were interesting. One person thought labor began when (1) the bag of water broke or (2) when the membranes ruptured. Apparently duplicate vocabulary had been learned with no understanding of the overlap. Many people thought hyperventilation should be corrected by speeding instead of slowing breathing. Many thought that tensing a right arm was a technique to be used in the labor room. One father thought a "paperback" instead of "paper bag" should be used to breathe into to correct hyperventilation. For one teacher both classes monitored thought laboring flat on the back was most comfortable in spite of the fact that she emphasized otherwise during lecture. She differed, however, from other teachers in that she showed classes slides of a laboring woman on her back. It seemed that pictures spoke louder than words, because couples remembered what they had seen rather than what she said. Through the evaluation process she identified this problem.

Affective Domain. Objectives in the affective domain (values, emotions) are hardest to measure. Attitudes may be assessed in group discussion. The teacher should not feel that it is her role to change an attitude as much as to see evidence that the person is open to considering a variety of options and then making an informed choice. The choice could be in relation to breastfeeding, rooming-in, use of medication and the like.

Ordinarily, evaluation of the affective domain is accomplished through informal formative evaluation. Through designing class activities and controlling class size, the teacher can create an evironment in which learners do explore their values and feelings. Observation of active participation by class members in the activities may be as far as the teacher takes evaluation. Having couples create and share a tentative birth plan is an activity that may help the teacher evaluate class members in the affective domain. Classes that consist of primarily lecture and that leave little time for active participation of class members are typically inadequate in the affective domain from both an instructional and evaluation perspective.

Psychomotor Domain. Evaluation in the psychomotor (skill) domain usually takes place through having the expectant parents return demonstrations of skills such as relaxation, patterned breathing, and expulsion efforts. Repeated formative evaluation is usually important, since most psychomotor skills are learned only with repeated practice. The frequent evaluation of progress toward these skills not only guides the learner in making progress but may also motivate the learner to practice.

Childbirth educators sometimes express concern about the amount of time it takes to go around the class and repeatedly evaluate skills. Yet this is a part of the class that the couples cannot get from a textbook. This is one reason why it is important to attend a childbirth preparation class. Humenick and Marchbanks[5] as well as Humenick[4] have reported attending classes at the end of the last session and finding individual women who can demonstrate very little or no skill attainment in relaxation. Can such women be said to be prepared for childbirth? Should not this have been caught earlier so that extra attention could have been provided during class, after class, or in extra sessions as needed?

IMPLICATIONS FOR PRACTICE

Determining whether or not the objectives for the learner have been met is most commonly associated with educational evaluation. If the objectives have been written in terms describing the behavior of the learner, the blueprint for evaluating objectives is already in place.

However, the goals and objectives of the class are not always appropriate. Important areas may be left out and some of the areas covered may not be important. Examples of questions that evaluate this issue:

> "What, if any, material would you suggest adding to or deleting from the classes?"

or

> "What would you add to the class? What would you leave out of the class?"

The specific wording of a question depends in part on the education level of the clientele one typically serves. A question such as that above might best be asked in follow-up evaluation. Couples can answer with more perspective after they have been through the birth.

When evaluating the learning activities, it is important to remember that given individual learning preferences, no activity is likely to please everyone. It is hoped, however, that each person could relate well to many of the learning activities. In most cases, people can give good information about class activities during summative evaluation. An example for evaluating learning activities might be:

> "Which activities did you like best or find most useful?"

> "Which if any activities did you not enjoy?"

or

"Comment on the balance and variety of activities in class."

or

"Comment on the degree to which the class activities were interesting and aided learning."

and

"To what extent did the class activities encourage you to become acquainted with other class members?"

Questions might be more specific if one wanted to evaluate a specific activity, such as role playing. Again the actual wording will depend on the clientele as well as on the question one wants answered.

Teacher Characteristics. The evaluation of teacher characteristics is the most sensitive area of evaluation. The types of information often sought are:

"What are this teacher's strengths?"

"What distracting characteristics, if any, should she work on?"

and

"Which class activities does this teacher do especially well?"

Teachers may want to evaluate themselves by audiotaping or having someone videotape their classes. Watching or listening to oneself can be very illuminating. Having a peer teacher observe and comment may also be a good source of information. Expectant parents, of course, are the other source of information.

Scheduling. Scheduling concerns can encompass several areas. Questions are often asked about the length of the course as well as the length of the individual class. Additional questions might be:

"How convenient was the time of day?"

"Were there adequate breaks during class?"

"Were there meaningful activities at the beginning of class for those who were on time?"

Program Administration. Evaluation questions that program administration may seek to answer are:

"How adequate was the pre-program information?"

> If evaluation is seen as a process around which change develops, then it loses some of its awesomeness as a final proof of merit.
>
> JEANNETTE SASMOR[1]
>
> The success of the evaluation effort depends on the active and informed participation of all potential respondents. Therefore, the educator must plan each aspect of the evaluation procedure with care, to ensure that the data collected are as accurate and complete as possible.
>
> ANDREA O'CONNOR[2]
>
> For centuries, the mystique associated with all of the healing arts intimidated patients and professional alike, so that systematic evaluation of care has only recently been attempted. Valid and reliable methodologies are being developed and tested as part of a major ongoing effort among health care professionals.
>
> MARLENE G. MAYERS[3]

"How well attended to were details such as directions and parking?"

"Were there adequate restrooms, water fountains, etc.?"

"How reasonable was the cost of the course for the benefit received?"

"Comment on the evaluation methods used as appropriate and nondisruptive to learning."

Timing of Questions. Some questions should be asked every series at the end of the class. Some should be asked every series after the birth. Other questions that measure relatively stable class attributes need be measured only periodically. For example, once the parking and building directions are clear, and the pre-class information developed, these aspects of class may need to be re-evaluated only yearly or when a change is made. Every effort should be made to keep the evaluation form short. A question should be judged by whether or not it provides useful information. Whenever some aspect of the class consistently gets an excellent rating, that question might well be routed to the group of questions that are asked only occasionally. This keeps the list of routine questions shorter.

Writing Questions. Avoid questions that ask for yes or no answers. "Did this course meet your needs?" could be replaced by "Are there some ways in which this course could have better met your needs?" Yes or no answers seldom give constructive, useful information. If someone says the course did not meet his or her needs but gives no details beyond a NO, the teacher has no direction for change.

Questions should be worded to call for constructive suggestions rather than complaints. For your own sake, do not force negative comments which you may interpret more negatively than intended

LABOR REPORT

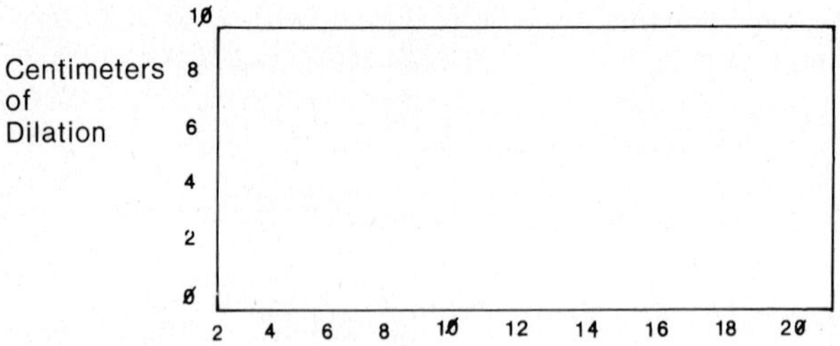

Chart the course of your labor

Plan an "X" where bag of waters broke and an "O" when you arrived at place of birth.

Childbirth Educator ____________ Site of Birth ____________

Birth Attendant ____________ # Previous Pregnancies ____________

1. How did your experience compare with your expectations?

2. What comments do you have for future class members?

3. What comments do you have for your childbirth educator?

4. What comments do you have for your care providers/birth attendants?

Continue on another page if needed. Give details about your baby.

FIGURE 28–2. Sample questionnaire for follow-up evaluation.

by the learner. For example: "Name three things you liked least about the course" forces a complaint where there may be none. Students may recognize full well that the things they liked least were nonetheless important, but the question does not make that distinction. A better approach might be "Name some things you might do differently if you were teaching the course" or "What suggestions do you have for future courses?"

A question that produces an overall rating of the course is, "On a scale of 1–10 (with 10 high), how strongly would you recommend this series to a friend?" Such a question should be followed with "What changes might enable you to rate the class higher?"

Figures 28–2 and 28–3 are the front and back side of a questionnaire that has been useful after the birth. The use of the Friedman labor graph[3] seems easily accomplished by couples when they have been exposed to this concept in class. The form gives one a quick overview of what type of labor the woman experienced. The comments made to future class members as called for on the form typically urge them to practice more.

The labor experience summary in Figure 28–3 has proved useful. When people are asked in general for what were they unprepared, they tend to not think of anything. When they are asked to review their labor phase by phase, they often give very good answers to this question. The teacher will probably remember that she did indeed cover the situation that the couple says they did not hear. The point is, however, that if some couples are not hearing some information, it needs to be covered more emphatically or in a more active way.

A form like that shown in Figures 28–2 and 28–3 has been used *anonymously* and then the filled-out questionnaires placed in the classroom. Couples seemed to enjoy reading them. The variety of the Friedman labor graphs in a stack of returned eval-

PROGRESS	What if anything bothered or hindered you?	What did you find helpful?	What if anything were you unprepared for?	What medication if any did you have?
0-3 cm				
4 -5 cm				
6 -7 cm				
8-10 cm				
Birth				
1st Hour After Birth				

FIGURE 28–3. Sample questionnaire for follow-up evaluation.

uation forms helps class members better understand that there is no "textbook" labor. Some couples arrive early or stay late to go through the stack of evaluations. They pay special attention to the ones pertaining to their hospital or their care provider. Previous class members typically show good sensitivity to the type of comments that would be constructive for future class members as well as their childbirth educator, and those put out for display should be selected for their frank yet constructive comments. Since couples know their form will be made available to future couples, they seem particularly motivated to return their evaluation forms. They of course have the option not to have their form displayed to future classes.

Because it includes questions about care providers, this form can also be used to present problems and suggestions to community care providers. The childbirth educator is in a better position to promote change if she can produce written spontaneous comments from consumers asking for that change. She can informally function as one channel through which couples can send messages to care providers. Also, these forms can be used to communicate positive evaluations to staff. One can copy some positive comments to send to a unit with a note. This builds rapport and stimulates further positive changes.

IMPLICATIONS FOR RESEARCH

Research on evaluation methods is very scant in the general research literature and essentially nonexistent in the childbirth education literature. Some research questions for projects that could be undertaken in the childbirth education setting include:

- What types of evaluation are used most frequently by childbirth educators?
- How is evaluation data used by childbirth educators?
- Which questions provide the most useful information for making decisions about childbirth education courses?
- What are the most effective ways to motivate childbirth educators to use evaluation data to improve their classes?

One could also develop scales that evaluate some aspect of childbirth education and test the scales for reliability and validity. If good evaluation strategies are developed so that one can reliably determine that class members learned what they needed to learn and enjoyed the learning process, then the childbirth educator will have all that is necessary to produce excellent classes.

SUMMARY

Program evaluation in childbirth education is an integral part of teaching. To the extent that the data collected are designed to answer questions about which someone generally cares and which can be used to improve classes, it will be seen as helpful rather than burdensome.

References

1. Bland, C. J., Ullian, J. S., Frober, D. G. User-centered evaluation. *Evaluation and the Health Professions* 7:53, March 1984.
2. Fine, N. J. *Handbook of Parent Education*. New York: Academic Press, 1980.

3. Friedman, E. A. The functional divisions of labor. *American Journal of Obstetrics and Gynecology* 109:274, 1971.
4. Humenick, S. S. Assessing the quality of childbirth education: Can teachers change? *Birth and the Family Journal* 7:82, 1980.
5. Humenick, S. S., and Marchbanks, P. Validation of a scale to measure relaxation in childbirth education classes. *Birth and the Family Journal* 8:145, 1981.
6. Knowles, M. Workshop on Teaching Adults. University of Wyoming, January 1985.
7. MacNaughton, R. H., Tracy, S., and Rogus, J. F. Effective teacher-evaluation-process must be individualized. *NASSP Bulletin* 68 (475), pp. 1–4, 1984.
8. Morgan, M. K., and Irby, D. M. *Evaluating Clinical Competence in the Health Professions*. St. Louis: C. V. Mosby Co., 1978.
9. Patton, M. Q. *Utilization-Focused Evaluation*. Beverly Hills, CA: Sage, 1978.
10. Saracho, O. New dimensions of evaluating the worth of a program. *Education* 103:74, 1982.
11. Singh, M. *Maxims*. Hyderabad: Trans-Indra Educational Press, 1973.
12. Stufflebaum, D. L. The use of experimental design in educational education. *Journal of Educational Measurement* 8 (4):267, 1971.
13. Tobin, H. M., Wise, P. S. and Hull, P. K. *The Process of Staff Development*. St. Louis: C. V. Mosby Co., 1979.

Beginning Quote

Singh, M. *Maxims*. Hyderabad: Trans-Indra Educational Press, 1973.

Boxed Quotes

1. Sasmor, J. *Childbirth Education: A Nursing Perspective*. New York: John Wiley & Sons, 1979, p. 121.
2. O'Connor, A. *Nursing Staff Development and Continuing Education*. Boston: Little, Brown and Company, 1986, p. 252.
3. Mayers, M. *A Systematic Approach to the Nursing Care Plan*. Norwalk, CT: Appleton-Century-Crofts, 1983.

Section

6

THE COMMUNITY

Maternity care is continually changing. During the past two or three decades, many communities have provided more options in maternity care in contrast to the traditional approach to maternity care services. Routine procedures, such as enemas and perineal shaves, are less likely to be performed. In most settings, the presence of husbands or other support persons during birth is a commonplace event. Sometimes siblings are present at the birth as well. More attention is given to keeping the family together after the birth. The effects of noise, temperature, and light on the newborn are considered and the environment adjusted accordingly.

Choices in the setting where birth takes place and the type of care provider have increased. Class members may be planning births in a traditional hospital delivery room, in a hospital birthing room, in a hospital single room maternity care unit, in an alternative birthing center, in a free-standing birthing center, or at home. They may be receiving prenatal care from a physician or a certified nurse midwife.

While choices have increased, simultaneously technology has increased. Some forms of technology have improved infant outcomes in high-risk situations. In some settings, however, these same interventions are used on a routine basis with low-risk situations with questionable results. For example, when all laboring women regardless of risk status are required to remain in bed, the mobility of many of these woman may be unnecessarily limited. Stimulation or augmentation of labor with Pitocin is an almost-routine occurrence in some labor units. The low-risk woman who has limited mobility and experiences Pitocin stimulation generally requires more analgesics, is more likely to have a regional block, and is even more likely to require a cesarean birth. Classes in which choices during childbirth are discussed may be more difficult to teach in some communities and will take careful planning as well as skillful implementation.

In the following chapters, skills are discussed which the childbirth educator may use to relate to the community in which she practices. These include consumer-provider relationships, conflict resolution, and negotiation. Also discussed is organizing a practice and marketing strategies. In many communities, childbirth education has become a marketing tool of large hospitals. When classes are offered below actual cost as a market strategy of a large corporation, the independent childbirth educator is threatened with extinction. Yet her presence in a community may be critical to assuring that a strong voice supporting choices for expectant couples remains.

In summary, the context in which childbirth occurs has changed, becoming more diverse and often presenting conflicting situations. While families may find it easier to be together during childbirth than in past years, they may also find it more difficult to avoid a series of routine medical or surgical interventions. Encouraging consumer activism and helping families plan how they can participate in their birth experience within the health care system they have chosen while promoting changes needed in the health care system require a sensitive and knowledgeable childbirth educator. She will need the skills of marketing and conflict resolution.

chapter 29

CONSUMER-PROVIDER RELATIONSHIPS

SUSAN McKAY

Let's say you have a craving for a chocolate ice cream cone and you go into the nearest ice cream shop and order one. The clerk hands you a tomato-onion ice cream cone. Do you accept it quietly, pay, and try to choke it down? Not if you feel the way the average person feels about ice cream.

People also feel strongly about childbirth experiences and outcomes. Why, then, are they willing to "choke down" many undesirable situations and interventions imposed on them by health care providers and institutions in this country? After all, aren't these providers and institutions in the business of service? And doesn't the word service imply that the server willingly tries to respond to the wants and needs of the person being served?

Charles Mahan

The heart of family-centered obstetrics is the relationships that develop during the childbearing year. These include relationships among family members, relationships that link the family with society and its support systems, and relationships that occur between childbearing families and those who provide care. Each of these has important implications for the healthy development of the family unit. In addition to forming relationships with expectant parents, childbirth educators frequently are asked to help families work out relationships with other care providers. Thus childbirth educators must be familiar with the literature that describes care provider-consumer communication and rela-

Editor's note: The terms client, patient, and health care consumer are used interchangeably in this chapter because the medical and sociology literature have yet to come to a common understanding about their definitions and the implications of calling people patients, clients, or consumers.

tionships so that they are knowledgeable about strategies that have been identified as promoting the development of collaborative provider-consumer interactions.

This chapter's focus is upon historical and contemporary issues surrounding the development of collaborative relationships between obstetrical care providers and childbearing families. Because the research literature is heavily loaded with discussion of physician-patient relationships, this is the predominant focus of the review of the literature. The information presented, however, is applicable to the childbirth educator or any health care provider-consumer relationship. Practical communication strategies also are discussed, based upon the process of shared decision-making.

REVIEW OF THE LITERATURE

Consumer-Provider Relationships

Many hospitals are rapidly making architectural and procedural changes in an effort to entice couples to seek their "family-centered" services. The most enduring problem in actualizing family-centered obstetrics is the asymmetrical communication patterns that still exist between providers and the families for whom they care. Both parties have been highly socialized to understand each other's roles and statuses—for example, who requests help and who provides it.[8] Furthermore, the interactions that occur are instrumental in the process of medical decision-making.[9] Providers and users of health care services often give lip service to the notion that professional autonomy and patient subservience are obsolete; nevertheless, they usually find it hard to change to more egalitarian relationships.

Gadow[11] observed that, despite the notion of shared autonomy (with professionals becoming increasingly human and patients increasingly professional), in reality many physicians (and often nurses) continue to maintain authority while patients resort to the legal system in order to have control over health professionals, and gather information about how to maintain control in the face of professional dominance.[3,19] This assert-and-counterassert struggle will continue, according to Gadow, unless there is a complete philosophical reorientation of the health professions. Fortunately, momentum for change is gradually occurring. Medical, nursing, and other health professional education programs are promoting experimentation with innovative ways of teaching communication skills. Practitioners in care settings are developing systematic methods by which negotiation between care providers and those who seek their services is included as part of the treatment process rather than as a bothersome and poorly implemented addendum.

Szasz and Hollender described a human relationship as an abstraction embodying the activities of two interacting systems (persons).[27] In their classic article that appeared in the medical literature 30 years ago, they observed that the concept of a relationship was a novel one in medicine because physicians have traditionally been more concerned with "things" (for example, anatomical structure and bacteria) and functions, neither of which can adequately describe the joint participation of two persons involved in a relationship. This tendency to depersonalize the consumer through placing the emphasis on the problem (diagnosis) has at times been a concern among all health care professionals.

Szasz and Hollender conceptualized three models of the physician-patient relationship. These are Activity-Passivity, Guidance-Cooperation, and Mutual Participation. Fink extended the spectrum of relationships defined by Szasz and Hollender to include two additional ones: Patient as Primary Provider and Self-Care.[5] These five models are further defined in Table 29–1.

Fink observed that the form the relationship takes is always mutually selected and agreed upon, even though this is often done at an unconscious level and is not explicitly stated. He believes that it is important to question to what degree the con-

TABLE 29–1. MODELS OF CARE PROVIDER-CONSUMER RELATIONSHIP

1. *Activity-Passivity:* Not an interaction, but based on the effect of one person on another so the person acted upon is unable to contribute actively or is considered inanimate; physician is active and in absolute control of the situation whereas patient is passive. Szasz and Hollender liken this relationship to the one existing between parent and helpless infant.
2. *Guidance-Cooperation:* Much of medical practice utilizes this model whereby the patient seeks help and is willing to cooperate with the physician, who possesses the position of power. Physician expects cooperation from patient, who is expected to "look up to" and "obey" the doctor without questioning, arguing, or disagreeing with orders received. The prototype of this relationship is that which exists between parent and adolescent child. (It may be wishful thinking on Szasz and Hollender's part to equate adolescent behavior with this level of cooperation!) The guidance-cooperation model requires that physicians be convinced they are "right" in their notion of what is "best" for patients and will therefore try to induce patients to accept their aims as the patient's own.
3. *Mutual Participation:* In this type of relationship there exists approximately equal power between participants, they are mutually interdependent (need each other), and they engage in activities that will be in some ways satisfying to both. For patients who want to take care of themselves—at least in part—this model will be favored. Essentially the physician assists the patient to help herself. There is a high degree of empathy and characteristics often associated with the notions of friendship and partnership as well as the imparting of expert advice. It requires that provider gratification not stem from power or control of someone else and that the relationship be that of adult to adult. Because this type of relationship is more complex psychologically and socially for both participants, it is rarely appropriate for children or for those who are mentally deficient, very poorly educated, or profoundly immature. According to Szasz and Hollender, the greater the intellectual, educational, and general experiential similarity between physician and patient, the more appropriate this relationship.
4. *Patient as primary provider:* The center of responsibility lies within the person, who is recognized as the healer. The provider, according to Fink, is a helper who gives counsel and technical assistance.
5. *Self-Care:* In this model, Fink describes the person as needing no outside assistance and totally able to care for a health problem or issue by herself. Even when a provider may be consulted, the total responsibility and choice, including outcome, clearly rests with the individual.

Adapted from Bursztajn, H., Feinbloom, R., Hamm, R., and Brodsky, A. *Medical Choices, Medical Chances.* New York: Delta/Seymour Lawrence, 1983, p. 1976; and Fink, D. L. Provider-Patient Relationships in Illness and Wellness. Presented at High-Level Wellness Seminar, Estes Park Institute, Asiolmar, CA, March 6–9, 1977.

tract is consciously established, to what degree from a sense of choice, and the explicitness of its terms. Labeling relationshps "right or wrong" is inappropriate; instead, providers and health care consumers need to be able to discern each other's needs and to select with wisdom the most effective relationship.

Whether individuals and families interacting with the health care system will soon be able to cast aside customary behavior patterns to do what Fink suggests is open to question. Furthermore, it may be wishful thinking to hope that most people will sort through their relationships and select one appropriate to the needs of the situation. Behavior is resistant to change and this is patently obvious in provider-consumer interactions within the health care system. However, obstetrical care providers can influence the behavior of consumer families and have as a responsibility facilitation of a relationship that incorporates mutual participation and shared decision-making. Accepting less or expecting this form of relationship (as defined by Szasz and Hollender) to occur only between people who are similar in characteristics to their care providers is an inadequate model.

Those with less education and lower social status need to be encouraged to be more participatory, just as does the middle class, well-educated population. This is not a philosophical nicety but a necessity, because evidence indicates that persons who obtain the best medical care are those who strive for mastery over their health needs, are experienced in dealing with professionals and formal agencies, and are ready to negotiate assertively to obtain good care.[23]

Of special relevance to family-centered care is the additional observation that persons who, in addition to their own coping ability and effort, have family members who are capable of expressing their needs to professionals. These persons have an even greater advantage in obtaining good professional care. The family's pool of social skills and collaboration in problem-solving serve to back up each individual member.[23] Research by Pratt[23] concluded that in families in which all members were experienced in interpersonal negotiations, over one-half (53 per cent) received excellent preventive medical services, compared to only one-fourth of the families in which members were generally inexperienced in negotiating.

Shared Decision-Making

As defined by the President's Commission for the Study of Ethical Problems in Medicine and Biomedical and Behavioral Research,[24] shared decision-making "requires that a practitioner seek not only to understand each patient's needs and develop reasonable alternatives to meet these needs but also to present the alternatives in a way that enables patients to choose ones they prefer. To participate in this process, patients must engage in a dialogue with the practitioner and make their views of well-being clear." The process is clearly a reciprocal one. To establish this relationship, the health professional invites the patient to participate in a dialogue in which the professional seeks to help the patient understand the medical situation and available courses of action, and the patient conveys his or her concerns and wishes.[24]

Gadow[11] asserted that shared autonomy can occur only when consideration of control and power is not pivotal—from either of two power extremes, consumerism and paternalism. The contribution of the clinician is not to reach a unilateral clinical judgment about the patient but to engage with the patient in an endeavor to reach a joint understanding of the situation and to frankly support the patient in exercising self-determination. Patients are gently drawn into the decision-making process to preserve their freedom of self-determination.

Katz[14] viewed it as odd to have to justify greater patient participation in decision-making. Physicians, according to Katz, have shown a keen sensitivity to patients' decision-making limitations but considerable insensitivity to patient's capabilities to decide. Katz related this to the educational process in which physicians are not prepared to attend caringly to patients' decision-making needs. Katz observed that significantly more can be explained by physicians than is the general custom, and doing that would improve the climate of physician-patient decision-making. Unfortunately, initiating the process of shared decision-making is often difficult for health professionals, who are accustomed to making autonomous decisions and are supported by the ready acquiescence of the patient.

For pregnant women seeking a greater share of decision-making, the responsibility has often been theirs to shift the decision-making process so that it is less unilateral. Toward this end, some childbirth educators have promoted birth plans as a means of trying to equalize power, frequently with

In mutual participation and shared decision-making, power is transferred to expectant parents and is shared more equally in provider-consumer relationships. (Photograph by Rodger Ewy, Educational Graphic Aids, Inc.)

mixed results. Obstetrical care providers have sometimes regarded patient checklists and birth plans less as a vehicle for shared decision-making than as a tool of coercion and evidence of lack of trust in the provider. Even when birth plans or checklists are not used, requests for information on the part of expectant parents have often been met with resistance or negative responses to the original source of the information, often the childbirth educator. An example of this is the resentment of obstetrical health care providers when childbirth educators provide risk-to-benefit information about commonly used and routine procedures. But if families are to share in decision-making, they must have information; it is unfortunate that more obstetrical care providers are not now considering providing this information as an essential part of their role. This is important because treatment refusals are usually triggered by too little information.[24]

A summary of a relationship characterized by mutual participation and notable for its emphasis upon the sharing of information and mutual decision-making is shown in Table 29–2.

Therapeutic Communication

Fisher[7] described therapeutic discourse (therapeutic communication) as a routinized form of behavior with well-defined boundaries. The interview is structured by the person who initiates the event and who is helped by it. The person initiating the event and helped by it is in a subordinate position. In traditional provider-patient interviews patients are not expected to expand on, or amend the topic or disagree with what the provider says on it. Therefore, the only conversational strategies left for patients are to request clarification, interrupt, pause, express hesitation or uncertainty, and agree or respond directly.[25]

Shuy[25] observed that the physician-patient interview is *not* the same as social conversation and that patients are seldom used to being interviewed. They are used to normal, social conversation with the expectation of balanced participation whereby participants talk, introduce topics, and respond to topics in about the same proportions.[14] Therefore, if the provider wishes to make the patient comfortable, reduce anxiety, and increase the probability of acquiring complete and accurate information about the patient, the interview style needs to be modified to be more conversational and less like an interview. For this to occur, providers need to communicate in the patient's language rather than the other way around, which is traditionally presumed appropriate. Furthermore, cues given by the provider can open up the conversation and show that asking questions is permissible. Cues that have been identified by consumers as encouraging or discouraging the continuation of an interview are shown in Table 29–3.

Factors affecting whether patients perceived that their questions were welcomed and ensuing discussion encouraged were related to the setting.[25] For example, an "assembly line" method of care whereby patients are stationary but the physician moves back and forth among the treatment rooms inhibited open discussion because of the message that there was "time pressure" upon the physician to see other patients. Lack of privacy in the treatment room also inhibited discussion. However, if the patient was clothed and there was a chair for the physician to sit in, conversation was fostered.

TABLE 29–2. CONSUMER-PROVIDER ROLES IN MUTUAL DECISION-MAKING

CONSUMER	PROVIDER
Talk to the health care professional.	Listen actively to the health care consumer.
Listen and learn from the health care professional.	Educate the health care consumer.
Ask questions of the health care professional.	Motivate the health care consumer to ask questions.
Decide with the health care professional what to do about a health problem or how to meet a health-related goal.	Share decision-making with the health care consumer.
Do what was decided upon.	Reinforce the health care consumer's efforts to achieve self-responsibility.

Developed at the University of Colorado Health Sciences Center, Health PACT Program, Denver, CO.

TABLE 29–3. CUES ENCOURAGING OR DISCOURAGING CONSUMER QUESTIONS

CUES ENCOURAGING QUESTIONS

- The provider providing literature in the context of a prolonged relationship is seen as inviting questions
- The provider says "come, let's talk," thereby putting the patient on a more equal footing
- The provider who walks the patient to the door of the outer office is seen as accessible and caring outside the confines of the office

CUES DISCOURAGING QUESTIONS

- The provider who closes the folder, stands up or says "Call if there are any problems" is saying that the interview is over
- The provider who uses "medispeak" (technical jargon) conveys the information that the physician's authority is not to be questioned
- Lack of concrete advice communicates that either the provider does not know or does not want to tell
- The provider asking "Do you have any questions?" tends to reinforce power and status differences

Conversation was inhibited if the physician was interrupted by phone calls or by other staff members.

How language is used by the provider is also important in influencing therapeutic communication and subsequent treatment decisions. Providers, for example, use presentation strategies that provide information while simultaneously suggesting how patients should make sense of it.[7] An example is, "We usually monitor the baby's heartbeat electronically once labor is well-established." This method of presenting information tells the patient about treatment procedures while suggesting that this is the normal or usual way to provide care. Presentational strategies are considered "soft sell"; persuasional strategies are "hard sell" that provide information while specifying how it should be understood.[7] The patient is told about the treatment that she should have and why she should have it.

"What you should do is come to the hospital and have your labor induced before your blood pressure goes any higher." This strategy can be justified by the argument that presumably the professional has good reason for preferring a recommended course of action.[24] On the other hand, such a strategy can be a method to package and present information in a manner that leaves patients with no real choice. Manipulation of information can be extreme—for example, withholding or distorting information in order to affect the patient's beliefs and decisions. It can also be more subtle, such as a professional's careful choice of words or nuances of tone and emphasis that might present the situation in a manner that heightens the appeal of a certain choice of action.[24] It has been found, for example, that presenting risk-to-benefit information in certain ways increases the likelihood that a therapeutic choice will or will not be accepted.[20,29]

To summarize, questioning and presentational and persuasional strategies are interactional mechanisms used to aid in making treatment decisions. Both providers and patients use questioning strategies, with patients asking questions to varying degrees, depending upon the provider's encouragement. Only practitioners use presentational and persuasional strategies, according to Fisher.[7]

Strategies for Promoting Shared Decision-Making

Thus far, this discussion has centered primarily upon the role of the provider in encouraging therapeutic communication. Because pregnant women usually have many opportunities to interact with their obstetrical care providers about preferred treatment decisions, the way they approach the process is important in moving toward shared decision-making. Health care consumers, too, profoundly affect the interactional process by the strategies they use. Childbirth educators can become aware of how to help couples communicate more effectively. Effective and ineffective consumer communication strategies are shown in Table 29–4. Further discussion of this topic is included in Chapter 30.

The Issues of Choice

In the book *How We Live,* Fuchs notes:

> Of all of life choices, none is more important to society, none has more far reaching consequences, none represents a more complete blending of social, biological, and emotional forces than bringing another life into the world.[10]

If family-centered care is the philosophical framework that has been adopted by an institution

TABLE 29–4. EFFECTIVE AND INEFFECTIVE CONSUMER COMMUNICATION STRATEGIES

EFFECTIVE

- Acknowledging the provider's expertise in the medical field and soliciting his or her viewpoint while adding the unique perspective she possesses about herself, her needs, and those of her family.
- Being positive in approach instead of overwhelming the provider with "I don't want" statements; spontaneously verbalizes her requests.
- Being friendly but firm.
- Using questioning strategies that encourage the sharing of information between both provider and expectant parent(s).
- Writing down questions in advance of the appointment.
- Taking notes about what the provider says or asking him or her to write it down.
- Summarizing what was understood about the information given by the provider.
- Being flexible enough to consider various alternatives to a treatment problem.
- Following up the appointment with a phone call if unanswered questions arise.
- Expressing appreciation to the provider.

INEFFECTIVE

- As the provider enters the treatment room where she is waiting, he sees a long list dangling from her hands and is immediately "hit" with a series of demands about what she wants to have him do or not do. (Nurses often comment about labor patients who upon admission whip out their lists.) The response on the part of providers is usually defensive.
- Her behavior is from the outset hostile.
- She chooses not to participate in any way in the decision-making process, abdicating responsibility. She doesn't question or make efforts to obtain information as a basis for shared decision-making.
- She is not sensitive to the value of timing—saving her requests for later in the interview, requesting a separate appointment to discuss specific concerns, deferring discussion when she learns her provider is unusually rushed or tired.

and the providers who work within it, commitment to family participation in making choices will be inherent in the care process of this institution. It appears from the preceding discussion that there are some relatively simple ways that the childbirth educator can communicate and encourage other care providers and expectant parents to communicate. This can improve the climate for questions to be asked and for information to be exchanged. The stage is thereby set for discussion of choices.

Whether choice is in reality a possibility for childbearing families (or other users of the health care system) is debatable because adequate information for making informed choices is usually hard to obtain. Even if it is acquired, assessing the utility of care relative to its cost is difficult. Hamilton asserted that the only real choices for consumers are whether and when to seek existing services.[12]

There also exist powerful constraints upon decision-making because of outside influences such as federal health regulations, physician-patient relationships that are structured by the team practice of medical care providers,[26] the legal profession, and the insurance industry. The net effect is that providers increasingly are finding that they, too, have fewer and fewer choices about practice issues.

Finally, in considering choices for childbearing families (assuming both provider and family members are willing to share in this process), recognition must exist on the part of both parties that uncertainty is an inherent part of the choice process. "All choices in life are gambles; we act with hope but there are no guarantees," says one writer.[2] Providers are well aware of the uncertainty that is an inherent part of health care practice but may at times be hesitant to admit it. Pregnant women who rigidly plan the intricacies of their childbearing experience, denying the reality that it is possible to anticipate but not to precisely predict in advance the exact process of labor and birth, are not choosing either wisely or realistically. *Both provider and family members must join together in realizing the need not only to acknowledge that uncertainty exists but also to plan flexibly to share in decision-making as the course of events unfolds.*

Using Negotiation for Shared Decision-Making

Negotiation has been called the heart of the clinical encounter.[15] Its aims are to maintain the highest professional standards, not to surrender them. For the pregnant woman and her care provider, negotiation is a means for both parties to develop a partnership. Lazare and colleagues[15] concluded on the basis of their studies that conflict is inherent in the relationship between clinician and patient and that conflict resolution by negotiation is a critical part of successful helping relationships. Pregnant women and their family members are in an ideal position to negotiate and discuss because of the long span of time that is usually available before active assistance is needed.[1]

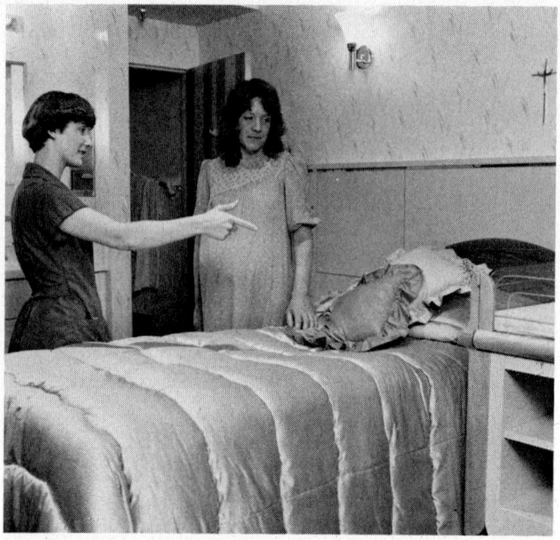

Pregnant women should be encouraged to discuss birthing options with obstetrical health care providers in the community. (Photo by Bill Youmans.)

Although negotiation may be viewed by many as a process between adversaries, it is more useful to think of it as a cooperative enterprise, the objective of which is to achieve agreement.[22] It requires that both parties agree they need a solution; not much can be done if one party refuses to negotiate.[29] When attempts to negotiate fail, the result may be patient dissatisfaction, noncompliance with treatment recommendations, changing care providers, or litigation. On the provider's part, when a negotiated approach to patienthood is not achievable, the result may be referral elsewhere or the withholding of goodwill and support that would otherwise be offered.[15]

In order for the negotiation process to be initiated in the clinical encounter, the pregnant woman's requests need to be elicited. Lazare and colleagues[15] view this as a means of learning the patient's perspective and as an important part of the negotiation process. Unless requests are encouraged to be expressed, many patients will not spontaneously verbalize these, thereby joining the provider in an apparent conspiracy of not sharing and exploring options.[15]

When the provider elicits requests in an empathetic manner there is less need on the part of the patient to engage in evasive activities meant to test the provider's flexibility, interest, and concern. The patient is made aware of the collaborative nature of the interview, a therapeutic alliance is fostered, and the focus of the interview is changed toward the task. Furthermore, the patient is encouraged to express more personal requests, such as the desire to avoid a routine episiotomy. Finally, when requests are voiced by patients, providers are relieved of the fear that they will be overwhelmed by demands that are impossible to respond to, a fear that is not likely to be justified.

To encourage patient requests, Lazare and colleagues suggest that rapport be established through meaningful interaction but *not* at the end of the interview, when neither party has time for the opportunity to enter into negotiations over the request. They recommend using questioning strategies that encourage the elicitation of requests—for example, "What do you hope (or wish) that I would do to help you?" Some patients will respond with "I don't know" or "You tell me; I wouldn't be here if I knew." Then providers can convey that the patient is not being asked to determine or control the treatment but rather that her wishes and hopes are important to know so that her needs are understood and the best care can be provided.

For expectant parents, who often have many requests, a written plan updated with each prenatal discussion can ensure that understanding of what

The pregnant woman needs to discuss her concerns with her health care provider. (Photo by Marjorie Pyle, RNC. © Lifecircle, Costa Mesa, CA.)

is agreed upon is reciprocal. This becomes especially important when many providers will have contact with the pregnant woman, such as in a group practice. The burden should not be on the woman to have to negotiate separately with each care provider about her requests. And yet this is what many women complain about when they are rotated for visits among providers in a group practice—that they have to find out each individual provider's approach to childbirth and try to work out a separate agreement with each practitioner. Health care providers who value mutual participation and shared decision-making have an obligation to "get their act together" as a group, coming to some consensus about practice issues so that the pregnant woman is not burdened with the responsibility of negotiating among her obstetrical care providers.

One of the concerns of providers is that if requests are made, they are bound to abide by them. Eisenthal and colleagues, in a study examining the relationships between patient and practitioner satisfaction ratings and the use of a negotiated approach to the initial psychiatric interview, found that clinicians overemphasized patients' desire to win in the end, to be in control, and to have the treatment plan they originally requested.[4] Apparently what is more important is the opportunity to share in decision-making through negotiation.

Katon and Kleinman[13] advocated a negotiation model to discuss the conflicts occurring in physician-patient relationships and to provide the day-to-day subject matter for clinical negotiation. The process is sequential and includes:

1. The development of the therapeutic or working alliance. Empathy, as previously discussed, and the development of an affective bond between care provider and client are regarded as crucial to the negotiation process. Again, the implications are substantial in group practices or similar setups in which multiple caregivers see pregnant women on a rotating basis, making it difficult for therapeutic relationships to be developed. If family-centered care is practiced in the prenatal setting, there must be provision for continuity of the caregiving process. Pregnant women usually prefer establishing a continuing relationship with one practitioner even if assurance cannot be provided that this person will be her birth attendant.

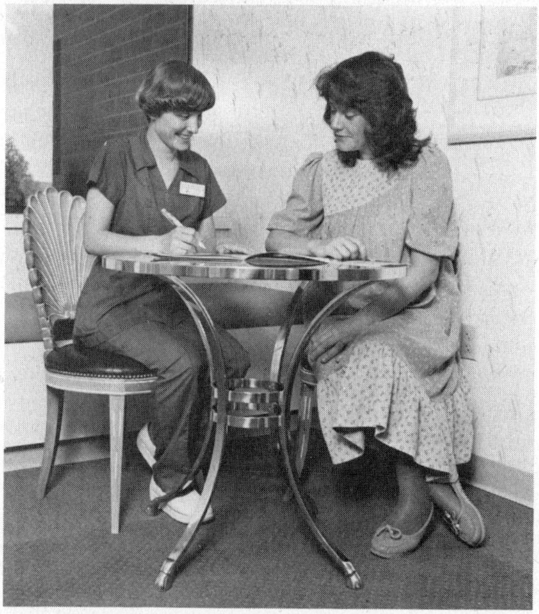

A written birth plan can be developed and discussed with a nurse at the birthing agency. (Photo by Bill Youmans.)

2. The care provider elicits the client's explanatory model, which is her understanding of the illness problem, its cause, expected course, and prognosis and the treatment believed to be useful. Obviously this model must be altered for the majority of pregnant women who are healthy to include an understanding of what pregnancy and the upcoming birth of a child means in the life of this family. The explanatory model for childbearing families would logically also include their requests with respect to care options.

3. The care provider's explanations may cause shifts in the patient's explanatory model so that they are closer to the provider's or the reverse may occur—the providers increased understanding of the consumer's perspective may result in a shift in recommendations that are closer to those of the client.

4. Discrepancies between the provider's and the consumer's viewpoints may remain with respect to expectations for treatment. The conflict should be openly acknowledged and clarified by the provider, providing references and data to argue on behalf of his or her perspective and the treatment it entails. The woman and her family should have

the same opportunity to present their alternatives and assess their arguments in support of them. For childbearing families, this seems a particularly salient stage of the negotiation process and one that often is ignored or neglected because the conflict is not openly discussed and an attempt made to work it out.

Providers at this phase sometimes make promises to pregnant women concerning their treatment options, but covertly they may have no intention of carrying them out. Thus after their baby's birth, the couple may be faced with the disappointment and anger of not having had their choices respected but unable to do anything about it. Both provider and family members must flexibly recognize that choices sometimes cannot be actualized because of unexpected outcomes. When this happens, the reasons can be discussed and are usually understood.

What is not acceptable is the provider's agreement to a care option—for example, ''I won't do an episiotomy unless it's necessary'' (but it is necessary 99.9 per cent of the time) with little or no intention of following through.

When the pregnant woman has ideas about treatment alternatives that differ from her provider's, she may need more information than she has about risks and benefits. The provider can lead her to information sources—specific books, other providers in the community such as pharmacists or childbirth educators, journal articles, hospital libraries, organizations such as ASPO/Lamaze and the International Childbirth Education Association, childbirth education classes in the community, and consumer health information sources. Many women and their partners will appreciate knowing where they can obtain more complete information. Although others will not follow through, the opportunity should still be provided.

5. Because of their understanding of one another's conflicting viewpoints about treatment, often the provider, consumer, or both will change their position so that a mutually desired treatment can be agreed upon. Katon and Kleinman believed that this was the end result in most cases.

6. When the conflict cannot be resolved, the provider should decide upon an acceptable treatment based upon biomedical knowledge, knowledge of the explanatory model of the patient, and his or her ethical standards. Input can be requested from other agencies, health professionals, and family members. Consumers, too, have the right to involve members of their social network and key others. For the pregnant woman this will usually be her husband, but it may be an advocate, other health professional, childbirth educator, or family member.

This is a critical juncture of the negotiation process that, when it occurs, will require the best communication skills on the part of both parties and a commitment to trying to resolve the situation. Reverting to using power tactics to influence decision-making seemingly would be a great temptation at this point when both parties are sure to be feeling frustration.

7. The provider's role throughout is to give expert advice and rationale for treatment recommendations, arguing strongly sometimes on behalf of a particular treatment (but ideally also including an objective discussion of risk information, something that often is not done when persuasional communication strategies are being used). The consumer may respond with a counterproposal. For example, if the woman requests that no intravenous solution be used during labor and the provider routinely starts an IV upon admission, they may be able to reach a compromise whereby she agrees to have a heparin lock inserted with IVs added only in the event of certain well-defined situations. The patient is the final arbiter of whatever choice is made. However, if the provider finds this untenable on biomedical and ethical grounds, the therapeutic alliance is broken and referral to another care provider should be offered. Based upon her own explanatory model and value system, the patient may at any time decide to seek care elsewhere, which Katon and Kleinman regarded not as ''doctor shopping'' or noncompliance but as an absolutely legitimate option.

Given today's economic climate and the ''scramble'' for consumers that typifies obstetrical care, ''letting patients go'' may be a difficult task. There is the potential for personal disappointment that may unleash a Pandora's box of emotions when provider and consumers cannot come to an agreement. Nevertheless, an inevitable part of human relationships is that sometimes they just do not work out. Both provider and consumer need to understand this and be able to move on, knowing they did what they could to reach a compromise and that it is time to search for another caregiver whose values, perspective, and medical treatment are more congruent with those of the pregnant woman.

One of the drawbacks of negotiation is that it takes time. People cannot be processed through the system rapidly if there is a commitment to this process. Katon and Kleinman asserted that although the time factor does not exonerate the provider from the negotiation process, surely it is an argument for the necessity of macrosocial structural change in the organization and financing of care.[13] Although it is beyond the scope of this chapter to discuss the implications of this statement for obstetric care providers, reorganization of many of the aspects of routine prenatal care as discussed by Mahan and McKay[16] could release significant amounts of time. Care could be planned to be far more relevant to today's families' needs.

Sharing Power

Fisher and Ury in *Getting to Yes* emphasized the importance of not becoming locked into positions and instead orienting the negotiation process toward mutual interests.[6] When "winning" becomes pivotal, the power struggle between consumer and provider asserts itself. Fisher and Ury's perspective is that the question "Who's winning?" is as inappropriate as asking who's winning in a marriage. When that question is asked about marriage, the more important negotiation has already been lost—". . . the one about what kind of game to play, about the way you deal with each other and your shared and differing interests." Similarly the question "Who's winning?" is equally unsuitable when talking about the experience of childbirth. Instead, the emphasis should be on working side by side toward solutions that are mutually acceptable.

Changing old habits, disentangling emotions from the merits of various alternatives, and enlisting others in the task of working out wise solutions to shared problems are difficult tasks for most of us. Fisher and Ury suggested that occasionally it helps to remind ourselves that the first thing we are trying to win is a better way to negotiate—one that avoids having to choose between the satisfactions of getting what we deserve and of behaving decently. Their contention is that both are possible.

To move toward mutual participation and shared decision-making means that power is transferred to families and shared more equally in provider-consumer relationships. Family members are informed. They are enabled to take control when providers listen carefully to them, helping them to clarify their needs and goals for childbearing and parenting. Finally, they are supported in their right to have choices and assisted in actualizing these.

IMPLICATIONS FOR PRACTICE

As a professional, the childbirth educator can have a unique influence in the development of the relationship between obstetrical care provider and expectant parents. This influence may be exerted to conserve the existing system (for example, it may be difficult for "in-house" childbirth educators to encourage change in an institution that is paying them to promulgate maintaining the status quo) or to help expectant parents to think, to develop new skills of communicating with their providers, and to understand the limitations of the system as well as its flexibility.

For the childbirth educator who is seriously concerned with helping expectant parents understand the options that exist, the effort must also involve providers and helping them to understand the most frequently expressed concerns of consumers and working as a team (obstetrical care provider, childbirth educator, and expectant parents) to mediate some of the complexities of developing a plan of care that is satisfactory for all concerned. Not only can the childbirth educator help care providers understand what parents want, but she can educate expectant parent-clients about the special stresses

ASSERTIVE HEALTH-CARE CONSUMER QUESTIONNAIRE

Below are a series of statements made by health-care consumers. In the blank to the left, put a number from 1 to 5 that best describes you.

1 2 3 4 5

Most unlike me or my situation — **Most like me or my situation**

1. _____ When I go to a health-care provider, I want him or her to tell me what to do.
2. _____ If I feel unsure about what the health-care provider has said, even after an explanation, I will usually seek a second opinion from another provider.
3. _____ I have questions when I see the health-care provider, and I see to it that I get answers.
4. _____ I adhere to the health-care provider's orders more often than not.
5. _____ My rights as a patient are most important to me. I stand up for my rights in dealing with most health-care providers, hospitals, health-insurance companies.
6. _____ Health-care providers are busy people. We really shouldn't take up their time. I'll find answers to my questions somewhere else.
7. _____ My health-care provider almost always has something new to teach me about my health, and I always have some new information to share with my health-care provider about my health.
8. _____ I can't remember the last time a health-care provider had time to really explain something new to me about my state of health.
9. _____ When I disagree with a health-care provider or want another opinion, I always tell him/her directly.
10. _____ Frankly it's not my place to tell the health-care provider what to do. If I don't agree with his or her recommendation, I'd rather not say this to the health-care provider directly. I'll handle it on my own.
11. _____ It's a mess when I want another medical opinion. I never know how to handle the situation with my own health-care provider.
12. _____ I usually will do what the health-care provider recommends, but I also add my own ideas. I've told my doctor I do this.
13. _____ I have questions when I see the health-care provider, but frequently they don't get asked or they go unanswered.
14. _____ I'd like to share decision making with a health-care provider, but I usually don't try it.
15. _____ I am well aware of the fees for services from my health-care provider. If I don't know I always ask before consenting to the service.
16. _____ I'm uncomfortable disagreeing with a health-care provider.
17. _____ I like to share decision making with my health-care provider and do so.
18. _____ There's too much risk in disagreeing with a health-care provider.
19. _____ My health-care provider and I have a relationship in which he or she always asks if I agree with the recommendations or if I would like to change them in some ways. Sometimes I suggest a change, which is OK with my health-care provider.
20. _____ If a health-care provider prescribes something for me, I want to know what it is, why it's needed, and what do watch for.

FIGURE 29–1. Developed at the University of Colorado Health Sciences Center, Health PACT Program, Denver, CO.

TABLE 29–5. A SUMMARY OF NONASSERTIVE, ASSERTIVE, AND AGGRESSIVE BEHAVIORS

NONASSERTIVE	ASSERTIVE	AGGRESSIVE
Avoids problem	Faces problem	Attacks person instead of dealing with problem
Allows manipulation by others	Lets others know what he or she thinks and feels and gains their respect	Takes advantage of others; others fear and avoid him
Gives up rights	Claims rights	Considers own rights superior to those of others
Lets others choose activities	Makes own choices	Chooses activities for others
Hopes goals will be accomplished	Expresses goals and works toward them	Works toward goals
Lacks confidence	Possesses self-confidence	Exhibits demanding, hostile, egotistical behavior
Develops a pattern of self-denial; feels inadequate to express thoughts and feelings; unable to achieve goals	Thinks and behaves in ways that coincide with his rights; often able to achieve goals	Behaves verbally or physically in a way that expresses own rights, but at expense of others

From McKay, S. Assertive childbirth. *Childbirth Educator* Winter 1984/1985, p. 40.

obstetrical care providers face, the multifaceted nature of good decision-making, and the need to work adaptively with the circumstances that arise. The childbirth educator can use the Assertive Health-Care Consumer Questionnaire (Fig. 29–1) to assist couples to examine their interactions with health care providers. If birth plans are part of the curriculum, these should be flexibly planned to include the possibility of unexpected outcomes; in developing these, expectant parents need assistance in communicating with their providers so that decision-making is collaborative rather than unilateral on the part of either party. In assisting expectant parents to accomplish this, specific help may be necessary in teaching questioning strategies that are effective (Table 29–5), how to be firm and assertive while not being aggressive (which is unfortunately too often the only way parents determined to see their choices actualized know how to behave), and developing good listening skills that enable expectant parents to understand their provider's perspective.

> Most expectant couples need to be taught to be as assertive with their health-care providers as they are in other aspects of their lives.
>
> SUSAN McKAY[1]
>
> Teaching assertive behavior and its companion, effective listening skills, should be integrated into the total curriculum instead of being presented as a single subject to be forgotten for the duration of the course.
>
> SUSAN McKAY[1]
>
> Informed parents ask more questions, express their preferences and concerns, make better choices, and raise the consciousness of attending professionals. This leads to re-examination and eventual changes in policies and procedures.
>
> DIONY YOUNG[2]

TABLE 29–6. DEVELOPING A BIRTH PLAN: CHILDBIRTH ALTERNATIVES

You will want to be involved in making decisions about the following aspects of childbirth. Be sure your birth attendant writes your preferences on your medical records so the information will be available when you enter your birth facility.

SUBJECT	DATE DISCUSSED	OPTIONS

Birthing Place		Hospital
		  Traditional labor and delivery room
		  Birthing or childbirth room
		Birth Center
		Home

Birth Attendant		Midwife
		  nurse-midwife
		  empirical or lay midwife
		Physician
		  obstetrician
		  family practitioner

Childbirth Preparation		Consumer-based classes Independent classes Red Cross or public health classes Hospital or clinic classes Classes for siblings Cesarean birth classes Grandparents' classes

Family Participation in Labor		Partner participation during
		  labor
		  birth
		  admission and other obstetrical procedures
		  complications
		Sibling participation during
		  labor
		  birth
		Policies about relatives' and friends' presence during labor and birth

Labor Procedures		IV's
		  routine
		  only as needed
		Perineal shave
		  partial
		  clip
		  complete
		  no shave
		Enema
		  soapsuds
		  phosphate solution
		  none or only if requested
		Vaginal exams
		  frequency
		  indications
		Electronic fetal monitoring
		  frequency (intermittent or continuous)
		  internal or external monitoring of heart rate
		  internal or external monitoring of uterine contractions
		  time in labor when attached
		    upon hospital admission
		    during active or late labor
		    only if indicated
		  radio telemetry option available

TABLE 29–6. DEVELOPING A BIRTH PLAN: CHILDBIRTH ALTERNATIVES *Continued*

	Medications names of commonly used medications percentage of time used and usual dosage time of administration early labor active labor transition second stage third stage
	Fetal scalp pH frequency used indications
	Amniotomy time in labor when done frequency of leaving membranes intact until second stage of labor ambulation allowed after membranes rupture
	Induction of labor frequency indications method Pitocin amniotomy stripping membranes other
Labor Behavior	Encouragement of alternative positions during labor walking sitting alternated with standing, walking, lying, or kneeling bean bag chair special labor–birth bed or chair other
	Birth positions squatting kneeling semisitting sidelying all fours position other
	Access to toilet
	Food and fluids allowed in labor
	Shower during labor with intact membranes
	Labor lounge for early labor
	Camera, tape recorder permitted
	Staff support for breathing and relaxation methods
Birth Procedures	Forceps or vacuum extraction frequency used indications
	Episiotomy frequency used type (midline or mediolateral) perineal massage/compresses used during labor to stretch perineal tissue

Table continued on following page.

TABLE 29–6. DEVELOPING A BIRTH PLAN: CHILDBIRTH ALTERNATIVES *Continued*

You will want to be involved in making decisions about the following aspects of childbirth. Be sure your birth attendant writes your preferences on your medical records so the information will be available when you enter your birth facility.

SUBJECT	DATE DISCUSSED	OPTIONS

		Stirrups
		  frequency used
		    delivery room
		    birthing room
		  Position of stirrups
		    high and wide or low and comfortably spaced

		Fundal pressure
		  frequency and reason used
		  indications

		Father assistance with birth
		  cutting cord
		  delivering baby

Cesarean Birth		Spontaneous labor before cesarean Admission to hospital the day of delivery Father or support person present Screen down or lowered to allow view of baby's birth Option to omit preoperative medications Anesthesia options Horizontal skin and uterine incisions Parents hold baby immediately after birth Baby remains in operating room until operative procedure is completed Breastfeeding and partner visitation in recovery room Regular nursery for normal cesarean babies Early removal of urinary catheter Nonseparation of mother and baby if a postoperative fever develops Vaginal birth after a previous cesarean

Immediate Postbirth		Cord clamping
		  average time before clamping
		Leboyer procedures
		  baby bath and massage
		  quiet environment
		  gentle handling
		Bonding
		  uninterrupted time alone with baby
		  skin-to-skin contact
		  presence of siblings or other family members and friends

Baby Care		Nursery observation of baby or baby stays with parents if desired Delay of administration of ophthalmic ointment Immediate breastfeeding without administration of glucose water Circumcision pros and cons

Postpartum Stay		Family-centered program
		  father welcome at all times
		  sibling visitation
		  provisions for other family and friends to visit
		  care for baby in mother's room
		  infant feeding according to baby's sucking cues
		educational programs for parents
		parents permitted in the nursery with special problems or with jaundiced infants
		early discharge
		home visit or telephone follow-up by member of birth facility staff or public health nurse

From McKay, S. *The Assertive Approach to Childbirth: Using Communication and Information Strategies to Increase Birthing Options*. Minneapolis, MN: International Childbirth Education Association, 1986.

IMPLICATIONS FOR RESEARCH

Finally, the childbirth educator needs to be aware that although much "ballyhooing" has taken place in the last decade about the need for women to make childbirth care choices, little systematic scrutiny has been applied to the process of decision-making about childbirth options. An exception has been the work of McClain, who has examined, in anthropologic research, choices of childbirth service and of repeat cesarean or a trial of labor.[17,18] Studies such as McClain's are important steps in helping childbirth educators understand how women make choices and in challenging preconceived notions that the childbirth educator may have that decision-making is straightforward once benefits and risks are presented to the expectant parents. Childbirth educators could contribute significantly to research in how expectant parents make decisions and the multifaceted factors that come into play. If this knowledge were available, its application to the teaching process would provide learning experiences that would tap into a variety of decision-making styles.

Another major implication for research relates to teaching expectant parents assertiveness and negotiation skills. Although there has been much general discussion of late among childbirth educators and other obstetrical care providers on the importance of collaborative decision-making and symmetrical communication patterns, in fact, most health care consumers—unless they have learned otherwise at a young age—have adopted socially acceptable patterns of interacting with their care providers that, more often than not, cast them in a role that is less than collaborative. Numerous questions need to be answered:

- How can this pattern of behavior (less than collaborative decision-making and asymmetrical communication patterns) be reversed?
- Is expectant parenthood a time when collaborative decision-making and symmetrical communication behavior can be taught?
- Would role playing, video demonstration, or other experiential teaching methods in childbirth education classes result in demonstrable behavior change when expectant parents interact with their care providers?
- What is the most effective way to stimulate more participatory health consumer behavior?
- How can obstetric care providers also be drawn into this process in a way that is mutually beneficial?

The research possibilities are virtually unlimited because there are so many questions that have never been asked about process issues in childbirth care decisions. Small pilot projects can guide the childbirth educator in formulating the questions to be answered and then systematic research protocols can be developed in an attempt to identify effective teaching strategies that can produce changes in interactional behavior.

SUMMARY

The foundation of family-centered obstetrics is the relationships that link the family with society and its support systems, and the relationships that occur between childbearing families and those who provide care. A continuing problem that hinders the development of true family-centered obstetrics is the asymmetrical communication patterns that still exist between care providers, who typically assume a superior role, and childbearing families, who often assume a passive role. The childbirth educator can have a unique influence on the development of a collegial relationship between obstetrical care providers and expectant parents through educating both providers and consumers about shared decision-making and the need to be flexible and work together. In classes, expectant parents can also be helped to develop assertive communication skills that will enable them to interact more effectively with care providers.

References

1. Banta, H. D., and Marinoff, S. C. Effective consumer participation in obstetric care. *Birth and the Family Journal* 2:137, Fall/Winter, 1975–1976.
2. Bursztajn, H., Feinbloom, R., Hamm, R., and Brodsky, A. *Medical Choices, Medical Chances*. New York: Delta/Seymour Lawrence, 1983, p. 176.
3. Carver, C. *Patients Beware. Dealing with Doctors and Other Medical Dilemmas*. Englewood Cliffs, NJ: Prentice-Hall, 1984.
4. Eisenthal, S., Koopman, C., and Lazare, A. Process analysis of two dimensions of the negotiated approach in relation to satisfaction in the initial interview. *The Journal of Nervous and Mental Disease* 171:49, 1983.
5. Fink, D. L. Provider-patient relationships in illness and wellness. Presented at High Level Wellness Seminar, Estes Park Institute, Asiolmar, CA, March 6–9, 1977.
6. Fisher, R., and Ury, W. *Getting to Yes*. Middlesex, England: Penguin Books, 1981, p. 154.
7. Fisher, S. Doctor talk/patient talk: How treatment decisions are negotiated in doctor-patient communication. *In* Fisher, S., and Todd, A. (eds.) *The Social Organization of Doctor-Patient Communication*. Washington, DC: Center for Applied Linguistics, 1983.
8. Fisher, S. Institutional authority and the structure of discourse. *Discourse Processes* 7:202, 1984.
9. Fisher, S. Doctor-patient communication: A social and micropolitical performance. *Sociology of Health and Illness* 6:5, 1984.
10. Fuchs, V. *How We Live*. Cambridge, MA: Harvard University Press, 1983.
11. Gadow, S. Allocating autonomy. Can patients and practitioners share? *In* Bell, N. (ed.) *Who Decides? Conflicts of Rights in Health Care*. Clifton, NJ: Humana Press, 1982.
12. Hamilton, P. *Health Care Consumerism*. St. Louis: C. V. Mosby, 1982.
13. Katon, W., and Kleinman, A. Doctor-Patient Negotiation and the Social Science Strategies in Patient Care. *In* Eisenberg, L., and Kleinman, A. (eds.) *The Relevance of Social Science for Medicine*. Boston: Reidel, 1981.
14. Katz, J. *The Silent World of Doctor and Patient*. New York: The Free Press, 1984.
15. Lazare, A., Eisenthal, S., Frank, A., and Stoeckle, J. Studies on a negotiated approach to patienthood. *In* Gallagher, E. *The Doctor-Patient Relationship in the Changing Health Scene*. Washington, DC: U.S. Government Printing Office, 1976.
16. Mahan, C., and McKay, S. Let's reform our antenatal care methods. *Contemporary OB/GYN* 23:147, 1984.
17. McClain, C. S. Perceived risk and choice of childbirth service. *Social Science and Medicine* 17:1857, 1983.
18. McClain, C. S. Why women choose trial of labor or repeat cesarean section. *Journal of Family Practice* 21:210, 1985.
19. McKay, S. *Assertive Childbirth*. Englewood Cliffs, NJ: Prentice-Hall, 1983.
20. McNeil, B., Pauker, S., Sox, H., and Tversky, A. Preferences for alternative therapies. *New England Journal of Medicine* 21:1259, 1262, 1982.
21. Morris, L. A., Barkdoll, G., Gordon, E., Rivera, C., and Soviero, C. Talking with the doctor: A focus group analysis. Rockville, MD: Food and Drug Administration, unpublished manuscript.
22. Nierenberg, G. *The Art of Negotiating*. New York: Hawthorn Books, 1968, p. 38.
23. Pratt, L. Reshaping the consumer's posture in health care. *In* Gallagher, E. (ed.) *The Doctor-Patient Relationship in the Changing Health Scene*. Washington, DC: U.S. Government Printing Office, 1976.
24. President's Commission for the Study of Ethical Problems in Medicine and Biomedical and Behavioral Research. *Making Health Care Decisions. The Ethical and Legal Implications of Informed Consent in the Patient-Practitioner Relationship. Vol. 1: Report*. Washington, DC: U.S. Government Printing Office, 1982.
25. Shuy, R. Three Types of Interference to an Effective Exchange of Information in the Medical Interview. *In* Fisher, S., and Todd, A. (eds.) *The Social Organization of Doctor-Patient Communication*. Washington, DC: Center for Applied Linguistics, 1983.
26. Stone, A. Foreword. *In* Lidz, C.W., Meisel, A., Zerubavel, E., Carter, M., Sestak, R., and Roth L. (eds.) *Informed Consent, A Study in Decisionmaking in Psychiatry.* New York: Guilford, 1984.
27. Szasz, T., and Hollender, M. A contribution to the philosophy of medicine. *Archives of Internal Medicine* 97:585, 1956.
28. Tversky, A., and Kahneman, D. The Framing of Decisions and the Psychology of Choice. *Science* 211:453, 1981.
29. Zartman, I. W. and Berman, M. *The Practical Negotiator.* New Haven: Yale University Press, 1982.

Beginning Quote

McKay, S. *The Assertive Approach to Childbirth*. Minneapolis, MN: International Childbirth Education Association, 1986, p. 1.

Boxed Quotes

1. McKay, S. Assertive childbirth. *Childbirth Educator* Winter 1984/1985, pp. 33–34.
2. Young, D. Activism: A necessary rule of childbirth educators. *Birth* 11:110, 1987.

chapter 30

CONFLICT RESOLUTION AND NEGOTIATION

MARY LOU MOORE

Like it or not, you are a negotiator.

Roger Fisher and William Ury

Conflict is not new to childbirth educators. In the 1950's in both Europe and the United States, the ideas of Grantly Dick-Read and Fernand Lamaze were matters of public debate. There was particular concern because Lamaze had imported his ideas from the "godless Russian culture." The conflict became so heated that in 1956 Pope Pius XII presented a paper on the subject of Lamaze techniques to 700 obstetricians at the Vatican. The Pope noted that sacred scripture did not prevent science from eliminating the pain of birth; moreover, ". . . bonds of motherly affection would surely be enhanced if the woman was fully conscious."[11]

In the United States, conflict was equally vehement. The ideas of the early proponents of childbirth education, Majorie Karmel and Elizabeth Bing, were met with resentment and hostility. Today's conflicts are frequently far more subtle than those of 30 years ago, but because conflict is always a part of a dynamic, changing field, childbirth educators will continue to experience conflict. For this reason development of skills in negotiation and conflict resolution is essential for all childbirth educators.

One can see in childbirth journals the continuing debate on a variety of issues; examples include "The Bonding Controversy,"[34] "Debate: Which

Position for Second Stage?''[37] and ''Risks and Benefits of Obstetric Epidural Analgesia: A Review.''[2] The medical obstetrical literature also reflects conflict on issues related to childbirth education: ''Home or Hospital Births,''[1] ''Home Delivery and Neonatal Mortality in North Carolina,''[8] ''Bathing or Washing Babies after Birth,''[18] and ''Toward a Middle Ground in the Technology Debate in Obstetric Care.''[14]

Knowledge of several concepts (conflict, power, and varying approaches to the management and resolution of conflict, including negotiation) is basic to understanding the process of negotiation and the ability to use that process successfully.

REVIEW OF THE LITERATURE

Conflict

Conflict exists when incompatible goals and/or activities are present together. For example, a childbearing couple and a health care provider may share the goal of a healthy pregnancy and a healthy baby but have different ideas on the activities that will lead to that healthy outcome.

Concepts regarding conflict have been developed from the perspective of many disciplines—history, international relationships, economics, and social psychology. Deutsch identifies five ''key notations'' in the social-psychological approach to conflict.[10]

1. Each participant in a social interaction responds to the other in terms of his perceptions and cognitions of the other's actions. These may or may not correspond to the other's actualities.
2. Each participant in social interaction is influenced by his own expectations concerning the other's actions.
3. Each participant in a social interaction is influenced by his perceptions of the other's conduct.
4. In the process of rationalizing and justifying actions that have been taken and effects that have been produced, new values and motives emerge.
5. Social interaction takes place in a social environment. In order to understand the events that occur in social interactions, one must understand the interplay of these events within the broader social context in which they occur, such as the total health care system in a community.

Causes of Conflict

Moore describes five spheres of conflict:[23]

1. *Data conflicts,* caused by lack of information, misinformation, differing views of what is relevant, differing interpretations of data, and different assessment procedures;
2. *Interest conflicts,* caused by perceived or actual competitive interests;
3. *Structural conflicts,* caused by unequal control ownership or distribution of resources, unequal power and authority, geographical, physical or environment factors that hinder cooperation, and time constraints;
4. *Value conflicts,* caused by different criteria for evaluating ideas or behavior, different ways of life, etiology, and religion; and
5. *Relationship conflicts,* caused by strong emotions, misperceptions or stereotypes, poor communication or miscommunication, and repetitive negative behavior.

Most conflicts have multiple causes and involve a combination of problems. For example, a conflict between a childbearing couple and the health care system in a particular community could involve data conflict (differing views of what is relevant), structural conflict (unequal power and authority), value conflict (family-oriented values versus the values of a traditional medical model), and relationship conflict (misperceptions and poor communication).

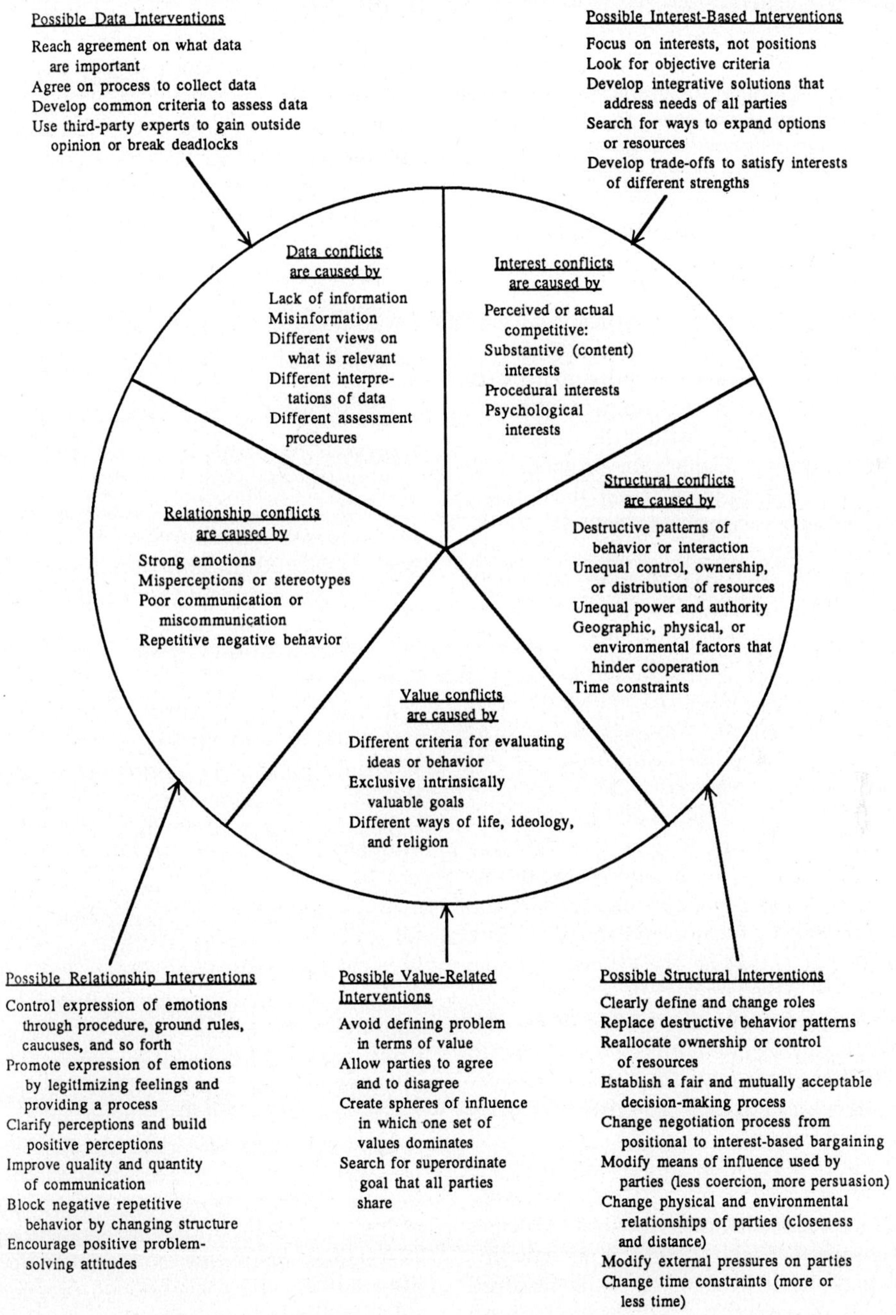

FIGURE 30–1. Sphere of conflict—causes and interventions. (From Moore, C. *The Mediation Process: Practical Strategies for Resolving Conflict.* San Francisco: Jossey-Bass Publishers, 1968, p. 27.)

Understanding the Nature of Conflict

To better understand the nature of a conflict, particular characteristics can be assessed by asking a series of questions. First, *what are the characteristics of the parties involved in the conflict?* Negotiation involves two or more ''parties,'' either groups or individuals; terms such as ''sides'' or ''actors'' are also used to describe groups or individuals.[17,35] For example, a dispute about a choice for consumers in childbirth in a local community may involve at least three parties, each with a somewhat different perspective: administrators of a hospital or birthing center, an individual child-bearing couple or a group of couples, and health care providers who practice within the institution. In addition, individual health care providers, or health care providers from different disciplines, may also represent varying perspectives. In the context of negotiating specific issues, all of the parties involved in the issue must be identified. Other questions to ask about the parties include: What are their values? What are their motives? What are their objectives? What kinds of resources (physical, intellectual, and social) do they possess? What are their conceptions of strategy and tactics?

Second, *what is the prior relationship of one party in a conflict to another party in the conflict?* What are their attitudes, beliefs, and expectations about one another? How do they believe the other parties view themselves? Is their relationship one of trustworthiness? The pre-existing relationship between a childbirth educator and the staff of a local birthing agency may be one of long-standing mutual respect in which each party has generally respected the contributions of the other to the outcome of pregnancy. A childbirth educator new to the community will not have that ''track record'' when she enters a negotiation, and the other party (or parties) may not know what to expect.

A third question is, *what is the nature of the issue giving rise to the conflict?* How rigid is it? How broad is its scope? A relatively limited issue, such as a proposal to allow mothers to have ice chips during labor, will be more easily resolved than a complex issue such as a proposal to increase the number of birthing rooms.

Fourth, *what is the social environment within which the conflict is occurring?* How does that social environment affect the conflict? Is the environment a university teaching hospital, in which women with complex social and physiological needs receive care from a large number of health care providers, or a community hospital that serves primarily women with low-risk pregnancies who receive care from private physicians?

Fifth, *who is the interested audience to the conflict?* Is the conflict taking place in the public spotlight or is it a private matter between the parties? While some conflicts will be most readily resolved away from the public spotlight, the knowledge that a large number of families are interested in the outcome and the implications of that knowledge for public relations may also be a factor in conflict resolution. For example, many couples may be interested in negotiations concerning a change in sibling visiting policies.

Sixth, *what are the strategies and tactics used by the parties in the conflict?* What strategies have been employed up until this time? What are the positive and the negative incentives, promises, rewards, threats, and punishment that are part of the strategies involved? Some conflicts concerning childbearing issues may have produced strong statements from all parties, causing current negotiations to be more difficult or bending to promises to change policies at a propitious time (e.g., when the hospital is remodeled; when staff increases), which may have been made and broken. In the current negotiation, these strategies and tactics will be part of the context in which deliberation occurs.

Seventh, *what is the consequence of the conflict to each of the parties?* What gains or losses do they perceive? What precedent will be established? What internal changes may result from the conflict? How does the conflict affect the long-term relationship between the parties involved? Many of the changes that childbearing couples desire do involve major alterations in traditional relationships between health care providers and families. As families become more active decision makers, they must recognize responsibility for the consequences of those decisions. At a time when the legal system is holding health care providers increasingly responsible for the outcome of pregnancy, many providers may perceive the potential long-term consequences of changes that involve decreased technology as extremely threatening. Yet, this very resistance to consumer desire may affect the provider-client relationship in such an adverse way that the likelihood of litigation may be increased.

Conflict: Positive or Negative

Because most individuals relish peaceful and harmonious relationships, conflict is frequently perceived as negative. Several writers suggest, however, that conflict has the potential for social and individual rewards.[9,10,29] Conflict may be the basis of both personal and social change. Conflict raises new issues, creates new norms, and modifies existing norms, and enables problems to be discussed and solutions to be explored and achieved by various individuals and loosely structured groups together. Conflict can lead to growth and can be productive for all parties.[23] Conflict can also strengthen the bonds of a social relationship and make it more rewarding. "Opposition is a regenerative force that introjects new vitality into a social structure."[5] While both sides may suffer during the conflict, both may benefit when the conflict is resolved satisfactorily.[28]

Power

Power is a key concept in understanding negotiation. Power has been defined as "the ability to influence the behavior of another in an intended direction."[30] Social power has been defined as "the ability or capacity of one person (or group) to produce (consciously or unconsciously) intended effects on the behavior or emotions of another person (or group). . . ."[33] The word *power* is derived from the Latin *potere* and involves the sense of ability and control.[28] These words seem particularly applicable to the sense of power we would wish for childbearing couples and for ourselves. " 'I can' " is the essence of power. "I can do something rather than be at the mercy of other forces. I can produce an effect on something or someone else."[28]

Power is an attribute of a relationship.[3,10,23] Power does not reside in an individual per se, nor does it necessarily remain constant across all situations. One may be powerful in one situation without being powerful in all situations. Six types of power (Table 30–1) have been described: coercive, reward, ecological, normative, referent, and expert.[13]

TABLE 30–1. TYPES OF POWER

TYPE	SOURCE
Coercive	Threats
Reward	Promise of gain
Ecological	Controlling social or political environment
Normative (legitimate)	Social norms governing relationship
Referent	Desire to identify with a person or group
Expert	Acceptance of another's superior knowledge or skill

From French, J., and Ravin, B. The Basis of Social Power. *In* Cartright, D. (ed.) *Studies in Social Power.* Ann Arbor: University of Michigan Press, 1959.

It is obvious that some persons or groups have more power than other persons or groups. How is power obtained and, once obtained, how does an individual or group maintain power? The concept that resources are a source of power is basic in sociology. Resources include tangible or acquired items such as economic wealth and knowledge but also include intangible items such as reputation, character, stamina, patience, and talent.

Deutsch describes the following as key elements of effective power:[10]

1. The control and possession of resources to generate power;
2. The motivation to employ these resources to influence others;
3. Skill in converting the resources into usable power;
4. Good judgment in employing power so that its use is appropriate in type and magnitude to the situation in which it is used.

Knowledge is a potent resource. Power in health care rests in providers who control information (knowledge) and thereby limit the choices of the consumer.[16] An individual (couple or group) can increase power by increasing resources (organization, knowledge, skill or respect, for example) and by increasing effectiveness in the use of power, as proposed by Kotter.[10]

Individuals might evaluate their own developing

power by asking themselves the following questions:[21]

1. Over the past 12 months, how much have I really learned about products or services, the markets, the technologies, and the people with whom I deal?
2. In the past year, how many new people have I gotten to know? With how many people have I strengthened or improved my relationship? Have I alienated anyone?
3. What new skills have I developed in the past year?
4. If I were to update last year's resume, what would I add?
5. Is my reputation as good as or better than a year ago?

Approaches to the Management and Resolution of Conflict

Differences are resolved through a variety of means. Figure 30–2 illustrates common ways of dealing with conflict. Frequently, conflicts are *avoided* by failure of a party to raise an issue when there is a disagreement. Avoidance may occur when neither party feels the issue is very important, but avoidance may also result when one party does not feel he or she has the power to effect a change or when one party does not feel that change for the better is possible.

When one or both parties is unwilling to avoid an issue, the next step frequently involves *informal problem-solving discussions*. Informal discussions and problem solving frequently are successfully used to solve the majority of differences in daily life, but when there is a perceived or actual conflict of interest, the more intentional and structured dispute resolution process of *negotiation* will be required.[23]

Mediation differs from negotation in that mediation involves the assistance of a neutral or impartial third party in helping people resolve differences. The third party must be acceptable to the disputing parties and viewed as impartial.

Beyond negotiation and mediation, several tech-

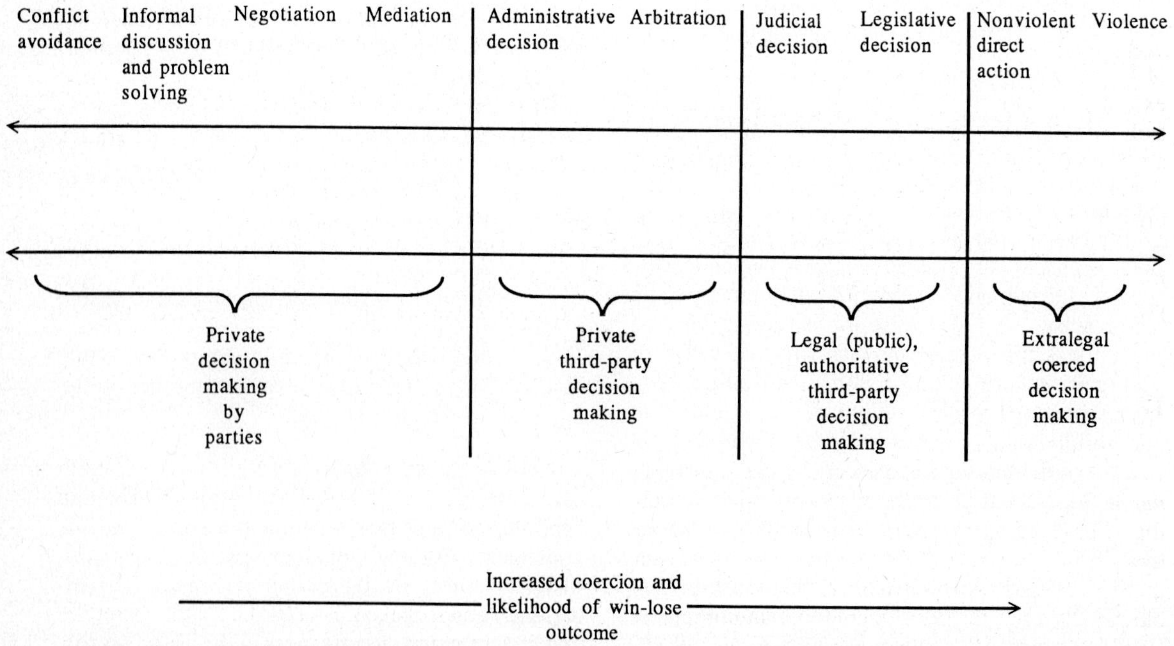

FIGURE 30–2. Common ways of dealing with conflict. (From Moore, C. *The Mediation Process. Practical Strategies for Resolving Conflict.* San Francisco: Jossey Bass Publishers, 1986.)

When there is perceived or actual conflict of interest, the process of negotiation may be required. Negotiation is not a contest of power, but it is the opportunity to create positive solutions and agreements that will be kept by all sides. (Photograph by Rodger Ewy, Educational Graphic Aids, Inc.)

niques exist. As one moves toward the right side of Figure 30–2, there is increasing involvement of external decision makers, decreasing personal control on the part of the parties to the dispute, and an increased likelihood of win-or-lose situations.

Negotiation is an approach most frequently utilized by childbirth educators and childbearing couples. While involvement of a third party as a mediator and other techniques may occasionally be used, they will be far less frequent.

The Process of Negotiation

The word *negotiation* is derived from the Latin *negotiari* and can involve doing business or trading. Negotiation has been defined as "arranging the terms of a contract, transaction, or agreement through talking matters over and working things out."[28] The aim of negotiation is the attainment of "a convergence of interests between previously conflicting parties."[30] "Negotiation is a process of building on common interests and reducing differences in order to arrive at agreement which is at least minimally acceptable to all parties concerned."[17] "Whenever people exchange ideas with the intention of changing relationships, whenever they confer for agreement, they are negotiating."[24]

A key word in the description of negotation is *process*. Process is defined as "a systematic series of actions directed to some end."[26] Three stages have been identified in process; in stages 2 and 3 the lines of demarcation between phases are not absolute.[37]

Stage 1: The diagnosis of the situation combined with the decision to try negotiation (diagnostic phase).

Stage 2: The negotiation of a formula or common definition of the conflict in terms amenable to a solution (formula phase).

Stage 3: Negotiation of the details of dispute (detail phase).

Diagnostic Phase: Preparation for Negotiation. "There are any number of life situations for which preparation is necessary. Negotiation is one of these."[24] As professionals who prepare families for childbirth, childbirth educators understand the value of preparation. How does one prepare for negotiation?

Preparation is both long range and short range.[24] Long-range preparation involves objective self-evaluation, first. An individual identifies traits and biases that would interfere with the ability to negotiate. For example, if one knows oneself to be quick to anger, this trait must be mastered if negotiation is to be successful.

Developing the art of listening, a second facet of long-range preparation, in which one concentrates on what is being said as well as what is not being said,[24] is a skill that, developed over time, can enhance a negotiator's ability.

Short-range preparation includes research through which the negotiator gathers information about both the issues and the persons with whom the negotiation is done. Through this research, one would answer questions such as those below:

- Have you recognized all of the interested parties to the negotiation?
- Is there a time limit?
- Who would like to maintain the status quo and who would like to change it?
- What would be the cost of a stalemate?
- What will be the means of communication between the parties?
- Can many items be introduced into the negotiation simultaneously?[24]

Following data gathering, a brainstorming session involving a group of people who share your goals is useful. In a brainstorming session the individual's thinking is quickened and many fresh, original ideas are obtained that far excel those produced in a conventional conference.[24]

Group drama or role playing is another technique useful in preparation for negotiation. There are several advantages. ''Group dramas give opportunity for self analysis. A study of your own motivation and thinking often gives you clues to the probable point of view of your opponent. This gives you the chance to ask yourself exactly what you want from the forthcoming negotiation. A thorough exploration of this question will serve to clarify your thinking on acceptable solutions to the problems to be negotiated, and will also suggest possible compromises that might be made.''[24]

Formula Phase. A formula provides a substantive framework for agreement and a set of criteria for resolving details.[37] This is the time in a negotiation when agreement on major points is sought. If a formula is carefully constructed or devised, it will provide a helpful means of proceeding to the next phase and of creating specific agreements on details.

Skilled negotiators build on common ground before attempting to reduce differences (Fig. 30–3). The following checklist is useful during this phase:

- Keep a flexible and comprehensive mind set, open to slightly or greatly different ways of encompassing like things, or alternatively of including most in the same package while isolating ''the one that does not belong'' for separate treatment or for postponement.
- Remember that the problem, not the opponent, is the ''enemy'' to be overcome.
- Do not be deterred by unfriendly behavior.

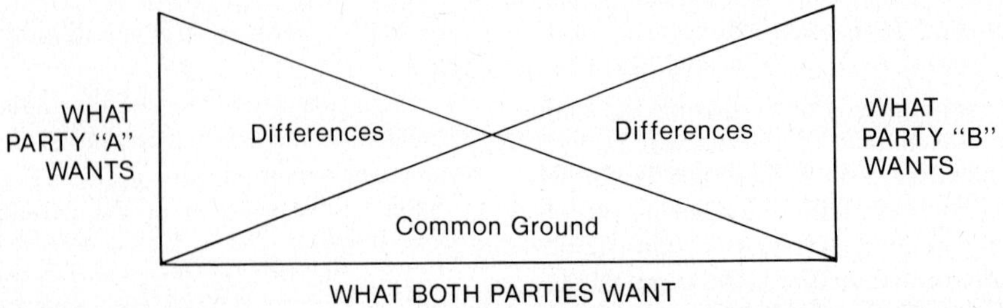

FIGURE 30–3. The Foundation of Negotiation. (From Hawver, D. *How to Improve Your Negotiation Skills.* New York: Modern Business Reports, 1982.)

- Keep talking.
- Think of detailed applications while thinking of broader formulas.[37]

Detail Phase: Working Out Agreements. The detail phase consists of a search for agreement on details to implement the general framework that was developed in the previous phases.[37] As in the formula phase, a checklist is suggested. Two items seem particularly relevant to this discussion:

1. Be clear from the beginning about objectives; do not confuse means with ends.
2. Do not lose the big picture in the little picture.

Oral Communication: The Cornerstone of the Negotiation Process

Most negotiation involves oral communication. The following categories of oral behavior are critical in the negotiating process:[17]

- Seeking information
- Giving information
- Proposing
- Agreeing
- Disagreeing
- Testing understanding
- Summarizing
- Labeling

All negotiations have two parts: *seeking information,* usually by asking questions, and *giving information,* by stating facts alone (external information giving), qualifying facts, or expressing feelings (both forms of internal information giving). Less skilled negotiators give more information and seek less than do those skilled at negotiation.[17] Skilled negotiators, on the other hand, use questions to identify the reasons for resistance by the other party, to politely disagree when direct disagreement may not be appropriate, to build mutual respect by showing interest in the position of the other party, and to lead the discussion into new areas. Skilled negotiators also provide both factual information and opinion, clearly identifying opinion as such and being careful not to present opinions as facts.

Making proposals is basic to negotiation; each party makes proposals to the other. Proposals may involve content (the party's position) or the negotiation process (what will be discussed first, for example, and what may be deferred until later). Skilled negotiators put virtually equal emphasis on content and process proposals and thereby exercise better control over negotiations.[17]

Achieving a balance between *agreement* and *disagreement* is another characteristic of the skilled negotiator. Finding common ground upon which both (all) parties can agree is necessary to successful negotiation. Stating disagreement is also important; when disagreement occurs, the reason for the disagreement must be clearly stated. *Blocking* and *attacking* or *defending* are two common disagreement behaviors. Blocking is disagreeing without giving the reason for the disagreement. Blocking dismisses the position of the other party without examining that position and thereby eliminates the possibility of joint problem solving. Attacking the motives or methods of the other party is a technique rarely used by skilled negotiators. Attacking is generally destructive, but occasionally an attacking statement may serve to indicate displeasure with certain tactics of the other party.

Testing understanding, summarizing, and labeling are *clarifying techniques*. Testing understanding is similar to seeking information in that questions are involved. One party may ask the other "Are you going to do . . . ?" Summarizing at intervals during negotiation can help to refocus attention on the principal issue. A summary is a brief, concise statement of what has transpired to date in a negotiation. The longer and more complex the negotiation, the more important summarizing at intervals becomes.

Labeling, a third clarifying technique, is an attention-getting device. Labeling, through a statement such as, "I want to ask a very important question," helps to focus attention on what you are going to say next. Skilled negotiators label far more frequently than less skilled negotiators.

Not only do skilled negotiators use certain verbal behaviors more frequently but also skilled negotiators use a much greater variety of verbal behaviors, whereas less skilled negotiators have a limited repertoire.[17]

Possible Outcomes of Negotiation

In any conflict situation, there are three possible outcomes. First, one side may win and the other may lose. The term "zero-sum" is used to describe this situation.[37] In a zero-sum situation the person or group on the losing side gains no apparent benefits. The winner "takes all."[28] This is a win-lose situation.[17] A zero-sum outcome is more common in legislative decision-making than in negotiation.

In social interaction, a "mixed-motive" situation[28,35] is more frequent. A mixed-motive situation is one in which "each party may be partly motivated by a desire to cooperate around the common interests in the relationship and partly motivated by a desire to compete . . . ."[7] In relationships between families and the health care system, between a childbirth educator and the health care system, and between a woman and her partner, a mixed-motive situation is far more likely than a zero-sum (win-lose) situation. In a mixed-motive situation, each party gets something they desire. All parties to a negotiation should come out with some needs satisfied.[24]

A third possibility involves an outcome of maximum joint profit (MJP), a term borrowed from economics by sociologists such as the Scanzonis. In MJP, "each individual and the relationship as a whole benefit."[28] At the same time, the transaction sets up a bond between the bargainers and a climate conducive to doing further business together. The term "win-win" describes this situation, in which each party not only gets something that is desired but also feels good about the outcome.

Ongoing relationships between families and childbirth educators and the health care system and between partners make MJP or a win-win situation the most desirable outcome for negotiations related to childbirth. *Negotiation should not be a contest of power, but it should present the opportunity to be supportive and positive in creating solutions and agreements that will be kept by all sides.*[25]

IMPLICATIONS FOR PRACTICE

A childbirth educator may be involved in a negotiation situation as an individual or part of a group. Childbirth educators can also teach women and families skills that will help them negotiate with the health care system on issues important to them. Childbirth educators can analyze and help others to analyze a conflict, increase their own power in a negotiation and empower others, prepare themselves and others for negotiating a specific issue, and increase skills in negotiating.

Analyzing the Conflict

In Hospital Y, the only hospital in your community, it is the policy to monitor all mothers throughout labor using electronic fetal monitoring (EFM). In childbirth education classes you teach couples the value of ambulation during labor and the use of multiple positions for comfort, but continuous fetal monitoring makes it difficult for women to utilize these techniques. In childbirth class, a couple (Mr. and Mrs. J.) asked how this conflict might be negotiated. This is the second child for Mr. and Mrs. J. Mrs. J. has had a healthy pregnancy and is considered at low risk for complications. Using Zartman's notion of stage, this conflict will be considered from the perspective of a (1) diagnostic phase, (2) formula phase, and (3) detail phase.[36]

Diagnostic Phase

The conflict here would appear to be over activities rather than goals. We can assume that all parties clearly share the goal of a healthy baby. However, some parties think that goal is best achieved by continuous electronic fetal monitoring, so that signs of fetal distress may readily be recognized. Other parties believe the mother's comfort, which may reduce the need for medication, and ambulation, which may facilitate labor, are important.

This is primarily data conflict (differing views of what is relevant). There may also be structural conflict (unequal power and authority), value conflict (different criteria for evaluating ideas or behavior), and relationship conflict due to poor communication, misperceptions, stereotypes, or even repetitive negative behavior. In preparing for negotiation, these possibilities need to be considered.

Next, the conflict should be analyzed. First, identify the parties involved in the conflict. You, the childbirth educator, the childbearing couple (Mr. and Mrs. J.), and the physician and hospital nurses are the principal parties. Not all parties may be present together. The J.'s may directly negotiate with their physician, but other parties may be negotiating as well. For example, the J.'s might decide to write to the hospital administration or nursing administration about their desires, and may indeed meet with representatives of one or both groups. The childbirth educator may meet independently with hospital staff.

Each of these parties will have his or her own needs, values, motives, and objectives. For example, nurses in Hospital Y may be very interested in more family-centered care and be supportive of the J.'s position. Mrs. J.'s physician may be sympathetic but, mindful of medical-legal concerns, may believe that allowing any patient to labor without continuous EFM puts him at risk for a liability suit. The childbirth educator may not only support the J.'s but may also be very aware of the long-term potential of the outcome of this negotiation for the other couples she teaches. Be clear about which of the parties would like to maintain the status quo and which would like or be open to change.

In assessing the parties, it will be crucial to understand the sources of power among them. Traditionally physicians have had considerable power in the health care setting; the power of physicians has been both normative (derived from social norms) and expert (derived from the acceptance by others of superior skill and knowledge).

Other parties also have power. The nurses and childbirth educator also have specialized knowledge that is an established resource and thus an important source of power. One way in which childbirth educators empower couples is by increasing the couples' knowledge. In preparation for negotiation, knowledge specific to the issue in conflict is essential. This kind of information is discussed in the section of this chapter called ''Gathering the Facts.'' Be aware of pre-existing relationships between parties. There are a number of relationships important to the resolution of this conflict (Fig. 30–4).

If Mrs. J. is a newcomer to the community, she is less likely to have power to facilitate change in traditional practice in Hospital Y than if she has a personal as well as a professional relationship with the physician and/or hospital nurses. Pre-existing relationships between the childbirth educator and hospital nurses and/or physicians can affect conflict resolution either positively or negatively.

You have already identified some values and goals in thinking about the nature of the conflict—the value of continuous EFM versus the value of ambulation and multiple positions. Another value may be the opportunity to make choices about childbearing. Each party may feel that he or she is the person who should have this opportunity.

The issue is potentially broad in scope. If the current policy is modified for Mr. and Mrs. J., other couples may ask for modification as well. Certainly the interested parties will be aware of this.

In assessing the social environment of Hospital Y, one would be interested in how policy decisions are made. Do nurses, physicians, and administra-

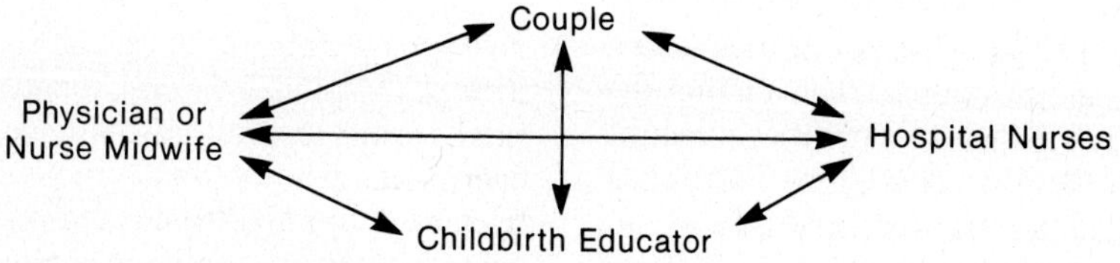

FIGURE 30–4. Relationships among parties.

> The truth is that we are all, men and women, negotiating all the time.
>
> JULIET NIERENBERG and IRENE ROSS[1]
> *Women on the Art of Negotiating*
>
> Although it may meet some of her own needs, a montrice who engages in pitched battles over a mother's body may not be best serving her client. . . . It takes far more patience and skill in the art of human relations and politics to be an effective advocate and negotiator than to fight openly.
>
> BETH SHEARER[2]
>
> Do veterans as compared to less experienced teachers avoid drawing expectant parents into their battles to change obstetric practices? Does this reflect a selling out to the medical establishment or an acceptance of each person as an individual responsible for his or her own decisions?
>
> ELSIE FLEMMING[3]

tors meet jointly to develop and review policy? Does one group make policy and another group administer it? In other words, how does the system work?

A large potential audience may exist for this conflict. Other couples may share the J.'s desire for more flexibility in the conduct of labor. One needs to evaluate carefully, however, whether this particular conflict is best negotiated in the public spotlight or as a private matter. The public spotlight may cause some parties to be more rigid than they might otherwise be. On the other hand, the weight of public opinion might prove helpful.

Find out if others have attempted similar negotiations previously. If so, what were their strategies? What were the responses? The finding that others have tried and failed does not mean that this attempt will fail. Perhaps they were unprepared before, or unskilled during, the negotiation.

The idea of time limits has at least two parts. First, for a couple approaching the time of birth, there are a limited number of weeks in which to prepare and negotiate. Second, finding a time in which the appropriate parties agree to sit down and talk is obviously essential. One cannot negotiate much of anything during the typical office prenatal visit. A physician with an office filled with pregnant women scheduled every 15 minutes is not likely to be very open to even the best of arguments. So time apart from the regular prenatal visit, or additional time prescheduled at the time of the office visit, is essential.

Gathering the Facts

In addition to understanding the dynamics of the situation, preparing for negotiation also involves gathering data specific to the issue. These data might include:

1. The results of research studies published in professional literature.
2. Policies from similar institutions.
3. Written policies and procedures from the institution in question.

The childbirth educator can help childbearing families by providing them with *current information* from studies in childbirth education, nursing, and medical literature. This means, of course, that childbirth educators must themselves keep their knowledge up-to-date through reading and attendance at professional meetings. ASPO/Lamaze, ICEA, and NAACOG frequently review the literature on topics in which conflict exists, which is particularly helpful to childbirth educators who may not have access to nursing and/or medical libraries. Many nursing and medical libraries will allow persons with legitimate interests to use the library. Also, many states have regional systems (e.g., Area Health Education Centers or AHEC's) to bring recent materials to areas away from medical centers.

One of the most persuasive arguments for policy change is *change in similar institutions*. Even though Hospital Y in our example is the only hospital in that community, competition from institutions in neighboring communities may be important. In comparing institutions, one must make sure that they are similar in personnel and facilities. Some practices that may be easily implemented in a small community hospital from which women with complicated pregnancies are transferred early in labor to a regional treatment facility may be implemented with greater difficulty on the high-risk service of a large medical center.

In our example, the childbirth educator may discover that Hospital Q and Hospital Z, both similar in size and population served by Hospital Y, have used intermittent fetal monitoring for two years for women at low risk and have had no adverse fetal or maternal outcomes. In addition, they are willing to discuss their results with appropriate persons at Hospital Y.

Asking for copies of *written policies and procedures* related to the issue under discussion is a third step in data gathering. It is not unusual to find that a practice, while common, is not a written policy and thus may be far more amenable to change. Or the written policy may specify particular conditions such as ''Continuous electronic fetal monitoring will be instituted through order of the attending physician'' or ''Continuous electronic fetal monitoring will be used for all women with admission blood pressure greater than 140/90, diabetes mellitus, Rh disease . . . and for any other woman at the discretion of the attending physician.'' The person negotiating for change is now in a much better position to proceed.

Few childbearing families will have access to policies, although they may request and receive them. Childbirth educators may gain access to policies through letters, meetings with staff, or simple

TABLE 30–2. NEGOTIATING BEHAVIORS* FOR CHILDBIRTH EDUCATORS AND CHILDBEARING FAMILIES

NEGOTIATING BEHAVIORS	EXAMPLES
(From most effective to least effective)	
Listen	
Ask questions	Is fetal monitoring required for all mothers-to-be?
Test understanding	Are you saying that all women in labor must have an IV?
Summarize	Then we agree that . . . .
Give information (external)	I did not have an episiotomy with my two previous births.
Give information (internal)	Having my coach with me during a cesarean delivery is very important to me.
Label	I want to ask a very important question.
Be open	
Agree	Can we agree that the needs of mothers identified as low risk are different from the needs of high-risk mothers?
Develop	Let me explain my reasons for . . .
Disagree	Because of these reasons, I can't agree with you.
Persuade	This solution has advantages for all of us.
Cite common ground	We all have the same goal; a healthy mother and a healthy baby.
Cite limits	Because my time is limited, I can't agree to a six-month delay.
Compromise	(Fetal monitoring intermittently rather than continuously.)
Counterpropose	I can't agree with your proposal, but let me offer another.
Ignore	
Divert	Let's discuss that later.
Postpone	Let's discuss that later.
Block	I don't agree with your position (no reason given).
Confront	That statement is incorrect.
Stop negotiating	(Physically prepare to leave.)

*Negotiating Behaviors are from Hawver, D. *How to Improve Your Negotiating Skills.* New York: Modern Business Reports, 1982.

requests when good working relationships have been established.

When all of the data have been collected, a brainstorming session may be appropriate to consider all possible strategies relevant to the negotiation of the issue. Interested couples, childbirth educators, and other advocates of family-centered childbirth may be part of this group.

Role play of a negotiation—either with a small group or in a childbirth class—is another way to prepare for negotiation. In Table 30–2 examples of a variety of negotiating behaviors described by Hawver[17] are summarized in the context of childbirth education issues. These behaviors can be practiced ahead of time as well as utilized in the negotiation itself. Each childbirth educator would also do well to evaluate her own developing power using Kotter's questions listed earlier in this chapter (p. 508).

Participating in the Negotiation: Formula Phase and Detail Phase

The negotiation has begun. Agreement on major points is being sought. Building on common ground, discussed earlier in this chapter, is a good beginning. No one can anticipate every turn in the negotiating, but the well-prepared party who is able to be flexible is likely to achieve some, if not all,

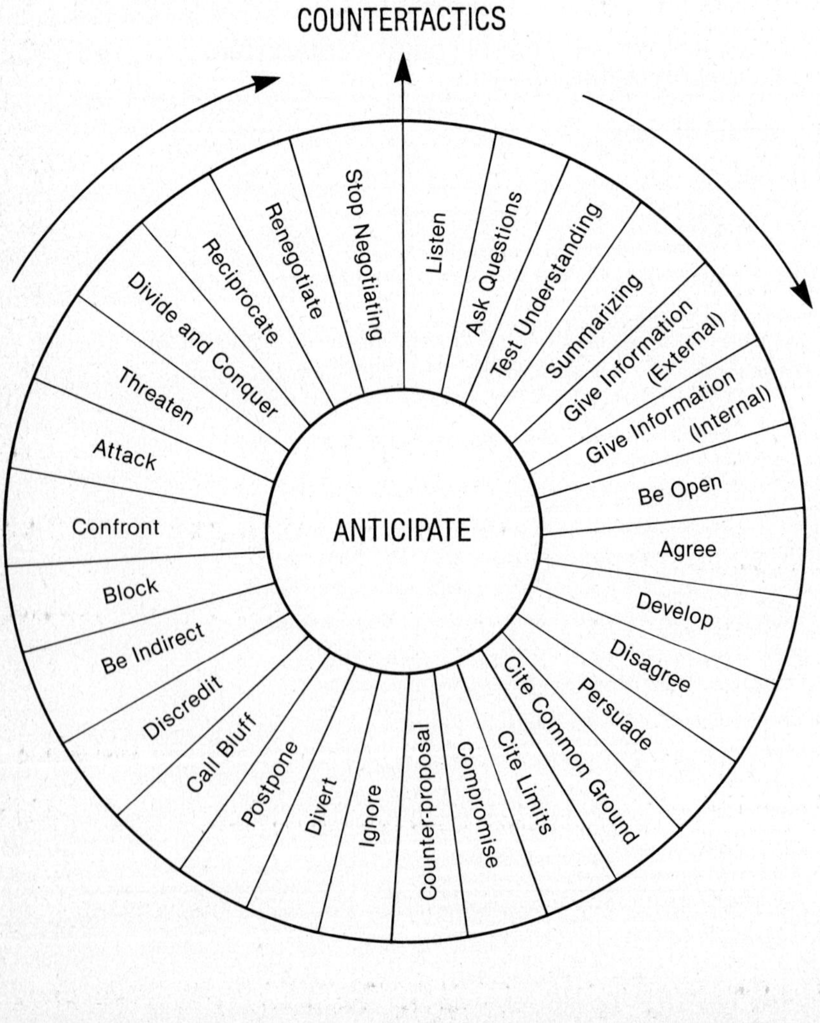

FIGURE 30–5. Countertactics to anticipate during negotiations and approaches that can be used. From Hawver, D. *How to Improve your Negotiation Skills.* New York: Modern Business Reports, 1982.

goals. Hawver[17] has identified many countertactics that can be anticipated and approaches that can be used during negotiations (Fig. 30–5).

During the formula phase: (1) the parties may agree on a goal, the healthy outcome of pregnancy; (2) the J.'s may present the data they have gathered; and (3) the providers representing the institution may agree to review their policies in relation to EFM, particularly as it relates to low-risk and high-risk pregnancies.

During the detail phase: (1) policy review may occur, and (2) changes may be made. Because the activities of the detail phase will probably take weeks to months, the J.'s also ask for a modification of the current policy during their labor. While a firm commitment is not made, a note is placed on Mrs. J.'s prenatal record concerning her wishes. The topic is also placed on the agenda for the next staff meeting.

Evaluating the Outcome

Mr. and Mrs. J. have no desire to ''win'' at all costs; they perceive, rather, that a modification of the present policy will result in maximum joint profit (MJP) for all concerned. Women at high risk and other women identified during the course of labor as potentially benefiting from EFM will be monitored electronically. Women at low risk will be followed with auscultation and intermittent EFM, allowing them the opportunity for increased mobility. The hospital and physician will benefit from community perception of sensitivity to the desire of many childbearing couples. Mr. and Mrs. J. feel satisfied that their desire has been noted and will be considered during their labor, and that a potential policy change will be considered.

IMPLICATIONS FOR RESEARCH

Conflict resolution and negotiation in relation to childbirth education and the experience of childbearing couples have not been a focus of research. Negotiation research, in general, has proceeded along several lines of inquiry. One type of research has focused on interviews with successful negotiators. An appropriate question is, ''What do you know now about negotiations that you wish you had known when you first started?''[37] Among childbirth educators there are successful negotiators who could illuminate the process of negotiation for us. Some of these professionals may have conducted many negotiations, although they may not have conceptualized their efforts in formal terms.

In a second type of research, data on individual negotiations in specific communities addressing particular issues could also be analyzed. In this analysis, questions are used that identify the parties involved, examine the sources of power (e.g., tangible and intangible resources), explore the process, and consider the outcome. Following the model (Fig. 30–6), the parties to the negotiation would first be identified. There would be at least two parties, but there could be three or more. The number of parties may be a variable on understanding the negotiation process. Next, the resources, both tangible and intangible, of each party can be identified. This can be done in a variety of ways. A list of resources to be explored can be developed which might include knowledge and socioeconomic status and self-esteem and patience. Partic-

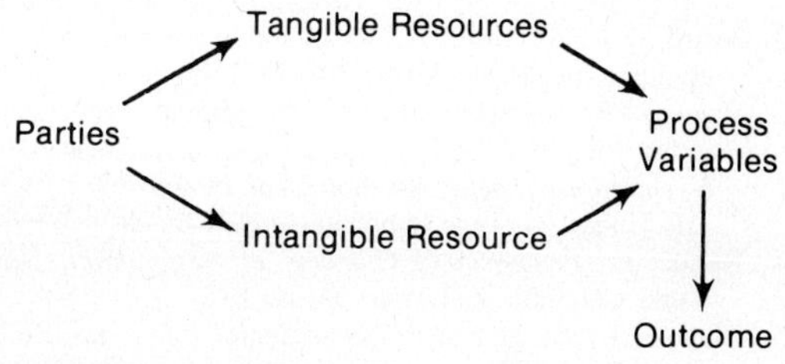

FIGURE 30–6. A research model for negotiation and conflict resolution.

ipants can rate themselves or be rated by an interviewer or observer. Evaluation of the process can also be developed from several perspectives. For example, an observer might utilize a list of negotiating behaviors, such as that found in Table 30–2, and identify each time a particular behavior was used by a party to the negotiation. The outcome of negotiation can also be evaluated. Was there a clear "winner" or did each side achieve certain goals?

The answers to the questions above constitute the raw data for the analysis of the negotiation. The researcher can now ask a number of further questions.

- What was the relationship between resources and negotiating behaviors? between resources and outcome?
- What was the relationship between negotiating behaviors and outcome?
- Were internal or external resources more important?
- Which negotiating behaviors were most successful?

Still another type of research that has potential for exploring negotiation in childbirth education issues involves the use of a simulated negotiating experience. A group of parents and/or childbirth educators and/or health care providers is presented with a hypothetical conflict situation; observers analyze and evaluate the process.

SUMMARY

Conflict is an integral part of life. The study of conflict resolution and negotiation is ongoing in many disciplines. A body of knowledge has been developed that includes understanding of the role of resources, power, specific skills, and the negotiation process. When childbirth educators incorporate this knowledge into their classes and their advocacy for change in childbirth practices, they increase the likelihood of successful negotiations and outcomes in which all parties feel like winners.

References

1. Adamson, G., and Gore, D. Home or hospital births. *Journal of American Medical Association* 243:1731, 1980.
2. Avard, D., and Nemrod, C. Risks and benefits of obstetric epidural anesthesia. *Birth* 12(4):215, 1985.
3. Bagozzi, R., and Dholakia, R. Mediational mechanisms in interorganizational conflict. *In* D. Druckman (ed.) *Negotiations; Social Psychological Perspectives*. Beverly Hills, CA: Sage Publications, 1977.
4. Bartos, O. *Process and Outcome of Negotiation*. New York: Columbia University Press, 1974.
5. Blau, P. *Exchange and Power in Social Life*. New York: John Wiley & Sons, 1964.
6. Bostrom, R. *Persuasion*. Englewood Cliffs, NJ: Prentice-Hall, 1983.
7. Brickman, P. *Social Conflict*. Lexington, MA: D.C. Heath, 1974.
8. Burnett, C. Home delivery and neonatal mortality in North Carolina. *Journal of American Medical Association* 244:2741, 1980.
9. Coser, L. *The Function of Social Conflict*. Glencoe, IL: Free Press, 1956.
10. Deutsch, M. *The Resolution of Conflict*. New Haven: Yale University Press, 1973.
11. Edwards, M., and Waldorf, M. Reclaiming birth: History of heroines of American childbirth reform. *Genesis* 6:11, December, 1984/January, 1985.
12. Fisher, R., and Ury, W. *Getting to Yes*. Boston: Houghton Mifflin, 1981.
13. French, J., and Ravin, B. The basis of social power. *In* D. Cartright (ed.) *Studies in Social Power*. Ann Arbor: University of Michigan Press, 1959.
14. Geyman, J. Toward a middle ground in the technology debate in obstetric care. *The Journal of Family Practice* 12:971, 1981.
15. Gulliver, P. *Disputes and Negotiations: A Cross-Cultural Perspective*. New York: Academic Press, 1979.
16. Hamilton, P. *Health Care Consumerism*. St. Louis: C. V. Mosby, 1982.
17. Hawver, D. *How to Improve Your Negotiation Skills*. New York: Modern Business Reports, 1982.
18. Henningsson, A., Nystrom, B., and Tunnell, R. Bathing or washing babies after birth. *Lancet* 2:1401, 1981.
19. Ilick, J. *Power Negotiating*. Reading, MA: Addison-Wesley, 1980.
20. Karrass, C. *The Negotiating Game*. New York: World Publishing Company, 1970.

21. Kotter, J. *Power and Influence: Beyond Formal Authority.* New York: The Free Press, 1985.
22. McKay, S. The limits of choice in childbirth. *Genesis* 7:8, 1985.
23. Moore, R. *The Mediation Process. Practical Strategies for Resolving Conflict*. San Francisco: Jossey-Bass, 1986.
24. Nierenberg, G. *The Art of Negotiating*. New York: Hawthorn Books, 1968.
25. Nierenberg, J., and Ross, J. *Women and the Art of Negotiating*. New York: Simon and Schuster, 1985.
26. *Random House Dictionary of the English Language*. New York: Random House, 1967.
27. Roberts, J., and Van Lier, D. Debate: Which position for second stage? *Childbirth Educator* 3:33, 1984.
28. Scanzoni, J., and Scanzoni, L. *Men, Women and Change. A Sociology of Marriage and Family.* New York: McGraw-Hill, 1976.
29. Simmel, G. *Conflict*. New York: Free Press, 1955.
30. Spector, B. A Social-Psychological Model of Position Modification: Asuan. *In* Zartman, I. W. (ed.) *The 50% Solution*. New York: Anchor Books, 1976.
31. Strauss, A. *Negotiations: Varieties, Contexts, Processes, and Social Order.* San Francisco: Jossey-Bass, 1978.
32. Swingle, P. *The Structure of Conflict*. New York: Academic Press, 1970.
33. Winter, D. *The Power Motive*. New York: Free Press, 1973.
34. Young, D. The bonding controversy. *Childbirth Educator* 3:44, 1984.
35. Zartman, I. W. The Analysis of Negotiation. *In* Zartman, I. W. (ed.) *The 50% Solution*. New York: Anchor Books, 1976.
36. Zartman, I. W. *The Negotiation Process: Theories and Applications*. Beverly Hills: Sage Publications, 1978.
37. Zartman, I. W., and Berman, M. *The Practical Negotiator.* New Haven: Yale University Press, 1982.

Beginning Quote

Fisher, R., and Ury, W. *Getting to Yes*. Boston: Houghton Mifflin, 1981.

Boxed Quotes

1. Nierenberg J., and Ross, I. *Women on the Art of Negotiating*. New York: Simon and Schuster, 1985.
2. Shearer, B. Whose Birth, Whose Body, Whose Baby is it? *Birth* 11:174, 1984.
3. Flemming, E. Needed: More Study of Veteran Childbirth Educators. *Birth* 11:173, 1984.

chapter 31

SETTING UP A PRACTICE

NORMA NEAHR WILKERSON and SHARRON SMITH HUMENICK

Teaching Lamaze classes is a professional business that requires a commitment of considerable time and enthusiasm. Students will quickly assess the validity of your interest. This interest in your students, coupled with your competency as a teacher, is your most powerful business asset.

Sharyn Huffman

Twenty to thirty years ago, childbirth education had limited acceptance in the medical community, and hence most childbirth educators began in private practice, often in their living rooms. Now the "living room" class is the minority. However, some fear that the childbirth education movement is becoming co-opted by big business in the health care industry. Now that the cost of health care is higher than it ever has been, community-based obstetricians and hospitals are also concerned with markets for their practices and services (see Chapter 32 on Marketing Strategies). Projections have been made that by the year 2000 there will be a 145 per cent excess of obstetricians and gynecologists in the United States.[9] Nevertheless, despite a relatively low birth rate, family physicians and nurse-midwives are re-emerging as primary care providers. Independent community birth centers are being built and maintained by family practice physicians and nurse-midwives.

Physicians and hospitals are more motivated than ever to offer packaged services, including childbirth education classes, in order to entice the consumer to utilize their services and their institutional facilities. Thus, childbirth education classes have been recognized as a valuable means for health care providers and institutions to compete for maternity clients. Is it any surprise that today there are numerous debates over the changing nature of organizational practice patterns for childbirth educators?

Scenarios such as the following are being encountered daily by childbirth educators.

Case: Suppose you are a new childbirth educator who is ready to begin teaching. Where should you teach, in a private practice? For a local parent-child association? For a hospital? Are there other options?

Case: Suppose you are an established childbirth educator who has worked hard for years to build a strong community-based group of childbirth educators who teach together. Two newer teachers, however, are making plans to break from the group to begin their own private practice. What is your response?

Case: Suppose the classes in your community have been provided by several groups such as a childbirth and parent education association, a community hospital, and teachers in private practice. All these teachers meet regularly and share a consumer-oriented philosophy. A new hospital is being built by a large national chain. Their well-financed advertising campaign states that they will offer free childbirth education classes. What are your feelings? What will you do?

An ethnographic approach was used to study organizational patterns in childbirth education for 10 years, in consultation with childbirth educators throughout the country. The advantages and disadvantages of four childbirth education practice patterns were identified. Although combinations or modifications of these patterns also exist, the four primary practice patterns are (1) agency employee practice, (2) private practice of one or more childbirth educators, (3) open-ended group practice accepting all qualified childbirth educators, and (4) associated practice networks.

In this chapter, the major issues facing childbirth educators as they determine the type of practice that is most appropriate for their professional goals and resources will be discussed. In addition, actual and potential solutions to problems encountered by individuals within the four major organizational patterns will be analyzed. Although there are no "cookbook" answers to the issues raised, recommendations are made for childbirth education practice and research.

REVIEW OF THE LITERATURE

There are major issues and current trends in the health care industry that influence all health care providers, including childbirth educators. Recognition and analysis of these factors is vital in order to make informed decisions regarding the type of practice to choose. Issues to be described here include the following: economics and cost-containment and reimbursement mechanisms; entrepreneurialship; current definitions of professionalism; competition among existing institutions; national health corporations (corporate power); oversupply and/or maldistribution of services; and politics or vested interests.

Economics, Cost-Containment, and Reimbursement Issues

Health care services are becoming increasingly expensive for the consumer. Furthermore, consumers have come to expect their insurance to pay for most of their required health care services and may prefer services that are covered. Therefore, nurses and childbirth educators who are in private practice are at a competitive disadvantage economically if they are not defined as eligible for third-party payment for services rendered.[4]

Hershey describes "free choice laws" as the mechanism that many states have enacted in order to require health care insurers to pay for services rendered by providers other than physicians. Where they exist, such laws require the insurer to pay for services that "would be paid for if rendered by a physician."[4] Professionals who seek to benefit from these laws will need to determine if their state has such a law. Even when covered by such a law, childbirth educators often need to mount campaigns to become eligible for these benefits.

Nurse-midwives and certified registered nurse anesthetists have become primary beneficiaries of changes in third-party payment practices resulting from these free choice laws. Therefore, it would appear that delivery of prenatal services, childbirth, and administration of anesthesia are considered to be services identical or equivalent to aspects of physicians' services. However, as Hershey further points out, inclusion of other benefits (such as childbirth education) by an insurance company depends on business decisions made by the insurers or on "existence of legislation concerning mandatory options or mandatory benefits."[4]

A mandatory *option* in a given state requires the insurer to offer the benefit as an option for which the consumer must pay additional premiums. A mandatory *benefit* is a requirement that all insurers in that state must provide a specific benefit to everyone. Needless to say, the insurance industry is opposed to both forms of legislation. Childbirth educators provide services that theoretically could be included under either category where such laws exist. If childbirth education classes can be shown to be cost effective, insurers will be more eager to include them as benefits to the health consumer.

In any study of cost containment, it must be realized that the United States does not have a "health care delivery system," but rather a very expensive "sickness care system."[2] Childbirth education is truly within the realm of health and wellness. If rising costs and consumer dissatisfaction with fragmented maternity care are to be changed, new models of health care delivery need to be developed. Childbirth educators are encouraged to be innovative and flexible as they explore ways to work with society in developing more holistic models of maternity care.

Entrepreneurialship

One health care provider model is that of the entrepreneur. A definition of an entrepreneur is "a person who organizes, operates, and assumes the risk for business ventures, especially an impresario."[10] Since the root of the word impresario implies the undertaking of a brave and honest deed in the service of the public, in one sense it seems especially appropriate for childbirth educators to become entrepreneurs.

Entrepreneurs are also described as comprehending the correlation between effort expended and productivity measured in terms of outcomes. They wish to earn their dollars for specific services rather than earn a wage for appearing at work and going through motions that may or may not lead to consistent results. Autonomy, freedom, risk-taking, self-motivation, accountability, and perpetual change are essential values of entrepreneurs, who perceive themselves as agents of their own success or failure.

The entrepreneurial process has been defined specifically by those who have developed their own practices;[2,5] however, there are common elements for any entrepreneurial business venture. The following elements seem to be especially appropriate to childbirth education.

Initially, there must be identification of the opportunity. A problem must exist that the business will solve, or a need must exist that can be filled. In childbirth education, there is the need for non-illness-oriented, consumer (expectant parent)-controlled childbirth experiences. The entrepreneur then analyzes the business risks involved in creating a means to fill this need. Many times this is referred to as a "needs assessment" approach to a problem. This process is more completely described in Chapter 32 on marketing.

Following the needs assessment, a planning process must occur. One example of such a planning process[2] includes a proposal documenting the purpose of the practice, the need for it, the philosophical framework on which it will be based, and the anticipated services. For example, exploration of a contract between entrepreneurs and hospitals potentially can offer affiliation within a private practice framework. In deciding on specific services, it is vital to consider how a private practice (free-standing or affiliated) can compete with free (no fee) classes that might be provided by hospitals or other agencies in the community.

Examples of such additional services (beyond standard classes) which could make a private practice competitive might include the expertise of the instructor in a specific area; smaller class size; accountability in measuring learner outcomes; classes for the entire childbearing year; and additional services such as lending library, infant care supplies such as developmental toys, self-care items such as breast pumps, and referral service for child care.

Financial considerations must also be part of the planning process. How much money does the entrepreneur have to invest? How much would be needed for start-up costs? How much for day-to-day operations? A thorough business plan will be required in order to obtain financing. A business plan includes information about the practice, the childbirth educator's professional and financial goals, a marketing plan, an itemization of costs, profit and loss projections for two or three years, resumes, and personal financial statements.

It is vital to select the entrepreneurial team most suited to the business venture. Is the business going to be a "one-man-show," or will there be partners and associates? Thorough consideration of the pros and cons of either enterprise is important for making the most profitable decision given available human resources. One entrepreneur describes partnership in private practice as being like a marriage.[8] The interpersonal factors are essential, and personalities must be carefully considered. Compatibility in terms of values and philosophical orientation is more important than expediency. Success will depend upon ability to keep lines of communication open.

Evaluation of the practice business is an on-going process. The most obvious consideration is documentation of monthly profit and loss. Marketing efforts and community visibility must be evaluated periodically. Revisions are made according to the data. The person in private practice will need to consult a bookkeeper or accountant, an insurance agent, and an attorney for assistance in keeping abreast of the latest regulations.

On-going classes should be evaluated with both objective business and learner data. Business-oriented data include such information as the number of couples registered for the classes, the number of classes offered per instructor, and the number of instructors required. Learner-oriented data are collected by using evaluation forms during the classes. Many variations exist, including such components as personal satisfaction as well as achievement of learning objectives.

Issues of Professionalism

The issue of entering independent private practice as an individual professional as opposed to serving the public as an agency employee is of particular concern to many childbirth educators. In a discussion of the historical perspectives of nursing's professionalism, Crowder has identified four essential elements as requirements for successful professional practice: education, commitment to the profession, community sanction, and professional organization.[1] These have particular application to childbirth education.

First, childbirth educators in any practice setting ideally must have strong educational qualifications for the teaching of childbirth education and birthing skills to expectant parents. It is now generally accepted that professional childbirth educators should be able to provide information about the physical and emotional events that might occur during the childbearing year, as well as the skills needed for labor, birth, and the early postpartal period.[3] Furthermore, high-quality childbirth education is based on the philosophy that providing childbirth education will also enhance the wellness behaviors of expectant parents as well as their skill for coping with life in general. Transfer of learning to other areas of class members' lives is a secondary, but important, goal of such classes.

In addition to formal educational preparation for implementing these goals, the professional childbirth educator values continuing education. A qualified technician in some fields may function for an entire career on the basis of the instructions received in an apprenticeship. In contrast, a childbirth educator is a professional whose skills will soon be out of date and who will not be able to maintain competency if she does not keep up with developments in the field of childbirth education. Thus, an additional commitment of time and money will be required from the professional childbirth educator in order to maintain competency for the business of childbirth education.

The question of whether or not a childbirth educator can provide high-quality classes and still earn good money has been raised.[11] While high quality of instruction and an adequate level of income generated from class fees are not incompatible, the issue raised by this question relates to professional commitment. Childbirth educators who perceive their practice as either temporary (until something better comes along) or as a part of another profession such as nursing may not view childbirth education as a profit-making business. But, income is not the sole motivation for teaching. The childbirth educator with a professional identity views herself as a member of a professional group. Long-term commitment to the activities involved in childbirth education will motivate her to improve her methods and enhance her working conditions in order to obtain a sense of satisfaction from her work with expectant parents as well as monetary rewards.

On the other hand, as Steffes states, the professional teacher with a good income will be most likely "to keep her library and teaching aids updated, to attend continuing education programs regularly, to maintain professional contacts among community groups and in birthing agencies used by her clientele, attend births, and provide other services to parents and professionals."[11] Furthermore, the professional does not "feel guilty" charging for high-quality services provided to the consumer. Thus, adequate income and quality services are complementary, not opposing, forces in professional identity as a childbirth educator.

Community sanction is another hallmark of a professional.[1] When the childbearing public identifies childbirth educators as important to their lives as their physician, clergyman, dentist, or attorney, true professional status will have been attained. In order to reach this goal, childbirth educators must not only provide quality services but they must also be able to demonstrate that their services *make a difference* in childbearing outcomes.

Childbirth educators who develop valid and reliable methods of measuring parental, neonatal, and family outcomes will be providing truly professional services. Furthermore, they will be able to improve their practices on the basis of scientifically obtained data. Humenick[6] outlines the major outcomes to be measured as follows: assessment of skills class members are learning, knowledge gained, attitudinal change, couples' satisfaction with classes and instructor, and birth outcomes.

Not only will consumers be meeting their initially perceived learning needs, they will have developed measurable skills to use during the childbearing year. Quality outcomes beget consumer satisfaction; consumer satisfaction is a good form of advertising; advertising attracts clients; and the final result will be productive income as well as quality education.

Skilled childbirth educators with well-developed professional role identity are motivated to develop additional services for expectant parents. For example, they will perceive themselves as able to offer emotional support to their clients, make home visits during the childbearing year, and prepare educational programs related to the childbearing year and beyond. Such programs could include topics related to parenting, breastfeeding, sibling rivalry, nutrition, and sexuality.

In summary, an analysis of the issues involved in private nursing practice shows both positive and negative aspects of independent professional practice. The focus in this literature review has been on private practice issues because that is a form of practice that few childbirth educators were socialized to consider in their basic education, be it nursing, physical therapy, education, or another field. It is therefore a new concept to many childbirth educators as they enter the field and consider their options. The following positive aspects presented in Koltz's[7] analysis of private practice in general have been adapted here for professional childbirth educators.

1. For consumers who want greater access to options in childbirth education, private practice can create services from which communities will benefit.
2. Childbirth education is preventive care; it has the potential to lower health costs and ultimately reduce insurance premiums.
3. Private practice can be rewarding and satisfying; a wide variety of expanded services can be made available. Childbirth educators can make home visits or offer many types of classes and can spend more time with clients who need it.
4. There are few restrictions for childbirth educators as to geographic location; practice can be established in a variety of settings—home, store front, professional building, and the like.
5. Childbirth educators in private practice may achieve greater self-esteem, confidence, and assertiveness. They may have more time available for teaching and may have the potential for greater collaboration with physicians and acquisition of new skills.

In the next section, the advantages and disadvantages of a variety of types of practice for childbirth education are reviewed.

IMPLICATIONS FOR PRACTICE

Childbirth educators develop personal goals for practice on the basis of their own value systems as well as the resources within their unique community environments. Having analyzed related issues as described in the previous literature review, childbirth educators can choose from several practice patterns. The purpose of this section of the chapter is to offer guidelines for practice in regard to the advantages and disadvantages of four primary practice patterns: (1) agency practice as an employee, (2) private practice of one or more childbirth educators, (3) open-ended group practice accepting all qualified childbirth educators, and (4) associated practice networks.

The Agency Employee

The agency employee pattern is advantageous to the childbirth educator who does not want to spend the time necessary to build a private practice. A childbirth educator who moves frequently or is committed to another job may prefer to work for an agency. Typically, the agency assumes responsibility for recruitment of expectant couples, registering students, buying equipment, collecting fees, and handling bookkeeping. The childbirth educator is free to spend her energy teaching.

Case: Jane, a graduate student, found teaching childbirth classes for a local hospital a convenient way to supplement the family income. She planned to move to a new community at the end of her program.

Disadvantages of the agency employee pattern are similar to those of any salaried position. Disagreements may arise about salary, benefits, or policies. More seriously, there may be interference by agency supervisory personnel or medical staff in the curriculum for classes. The employed childbirth educator may feel primarily accountable to the employing agency and only secondarily to the expectant couples in the classes. It may take an assertive teacher to successfully maintain a consumer-oriented class series or to control class size. Some teachers work out satisfactory agreements with employing agencies; others have not been able to do so.

Case: In one large hospital, childbirth educators were expected to emphasize the merits of epidural anesthesia, which was used routinely. Only when the instructors documented decreasing enrollment in their classes, as opposed to an increase in enrollment in a more consumer-oriented class being taught by a private practice group, were they able to change the hospital curriculum. The curriculum was modified to emphasize choices that an

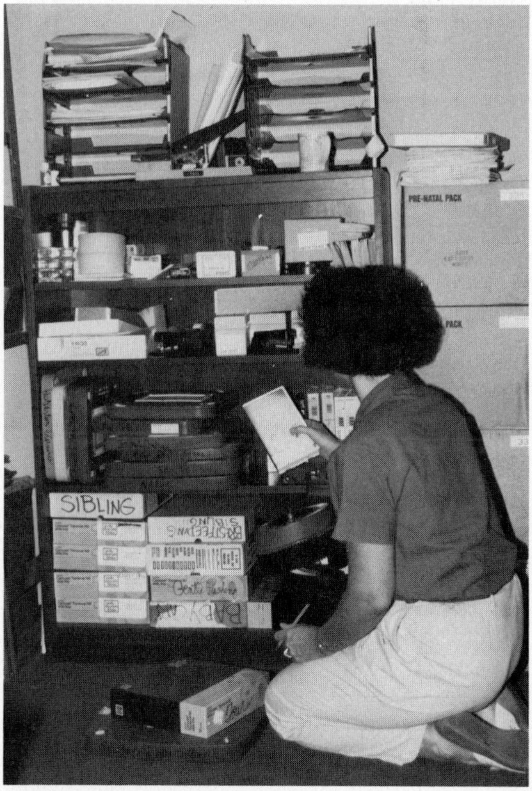

FIGURE 31–1. Taking inventory. An adequate supply of audiovisual materials and other teaching resources such as a childbirth lending library is essential. Audiovisual aids and supplies should be checked regularly, to determine if additional ones are needed or if current ones need to be replaced. (Photograph by Francine H. Nichols. Courtesy of Equicor Health Plan, Inc., Wichita, KS.)

informed couple could make during their birth experience.

Rarely does an agency employ a childbirth educator in a full-time position as childbirth or parent educator. Thus, those who want a full-time salary will often divide their energy between childbirth education and another job. Opportunities for advancement will typically lie with the "other job." This situation may eventually encourage the childbirth educator to leave the field of childbirth education.

Case: When Susan was promoted to supervisor on her job, she reluctantly gave up teaching childbirth classes and focused her career toward her new administrative position. Subsequently, the other childbirth educators missed her leadership skills, which had been helpful on many occasions.

Private Practice

Private practice may consist of one individual or a partnership. An advantage of private practice is professional independence. If the practice is highly successful, it may pay better than an agency salary or the income derived from membership in a larger group practice. Initially, however, the costs of supplies, films, accounting, and other administrative functions—as well as the time spent on details of putting the practice together—may result in meager profits. However, the childbirth educator in private practice has the opportunity to benefit from establishing a reputation for excellence. If the childbirth educator is motivated to provide quality, consumer-oriented, outstanding classes, referrals from satisfied clients will begin to accumulate. Childbirth educators wishing to expand their business may use the practice as a base from which to offer related services.

Case: As her children entered school, Loretta wished to work more hours without increasing her evenings away from home. She rented classroom space and expanded her business to include daytime prenatal exercise classes, mother-infant exercise classes, and classes on menopausal adjustments for women. Selling a selection of related books, tapes, and products provided additional profit.

The greatest disadvantage of private practice is the risk involved. There is no guaranteed profit. Private practitioners must be assertive, energetic, creative, dedicated individuals who are able to network effectively throughout their community. If private practitioners are to survive competition with hospitals and large, established, open-ended and associated group practices, they must learn some survival skills.

Case: JoAnn, who loved teaching, nearly quit private teaching after facing up to the fact that she was working for $.50 per hour. However, she took a course in small business management, simplified her registration and bookkeeping systems, produced attractive, high-quality brochures explaining her services, and assertively called upon local physicians who might make referrals to her. Ultimately, she found she could profitably continue the work she loved so well.

Open-Ended Group Practice

In an open-ended practice pattern, all teachers who are certified by the group's national certifying body and move to town are eligible to join a practice and be assigned expectant parents as students. This pattern has been especially effective in areas with transient populations. Open-ended group practice has some of the advantages of the agency employee pattern. Childbirth educators may incorporate, employ themselves, and hire others to manage many of the administrative and business details. This pattern also has an advantage similar to private practice in that control of the practice belongs to childbirth educator members. They set their own class size, fees, and curriculum. Such groups tend to be highly consumer-oriented.

Case: Ruth, an experienced childbirth educator, was married to an Air Force captain. They moved, on the average, every two years. Her national childbirth education group usually had an open-ended practice group into which she was automatically accepted in the new town. It made getting started teaching in a new town so much easier.

Some open-ended groups have as many as 40 childbirth educators. In the early years when childbirth education was new and controversial, this pattern served the community and childbirth educators well. There was strength in numbers. Many groups have now modified this pattern. However, when several members function as a single practice, organizational problems can easily develop.

Individuals who have left such group practices report that their two main reasons for doing so were desire for financial independence and need for professional autonomy. When need for professional autonomy is a strong reason for members considering leaving, it would serve the group well to examine its bylaws and policies. If the group is rigid, requiring members to teach in the same way and thereby stifling creativity, it will probably not survive growing competition.

Case: Juanita, an experienced childbirth educator who belonged to a well-established, open-ended group practice, left it because she felt stifled by group policies on class fees, size, and content. She believed that on her own she could offer a superior service.

Case: Members of an open-ended group practice were concerned when several discussed leaving the group. The group responded by working to accommodate individual teachers. Referrals from physicians and midwives for particular instructors were honored. Instructors who were ''popular'' and who received personal requests for services were evaluated as excellent practitioners and allowed to benefit from their excellence. Members were free to incorporate their preferred methods. The only group expectation was that members maintain a consumer-oriented standard, attend monthly in-service education sessions, and participate in peer review.

Contracting

Childbirth education has become widely accepted and increasingly profitable as a marketing strategy; thus, more hospitals and agencies can be expected to hire teachers and offer childbirth preparation classes. Groups—whether open-ended or in private practice—should consider negotiating to offer services through hospitals, health departments, health maintenance organizations, and physician practice groups. Contracting is a survival skill that is proving useful.

It may be advantageous for childbirth educators to assess community needs and be prepared to make the first move toward proposing contracts. Childbirth educators who contract their services function similarly to those providing private laboratory or anesthesia services who contract with a hospital but retain more autonomy than do regular employees. They thus have the advantages of promoting their philosophy while benefiting financially from the additional classes.

Case: Vernella, an excellent, popular instructor for an established childbirth educators group, was actively recruited to teach for a local physician group practice. She did not really wish to leave the group; however, the higher salary was an important factor in her consideration of the offer. With her permission, the group approached the physicians and offered to have her teach all of their classes through contractual arrangements with the organization. All were benefited by the final contract—the physicians obtained the services they desired, the instructor was able to earn additional money, and the organization gained financially from the additional classes while retaining a valuable member.

Case: In a large urban community a local hospital decided to become more family-oriented in order to salvage its maternity service. They remodeled, built birthing suites, replaced traditional delivery rooms with labor-delivery-recovery suites, and approached the group practice to ''train'' their nurses in childbirth education. The group presented a counterproposal offering to ''educate'' the nurses, who would then become members of the childbirth educator group practice and would teach classes in the hospital through the organization.

Mutual benefits from these contracts include new members, financial gain for the group practice from additional classes, well-prepared instructors for the hospital contributing to larger numbers of private patients for their maternity service, and educational benefits for the nurses, including continuing inservice and peer review. Ultimately, these innovative arrangements improve the quality of childbirth education for expectant couples.

Associated Practice Networks

The associated practice pattern allows for many types of practice to exist in competition in a community while maintaining a level of cooperation. The associated practice may be organized around members being certified by the same national group. In some communities membership represents a variety of national groups and the focus of the organization is that all teach in one community.

The degree of cooperation in such an association may be as low as holding meetings and sponsoring speakers of interest. It may be as high as maintaining an office through which lists of member-

> Implementing the plan in putting into action the goals and objectives of a program depends on careful consideration of human, financial and material resources. The childbirth educator must carefully weigh the advantages and disadvantages of private practice versus employment status in terms of the educator's own personality and ability to cope with the outcome of each. Examination of funding resources is necessary to build a full program that can supply adequate material resources such as childbirth education library, films, slides, charts, and other teaching tools.
>
> JEANNETTE SASMOR

teachers and their services are distributed. Such groups often set standards of practice for childbirth education for the community.

The advantage of this organizational pattern is that it allows for association and cooperation of childbirth educators from diverse organizational patterns. The right and desirability of each childbirth educator to select a practice pattern that best meets her needs is recognized. Private practice is supported but not required. When private practice teachers are clearly accountable to the clients they teach, they have built-in motivation to remain consumer-oriented. The coexistence of teachers in many types of practice patterns adds impetus to keeping childbirth education consumer-oriented throughout the community.

A disadvantage of this pattern may be that it takes strong leadership to keep diverse groups working together. It takes skill to achieve the fine balance of associating and cooperating without stifling one another. Groups may need outside consultation to achieve their goals. However, successful networks are more apt to survive and flourish than isolated group practices, which may stagnate.

Case: The Regional Education Association of Childbirth Educators of Puget Sound (REACH) is a prototype for the associated practice. This group is organized solely for improvement of the quality of childbirth education in the area. Membership is varied (for example, it may include both Lamaze and Bradley advocates, hospital teachers, independent private teachers, and Red Cross teachers). There is no membership fee; anyone who considers herself a member is a member. The association recruits well-prepared speakers and sponsors two inexpensive continuing education programs yearly that have been highly successful in attracting both lay and professional attendance. The association operates on a ''pay as we go,'' nonprofit basis.

IMPLICATIONS FOR RESEARCH

The following studies would be useful to childbirth educators:

- What is the organizational pattern of flourishing practices?
- What variables are predictive of success in delivering comprehensive, family-centered maternity services?
- What is the cost effectiveness within a given health care delivery system of one childbirth education pattern versus another?
- What support is necessary for childbirth educators to compete in private practice?
- What are the differences between the organizational policies of open-ended groups and group private practice?
- What are the characteristics of associated practice patterns with special attention to the collaboration across different types of practice?

SUMMARY

There is no organizational pattern that is best for providing childbirth education. Instructors, those affiliated with maternity services, and consumers all have particular needs to be considered. Childbirth educators will benefit from carefully considering the alternatives and making informed decisions regarding the type of practice in which they engage. As the field of childbirth education continues to grow, more communities will have a variety of organizational patterns for delivering childbirth education.

The quality of service offered to both expectant parents and the community as a whole should be the guiding principle in judging the practice of childbirth education. Through united efforts, childbirth educators can continue to work toward high standards of childbirth education and, subsequently, optimal birth practices across the United States. Therefore, research identifying quality outcomes is most vital in order to develop standards for childbirth education regardless of the type of practice.

References

1. Crowder, E. Historical perspectives of nursing's professionalism. *Occupational Health Nursing* 33:184, 1985.
2. Dickerson, P., and Nash, B. The business of nursing: Development of a private practice. *Nursing and Health Care* 6:327, 1985.
3. Dzurec, L. Childbirth educators: Are they helpful? *MCN: American Journal of Maternal/Child Nursing* 6:329, 1981.
4. Hershey, N. Entrepreneurial practice for nurses: An assessment of the issues. *Law and Medical Health Care* 11:253, 1983.
5. Hoeffer, B. The private practice model: An ethical perspective. *Journal of Psychosocial Nursing and Mental Health Services* 21:31, 1985.
6. Humenick, S. Measuring quality in childbirth education. *Birth* 11:174, 1984.
7. Koltz, C.K. *Private Practice in Nursing*. Germantown, MD: Aspen Systems Corporation, 1979.
8. Kraus, N. The success and failure of a nurse-midwifery practice. *Journal of Nurse Midwifery* 30:311, 1985.
9. McCord, G. Enlarging the market for perinatal procedures. *Birth* 12:40, 1985.
10. Morris, W. (ed.) *The American Heritage Dictionary of the English Language*. New York: Houghton Mifflin Co., 1970.
11. Steffes, S. Quality and money—can they go together in childbirth education? *Birth* 11:177, 1984.
12. Thayer, M. Strategies for creating a job: Collaborative practice. *Pediatric Nursing* 11:60, 1985.

Beginning Quote

Huffman, S. Guidelines for establishing An independent Lamaze practice. *Genesis* 5:11, 1984.

Boxed Quotes

Sasmor, J. *Childbirth Education: A Nursing Perspective*. New York: John Wiley & Sons, 1979, p. 119.

chapter 32

MARKETING STRATEGIES

DONNA J. HAWLEY and CELESTE PHILLIPS

If you're going to play the game properly, you'd better know every rule.

Barbara Jordan

Until recently, health care was delivered within a seller's market and provided in an atmosphere of plenty. Physicians, hospitals, and other health care professionals functioned in an arena in which third parties paid most of the costs of providing services. Generally money, services, and patients were plentiful; more money was available as more services were provided. The preferences of consumers were not sought or considered useful.

Today, however, the emphasis is changing, with monetary rewards available when less service is provided, especially in the area of inpatient hospital care. Patients are directly paying part of the costs of health care, and third parties are paying less. Competition for both limited dollars and patients is increasing. All parties in the system—hospitals, physicians, other health professionals—are examining what the consumer wants and are beginning to market their services to the consumer. Maternity care and childbirth education are part of this change.[10,32,33,36,38,40] Learning and using the tools of marketing are becoming essential for the childbirth educator.

REVIEW OF THE LITERATURE

Trends in Health Care Delivery

Historically, the major goal of every hospital in the United States was to provide service to the people of the community. The hospital's principal agents were its medical staff, who served as gatekeepers for admission of patients to the hospital.

Hospitals of the past literally marketed to the physicians in the community, relying on their judgment to determine what to offer in the way of services. Marketing to the actual consumer of the service was considered unnecessary and unproductive. The assumption was that the health care professional knew what the community needed and if this identified service was provided in a professionally satisfactory way, the hospital would flourish . . . and flourish it did.

Health care is now the nation's third largest industry and with the industry growth have come staggering costs. Health costs have increased more than 250 per cent since 1970. In 1970, 7.2 per cent of the gross national product (GNP), or $69 billion, was spent for health care, while in 1982, 10.5 per cent of the GNP, or $322 billion, was spent. At this rate of growth, we could reach $1 trillion in health care expenditures by 1990.[39] As a result of excesses in hospital capital investments, overstaffing, and a lack of attention to productivity management, hospital unit costs became a significant problem during the 1970's. At the same time, dramatic expansion in insurance coverage for all people reinforced the belief of U.S. citizens that highest quality health care was a right and should be accessible to all, regardless of the costs. Reimbursement policies often rewarded health service providers who prescribed more treatment rather than less, and who used the most costly health care delivery systems.

However, the more-is-better era came to an abrupt end in 1983 with the implementation of the new Medicare prospective pricing systems—prices set by diagnostic-related groups (DRG's). The change is prepayment of set fees according to 467 DRG's for a person or family for a defined period of time. If a hospital spends more, it must absorb the cost. With DRG's the entire approach to spending changed from more-is-better to cost containment.[14]

Although quality and access of care for all people remain important, this is a time of retrenchment or shakedown as hospital occupancy rates and reimbursements fall dramatically. Competitive pricing, modifications of traditional hospital services, and out-of-hospital alternatives to hospitalization are pressuring hospitals to change. As a result, decisions about needs, wants, and services are now being driven by the market, whether it be the consumer, the government, local employers, or other purchasers of care. What the market wants and is willing to pay is now of major concern. Hospitals are fast becoming market driven as the health care delivery system moves from a seller's to a buyer's market.[16]

This new emphasis on cost containment provided an optimal climate for proliferation of private insurance plans such as health maintenance organizations (HMO's), preferred provider organizations (PPO's), and preferred provider arrangements (PPA's). These new delivery systems are really new financing systems that are also geared to prospective payment. In all of health care there is a shift from economic incentives that reward providers for giving maximum care toward new incentives that reward minimum care.

Maternity Care

Maternity care has not escaped this movement. For the last 50 years most hospital maternity units have been loss leaders. Their dramatically fluctuating censuses and totally inefficient structure contributed to maternity units not being profit making. Consequently, hospital administrators literally subsidized these units to attract obstetricians, pediatricians, and family practice physicians. The goal was to capture the gynecological surgery and family clientele of these medical practitioners to assure admissions for future medical and surgical care. This goal remains an important component of marketing, and marketing to physicians continues.[19] However, the desire of third-party payers to reduce costs, and the demand by consumers for an important role in their own maternity care, have led hospital administrators to broaden the market. They now market to insurance carriers and consumers.

The average length of stay (ALOS) for maternity care has been reduced from six days in 1950 to two days in 1986. It is estimated that the ALOS for normal maternity care will be 24 hours by 1995. In many communities this trend is being accelerated by third party payers giving incentives to families who elect early discharge for maternity care. Therefore, demonstration of efficiency through shortened stay is an important component for marketing to insurers.

The consumer of maternity services is in a unique position as a patient within the health care delivery system. With an increasing emphasis on preventive health care in this society, women in larger numbers are seeking information on how to be better prepared for birth and parenting. In 1984, approximately 70 per cent of all pregnant women in the U.S. attended some type of prenatal class.[3] These women and their families represent a new childbearing population of better informed consumers of health care.

Box 32–1

MARKETING DEFINITIONS

GOODS MARKETING: Marketing of products or tangible items; oldest type of marketing.

MACRO MARKETING: A level of marketing that operates at the societal level rather than at the individual or company level and involves the total economic system.

MARKET: Target of the marketing plan. The market is composed of the consumers or customers. These consumers or customers are the recipients of the goods, services, or knowledge offered by the marketer.

MARKETER: A person, firm, company, or social agency trying to influence another party.

MARKETING: A social process including three phases: a transaction or exchange between the marketer and the market, the tangible and intangible entities that are exchanged, and the systematic efforts made to influence these transactions.

MARKETING MIX: One part of the marketing plan that includes the four ingredients of product, place, promotion, and price. The proportion of each that enters this mix varies with the situation and is determined by the marketer. The fit of the pieces and the harmonious interaction among the elements is important.

MARKETING PLAN: Strategies used to market a product, service, or program. The plan has two parts: the target market and the marketing mix.

MICRO MARKETING: A level of marketing that includes those activities by individual firms, organizations, or companies. The goal is to meet the objectives of a particular agency and the focus is narrow and specific.

NONPROFIT MARKETING: Marketing by agencies, companies, or firms who do not have profit as a goal.

PROFIT SECTOR MARKETING: Marketing by organizations, companies, and institutions for the specific purpose of maximizing profits.

SEGMENTATION: Division of the target market into homogeneous groups or subsets of consumers. The four major categories that can be used to segment the market are geographic, demographic, volume, and benefit.

SERVICES MARKETING: A type of marketing that includes the marketing of intangible products.

SOCIAL MARKETING: Newest type of marketing; includes the marketing of socially desirable ideas and activities.

TARGET MARKET: Consumer of the product or service that is being marketed.

The maternity service in acute care hospitals is different from other health services in these same hospitals. The urgency and pain and suffering of most illnesses prompts people to seek immediate care. Also, fear and anxiety that accompany serious illness often prompts people to delegate much of the decision-making about health care to health professionals. This is not true of pregnancy.

Since pregnancy is not a disease but is instead a normal physiological process lasting nine months, the consumer has an unusual opportunity to inform herself about the care alternatives. She and her family also have adequate time and motivation to learn certain useful coping skills. In many communities where choices exist, women select the facility in which they want to give birth and then find a physician who has privileges there.

Since women also make most of the purchase decisions for their families, they often decide where other family members will go for health care. A survey conducted by Professional Research Consultants, Inc., Omaha, Nebraska, and American Hospital Publishing, Inc. found that consumers tend to associate maternity services with a particular hospital, and in 67 per cent of the households surveyed women were responsible for making most health care decisions.[20] This information is very important to providers of maternity care because hospital procedures related to childbirth are the most common procedures performed on women. With approximately 3.6 million babies born in the U.S. each year, childbearing women have become targets of hospital marketing programs.

Definition of Marketing

Before discussing the concept of marketing, it is useful to review the differences between marketing and selling. Marketing is an ongoing, sophisticated, and complex process and is much more complicated than selling. Selling is a part of the broader concept of marketing. Table 32–1 illustrates these differences.

Although marketing was originally conceptualized as a business process involving the "flow of goods and services from producer to consumer or user,"[11] definitions of marketing in the current literature describe a social process.[22] The process involves three phases: a transaction or exchange between the marketer and the market, the tangible and intangible entities that are exchanged, and the systematic efforts made to influence these transactions.

TABLE 32–1. COMPARISON OF SELLING AND MARKETING

SELLING	MARKETING
Focus is on needs of the seller.	Focus is on the needs of the buyer.
Emphasis is on seller's need to convert a product to cash.	Emphasis is on satisfying needs of the consumer by means of the product.
The product for sale is determined by the seller.	The product for sale is determined by the buyer.
Customer is offered what the seller wants to sell.	Seller researches customers' desires and preferences.
The sale is considered final.	Marketing is an ongoing process with follow-up.

The two parties participating in the marketing process are the marketer and the market. The marketer is the person, firm, company, or social agency trying to influence the other party. The marketers collectively or independently develop a systematic plan designed to influence the market. The market is the target of the plan and is composed of the consumers or customers. These consumers or customers are the recipients of the goods, services, or knowledge offered by the marketer. Kotler summarizes the complex nature of marketing when he states, "Marketing is specifically concerned with transactions that are created, stimulated, facilitated, and valued."[25] In the next section we describe the types of marketing and the development of the plan for marketing.

Divisions of Marketing

Marketing may be divided into three divisions. These divisions are composed of two levels, three basic types, and two sectors. The two levels are micro or macro marketing. The three types are goods, services, and social marketing. The sectors are divided into profit and nonprofit enterprises. Table 32–2 illustrates the divisions and gives examples of each.

The levels in marketing comprise the macro/micro dichotomy. Macro marketing operates at the

TABLE 32–2. MARKETING DIVISIONS

Levels	
Micro	Individual companies, schools, firms, agencies
Macro	National economic system
Type	
Goods	Steel, farm products, toothpaste
Services	Airplane travel, restaurants, health care
Social	Prevent forest fires, using seat belts, promote breastfeeding
Sectors	
Profit	Manufacturing companies, most insurance companies, some hospitals
Nonprofit	Public education, some hospitals, some insurance companies, charities

societal level rather than the individual firm level and involves the total economic system. McCarthy defines macro marketing as "a social process which directs an economy's flow of goods and services from producers to consumers in a way which effectively matches supply and demand and accomplishes the objectives of the society."[31]

Micro marketing includes those activities by individual firms, organizations, or companies. The goal is to meet the objectives of a particular agency by ". . . anticipating customer or client needs and directing a flow of need-satisfying goods and services from producer to customer or client."[31] The focus is narrow and specific. Since marketing of childbirth education classes falls under the general rubric of micro marketing, the discussion in this chapter focuses at this level of marketing.

Marketing of goods is the oldest type of marketing, the best established, and the model for other types. Goods are such entities as farm products and manufactured items that are available to the consuming public in exchange for money. Examples include items ranging from food to clothing to land to cars to steel. These products are tangible, readily describable, and generally reproducible.[35] They can be touched, felt, held, seen, tasted, or worn.

Service marketing, the second type, includes the marketing of intangible products. The marketing of childbirth education programs falls under this type of marketing. Services are experienced but cannot be touched, felt, or smelled.[41]

Lovelock and Young[30] identify three unique aspects to service marketing. First, like goods, services are produced and made available to the consumer; however, unlike goods, services are "time-bound."[30] At the time services are offered, they must be used. Services cannot be held in inventory or placed on a shelf. Second, unlike the manufacture of goods, services involve the consumer in the production of the product.[30] The consumer goes to the hospital, to the childbirth education class, to the beauty salon, and to the museum and remains during the rendering of the service. Last, the services are labor intensive and the employees are part of the product. Future patronage is determined by the people and the quality of service provided, not by the quality of the tangible good.[5] Nurses are vital in the provision of health services in a hospital, the waitress is part of the product in a restaurant, and the childbirth educator is immersed within the teaching process.

Social marketing is the third, and newest, type of marketing.[18] It includes the marketing of socially desirable activities. Kotler and Zaltman define social marketing as follows: "the designing, implementation, and control of programs calculated to influence the acceptability of social ideas and involving considerations of product planning, pricing, communication, distribution, and marketing research."[26] Examples include preventing forest fires, promoting desirability of breastfeeding, wearing seat belts, the dangers of drinking and driving, the dangers of smoking and drinking alcohol during pregnancy, and so on. Social marketing encompasses the collective beliefs and values of a society. These beliefs and values are basic and almost unanimous within a society. Kotler and Zaltman indicate that social marketing then involves the "core" of the market. On the other hand, traditional marketing of goods and services often deals with "superficial preferences and opinions."[26]

While social marketing is limited to ideas of perceived social value, the concept is not limited to only those universally accepted practices whose value is not open to debate by reasonable persons. Instead, social marketing is delineated by the social nature of the intangible product to be marketed. Fine lists 116 social ideas that are being marketed to the consuming public.[17] The list, literally from A to W, has such varied concepts as abortion rights, car-pooling, energy conservation, fluoridation, gay rights, the metric system, nudism, prayer in schools, saving the whales, suicide hotlines, voter registration, and women's rights.[17]

Two sectors within the marketing concept are

profit and nonprofit. The profit sector includes organizations, companies, and institutions whose major objective is profit. Maximization of profit is the goal of marketing. Profit-making organizations can participate in all three types of marketing. For example, fine restaurants market two products—food and service. Manufacturers of alcoholic beverages participate in social marketing by supporting advertising that warns against driving after drinking their products.[6]

The nonprofit sector is marketing by agencies, companies, or firms that do not have profit as a goal. Generally this sector includes provision of services rather than products. Examples of nonprofit agencies include public health departments, museums, many educational institutions, government agencies, and charities.

These types, levels, and sectors are not distinct entities, and overlap exists. Automobiles are products but companies market more than cars—they also market pleasurable and dependable transportation. Airlines, on the other hand, market primarily travel services, with the airplane being the vital product within the service. Likewise the marketing of car seats for infants or birth control for third world countries is primarily social marketing with the elements of service (teaching) and product (the car seats, the contraceptive device) still evident. Further, one could argue that urging parents to use infant car seats is macro marketing aimed at meeting the societal objective for safe infant care. However, the manufacturers of infant car seats have a profit objective at the micro level.

The main difference between marketing types lies in the tangibility of the ''product.'' Shostack[41] places a perspective on this overlap with her conceptualization of marketing on a continuum. She uses the concept of tangibility for the continuum and sees marketing entities existing as tangible to intangible dominant. (Figure 32–1 illustrates this continuum.) While her discussion centers primarily on differentiation between product and service marketing, the concept can be extended to include social marketing. Entities have a degree of tangibility that is important to identify when determining the methodology used to market. Farm products and basic manufacturing products are the most tangible, restaurants are about in the middle, and teaching and persuading others toward socially desirable habits the least tangible.

The Marketing Plan

The marketing plan is the strategies used to market a product, service, or program. The target market and the marketing mix together form the plan. Each part supports the other and they interact. Targeting the market and developing the marketing mix represent the two parts in the plan. The marketing mix is composed of four basic components called product, place, price, and promotion (or the four p's).[31] The marketing plan can be visualized as a wheel with the target market seen as the center and the four areas of the mix as the spokes. (Figure 32–2 illustrates this model.)

The center of the marketing plan is the target market or consumer of the product or service. The importance of the desires, interests, and behaviors of this group of people is paramount to the success of the marketing plan. Thus the first step in developing a marketing plan is defining or targeting the market. This process is known as segmenting the market.

Segmentation

Basically, segmentation of the market is the division of the target market into homogeneous groups or subsets of consumers.[31] Explicitly, carefully and completely defining those groups of people who are most interested in a product or service is the first step in marketing.[25] The four major categories that can be used to segment the market are:

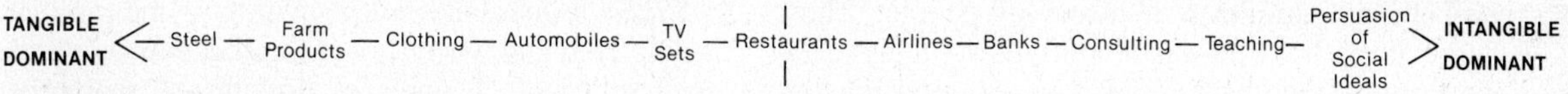

FIGURE 32–1. Marketing of goods and services. (Adapted from Shostack, G.L. Breaking Free from Product Marketing. *Journal of Marketing* 41:73, 1977.)

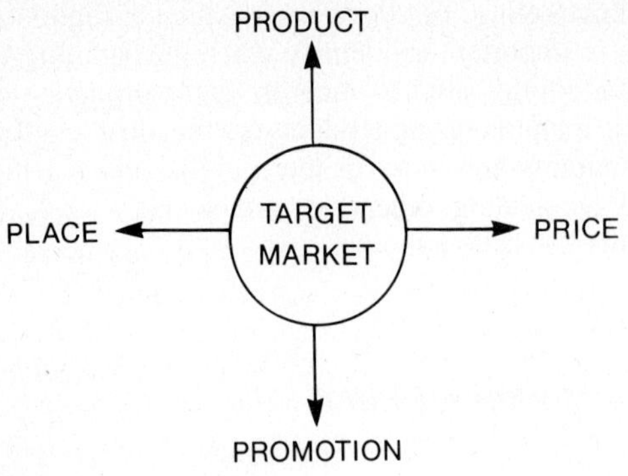

FIGURE 32–2. Marketing model. (Adapted from McCarthy, E.J. *Basic Marketing*. 7th ed. Homewood, IL: Richard D. Irwin, Inc., 1981.)

geographic, demographic, volume, and benefit.[21] Geographic segmentation is division by region of the country (e.g., north, southeast, mountain, New England), state, county, city, or even neighborhoods within communities. Demographic factors used to segment include age, sex, family size, life style (singles, widows, young married couples, children under 12, adolescents), occupations, educational levels, and socioeconomic class.[31]

Volume segmentation aims marketing efforts at the highest users of a product or the most valuable customers. For example, the greatest share of funds for advertising can be aimed at those most likely to purchase a commodity.

Benefit segmentation is a complex process that attempts to examine why people buy certain products or what benefit they seek from products or services. Haley[21] uses the example of toothpaste. What segment of the market is most interested in decay prevention, brightness of teeth, taste, or cost? The demographic and geographic commonalities for each of the four interest groups is then described. Advertising is targeted at the individual groups.[21]

Segmenting the market is a process that appears logical and on the surface simple. However, the process becomes complex when one is considering a product distributed nationally or a service designed for significant numbers of people. Thus large firms have research units that supply data concerning the characteristics of the total market and its identified segments.

The need for marketing research at the national level is obvious; however, research is necessary for segmenting the market at any level. One example will be used to illustrate the process. A college in Ohio, offering health education programs, surveyed a random sample of households within the geographic area served by the college. Through this survey, the authors were able to separate the population into four segments: health learners, health enhancers, health complainers, and health loners.

They found that the segment most likely to attend classes was the health enhancers. These included the higher income families whose members were employed full time, generally in good health, and 35 to 45 years old. The health loners included those people 35 to 45 years old with lower incomes than the enhancers. Further, they seldom saw a physician and believed that individuals were responsible for their own health. This group was least likely to attend educational programs.[7]

With the benefit characteristics defined, the demographics identified for each benefit group, and the geographic area predetermined, the marketers were able to plan programs that had the highest probability of attendance for each group. They targeted specific programs for specific groups.

Marketing Mix

Following segmentation of the market and definition of the target group, the marketing mix is determined. The marketing mix has the four ingredients of product, place, promotion, and price; however, the proportion of each that enters this mix varies and must be determined by the marketer. The fit of the pieces and the harmonious interaction among the elements are most important.[35]

Product, or the first of the p's, is broadly defined as anything of value that may be exchanged.[15] Thus the product may be a tangible item, a service, or a socially acceptable idea. In the area of childbirth education, the classes are, of course, the product. The quality, type, content, and benefits of these classes are the products offered to expectant parents and the commodity exchanged for a fee.

Place or distribution deals with how the product is delivered and where it is delivered. For products one speaks of channels of distribution from the producer to the wholesaler, retailer, and consumer. For service marketing, the location of the service becomes the major factor. The location and the times of day the service is offered are critical. Conveniences become paramount.[16,31]

Promotion, the third ingredient in the marketing mix, involves communicating about the product with the consumer and stimulating interest in the product.[34] It is composed of personal selling, mass selling, and sales promotion. Personal selling is the one-to-one interaction and may include activities of a professional salesperson or word-of-mouth promotion by previous and present clients. While it is a valuable method of promotion, the high cost involved in personal selling limits its use in many marketing settings.

Mass selling, on the other hand, necessitates communication with large numbers of people at the same time. Advertising, the most common type of mass selling, is "any paid form of nonpersonal presentation" about the goods or services being marketed.[31] Television, newspaper, radio, magazines, signs or posters, and mass mailings are used for advertising.

Publicity, another form of mass selling, differs from advertising only in fees paid. Examples of publicity include newspaper features about the benefits of childbirth education classes, radio interviews on local talk shows concerning the dangers of not placing infants in car seats, and an item on a television news program about a newly available medication.

Sales promotion, the third component to promotion, includes various activities that complement the personal and mass selling programs of an agency. These are the tools available to the promoter. Examples range from brochures and ad copy to the promotional strategies of "end-of-the-season sales," discounts for paying early, coupons, and free samples.

The last ingredient in the marketing mix is the *price* of the product or service. The importance of the "right" price cannot be overestimated. Pricing depends on the costs of production, distribution, and promotion of the product or service. It is related to the cost of similar products offered by competitors as well as the objectives of the agency offering the product. For example, childbirth education classes may be used by hospitals as one means to encourage women to give birth within that hospital. The classes, therefore, may be offered at a price below the cost needed to operate them. In this case, the classes are part of the promotion program of the hospital. On the other hand, some agencies may see these classes as a community service but demand that they at least "break even." Others may want to make a profit.

The actual mix used by an agency will vary at any particular time and may change frequently.[8] Competitors, the options of consumers, government regulations, and the evolving nature of the health care delivery system will impinge on the marketing mix. The goal is to create the best mix for the situation and be prepared to modify as necessary. The remaining part of this chapter looks at designing a marketing plan for childbirth education classes, including segmenting the market and describing the marketing mix.

IMPLICATIONS FOR PRACTICE

Nature of Childbirth Education

The decision to market one's childbirth education classes must be a conscious one. Some health professionals may have misgivings about the appropriateness of marketing their professional services. They may believe that professional services are provided only in response to a specific client's need. The attempt to influence, persuade, or even create demand for a health service may be seen as inappropriate by some health care professionals. Some believe that health care is provided for the benefit of the client and is not sold like toothpaste, television sets, or airline tickets. Armstrong states, when referring to nursing, "because the profession was founded on the philosophy of charity and compassion, it seems almost disloyal to sell it for silver."[2] This is certainly applicable to all the health professions.

The need to market professional services is not

unique to health care. Colleges and universities are marketing the values of higher education and actively recruiting adults returning to school as well as high school students.[27] The American Bar Association has approved advertising by attorneys. The American Hospital Association published guidelines for responsible advertising as early as 1977.[19] Charities, museums, and art galleries have marketed for years.

Marketing is not inherently bad or good; it is not coercion or brainwashing. Instead, it is the process of producing a desired response by "creating and offering values to the market."[25] The process, under appropriate direction and leadership, is an honest, ethical act.

Childbirth education has been identified to be an important product line for hospitals in these competitive times. Because such programs attract private pay patients, childbirth education is often used to make the public aware of the services of the hospital and to establish hospital name recognition. Childbirth education has been shown to reduce length of stay (LOS) and thus cut costs for hospital maternity care.[4] Childbirth education also provides feedback for understanding what consumers want from the maternity service. In addition, classes in women's health concerns and health promotion (wellness and fitness programs) channel potential customers to hospitals before they are in need of hospitalization.

There is a huge marketing potential for childbirth education; therefore, this is an excellent time to be a childbirth educator. Whether childbirth educators join a hospital maternity "team" or teach on an independent basis, survival in the increasingly competitive marketplace will be aided when they understand marketing and utilize appropriate marketing techniques as part of their practice.

In order to influence health care for the childbearing family in a positive way, it is essential for childbirth educators to establish good working relationships with health care facilities. In the past, adversarial relationships have often existed between childbirth educators and health care providers. When the educator was solely community based, it could be difficult for her to be totally familiar with constantly changing hospital childbirth practices. At the same time, many hospital staffs' perspectives on maternity care were very narrow, identifying the hospitals' responsibility as encompassing only intrapartum and early postpartum care. Just as community educators had difficulty in keeping current with changing hospital practices, oftentimes hospital nurses were uninformed about content and goals of childbirth education classes. This lack of communication sometimes contributed to fear and suspicion and lack of understanding about each other's roles, rights, and responsibilities.

Although actions of both childbirth educators and hospital personnel may have contributed to communication gaps in the past, it is imperative that these gaps be closed. Because of the dramatic changes in health care delivery briefly described in this chapter, most hospitals will eventually utilize childbirth education as a marketing tool. Many insurance plans and new delivery systems will encourage and reimburse maternity hospitalization packages that include childbirth education. Thus, unless they are hospital affiliated, many community-based educators will find fewer and fewer clients for their classes.

In these changing times, it is possible for childbirth educators to work with hospitals and not be coopted. It is neither necessary to "sell one's soul" or "sell the party line." Since childbirth education began as a consumer movement 25 years ago, its thrust has been consumer advocacy. Just as hospitals have historically assumed what people wanted from them, many childbirth educators have assumed that they knew what is best for people. Both hospitals and educators may have been working on invalid assumptions.

Marketing Plan

Following the conscious decision to market, marketing of a professional service such as childbirth education requires a systematic approach—that is, development of a plan. The plan consists of the segmented target market, the description of the "four p's," and the evaluation of the plan. The plan should be written and revised as necessary. One author suggests preparing a flow sheet on a large piece of paper that can be used as a wall chart.[9] A simple, straightforward plan is best.[35] A form that has been adapted from the Buttle[9] idea for use with childbirth education marketing plans is given in Fig. 32–3.

MARKETING PLAN WORKSHEET

Class ______________________ Instructor(s) ______________________

Agency ______________________ Dates ______________________

ANALYSIS	DECISIONS	STRATEGIES	EVALUATION
Community Description:	Agency Objectives:	Product:	Strengths:
	Market Objectives:	Budget:	
Maternity Care:	Demand Market:	Place:	Weaknesses:
	Competition:	Budget:	
Consumer Preferences:	Target Market:	Price:	Changes:
		Budget:	
Funds:		Promotion:	
		Budget:	

FIGURE 32–3. Worksheet for a marketing plan. (Adapted from Buttle, F. The Marketing Worksheet—A Practical Planning Tool. *Long Range Planning* 18:80, 1985.)

Developing a marketing plan. A planning conference is the first step in the development of a comprehensive and realistic marketing plan. (Photograph by Francine Nichols. Courtesy of Equicor Health Plan, Inc.)

Segmenting the Market

The first step in writing the marketing plan is segmenting the market. The target market is, of course, the pregnant women in the community and their families. However, prior to actual marketing efforts, this total market is divided into segments. Assessment of the community and the maternity care in the community is the initial part of the process of segmenting the target market.

The first step is to determine the number of births in the community, where they occur, and to whom. What percentage of total community births occurs in each location identified? Who delivers the maternity care—obstetricians, nurse-midwives, family practice physicians? What cultures, ethnic groups, ages, socioeconomic groups, and education levels are represented?

Next, determine the clinical care programs provided for segmented groups identified. Is family-centered care offered and how is it implemented? Where are the childbirth education programs located and what is taught? For each facility, what are the obstetrical acuity levels, percentages of cesarean births, and types and percentages of episiotomies, length of stay, and analgesia and anesthesia administered?

Essential information will include sources of reimbursement for maternity care. Which percentage is indigent care and which is government and/or private insurance reimbursed? Is there health care contracting with HMO's, PPO's, PPA's, and similar groups? Are financial incentives being offered for early discharge and/or reduced use of analgesia and anesthesia? What are the reimbursement trends and prediction for future funding of maternity care in the community? Is there competition among or between facilities and providers of maternity care? Who has the largest percentage of the market share and why?

After gathering the data on the total market, a decision is made as to which segment or segments one wants to target. If one's major goal or the goal of the employing agency is the most profitable program, one should target those individuals most likely to attend health education programs and those with adequate incomes. Data suggest that highly educated, white-collar professionals in their late twenties to early forties are the more likely to attend health education wellness programs.[7,23] On the other hand, if one's goal is service and one is working with a charity, public health agency, or other nonprofit group, one might target classes at the adolescent population or the poor.

Before completing the assessment phase, determine what the childbearing people of the community want in their maternity care. Do they desire classes or programs or services not being offered in the community? Are there groups in the community not being served through any type of educational program? Are there groups desiring specific information that is not available within presently operating classes? Where are the gaps in childbirth education and how can one fill these gaps?

These questions are answered through market research. A variety of methods can be used. Initially, identification of data already available is useful. In market research, data can be divided into two groups, primary and secondary data. Primary data are new facts gathered for a specific purpose or marketing project. Secondary data include materials that have been gathered for another purpose. Secondary data are valuable sources of inexpensive information and should be used whenever available.[29]

For example, if one is working within a hospital, its administration has data descriptive of the community it serves, demographic characteristics of the patients who use the hospital, and information about the medical staff. Statistics descriptive of maternity care in that institution are also available. Hospitals frequently send questionnaires to former patients soliciting their positive and negative reactins to their hospital stay. These kinds of data are available at no or minimal cost.

The federal government, as one of the world's largest publishers, often has useful information. The U.S. Printing Office publishes a free catalog of major publications.* The Bureau of Census of the Department of Commerce has sales and revenue information on almost every industry—including the health care industry—by state, county, and metropolitan areas.† Specific information about maternal and infant health is available from the Division of Maternal and Child Health at both the federal and state levels.

State and local government agencies, the research department of the local newspaper, and state and local libraries may have information that can assist the childbirth educator to identify the location and needs of the potential and actual childbearing population in a particular region.[12] Again, these data are available inexpensively and frequently through a phone call.

> Thinking in business terms involves more than keeping track of expenses. It requires the art of selling or marketing yourself and your programs to the consumer. Childbirth educators are often deficient in this area. Knowledge of marketing strategies can help you present your programs in a positive way, and can contribute to an increase in your self-esteem.
>
> PATTIE KEARNS

After the secondary sources are examined, additional information may need to be collected specifically related to childbirth education for a particular geographic area. Marketing research or the collection of primary data is useful in identifying consumer preference. Surveys of a random sample of households in a catchment area are valuable. Questionnaires mailed to former participants may be used to gather information about strengths and weaknesses within the classes or for identifying additional areas of interest to the pregnant woman and her family.

If there is sufficient funds, focus groups are useful.[13,29] A *focus group* is a small number of people brought together to discuss childbirth education in a region. Under the leadership of a moderator this group discusses a particular topic. Lovelock estimates that a focus group may cost one thousand dollars or more when moderator fees, cost of recruiting group members, space rental, and fees for analysis of data are included.[29]

Marketing Mix

Following segmentation of the market and gathering of data, the next step in the development of the strategic marketing plan is defining the marketing mix. Each of the four p's—product, place, price, and promotion—is considered and the proportion of emphasis placed on each determined. This phase includes planning and implementation of the childbirth education class.

---

*Address: Superintendent of Documents, U.S. Government Printing Office, Washington, D.C. 20401.

†Address: Public Information Office, Bureau of Census, Department of Commerce, Washington, D.C. 20233, (301-763-4051).

Box 32–2

MARKETING SUCCESS STORY

When developing a childbirth education program for implementation in a community hospital, the education coordinator first segmented the market by reviewing that hospital's obstetrical statistics for the previous three years. She identified such important data as percentage of cesareans, anesthesia given for vaginal births, and average length of stay. Interviews with new parents and physicians randomly selected in the service area provided information on birth preferences and of existing childbirth education programs. In addition, she collected projections on numbers of births expected in the next three years and economic trends, and also interviewed pregnant women and their families in clinics, physicians' offices, laundromats, and grocery stores.

With this extensive collection of information, it was possible to develop a customized product of education with place and price for the target market that had been identified and researched.

The program was designed to be both a frontline marketing and education program for the hospital. A coupon good toward $100 of class credit was distributed as a program promotion. This coupon had an expiration date and could be exchanged in a variety of ways:

- Early Pregnancy Class—$10 per couple
- Prenatal Class Series—$25 per couple or family
- Prepared Childbirth Classes—$50 per couple or family
- Prepared Childbirth Refresher Course—$25 (two weeks)
- Prenatal Exercise Program—$15 (six classes)
- Sibling Preparation Class—$10 (one child)
—$15 (two or more children)
- New Mother Support Group—$50 (eight sessions)

This strategy was chosen because people interviewed had placed a value on charges for services, while at the same time the income level of the target group was low.

Other promotion emphasized the hospital's commitment to comprehensive care of the childbearing family as evidenced by the childbirth education program. The childbirth education philosophy statement flowed from the hospital maternity service philosophy and was integrated into the hospital marketing program.

Evaluation disclosed consumer satisfaction with the continuity in both philosophy and content of the childbirth education and intra-postpartum experience. A study disclosed that the hospital maternity census had increased by 20 per cent as a result of the childbirth education program. This increase in volume of births subsidized the childbirth classes so that the coupon for class credit could be continued.

Since the product and the place are so closely intertwined in a service industry, we will examine these two areas of the marketing mix together. The product offered is education, specifically childbirth education. The place includes the actual surroundings in which the program is presented and the dates and times of the classes. Using the data gathered, one must determine how to ''package'' the product in the most appealing and consumer-satisfying way.[25] The packaging includes both the program itself and circumstances under which it is presented.

Of course, the most important part of any educational program is quality—including appropriate and relevant content and excellent teaching by qualified instructors. The best marketing strategy lies in the quality of the offering.[1] Without this basic ingredient, further efforts are of little value. The essence of quality programs is discussed elsewhere in ths book. In this discussion we pose some questions that might be considered, assuming the initial high quality of classes.

Could the current classes be improved? Is there subject matter that should be added or deleted? Are the classes appropriate to the consuming group? For example, is the same material taught to a group of pregnant teenagers and a group of young middle-class couples? Could changes be made that make the material particularly relevant to the audience? Does the content fit the type of maternity care available in the community? Is the material presented to participants who are planning an in-hospital delivery the same as that taught in a class in which participants are anticipating home delivery? If almost all infants in the community are delivered by physicians, are the physicians knowledgeable about the program and do they agree with the content presented? Are the participants receiving the information they want or does the material taught reflect the instructors' biases? What material requested by a group of participants could be added to the program without sacrificing quality? What could be deleted?

Next, look at the location of the classes. Are the programs offered in physically attractive surroundings? Are the rooms well ventilated, heated, and cooled according to the seasons? Are the wall hangings related to childbearing and aesthetically pleasing? Are the classes offered at locations convenient to the participants? Could some classes be offered in neighborhood centers rather than at the hospital? Is there ample parking? Is child care available for the siblings-to-be? Could classes be offered in the public schools for pregnant teens? Could classes be offered in a physician's office, thereby capturing essentially all of that physician's patients for classes? Are classes being offered in rural areas? Is there a central location that could draw individuals from several smaller surrounding communities?

The scheduling of classes is also important. Are they available at convenient times of the day and week? Long-range scheduling of classes six months to one year in advance will provide a framework for positioning classes.

Pricing, the third component of the marketing mix, encompasses the issue of operating costs and charges to participants. The mechanism for paying for the classes varies with the sponsorship. If the programs are used as a marketing tool by a hospital, it may absorb the costs. In this case, the hospital is using the classes to encourage births at that institution, as a public relations tool to enhance the hospital's image, or as a long-range plan that includes future use of inpatient services by participants and their families. Costs to the participants in this case may be minimal.

Box 32–3

MARKETING FAILURE STORY

When organizing childbirth education programs, educators offering community classes met to plan. Discussion centered on fees charged, instructor costs, instructor capabilities, sizes of classes, and variety of class content.

Market research consisted of a sharing of experiences and poll of what each perceived to be needed in the way of classes. There was agreement that the current offerings were fragmented in the community and that a more extensive program was needed. Special emphasis was placed on the lack of postpartum support and parenting education.

Product decisions were made to increase the community offerings in postpartum classes and to develop a standard fee structure for all educators' classes. Promotion was to be by word of mouth with instructors referring to each other after their individual classes filled.

Within one year of this planning meeting, a local hospital developed a comprehensive prenatal and parenting education program. The extensive curriculum was marketing through physicians' offices, hospital newsletters, and newspaper articles. The program was developed after market study that included an analysis of current classes offered in the community.

The hospital classes are well attended today and most of the community educators are on the hospital teaching staff at greatly reduced hourly compensation.

Segmenting the market and developing a market mix were never considered by these individual educators. With all their extensive combined experience in teaching childbirth preparation, they fell victim to the belief that they knew what was best for childbearing families. Or were they really only aware of what was best for them, the childbirth educators?

If the programs are expected to be self-supporting, the marketing approach is different. Costs of presenting the programs, including instructor salary, promotional materials, space rental and the like, must be calculated and revenue raised to meet these costs. Charging participants is the most obvious means for meeting these costs. If one is offering programs to those who are able to pay, this mechanism is very appropriate.

However, one may also look at other sources of funding. Is it possible for a new or different childbirth education approach to reduce length of hospital stay and reduce health care costs? If this were documented, one possible source of revenue would be third party payers. Some childbirth educators are increasing their incomes by diversification. For a fee, they are offering classes for special interest groups. Examples include classes in exercise during the pregnancy and post partum periods, breast feeding, cesarean births, grandparenting, fathering, and being a sibling. Private lessons are also an idea.[38] Charging for attendance during labor is another option, although one recent survey indicated that few childbirth educators charged for this service.[38]

If one desires to provide a service to those not able to pay (e.g., pregnant teens, the unemployed), other sources of revenue need to be considered. In this situation, one needs to secure donations from businesses, community leaders, and private citizens or seek funds from private and government agency sources. Conceivably one could operate

Box 32–4

PUBLIC SERVICE ANNOUNCEMENTS

A public service announcement is a brief announcement of information, usually made on the radio. By law, radio stations are required to set aside a certain amount of time each day for PSAs, including those from nonprofit organizations such as ASPO/Lamaze. You cannot dictate the time of day during which your announcement will be read, but if you write one in the correct format and send it to the appropriate person (usually the Public Service Director), then your chances of getting it read over the air are good.

PSAs can vary in length from ten to thirty seconds. This is the time it takes to read the entire announcement in an unhurried manner. It must be typed, double-spaced and include the following information (in this order):

***What*—Name of event/activity (with one line explanation)**
***When*—Time and day(s) of week**
***Where*—Name of building, street address**
***Cost*—Fee, if any, and information on advance ticket sales**
***Sponsored by*—Who the event is sponsored by, name of organization, with a brief explanation**
***Contact*—Name of person or organization to be called**
***Telephone*—Number to be called**

After this has been typed up, read it out loud in an unhurried voice and time yourself. If it is longer than 30 seconds, cut it down. Most radio stations will not air a PSA longer than 30 seconds; some will not even go that long.

It is worth a phone call to the station to determine who the public service director is. Talk to that person and ask about the specifics, such as how long their PSAs usually are, and what format they prefer. When you send in your PSA, attach a hand-written or typed note addressed to the person you spoke with, mentioning that this is the PSA you discussed over the phone. This technique will get your PSA past the person who does the initial screening, and into the hands of the person who makes the final decision—the public service director.

After the PSA has been aired, send a thank-you note acknowledging your PSA was used. This helps the radio station prove it has fulfilled its legal requirements, and shows the public service director you appreciate his efforts on your behalf.

From Berman, A. The art and science of good public relations. *Genesis* February/March 1983.

fund drives or become part of community groups such as the United Fund or Community Chest.

Promotion, the last ingredient in the mix, informs the market about the service. One builds a reputation for quality and then makes this quality known to as many people as is feasible. This area includes personal selling, mass selling, and sales promotion.

Personal selling, one-to-one contact with the consumer, is vital, but the scope is limited. Childbirth education is not marketed through a professional sales force that goes door to door. However, the childbirth educator can do personal selling by selling her professional knowledge and skills. Wittreich[42] makes two important points concerning the marketing of professional services. First, knowledge and skills of the professional are being sold, not a product. Wittreich states, "A professional service can only be purchased from someone who is capable of rendering the service. Selling

Box 32–5

WRITING A PRESS RELEASE

A press release has a standard format which is understood and accepted by the media. It contains hard news, such as the announcement of an event of some kind. Press releases must be typed, double-spaced, and written so that the most important information is at the beginning, followed by less important information. This allows the editor to cut out parts at the end, when space requirements dictate, without losing any of the vital information provided in the beginning.

The following questions should be answered near the beginning of your press release:

Who?
What?
Where?
When?
How?
Why?

This information can be followed by other details, such as background information on your speakers, etc.

Press releases should be typed on your official letterhead. In the upper left-hand corner you should type:

PRESS RELEASE: For immediate release.
For more information, contact:
Suzy Q. Jones, (123) 456-7890.

The goal of your press release is to have it used. This will happen only if you provide information that is valuable and clearly written. You will have a greater chance of seeing your material published if you call the newspaper (or other media) you are directing your press release to and obtain the name of the person you should send the release to. If there is a specific page (e.g., a Lifestyle Page) you are aiming for, address it to the appropriate person, usually the editor, for that particular page.

If you think the editor might be interested in more information about your program or ASPO/Lamaze in general, create and include a *Fact Sheet*. This can give background information on the organization, statistics which can be quoted (such as how many couples are taught Lamaze childbirth each year, etc.). Providing extra details like this can lead to an additional query and perhaps a feature story. But don't overload your press release with this kind of material—it will only get pitched.

Be sure the person you list on the press release as the contact for more information will actually be available, and can answer questions (or knows where to go for the answers). It is important for your chapter to establish and maintain local contacts with the media, and to establish your credibility as a reliable source of information. Don't jeopardize your position by providing shaky statistics, or by listing a contact person who can't be reached, or who can't answer questions put forth by a reporter.

All in all, a press release is for hard news—announcing an event of some kind. It should usually be limited to one page, at most two pages.

From Berman, A. The art and science of good public relations. *Genesis* February/March 1983.

ability and personality by themselves are meaningless.''[42] Second, what is needed is the professional who sells, not the professional salesman.[42]

One of the best ways to sell an educational program is through its former students. *Recommendations* (word-of-mouth) by former participants to friends, neighbors, and relatives is an indispensable source of future participants.

The importance of *networking* with professionals in the community cannot be minimized. Establishing a network with colleagues through reciprocal referrals will contribute significantly to the volume of childbearing families attending classes. Knowing and communicating with the physicians and midwives in the community is another source of participant referrals.

Mass selling or communication through the media is another means to publicize one's classes. Public service announcements on local radio and television stations are usually free and represent an inexpensive means for reaching large numbers of people.[24] If funds are available, tastefully worded advertisements in the telephone book and local newspapers and magazines are useful. Posters in neighborhood stores describing classes are another means. Laundromats, grocery stores, convenience stores, baby clothing and furniture stores, and maternity shops are a few places where materials may be distributed or posted.

Sales promotion encompasses all the ''little'' but important aspects of communicating the service and the quality of that service. In establishing identity and visibility, promotional materials need to be of high quality. A 24-hour answering service is useful in developing positive customer relations. Utilization of a logo and an identifiable name will help in achieving visibility in the community. Business cards, stationery, brochures, badges, and name tags are also important tools for identification of both the provider and service offered. The use of a good grade of paper, professional printing rather than the mimeograph, and well-written advertisements and brochures give an image of quality that reflects on the educational program. A newsletter with dates, locations, and times of future classes, announcements of the births of participants' babies, and news about changes in classes is another promotional method. The mailing list could include names of local physicians, midwives, former participants, present participants, hospital maternity units, local baby and maternity shops, and other childbirth educators.

Marketing is an ongoing process requiring continuing research and follow-up. Determining whether or not the consumers are satisfied with the product is crucial. A willingness to be open and honest in determining satisfaction will require ego strength and a true belief that both health care and childbirth education are now market-driven.

Constant evaluation of the marketing plan and changes in emphasis within the marketing mix is essential. Is it possible to deliver different content, repackage content, and change times and locations or instructors if necessary? Are promotional materials adequate and of appropriate quality? How do they need to be modified? Are additional or different mass advertising campaigns needed? The evaluation phase of marketing returns full circle to marketing segmentation and marketing research. The process continues indefinitely.

IMPLICATIONS FOR RESEARCH

Research is an essential component of marketing and one of the initial steps in the process. Descriptive studies designed to provide data about various segments present within the total childbearing population would be one area of interest. Exploratory studies and descriptive investigations are needed to identify the educational needs of this population as perceived by the consumers. Determining the preferences of the consumer of our service has been lacking and is a major area for study. Experimental designs that look at the effectiveness of various teaching strategies is another area open for investigation. Specific questions that can be asked are:

1. What are the characteristics of the childbearing families (e.g., age, marital status, income levels) and what are the types of obstetrical facilities (e.g., traditional maternity care units, birthing rooms, or single-room maternity care units) available within a given geographic area?

2. What are the educational needs of childbearing families and what types of programs are available to meet those needs within a given geographic area?

3. Are there any differences in costs, participant satisfaction, and participant knowledge among childbirth education classes offered by hospitals, community agencies, physicians' offices, and childbirth educators in private practice?

4. Is computer-assisted instruction as effective as traditional teaching methods for the presentation of factual content in childbirth education classes? Suggested outcome measures include participant satisfaction and participant knowledge using both types of teaching methods.

SUMMARY

It is an all-new world of health care. Despite old myths, American health care is a business, and so is childbirth education. The best hope for the future lies with childbirth educators attempting to understand this business and working together to make it the best competitive, market-driven industry possible. Childbearing consumers and their children will be the benefactors.

References

1. Andreasen, A. R. Nonprofits: check your attention to customers. *Harvard Business Review* 60:105, 1982.
2. Armstrong, D. M., Amo, E., Duer, A. L., Hanson, M., Hijeck, T, Karwoski, P., and Young, S. Marketing opportunities for a nursing department in a changing economic environment. *Nursing Administration Quarterly* 10:1, 1985.
3. Bajo, K., and Doodan, J. Innovations in obstetric design: single room maternity care. *Hospital Administration Currents* 30:6, 1986.
4. Bartlett, E. E. *Assessing the benefits of patient education under prospective pricing*. Birmingham, AL: Resource Packet No. 4, University of Alabama in Birmingham, 1984.
5. Berry, L. L. Service marketing is different. *In* Lovelock, C. H. (ed.) *Services Marketing*. Englewood Cliffs, NJ: Prentice-Hall, 1984, pp. 29–36.
6. Bloom, P. N., and Novelli, W. D. Problems and challenges in social marketing. *Journal of Marketing* 45:79, 1981.
7. Bonaguro, J. A., and Bonaguro, E. W. Use of benefit segmentation in designing family health programs. *Family and Community Health* 8:5, February, 1985.
8. Borden, N. H. The concept of the marketing mix. *Journal of Advertising Research* 4:2, 1964.
9. Buttle, F. The marketing strategy worksheet—a practical planning tool. *Long Range Planning* 18:80, 1985.
10. Chez, R. A. Roundtable: Reconsidering the "market model" in Obstetrics. Part II. Marketing is identifying and meeting the needs of our patients. *Birth* 12:39, 1985.
11. Committee on Terms. *Marketing Definitions: A Glossary of Marketing Terms*. Chicago: American Marketing Association, 1960.
12. Connor, R. A., and Davidson, J. P.: *Marketing Your Consulting and Professional Services*. New York: John Wiley & Sons, 1986.
13. DeWolf, L. Focus groups: assessing patient satisfaction and targeting new services. *Hospital Topics* 63:24, 1985.
14. Edwardson, S. R. Shedding light on a shifting marketplace: competition in maternity care. *Nursing and Health Care* 6:73, 1985.
15. Enis, B. M. Deepening the concept of marketing. *Journal of Marketing* 37:57, 1973.
16. Fine, S. H. The health product: a social marketing perspective. *Hospitals* 58:66, June 16, 1984.
17. Fine, S. H. *The Marketing of Ideas and Social Issues*. New York: Praeger Publishers, 1981.
18. Fox, K. F. A., and Kotler, P. The marketing of social causes: the first 10 years. *Journal of Marketing* 44:24, 1980.
19. Goldsmith, J. C. The health care market: Can hospitals survive: *Harvard Business Review* 58:100, 1980.
20. Graham, J. Radical changes are continuing in health care industry. *Modern Health Care* 15:134, 1985.
21. Haley, R. I. Benefit segmentation: A decision-oriented research tool. *Journal of Marketing* 32:30, 1968.
22. Hunt, S. D. The nature and scope of marketing. *Journal of Marketing* 40:17, 1976.
23. Jensen, J. Health care alternatives. *American Demographics* 8:36, 1986.
24. Kitaeff, A. Public service television spots: Avenue for social responsibility. *Public Relations Journal* 46:10, 20, December 1975.

25. Kotler, P. A generic concept of marketing. *Journal of Marketing* 36:46, 1972.
26. Kotler, P., and Zaltman, G. Social Marketing: An Approach to planned social change. *Journal of Marketing* 35:3, 1971.
27. Krachenberg, A. R. Bringing the concept of marketing to higher education. *Journal of Higher Education* 43:369, 1972.
28. Lovelock, C. H. Developing frameworks for understanding services marketing. *In* Lovelock, C. H. (ed.) *Services Marketing*. Englewood Cliffs, NJ: Prentice-Hall, 1984, pp. 49–64.
29. Lovelock, C. H., and Weinberg, C. B. *Marketing for Public and Nonprofit Managers*. New York: John Wiley & Sons, 1984.
30. Lovelock, C. H., and Young, R. F. Look to consumers to increase productivity. *Harvard Business Review* 57:168, May–June 1979.
31. McCarthy, E. J. *Basic Marketing,* 7th Ed. Homewood, IL: Richard D. Irwin, Inc., 1981.
32. McCord, G. Roundtable: Reconsidering the ''market model'' in Obstetrics. Part II. Enlarging the market for perinatal procedures. *Birth* 12:40, 1985.
33. McKay, S. Roundtable: Reconsidering the ''market model'' in Obstetrics. Part II. Are patients customers? *Birth* 12:40, 1985.
34. Shapiro, B. P. Marketing for nonprofit organizations. *Harvard Business Review* 51:123, 1973.
35. Shapiro, B. P. Rejuvenating the marketing mix. *Harvard Business Review* 63:28, 1985.
36. Shearer, M. H. Editorial: Reconsidering the 'market model' in Obstetrics. Part I. *Birth* 11:213, 1984.
37. Shearer, M. H. Editorial: Reconsidering the ''market model'' in Obstetrics. Nursing. Part III. *Birth* 12:75, 1985.
38. Shearer, M. H. and Bunnin, N. Childbirth Educators in the 1980's: A survey of 25 veterans. *Birth* 10:251, 1983.
39. Shelton, J. Can nursing options cut health care's bottom line? *Nursing and Health Care* 6:251, 1985.
40. Sheps, C. G. Roundtable: Reconsidering the 'market model' in obstetrics. Part II. Private profit and investment in perinatal services. *Birth* 12:37, 1985.
41. Shostack, G. L. Breaking free from product marketing. *Journal of Marketing* 41:73, 1977.
42. Wittreich, W. J. *Selling—A Perspective to Success as a Professional*. Philadelphia: Wittreich Associates, 1969.

Beginning Quote

Ellerbee, L. *''And So It Goes,'' Adventures in Television*. New York: G. P. Putnam's Sons, 1986.

Boxed Quote

Kearns, P. Childbirth education as a profession: Increasing your business awareness. *Genesis* December 1983/1984, p. 12.

EPILOGUE

As this book developed, the air became ''pregnant'' with ideas, some of which we were able to incorporate into this book while others will have to wait until the next edition. The enthusiasm of childbirth educators and other childbirth professionals we talked with as we were writing the book and their eagerness to share their knowledge and experience have been exciting. *We see this book as a beginning.* It will continue to grow and develop as we hear from childbirth educators, practitioners, and researchers who share with us their ideas, teaching strategies, and results of research projects. We look forward to hearing from you!

FRANCINE H. NICHOLS, PhD, ACCE
Department of Nursing
The Wichita State University
Wichita, Kansas 67208

SHARRON S. HUMENICK, PhD, ACCE
School of Nursing
Box 3065, University Station
The University of Wyoming
Laramie, WY 82071

APPENDICES

A
MATERNAL-CHILD HEALTH ORGANIZATIONS

American Academy of Family Physicians
1740 West 92nd Street,
Kansas City, MO 64114
(816) 333-9700
Offers listings of family physicians in each area of U.S.

American Academy of Husband-Coached Childbirth (AAHCC)
P. O. Box 5224,
Sherman Oaks, CA 91413
(818) 788-6662 or (800) 423-2397 (outside CA)
The official Bradley method organization. Offers information about the Bradley method and childbirth classes.

American Academy of Pediatrics
141 Northwest Point Road,
Elk Grove Village, IL 60007
(312) 228-5005
Largest U.S. organization of pediatricians. Offers information and support related to children's health from infancy through young adulthood.

American Association for Maternal and Child Health
233 Prospect, P-204,
La Jolla, CA 92037
(619) 459-9308
Provides information and reprints and has perinatal conferences. The AAMCH is active in several states and has chapters in others.

American College of Home Obstetrics (ACHO)
P. O. Box 25,
River Forest, IL 60305
(312) 383-1461
Offers listing of physicians available for home births.

American College of Nurse-Midwives (ACNM)
1522 K Street NW,
Suite 1120,
Washington, DC 20005
(202) 347-5445
Offers listing of certified nurse-midwives and where they attend births. Provides information about nurse-midwifery training programs.

American College of Obstetricians and Gynecologists (ACOG)
600 Maryland Avenue, SW,
Suite 300 East,
Washington, DC 20024
(202) 638-5577
The professional organization of obstetricians and gynecologists. Provides both professional and lay educational materials related to pregnancy and childbirth.

American Foundation for Maternal and Child Health
Doris Haire,
30 Beekman Place,
New York, NY 10022
(212) 759-5511
Clearinghouse for information on drug research and technology related to pregnancy, childbirth, and the newborn period.

American Fertility Society
2131 Magnolia Avenue,
Suite 201,
Birmingham, AL 35256
(205) 251-9764
Provides information related to fertility.

Eylene Teichgraeber, Research Assistant, Department of Nursing, The Wichita State University, assisted with compiling the appendices materials.

American Hospital Association
840 North Lake Shore Drive,
Chicago, IL 60611
(312) 280-6000
Provides information about hospitals and other health care facilities. Publishes a Guide to the Health Care Field *that lists the names and addresses of all hospitals, the number of births per year, and other information.*

American Indian Health Care Association
California Urban Indian Health Council,
2422 Arden Way,
Sacramento, CA 95825
(916) 920-0310
Sponsors administrative, clinical, and fiscal training related to urban Indian health.

American Medical Association
535 North Dearborn Street,
Chicago, IL 60610
(312) 645-5000
The professional organization of physicians. Operates a library that lends materials and provides medical information to physicians.

American Natural Hygiene Society
12816 Race Track Road,
Tampa, FL 33625
(813) 855-6607
Publishes the Health Science Magazine *and various books, pamphlets, and tapes.*

American Nurses' Association
2420 Pershing Road,
Kansas City, MO 64108
(816) 474-5720
The professional organization of registered nurses. Provides publications related to maternal-child health and information on current issues in the area.

American Physical Therapy Association
(OB-GYN Section)
1111 North Fairfax Street,
Alexandria, VA 22314
(703) 684-2782
Holds meetings of interest to childbirth educators and publishes a quarterly bulletin.

American Public Health Association
1015 15th Street, NW,
Washington, DC 20005
(202) 789-5600
Has a maternal-child health section. Provides information on maternal-child health legislative and policy issues. Has many publications on maternal and child health.

American Society for Psychoprophylaxis in Obstetrics
(ASPO/Lamaze)
1840 Wilson Boulevard,
Suite 204,
Arlington, VA 22201
(800) 368-4404 or (703) 524-7802
The official Lamaze method organization. Certifies childbirth educators in the Lamaze method of childbirth preparation. Provides information about the Lamaze method and other pregnancy and childbirth-related topics to health professionals and consumers. Provides referrals to ASPO-Lamaze certified childbirth educators (ACCE's) and physicians who support the Lamaze method of childbirth. Publishes the Lamaze Parents Magazine, *a Lamaze class supplement, which is offered free to childbirth educators, physicians, and hospitals.*

Association for Childbirth at Home, International
P. O. Box 39498,
Los Angeles, CA 90039
(213) 667-0839
Provides information and support for home births.

Association for the Care of Children's Health
3615 Wisconsin Avenue,
Washington, DC 20016
(202) 244-1801
Offers resources and supports research related to children's health.

Birth & Life Bookstore
7001 Alonzo Avenue NW,
P. O. Box 70625,
Seattle, WA 98107-0627
(206) 789-4444
Mail order bookstore which has catalog of books, including reviews, entitled ''Imprints.''

Birth Works
P. O. Box 152,
Syracuse, NY 13210
(609) 953-0371
Supports the holistic approach to childbirth. Provides information about the holistic approach and childbirth classes.

Boston Women's Health Book Collective (BWHBC)
47 Nichols Avenue,
Watertown, MA 02172
(617) 942-0271
Distributes a list of feminist women's health centers. Provides information about women's health and women's health issues.

Canadian Physiotherapy Association
Obstetrical Division,
6 Wimpole Road,
Willowdale, Ontario M2L 2L3
Offers exercise charts, book lists, and other information related to pregnancy and childbirth.

Centers for Disease Control (CDC)
1600 Clifton Road,
Room 345,
Atlanta, GA 30333
(404) 329-1830
Concerned with control of diseases. Develops diagnostic criteria for diseases and provides information about specific diseases.

Center for Medical Consumers and Health Care Information
237 Thompson Street,
New York, NY 10012
(212) 674-7105
Publishes bulletin called "Health Facts."

Center for Study of Multiple Births
333 E. Superior, #463-5,
Chicago, IL 60611
(312) 266-9093
Provides information and publications on multiple births.

Cesarean Prevention Movement, Inc. (CPM)
P. O. Box 152,
Syracuse, NY 13210
(315) 424-1942
Offers information, support, and childbirth education classes through 30 national chapters for cesarean prevention and vaginal birth after cesarean (VBAC).

Cesareans/Support, Education and Concern (C/SEC)
22 Forest Road,
Framingham, MA 01701
(617) 877-8266
Provides information and support to parents who have had or anticipate a cesarean birth and to those who want to prevent one, as well as parents seeking a vaginal birth after cesarean birth.

Children's Defense Fund (CDF)
1520 New Hampshire Avenue NW,
Washington, DC 20036
(202) 628-8787
A national public charity created to provide a long-range and systematic advocacy for the nation's children. The goal of the CDF is to put children's needs high on the nation's public policy agenda. Provides many publications.

The Children's Foundation
1420 New York Avenue NW,
Washington, DC 20005
Provides information and publications to consumers and health professionals about children.

Coalition for the Medical Rights of Women
2845 25th Street,
San Francisco, CA 94110
(415) 826-4401
Provides information on several prenatal issues and is active in consumer rights in perinatal issues.

Compassionate Friends
P. O. Box 3696,
Oakbrook, IL 60522
(312) 323-5010
Offers emotional support for parents who have had a miscarriage or whose child has died. Has over 450 chapters in the U.S.

Consumer Coalition for Health
P. O. Box 50088,
930 F Street NW,
Suite 617,
Washington, DC 20004
(202) 638-5828
National alliance of labor, civil rights, and other organizations working for consumer control of health care resources. Publishes a bimonthly newsletter.

COPE—Coping with the Overall Parenting/ Pregnancy Experience
37 Clarendon Street,
Boston, MA 02116
(617) 357-5588
The nation's first licensed parenting center. Provides support groups, counseling for individuals and couples, workshops, telephone information and referral, and consultations.

Council for Cesarean Awareness
5520 SW 92nd Avenue,
Miami, FL 33165
(305) 596-2699
Provides information on cesarean prevention, vaginal birth after cesarean (VBAC), and prepared cesarean birth.

Family of Americas Foundation
P. O. Box 219,
1150 Lovers Lane
Mandeville, LA 70488
(504) 626-7724
Promotes teachings of the Billings Ovulation Method of family planning. Provides referral services and technical assistance. Maintains library of natural family planning reference materials.

Family Resource Coalition
230 North Michigan Avenue,
Suite 1625,
Chicago, IL 60601
(312) 726-1750
Nationwide community-based family support organizations concerned with child development.

The Farm
P. O. Box 157,
Summertown, TN 38483
(615) 964-3574
Offers information and many resources related to childbirth.

The Fatherhood Project
Bank Street College of Education,
610 West 112th Street,
New York, NY 10036
(212) 663-7200
Clearinghouse for information and support for fathers.

Health Research Group
2000 P Street,
Suite 708, NW,
Washington, DC 20036
(212) 872-0320
Ralph Nader's citizen lobby and research group on drug testing and marketing, safety of medical devices.

Infants Need to Avoid Circumcision Trauma
P. O. Box 5,
Wilbraham, MA 01095
(413) 596-8959
Provides information regarding circumcision and proper care of an infant's uncircumcised penis.

Informed Consent
P. O. Box 369,
Corte Madera, CA 94925-0369
(415) 927-0664
Provides information regarding circumcision and proper care of an infant's uncircumcised penis.

Informal Homebirth/Informed Birth and Parenting
Box 3675,
Ann Arbor, MI 48106
(313) 662-6857
Offers information and publications about home birth. Focuses on educating parents and health care providers on safe home birth methods and services.

International Childbirth Education Association (ICEA)
P. O. Box 20048,
Minneapolis, MN 55420
(612) 854-8660

One of the largest federations of consumer-oriented groups providing information about pregnancy, birth, and childbirth education. Certifies childbirth educators and offers referrals to them, as well as referrals to birth attendants who focus on a family-oriented approach. Has mail order bookstore and publishes free catalog "Bookmarks" that includes book reviews.

LaLeche League International
9616 Minneapolis Avenue,
P. O. Box 1209,
Franklin Park, IL 60131
(312) 455-7730
Headquarters for over 3000 groups worldwide offering education, individual counseling, and support for breastfeeding.

March of Dimes Birth Defects Foundation
1275 Mamaroneck Avenue,
White Plains, NY 10605
(914) 428-7100
National headquarters for 650 chapters who provide programs, research, medical services, and education aimed at the prevention of birth defects.

Maternal Health Society
P. O. Box 46563, Station G,
Vancouver, British Columbia, Canada VGR4G8
(604) 438-5365
Consumer group dedicated to improving health care for childbearing women and their families. Provides written and telephone information to groups and individuals and teaching resources, films, and publications related to childbearing.

Maternity Center Association (MCA)
48 East 92nd Street,
New York, NY 10028
(212) 369-7300
Provides education and information regarding family-oriented maternity care. Has many publications and teaching resources for childbirth educators.

Midwest Parentcraft Center
627 Beaver Road,
Glenview, IL 60025
(312) 998-6547
The official Gamper method organization. Offers information about the Gamper method and childbirth preparation classes.

Midwife Alliance of North America (MANA)
309 Main Street,
Concord, NH 03301
(603) 225-9586
National support network for all midwives (CNM's licensed and lay). Provides information and publications related to midwifery and childbirth.

Nurses Association of the American College of Obstetricians and Gynecologists (NAACOG)
600 Maryland Avenue, SW,
Suite 200 East,
Washington, DC 20024
(202) 638-5577
A specialty organization for registered nurses specializing in obstetric, gynecological, and neonatal nursing. Provides many publications related to pregnancy and childbirth, continuing education programs, and information related to current maternal and child health issues.

National Association of Childbearing Centers
Route 1, Box 1,
Perkiomenville, PA 18074
(215) 234-8068
Offers information on freestanding birth centers.

National Association of Childbirth Education (NACE)
3940 Eleventh Street,
Riverside, CA 92501
(714) 686-0422
Promotes the Lamaze method of childbirth education. Offers information about the Lamaze method and childbirth classes.

National Association of Parents and Professionals For Safe Alternatives in Childbirth
P. O. Box 428,
Marble Hill, MO 63764
(314) 238-2010
Offers literature, statistics, and referrals for home birth programs, freestanding birth centers, and family-oriented hospitals, as well as referrals for midwives.

National Center for Education in Maternal and Child Health

38th and R Streets, NW,
Washington, DC 20057
(202) 625-8400

Has a variety of publications on the topic of maternal and child health.

National Center for Health and Medical Information, Inc.

Consumer's Health and Medical Information,
P. O. Box 390,
Clearwater, FL 33517
(813) 734-9016 or (813) 531-6047

National clearinghouse of traditional and nontraditional, unproven and late-breaking health information from health and medical organizations, journals, and other sources. Provides current reports about treatment options for specific diseases.

National Clearinghouse for Alcohol Information

United States Department of Health Services,
P. O. Box 2345,
Department AFT-FAS,
Rockville, MD 20852
(301) 468-2600

Provides information on the effects of alcohol.

National Clearinghouse on Child Abuse and Neglect Information

P. O. Box 1182,
Washington, DC 20013
(301) 251-5157

National clearinghouse on child abuse and neglect. Provides information and many types of resource materials—research projects, published documents, state laws, court case decisions, and audiovisual material on the subject.

National Down's Syndrome Congress

1640 West Roosevelt Road,
Chicago, IL 60608
(312) 226-0416

Offers information and referrals to parents with Down's syndrome children.

National Genetics Foundation

555 West 57th Street,
New York, NY 10019
(212) 586-5800

Provides information and referrals to a network of 60 university-oriented genetic centers.

National Health Information Clearinghouse

P. O. Box 1133,
Washington, DC 20013-1133
(800) 336-4797

Provides information and referrals to over 1500 health information resources.

National Institute of Child Health & Human Development (NICHD)

9000 Rockville Pike,
Building 31, Room 2A-32,
Bethesda, MD 20205
(301) 496-4000

Provides current information on a variety of topics related to pregnancy, childbirth, and parenting.

National Maternal and Child Health Clearinghouse

U.S. Department of Health and Human Services,
38th and R Streets, NW,
Washington, DC 20057
(202) 625-8410

Clearinghouse provides current information on maternal and child health through distribution of publications.

National Perinatal Association (NPA)

101½ South Union Street,
Alexandria, VA 22314
(703) 549-5523

Composed of regional and state perinatal organizations that are committed to improving perinatal health care. Offers information and publications on perinatal health care.

National Safety Council (NSC)

444 North Michigan Avenue,
Chicago, IL 60611
(312) 527-4800

Provides information on infant safety.

National Self-Help Clearinghouse
33 West 42nd Street,
New York, NY 10036
(212) 840-1259
Provides information and support including names of parent self-help groups throughout the United States.

National Women's Health Network
224 7th Street, SE,
Washington, DC 20003
(202) 543-9222
Nation's only national membership organization for women's health. Focuses on women's health issues.

National Institutes of Health
U.S. Department of Health and Human Services,
Building 31, Room 7A-32,
Bethesda, MD 20205
(301) 496-4000
Provides information on toxoplasmosis and the task force report on antenatal diagnosis, cesarean birth, and ultrasound imaging. Information on all major NIH publications can be obtained from this source.

National Institute of Mental Health (NIMH)
Public Inquiries,
5600 Fishers Lane,
Rockville, MD 20805
Offers a variety of resources and references related to low birth weight infants and parenting behaviors that foster infants' growth and development.

Pan American Health Organizations (PAHO)
525 23rd Street, NW,
Washington, DC 20037
(202) 861-3200
Has many publications related to pregnancy and childbirth.

Parenthood After Thirty
451 Vermont Avenue,
Berkeley, CA 94707
(415) 524-6635
Provides information and resources for couples who are considering having a baby after the woman has reached age 30.

Parents Without Partners
Information Center,
7910 Woodmont Avenue,
Bethesda, MD 20814
(800) 638-8078
National network that provides information and support for single parents.

Planned Parenthood Federation of America
810 Seventh Avenue,
New York, NY 10019
(212) 541-7800
Operates over 700 clinics in U.S. which provide information and services for family planning, birth control, abortion, female sterilization, vasectomies, infertility, and prenatal care.

Pregnancy Environmental Hotline National Birth Defects Center
30 Warren Street,
Brighton, MA 02135
(800) 322-5014
Hotline for information on pregnancy.

Read Natural Childbirth Foundation
P. O. Box 956,
San Rafael, CA 94915
(415) 456-8462
The official Read method organization. Offers information about the Read method and childbirth classes.

Refugee Materials Center
U.S. Department of Education,
324 East 11th Street, 9th Floor,
Kansas City, MO 64106
(816) 734-7081
Offers information sheets on breastfeeding in Vietnamese and English.

Resolve Inc.
P. O. Box 474,
Belmont, MA 02178
(617) 484-2424
Offers referrals to specialists and support services for couples with infertility problems.

Sex Information and Education Council of the United States (SIECUS)

80 Fifth Avenue, Suite 801,
New York, NY 10011
(212) 929-2300

Provides information and resource information on sex education.

Share

St. John's Hospital,
800 East Carpenter,
Springfield, IL 62769
(217) 544-6464, ext. 5275

Provides referrals to a national network of 125 Share organizations and over 400 support groups for couples who have had a miscarriage, a tubal pregnancy, stillbirth, or baby who dies.

Society for Nutrition Education

1736 Franklin Street, Suite 900,
Oakland, CA 94612
(415) 444-7133

Provides information regarding nutrition, especially for high-risk pregnancies.

Superintendent of Documents. U.S. Government Printing Office

Washington, DC 20402
(202) 783-3238

U.S. printing office. Has many books and pamphlets on a wide variety of topics related to pregnancy, childbirth, and parenting.

The United States Department of Agriculture

WIC Supplemental Food Section,
1103 North B Street, Suite E,
Sacramento, CA 95814
(916) 322-5277

Offers information on the importance of nutrition for pregnant and nursing women.

The United States Department of Agriculture

FNS Western Region,
550 Kearny Street,
San Francisco, CA 94108
(415) 556-4950

Has materials available on working with the pregnant teenager, promoting breastfeeding among low-income women, and several others to choose from.

World Health Organization Publications Center

49 Sheridan Avenue,
Albany, NY 12210
(518) 436-9686

Has a wide variety of publications related to pregnancy, childbirth, and parenting.

B
AUDIOVISUAL RESOURCES FOR CHILDBIRTH EDUCATION

The following organizations provide audiovisual resources for childbirth education classes in all settings. Since new films, videotapes and audiotapes are continually being produced, a list of current audiovisual resources is not included. The childbirth educator can write to these companies to obtain a current catalog of materials and can request to be placed on the mailing list for notification of future releases.

ASPO/Lamaze

1840 Wilson Boulevard,
Suite 204, Arlington, VA 22201
(800) 368-4404

Artemis
Distributed by Childbirth Graphics,
1210 Culver Road,
Rochester, NY 14609-5454
(716) 482-7940

Joseph T. Anzalone Foundation
P. O. Box 5206,
Santa Cruz, CA 95063
(408) 476-7676

BABES (Bay Area Birth Education Service)
Distributed by Childbirth Graphics,
1210 Culver Road,
Rochester, NY 14609-5454
(716) 482-7940

Baby Dance Institute
4110 Duquesne Avenue,
Culver City, CA 90230
(213) 204-6746 (Mail Order Dept.)

Barlas/Walker Associates
15 La Costa Drive,
Natick, MA 01760
(617) 893-3553

Big Productions
2807 32nd Avenue South,
Seattle, WA 98144

Birthing Education Services
P. O. Box 22055,
Indianapolis, IN 46222
(317) 291-3375

Centre Films, Inc.
1103 North El Centro Avenue,
Hollywood, CA 90038
(213) 466-5123

Centre Productions, Inc.
1800 30th Street,
Boulder, CO 80301
(800) 824-1166

Childbirth Graphics
P. O. Box 17025, Irondequoit Post Office,
Rochester, NY 14617
(716) 266-6769

Churchill Films
662 North Robertson Blvd.,
Los Angeles, CA 90069
(800) 334-7830 for previews and sales; in CA
(213) 657-5110; for rentals (800) 624-8613; in CA
(818) 884-3100.

Cinema Medica
6652 North Western Avenue,
Chicago, IL 60645
(312) 973-2297 or (800) 621-5147 (IL residents call collect.)

Educational Graphics Aids, Inc.
7762 Brentwood Court, Suite 101,
Arvada, CO 80005
(303) 424-9221

Evenflo
Juvenile Furniture Company,
Division of Spalding & EvenFlo Companies, Inc.
1801 Commerce Drive,
Piqua, OH 45356
(513) 773-3971

Fairview Audio-Visuals
17909 Groveland,
Cleveland, OH 44111-5656
(216) 476-7054

Family-Centered Childbirth Education Association
c/o Terri Peterson,
P. O. Box 2243,
Des Moines, IA 50310
(515) 255-0674 (ask for Carla)

Fanlight Productions
47 Halifax Street,
Boston, MA 02130
(617) 524-0980

Farm Tapes
P.O. Box 247,
Summertown, TN 38483
(615) 964-3574

Feeling Fine Programs, Inc.
3575 Cahuenga Boulevard West,
Suite 425,
Los Angeles, CA 90068
(800) 443-4040; (800) 531-1212 in CA

Foresight Productions
405 North Salem Street,
Apex, NC 27502
(919) 362-4790

The Glendon Association
2409 Century Park East,
Suite 3000,
Los Angeles, CA 90067
(213) 837-5837

Ferde Grofe Films
3100 Airport Avenue,
Santa Monica, CA 90405
(213) 397-7520

Health Systems Alternatives
c/o Rosalys Peel,
1520 Avenil Park Drive,
San Pedro, CA 90732
(213) 831-1439

Inner Guidance Systems
Gwynedd Plaza, II Suite 301,
Springhouse, PA 19477
(215) 643-7220

International Childbirth Educators Association, Inc. (ICEA)
P.O. Box 20048,
Minneapolis, MN 55420-0048
(612) 854-8660 or (800) 624-4934

Iris Productions
Available from Nicolas J. Kaufman Productions,
14 Clyde Street,
Newtonville, MA 02160
(617) 964-4466

Johnson and Johnson Baby Products Company
Grandview Road,
Skillman, NJ 08558
(800) 526-3967

Lawren Productions Inc.
P. O. Box 666,
Mendocino, CA 94560
(707) 937-0536

Lifecircle
c/o Marjorie Pyle, RNC
2378 Cornell Drive,
Costa Mesa, CA 92626
(714) 546-1427

Lifecycle Productions
P. O. Box 183,
Newton, MA 02165
(617) 890-2303

Medrier
4731 South State Street,
Murray, VT 84107
(801) 266-1114

Milner-Fenwick Inc.
2125 Greenspring Drive,
Timonium, MD 21093
(800) 638-8652

Motavision Media
2 Parktree Court,
Chico, CA 95926
(916) 891-8475

Motion Inc.
3138 Highland Place, NW,
Washington, DC 20008
(202) 363-9450

National Center for Education in Maternal and Child Health
38th and R Streets, NW,
Georgetown University,
Washington, DC 20036
(202) 625-8400

National Foundation/March of Dimes Birth Defects Foundation
Professional Education Department,
1275 Mamaroneck Avenue,
White Plains, NY 10605
(914) 428-7100

National Sudden Infant Death Syndrome Foundation
Two Metro Plaza, Suite 205,
8240 Professional Place,
Landover, MD 20785
(301) 459-3388 or (800) 221-SIDS

New Day Films
22 Riverview Drive,
Wayne, NJ 07470
(201) 633-0212

New Horizons for Learning
P.O. Box 51140,
Seattle, WA 98115-1140

Omega Films Limited
70 Milner Avenue, Unit 5A,
Scarborough, Ontario, Canada MIS 3P8
(416) 291-4733

Parenting Pictures
121 N.W. Crystal Street,
Crystal River, FL 32629
(904) 795-2156

Parenting Resources and Education Program
P.O. Box 36024,
San Jose, CA 95158-6024

Parents with Careers Inc.
2513 Oakenshield Drive,
Rockville, MD 20854
(800) 446-4462 following dial tone 369-1600

Pennypress
1100 23rd Avenue East,
Seattle, WA 98112
(206) 325-1419

Perennial Education Inc.
930 Pitner Avenue,
Evanston, IL 60202
(312) 328-6700 or (800) 323-9084

Polymorph Films Inc.
118 South Street,
Boston, MA 02111
(617) 542-2004

Prepared Childbirth Association
1616 S.W. Sunset Boulevard, Suite G,
Portland, OR 97201
(503) 245-3196

Professional Research Inc.
930 Pitner Avenue,
Evanston, IL 60202
(312) 328-6700 or (800) 421-2363

Read Natural Childbirth Foundation, Inc.
P.O. Box 956,
San Rafael, CA 94915
(415) 456-8462

The Prenatal University
Rene Vande Carr
27255 Calaroga Avenue,
Hayward, CA 94545
(415) 786-3792

Ross Laboratories
Division of Abbott Laboratories,
625 Cleveland Avenue,
Columbia, OH 43216
(614) 227-3333

Society of Nutrition Education
1736 Franklin Street, Suite 900,
Oakland, CA 94612
(415) 444-7133

Star Publishing
P.O. Box 161113,
Austin, TX 78746
(512) 327-8310

3-West Productions Inc.
P.O. Box 12317,
Birmingham, MI 48612

Vida Health Communications
335 Huron Avenue,
Cambridge, MA 02138
(617) 864-4334

Video-Farm
156 Drakes Lane,
Summertown, TN 38483
(615) 964-2286 or (615) 964-3574

Videograph
2833 25th Street,
San Francisco, CA 94110
(415) 282-6001

Videotalk
220 Shrewsbury Avenue,
Red Bank, NJ 07701
(201) 747-2444 or (800) 526-7002

Wesley Women's Hospital
Wesley Medical Center
550 N. Hillside
Wichita, Kansas 67208

Women's Hospital of Texas
Education Department,
7600 Fannin,
Houston, TX 77084
(713) 791-5895

C
SELECTED PUBLICATIONS FOR CHILDBIRTH EDUCATORS

Publications from the behavioral and health sciences literature that frequently have articles related to childbirth and parent education are included in this section. It is useful to review these journals on a routine basis and then refer to the current issue of each of the following indexes to identify other articles related to childbirth and parent education: *Cumulative Index to Nursing and Allied Health Literature, Index Medicus, Psychological Abstracts,* and *Sociological Abstracts.*

Keeping abreast of the current literature is a formidable task and can best be accomplished when childbirth educators form a journal club. Each member is responsible for reviewing specific journals monthly and making a copy of each article related to childbirth and parent education. During journal club meetings, members discuss the articles and their implications for practice. The articles can be compiled in a notebook and members can check them out as needed.

American Baby Magazine
249 W. 17th Street
New York, NY 10011

American Journal of Maternal/Child Nursing (MCN)
555 W. 57th Street
New York, NY 10019-2961

American Journal of Nurse-Midwifery
Elsevier Scientific Publishing Company, Inc.
52 Vanderbilt Avenue
New York, NY 10017

American Journal of Obstetrics and Gynecology
C. V. Mosby Company
11830 Westline Drive
St. Louis, MO 63146

American Journal of Orthopsychiatry
American Orthopsychiatric Association
19 West 44th Street
New York, NY 10036

American Journal of Public Health
1015 Fifteenth Street, NW
Washington, DC 20005

The Birth Gazette
42 The Farm
Summertown, TN 38483

Birth: Issues in Perinatal Care and Education
Blackwell Scientific Publications, Inc.
52 Beacon Street
Boston, MA 02108

Breastfeeding Abstracts
LaLeche League International, Inc.
9616 Minneapolis Avenue
P. O. Box 1209
Franklin Park, IL 60131-8209

Bulletin of the APTA Section on Obstetrics and Gynecology
American Physical Therapy Association (APTA)
662 Big Foot Court
Fremont, CA 94539

Childbirth Educator
249 West 17th Street
New York, NY 10011

Clinical Obstetrics and Gynecology
J. B. Lippincott
East Washington Square
Philadelphia, PA 19105

Contemporary Obstetrics and Gynecology
Medical Economic Publishers
Box 552
Oradell, NJ 07649

Genesis
ASPO/Lamaze
1840 Wilson Boulevard
Suite 204
Arlington, VA 22201

Health Care for Women International
Hemisphere Publishing Corporation
1010 Vermont Avenue, NW
Washington, DC 20005

International Journal of Childbirth Education
International Childbirth Education Association
P. O. Box 20048
Minneapolis, MN 55420-0048

Journal of Health and Social Behavior
American Sociological Association
1722 N Street, NW
Washington, DC 20036

Journal of Obstetric, Gynecologic, and Neonatal Nursing (JOGNN)
600 Maryland Avenue, SW, Suite 200
Washington, DC 20024

Journal of Perinatal and Neonatal Nursing
Aspen Publishers, Inc.
1600 Research Boulevard
Rockville, MD 20850

Journal of Psychosomatic Obstetrics and Gynecology
Elsevier Science Publishers BV
Box 211, 1000 AE
Amsterdam, Netherlands

Journal of Psychosomatic Research
Pergamon Press, Inc., Journal Division
Maxwell House, Fairview Park
Elmsford, NY 10523

Lamaze Parents' Magazine
1840 Wilson Boulevard, Suite 204
Arlington, VA 22201

Maternal-Child Nursing Currents
Ross Laboratories
625 Cleveland Avenue
Columbus, OH 43216

Maternal-Child Nursing Journal
University of Pittsburgh
Maternity Nursing and Nursing of Child Departments
437 Victoria Bldg.
3500 Victoria Street
Pittsburgh, PA 15261

New England Journal of Medicine
10 Shattuck Street
Boston, MA 02115

Nursing Research
555 W. 57th Street
New York, NY 10019

Obstetrics and Gynecology
Elsevier Science Publishing Co., Inc.
52 Vanderbilt Avenue
New York, NY 10017

Psychosomatic Medicine
Elsevier Science Publishing Co., Inc.
52 Vanderbilt Avenue
New York, NY 10017

Research in Nursing and Health
John Wiley and Sons, Inc.
605 3rd Avenue
New York, NY 10158

D
SELECTED FUNDING RESOURCES FOR RESEARCH RELATED TO CHILDBIRTH AND PARENT EDUCATION

There are a number of *local* potential funding agencies that childbirth educators can contact when seeking resources for a planned study. These are community agencies such as a chapter of the March of Dimes Birth Defects Foundation, health care agencies, insurance agencies, private foundations, and universities. Also, corporations that produce baby products will often fund research projects related to their interest areas. Selected *national and federal government* agencies and *private foundations* that provide funding for research in the area of childbirth and parent education are listed below. The childbirth educator can write these agencies and request a copy of the application guidelines.

For a comprehensive listing of private funding agencies the reader is referred to *The Foundation Directory*.[1] Researchers can also write and ask to have their names placed on the mailing list to receive the *NIH Guide for Grants and Contracts*[2] that is published on a biweekly basis. It contains descriptions of grants and contracts that are being solicited.

National Agencies and Private Foundations

Allstate Foundation
Allstate Plaza, F–3
Northbrook, IL 60062
(312) 291-5502

American Nurses' Foundation
2420 Pershing Road
Kansas City, MO 64108
(816) 474-5720

Atlantic Richfield Foundation
515 South Flower Street
Los Angeles, CA 90071
(213) 486-3342

Carnegie Corporation of New York
437 Madison Avenue
New York, NY 10022
(212) 371-3200

Edna McConnell Clark Foundation
250 Park Avenue
New York, NY 10017
(212) 986-7050

Ford Foundation
320 East 43rd Street
New York, NY 10017
(212) 573-5000

Foundation for Child Development
345 East 46th Street
New York, NY 10017
(212) 697-3150

Foundation of the National Association of Pediatric Nurse Associates and Practitioners (NAPNAP)
1000 Maplewood Drive, Suite 104
Maple Shade, NJ 08052
(609) 667-1773

Hearst Foundation
888 Seventh Avenue
27th Floor
New York, NY 10106
(212) 586-5404

International Childbirth Education Association
ICEA Virginia Larson Research Fund
P. O. Box 20048
Minneapolis, MN 55420
(612) 854-8660

Robert Wood Johnson Foundation
P. O. Box 2316
Princeton, NJ 08543
(609) 452-8701

W. K. Kellogg Foundation
400 North Avenue
Battle Creek, MI 49017-3398
(616) 968-1611

March of Dimes
Birth Defects Foundation
1275 Mamaroneck Avenue
White Plains, NY 10605
(914) 428-7100

Andrew W. Mellon Foundation
140 East 62nd Street
New York, NY 10021
(212) 838-8400

Metropolitan Life Foundation
One Madison Avenue
New York, NY 10010
(212) 578-7049

Nurses' Association of the American College of Obstetricians and Gynecologists (NAACOG)
600 Maryland Avenue, SW, Suite 200 East
Washington, DC 20024
(202) 638-0026

National Association of Neonatal Nurses (NANN)
55 Maria Drive, Suite 842
Petaluma, CA 94952
(707) 762-5588

Helena Rubinstein Foundation
405 Lexington Avenue
New York, NY 10174
(212) 986-0806

Sigma Theta Tau
National Honor Society of Nursing
1100 Waterway Boulevard
Indianapolis, IN 46202
(317) 634-8171

Federal Government Agencies

Office of Adolescent Pregnancy Programs
Office of Population Affairs
Grants Management Office
Room 736E, Hubert H. Humphrey Building
200 Independence Avenue, SW
Washington, DC 20201
(202) 245-0146

HRSA–Bureau of Maternal and Child Health and Resources Division
Office of the Director
Parklawn Building, Room 6-05
5600 Fishers Lane
Rockville, MD 20857
(301) 443-2170

National Center for Health Services Research
Division of Extramural Research
3-30 Park Building
5600 Fishers Lane
Rockville, MD 20857
(301) 443-2345 or (301) 443-5656

National Center for Nursing Research (NCNR)
National Institutes of Health
Building 38A/B2E17
Bethesda, MD 20894
(301) 496-0526

National Institute of Child Health and Human Development (NICHD)
National Institutes of Health
Center for Research on Mothers and Children
Landow Building, Room 7C-03
Bethesda, MD 20892
(301) 496-5097

National Institute of Mental Health (NIMH)
National Institutes of Health
Health and Behavior Research Branch
Room 11C-06
Parklawn Building
5600 Fishers Lane
Rockville, MD 20857
(301) 443-4337

References

1. *The Foundation Directory* (10th ed.) New York: The Foundation Center, 1985.
2. *NIH Guide for Grants and Contracts,* Office of Extramural Research and Training, Building 1, Room 111, National Institutes of Health, Bethesda, MD 20205.

NAME INDEX

Numbers in *italics* refer to illustrations; numbers followed by t refer to tables.

SUBJECT INDEX

Numbers in *italics* refer to illustrations; numbers followed by t refer to tables.

Working mothers, returning to outside employment, 72, 87